· Dictionary of Opera and Operetta ·

DICTIONARY *of* OPERA *and* OPERETTA

James Anderson

Foreword by the Rt. Hon. David Mellor QC MP

BLOOMSBURY

This book is dedicated to my mother and to the memory of my father L. Guy Anderson, DVM, FRCVS, who sadly did not live to see it finished.

The publishers would like to thank Alison Emmett and Kate Bouverie for their work on this book.

First published 1989
Second edition first published 1995

Bloomsbury Publishing Plc, 2 Soho Square, London W1V 6HB

10 9 8 7 6 5 4 3 2 1

A CIP record for this book is available from the British Library

ISBN 0 7475 2094 1

Designed by Hugh Adams, AB3
Typeset by Hewer Text Composition Services, Edinburgh
Printed in Great Britain by Clay Ltd, St Ives plc

· Contents ·

Foreword	vii
Introduction	ix
Preface to Second Edition	xi
Acknowlegements	xiii
Abbreviations	xv
A–Z SECTION	1
Appendix I: Opera on Record	629
Appendix II: Operatic Chronology	641
Bibliography	649

· Foreword ·

At the end of the last century Britain was derided as 'The land without music', but no longer. This century has seen a remarkable renaissance in every aspect of musical creativity, not least in the composition of opera. Britten, Tippett, Birtwistle, Walton, Vaughan Williams, Delius and others have all produced operas of international note which have in some cases – like Britten's *Peter Grimes* whose 50th birthday we celebrate this year (1995) – become standard repertory around the world.

The work of these composers has been complemented by a tremendous increase in operatic performances, not just in London but across the nation. Today, almost every region is well served by permanent or touring companies. To give but two examples, Opera North, founded as recently as 1979, fills a huge gap in the north of England magnificently, while the Welsh National Opera has, in recent years, achieved world renown.

Today, the British are increasingly a nation of opera goers. Some people know a lot about it, others next to nothing. The latter go for the spectacle, revelling in the fact that you don't have to be particularly musical to appreciate opera – nor indeed, I'm often compelled to think, to perform in it either!

Whether you wallow in a pit of ignorance or dwell on the highest peak of sophistication in these matters, this is very much the book for you. No technical training is needed to get the best out of it, but even those who have immersed themselves in opera for many years will find not just something, but lots of things of real interest within these covers.

Treat this book as a friend and mentor, and it will serve you well. It doesn't talk down to you as one or two misconceived forays into this territory have done recently. What it will do is expertly convey information and above all enthusiasm for this great art form and all its various branches and tributaries, notably operetta, which the author rightly feels has been undervalued for too long.

To pack all this information into one modest volume is a remarkable piece of compression, which reflects great credit on James Anderson's literary skills as well as his musical knowledge. When I think that much of this work has been done whilst he has been struggling against grave illness, my admiration becomes boundless.

This book is a testimony to his courage and is a substantial monument to his life and work.

The Rt. Hon. David Mellor QC MP
January 1995

· Introduction ·

This book has been undertaken partly as an act of self-defence: for many years, friends had been urging me to put my knowledge of opera to some practical use. This book is the result of that urging, and I hope that it will stop them nagging me.

'An irrational and exotic entertainment' pronounced the redoutable Dr Johnson on the subject of opera, and the form has never lacked its detractors or satirists, from Tolstoy to the Marx Brothers. Fond of it though I am, opera is not actually my favourite form of music: I would happily exchange every opera ever written for one symphony by Sibelius (or to be strictly honest, every opera except *Falstaff*). The exercise of providing over 750 operatic plot summaries for this dictionary has led me to the conclusion that Mark Twain was not exactly exaggerating when he said that anything too stupid to be spoken is sung. It must be admitted that opera is an inherently 'unnatural' form of drama, but then so too are theatre, ballet and the cinema. After all, in real life people do not express themselves in Shakespearian blank verse or Aeschylean hexameters, they do not communicate their emotions through the use of pliés and entrechats, nor (in the case of the cinema) do they happen to have faces 'half a block wide', as Gian-Carlo Menotti once observed. What makes opera sometimes appear more 'unnatural' than other dramatic forms is the fact that it is much the most complex, incorporating parts of nearly all other forms of the arts. It is thus by far the most difficult form to bring off: Wagner's vision of *Gesamtkunstwerk* (a work of art uniting all the artistic disciplines) has seldom been realized. Of the hundreds of thousands of operas which have been written there are perhaps a dozen which can be taken seriously as true music-drama. Only Verdi, Wagner and Moussorgsky, it has been argued, were real musico-dramatists rather than just composers. This view is rather hard on Gluck, Beethoven and Berg, but I would subscribe to it. There is a compensation, however: there are an enormous number of operas which are magnificent on purely musical, if not dramatic, grounds.

I was persuaded to write this dictionary for a number of reasons. Firstly, I wanted to provide an affordable one-volume work: at £550 the four-volume *Grove Dictionary of Opera* is outside the pockets of all but the very wealthiest. In addition, I have attempted (as is reflected in the book's title) to give a comprehensive coverage to operetta, a genre which seems to receive short shrift in most reference works, despite its great popularity. I have, as well, provided considerable material on the most significant modern operas which are, naturally, not dealt with in older reference works. I have thus included the recent works of composers such as Reimann, Birtwistle and Glass, as well as covering the remarkable operatic flowering currently taking place in Finland. Finally, my coverage has attempted to reflect contemporary trends in operatic performance and in public taste, such as the major renewal of interest in early opera (especially the works of Rameau, Lully, Cavalli and Charpentier), the continuing and still-growing interest in the Czech and the Italian bel canto repertories, and the recent revival of interest in the operas of individual composers, such as Haydn, Zemlinsky and Massenet. If the attentive reader wishes to know what trend is represented by the inclusion of nearly all of Schubert's operas, I can only say that I hope it is a future trend: there is more real music in a single Schubert song than in the entire combined output of the Italian verismo composers.

I have tried to write this book with a younger audience in mind. To this end I have included more composers, more operas and more contemporary artists at the expense of many singers of the past. Apart from the very greatest, who are of course included, audiences of the 1990s have never heard of most pre-1945 singers.

Authorial prejudice is an important issue as it can colour the text, so I must come clean at the outset. My operatic dislikes I have endeavoured to suppress ruthlessly (even my low opinion of Puccini), and only in the case of Menotti have I allowed myself to speak my mind. On the other side, I have availed myself of the authorial privilege of occasionally doing some special pleading in the case of individual operas: Enescu's *Oedipe*, Smetana's *Dalibor*, Vaughan Williams's *The Pilgrim's Progress* and Nielsen's *Saul og David*, all of which are grossly ignored. There is something seriously wrong with an operatic system which ignores such masterpieces in favour of the works of lesser Italian composers.

My own personal experience of reference books of any kind (an experience which I should imagine is shared by most people) is that they are frequently difficult to use, and I often cannot find what I want even if it is actually there somewhere. Bearing this in mind I have endeavoured at all times to make this dictionary user-friendly. As a general rule, this means that entries are placed where I believe that the average user would look for them; where there might be confusion they are cross-referenced. I have laid down a few ground rules for where things should go, which I hope will assist the reader. Rules are, of course, made to be broken, and I have not followed them slavishly where common sense or logic dictated otherwise.

Perhaps the most important of these ground rules is the thorny old question of languages, about which I have decided as follows. When the original language concerned is French, German, Italian or Spanish, the entry is listed under its original language and the titles of operas are given in translation in brackets afterwards. For the reader's convenience, some works which are frequently referred to by their English translation are cross-referenced (for example, *The Merry Widow*: see *Die Lustige Witwe*). When any other language, such as Russian or Czech is concerned, the entry is listed under its English translation unless the original is so near to English as to render a translation superfluous (for example, *Káťa Kabanová*). In a few cases where logic dictates, I have ignored this rule: for example, it would not have made sense to have listed Moniuszko's best-known opera as *Helen* rather than *Halka*. A special note about operas written by Italian composers to French libretti: all references to them are listed under their original French. This applies particularly to Rossini's *Guillaume Tell* and *Le Comte Ory*, Cherubini's *Médée*, Donizetti's *La Favorite* and *La Fille du Régiment* and Verdi's *Les Vêpres Siciliennes*. Again, common sense has dictated one exception: Verdi's *Don Carlos* is almost universally known and performed in Italian, and to have referred to it in French would have been perverse.

I have also laid down an immutable rule on names which contain prefixes such as van, von, de and so on. While one would never look up Ludwig van Beethoven or Carl Maria von Weber under letter V, in some reference books Richard van Allan and Frederica von Stade are listed under V. In this dictionary, for the sake of consistency, all names with a prefix are listed under the letter of the main surname. A note on Strausses might also help the reader. Where Strauss, plain and unadorned, is mentioned, this refers without exception to Richard Strauss. Where Johann or Oskar are intended, they are written as J. Strauss and O. Strauss.

Opera is now one of the most rapidly growing entertainments as far as popularity is concerned. Now coming up to its 400th birthday, what was originally an exercise in the recreation of classical Greek drama has developed into a complex, intriguing, often infuriating and sometimes exhilarating art form which is nowadays appealing to a wider section of society than ever before. I offer this book as a small contribution to today's audiences, in the hope that it may help them a little toward a further enjoyment and understanding of opera.

James Anderson
London, 1995

· *Preface* ·

I have taken the opportunity of this second edition to undertake a major revision and expansion of this dictionary. As well as trying to correct any errors that crept in originally, I have gone through each entry adjusting, expanding or changing, with the result that almost every entry has been improved in some respect. The most substantial additions I have made include:

- The addition of another 120 operas, bringing the total number covered to over 1,000.
- The addition of a further 250 plot summaries to operas that were already listed.
- The addition of a bibliography.
- The inclusion of a further 55 singers and conductors.
- The inclusion of a further 75 composers, with an emphasis on the 18th and 20th centuries.

The basic structure of the book remains the same with one important exception, which is the reflection of the break-up of the former Soviet Union, the former Yugoslavia and the former Czechoslovakia. All references to these countries are now under their various successor states.

James Anderson
London, 1995

· *Acknowledgements* ·

I should like to take this opportunity to thank the many people, both personal friends and professional musicians, who have given me advice, information and encouragement during the several years that the production of two editions of this dictionary have taken. Many individual musicians and musical organizations have provided me with assitance and invaluable comment. I am particularly indebted to the conductor Ronald Corp and to Eileen and Terence Hilton (on whose dining-room table a fair proportion of the first edition was written). Many thanks are also due to the baritone William Elvin, to John Hughes for unearthing some very obscure dates for me, and to Roger Hewland of Gramex for finding me several very rare recordings. I should also like to acknowledge the aid provided by the unfailingly helpful staff of the Putney and Barbican music libraries, by the *Times* obituary service, by the cultural department of the Russian Embassy, and by the press offices of the English National Opera and the Royal Opera House, Covent Garden.

To my immediate family I owe an enormous debt of thanks for their never flagging support and encouragement, even after the project had gone on so long as to have driven them mad. To my friends I also owe a big debt of thanks for constant encouragement and for help and support during several periods of illness. Special thanks to Robert Taylor, Quincy Julien, Viv Packer, d'Artagnan and Marisa Arbuah, Everton Nelson, Martina Berne and Greg Johnson. I must also express my appreciation for the staff of St Thomas's Hospital, particularly Dr Caroline Bradbeer and Dr Meg Campbell, for keeping me going for so long against all the odds; without them, this book would never have been finished.

Finally, I would like to thank everyone at Bloomsbury – if only every author had such considerate publishers! My especial thanks to Kathy Rooney, the perfect editorial boss, to Kate Quarry, and to Tracey Smith, whose own love of opera has been a great encouragement. I am also most grateful that the Rt Hon David Mellor kindly agreed to write a foreword for the second edition.

James Anderson
London, 1995

· Abbreviations ·

b	born	NBC	National Broadcasting Company
bar	baritone	Op	opus number (Mozart, Schubert and Weber have K, D and J numbers)
b-bar	bass-baritone	perf	performed; performance
BBC	British Broadcasting Corporation	R	Commercially recorded
cap	seating capacity	RAI	Radio-televisione Italiana
CBS	Columbia Broadcasting System	sop	soprano
cont	contralto	ten	tenor
c-ten	counter-tenor	TV	television
d	died	U	unfinished
Exc	excerpts		
libr	libretto		

· Nationalities ·

Arg	Argentinian	Jam	Jamaican
Arm	Armenian	Jap	Japanese
Aus	Austrian	Mart	Martiniquan
Aust	Australian	Mex	Mexican
Belg	Belgian/Flemish	Neth	Dutch
Br	British/Welsh/Scottish	Nor	Norwegian
Braz	Brazilian	NZ	New Zealand
Bulg	Bulgarian	Per	Peruvian
Can	Canadian	Pol	Polish
Chil	Chilean	Port	Portuguese
Cro	Croatian	PR	Puerto Rican
Cz	Czech	Rom	Romanian
Den	Danish	Russ	Russian
Est	Estonian	Ser	Serbian
Fin	Finnish	Slo	Slovakian
Fr	French	Slv	Slovenian
Geo	Georgian	Sp	Spanish
Ger	German	Swe	Swedish
Gk	Greek	Swit	Swiss
Hung	Hungarian	Turk	Turkish
Ind	Indian	Ukr	Ukrainian
Ire	Irish	Ur	Uruguayan
Isr	Israeli	US	American
It	Italian		

· Alphabetization ·

Titles which begin with a definite or indefinite article are listed under the letter of the first main word. Names which contain a prefix (such as de, van, von or di) are listed under the letter of the main surname.

A

A, An
Titles beginning with the English indefinite article are listed under the letter of the first main word. For example, *A Hand of Bridge* is listed under H.

Aachen Opera
(Aachen was known as Aix-la-Chapelle when it was part of France). The present opera house (cap 944) in this German city in North Rhine Westphalia was opened in 1951. One of Germany's most important provincial houses, it has long had a fine reputation for fostering major talent. Musical directors have included Fritz Busch, Herbert von Karajan, Wolfgang Sawallisch, Gabriel Chmura and Bruce Ferden.

Abbado, Claudio (b 1933)
Italian conductor, particularly associated with Rossini, Verdi and Moussorgsky operas. Also a champion of contemporary Italian composers, he conducted the first performances of Nono's *Al Gran Sole Carico d'Amore* and Giacomo Manzoni's *Atomtod*. He is one of the outstanding operatic conductors of recent times, whose performances are notable for their muscular attack, strong dramatic tension and scrupulous observance of the composer's intentions. He was musical director of La Scala, Milan (1971–86) and the Vienna State Opera (1986–91). His nephew **Roberto** is also a conductor, and his brother **Marcello** (*b* 1926) is a composer who has written two operas.

Abbatini, Antonio Maria (1595–c 1679)
Italian composer. His first opera, written in collaboration with Marazzoli, was *Dal Male il Bene* (Rome, 12 Feb 1654; libr Giulio Rospigliosi, after Sigler de Huerta's *No Ay Bien*). One of the earliest comic operas, it introduced the ensemble finale and contains the first SOUBRETTE role in opera. His subsequent operas were *Ione* (Vienna 1664; libr Antonio Draghi) and *La Comica del Cielo* (Rome, 1 Feb 1668; libr Rospigliosi, after Luis Vélez de Guevara's *La Baltasara*).

Abencérages, Les or **L'Étandard de Grenade** (*The Standard of Granada*)
Opera in three acts by Cherubini. 1st perf Paris, 6 April 1813; libr by Victor Joseph Étienne de Jouy, after Jean-Pierre-Claris de Florian's *Gonzalve de Cordove ou Grenade Reconquise*. Principal roles: Almansor (ten), Noraima (sop), Gonzalve (ten), Alémar (bass), Alamir (bass). It concerns the victories and final defeat in 1492 of Almansor, the last of the Moorish Abenceragi warriors in Spain. Cherubini's grandest opera, it was only moderately successful in its time and is nowadays only very rarely performed.

Abduction from the Seraglio, The
see ENTFÜHRUNG AUS DEM SERAIL, DIE

Abigaille
Soprano role in Verdi's *Nabucco*. She is Nabucco's elder but illegitimate daughter.

Ábrányi, Emil (1882–1970)
Hungarian composer and conductor. He wrote a number of operas, all of them now long forgotten, including *Monna Vanna* (Budapest, 2 Mar 1907; libr Emil Ábrányi, after Maurice Maeterlinck), *Paolo és Francesca* (Budapest, 13 Jan 1912; libr Ábrányi, after Dante's *La Divina Commedia*), *Don Kichóte* (Budapest, 30 Nov 1917; libr Ábrányi, after Miguel Cervantes's *Don Quixote*) and the unperformed *The Cantor of St Thomas Church* (*A Tamás Templon Karnagya*, 1947; libr György Láng), which is about J.S. Bach. One of the leading conductors of the early 20th century, he was musical director of the Cologne Opera (1904–06) and the Hanover State Opera (1907–11). His father **Emil** (1851–1920) was a librettist and translator, whose texts included several for his son.

Abreise, Die (*The Departure*)
Comic opera in one act by d'Albert. 1st

perf Frankfurt, 20 Oct 1898; libr by Ferdinand von Sporck, after August von Steinentsech's play. Principal roles: Luise (sop), Trott (ten), Gilfen (bar). D'Albert's only opera other than *Tiefland* to have survived, it is still occasionally performed in Germany.
Plot: Central Germany, late 18th century. Trott tries to persuade Gilfen to set out on a journey so that he can make advances to Gilfen's neglected wife Luise. However, it is Trott who is finally despatched, and Gilfen's jealousy reawakens his own love for his wife. [R]

Absalom and Etery (*Abesalom da Eteri*)
Opera in four acts by Paliashvili. 1st perf Tiflis, 21 Feb 1919; libr by P. Mirianashvili, after the traditional Georgian poem *Eteriani*. Principal roles: Etery (sop), Absalom (ten), Abio (bass), Natela (mezzo), Murman (bar), Marich (sop). Notable for its rich orchestration and for its superb choral scenes, it is arguably the finest opera by a Georgian composer, and incorporates traditional Georgian material. Unaccountably, it is virtually unknown in the West.
Plot: Legendary Georgia. King Abio's son Absalom weds the shepherdess Etery, who is desired by the vizier Murman. He gives her a poisoned necklace which destroys her beauty. She insists on leaving Absalom and turns to Murman. When her beauty returns, she rejects the pleas of Queen Natela that she return to Absalom as he has broken his vows of fidelity to her. Absalom's sister Marich succeeds in changing her mind, but soon after they are reunited Absalom dies and Etery stabs herself in grief. [R]

Abscheulicher!
Soprano aria for Leonore in Act I of Beethoven's *Fidelio*, in which she vents her fury at Don Pizarro's imprisonment of her husband.

Abu Hassan
Comic opera in one act by Weber (J 106). 1st perf Munich, 4 June 1811; libr by Franz Karl Hiemer, after Antoine Galland's *Le Dormeur Éveillé*, an addition to *The Thousand and One Nights*. Principal roles: Fatime (sop), Abu Hassan (ten), Omar (bass). The most successful of Weber's early SINGSPIELS, it is a delightful little piece which is still quite often performed.
Plot: Legendary Baghdad. The poet Abu Hassan and his wife Fatime each pretend that the other is dead, so as to collect the funeral money which will pay their debts. When the deception is revealed, their ruler, the Caliph, forgives their audacity, and their creditor Omar is disgraced for having tried to purchase Fatime's love. [R]

Ach, ich fühl's
Soprano aria for Pamina in Act II of Mozart's *Die Zauberflöte*, in which she grieves over Tamino's seeming indifference towards her.

Ach ich liebte
Soprano aria for Constanze in Act I of Mozart's *Die Entführung aus dem Serail*, in which she laments her separation from Belmonte.

Ach so fromm (often sung in Italian as 'M'apparì')
Tenor aria for Lionel in Act III of Flotow's *Martha*, in which he agonizes over his hopeless love for Lady Harriet. It was not in the original score, and Flotow inserted it from his earlier *L'Âme en Peine*.

Achilles
The Homeric Greek hero appears in many operas, including: **1** Tenor role in Tippett's *King Priam*. **2** Tenor role in Offenbach's *La Belle Hélène*. **3** Soprano trouser role in Händel's *Deidamia*. **4** Baritone role in Schoeck's *Penthesilea*. **5** Tenor role in Paer's *Achille*. **6** Tenor role in Manfroce's *Ecuba*. **7** A role in the many settings of Pietro Metastasio's OPERA SERIA text *Achille in Sciro*.

Acis and Galatea
Masque in two acts by Händel. 1st perf (privately) Cannons (Edgware), c 1718; 1st public perf London, 10 June 1732; libr by John Gay, Alexander Pope and John Hughes, after John Dryden's translation of Ovid's *Metamorphoses*. Version by Mozart 1st perf Vienna, Dec 1788. Principal roles: Galatea (sop), Acis (ten), Polyphemus (bass), Damon (ten). Always one of Händel's most popular stage works, still regularly performed, it is notable both for the skill with which Händel adapts his style to the requirements of the English

masque, and for its delightful sense of characterization, for example, the giant is represented by the smallest instrument in the orchestra.
Plot: Legendary Greece. Galatea laments the absence of her husband Acis. He returns followed by the giant Polyphemus, who also loves Galatea. Polyphemus crushes Acis under a rock, but Galatea uses her divine powers to transform him into a spring. [R original and Mozart versions]

Ackermann, Otto (1909–60)
Swiss conductor, particularly associated with the German repertory, especially Mozart and J. Strauss. He was musical director of the Cologne Opera (1953–58) and the Zürich Opernhaus (1958–60).

Ackté, Aïno (b Achté) (1876–1944)
Finnish soprano, particularly associated with Wagner and Strauss roles. She had a pure and radiant voice of considerable power, and a strong stage presence. She was director of the Finnish National Opera (1938–39), of which she had been a co-founder in 1911. She wrote the libretto for Merikanto's *Juha* as well as two volumes of autobiography, *The Book of My Recollections* (1925) and *My Life as an Artist* (1935). Her sister **Irma Tervani** (1887–1936) was a successful mezzo; their mother **Emmy Strömer–Achté** (1850–1924) was also a mezzo, and created the Chatelaine in Sibelius's *The Maiden in the Tower*.

Adalgisa
Soprano role in Bellini's *Norma*. She is Norma's confidante and rival for Pollione's love. The role is frequently sung by a mezzo.

Adam, Adolphe (1803–56)
French composer. His first stage work, *Pierre et Catherine* (Paris, 22 Jan 1829; libr Jules-Henri Vernoy de Saint-Georges), was followed by 23 other OPÉRA-COMIQUES notable for their grace and tunefulness. The most important include LE CHÂLET, LE POSTILLON DE LONGJUMEAU, by far his most successful and enduring work, *Lambert Simnel* (Paris, 14 Sept 1843; libr Eugène Scribe and Anne-Honoré Joseph de Mélesville), a completion of an unfinished work by Monpou, *Le Toréador* (Paris, 18 May 1849; libr Thomas Sauvage), *Giralda* (Paris, 20 July 1850; libr Scribe), *La Poupée de Nuremberg* (Paris, 21 Feb 1852; libr Adolphe de Leuven and Arthur de Beauplan, after E.T.A. Hoffmann's *Der Sandmann*), the successful SI J'ÉTAIS ROI, *Le Muletier de Tolède* (Paris, 16 Dec 1854; libr Louis François Clairville and Adolphe Philippe d'Ennery) and *Falstaff* (Paris, 18 Jan 1856; libr Saint-Georges and de Leuven, after Shakespeare's *The Merry Wives of Windsor*). His autobiography, *Souvenirs d'un Musicien*, was published in 1857.

Adam, Theo (b 1926)
German bass-baritone, particularly associated with Wagnerian roles, especially Wotan (*Das Rheingold*, *Die Walküre* and *Siegfried*) and Hans Sachs (*Die Meistersinger von Nürnberg*). An intelligent singing-actor with a powerful if not intrinsically beautiful voice, he also achieved success in contemporary operas, creating Prospero in Berio's *Un Rè in Ascolto* and the title-roles in Cerha's *Baal* and Dessau's *Einstein*. He enjoyed a remarkably long career, singing into his late 60s, and has also produced a number of operas.

Adamastor
Baritone aria for Nélusko in Act III of Meyerbeer's *L'Africaine*, sung in praise of the god of the sea.

Adami, Giuseppe (1878–1946)
Italian librettist and critic. He provided texts for Alfano (the unfinished *I Cavalieri e la Bella*), Puccini (*La Rondine*, *Il Tabarro* and *Turandot*), Vittadini (*Anima Allegra*, *Nazareth*, *La Sagredo* and *Fiametta e l'Avaro*) and Zandonai (*La Via della Finestra*). He also wrote a biography of Puccini, *Il Romanzo della Vita di Giacomo Puccini* (1935).

Adams, Donald (b 1928)
British bass, particularly associated with Sullivan and other BUFFO roles. He was for long a principal of the D'Oyly Carte Opera Company, becoming one of the best-loved Gilbert and Sullivan artists, and also founded the company Gilbert and Sullivan For All. Later, he enjoyed a second, highly successful career in opera. An outstanding

singing-actor, he has a good voice, superb diction and excellent comic timing. His wife **Muriel Harding** was a soprano noted for her Sullivan performances.

Adams, John (b 1947)
American composer, writing in minimalist style which he has developed into a readily accessible system of continuous modulation. His two operas are the highly successful NIXON IN CHINA and THE DEATH OF KLINGHOFFER.

Addio, addio speranza ad anima
Soprano/tenor duet for Gilda and the Duke of Mantua in Act I of Verdi's *Rigoletto*, in which they take leave of each other after their first meeting.

Addio del passato
Soprano aria for Violetta in Act III of Verdi's *La Traviata*, in which she bids farewell to her former happiness with Alfredo.

Addio fiorito asil
Tenor aria for Pinkerton in Act II of Puccini's *Madama Butterfly*, in which he takes leave of the home which he has shared with Cio-Cio-San.

Adelaide
see STATE OPERA OF SOUTH AUSTRALIA

Adelaide
Mezzo role in Strauss's *Arabella*. Count Waldner's wife, she is Arabella's and Zdenka's mother.

Adelaide di Borgogna (*Adelaide of Burgundy*)
Opera in two acts by Rossini. 1st perf Rome, 27 Dec 1817; libr by Giovanni Federico Schmidt. Principal roles: Adelaide (sop), Adelberto (ten), Ottone (mezzo), Berengario (bass). Unsuccessful at its appearance, it is hardly ever performed.
Plot: 10th-century Italy. Berengario has killed the king and is besieging his widow Adelaide, who rejects his proposal that she wed his son Adelberto. The German King Otto arrives to aid Adelaide, but is captured and imprisoned by Adelberto. He escapes and leads loyal forces in the defeat of Berengario. Otto is crowned King of Italy.

Adele
1 Soprano role in Rossini's *Le Comte Ory*. She is the countess who is the object of Ory's amorous intentions. **2** Soprano role in J. Strauss's *Die Fledermaus*. She is Rosalinde's parlourmaid. **3** Mezzo comprimario role in Bellini's *Il Pirata*. She is Imogene's companion.

Adelson e Salvini
Opera in three acts by Bellini. 1st perf Naples, 12 Jan 1825; libr by Andrea Leone Tottola, after François-Thomas de Baculard d'Arnaud's novella and Prospère Delamarre's play. Principal roles: Nelly (sop), Salvini (ten), Adelson (bar), Fanny (mezzo), Struley (bass), Bonifacio (bass). Bellini's first opera, stylistically heavily influenced by Rossini, it is hardly ever performed.
Plot: 17th-century Ireland. The painter Salvini loves Nelly, the fiancée of his patron Lord Adelson. He foils an attempt by her uncle Struley to abduct her, but hearing a shot believes that she has been killed. He is dissuaded from suicide when he discovers that she is still alive. Cured of his infatuation, he becomes engaged to his pupil Fanny, whilst Adelson marries Nelly.

Adieu Mignon
Tenor aria for Wilhelm in Act II of Thomas's *Mignon*, in which he takes leave of Mignon.

Adieu, notre petite table
Soprano aria for Manon in Act II of Massenet's *Manon*, in which she bids farewell to the room which she has shared with des Grieux.

Adina
Soprano role in Donizetti's *L'Elisir d'Amore*. She is a capricious landowner loved by Nemorino.

Adler, Kurt Herbert (1905–88)
Austrian conductor, resident in the USA from 1938. He had a wide-ranging repertory and was musical director of the San Francisco Opera Association (1953–81).

Admeto, Rè di Tessaglia (*Admetus, King of Thessaly*)
Opera in three acts by Händel. 1st perf

London, 31 Jan 1727; libr possibly by Nicola Francesco Haym, after Aurelio Aureli's *L'Antigone Delusa da Alceste.* Principal roles: Admeto (c-ten), Alceste (sop), Antigone (sop), Hercules (bass), Apollo (bass), Orindo (mezzo), Trasimede (c-ten). Telling much the same story as Gluck's *Alceste*, it is only infrequently performed. [R]

Admetus
The King of Thessaly and husband of Alkestis appears in a number of operas, including: **1** Tenor role in Gluck's and Lully's *Alceste.* **2** Counter-tenor role in Händel's *Admeto.*

Administrator
see panel below

Adolar
Tenor role in Weber's *Euryanthe.* Euryanthe's lover, he is the Count of Nevers.

Adriana Lecouvreur
Opera in four acts by Cilea. 1st perf Milan, 6 Nov 1902; libr by Arturo Colautti, after Eugène Scribe and Ernest Legouvé's *Adrienne Lecouvreur.* Principal roles: Adriana (sop), Maurizio (ten), Michonnet (bar), Prince and Princess de Bouillon (bass and mezzo), Abbé de Chazeuil (ten). Much the most successful and enduring of Cilea's operas, it is based on the life of an actress in the Comédie-Française, Adrienne Lecouvreur (1692–1730).
Plot: Paris, 1730. Adriana is in love with Maurizio, Count of Saxony, who for political reasons is having a liaison with the Princess de Bouillon. Adriana saves her rival from a compromising situation, but later insults her under cover of a recitation of Racine. The Princess sends Adriana a bunch of poisoned violets, which she smells. She dies in Maurizio's arms, watched by the stage manager Michonnet, who also loves her. [R]

Aegisthus
Tenor role in Strauss's *Elektra.* He is Clytemnestra's foppish paramour.

Aeneas
The Virgilian hero appears in several operas, including: **1** Tenor role in Berlioz's *Les Troyens.* **2** Baritone role in Purcell's *Dido and Aeneas.* **3** Tenor role in Cavalli's *Didone.* **4** Tenor role in Piccinni's *Didon.*

Aeschylus
see panel on page 6

Africaine, L' (*The African Girl*)
Opera in five acts by Meyerbeer. 1st perf Paris, 28 April 1865; libr by Eugène Scribe. Principal roles: Sélika (mezzo), Vasco da Gama (ten), Nélusko (bar), Inès (sop), Don Pédro (bass), Don Alvar (ten),

· *Administrator* ·

The administrator or general director of an opera house has responsibility both for the day-to-day functioning of the theatre and for long-term planning. The post is not the same as either artistic director or musical director, although they have occasionally been combined. The administrator is called *Intendant* in Germany and Austria, General Manager in the USA and *Sovrintendente* in Italy.

Below are listed the 16 administrators with entries in this dictionary. Their nationalities are given in brackets afterwards.

Arlen, Stephen (Br)
Barbaia, Domenico (It)
Baylis, Lilian (Br)
Bing, Sir Rudolf (Aus)
Carte, Richard d'Oyly (Br)
Carvalho, Léon (Fr)
Fox, Carol (US)
Gatti-Casazza, Giulio (It)
Gentele, Göran (Swe)
Harewood, Earl of (Br)
Harris, Sir Augustus (Br)
Liebermann, Rolf (Swit)
Mapleson, James (Br)
Morelli, Bartolomeo (It)
Tooley, Sir John (Br)
Webster, Sir David (Br)

· Aeschylus ·

The works of the Greek tragic playwright Aeschylus (525–*c* 456 BC), the earliest dramatist whose writing survives, have inspired some 30 operas. Below are listed, by play, those operas by composers with entries in this dictionary.

Agamemnon		
Brian	*Agamemnon*	1957
Hamilton	*Agamemnon*	1969
Eaton	*The Cry of Clytaemnestra*	1980
The Libation Bearers		
Milhaud	*Les Choëphores*	1919
Oresteian Trilogy		
Taneyev	*Oresteia*	1895
The Persians		
Prodromidès	*Les Perses*	1961
Prometheus		
Fauré	*Prométhée*	1900
Wagner-Régeny	*Prometheus*	1959
Hanuš	*The Torch of Prometheus*	1963
Orff	*Prometheus*	1968

High Priest of Brahma (b-bar), Grand Inquisitor (bass). Meyerbeer's last opera, produced posthumously, it is one of the longest operas ever written. It was enormously popular throughout the second half of the 19th century, but is nowadays only intermittently performed.
Plot: Late-15th-century Lisbon and Madagascar. Vasco da Gama returns from an expedition to Africa with two native captives, Nélusko and Sélika. He is accused of heresy and imprisoned with them. In his absence, his beloved Inès has been promised to Don Pédro. She and Sélika, who also loves Vasco, conspire for his release. Vasco returns to Africa with Sélika, but cannot forget Inès. Sélika releases him so that he can return to Inès and – despite Nélusko's offer of love – commits suicide under the poisonous Manchineel tree. [R Exc]

Agamemnon
The Homeric Greek king appears in several operas, including: **1** Baritone role in Gluck's *Iphigénie en Aulide*. **2** Bass-baritone role in Offenbach's *La Belle Hélène*. **3** Bass role in Taneyev's *Oresteia*.

Agathe
Soprano role in Weber's *Der Freischütz*. Cuno's daughter, she is in love with Max.

Agnes von Hohenstaufen
Opera in three acts by Spontini. 1st perf Berlin, 12 June 1829; libr by Ernst Raupach. Revised version 1st perf Berlin, 6 Dec 1837. Principal roles: Agnes (sop), Henry of Brunswick (ten), Henry VI (bass), Ermengard (sop), King of France (bar). Spontini's last opera, it was successful in its time but is nowadays only rarely performed.
Plot: Mainz, 1194. Agnes, daughter of Countess Ermengard, loves Henry of Brunswick, son of the rebel Duke of Saxony. The Emperor Henry VI and the King of France (disguised as the Duke of Burgundy) intrigue to prevent the lovers from marrying.

Agricola, Johann Friedrich (1720–74)
German composer, Graun's successor as court composer to Frederick the Great, Agricola wrote nine operas, both INTERMEZZI and OPERA SERIAS, all of which are now forgotten. The most successful was *Achille in Sciro* (Berlin, 16 Sept 1765;

libr Pietro Metastasio). His wife **Benedetta Molteni** (1722–80) was one of the leading sopranos of her age.

Agrippina
Opera in three acts by Händel. 1st perf Venice, 26 Dec 1709; libr by Cardinal Vincenzo Grimani, after Tacitus's *Annals*. Principal roles: Agrippina (sop), Poppea (sop), Ottone (mezzo), Nerone (c-ten), Pallante (bass), Narciso (c-ten), Claudio (bass). It is the earliest of Händel's operas still to be occasionally performed.
Plot: Rome, *c* AD 50. In the absence of her husband, the Emperor Claudius, Agrippina intrigues to ensure the succession of her son Nero. Following Claudius's unexpected return, she poisons his mind against Ottone, whom he has chosen as his successor. Exploiting the fact that both Claudius and Nero love her, Ottone's fiancée Poppea sets out to thwart Agrippina. Compromising both her admirers, she obtains Claudius's permission to wed Ottone, but he then renounces the succession for her sake. Agrippina extricates herself and sees Nero declared Claudius's heir. [R]

Ägyptische Helena, Die (*The Egyptian Helen*)
Opera in two acts by Strauss (Op 75). 1st perf Dresden, 6 June 1928; libr by Hugo von Hofmannsthal, after Euripides's *Helen in Egypt* and other classical legends. Revised version 1st perf Salzburg, 14 Aug 1933. Principal roles: Helena (sop), Menelaus (ten), Altair (bar), Aithra (sop), Da-Ud (ten). Despite the lush beauty of its score, it has never been one of Strauss's more popular operas and is only infrequently performed.
Plot: Legendary Egypt. Menelaus intends to kill his wife Helen because of the slaughter of the Trojan War, of which she was the cause. However, the sorceress Aithra persuades him that Helen was never in Troy and gives Helen a potion to forget past evils. They are sent to a land which knows nothing of the war, where the desert chieftain Altair and his son Da-Ud both fall in love with Helen. Menelaus kills Da-Ud. He and Helen take an antidote to the potion of forgetfulness and their life begins afresh after Aithra intervenes to thwart the vengeance of Altair. [R]

Ah chi mi dice mai
Soprano aria for Donna Elvira in Act I of Mozart's *Don Giovanni*, in which she laments her abandonment by her lover.

Ah! fors'è lui
Soprano aria for Violetta in Act I of Verdi's *La Traviata*, in which she wonders if she is falling genuinely in love. Its CABALETTA is the famous 'Sempre libera'.

Ah, fuyez douce image
Tenor aria for des Grieux in Act III of Massenet's *Manon*, in which he tells of his inability to exorcise the image of Manon from his mind.

Ah je ris
Soprano aria (the Jewel Song) for Marguerite in Act III of Gounod's *Faust*, in which she admires the jewels in Méphistophélès's casket.

Ah, la paterna mano
Tenor aria for Macduff in Act IV of Verdi's *Macbeth*, in which he laments the murder of his children.

Ahlersmeyer, Mathieu (1896–1979)
German baritone, particularly associated with the German repertory. One of the leading Germanic baritones of the inter-war and immediate post-war periods, he enjoyed a remarkably long career, singing into his mid-70s. An admired singing-actor, he created the Barber in *Die Schweigsame Frau*, the title-role in Einem's *Dantons Tod*, a role in Haas's *Die Hochzeit des Jobs* and Count Almaviva in Klebe's *Figaro lässt sich Scheiden*.

Ah mes amis
Tenor aria for Tonie in Act I of Donizetti's *La Fille du Régiment*, in which he announces his enlistment in the regiment. Its CABALETTA, 'Pour mon âme', contains nine high Cs, which, unlike most tenor high Cs, were written by the composer, not added later by the performer.

Ah! non credea mirarti
Soprano aria for Amina in Act II of Bellini's *La Sonnambula*. The sleep-walking scene, its CABALETTA, 'Ah! non giunge', is the final scene of the opera.

Ah que j'aime les militaires
Soprano aria for the Grand-Duchess in Act I of Offenbach's *La Grande-Duchesse de Gérolstein*, in which she tells of her attraction to men in uniform.

Ahronovich, Yuri (b 1932)
Russian conductor, particularly associated with the Russian and Scandinavian repertories. An exciting orchestral conductor, his operatic appearances have been infrequent. He left the then Soviet Union in 1972 and is now an Israeli citizen.

Ah! se tu dormi
Mezzo aria for Romeo in Act II of Vaccai's *Giulietta e Romeo*, sung on his finding Giulietta in the tomb. During the 19th century it was often inserted into the final scene of Bellini's *I Capuleti e i Montecchi*.

Ah sì, ben mio
Tenor aria for Manrico in Act III of Verdi's *Il Trovatore*, in which he consoles Leonora. Its warlike CABALETTA is the notorious 'Di quella pira'.

Aida
Opera in four acts by Verdi. 1st perf Cairo, 24 Dec 1871; libr by Antonio Ghislanzoni and Camille du Locle, after a synopsis by the Egyptologist Auguste Mariette Bey. Principal roles: Aida (sop), Radamès (ten), Amneris (mezzo), Amonasro (bar), Ramphis (bass), King of Egypt (bass), High Priestess (sop). Dealing with the conflict between love and patriotism, it was an instant success and remains one of the most enduringly popular of all operas. Marking the transition between Verdi's middle and late periods, it is notable for its orchestral and harmonic richness, for its magnificent choral scenes and for Verdi's psychological penetration in his depiction of the jealous Amneris. The opera was not, as is so often thought, commissioned to celebrate the opening of the Suez Canal. For the Milan premiere, Verdi wrote an overture which was cut before the first performance; it has been recorded but has never been performed in the theatre.
Plot: Legendary Egypt. Aida, an Ethiopian slave to Pharaoh's daughter Amneris is emotionally torn over her love for the general Radamès when he is named as commander of a campaign against Ethiopia. Amneris also loves Radamès, and tricks Aida into revealing her feelings. The victorious Radamès returns in triumph and is rewarded with the hand of Amneris. Disguised amongst the prisoners is Aida's father Amonasro, the Ethiopian king. He persuades his daughter to wheedle out of Radamès the route of the next army campaign. Radamès's inadvertent betrayal is overheard, and the priests, led by Ramphis, the high priest, condemn him to be buried alive. Aida joins him in the tomb. [R]

Aida trumpet
An instrument invented by Verdi for the Triumph Scene in *Aida*. It is much longer than a normal orchestral trumpet. The score of *Aida* requires six, three in A♭ and three in B.

Aiglon, L' (*The Eaglet*)
Opera in five acts by Honegger (who wrote the three inner acts) and Ibert (who wrote the two outer acts). 1st perf Monte Carlo, 11 March 1937; libr by Henri Cain, after Edmond Rostand's play. Principal roles: Aiglon (sop), Flambeau (bar), Metternich (bar), Thérèse (mezzo), Frédéric (ten), Marie–Louise (mezzo), Marmont (bass). Dealing with events in the life of Napoleon's son, the Duke of Reichstadt (1811–32), it is the finest of the three operas on which Honegger and Ibert collaborated. Reasonably successful at its appearance, it is nowadays hardly ever performed.
Plot: Schönbrunn and Wagram (Austria), 1831–2. Despite the efforts of Metternich, the heart of the young Duke (known as L'Aiglon) remains wedded to France. He shuns love and ignores the feelings of Thérèse, the companion of his mother Marie-Louise. He is persuaded to escape by the old Napoleonic soldier Flambeau, and the two abscond under the cover of a fancy-dress ball. On the field of Wagram, the two relive the glory of Napoleon's great victory. The police arrive and Flambeau kills himself. The Duke is taken back to Schönbrunn, where he dies of phtisis whilst listening to Thérèse singing of France.

Ai nostri monti
Mezzo/tenor duet for Azucena and Manrico in Act IV of Verdi's *Il Trovatore*, in which the imprisoned pair console one another with memories of their homeland.

Aio nell'Imbarazzo, L' (*The Embarrassed Tutor*)
Comic opera in two acts by Donizetti. 1st perf Rome, 4 Feb 1824; libr by Jacopo Ferretti, after Giovanni Giraud's play. Revised version *Don Gregorio*, 1st perf Naples, 11 June 1826. Principal roles: Gregorio (bass), Enrico (ten), Gilda (sop), Don Giulio (bar), Pippetto (ten), Leonarda (mezzo). An entertaining little piece in Rossinian style, it is the earliest of Donizetti's operas which is still occasionally performed.
Plot: 18th-century Italy. On the orders of their puritanical father Don Giulio, the tutor Don Gregorio has educated Enrico and Pippetto so strictly that they know nothing of the opposite sex. Pippetto falls for the only female he has ever seen, the senile housekeeper Leonarda. Enrico, meanwhile, has secretly married their neighbour Gilda, and has a son. Through Gilda's machinations, Giulio is led to bless the marriage and to admit the stupidity of his educational ideas. [R]

Air
The term has two meanings in opera: **1** The French term for aria. **2** A term used in ballad operas to indicate the source of a melody. For example, 'Since laws were made' in Act III of *The Beggar's Opera* carries the superscription 'Air: Green Sleeves'.

Aix-en-Provence Festival
An annual summer opera festival in Bouches-du-Rhône (France), which was founded in 1948 by Gabriel Dussurget and André Bigonnet. Performances are given at the open-air theatre (cap 1,639) in the Archbishop's palace, which was designed by A.M. Cassandre. The repertory is notable for its Mozart and Rossini productions. Musical directors have included Hans Rosbaud.

Akhnaten
Opera in three acts by Glass. 1st perf Stuttgart, 24 March 1984; libr by the composer, Robert Israel, Richard Riddell and Shalom Goldman. Principal roles: Akhnaten (c-ten), Tye (sop), Nefertiti (mezzo), Aye (bass), High Priest (ten), Horemhab (bar). The third of Glass's minimalist stage works, it concerns the 'heretic' Pharaoh Akhnaten (*d c* 1358 BC), sometimes regarded as the first monotheist. The text consists of Akkadian, ancient Egyptian and Hebrew. One of the most successful operas of the 1980s, it has been widely performed.
Plot: 18th-dynasty Egypt. Akhnaten abandons polygamy for the love of his beautiful wife Nefertiti, and builds a city in honour of his new god, the Aten. Failing to produce a male heir and oblivious to the sufferings of his people, he sees his family carried off and his temple to the Aten destroyed by the traditional priesthood led by Aye. Egypt's immemorial old order is restored. [R]

À la faveur
Soprano/mezzo/tenor trio for Countess Adèle, Isolier and Ory in Act II of Rossini's *Le Comte Ory*, in which Ory's wooing of the Countess is cynically observed by his page. One of the most beautiful individual numbers Rossini ever wrote.

Albanese, Licia (b 1913)
Italian soprano, particularly associated with Verdi and Puccini roles, especially Cio-Cio-San (*Madama Butterfly*). She was an intense singer who used her beautiful voice with a fine technique.

Albani, Dame Emma (b Marie Louise Lajeunesse) (1847–1930)
Canadian soprano, particularly associated with Wagnerian roles. One of the leading sopranos of the late 19th century, she was a rich-voiced singer of great personal beauty. Her fine technique enabled her to sing roles as diverse as Lucia (in Donizetti's *Lucia di Lammermoor*) and Isolde (in Wagner's *Tristan and Isolde*). Her autobiography, *Forty Years of Song*, was published in 1911.

Albanian opera composers
These include Tish Daija (*b* 1926), Pjeter Gaci (*b* 1939), Martin Gjoka (1890–1940), Tonin Harapi (*b* 1928), Prenkë Jakova (1917–69), whose *Mrika* (1958)

was the first completed Albanian opera, Kristo Kono (1907–91), Avni Mula (*b* 1928), Vangjo Nova (*b* 1927) and Nikolla Zoraqi (*b* 1929).

Albéniz, Isaac (1860–1909)
Spanish composer. He wrote several stage works, nearly all of them now forgotten. They include *The Magic Opal* (London, 19 Jan 1893; libr Arthur Law), the ZARZUELA *San Antonio de Flórida* (Madrid, 26 Oct 1894; libr Eusebio Sierra), *Enrico Clifford* (Barcelona, 8 May 1895; libr Francis Burdett Money-Coutts), PEPITA JIMÉNEZ, his most successful work, and the unperformed *Merlin* (1906; libr Money-Coutts, after Thomas Mallory's *Morte d'Arthur*), part of a projected Arthurian trilogy.

Alberich
Baritone role in Wagner's *Das Rheingold*, *Siegfried* and *Götterdämmerung*. The leader of the Nibelung dwarfs, he steals the gold from the Rhine and fashions the Ring after renouncing love.

Albert
Baritone role in Massenet's *Werther*. He is Charlotte's fiancé.

Albert, Eugen d' (b Francis Charles) (1864–1932)
Scottish-born German composer and pianist. His first opera, *Der Rubin* (Karlsruhe, 12 Oct 1893; libr composer, after Christian Friedrich Hebbel), was followed by 19 others, of which only the comedy DIE ABREISE and the VERISMO-style TIEFLAND are still remembered. Of the rest, *Flauto Solo* (Prague, 12 Nov 1905; libr Ernst von Wolzogen), which is about Frederick the Great, and DIE TOTEN AUGEN enjoyed brief successes.

Albert Herring
Comic opera in three acts by Britten (Op 39). 1st perf Glyndebourne, 20 June 1947; libr by Eric Crozier, after Guy de Maupassant's *Le Rosier de Madame Husson*. Principal roles: Albert (ten), Lady Billows (sop), Sid (bar), Nancy (mezzo), Florence Pike (mezzo), Superintendent Budd (bass), Mr Gedge (bar), Miss Wordsworth (sop), Mr Upfold (ten), Mrs Herring (mezzo), Emmie (sop). One of Britten's most popular operas, it contains a magnificent gallery of local characters from the composer's native Suffolk.
Plot: Loxford (East Suffolk), 1900. Lady Billows and a committee of local notables are unable to find a suitably chaste girl to crown as Queen of the May, so they decide upon a May King, the virtuous Albert. At his coronation, Sid and his girlfriend Nancy spike Albert's lemonade. Thus emboldened, Albert sets out with his prize money to sample the delights of alcohol and female companionship, blaming his mother for a repressive upbringing. The dignitories are scandalized when he rolls up distinctly the worse for wear, but his friends cheer his emancipation from Mrs Herring's apron strings. [R]

Albinoni, Tomaso (1671–1750)
Italian composer. He wrote 55 operas, including *Astarto* (Venice 1708; libr Apostolo Zeno and Pietro Pariati) and *Il Nascimento dell'Aurora* (*c* 1716) [R], but only the comic intermezzo PIMPINONE is in any way still remembered.

Alboni, Marietta (b Maria Anna Marizia) (1823–94)
Italian contralto, particularly associated with the French and Italian repertories. One of the greatest contraltos in history, she possessed a range so wide that she was able to sing Don Carlo in the first London performance of *Ernani* after baritones had refused to sing it. She created the title-role in Auber's *Zerline*.

Albrecht, Gerd (b 1935)
German conductor, particularly associated with Wagner, Strauss and Zemlinsky operas and with lesser-known 19th-century works. He was musical director of the Lübeck Opera (1963–6), the Kassel Staatstheater (1966–72), the Hamburg State Opera (1988–94) and the Darmstadt Opera (1995–). He conducted the first performances of Fortner's *Elisabeth Tudor* and Reimann's *Lear* and *Troades* (of which he was co-author of the libretto).

Alceste or **Le Triomphe d'Alcide** (*The Triumph of Hercules*)
Opera in prologue and five acts by Lully. 1st perf Paris, 10 Jan 1674; libr by

Philippe Quinault, after Euripides's *Alkestis*. Principal roles: Alceste (sop), Admète (ten), Alcide (bar), Céphise (sop), Apollo (ten), Charon (bass). Often regarded as Lully's finest opera, and described by the 17th-century French writer Madame de Sévigné as a 'prodigy of beauty', it has been his most regularly performed work in recent years.
Plot: Legendary Thessaly. It is decreed that King Admetus must die unless someone else will give up his life in his place. His devoted wife Alceste volunteers and dies in his stead. She is brought back from Hades by Alcide (Hercules) and Apollo restores her to life to live with Admetus. [R]

Alceste
Opera in three acts by Gluck. 1st perf Vienna, 26 Dec 1767; libr by Ranieri de' Calzabigi, after Philippe Quinault's libretto for Lully, itself based on Euripides's *Alkestis*. Revised version 1st perf Paris, 23 April 1776; libr revised by Bailli Leblanc du Roullet. Principal roles: Alceste (sop), Admète (ten), High Priest (bar), Oracle (bass), Hercule (bar), Apollo (bar), Évandre (ten). One of Gluck's greatest works, the famous preface to the score – one of the most important documents in the history of opera – contains Gluck's insistence that opera should be serious music-drama and not the elaborate and artificial concert-in-costume which it had become. The most important of Gluck's reform operas and a work which effectively announces opera's second birth, *Alceste* is still regularly performed and is a seminal work in the history of music.
Plot: Legendary Thessaly. The Oracle decrees that the ailing King Admetus must die unless someone will take his place, and his wife Alceste offers herself. When Admetus recovers, he does not wish to live without Alceste and joins her at the entrance to Hades. Determined to save his king, Hercules arrives to defy the rulers of Hades. Apollo raises Hercules to godhead for his actions and decrees that Alceste and Admetus shall live to serve as an example of perfect conjugal love. [R]

Alcina
Opera in three acts by Händel. 1st perf London, 16 April 1735; libr by Antonio Marchi, after Lodovico Ariosto's *Orlando Furioso*. Principal roles: Alcina (sop), Ruggiero (c-ten), Bradamante (mezzo), Morgana (sop), Oronte (ten), Melisso (bass). Händel's last fully successful Italian opera for London, it has in recent years been one of his most frequently performed works.
Plot: The enchantress Alcina rules over a magic island, where she lives with her sister Morgana and her general Oronte. She has transformed the knights who have courted her into inhuman creatures, but has allowed her current suitor Ruggiero to remain a man. Infatuated with Alcina, Ruggiero has forgotten his fiancée Bradamante who, disguised as her own brother Ricciardo, arrives in search of him, after being shipwrecked on the island with her guardian Melisso. There follows a series of complications and misunderstandings: Morgana falls for 'Ricciardo', rejecting Oronte; an infuriated Oronte tells the besotted Ruggiero that Alcina has fallen for 'Ricciardo'; and Bradamante and Melisso try in vain to convince Ruggiero that his supposed rival is in reality his own fiancée. Eventually, all is resolved: Alcina's powers are destroyed, the captured knights are returned to their proper form, and Ruggiero returns to Bradamante. [R]

Alcindoro
Bass comprimario role in Puccini's *La Bohème*. He is Musetta's elderly admirer.

Alda, Frances (b Davies) (1883–1952)
New Zealand soprano, renowned for her explosive temper and for her involvement in several lawsuits. Particularly associated with the French and Italian repertories, she also created Roxane in Damrosch's *Cyrano de Bergerac* and the title-roles in Herbert's *Madeleine* and Hadley's *Cleopatra's Night*. Married for a time to the administrator GIULIO GATTI-CASAZZA, her autobiography, *Men, Women and Tenors*, was published in 1937.

Aldeburgh Festival
An annual British summer music festival in Suffolk, founded in 1948 by Britten, Eric Crozier and Peter Pears. It is largely devoted to the music of Britten and other English composers. Since 1970, opera has been given at the Maltings (cap 840) in

nearby Snape, redesigned by Ove Arup after the original building burnt down in 1969 after the opening night of the festival. Artistic directors have included Britten, Steuart Bedford, Mstislav Rostropovich and Oliver Knussen.

Al dolce guidami
Soprano aria (the Mad Scene) for Anna in Act II of Donizetti's *Anna Bolena*. The melody is derived from 'Home, sweet home' from Bishop's *Clari*, and Bishop unsuccessfully brought an action against Donizetti for 'piracy and breach of copyright'. Its CABALETTA, 'Coppia iniqua', is the final scene of the opera.

Aleko
Opera in one act by Rachmaninov. 1st perf Moscow, 27 April 1893; libr by Vladimir Nemirovich-Danchenko, after Alexander Pushkin's *The Gypsies*. Principal roles: Aleko (bass), Zemfira (sop), Young Gypsy (ten), Gypsy Chief (bass). Rachmaninov's first opera, written as a student graduation exercise, it is seldom performed outside Russia.
Plot: 19th-century Russia. Aleko gives up his quiet life to join a band of gypsies. When his lover Zemfira grows bored with him and plans to run off with one of the other gypsies, Aleko kills her and is abandoned by the others. [R]

Aler, John (b 1949)
American tenor, particularly associated with Italian BEL CANTO roles and with the 18th- and 19th-century French repertories. His voice, if not over-large, is agile and pleasing, and is used with style, taste and an assured technique. He has a good stage presence.

Alerta! Alerta!
Bass aria for Ferrando in Act I of Verdi's *Il Trovatore*, in which he tells how Conte di Luna's baby brother was killed by an old gypsy. It is one of the longest bass arias ever written.

Alessandro (*Alexander*)
Opera in three acts by Händel. 1st perf London, 5 May 1726; libr by Paolo Antonio Rolli, after Ortensio Mauro's libretto for Steffani's *La Superbia d'Alessandro*. Principal roles: Alessandro (c-ten), Rossane (sop), Lisaura (sop), Clito (bass), Leonato (ten), Tassile (c-ten). Never one of Händel's more popular operas, it is only infrequently performed.
Plot: Oxidraca (India), late 3rd century BC. The Scythian princess Lisaura and the Persian princess Roxana are both in love with Alexander the Great. Lisaura is loved by the Indian King Taxiles. Alexander, unable to chose between the princesses, grows ever more arrogant, allowing himself to be worshipped as divine, and General Leonatus plans to depose him. However, Alexander escapes unhurt from an assassination attempt. He persuades Lisaura to transfer her love to Taxiles, thereby winning the latter's support, with the aid of which he defeats Leonatus's forces. The conspirators plead for mercy, which Alexander magnanimously grants. [R]

Alessandro Stradella
Opera in three acts by Flotow. 1st perf Hamburg, 30 Dec 1844; libr by Friedrich Wilhelm Riese, after P.A.A. Pittaud de Forges and Paul Duport's *Stradella*. Principal roles: Stradella (sop), Leonore (sop), Bassi (bass), Malvolio (bass), Barbarino (ten). Dealing with supposed events in the colourful life of the composer STRADELLA, it is Flotow's only opera apart from *Martha* still to be in any way remembered, and that mainly for the tenor's prayer 'Jungfrau Maria'.
Plot: Venice and Rome, *c* 1670. Leonore, the ward of Bassi, is carried off by Stradella during a Venetian carnival and taken to Rome. They are pursued by Bassi's hired assassins Malvolio and Barbarino, but the composer wins them over with his musical genius, later having the same effect on Bassi.

Alexander the Great
King Alexander of Macedon (356–23 BC) appears in a number of operas, including: **1** Tenor role in Mozart's *Il Rè Pastore*. **2** Counter-tenor role in Händel's *Alessandro*. **3** A role in the many settings of Pietro Metastasio's OPERA SERIA text *Alessandro nell'Indie*. **4** Counter-tenor role in Hasse's *Cleofide*. **5** Tenor role in Händel's *Poro*.

Alexei
1 Tenor role in Prokofiev's *The Gambler*.

He is tutor to the General's children. **2** Baritone role in Prokofiev's *The Story of a Real Man*. He is an aviator.

Alfano, Franco (1876–1954)
Italian composer. He wrote 11 operas, firstly in VERISMO and later in romantic style. Some are still occasionally performed in Italy, but are virtually unknown elsewhere. His operas are the unperformed *Miranda* (1896; libr composer, after A. Fogazzaro), *La Fonte di Enschir* (Breslau, 8 Nov 1898; libr Luigi Illica), the successful RISURREZIONE, *Il Principe Zilah* (Genoa, 3 Feb 1909; libr Illica, after Jules Clarétie), the unfinished *I Cavalieri e la Bella* (1910; libr Giuseppe Adami and T. Monicelli), *L'Ombra di Don Giovanni* (Milan, 2 Apr 1914; libr Ettore Moschino, after Prosper Mérimée's *Les Âmes du Purgatoire*; revised version *Don Juan de Mañara*, (Florence, 28 May 1941), the impressive SAKÙNTALA, *Madonna Imperia* (Turin, 5 May 1927; libr Arturo Rossato, after Anne-Honoré de Balzac's *Contes Drôlatiques*), *L'Ultimo Lord* (Naples, 19 Apr 1930; libr Rossato and Ugo Falena), CYRANO DE BERGERAC, possibly his finest work, and *Il Dottor Antonio* (Rome, 30 Apr 1949; libr Mario Ghisalberti, after Giovanni Ruffini). Outside Italy, Alfano is best known for having completed Puccini's *Turandot*.

Alfio
Baritone role in Mascagni's *Cavalleria Rusticana*. A carter, he is Lola's husband.

Alfonso
1 Baritone role in Mozart's *Così fan Tutte*. He is a cynical bachelor. **2** Bass role in Donizetti's *Lucrezia Borgia*. Lucrezia's husband, he is Alfonso d'Este (1476–1534), Duke of Ferrara. **3** Baritone role in Donizetti's *La Favorite*. He is King Alfonso IX of Castile. **4** Tenor role in Hérold's *Zampa*. He is Camilla's fiancé. **5** Tenor role in Korngold's *Violanta*. He is the seducer of Violanta's sister. **6** Baritone role in Donizetti's *Torquato Tasso*. He is the Duke of Ferrara. **7** Tenor role in Schubert's *Alfonso und Estrella*. He is Troila's son. **8** Tenor role in Auber's *La Muette de Portici*. He is the viceroy of Naples.

Alfonso und Estrella
Opera in three acts by Schubert (D 732). 1st perf Weimar, 24 June 1854 (composed 1822); libr by Franz von Schober. Principal roles: Estrella (sop), Alfonso (ten), Troila (bar), Mauregato (bar), Adolfo (b-bar). It is Schubert's only THROUGH-COMPOSED opera, containing neither dialogue nor SECCO rectitative. Despite its weak libretto, it is arguably Schubert's finest and most important opera, containing some of his greatest music. Quite unaccountably, it is almost never performed.
Plot: Legendary Asturia. Troila, King of León, his throne usurped by Mauregato, lives with his son Alfonso in an idyllic valley filled with wisdom and kindness. Alfonso meets and falls in love with Mauregato's daughter Estrella. Her rejected suitor Adolfo attempts to overthrow Mauregato, but is defeated by Alfonso. Troila and Mauregato are reconciled in the face of a common enemy, and Alfonso weds Estrella. [R]

Alfred
1 Tenor role in J. Strauss's *Die Fledermaus*. He is an Italian tenor in love with Rosalinde. **2** Tenor role in Liebermann's *Leonore 40/45*. He is a German soldier. **3** Baritone role in Einem's *Der Besuch der Alten Dame*. He is Claire's former lover. **4** Baritone role in Offenbach's *La Vie Parisienne*. He is the head waiter.

Alfredo
Tenor role in Verdi's *La Traviata*. Giorgio Germont's son, he is Violetta's lover.

Ali
Bass role in Rossini's *L'Italiana in Algieri*. He is captain of the Algerian corsairs.

Ali Baba or **Les Quarante Voleurs** (*The Forty Thieves*)
Comic opera in prologue and four acts by Cherubini. 1st perf Paris, 22 July 1833; libr by Eugène Scribe and Anne-Honoré Joseph de Mélesville, after *The Arabian Nights*. Principal roles: Ali Baba (bar), Delia (sop), Nadir (ten), Aboul Hassan (bass), Morgiane (mezzo). Cherubini's last opera, it is a revision of his unperformed *Koukourgi* (1793). Successful at its appearance, it is nowadays only very rarely performed.
Plot: Legendary Persia. Ali Baba's daughter

Delia loves Nadir, but for financial reasons her father has promised her to Aboul Hassan. Nadir outbids Hassan, who in fury threatens to expose Ali's coffee-smuggling operations. Nadir buys off Hassan, but news arrives of Delia's abduction by the Forty Thieves. Nadir has given Ali the password to their cave, where he is recognized and held to ransom. After much intrigue, Ali and Delia are rescued and the lovers are united.

Alice
1 Soprano role in Verdi's *Falstaff*. Ford's wife, she is Nannetta's mother. **2** Soprano role in Meyerbeer's *Robert le Diable*. She is Bertram's sister. **3** Mezzo role in Goehr's *Arden Must Die*. She is Arden's wife. **4** Soprano COMPRIMARIO role in Rossini's *Le Comte Ory*. She is a peasant girl.

Alidoro
Bass role in Rossini's *La Cenerentola*. A philosopher and tutor to Don Ramiro, he takes the place of the traditional fairy godmother.

Alkmene
Opera in three acts by Klebe. 1st perf Berlin, 25 Sept 1961; libr by the composer after Heinrich Wilhelm von Kleist's play. Principal roles: Alkmene (sop), Jupiter (bass), Amphitryon (ten), Cleanthis (sop), Sosias (bar), Mercury (bass). Klebe's most successful opera, it tells how Jupiter assumes the form of the Theban general Amphitryon in order to pursue his conquest of Alkmene.

Allan, Richard Van (b Alan Jones) (b 1935)
British bass, particularly associated with Verdi, Britten and Mozart roles, especially Leporello (*Don Giovanni*) and Don Alfonso (*Così fan Tutte*). One of the finest contemporary British singing-actors, with a repertory of over 120 roles ranging from the title-role in *Boris Godunov* to Pooh-Bah in *The Mikado*, he is equally at home in serious or comic roles. He created Col Jowler in Maw's *The Rising of the Moon*, the Marquis in Osborne's *Terrible Mouth*, the Abbot in Harvey's *Inquest of Love* and Tiresias in Buller's *The Bacchae*. Director of the National Opera Studio (1986–).

Alla vita
Baritone aria for Ankerström in Act I of Verdi's *Un Ballo in Maschera*, in which he urges Gustavus to preserve his life for the good of his country.

Allen, Thomas (b 1944)
British baritone, particularly associated with Mozart roles and with the title-roles in *Billy Budd* and *Eugene Onegin* and Pelléas in *Pelléas et Mélisande*. Possessing a beautiful voice and excellent diction, he is an artist of outstanding intelligence and musicianship and is one of the finest British singing-actors of the post-war era, especially effective in comedy. He created Valerio in Musgrave's *The Voice of Ariadne*.

All'idea
Tenor/baritone duet for Count Almaviva and Figaro in Act I of Rossini's *Il Barbiere di Siviglia*, in which Figaro tells the Count how to gain access to Bartolo's house.

Allmächt'ger Vater
Tenor aria for Rienzi in Act V of Wagner's *Rienzi*. Rienzi's prayer.

Almaviva, Count
The amorous nobleman of Beaumarchais's plays appears as: **1** Tenor role in Rossini's and Paisiello's *Il Barbiere di Siviglia*. **2** Baritone role in Mozart's *Le Nozze di Figaro*. **3** Baritone role in Klebe's *Figaro lässt sich Scheiden*. **4** Tenor role in Corigliano's *The Ghosts of Versailles*.

Almaviva, Countess
Soprano role in Mozart's *Le Nozze di Figaro*. She is Dr Bartolo's former ward.

Almeida, António de (c 1702–55)
Portuguese composer. He wrote many operas, now largely forgotten, including *La Pazienza di Socrate* (Lisbon 1733; libr Nicolò Minato), *La Spinalba* (Lisbon 1739) an *L'Ippolito* (Lisbon, 4 Dec 1752; libr A. Tedeschi).

Almira
Opera in three acts by Händel. 1st perf Hamburg, 8 Jan 1705; libr by Friedrich Christian Feustking, after Giulio Pancieri's *L'Almira*. Principal roles: Almira (sop), Fernando (ten), Osman (ten), Bellante (sop), Tabarco (ten), Raymondo (bass),

Consalvo (bass). Händel's first opera, nowadays virtually forgotten, it includes 15 arias in Italian and a further 41 in German.
Plot: Medieval Valladolid. On coming of age, Almira is crowned Queen of Castile by her guardian Consalvo, whose son Osman she is under obligation to marry. Osman abandons his former love Edilia to gain the throne. Almira, however, is in love with her secretary, the orphan Fernando, who has been brought up by Consalvo. The situation is complicated by the appearance of Raymondo, King of Mauritania, as a suitor for Almira, and by the activities of Fernando's servant Tabarco. Eventually, Fernando is revealed as Consalvo's youngest son, long believed dead, and is united with Almira. At the same time, Raymondo marries Edilia and Osman weds the princess Bellante.

Alpaerts, Flor (1876–1954)
Belgian composer and conductor. He wrote one opera, *Shylock* (Antwerp, 22 Dec 1913; libr after Shakespeare's *The Merchant of Venice*). He was director of the Antwerp Conservatory (1933–41).

Alt (German for 'high')
The German term for the contralto voice.

Alte Stürme, Der
Mezzo/baritone scene for Fricka and Wotan in Act II of Wagner's *Die Walküre*, in which they debate the morality of the love of Siegmund and Sieglinde.

Altistin
The German term for a contralto singer.

Alto (Italian for 'high')
The term is applied to two voice types: **1** Female: a contralto or low mezzo. **2** Male: a bass or baritone singing falsetto. The term is also often used in reference to a modern counter-tenor, although this is not strictly correct.

Altoum
Tenor COMPRIMARIO role in Puccini's *Turandot* and bass role in Busoni's version. He is the aged Emperor of China.

Altra notte, L'
Soprano aria for Margherita in Act III of Boito's *Mefistofele*, in which she tells how she drowned her child.

Alva, Luigi (b Luis) (b 1927)
Peruvian tenor, particularly associated with Mozart, lighter Donizetti and Rossini roles, especially Count Almaviva (*Il Barbiere di Siviglia*). One of the leading TENORE DI GRAZIAS of the post-war era, with a fine technique and excellent diction, he was also an accomplished comic actor. He created Lomov in Chailly's *Una Domanda di Matrimonio* and a role in R. Malipiero's *La Donna è Mobile*. In 1981 he founded Peru's opera company, Fundación para Arte Lirica, of which he is producer and artistic director.

Alvaro, Don
1 Tenor role in Verdi's *La Forza del Destino*. A Peruvian with Inca blood, he is Leonora's lover. **2** Baritone role in Rossini's *Il Viaggio a Reims*. He is a Spanish admiral. **3** Tenor role in Gomes's *Il Guarany*. He is a hunter in love with Cecilia. **4** Tenor role in Spontini's *Fernand Cortez*. He is Cortez's brother. **5** Baritone role in Wolf-Ferrari's *La Vedova Scaltra*. He is Rosaura's Spanish suitor.

Alvise
Bass role in Ponchielli's *La Gioconda*. He is a nobleman married to Laura.

Alwa
Tenor role in Berg's *Lulu*. Dr Schön's son, he is one of Lulu's lovers.

Alwyn, William (1905–85)
British composer and conductor. His four operas are *The Fairy Fiddler* (1917), *Farewell Companions* (BBC Radio, 1955), *The Libertine* (1971; libr after James Elroy Flecker) and MISS JULIE, his finest work.

Alyabyev, Alexander (1787–1851)
Russian composer. His study of folk music and his knowledge of Caucasian and Oriental subjects (mostly acquired during a period of political exile) helped to shape the development of Russian opera, of which he was possibly the most important composer before Glinka. His operas, nowadays all but forgotten, include the comedy *The Moonlit Night* (*Lunnaya Noch*, St Petersberg, 7 June 1823; libr P.A.

Mukhanov and P.N. Arapov), *The Tempest* (*Burya*, 1835; libr after Shakespeare), *The Enchanted Night* (*Volshebnaya Noch*, 1839; libr Alexander Veltman, after Shakespeare's *A Midsummer Night's Dream*), *The Fisherman and the Water-Nymph* (*Rybak i Rusalka*, Moscow 1865, composed 1843; libr Veltman, after Alexander Pushkin's *Rusalka*) and *Ammalet-Bek* (1847; libr Veltman, after Bestuzhev-Marlinsky).

Alzira
Opera in prologue and two acts by Verdi. 1st perf Naples, 12 Aug 1845; libr by Salvatore Cammarano, after Voltaire's *Alzire ou Les Américains*. Principal roles: Alzira (sop), Zamoro (ten), Gusmano (bar), Ataliba (bass). Possibly Verdi's least successful opera (he himself later described it as '*brutta*'), it is only rarely performed.
Plot: Mid-16th-century Peru. The Inca chief Zamoro returns to his tribe after being tortured by the Christians. He discovers that his beloved Alzira, daughter of the tribal leader Ataliba, has been abducted by the Christian governor Gusmano, who attempts to arrange peace with the Incas whilst keeping Alzira for himself. Zamoro is recaptured, and to gain his release Alzira agrees to marry Gusmano. Zamoro appears in disguise at the wedding and kills Gusmano. [R]

Amadigi di Gaula (*Amadis of Gaul*)
Opera in three acts by Händel. 1st perf London, 25 May 1715; libr by Nicola Francesco Haym, after Antoine Houdart de la Motte's libretto for Destouches's *Amadis de Grèce*. Principal roles: Amadigi (mezzo), Oriana (sop), Melissa (sop), Dardano (mezzo). Never one of Händel's more successful operas, it is only very rarely performed.
Plot: Amadigi and Dardano, Prince of Thrace, are attempting to flee the enchanted realm of the sorceress Melissa. Dardano learns that Amadigi loves Princess Oriana, who he also loves. Amadigi rejects Melissa's love, and he and Dardano undergo a series of ordeals to rescue Oriana, imprisoned by Melissa. Amadigi and Oriana are united, and a jealous Dardano is killed fighting Amadigi. Again rejected by Amadigi, Melissa vows vengeance. She summons up the ghost of Dardano, but he announces that the gods have decreed that her powers are ended. Melissa stabs herself and Amadigi and Oriana swear eternal love. [R]

Amadis
Opera in prologue and five acts by Lully. 1st perf Paris, 18 Jan 1684; libr by Philippe Quinault, after García Rodríguez de Montalvo's *Amadís de Gaula*. Principal roles: Amadis (ten), Oriane (sop), Florestan (bar), Corisande (sop), Arcabonne (sop), Arcalaus (bass). It is historically important, being the first French opera to be based on a subject other than classical mythology. It is hardly ever performed.
Plot: Medieval Britain. Amadis falls in love with Princess Oriane and embarks upon his chivalric adventures to prove himself worthy of her hand. He accomplishes many heroic deeds, including the rescue of Oriane and her father and also that of his parents and brother, who he does not recognize, having not seen them since they set him adrift on the sea in infancy because of his illegitimacy. After many victories, Amadis receives his knighthood and is united with Oriane.

Amahl and the Night Visitors
Opera in one act by Menotti. 1st perf NBC TV, 24 Dec 1951; 1st stage perf Indiana 21 Feb 1952; libr by the composer, inspired by Hieronymus Bosch's painting *The Adoration of the Magi*. Principal roles: Amahl (treble), Mother (sop), Melchior (bar), Kaspar (ten), Balthazar (bass). The first opera written specifically for television, it has always been one of Menotti's most popular works and is regularly performed.
Plot: The crippled boy Amahl lives in poverty with his mother. They are visited by the Magi, Kaspar, Melchior and Balthazar, on their way to see the infant Jesus. During the night, the mother succumbs to temptation and steals some of their gold. She is caught, but explains that the money is for her boy. The Magi tell her to keep it, since Jesus will build his kingdom on love. Amahl offers his crutch as a gift to the child, and discovers that he can walk unaided. The mother allows him to accompany the Magi on their journey. [R]

Amalia
Soprano role in Verdi's *I Masnadieri*. She is Carlo Moor's beloved.

Amara, Lucine (b Armaganian) (b 1927)
American soprano, particularly associated with the Italian repertory. A versatile singer with a fine voice, she was largely based at the Metropolitan Opera, New York.

Amato, Pasquale (1878–1942)
Italian baritone, particularly associated with the Italian repertory. Possessing a rich and vibrant voice and exemplary diction, he created Jack Rance in *La Fanciulla del West*, Napoleon in Giordano's *Madame Sans-Gêne*, the title-role in Damrosch's *Cyrano de Bergerac* and Bardo in Cilea's *Gloria*.

Ambo nati
Baritone aria for Antonio in Act I of Donizetti's *Linda di Chamounix*, in which he expresses his nostalgia for his birthplace.

Amelia
Soprano role in: **1** Verdi's *Un Ballo in Maschera*. Ankerström's wife, she is loved by Gustavus. **2** Verdi's *Simon Boccanegra*. In reality Boccanegra's daughter Maria, she has been brought up as Amelia Grimaldi. **3** Donizetti's *Il Castello di Kenilworth*. She is the historical Amy Robsart (*d* 1560). **4** Menotti's *Amelia al Ballo*.

Amelia al Ballo (*Amelia Goes to the Ball*)
Comic opera in one act by Menotti. 1st perf Philadelphia, 1 April 1937; libr by the composer. Principal roles: Amelia (sop), Husband (bar), Lover (ten), Police Chief (bass). Menotti's first opera, it is a satire on social priorities.
Plot: Amelia, about to leave to attend a ball, is detained by a showdown between her husband and her lover. She strikes her husband, leaving him unconscious, has the lover arrested, and proceeds to the ball with the police chief. [R]

Ameling, Elly (b Elisabeth) (b 1938)
Dutch soprano. Best known as one of the finest contemporary lieder singers, her operatic appearances have sadly been very rare, largely restricted to an occasional Mozart performance. She created a role in Martin's *Le Mystère de la Nativité*.

America
see UNITED STATES OF AMERICA

American opera composers
see ADAMS; ANTHEIL; ARGENTO; BARBER; BEESON; BERNSTEIN; BLITZSTEIN; CONVERSE; COPLAND; CORIGLIANO; DAMROSCH; DAVIS; EATON; FLOYD; FOSS; FRIML; GERSHWIN; GIANNINI; GLASS; GRUENBERG; HADLEY; HANSON; HERBERT; HERRMANN; JOPLIN; KAY; KURKA; LEVY; MENOTTI; MOORE; NABAKOV; PASATIERI; ROMBERG; SCHULLER; SCHUMAN; SESSIONS; SOUSA; STILL; TAYLOR; THOMSON; WARD; WEISGALL

Other national opera composers include Samuel Adler (*b* 1928), William Bergsma (*b* 1921), William Bolcom (*b* 1938), Paul Bowles (*b* 1910), George Bristow (1825–98), Charles Cadman (1881–1946), Benjamin Carr (1768–1831), whose *The Archers* (New York, 18 Apr 1796; libr William Dunlap) was the first American opera, William Henry Fry (1813–64), Horatio William Parker (1863–1919), Bernard Rogers (1893–1968) and John Laurence Seymour (1893–1986).

American Opera Society
Founded in 1951 by Allen Sven Oxenburg, it operated until 1970 and was devoted to giving concert performances of little-known operas. Most of these were given at Carnegie Hall in New York with top international casts.

Amerò sarò costante, L'
Soprano aria for Amintas in Act II of Mozart's *Il Rè Pastore*, in which he vows to remain always in love with Elisa.

Amfiparnaso, L' (rough translation: *The Lower Slopes of Parnassus*)
Musical comedy in prologue and three acts by Vecchi. 1st perf (?) Modena, 1594; libr by the composer and (possibly) Giulio Cesare Croce. One of the most important 'proto-operas', it is a madrigal cycle for five voices, and is one of the earliest attempts to combine farce with music. Its plot, comprising various episodes relating to love, as well as its character types and

use of dialect, derive from the COMMEDIA DELL'ARTE tradition. The piece has occasionally been staged as an opera in recent times. [R]

Amfortas
Baritone role in Wagner's *Parsifal*. Titurel's son, he is the guardian of the Holy Grail.

Amico Fritz, L' (*Friend Fritz*)
Opera in three acts by Mascagni. 1st perf Rome, 31 Oct 1891; libr by Nicola Daspuro, after Émile Erckmann and Alexandre Chatrian's *L'Ami Fritz*. Principal roles: Fritz (ten), Suzel (sop), David (bar), Beppe (mezzo). Mascagni's most successful opera apart from *Cavalleria Rusticana*, it is a pastoral comedy.
Plot: Late-19th-century Alsace. The wealthy middle-aged landowner Fritz has bet with the Rabbi David that he will always remain a bachelor. However, David notices that Fritz is captivated by Suzel, the daughter of one of his tenants. When David mischievously tells Fritz that he has found a young husband for Suzel, Fritz is so upset that he leaves without a word to Suzel, who loves him. Despairing, she appeals to him to save her from the supposed marriage, and he finally confesses that he loves her. David has won his bet and donates his winnings – a vineyard – to Suzel. [R]

Amina
Soprano role in Bellini's *La Sonnambula*. Teresa's foster-daughter, she is the sleep-walking girl of the opera's title.

Amis, l'amour tendre
Tenor aria for Hoffmann in the Giulietta Act of Offenbach's *Les Contes d'Hoffmann*. Hoffmann's drinking song.

Amneris
Mezzo role in Verdi's *Aida*. Pharaoh's daughter, she loves Radamès.

Amonasro
Baritone role in Verdi's *Aida*. Aida's father, he is the Ethiopian king.

Amore dei Tre Re, L' (*The Love of Three Kings*)
Opera in three acts by Montemezzi. 1st perf Milan, 10 April 1913; libr by Sem Benelli, after his own verse play. Principal roles: Archibaldo (bass), Fiora (sop), Manfredo (bar), Avito (ten), Flaminio (ten). A hauntingly beautiful work, it is Montemezzi's masterpiece and one of the finest of all 20th-century Italian operas. It is especially notable for its magnificent orchestration and for its remarkable characterization of the blind old king.
Plot: 10th-century Italy. The Italian princess Fiora, originally betrothed to Avito, has been forced to marry Manfredo, son of the blind old barbarian king Archibaldo. Already suspecting her of infidelity, Archibaldo chances on her and Avito declaring their love, but Avito escapes. Archibaldo strangles Fiora, who dies refusing to reveal her lover's identity. Archibaldo lays a trap by smearing Fiora's lips with poison. Avito kisses her lips and dies, but Manfredo, who has forgiven her and who no longer wishes to live, does the same. Archibaldo, finding the body which he thinks is Fiora's lover, discovers that he has also killed his son. Everything is now darkness, to which Archibaldo has so long been accustomed. [R]

Amore Medico, L' (*Love the Doctor*)
Comic opera in two acts by Wolf-Ferrari. 1st perf Dresden, 4 Dec 1913; libr by Enrico Golisciani, after Molière's *L'Amour Médecin*. Principal roles: Lucinda (sop), Clitandro (ten), Arnolfo (bass). An elegant example of Wolf-Ferrari's neo-classical comic style, it was successful at its appearance but is nowadays only rarely performed.
Plot: 17th-century Paris. Arnolfo has forbidden his lovesick daughter Lucinda to marry. However, her secret lover Clitandro disguises himself as a doctor and prescribes a mock marriage as the cure for her condition. Needless to say, it turns out to be a real marriage, to which Arnolfo eventually gives his blessing.

Amor ti vieta
Tenor aria for Loris in Act II of Giordano's *Fedora*, in which he tells Fedora that she loves him even though she will not admit it.

Amour est un oiseau rebelle, L'
Mezzo aria (the *Habañera*) for Carmen in Act I of Bizet's *Carmen*, in which she sings

of the capriciousness of love. It is adapted from the song 'El Arregilito' by the Spanish composer Sebastián Yradier (1808–65).

Amsterdam
see NETHERLANDS OPERA

Am stillen Herd
Tenor aria for Walther von Stolzing in Act I of Wagner's *Die Meistersinger von Nürnberg*, in which he relates where and how he learnt to sing.

Anacréon
Opera-ballet in one act by Rameau. 1st perf Fontainebleau, 23 Oct 1754; libr by Louis de Cahusac. Principal roles: Anacréon (bar), Cupid (sop), Agathocle (mezzo), Priestess (sop). Forming the third entrée of *Les Surprises de l'Amour*, it is only very rarely performed. [R]

Anacréon or **L'Amour Fugitif** (*Love the Fugitive*)
Opera in two acts by Cherubini. 1st perf Paris, 4 Oct 1803; libr by R. Mendouze. Principal roles: Anacréon (ten), Corine (sop), Amour (sop). Telling a fictitious story about the Greek poet Anakreon (*c* 572–487 BC), it was successful in its time, but nowadays only the magnificent overture is remembered.
Plot: Legendary Greece. Despite the difference in their ages, Corine and the poet Anacréon love one another. They befriend Cupid, who is playing truant from his mother Venus, who offers to fulfil any wish of the person who restores Cupid to her. Anacréon's songs, inspired by Cupid, draw Venus to the area. She grants Anacréon's wish: the perennial love of Corine.

Anch'io dischiuso
Soprano aria for Abigaille in Act II of Verdi's *Nabucco*, in which she recalls the time when she opened her heart to love. Its spectacular CABALETTA is the warlike 'Salgo già il trono aurato'.

Ancona, Mario (1860–1931)
Italian baritone, particularly associated with the Italian repertory. One of the leading baritones of the early 20th century, he had a beautiful voice used with elegance and a superb technique. He created Silvio in *Pagliacci*.

Andersen, Hans Christian
see panel on page 20

Anderson, June (b 1952)
American soprano, particularly associated with French and Italian COLORATURA roles. Possessing a beautiful voice which is both large and extraordinarily agile, coupled with a superb technique, she is possibly the finest coloratura to have emerged since Joan Sutherland.

Anderson, Marian (1897–1993)
American contralto with a large and rich voice of great beauty. In 1955, she became the first black singer ever to appear at the Metropolitan Opera, New York (as Ulrica in Verdi's *Un Ballo in Maschera*). Described by the conductor Toscanini as 'the voice that comes once in a hundred years', her career was almost exclusively confined to the concert platform. Her autobiography, *My Lord What a Morning*, was published in 1956.

Andrea Chénier
Opera in four acts by Giordano. 1st perf Milan, 28 March 1896; libr by Luigi Illica. Principal roles: Chénier (ten), Madeleine (sop), Gérard (bar), Bersi (mezzo), Countess Coigny (mezzo), Madelon (mezzo). Giordano's most successful and enduring work, it is based on events in the life of the French poet André Chénier (1762–94).
Plot: France, 1789–94. At a party, the poet Chénier rebukes the wealthy Madeleine, daughter of Countess Coigny, for scorning love. They meet again after the Revolution and fall in love. Carlo Gérard, who had loved Madeleine when he was a servant in the Coigny household, is now a revolutionary leader and denounces Chénier. To save Chénier, Madeleine offers herself to Gérard, who repents and intervenes on the poet's behalf. However, he is unsuccessful. Madeleine bribes the jailer to let her take the place of a condemned woman, and she and Chénier go to death together. [R]

Andrei
1 Baritone role in Prokofiev's *War and*

· Hans Christian Andersen ·

The Danish writer Hans Christian Andersen (1805–75) was keenly interested in opera: he had originally hoped to be an actor or a singer, and he worked at the Theatre Royal, Copenhagen. He wrote a number of opera libretti, including *The Watersprites* (*Nøkken*, 1835) and *The Wedding on Lake Como* (*Bryllupet ved Como-Søen*, 1849, after Alessandro Manzoni's *I Promessi Sposi*) for Franz Gläser, and adaptations of Sir Walter Scott's *Kenilworth* (*Festen på Kenilworth*, 1836) for Weyse and *The Bride of Lammermoor* (*Bruden fra Lammermoor*, 1832) for Bredal. His fairy tales have inspired some 50 operas. Below are listed, by story, those operas by composers with entries in this dictionary.

The Emperor and the Nightingale		
Enna	*The Nightingale*	1912
Stravinsky	*The Nightingale*	1914
The Emperor's New Clothes		
Wagner–Régeny	*Der Nachte König*	1928
Moore	*The Emperor's New Clothes*	1948
The Garden of Paradise		
Bruneau	*Le Jardin du Paradis*	1923
Little Christina		
Leoni	*Ib and Little Christina*	1901
The Match Girl		
Enna	*The Little Match Girl*	1897
Veretti	*Una Favola di Andersen*	1934
The Prince and the Swineherd		
Rota	*Il Principe Porcaro*	1925
The Princess and the Pea		
Enna	*The Princess and the Pea*	1900
The Travelling Companion		
Stanford	*The Travelling Companion*	1919
What the Old Man Does is Always Right		
Hoddinott	*What the Old Man Does is Always Right*	1977

Peace. He is a prince loved by Natasha. **2** Tenor role in Tchaikovsky's *Mazeppa*. He is in love with Maria. **3** Tenor role in Moussorgsky's *Khovanschina*. He is Ivan Khovansky's son. **4** Bass role in Prokofiev's *The Story of a Real Man*. **5** Tenor role in Tchaikovsky's *The Oprichnik*. The oprichnik guard of the opera's title, he loves Natasha.

Andres
1 Baritone role in Offenbach's *La Périchole*. He is the viceroy of Peru. **2** Tenor role in Berg's *Wozzeck*. He is Wozzeck's companion. **3** Tenor COMPRIMARIO role in Offenbach's *Les Contes d'Hoffmann*. He is the stage-door keeper of the opera house.

Anelli, Angelo (1761–1820)
Italian librettist, sometimes writing under the pseudonyms Nicolò Liprandi and Marco Landi. One of the best Italian librettists of his day, excelling in comedy, he provided texts for Cimarosa, Coccia, Gazzaniga, Guglielmi, Martín y Soler, Mayr, Mosca, Pacini, Paer, Pavesi, Portugal, Rossini (*L'Italiana in Algieri*) and Zingarelli amongst others.

Anfossi, Pasquale (1727–97)
Italian composer. He wrote some 70 operas, beginning with *La Serva Spiritosa* (Rome, 1763). Many of his operas enjoyed considerable success in their day, but they are all now largely forgotten. His most

important works include *L'Incognita Perseguitata* (Rome 1773; libr Giuseppe Petrosellini, after Carlo Goldoni), his most successful work, *La Finta Giardiniera* (Rome, 1774; libr Marco Coltellini), *L'Avaro* (Venice, 1775; libr Giovanni Bertati), *La Vera Costanza* (Rome, 2 Jan 1776; libr Francesco Puttini), *Il Curioso Indiscreto* (Rome, Feb 1777; libr Bertati) and *La Maga Circe* (Rome 1788).

Angeles, Victoria de los (b López Chima) (b 1923)
Spanish soprano, particularly associated with lyric Italian and French roles. An artist of outstanding musicianship, she possessed one of the loveliest voices of the immediate post-war era. Her affecting stage presence and her warm personality made her a great favourite with audiences everywhere. She enjoyed a remarkably long career, continuing to appear as a recitalist into her late 60s.

Angélique
Comic opera in one act by Ibert. 1st perf Paris, 28 July 1927; libr by Michel Veber under the pen-name of Nino. Principal roles: Angélique (sop), Boniface (ten), Charlot (bar), Devil (ten). Ibert's most successful opera, it still receives an occasional performance.
Plot: France. The china-shop owner Boniface is made miserable by his ill-natured and sharp-tongued wife Angélique. His friend Charlot tells him that the only way to be rid of her is to put her up for sale. She is purchased by three people, including the Devil, all of whom soon return her.

Angelotti, Cesare
Bass role in Puccini's *Tosca*. He is an escaped political prisoner. In history, he was Liberio Angelucci, Consul of the short-lived Roman Republic.

Anges du Paradis
Tenor aria for Vincent in Act III of Gounod's *Mireille*, in which he entreats heaven to protect Mireille.

Ange si pure (often sung in Italian as 'Spirito gentil')
Tenor aria for Fernand in Act IV of Donizetti's *La Favorite*, in which he recalls his love for Léonor as he is about to take his monastic vows. It was originally written for the unfinished *Le Duc d'Albe*.

Aniara
Opera in two acts by Blomdahl. 1st perf Stockholm, 31 May 1959; libr by Erik Lindegren, after Harry Martinson's epic poem. Principal roles: Daisy Doodle (sop), Mimarobe (bar), Blind Poetess (sop), Blind Man (ten). Employing electronic music, it has proved to be one of the most successful post-war operas and has been widely performed.
Plot: A spaceship is carrying refugees from an Earth devastated by a nuclear holocaust to a settlement on Mars. The ship collides with an asteroid and is knocked off course, doomed to journey through space for eternity. [R]

Anima Allegra (*The Joyous Spirit*)
Comic opera in three acts by Vittadini. 1st perf Rome, 15 April 1921; libr by Giuseppe Adami and Luigi Motta, after Joaquín and Serafín Álvarez Quintero's *Genio Alegre*. Principal roles: Consuela (sop), Pedro (ten), Donna Sacramento (mezzo), Don Eligio (bass). Set in Spain in the 1830s, it tells of a vivacious girl who transforms the dark and cheerless household of her lover's family. Very successful at its appearance, it is nowadays virtually forgotten.

Anima del Filosofo, L'
see ORFEO ED EURIDICE (Haydn)

Ankerström
The advisor to Gustavus III of Sweden, he appears as: **1** Baritone role in Verdi's *Un Ballo in Maschera*. Amelia's husband, he is Renato in the Boston setting. **2** Baritone role in Auber's *Gustave III*. **3** Bass role in Werle's *Tintomara*. In history, Jakob Johan Ankerström was indeed Gustavus's assassin, but he did not know him personally.

Anna
1 Mezzo role in Berlioz's *Les Troyens*. She is Dido's sister. **2** Soprano role Donizetti's *Anna Bolena*. She is Anne Boleyn (*c* 1507–36), second wife of Henry VIII. **3** Soprano role in Catalani's *Loreley*. She is Walther's fiancée. **4** Soprano role in Puccini's *Le*

Villi. She is Robert's fiancée. **5** Soprano role in Sallinen's *The Horseman.* She is Antti's wife. **6** Soprano role in Strauss's *Intermezzo.* She is Christine's maid. **7** Soprano role in Boïeldieu's *La Dame Blanche.* She is Gaveston's ward. **8** Soprano role in Rossini's *Maometto II.* She is Erisso's daughter. **9** Soprano role in Zandonai's *I Cavalieri di Ekebù.* Sintram's daughter, she is loved by Berling. **10** Soprano role in Marschner's *Hans Heiling.* She is loved by Heiling. **11** Mezzo role in Egk's *Der Revisor.* She is the militia captain's wife. **12** Mezzo COMPRIMARIO role in Donizetti's *Maria Stuarda.* She is Hannah Kennedy, Mary's companion. **13** Soprano comprimario role in Verdi's *Nabucco.* She is Zaccaria's sister.

Anna, Donna
Soprano role in Mozart's and Gazzaniga's *Don Giovanni* and Dargomijsky's *The Stone Guest.* She is the Commendatore's daughter.

Anna Bolena (*Anne Boleyn*)
Opera in two acts by Donizetti. 1st perf Milan, 26 Dec 1830; libr by Felice Romani, partly after Alessandro Pepoli's play and Ippolito Pindemonte's *Enrico VIII.* Principal roles: Anna (sop), Giovanna (mezzo), Enrico (bass), Riccardo (ten), Smeton (mezzo), Rochefort (bass), Harvey (ten). Donizetti's 33rd opera, it was his first major success and established his European reputation. Historically a great deal more accurate than most Italian operas based on British history, it is one of Donizetti's finest works, both musically and dramatically, and has been a key opera in the post-war Donizetti revival, particularly the 1957 La Scala production with Maria Callas.
Plot: Windsor, 1536. Henry VIII has tired of his wife Anne and has transferred his attentions to her lady-in-waiting Jane Seymour. Hoping to compromise Anne, he recalls her first love Richard Percy from exile. It is, however, through the unintentional indiscretion of the young musician Mark Smeaton that Henry is able to order Anne's trial for adultery. Learning that Jane is her rival, Anne forgives her. Despite Jane's pleas to Henry for mercy, Anne is condemned to death along with Smeaton, Percy and her brother Rochford. She loses her reason, but on hearing the music for Henry's new wedding she recovers her senses and forgives the pair. [R]

Ännchen
Soprano role in Weber's *Der Freischütz.* She is Agathe's cousin.

Annina
1 Soprano role in J. Strauss's *Eine Nacht in Venedig.* She is Barbara's friend. **2** Mezzo role in Strauss's *Der Rosenkavalier.* Valzacchi's colleague, she is an Italian schemer. **3** Mezzo COMPRIMARIO role in Verdi's *La Traviata.* She is Violetta's maid.

Annius
Mezzo trouser-role in Mozart's *La Clemenza di Tito.* He is loved by Servilia.

Annunzio, Gabriele d'
see panel on page 23

Ansermet, Ernest (1883–1969)
Swiss conductor, particularly associated with the French repertory. Founder of L'Orchestre de la Suisse Romande, he was musical director of the Grand Théâtre, Geneva (1962–69). He conducted the first performances of Britten's *The Rape of Lucretia*, Stravinsky's *Renard* and Martin's *Der Sturm, Le Mystère de la Nativité* and *Monsieur de Pourceaugnac.*

Antheil, George (1900–59)
American composer. His operas, written in a varity of styles, are the jazz-influenced *Transatlantic* (Frankfurt, 25 May 1930; libr composer), *Helen Retires* (New York, 28 Feb 1934; libr James Erskine), *Volpone* (Los Angeles, 9 Feb 1953; libr A. Perry, after Ben Jonson), *The Brothers* (Denver, 28 July 1954; libr composer), *Venus in Africa* (Denver, 24 May 1957, composed 1954; libr M. Dyne) and *The Wish* (Louisville, 2 Apr 1955; libr composer). A colourful figure, he wrote detective stories, a syndicated agony column and his autobiography, *Bad Boy of Music*, which was published in 1945.

Antigonae
Opera in five acts by Orff. 1st perf Salzburg, 9 Aug 1949; a setting of Friedrich Hölderlin's translation of

Sophocles's play. Principal roles: Antigonae (sop), Kreon (bar), Hämon (ten), Tiresias (ten), Eurydice (mezzo), Messenger (bass), Ismene (sop). An austere and powerful setting, it consists of heightened declamation of the text over a percussive and largely rhythmical accompaniment. It is only infrequently performed.
Plot: Legendary Thebes. King Creon has ordered that the body of the defeated rebel Eteocles be left to rot, and decrees death for anyone attempting to bury it. Despite warnings from her sister Ismene, Antigonae determines to give her brother burial. She throws earth over the body and confesses to Creon. Despite pleas for mercy from her beloved, Creon's son Haemon, she is immured in a cave. Warned by the seer Tiresias of impending doom, Creon relents. But Antigonae has hung herself and Haemon falls on his sword. When the Messenger relates the news to Creon's wife Eurydice, she kills herself. Creon's barbarous decree has thus lost him all that he cherished. [R]

Antigone
Opera in three acts by Honegger. 1st perf Brussels, 28 Dec 1927; libr by Jean Cocteau, after Sophocles's play. Principal roles: Antigone (mezzo), Ismène (sop), Hamon (bar), Créon (bar), Tirésias (bass). Although it contains some fine music, it is hardly ever performed. For plot see *Antigonae*.

Antonia
Soprano role in Offenbach's *Les Contes d'Hoffmann*. Crespel's daughter, she is a consumptive singer.

Antonida
Soprano role in Glinka's *A Life for the Tsar*. She is in love with Sobinin.

Antonio
1 Baritone role in Donizetti's *Linda di Chamounix*. Maddalena's husband, he is Linda's father. **2** Baritone role in Lehár's *Giuditta*. He is an army lieutenant. **3** Tenor role in Prokofiev's and Gerhard's *The*

· *Gabriele d'Annunzio* ·

The Italian poet, playwright and patriot Gabriele d'Annunzio (1863–1938) has an important place in operatic history. He was a close associate of Pizzetti and wrote the libretto for his *Fedra*, as well as that for Mascagni's *Parisina*. With Pizzetti, Casella and Malipiero, he was editor of the *Roccolta Nazionale della Musica Italiana*. An opponent of VERISMO and a qualified admirer of Wagner, he was an advocate of classical and pre-classical opera. The constitution which he drew up during his military occupation of Fiume in 1920 contained two clauses giving music a central position in the life of the state. His plays have inspired a number of operas. Below are listed, by play, those operas by composers with entries in this dictionary.

Fedra		
Pizzetti	*Fedra*	1915
La Fiaccola Sotto il Moggio		
Pizzetti	*Gigliola*	1915 (U)
La Figlia di Iorio		
Franchetti	*La Figlia di Iorio*	1906
Pizzetti	*La Figlia di Iorio*	1954
Francesca da Rimini		
Zandonai	*Francesca da Rimini*	1914
La Nave		
Montemezzi	*La Nave*	1918
Parisina		
Mascagni	*Parisina*	1913
Il Sogno d'un Tramonto		
Malipiero	*Il Sogno d'un Tramonto*	1913

Duenna. He is loved by Louisa. **4** Bass role in Mascagni's *Lodoletta*. He gives Lodoletta her red shoes. **5** Bass role in Gomes's *Il Guarany*. He is Cecilia's father. **6** Bass role in Mozart's *Le Nozze de Figaro*. Susanna's uncle, he is a drunken gardener. **7** Baritone role in Sullivan's *The Gondoliers*. He is a Venetian gondolier. **8** Tenor role in Offenbach's *Le Brigands*. He is the ducal treasurer. **9** Tenor COMPRIMARIO role in Rossini's *La Gazza Ladra*. He is the jailer.

Antony and Cleopatra
Opera in three acts by Barber (Op 40). 1st perf New York, 16 Sept 1966; libr by Franco Zeffirelli, after William Shakespeare's play. Revised version 1st perf New York, 6 Feb 1975; libr revised by Gian-Carlo Menotti. Principal roles: Cleopatra (sop), Antony (b-bar), Augustus Caesar (ten), Iras (mezzo), Enobarbus (bass). Commissioned to open the new Metropolitan Opera House, it was unsuccessful, but was subsequently revised and revived with better fortune.
Plot: Egypt and Rome, 41–31 BC. Antony takes leave of his mistress, Queen Cleopatra, and returns to Rome, where he is forced to marry Augustus's sister Octavia. When he returns to Cleopatra, Augustus goes to war against him. Defeated, Antony commits suicide and dies in Cleopatra's arms. To avoid being paraded in Augustus's triumph, Cleopatra kills herself by means of being bitten by a venomous snake. [R]

Antwerp
see ROYAL FLEMISH OPERA

Anvil Chorus
Chorus of gypsies ('Vedi le fosche') in Act II of Verdi's *Il Trovatore*, during which on-stage anvils are struck rhythmically.

Apollo
The Graeco-Roman sun god appears in many operas, including: **1** Tenor role in Lully's *Alceste*. **2** Baritone role in Gluck's *Alceste*. **3** Mezzo trouser role in Mozart's *Apollo et Hyacinthus*. **4** COUNTER-TENOR role in Britten's *Death in Venice*. **5** Tenor role in Händel's *Semele*. **6** Baritone role in Rameau's *Les Boréades*. **7** Tenor role in Strauss's *Daphne*. **8** Bass role in Händel's *Admeto*. **9** Baritone role in Taneyev's *Oresteia*. **10** Tenor role in Boughton's *Alkestis*.

Apollo et Hyacinthus or **Hyacinthi Metamorphosis**
Opera in one act by Mozart (K 38). 1st perf Salzburg, 13 May 1767; libr (in Latin) by Rufinus Widl. Principal roles: Melia (sop), Oebalus (ten), Apollo (mezzo), Zephyrus (mezzo), Hyacinthus (sop). Mozart's second stage work, written at the age of 11, it is an INTERMEZZO comprising a prologue and nine musical numbers, originally designed for insertion into Widl's *Clementia Croesi*. A work of remarkable precocity and assurance, it still receives an occasional performance.
Plot: Legendary Greece. Melia, sister of Hyacinth, is loved by Apollo and Zephyrus. Apollo's plan to wed Melia prompts Zephyrus to kill Hyacinth in a jealous rage. Zephyrus tries to blame Apollo so as to discredit the god in the eyes of Melia and her father Oebalus. Apollo summons the winds to remove Zephyrus, and the dying Hyacinth reveals his murderer's true identity. Apollo transforms Hyacinth into a flower and prepares to wed Melia. [R]

Apolloni, Giuseppe (1822–89)
Italian composer. Beginning with *Adelchi* (Vicenza, 14 Aug 1852; libr Gian Battista Niccolini, after Alessandro Manzoni), he wrote six operas in a style influenced by Verdi's early works. Much the most successful was *L'Ebreo* (Venice, 23 Jan 1855; libr Antonio Boni, after Edward Bulwer-Lytton's *Leila*), which was widely performed in Italy in the later 19th century.

Appia, Adolphe (1862–1928)
Swiss designer. Sometimes regarded as the father of modern operatic staging, he was a pupil of Liszt and a fanatical admirer of Wagner. Horrified by the old-fashioned naturalism favoured at Bayreuth, he advocated three-dimensional, sculptural stagings with abstract scenery. Regarding lighting as 'the supreme scene painter, the interpreter, the most significant plastic medium on stage', his sets were always grey awaiting light to give them colour. His actual theatre work was limited, but

included principally a controversial *Tristan und Isolde* at La Scala in 1923 and a *Ring* in Basel which was abandoned halfway through. His theories, expounded in the books *La Mise-en-Scène du Drame Wagnérien* (1895) and *Die Musik und die Inszenierung* (1899), exerted a powerful influence on 20th-century designers and producers such as Max Reinhardt, Konstantin Stanislavsky, Josef Svoboda and, particularly, Wieland Wagner.

Appoggiatura (Italian for 'leaning')
A vocal ornament or 'grace note', mainly used in the 18th century, consisting of an unharmonized auxiliary note falling (or, less frequently, rising) to an adjacent note which is harmonized or which is implied to be so.

Aprite un po'
Bass-baritone aria for Figaro in Act IV of Mozart's *Le Nozze di Figaro*, in which he complains of women's deceitfulness.

Arabella
Opera in three acts by Strauss (Op 79). 1st perf Dresden, 1 July 1933; libr by Hugo von Hofmannsthal. Principal roles: Arabella (sop), Mandryka (bar), Zdenka (sop), Matteo (ten), Count Waldner (bass), Adelaide (mezzo), Count Elemer (ten), Fiakermilli (sop), Count Dominik (bar), Count Lamoral (bass). One of Strauss's lushest neo-classical scores, it was an immediate success and has always been one of his most popular operas.
Plot: Vienna, 1860. Pressed by his creditors, Count Waldner needs to arrange a financially satisfactory marriage for his elder daughter Arabella, and has sent her picture to a rich but elderly friend. It is, however, the friend's son Mandryka who arrives, wishing to marry Arabella. The two meet at a ball and fall in love. Arabella parts from her other suitors, particularly the officer Matteo, who is desolated. Arabella's sister Zdenka, brought up as a boy as an economy measure, is secretly in love with Matteo. She promises him a meeting with Arabella, and gives him a letter and a key. Mandryka overhears and, thinking himself betrayed, flirts with the regimental mascot Fiakermilli. Confusion reigns until Zdenka explains that the key was to her own room, whereupon Matteo transfers his affections to her, whilst Arabella and Mandryka are engaged. [R]

Aragall, Giacomo (b Jaime) (b 1940)
Spanish tenor, particularly associated with Verdi and Puccini roles and with the French repertory. He possesses an extremely pleasing and easily produced voice, used with fine musicianship, and has a handsome stage presence.

Araiza, Francisco (b 1950)
Mexican tenor, particularly associated with Mozart, Rossini and Donizetti roles. One of the most stylish and musicianly contemporary lyric tenors, with an exciting upper register, he has recently undertaken a number of heavier Italian and German roles.

Arbace
Tenor role in Mozart's *Idomeneo*. He is Idomeneo's counsellor.

Arcadians, The
Operetta in three acts by Monckton and Talbot. 1st perf London, 28 April 1909; libr by Mark Ambient, Alexander M. Thompson, Robert Courtenidge and Arthur Wimperis. Principal roles: Sombra (sop), Jack Meadows (bar), Eileen (mezzo), Smith/Simplicitas (ten), Doody (bass). Possibly the most tuneful of all non-Sullivan British operettas, it was sensationally successful at its appearance and is still sometimes performed, despite its dated quality.
Plot: Arcadia and London, early 20th century. The Arcadians wish to meet an Englishman and are sent the caterer James Smith, who is befriended by Sombra. After he has been caught in a lie, he is washed in the Well of Truth and emerges as Simplicitas. The Arcadians decide to go to London to purify its wicked inhabitants. At the races, Jack Meadows, who loves Eileen, the niece of Smith's wife, has staked his all on a horse. The horse savages its melancholic rider Doody, but the Arcadians appear, and Simplicitas rides the horse to victory. Now running an Arcadian restaurant, Simplicitas tells another lie and falls back into the Well of Truth, re-emerging as Smith once more. Sombra

realizes that there is no chance of civilizing the English, and she and her companions return to Arcadia. [R Exc]

Archibaldo
Bass role in Montemezzi's *L'Amore dei Tre Re*. Manfredo's father, he is the blind old king of Altura.

Arden Must Die
Opera in two acts by Goehr (Op 21). 1st perf Hamburg, 5 March 1967; libr by Eric Fried, after the anonymous 16th-century play *Arden of Faversham*. Principal roles: Arden (bar), Alice (mezzo), Mosbie (ten), Mrs Bradshaw (mezzo), Franklin (bass), Susan (sop), Michael (ten), Reede (bass), Shakebag (bass), Black Will (bass). Goehr's most important opera, it is a black comedy based on an historical incident. **Plot**: Faversham (Kent), 1551. Alice and her lover Mosbie plan to murder her husband, the rich businessman Arden, and are joined by the disgruntled servants Michael and Susan and by Franklin and Reede, landowners ruined by Arden. The hired killers Shakebag and Black Will make three unsuccessful attempts on Arden's life before succeeding at a reconciliation dinner with his enemies. At their trial, Alice and Mosbie admit responsibility, while the others try to deny their roles in the plot.

Arditi, Luigi (1822–1903)
Italian conductor and composer. Largely based in London, he was one of the leading operatic conductors of the 19th century, particularly of the Italian repertory. Best known as a song composer, he also wrote three operas: *I Briganti* (Milan, 1841), *Il Corsaro* (Havana, 1847; libr after Lord Byron's *The Corsair*) and *La Spia* (New York, 24 Mar 1856; libr F. Manetta, after James Fenimore Cooper's *The Spy*). His autobiography, *My Reminiscences*, was published in 1896.

Ardon gl'incesi
Soprano aria (the 'Mad Scene') for Lucia in Act III of Donizetti's *Lucia di Lammermoor*, in which Lucia, having murdered Arturo, hallucinates about a marriage with Edgardo. It is one of the most famous and demanding soprano scenes in all opera. The long central duet between voice and flute before the CABALETTA 'Spargi d'amaro pianto' is not in the original score. The original OBBLIGATO instruments were glass harmonica and glockenspiel, but Donizetti was forced to abandon them as impractical and replaced them with the flute.

Arensky, Anton (1861–1906)
Russian composer. His first opera, *A Dream on the Volga* (*Son na Volge*, Moscow, 2 Jan 1891; libr after Alexander Nikolayevich Ostrovsky), enjoyed very considerable success. This was not shared by his two subsequent operas *Rafael* (Moscow, 18 May 1894; libr A.A. Kryukov) [R] and *Nal and Damayanti* (Moscow, 22 Jan 1904; libr Modest Tchaikovsky, after Vasily Zhukovsky). He was also a distinguished teacher, whose pupils included Rachmaninov and Scriabin.

Argentina
see TEATRO COLÓN, BUENOS AIRES

Argentinian opera composers
see BERUTI; CASTRO; GAITO; GINASTERA; PANIZZA

Other national opera composers include Felipe Boero (1884–1958), Enrique Mario Casella (1891–1948), Raúl Espoile (1888–1958), Arnoldo d'Espósito (1907–45), Gilardo Gilardi (1889–1963), Mauricio Kagel (*b* 1931), Valdo Sciammerella (*b* 1924), Alfredo L. Schiuma (1885–1963), Antonio Tauriello (*b* 1931), Floro M. Ugarte (1884–1975), Héctor Iglésias Villoud (*b* 1913) and Juan Carlos Zorzi (*b* 1936).

Argento, Dominick (b 1927)
American composer. His operas, written in a conservative and readily accessible idiom, include *Sicilian Limes* (Baltimore, 1954; libr John Olon-Scrymgeour), *The Boor* (Rochester, 6 May 1957; libr Olon-Scrymgeour, after Anton Chekhov's *The Bear*), *Christopher Sly* (Minneapolis, 31 May 1963; libr John Manlove, after Shakespeare's *The Taming of the Shrew*), *The Masque of Angels* (Minneapolis, 9 Jan 1964; libr Olon-Scrymgeour), *The Shoemaker's Holiday* (Minneapolis, 1 June 1967; libr Olon-Scrymgeour, after T. Dekker), the successful *Postcard From Morocco* (Minneapolis, 14 Oct 1971; libr

John Donahue), *The Voyage of Edgar Allan Poe* (Minneapolis, 24 Apr 1976; libr Charles Nolte), *Miss Havisham's Fire* (New York, 22 Mar 1979; libr Olon-Scrymgeour, after Charles Dickens's *Great Expectations*), *Casanova's Homecoming* (St Paul, 12 Apr 1985; libr composer, after Casanova's autobiography), *The Aspern Papers* (Dallas, 19 Nov 1988; libr composer, after Henry James) and *The Dream of Valentino* (Washington, 15 Jan 1994; libr Nolte). He was co-founder in 1964 of the Center Opera Company (now the Minnesota Opera).

Argomento (Italian for 'argument')
A term describing the summary of the plot that precedes the text in the printed libretto of an opera.

Århus
see JUTLAND OPERA

Aria (Italian for 'air')
A musical number for solo singers. Until the end of the 17th century, the term was used for a piece with any number of soloists, but since then it has denoted a solo piece. The aria developed from the early RECITATIVE-style operas as a point of heightened emotional and musical tension, and soon became a fully self-contained number. It reached its first period of rigid formality in the late baroque OPERA SERIAS, with the DA CAPO form (A–B–A decorated). Gluck and Mozart loosened the rigidity, but by the early 19th century a second formal structure had developed in Italy. This was the 'aria and CABALETTA', which comprised a lyrical (usually slow) aria, followed by a contrasting (usually fast) two-verse cabaletta, in which singers displayed their virtuosity by decorating the second verse. The form was dramatically suffocating, and it was left to Verdi and Wagner to loosen the structure once more, and eventually almost to dispense with formal arias altogether.

Many different types of aria, usually relating to specific dramatic situations, came into being, especially in 18th-century opera seria. They included Aria di Infuriata (for anger), Aria di Sentimento, Aria di Lamento and many others (including the seven following entries). They refer more to the sentiment of the aria rather than to any specific structure.

see also AIR; ARIA DEL SORBETTO; ARIA DI BAULE; ARIA DI BRAVURA; ARIA DI CATALOGO; ARIA DI IMITAZIONE; ARIA DI PORTAMENTO; ARIA DI SORTITA; ARIE; ARIE ANTICHE; ARIETTA; ARIOSO; AUBADE; AUFTRITTSLIED; BALLAD; BALLATA; BERCEUSE; BRINDISI; CABALETTA; CANZONA; CANZONETTA; CAVATINA; DA CAPO; DAL SEGNO; LAMENTO; LIED; METAPHOR ARIA; ROMANZA; SERENADE; VENGEANCE ARIA

Aria del Sorbetto (Italian for 'sorbet air')
An aria in an early 19th-century Italian opera for a secondary character, during which the audience would often leave their seats to buy their ices and chat with their friends. An example is Berta's 'Il vecchioto' in Rossini's *Il Barbiere di Siviglia*. Nowadays, the audience is expected to listen to them.

Aria di Baule (Italian for 'trunk air')
An individual singer's favourite aria, which they would carry around with them in their luggage and insert into whatever opera they happened to be appearing in at the time. In the 19th century, many great singers indulged in this, but nowadays the practice is frowned upon.

Aria di Bravura (Italian for 'swagger air')
Also known as Aria d'Agilità, it is an aria specifically designed to show off a singer's virtuosity. Typically, such arias are of great technical difficulty, involving wide intervals, long runs and elaborate COLORATURA.

Aria di Catalogo (Italian for 'catalogue air')
An aria in an 18th or early 19th-century Italian comic opera, in which the singer reels off a long list of names, places or items, usually at high speed (*see* PATTER). Had Rossini carried out his famous offer to set a laundary list to music it would have been an aria di catalogo. Perhaps the most famous example is Leporello's Catalogue Aria ('Madamina, il catalogo è questo') in Mozart's *Don Giovanni*, although it is atypical. Possibly the finest examples are by Donizetti: Dulcamara's proclamation of his wares in *L'Elisir d'Amore* and, particularly, Enrico's unbelievable prescription in *Il Campanello*, which is so

long and goes so fast that Donizetti recommended the singer to take the words on stage with him. Non-Italian composers also used the form occasionally, for example Sullivan with Col Calverley's 'If you want a receipt' in *Patience*.

Aria di Imitazione (Italian for 'imitation air')
Two types of aria: **1** In which the voice and/or the orchestra imitate the sounds of nature. **2** In which the singer imitates the sounds of the orchestra. Much the most famous example is Cimarosa's *Il Maestro di Cappella*.

Aria di Portamento (Italian for 'carrying air')
A type of aria in which the primary vocal requirement is a smooth, expressive and full-toned delivery. Always in slow tempo, these arias lay great stress on pure vocal beauty and are vehicles to express the singer's dignity of bearing, rather than to impress with ornamentation and showiness. An example is 'O del mio dolce ardor' in Gluck's *Paride ed Elena*.

Aria di Sortita (Italian for 'departure air')
An aria for a character about to leave the stage. Very popular in 18th century OPERA SERIA.

Ariadne auf Naxos
Opera in prologue and one act by Strauss (Op 60). 1st perf (second part only) Stuttgart, 25 Oct 1912; libr by Hugo von Hofmannsthal, partly after Molière's *Le Bourgeois Gentilhomme*. Revised version 1st perf Vienna, 4 Oct 1916. Principal roles: Prima Donna/Ariadne (sop), Zerbinetta (sop), Composer (mezzo), Tenor/Bacchus (ten), Music Master (bar), Harlequin (bar), Major-Domo (speaker), Dancing Master (ten), Truffaldino (bass), Brighella (ten), Scaramuccio (ten), Naiad (sop), Dryad (mezzo), Echo (sop). A popular and highly sophisticated work in Strauss's neo-Mozartian vein, it gave him the opportunity to put on the stage some of his ideas concerning music and drama.
Plot: 18th-century Vienna and legendary Naxos. In the prologue, a wealthy gentleman has hired a COMMEDIA DELL'ARTE troupe, led by Harlequin and Zerbinetta, and an opera company to provide entertainment for his guests. The Major-Domo informs the two groups that time limitations mean that they must perform their offerings simultaneously. Despite the protests of the Composer, cuts are made in the OPERA SERIA *Ariadne*, which the comedians plan to enliven. In the opera, Ariadne bemoans the fact that Theseus has abandoned her, and resists all attempts by the comedians to cheer her up. Bacchus arrives and Ariadne believes him to be the god of death. He persuades her that life is just beginning, and they depart together with the approval of Zerbinetta. [R]

Ariane (*Ariadne*)
Opera in one act by Martinů. 1st perf Gelsenkirchen, 2 March 1961; libr by the composer, after Georges Neveux's *Le Voyage de Thésée*. Principal roles: Ariane (sop), Thésée (bar), Minotaure (bass), Bouroun (ten). Martinů's last opera, said to have been inspired by the art of Maria Callas, it is a work of great beauty and misleading simplicity, with the orchestral passages and the final aria written in neo-classical style and the remainder in the form of a baroque monody. [R]

Ariane et Barbe-Bleue (*Ariadne and Bluebeard*)
Opera in three acts by Dukas. 1st perf Paris, 10 May 1907; libr by Maurice Maeterlinck, after Charles Perrault's story. Principal roles: Ariane (mezzo), Barbe-Bleue (b-bar), Nurse (mezzo), Ygraine (sop), Selysette (mezzo), Mélisande (sop), Bellangère (sop). Dukas's sole opera, it is only rarely performed.
Plot: At his castle, Bluebeard gives his new wife Ariadne six silver keys and one of gold, but forbids her to use them. The silver keys open doors to Bluebeard's treasure and the golden key a door to a staircase. She opens this door and, hearing the wailing of women, discovers Bluebeard's five former wives imprisoned. Bluebeard tries to drag her away but later, when he is away, she and her Nurse unlock the prison vault. Bluebeard is captured by peasants, but Ariadne releases him and, freeing the captive women, encourages them to emerge into a world of hope. However, they hesitate and remain inside the castle. [R]

Arianna (*Ariadne*)
Opera in prologue and eight scenes by Monteverdi. 1st perf Mantua, 28 May 1608; libr by Ottavio Rinuccini. Virtually all of the music is lost, the famous lament being the only substantial portion to survive.

Arianna in Creta (*Ariadne in Crete*)
Opera in three acts by Händel. 1st perf London, 26 Jan 1734; libr by Francis Colman, after Pietro Pariati's libretto for Porpora's *Arianna e Teseo*. Principal roles: Arianna (sop), Teseo (c-ten), Alceste (c-ten), Tauride (mezzo), Minos (bass), Carilda (mezzo). Telling of Theseus's love for Ariadne and of his slaying of the Minotaur, it has never been one of Händel's more successful operas and is only very rarely performed.

Arie (German for 'air')
The German term for aria.

Arié, Raphael (1920–88)
Bulgarian bass, particularly associated with the Italian and Russian repertories. A rich-voiced singer with a good stage presence, he created Truelove in *The Rake's Progress*.

Arie Antiche (Italian for 'ancient airs')
Songs and arias by 17th- and early-18th-century composers (mainly Italian), a group of which often opens a solo recital by a singer. These often include operatic arias, of which two popular examples are 'O cessate di piagarmi' from A. Scarlatti's *Il Pompeo* and 'Nel cor più' from Paisiello's *La Molinara*.

Arietta (Italian for 'little air')
A short aria, such as 'Quand'ero paggio' in Verdi's *Falstaff*.

Ariodant
Opera in three acts by Méhul. 1st perf Paris, 11 Oct 1799; libr by François Benoît Hoffman, after Lodovico Ariosto's *Orlando Furioso*. Principal roles: Ariodant (ten), Ina (sep), Othon (ten). Méhul's own favourite amongst his operas and notable for its dark orchestration, it is nowadays all but forgotten.

Ariodante
Opera in three acts by Händel. 1st perf London, 8 Jan 1735; libr by Antonio Salvi, after Lodovico Ariosto's *Orlando Furioso*. Principal roles: Ariodante (mezzo), Ginevra (sop), Polinesso (c-ten), Lurcanio (ten), Dalinda (sop), King (bass), Odardo (ten). In recent years it has become one of the most frequently performed of Händel's operas.
Plot: Medieval Scotland. Ariodante is betrothed to Ginevra, daughter of the King, but has a rival in Polinesso, Duke of Albany. Polinesso uses the maid Dalinda to help him contrive false evidence that Ginevra is unchaste. Ginevra is saved from execution by a dying confession from Polinesso and by the return of Ariodante who had been thought dead. [R]

Arioso (Italian for 'song-like')
Something which is midway between an aria and plain RECITATIVE, lacking the formal structure of an aria. It is epitomized in early opera by Monteverdi and in the 19th century by Wagner and Moussorgsky.

Ariosto
see panel on page 30

Arkel
Bass role in Debussy's *Pelléas et Mélisande*. He is the blind old king of Allemonde.

Arkhipova, Irina (b 1925)
Russian mezzo, particularly associated with the Russian and Italian repertories. One of the outstanding mezzos of the post-war period, she possessed a rich and beautiful voice, used with outstanding musicianship, and she had a keen dramatic sense. She enjoyed a remarkably long career, singing into her late 60s. She created Klavdiya in Prokofiev's *The Story of a Real Man*, the Commissar in Kholminov's *An Optimistic Tragedy*, Nilovna in Khrennikov's *The Mother* and Varvara in Shchedrin's *Not Love Alone*.

Arlecchino (*Harlequin*) or **Die Fenster** (*The Windows*)
Comic opera in prologue, one act and epilogue by Busoni (Op 50). 1st perf Zürich, 11 May 1917; libr by the composer. Principal roles: Arlecchino (speaker), Matteo (bass), Abbot Cospicuo (bar), Columbina (mezzo), Dr Bombasto (bass), Leandro (ten). Dealing with the

· Lodovico Ariosto ·

The epic poem *Orlando Furioso* (1516/32) by the Italian poet Lodovico Ariosto (1474–1535) has inspired more operas than any other single literary work. About 100 operas are based on incidents in the epic; those by composers with entries in this dictionary are listed below.

Rossi	*Il Palazzo Incantato*	1642
Lully	*Roland*	1685
A. Scarlatti	*Olimpia Vendicata*	1685
Steffani	*Orlando Generoso*	1691
Campra	*Alcine*	1705
A. Scarlatti	*Orlando*	1711
Gasparini	*Rodomonte Sdegnate*	1714
Vivaldi	*Orlando Finto Pazzo*	1714
Fux	*Angelica Vincatrice di Alcina*	1716
Porpora	*Angelica*	1720
Albinoni	*Angelica Delusa da Ruggero*	1725
Vivaldi	*Orlando Furioso*	1727
Händel	*Orlando*	1733
Händel	*Ariodante*	1735
Händel	*Alcina*	1735
Vivaldi	*Ginevra*	1736
Graun	*Angelica e Medoro*	1742
Sacchini	*Olimpia Tradita*	1758
Piccinni	*Il Nuovo Orlando*	1764
Paisiello	*Alceste in Eduba*	1768
Guglielmi	*Ruggiero*	1769
Guglielmi	*Le Pazzie di Orlando*	1771
Hasse	*Ruggiero*	1771
Gazzaniga	*L'Isola d'Alcina*	1772
Piccinni	*Roland*	1778
Haydn	*Orlando Paladino*	1782
Isouard	*Ginevra di Scozia*	1798
Méhul	*Ariodant*	1799
Guglielmi	*Alcina*	1800
Mayr	*Ginevra di Scozia*	1801
G. Mosca	*Ginevra di Scozia*	1802
Portugal	*Ginevra di Scozia*	1805
Nicolini	*Orlando*	1811
G. Mosca	*Le Bestie in Uomini*	1812
Thomas	*Angélique et Médore*	1843

traditional COMMEDIA DELL'ARTE figures and containing a number of operatic quotations and send-ups, it is Busoni's most accessible opera and still receives an occasional performance.

Plot: 18th-century Bergamo. Arlecchino flirts with the mute Annunziata under the nose of her husband Matteo the tailor, trying various ploys to get rid of him. His disgusted wife Columbina berates him and he leaves her in the hands of Leandro, a bombastic cavalier much prone to operatic outbursts in Italian. Arlecchino injures Leandro in a duel, and while Columbina takes him to hospital, Arlecchino elopes with Annunziata. Matteo remains blissfully unaware of the goings-on and calmly continues his sewing and his reading of Dante. [R]

Arlen, Stephen (1913–72)
British administrator. As administrator of Sadler's Wells Opera from 1966, he planned and began both the company's move from Sadler's Wells Theatre to the London Coliseum and the project of an English-language *Ring*. He persisted despite bitter opposition and prophecies of doom, but, tragically, did not live to see the triumphant success of both ventures.

Arlesiana, L' (*The Girl from Arles*)
Opera in three (originally four) acts by Cilea. 1st perf Milan, 27 Nov 1897; libr by Leopoldo Marenco, after Alphonse Daudet's *L'Arlésienne*. Revised version 1st perf Milan, 22 Oct 1898. Principal roles: Federico (ten), Rosa Mamai (mezzo), Vivetta (sop), Metifio (bar), Baldassarre (bass). Cilea's only opera other than *Adriana Lecouvreur* still to be remembered.
Plot: 19th-century Provence. Rosa Mamai's son Federico is in love with a girl from Arles, whilst his mother's godchild Vivetta is in love with him. Rosa and Vivetta produce letters which reveal that Federico's girl has been the mistress of Metifio. Federico decides to forget her and marry Vivetta, but Metifio arouses him to a jealous rage and he finally kills himself in despair. [R]

Arme Heinrich, Der (*Poor Henry*)
Opera in three acts by Pfitzner. 1st perf Mainz, 2 April 1895; libr by James Grun, after the medieval poem by Hartmann von Aue. Principal roles: Heinrich (ten), Agnes (sop), Dietrich (bar), Hilde (sop). Pfitzner's first opera and his only one apart from *Palestrina* still to be remembered.
Plot: Medieval Swabia and Salerno. The minstrel-knight Heinrich has been visited by a divinely-sent illness because of his arrogance, and may only recover if a virgin sacrifices herself on his behalf. Agnes, daughter of Heinrich's faithful servants Dietrich and Hilde, offers herself. However, at the last moment Heinrich receives the strength to snatch away the sacrificial knife descending on Agnes.

Armenian opera composers
see CHUKHADJIAN; TIGRANIAN
Other national opera composers include Artemy Ayvazian (1902–75), Andrey Babayev (1923–64), Alexander Spendiarov (*b* Spendiarian) (1871–1928) and Aro Atepanian (1897–1966).
see also TURKISH OPERA COMPOSERS

Armida
Opera in three acts by Sacchini. 1st perf Milan, 1772; libr by Giovanni de Gamerra, after Torquato Tasso's *Gerusalemme Liberata*. Revised version *Renaud*, 1st perf Paris, 28 Feb 1783; libr revised by J. Leboeuf and Abbé Simon Joseph de Pellegrin. Principal roles: Renaud (ten), Armide (sop), Hidraot (bar), Adraste (bar), Antiope (sop). One of Sacchini's finest operas, it is nowadays virtually forgotten.

Armida
Opera in three acts by Haydn. 1st perf Esterháza, 26 Feb 1784; libr by Jacopo Durandi, after Torquato Tasso's *Gerusalemme Liberata*. Principal roles: Armida (sop), Rinaldo (ten), Zelmira (sop), Idreno (bass), Ubaldo (ten), Clotarco (ten). Haydn's last completed opera, it suffered a long period of total neglect but has received an occasional performance in the last decade. [R]

Armida
Opera in three acts by Rossini. 1st perf Naples, 11 Nov 1817; libr by Giovanni Federico Schmidt, after Torquato Tasso's *Gerusalemme Liberata*. Principal roles: Armida (sop), Rinaldo (ten), Carlo (ten), Goffredo (ten), Astarotte (bass). One of Rossini's best serious operas, notable for its large number of tenor roles, it still receives an occasional performance.
Plot: The sorceress Armida, unable to vanquish the heart of Rinaldo, spirits him away to an enchanted island and falls in love with him. He reciprocates her passion until he realizes that he has been enslaved by magic, whereupon he rejects her. [R]

Armida
Opera in four acts by Dvořák (Op 115). 1st perf Prague, 25 Mar 1904; libr by Jaroslav Vrchlický, after Torquato Tasso's *Gerusalemme Liberata*. Principal roles: Armida (sop), Rinald (ten), Ismen (bar), Hydraot (bass), Petr (bass). Dvořák's last opera, it has some beautiful passages but is only very rarely performed.

Armide
Opera in five acts by Gluck. 1st perf Paris, 23 Sept 1777; libr by Philippe Quinault, after Torquato Tasso's *Gerusalemme Liberata*. Principal roles: Armide (sop), Renaud (ten), Phénice (mezzo), Sidonie (sop), Hidraot (b-bar), Ubalde (bar). Although it contains much fine music, it is one of the least often performed of Gluck's mature operas.
Plot: Damascus, 1099. During the First Crusade, King Hidraot and the sorceress Armida plan to kill Roland, general of the victorious crusaders, but Armida falls in love with him. Roland, ensnared by her magic, is eventually rescued by his fellow knights. [R]

Armide et Renaud (*Armida and Roland*)
Opera in prologue and five acts by Lully. 1st perf Paris, 15 Feb 1686; libr by Philippe Quinault, after Torquato Tasso's *Gerusalemme Liberata*. Principal roles: Armide (sop), Renaud (ten), Hidraot (bass), Ubalde (bar), Phénice (sop), Sidonie (sop), Aronte (bar). One of Lully's greatest operas, it still receives an occasional performance. For plot see *Armide*. [R]

Arminio
Opera in three acts by Händel. 1st perf London, 12 Jan 1737; libr by Antonio Salvi. Principal roles: Arminio (c-ten), Tusnelda (sop), Ramise (mezzo), Varo (ten), Segeste (bass), Sigismondo (c-ten). Dealing with events in the Germano-Roman wars of AD 15–16, it has never been one of Händel's more successful operas and is only very rarely performed.

Armstrong, Richard (b 1943)
British conductor, particularly associated with the Italian repertory, especially Verdi, and with Janáček. He was musical director of the Welsh National Opera (1973–86) and Scottish Opera (1993–). He conducted the first performances of Hoddinott's *The Beach at Falesá* and John Metcalf's *Tornrak*.

Arne, Thomas (1710–78)
British composer. His many stage works, in various forms, include *Rosamond* (London, 7 Mar 1733; libr Joseph Addison), the masque *Comus* (London, 4 Mar 1738; libr John Dalton, after John Milton) [R], *The Judgement of Paris* (London, 1 Aug 1740; libr William Congreve), the masque *Alfred* (Clivedon, 1 Aug 1740; libr James Thomson and David Mallet), in which 'Rule Britannia' appears, ARTAXERXES, THOMAS AND SALLY, the ballad opera *Love in a Village* (London 8 Dec 1762; libr Isaac Bickerstaffe), *Olimpiade* (London 27 Apr 1764; libr Giovanni Gualberto Bottarelli, after Pietro Metastasio) and *The Cooper* (London 9 June 1772; libr composer, after Nicolas-Médard Audinot and François Antoine Quêtant's *Le Tonnelier*) [R]. He made a crucial contribution to the development of British opera, but nowadays his works are only very rarely performed. His illegitimate son **Michael** (*c* 1740–86) was also a composer of several stage works.

Arnold
Tenor role in Rossini's *Guillaume Tell*. Melchtal's son, he is in love with Mathilde.

Arnold, Sir Malcolm (b 1921)
British composer. He has written two operas: *The Dancing Master* (London, 1 Mar 1962, composed 1952; libr J. Mendoza, after W. Wycherley) and *The Open Window* (BBC TV, 14 Dec 1956; libr Sydney Gilliat, after Saki).

Arnould, Sophie (1740–1802)
French soprano. The leading soprano at the Paris Opéra from 1757 until 1778, she was said to have had a fine, if not over large, voice and to have been a passionate singing-actress. Excelling in Rameau and Monsigny roles, she also created, for Gluck, the title-role in *Iphigénie en Aulide* and Eurydice in the revised French version of *Orfeo ed Euridice*. She was a famous wit and conversationalist, much sought after in high society, and attracted the comment 'with such talents you may become a princess' from Mme de Pompadour, Louis XV's mistress. A famous portrait of her by Jean-Baptiste Greuze is in the Wallace Collection, and Pierné's opera *Sophie Arnould* is based on incidents in her life.

Aroldo (*Harold*)
Opera in four acts by Verdi. 1st perf

Rimini, 16 Aug 1857; libr by Francesco Maria Piave. The revised version of STIFFELIO. Principal roles: Aroldo (ten), Mina (sop), Egberto (bar), Briano (bass), Godvino (ten). It contains a considerable amount of new music, including the whole of Act IV. Since the rediscovery of its orchestral score, *Stiffelio* – far the superior work – has nearly always been performed in preference to *Aroldo*.
Plot: Kent and Scotland, 1189–92. The Saxon warrior Aroldo returns from the Crusades to discover that his wife Mina has been seduced by the knight Godvino. Mina's father Egberto avenges the stain on his honour by killing Godvino, whilst Aroldo puts aside his wife. Mina swears eternal love for Aroldo, but he becomes a hermit on the edge of Loch Lomond. When Mina and Egberto are cast ashore there by a storm, husband and wife are reunited. [R]

Arriaga y Balzola, Juan (1806–26)
Spanish composer, whose early death cut short a career of great promise. He wrote one opera, *Los Esclavos Felices* (*The Happy Slaves*, Bilbao, 1820; libr L.F. Comella y Comella).

Arrieta y Corera, Emilio (1823–94)
Spanish composer. He wrote a number of operas, including *Ildegonda* (Milan, 1845; libr Temistocle Solera) and *La Conquista di Granada* (Madrid, 10 Feb 1850; libr Solera), but he is chiefly remembered as a ZARZUELA composer. He wrote over 50 works in this genre, some of which are still performed in Spain. The most successful were *El Dominó Azul* (Madrid, 12 Feb 1853; libr Francisco Comprodón) and *Marina* (Madrid 21 Sept 1855; libr Comprodón), which was later revised as an opera (Madrid, 16 Apr 1871) [R].

Arroyo, Martina (b 1936)
American soprano, particularly associated with the Italian repertory, especially Verdi. One of the finest Verdi sopranos of the 1970s, she possessed a rich and beautiful voice of considerable power, range and agility, which she used with fine musicianship. She had a dignified stage presence.

Arsace
1 Mezzo trouser role in Rossini's *Semiramide*. He turns out to be Semiramide's long-lost son. **2** COUNTER-TENOR role in Händel's *Berenice*. **3** CASTRATO (now mezzo) role in Rossini's *Aureliano in Palmira*. One of the last roles to be written for a castrato. **4** Counter-tenor role in Händel's *Partenope*. He is Rosmira's fiancé.

Arsena
Soprano role in J. Strauss's *Der Zigeunerbaron*. She is Zsupán's daughter.

Artaserse (*Artaxerxes*)
Opera in three acts by Jommelli. 1st perf Rome, 4 Feb 1749; libr by Pietro Metastasio. One of the more than 100 settings of Metastasio's text, Jommelli's version – nowadays forgotten – is significant in that he excluded the DA CAPO aria, thus partly anticipating Gluck's reforms.
Plot: Legendary Babylon. In an attempt to seize the throne, Artabanes kills King Xerxes, whose daughter Mandane is loved by his son Arbace. Artabanes next attempts to poison Xerxes's son Artaxerxes, who loves his daughter Semira. After much complication caused by the divided loyalties involved, Arbace foils his father's machinations. Artabanes is exiled and the two pairs of lovers are united.

Artaxerxes
Opera in three acts by Arne. 1st perf London, 2 Feb 1762; libr by the composer, after Pietro Metastasio's *Artaserse*. Principal roles: Artaxerxes (mezzo), Artabanes (ten), Arbaces (sop), Rimenes (ten), Mandane (sop), Semira (sop). Possibly the finest of Arne's full-scale operas, it is nowadays virtually forgotten. For plot see *Artaserse*.

Arts Florissants, Les
A vocal and instrumental ensemble founded in France in 1979 by the American conductor and harpsichordist William Christie (*b* 1944), which takes its name from a work by M.-A. Charpentier. It is devoted to the performance of works by 17th- and early-18th-century composers, especially Monteverdi, Lully, Charpentier and Rameau. One of Europe's finest early music ensembles, mixing scholarship and fine musicianship with an infectious

· Artists in opera ·

The lives of a number of painters, sculptors and metalsmiths have been the subject of operatic treatment. Amongst the artists who appear as operatic characters are:

- Benvenuto Cellini in Berlioz's *Benvenuto Cellini*, Saint-Saëns's *Ascanio*, Lachner's *Benvenuto Cellini* and Rossi's *Cellini a Parigi*.
- Paul Gauguin in Gardner's *The Moon and Sixpence* and Elizalde's *Paul Gauguin*.
- Vincent van Gogh in Rautavaara's *Vincent*.
- Francisco Goya in Menotti's *Goya*, Osborne's *Terrible Mouth* and Barbieri's *Pan y Toros*.
- Matthias Grünewald in Hindemith's *Mathis der Maler*.
- Michelangelo in F. Ricci's *Luigi Rolla e Michelangelo*.
- Phidias in Christiné's *Phi-Phi*.
- Raphael in Arensky's *Rafael*.
- Rembrandt in Klenau's *Rembrandt van Rijn*.
- Salvator Rosa in Gomes's *Salvator Rosa* and Sobolewski's *Salvator Rosa*.
- Andrea del Sarto in Lesur's *Andrea del Sarto*.
- Cornil Schut in Smareglia's *Cornil Schut*.
- Titian in Kubelík's *Cornelia Faroli*.
- Leonardo da Vinci in Hamerik's *Leonardo da Vinci* and Werle's *Lionardo*.

enthusiasm, it has been responsible for performances and recordings of many early French operas.

Arturo
1 Tenor role in Bellini's *I Puritani*. He is Lord Arthur Talbot, a Cavalier in love with Elvira. **2** Tenor role in Bellini's *La Straniera*. He is in love with Alaide. **3** Mezzo trouser role in Donizetti's *Rosmonda d'Inghilterra*. **4** Tenor comprimario role in Donizetti's *Lucia di Lammermoor*. He is Lord Arthur Bucklaw, whom Lucia is forced to marry.

Arundell, Dennis (1898–1988)
British producer, actor, writer and composer. He directed many notable productions for Sadler's Wells Opera in the immediate post-war period, particularly *Der Fliegende Holländer*, as well as directing the first performances of Vaughan Williams's *The Pilgrim's Progress* and Delius's *Irmelin*. He wrote three books on musical topics: on Purcell, on Sadler's Wells, and his witty *The Critic at the Opera* (1957). He also composed two operas: *Ghost of Abel* (libr after William Blake) and *A Midsummer Night's Dream* (1930; libr after Shakespeare).

Arvidson, Madame
A Swedish fortune-teller, she appears as: **1** Contralto role in Verdi's *Un Ballo in Maschera*. She is Ulrica in the Boston setting. **2** Soprano role in Auber's *Gustave III*.

Ascanio
Mezzo trouser role in Berlioz's *Benvenuto Cellini*. He is Cellini's young apprentice. He is also the subject of Saint-Saëns's *Ascanio*.

Ascanio in Alba
Opera in two acts by Mozart (K 111). 1st perf Milan, 17 Oct 1771; libr by Giuseppe Parini, after Count Claudio Nicolò Stampa's play. Principal roles: Ascanio (sop), Sìlvia (sop), Venere (sop), Aceste (ten). One of Mozart's earliest operas, it prompted Hasse (whose own last opera had had its first performance the previous day) to remark 'this boy will make us all be forgotten'. It is only very rarely performed.
Plot: Legendary Greece. Ascanio has been promised the Arcadian nymph Silvia by his grandmother Venus. Happily, Ascanio turns out to be the young man whom Silvia has loved in her dreams. [R]

Aschenbach, Gustav von
Tenor role in Britten's *Death in Venice*. He is a writer whose love for a beautiful boy leads to his death.

Asile héréditaire
Tenor aria for Arnold in Act IV of Rossini's *Guillaume Tell*, in which he laments the death of his father. Its CABALETTA 'Amis, amis, secondez ma vengeance' is one of the most fearsomely difficult heroic tenor arias ever written.

Assassinio nella Cattedrale, L' (*The Murder in the Cathedral*)
Opera in two acts with intermezzo by Pizzetti. 1st perf Milan, 1 March 1958; libr by the composer and Alberto Castelli, after T.S. Eliot's play. Principal roles: Thomas (bass), four Knights (ten, two bars, bass), four Tempters (ten, three bars). Dealing with the murder of Archbishop Thomas à Becket on 29 Dec 1170, it is one of Pizzetti's finest works and has been widely performed.

Assedio di Calais, L' (*The Siege of Calais*)
Opera in three acts by Donizetti. 1st perf Naples, 19 Nov 1836; libr by Salvatore Cammarano, after Pierre de Belloy's *Le Siège de Calais*. Principal roles: Eustachio (bar), Aurelio (mezzo), Eleonora (sop), Edoardo (bar), Isabella (sop), Incognito (b-bar). One of Donizetti's richest scores, which unusually includes a ballet, it has recently been successfully revived after 150 years of total neglect.
Plot: Calais, 1347. King Edward III offers to raise the English siege of the town if seven leading citizens will sacrifice themselves. The seven burghers who offer themselves include the mayor Eustachio and his young son Aurelio. Their bravery deeply moves Queen Isabella, who pleads with her husband to spare them. Edward magnanimously consents. [R]

Assisa al piè d'un salice
Soprano aria (the Willow Song) for Desdemona in Act III of Rossini's *Otello*.

Assur
Bass role in Rossini's *Semiramide*. He is Semiramide's lover.

Astrologer
1 Tenor role in Rimsky-Korsakov's *The Golden Cockerel*. Possibly the highest-lying tenor role ever written. **2** Baritone role in Britten's *The Burning Fiery Furnace*.

Astuzie Femminile, Le (*Female Wiles*)
Comic opera in two acts by Cimarosa. 1st perf Naples, 26 Aug 1794; libr by Giovanni Palomba. Principal roles: Bellina (sop), Leonora (mezzo), Giampaolo (bass), Dr Romualdo (bass), Filandro (ten). Cimarosa's only full-length work apart from *Il Matrimonio Segreto* still to be remembered.
Plot: 18th-century Rome. According to her father's will, Rome's wealthiest heiress Bellina has to marry the elderly Bergamo merchant Giampaolo. Her tutor Romualdo (although engaged to her governess Leonora) also wishes to marry her. She herself loves Filandro, and the two run away together. Returning in the guise of Cossack officers, the lovers succeed in a subterfuge which enables them to marry.

Atalanta
Opera in three acts by Händel. 1st perf London, 12 May 1736; libr after Belisario Valeriani's *La Caccia in Etolia*. Principal roles: Atalanta (sop), Meleagro (sop), Aminta (ten), Irene (mezzo), Nicandro (bass), Mercury (bass). Written to celebrate the wedding of Frederick, Prince of Wales and Princess Augusta of Saxe-Gotha, it was successful at its appearance but is nowadays only infrequently performed.
Plot: Legendary Arcadia. Disguised as a shepherd, King Meleagro of Aetolia is pursuing his beloved, the princess Atalanta, who feels unable to return his love as she is unaware of his royal status. At the same time, Irene, daughter of Meleagro's confidant Nicandro, plans to test the fidelity of her lover, the shepherd Aminta. After many amorous misunderstandings and complications, the two pairs of lovers are united and Mercury descends to bestow a divine blessing on their union. [R]

Atanasov, Georgy (1882–1931)
Bulgarian composer and conductor. Effectively the founder of Bulgarian opera, and always known as 'the

Maestro', many of his operas are still performed in Bulgaria but are unknown elsewhere. His stage works include the children's opera *For the Birds* (*Za Ptichy*, 1909), the historical *Borislav* (Sofia, 4 Mar 1911; libr N. Popov, after I. Wasov), the further children's operas *The Fountain of Samodiva* (*Samodiskoto Izvorche*, 1911) and *The Golden Girl* (*Zlatnoto Momiche*, 1915), *Moralisti* (Sofia, Jan 1916; libr A. Milenkov), which was the first Bulgarian operetta, *Gergana* (Sofia, 6 June 1917; libr P. Bobevski, after P.R. Slaweikov), *The Abandoned Mill* (*Zapustyalata Vodenitsa*, Sofia, 21 Mar 1923; libr A. Morfov), *The Flower* (*Tsveta*, 1925; libr Chernodrinsky), *Kosara* (1927; libr Danovsky) and *Altsek* (Sofia, 15 Sept 1930; libr P. Karapetrov).

A te, o cara
Tenor aria for Arturo in Act I of Bellini's *I Puritani*, in which he sings of his joy at his approaching marriage with Elvira.

Athalia
Dramatic oratorio in three parts by Händel. 1st perf Oxford, 10 July 1733; libr by Samuel Humphreys, after Jean Baptiste Racine's *Athalie*. Principal roles: Athalia (sop), Josabeth (sop), Joad (c-ten), Joas (treble), Abner (bass), Mathan (ten). Although it is not strictly speaking an opera, it has occasionally been staged.
Plot: Ancient Jerusalem. The Baalite Queen Athalia, daughter of Jezebel, is terrified by a dream of a boy who will effect her downfall. Mathan, priest of Baal, goes to the Temple in search of the boy. The high priest Joad and his wife Josabeth tell the people that Joas, the child they have brought up, is the rightful King of Judea. Promised the support of Abner, captain of the guard, Joad asks Joas who he would take as a model. When Joas replies that his model would be David, he is acclaimed as king. [R]

Athanaël
Baritone role in Massenet's *Thaïs*. A Coenobite monk, he attempts to redeem the courtesan Thaïs but ends up falling in love with her.

Athens
see GREEK NATIONAL OPERA

Atherton, David (b 1944)
British conductor, particularly associated with the French repertory and with 20th-century works. He was a co-founder of the London Sinfonietta, and at his Covent Garden debut was the youngest conductor ever to have appeared in the house. One of the leading exponents of modern opera, he conducted the first performances of Henze's *We Come to the River*, Birtwistle's *Punch and Judy* and *Down By the Greenwood Side* and Crosse's *The Grace of Todd*.

Atlántida, L' (*Atlantis*)
Scenic oratorio in prologue and three parts by de Falla. 1st perf (in concert) Barcelona, 24 Nov 1961 (composed 1929); 1st stage perf Milan, 18 June 1962; libr (in Catalan) by the composer, after Mosén Jacinto Verdaguer and other sources. Principal roles: Queen Isabella (sop), Pyrene (mezzo), Narrator (bar), Archangel (ten). A vast Spanish epic, calling for enormous resources, it was left unfinished at de Falla's death and was completed by Ernesto Halffter.
Plot: Covering a wide range of Spanish myth and history, it includes the immersion of Atlantis, the rescue of Spain by Hercules from the monster Geryon, the foundation of Barcelona, and the discovery of the New World by Columbus. [R]

Atlantov, Vladimir (b 1939)
Russian tenor with a dark and powerful voice. He is particularly associated with heavier Russian and Italian roles, especially the title-role in Verdi's *Otello* and Canio in Leoncavallo's *Pagliacci*, but his technique is such that he has also sung more lyrical roles such as Lensky in Tchaikovsky's *Eugene Onegin* with success. The leading contemporary Russian tenor, he has a restrained stage presence. His wife **Tamara Milashkina** (*b* 1934) was a successful soprano.

Attaque du Moulin, L' (*The Attack on the Mill*)
Opera in four acts by Bruneau. 1st perf Paris, 23 Nov 1893; libr by Louis Gallet, after Émile Zola's *Les Soirées de Medan*. Principal roles: Merlier (bar), Françoise (sop), Dominique (ten), Marcelline (mezzo). An anti-war protest, based on an

incident in the Franco-Prussian War, it is Bruneau's most successful opera, but it is nowadays almost never performed.
Plot: France, 1870. The betrothal of the Flemish peasant Dominique to Françoise, daughter of the miller Merlier and his wife Marcelline, is interrupted by the sounds of war. The Germans attack the mill and seize Dominique, who is condemned to be shot at dawn. He escapes by stabbing a sentry. Merlier is taken out and shot in his place, but almost at once, Dominique – who has joined the French forces – arrives with a squadron proclaiming 'Victory'.

Atterberg, Kurt (1887–1974)
Swedish composer. His five operas met with some success in Sweden, but have not been performed elsewhere. They are *Harvard the Harper* (*Härvard Harpolekare*, Stockholm, 29 Sept 1919; libr composer), *The River Horse* (*Bäckahästen*, Stockholm, 23 Jan 1925; libr A. Österling), *The Burning Land* (*Fanal*, Stockholm, 27 Jan 1934; libr O. Ritter and I.M. Willeminsky, after Heinrich Heine's *Der Schlem von Bergen*), *Aladdin* (Stockholm, 18 Apr 1941; libr Willeminsky and B. Hard-Warden) and *Stormen* (Stockholm, 9 Sept 1948; libr composer, after Shakespeare's *The Tempest*).

At the Boar's Head
Comic opera in one act by Holst (Op 42). 1st perf Manchester, 3 April 1925; libr by the composer, after William Shakespeare's *King Henry IV*. Principal roles: Falstaff (bass), Prince Hal (ten), Doll Tearsheet (mezzo), Mistress Quickly (sop), Pistol (bar). One of Holst's finest stage works, but almost never performed.
Plot: 15th-century Eastcheap (London). Falstaff boasts of his exploits during an attempted highway robbery, until Prince Hal reveals that it was staged by himself. Hal is summoned to Court and practices his answers to his father with Falstaff. Falstaff woos Doll Tearsheet, until, summoned by Pistol, he marches off to the wars. [R]

Attila
Opera in prologue and three acts by Verdi. 1st perf Venice, 17 March 1846; libr by Temistocle Solera, after Zacharias Werner's *Attila, König der Hunnen*. Principal roles: Attila (bass), Odabella (sop), Ezio (bar), Foresto (ten), Leone (bass). One of the most vigorous (if not exactly the most subtle) of Verdi's early works, it is notable for its full-blooded patriotic choruses. It has been regularly performed in recent years.
Plot: Italy, AD 452. Attila has invaded Italy and conquered Aquileia. The captured Odabella pretends loyalty to Attila, but secretly plans revenge for the death of her father, and persuades her lover Foresto to aid her. Ignoring the warning of a dream, and halted at the gates of Rome by Leone, Attila entertains the general Ezio and other Romans to a feast, where Odabella saves him from being poisoned by Foresto so that she can kill him herself. She persuades Attila to spare Foresto and he promises to marry her. Foresto and Ezio now doubt Odabella, but when Attila joins them, she stabs him to death. [R]

Atys
Opera in prologue and five acts by Lully. 1st perf St Germain, 10 Jan 1676; libr by Philippe Quinault, after Ovid's *Fasti*. Principal roles: Atys (ten), Cybèle (mezzo), Sangaride (sop), Célénus (bass). After 300 years of almost complete neglect, it has received a number of performances in the last decade.
Plot: Legendary Phrygia. The nymph Sangaride is betrothed to King Célénus, but she is in love with Atys, as is Cybèle, Queen of the Gods. Atys returns Sangaride's affections and Célénus asks Cybèle for assistance in gaining revenge. Cybèle sends Atys insane and he stabs Sangaride. Recovering his senses, he attempts to kill himself, but Cybèle prevents him and transforms him into a pine tree. [R]

Aubade
A French term meaning a song for the morning (as opposed to a serenade, which is a song for the evening). The best known operatic example is Mylio's 'Vainement ma bien-aimée' in Lalo's *Le Roi d'Ys*.

Auber, Daniel François Ésprit (1782–1871)
French composer. He wrote 46 operas, one of them in collaboration with

Boïeldieu and one with Halévy. The large majority are OPÉRA-COMIQUES, notable for their elegance and sparkling melodies. Many were great successes in their day, but apart from several of their overtures, they are now very seldom performed. The most important include *Leicester* (Paris, 25 Jan 1823; libr Eugène Scribe and Anne-Honoré Joseph de Mélesville, after Sir Walter Scott's *Kenilworth*), FRA DIAVOLO, his most popular and enduring work, GUSTAVE III, the delightful LE CHEVAL DE BRONZE, *L'Ambassadrice* (Paris, 21 Dec 1836; libr Scribe), LE DOMINO NOIR, *Le Lac des Fées* (Paris, 1 Apr 1839; libr Scribe and Mélesville), *Zanetta* (Paris, 18 May 1840; libr Scribe and Jules-Henri Vernoy de Saint-Georges), the highly successful LES DIAMANTS DE LA COURONNE, *L'Enfant Prodigue* (Paris, 6 Dec 1850; libr Scribe), *Zerline* (Paris, 16 May 1851; libr Scribe), *Marco Spada* (Paris, 21 Dec 1852; libr Scribe and Germain Delavigne), which was late revised as a ballet, and the fine MANON LESCAUT. In an altogether different category is his masterpiece LA MUETTE DE PORTICI (or *Masaniello*), which is in effect the first French GRAND OPERA.

Auber's contemporaries, including Wagner, thought highly of him: Rossini – referring to his diminutive stature – called him 'a small musician, but a great music-maker'. He had a considerable influence on other composers, such as Offenbach, Thomas and Sullivan. An almost pathalogically shy man, he was a respected director of the Paris Conservatory (1842–70).

Auden, W.H. (1907–73)
British poet and librettist. He provided texts for Britten (*Paul Bunyan*), Henze (*Elegie für Junge Liebende* and *The Bassarids*), Nabokov (*Love's Labour's Lost*) and Stravinsky (*The Rake's Progress*). All but the first were written in collaboration with Chester Kallman.

Audran, Edmond (1840–1901)
French composer. He wrote some 20 operettas, of which the most important are LA MASCOTTE, his most successful work, *Gillette de Narbonne* (Paris, 11 Nov 1882; libr Henri Charles Chivot and Alfred Duru, after Shakespeare's *All's Well That Ends Well*) and *La Poupée* (Paris, 21 Oct 1896; libr Maurice Ordonneau, after E.T.A. Hoffmann's *Der Sandman*). He also wrote one opera, the unsuccessful *Photis* (Geneva, Feb 1896; libr Louis Gallet).

Au fond du temple saint
Tenor/baritone duet for Nadir and Zurga in Act I of Bizet's *Les Pêcheurs de Perles*, in which they recall the woman with whom they both fell in love and then swear eternal friendship. One of the most famous duets in all opera.

Aufstieg und Fall der Stadt Mahagonny
(*Rise and Fall of the City of Mahagonny*)
Opera in three acts by Weill. 1st perf Leipzig, 9 March 1930; libr by Bertolt Brecht. Principal roles: Jenny (sop), Jimmy Mahoney (ten), Trinity Moses (bar), Mrs Begbick (sop), Jake (ten). One of the most popular of all Weill's stage works, it is an expansion of his earlier MAHAGONNY SONGSPIEL.

Plot: The escaped convicts Mrs Begbick, Trinity Moses and Jake establish Mahagonny, where pleasure will hold sway. To the city come Jenny and her fellow prostitutes, as well as Jimmy and his friends from Alaska. After a close shave with a hurricane, Jimmy decrees anarchy, and the inhabitants have unlimited licence to enjoy themselves. The only condition to be outlawed is that of shortage of money. When Jimmy cannot pay for his drinks, he is arrested, tried and executed. Inflation and disorder cause the citizenry to demonstrate and riot and Mahagonny burns. [R]

Auftrittslied (German for 'entry song')
The name given to an aria, usually in a SINGSPIEL, in which a character introduces himself to the audience at his first appearance. A famous example is Papageno's 'Der Vogelfänger bin ich ja' in Mozart's *Die Zauberflöte*.

Augér, Arleen (1939–93)
American soprano, particularly associated with Mozart and Händel roles. She possessed a beautiful and agile voice, which she used with a fine technique, intelligence and musicianship. Best known as a concert singer and as an outstanding recitalist, her operatic appearances were intermittent.

Augsburg Stadttheater
The present opera house (cap 1,010) in this German city in Bavaria opened in 1877. Destroyed by bombs in 1944, it reopened in 1956. Musical directors have included Heinz Wallberg, István Kertesz, Gabor Otväs and Michael Luig.

Au Mont Ida
Tenor aria for Paris in Act I of Offenbach's *La Belle Hélène*, in which he tells how he made his judgement between the three goddesses.

A un dottor
Bass aria for Dr Bartolo in Act I of Rossini's *Il Barbiere di Siviglia*, in which he threatens to have Rosina locked up in her room. In the past, it was often replaced by a less demanding alternative, 'Manca un foglio', which was composed by Pietro Romani (1791–1877).

Auntie
Mezzo role in Britten's *Peter Grimes*. She manages the local pub, where her nieces are the principal attractions.

Aura amorosa, Un
Tenor aria for Ferrando in Act I of Mozart's *Così fan Tutte*, in which he describes the beauty of Dorabella's love.

Aureliano in Palmira
Opera in two acts by Rossini. 1st perf Milan, 26 Dec 1813; libr by Gian Francesco Romanelli, after Gaetano Senrtor's libretto for Anfossi's *Zenobia di Palmira*. Principal roles: Aureliano (ten), Zenobia (sop), Arsace (mezzo), Publia (sop), Oraspe (ten), Licinio (bass). Telling of the Roman Emperor Lucius Domitius Aurelian (AD 215–75), it is one of Rossini's least successful operas and is nowadays very rarely performed. The overture, however, is well-known as Rossini reused it for both *Elisabetta Regina d'Inghilterra* and *Il Barbiere di Siviglia*. Arsace was one of the last major roles to be written for a CASTRATO.

Auric, Georges (1899–1983)
French composer and administrator. A member of the group 'Les Six', he wrote one opera: *Sous le Masque* (1927; libr Louis Laloy). He was administrator of the Opéra-Comique, Paris (1962–68) and his autobiography, *Quand J'Étais Là*, was published in 1979.

Austin, Frederic (1872–1952)
British baritone. One of the leading British singers of the inter-war period, his 1920 edition of *The Beggar's Opera* enjoyed the longest run in operatic history. He created Eochaidh in Boughton's *The Immortal Hour* and was artistic director of the British National Opera Company (1924–9). His son **Richard** (1903–89) was a conductor.

Austral, Florence (b Mary Wilson) (1894–1968)
Australian soprano, particularly associated with Wagnerian roles. One of the leading Wagnerians of the inter-war period, she possessed a rich and warm voice used with a fine technique and was one of the few Wagnerians of her age to approach Wagner vocally in the same way as BEL CANTO music.

Australia
see AUSTRALIAN OPERA; STATE OPERA OF SOUTH AUSTRALIA; SYDNEY OPERA HOUSE

Australian Opera
Australia's principal opera company, it was founded in 1954 as the Elizabethan Trust following the amalgamation of the New South Wales National Opera and Melbourne's National Theatre Opera Company. It acquired its present name in 1969, and since 1973 has been based at the SYDNEY OPERA HOUSE. Musical directors have been Karl Rankl, Carlo Felice Cillario, Sir Edward Downes, Richard Bonynge and Moffatt Oxenbould.

Australian opera composers
see BENJAMIN; GLANVILLE-HICKS; WILLIAMSON

Other national opera composers include John Antill (1904–86), Richard Meale (*b* 1932) and Peter Sculthorpe (*b* 1929).

Austria
see BREGENZ FESTIVAL; GRAZ OPERNHAUS; LINZ LANDESTHEATER; SALZBURG EASTER FESTIVAL; SALZBURG FESTIVAL; THEATER AN DER WIEN, VIENNA; TIROLESE LANDESTHEATER, INNSBRUCK; VIENNA CHAMBER OPERA; VIENNA STATE OPERA; VIENNA VOLKSOPER

Austrian opera composers
see BERG; BIBER; CERHA; DITTERSDORF; EINEM; FALL; FUX; HAYDN; HAYDN, M.; HEUBERGER; HOLZBAUER; HUMMEL; KAUER; KIENZL; KORNGOLD; KŘENEK; MAHLER; MILLÖCKER; MOZART; MÜLLER; REZNIČEK; SCHENK; SCHMIDT; SCHÖNBERG; SCHUBERT; SEYFRIED; STOLZ; STRAUS, O.; STRAUSS II, J.; SUPPÉ; SÜSSMAYR; WELLESZ; ZELLER; ZEMLINSKY; ZIEHRER

Auto-da-Fé Scene
Act III Scene 2 of Verdi's *Don Carlos*. The grand public scene, which includes the ballet and ends with the burning of the heretics.

Avant de quitter ces lieux
Baritone aria for Valentin in Act II of Gounod's *Faust*, in which he calls on heaven to protect Marguerite whilst he is at the wars. It was added by Gounod for Charles Santley to sing in the first British performance in 1863.

Ave Maria
Soprano aria for: **1** Desdemona in Act IV of Verdi's *Otello*. **2** Giselda in Act II of Verdi's *I Lombardi*.

Ave Signor
Chorus in the prologue of Boito's *Mefistofele*, in which the heavenly host sings praise to God.

Avito
Tenor role in Montemezzi's *L'Amore dei Tre Re*. He is a prince in love with Fiora.

Axur, Rè d'Ormus
see TARARE

Azerbaijan
see BAKU OPERA AND BALLET THEATRE

Azerbaijani opera composers
see HADJIBEYOV
Other national opera composers include Shafiga Akhundova (*b* 1924), Fikret Amirov (1922–84), Afrasiyab Badalbeyli (1907–76), Kara Kareyev (1918–82), Abdul Muslim Mahomeyev (1885–1937) and Boris Zaidman (*b* 1908).

Azione sacra (Italian for 'sacred action')
A term used in the late 17th and early 18th centuries to describe an opera on a religious subject, such as some of those written for Vienna by Draghi. It subsequently came to be used almost entirely in reference to oratorios but was still occasionally used to describe an opera, such as Refice's *Cecilia*.

Azione teatrale (Italian for 'theatrical action')
A term used in the 18th century to describe an opera written for small forces and intended for performance in private aristocratic theatres. Examples include Mozart's *Il Sogno di Scipione* and Gluck's *Il Parnasso Confuso*.

Azucena
Mezzo role in Verdi's *Il Trovatore*. She is an old gypsy who is presumed to be Manrico's mother.

B

Baba the Turk
Mezzo role in Stravinsky's *The Rake's Progress*. She is the bearded lady.

Baccaloni, Salvatore (1909–69)
Italian bass, particularly associated with Italian BUFFO roles, especially the title-role in Donizetti's *Don Pasquale* and Dr Bartolo in Rossini's *Il Barbiere di Siviglia*. Possessing a rich voice and abundant (if occasionally rather broad) comic talents, he is often regarded as the greatest buffo artist of the 20th century. He created Gorgibus in Lattuada's *Le Preziose Ridicole*, Astolfi in Wolf-Ferrari's *Il Campiello* and a role in Pizzetti's *Fra Gherardo*.

Bacchus
The Graeco-Roman god of wine appears in a number of operas, including tenor roles in: **1** Strauss's *Ariadne auf Naxos*. The tenor of the prologue, he rescues the abandoned Ariadne. **2** Bliss's *The Olympians*.

Bach, Johann Christian (1735–82)
German composer. The youngest son of Johann Sebastian Bach, he spent much time in Britain and is sometimes referred to as the 'English Bach'. He wrote 12 operas, all on tragic subjects, notable for their grace, their delicate orchestration, and for their introduction of German techniques into the Italian OPERA SERIA style. His operas, which had some influence on Mozart and which are today surprisingly neglected, are *Artaserse* (Turin, 26 Dec 1760; libr Pietro Metastasio), *Catone in Utica* (Naples, 4 Nov 1761; libr Metastasio), *Alessandro nell'Indie* (Naples, 20 Jan 1762; libr Metastasio), *Orione* (London, 19 Feb 1763; libr Giovanni Gualberto Bottarelli), *Zanaida* (London, 7 May 1763; libr Bottarelli), *Adriano in Siria* (London, 26 Jan 1765; libr Metastasio), *Carattaco* (London, 14 Feb 1767; libr Bottarelli), *Gioas Rè di Giuda* (London, 22 Mar 1770; libr Metastasio), *Temistocle* (Mannheim, 4 Nov 1772; libr Mattia Verazi, after Metastasio), *Lucio Silla* (Mannheim, 4 Nov 1774; libr Verazi, after Giovanni de Gamerra), *La Clemenza di Scipione* (London, 4 Apr 1778; libr composer), perhaps his finest and most successful work, and *Amadis des Gaules* (Paris, 14 Dec 1779; libr Alphonse-Denis-Marie de Vismes du Valgay, after Philippe Quinault) [R]. His brother **Johann Christian Friedrich** (1732–95) also wrote some operas.

Bacquier, Gabriel (b 1924)
French baritone, particularly associated with the Italian and French repertories. He possessed an incisive voice, used with intelligence and musicianship, and was a fine singing-actor, equally at home in serious or comic roles. He created Abdul in Menotti's *The Last Savage*, a role in Rivière's *Pour un Don Quichotte* and the title-role in Lesur's *Andrea del Sarto*. He enjoyed a remarkably long career, singing into his 70s.

Bailey, Norman (b 1933)
British baritone, particularly associated with Wagnerian roles (especially Wotan, Hans Sachs and the Dutchman) and with Giorgio Germont and Kutuzov in *War and Peace*. One of the outstanding post-war British operatic artists, he possesses exemplary diction and a rich and grainy voice of considerable power, which he uses with unfailing intelligence and musicianship. He has recently successfully undertaken a number of bass roles, and is a singing-actor of remarkable insight, nobility and humanity. He created Johann Matthys in Goehr's *Behold the Sun*. His wife **Kristine Ciesinski** (*b* 1952) is a dramatic soprano; her sister **Katherine** (*b* 1950) is a successful mezzo.

Baillie, Dame Isobel (b Bella) (1895–1983)
British soprano. One of the leading British concert artists of her age, with a beautiful

if small voice, her operatic appearances were very rare. Her autobiography, *Never Sing Louder Than Lovely*, was published in 1982.

Baker, Dame Janet (b 1933)
British mezzo, particularly associated with Mozart, Händel, Gluck and Monteverdi roles and with Dido in *Les Troyens* and the title-role in *Maria Stuarda*. Often regarded as the finest British mezzo of the post-war era, she possessed a voice of great beauty and considerable power and range, which she used with intelligence and outstanding musicianship, and she was a compelling singing-actress. Also associated with British opera, she created Kate Julian in *Owen Wingrave* and Cressida in the revised version of *Troilus and Cressida*. She retired from the stage in 1982 and her account of her final operatic year, *Full Circle*, was published in 1983.

Baku Opera and Ballet Theatre
Built in 1911 and reconstructed (cap 1,281) in 1938, it is the principal opera house in Azerbaijan. Works in Russian and Azerbaijani are performed separately.

Balassa, Sándor (b 1935)
Hungarian composer. He has written one opera: *The Man Outside* (*Az Ajtón Kivül*, Budapest, 20 Oct 1978; libr Géza Fodor, after Wolfgang Borchert) [R]. He is musical director of Hungarian Radio.

Balducci
Bass role in Berlioz's *Benvenuto Cellini*. Teresa's father, he is the Papal Treasurer.

Balen, Il
Baritone aria for Conte di Luna in Act II of Verdi's *Il Trovatore*, in which he sings of the tempest raging in his heart caused by his love for Leonora. The highest-lying of all Verdi's baritone arias.

Balfe, Michael (1808–70)
Irish composer and baritone. Following a short but successful singing career, he turned to composition, making a crucial contribution to the development of British opera and becoming its most important composer of the mid-19th century. His operas, largely forgotten nowadays, are notable for their graceful and tuneful melodies and their deft orchestration. His 26 stage works, beginning with *I Rivali di Se Stesso* (Palermo, 1829; libr A. Alcazar, after Friedrich Wilhelm von Ziegler's *Liebhaber und Nebenbuhler in einer Person*), include *The Siege of Rochelle* (London, 29 Oct 1835; libr Edward Fitzball, after Comtesse de Genlis), which established his British reputation, *The Maid of Artois* (London, 27 May 1836; libr Alfred Bunn, after Abbé Antoine-François Prévost's *Histoire du Chevalier des Grieux et de Manon Lescaut*), *Catherine Grey* (London, 27 May 1837; libr George Linley), which was the first British opera without spoken dialogue, *Joan of Arc* (London, 30 Nov 1837; libr Fitzball, after Friedrich von Schiller's *Die Jungfrau von Orleans*), *Falstaff* (London, 19 July 1838; libr S.M. Maggioni, after Shakespeare's *The Merry Wives of Windsor*), THE BOHEMIAN GIRL, the most successful British opera of the 19th century, *The Daughter of St Mark* (London, 27 Nov 1844; libr Bunn, after Jules-Henri Vernoy de Saint-Georges's *La Reine de Chypre*), the very successful *The Rose of Castille* (London, 29 Oct 1857; libr Augustus Harris and Edmund Falconer, after Adolphe Philippe d'Ennery's *Le Muletier de Tolède*), *Satanella* (London, 14 May 1858; libr Harris and Falconer, after Alain René le Sage's *Le Diable Boîteux*), which was long popular, *The Armourer of Nantes* (London, 12 Feb 1863; libr J.V. Bridgeman, after Victor Hugo's *Marie Tudor*) and *Il Talismano* (originally written as *The Knight of the Leopard*, London, 11 June 1874; libr A. Matthison, after Sir Walter Scott's *The Talisman*), which was completed after Balfe's death by MacFarren. His wife **Lina Roser** was a successful soprano.

Ballad
Strictly speaking, the term describes an old song, such as a folk song, which tells a story. It thus came to refer to a self-contained narrative song. Although the most famous operatic ballad is Senta's Ballad in Wagner's *Der Fliegende Holländer*, they are most usually found in French opera. The term is also used to refer to the sentimental songs so popular in English drawing rooms in Victorian times, of which there are a number in opera, particularly by Sullivan.

Ballad of Baby Doe, The
Opera in two acts by Moore. 1st perf Central City, 7 July 1956; libr by John Latouche. Principal roles: Baby Doe (sop), Tabor (bar), Augusta (mezzo), Mama McCourt (mezzo), Wm. J. Bryan (bass). One of the most successful post-war American operas and arguably Moore's finest work, it incorporates American folk melodies. Set during the Colorado gold rush, it recounts the life of the historical Baby Doe Tabor (1854–1935).
Plot: Denver and Washington, 1880–99. Elizabeth 'Baby' Doe has left her husband. She goes to Colorado and falls in love with Horace Tabor, a wealthy man 30 years her senior. Horace divorces his wife Augusta and marries Baby, but the new Mrs Tabor is not accepted in society. Augusta warns Horace that the price of silver is about to collapse, but he ignores her and is ruined. When he dies, Baby retreats to his Matchless Mine, which she has sworn never to sell, to remain there for the rest of her life. [R]

Ballad opera
An 18th-century English theatrical form, which consisted of a play interspersed with songs whose music was arranged from popular melodies by various composers. Nearly always of a comic nature, it usually ridiculed the excesses of contemporary opera and contained political satire. Much the most famous is John Gay's THE BEGGAR'S OPERA, but there are also fine examples by Arne, whilst Allan Ramsey's *The Gentle Shepherd* (Edinburgh, 29 Jan 1729) enjoyed great success in Scotland. The form also flourished slightly later in America, the earliest example being Andrew Barton's *The Disappointment* (Philadelphia, Apr 1767) [R]. The term has occasionally been used in the 20th century by composers to describe a pastoral piece in relatively simple style, such as Vaughan Williams's *Hugh the Drover*.

Ballata (Italian for 'ballad')
A term often used in 19th-century Italian opera to refer to an aria written in dance rhythm. Two Verdi examples are 'Questa o quella' in *Rigoletto* and 'Son Pereda' in *La Forza del Destino*.

Ballet
In early opera, particularly in France, dance was an integral part of the drama (as it had been in Greek drama, which early opera sought to recreate). Only in the early 18th century did opera and ballet become two totally independent art forms. Subsequently, dance has formed an important part of the operatic tradition of only two countries. In Russia, the 19th-century nationalist composers (particularly Borodin, Rimsky-Korsakov and Tchaikovsky) made extensive use of traditional national and regional dances. In France, the rigid structure of 19th-century grand opera at the Paris Opéra demanded a ballet in Act III. This is epitomized in the works of Meyerbeer, but the best examples are actually by Italian composers: Verdi in *Les Vêpres Siciliennes* and *Macbeth* and Rossini in *Guillaume Tell*.

Famous operatic dances are listed under their various titles, as also are specific dance types.

Ballet-héroïque (French for 'heroic ballet')
A French theatrical form, popular in the early and mid-18th century, it was a variety of opera-ballet which laid increased emphasis on the exotic and heroic. It comprised a prologue followed by either three or four acts (or *entrées*), each set in a different location and each telling self-contained and unconnected stories. An example is Rameau's *Les Indes Galantes*.

Ballo delle Ingrate, Il (*The Ball of the Ungratefuls*)
Opera-ballet in one act by Monteverdi. 1st perf Mantua, 4 June 1608; libr by Ottavio Rinuccini. Principal roles: Pluto (bass), Venus (mezzo), Cupid (sop). Really a 'proto-opera' and a forerunner of Lully's early works, it has been regularly performed in recent years.
Plot: Venus and Cupid entreat Pluto to release some of the ungrateful women who have rejected the attentions of their suitors. Their spirits are summoned from Hades and perform a melancholy dance. Pluto warns the ladies of the audience not to follow the example of these pitiful creatures. [R]

Ballo in Maschera, Un (*A Masked Ball*)
Opera in three acts by Verdi. 1st perf

Rome, 17 Feb 1859; libr by Antonio Somma, after Eugène Scribe's libretto for Auber's *Gustave III ou le Bal Masqué*. Principal roles (with the Swedish names first): Gustavus/Riccardo (ten), Amelia (sop), Ankerström/Renato (bar), Oscar (sop), Madame Arvidson/Ulrica (cont), Count Ribbing/Samuel (bass), Count Horn/Tom (bass), Christian/Silvano (bar). One of Verdi's finest and richest middle-period operas, distinguished by a precisely balanced score, it deals with largely fictional events surrounding the assassination of Gustavus III of Sweden on 16 March 1792. Censorship troubles forced Verdi to transpose the action to 17th-century Boston, with Gustavus becoming the English governor Richard Earl of Warwick and Ankerström becoming his Creole secretary Renato. Most modern productions revert to the Swedish setting.
Plot: Stockholm, March 1792. Gustavus is in love with Amelia, the wife of his friend and advisor Ankerström. He is warned by the fortune-teller Madame Arvidson that he will be killed by the next man to shake his hand. In the event, this is Ankerström. Amelia returns Gustavus's love, and Arvidson tells her of a magic herb which will cure her of her feelings. As Amelia is gathering the herb near the scaffold, she is joined by Gustavus and, later, by Ankerström. When the latter discovers that the veiled woman he had agreed to escort back to town is his own wife, he joins Counts Ribbing and Horn in their conspiracy to kill Gustavus. He is chosen for the act and at a masked ball at the opera house discovers Gustavus's identity from the page Oscar and shoots him. Gustavus dies declaring Amelia's innocence and forgiving his enemies. [R]

Balstrode
Baritone role in Britten's *Peter Grimes*. He is a retired sea captain.

Baltimore Civic Opera
Originally founded in 1932 as an opera workshop, the company became fully professional in 1950, with Rosa Ponselle as artistic director. Performances are given at the Lyric Opera House (cap 2,600).

Baltsa, Agnes (b 1944)
Greek mezzo, particularly associated with Rossini, Mozart, Strauss and Verdi roles. She is a fine singing-actress and possesses a rich and flexible voice, even if some may feel that her registers are not entirely knitted together. Sadly, the heavier roles which she has recently undertaken may have caused her voice to coarsen. Married for a time to the bass **Günter Missenhardt** (*b* 1938).

Bampton, Rose (b 1909)
American mezzo and later soprano. A musicianly and sympathetic singer, largely based at the Metropolitan Opera, New York, she enjoyed a successful career as a mezzo, mainly in the Italian repertory, before changing to soprano in 1937 and achieving success in Wagnerian roles. Her husband **Wilfrid Pelletier** (1896–1982) was a successful conductor.

Banda (Italian for 'band')
The off-stage instrumental ensemble in a 19th-century Italian opera, it usually comprised wind and brass only. An example of its use is the arrival of King Duncan in Verdi's *Macbeth*.

Banfield, Raffaello de (b 1922)
Italian composer and administrator. His most important operas are the successful *Lord Byron's Love Letter* (New Orleans, 1955; libr Tennessee Williams) [R] and *Alissa* (Geneva, 4 May 1965; libr Richard Millar). Artistic director of the Teatro Comunale Giuseppe Verdi, Trieste (1972–).

Bánk Bán
Opera in three acts by Erkel. 1st perf Budapest, 9 March 1861; libr by Béni Egressy, after József Katona's play. Principal roles: Bánk Bán (ten), Melinda (sop), Otto (ten), Petur Bán (bass), Gertrude (mezzo), Endre (bar). Erkel's most successful opera, it is a strongly nationalist work still very popular in Hungary but only seldom performed elsewhere.
Plot: Visegrád (Hungary), 1213. In the absence of her warring husband King Endre, Gertrude oppresses the country. Her brother Otto tries to seduce Bánk Bán's wife Melinda. Bánk is troubled by the sad state of the country and goes to confront Gertrude. She attempts to stab

him, but he seizes the weapon and kills her. Meanwhile, Melinda has gone mad and drowned herself. King Endre orders Bánk to be tried, but at this moment servants bring in Melinda's body. Bánk tells Endre that he has had his vengeance for Gertrude's death. [R]

Bantock, Sir Granville (1868–1946)
British composer. He wrote three operas, the first two of which, *Caedmar* (London, 18 Oct 1892; libr Frederick Corder) and *The Pearl of Iran* (Leipzig, 1894; libr composer), were student works. *The Seal Woman* (Birmingham, 28 Sept 1924; libr Marjory Kennedy-Fraser) reflected his long-standing interest in Hebridean folklore. It was successful in its time but is nowadays virtually forgotten.

Banquo
Bass role in Verdi's *Macbeth* and tenor role in Bloch's version. He is Macbeth's co-general.

Bär, Olaf (b 1957)
German baritone, particularly associated with Mozart and lighter Strauss roles. Also a noted recitalist, his warm and attractive voice, used with outstanding intelligence and musicianship, and his good stage presence, have made him one of the finest artists to have come to the fore in recent years. He created the Marquis in Matthus's *Die Weise von Liebe und Tod.*

Barak
Baritone role in: **1** Strauss's *Die Frau ohne Schatten*. He is a dyer. **2** Busoni's *Turandot*. He is Calaf's servant.

Baranović, Krešimir (1894–1975)
Croatian conductor and composer. Particularly associated with the Russian repertory, he was musical director of the Zagreb Opera (1915–25), the Belgrade Opera (1927–9) and the Bratislava Opera (1945–6). He composed two operas: *Shaven and Shorn* (*Striženo-Košeno*, Zagreb, 4 May 1932; libr G. Krklec), a nationalist work incorporating folk material, and the comedy *The Bride of Cetingrad* (*Nevjesta od Cetingrada*, Belgrade, 12 May 1951, composed 1942; libr M. Fotez, after A. Šenoa's *Turci Idu*).

Barbaia, Domenico (1778–1841)
Italian impresario and administrator. One of the most colourful figures in operatic history, he started life as a waiter, inventing the *barbaiata* – chocolate or coffee with a head of whipped cream. Turning to opera management, he ran the Teatro San Carlo, Naples, almost continuously from 1809 to 1840. In the 1820s, he also ran the Theater an der Wien and the Kärtnertortheater in Vienna and both La Scala and the Teatro Canobbiana in Milan. Possessing a remarkable nose for talent, he commissioned many of the finest works of Rossini and Donizetti, as well as Mayr's *Medea in Corinto* and Weber's *Euryanthe*. He lived for some time with the soprano ISABELLA COLBRAN until Rossini relieved him of her. He appears as a character in Auber's *La Sirène*, and was the inspiration of Emil Luka's novel *Der Impresario*.

Barbarina
Soprano role in Mozart's *Le Nozze di Figaro*. She is Antonio's daughter.

Barbe-Bleue (*Bluebeard*)
Operetta in three acts by Offenbach. 1st perf Paris, 5 Feb 1866; libr by Henri Meilhac and Ludovic Halévy. Principal roles: Barbe-Bleue (ten), Boulotte (mezzo), Fleurette (sop), Daphnis (ten), Count Oscar (bar), King Bobèche (ten), Popolani (bar), Clementine (mezzo). Although never one of his most popular works, Offenbach's irreverent view of the Bluebeard legend is still quite often performed.
Plot: Count Oscar discovers that the shepherdess Fleurette is the long-lost daughter of his master King Bobèche. When it turns out that her rustic admirer Daphnis is a prince in disguise, they are able to marry. Meanwhile, Duke Bluebeard, having already lost four wives, is in search of a new bride. A lottery to select one is won by the earthy and worldly-wise Boulotte, who causes a scandal when presented to Bobèche and his queen Clementine. Bluebeard soon tires of her and asks his alchemist Popolani to prepare the usual poison. Boulotte outwits Bluebeard, however, and Popolani reveals that he never carried out his orders, and that all the previous wives are still alive.

Barber, Samuel (1910–81)
American composer. He wrote three operas in a readily accessible late romantic style. They are VANESSA, the mini-opera A HAND OF BRIDGE and ANTONY AND CLEOPATRA. His aunt was the mezzo LOUISE HOMER.

Barberillo de Lavapiés, El (*The Little Barber of Lavapiés*)
ZARZUELA in three acts by Barbieri. 1st perf Madrid, 19 Dec 1874; libr by Luis Mariano de Larra. Principal roles: Paloma (sop), Lamparilla (bar), Marquesita del Bierzo (sop), Don Luis (ten). One of the finest and most popular of all zarzuelas, it is a delightful and tuneful comedy set in Madrid in 1770. [R]

Barber of Seville, The
see BARBIERE DI SIVIGLIA, IL

Barbier, Jules (1822–1901)
French librettist. He wrote a large number of libretti, frequently in collaboration with MICHEL CARRÉ. He provided texts for Gounod (*Le Médecin Malgré Lui*, *Faust*, *Roméo et Juliette*, *La Colombe*, *Polyeucte* and *Philémon et Baucis*), Massé (*Les Noces de Jeanette*, *Pygmalion*, *Paul et Virginie* and *Galathée*), Meyerbeer (*Dinorah*), Offenbach (*Les Contes d'Hoffmann*), Reyer (*La Statue*), Rubinstein (*Nero*), Saint-Saëns (*Le Timbre d'Argent*) and Thomas (*Mignon*, *Psyché*, *Hamlet* and *Françoise de Rimini*).

Barbiere di Siviglia, Il (*The Barber of Seville*) or **L'Inutile Precauzione** (*The Useless Precaution*)
Comic opera in four acts by Paisiello. 1st perf St Petersburg, 26 Sept 1782; libr by Giuseppe Petrosellini, after Pierre Augustin Caron de Beaumarchais's *Le Barbier de Séville*. Principal roles: Figaro (bar), Rosina (sop), Count Almaviva (ten), Dr Bartolo (b-bar), Don Basilio (bass). Enormously popular until eclipsed by Rossini's version, it is still occasionally performed. However, its merits deserve more frequent hearings: the trio for Bartolo and his sneezing and yawning servants is one of the gems of OPERA BUFFA. [R]

Barbiere di Siviglia, Il (*The Barber of Seville*) or **L'Inutile Precauzione** (*The Useless Precaution*)
Comic opera in two acts by Rossini. 1st perf (as *Almaviva*) Rome, 20 Feb 1816; libr by Cesare Sterbini, after Pierre Augustin Caron de Beaumarchais's *Le Barbier de Séville*. Principal roles: Figaro (bar), Count Almaviva (ten), Rosina (mezzo), Dr Bartolo (b-bar), Don Basilio (bass), Berta (sop). Although its first performance was one of the most famous fiascos in operatic history, the piece soon established itself and has remained ever since arguably the most popular of all comic operas.
Plot: 18th-century Seville. Rosina is kept under lock and key by her guardian, the crusty old physician Bartolo, who intends to marry her with the aid of the unscrupulous priest Don Basilio, Rosina's singing teacher. Count Almaviva, disguised as a student, Lindoro, woos her with the aid of Figaro, the local barber and general busybody. Almaviva gains entry to Bartolo's house, disguised firstly as a drunken soldier and secondly as an oily priest, supposedly deputed by Basilio to give Rosina a singing lesson. He manages to cause total confusion each time, but does succeed in letting Rosina know his intentions. Figaro and Almaviva plan Rosina's escape, and after various confusions and misunderstandings have been ironed out, the lovers are united and Bartolo is outwitted. [R]

Barbieri, Fedora (b 1920)
Italian mezzo, particularly associated with the Italian repertory. Possessing a powerful and exciting voice, she was the leading Italian mezzo of the 1950s, excelling in Verdi. Her repertory ran to over 100 roles and she continued singing into her mid-60s. She created Dariola in Alfano's *Don Juan de Mañara*, Lizaveta in Chailly's *L'Idiota* and the Governess in Rossellini's *Il Linguaggio dei Fiori*.

Barbieri, Francisco Asenjo (1823–94)
Spanish composer. The leading exponent of the ZARZUELA revival of the mid-19th century, he wrote 77 stage works. The most successful include *Jugar con Fuego* (*Playing With Fire*, Madrid, 6 Oct 1851; libr Ventura de la Vega) [R], *Los Diamantés de la Corona* (Madrid, 15 Sept 1854; libr Francisco Comprodón, after Eugène Scribe's libretto for Auber) [R], *Pan y Toros* (*Bread and Bulls*, Madrid, 22 Dec 1864;

libr José Picón) and EL BARBERILLO DE LAVAPIÉS, one of the most enduringly popular of all zarzuelas.

Barbier von Bagdad, Der (*The Barber of Baghdad*)
Comic opera in two acts by Cornelius. 1st perf Weimar, 15 Dec 1858; libr by the composer, after *The Tale of the Tailor* in *The Thousand and One Nights*. Principal roles: Abul Hassan Ali Ebn Bekar (bass), Nureddin (ten), Margiana (sop), Caliph (bar), Bostana (mezzo), Cady (ten). By far Cornelius's most successful work, it is a delightful piece which is still regularly performed in Germany but only seldom elsewhere.
Plot: Legendary Baghdad. Nureddin is madly in love with the Cady's daughter Margiana. A meeting is arranged by Bostana, who stipulates the involvement of the barber Abul Hassan to prepare Nureddin. Unfortunately, the barber's unstoppable vocal flow almost causes Nureddin to miss the rendezvous, to which Abul insists on accompanying him. However, when the lovers' meeting is interrupted and Nureddin is shut into a stifling chest, the barber's resourcefulness is instrumental in reviving him. Eventually, the Cady agrees to the lovers' marriage. [R]

Barbirolli, Sir John (1899–1970)
British conductor. He conducted a number of operas, mainly Italian, during the early part of his career, but, sadly (apart from two recordings), none at all after 1954.

Barcarolle (from the Italian *barcaruola*, 'boat song')
A French term, used internationally, it refers to a boating song, particularly of Venetian gondoliers. In 6/8 time and with alternating weak and strong beats, the rhythm is suggestive of the motion of a boat. There are many examples in opera, much the most famous being 'Belle nuit, ô nuit d'amour' in Offenbach's *Les Contes d'Hoffmann*.

Barcelona
see TEATRO LICEO, BARCELONA

Bardolph
Falstaff's henchman appears in a number of operas, including: **1** Tenor role in Verdi's *Falstaff*. **2** Baritone role in Holst's *At the Boar's Head*. **3** Baritone role in Salieri's *Falstaff*.

Barenboim, Daniel (b 1942)
Argentine-born Israeli conductor and pianist. His operatic appearances, infrequent until recently, have included a number of notable Mozart and Wagner performances. He was appointed musical director of the Opéra Bastille, Paris, but was dismissed in Jan 1989 because of artistic disagreements. Artistic director of the Berlin State Opera (1992–). His autobiography, *A Life in Music*, was published in 1991. He was married to the cellist Jacqueline du Pré.

Bari
see TEATRO PETRUZZELLI, BARI

Baritone
see panel on page 48. See also BASS-BARITONE; BASSE-TAILLE; MARTIN; VERDI BARITONE

Barnaba
Baritone role in Ponchielli's *La Gioconda*. He is a spy for the Inquisition.

Barnett, John (b Beer) (1802–90)
British composer. Although none of his works are remembered nowadays, he played an important part in the development of British opera. *The Mountain Sylph* (London, 25 Aug 1834; libr James Thomas Thackeray, after Jean Charles Émmanuel Nodier's *Trilby*), his finest work, which was long popular, is the first significant British romantic opera. In his later, less distinguished works, such as *Fair Rosamond* (London, 28 Feb 1837; libr Zarah Barnett and F. Shannon) and *Farinelli* (London, 8 Feb 1839; libr Barnett), he returned to a simpler, ballad opera style. His autobiography, *Musical Reminiscences and Impressions*, was published in 1906.

Baroque
A term which music has borrowed from architecture, where it describes an elaborate and heavily ornamented style. In music, it describes the style of the late 17th and early 18th centuries; broadly speaking from Lully to Händel in opera.

· *Baritone* ·

From the Greek βαρύτονος, meaning 'heavy-tone', baritone is the middle of the three natural male vocal ranges, between tenor and bass. Its tonal quality is nearer to bass than to tenor. Baritone became regarded as a separate vocal range only in the early 19th century; until then, all non-tenors were called basses of one type or another. Many different subdivisions of the baritone voice have evolved, particularly in Germany. They often overlap and do not correspond precisely from one country to another. They are seldom used by composers, but are useful as an indication of the character of a role, even if rather less so for its exact TESSITURA. The main French, German and Italian categories are as follows:

	Name	Range	Examples
FRANCE	*basse-taille*	g to f	Theseus in *Hippolyte et Aricie*
	baryton	C to $a^{\flat\prime}$	Athanaël in *Thaïs*
	Martin	C to a'	Pelléas in *Pelléas et Mélisande*
GERMANY	*Bass-bariton*	$A^{\flat}$ to f	Wotan in *Das Rheingold*
	Spielbariton	$A^{\flat}$ to g	Title-role in *Don Giovanni*
	Heldenbariton	C to $a^{\flat\prime}$	Jokanaan in *Salome*
	hoher Bariton	C to $a^{\flat\prime}$	Sir Ruthven in *Der Vampyr*
	Kavalierbariton	C to $a^{\flat\prime}$	Count in *Capriccio*
ITALY	*baritono cantante*	C to g	Title-role in *Belisario*
	baritono brillante	C to $a^{\flat\prime}$	Dr Malatesta in *Don Pasquale*
	Verdi baritone	C to a'	Conte di Luna in *Il Trovatore*

Below are listed the 115 baritones with entries in this dictionary. Their nationalities are given in brackets afterwards.

Adam, Theo (Ger)
Ahlersmeyer, Mathieu (Ger)
Allen, Thomas (Br)
Amato, Pasquale (It)
Ancona, Mario (It)
Austin, Frederic (Br)
Bacquier, Gabriel (Fr)
Bailey, Norman (Br)
Bär, Olaf (Ger)
Bastianini, Ettore (It)
Battistini, Mattia (It)
Bechi, Gino (It)
Berry, Walter (Aus)
Blanc, Ernest (Fr)
Bockelmann, Rudolf (Ger)
Bösch, Christian (Aus)
Bruscantini, Sesto (It)
Bruson, Renato (It)
Capecchi, Renato (It)
Cappuccilli, Piero (It)
Dam, José van (Belg)
Dens, Michel (Fr)
Desderi, Claudio (It)
Domgraf-Fassbaender, Willi (Ger)
Evans, Sir Geraint (Br)
Faure, Jean-Baptiste (Fr)
Fischer-Dieskau, Dietrich (Ger)
Forsell, John (Swe)
Frantz, Ferdinand (Ger)
Fugère, Lucien (Fr)
Galeffi, Carlo (It)
García, Manuel (Sp)
Glossop, Peter (Br)
Gobbi, Tito (It)
Gramm, Donald (US)
Guelfi, Giangiacomo (It)
Hagegård, Håkan (Swe)
Hammond-Stroud, Derek (Br)
Hampson, Thomas (US)
Hemsley, Thomas (Br)
Herincx, Raimund (Br)
Hotter, Hans (Ger)
Hvorostovsky, Dmitri (Russ)
Hynninen, Jorma (Fin)
Inghillieri, Giovanni (It)
Jerger, Alfred (Aus)
Kéléman, Zoltán (Hung)
Kraus, Otakar (Cz)
Krause, Tom (Fin)
Kunz, Erich (Aus)
Kusche, Benno (Ger)
Leiferkus, Sergei (Russ)
Lisitsian, Pavel (Arm)
London, George (US)
Luca, Giuseppe de (It)
Luxon, Benjamin (Br)
Lytton, Sir Henry (Br)
McIntyre, Sir Donald (NZ)
MacNeil, Cornell (US)
Manuguerra, Matteo (Fr)
Marcoux, Vanni (Fr)
Martin, Jean-Blaise (Fr)
Massard, Robert (Fr)
Maurel, Victor (Fr)
Mazurok, Yuri (Russ)
Merrill, Robert (US)
Milnes, Sherrill (US)
Neidlinger, Gustav (Ger)
Nimsgern, Siegmund (Ger)
Nissen, Hans Hermann (Ger)
Noble, Dennis (Br)
Noble, John (Br)
Nucci, Leo (It)
Panerai, Rolando (It)
Paskalis, Kostas (Gk)
Pini-Corsi, Antonio (It)
Prey, Hermann (Ger)
Quilico, Louis (Can)
Reardon, John (US)
Reich, Günter (Ger)
Ronconi, Giorgio (It)
Rothmüller, Marko (Cro)
Ruffo, Titta (It)
Saedén, Erik (Swe)
Santley, Sir Charles (Br)
Schlusnus, Heinrich (Ger)
Schöffler, Paul (Ger)
Schorr, Friedrich (Hung)
Scotti, Antonio (It)
Sereni, Mario (It)
Shilling, Eric (Br)
Shirley-Quirk, John (Br)
Silveri, Paolo (It)
Singher, Martial (Fr)
Souzay, Gérard (Fr)
Stabile, Mariano (It)
Stewart, Thomas (US)
Stracciari, Riccardo (It)
Taddei, Giuseppe (It)
Tagliabue, Carlo (It)
Tamburini, Antonio (It)
Terfel, Bryn (Br)
Tibbett, Lawrence (US)
Trimarchi, Domenico (It)
Uhde, Hermann (Ger)
Uppman, Theodore (US)
Valdegno, Giuseppe (It)
Varesi, Felice (It)
Wächter, Eberhard (Aus)
Warren, Leonard (US)
Weikl, Bernd (Aus)
Wilson–Johnson, David (Br)
Wixell, Ingvar (Swe)
Yurisich, Gregory (Aust)
Zancanaro, Giorgio (It)

Barraud, Henry (b 1900)
French composer. His five operas, which have had some success in France, are *La Farce de Maître Pathelin* (Paris, 24 June 1948, composed 1937; libr Gustave Cohen), *Numance* (Paris, 15 Apr 1955, composed 1950; libr Salvador de Madariaga, after Miguel Cervantes's *La Numancia*), the comedy *Lavinia* (Aix-en-Provence, 20 July 1961, composed 1958; libr Félicien Marceau), the radio opera *La Fée aux Miettes* (1967; libr after Charles Nodier) and *Tête d'Or* (Paris Radio, 1985, composed 1980; libr after Paul Claudel). He was musical director of Radio France (1937–44).

Barstow, Josephine (b 1940)
British soprano, particularly associated with Verdi, Strauss and Janáček roles and with contemporary operas. She possesses a good voice, and is a powerful, intense and deeply committed singing-actress, however occasionally the clarity of her diction is less than perfect. She created Denise in *The Knot Garden*, Gayle in *The Ice Break*, the Young Woman in Henze's *We Come to the River*, Marguerite in Crosse's *The Story of Vasco* and Benigna in Penderecki's *Die Schwarze Maske*. Her husband **Ande Anderson** was a staff producer at Covent Garden.

Bartered Bride, The (*Prodaná Nevěsta*)
Comic opera in three acts by Smetana. 1st perf Prague, 30 May 1866; libr by Karel Sabina. Revised version 1st perf Prague, 25 Sept 1870. Principal roles: Mařenka (sop), Jeník (ten), Kecal (bass), Vašek (ten), Krušina (bar), Ludmila (mezzo), Circus Master (ten), Tobiaš Mícha (bass), Esmeralda (sop), Háta (mezzo). Smetana's most successful work and the most popular of all Czech operas, it combines much traditional Czech material with its charm and humour, and is one of the very few intensely nationalist operas to have transcended national boundaries.
Plot: 19th-century Bohemia. The peasant girl Mařenka is in love with the handsome but poor Jeník, whose family origins are unknown. Working with the persuasive and avaricious marriage-broker Kecal, Mařenka's parents, Krušina and Ludmila, are adamant that she must marry the son of a wealthy man, and agree to Vašek, the son of Tobiaš Mícha and Háta. Furious, Mařenka seeks out Vašek, whom she has never met – and who is something of a simpleton with a nervous stammer – and, pretending to be someone else, discourages him from marrying her. Meanwhile, Kecal persuades Jeník to relinquish Mařenka in exchange for money. Jeník agrees on condition that Mařenka marries 'the eldest son of Tobiaš Mícha'. Both Mařenka's wiles and Jeník's apparent disregard for her lead to numerous misunderstandings, until it is revealed that Mícha's eldest son, long supposed dead, is, in fact, Jeník. Kecal is outwitted, the lovers are united, and Vašek marries Esmeralda of the travelling circus, which he joins. [R]

Bartók, Béla (1881–1945)
Hungarian composer. One of the most important composers of the 20th century, he wrote only one opera, the symbolist DUKE BLUEBEARD'S CASTLE. However, his contribution to opera is out of all proportion to the amount he actually wrote: his harmonic audacity and his richness of orchestration had wide international influence, and his vocal writing – based on Hungarian speech rhythms – had a profound influence on subsequent Hungarian composers such as Kodály.

Bartoletti, Bruno (b 1926)
Italian conductor, particularly associated with the Italian repertory and with contemporary operas. He was musical director of the Rome Opera (1965–9), the Maggio Musicale Fiorentino (1986–91) and the Chicago Lyric Opera (1964–). He conducted the first performances of Rocca's *Antiche Iscrizioni*, Malipiero's *Il Figliuol Prodigo* and *Venere Prigioniera*, Mortari's *La Scuola delle Mogli*, Penderecki's *Paradise Lost* and Ginastera's *Don Rodrigo*.

Bartoli, Cecilia (b 1966)
Italian mezzo, particularly associated with Rossini and Mozart roles. One of the most exciting talents to have emerged in recent years, she possesses a rich, warm voice of considerable range and remarkable agility. She has a good stage

presence which is enhanced by her personal beauty.

Bartolo, Dr
The pompous physician of Beaumarchais's plays appears as a bass role in Rossini's and Paisiello's *Il Barbiere di Siviglia* and Mozart's *Le Nozze di Figaro.*

Basel Stadttheater
The opera house (cap 1,000) in this Swiss city opened on 20 Sept 1909. Musical directors have included Silvio Varviso, Armin Jordan, Michael Boder and Walter Weller.

Basilio, Don
The intriguing priest of Beaumarchais's plays appears as: **1** Bass role in Rossini's and Paisiello's *Il Barbiere di Siviglia.* **2** Tenor role in Mozart's *Le Nozze di Figaro.*

Basoche, La
Operetta in three acts by Messager. 1st perf Paris, 30 May 1890; libr by Albert Carré. Principal roles: Clément (ten), Colette (sop), Marie (mezzo), Duc de Longueville (bar). One of Messager's most successful works, it is still occasionally performed in France.
Plot: Paris, 1514. Clément Marot is elected 'King of the Basoche', the guild of young legal clerks. The post must only be filled by a bachelor, and Clément is already married to Colette, whose existence he has kept secret. When Colette arrives and sees Clément acting as a king, she believes that she has married Louis XII, who has in fact contracted a morganatic marriage with Marie, an English princess. When Marie, chaperoned by the Duc de Longueville, arrives incognito, she too mistakes Clément for the real king. After much confusion, everything is sorted out when the real Louis appears. At Marie's insistence, he forgives Clément for his duplicity in keeping his marriage to Colette a secret. [R Exc]

Bass
see panel on page 51. See also BASS-BARITONE; BASSO-BUFFO

Bassarids, The
Opera in one act with INTERMEZZO by Henze. 1st perf Salzburg, 6 Aug 1966; libr by W.H. Auden and Chester Kallman, after Euripides's *The Bacchae.* Principal roles: Pentheus (bar), Dionysus (ten), Agave (mezzo), Tiresias (ten), Autonoë (sop), Cadmus (bass), Captain of the Guard (bar), Beroë (mezzo). Structured on the lines of a symphony, it is one of the most powerful post-war operas and is arguably Henze's masterpiece. In the contrasting intermezzo, four of the characters enact the Judgement of Calliope.
Plot: Legendary Thebes. In a situation representing the conflict between social repression and sexual liberation, King Pentheus attempts to suppress the worship of Dionysus. He dresses as a woman to spy upon the activities of Dionysus's frenzied followers, but is discovered and is torn to pieces by the women, who include his mother Agave. [R]

Bass-baritone
A loose term which describes a voice or a role (such as the Dutchman in Wagner's *Der Fliegende Holländer*) which contains both bass and baritone elements.

Basse-taille (French for 'low edge')
A term used in France in the 17th and 18th centuries to describe a low tenor (who would nowadays be called a baritone).

Basso-buffo
An Italian term which describes a role (such as Bartolo in *Il Barbiere di Siviglia* and *Le Nozze di Figaro* or Dulcamara in Donizetti's *L'Elisir d'Amore*) of a comic nature which usually requires a voice with a facility in patter. It is called *basse-bouffe* in France. Famous basso-buffos have included Salvatore Baccaloni, Fernando Corena and Enzo Dara.

Basso continuo
see CONTINUO

Bastianini, Ettore (1922–67)
Italian baritone, particularly associated with the Italian repertory. Beginning as a bass, he turned to baritone roles in 1952 and developed a rich, dark and velvety voice which he used with a fine technique. His early death from cancer removed one of the finest Verdi baritones of the post-war era.

· *Bass* ·

From the Italian *basso*, meaning 'low', bass is the lowest male vocal range. Until the early 19th century, baritones were also classed as basses, but are now regarded as a seperate species. Many different subdivisions of the bass voice have evolved, particularly in France and Germany. They often overlap and do not correspond precisely from one country to another. They are seldom used by composers, but are useful as an indication of the character of a role, even if rather less so for its exact TESSITURA. The main French, German and Italian categories are as follows:

	Name	Range	Example
FRANCE	*basse-bouffe*	F to f	Agamemnon in *La Belle Hélène*
	basse de caractère	G to e	Méphistophélès in *Faust*
	basse noble or *basse chantante*	F to f	Bertram in *Robert le Diable*
	basse-contre	$E^\flat$ to d	Pluto in *Hippolyte et Aricie*
GERMANY	*Bass-bariton*	$A^\flat$ to f	Wotan in *Das Rheingold*
	hoher Bass	G to f	Caspar in *Der Freischütz*
	komischer Bass	F to f	Osmin in *Die Entführung aus dem Serail*
	tiefer Bass	E to e	Sarastro in *Die Zauberflöte*
ITALY	*basso cantante*	F to f	King Philip in *Don Carlos*
	basso-buffo	F to f	Don Magnifico in *La Cenerentola*
	basso profondo	D to e	Grand Inquisitor in *Don Carlos*

Below are listed the 78 basses with entries in this dictionary. Their nationalities are given in brackets afterwards.

Adams, Donald (Br)
Allan, Richard Van (Br)
Arié, Raphael (Bulg)
Baccaloni, Salvatore (It)
Bastin, Jules (Belg)
Böhme, Kurt (Ger)
Borg, Kim (Fin)
Brannigan, Owen (Br)
Burchuladze, Paata (Geo)
Chaliapin, Fyodor (Russ)
Christoff, Boris (Bulg)
Corena, Fernando (Swit)
Czerwenka, Oskar (Aus)
Dara, Enzo (It)
Díaz, Justino (PR)
Edelmann, Otto (Aus)
Estes, Simon (US)
Flagello, Ezio (US)
Franklin, David (Br)
Frick, Gottlob (Ger)
Galli, Filippo (It)
Ghiaurov, Nicolai (Bulg)
Ghiuselev, Nicola (Bulg)
Greindl, Josef (Ger)
Haken, Eduard (Cz)
Haugland, Aage (Den)
Hines, Jerome (US)
Howell, Gwynne (Br)
Journet, Marcel (Fr)
Jungwirth, Manfred (Aus)
Kipnis, Alexander (Ukr)
Lablache, Luigi (It)
Langdon, Michael (Br)
Lazzari, Virgilio (It)
Lloyd, Robert (Br)
Malas, Spiro (US)
Manners, Charles (Ire)
Mayr, Richard (Aus)
Moll, Kurt (Ger)
Montarsolo, Paolo (It)
Morris, James (US)
Navarini, Francesco (It)
Neri, Giulio (It)
Nesterenko, Yevgeny (Russ)
Ognivstev, Alexander (Russ)
Pasero, Tancredi (It)
Petrov, Ivan (Russ)
Petrov, Osip (Russ)
Pinza, Ezio (It)
Plançon, Pol (Fr)
Plishka, Paul (US)
Raimondi, Ruggero (It)
Ramey, Samuel (US)
Reizen, Mark (Ukr)
Reszke, Édouard de (Pol)
Ridderbusch, Karl (Ger)
Robinson, Forbes (Br)
Rossi-Lemeni, Nicola (It)
Rouleau, Joseph (Can)
Salminen, Matti (Fin)
Siepi, Cesare (It)
Sotin, Hans (Ger)
Soyer, Roger (Fr)
Tajo, Italo (It)
Talvela, Martti (Fin)
Tomlinson, John (Br)
Tozzi, Giorgio (US)
Treigle, Norman (US)
Uhde, Hermann (Ger)
Vedernikov, Alexander (Russ)
Vieuille, Félix (Fr)
Vinco, Ivo (It)
Wallace, Ian (Br)
Ward, David (Br)
Weber, Ludwig (Ger)
White, Willard (Jam)
Zaccaria, Nicola (Gk)
Zítek, Vilém (Cz)

Bastien und Bastienne
Comic opera in one act by Mozart (K 50). 1st perf Vienna, Sept 1786; libr by Friedrich Wilhelm Weiskern, after Charles-Simon Favart's *Les Amours de Bastien et Bastienne*, itself a parody of Jean-Jacques Rousseau's LE DEVIN DU VILLAGE. Principal roles: Bastien (ten), Bastienne (sop), Colas (bass). One of Mozart's earliest stage works, written when he was 12 and first performed at the home of the hypnotist Anton Mesmer, it is musically astonishingly assured. It is still quite often performed, sometimes with a cast of children.
Plot: 18th-century France. Bastienne, believing that Bastien no longer loves her, seeks the help of the soothsayer Colas to win him back. Colas advises her to pretend indifference towards Bastien, and at the same time he tells Bastien that Bastienne's ardour has cooled. The ploy succeeds: Bastien woos Bastienne with renewed fervour and wins his suit. [R]

Bastin, Jules (b 1933)
Belgian bass, particularly associated with the French repertory, and with Baron Ochs in *Der Rosenkavalier*. He possessed a warm, lyric voice and on stage was at his best in comedy, in which he used his substantial physique to good effect. He created the Banker in the three-act version of *Lulu* and Don Diègue in Debussy's *Rodrigue et Chimène*.

Battaglia di Legnano, La (*The Battle of Legnano*)
Opera in three acts by Verdi. 1st perf Rome, 27 Jan 1849; libr by Salvatore Cammarano, after Joseph Méry's *La Battaille de Toulouse*. Principal roles: Arrigo (ten), Lida (sop), Rolando (bar), Federico (bass). A strongly nationalist work, telling of the defeat of the Emperor Frederick Barbarossa by the Lombard League on 29 May 1176, it was Verdi's gift to the Risorgimento, which was at that time attempting to expel the Austrians from Lombardy. It is still occasionally performed.
Plot: Milan and Como, 1176. Arrigo returns wounded from war to discover that his beloved Lida has married Rolando, a Milanese army captain. Federico invades Italy, and Arrigo joins the Knights of Death, who vow to die in the defence of Milan. Lida tries to dissuade him and the two are discovered together by Rolando, who denounces them. Arrigo kills Federico but is himself mortally wounded. He dies swearing to Rolando that Lida's honour is intact. [R]

Batti, batti
Soprano aria for Zerlina in Act I of Mozart's *Don Giovanni*, in which she invites Masetto's anger and thus regains his affection.

Battistini, Mattia (1856–1928)
Italian baritone, particularly associated with Verdi and Donizetti roles. One of the greatest baritones of all time, he possessed a voice of great beauty and flexibility, used with style and a matchless technique. His range was so wide that Massenet adapted the title-role of Werther for him. He enjoyed an exceptionally long career, singing well into his 70s, and was the one great singer of the late BEL CANTO period who lived to preserve his singing on records. He created Giacomo in Mascagni's *I Rantzau*.

Battle, Kathleen (b 1948)
American soprano, particularly associated with Mozart and lighter Italian roles and with Zerbinetta. Possessing a lovely and agile voice used with a fine technique, she has an enchanting stage presence which is heightened by her personal beauty. One of the foremost contemporary light lyric sopranos, despite a temperament which has from time to time presented a challenge to her colleagues.

Baudo, Serge (b 1927)
French conductor, nephew of the cellist Paul Tortelier. Particularly associated with the French repertory, he was musical director of the Paris Opéra (1967–9) and the Opéra de Lyon (1969–71) and founded the Lyon Berlioz Festival in 1979. He conducted the first performances of Milhaud's *La Mère Coupable*, Menotti's *The Last Savage* and Barraud's *Lavinia*.

Bavarian State Opera
One of Germany's leading companies, it is based at the Nationaltheater (cap 2,100) in Munich, which originally opened in 1818. It was destroyed by bombs on 3 Oct 1943 and reopened on 21 Nov 1963. The

annual season runs from September to July, and the repertory is notable for its strong Wagner and Strauss traditions. Musical directors have included Hans von Bülow, Franz Wüllner, Hermann Levi, Felix Mottl, Bruno Walter, Hans Knappertsbusch, Clemens Krauss, Ferdinand Leitner, Sir Georg Solti, Rudolf Kempe, Ferenc Fricsay, Joseph Keilberth, Wolfgang Sawallisch and Peter Schneider.

Baylis, Lilian (1874–1937)
British administrator. As manager of London's Old Vic Theatre from 1898 to 1937 and by her reopening of Sadler's Wells Theatre in 1931 (where she presented opera in English with British singers), she laid the foundations from which grew Britain's two great national companies: the Royal Ballet and the English National Opera.

Bayreuth Festival
The annual summer festival at this German town in Franconia is devoted to the operas of Wagner. Performances are given at the Festpielhaus (cap 1,800), which opened on 13 Aug 1876. Because of financial problems there were no further performances until 1882, when *Parsifal* received its first performance. Since then, there have been performances every year, except during World War II. Designed by Wagner himself, the theatre resembles a classical amphitheatre and has a superb acoustic, owing to the fact that the orchestra is covered. The hard benches which serve as seating have been a trial for audiences for over a century! Control of the festival has always remained with the Wagner family: the artistic directors have been Cosima Wagner (1883–1906), Siegfried Wagner (1906–30), Winifred Wagner (1931–44), Wieland and Wolfgang Wagner (1951–66) and Wolfgang Wagner alone (1966–).

Bear, The
Comic opera in one act by Walton. 1st perf Aldeburgh, 3 June 1967; libr by Paul Dehn, after Anton Chekhov's play. Principal roles: Madame Popova (mezzo), Smirnov (bar), Luka (bass). Walton's second opera, it is an amusing little piece which contains affectionate parodies of several contemporary composers, including Britten.
Plot: Russia, 1890. Madame Popova, who is in mourning, and the boorish Smirnov, a creditor of her late husband, quarrel violently over the payment of the debt and decide to fight a duel. Whilst he is instructing the widow in the use of firearms, Smirnov – to his astonishment – falls in love with her. [R]

Beaton, Sir Cecil (1907–79)
British designer and photographer. His widespread theatrical work included the designs for three notable productions at the Metropolitan Opera, New York: *La Traviata*, *Turandot* and the first performance of Barber's *Vanessa*. He also designed a *Turandot* for Covent Garden.

Beatrice di Tenda
Opera in two acts by Bellini. 1st perf Venice, 16 March 1833; libr by Felice Romani, after Carlo Tebaldi-Fores's play. Principal roles: Beatrice (sop), Filippo (bar), Orombello (ten), Agnese (mezzo). Bellini's penultimate opera, it tells of Filippo Maria Visconti (1392–1447), Duke of Milan. It was a failure at its appearance and although it is musically one of his finest works, it has been performed only infrequently ever since.
Plot: Milan, 1418. Having gained his dukedom by marriage to Beatrice, whose subjects he rules by oppression, Filippo Visconti tires of his wife and falls in love with Agnese del Maino. Beatrice has rejected the advances of Orombello, whom Agnese secretly loves but whom she eventually betrays to Filippo. Under torture, Orombello falsely testifies against Beatrice. He subsequently recants, but Filippo remains obdurate in condemning his wife to death. As she is led to her execution, Beatrice forgives the distraught and now repentant Agnese. [R]

Béatrice et Bénédict
Comic opera in two acts by Berlioz. 1st perf Baden-Baden, 9 Aug 1862; libr by the composer, after William Shakespeare's *Much Ado About Nothing*. Principal roles: Béatrice (mezzo), Bénédict (ten), Héro (sop), Ursule (mezzo), Claudio (bar), Somarone (b-bar), Don Pédro (bass). Berlioz's last opera, it follows Shakespeare reasonably closely, but omits the darker

Don John sub-plot and replaces Verges and Dogberry with the pedantic *Kapellmeister* Somarone. Despite the great beauty of much of the music, it is only intermittently performed.

Plot: Messina, *c* 1700. Claudio is warmly welcomed home from the wars by his beloved Héro, but his friend Bénédict invites only disdain from Béatrice. Bénédict is as scornful of marriage as Béatrice is of him, and the two develop a relationship based on verbal sparring. They eventually capitulate to the growing feelings of love for one another and marry in a double wedding with Claudio and Héro. [R]

Beatrix Cenci

Opera in two acts by Ginastera (Op 38). 1st perf Washington, 10 Sept 1971; libr by Alberto Girri and William Shand, after Stendhal's *Chroniques Italiennes* and Percy Bysshe Shelley's *The Cenci*. Principal roles: Beatrix (sop), Count Francesco (b-bar), Lucrecia (mezzo), Orsino (ten), Bernardo (treble). Possibly Ginastera's finest opera, it tells of the gory events surrounding the execution of a 22-year-old girl in Rome in 1599 for complicity in the murder of her father.

Beaumarchais

see panel below

· *Beaumarchais* ·

The French playwright, adventurer and musician Pierre Augustin Caron de Beaumarchais (1732–99) occupies an important place in operatic history. He wrote a number of libretti, of which the most important is Salieri's *Tarare* (1787), whose second edition contains a preface discussing opera's musico-dramatic parameters and claiming that greater weight should be given to the words. Beaumarchais is himself the subject of an operetta by a minor composer, and also appears as a character in Corigliano's *The Ghosts of Versailles*. His trilogy of Figaro plays has attracted more composers than almost any other single literary subject. Those operas by composers with entries in this dictionary are listed below.

Le Barbier de Séville		
F. Benda	*Der Barbier von Sevilla*	1776
Paisiello	*Il Barbiere di Siviglia*	1782
Isouard	*Il Barbiere di Siviglia*	1796
Rossini	*Il Barbiere di Siviglia*	1816
Morlacchi	*Il Barbiere di Siviglia*	1816
Giménez	*El Barbero de Sevilla*	1901
La Folle Journée ou Le Mariage de Figaro		
Mozart	*Le Nozze di Figaro*	1786
Dittersdorf	*Die Hochzeit des Figaro*	1789
Portugal	*La Pazza Giornata*	1799
L. Ricci	*Le Nozze di Figaro*	1838
La Mère Coupable		
Milhaud	*La Mère Coupable*	1966

Operas not based directly on the trilogy but using their characters include:

Paer	*Il Nuovo Figaro*	1794
Carafa	*Les Deux Figaros*	1827
Rossi	*La Figlia di Figaro*	1846
Cagnoni	*Il Testamento di Figaro*	1848
Massenet	*Chérubin*	1905
Leroux	*La Fille de Figaro*	1914
Klebe	*Figaro lässt sich Scheiden*	1964
Corigliano	*The Ghosts of Versailles*	1991

Bécaud, Gilbert (b 1927)
French composer. Best known as a prolific song composer, he has also written one opera, the successful *Opéra d'Aran* (Paris, 25 Oct 1962; libr Jacques Émmanuel, Pierre Delanoë and Louis Amade) [R].

Bechi, Gino (1913–93)
Italian baritone, particularly associated with the Italian repertory, especially Verdi. One of the leading baritones of the immediate post-war period, and an admired singing-actor, he created roles in Rocca's *Monte Ivnor* and Alfano's *Don Juan de Mañara.*

Beckmesser, Sixtus
Baritone role in Wagner's *Die Meistersinger von Nürnberg.* The pedantic town clerk, he is a caricature of the critic EDUARD HANSLICK.

Bedford, Steuart (b 1939)
British conductor, particularly associated with Mozart operas and with the English repertory, especially Britten. Musical director of the English Music Theatre (1975–79) and artistic director of the Aldeburgh Festival, he conducted the first performances of *Death in Venice*, Gardner's *The Visitors* and Oliver's *Tom Jones.* Married for a time to the soprano **Norma Burrowes**.

Beecham, Sir Thomas (1879–1961)
British conductor. His repertory was vast, but he was particularly associated with Mozart operas and with Delius, of whose music he was a tireless champion. Dictatorial, controversial, and possessing a brilliant if often cruel wit, he was one of the greatest of all British conductors. His interpretations were often highly idiosyncratic, but were always illuminating. He founded the Beecham Opera Company and was musical director of Covent Garden (1932–9). He conducted the first performances of Delius's *Irmelin*, Benjamin's *The Devil Take Her* and Holbrooke's *The Children of Don.* His autobiography, *A Mingled Chime*, was published in 1944.

Beecham Opera Company
Founded by Sir Thomas Beecham, the company operated from 1915 until 1920, when financial difficulties forced it into liquidation. It was then reorganized as the BRITISH NATIONAL OPERA COMPANY.

Beeson, Jack (b 1921)
American composer. He has written a number of operas, mainly on American subjects, in a readily accessible style, several of which have had success in the USA but which have been little performed elsewhere. His operas include *Jonah* (1950; libr composer, after Paul Goodman), *Hello Out There* (New York, 27 May 1954; libr composer, after William Saroyan) [R], *The Sweet Bye and Bye* (New York, 21 Nov 1957; libr Kenward Elmslie) [R], LIZZIE BORDEN, his most successful work, *My Heart's in the Highlands* (New York TV, 17 Mar 1970; libr composer, after Saroyan), *Captain Jinks of the Horse Marines* (Kansas City, 20 Sept 1975; libr Sheldon Harnick, after Clyde Fitch) [R], *Dr Heidegger's Fountain of Youth* (New York, 17 Nov 1978; libr Harnick, after Nathaniel Hawthorne's *Dr Heidegger's Experiment*) [R] and *Cyrano* (Hagen, 10 Sept 1994; libr after Edmond Rostand's *Cyrano de Bergerac*).

Beethoven, Ludwig van (1770–1827)
German composer. His only completed opera is FIDELIO, in which Beethoven's genius and burning humanity transform the simple structures of SINGSPIEL into a powerful drama and one of the greatest of pleas for liberty. He toyed with many other operatic projects, but only two – *Macbeth* and Emanuel Schikaneder's *Vestas Feuer* (1803) – ever progressed even to the stage of preliminary sketches. Nevertheless, Beethoven's contribution to opera is vast – out of all proportion to the quantity which he actually wrote.

Beggar's Opera, The
Ballad opera in three acts arranged by Pepusch. 1st perf London, 29 Jan 1728; libr by John Gay. Principal roles: Macheath (bar), Lucy (sop), Polly (sop), Mr and Mrs Peachum (bass and mezzo), Lockit (bass). By far the most successful of all ballad operas, it satirizes both music (the conventions of Italian OPERA SERIA and the rivalries of prima donnas) and politics – Macheath is a caricature of Horace Walpole (1717–97). Innumerable editions

of the work have been made in the 20th century. They include versions by Frederic Austin (whose initial run of 1,463 performances from 5 June 1920 was the longest run in operatic history), Brecht and Weill (DIE DREIGROSCHENOPER), Edward J. Dent (1944), Britten (1948), Manfred Bukofzer, Bliss (for the 1953 film starring Laurence Olivier and Stanley Holloway) and Blitzstein (1954).
Plot: London, 1727. The womanizing highwayman Macheath has seduced both Polly (daughter of the criminal Peachum) and Lucy, daughter of the jailer Lockit. In Newgate prison after he has been arrested at his favourite bordello, Lucy and Polly vie for his affections and vow to die with him. The beggar of the work's title (a speaking role) intervenes and, with the threat of Macheath's execution removed, ensures a happy ending. [R original and Britten versions]

Beginning of a Romance, The (*Pocátek Románu*)
Opera in one act by Janáček. 1st perf Brno, 10 Feb 1894 (composed 1891); libr by Jaroslav Tichý, after Gabriela Priessová's story. Janáček's second opera, almost never performed, it is a light comedy in traditional Czech style. Janáček later destroyed some of the music, which was reconstructed by Břetislav Bakala.

Begnis, Giuseppina Ronzi de (1800–53)
Italian soprano. One of the leading lyric sopranos of the first half of the 19th century, she created the title-role in Mercadante's *Zaira* and, for Donizetti, Elizabeth I in *Roberto Devereux* and the title-roles in *Maria Stuarda*, *Gemma di Vergy*, *Fausta* and *Sancia di Castiglia*. Her husband **Giuseppe** (1793–1849) was a leading BUFFO, who created Dandini in *La Cenerentola*.

Behrens, Hildegard (b 1937)
German soprano, particularly associated with Wagner and Strauss roles. Her bright, powerful and intelligently-used voice has made her one of the finest contemporary Brünnhildes, Isoldes and Elektras. She also has a strong stage presence.

Bei Männern
Soprano/baritone duet for Pamina and Papagena in Act I of Mozart's *Die Zauberflöte* in which they sing of the power of love.

Bel canto (Italian for 'beautiful singing') An imprecise term which refers to the art of singing in the Italian style: with beauty, elegance, flexibility, an assured technique and a certain bravura, often in COLORATURA. The term is also used to refer to the type of operas written in Italy in the first half of the 19th century, principally by Rossini, Bellini, Donizetti, Pacini and Mercadante. It is fashionable to maintain that the art of bel canto is long dead, but the voices and artistry of Montserrat Caballé, Marilyn Horne, Alfredo Kraus and Renato Bruson – to name but four – would suggest otherwise.

Belcore
Baritone role in Donizetti's *L'Elisir d'Amore*. He is the bumptious sergeant who takes a fancy to Adina.

Bel dì, Un
Soprano aria for Cio-Cio-San in Act II of Puccini's *Madama Butterfly*, in which she sings of the day when Pinkerton will return. It is often referred to by its English translation 'One fine day'.

Belfagor
Comic opera in prologue, two acts and epilogue by Respighi. 1st perf Milan, 26 April 1923; libr by Claudio Guastalla, after Ercole Luigi Morselli's play.
Principal roles: Belfagor (bar), Candida (sop), Baldo (ten), Mirocleto (bass), Olimpia (mezzo). Respighi's first major success, it is nowadays only very rarely performed.
Plot: Legendary Tuscany. The arch-devil Belfagor wishes to discover if marriage is the cause of all earthly troubles. He strikes a bargain with the quack Mirocleto and his wife Olimpia: he takes human shape, gives them money and is given their daughter Candida as bride. She, however, loves the sailor Baldo, and will not allow her marriage to Belfagor to be consummated. Candida's prayers prompt a miraculous nullification of the marriage. She escapes with Baldo, who beats up Belfagor and sends him packing. [R]

Belgian opera composers
see ALPAERTS; BLOCKX; FRANCK; GOSSEC; GRÉTRY; YSAŸE

Other national opera composers include Jean Absil (1893–1974), Auguste de Boeck (1865–1937), Jan van der Eeden (1842–1913), Antoine Frédéric Gresnick (1755–99), Albert Grisar (1808–69), Léon Jongen (1885–1969), Henri Pousseur (*b* 1929), Eugène Samuel-Holeman (1863–1944) and Victor Vreuls (1876–1944). *See also* FLEMISH OPERA COMPOSERS

Belgium
See GRAND THÉÂTRE, LIÈGE; ROYAL FLEMISH OPERA; ROYAL OPERA, GHENT; THÉÂTRE ROYAL DE LA MONNAIE, BRUSSELS

Belgrade Opera
Serbia's principal opera company, it was founded in 1920 and soon achieved the high artistic standards which it has maintained, almost uninterrupted, since. Performances are given at the National Theatre (cap 993), and the repertory has a preponderance of Slavonic works. The annual season runs from September to June. Musical directors have included Stanislav Binički, Stevan Hristić, Krešimir Baranović and Oskar Danon.

Belisario
Opera in three acts by Donizetti. 1st perf Venice, 4 Feb 1836; libr by Salvatore Cammarano, after Eduard von Schenk's *Belisarius*. Principal roles: Belisario (bar), Antonina (sop), Irene (mezzo), Alamiro (ten), Justiniano (bass), Eutropio (ten). Telling of Justinian's general Belisarius (*c* AD 505–65), it is one of Donizetti's finest operas, notable for the father-daughter exile scene, on which Verdi based the similar scene in *Luisa Miller*. It is still quite often performed.
Plot: 6th-century Byzantium and Mount Emo. Belisarius enjoys a triumphal homecoming after vanquishing the Bulgarians. His wife Antonina, however, believes him to have murdered their son. This – added to the fact that she is in love with Eutropius, the captain of the imperial guard – leads her to manufacture false evidence that Belisarius plans to kill Justinian. Belisarius is blinded and exiled and departs with his daughter Irene. His son, Alamirus, is in fact alive and the two are reunited. Alamirus helps Justinian's troops to victory, but Belisarius is fatally wounded. Before he dies, Antonina confesses her perjury to the horrified Justinian.

Bella
Soprano role in Tippett's *The Midsummer Marriage*. King Fisher's secretary, she is Jack's girlfriend.

Bella figlia dell'amore
Soprano/mezzo/tenor/baritone quartet for Gilda, Maddalena, the Duke of Mantua and Rigoletto in Act III of Verdi's *Rigoletto*, in which Gilda watches her lover flirt with Maddalena. One of the finest ensembles in all opera, Verdi himself admitted that he never expected to surpass it.

Bella siccome un angelo
Baritone aria for Dr Malatesta in Act I of Donizetti's *Don Pasquale*, in which he describes the virtues of the bride he has found for Pasquale.

Belle Hélène, La (*Beautiful Helen*)
Operetta in three acts by Offenbach. 1st perf Paris, 17 Dec 1864; libr by Henri Meilhac and Ludovic Halévy. Principal roles: Hélène (mezzo), Paris (ten), Agamemnon (b-bar), Ménélas (ten), Calchas (bar), Oreste (mezzo), Achille (ten), Ajax I and II (ten and bar). An hilarious send-up of the legend of Helen of Troy, it provided Offenbach with a superb vehicle for one of his favourite occupations: satirizing Second Empire society whilst simultaneously debunking mythological personages. It also contains some splendid musical satire. Triumphantly successful at its appearance, it remains one of the most popular of all operettas.
Plot: Legendary Sparta. Queen Helen and her ladies pray to Venus to send them lovers. The goddess obliges Helen in the shape of Paris, to the delight of the queen, who is bored with her wimpish husband Menelaus. She attempts the experiment of yielding to Paris emotionally whilst resisting him rationally. She finds the experience most stimulating, and pleases the young blade Orestes, since her example has now made all Greek wives unfaithful. Agamemnon and the high priest

Calchas are horrified by this moral laxity and round on Menelaus for his conjugal inadequacy. Paris disguises himself as a priest of Venus, telling the people that the only way for normality to return is for Helen to leave with him so that they may worship Venus together on her island. When he reveals his identity, the Greeks swear to wage a war of vengeance, but Helen finds the arrangement eminently satisfactory. [R]

Belle insecte à l'aile adorée
Soprano/baritone duet (the Fly Duet) for Eurydice and Jupiter in Act III of Offenbach's *Orphée aux Enfers*, in which Jupiter woos Eurydice in the guise of a fly.

Belle nuit, ô nuit d'amour
Soprano/mezzo duet (the Barcarolle) for two voices on the lagoon in the Giulietta Act of Offenbach's *Les Contes d'Hoffmann*. It is usually sung by Giulietta and Nicklaus. One of the most famous melodies in all opera, Offenbach incorporated it from his earlier *Die Rheinnixen*.

Bellezza, Vincenzo (1888–1964)
Italian conductor, particularly associated with the Italian repertory. Working principally at the Teatro Colón, Buenos Aires, the Rome Opera and the Metropolitan Opera, New York, he was one of the leading Italian conductors of the inter-war period.

Bellincioni, Gemma (1864–1950)
Italian soprano, particularly associated with Italian VERISMO roles and with the title-role in Strauss's *Salome*. An emotionally intense singing-actress, she created Santuzza in *Cavalleria Rusticana* and the title-role in Giordano's *Fedora*. Her autobiography, *Io e il Palcoscenico*, was published in 1920. Her husband **Roberto Stagno** (1840–97) was a successful tenor, who created Turiddù in *Cavalleria Rusticana*. Their daughter **Bianca** (1888–1980) was a soprano.

Bellini, Vincenzo (1801–35)
Italian composer. His ten completed operas, nearly all of which have libretti by Felice Romani, mark a move away from the florid style of Rossini to something simpler, more lyrical and more intense. His melodies are notable for their great beauty and for their long, arching phrases, and are the very epitome of the romantic period in opera. His first two operas, ADELSON E SALVINI and BIANCA E FERNANDO, are unremarkable and are heavily influenced by Rossini. However, IL PIRATA, which established his reputation, marks a new departure in Italian opera. LA STRANIERA and ZAIRA are less impressive, but I CAPULETI E I MONTECCHI marks a further advance. His *Ernani* (1830; libr Romani, after Victor Hugo's *Hernani*) was abandoned halfway through because of censorship problems, and he turned instead to the pastoral LA SONNAMBULA, one of his most popular works. This was followed by his masterpiece NORMA. The fine BEATRICE DI TENDA has never achieved the success which it deserves, but his last opera I PURITANI was a triumphant success.

Bellini's genius was almost exclusively musical: it has to be admitted that his melodies, for all their elegiac beauty, often have minimal relevance to the dramatic situation, and there is little true dramatic insight in any of his operas. The exception to this is *Norma*, which – despite its almost total lack of 'action' – is intensely powerful and dramatic; here the music not only reflects the dramatic situation, but also heightens it, encouraging reflection on what Bellini might have achieved had he not died so tragically young. His music was highly esteemed by his contemporaries, particularly by Wagner, Berlioz and Donizetti, and exercised a powerful influence on many composers, especially Chopin.

Bell Song
Soprano aria ('Où va la jeune Hindoue?') for Lakmé in Act II of Delibes's *Lakmé*.

Belmonte
Tenor role in Mozart's *Die Entführung aus dem Serail*. He is in love with Constanze.

Belshazzar
Dramatic oratorio in three parts by Händel. 1st perf London, 27 March 1745; libr by Charles Jennens, after the Book of Daniel in the Old Testament. Principal roles: Belshazzar (ten), Nitocris (sop),

Daniel (c-ten), Cyrus (mezzo), Gobrias (bass). Telling the famous biblical story of Belshazzar's Feast, it is not strictly speaking an opera, but it is often staged. [R]

Beňačková-Čápová, Gabriela (b 1947)
Slovakian soprano, particularly associated with the Czech and German repertories. One of the finest Slavic sopranos of recent times, she has a full and warm voice used with fine musicianship. On stage, she can sometimes seem a little distant and uninvolved. Her cousin **Marta** is a mezzo.

Benatzky, Ralph (b Rudolf Josef František) (1887–1952)
Czech (Moravian) composer. He wrote over 20 operettas, of which the most successful were the J. Strauss pastiche *Casanova* (Berlin, 1 Sept 1928; libr Robert Schanzer and E. Welisch), *Die Drei Musketiere* (Berlin, 31 Aug 1929; libr Schanzer and Welisch, after Alexandre Dumas's *Les Trois Mousquetaires*), the hugely successful *Im Weissen Rössl* (*At the White Horse Inn*, Berlin, 8 Nov 1930; libr Hans Müller and Robert Gilbert, after Oskar Blumenthal and Gustav Kadelburg) [R] and *Bezaubernde Fräulein* (Vienna, 24 May 1933; libr composer, after P. Gervault's *La Petite Chocolatière*).

Benda, Jiří Antonín (1722–95)
Czech composer. He wrote a number of operas and SINGSPIELS, of which the most successful were *Der Dorfjahrmarkt* (*The Village Fair*, Gotha, 10 Feb 1775; libr Friedrich Wilhelm Gotter) [R] and *Romeo und Julie* (Gotha, 25 Sept 1776; libr Gotter, after Shakespeare). Benda is chiefly remembered, however, for his four melodramas (which he called duodramas): spoken texts to an orchestral accompaniment. The finest were *Ariadne auf Naxos* (Gotha, 27 Jan 1775; libr Johann Christian Brandes) and *Medea* (Leipzig, 17 May 1775; libr Gotter). They made a considerable impression on his contemporaries, including Mozart, and influenced several later Czech composers, particularly Fibich. His nephew **Friedrich** (1745–1814) was also a composer who wrote a number of singspiels. The most successful was *Das Blumenmädchen* (Berlin, 16 July 1806; libr F. Rochlitz).

Bendl, Karel (1839–97)
Czech composer and conductor. He wrote 12 operas in a wide variety of styles, the musical qualities of which make the virtual oblivion into which they have fallen difficult to understand. The Meyerbeerian *Lejla* (Prague, 4 Jan 1868; libr Eliška Krásnohorská, after Edward Bulwer Lytton's *Leila*) was successful, and *Břetislav* (Prague, 18 Sept 1870; libr Krásnohorská) established his reputation. His subsequent operas include *The Indian Princess* (*Indická Princezna*, Prague, 26 Aug 1877; libr A. Pulda), which is the first Czech operetta, the VERISMO *The Montenegrins* (*Černohorci*, Prague, 11 Oct 1881; libr Josef Otakar Veselý), *The Old Bridegroom* (*Starý Ženich*, Chrudim, 4 Feb 1882, composed 1874; libr Karel Sabina), which was considered to be too similar to Smetana's *The Bartered Bride*, the comedy *Karel Škréta* (Prague, 11 Dec 1883; libr Krásnohorská), the tragedy *The Child of Tabor* (*Dítě Tábora*, Prague, 13 Mar 1888; libr Krásnohorská) and the verismo *Máti Míla* (Prague, 25 June 1895; libr A. Delmar and V.J. Novotný).

Benedict, Sir Julius (1804–85)
German-born British composer and conductor. He wrote eight operas, in all of which the influence of Weber is strong. His first three operas were unsuccessful: *Giacinta ed Ernesto* (Naples, 31 Mar 1827; libr L. Riciutti), *I Portughesi in Goa* (Stuttgart, 28 June 1830; libr V. Torelli) and *Un Anno ed un Giorno* (Naples, 19 Oct 1836; libr D. Andreotti). After settling in Britain, he played an important part in the development of native British opera. *The Gypsy's Warning* (London, 19 Apr 1838; libr George Linley and R.B. Peake) was followed by *The Brides of Venice* (London, 22 Apr 1844; libr Alfred Bunn), *The Crusaders* (London, 26 Feb 1846; libr Bunn), THE LILY OF KILLARNEY, by far his most successful and enduring work, and *The Bride of Song* (London, 3 Dec 1864; libr H.B. Farnie).

Benelli, Ugo (b 1935)
Italian tenor, particularly associated with Rossini, Mozart and lighter Donizetti roles. One of the leading TENORE DI GRAZIAS of the 1960s and 1970s and subsequently a fine character tenor, he was also an accomplished comic actor.

Beneš
Bass role in: **1** Smetana's *Dalibor*. He is the jailer. **2** Smetana's *The Devil's Wall*. He is the Devil disguised as a hermit.

Benjamin, Arthur (1893–1960)
Australian composer. He wrote five operas, all of which enjoyed some initial success. They are the comedy *The Devil Take Her* (London, 1 Dec 1931; libr Alan Collard and John B. Gordon, after Ben Jonson), PRIMA DONNA, A TALE OF TWO CITIES, *Mañana* (BBC Radio, 1 Feb 1956; libr Carol Brahms and G. Foa) and *Tartuffe* (London, 30 Nov 1964; libr Cedric Cliffe, after Molière), of which only the vocal score had been completed at his death; it was orchestrated by Alan Boustead.

Bennett, Richard Rodney (b 1936)
British composer. He has written five operas in a fluent and readily accessible style. They are *The Ledge* (London, 12 Sept 1951; libr Adrian Mitchell), THE MINES OF SULPHUR, his most successful work, *A Penny For a Song* (London, 31 Nov 1967; libr Colin Graham, after John Whiting), the children's opera *All the King's Men* (Coventry, 28 Mar 1969; libr Beverley Cross) [R] and *Victory* (London, 13 Apr 1970; libr Cross, after Joseph Conrad).

Benois, Alexandre (b Alexander Nikolayevich) (1870–1960)
Russian designer, great-uncle of actor and producer SIR PETER USTINOV. Principally associated with Sergei Diaghilev's Russian Ballet, he also designed a number of operas. His vivid sense of colour and his taste for the spectacular were best exemplified in his Paris designs for *The Golden Cockerel* in 1927. His *Mémoires* were published in 1964. His son **Nicola** (1901–88) was also a distinguished designer. He was chief designer at the Rome Opera (1927–32) and La Scala, Milan (1936–70). His wife **Disma de Cecco** (*b* 1926) was a soprano.

Benoit
Bass COMPRIMARIO role in Puccini's *La Bohème*. He is the bohemians' landlord.

Benvenuto Cellini
Opera in two acts by Berlioz (Op 23). 1st perf Paris, 10 Sept 1838; libr by Léon de Wailly and Auguste Barbier, after Benvenuto Cellini's autobiography.
Principal roles: Cellini (ten), Teresa (sop), Fieramosca (bar), Ascanio (mezzo), Balducci (bass), Cardinal Salviati or Pope Clement VII (bass), Pompeo (bar).
Berlioz's first completed opera, based on events in the life of the goldsmith Benvenuto Cellini (1500–71), it was a failure at its appearance and it is only in recent years that it has been much performed. The concert overture *Le Carnaval Romain* is drawn from music from the opera.
Plot: Rome, 1532. Cellini and Fieramosca are rivals both in their art and in their love for Teresa, daughter of the papal treasurer Balducci. A fight develops during Carnival in which Cellini, disguised as a friar and planning to elope with Teresa, kills Pompeo. The Cardinal comes to Cellini's studio, where Teresa has been brought by Cellini's apprentice Ascanio, and insists that a statue which he has commissioned must be completed by midnight. Otherwise Cellini will be handed over to the authorities for murder and abduction. Despite a strike organized by Fieramosca, Cellini – using every piece of precious metal he has – succeeds in casting his Perseus and so is pardoned and wins Teresa. [R]

Beppe
1 Tenor role in Leoncavallo's *Pagliacci*. He is a member of Canio's theatrical troupe. **2** Mezzo trouser-role in Mascagni's *L'Amico Fritz*. He is a young gypsy. **3** Tenor role in Donizetti's *Rita*. He is Rita's first husband.

Berbié, Jane (b Jeanne Marie Louise Bergougne) (b 1934)
French mezzo, particularly associated with the French repertory and with Mozart and Rossini roles. She had a fine voice of considerable range and agility, used with an assured technique, and was an accomplished comic actress. She created Oulita in Liebermann's *La Forêt*.

Berceuse
A French term for a lullaby or cradle song. There are operatic examples in Godard's *Jocelyn* and Gounod's *Philémon et Baucis*.

Berenice, Regina d'Egitto (*Berenice, Queen of Egypt*)
Opera in three acts by Händel. 1st perf London, 18 May 1737; libr by Antonio Salvi. Principal roles: Berenice (sop), Selene (mezzo), Arsace (mezzo), Alessandro (sop), Demetrio (bass). Unsuccessful at its appearance, it is nowadays only rarely performed.
Plot: Egypt, 1st century BC. Queen Berenice is under pressure from Rome to marry Alessandro, but is in love with Demetrio, who himself loves her sister Selene. Berenice orders Selene to marry Arsace. Demetrio believes Selene faithless and conspires with the enemy, for which Berenice has him condemned to death. However, impressed with Alessandro's nobility, she agrees to marry him and pardons Demetrio and allows him to wed Selene.

Berg, Alban (1885–1935)
Austrian composer. Strongly influenced by Schönberg, he wrote two operas: WOZZECK and the unfinished LULU. Both deal with the plight and the exploitation of the dregs of humanity and are amongst the greatest, most powerful and most disturbing of 20th century operas.

Bergamo
see TEATRO DONIZETTI, BERGAMO

Berganza, Teresa (b Vargas) (b 1935)
Spanish mezzo, particularly associated with Rossini and Mozart roles and with the French and Spanish repertories, including ZARZUELA. Possessing a rich and alluring voice of considerable range and great agility, together with an outstanding technique, she was one of the finest mezzos of the post-war era. Her autobiography, *Flor de Soledad y Silencio*, was published in 1984. Married for a time to the composer and pianist **Felix Lavilla**.

Berger, Erna (1900–90)
German soprano, particularly associated with Mozart roles, especially the Queen of the Night in *Die Zauberflöte*. She had a beautiful voice which retained its fresh and girlish quality throughout her career. A singer of fine artistry, she was also a noted teacher, whose pupils included Rita Streich.

Bergonzi, Carlo (b 1924)
Italian tenor, particularly associated with the Italian repertory, especially Verdi. Beginning as a baritone, he retrained himself as a tenor in 1951. One of the greatest operatic tenors of the 20th century (despite his total inability to act), he possessed a smooth, velvety and gloriously-toned voice, used with impeccable taste and style and with an almost flawless technique which allowed him to continue singing into his late 60s. His recording of Verdi's complete tenor arias was an extraordinary achievement which is likely to remain unique. He created the title-role in Napoli's *Masaniello*.

Berio, Luciano (b 1925)
Italian composer. One of the most important contemporary avant-garde composers, his stage works include *Opera* (Santa Fe, 12 Aug 1970; libr composer and Umberto Eco), LA VERA STORIA and the fine UN RÈ IN ASCOLTO. Artistic director of the Maggio Musicale Fiorentino (1984–). His wife **Cathy Berberian** (1925–83) was a successful soprano who specialized in early and contemporary works.

Berkeley, Sir Lennox (1903–89)
British composer. He wrote five operas which, somewhat unjustly, have been rarely performed. They are *Nelson* (London 22 Sept 1954; libr Alan Pryce-Jones), the comedy A DINNER ENGAGEMENT, his most successful work, *Ruth* (London, 2 Oct 1956; libr Eric Crozier, after the Old Testament), *The Castaway* (Aldeburgh, 3 June 1967; libr Paul Dehn) and the unfinished *Faldon Park* (1980; libr Winton Dean). His son **Michael** (*b* 1948) is also a composer, who has written one opera: *Baa Baa Black Sheep* (Cheltenham, 3 July 1993; libr David Malouf, after Rudyard Kipling's *Jungle Book*) [R].

Berlin
see BERLIN STATE OPERA; DEUTSCHE OPER, BERLIN; KOMISCHE OPER, BERLIN

Berlin State Opera
Originally called the Königliche Oper, the theatre was destroyed in World War II and rebuilt (cap 1,452) only in 1954, reopening in Sept 1955. The principal

opera house of the former East Germany, it pursues a traditional repertory policy. The annual season runs from September to July. Musical directors have included Leo Blech, Erich Kleiber, Wilhelm Furtwängler, Clemens Krauss, Robert Heger, Franz Konwitschny, Otmar Suitner and Daniel Barenboim.

Berlioz, Héctor (1803–69)
French composer and critic. One of the greatest, most original and most innovative composers of the 19th century (sometimes said to be the inventor of the modern orchestra), Berlioz had little luck with his operas in his own lifetime. His first opera *Estelle et Némorin* (1823; libr H.-C. Gerono) is lost, and *Les Francs Juges* (1826; libr Humbert Ferrand) was abandoned; only the well-known overture survives. His first completed opera, BENVENUTO CELLINI, was a failure despite its fine music. LA DAMNATION DE FAUST, described by Berlioz as a 'dramatic legend', is – despite its elements of great theatricality – not really an opera, although it has often been staged. His operatic masterpiece (and perhaps his greatest piece of music) is the vast and spectacular LES TROYENS, but he saw only half of it performed in his lifetime: it had to wait until 1969 for its first uncut performance in French. His last opera, the Shakespearian BÉATRICE ET BÉNÉDICT, had only moderate success.

Only in the last 30 years or so have Berlioz's dramatic works been appreciated at their true value, especially *Les Troyens*. All of his operas are now regularly performed, particularly in Britain as a result of the tireless championing of them by Sir Colin Davis, perhaps the greatest modern interpreter of Berlioz's music. Berlioz's fascinating *Mémoires* were published in 1870.

Bernauerin, Die: ein Bayrisches Stück
(The Bernauer Girl: a Bavarian Tale)
Opera in two acts by Orff. 1st perf Stuttgart, 15 June 1947; libr (in Bavarian dialect) by the composer, after a 17th-century ballad. Really more of a play with music than an opera, it is only rarely performed.
Plot: 17th-century Bavaria. Agnes, daughter of the public baths owner Bernauerin, marries the nobleman Albrecht. She is accused of witchcraft and is eventually murdered. [R]

Berners, Lord (b Sir Gerald Hugh Tyrwhitt-Wilson) (1883–1950)
British composer, diplomat, writer and painter. Best known as a ballet composer, his music exhibits the same wit and irony as his writings. He wrote one opera: *La Carosse du Saint Sacrement* (Paris, 24 Apr 1924; libr after Prosper Mérimée).

Berne Stadttheater
The opera house (cap 770) in the capital of Switzerland opened on 25 Sept 1903. Musical directors have included Klaus Weise, Roderick Brydon, Gustav Kuhn and Christian Delfs.

Bernstein, Leonard (1918–90)
American conductor and composer. One of the leading (and most flamboyant) conductors of the post-war era, with a wide-ranging repertory, his operatic appearances were infrequent, but included *Médée* at La Scala with Maria Callas and *Carmen* at the Metropolitan Opera, New York. Apart from the musicals *On the Town* (New York, 28 Apr 1944; libr Adolph Green and Betty Comden) [R], *Wonderful Town* (New York, 25 Feb 1953; libr Green and Comden, after Joseph Fields and Joseph Chodorov's *My Sister Eileen*) and the enormously successful WEST SIDE STORY, his operatic stage works are the duodrama TROUBLE IN TAHITI, the operetta CANDIDE and the opera A QUIET PLACE (which incorporates *Trouble in Tahiti*). His writings include *The Joy of Music* (1954) and *The Unanswered Question* (1976).

Berry, Walter (b 1929)
Austrian baritone, particularly associated with Mozart and Strauss roles and with the title-role in Berg's *Wozzeck*. His incisive and expressive voice was matched by a strong stage presence, intense in tragedy and ebullient in comedy. He created roles in Egk's *Irische Legende*, Liebermann's *Penelope* and Einem's *Der Prozess* and *Kabale und Liebe*. Married for a time to the mezzo CHRISTA LUDWIG.

Berta
Soprano role in Rossini's *Il Barbiere di Siviglia*. She is Dr Bartolo's housekeeper. The role is often sung by a mezzo.

Bertati, Giovanni (1735–1815)
Italian poet and librettist. He wrote some 70 libretti, the best being comedies notable for their sharp social comment. He provided texts for Anfossi, Cimarosa (*Il Matrimonio Segreto*), Galuppi, Gazzaniga (*Don Giovanni*), Guglielmi, Mayr, Naumann, Paer, Paisiello, Portugal, Sacchini, Salieri, Spontini, Traetta, Winter and Zingarelli amongst others.

Bertini, Gary (b 1927)
Russian-born Israeli conductor and composer, particularly associated with Rossini operas and with contemporary works. He founded the Israeli Chamber Ensemble in 1966 and was musical director of the Frankfurt Opera (1988–90). He conducted the first performances of Tal's *Masada 967*, *Ashmedai* and *Die Versuchung*.

Beruti, Arturo (1862–1938)
Argentinian composer. He wrote eight operas, some of which are still performed in Argentina. They are *Vendetta* (Vercelli, 21 May 1892; libr D. Crisafuli), *Evangelina* (Milan, 19 Sept 1893; libr A. Cortella, after Henry Longfellow), *Taras Bulba* (Turin, 9 Mar 1895; libr G. Godio, after Nikolai Gogol), *Pampa* (Buenos Aires, 27 July 1897; libr G. Borra, after Eduardo Gutiérrez's *Juan Moreira*), which is the first Argentine national opera, *Yupanki* (Buenos Aires, 25 July 1899; libr Enrique Rodríguez Larreta, after V.F. López's *El Hijo del Sol*), *Khrysé* (Buenos Aires, 20 June 1903; libr J. Pacchierotti, after Pierre Louÿs's *Aphrodite*), *Horrida Nox* (Buenos Aires, 7 July 1908) and *Los Héroes* (Buenos Aires, 23 Aug 1919; libr after López's *La Loca de la Guardia*).

Berwald, Franz (1796–1868)
Swedish composer. Although best known as a symphonic composer, he also wrote a number of stage works, most of them now largely forgotten. His first work was an unfinished opera, *Gustaf Vasa* (Stockholm, 12 Feb 1828; libr after Johan Henrik Kellgren). His first completed work was *Estrella de Soria* (Stockholm, 9 Apr 1862, composed 1840; libr Otto Pretchler) [R Exc], whose overture is still remembered. It was followed by two operettas: *I Enter the Monastery* (*Jag Går i Kloster*, Stockholm, 2 Dec 1843; libr composer and H. Sätherberg) and *The Modiste* (*Modehandlerskan*, Stockholm, 26 Mar 1845; libr composer). Two further operas followed: *Ein Ländliches Verlobungfest in Schweden* (*A Swedish Country Betrothal*, Vienna 26 Jan 1847; libr Pretchler) and THE QUEEN OF GOLCONDA.

Bess
Soprano role in Gershwin's *Porgy and Bess*. She is Crown's and later Porgy's woman.

Besuch der Alten Dame, Der (*The Visit of the Old Lady*)
Opera in three acts by Einem (Op 35). 1st perf Vienna, 23 May 1971; libr by Friedrich Dürrenmatt, after his own *Der Besuch*. Principal roles: Claire (mezzo), Alfred (bar), Mayor (ten). Perhaps Einem's most successful opera, it has been widely performed.
Plot: Central Europe, 20th century. The once poor Klara Wäscher returns to her home town of Güllen as Claire Zachanassian, the world's richest woman. She encounters Alfred, her former lover and the father of her illegitimate child, who had abandoned her. She offers a fortune to the town in return for his death. Alfred is duly killed, but the cause of death is given as heart failure. Claire claims the body and hands the Mayor a cheque. [R]

Betly or **La Capanna Svizzera** (*The Swiss Cabin*)
Comic opera in one act by Donizetti. 1st perf Naples, 24 Aug 1836; libr by the composer, after Eugène Scribe and Anne-Honoré Joseph de Mélesville's libretto for Adam's LE CHÂLET, itself based on Johann von Goethe's *Jery und Bätely*. Principal roles: Betly (sop), Daniele (ten), Max (bar). A delightful little work, it is still performed from time to time.
Plot: 18th-century Switzerland. Local jokers have sent Daniele a letter purporting to be from Betly, accepting him

in marriage. When Daniele arrives, Betly rejects him, preferring her independence. Her brother Max returns incognito after a long spell in the army and decides to aid Daniele. He gets Daniele to show his spirit by letting his troops loose in Betly's house and by challenging him to a duel. Daniele's pluck has the desired effect on Betly, who accepts him. [R]

Betrothal in a Monastery
see DUENNA, THE

Bettelstudent, Der (*The Beggar Student*)
Operetta in three acts by Millöcker. 1st perf Vienna, 6 Dec 1882; libr by F. Zell (Camillo Walzel) and Richard Genée, after Victorien Sardou's *Les Noces de Fernande* and Edward Bulwer Lytton's *The Lady of Lyons*. Principal roles: Simon (ten), Laura (sop), Palmatica (mezzo), Bronislawa (sop), Col Ollendorf (bass), Enterich (bar), Jan (ten). Millöcker's most successful and enduring work, it received over 5,000 performances in Germany alone in its first 25 years of life and is still regularly performed.
Plot: Cracow, 1704. Rejected by the young Countess Laura, Col Ollendorf plans revenge. He has two prisoners released, the 'beggar student' Simon and the political activist Jan, equips them with money and finery, and hopes that they will captivate Laura. Laura falls for Simon, who finds himself returning her feelings and unable to respond to Jan's patriotic urgings. After much complication and intrigue, Jan's plans come to fruition. Poland is liberated, and Simon and Laura are united to the discomfiture of Ollendorf. [R]

Bianca
1 Mezzo role in Britten's *The Rape of Lucretia*. She is Lucretia's nurse. **2** Soprano role in Bellini's *Bianca e Fernando*. She is Filippo's sister. **3** Mezzo role in Zemlinsky's *Eine Florentinische Tragödie*. She is Simone's wife. **4** Soprano role in Donizetti's *Ugo Conte di Parigi*. She is Louis V's fiancée. **5** Soprano role in Musgrave's *The Voice of Ariadne*. **6** Soprano role in Rossini's *Bianca e Faliero*. She is Contareno's daughter. **7** Soprano role in Mercadante's *Le Due Illustri Rivali*. She is the Queen of Navarre.

Bianca e Faliero or **Il Consiglio dei Tre** (*The Council of Three*)
Opera in two acts by Rossini. 1st perf Milan, 26 Dec 1819; libr by Felice Romani, after Antoine-Vincent Arnault's *Blanche et Montcassin*. Principal roles: Bianca (sop), Faliero (mezzo), Contareno (ten), Capellio (bass). After a long period of total neglect, it has recently had a number of successful revivals.
Plot: 18th-century Venice. To resolve a feud which has divided their senatorial families, Capellio requests the hand of Contareno's daughter Bianca. She, however, loves the general Faliero, who returns in triumph after defeating a foreign conspiracy. Contareno forces Bianca to accept Capellio and she reluctantly agrees, suffering Faliero's accusations of infidelity. Faliero takes a tender leave of her and on the approach of Contareno escapes over a wall into the Spanish Embassy. Discovered there, he is believed to be a traitor, and is tried before the Senate. Bianca tells the true version of events, and Capellio nobly refuses to give his vote for the death sentence. Contareno finally gives his consent to Bianca's union with Faliero.

Bianca e Fernando
Opera in two acts by Bellini. 1st perf (as *Bianca e Gernando*) Naples, 30 May 1826; libr by Domenico Gilardoni, after Carlo Roti's *Bianca e Fernando alla Tomba di Carlo IV*. Revised version 1st perf Genoa, 7 April 1828; libr revised by Felice Romani. Principal roles: Bianca (sop), Fernando (ten), Filippo (bar), Carlo (b-bar). Bellini's second opera, Rossinian in style, it is only very rarely performed.
Plot: 13th-century Agrigento (Sicily). Fernando, son of Duke Carlo (imprisoned by the usurper Filippo), visits the court of his enemy in disguise. Together with his sister Bianca, whom Filippo wishes to marry, he gains access to his father's dungeon just as the populace rise up against Filippo.

Biber, Heinrich Johann (1644–1704)
Austrian composer and violinist. He wrote two operas: *Chi la Dura la Vince* (Salzburg, 1687; libr Francesco Maria Raffaelini) and the lost *Alessandro in Pietra* (Salzburg, 1689; libr Raffaelini).

Bielefeld Stadttheater
The opera house (cap 890) in this German town in Westphalia opened in 1904. Musical directors have included Bernhard Conz and Rainer Koch.

Billows, Lady
Soprano role in Britten's *Albert Herring*. She is the local aristocrat.

Billy Budd
Opera in two (originally four) acts by Britten (Op 50). 1st perf London, 1 Dec 1951; libr by E.M. Forster and Eric Crozier, after Herman Melville's *Billy Budd, Sailor*. Revised version 1st perf BBC TV, 13 Nov 1960. Principal roles: Billy (bar), Capt Vere (ten), Claggart (bass), Mr Redburn (bar), Mr Flint (bass), Dansker (bass), Novice (ten), Mr Ratcliffe (bass), Squeak (ten), Donald (bar), Red Whiskers (ten). Notable for its all-male cast and for its atmospheric orchestration, it explores Britten's favourite theme of the corruption of innocence and is one of the finest of all post-war operas.
Plot: H.M.S. Indomitable, 1797. Capt Vere, haunted by the past, recalls the case of Billy Budd. Young and handsome Billy, an impressed man, is liked by all except the evil master-at-arms John Claggart, who envies his beauty and popularity and who vows to destroy him. Claggart systematically persecutes Billy, tries to incite him to mutiny and finally accuses him before Vere. Billy, suffering from a stammer, is unable to speak in his defence and strikes out at Claggart, who dies from the blow. Although Vere is deeply troubled in his conscience, he has to obey the law: a drumhead court under Mr Redburn convicts Billy, and he is hanged from the yardarm. [R]

Bing, Sir Rudolf (b 1902)
Austrian administrator (a British citizen since 1946). He was general manager of the Glyndebourne Festival (1936–46), artistic director of the Edinburgh Festival (1947–9), of which he was a co-founder, and general manager of the Metropolitan Opera, New York (1950–72). His autobiography, *5,000 Nights at the Opera*, was published in 1972.

Birtwistle, Sir Harrison (b 1934)
British composer. One of the most talented and original contemporary opera composers, several of his stage works have met with considerable success. The violent PUNCH AND JUDY was followed by the macabre cabaret-style *Down By the Greenwood Side* (Brighton, 8 May 1969; libr Michael Nyman), *The Mask of Orpheus* (London, 21 May 1986, composed 1977; libr Peter Zinovieff), YAN TAN TETHERA, the epic GAWAIN and *The Second Mrs Kong* (Glyndebourne 24 Oct 1994; libr Russell Hoban).

Bis (Latin for 'twice')
Audiences in European opera houses shout 'bis' when they want an encore.

Bishop, Sir Henry (1786–1855)
British composer and conductor. He is credited with having written 57 operas, but the vast majority consist of little more than musical numbers inserted into plays. Shallow and sentimental – epitomized by 'Home, sweet home' in *Clari* (London, 8 May 1823; libr J.H. Payne) – his stage works are justifiably forgotten. His most important opera was *Aladdin* (London, 29 Apr 1826; libr G. Soane). He was musical director of Covent Garden (1810–24), where he was responsible for the rearrangement and 'improvement' (in other words mutilation) of many major operas. His wife **Ann Riviere** (1810–84) was a successful soprano, who led a colourful life and who created a role in Mercadante's *Il Vascello di Gama*.

Biterolf
Bass role in Wagner's *Tannhäuser*. He is a minstrel-knight.

Bizet, Georges (1838–75)
French composer. One of the greatest French opera composers, although slow to reach his full potential, it is not exactly certain how many operas he actually wrote, as several remain unperformed, lost or incomplete. His first opera was *La Maison du Docteur* (1855; libr Henry Boitteaux), which has never been published. His earliest extant work is the delightful LE DOCTEUR MIRACLE, joint winner with Lecoq of a competition organized by Offenbach for a one-act

OPÉRA-COMIQUE. This was followed by the Italian-style comedy DON PROCOPIO. Of greater substance is his one grand opera IVAN IV, which was not performed until 1946; Bizet incorporated parts of it into later works. His first real success was the gloriously melodious LES PÊCHEURS DE PERLES, where his dramatic gifts are first apparent. These gifts are still further evident in the unjustly neglected LA JOLIE FILLE DE PERTH. The incomplete *La Coupe du Roi de Thulé* (1868; libr Louis Gallet and Édouard Blau) survives only in fragments; scholars believe that it might have been one of his finest works. Three opéra-comiques followed, all of which are lost except for fragments of the second: *Calendal* (1870; libr Paul Fernier), *Clarissa Harlowe* (1871; libr Philippe Gille, after Samuel Richardson) and *Grisélidis* (1871; libr Victorien Sardou). His next work DJAMILEH was a failure and was followed by the operetta *Don Rodrigue* (1873; libr Gallet and Blau, after Guilhem de Castro's *Las Mocedades del Cid*), of which only a fragment survives.

Much of Bizet's operatic failure can be attributed to poor libretti or to subjects which failed to fire his imagination sufficiently. Finally, for his last opera, he found both the right subject and a superb libretto in CARMEN. Although it failed at its appearance, it soon came to be regarded by both public and musicians alike as one of the finest of all music-dramas; Tchaikovsky was not far out when he predicted that in ten years it would be the most popular of all operas. Bizet also completed the unfinished *Noé* by his father-in-law **Halévy**.

Bjoner, Ingrid (b 1927)
Norwegian soprano, particularly associated with Wagner and Strauss roles. She possessed a radiant voice of great beauty and considerable power, which she combined with a strong stage presence.

Björling, Jussi (b Johan) (1911–60)
Swedish tenor, particularly associated with the Italian, French and Russian repertories. He possessed a voice of rare warmth and sweetness, considered one of the finest of the 20th century, which he used with matchless style and technique and with impeccable good taste. His wife **Anna-Lisa Berg** was a successful soprano; their son **Rolf** (*b* 1937) was also a tenor.

Blacher, Boris (1903–75)
German composer and librettist. One of the leading post-war German opera composers, many of his stage works met with success in Germany but are little known elsewhere. His operas are: *Fürstin Tarakanova* (Wuppertal, 5 Feb 1941; libr K.O. Koch), the chamber opera *Die Flut* (*The Tide*, Berlin Radio, 20 Dec 1946; libr Heinz von Cramer), the scenic oratorios *Romeo und Julia* (Berlin Radio, 1947; libr after Shakespeare) and *Der Grossinquisitor* (Berlin, 14 Oct 1947; libr Leo Borchard, after Fyodor Dostoyevsky's *The Brothers Karamazov*) [R], *Die Nachtschwalbe* (*The Night Swallow*, Leipzig, 22 Feb 1948; libr F. Wolf), *Preussisches Märchen* (*Prussian Tale*, Berlin, 23 Sept 1952; libr von Cramer, after Carl Zuckmayer's *Der Hauptmann von Köpenick*), *Abstrakte Oper No 1* (Frankfurt Radio, 28 June 1953; libr Werner Egk), *Rosamunde Floris* (Berlin, 21 Sept 1960; libr G. von Westerman, after Georg Kaiser), *Zwischenfälle bei einer Nottlandung* (*Incidents at a Forced Landing*, Hamburg, 4 Feb 1966; libr von Cramer), ZWEIHUNDERTTAUSEND TALER, *Yvonne, Prinzessin von Burgund* (Wuppertal, 15 Sept 1973; libr composer, after Gombrowicz) and *Das Geheimnis des Entwendeten Briefes* (Berlin, 2 Feb 1975; libr H. Brauer, after Edgar Allan Poe's *The Purloined Letter*). He also wrote the libretti for Einem's *Dantons Tod*, *Der Zerissene*, *Der Prozess* and *Kabale und Liebe*. He was married to the pianist **Gerty Herzog**, and his son is the violinist **Kolja Blacher**.

Blachut, Beno (1913–85)
Czech tenor, particularly associated with the Czech repertory. One of the finest tenors of his time, he never achieved the international recognition which should have been his. Later in his career he excelled in comic character roles. He created Diafoirus in Pauer's *The Hypochondriac*.

Blake, David (b 1936)
British composer. He has written two operas: the epic *Toussaint* (London, 29 Sept 1977; libr Anthony Ward, after C.L.R. James's *The Black Jacobins*: *Toussaint*

l'Ouverture and the San Domingo Revolution; revised version London, 1983) and the comedy of manners *The Plumber's Gift* (London, 25 May 1989; libr John Birtwhistle).

Blanc, Ernest (b 1923)
French baritone, particularly associated with the French repertory. He possessed a rich and beautiful voice, marred only by his tendency to sing flat. His international career was limited by his disinclination to leave France. He created Theogène in Barraud's *Numance*.

Blavet, Michel (1700–68)
French composer. He wrote two operas: the pastiche INTERMEZZO *Le Jaloux Corrigé* (Château-de-Berney, 18 Nov 1752; libr G. Collé) [R] and *La Fête de Cythère* (Château-de-Berney, 19 Nov 1753; libr A. de Laurès).

Bleat
A vocal device consisting of the rapid repetition of a single note with varied pressures of the breath. It is usually found in early opera, but Wagner calls for it in the final scene of *Die Meistersinger von Nürnberg*. Also known as the goat's trill, it is called *trillo caprino* in Italy, *Bockstriller* in Germany, *trino de cabra* in Spain and *chèvrotement* in France.

Blech, Leo (1871–1958)
German conductor and composer. An outstanding Wagnerian interpreter, he was also associated with Verdi operas and with *Carmen*, which he conducted over 600 times. He was musical director of the Berlin State Opera (1913–23 and 1926–37) and conducted the first performance of d'Albert's *Tiefland*. He also composed several operas, of which the most successful were *Das War Ich* (Dresden, 6 Oct 1902; libr Richard Batka, after J. Hutt), *Alpenkönig und Menschenfeind* (Dresden, 1 Oct 1903; libr Batka, after F. Raimund) and the comedy *Versiegelt* (Hamburg, 4 Nov 1908; libr Batka and A.S. Pordes-Milo, after S. Rauppach). He also completed d'Albert's unfinished *Mister Wu*.

Blegen, Judith (b 1941)
American soprano, particularly associated with Mozart roles and with the lighter Italian repertory. She uses her appealing voice with intelligence and musicianship and has a delightful stage presence. She is also a creditable violinist.

Blind, Dr
Tenor COMPRIMARIO role in J. Strauss's *Die Fledermaus*. He is Eisenstein's stammering lawyer.

Bliss, Sir Arthur (1891–1975)
British composer. He wrote two operas: THE OLYMPIANS and the television opera *Tobias and the Angel* (BBC TV, 19 May 1960; libr Christopher Hassall, after the Apocrypha). He also prepared an edition of *The Beggar's Opera* for the 1953 film starring Laurence Olivier. His autobiography, *As I Remember*, was published in 1970.

Blitzstein, Marc (1905–64)
American composer. Starting as a disciple of Schönberg, he soon abandoned his experimental style in favour of a direct and easily accessible vein in which he could communicate his left-wing political views to the widest possible audience. His first opera was the satirical one-act *Triple Sec* (Philadelphia, 6 May 1929; libr R. Jeans), which was followed by *The Harpies* (New York, 25 May 1931; libr composer) [R]. His first major stage work was *The Cradle Will Rock* (New York, 3 Jan 1938; libr composer), which was originally banned by the US government because of its advocacy of social revolution. His next opera, *No For an Answer* (New York, 5 Jan 1941; libr composer), was also banned for similar reasons. His last completed opera, less overtly political, was the successful REGINA. *Sacco and Vanzetti* was left unfinished at the time of his murder in Martinique. He also produced an adaptation of Weill's *Die Dreigroschenoper* in 1954 which enjoyed great success.

Bloch, Ernest (1880–1959)
Swiss composer. Best known as an orchestral composer, he also wrote one opera, the unjustly neglected MACBETH. A second opera, *Jézabel* (libr Edmond Fleg), was only sketched.

Blockx, Jan (1851–1912)
Flemish composer. He wrote seven operas,

several of which enjoyed considerable success in their time, but which are now largely forgotten. The comedy *To Forget Something* (*Iets Vergeten*, Antwerp, 19 Feb 1877; libr V. de la Montagne) was followed by *Maître Martin* (Brussels, 30 Nov 1892; libr E. Landoy, after E.T.A. Hoffmann's *Meister Martin*) and *The Princess of the Inn* (*Herbergprinses*, Antwerp, 10 Oct 1896; libr Nestor de Tière), his most successful work. There followed *Thyl Uilenspiegel* (Brussels, 12 Jan 1900; libr Henri Cain and L. Solvay, after Charles de Coster), the successful *The Bride of the Sea* (*Der Bruid der Zee*, Antwerp, 30 Nov 1901; libr de Tière), *The Chapel* (*De Kapel*, Antwerp, 7 Nov 1903; libr de Tière) and *Baldie* (Antwerp, 25 Jan 1908; libr de Tière; revised version *Liefdelied*, Antwerp, 6 Jan 1912).

Blodek, Vilém (1834–74)
Czech composer and flautist. He is chiefly remembered for the highly successful comedy IN THE WELL. The historico-romantic *Zítek* (Prague, 3 Oct 1934, composed 1869; libr Karel Sabina) [R Exc] was left unfinished at his death and was completed by F.X. Váňa.

Blomdahl, Karl-Birger (1916–68)
Swedish composer. He wrote three operas employing electronic music, of which ANIARA has proved to be one of the most successful modern operas. His other two operas are *Herr von Hancken* (Stockholm, 2 Sept 1965; libr Erik Lindegren, after Hjalmar Bergman) and the unfinished *The Tale of the Big Computer* (*Sagan om den Stora Datan*, libr after Hannas Alfvén). He was musical director of Swedish Radio (1965–68).

Blönchen (or **Blonde**)
Soprano role in Mozart's *Die Entführung aus dem Serail*. She is Constanze's English maid.

Blood Wedding (*Vérnász*)
Opera in three acts by Szokolay (Op 19). 1st perf Budapest, 31 Oct 1964; libr by Gyula Illyés, after Federico García Lorca's *Bodas de Sangre*. Principal roles: Mother (mezzo), Bridegroom (ten), Bride (sop), Leandro (bar), Neighbour (sop), Wife (sop). A powerful work which has been widely performed, it is perhaps the finest modern Hungarian opera. For plot see DIE BLUTHOCHZEIT. [R]

Blow, John (1649–1708)
British composer. His one stage work, VENUS AND ADONIS, is usually regarded as the earliest British opera.

Bluebeard's Castle
see DUKE BLUEBEARD'S CASTLE

Bluthochzeit, Die (*The Blood Wedding*)
Opera in two acts by Fortner. 1st perf Cologne, 8 June 1957; libr by Enrique Beck, after Federico García Lorca's *Bodas de Sangre*. Principal roles: Mother (sop), Leandro (bar), Bride (sop), Bridegroom (speaker), Leandro's Wife (mezzo). Fortner's most successful opera, it is written in TWELVE-TONE form, interspersed with traditional Spanish melodies and long stretches of spoken dialogue.
Plot: Early-20th-century Spain. The Mother's husband and elder son have been murdered, and she only reluctantly agrees to her remaining son's engagement, the more so as the Bride had previously been affianced to Leandro, kin of the murderers. Although Leandro is now married, he still loves the intended Bride. After the wedding, it is discovered that Leandro and the Bride have fled into the woods together. In an ensuing duel, Leandro and the Bridegroom are both killed, and the women are left to acknowledge that Fate was responsible for the tragedy.

Boatswain's Mate, The
Comic opera in one act by Smyth. 1st perf London, 28 Jan 1916; libr by the composer, after William Wymark Jacob's *Captains All*. Principal roles: Mrs Waters (sop), Harry (ten), Ned (bar). Smyth's most successful opera, it was long popular but is nowadays virtually never performed.
Plot: Early-20th-century England. The widowed Mrs Waters, landlady of 'The Beehive', rejects a marriage proposal from the ex-boatswain Harry Ben. His friend Ned Travers pretends to be a burglar so that Harry can impress Mrs Waters by playing the hero. Mrs Waters captures Ned, and to teach Harry a lesson she tells him that she shot the intruder. Harry gives himself up and the affair is sorted out, with Mrs Waters taking a fancy to Ned.

Bobinet
Baritone role in Offenbach's *La Vie Parisienne.* He is one of the two rakes in love with Métella.

Boccaccio
Operetta in three acts by Suppé. 1st perf Vienna, 1 Feb 1879; libr by F. Zell (Camillo Walzel) and Richard Genée, after Jean-François-Antoine Bayard, Adolphe de Leuven, Léon Lévy Brunswick and Arthur de Beauplan's play. Principal roles: Boccaccio (bar), Fiametta (sop), Beatrice (sop), Lotteringhi (ten), Leonetto (bar), Isabella (mezzo), Pietro (ten), Petronella (sop), Scalza (bass). Suppé's finest operetta, it is based on the life of the Italian poet Giovanni Boccaccio (1313–75). An immediate success, it is still regularly performed.
Plot: Florence, 1331. The husbands of Florence, led by Isabella's spouse Lotteringhi, are angered at Boccaccio's verses scorning female fidelity, and wish to give the poet a thrashing. Pietro, Prince of Palermo, has come to Florence to wed the Duke's natural daughter Fiametta. However, he prefers Isabella and accidentally receives the chastisement intended for Boccaccio, to whom Fiametta is drawn. The husbands force a beggar to burn Boccaccio's poems in public, but the beggar turns out to be the poet in disguise. Boccaccio finds favour with the Duke, and is eventually able to marry Fiametta. [R]

Bocca chiusa (Italian for 'closed mouth')
The musical term for humming. It is a vocal technique used predominantly for teaching purposes to encourage breath preservation. Its most famous operatic usages are the Humming Chorus in Puccini's *Madama Butterfly* and the off-stage chorus in the storm music in the last act of Verdi's *Rigoletto.*

Boccherini, Luigi (1743–1805)
Italian composer and cellist. Although best known as an orchestral composer, he also wrote one stage work, the ZARZUELA la clementina (Madrid 1786; libr Ramón de la Cruz). His brother **Giovanni** was a librettist who provided texts for Salieri amongst others.

Bockelmann, Rudolf (1892–1958)
German baritone, particularly associated with Wagnerian roles, especially Wotan and Hans Sachs. An outstanding *Heldenbariton* (see BARITONE), he was widely regarded in the inter-war period as Friedrich Schorr's only serious rival. He created Orestes in Křenek's *Leben des Orest* and the Ruler in Korngold's *Das Wunder der Heliane.* His Nazi sympathies brought his career to an abrupt halt in 1945.

Bockstriller
see BLEAT

Bohème, La
Opera in four acts by Puccini. 1st perf Turin, 1 Feb 1896; libr by Luigi Illica and Giuseppe Giacosa, after Henri Murger's *Scènes de la Vie de Bohème.* Principal roles: Mimì (sop), Rodolfo (ten), Marcello (bar), Musetta (sop), Colline (bass), Schaunard (bar), Benoit (bass), Alcindoro (bass). An immediate success, its mixture of high spirits, ardent love music and touching pathos have ensured that it has always remained one of the most enduringly popular of all operas.
Plot: Paris, *c* 1830. The young bohemians Rodolfo, Schaunard, Colline and Marcello live in penury in a garret owned by Benoit. Rodolfo meets and falls in love with the poor seamstress Mimì. Marcello gets back together with his old flame Musetta, who tricks her elderly admirer Alcindoro into paying their bill at the Café Momus. Rodolfo's jealousy is too much for Mimì, and they agree to part. In the winter, Mimì appears at the garret desperately ill with consumption. Her friends pawn their few paltry belongings to buy medicine for her and – her greatest wish – a warm muff. They return to find her dying in Rodolfo's arms. [R]

Bohème, La
Opera in four acts by Leoncavallo. 1st perf Venice, 6 May 1897; libr by the composer, after Henri Murger's *Scènes de la Vie de Bohème.* Principal roles: Mimì (sop), Marcello (ten), Musetta (mezzo), Rodolfo (bar), Schaunard (bar), Barbemuche (bass). Following Murger much more closely than Puccini's version, it is one of Leoncavallo's finest operas, but was almost

entirely eclipsed from the start by the huge success of Puccini's setting. It deserves more than the occasional performance which it currently receives.
Plot: Roughly the same as Puccini's version, except that in the central acts Mimì accepts the offer of a wealthy admirer to live with him, and that when she returns remorsefully to Rodolfo he violently rejects her. [R]

Bohemian Girl, The
Opera in three acts by Balfe. 1st perf London, 27 Nov 1843; libr by Alfred Bunn, after Joseph Marzilier and Jules-Henri Vernoy de Saint-Georges's ballet-pantomime *La Gypsy*, itself based on Miguel de Cervantes Saavedra's *La Gitanilla*. Principal roles: Arline (sop), Thaddeus (ten), Count Arnheim (bar), Gypsy Queen (mezzo), Devilshoof (bass). Balfe's finest work, it was the most successful British opera of the 19th century and retained its popularity for nearly 100 years. It is nowadays only infrequently performed.
Plot: 18th-century Pressburg. The noble Polish refugee Thaddeus loves Arline, who has been raised by a gypsy band. Accused of theft, Arline is brought for judgement to Count Arnheim, who recognizes her as his long-lost daughter. In spite of the attempts to prevent it by the vengeful Gypsy Queen, Arline and Thaddeus are united. [R]

Bohemios
ZARZUELA in one act by Vives. 1st perf Madrid, 24 March 1904; libr by Guillermo Perrín and Miguel de Palacios. Principal roles: Roberto (ten), Cossette (sop), Víctor (bar), Girard (bass). One of the most enduringly popular of all zarzuelas.
Plot: Paris, *c* 1830. The composer Roberto and the poet Víctor live in penury in a garret and are writing an opera together. Roberto meets and falls in love with the young singer Cossette. At an audition for the Opéra-Comique before the impresario Girard, Cossette sings music from Roberto and Víctor's opera with such success that the future of all three seems set fair. [R]

Böhm, Karl (1894–1981)
Austrian conductor, particularly associated with Mozart, Strauss and Wagner operas. One of the greatest conductors of the 20th century, he was musical director of the Darmstadt Opera (1927–31), the Hamburg State Opera (1931–3), the Dresden State Opera (1934–42) and the Vienna State Opera (1942–4 and 1954–5). He conducted the first performances of *Daphne*, *Die Schweigsame Frau*, Schoeck's *Massimilla Doni* and Einem's *Der Prozess*. His autobiography, *A Life Remembered*, was published in 1970.

Böhme, Kurt (1908–89)
German bass, particularly associated with the German repertory. One of the finest Wagnerian singers of the immediate post-war era, he was equally successful in comic roles, especially Baron Ochs in *Der Rosenkavalier*. He created Count Lamoral in *Arabella*, Vanuzzi in *Die Schweigsame Frau*, Odysseus in Liebermann's *Penelope*, Aleel in Egk's *Irische Legende* and, for Sutermeister, Capulet in *Romeo und Julia* and Prospero in *Die Zauberinsel*.

Boïeldieu, François-Adrien (1775–1834)
French composer. He wrote 32 operas, including one each in collaboration with Cherubini, Hérold and Auber. His early works are pleasing but derivative, but in his later operas, which were admired by Weber and Wagner, he developed a distinctive romantic style. His operas are notable for their charming melodies and for their deft orchestration. His first opera *La Fille Coupable* (Rouen, 2 Nov 1793; libr J.F.A. Boïeldieu) was a success. The most important of his later works were *Zoraime et Zulnar* (Paris, 10 May 1798; libr Claude Godard d'Aucour de Saint-Just), the very successful LE CALIFE DE BAGDAD, *Ma Tante Aurore* (Paris, 13 Jan 1803; libr Charles de Longchamps) [R], *Aline Reine de Golconde* (St Petersburg, 17 Mar 1804; libr Jean Vial and Étienne de Favières), *Télémaque* (St Petersburg, 28 Dec 1806; libr P. Dercy), the successful JEAN DE PARIS, *Angéla* (Paris, 13 June 1814; libr C. Montcloux d'Épinay), his masterpiece LA DAME BLANCHE and *Les Deux Nuits* (Paris, 20 May 1829; libr Eugène Scribe, after Jean Nicolas Bouilly), which contains a chorus filched by Wagner for the 'Bridal Chorus' in *Lohengrin*. His son **Adrien-Louis-Victor** (1816–83) was also a composer, whose most successful opera was *Marguerite* (Paris, 18 June 1838; libr Scribe).

Boito, Arrigo (b Enrico) (1842–1918)
Italian composer, poet, librettist and critic. One of the most remarkable and versatile figures in operatic history, he had imbibed transalpine culture, was an early admirer of Wagner, and was a leading member of the Scapigliatura, a Milanese movement for the reform of Italian art. As a composer, his fame rests chiefly on the extraordinary MEFISTOFELE. Few operas were (or have remained) so controversial: dismissed out of hand by some critics, regarded by others as one of the finest and most high-minded Italian operas since those of Gluck. In it, Boito attempted a synthesis of Italian lyricism and Germanic philosophy and dramatic theory; the result is like no other opera. He worked intermittently on his second opera NERONE for some 40 years, but it was still incomplete at his death and was prepared for performance by Toscanini and Vincenzo Tommasini.

Boito was one of the very few truly outstanding librettists, his best work being done for Verdi. In his youthful days, he had denigrated Verdi in an *Ode to Italian Art*, which had deeply hurt the composer. Later, Boito came to revere Verdi and the quarrel was patched up. Their remarkable artistic partnership produced the revised *Simon Boccanegra* (Boito wrote the Council Chamber Scene) and Verdi's last two Shakespearean masterpeices, *Otello* and *Falstaff*. The libretto for the latter is widely regarded as the finest which any composer has ever been given. He also began work on a *King Lear* libretto for Verdi, but the project failed to materialize. As well as those for his own operas, Boito also provided libretti for Bottesini, Catalani (*La Falce*), his close friend Faccio (*Amleto*), Mancinelli (*Ero e Leandro*), Pick-Mangiagalli (*Basi e Bote*) and Ponchielli (*La Gioconda*). Boito was for many years the companion of the actress **Eleonora Duse**.

Bolero
A Spanish dance, usually accompanied by voices, with a triplet on the second half of the first beat of the bar. The best known operatic number in bolero rhythm is Hélène's 'Merci, jeunes amies' in Act V of Verdi's *Les Vêpres Siciliennes*.

Boles, Bob
Tenor role in Britten's *Peter Grimes*. He is a bigoted Methodist preacher.

Bolivar
Opera in three acts by Milhaud (Op 236). 1st perf Paris, 12 May 1950 (composed 1943); libr by Madelaine Milhaud and Jules Supervielle. Principal roles: Bolivar (bar), Manuela (sop), Maria-Teresa (sop), Nicador (ten), Bovès (bass), Precipitation (mezzo). Dealing with events in the life of the South American liberator Simón Bolívar (1783–1830), it was received with respect rather than enthusiasm at its appearance and has since then been only very rarely performed.

Bologna
see TEATRO COMUNALE, BOLOGNA

Bolshoi Opera
The present theatre (cap 2,100) in Moscow was designed by Alberto Cavos and opened in 1856, replacing a previous theatre of the same name (which means 'grand') which had opened on 18 Jan 1825, but which burnt down in 1853. Usually regarded as Russia's principal opera company, its repertory and stagings are conservative, but its musical standards are very high. The annual season runs from September to July. Musical directors have included Ippolit Altani, Samuel Samosud, Gennadi Rozhdestvensky, Yuri Simonov and Alexander Lazarev.

Bomarzo
Opera in two acts by Ginastera (Op 34). 1st perf Washington, 19 May 1967; libr by Manuel Mujíca Láinez, after his own novel. Principal roles: Pier Francesco (ten), Silvio da Narni (bar), Diana (mezzo), Pantasilea (mezzo), Giulia Farnese (mezzo), Maerbale (bar), Girolamo (bar), Gian Corrado (bass), Niccolo Orsini (ten). One of the most controversial of all modern operas, it has enjoyed a *succès de scandale* in many countries, but was banned as immoral in Ginastera's native Argentina by President Onganía's government. An erotic and hallucinatory work, it is notable for the scene in which the chorus intones the word 'love' in 40 different languages.
Plot: 16th-century Italy. The astrologer Silvio da Narni gives Pier Francesco

Orsini, Duke of Bomarzo, a potion which he says will secure him immortality. It is in fact a fatal poison. After drinking it, Pier Francesco relives the secret, sordid and erotic episodes of his life and then dies. [R]

Bonci, Alessandro (1870–1940)
Italian tenor, particularly associated with lighter Italian roles. Possessor of an elegant and stylish voice, he was the first tenor to introduce the laughs into Gustavus's 'È scherzo od è follia' in Verdi's *Un Ballo in Maschera.*

Bondeville, Émmanuel (1898–1987)
French composer and administrator. His three operas met with some success in France but are unknown elsewhere. They are *L'École des Maris* (Paris, 15 June 1935; libr Jacques Laurent, after Molière) [R Exc], *Madame Bovary* (Paris, 1 June 1951; libr René Fauchois, after Gustave Flaubert) and *Antoine et Cléopâtre* (Rouen, 8 Mar 1974; libr composer, after Victor Hugo's translation of Shakespeare's *Antony and Cleopatra*). He was director of the Opéra-Comique, Paris (1948–51) and the Paris Opéra (1951–59). His wife **Viorica Cortez** (*b* 1935) was a successful mezzo.

Bonisolli, Franco (b 1938)
Italian tenor, particularly associated with heavier Italian roles such as Calaf in Puccini's *Turandot* and Manrico in Verdi's *Il Trovatore.* A sometimes exciting if not exactly subtle TENORE DI FORZA, he created the title-role in Rota's *Aladino e la Lampada Magica.*

Bonn Stadttheater
The opera house (cap 896) in the administrative capital of Germany opened in 1965. Musical directors have included Martin Turnovský, Ralf Weikert, Peter Maag, Gustav Kuhn and Dennis Russell Davies.

Bononcini, Giovanni Battista (1670–1747)
Italian composer and cellist. He composed some 20 operas, many of them being first performed in London, where the rivalry between himself and Händel was the main feature of operatic life at the time. This rivalry included a jointly-written opera, *Muzio Scevola* (London, 15 Apr 1721; libr Paolo Antonio Rolli, after Silvio Stampiglia), which has an act each by Bononcini, Händel and Filippo Mattei. His operas, now largely forgotten, include GRISELDA, perhaps his finest work, *Farnace* (London, 27 Nov 1723; libr after Lorenzo Morari), *Calfurnia* (London, 18 Apr 1724; libr Nicola Francesco Haym, after Orazio Braccioli) and *Astianatte* (London, 6 May 1727; libr Haym, after Antonio Salvi). His brother **Antonio Maria** (1677–1726) also composed several operas. *Camilla* (1696), usually attributed to him, is actually by Giovanni.

Bontempi, Giovanni (b Angelini) (c 1624–1705)
Italian composer, singer, musicologist, architect and historian. A remarkable polymath, he was one of the leading castrati of his time, was an accomplished architect and wrote two books on European history. His three operas are *Il Paride* (Dresden, 3 Nov 1662; libr composer), *Dafne* (Dresden, 3 Sept 1671; libr composer, after Ottavio Rinuccini) and the lost *Jupiter und Ino* (Dresden, 16 Jan 1673), which was written in collaboration with Marco Giuseppe Peranda. His *Historia Musica* (1695) was the first history of music written in Italian.

Bonynge, Richard (b 1930)
Australian conductor, pianist and musicologist, particularly associated with the Italian BEL CANTO and French repertories. A distinguished musicologist and coach but as a conductor seldom more than an accompanist, he was musical director of the Vancouver Opera Association (1973–78) and the Australian Opera (1976–85). Married to the soprano DAME JOAN SUTHERLAND.

Bonze
Bass role in: **1** Puccini's *Madama Butterfly.* He is Cio-Cio-San's uncle. **2** Stravinsky's *The Nightingale.*

Booing
This is a regrettably prevelant feature of operatic performances, especially on the continent (in Italy the audience usually hisses). People try to justify the practice on the grounds that the audience has paid for its seats and is thus entitled to register its disapproval. There is, however, no justification for booing; it is simply bad manners.

Bordeaux
see GRAND THÉÂTRE, BORDEAUX

Bordoni, Faustina (1700–81)
Italian soprano. One of the greatest singers of her age, she was famous for her impeccable technique and exciting delivery of fiery and florid music. For Händel she created Rossane in *Alessandro*, Pulcheria in *Riccardo Primo*, Emira in *Siroe*, Alceste in *Admeto* and Elisa in *Tolomeo*. Her rivalry with FRANCESCA CUZZONI led to the famous affray during Bononcini's *Astianatte*, when the two divas ended up pulling each other's hair. The incident is the basis for some of the satire in *The Beggar's Opera*. Married to the composer JOHANN HASSE, she is the subject of Louis Schubert's opera *Faustina Hasse* (1879).

Boréades, Les or **Abaris**
Opera in five acts by Rameau. 1st perf London, 19 April 1975 (composed 1764); libr possibly by Louis de Cahusac. Principal roles: Alphise (sop), Abaris (ten), Calisis (ten), Borilée (bar), Adamas (bar), Sémire (sop), Borée (bass), Apollo (bar). Rameau's last opera, it was edited and prepared for performance by John Eliot Gardiner.
Plot: Legendary Bactria. Tradition demands that Queen Alphise must wed a descendant of Boreas, god of the North Wind, but she loves the unknown foreigner Abaris. Rather than marry one of the Boread princes Borilée and Calisis, Alphise prepares to abdicate. Boreas is outraged: he unleashes a great storm and carries off Alphise. Abaris, with the aid of Apollo, attempts to rescue her. Finally, Apollo reveals that he himself is Abaris's father and that Abaris is therefore of royal blood and so may marry Alphise. [R]

Borg, Kim (b 1919)
Finnish bass (and also a qualified engineer), who also sang a number of baritone roles. Particularly associated with Mozart roles, he was a fine singing-actor with an effective if not intrinsically beautiful voice. He created a role in Schuller's *The Visitation*.

Borgatti, Giuseppe (1871–1950)
Italian tenor, particularly associated with Wagnerian roles. Italy's first and finest HELDENTENOR, he created the title-role in *Andrea Chénier*. He was forced to retire in 1914 because of blindness. His autobiography, *La Mia Vita d'Artista*, was published in 1927.

Borgioli, Dino (1891–1960)
Italian tenor, particularly associated with Mozart and Donizetti roles. He was one of the most stylish and musicianly lyric tenors of the inter-war period.

Bori, Lucrezia (b Lucrecia Borja y González de Riancho) (1887–1960)
Spanish soprano, particularly associated with the Italian and French repertories. One of the most stylish and elegant singers of the inter-war period, her lovely voice was enhanced by her personal beauty and by her considerable dramatic abilities, especially in the portrayal of vulnerable heroines such as Cio-Cio-San. She created the Duchess of Towers in Taylor's *Peter Ibbetson*.

Boris
1 Tenor role in Janáček's *Káťa Kabanová*. Dikoi's nephew, he is in love with Káťa. **2** Bass role in Moussorgsky's *Boris Godunov*. He is the Tsar of Russia (*c* 1550–1605). **3** Bass role in Shostakovich's *Lady Macbeth of Mtsensk*. Zinovy's father, he is Katerina's ill-tempered father-in-law.

Boris Godunov
Opera in prologue and four acts by Moussorgsky. 1st perf Leningrad, 16 Feb 1928 (composed 1869); libr by the composer, after Alexander Pushkin's *The Comedy of the Distress of the Muscovite State* and Nikolai Mikhailovich Karamzin's *History of the Russian State*. Revised version 1st perf St Petersburg, 17 Feb 1873; revised edition by Rimsky-Korsakov 1st perf St Petersburg, 10 Dec 1896; revised edition by Shostakovich 1st perf Leningrad, 4 Nov 1959. Principal roles: Boris (bass), Grigori/False Dimitri (ten), Pimyen (bass), Marina (mezzo), Varlaam (bass), Shuisky (ten), Rangoni (bar), Schelkhalov (bar), Hostess (mezzo), Simpleton (ten), Fyodor (mezzo), Misail (ten), Xenia (sop), Nurse (mezzo). Moussorgsky's masterpiece and his only completed opera, this vast sprawling tapestry of Russian life – whose central character is in fact the Russian

people rather than Tsar Boris – is the epitome of Russian nationalist opera. Neither the fact that it obeys none of the rules of dramatic structure, nor that the self-taught Moussorgsky commits what the academic world of music would regard as mistakes is in any way relevant: the opera is a work of genius, and has a vision and sense of purpose unequalled by almost any other composer. In recent years, Rimsky-Korsakov has come in for much criticism for his 'tidying-up' of the score. History should, however, be in some ways grateful to him: without his having made the music more readily digestible for conservative-minded audiences, the work would have remained largely unperformed. Nowadays, the original version is nearly always preferred, usually in the critical edition prepared by David Lloyd–Jones. The work's influence on the subsequent development of opera, not only in Russia, has been vast, and its acknowledgement as one of the greatest of all music-dramas at last seems to be assured.
Plot: Russia and Poland, 1598–1605. Exhorted by the police, the people entreat Boris to accept the vacant throne. At his coronation he experiences pangs of conscience, since the young Tsarevich Dimitri had been murdered on his orders. In the Chudov Monastery, the old chronicler Pimyen tells the young novice Grigori Otrepyev of these events, and Grigori vows to avenge the Tsarevich. He flees the monastery and joins the itinerant monks Varlaam and Misail. At an inn, he escapes from the police and crosses the Lithuanian frontier. The scheming Prince Vassili Shuisky, Boris's advisor, exacerbates the Tsar's feelings of guilt, and Boris begins to hallucinate. Grigori has gone to Poland and declared himself to be the Tsarevich Dimitri. Urged on by the Jesuit Rangoni, who wishes to convert Russia to Catholicism, Marina (daughter of a Sandomir noble) accepts Grigori's love. The tormented Boris is told by Pimyen of a miracle at the Tsarevich's tomb. This news induces a seizure in Boris who, naming his son Fyodor as his successor, dies begging for divine forgiveness. In the Kromy Forest, Varlaam and Misail incite the mob in support of Grigori, who invites all to join him on the march to Moscow. The Simpleton is left alone to lament the fate of Russia.

The original version did not include the Polish or Kromy Forest scenes, but did include a scene preceding the death of the Tsar in the square of St Basil's Cathedral, in which Boris is confronted by the Simpleton, who refuses to pray for him. [R original and Rimsky versions]

Borkh, Inge (b Ingeborg Simon) (b 1917)
Swiss soprano, particularly associated with Strauss roles and with the title-role in Puccini's *Turandot* and Lady Macbeth in Verdi's *Macbeth*. A magnificent singing-actress, she possessed a powerful and incisive voice. She created Cathleen in Egk's *Irische Legende* and the Queen in Tal's *Ashmedai*. In 1977 she returned to her original career as a straight actress.

Borodin, Alexander (1833–77)
Russian composer (and also a distinguished research chemist). Like the other members of the Mighty Handful, he was a musical amateur and was largely self-taught. Of his four operas, only the first was actually completed: *The Bogatyirs* (Moscow, 18 Nov 1867; libr Viktor Krylov), which is a pastiche based on a number of other composers' music. MLADA is an unfinished collective opera-ballet, written with Cui, Moussorgsky and Rimsky-Korsakov, for which Borodin was responsible for Act IV. *The Tsar's Bride*, begun in 1867, amounts to little more than sketches. Borodin's operatic reputation rests almost entirely on the magnificent PRINCE IGOR, which was completed by Glazunov and Rimsky-Korsakov. An epic of Russian nationalist opera, it may lack the tragedy and sense of vision of Moussorgsky, but it is more lyrical and spectacular, and few operas have made more thrilling use of dance and of the clash of different cultures.

Borromeo
Baritone role in Pfitzner's *Palestrina*. He is the historical Cardinal Carlo Borromeo (1538–84).

Borsa, Matteo
Tenor COMPRIMARIO role in Verdi's *Rigoletto*. He is a courtier.

Bortnyansky, Dimitri (1751–1825)
Russian (Ukrainian) composer. Like those of most pre-Glinka Russian composers, his operas contain no specifically Russian characteristics, but are imitations – skillfully and suavely written – of Italian models, mainly of his teacher Galuppi. His operas, now virtually all forgotten, include *Creonte* (Venice, 26 Nov 1776; libr Marco Coltellini), *Alcide* (Venice, 1778; libr Pietro Metastasio), *Quinto Fabio* (Modena, 26 Dec 1778; libr Apostolo Zeno), *Le Faucon* (St Petersburg, 22 Oct 1786; libr François Hermann Lafermière, after Jean-Marie Sedaine) [R], perhaps his finest work, *La Fête du Seigneur* (Pavlovsk, 1787) and *Le Fils Rival* (Pavlovsk, 22 Oct 1787; libr Lafermière) [R].

Bösch, Christian (b 1941)
Austrian baritone, particularly associated with Mozart roles, especially Papageno in *Die Zauberflöte*. He possesses a light, melodious and well-schooled voice and is an outstanding singing-actor with a handsome and engaging stage presence. His mother **Ruthilde** (*b* 1918) was a successful mezzo.

Boskovsky, Willi (1909–91)
Austrian conductor and violinist, particularly associated with the lighter Viennese repertory, especially J. Strauss II. Originally a violinist (leader of the Vienna Philharmonic and later of the orchestra of the Vienna State Opera), he turned increasingly to conducting, becoming one of the finest and most persuasive interpreters of Viennese operetta of the post-war era.

Boston
see OPERA COMPANY OF BOSTON

Bottesini, Giovanni (1821–89)
Italian composer, conductor and double bass player. Although best known as one of the greatest double bass virtuosi in history, he also composed a number of operas, all now forgotten. They include *Marion Delorme* (Palermo, 10 Jan 1862; libr Antonio Ghislanzoni, after Victor Hugo), *Alì Babà* (London, 18 Jan 1871; libr E. Taddei, after *The Arabian Nights*) and *Ero e Leandro* (Turin, 11 Jan 1879; libr Arrigo Boito). He conducted the first performance of *Aida*.

Bottom
Bass role in Britten's *A Midsummer Night's Dream*. A weaver, he is one of the mechanicals.

Boughton, Rutland (1878–1960)
British composer. An admirer of Wagner, he attempted to establish a British school of Wagnerian opera with its own Bayreuth, for which purpose he founded the Glastonbury Festival in 1914. Most of his operas were successful and were highly regarded by his contemporaries, including Elgar and Ernest Newman. Whilst hardly on Wagner's level, they are of considerable quality and of great melodic charm, and their current neglect is somewhat surprising. His most ambitious project was an Arthurian cycle to his own libretto, which comprises *The Birth of Arthur* (Glastonbury, 16 Aug 1920, composed 1909), *The Round Table* (Glastonbury, 14 Aug 1916), *The Lily Maid* (Stroud, 10 Sept 1934) and the unperformed *Galahad* (1944) and *Avalon* (1945). His other operas are THE IMMORTAL HOUR, his masterpiece, which enjoyed one of the greatest initial successes of any British opera, the choral drama *Bethlehem* (Somerset, 28 Dec 1915; libr composer, after a Coventry nativity play) [R], the successful *Alkestis* (Glastonbury, 26 Aug 1922; a setting of Gilbert Murray's translation of Euripides), THE QUEEN OF CORNWALL and *The Ever Young* (Bath, 9 Sept 1935; libr composer).

Bouillon, de
Roles in Cilea's *Adriana Lecouvreur*: the Prince (bass) and the Princess (mezzo), who is having an affair with Maurizio.

Bouilly, Jean Nicolas (1763–1842)
French librettist and writer of Jacobin sympathies. He is remembered as the inventor of the RESCUE OPERA libretto, especially that for Gaveaux's *Léonore ou l'Amour Conjugal*, which was the source for Paer's *Leonora*, Mayr's *L'Amor Conjugale* and Beethoven's *Fidelio*. Bouilly claimed that the story was based on a true event which he had witnessed as a civil administrator in Tours during the Revolution. He also provided texts for Auber (*Le Séjour Militaire*), Boïeldieu, Cherubini (*Les Deux Journées*), Dalayrac,

Isouard and Méhul (*La Chasse du Jeune Henri*). His autobiography, *Mes Récapitulations*, was published in 1837.

Boulevard Solitude
Opera in one act (seven tableaux) by Henze. 1st perf Hanover, 17 Feb 1952; libr by the composer and Grete Weil, after Walter Jockisch's adaptation of the Abbé Antoine-François Prévost's *Histoire du Chevalier des Grieux et de Manon Lescaut.* Principal roles: Manon (sop), des Grieux (ten), Lescaut (bar), Lilaque père et fils (ten and bar), Francis (bar). The most successful of Henze's early operas, it is still performed in Germany.
Plot: France, late 1940s. Manon meets des Grieux at a railway station and elopes with him. They move in together, but Manon agrees to her brother Lescaut's suggestion that she should live with a richer man. She lives in luxury with Lilaque, but Lescaut robs Lilaque's safe and the two flee. A desperate des Grieux has turned to drugs and Manon, after comforting him at an inn, leaves with Lilaque's son. During the latter's absence, Manon and des Grieux meet at the Lilaque home, Lescaut arrives and the three decide to steal a painting. Lilaque senior breaks in, notices the painting cut from its frame, and in an ensuing scuffle is killed by a shot from a gun handed by Lescaut to Manon. Manon is jailed and des Grieux is left alone.

Boulez, Pierre (b 1925)
French conductor and composer. A leader of the extreme avant-garde in composition, he is also one of the greatest living interpreters of other composers' music, all of which (however complex) he conducts from memory. He holds equivocal views on opera: he once advocated the blowing-up of all opera houses, but luckily this has not stopped him from giving magnificent, if sadly infrequent, performances in them, notably of Schönberg, Wagner, Berg and Debussy's *Pelléas et Mélisande*. He conducted the first performance of the three-act version of Berg's *Lulu*. He is director of the *Institut de Recherche et de Co-ordination Acoustique Musique*, which he established in Paris in 1977 for the exploration of modern compositional techniques.

Boum, Gen
Bass-baritone role in Offenbach's *La Grande-Duchesse de Gérolstein*. He is the Grand-Duchess's bombastic military commander.

Boult, Sir Adrian (1889–1983)
British conductor. One of the finest British conductors of the 20th century, and a tireless champion of English music, his operatic experiences were extensive in his early days but gradually became ever rarer. In his later years, his sole operatic project was a recording of Vaughan Williams's *The Pilgrim's Progress*. His autobiography, *My Own Trumpet*, was published in 1973.

Bourgeois Gentilhomme, Le (*The Bourgeois Gentleman*)
Comedy-ballet by Lully. 1st perf Château de Chambord, 14 Oct 1670; libr by Molière. A biting satire on the aping of the aristocracy by the nouveau riche, at its first performance Molière himself played Monsieur Jourdain and Lully sang the Turkish Mufti. Although it is really more of a play with songs and dances rather than a true opera, it is a crucial work in the early development of French OPERA-BALLET. [R]

Bowman, James (b 1941)
British COUNTER-TENOR, particularly associated with Händel and other baroque roles and with Oberon in *A Midsummer Night's Dream*. One of the finest modern counter-tenors, with a considerably more powerful voice than most, he created Astron in *The Ice Break*, the Voice of Apollo in *Death in Venice* and the Priest-Confessor in Maxwell Davies's *Taverner*.

Boyarinya Vera Sheloga
see under MAID OF PSKOV, THE

Boyce, William (1711–79)
British composer. His many stage works, now largely forgotten, include the masque *Peleus and Thetis* (*c* 1740; libr Lord Lansdowne).

Braithwaite, Warwick (1898–1971)
New Zealand conductor, particularly associated with the Italian and German repertories. He was musical director of the Australian Opera (1954–5) and the Welsh

National Opera (1956–60). His writings include *The Conductor's Art* (1952). His son **Nicholas** (*b* 1939) is also a conductor, who was musical director of Glyndebourne Touring Opera (1977–80) and the Göteborg Opera (1981–4).

Brambilla, Marietta (1807–75)
Italian contralto. One of the greatest singers of the 19th century, with an enormous vocal range, she created Maffio Orsini in *Lucrezia Borgia*, Pierotto in *Linda di Chamounix* and Paolo in Generali's *Francesa da Rimini*. Her sister **Teresa** (1813–95) was a successful soprano, who created Gilda in *Rigoletto*. Their niece **Teresina** (1845–1921) was also a soprano, who married Ponchielli.

Brandenburgers in Bohemia, The
(*Braniboři v Čechách*)
Opera in three acts by Smetana. 1st perf Prague, 5 Jan 1866; libr by Karel Sabina. Principal roles: Olbramovič (bass), Oldřich (bar), Junoš (ten), Ludiše (sop), Jíra (ten), Tausendmark (bar). Smetana's first opera, it is a strongly nationalist work which is virtually unknown outside the Czech lands.
Plot: Bohemia, 1279. Following the death of Přemysl II in battle against the Habsburgs, his widow has requested the aid of the Margrave of Brandenburg against the Habsburgs. Junoš brings news of a revolt in Prague and the knights under Oldřish Rokycarský and the mayor of Prague, Volfram Olbramovič, agree to resist the Brandenburg advance. Tausendmark, rejected in love by Volfram's daughter Ludiše, sides with the Brandenburgers and Ludiše is captured. The crowd chooses the runaway serf Jíra as its leader, but his attempt to rescue Ludiše fails, and he is jailed on false charges and condemned to death. Junoš, in love with Ludiše, discovers her whereabouts. He engineers Jíra's release and they and the crowd rescue Ludiše and arrest Tausendmark. [R]

Brander
Bass role in Berlioz's *La Damnation de Faust*. He is a student.

Brangäne
Mezzo role in Wagner's *Tristan und Isolde*. She is Isolde's companion.

Brannigan, Owen (1908–73)
British bass, particularly associated with Britten and Sullivan roles. One of the best-loved British singers of the post-war era, he combined a large and rich voice with fine acting ability (especially in comedy) and a superb personality. He created Swallow in *Peter Grimes*, the title-role in *Noye's Fludde*, Collatinus in *The Rape of Lucretia*, Bottom in *A Midsummer Night's Dream*, a role in Gardner's *The Moon and Sixpence* and, for Williamson, Dr Hasselbacher in *Our Man in Havana*, Agenor in *The Violins of St Jacques* and a role in *English Eccentrics*.

Bratislava Opera
(Pressburg or Pozsony when it was part of Austria-Hungary). Slovakia's principal opera company, it performs at the Slovak National Theatre (cap 611), which opened in 1919. The company's main founder was Nedbal, and musical directors have included Zdeněk Chalabala, Krešimir Baranović, Zdeněk Košler and Ondřej Lenárd. The company also has an operetta theatre, New Scene (*Nová Scéna*).

Brautwahl, Die (*The Bridal Lottery*)
Opera in three acts and epilogue by Busoni. 1st perf Hamburg, 13 April 1912; libr by the composer, after E.T.A. Hoffmann's story. Principal roles: Edmund (ten), Albertine (sop), Voswinkel (bass), Manasse (ten), Thusmann (bass). Busoni's first mature opera, it is hardly ever performed.
Plot: Berlin, *c* 1920. The artist Edmund Lehsen loves Albertine, daughter of the official Voswinkel, but she has been promised to Thusmann. Her father assumes Thusmann to have lost interest after reporting seeing Albertine dancing at an inn. However, he renews his suit when the old Jew Manasse asks for Albertine as a bride for his nephew. Voswinkel assembles the three suitors and offers Albertine to the man who choses the correct one of three caskets. Edmund chooses one containing a letter promising happiness and is united with Albertine.

Bravo, Il
Opera in three acts by Mercadante. 1st perf Milan, 9 March 1839; libr by Gaetano Rossi and Marco Marcello, after James

Fenimore Cooper's novel and Eugène Anicet-Bourgeois's *La Vénitienne*. Principal roles: Bravo (ten), Violetta (sop), Teodora (sop), Pisani (ten), Foscari (bass). One of Mercadante's finest operas, in which his reform ideas are put into practice, it was long popular and still receives an occasional performance in Italy.
Plot: 18th-century Venice. Violetta, abandoned by her mother Teodora, is loved by the nobleman Foscari, who has her guardian murdered. Teodora hires the official government assassin (the Bravo) to abduct Violetta. After reuniting her with her mother, the Bravo reveals that he is Violetta's father and that the government has ordered him to kill Teodora. Teodora snatches his dagger and stabs herself. Eventually, the Bravo is released from his grim profession, and Violetta leaves the city with her exiled beloved Pisani, who has secretly returned to elope with her. [R]

Bravura (Italian for 'courage' or 'swagger')
The term is used to describe a performance or a piece of music involving an assured display of great technical difficulty, as in an ARIA DI BRAVURA.

Brazil
see TEATRO AMAZONES, MANAUS; TEATRO MUNICIPAL, RIO DE JANEIRO

Brazilian opera composers
see GOMES; VILLA-LOBOS
Other national opera composers include Elías Álvares Lôbo (1834–1901), whose *A Noite de São João* (Rio de Janeiro, 14 Dec 1860; libr José Martiniano de Alençar) was the first Brazilian opera on a native subject, Francisco Braga (1868–1945), Delgado de Carvalho (1872–1921), Itiberê da Cunha (1848–1913), José de Lima Siqueira (1907–85), Oscar Lorenzo Fernândez (1897–1948), Manuel Joaquim de Macedo (1847–1925), Francisco Mignone (1897–1986), Leopoldo Miguez (1850–1902), Alberto Nepomuceno (1864–1920), Henrique Oswald (1854–1931) and Assís Pacheco (1865–1937).

Break
The place in the voice where the tonal quality changes between the chest and head registers.

Brecht, Bertolt (b Berthold) (1898–1956)
German playwright and librettist. A biting satirist of both Nazi Germany and of capitalism, he is best known for his collaborations with Eisler and with Weill, for whom he wrote *Die Dreigroschenoper*, *Mahagonny Songspiel*, *Happy End*, *Der Jasager*, *Aufstieg und Fall der Stadt Mahagonny* and *Die Sieben Todsünden*. With Caspar Neher, he also wrote the libretto for Wagner-Régeny's *Der Därmwascher*. His *Herr Puntila und sein Necht Marti* and *Die Verurteilung des Lukullus* were both set by Dessau.

Breeches role
An alternative British term for TROUSER ROLE.

Bregenz Festival
An annual summer festival in Vorarlberg (Austria) which was founded in 1956. Star casts perform at the open-air lakeside theatre (cap 4,388) and smaller-scale works are given at the Theater am Kornmarkt. Ranking as one of Europe's leading opera festivals, the resident orchestra is the Vienna Symphony.

Bremen Opera
The original Staatstheater in this German city in Lower Saxony was destroyed in World War II. Its successor, the Theater am Goetheplatz (cap 900), opened on 27 Aug 1950. With a long tradition of fostering major talent, musical directors have included Anton Seidl, Heinz Wallberg, Manfred Gurlitt, Peter Schneider, Peter Herman Adler, Marcello Viotti and Markus Stenz.

Brétigny, de
Baritone role in Massenet's *Manon*. He is a tax farmer.

Bretón y Hernández, Tomás (1850–1923)
Spanish composer. He wrote six operas, some of which enjoyed success in their time, including *Los Amantes de Teruel* (Madrid, 12 Feb 1889; libr composer), *Garín* (Barcelona, 14 May 1892; libr C. Fereal) and *La Dolores* (Madrid, 16 Mar 1895; libr composer, after José Filíu y Codina), with its famous JOTA. His reputation rests chiefly, however, on his ZARZUELAS. Of these, LA VERBENA DE LA

PALOMA has proved to be one of the most enduringly popular of all zarzuelas.

Brian, Havergal (1876–1972)
British composer. One of the strangest and most isolated figures in British music, he wrote a considerable amount of his large output after the age of 80. Best known as a symphonic composer, he also wrote five operas, only two of which have ever been performed. They are *The Tigers* (BBC Radio, 3 May 1983, composed 1930; libr composer), *Turandot* (1950; libr after Carlo Gozzi), *The Cenci* (1952; libr after Percy Bysshe Shelley), *Faust* (1956; libr after Goethe) and *Agamemnon* (London, 28 Jan 1971, composed 1957; libr composer, after Aeschylus). Despite the ardent and vociferous advocacy of his music by his admirers, Brian remains in musical limbo.

Bride of Messina, The (*Nevěsta Messinská*)
Opera in three acts by Fibich. (Op 18). 1st perf Prague, 28 March 1884; libr by Otakar Hostinský, after Friedrich von Schiller's *Die Braut von Messina*. Principal roles: Isabella (mezzo), Manuel (bar), Cesar (ten), Beatrice (sop), Kajetán (bass) Diego (bass). Fibich's first major success, it is still performed in the Czech lands but is little known elsewhere.
Plot: Sicily. The widowed Princess Isabella wishes to reconcile her estranged sons Manuel and Cesar, and abdicates in their favour. She also has her unknown daughter Beatrice brought from a nearby convent. Kajetán, leader of Manuel's followers, effects a truce between the brothers, both of whom are secretly in love with an unknown woman. When Isabella tells him of Beatrice, Manuel realizes that she is the girl he loves. He greets Beatrice as a sister, but Cesar enters and sees him embracing his own secret love. Cesar kills Manuel out of jealousy and stabs himself when he learns that Beatrice is his sister. [R]

Bridge, Frank (1879–1941)
British composer. Although best known as a composer of chamber and orchestral music, he also wrote one opera, THE CHRISTMAS ROSE. He was also a noted teacher, whose pupils included Britten.

Brigands, Les (*The Bandits*)
Operetta in three acts by Offenbach. 1st perf Paris, 10 Dec 1869; libr by Henri Meilhac and Ludovic Halévy. Principal roles: Falsacappa (ten), Fiorella (sop), Antonio (ten), Fragoletto (mezzo), Pietro (bar), Campotasso (bar). Perhaps the best of all the texts which Meilhac and Halévy gave Offenbach, it is set on the Italian-Spanish border (*sic*) and tells of a robber chief who discovers that the ducal treasurer whom he is trying to rob is even more dishonest than he is. Although never one of Offenbach's most popular works, it is still performed quite often. [R]

Brighella
The traditional COMMEDIA DELL'ARTE figure appears in a number of operas, including: **1** Tenor role in Strauss's *Ariadne auf Naxos*. **2** Bass role in Wagner's *Das Liebesverbot*. **3** Baritone role in Cowie's *Commedia*.

Brilioth, Helge (b 1931)
Swedish tenor, particularly associated with the German repertory. He began as a baritone, turning to tenor roles in 1965. Although he was not a true HELDENTENOR, he became one of the leading Wagnerian tenors of the 1970s, especially noted for his Siegfried. Later in his career he undertook character roles.

Brindisi (from the Italian *far brindisi*, 'to drink one's health')
A drinking song. There are many famous examples in opera, notably 'Il segreto per esser felice' in Donizetti's *Lucrezia Borgia* and 'Libiamo, libiamo' in Verdi's *La Traviata*.

Britain
see GREAT BRITAIN

British Broadcasting Corporation
The BBC has played a large and invaluable part in British operatic life. The first opera on radio was *Hänsel und Gretel* on 6 Jan 1923 from Covent Garden, which was also the first broadcast from a European opera house. The first studio performance was *Roméo et Juliette* in October of the same year. With the advent of the Third Programme (later Radio Three), a vast amount of opera has been broadcast. It has included studio recordings (with many

· *British royalty in opera* ·

The English and Scottish monarchies, particularly the Tudors (1485–1603), have frequently fascinated opera composers, especially in Italy in the first half of the 19th century. The many British kings and queens who appear as operatic characters include:

ENGLAND

- Alfred the Great in Donizetti's *Alfredo il Grande*, Arne's *Alfred*, Gatty's *King Alfred and the Cakes*, Dvořák's *Alfred* and Mayr's *Alfredo il Grande*.
- William I in Nápravník's *Harold*.
- Henry II in Donizetti's *Rosmonda d'Inghilterra* and Nicolaï's *Enrico II*.
- Richard I in Lotti's *Isacio Tiranno*, Adam's *Richard à Palestine*, Sullivan's *Ivanhoe*, Marschner's *Der Templer und die Jüdin*, Grétry's *Richard Coeur de Lion* and Händel's *Riccardo Primo*.
- John in Sullivan's *Ivanhoe*.
- Richard II in Bush's *Wat Tyler*.
- Edward III in Donizetti's *L'Assedio di Calais*.
- Henry V in Hérold's *La Gioventù di Enrico V*, Holst's *At the Boar's Head*, Mercadante's *La Gioventù di Enrico V* and Pacini's *La Gioventù di Enrico V*.
- Edward IV in Testi's *Riccardo III*.
- Richard III in Meyerbeer's *Margherita d'Anjou* and Testi's *Riccardo III*.
- Henry VIII in Donizetti's *Anna Bolena*, Maxwell Davies's *Taverner* and Saint-Saëns's *Henri VIII*.
- Mary I in Gomes's *Maria Tudor*, Wagner-Régeny's *Der Günstling* and Pacini's *Maria Tudor*.
- Lady Jane Grey in Vaccai's *Giovanna Grey*.
- Elizabeth I in Britten's *Gloriana*, Carafa's *Elisabetta in Derbyshire*, Donizetti's *Il Castello di Kenilworth*, *Maria Stuarda* and *Roberto Devereux*, Fortner's *Elisabeth Tudor*, German's *Merrie England*, Klenau's *Elizabeth von England*, Mercadante's *Il Conte d'Essex*, Pavesi's *Elisabetta d'Inghilterra*, Thomas's *Le Songe d'une Nuit d'Été* and Rossini's *Elisabetta Regina d'Inghilterra*.
- Charles I in Bennett's *All the King's Men*.
- Charles II in MacFarren's *King Charles II*.

SCOTLAND

- Duncan in Bloch's *Macbeth*.
- Macbeth in Verdi's *Macbeth* and Bloch's *Macbeth*.
- James V in Rossini's *La Donna del Lago*.
- Mary in Donizetti's *Maria Stuarda*, Carafa's *Elisabetta in Derbyshire*, Coccia's *Maria Stuarda*, Musgrave's *Mary Queen of Scots*, Mercadante's *Maria Stuarda* and Slonimsky's *Mariya Stywart*.
- Bonnie Prince Charlie in Coccia's *Edoardo in Iscozia*.

first performances), relays from the BBC-run Promenade Concerts and from British opera companies, recordings of European performances and studio recordings from other European broadcasting authorities. These broadcasts have included many rare works that could never otherwise have been heard.

In the field of television, the BBC gave the world's first opera performance on TV when it broadcast excerpts from Coates's *Pickwick* in 1936. Only in the last decade or so, however, has opera been a regular feature on BBC television. Performances are now frequently relayed from both Britain and abroad. The BBC has also mounted a number of its own productions, most notably the world premiere of

Britten's *Owen Wingrave* (the most important opera specifically commissioned for television) and an award-winning production of Wagner's *Der Fliegende Holländer* with Norman Bailey and Dame Gwyneth Jones.

British National Opera Company
Founded in 1922 from the membership of the bankrupt Beecham Opera Company, it performed in London and the provinces under the artistic direction of the conductor Percy Pitt (1870–1932) and the baritone FREDERIC AUSTIN. It was taken over in 1929 as the Covent Garden English Company, continuing as such until 1931.

British opera composers
see ALWYN; ARNE; ARNOLD; BALFE; BANTOCK; BARNETT; BENEDICT; BENNETT; BERKELEY; BERNERS; BIRTWISTLE; BISHOP; BLAKE; BLISS; BLOW; BOUGHTON; BOYCE; BRIAN; BRIDGE; BRITTEN; BULLER; BUSH; CELLIER; CHISHOLM; COATES; COLERIDGE-TAYLOR; COLLINGWOOD; COSTA; COWEN; COWIE; CROSSE; DELIUS; DIBDIN; ELGAR; D'ERLANGER; GARDNER; GATTY; GERMAN; GOEHR; GOOSSENS; HAMILTON; HARVEY; HODDINOTT; HOLBROOKE; HOLST; HOPKINS; HUGHES; JOUBERT; KNUSSEN; LARA; LINLEY; LITOLFF; LLOYD; LOCKE; LUTYENS; MACCUNN; MACFARREN; MACONCHY; MAW; MAXWELL DAVIES; MONCKTON; MUSGRAVE; NYMAN; OLIVER; ORR; OSBORNE; PARRY; J. PARRY; PEPUSCH; PURCELL; QUILTER; SAXTON; SCOTT; SEARLE; SHIELD; SMYTH; STANFORD; STORACE; SULLIVAN; TALBOT; TAVENER; A.G. THOMAS; TIPPETT; TURNAGE; VAUGHAN WILLIAMS; WALLACE; WALTON; WEIR; WISHART
see also AUSTRALIAN OPERA COMPOSERS; IRISH OPERA COMPOSERS

British royalty in opera
see panel on page 80

Britten, Benjamin (later Lord Britten of Aldeburgh) (1913–76)
British composer and conductor. More than any other musician, Britten may be regarded as the central figure in the British musical renaissance of the post-war era, and of the international repute in which British music is now held. His music, although rooted in tradition, is strikingly original, and almost no composer since Verdi possessed such dramatic flair and insight. Two themes which run through many of his operas are the corruption of innocence and the position of the outsider in society. Most of his operas were written for the tenor SIR PETER PEARS, with whom Britten enjoyed a lifelong relationship. Their artistic partnership, one of the most remarkable in musical history, resulted not only in some of Britten's greatest music, but also in the establishment of the English Opera Group, the Aldeburgh Festival and the Britten-Pears School.

Britten's first stage work was the operetta PAUL BUNYAN, which he soon withdrew and which was not heard again until the 1970s. The production of PETER GRIMES, which marked the reopening of Sadler's Wells after the war, was a milestone in the history of British opera. Regarded by many as his masterpiece, it established Britten overnight in the forefront of European opera composers and was the first British opera to enter the international repertory. He then turned to chamber opera with THE RAPE OF LUCRETIA and the comedy ALBERT HERRING. He next produced a version of THE BEGGAR'S OPERA (Cambridge, 24 May 1948) [R], an edition so radical as to amount virtually to a separate work, the children's opera THE LITTLE SWEEP (the second part of the play *Let's Make an Opera*) and a realization of Purcell's *Dido and Aeneas* in 1951. He returned to full-scale opera with the powerful, all-male BILLY BUDD and the initially unsuccessful GLORIANA, written for the coronation of Queen Elizabeth II. Returning to chamber opera, he wrote the deeply disturbing THE TURN OF THE SCREW, one of his finest and most complex works. It was followed by his first church work NOYE'S FLUDDE, a setting of a Chester mystery play, and the Shakespearian A MIDSUMMER NIGHT'S DREAM. He then wrote, for very small forces, his *Three Church Parables*: CURLEW RIVER, THE BURNING FIERY FURNACE and THE PRODIGAL SON. The television opera OWEN WINGRAVE gave Britten an opportunity to advocate his long-held views on pacifism, and in his last opera, DEATH IN VENICE, he introduced dance as an integral part of the drama.

As well as directing his own works, Britten was also an outstanding conductor of other composers' music, particularly English composers. His appearances as an operatic conductor were sadly infrequent. He was also a fine pianist.

Brno Opera
(Brünn when it was part of Austria-Hungary). The second most important Czech opera company, in the capital of Moravia, it performs at the Janáček Opera House (cap 1,317), which opened in 1965. Its repertory is notable for its advocacy of contemporary works and for its long Janáček tradition. The annual season runs from September to June. Musical directors have included František Neumann, Milan Sachs, Zdeněk Chalabala, Václav Kašlík, František Jílek, Jiří Pinkas and Graham Buckland. There is also a chamber house, Miloš Wasserbauer Chamber Opera (*Komorní Opera Miloše Wasserbauera*), which opened in 1957.

Brogni, Cardinal de
Bass role in Halévy's *La Juive*. He turns out to be Rachel's father.

Brouwenstijn, Gré (b Gerda) (b 1915)
Dutch soprano, particularly associated with Wagner and Verdi roles. One of the finest and most musically sensitive and intelligent sopranos of the immediate post-war era, she had a lovely voice and a fine stage presence.

Bruch, Max (1838–1920)
German composer. Best known as an orchestral composer, he also wrote three operas, all now largely forgotten, in a conservative and lyrical style. They are the SINGSPIEL *Scherz, List und Rache* (Cologne, 14 Jan 1858; libr Ludwig Bischoff, after Goethe), DIE LORELEY, his best opera, and *Hermione* (Berlin, 21 Mar 1872; libr Emil Hopffer, after Shakespeare's *A Winter's Tale*).

Bruneau, Alfred (1857–1934)
French composer. He wrote 12 operas, some of them very successful in their time, in which he attempted a reform of French opera on Wagnerian lines. Strongly influenced by his friend ÉMILE ZOLA, Bruneau addressed social and political issues in many of his works. His operas include *Le Rêve* (Paris 18 June 1891; libr Louis Gallet, after Zola), the anti-war L'ATTAQUE DU MOULIN, his most successful work, *Messidor* (Paris, 19 Feb 1897; libr Zola), *L'Ouragan* (Paris, 29 Apr 1901; libr Zola), *Lazare* (French Radio, 15 Apr 1957, composed 1903; libr Zola, after the New Testament), *L'Enfant Roi* (Paris, 3 Mar 1905; libr Zola) and *Les Quatre Journées* (Paris, 2 Dec 1916; libr composer, after Zola).

Brünnhilde
Soprano role in Wagner's *Die Walküre*, *Siegfried* and *Götterdämmerung*. The daughter of Wotan and Erda, she is the rebellious leader of the Valkyries.

Brunswick Staatstheater
The opera house (cap 1,370) in this German city in Lower Saxony opened in 1948, replacing the previous Landestheater, which was destroyed in World War II. Musical directors have included Stefan Soltesz.

Bruscantini, Sesto (b 1919)
Italian baritone, particularly associated with the Italian repertory and with Mozart roles. One of the greatest BUFFOS of the post-war era, especially renowned in Rossini and Cimarosa's *Il Maestro di Cappella*, he enjoyed a remarkably long career, singing into his 70s, and also had success in a number of serious roles, notably Giorgio Germont. His somewhat dry voice was good, if not outstanding, and was allied to fine musicianship, superlative diction and great dramatic ability. Married for a time to the soprano SENA JURINAC.

Bruson, Renato (b 1936)
Italian baritone, particularly associated with Donizetti and Verdi roles. One of the finest baritones of the 20th century, he possesses a gloriously rich and even-toned voice, used with intelligence, a superb technique and scrupulous good taste. He is a restrained and dignified singing-actor, seen to best advantage in the title-role in Verdi's *Macbeth*.

Brussels
see THÉÂTRE ROYAL DE LA MONNAIE, BRUSSELS

Bucharest Opera
Romania's principal opera house (cap 1,000), designed by D. Diocescu, opened in 1953, replacing the previous theatre which had been wrecked by an earthquake in 1940 and then severely damaged by

bombs in 1944. The repertory is strong in Italian works and Romanian operas are also championed. The annual season runs from September to June. Musical directors have included Enescu, George Stephanescu, George Georgescu, Jonel Perlea and Cornel Trailescu.

Budapest State Opera
Hungary's principal opera company, which currently enjoys a high international reputation, it performs at either the Operaház (cap 1,310), designed by Miklós Ybl and one of the world's most beautiful opera houses, or at the Erkel Theatre (cap 2,450). It pursues an enterprising repertory policy, with a strong emphasis on Italian and Hungarian operas. The annual season runs from September to June. Musical directors have included Erkel, Hans Richter, Mahler, Artur Nikisch, Miklós Bánffi, Sergio Failoni, Ferenc Fricsay, János Ferencsik, Ervin Lukács, Ádám Medveczky and Géza Oberfrank.

Budd, Supt
Bass role in Britten's *Albert Herring*. He is the local police chief.

Buenos Aires
see TEATRO COLÓN, BUENOS AIRES

Buffo (from the Italian *buffone*, 'buffoon')
A buffo is a singer of comic roles, as in a BASSO-BUFFO. OPERA BUFFA is comic opera. The French term *bouffe* has the same meaning.

Bühnenfestspiel (German for 'stage festival play')
The term used by Wagner to describe *Der Ring des Nibelungen*. He described *Parsifal* as *Bühnenweihfestspiel* (German for 'stage consecration festival play').

Bulgaria
see SOFIA NATIONAL OPERA

Bulgarian opera composers
see ATANASOV

Other national opera composers include Marin Goleminov (*b* 1908), Parashkev Hadjiev (1912–92), Ivan Ivanov (1862–1917), Emanuil Manolov (1860–1902), whose *The Poor Woman* (*Siromakhkinya*, Kazanluk, Dec 1900; libr composer, after Ivan Vazov) was the first Bulgarian opera, Lyobomir Pipkov (1904–74), Veselin Stoyanov (1902–69) and Pancho Vladigerov (1899–1978).

Buller, John (b 1927)
British composer. He has written one opera, the fine *The Bacchae* (*Bakxai*, London, 5 May 1992; a setting of Euripides), which is sung predominantly in ancient Greek.

Bülow, Hans von (1830–94)
German conductor and pianist. Often regarded as the first modern-style conductor, he was an ardent champion of Wagner, and conducted the first performances of *Tristan und Isolde* and *Die Meistersinger von Nürnberg*. He was musical director of the Hamburg Opera (1888–91) and the Hanover Opera. He was married to Liszt's daughter **Cosima** until she deserted him for Wagner.

Bumbry, Grace (b 1937)
American mezzo and later soprano, particularly associated with the Italian and French repertories. Possessing a rich and powerful voice and a strong, if somewhat generalized, stage presence, she began as a mezzo, especially notable as Eboli in Verdi's *Don Carlos*, and later developed into a dramatic soprano, excelling in roles such as Tosca and Lady Macbeth. In 1961, she became the first black singer ever to appear at the Bayreuth Festival.

Buona Figliuola, La (*The Good Daughter*) or **La Cecchina**
Comic opera in three acts by Piccinni. 1st perf Rome, 6 Feb 1760; libr by Carlo Goldoni, after Samuel Richardson's *Pamela or Virtue Rewarded*. Principal roles: Cecchina (sop), Armindoro (ten), Marchese (ten), Lucinda (sop), Sandrina (sop), Paoluccia (sop), Tagliaferro (bar), Mengotto (bass). Piccinni's most successful work and his only opera which is still remembered, it founded the genre of OPERA SEMISERIA. Piccinni wrote a less successful follow-up, *La Buona Figliuola Maritata* (Bologna, 10 June 1761; libr Goldoni), which is now forgotten.
Plot: 18th-century Italy. The orphan Cecchina loves and is loved by her master the Marchese. This provokes the jealousy

of her fellow servants Sandrina and Paoluccia, and of Mengotto who also loves her. Also angered is the Marchese's sister Lucinda, who fears that her own marriage prospects will be compromised if her brother marries beneath himself. The German soldier Tagliaferro arrives and reveals that Cecchina is in fact a baroness, thus allowing all to end happily.

Buona sera, mio signore
Mezzo/tenor/baritone/bass/bass quintet for Rosina, Count Almaviva, Figaro, Dr Bartolo and Don Basilio in Act II of Rossini's *Il Barbiere di Siviglia*, in which the others try to get Basilio to go home to bed.

Burchuladze, Paata (b 1951)
Georgian bass, particularly associated with the Italian and Russian repertories, even if his voice is not ideally suited to the former. He possesses a rich and soaring voice of vast proportions, even if occasionally wayward of pitch. He has a strong, if somewhat generalized, stage presence.

Burian, František (1904–59)
Czech composer and producer, nephew of the tenor KAREL BURIAN. As a producer, he was noted for his work in avant-garde theatre techniques. He also wrote eight operas, of which the folk tragedy *Maryša* (Brno, 16 Apr 1940; libr composer, after Alois and Vilém Mrštík) still receives an occasional performance.

Burian, Karel (often Germanized as Carl Burrian) (1870–1924)
Czech tenor, particularly associated with the German and Czech repertories. One of the greatest singing-actors of his age, he was an outstanding linguist and was an artist of remarkable intelligence and musicality. Some contemporary critics rated his voice above Caruso's. He created Herod in *Salome*, an interpretation described by the composer Arnold Bax as 'horrifying, slobbering with lust and apparently almost decomposing before our eyes'. His autobiography, *Z Mých Pamětí*, was published in 1913. His brother **Emil** (1876–1926) was a successful baritone, and his nephew was the composer FRANTIŠEK BURIAN.

Burletta (Italian for 'little joke')
A term which was used loosely in the 18th century to refer to an INTERMEZZO.

Burmeister, Annelies (1929–88)
German mezzo, particularly associated with Wagnerian roles. A dramatic and warm-voiced singer, she created, for Dessau, the Fishwife in *Die Verurteilung des Lukullus* and Laina in *Puntila*.

Burning Fiery Furnance, The
Opera in one act by Britten (Op 77). 1st perf Orford, 9 June 1966; libr by William Plomer, after the Book of Daniel in the Old Testament. Principal roles: Nebuchadnezzar (ten), Abbot/Astrologer (bar), Misael (ten), Azarias (bass), Ananias (bar). The second of Britten's *Three Church Parables*, written for church performance by very small forces, it tells the famous biblical story. [R]

Burrian, Carl
see BURIAN, KAREL

Burrowes, Norma (b 1944)
British soprano, particularly associated with Mozart and other SOUBRETTE roles. She possessed a lovely and well-schooled voice and had a delightful stage presence, especially in comedy. Married for a time to the conductor STEUART BEDFORD; her second husband **Emile Belcourt** (*b* 1926) was a tenor who had particular success in operetta.

Burrows, Stuart (b 1933)
British tenor, particularly associated with Mozart roles. He possessed a small but attractive and well-focused voice, a fine technique, and phenomenal breath control. He was one of the most elegant and stylish Mozartian vocal interpreters of the post-war era, but was considered distinctly dull on stage.

Busch, Fritz (1890–1951)
German conductor, particularly associated with the German repertory and with Mozart operas. He was musical director of the Aachen Opera (1912–19), the Stuttgart Opera (1920–22), the Dresden State Opera (1922–33) and the Glyndebourne Festival (1934–51), where he built up the infant company. He conducted the first

performances of Busoni's *Doktor Faust*, Strauss's *Die Ägyptische Helena* and *Intermezzo*, Weill's *Der Protagonist*, Schoeck's *Vom Fischer un syner Fru* and Hindemith's *Mörder, Hoffnung der Frauen*, *Das Nusch-Nuschi* and *Cardillac*. His autobiography, *Aus dem Leben eines Musikers*, was published in 1949.

Bush, Alan (b 1900)
British composer. His operas, written in a traditional and readily accessible style and all but one with libretti by his wife Nancy, reflect his left-wing political views, and it was in the former East Germany that they met with most success. His stage works include the children's opera *The Press Gang* (Letchworth, 7 Mar 1947), WAT TYLER, his finest opera and a joint winner of the 1951 Festival of Britain competition, the operetta *The Spell Unbound* (Bournemouth, 6 Mar 1955), *The Men of*

· Lord Byron ·

The British romantic poet and playwright George Gordon, Lord Byron (1788–1824) appears as a character in Meale's *Mer de Glace* and Thomson's *Lord Byron*. His writings have inspired nearly 50 operas. Below are listed, by work, those operas by composers with entries in this dictionary.

The Bride of Abydos		
Poniatowski	*La Sposa d'Abido*	1845
Cain		
Lattuada	*Caino*	1957
The Corsair		
Pacini	*Il Corsaro*	1831
Schumann	*Der Korsar*	1844 (U)
Arditi	*Il Corsaro*	1847
Verdi	*Il Corsaro*	1848
Don Juan		
Fibich	*Hedy*	1896
Heaven and Earth		
Donizetti	*Il Diluvio Universale*	1830
Glière	*Earth and Sky*	1900
The Lament of Tasso		
Donizetti	*Torquato Tasso*	1833
Lara		
Maillart	*Lara*	1864
Manfred		
Reinecke	*König Manfred*	1867
Petrella	*Manfredo*	1872
Marino Faliero		
Donizetti	*Marino Faliero*	1835
Parisina		
Donizetti	*Parisina d'Este*	1833
Orefice	*Ugo e Parisina*	1915
The Two Foscari		
Verdi	*I Due Foscari*	1844

Blackmoor (Weimar, 18 Nov 1956), *The Sugar Reapers* or *Guyana Johnny* (Leipzig, 11 Dec 1966) and *Joe Hill* (Berlin, 29 Sept 1970; libr B. Stavis). His autobiography, *In My Eighth Decade*, was published in 1980.

Busoni, Ferruccio (1866–1924)
Italian composer and pianist. His five operas, far more Germanic than Italian in style and outlook, are the unperformed *Sigune* (1889; libr L. and F. Soyaux, after Rudolf Baumbach), DIE BRAUTWAHL, the comedy ARLECCHINO, TURANDOT and his masterpiece DOKTOR FAUST, which was left unfinished at his death and which was completed by his pupil Philipp Jarnach. Although much admired by specialists and musicologists, his operas are only rarely performed.

Bussotti, Sylvano (b 1931)
Italian composer. His stage works, in avant-garde style, include *La Passion Selon Sade* (Palermo, 5 Sept 1965; libr composer, after Louise Labé), *Lorenzaccio* (Venice, 7 Sept 1972; libr composer and Fred Philippe, after Alfred de Musset), *Nottetempo* (Milan, 7 Apr 1976; libr composer and Romano Amidei), *Fedra* (Rome, 19 Apr 1988; libr composer, after Jean Baptiste Racine's *Phèdre*) and *L'Ispirazione* (Florence, 26 May 1988; libr composer, after Ernst Bloch's *Die Gutmachende Muse*). He has also written three marionette operas: *Nottetempolunapark* (Florence, 1954), *Arlechinbatocieria* (Florence, 1955) and *Masacre in Gloria* (Aix-en-Provence, 1956).

Butt, Dame Clara (1873–1936)
British contralto. A greatly loved concert singer, she made only one operatic appearance in her entire career: in Gluck's *Orfeo ed Euridice* at Covent Garden in 1920.

Buxton Festival
An annual summer festival in the Peak District of England, it was founded in 1979. Opera is given at the Buxton Opera House (cap 980), which was designed by Frank Matcham and which opened in 1903. Musical directors have been Anthony Hose and Jane Glover.

Byron, Lord
see panel on page 85

C

Cabaletta (from the Italian *cavatinetta*, 'short melodic air')
The term refers to two similar types of aria: **1** A short aria in simple rhythm with repeats. These arias are mostly found in Rossini, who stipulated that the first statement should be sung as written and that the second could be embellished at the singer's discretion. **2** The second part of a formal two-part aria in a mid-19th-century Italian opera. Typically found in Bellini, Donizetti, Pacini and early Verdi, they are of two stanzas (with the same words each time) and are in fast tempo, being designed to show off a singer's virtuosity and to provide a musical contrast with the slower first part of the full aria. The slow/fast structure of a full aria was occasionally reversed: Donizetti was a master of the slow cabaletta, writing fine examples in the final scenes of *Roberto Devereux*, *Maria Stuarda* and *Parisina d'Este*.

The cabaletta was a dramatically suffocating convention: apart from 'Sempre libera' in *La Traviata* and 'Salgo già il trono aurato' in *Nabucco*, few serve any function other than to provide a singer with a dazzling display piece. Verdi eventually suppressed the cabaletta altogether, and it has subsequently been used only very rarely (as, for example, in *The Rake's Progress*).

Caballé, Montserrat (b 1933)
Spanish soprano, particularly associated with Verdi, Donizetti and Bellini roles. One of the greatest singers of the 20th century, she sang a wide variety of roles until 1965, when her sensational success in the title-role of Donizetti's *Lucrezia Borgia* led her to specialize in the BEL CANTO repertory, of which she became one of the finest modern exponents. Her unfailing musicianship and virtually flawless technique were at the service of a beautiful voice of considerable range and power. Especially noted for the aristocracy of her phrasing and for her sustained pianissimi, she was at her best in concert, where her substantial physique was not the handicap it occasionally proved on stage. Her husband **Bernabé Martí** (*b* 1934) was a successful tenor; their daughter **Montserrat** (*b* 1973) is a soprano.

Caballero, Manuel Fernández (1835–1906)
Spanish composer. One of the most successful and prolific composers of ZARZUELA, he wrote some 220 stage works. The most popular include *Los Sobrinos del Capitán Grant* (Madrid, 25 Aug 1877; libr Miguel Ramos Carrión, after Jules Verne) [R], *El Salto del Pasiego* (Madrid, 17 Mar 1878; libr L. Eguílaz), *Château Margaux* (Madrid, 5 Oct 1887; libr J. Jackson Veyán), *El Dúo de la Africana* (Madrid, 13 May 1893; libr Miguel Echegaray) [R], *La Viejecita* (Madrid, 29 Apr 1897; libr Echegaray) [R], *El Señor Joaquín* (Madrid, 18 Feb 1898; libr Julián Romea) and *Gigantes y Cabezudos* (Madrid, 29 Nov 1898; libr Echegaray) [R].

Caccini, Giulio (c 1545–1618)
Italian composer and lutenist. A member of the FLORENTINE CAMERATA, he was largely responsible for the development of accompanied recitative, and thus of opera. His DAFNE was one of the first two operas, although it may never have been performed and its music is lost. This was followed by *Il Rapimento di Cefalo* (Florence, 9 Oct 1600; libr Gabriello Chiabrera), written with three other composers, almost all of which is lost. He contributed some music to Peri's EURIDICE and subsequently made his own setting of the text, which was the first opera to be published. His elder daughter **Francesca** (1587–*c* 1640) was also a composer, who wrote the opera-ballet *La Liberazione di Ruggero dall'Isola d'Alcina* (Florence, 3 Feb 1625; libr Ferdinando Saracinelli, after Lodovico Ariosto's *Orlando Furioso*). His second daughter **Settimia** (1591–*c* 1660) was a singer who created Venus in Monteverdi's *Arianna*.

Cadenza (Italian for 'cadence')
An improvized passage in free time inserted by a singer before the final cadence of an 18th- or 19th-century aria. The licence for extravagent vocal gymnastics which the convention provided led composers increasingly to write out the cadenzas themselves, sometimes tailored to the abilities of particular singers.

Cadi Dupé, Le (*The Deceived Cady*)
Comic opera in one act by Gluck. 1st perf Vienna, 8 Dec 1761; libr by Pierre René Lemonnier, after *The Arabian Nights*. Principal roles: Cady (bar), Fatime (sop), Nuradin (ten), Zelmire (sop), Omar (ten), Omega (mezzo). Gluck's last pre-reform opera, it is an entertaining little piece which still receives an occasional performance.
Plot: Legendary Baghdad. The attentions of the Cady have turned from his wife Fatime to Zelmire. Despite all his subterfuges, Zelmire rejects his advances as she is in love with Nuradin. Finally, Zelmire pretends to be Omega, daughter of Omar the dyer, who – according to Omar – is appallingly ugly. The Cady enters into a marriage contract with the supposed Omega, but when the real one arrives she proves to be plain indeed. The Cady has to pay through the nose to get out of the contract, whilst Zelmire and Nuradin are united. [R]

Caffarelli (b Gaetano Majorano) (1710–83)
Italian CASTRATO. A male alto and one of the most famous of all castrati (mentioned by Dr Bartolo in *Il Barbiere di Siviglia*), he was believed to be the first singer to introduce chromatic scales as vocal decorations in fast sections. He created the title-roles in Händel's *Serse* and *Faramondo* and Sextus in Gluck's *La Clemenza di Tito*. Commanding the highest fees ever then paid to a singer, he amassed a vast fortune, out of which he purchased two palaces and a dukedom. A highly temperamental man, who had been both jailed and placed under house arrest for his behaviour towards other singers, he wounded the poet Ballot de Sauvot in a duel over the respective merits of Italian and French music.

Cagnoni, Antonio (1828–96)
Italian composer. He wrote 19 operas, some of them successful in their time but all of them now forgotten. His most important operas are *Don Bucefalo* (Milan, 28 June 1847; libr C. Bassi), *Michele Perrin* (Milan, 7 May 1864; libr Marco Marcello), *Claudia* (Milan, 20 May 1866; libr Marcello), *Papà Martin* (Genoa, 4 Mar 1871; libr Antonio Ghislanzoni) and *Francesca da Rimini* (Turin, 19 Feb 1878; libr Ghislanzoni, after Dante's *La Divina Commedia*), his most successful work, which makes considerable use of LEITMOTIVS. His *Rè Lear* (1893; libr Ghislanzoni, after Shakespeare's *King Lear*) was unperformed.

Cain, Henri (1857–1922)
French librettist. He provided texts for several composers, including Alfano (*Cyrano de Bergerac*), Blockx (*Thyl Uilenspiegel*), Erlanger (*Le Juif Polonaise*), Godard (*La Vivandière*), Honegger and Ibert (*L'Aiglon*), Massenet (*Roma, Cendrillon, Chérubin, Don Quichotte, La Navarraise* and *Sapho*), Nouguès (*Quo Vadis?*), Widor (*Les Pêcheurs de Saint-Jean*), Février (*Carmosine* and *Gismonda*) and Lara (*Les Trois Mousquetaires*).

Caius, Dr
Tenor role in Verdi's *Falstaff*. He is the pedant who aspires to marry Nannetta.

Calaf
Tenor role in Puccini's and Busoni's *Turandot*. Timur's son, he is a Tartar prince.

Calchas
The mythical Greek high priest and augur appears in a number of operas, including: **1** Baritone role in Offenbach's *La Belle Hélène*. **2** Bass role in Walton's *Troilus and Cressida*. **3** Bass role in Gluck's *Iphigénie en Aulide*.

Caldara, Antonio (1670–1736)
Italian composer. He wrote 60 operas, virtually all of them now forgotten, including *Ifigenia in Aulide* (Vienna, 4 Nov 1718; libr Apostolo Zeno, after Euripides), *La Clemenza di Tito* (Vienna, 4 Nov 1734; libr Pietro Metastasio) and *Achille in Sciro* (Vienna, 13 Feb 1739; libr Metastasio).

Caldwell, Sarah (b 1924)
American conductor and producer. The first woman American conductor of significance, she founded the Opera Company of Boston in 1957 and has been its director ever since. She also produces most of its performances. She conducted the first performance of Schuller's *The Fisherman and his Wife* and in 1973 became the first woman to conduct at the Metropolitan Opera, New York.

Calife de Bagdad, Le (*The Caliph of Baghdad*)
Comic opera in one act by Boïeldieu. 1st perf Paris, 16 Sept 1800; libr by Claude Godard d'Aucour de Saint-Just, after *The Arabian Nights*. Principal roles: Zémaïde (sop), Zétulbé (sop), Késie (mezzo), Isauun (bass). Very successful in its time, nowadays only its delightful overture is still remembered.
Plot: Legendary Baghdad. The Caliph Harun al Rashid, disguised as Isauun, rescues Zétulbé from robbers. Himself suspected of being a robber, he privately confesses his real identity to the Cady at the house of Zétulbé's mother Zémaïde. After much confusion, he wins Zétulbé as his bride.

Calinda, La
Orchestral piece in Act II of Delius's *Koanga*. It is a dance that takes its name from an African dance brought to America by slaves.

Calisto, La
Opera in prologue and three acts by Cavalli. 1st perf Venice, 28 Nov 1651; libr by Giovanni Battista Faustini, after Ovid's *Metamorphoses*. Principal roles: Calisto (sop), Diana (mezzo), Giove (bass), Linfea (ten), Endimione (c-ten), Pane (bass), Mercurio (bass), Giunone (sop), Silvano (bass). Unperformed for over 300 years, it has nowadays become Cavalli's most frequently performed opera, usually given in the version prepared by the conductor and musicologist Raymond Leppard.
Plot: Legendary Greece. Jove, having decided that Calisto should become an immortal, comes down to earth to claim her, only to find that she has become one of Diana's nymphs. He disguises himself as Diana so as to win Calisto, but Juno turns her into a bear. Meanwhile Endymion, in love with the real Diana, is captured by Pan. He is eventually reunited with Diana, and Jove gives Calisto her immortality by placing her in the heavens as the constellation Ursa Minor. [R]

Callas, Maria (b Kalogeropoulou) (1923–77)
Greek soprano. The most famous – and the most controversial – opera singer of the 20th century, Callas was one of the finest singing-actresses the operatic stage has ever known. She was mainly associated with the Italian repertory, particularly the title-roles in *Tosca*, Bellini's *Norma*, Donizetti's *Anna Bolena* and Cherubini's *Médée*, but also sang the German repertory early in her career. Largely responsible for the modern revival and re-evaluation of the BEL CANTO repertory, she possessed a unique ability to illuminate and communicate the true meaning of a composer's music. Particularly when in partnership with Tito Gobbi, she set entirely new dramatic standards in operatic performance. Her actual singing was variable and her technique was imperfect, but at its best, her voice was large, agile and very beautiful. She retired from the stage in 1965 and – apart from an ill-advised concert tour with Giuseppe di Stefano in 1972–3 – she never sang again in public. She played the title-role in Pasolini's film of Euripides's *Medea* in 1970 and made one appearance as a producer, with *Les Vêpres Siciliennes* in Turin in 1973.

Calunnia, La
Bass aria for Don Basilio in Act I of Rossini's *Il Barbiere di Siviglia*, in which he explains his system of starting a slander campaign.

Calvé, Emma (b Rosa Calvet de Roquer) (1858–1942)
French soprano, particularly associated with the Italian and French repertories, especially Carmen. One of the finest sopranos of her age, and a tempestuous actress, she created Suzel in Mascagni's *L'Amico Fritz*, the title-role in Hahn's *La Carmélite* and, for Massenet, Anita in *La Navarraise* and the title role in *Sapho*. Her

autobiography, *Sous les Ciels J'ai Chanté*, was published in 1940.

Calzabigi, Ranieri de' (1714–95)
Italian librettist. After an adventurous period in Paris as an associate of Casanova, during which he edited Pietro Metastasio's works, he settled in Vienna, where he collaborated with Gluck. As well as the later *Paride ed Elena*, he wrote the texts for the two 'reform' operas: *Orfeo ed Euridice* and *Alceste*, in which his verses reflect Gluck's desire for dramatic truth and the banishment of artificiality. He also wrote the libretti for Paisiello's *Elfrida* and *Elvira*, Gassmann's *La Critica Teatrali* and Morandi's *Comala* (1780), which was the first OSIANIC opera. His *Ippermestra* was the source for Salieri's *Les Danaïdes*.

Cambert, Robert (c 1628–77)
French composer. His *Pomone* (Paris, 19 Mar 1671; libr Abbé Pierre Perrin) is usually regarded as the first opera by a French composer. He also wrote *Les Peines et les Plaisirs d'Amour* (Paris, Feb 1672; libr Gabrial Gilbert). Only a small portion of the music of either work survives.

Cambiale di Matrimonio, La (*The Marriage Contract*)
Comic opera in one act by Rossini. 1st perf Venice, 3 Nov 1810; libr by Gaetano Rossi, after Camillo Federici's play. Principal roles: Tobias Mill (b-bar), Fanny (sop), Slook (bar), Edoardo (ten), Norton (bass). Rossini's first opera to be staged, it is a melodically fresh and entertaining little piece which is still quite often performed.
Plot: 18th-century England. The wealthy Canadian merchant Slook offers the businessman Sir Tobias Mill a large sum of money if he will find him a wife. Mill suggests his daughter Fanny, who is, however, in love with Edoardo Milfort. Slook is impressed by the lovers' determination, sacrifices Fanny and helps them to win Mill's approval for their marriage. [R]

Camden Festival
An annual spring festival in London, founded in 1954 and continuing until 1987, of which opera was the central feature. Called the St Pancras Festival until 1965, it specialized in the revival of long-forgotten operas – some of which subsequently made their way back into the general repertory. Performances were given at St Pancras Town Hall until 1969, and thereafter at the Bloomsbury (formerly Collegiate) Theatre.

Camerata
see FLORENTINE CAMERATA

Camille de Rosillon
Tenor role in Lehár's *Die Lustige Witwe*. He is in love with Valencienne.

Cammarano, Salvatore (1801–52)
Italian librettist. Long resident at the Teatro San Carlo, Naples (where he was stage manager), he was one of the better Italian librettists of his day. Without being inspired, his work is direct, effective and often skilfully constructed. He wrote some 50 libretti in all, including texts for Donizetti (*Lucia di Lammermoor*, *Roberto Devereux*, *Poliuto*, *L'Assedio di Calais*, *Maria di Rohan*, *Maria de Rudenz*, *Belisario* and *Pia de' Tolomei*), Mercadante (nine, including *La Vestale*, *Orazi e Curiazi* and *Il Reggente*), Pacini (six, including *Saffo*), Persiani, Ricci and Verdi (*Alzira*, *La Battaglia di Legnano*, *Luisa Miller* and *Il Trovatore*, which last he had not completed at his death).

Campana Sommersa, La (*The Sunken Bell*)
Opera in four acts by Respighi. 1st perf Hamburg, 18 Nov 1927; libr by Claudio Guastalla, after Gerhard Hauptmann's *Die Versunkene Glocke*. Principal roles: Enrico (ten), Rautendelein (sop), Magda (sop), Ondino (bar). The second of Respighi's mature operas, it was successful at its appearance but is nowadays almost forgotten.
Plot: Legendary Germany. The bell-founder Enrico is bewitched by the fairy Rautendelein and follows her into the mountains. He returns home on the death of his wife Magda, but is unable to erase the memory of Rautendelein, who marries Ondino, King of the Frogs. Later, as he himself lies dying, Enrico calls to her and she returns to comfort him.

Campanello di Notte, Il (*The Little Night Bell*)
Comic opera in one act by Donizetti. 1st perf Naples, 1 June 1836; libr by the composer, after Léon Lévy Brunswick, Mathieu-Barthélemy Troin and Victor Lhérie's *La Sonnette de Nuit*. Principal roles: Enrico (bar), Don Annibale (b-bar), Serafina (sop). A delightfully funny and tuneful little piece, containing some of the longest and fastest patter in all opera, it is still regularly performed.
Plot: Early-19th-century Naples. The elderly apothecary Don Annibale Pistacchio marries the young Serafina. After they have retired to bed, Serafina's rejected lover Enrico interrupts the wedding night by donning a series of disguises (including that of an opera singer) and repeatedly ringing the apothecary's bell and demanding ever more complicated and fantastic prescriptions to be dispensed. [R]

Campanini, Cleofonte (1860–1919)
Italian conductor, particularly associated with the Italian repertory. One of the finest conductors of the early 20th century, he was artistic director of the Manhatten Opera (1906–9) and general manager of the Chicago Opera (1910–19). He conducted the first performances of *Madama Butterfly*, *Adriana Lecouvreur* and Giordano's *Siberia*. Married to the soprano EVA TETRAZZINI. His brother **Italo** (1845–96) was a successful tenor, who created Kenneth in Balfe's *Il Talismano*.

Campiello, Il (*The Little Square*)
Comic opera in three acts by Wolf-Ferrari. 1st perf Milan, 12 Feb 1936; libr by Mario Ghisalberti, after Carlo Goldoni's play. Principal roles: Gasparina (sop), Lucieta (mezzo), Anzoleto (bass), Astolfi (bar), Gnese (sop), Fabrizio (bass). Wolf-Ferrari's last major success, still occasionally performed, it culminates in a street fight between two old women played and sung by tenors.
Plot: Mid-18th-century Venice. Gasparina, Lucieta and Gnese are all the objects of the attentions of the Neapolitan Astolfi. Lucieta and Gnese already have admirers, and Gasparina is unwilling to wed Astolfi. However, her uncle Fabrizio aids his suit, and after much confusion and quarrelling involving the old women who live on the square, Gasparina accepts Astolfi.

Campra, André (1660–1744)
French composer. The historical link between Lully and Rameau, Campra's operas represent a synthesis of what he considered best in the French and Italian schools. His operas and opera-ballets include L'EUROPE GALANTE, *Le Carnaval de Venise* (Paris, 20 Jan 1699; libr Jean François Regnard), *Tancrède* (Paris, 7 Nov 1702; libr Antoine Danchet, after Torquato Tasso's *Gerusalemme Liberata*) [R], possibly his finest work, *Iphigénie en Tauride* (Paris, 6 May 1704; libr Joseph François Duché de Vancy and Danchet, after Euripides), the fine IDOMÉNÉE, *Les Ages* (Paris, 9 Oct 1718; libr Louis Fuzelier) and *Achille et Deidamie* (Paris, 24 Feb 1735; libr Danchet). Virtually ignored for over 200 years, his operas have been much underrated. The last decade has witnessed a considerable revival of interest in his works.

Canada
see CANADIAN OPERA COMPANY; OPÉRA DE MONTRÉAL; VANCOUVER OPERA ASSOCIATION

Canadian Opera Company
Founded in 1950, it is based at the O'Keefe Centre (cap 3,200) in Toronto, and also vists Ottawa and other towns. The annual season is January to June and September and October. Musical directors have included Mario Bernardi.

Canadian opera composers
These include John Beckwith (*b* 1927), John Oliver, R. Murray Schafer (*b* 1933), Harry Somers (*b* 1925), Healey Willan (1880–1968) and Charles Wilson (*b* 1931).

Can-Can
A fast and energetic Parisian dance in 2/4 time, involving much high kicking. It has become almost synonymous with Offenbach, who wrote many exhilarating can-cans. The most famous is the finale to *Orphée aux Enfers*.

Candide
Operetta in three acts by Bernstein. 1st perf Boston, 29 Oct 1956; libr by Lillian

Hellman, Richard Wilbur, Dorothy Parker and John Latouche, after Voltaire's novel. Revised version 1st perf New York, 20 Dec 1973; libr revised by Hugh Callingham Wheeler and Stephen Sondheim. Principal roles: Candide (ten), Cunigonde (sop), Maximilian (bar), Paquette (mezzo), Voltaire (speaker). Initially a failure, the revised version met with great success and has been widely performed.
Plot: Dr Pangloss has taught the Westphalian nobleman Candide and his beloved Cunegonde that this is 'the best of all possible worlds'. In this belief they go off on their travels – and experience exile, war, rape, the Inquisition and frequent betrayals. In the end, they realize that they must come to terms with reality and 'make their gardens grow'. [R]

Caniglia, Maria (1905–79)
Italian soprano, particularly associated with dramatic Italian roles, especially the title-roles in *Tosca*, Cilea's *Adriana Lecouvreur* and *Aida*. Possessing a powerful if sometimes squally voice, she created Roxane in Alfano's *Cyrano de Bergerac*, the title-role in Respighi's *Lucrezia* and Manuela in Montemezzi's *La Notte di Zoraima*. Her husband **Pino Donati** (1907–75) was artistic director of the Verona Arena, the Chicago Lyric Opera and the Teatro Comunale, Bologna.

Canio
Tenor role in Leoncavallo's *Pagliacci*. Nedda's husband, he is the leader of the theatrical troupe.

Canon
A contrapuntal piece of music, in which the melody sung by one voice is repeated by others, each of them entering before the previous one has finished. A famous operatic example is the quartet 'S'appressan gl'isante' in Verdi's *Nabucco*.

Cantabile (Italian for 'singable')
The term has two meanings: **1** In general musical usage it means a flowing style of performance. **2** In opera, it can also mean the first (slow) movement of an 18th- or 19th-century double aria in an Italian opera.

Cantata
An extended choral work, often featuring soloists and nearly always with orchestra. Composers have occasionally used the term to describe stage works which are really fully operatic. For example, Sullivan's *Trial By Jury* and Schoeck's *Vom Fischer un syner Fru* are described as 'dramatic cantatas'.

Cantatrici Villane, Le (*The Village Singers*)
Comic opera in two acts by Fioravanti. 1st perf Naples, Jan 1799; libr by Giovanni Palomba. Principal roles: Rosa (sop), Don Bucefalo (b-bar), Giannetta (mezzo), Agata (sop), Don Marco (bass), Carlino (ten). Fioravanti's only opera still to be in any way remembered.
Plot: 18th-century Italy. The pompous musician Don Bucefalo Zibaldone hears Rosa, Agata and Giannetta singing and offers to teach them. Rosa's husband Carlino has fled the country, and she is wooed by the gouty Don Marco Mbomma. The locals decide to perform an opera (a setting of Metastasio's *Ezio*), and during the already unruly rehearsals, Carlino arrives in disguise and causes chaos. Eventually, he reveals himself to Rosa and all ends happily. [R Exc]

Cantelli, Guido (1920–56)
Italian conductor. One of the most brilliant conductors of the 1950s, he turned to opera only in the last year of his life. He was killed in an air crash a few days after the announcement of his appointment as musical director of La Scala, Milan.

Canteloube, Joseph (1879–1957)
French composer. Although best known as a composer and arranger of songs (mainly from his native Auvergne), he also wrote two unsuccessful operas: *Le Mas* (Paris, 3 Apr 1929; libr composer) and *Vercingétorix* (Paris, 26 June 1933; libr E. Clémental and J.-H. Louwyck).

Canterbury Pilgrims, The
Opera in three acts by Stanford. 1st perf London, 28 April 1884; libr by Gilbert Arthur A'Beckett, after Geoffrey Chaucer's *The Canterbury Tales*. Principal roles: Sir Christopher (bar), Cicely (sop), Hubert

Lovel (ten), Hal O' the Chepe (bar), Dame Margery (mezzo), Geoffrey Blount (bass). Reasonably successful at its appearance, it is nowadays virtually forgotten.

Cantilena (Italian for 'singsong')
The term describes a smoothly flowing vocal line, and is thus also a direction that a passage should be so sung.

Canto figuraturo (Italian for 'figured singing')
An obsolete term which was the original description of COLORATURA.

Canzona (from the Provençal *canzo*, a type of song)
A song which is outside the general dramatic action; in other words, a song within a sung drama. Examples include the 'Canzon del Salice' (the Willow Song) in Verdi's *Otello*, Cherubino's 'Voi che sapete' in Mozart's *Le Nozze di Figaro* and the Veil Song in Verdi's *Don Carlos*.

Canzonetta
The diminutive form of CANZONA, it describes a short song in simple style.

Capecchi, Renato (b 1923)
Italian baritone, particularly associated with the Italian repertory. Although best known as one of the greatest BUFFO artists of the post-war era (and one of the few with a really first-rate voice), his enormous repertory of over 280 roles encompassed Verdi, BEL CANTO, VERISMO and, many 20th-century works, both comic and serious. He created roles in Malipiero's *L'Allegra Brigata*, Ghedini's *Billy Budd* and *Lord Inferno*, Napoli's *Un Curioso Accidente*, Tosatti's *Il Giudizio Universale*, R. Malipiero's *La Donna è Mobile* and Bussotti's *L'Ispirazione*. An outstanding singing-actor with superb diction, a great wit and a fine musician, he enjoyed a remarkably long career, singing into his early 70s. He has also produced a number of operas.

Capellio
Bass role in: **1** Bellini's *I Capuleti e i Montecchi*. He is the leader of the Capulets. **2** Rossini's *Bianca e Faliero*. He is a Venetian senator.

Capobianco, Tito (b 1931)
Argentinian producer and administrator. His traditional but strongly staged productions have been seen mainly in the United States, particularly at the New York City Opera. He was artistic director of the Cincinnati Opera Association (1961–5) and the San Diego Opera Giuld (1977–) and general director of the Pittsburgh Opera (1983–).

Cappello di Paglia di Firenze, Il (*The Florentine Straw Hat*; usually known as *The Italian Straw Hat*)
Comic opera in four acts by Rota. 1st perf Palermo, 21 April 1955; libr by the composer and Ernesta Rota, after Eugène Labiche and Marc-Michel's *Un Chapeau de Paille d'Italie*. Principal roles: Fadinard (ten), Elena (sop), Nonancourt (bass), Beaupertuis (bass), Baroness (mezzo), Anaida (mezzo), Emilio (bar), Vezinet (ten), Felice (ten). Perhaps the last true Italian OPERA BUFFA, it has proved by far Rota's most successful work and has been widely performed.
Plot: Paris, 1850. Fadinard is to wed Elena, daughter of the bumpkin Nonancourt. His horse eats an expensive Florentine straw hat belonging to Anaida, who pursues him with her lover Emilio. Anaida confesses that the hat was given to her by her jealous husband and demands a replacement. Fadinard learns that the only identical hat was sold to the Baroness Champigny. Visiting her, he is mistaken for a famous violinist, pretends to be a suitor to the Baroness, and asks for the hat as a memento, only to learn that the Baroness has given it to her god-daughter Madame Beaupertuis. After leaving a trail of chaos at the home of Beaupertuis (who is Anaida's husband), Fadinard decides to cancel his wedding. However, a replacement hat is finally found and all ends happily. [R]

Cappuccilli, Piero (b 1929)
Italian baritone, particularly associated with the Italian repertory, especially Verdi. One of the finest Verdi baritones of the post-war era, if a little dull on stage, he possessed a beautiful, rich, smooth voice, used with musicianship, a fine technique and scrupulous good taste. He was noted for his phenomenal breath control.

Capriccio
Opera in one act by Strauss (Op 85). 1st perf Munich, 28 Oct 1942; libr by the composer and Clemens Krauss. Principal roles: Countess Madeleine (sop), Count (bar), Flamand (ten), Oliver (bar), La Roche (bass), Clairon (mezzo), Italian Singers (sop and ten), Taupe (ten). Strauss's last opera, set at the time of Gluck's reforms, it is described as a 'conversation piece with music' and discusses the relative importance of words and music in opera.
Plot: Paris, *c* 1775. At her château, the Countess is wooed by the composer Flamand and by the poet Olivier. While waiting for her to chose between them, the two men argue over the respective merits of their arts. It is decided that they will jointly write a work discussing whether music or poetry comes first in opera, and which will involve Madeleine's brother the Count, the theatre manager La Roche, the actress Clairon and others. At the close, the Countess muses over whether the question has any answer that is of the slightest importance. [R]

Capro e la capretta, Il
Mezzo aria for Marcellina in Act IV of Mozart's *Le Nozze di Figaro*. It is nearly always cut.

Capuana, Franco (1894–1969)
Italian conductor and composer, particularly associated with the Italian and German repertories and with contemporary operas. He was musical director of La Scala, Milan (1949–52) and conducted the first performances of Alfano's *L'Ultimo Lord*, Lattuada's *Sandha*, Refice's *Margherita da Cortona*, Malipiero's *Sette Canzoni* and Ghedini's *Rè Hassan* and *La Pulche d'Oro*. He also composed an operetta, *La Piccola Irredenta* (Naples 1915). He died whilst conducting *Mosè in Egitto* in Naples. His sister **Maria** (1891–1955) was a Wagnerian mezzo.

Capuleti e i Montecchi, I (*The Capulets and the Montagues*)
Opera in two acts by Bellini. 1st perf Venice, 11 March 1830; libr by Felice Romani, after Matteo Bandello's novel, itself based on William Shakespeare's *Romeo and Juliet*. Principal roles: Giulietta (sop), Romeo (mezzo), Tebaldo (ten), Capellio (bass), Lorenzo (bass). One of Bellini's finest operas, into which he incorporated much music from the unsuccessful ZAIRA, it was widely performed in the 19th century, when part of the final act of Vaccai's *Giulietta e Romeo* was often substituted for Bellini's. Following a long period of neglect, it has been regularly performed in recent years. In this version of the story, Giulietta's kinsman Tebaldo combines the functions of Tybalt and Paris.
Plot: 13th-century Verona. Tebaldo and the other Capulet supporters swear vengeance on the Montagues, and Capellio promises Tebaldo the hand of his daughter Giulietta. A Montague peace offer, brought by a disguised Romeo, is rejected. Giulietta and Romeo are in love, and Romeo and his supporters interrupt the wedding of Giulietta and Tebaldo. The Capulet doctor Lorenzo gives Giulietta a potion that will simulate death. Romeo and Tebaldo meet and insult one another, but their intended duel is forestalled by a funeral dirge for Giulietta. Romeo enters the vault where she has been laid and, believing her to be dead, takes poison. Giulietta awakens and, after Romeo has expired in her arms, dies of grief. [R]

Carafa, Michele Enrico (1787–1872)
Italian composer. He wrote 35 operas, in which may be seen the influence of both Cherubini and his close friend Rossini, who remarked that Carafa 'made the mistake of being born my contemporary'. His operas, several of them successful in their time but all now forgotten, are solidly written but largely lacking in individuality. He was also unfortunate in often chosing subjects on which other composers soon afterwards based some of their finest works. His most successful operas were *Gabriella di Vergy* (Naples, 5 July 1816; libr Andrea Leone Tottola), *Jeanne d'Arc à Orléans* (Paris, 10 Mar 1821), *Le Solitaire* (Paris, 22 Aug 1822; libr François-Antoine-Eugène de Planard), *Le Valet de Chambre* (Paris, 16 Sept 1823; libr Eugène Scribe and Anne-Honoré Joseph de Mélesville), *Masaniello* (Paris, 27 Dec 1827; libr C. Moreau and A.M. Lafortelle), written just two months before Auber's version, *Le Nozze di Lammermoor* (Paris,

12 Dec 1829; libr Luigi Balocchi, after Sir Walter Scott's *The Bride of Lammermoor*), *La Prison d'Édimbourg* (Paris, 20 July 1833; libr Scribe and Planard, after Scott's *The Heart of Midlothian*) and *Thérèse* (Paris, 26 Sept 1838; libr Planard and Adolphe de Leuven).

Caramello
Tenor role in J. Strauss's *Eine Nacht in Venedig*. He is the Duke of Urbino's barber.

Caramoor Festival
An annual summer festival, founded in 1946, which is held at a private estate in Katonah (New York). Opera is the central feature, and the repertory is notable for its 17th-century and contemporary works. Musical directors have included Julius Rudel.

Cara selve
Soprano aria for Meleagro in Act I of Händel's *Atalanta*, in which he tells that he is seeking his love in the dark woods.

Cardillac
Opera in three acts by Hindemith (Op 39). 1st perf Dresden, 9 Nov 1926; libr by Ferdinand Lion, after E.T.A. Hoffmann's *Das Fräulein von Scuderi*. Revised version 1st perf, Zürich, 20 June 1952. Principal roles: Cardillac (bar), Daughter (sop), Lady (sop), Officer (ten), Cavalier (ten). Hindemith's first full-length opera, it embodies the 'new objectivist' movement in German art and is his most frequently performed stage work.
Plot: 17th-century Paris. The master jeweller Cardillac is so obssessed with his creations that he cannot bear to part with them, believing that the artist and his work should never be seperated. Consequently, he murders each of his customers after a sale. Things get out of hand with the involvement of an opera singer whose lover buys a belt from Cardillac, and the involvement of his own daughter's army-officer lover. Cardillac finally loses his reason, confesses to the killings and is murdered by the mob. [R]

Carlo
1 Baritone role in Verdi's *Ernani*. He is the Emperor Charles V (1500–58). **2** Tenor role in Verdi's *Don Carlos*. King Philip's son, he is the Infante of Spain (1545–68). **3** Tenor role in Verdi's *Giovanna d'Arco*. He is King Charles VII of France (1403–61). **4** Baritone role in Verdi's *La Forza del Destino*. Don Carlo de Vargas, he is Leonora's vengeful brother. **5** Tenor role in Verdi's *I Masnadieri*. Massamiliano's son, he is Amalia's lover. **6** Bass role in Bellini's *Bianca e Fernando*. He is the deposed Duke of Agrigento. **7** Tenor role in Donizetti's *Linda di Chamounix*. The Vicomte de Sirval, he is in love with Linda. **8** Tenor role in Rossini's *Armida*. He is a Christian knight.

Carl Rosa Opera Company
Founded by the German violinist Karl August Nicolaus Rose (1842–89), and dedicated to performing opera in English, the company gave its first performance in Sept 1875. The longest-lived British touring opera company, it continued to operate until 1958, when most of its membership was incorporated into Sadler's Wells Opera. Musical directors included Eugène Goossens, Arthur Hammond and Vilém Tausky.

Carmen
Opera in four acts by Bizet. 1st perf Paris, 3 March 1875; libr by Henri Meilhac and Ludovic Halévy, after Prosper Mérimée's novella. Principal roles: Carmen (mezzo), Don José (ten), Micaëla (sop), Escamillo (bar), Zuniga (bass), Frasquita (sop), Mercédès (mezzo), Remendado (ten), Dancairo (bar). A failure at its first appearance, it soon came to be appreciated not only as Bizet's masterpiece, but as one of the greatest of all music-dramas, and it can lay a strong claim to be the most popular opera ever written. With its spectacle, its powerful theatrical drive, its rich orchestration and its inexhaustible melody, its appeal is timeless. For many years, the spoken dialogue was replaced by recitatives written by Guiraud, but nearly all modern productions revert to the original OPÉRA-COMIQUE structure.
Plot: Spain, 1820. The beautiful and tempestuous Carmen works in a Seville cigarette factory. Arrested after a fight with a fellow worker, she is assigned to the custody of Don José, a corporal in the local barracks, whose sweetheart Micaëla

has just arrived from their village in search of him. Bewitched by Carmen, he allows her to escape and is himself placed under arrest. At the tavern of Lilas Pastia, the glamorous toreador Escamillo arrives with his entourage and sets his sights on Carmen. Although attracted, she decides to wait for José, who is due for release. He arrives and becomes involved in a fight with the officer Zuniga. He is persuaded to desert from the army and join Carmen and her smuggling companions in the mountains. Carmen grows bored with José and, when Escamillo arrives in search of her, she agrees to attend his forthcoming bullfight. When Micaëla appears, pleading with José to return home with her, Carmen urges him to go. However, the unhappy José spurns Micaëla and follows Carmen back to Seville. He accosts her outside the bull ring and begs her to start a new life with him. She refuses and, just as the crowd erupts in acclamation of Escamillo's triumph, the half-crazed José stabs Carmen to death. [R]

Carnival (from the Latin *carnem levare*, 'to put away meat')
The festive season before the beginning of Lent. Carnival was – and in Italy still is – the period of the main operatic season, starting on 26 Dec and lasting until Shrove Tuesday.

Carolina
1 Soprano role in Cimarosa's *Il Matrimonio Segreto*. She is Geronimo's daughter. **2** Mezzo role in Henze's *Elegie für Junge Liebende*. She is Mittenhofer's patroness and secretary.

Caro nome
Soprano aria for Gilda in Act I of Verdi's *Rigoletto*, in which she repeats the name 'Gualtier Maldè' which the Duke has used to woo her.

Carosio, Margherita (b 1908)
Italian soprano, particularly associated with lighter Italian roles, especially Violetta. One of the leading lyric sopranos of the inter-war period, she had a light and agile voice and was a singing-actress of charm and pathos. She created Ègloge in Mascagni's *Nerone* and Gnese in Wolf-Ferrari's *Il Campiello*.

Carré, Michel (1819–72)
French librettist. One of the most prolific 19th century French librettists, often writing in collaboration with JULES BARBIER, he provided texts for Bizet (*Les Pêcheurs de Perles*), David (*Lalla Roukh*, *La Captive* and *Le Saphir*), Gounod (*Faust*, *Le Médecin Malgré Lui*, *Mireille*, *La Colombe*, *Philémon et Baucis*, *Polyeucte* and *Roméo et Juliette*), Lecocq (*Nos Bons Chasseurs*), Maillart (*Lara* and *Les Pêcheurs de Catane*), Massé (*Les Noces de Jeanette* and *Galathée*), Messager (*Mirette*), Meyerbeer (*Dinorah*), Offenbach (*Le Mariage aux Lanternes*, *La Rose de Saint-Flour* and *Les Contes d'Hoffmann*), Reyer (*La Statue*) and Thomas (*Hamlet*, *Mignon*, *Françoise de Rimini* and *Psyché*) amongst others. His nephew **Albert** (1852–1938) was director of the Opéra-Comique, Paris (1896–1914) and himself wrote some libretti, including that for Messager's *La Basoche*. His autobiography, *Souvenirs de Théâtre*, was published in 1950. His wife **Marguerite Giraud** (1880–1947) was a successful soprano.

Carreras, José (b 1946)
Spanish tenor, particularly associated with the 19th-century Italian and French repertories. One of the finest lyric tenors of the post-war era, he possesses a warm, rich and liquid voice, used with fine musicianship, and has a dignified stage presence. Outstanding in Donizetti and lighter Verdi roles, he has subsequently turned successfully to heavier roles, such as Samson, Chénier and Stiffelio. His career was sadly interrupted in the late 1980s by his long and remarkable struggle against leukaemia. His autobiography, *El Placer de Cantar*, was published in 1989.

Carry Nation
Opera in two acts by Moore. 1st perf Lawrence (Kansas), 28 April 1966; libr by William North Jayme. Principal roles: Carry (mezzo), Charles (bar), Father (bass), Mother (sop). Telling of the historical prohibition campaigner Carry Nation (1846–1911), it has been successful in the United States but is little known elsewhere. [R]

Carte, Richard d'Oyly (1844–1901)
British impresario and administrator. The

builder of both the Savoy Theatre and the Royal English Opera House (now the Palace Theatre), he was responsible for bringing about the Gilbert and Sullivan partnership and for founding the D'Oyly Carte Opera Company to perform their works. After his death, the company was run by his wife **Helen** (1852–1913), then by his son **Rupert** (1876–1948), and finally by his granddaughter **Dame Bridget** (1908–85).

Caruso, Enrico (1873–1921)
Italian tenor. Generally regarded as the greatest tenor in operatic history, his most famous roles were Nemorino in Donizetti's *L'Elisir d'Amore*, the Duke of Mantua in *Rigoletto* and Éléazar in *La Juive* by Halévy (the last role he undertook). His glorious, rich voice had a dark and powerful lower register, and his phrasing, diction and technique remain an object lesson to all singers. He created Maurizio in *Adriana Lecouvreur*, Dick Johnson in *La Fanciulla del West*, Federico in Cilea's *L'Arlesiana*, Loris in Giordano's *Fedora* and Loewe in Franchetti's *Germania*. The film made of his life, *The Great Caruso* (1950) starring Mario Lanza, is a typical Hollywood biopic, crammed with inaccuracies and sheer invention.

Carvalho, Léon (b Carvaille) (1825–97)
French administrator. The leading 19th-century French impresario, he was director of the Théâtre Lyrique, Paris (1856–8), the Cairo Opera House (1868–72) and the Opéra-Comique, Paris (1876–87), where he was responsible for introducing many major new French operas. In 1887, he was fined and jailed for negligence after 131 people were killed in a fire which destroyed the Opéra-Comique, but he was reinstated after an appeal in 1891. Married to the soprano MARIE MIOLAN–CARVALHO.

Casa, Lisa della (b 1919)
Swiss soprano, particularly associated with Mozart and Strauss roles. One of the loveliest singers of the immediate post-war era, she possessed a rich and creamy voice – heard to perfection in the title-role of *Arabella* – which she used with unfailing style, musicianship and good taste. She created the Young Woman in Burkhard's *Die Schwarze Spinne* and three roles in Einem's *Der Prozess*.

Casella, Alfredo (1883–1947)
Italian composer. One of the most influential Italian musicians of the inter-war period, his three operas met with considerable success in their time but are nowadays virtually forgotten. They are *La Donna Serpente* (Rome, 17 Mar 1932; libr Cesare Lodovici, after Carlo Gozzi), the chamber opera *La Favola d'Orfeo* (Venice, 6 Sept 1932; libr Corrado Pavolini, after Angelo Poliziano) and *Il Deserto Tentato* (*The Desert Challenged*, Florence, 19 May 1937; libr Pavolini), which idealized Mussolini's conquest of Ethiopia.

Caspar
Bass role in Weber's *Der Freischütz*. He is an evil huntsman.

Cassandra
Soprano role in Berlioz's *Les Troyens*. She is a Trojan prophetess loved by Chorebus. The role in sometimes sung by a mezzo.

Cassel
See KASSEL STAATSTHEATER

Cassilly, Richard (b 1927)
American tenor, particularly associated with heroic roles, for which his powerful physique well suited him. He possessed a strong if not intrinsically beautiful voice and was a committed singing-actor. He created the Young Man in Menotti's *The Saint of Bleecker Street*, the title-role in Weisgall's *The Tenor* and Troilus in the revised version of *Troilus and Cressida*.

Cassio
Tenor role in Verdi's *Otello*. He is Otello's lieutenant.

Casta diva
Soprano aria for Norma in Act I of Bellini's *Norma*, in which she prays to the moon for peace in Gaul.

Castelnuovo-Tedesco, Mario (1895–1968)
Italian composer. He wrote eight operas, some initially successful but all now largely forgotten. They include *La Mandragola* (Venice, 4 May 1926; libr composer, after Machiavelli), the

MARIONETTE OPERA *Aucassin et Nicolette* (Florence, 2 June 1952), the unperformed *Giglietta di Narbona* (1959; libr after Shakespeare's *All's Well That Ends Well*), *Il Mercante di Venezia* (Florence, 25 May 1961; libr after Shakespeare's *The Merchant of Venice*) and *L'Importanza di Esser Franco* (New York, 22 Feb 1975; libr after Oscar Wilde's *The Importance of Being Ernest*).

Castor et Pollux
Opera in prologue and five acts by Rameau. 1st perf Paris, 24 Oct 1737; libr by Pierre-Joseph Bernard. Revised version 1st perf Paris, 11 Jan 1754. Principal roles: Pollux (bar), Castor (ten), Thélaïre (sop), Jupiter (bass), Phébé (mezzo), Cléone (sop). Sometimes regarded as Rameau's finest opera, it is still quite often performed.
Plot: Legendary Sparta. The Heavenly Twins Castor and Pollux both love Thélaïre. Castor is killed and Thélaïre begs Pollux to ask Jupiter to restore him to life. Jupiter agrees on the condition that Pollux renounces immortality, and that he and Thélaïre take Castor's place. Pollux agrees, but Castor – returning for a day – refuses. Despite Thélaïre's pleas, he insists on returning to the underworld. In the face of such fraternal devotion, Jupiter relents and restores Castor to life without conditions. [R]

Castrato
see panel below

Castro, Juan José (1895–1968)
Argentinian composer and conductor. He wrote four operas: *La Zapatiera Prodigosa* (Montevideo, 22 Oct 1949; libr composer, after Federico García Lorca), *Proserpina y*

· *Castrato* ·

The castrato was a eunuch male singer, whose sexual organs were 'modified' before puberty to preserve and develop a soprano or contralto vocal range: hence the terms 'male soprano' and 'male alto'. The word is derived from the Italian *castrare*, 'to castrate'. An alternative term occasionally encountered is *evirato*, from the Italian *evirare*, 'to emasculate'.

The voice first appeared in the 17th century in church choirs, when boys were regularly castrated to preserve their voices. The Roman Catholic Church condoned the practice on the grounds that St Paul in one of his epistles had enjoined that women should remain silent in church. Castrati soon made their appearance in opera, and in the late baroque they were perhaps the most important singers: their voices were more powerful, rich and flexible than women's, and the sheer unnaturalness of them epitomized the artificiality of opera at the time. By the early 19th century, a more humane age had come to appreciate the barbarity of the practice, and it was finally made illegal – Rossini only just escaped the indignity. The last major composers to write roles for castrati were Rossini himself and Meyerbeer in the early 1820s, by which time the voice was already considered strange and somehow unpleasant. The very last professional castrato was Alessandro Moreschi (1858–1922), whose voice is preserved on records, but he never appeared in opera.

In later years, roles which had been written for castrati were either transposed for tenors or were taken by sopranos or mezzos *in travesti*. More recently, many of these roles have been sung by counter-tenors, who produce a similar (if far less powerful) sound without recourse to the surgeon's knife.

The following six castrati, all Italian, have entries in this dictionary:

Caffarelli	Guadagni, Gaetano	Senesino
Farinelli	Nicolini	Velluti, Giovanni Battista

el Extranjero (Milan, 17 Mar 1952; libr Omar del Carlo), a winner of the 1951 Verdi competition, *Bodas de Sangre* (*Blood Wedding*, Buenos Aires, 9 Aug 1956; libr composer, after Lorca) and the unfinished and unperformed *Cosecha Negra* (1961; libr composer), which was orchestrated by Eduardo Ogando.

Catalani, Alfredo (1854–93)
Italian composer, whose early death cut short a career of great promise. An admirer of Wagner and a friend of Boito, his operas are romantic in style but have an orchestral prominence unusual in Italian opera. His first opera, *La Falce* (Milan, 19 July 1875; libr Arrigo Boito), was followed by *Elda* (1876), later revised as the successful LORELEY, *Dejanice* (Milan 17 Mar 1883; libr Antonio Zanardini), *Edmea* (Milan, 27 Feb 1886; libr Antonio Ghislanzoni, after Alexandre Dumas fils's *Les Danicheff*), which was successful in its time, and LA WALLY, by far his finest and most enduring work.

Catalogue Aria
Bass-baritone aria ('Madamina') for Leporello in Act I of Mozart's *Don Giovanni*, in which he shows Elvira his book of Giovanni's conquests. *See also* ARIA DI CATALOGO

Catania
See TEATRO MASSIMO BELLINI, CATANIA

Caterina Cornaro
Opera in prologue and two acts by Donizetti. 1st perf Naples, 12 Jan 1844; libr by Giacomo Sacchero, after Jules-Henri Vernoy de Saint-Georges's libretto for Halévy's *La Reine de Chypre*. Principal roles: Caterina (sop), Gerardo (ten), Lusignano (bar), Mocenigo (bass), Andrea (bass). Donizetti's last opera, it is based on incidents in the life of the historical Venetian aristocrat Caterina Cornaro (1454–1510). It contains some fine music but is only infrequently performed.
Plot: Venice and Nicosia, 1472. Caterina, daughter of Andrea, is betrothed to the young Frenchman Gerardo, but the marriage is postponed when Mocenigo reports that King Lusignano of Cyprus wishes to marry Caterina himself. After a great deal of intrigue, which includes the slow poisoning of Lusignano by Mocenigo, Gerardo joins the Knights of the Cross to help Lusignano defend Cyprus against Venice. Lusignano is mortally injured and dies commending the Cypriots to Caterina's care, whilst Gerardo returns to Rhodes.

Catiline Conspiracy, The
Opera in two acts by Hamilton. 1st perf Sterling, 16 March 1974; libr by the composer, after Ben Jonson. Principal roles: Catiline (bar), Cicero (ten), Fulvia (sop), Quintus (ten), Sempronia (mezzo), Crassus (bass), Aurelia (mezzo). Hamilton's first major opera to be performed, it is written in serial style, but employs traditional operatic devices.
Plot: Rome, 64–62 BC. The unscrupulous Catiline gains patrician support for his election as consul as a step towards overthrowing the republic and establishing a personal dictatorship. He is defeated in the election, however, by the democrat Cicero, on whom he vows to take revenge. He forms a secret conspiracy which is betrayed by Quintus (by way of Fulvia), and is expelled after Cicero exposes him in the Senate. He leads a rebel army against Rome, but is killed in battle. The republic is thus preserved.

Cauldron of Annwn, The
Operatic trilogy by Holbrooke (Op 53, 56 and 75). A setting of Lord Howard de Walden's dramatic poem based on the *Mabinogion*, the three operas are *The Children of Don* (London, 15 June 1912), *Dylan, Son of the Wave* (London, 4 July 1914) and *Bronwen* (Huddersfield, 1 Feb 1929). A vast Wagnerian-style work based on Celtic mythology, it is a cycle of some imaginative scope and does not fully deserve the total obscurity into which it has fallen.

Cavalieri, Emilio de' (c 1550–1602)
Italian composer. A member of the FLORENTINE CAMERATA, his LA RAPPRESENTAZIONE DI ANIMA E DI CORPO is a sacred stage oratorio and is perhaps the most important 'proto-opera'.

Cavalieri, Lina (b Natalina) (1874–1944)
Italian soprano, particularly associated with lyrical Italian and French roles. Said to

have been one of the most beautiful women ever to sing in opera, her colourful life led from childhood deprivation, through a liaison with a Russian prince, to operatic failure and then triumph, four marriages, tokens of royal esteem (many of them running to several carats), to her death in an air raid. She created L'Ensoleillad in Massenet's *Chérubin*. Her autobiography, *Le Mie Verità*, was published in 1936, and she was the subject of a film biography, *La Donna più Bella del Mondo* starring Gina Lollobrigida, which was made in 1957.

Cavalieri di Ekebù, I (*The Knights of Ekebù*)
Opera in four acts by Zandonai. 1st perf Milan, 7 March 1925; libr by Arturo Rossato, after Selma Lagerlöf's *Gösta Berlings Saga*. Principal roles: Berling (ten), Comandante (mezzo), Anna (sop), Cristiano (bar), Sintram (bass). Possibly Zandonai's finest opera, it was successful in its time but is nowadays only very rarely performed.
Plot: Legendary Sweden. The drunken Berling loves Anna. The Devil, in the guise of Anna's father Sintram, offers him drink in exchange for his soul the next day. Berling meets the strange quasi-masculine Commandant of the Ekebù mines, who collects dropouts and turns them into knights. The knights, led by Cristiano, initiate Berling. Asked to enact a playlet with Anna, Berling professes his love, and the two fall into each other's arms to the fury of Sintram. Sintram reminds the Commandant of the pact whereby she acquired the mines in return for one of her knights descending to hell each year. The Commandant renounces the mines and departs, but without her they fall into decay. Old and feeble, she is persuaded to return. She restores the mines, gives them to Cristiano and the knights, blesses the union of Anna and Berling and dies in peace.

Cavalleria Rusticana (*Rustic Chivalry*)
Opera in one act by Mascagni. 1st perf Rome, 17 May 1890; libr by Giovanni Targioni-Tozzetti and Guido Menasci, after Giovanni Verga's play. Principal roles: Santuzza (sop), Turiddù (ten), Alfio (bar), Lola (mezzo), Mamma Lucia (mezzo). By far Mascagni's best known work, it was the winner of a competition organized by the publisher Sonzogno. An instant success, it has remained ever since one of the most popular of all operas. Marking the advent of the VERISMO style in Italian opera, it is almost invariably coupled with Leoncavallo's *Pagliacci*; the two are sometimes referred to as the 'heavenly twins'.
Plot: Sicily, 1880. Turiddù has returned from the army to discover that his love Lola has married the village carter Alfio. After a brief fling with Santuzza, who is expecting his child, he restarts his affair with Lola. Santuzza begs him not to abandon her, but when he scornfully rejects her she reveals the entire story to Alfio. Alfio challenges Turriddù to a duel by the Sicilian custom of biting his ear. Turiddù bids farewell to his mother Mamma Lucia and goes to face Alfio, who kills him. [R]

Cavalli, Pier Francesco (b Caletti-Bruni) (1602–76)
Italian composer. He wrote over 40 operas, of which 28 are still extant. For nearly 300 years, Cavalli was little more than a name in the history books, but with the recent revival of interest in early music many of his operas have been staged in the last 20 years. His operas lack the dramatic power and insight of Monteverdi, but contain much beautiful and charming music. Many modern performances are given in realizations by musicologists Raymond Leppard or Jane Glover, the latter being the more scrupulous observer of Cavalli's intentions. His first opera was *Le Nozze di Teti e di Peleo* (Venice, 24 Jan 1639; libr Orazio Persiani). Of its successors, the most important are L'EGISTO, L'ORMINDO, GIASONE, the most successful of his operas in his own lifetime, *Rosinda* (Venice, 1651; libr Giovanni Battista Faustini), LA CALISTO, *Eritrea* (Venice, 17 Jan 1752; libr Faustini), SERSE, L'ERISMENA, ERCOLE AMANTE and *Scipione Affricano* (Venice, 9 Feb 1664; libr Nicolò Minato).

Cavaradossi, Mario
Tenor role in Puccini's *Tosca*. Tosca's lover, he is a painter of republican sympathies.

Cavatina (diminutive of the Italian *cavata*, 'extraction')
In 18th-century opera, a cavata was a short ARIOSO at the end of a recitative, the melody being 'carved out' of the preceding music. The diminutive form describes an 18th or 19th century single-part aria in relatively simple style.

Cebotari, Maria (b Cebutaru) (1910–49)
Russian (Bessarabian) soprano, particularly associated with Mozart and lighter Strauss roles. Her attractive voice was matched by a delightful stage presence, and her early death robbed the immediate post-war era of one of its finest light lyric sopranos. She created Aminta in *Die Schweigsame Frau*, Julia in Sutermeister's *Romeo und Julia*, Lucille in Einem's *Dantons Tod* and Iseut in Martin's *Le Vin Herbé*.

Cecchina, La
see BUONA FIGLIUOLA, LA

Cecil
Baritone role in Donizetti's *Maria Stuarda*. He is the historical William Cecil, Lord Burghley (1520–98). His son Sir Robert Cecil (1563–1612) appears as a baritone role in Britten's *Gloriana*.

Cecilia
Opera in prologue and three acts by Refice. 1st perf Rome, 15 Feb 1934; libr by Emidio Mucci. Principal roles: Cecilia (sop), Valeriano (ten), Tiburzio (bar), Urbano (bass). Refice's finest opera, described as an AZIONE SACRA, it tells of the legend of St Cecilia, the patron saint of music.
Plot: 2nd-century Rome. The Christian Cecilia is married to the pagan Valeriano. She asks him to respect her virginity, but his ardour is only halted by the intervention of an angel. Cecilia takes Valeriano to the catacombs, where the Christians under Bishop Urbano are praying. A vision of St Paul converts Valeriano. The prefect Tiburzio orders Cecilia's execution, and after her martyrdom she appears in glory as a saint.

Celeste Aida
Tenor aria for Radamès in Act I of Verdi's *Aida*, in which he apostrophizes Aida's beauty.

Cellier, Alfred (1844–91)
British composer and conductor. He wrote many operettas, some of which enjoyed considerable success in their day. They include *Nell Gwynne* (Manchester, 16 Oct 1876; libr H.B. Farnie, after W.G.T. Moncrieff's *Rochester*), later revised as the highly successful DOROTHY, *The Spectre Knight* (London, 9 Feb 1878; libr James Albery) and *The Mountebanks* (London, 4 Jan 1892; libr W.S. Gilbert), which was completed by Ivan Caryll and produced posthumously. As a conductor, he prepared many of the Savoy Operas for their first performances and arranged several of the overtures. His brother **François** (1849–1914) was also a conductor closely associated with Sullivan's stage works.

Cena delle Beffe, La (*The Jesters' Supper*)
Opera in four acts by Giordano. 1st perf Milan, 20 Dec 1924; libr by Sem Benelli, after his own play. Principal roles: Ginevra (sop), Gabriello (ten), Neri (bar), Gianetto (ten). One of the most unpleasant and sadistic of all VERISMO pieces, it enjoyed some success at its appearance but is nowadays only very rarely performed.
Plot: 15th-century Florence. Gianetto is brutally treated by the brothers Neri and Gabriello because he is in love with Neri's mistress Ginevra. Gianetto manoeuvres Neri into killing his own brother, who is revealed as another of Ginevra's lovers.

Cendrillon (*Cinderella*)
Opera in four acts by Massenet. 1st perf Paris, 24 May 1899; libr by Henri Cain, after Charles Perrault's version of the fairy tale. Principal roles: Cendrillon (mezzo), Prince (sop), La Fée (sop), Pandolfe (b-bar), Haltière (mezzo), Noémie (sop), Dorothée (mezzo), King (ten). After a long period of neglect, Massenet's charming if somewhat stickily romantic setting of the story is now quite often performed.
Plot: Pandolfe regrets his second marriage to Madame de la Haltière, who – with her daughters Noémie and Dorothée – mistreats his daughter Cendrillon. The women leave for the Prince's ball, leaving Cendrillon behind. The Fairy appears, dresses Cendrillon in gorgeous clothes,

gives her a crystal slipper to render her unrecognizable and sends her to the ball, where she captivates the Prince. They declare their love, but she is forced to leave hurriedly at midnight, and loses the slipper. Believing the lies of her stepsisters that the Prince was not serious, Cendrillon decides to leave with Pandolfe for the country. She becomes distracted, but the Fairy intervenes and sends her to court, where the Prince has found the slipper. It fits Cendrillon, and she and the Prince are united. [R]

Cenerentola, La (*Cinderella*) or **La Bontà in Trionfo** (*Goodness Triumphant*)
Comic opera in two acts by Rossini. 1st perf Rome, 25 Jan 1817; libr by Jacopo Ferretti, after Charles-Guillaume Étienne's libretto for Isouard's *Cendrillon*, itself based on Charles Perrault's version of the fairy tale. Principal roles: Cenerentola (mezzo), Don Ramiro (ten), Don Magnifico (bass), Dandini (bar), Alidoro (bass), Tisbe (sop), Clorinda (mezzo). Purged of the supernatural element which Rossini so disliked, it is one of the greatest of all comic operas, and is Rossini's only comedy to contain moments of genuine pathos.
Plot: 18th-century Salerno. Angelina, known as Cenerentola, is maltreated by her step-father Don Magnifico and by her nasty stepsisters Tisbe and Clorinda. The family is awaiting the arrival of the prince Don Ramiro, who is searching for a bride. He arrives, disguised as his own valet, meets Cenerentola and falls in love with her. His valet Dandini, disguised as the prince, is meanwhile fawned over by the rest of the family. Ramiro's tutor, the philosopher Alidoro, knows of Cenerentola's goodness and arranges for her to attend the ball, where she dazzles everyone. Before leaving, she gives Ramiro one of a pair of bracelets given her by Alidoro. The next day, Ramiro finds her at home, recognizes her despite her rags, matches the bracelet and insists on marrying her. She ascends the throne and forgives the cruelty of her family. [R]

Ceprano, Count
Bass COMPRIMARIO role in Verdi's *Rigoletto*. He is a courtier.

Cerha, Friedrich (b 1926)
Austrian composer. A leader of the Austrian avant-garde in the immediate post-war period, he is best known for his completion of Berg's *Lulu*. He has also written two operas: *Baal* (Salzburg, 16 Aug 1981; libr composer, after Bertolt Brecht) and *Der Rattenfänger* (Graz, 26 Sept 1987; libr composer, after Carl Zuckmayer).

Cerquetti, Anita (b 1931)
Italian soprano, particularly associated with heavier Italian roles. She enjoyed a brilliant career playing dramatic roles such as the title-roles in *Turandot* and Ponchielli's *La Gioconda*, but after only a short time she was sadly forced by ill-health to retire.

Cervantes, Miguel
see panel on page 103

Cesti, Pietro Antonio (1623–69)
Italian composer. With Cavalli, he ranks as the most important of Monteverdi's successors and, also like Cavalli, his music was long forgotten. However, a number of his works have been revived in recent years. His 11 operas are ORONTEA, *Cesare Amante* (Venice, 1651; libr Dario Varotari), *Alessandro il Vincitor* (Venice, 20 Jan 1651; libr Francesco Sbarra), *L'Argia* (Innsbruck, 4 Nov 1655; libr Giovanni Filippo Apolloni), *La Magnanimità d'Alessandro* (Innsbruck, 4 June 1662; libr Sbarra), *Il Tito* (Venice, 13 Feb 1666; libr Niccolò Berengani), *Nettuno e Flora* (Vienna, 12 July 1666; libr Sbarra), the spectacular IL POMO D'ORO, *Le Disgrazie d'Amore* (Vienna, 19 Feb 1667; libr Sbarra) and *La Semirami* (Vienna, 9 July 1667; libr Giovanni Andrea Moniglia). His nephew **Remigio** (*c* 1635–*c* 1715) was also a composer, who wrote one opera, *Il Principe Generoso* (Innsbruck, 1665).

C'est une chanson d'amour
Soprano/tenor duet for Antonia and Hoffmann in the Antonia Act of Offenbach's *Les Contes d'Hoffmann*, in which they recall how often they had sung together in the past.

Chabrier, Émmanuel (1841–94)
French composer and pianist. He wrote a number of stage works, but completed only four of them. Composed in various

· Miguel Cervantes ·

The Spanish writer Miguel de Cervantes Saavedra (1547–1616) himself appears as a character in a number of works, including J. Strauss's *Das Spitzentuch der Königin.* His writings, especially *Don Quixote*, have inspired over 100 operas and ZARZUELAS. Below are listed, by work, those operas by composers with entries in this dictionary.

El Celoso Extremeño		
Dibdin	*The Padlock*	1768
La Cueva de Salamanca		
Winter	*Der Bettelstudent*	1785
Lattuada	*La Caverna di Salamanca*	1938
Don Quixote		
Caldara	*Sancio Panza*	1733
Piccinni	*Il Curioso*	1756
Telemann	*Don Quichotte der Löwenritter*	1761
Philidor	*Sancho Pança dans son Île*	1762
Paisiello	*Don Chisciotte della Mancia*	1769
Salieri	*Don Chisciotte alle Nozze di Gamace*	1770
Dittersdorf	*Don Quixote der Zweyte*	1779
Mendelssohn	*Die Hochzeit des Camacho*	1827
Mercadante	*Don Chisciotte*	1829
MacFarren	*An Adventure of Don Quixote*	1846
Hervé	*Don Quichotte et Sancho Pança*	1848
Kienzl	*Don Quixote*	1898
Chapí	*La Venta di Don Quijote*	1902
Heuberger	*Don Quixote*	1910
Massenet	*Don Quichotte*	1910
Abrányi	*Don Kichóte*	1917
de Falla	*El Retablo de Maese Pedro*	1923
Frazzi	*Don Chisciotte*	1952
Henze/Paisiello	*Don Quixote*	1976
U. Zimmermann	*Don Quichotte*	1992
La Fuerza de la Sangre		
Auber	*Léocadie*	1824
La Gitanilla		
Balfe	*The Bohemian Girl*	1843
Los Habladores		
Offenbach	*Les Bavards*	1862
La Ilustre Fregona		
Guerrero	*El Huésped del Sevillano*	1926
La Numancia		
Barraud	*Numance*	1955
El Viejo Celoso		
Petrassi	*Il Cordovano*	1949

styles, his operas are notable for their sparkling melodies, their brilliant orchestration and their sharp sense of characterization. His first two stage works were unfinished operettas, both with libretti by his friend Paul Verlaine: *Fisch-Ton-Kan* (Paris, 22 Apr 1941, composed 1863) and *Vaucochard et Fils Premier* (Paris, 22 Apr 1941, composed 1864). Next came an unfinished opera, *Jean Hunyade* (1867; libr Henri Fouquier), much of which he reused in later works. His first completed operas were the comedies L'ÉTOILE and UNE ÉDUCATION MANQUÉE. Coming under the spell of Wagner, he then wrote the heroic GWENDOLINE. It was followed by the comedy LE ROI MALGRÉ LUI, perhaps his most successful opera. He completed only one act of his last opera *Briséïs* (Paris, 8 May 1899; libr Catulle Mendès and Georges Ephraïm Mikhaël, after Goethe's *Die Braut von Korinth*).

A man of wide artistic tastes, he was one of the first to appreciate the Impressionist school of painting. He was a personal friend of Manet and possessed one of the finest ever private collections of Impressionist paintings.

Chaconne (once called Chacony in Britain)
A French term which describes a piece of music, either vocal or instrumental and originally for dancing, in slow three-beat time, in which a single theme is repeated again and again in the bass. An operatic example is 'When I am laid in earth' in Purcell's *Dido and Aeneas*.

Chacun le sait
Soprano aria for Marie in Act I of Donizetti's *La Fille du Régiment*. It is the regimental song.

Chagall, Marc (1887–1985)
Russian painter and designer. One of the greatest 20th-century artists, he undertook a number of operatic designs, most notably for *Die Zauberflöte* at the Metropolitan Opera, New York, in 1967. He also designed the murals for the ceiling of the Paris Opéra and for the foyer of the new Metropolitan Opera at Lincoln Center.

Chailly, Luciano (b 1920)
Italian composer, father of the conductor RICCARDO CHAILLY. Several of his operas have met with some success in Italy but are unknown elsewhere. They are *Ferrovia Sopraelevata* (Bergamo, 1 Oct 1955; libr Dino Buzzati), *Una Domanda di Matrimonio* (Milan, 22 May 1957; libr Claudio Fino and Saverio Vertone, after Anton Chekhov's *The Proposal*), *Il Canto del Cigno* (Bologna, 16 Nov 1957; libr composer, after Chekhov's *Swan Song*), *La Riva delle Sirti* (Monte Carlo, 1 Mar 1959; libr R. Prinzhofer, after J. Gracq), *Procedura Penale* (Como, 30 Sept 1959; libr Buzzati), *Il Mantello* (Florence, 11 May 1960; libr Buzzati), *Era Proibito* (Milan, 5 Mar 1963; libr Buzzati), *Vassiliev* (Genoa, 16 Mar 1967; libr composer, after Chekhov's *The Crisis*), *Markheim* (Spoleto, 14 July 1967; libr Prinzhofer, after Robert Louis Stevenson), *L'Idiota* (Rome, 18 Feb 1970; libr Gilberto Loverso, after Fyodor Dostoyevsky's *The Idiot*), *Sogno, Ma Forse No* (Trieste, 28 Jan 1974; libr Prinzhofer, after Luigi Pirandello), *Il Libro dei Reclami* (Vienna, 29 May 1975; libr Prinzhofer, after Chekhov) and *La Cantatrice Calva* (Vienna, 8 Nov 1986; libr composer, after Eugene Ionesco). He was artistic director of La Scala, Milan (1968–71) and the Teatro Regio, Turin (1973–5).

Chailly, Riccardo (b 1953)
Italian conductor, son of the composer LUCIANO CHAILLY. One of the leading Italian conductors of the younger generation, he is particularly associated with Verdi and Rossini operas. Musical director of the Teatro Comunale, Bologna (1986–).

Chalabala, Zdeňek (1899–1962)
Czech conductor, particularly associated with the Czech and Russian repertories. One of the finest post-war Czech opera conductors, he was musical director of the Ostrava Opera (1945–7), the Brno Opera (1949–52), the Bratislava opera (1952–3) and the Prague National Theatre (1953–62). He conducted the first performance of Škroup's *Columbus*. His wife **Běla Ruzumová** (*b* 1903) was a successful COLORATURA soprano.

Châlet, Le (*The Cabin*)
Comic opera in one act by Adam. 1st perf Paris, 25 Sept 1834; libr by Eugène Scribe and Anne-Honoré Joseph de Mélesville, after Johann von Goethe's *Jery und Bätely*.

Principal roles: Bettly (sop), Max (bass), Daniel (ten). A delightful and tuneful little piece, it was long popular but is nowadays hardly ever performed. For plot see BETLY.

Chaliapin, Fyodor (1873–1938)
Russian bass, particularly associated with the Russian repertory. Sometimes regarded as the greatest bass in operatic history, he had a majestic voice of great power and range, and was a well-nigh unrivalled singing-actor. His portrayals, especially of Boris Godunov, exerted a strong influence on subsequent generations of singers. He created the title-role in Massenet's *Don Quichotte* and Salieri in Rimsky-Korsakov's *Mozart and Salieri*, and also made two films: *Tsar Ivan the Terrible* (1915) and *Don Quixote* (1933). His two volumes of autobiography, *Pages From My Life* and *Man and Mask*, were published in 1927 and 1932, and he also wrote a biography of Maxim Gorky. His son **Fyodor** was a successful actor.

Chamber opera
A loose term signifying an opera written for small forces – often without chorus – for performance in smaller theatres. The 18th-century INTERMEZZI fall into this category, as also do Rossini's early farces, and many chamber operas have been written in the 20th century by composers such as Britten and Holst.

Champagne Aria
Baritone aria ('Finch' han dal vino') for the Don in Act I of Mozart's *Don Giovanni*, in which he tells Leporello that after the forthcoming party there will be a dozen or more names for his list. The name has no relevance whatsoever to the subject matter of the aria, but for some reason it has become the standard way of referring to it.

Chanson de la Puce
Bass aria for Méphistophélès in Part II of Berlioz's *La Damnation de Faust*. It is the Song of the Flea.

Chapí y Lorente, Ruperto (1851–1909)
Spanish composer. He wrote eight operas, including *Las Naves de Cortés* (Madrid, 19 Apr 1874; libr A. Arnao) and *Roger de Flor* (Madrid, 25 Jan 1878; libr M. Capdepón). His reputation rests chiefly, however, on his 155 ZARZUELAS, several of which are still popular in Spain. The most successful include *La Tempestad* (Madrid, 11 Mar 1882; libr Miguel Ramos Carrión, after Émile Erckmann and Alexandre Chatrian's *Le Juif Polonais*) [R], *El Milagro de la Virgen* (Madrid, Oct 1884; libr M. Piña Domínguez), *La Bruja* (Madrid, 10 Dec 1887; libr Ramos Carrión and Vital Aza) [R], *Las Hijas del Zebedeo* (Madrid, 9 July 1889; libr J. Estremera), *Las Bravías* (Madrid, 12 Dec 1896; libr Carlos Fernández Shaw and José López Silva, after Shakespeare's *The Taming of the Shrew*), *La Revoltosa* (Madrid, 25 Nov 1897; libr Fernández Shaw and López Silva) [R], his most popular work, *La Chavala* (Madrid, 23 Oct 1898; libr Fernández Shaw and López Silva) and *La Patria Chica* (Madrid, 15 Oct 1907; libr Serafín and Joaquín Álvarez Quintero).

Charlotte
Mezzo role in Massenet's *Werther*. The Bailie's eldest daughter, she is Albert's fiancée.

Charpentier, Gustave (1860–1956)
French composer who brought elements of VERISMO into French opera, and whose works show his socialist leanings. His first opera *La Couronnement de la Muse* (Paris, 1898) was later incorporated into the sensationally successful LOUISE, on which his reputation chiefly rests. His follow-up to the story, JULIEN, was a total failure.

Charpentier, Marc-Antoine (1636–1704)
French composer. He wrote 17 stage works, a number of which enjoyed great success. Subsequently they lay long forgotten, but there has recently been a major revival of interest in his music. His operas and opera-ballets include *Le Malade Imaginaire* (Paris, 10 Feb 1673; libr Molière) [R], *Les Amours d'Acis et de Galathée* (Paris, Jan 1678), *Endimion* (Paris 22 July 1681), *Andromède* (1682; libr Pierre Corneille), *Actéon* (1683) [R], the magnificent DAVID ET JONATHAS and his masterpiece MÉDÉE.

Chausson, Ernest (1855–99)
French composer. Best known as an orchestral composer, he also wrote three operas. They are *Les Caprices de Marianne*

(1882; libr after Alfred de Musset), *Hélène* (1884; libr after Charles Leconte de Lisle) – neither of which have ever been performed – and the richly-scored Wagnerian LE ROI ARTHUS. He also helped to complete Franck's unfinished *Ghisèle*. He died as a result of riding his bicycle into a wall.

Chaynes, Charles (b 1925)
French composer. His stage works include the soprano MONODRAMA *Erzsebet* (Paris, 4 Apr 1983; libr after Ludovic Janvier's *Vers Bathory*) [R] and *Noces de Sang* (Montpellier, 15 Mar 1988; libr composer, after Federico García Lorca's *Bodas de Sangre*).

Che farò senza Euridice?
Mezzo aria for Orfeo in Act III of Gluck's *Orfeo ed Euridice*, in which he asks how he can be expected to live without his beloved wife.

Che gelida manina
Tenor aria for Rodolfo in Act I of Puccini's *La Bohème*, in which he tell Mimì who he is and what he does.

Chekhov, Anton
see panel on page 107

Ch'ella mi creda
Tenor aria for Dick Johnson in Act III of Puccini's *La Fanciulla del West*, in which he asks that Minnie be told that he has been released, not lynched.

Chelsea Opera Group
Founded in 1950 by Sir Colin Davis and others, it gives three concert performances a year, usually at the Queen Elizabeth Hall in London, with amateur orchestra and chorus and professional soloists. It has presented many lesser-known works and has given many of Britain's finest singers some of their earliest major roles.

Che puro ciel
Mezzo aria for Orfeo in Act II of Gluck's *Orfeo ed Euridice*, in which he responds to the beauty of the Elysian Fields.

Chéreau, Patrice (b 1944)
French producer. His highly controversial and radically 'deconstructionist' productions are epitomized by the Bayreuth centenary *Ring* of 1976. He directed the first performance of the three-act version of Berg's *Lulu*.

Chère enfant que j'appelle
Soprano/mezzo/bass trio for Antonia, the Mother and Dr Miracle in the Antonia Act of Offenbach's *Les Contes d'Hoffmann*, in which Miracle brings the portrait of Antonia's mother to life.

Cherry Duet
Soprano/tenor duet ('Suzel, buon dì') for Suzel and Fritz in Act II of Mascagni's *L'Amico Fritz*, in which Suzel gives Fritz a gift of cherries that she has picked.

Chérubin
Opera in three acts by Massenet. 1st perf Monte Carlo, 14 Feb 1905; libr by Henri Cain and Francis de Croisset, after the latter's play. Principal roles: Chérubin (mezzo), Nina (sop), Philosopher (bass), L'Ensoleillad (sop), Duke (ten), Baron (bar). Telling of the subsequent doings of Beaumarchais's Cherubino, it has never been one of Massenet's more popular operas and is only infrequently performed, despite its delightful score which incorporates some Andalusian material.
Plot: Late-18th-century Andalusia. Chérubin, now 17, is graduating as an officer. His childhood sweetheart Nina complains to his tutor the Philosopher that he no longer cares for her. He is carrying on with three women: a countess, a baroness and the great dancer Ensoleillad. After many scrapes and confusions, which seem set to necessitate him fighting three duels, Chérubin sees the error of his ways when Nina threatens to enter a convent. The two are finally united. [R]

Cherubini, Luigi (1760–1842)
Italian composer. He wrote 25 operas, beginning with *Il Quinto Fabio* (Alessandria, 1779; libr Apostolo Zeno). His next 12 works are unremarkable OPERA SERIAS, mainly to Metastasian texts. His mature style developed when he moved to Paris in 1788. His later operas, beginning with *Démophon* (Paris, 2 Dec 1788; libr Jean-François Marmontel), mark the foundation both of French grand opera and of romantic opera in general. His

· Anton Chekhov ·

The works of the Russian writer and playwright Anton Chekhov (1860–1904) have inspired some 40 operas. Below are listed, by work, those operas by composers with entries in this dictionary.

The Bear		
Argento	*The Boor*	1957
Kay	*The Boor*	1960
Walton	*The Bear*	1967
The Crisis		
Chailly	*Vassiliev*	1967
The Kiss		
Oliver	*The Kiss*	1973
The Proposal		
Chailly	*Una Domanda di Matrimonio*	1957
Romance with a Double Bass		
Sauget	*La Contrebasse*	1930
Rothschild's Violin		
Fleishman/Shostakovich	*Rothschild's Violin*	1941 (U)
The Seagull		
Pasatieri	*The Seagull*	1974
Swan Song		
Chailly	*Il Canto del Cigno*	1957
Pauer	*Swan Song*	1974
The Three Sisters		
Pasatieri	*Three Sisters*	1986

mature works are notable for their complex ensembles, their rich orchestration (especially in the fine overtures), their dramatic effects, and for the nobility and beauty of the vocal writing. The unfinished *Marguerite d'Anjou* (1790) was followed by his first major work LODOÏSKA, the once-popular ÉLISA and his masterpiece MÉDÉE. There followed *L'Hôtellerie Portughaise* (Paris, 25 July 1798; libr Étienne Aignan), *Le Punition* (Paris, 23 Feb 1799; libr Jean Louis Brousse Desfaucherets), *La Prisonnière* (Paris, 12 Sept 1799; libr Victor Joseph Étienne de Jouy, Charles de Longchamps and Claude Godard d'Aucour de Saint-Just), which was written in collaboration with Boïeldieu, LES DEUX JOURNÉES, *Épicure* (Paris, 14 Mar 1800; libr Charles Albert Demoustier), ANACRÉON, *Faniska* (Vienna, 25 Feb 1806; libr Josef Sonnleithner), *Pimmalione* (Paris, 30 Nov 1809; libr Stefano Vestris, after Jean-Jacques Rousseau), *Le Crescendo* (Paris, 30 Sept 1810; libr Charles Augustin Sewrin), the grandiose LES ABENCÉRAGES and ALI BABA.

Cherubini's influence on the subsequent development of opera was enormous. Beethoven regarded him more highly than almost any other composer, and he had a strong influence on Weber, Wagner, Spontini and many French composers including Auber. He was an austere and somewhat pedantic director of the Paris Conservatory (1821–41), where his pupils included Auber, Carafa, Halévy and Offenbach.

Cherubino
Soprano trouser role in Mozart's *Le Nozze*

di Figaro. He is an amorous pageboy in the Almaviva household. The role is frequently sung by a mezzo. His subsequent career is the subject of Massenet's *Chérubin*.

Chest voice
The lowest of the three vocal registers, below 'middle' and 'head', and the richest in tone. It is often overindulged by singers, particularly dramatic mezzos.

Cheti, cheti
Baritone/bass duet for Dr Malatesta and Pasquale in Act III of Donizetti's *Don Pasquale*, in which they work out how to catch the young lovers together. Perhaps the greatest of all BUFFO duets.

Cheval de Bronze, Le (*The Bronze Horse*)
Opera in three acts by Auber. 1st perf Paris, 23 March 1835; libr by Eugène Scribe. Principal roles: Yang (ten), Péki (sop), Tsing-Sing (bass), Stella (sop), Tchin-Kao (bass), Tao-Jin (sop). A delightful and sparkling work, notable for Auber's 'Oriental' touches, it was long popular, but nowadays only the famous overture is remembered.
Plot: Legendary Chatong (China). The mandarin Tsing-Sing is turned to stone by one of his wives. Another wife, Péki, flies on the magical bronze horse to seek the help of the fairy princess Stella. Stella gives Péki a magic bracelet with which to break the spell. She does so on condition that Tsing-Sing divorce her, thus freeing her to marry her true love, Prince Yang.

Chevrotement
see BLEAT

Chiara, Maria (b 1939)
Italian soprano, particularly associated with Verdi and Puccini roles. One of the leading contemporary Italian lyric sopranos, she possesses a smooth and beautiful voice used with fine musicianship and has an affecting stage presence.

Chicago Lyric Opera
One of the leading American opera companies, it was founded in 1954 by Carol Fox, who was its administrator until her death in 1981. Performances are given at the Civic Opera House (cap 3,563) and the annual season runs from September to February. The repertory tends to be traditional with an emphasis on Italian works. Musical directors have included Bruno Bartoletti.

Children's operas
Although there were companies of child performers in the 18th century, especially in Austria, it is really only in the 20th century that operas have been written specifically for casts of children. Britten, Williamson, Bennett, Crosse, Menotti, Fortner, Hindemith, Milhaud, Cui and Copland all wrote stage works for children.

Chile
see TEATRO MUNICIPAL, SANTIAGO

Chilean opera composers
These include Remigio Acevedo Guajardo (1863–1911), Pablo Garrido Vargas (1905–82), Juan Orrego Salas (*b* 1919) and Eleodoro Ortíz de Zárate (1865–1953), whose *La Florista de Lugano* (1895) was the first opera by a Chilean composer.

Chimène
Soprano role in Massenet's *Le Cid*. She is Count Gormas's daughter.

Chi mi frena
Soprano/mezzo/tenor/tenor/baritone/bass sextet for Lucia, Alisa, Edgardo, Arturo, Enrico and Raimondo in Act II of Donizetti's *Lucia di Lammermoor*, which follows Edgardo's appearance at the wedding ceremony. One of the greatest ensembles in all opera.

Chisholm, Erik (1904–65)
British conductor, composer and musicologist. One of the leading British conductors of the inter-war period, he also wrote ten operas. They include *The Feast of Samhain* (1941; libr composer, after J. Stephen), the trilogy *Murder in Three Keys* (New York, 6 July 1954; libr composer, after Eugene O'Neill, T.S. Eliot and August Strindberg), *The Inland Woman* (Cape Town, 21 Oct 1953; libr composer, after Mary Lavin) and *The Pardoner's Tale* (Cape

Town, Nov 1961; libr composer, after Geoffrey Chaucer's *The Canterbury Tales*). His writings include a book on Janáček's operas.

Chocolate Soldier, The
see TAPFERE SOLDAT, DER

Choëphores, Les (*The Libation Bearers*)
Opera in one act by Milhaud. 1st perf Paris, 15 June 1919; libr by Paul Claudel, after *The Choephori* in Aeschylus's *Oresteia*. Principal roles: Elektra (sop), Orestes (bar), Clytemnestra (sop). The second part of Milhaud's projected Aeschylean trilogy, it deals with the relationship between Elektra and Orestes. It is only very rarely performed. [R]

Chorebus
Baritone role in Berlioz's *Les Troyens*. He is a Trojan commander in love with Cassandra.

Chorley, Henry Fothergill (1808–72)
British critic. The leading British critic of his time, his *Thirty Years' Musical Recollections* (1862) is a prime source for information about operatic life in London at the time. He also wrote the libretti for Sullivan's *The Sapphire Necklace* and Wallace's *The Amber Witch*.

Chorus (from the Greek Χορός, a festive dance, and, thus, those who performed it)
In opera, chorus means either a group of singers who perform and sing as a single body, or the music written for it. Integral to French opera from its earliest days, the chorus became important in Italian opera only in the late 18th century.

Chorus
Roles in Britten's *The Rape of Lucretia*: Male (ten) and Female (sop).

Christie, John (1882–1962)
British patron and administrator. Married to the soprano AUDREY MILDMAY, he founded and built the Glyndebourne Opera House in 1934 at his country seat in Sussex. His son **Sir George** (*b* 1934) succeeded him as principal administrator.

Christie, William
see under ARTS FLORISSANTS, LES

Christiné, Henri (1867–1941)
Swiss-born French composer. He wrote a number of light operettas, of which much the most successful was *Phi-Phi* (Paris, 12 Nov 1918; libr F. Sollar and Albert Willemetz) [R], which is about the Greek sculptor Phidias.

Christmas Carol, A
Opera in two acts by Musgrave. 1st perf Norfolk (Virginia), 7 Dec 1979; libr by the composer, after Charles Dickens's novel. Principal roles: Scrooge (bar), Belle (sop), Bob Cratchit (ten), Ben (bar), Mr Fezziwig (bass). One of Musgrave's most successful operas, which has been widely performed, the plot follows Dickens closely. [R]

Christmas Eve (*Notch Pered Rozhdestvom*)
Comic opera in four acts by Rimsky-Korsakov. 1st perf St Petersburg, 10 Dec 1895; libr by the composer, after Nikolai Gogol's story. Principal roles: Oksana (sop), Vakula (ten), Chub (bass), Solokha (mezzo), Devil (ten), Priest (ten), Panas (bass), Mayor (bar), Patsyuk (bass). Although it contains much colourful and delightful music, it has never been one of Rimsky-Korsakov's more popular works and is only rarely performed.
Plot: 18th-century Ukraine and St Petersburg. On Christmas Eve, the Devil and the witch Solokha decide to cause mischief by stealing the moon and whipping up a snow storm. The blacksmith Vakula comes to serenade Oksana, but bumps into the latter's father Chub in the storm and mistakes him for a rival. Oksana tells Vakula that she will marry him only if he brings her the empress's slippers as a present. At Solokha's cottage, the Devil, the Mayor, the Priest and Chub all arrive and hide in sacks so as not to be seen. Vakula carries them all away and the villagers are highly entertained when three of them are opened. Vakula visits the dumpling-eating medicine man Patsyuk to ask how to get the Devil's help in his quest. Patsyuk tells him to open his remaining sack, in which Vakula finds the Devil. Vakula forces him to take him to the imperial court, where he acquires the slippers. However, in his absence, Oksana has decided that she loves him anyway. [R]

Christmas Rose, The
Opera in three scenes by Bridge. 1st perf London, 8 Dec 1931; libr by Margaret Kemp-Welch and Constance Cotterell. Principal roles: Miriam (sop), Reuben (mezzo), three Shepherds (ten, bar and bass). Bridge's only opera, telling of the visit of the shepherds to the inn at Bethlehem to see the infant Jesus, it is nowadays virtually never performed. [R]

Christoff, Boris (1914–93)
Bulgarian bass, particularly associated with the Russian and Italian repertories, especially the title-role in Moussorgsky's *Boris Godunov*, Konchak in Borodin's *Prince Igor*, King Philip in Verdi's *Don Carlos* and Fiesco in Verdi's *Simon Boccanegra*. One of the finest singing-actors of the post-war era, his magnificent voice had a highly individual timbre, and his dramatic insight was remarkable. One of the truly great operatic artists, despite a temperament which many colleagues found a sore trial.

Christophe Colomb
Opera in two parts by Milhaud (Op 102). 1st perf Berlin, 5 May 1930; libr by Paul Claudel. Revised version 1st perf Graz, 27 June 1968. Principal roles: Columbus (bar), Queen Isabella (sop), King of Spain (bass), Narrator (speaker). The first work in Milhaud's so-called *New World Trilogy*, it is a religious allegory treating the events of Columbus's life in 27 short scenes connected by the use of a narrator, the chorus and film projections. It is only very rarely performed.

Christopher Columbus
Operetta in four acts by Offenbach. 1st perf Belfast, 3 July 1976; libr by Don White. Principal roles: Columbus (ten), Beatriz (sop), Fleurette (sop), Rosa (mezzo), Gretel (sop), Police Chief (bar), Luis de Torres (bar), Queen Isabella (sop), King Ferdinand (bar). A pastiche arranged by Patric Schmid of Opera Rara from 22 of Offenbach's forgotten operettas, it is an outrageous and riotously funny piece, telling of Columbus's voyage to the Americas to discover Coca-Cola! [R]

Chrysothemis
Soprano role in Strauss's *Elektra*. She is Elektra's sister.

Chueca, Federico (1848–1908)
Spanish composer. He wrote 37 ZARZUELAS, mostly in GÉNERO CHICO form. The most successful were *La Gran Vía* (Madrid, 2 July 1886; libr Felipe Pérez y González) [R], which was written in collaboration with Valverde and which is one of the very few zarzuelas to have been performed in Britain, and *Agua, Azucarillos y Aguardiente* (*Water, Sweets and Liquor*, Madrid, 23 June 1897; libr Miguel Ramos Carrión) [R].

Chukhadjian, Tigran (1837–98)
Armenian composer. The first Armenian composer to attempt a synthesis of Western musical styles with his national folk heritage, his ardent nationalism has ensured him a place in his tragic people's history. His operas are *Arshak II* (*Arshak Erkrord*, Yerevan, 1945, composed 1868; libr T. Terzyan), three comedies, *Arif* (Constantinople, 1872; libr H. Atjemian, after Nikolai Gogol's *The Inspector General*), *The Balding Elder* (*Kyose Kyokhava*, 1873; libr G. Rshtuni) and *The Chick-Pea Seller* (*Leblebidji*, Constantinople, 1876; libr T. Nalian), the fairy tale *Zemire* (Constantinople, 1891; libr T. Galymdjian) and *Indiana* (1897).

Church Parable
The term used by Britten to describe his three one-act operas written for very small forces and designed for church performance: CURLEW RIVER, THE BURNING FIERY FURNACE and THE PRODIGAL SON.

Chûte de la Maison Usher, La (*The Fall of the House of Usher*)
Unfinished opera in one act (two scenes) by Debussy. 1st perf New Haven (Connecticut), 25 Feb 1977 (composed *c* 1916); libr by the composer, after Edgar Allan Poe's short story. Principal roles: Friend (bar), Roderick (bar), Lady Madeline (sop), Doctor (bass). One of opera's greatest might-have-beens, Debussy worked on the score in 1909–10 and 1916–7, but only completed just under half-an-hour of music, a little over half of the opera. Three separate realizations have been made: by W. Harwood, by the American musicologists Carolyn Abbate and R. Kyr, and by the Chilean composer Juan Allende-Blin. The piece has had a

number of performances in the last decade. [R]

Ciboletta
Soprano role in J. Strauss's *Eine Nacht in Venedig*. She is Pappacoda's fiancée.

Ciboulette
Operetta in three acts by Hahn. 1st perf Paris, 7 April 1923; libr by Robert de Flers and Francis de Croisset. Principal roles: Ciboulette (sop), Antonin (ten), Duparquet (bar), Zénobie (mezzo), Roger (bar). By far Hahn's most successful work, it is still performed from time to time.
Plot: Paris, 1867. Ciboulette is told that she will marry a man found in a cabbage, after causing him to leave a woman capable of turning white instantly, and after receiving a proposal in a tambourine. The adventures of Antonin, his love Zénobie, the captain Roger (who is preferred by Zénobie) and of their friend Duparquet provide the fulfilment of the prophecy. [R]

Cid, Le
Opera in four acts by Massenet. 1st perf Paris, 30 Nov 1885; libr by Adolphe Philippe d'Ennery, Louis Gallet and Édouard Blau, after Pierre Corneille's play. Principal roles: Don Rodrigue (ten), Chimène (sop), Don Diègue (bass), Count Gormas (bass). An essay in Meyerbeerian grand opera, it is one of Massenet's most heroic and exciting scores, which includes his finest ballet music. It was very successful in its time but is nowadays only infrequently performed.
Plot: 12th-century Seville. To avenge the honour of his father Don Diègue, Rodrigue (known as 'The Cid') reluctantly fights a duel with Don Gormas, the father of his beloved Chimène. Gormas is killed, and Chimène is torn between her love and the honour of her family. Rodrigue fights heroically against the Moors, and when he returns he and Chimène are reconciled. [R]

Cieca, La
Mezzo role in Ponchielli's *La Gioconda*. She is Gioconda's blind mother.

Cielo e mar
Tenor aria for Enzo in Act II of Ponchielli's *La Gioconda*, in which he apostrophizes the sky and sea.

Cigna, Gina (b Ginetta Sens) (b 1900)
Italian soprano, particularly associated with heavier Italian roles, especially Turandot and Gioconda. The leading Italian dramatic soprano of the inter-war period, she was forced to retire in 1948 after being seriously injured in a car accident.

Cikker, Ján (1911–90)
Slovakian composer. The leading Slovak composer of the post-war era, his operas in post-romantic style met with success both in the former Czechoslovakia and in Germany. His operas are the nationalist *Juro Jánošík* (Bratislava, 10 Nov 1954; libr Štefan Hoza), *Mr Scrooge* (Kassel, 5 Oct 1963, composed 1954; libr composer and J. Smrek, after Charles Dickens's *A Christmas Carol*), the nationalist *Prince Bajazid* (*Beg Bajazid*, Bratislava, 16 Feb 1957; libr Smrek), *Resurrection* (*Vzkriesenie*, Prague, 18 May 1962; libr composer, after Tolstoy) [R], *The Play of Love and Death* (*Hra o Láske a Smrti*, Munich, 1 Aug 1969; libr composer, after Romain Rolland), *Coriolanus* (Prague, 4 Apr 1973; libr composer, after Shakespeare) [R], *The Sentence* (*Rozsudok*, Bratislava, 8 Oct 1979; libr composer, after Heinrich Wilhelm von Kleist's *Das Erdbeben in Chile*), *The Siege of Bystrica* (*Obliehanie Bystrice*, Bratislava, 8 Oct 1983; libr composer, after Kálmán Mikszáth) and *The Insect Play* (Bratislava, 21 Feb 1987; libr composer, after Karel Čapek).

Cilea, Francesco (1866–1950)
Italian composer. One of the leading VERISMO composers, his operas are notable for their somewhat cloying charm, but are largely innocent of any dramatic insight. His first opera *Gina* (Naples, 9 Feb 1889; libr Enrico Golisciani) was followed by *La Tilda* (Florence, 7 Apr 1892; libr Antonio Zanardini), the successful L'ARLESIANA, ADRIANA LECOUVREUR, his finest and most enduring work, *Gloria* (Milan, 15 Apr 1907; libr Arturo Colautti) and the unperformed *Il Matrimonio Selvaggio* (1909; libr G. di Bognasco).

Cimarosa, Domenico (1749–1801)
Italian composer. He wrote 63 operas, winning especial renown in comedy, in which field he was compared in his day to

Mozart. His comedies are notable for their pace and vivacity, their delightful melodies and their deft orchestration. His serious operas, whilst musically solid, are dramatically somewhat cold and formal. The most successful of his operas include *Il Fanatico per gli Antichi Romani* (Naples, 1777; libr Giovanni Palomba), *L'Italiana in Londra* (Rome, 28 Dec 1778; libr Giuseppe Petrosellini), *Il Pittor Parigino* (Rome, 4 Jan 1781; libr Petrosellini) [R], *I Due Baroni di Rocca Azzura* (Rome, Feb 1783; libr Palomba), *L'Olimpiade* (Vicenza, 10 July 1784; libr Pietro Metastasio), *Il Marito Disperato* (Naples, 1785; libr Giovanni Battista Lorenzi), L'IMPRESARIO IN ANGUSTIE, the hilarious intermezzo IL MAESTRO DI CAPPELLA, his masterpiece IL MATRIMONIO SEGRETO, *I Traci Amanti* (Naples, 19 June 1793; libr Palomba), LE ASTUZIE FEMMINILI, GLI ORAZI E I CURIAZI, perhaps his finest serious work, and *Artemisia* (Venice, 18 Jan 1801; libr Cratisto Jamejo). He appears as a character in Isouard's *Cimarosa*.

Cincinnati Opera Association
The second oldest opera company in the United States, it was founded in 1920. Until 1974 it performed in the open air at the local zoo, and thereafter has been based at the Music Hall (cap 3,630). It has a long reputation for fostering major talent, and is sometimes known as 'the cradle of American opera singers'. The annual season is held in June and July and the repertory is predominantly French and Italian. Musical directors have included Fausto Cleva.

Cinderella
see CENDRILLON; CENERENTOLA, LA

Cinesi, Le (*The Chinese*)
Comic opera in one act by Gluck. 1st perf Vienna, 24 Sept 1754; libr by Pietro Metastasio. Principal roles: Sivene (sop), Lisinga (mezzo), Silango (ten), Tangia (mezzo). Described as a serenade, it is a work of elegance and great charm. Totally unperformed for over 200 years, it has recently received a considerable number of performances.
Plot: 18th-century China. Sivene, Lisinga and Tangia discover Lisinga's brother Silango, who loves Sivene, hidden behind a screen as the women are planning to perform scenes from the classics. Silango refuses to leave and insists on taking part in the theatricals. Under the cover of his part in the play, he succeeds in furthering his suit with Sivene. [R]

Cinq-Mars
Opera in four acts by Gounod. 1st perf Paris, 5 April 1877; libr by Paul Poirson and Louis Gallet, after Alfred de Vigny's novel. Principal roles: Cinq-Mars (ten), Marie (sop), de Thou (bar), Marion (sop), Père Joseph (bass). Telling of Henri Coiffier de Ruzé, Marquis de Cinq-Mars (1620–42), executed for plotting against his friend Louis XIII, it was reasonably successful at its appearance but is nowadays virtually forgotten.
Plot: France, early 1640s. Cinq-Mars is rising to political prominence. He confides to his friend de Thou his love for Princess Marie de Gonzague, who – despite her engagement to the King of Poland – returns his love. Because Cardinal Richelieu insists on Marie making the political marriage, Cinq-Mars joins the conspiracy of the courtesan Marion Delorme against the cardinal. Secret marriage vows between Cinq-Mars and Marie are overheard by Fr Joseph, the cardinal's aide, and Cinq-Mars is condemned to death for his part in the conspiracy. An escape plan by de Thou comes to nothing and Cinq-Mars, after being told by Marie that she will always love him, is led to the gallows.

Cinta di fiori
Bass aria for Giorgio in Act II of Bellini's *I Puritani*, in which he describes Elvira's madness.

Cio-Cio-San
Soprano role in Puccini's *Madama Butterfly*. It is Butterfly's Japanese name.

Ciro in Babilonia (*Cyrus in Babylon*) or **La Caduta di Baldassare** (*The Fall of Belshazzar*)
Opera in two acts by Rossini. 1st perf Ferrara, 14 March 1812; libr by Francesco Aventi, partly after Xenophon's *Ciropedia* and the Book of Daniel in the Old Testament. Principal roles: Ciro (mezzo), Baldassare (ten), Amira (sop), Argene

(mezzo), Daniello (bass), Zambri (bass), Arbace (ten). Rossini's first mature serious opera, it is only very rarely performed. **Plot**: Babylon, 6th century BC. King Cyrus of Persia has been defeated by King Belshazzar (Baldassare) of Babylon, who makes advances to Cyrus's captured wife Amira. She rejects him, even after Cyrus is imprisoned after an unsuccessful attempt to rescue her. Belshazzar decides to wed Amira against her will and orders the wedding feast to be prepared. However, a violent storm breaks out and a mysterious hand writes upon the wall. The prophet Daniel interprets this as a sign of Divine anger, but Belshazzar ignores him and heeds the advice of his Magi that Cyrus and Amira must be sacrificed. As they are led to their deaths, news arrives of the total defeat of Belshazzar's forces by the Persians. Cyrus is released and ascends Belshazzar's throne.

Claggart, John
Bass role in Britten's *Billy Budd*. He is the evil master-at-arms of H.M.S. Indomitable.

Clairon
Mezzo role in Strauss's *Capriccio*. She is an actress.

Claque (French for 'clap' or 'smack')
One of opera's most colourful if not particularly attractive institutions, the claque is a group in the audience paid by the management to get the applause going and to stimulate enthusiasm. It is also sometimes paid by singers to cheer them and to hiss their rivals. Its leader is called the *chef de claque* in France and the *capo di claque* in Italy. The phenomenon is virtually as old as opera itself, but it became an established institution only at the beginning of the 19th century in Paris, which once even boasted a claque agency, *L'Assurance des Succès Dramatiques*, which offered specialist services, including *bisseurs* (who called for encores) and *pleureurs* (who used concealed smelling salts to induce crying). The claque soon became established in Italy, where by the end of the 19th century there was a regular tariff for its services: 5 lire for a bravo, 25 lire for applause at the singer's first entry and 50 lire for 'wild enthusiam'.

The claque members regard themselves as encouragers of talent and of high artistic standards: the story is often told of the notorious Parma claque which, hired to cheer a visiting tenor, was so appalled by his singing on the first night that it refunded his money and hissed all his subsequent performances. The fun really starts when there are rival claques at the same performance: a clash between pro- and anti-Callas claques once led to a serious riot at the Paris Opéra. The claque is still very much a feature of operatic life in Italy – the current rate to ensure a reasonable reception for a singer is around 50,000 lire. It also exists in Vienna, but in Britain – whatever Italian singers who have been given a hostile reception may maintain to the contrary – the claque does not really exist.

Claudel, Paul (1868–1965)
French poet and librettist. Closely linked to the Symbolist school, he provided libretti for Honegger (*Jeanne d'Arc au Bûcher*) and Milhaud (*Christophe Colomb*, *Saint Louis* and the *Orestie* trilogy). Rossellini's *L'Annonce Faite à Marie* is a setting of his verse play.

Claudine von Villa Bella
Opera in three acts by Schubert (D 239). 1st perf Vienna, 26 April 1913 (composed 1815); libr by Johann von Goethe. Principal roles: Claudine (sop), Pedro (ten), Lucinda (sop), Carlos (ten), Alonzo (bass), Basco (bass). One of Schubert's early SINGSPIELS, the music of Acts II and III was destroyed in a fire. The overture and Act I are very occasionally given in concert.

Claudio
1 Baritone role in Berlioz's *Béatrice et Bénédict* and tenor role in Stanford's *Much Ado About Nothing*. He is in love with Hero. **2** Tenor role in Wagner's *Das Liebesverbot*. He is Isabella's brother. **3** Bass role in Händel's *Agrippina*. He is the Roman Emperor Claudius.

Clemenza di Tito, La (*The Clemency of Titus*)
Opera in two acts by Mozart (K 621). 1st perf Prague, 6 Sept 1791; libr by Caterino Mazzolà, after Pietro Metastasio. Principal

roles: Tito (ten), Vitellia (sop), Sesto (mezzo), Annio (mezzo), Publio (bass), Servilia (sop). Mozart's last opera, dealing with the Roman Emperor Titus Vespasianus (AD 39–81), it was very popular so long as OPERA SERIA itself remained so, but thereafter was almost forgotten. In recent years, however, it has once again been widely performed. Despite the stiff formality of its structure, it is a work of great musical and dramatic quality.
Plot: Rome, AD 79–81. Furious that Titus has decided to marry Berenice, Vitellia persuades her admirer Sextus to assassinate him. However, Titus has a change of plan, and decides instead to marry Servilia. When he learns that she loves Sextus's friend Annius, he withdraws and determines to marry Vitellia. Vitellia finds out about this too late to stop Sextus's plot, but Titus escapes death. Sextus is arrested; tried and condemned to death, and Vitellia eventually confesses her part in the plot. In the end, Titus shows his clemency by forgiving both of them. [R]

Cleopatra
The Queen of Egypt (69–30 BC) appears in a number of operas, including soprano roles in: **1** Händel's *Giulio Cesare.* **2** Barber's *Antony and Cleopatra.* **3** Massenet's *Cléopâtre.* **4** Bondeville's *Antoine et Cléopâtre.*

Cléopâtre
Opera in four acts by Massenet. 1st perf Monte Carlo, 28 Feb 1914; libr by Albert Liénard under the pen-name of Louis Payen. Principal roles: Cléopâtre (sop), Octavie (sop), Charmion (mezzo), Marc-Antoine (bar), Spakos (ten), Ennius (bar). Massenet's last opera and one of his most exotically scored works, it is hardly ever performed. [R]

Cleva, Fausto (1902–71)
Italian conductor, particularly associated with the Italian repertory. Working predominantly in the United States, he was artistic director of the Cincinnati Summer Opera (1934–63) and the Chicago Opera (1944–6). He died whilst conducting *Orfeo ed Euridice* in Athens.

Cloches de Corneville, Les (*The Bells of Corneville*)
Operetta in three acts by Planquette. 1st perf Paris, 19 April 1877; libr by Charles Gabet and Louis François Clairville. Principal roles: Germaine (sop), Henri (ten), Serpolette (mezzo), Grenicheux (ten), Père Gaspard (bar), Bailie (bar). By far Planquette's most successful work, which enjoyed an initial run of 461 performances, it is still regularly performed in France.
Plot: Normandy, 1685. It is foretold that a set of bells will ring when Henri Marquis of Corneville, rightful owner of the château, returns to his home. The adventures of Germaine, Jean Grenicheux and his sweetheart Serpolette, the old blacksmith Gaspard and an unknown soldier (Henri) provide the fulfilment of the prophecy. Eventually, Henri enters into his own and weds Germaine. [R]

Clorinda
Mezzo role in Rossini's *La Cenerentola.* She is one of Cenerentola's two step-sisters.

Cluytens, André (1905–67)
Belgian conductor, particularly associated with the French repertory and with Wagner operas. He was musical director of the Toulouse Opera (1932–5) and the Opéra-Comique, Paris (1947–9). He conducted the first performance of Milhaud's *Bolivar.*

Clytemnestra
Agamemnon's wife and joint murderess appears in a number of operas, including: **1** Mezzo role in Strauss's *Elektra.* **2** Mezzo role in Gluck's *Iphigénie en Aulide.* **3** Soprano role in Milhaud's *Les Choëphores.* **4** Mezzo role in Taneyev's *Oresteia.* **5** Soprano role in Pizzetti's *Clitennestra.*

Coates, Albert (1882–1953)
British conductor and composer. One of the leading operatic conductors of his age, he was musical director of the Elberfeld Opera (1906–8) and the Maryinsky Theatre, St Petersburg (1912–7). He conducted the first performances of Quilter's *Julia* and Lloyd's *The Serf.* His three operas, nowadays long forgotten, are *Samuel Pepys* (Munich, 21 Dec 1929), *Pickwick* (London, 20 Nov 1936; libr after Charles Dickens's *The Pickwick Papers*), which was the first

opera to be televized, and *Von Hunks and His Devil* (Cape Town, 1952).

Coates, Edith (1908–83)
British mezzo, long resident at Covent Garden. An impressive singing-actress, she created Auntie in *Peter Grimes*, a role in *Gloriana*, Bardeau in Bliss's *The Olympians* and Grandma in Grace Williams's *The Parlour*.

Coccia, Carlo (1782–1873)
Italian composer. He wrote many operas, all of them now long forgotten, enjoying his best success with OPERA SEMISERIA. His most important operas include *Il Poeto Fortunato* (Florence, 1808; libr G. Gasbarri), *Clotilde* (Venice, 8 June 1815; libr Gaetano Rossi), *Maria Stuarda* (London, 7 June 1827; libr Pietro Giannone) and *Caterina di Guisa* (Milan, 14 Feb 1833; libr Felice Romani, after Alexandre Dumas's *Henri III et Sa Cour*), by far his finest work. He was director of the Turin Conservatory (1836–40).

Cochers au Relais, Les (*The Relay Coachmen*)
Comic opera in one act by Fomin. 1st perf St Petersburg, 1787; libr by Nikolai Lvov. Principal roles: Timofei (ten), Ianka (bar), Fadeievna (sop), Abraham (bass). Perhaps the finest late-18th-century Russian work written in OPÉRA-COMIQUE style, it is notable for its rich choral writing which prefigures Glinka.
Plot: 18th-century Russia. Ianka tries to trick the coachman Timofei into joining the army. With the help of his colleagues and of the visiting officer Abraham, Timofei succeeds in turning the tables, and it is Ianka who finds himself dragooned into the army. [R]

Cocteau, Jean (1889–1963)
French playwright, painter and librettist. He provided libretti for Honegger (*Antigone*), Milhaud (*Le Pauvre Matelot*), Poulenc (*La Voix Humaine* and *Le Gendarme Incompris*) and Stravinsky (*Oedipus Rex*), in which last he sometimes appeared as the Narrator.

Cola Rienzi, der letzte der Tribunen
see RIENZI

Colas Breugnon
Sometimes mistakenly used as the title of Kabalevsky's *The Craftsman of Clamecy*, Colas Breugnon is both the principal baritone role and the title of the overture.

Colbran, Isabella (1785–1845)
Spanish soprano, particularly associated with Rossini roles. Regarded as the finest dramatic COLORATURA soprano of the early 19th century, she was the mistress of both DOMENICO BARBAIA and the King of Naples, but left both of them for Rossini, whose first wife she became in 1822; they were separated in 1837. She created the title-roles in Carafa's *Gabriella di Vergi* and Mayr's *Medea in Corinto* and *Cora*, and, for Rossini, Desdemona in *Otello*, Elena in *La Donna del Lago*, Elcia in *Mosè in Egitto*, Zoraide in *Ricciardo e Zoraide*, Anna in *Maometto Secondo* and the title-roles in *Elisabetta Regina d'Inghilterra*, *Zelmira*, *Armida* and *Semiramide*.

Coleridge-Taylor, Samuel (1875–1912)
British composer of Sierra Leonean extraction. The first important black classical composer, he is best known as a choral composer, but he also wrote one opera, the unperformed *Thelma* (1909).

Colin
Tenor role in Rousseau's *Le Devin du Village*. He is Colette's lover. The name came to be used as a generic term for a sentimental rustic lover in 18th- and early-19th-century French opera.

Collatinus
Bass role in Britten's *The Rape of Lucretia*. He is Lucretia's husband.

Colla voce (Italian for 'with the voice')
An instruction to an instrument or to an accompanist to follow the voice closely, especially in a passage in free time.

Collier, Marie (1926–71)
Australian soprano, particularly associated with Puccini and Janáček roles, especially the title-role in *Tosca* and Emilia Marty in *The Macropolus Case*. She possessed a vibrant but not flawless voice and was a powerful – sometimes almost flamboyant – singing-actress. She created Hecuba in *King Priam* and Christine Mannon in

Levy's *Mourning Becomes Electra.* She died as a result of a fall from a window.

Colline
Bass role in Puccini's *La Bohème*. He is the philosopher of the four bohemians.

Collingwood, Lawrence (1887–1982)
British conductor and composer, particularly associated with Sadler's Wells Opera, of which he was musical director (1940–46). He wrote two operas: *Macbeth* (London, 12 Apr 1934; libr composer, after Shakespeare) and *The Death of Tintagiles* (London, 16 Apr 1950; libr Alfred Sutro, after Maurice Maeterlinck's *La Mort de Tintagiles*)

Colmar
see OPÉRA DU RHIN

Cologne Opera (Köln in German)
The present opera house in this German city in North Rhine Westphalia is the Grosses Haus (cap 1,346), designed by Wilhelm Riphahn, which opened in 1957. It replaced the previous building, which was destroyed by bombs in 1943. One of Germany's leading houses, with a long tradition of the highest artistic standards, it has recently been noted for its Mozart performances. The annual season runs from September to June. Musical directors have included Emil Ábrányi, Otto Lohse, Otto Klemperer, Eugene Szenkar, Günter Wand, Otto Ackermann, Wolfgang Sawallisch, István Kertesz, Sir John Pritchard and James Conlon.

Colombian opera composers
These include Luis Antonio Escóbar (*b* 1925), José María Ponce de León (1846–82), whose *Ester* (Bogotá, 12 July 1874) was the first Colombian opera, and Guillermo Uribe-Holguín (1880–1971).

Coloratura (from the German *Koloratur*, 'colouring')
An elaborate and brilliant ornamentation of the vocal line. The Italian term FIORITURA means virtually the same thing. It was originally called *canto figuraturo*.

Coloratura mezzo
A mezzo of considerable range and agility who specializes in florid roles, particularly many of those by Rossini. Famous coloratura mezzos have included Conchita Supervia, Marilyn Horne and Cecilia Bartoli.

Coloratura soprano
A soprano who specializes in florid, highly ornamented singing, and who performs such roles as Zerbinetta, the Queen of the Night, Lucia and Olympia. Famous coloratura sopranos have included Amelita Galli-Curci, Selma Kurtz, Dame Joan Sutherland and June Anderson.

Coltellini, Marco (1719–77)
Italian poet and librettist. He succeeded Pietro Metastasio as court poet in Vienna and later became official librettist in St Petersburg. He wrote some 20 libretti, many of which were used more than once. His texts were set by Bortnyansky, Galuppi, Gassmann (*La Contessina*), Gluck (*Telemaco*), Hasse, Haydn (*L'Infedeltà Delusa*), Mozart (*La Finta Semplice* and *La Finta Giardiniera*), Paisiello, Piccinni, Salieri (*Armida*), Sarti, D. Scarlatti, Traetta (*Antigonae*) and Winter amongst others. His daughter **Celeste** (1760–1828) was a successful mezzo, who created the title-role in Paisiello's *Nina* and Tonina in Salieri's *Prima la Musica e Poi le Parole.*

Combattimento di Tancredi e Clorinda, Il
(*The Duel of Tancred and Clorinda*)
Dramatic cantata in one act by Monteverdi. 1st perf Venice, 1624; a setting of part of Canto XII of Torquato Tasso's *Gerusalemme Liberata.* Principal roles: Narrator (ten), Clorinda (sop), Tancredi (ten). Although not strictly speaking an opera, the work was intended to be performed by costumed singers, and has been regularly staged in recent years. In his preface to the work, Monteverdi outlined some of his theories, particularly his innovative use of TREMOLO and pizzicato (plucked strings) to heighten musico-dramatic tension. A seminal work in the development of music-drama.
Plot: Late-11th-century Palestine. During the First Crusade, the Christian warrior Tancredi, in love with Clorinda, fights a long duel with a Saracen wearing full armour. Only after the Saracen is

vanquished and is dying does Tancredi discover that the warrior is in fact Clorinda. [R]

Come dal ciel precipita
Bass aria for Banquo in Act II of Verdi's *Macbeth*, in which he tells of his forebodings of disaster.

Com'è gentil
Tenor aria for Ernesto in Act III of Donizetti's *Don Pasquale*, in which he serenades Norina in the garden.

Come in quest'ora bruna
Soprano aria for Amelia in Act I of Verdi's *Simon Boccanegra*, in which she salutes the morning light over the sea.

Come Paride
Baritone aria for Belcore in Act I of Donizetti's *L'Elisir d'Amore*, in which he bumptiously introduces himself to Adina.

Come per me sereno
Soprano aria for Amina in Act I of Bellini's *La Sonnambula*, in which she tells of her happiness at her approaching wedding.

Come scoglio
Soprano aria for Fiordiligi in Act I of Mozart's *Così fan Tutte*, in which she vows to stand rock-like against the attentions of would-be suitors.

Come scritto (Italian for 'as written')
An instruction to a singer to perform the music exactly as it is written, without decoration and with no change in tempo.

Come un bel dì di Maggio
Tenor aria for Chénier in Act IV of Giordano's *Andrea Chénier*, sung as he awaits execution.

Comedy on the Bridge (*Veselohra no Mostě*)
Comic opera in one act by Martinů. 1st perf Czech Radio, 18 March 1937; libr by the composer, after Václav Kliment Klicpera's play. Principal roles: Popelka (sop), Ján (bar), Eva (mezzo), Brewer (bass), Schoolmaster (ten). A brilliant satire on bureaucracy and war, it tells of events on a bridge joining friendly and enemy territories. [R]

Comic opera
A loose term, simply meaning an opera on a comic subject. The first comic opera is believed to have been Marazzoli's *Chi Soffre, Speri* of 1639, which has a libretto by the future Pope Clement IX. Many other terms refer to comic opera, but are more specific as regards style and structure.
see also BALLAD OPERA; BURLETTA; DRAMMA EROICOMICO; DRAMMA GIOCOSO; FARSA; GÉNERO CHICO; INTERMEZZO; OPÉRA-BOUFFE; OPERA BUFFA; OPÉRA-COMIQUE; OPERA SEMISERIA; OPERETTA; SAINETE; SINGSPIEL; TONADILLA; ZARZUELA; ZAUBEROPER; ZWISCHENSPIEL

Comme autrefois
Soprano aria for Leïla in Act II of Bizet's *Les Pêcheurs de Perles*, in which she sings of the love filling her heart.

Commedia dell'Arte (Italian for 'comedy of art')
A dramatic form of uncertain origin which flourished in Italy in the 16th and 17th centuries. It involved stock characters (Harlequin, Colombine, Pantaloon etc) and stock situations (cunning servants, scheming doctors, duped employers and the like). It had an enormous influence on the development of comic opera (both *Il Barbiere di Siviglia* and *Don Pasquale*, for example, are pure Commedia dell'Arte plots) and its conventions are used to powerful effect in *Pagliacci*. The early 20th century witnessed a considerable revival of interest in its use, its characters being the basis of *The Love of Three Oranges*, *Ariadne auf Naxos*, Mascagni's *Le Maschere*, Rosenberg's *Marionettes* and Busoni's *Arlecchino* amongst others.

Commendatore
Bass role in Mozart's and Gazzaniga's *Don Giovanni* and Dargomijsky's *The Stone Guest*. He is Donna Anna's father.

Competitions
Competitions have sometimes been held for new operas. They have included that organized by Offenbach in 1857 for a one-act OPÉRA-COMIQUE (won jointly by Lecocq's and Bizet's *Le Docteur Miracle*), that of the Italian publisher Sonzogno in 1889 for a one-act opera (won by

· Composers in opera ·

The lives of a number of composers have been the subject of operatic treatment. Composers who appear as operatic characters include:

- J.S. Bach in Ábrányi's *The Cantor of St Thomas Church.*
- Chopin in Orefice's *Chopin.*
- Cimarosa in Isouard's *Cimarosa.*
- Grieg in Wright's *Song of Norway.*
- Haydn in Suppé's *Joseph Haydn.*
- Lully in Grétry's *Les Trois Âges de l'Opéra* and Isouard's *Lully et Quinault.*
- Mozart in Flotow's *Die Musikanten*, Rimsky-Korsakov's *Mozart and Salieri*, Hahn's *Mozart* and the Lortzing pastiche *Szenen aus Mozarts Leben.*
- Paganini in Lehár's *Paganini.*
- Palestrina in Pfitzner's *Palestrina.*
- Pergolesi in Serrao's *Pergolesi.*
- Rossini in Paumgartner's *Rossini in Neapel.*
- Rousseau in Dalayrac's *L'Enfance de Jean-Jacques Rousseau.*
- Salieri in Rimsky-Korsakov's *Mozart and Salieri* and the Lortzing pastiche *Szenen aus Mozarts Leben.*
- Schubert in Suppé's *Franz Schubert.*
- Stradella in Flotow's *Alessandro Stradella* and Niedermeyer's *Stradella.*
- Taverner in Maxwell Davies's *Taverner.*
- Tchaikovsky in Schat's *Symposion.*

Mascagni with *Cavalleria Rusticana*), that for the Festival of Britain in 1951 (jointly won by Bush's *Wat Tyler*, Goldschmidt's *Beatrice Cenci*, Benjamin's *A Tale of Two Cities* and Karl Rankl's *Deirdre of the Sorrows*) and that by La Scala, Milan, for the 1951 Verdi celebrations (jointly won by Napoli's *Masaniello* and Castro's *Proserpina y el Extranjero*). *See also* VOCAL COMPETITIONS

Composer
Mezzo trouser role in Strauss's *Ariadne auf Naxos*. Composer of the opera to be performed, he is the Music Master's pupil. The role is sometimes sung by a soprano.

Composer-librettists
Many composers have preferred to write their own libretti so as to ensure that the text provides them with exactly what they require. The most famous example is Wagner. Other composers who always (or nearly always) wrote their own libretti include Berg, Boito, Busoni, Cornelius, Dallapiccola, Floyd, Holst, Janáček, Klebe, Křenek, Leoncavallo, Lortzing, Lualdi, Menotti, Moussorgsky, Orff, Pizzetti, Schreker, Tippett and Viozzi. A number of other composers occasionally provided their own libretti; those who did so successfully include Berlioz, Charpentier, Delius, Donizetti, Hindemith, Martinů, Prokofiev, Rimsky-Korsakov, Schönberg, Strauss and Tchaikovsky. In addition, Blacher, Boito, Draghi, Egk, Leoncavallo, Marcello, Nyman and Menotti wrote libretti for other composers.

Comprimario (Italian for 'with the first')
A term used in the 19th century to describe a sub-principal role (such as Cecil in *Maria Stuarda*), it has more recently been used to describe any small, secondary role, such as confidantes, messengers, duennas and the like. Performing comprimario roles is not necessarily any less demanding than performing principal roles, and their contribution to an overall performance is crucial. Some famous comprimarios, such as Piero de Palma and Giuseppe Nessi, have been operatic artists of considerable stature.

Comte Ory, Le (*Count Ory*)
Comic opera in two acts by Rossini. 1st perf Paris, 20 Aug 1828; libr by Eugène Scribe and Charles-Gaspard Delestre-Poirson, after Pierre Antoine de la Place. Principal roles: Ory (ten), Countess Adèle (sop), Isolier (mezzo), Raimbaud (bar), Tutor (bass), Ragonde (mezzo), Alice (sop). Rossini's last and most sophisticated comedy, it incorporates much music from his earlier *Il Viaggio a Reims*. An immediate success, it is still regularly performed.
Plot: Touraine, *c* 1200. Countess Adèle, Ragonde and their companions have taken a vow of chastity whilst their menfolk are away on the Crusades. The amorous Count Ory, aided and abetted by his Tutor, his page Isolier and his friend Raimbaud, lays siege to the Countess, disguising himself first as a miraculous curer of love-sickness and secondly as a journeying nun. Raimbaud discovers the contents of the Countess's cellar and the 'nuns' get uproariously drunk, escaping only just in time as the ladies' husbands return. [R]

Concepción
Mezzo role in Ravel's *L'Heure Espagnole*. She is Torquemada's flirtatious wife.

Conductor
see panel on pages 120–1

Confession Scene
The title of Act III Scene II of Donizetti's *Maria Stuarda*, in which Mary confesses to Talbot before her execution.

Confrontation Scene
A title often given to the end of Act II of Donizetti's *Maria Stuarda*, when in a tremendous if historically fictitious scene Mary and Elizabeth meet and roundly insult one another.

Congiura (Italian for 'conspiracy')
A name sometimes given to a conspiracy scene in an Italian opera, such as that in Act III of Verdi's *Ernani*.

Conlon, James (b 1950)
American conductor, particularly associated with the Italian repertory, especially Verdi. One of the finest of the younger generation of American conductors, he is noted for his scrupulous preparation and muscular performances. Musical director of the Cologne Opera (1989–).

Connell, Elizabeth (b 1946)
South African-born Irish mezzo and later soprano, particularly associated with Mozart and with dramatic Italian and German roles. Beginning as a dramatic mezzo, she subsequently developed into a SPINTO soprano, excelling as Lady Macbeth in Verdi's *Macbeth*, Medea in Cherubini's *Medée* and Ortrud in Wagner's *Lohengrin*. Possessing a large, exciting and incisive voice, which she uses with considerable intelligence and musicianship, she is a committed – at times even flamboyant – singing-actress.

Constanze
Soprano role in Mozart's *Die Entführung aus dem Serail*. She is loved by Belmonte.

Consul, The
Opera in three acts by Menotti. 1st perf Philadelphia, 1 March 1950; libr by the composer. Principal roles: Magda and John Sorel (sop and bar), Secretary (mezzo), Agent (bar), Mother (mezzo), Magician (ten). Arguably Menotti's finest full-length opera, it is a VERISMO piece in which the title character never appears.
Plot: A European police state, late 1940s. The political dissident John Sorel is in hiding, waiting for his wife Magda, his child and his Mother to join him. Magda's attempts to obtain exit visas are continually hindered by the red tape at a foreign consulate. The Sorels' child dies and John resolves to return, even though Magda pleads with him not to come, warning that she will not be alive. John is arrested at the consulate and the Secretary at last promises help, but she rings Magda too late to prevent her from committing suicide. [R]

Contes d'Hoffmann, Les (*The Tales of Hoffmann*)
Opera in prologue, three acts and epilogue by Offenbach. 1st perf Paris, 10 Feb 1881; libr by Jules Barbier and Michel Carré, after E.T.A. Hoffmann's *Der Sandmann*, *Geschichte vom Verlorenen Spiegelbilde* and *Rat Krespel*. Principal roles: Hoffmann (ten), Antonia/Giulietta/Olympia/Stella

· *Conductor* ·

The conductor is in overall charge of the musical preparation of an opera production, both orchestrally and vocally, and leads the actual performance from the orchestra pit. It is the conductor who decides how the music will actually sound (in other words, all matters of tempo, balance, style and interpretation), and he is – whatever singers might think – the single most important person in an operatic performance. He thus also tends to be much the most powerful person, which goes some way to explain the dictatorial behaviour of some great conductors, such as Toscanini, Beecham and Karajan.

The modern orchestral conductor as we know him – and occasionally in recent years her – emerged in the 19th century. In the 17th century, the composer would beat time with a long pole, and in the 18th and early 19th centuries, either the first violinist or the harpsichordist would ensure the ensemble. Spohr may perhaps be regarded as the earliest modern-style conductor: he introduced the baton, now used by virtually all conductors. In the second half of the 19th century, the leading conductors tended to be composers: Mahler, Nápravník, Liszt, Messager and Strauss, for example. The conductor as a separate species is essentially a 20th-century phenomenon.

The conductor is called *dirigente* in Italy, *chef d'orchestre* in France and *dirigent* in Germany. Conductors are often addressed as and referred to by the courtesy title of *Maestro* (Italian for 'master').

Below are listed the 216 conductors with entries in this dictionary. Their nationalities are given in brackets afterwards.

Abbado, Claudio (It)
Ackermann, Otto (Swit)
Adler, Kurt Herbert (Aus)
Ahronovich, Yuri (Russ)
Albrecht, Gerd (Ger)
Ansermet, Ernest (Swit)
Arditi, Luigi (It)
Armstrong, Richard (Br)
Atherton, David (Br)
Baranović, Krešimir (Cro)
Barbirolli, Sir John (Br)
Barenboim, Daniel (Isr)
Bartoletti, Bruno (It)
Baudo, Serge (Fr)
Bedford, Steuart (Br)
Beecham, Sir Thomas (Br)
Bellezza, Vincenzo (It)
Bernstein, Leonard (US)
Bertini, Gary (Isr)
Blech, Leo (Ger)
Böhm, Karl (Aus)
Bonynge, Richard (Aust)
Boskovsky, Willi (Aus)
Boulez, Pierre (Fr)
Boult, Sir Adrian (Br)
Braithwaite, Warwick (NZ)
Bülow, Hans von (Ger)
Busch, Fritz (Ger)
Caldwell, Sarah (US)
Campanini, Cleofonte (It)
Cantelli, Guido (It)
Capuana, Franco (It)
Chailly, Riccardo (It)
Chalabala, Zdeněk (Cz)
Cleva, Fausto (It)
Cluytens, André (Belg)
Collingwood, Lawrence (Br)
Conlon, James (US)
Costa, Sir Michael (Br)
Damrosch, Walter (US)
Daniel, Paul (Br)
Danon, Oskar (Ser)
Davis, Andrew (Br)
Davis, Sir Colin (Br)
Désmorière, Roger (Fr)
Dobrowen, Issay (Russ)
Dohnányi, Christoph von (Ger)
Doráti, Antal (Hung)
Downes, Sir Edward (Br)
Dutoit, Charles (Swit)
Ehrling, Sixten (Swe)
Elder, Mark (Br)
Elmendorff, Karl (Ger)
Erede, Alberto (It)
Ermler, Mark (Russ)
Fabritiis, Oliviero de (It)
Faccio, Franco (It)
Farncombe, Charles (Br)
Fasano, Renato (It)
Ferencsik, János (Hung)
Ferro, Gabriele (It)
Fischer, Ádám (Hung)
Franci, Carlo (Arg)
Fricsay, Ferenc (Hung)
Frühbeck de Burgos, Rafael (Sp)
Furtwängler, Wilhelm (Ger)
Gardelli, Lamberto (It)
Gardiner, John Eliot (Br)
Gavazzeni, Gianandrea (It)
Gergiev, Valery (Russ)

Gibson, Sir Alexander (Br)
Gielen, Michael (Ger)
Giulini, Carlo Maria (It)
Glover, Jane (Br)
Goldovsky, Boris (Russo)
Goodall, Sir Reginald (Br)
Groves, Sir Charles (Br)
Guarnieri, Antonio (It)
Gui, Vittorio (It)
Hager, Leopold (Aus)
Haitink, Bernard (Neth)
Hallé, Sir Charles (Br)
Harnoncourt, Nickolas (Aus)
Heger, Robert (Ger)
Howarth, Elgar (Br)
Inbal, Eliahu (Isr)
Janowski, Marek (Pol)
Järnefelt, Armas (Fin)
Järvi, Neeme (Est)
Jochum, Eugen (Ger)
Jullien, Louis (Fr)
Karajan, Herbert von (Aus)
Keilberth, Joseph (Ger)
Kempe, Rudolf (Ger)
Kertesz, István (Hung)
Khaikin, Boris (Russ)
Kleiber, Carlos (Arg)
Kleiber, Erich (Aus)
Klemperer, Otto (Ger)
Knappertsbusch, Hans (Ger)
Kondrashin, Kiril (Russ)
Konwitschny, Franz (Ger)
Košler, Zdeněk (Cz)
Koussevitzky, Serge (Russ)
Kovařovic, Karel (Cz)
Krauss, Clemens (Aus)
Krips, Josef (Aus)
Krombholc, Jaroslav (Cz)
Kubelík, Rafael (Cz)
Lamoureux, Charles (Fr)
Leibowitz, René (Fr)
Leinsdorf, Erich (Aus)
Leitner, Ferdinand (Ger)
Leppard, Raymond (Br)
Levi, Hermann (Ger)
Levine, James (US)
Lewis, Sir Anthony (Br)
Lloyd Jones, David (Br)
Lockhart, James (Br)
Lombard, Alain (Fr)
López-Cobos, Jesús (Sp)
Loughran, James (Br)
Ludwig, Leopold (Aus)
Maag, Peter (Swit)
Maazel, Lorin (US)
Mackerras, Sir Charles (Aust)
Mahler, Gustav (Aus)
Malgoire, Jean-Claude (Fr)
Mancinelli, Luigi (It)
Mar, Norman del (Br)
Mariani, Angelo (It)
Marinuzzi, Gino (It)
Markevich, Igor (Russ)
Marriner, Sir Neville (Br)
Mascheroni, Edoardo (It)
Masur, Kurt (Ger)
Matačić Lovro von (Slv)
Mauceri, John (US)
Mehta, Zubin (Ind)
Messager, André (Fr)
Mitropoulos, Dimitri (Gk)
Molinari-Pradelli, Francesco (It)
Monteux, Pierre (Fr)
Mottl, Felix (Aus)
Muck, Karl (Ger)
Mugnone, Leopoldo (It)
Muti, Riccardo (It)
Nápravník, Eduard (Russ)
Neumann, František (Cz)
Neumann, Václav (Cz)
Nikisch, Artur (Hung)
Norrington, Roger (Br)
Ormandy, Eugene (Hung)
Östman, Arnold (Swe)
Ozawa, Seiji (Jap)
Panizza, Ettore (Arg)
Patanè, Giuseppe (It)
Perlea, Jonel (Rom)
Plasson, Michel (Fr)
Prêtre, Georges (Fr)
Previn, André (US)
Previtali, Fernando (It)
Pritchard, Sir John (Br)
Quadri, Argeo (It)
Queler, Eve (US)
Rankl, Karl (Aus)
Rattle, Sir Simon (Br)
Reiner, Fritz (Hung)
Rescigno, Nicola (US)
Richter, Hans (Aus)
Rizzi, Carlo (It)
Rosbaud, Hans (Aus)
Rostropovich, Mstislav (Russ)
Rozhdestvensky, Gennadi (Russ)
Rudel, Julius (Aus)
Sabata, Victor de (It)
Santi, Nello (It)
Santini, Gabriele (It)
Sanzogno, Nino (It)
Sargent, Sir Malcolm (Br)
Sawallisch, Wolfgang (Ger)
Schalk, Franz (Aus)
Scherchen, Hermann (Ger)
Schippers, Thomas (US)
Schmidt-Isserstedt, Hans (Ger)
Schuch, Ernst von (Aus)
Scimone, Claudio (It)
Seidl, Anton (Hung)
Serafin, Tullio (It)
Serebrier, José (Ur)
Simonetto, Alfredo (It)
Sinopoli, Giuseppe (It)
Söderblom, Ulf (Fin)
Solti, Sir Georg (Hung)
Stein, Horst (Ger)
Stiedry, Fritz (Aus)
Stokowski, Leopold (US)
Suitner, Otmar (Aus)
Svetlanov, Yevgeny (Russ)
Széll, George (Hung)
Talich, Václav (Cz)
Tate, Jeffrey (Br)
Temirkanov, Yuri (Russ)
Tennstedt, Klaus (Ger)
Toscanini, Arturo (It)
Varviso, Silvio (Swit)
Votto, Antonino (It)
Wallberg, Heinz (Ger)
Walter, Bruno (Ger)
Weingartner, Felix (Aus)
Weller, Walter (Aus)
Welser-Möst, Franz (Aus)
Wolff, Albert (Fr)
Wood, Sir Henry (Fr)
Zagrosek, Lothar (Ger)
Zedda, Alberto (It)

(sop), Dr Miracle/Dapertutto/Coppélius/ Lindorf (b-bar), Nicklausse/Muse (mezzo), Spalanzani (ten), Crespel (bass), Franz (ten), Mother (mezzo), Schlemil (bar). Offenbach's last and greatest work, it was not quite completed at his death. The final scoring was completed by Guiraud, who also provided recitatives, although it was intended to have spoken dialogue. A fascinating and at times disturbing work, it tells three interconnected stories in which Hoffmann is thwarted in love by his evil genius. Ideally, the four villains should be sung by the same man and the four heroines by the same woman, as they are aspects of the same persons. Contrary to most productions, the Antonia Act should be in the middle. The work was an immediate success and has remained ever since one of the most popular of all operas.

Plot: Early-19th-century Nuremburg, Paris, Munich and Venice. In Luther's beer cellar, the students await the end of a performance of *Don Giovanni*, starring Stella, who is loved by the poet Hoffmann and who is also pursued by the sinister Councillor Lindorf. To pass the time, Hoffman offers to tell the story of his three great loves, in all of which he was aided by his young friend Nicklausse (later revealed as the embodiment of the Muse of Poetry). In Paris, he is sold a magical pair of spectacles by Coppélius and falls in love with Olympia, the 'daughter' of the inventor Spalanzani. She turns out to be a mechanical doll, which Coppélius destroys when he discovers that Spalanzani has double-crossed him. In Munich, Hoffmann has fallen in love with the singer Antonia. Her father Crespel has forbidden her to sing, without telling her the reason: she is consumptive, as was her dead mother, also a great singer. After treating Antonia by remote control, the evil quack Dr Miracle brings to life the portrait of her mother and urges her to sing ever more ecstatically. The strain is too much, and she dies in Hoffmann's arms. In Venice, Hoffmann is having an affair with the courtesan Giulietta, who – at the behest of the magician Dapertutto who controls her – steals his reflection. Hoffmann kills Giulietta's former lover Peter Schlemil in a duel and flees for his life, having witnessed Giulietta leaving with another admirer. Back in the beer cellar, the students realize that the three women are aspects of Stella. Hoffmann is by now totally drunk, and a triumphant Lindorf escorts Stella away. Nicklausse as Hoffmann's muse urges him to return to his poetry. [R]

Continuo (Italian for 'continuous')
A shortening of *basso continuo*, it refers to the bass part which accompanies recitative in a 17th or 18th century opera. It is played by the harpsichord and sometimes also by the cello.

Contralto (Italian for 'against the high')
Meaning a contrast to a high voice, the term refers to the lowest female vocal range. It is similar to mezzo-soprano – the two terms are often used interchangeably – and is nowadays usually used to describe a voice (such as that of Dame Clara Butt) or a role (such as Ulrica in *Un Ballo in Maschera*) of exceptionally dark quality and low range. Only in Germany is contralto still regarded as a seperate range from mezzo. There, where it is called *Alt* and its singer *Altistin*, there are two recognized types: **1** *Dramatischer Alt*, such as Erda in *Siegfried*, with a range of f to f''; **2** *Komischer Alt*, such as Widow Browe in *Zar und Zimmermann*, with a range of f to g''. *See also* MEZZO-SOPRANO

Contro un cor
Mezzo aria for Rosina in Act II of Rossini's *Il Barbiere di Siviglia*. It is Rosina's singing lesson.

Convenienze (Italian for 'conveniences')
An Italian theatrical term which defies exact definition. Basically, it was used in 19th-century Italy to describe the way in which the operatic system worked, in particular the hierarchy of singers and the structure to which an opera had to conform so as to respect that heirarchy. The ludicrousness of much of the *convenienze* was gloriously sent up by Donizetti (see below).

Convenienze ed Inconvenienze Teatrali, Le (*Theatrical Conveniences and Inconveniences*; often given as *Viva la Mamma*)
Comic opera in two acts (originally one

act) by Donizetti. 1st perf Naples, 21 Nov 1827; libr by the composer, after Antonio Simone Sografi's *Le Convenienze Teatrali* and *Le Inconvenienze Teatrali*. Revised version 1st perf Milan, 20 April 1831. Principal roles: Mamm' Agata (bar), Composer (ten), Impresario (bass), Corilla (sop). An hilarious send-up of Italian opera's backstage intrigues, it contains in Mamm' Agata the greatest 'drag' role in opera. It has been regularly performed in recent years.
Plot: Early-19th-century Milan. A provincial company is rehearsing the new opera by Biscroma Strappaviscere ('Fast-Note Gut-Buster'). Luigia, the seconda donna, complains that her part is too small. Her formidable mother Mamm' Agata bursts in, ready for battle on Luigia's behalf. She demands a new aria for Luigia, and tells the Composer how to orchestrate it. The boasts of the bass Proclo about the prowess of his daughter Corilla, the prima donna, lead Mamm' Agata to lay into Corilla, who storms out for good. Mamm' Agata assures the by now distracted Impresario that she herself is more than capable of undertaking the leading role, and sings the Willow Song from Rossini's *Otello* to prove it. A new rehearsal is called, with all save Mamm' Agata convinced that the opera will be a disaster.

Converse, Frederick (1871–1940)
American composer. He wrote four operas, the most successful of which was *The Pipe of Desire* (Boston, 31 Jan 1906; libr George Edward Burton), which in 1910 became the first American opera to be performed at the Metropolitan Opera, New York. His other operas are *The Sacrifice* (Boston, 6 Jan 1911; libr composer and John Albert Macy), *Sinbad the Sailor* (1913; libr Percy Mackaye) and *The Immigrants* (1914; libr Mackaye), the last two of which were never performed.

Copenhagen
see ROYAL DANISH OPERA

Copland, Aaron (1900–90)
American composer. Best known as an orchestral composer, he also wrote two operas: the children's opera *The Second Hurricane* (New York, 21 Apr 1937; libr Edwin Denby) [R] and the successful THE TENDER LAND. He also wrote three books on music.

Copley, John (b 1933)
British producer, particularly associated with Mozart operas. He has been especially active at Covent Garden (where he was resident producer), the Australian Opera and the English National Opera, where his many notable successes included *La Traviata*, *Maria Stuarda* and *Il Trovatore*. His traditional-style productions are notable for their naturalness and great inventiveness in comedy, as well occasionally for a certain fussiness and campness.

Coppélius
Bass-baritone role in Offenbach's *Les Contes d'Hoffmann*. He is the sinister spectacle maker in the Olympia Act.

Coq d'Or, Le
see GOLDEN COCKEREL, THE

Corelli, Franco (b 1921)
Italian tenor, particularly associated with heroic Italian roles, especially Calaf in *Turandot*, the title-role in Donizetti's *Poliuto*, Pollione in *Norma* and, above all, Manrico in *Il Trovatore*. He was perhaps the most thrilling TENORE DI FORZA of the post-war era and was a great favourite with audiences everywhere with his good looks, magnificent voice and ringing high notes. He was, however, hardly the most subtle of singers: one critic aptly described him as 'an adept at tearing a passion to tatters'.

Corena, Fernando (1916–84)
Swiss bass, particularly associated with the Italian repertory and with Mozart roles, especially Leporello in *Don Giovanni* and Dr Bartolo in *Le Nozze di Figaro*. Usually regarded as Salvatore Baccaloni's natural successor, he was one of the greatest BUFFOS of the post-war era. He possessed a good voice and superb diction and was an hilarious (and occasionally slightly unpredictable) comic actor. From 1954, he was largely resident at the Metropolitan Opera, New York. He created a role in Petrassi's *Il Cordovano*.

Corigliano, John (b 1938)
American composer. He has written one

opera, *The Ghosts of Versailles* (New York, 14 Dec 1991; libr William M. Hoffman, partly after Pierre-Augustin Caron de Beaumarchais's *La Mère Coupable*).

Corneille, Pierre
see panel on page 125

Cornelius, Peter (1824–74)
German composer. A disciple of Liszt and Wagner, he wrote three operas, of which the comedy DER BARBIER VON BAGDAD was much the most successful. Neither *Der Cid* (Weimar, 21 May 1865; libr composer, after Pierre Corneille's *Le Cid*) nor *Gunlöd* (Weimar, 6 May 1891, composed *c* 1870; libr composer) are now remembered. The latter was left unfinished at his death and was completed by Carl Hoffbauer.

Corona (Italian for 'crown')
The term used in Italy for FERMATA.

Coronation March
March in Act IV of Meyerbeer's *Le Prophète*, played as Jean de Leyden has himself crowned king.

Coronation of Poppea, The
see INCORONAZIONE DI POPPEA, L'

Coronation Scene
The title usually given to Scene II of the Prologue of Moussorgsky's *Boris Godunov*, in which Boris is crowned Tsar.

Corregidor, Der (roughly *The Magistrate*)
Comic opera in four acts by Wolf. 1st perf Mannheim, 7 June 1896; libr by Rosa Mayreder, after Pedro de Alarcón's *El Sombrero de Tres Picos*. Principal roles: Frasquita (sop), Tio Lucas (bar), Corregidor (ten), Mercedes (sop). Wolf's only completed opera, it contains some delightful music (including two of his songs incorporated into the score), but is hampered by its weak libretto. It still receives an occasional performance.
Plot: Andalusia, 1804. Frasquita, wife of the miller Tio Lucas, dismisses her husband's jealousy as groundless, and uses the advances of the amorous elderly Corregidor to obtain a post for her nephew. The Corregidor, soaking wet from having fallen into the mill-stream, visits Frasquita, who defends her honour with a musket in the absence of Tio Lucas, who has been called into town on a false errand trumped up by the Corregidor. On his way home, he passes Frasquita who has gone to look for him, but fails to notice her in the dark. Lucas finds the Corregidor asleep in his bed and dressed in his clothes. When he wakens, the Corregidor is beaten by his own officers from the town and then refused entry into his own home by his wife Mercedes, who claims that she has mistaken Lucas for him. Lucas, suspected of murdering the Corregidor, also receives a sound beating. [R]

Corsaro, Il (*The Corsair*)
Opera in three acts by Verdi. 1st perf Trieste, 25 Oct 1848; libr by Francesco Maria Piave, after Lord Byron's poem. Principal roles: Corrado (ten), Gulnara (sop), Pasha Seid (bar), Medora (sop). One of the least successful of Verdi's early operas, vigorous but hardly subtle, it is only occasionally performed.
Plot: Coron and an Aegean island, early 19th century. The pirate captain Corrado leads an attack against the Turkish Pasha Seid and is captured and imprisoned. Seid's favourite slave Gulnara kills her master, thus rescuing Corrado, and persuades him to take her with him to his island. Returning home, Corrado finds that his beloved Medora, believing him dead, has taken poison. After she dies in his arms, Corrado hurls himself into the sea. [R]

Cortigiani
Baritone aria for Rigoletto in Act II of Verdi's *Rigoletto*, in which he rages against the courtiers for refusing to return his daughter to him.

Cosa Rara, Una (*A Rare Thing*) or **Bellezza ed Onestà** (*Beauty and Honesty*)
Comic opera in two acts by Martín y Soler. 1st perf Vienna, 17 Nov 1786; libr by Lorenzo da Ponte, after Luis Vélez de Guevara's *La Luna della Sierra*. Principal roles: Queen Isabella (sop), Lilla (sop), Ghita (sop), Giovanni (ten), Lubino (bar), Tita (b-bar), Corrado (ten), Lisargo (bass). By far Martín y Soler's most successful

· Pierre Corneille ·

The works of the French playwright Pierre Corneille (1606–84) have had an important influence on opera, both as source material and as the models – with their theme of the conflict between passion and duty – on which Apostolo Zeno and Pietro Metastasio based their OPERA SERIA libretti. Corneille's works have inspired some 50 operas. Below are listed, by play, those operas by composers with entries in this dictionary.

Andromède		
Lully	*Persée*	1682
Charpentier	*Andromède*	1682
Philidor	*Persée*	1780
Le Cid		
Händel	*Flavio*	1723
Piccinni	*Il Gran Cid*	1766
Sacchini	*Il Cidde/Chimène*	1769/83
Paisiello	*Il Gran Cid*	1775
Pacini	*Il Cid*	1853
Cornelius	*Der Cid*	1865
Massenet	*Le Cid*	1885
Debussy	*Rodrigue et Chimène*	1888 (U)
Cinna		
Hasse	*Tito Vespasiano*	1735
Graun	*Cinna*	1748
Portugal	*Cinna*	1793
Paer	*Il Cinna*	1795
Horace		
Salieri	*Les Horaces*	1786
Zingarelli	*Gli Orazi e i Curiazi*	1795
Cimarosa	*Gli Orazi e i Curiazi*	1796
Portugal	*Gli Orazi e i Curiazi*	1798
Mercadante	*Orazi e Curiazi*	1846
La Mort de Pompé		
Graun	*Cesare e Cleopatra*	1742
Pertharite		
Händel	*Rodelinda*	1725
Graun	*Rodelinda*	1741
Polyeucte		
Donizetti	*Poliuto/Les Martyrs*	1838/40
Gounod	*Polyeucte*	1878
Sofonisbe		
Caldara	*Sofonisba*	1708
Galuppi	*Sofonisba*	1753
Traetta	*Sofonisba*	1762
Paer	*Sofonisba*	1805
Tite et Bérénice		
Caldara	*Tito e Berenice*	1714
La Toison d'Or		
Keiser	*Jason*	1720

His brother **Thomas** (1625–1709) was also a playwright, whose *Médée* was the source for M.-A. Charpentier's *Médée* and Cherubini's *Médée*.

opera, it was hugely popular for over 50 years and still receives an occasional performance. Mozart quotes from it in the Supper Scene of *Don Giovanni*.
Plot: 15th-century Spain. The peasant girl Lilla, intended by her brother Tita as a bride for the magistrate Don Lisargo, is also pursued by Prince Giovanni and by his chamberlain Corrado. However, despite all threats and entreaties, she remains faithful to her lover Lubino.

Così fan Tutte (*Thus Do They All*) or **La Scuola degli Amanti** (*The School for Lovers*)
Comic opera in two acts by Mozart (K 588). 1st perf Vienna, 26 Jan 1790; libr by Lorenzo da Ponte. Principal roles: Fiordiligi (sop), Ferrando (ten), Dorabella (mezzo), Guglielmo (bar), Don Alfonso (b-bar), Despina (sop). One of the most human and heart-searching of all operas, it was only infrequently performed in the 19th century (and then only in adaptions) because the story was considered immoral. Nowadays, it is firmly established as one of the best-loved of all operas.
Plot: 18th-century Naples. The officers Ferrando and Guglielmo are engaged to the sisters Dorabella and Fiordiligi. Their cynical bachelor friend Don Alfonso makes a wager with them that the fidelity of their fiancées is as shaky as that of all other women. Pretending to be called away on active service, the men disguise themselves as a pair of Albanians, and each pays court to the other's lover. Alfonso enlists the aid of the girls' servant Despina to help in the deception, and she disguises herself first as a doctor of mesmerism and later as a notary. The girls do eventually succumb to the persistent ardour of their new 'admirers', Fiordiligi more gradually than Dorabella, and a double wedding is planned. Alfonso has won his bet, the 'Albanians' unmask themselves, and the girls throw themselves on their lovers' mercy. Alfonso reveals the plot, and all is eventually sorted out in a spirit of understanding and reconciliation. [R]

Cossotto, Fiorenza (b 1935)
Italian mezzo, particularly associated with the Italian repertory, especially Verdi. The leading Italian dramatic mezzo of recent decades, she possessed a rich and powerful voice and was a compelling SINGING-ACTRESS, especially in roles such as Azucena and Amneris. She created Sister Mathilde in *Dialogues des Carmélites*. Married to the bass IVO VINCO.

Cossutta, Carlo (b 1932)
Italian-born Argentinian tenor, particularly associated with the Italian repertory. After a period singing lyrical roles, he turned with great success to the dramatic repertory, particularly Otello. Not only an exciting TENORE DI FORZA, he was also a fine musician and a sensitive artist. He created the title-role in Ginastera's *Don Rodrigo*.

Costa, Sir Michael (b Michele Andrea Agniello) (1808–84)
Italian-born British conductor and composer. As musical director of the King's Theatre, London (1833–46) and then of Covent Garden (1847–69), he was responsible for a vast improvement in the standard of operatic performance in Britain. He also composed a number of operas, all now long forgotten. They include *Il Delitto Punito* (Naples 1826), *Il Carcere d'Ildegonda* (Naples, 1827; libr Domenico Gilardoni), *Malvina* (Naples, Jan 1829; libr Giovanni Federico Schmidt), *Malek Adhel* (Paris, 14 Jan 1837; libr Carlo Pepoli, after Sir Walter Scott's *The Talisman*) and *Don Carlo* (London, 29 June 1844; libr Leopoldo Tarantini, after Friedrich von Schiller).

Cotrubas, Ileana (b 1939)
Romanian soprano, particularly associated with Mozart and lighter Italian roles. She possessed a beautiful and agile voice used with fine musicianship, and had a fragile and most affecting stage presence, particularly as Violetta in *La Traviata* and Mélisande in *Pelléas et Mélisande*. She was also an accomplished comedienne. Her husband **Manfred Ramin** is a conductor.

Council Chamber Scene
Act I Scene II of Verdi's *Simon Boccanegra*. One of the finest musico-dramatic scenes in all Italian opera, it was added for the revised version.

Counter-tenor
see panel on page 127

Countess Madeleine
Soprano role in Strauss's *Capriccio*. The Count's sister, she is courted by Olivier and Flamand.

Countess Maritza
see GRÄFIN MARIZA

Count of Luxembourg, The
see GRAF VON LUXEMBURG, DER

Count Ory
see COMTE ORY, LE

Coup de glotte (French for 'stroke of the glottis')
A method of vocal 'attack', which consists of the closing and immediate reopening of the false vocal chords (the two membrances above the real chords).

Couplet
A French term used in the 18th and 19th centuries to denote a two-verse song or aria in STROPHIC form, usually of a comic nature. Mostly found in operetta, an example is 'Ah! que j'aime les militaires' in Offenbach's *La Grande-Duchesse de Gérolstein.*

Covent Garden
see ROYAL OPERA HOUSE, COVENT GARDEN

Cover
The term has two meanings in opera: **1** A 'cover' is the understudy of a role. **2** Vocal tone that is 'covered' is gentler and more veiled in quality than that produced by open tone. It is produced when the voice is pitched in the soft palate.

Covetous Knight, The (*Skupoy Ritsar*)
Opera in one act by Rachmaninov (Op 24). 1st perf Moscow, 24 Jan 1906; a setting of Alexander Pushkin's play. Principal roles: Baron (bar), Albert (ten), Usurer (ten), Duke (bar). It is hardly ever performed outside Russia.
Plot: 18th-century Russia. The rake Albert cannot afford court clothes because of the stinginess of his father the Baron, who fears that Albert will squander his hoarded wealth. The Usurer refuses him further money, but Albert strongly rejects the Usurer's advice that he poison his father. He takes his case to the Duke, who is sympathetic. The Duke halts a violent quarrel between father and son, and Albert is sent away. However, the Baron discovers that he has lost the keys to his hoard and dies of shock. [R]

Cowen, Sir Frederick (1852–1935)
British composer. He wrote five stage works, beginning with the operetta *Garibaldi* (1860; libr R. Cowen), written at the age of eight. His four mature operas are *Pauline* (London, 22 Nov 1876; libr Henry Hersee, after Edward Bulwer Lytton's *The*

· Counter-Tenor ·

Counter-tenor was a rare male voice which had a naturally produced tone consisting almost exclusively of head voice. It was relatively common in Britain in the early 18th century, but subsequently all but disappeared. The term has been revived in the post-war era to describe – not entirely accurately – a male alto singing baroque music originally written for a CASTRATO, whose voice is produced by singing falsetto. The voice's range falls roughly between those of tenor and mezzo-soprano. The first operatic role written specifically for the modern counter-tenor voice was Oberon in *A Midsummer Night's Dream*. Subsequently several contemporary composers have written roles for the voice, notably Maxwell Davies (the Priest-Confessor in *Taverner*), Glass (Akhnaten) and Reimann (Edgar in *Lear*).

Below are listed the six counter-tenors with entries in this dictionary. Their nationalities are given in brackets afterwards.

Bowman, James (Br)	Esswood, Paul (Br)	Kowalski, Jochen (Ger)
Deller, Alfred (Br)	Jacobs, René (Belg)	Ragin, Derek Lee (US)

Lady of Lyons), *Thorgrim* (London, 22 Apr 1890; libr Joseph Bennett, after an Icelandic saga), *Signa* (Milan, 12 Nov 1893; libr Gilbert Arthur A'Beckett, H.A. Rudall and Frederick Edward Weatherly, after Ouida) and *Harold* (London, 8 June 1895; libr Edward Malet). His operas are all nowadays forgotten.

Cowie, Edward (b 1943)
British composer. He has written one opera, *Commedia* (Kassel, 10 June 1979; libr D. Starsmeare).

Cox, Jean (b 1932)
American tenor, particularly associated with Wagnerian roles, especially the title-role in *Siegfried*. One of the leading HELDENTENORS of the 1970s, he had a strong if not particularly tonally attractive voice. He created Ted Leroux in Stolz's *Trauminsel*.

Cox, John (b 1935)
British producer, particularly associated with Glyndebourne and with the English National Opera, where his productions of *Così fan Tutte* and *Patience* displayed his keen sense of characterization and his witty eye for detail. He was director of productions at Glyndebourne (1971–81), general administrator of Scottish Opera (1981–7) and is now production director at Covent Garden (1988–).

Cox and Box or **The Long-Lost Brothers**
Operetta in one act by Sullivan. 1st perf London, 26 May 1866; libr by Francis Cowley Burnand, after John Maddison Morton's *Box and Cox*. Principal roles: Box (ten), Cox (bar), Bouncer (b-bar). An entertaining little curtain-raiser, it is the only one of Sullivan's non-Gilbertian stage works still to be performed with any regularity.
Plot: 19th-century England. The ex-soldier Bouncer is renting one room to two people at once: the journeyman hatter Cox (who works all day) and the journeyman printer Box (who works all night). All goes well until Cox is given a day off, returns home and finds Box in 'his' room. A heated argument ensues and a duel is arranged on the basis that the pistols remain unloaded. All is resolved when the two realize that they are brothers. [R]

Craftsman of Clamecy, The (*Master iz Klamsi*)
Opera in three acts by Kabalevsky (Op 24/90). 1st perf Leningrad, 22 Feb 1938; libr by the composer and V.G. Bragin, after Romain Rolland's *Colas Breugnon*. Revised version 1st perf Leningrad, 16 April 1970. Principal roles: Colas (bar), Selina (mezzo), Duke (ten), Jacqueline (sop), Gifflard (bass), Curé (bass), de Termes (sop). Kabalevsky's most successful opera, it is hardly ever performed outside Russia, although the exciting overture is well known. The opera is sometimes called *Colas Breugnon*, although strictly this is only the title of the overture and the name of the protagonist.
Plot: 16th-century Burgundy. The sculptor Colas loves Selina, but Gifflard, who also loves her, spreads a rumour that Colas loves Mlle de Termes, a guest whom the tyrannical Duke d'Asnois has brought from Paris. Blind with jealousy, Selina tells the drunken Curé to marry her to Gifflard. Thirty years later, during which Colas has lived with his old love Jacqueline, the Duke takes Colas's sculpture of Selina to his castle. His soldiers bring a plague to the town, in which Jacqueline dies. Colas and Selina meet and are reunited. Gifflard tells the Duke that Colas is a rebel, and the Duke destroys the statue of Selina. Colas, furious at such wanton destruction of art, vows revenge. Pretending to be repentant, he offers to make a sculpture of the Duke. At its unveiling, it shows the Duke sitting back-to-front on a donkey. Publicly ridiculed and humiliated, the Duke retreats in shame to his castle. [R]

Craig, Charles (b 1920)
British tenor, particularly associated with the Italian repertory. He was virtually the only post-war British tenor able to sing the heavier Italian roles such as Verdi's Otello and Don Alvaro in *La Forza del Destino*. He enjoyed a remarkably long career, still singing Otello in his early 60s.

Credo in un dio crudel
Baritone aria for Iago in Act II of Verdi's *Otello*, in which he propounds his belief in a god of cruelty who has created him in his image. It is the opera's one substantial textual addition to Shakespeare.

Creon
The mythical Greek king of Corinth appears in many operas, including: **1** Bass role in Cherubini's and M.-A. Charpentier's *Médée*. **2** Baritone role in Orff's *Antigonae*. **3** Bass role in Mayr's *Medea in Corinto*. **4** Baritone role in Stravinsky's *Oedipus Rex*. **5** Baritone role in Honegger's *Antigone*. **6** Bass role in Haydn's *Orfeo ed Euridice*. **7** Tenor role in Leoncavallo's *Edipo Rè*. **8** Baritone role in Enescu's *Oedipe*.

Crescendo (Italian for 'growing')
It denotes an increase in loudness, usually built up repetitively. Giuseppe Mosca claimed to have first used the device in his *I Pretendenti Delusi* of 1811, although it has since been discovered in Domènech Terradellas's *Bellerofonte* of 1747. By far the best known examples are by Rossini, who used the device frequently and who was nicknamed 'Signor Crescendo'. The most famous usage is in Don Basilio's 'La calunnia' in *Il Barbiere di Siviglia*.

Crespel
Bass role in Offenbach's *Les Contes d'Hoffmann*. He is Antonia's father.

Crespin, Régine (b 1927)
French soprano, particularly associated with the French repertory, Wagner and Offenbach and with the title-role in *Tosca* and the Marschallin in *Der Rosenkavalier*. One of the finest sopranos of the post-war era, she possessed a warm and powerful voice and her exemplary diction made her attention to the text a particular asset. A sensitive and highly intelligent musician, she was also an outstanding comedienne. Later in her career she turned successfully to mezzo roles, notably the Old Prioress in *Dialogues des Carmélites*. She created a role in Tomasi's *Sampiero Corso*.

Crimi, Giulio (1885–1939)
Italian tenor, particularly associated with the Italian repertory. One of the leading tenors of the inter-war period, he created Luigi in *Il Tabarro*, Rinuccio in *Gianni Schicchi* and Paolo in Zandonai's *Francesca da Rimini*. He was later a noted teacher, whose pupils included Tito Gobbi.

Crispino e la Comare (*Crispin and the Fairy*)
Comic opera in four acts by L. and F. Ricci. 1st perf Venice, 28 Feb 1850; libr by Francesco Maria Piave, after S. Fabbrichesi's *Il Medico e la Morte*. Principal roles: Crispino (bar), Annetta (sop), Fabrizio (bar), Mirabolano (b-bar), Comare (mezzo), Contino del Fiore (ten), Don Asdrubale (bass). A delightful work, it is much the most successful of the Ricci brothers' collaborations and is the only Italian comic opera of any importance between *Don Pasquale* and *Falstaff*. It still receives an occasional performance.
Plot: 17th-century Venice. With the help of a fairy, Crispino becomes a wealthy physician. However, he grows arrogant and maltreats his wife Annetta. Matters go from bad to worse and he almost loses his life before finally repenting his behaviour.

Cristoforo Colombo (*Christopher Columbus*)
Opera in three (originally four) acts and epilogue by Franchetti. 1st perf Genoa, 6 Oct 1892; libr by Luigi Illica. Revised version 1st perf Milan, 17 Jan 1923. Principal roles: Colombo (bar), Don Roldano (bass), Isabella (sop), Guevara (ten), Anacoana (mezzo), Iguamota (sop). Franchetti's most grandiose opera, notable for its choral writing, it provides a fine vehicle for a star baritone. Written to commemorate the 400th anniversary of the discovery of the Americas, it was successful at its appearance but was soon forgotten. However, it has recently had a few revivals in connection with the Columbus quincentennial.
Plot: Spain, the Atlantic and Xaragua (Mexico), 1487–1506. The Council rejects Columbus's plan to reach the Indies by sailing westwards, but Queen Isabella overrules the decision. After a long voyage, the crew are about to mutiny and return home when land is sighted. Led by Roldano, the Spaniards despoil the natives of their gold. Columbus, horrified by the repression of the natives, orders Roldano's arrest. A skirmish develops during which Roldano kills the Aztec princess Anacoana, whose daughter Iguamota is loved by Columbus's aide Guevara. Spanish envoys arrive and – deceived by Roldano – arrest Columbus for planning to make himself

king of Mexico. After many years in prison, Columbus's spirit is broken, and after visiting Isabella's grave he dies in Guevara's arms. [R]

Critic, The or **An Opera Rehearsal**
Comic opera in two acts by Stanford (Op 144). 1st perf London, 14 Jan 1916; libr by Lewis Cairns James, after Richard Brindsley Sheridan's play. Principal roles: Puff (speaker), Tilburina (sop), Don Ferolo Wiskerandos (ten), Governor (bar), Sneer (speaker). Disposing of Sheridan's first act, it otherwise follows the play closely, with Puff becoming the composer and only *The Spanish Armada* sections being sung. Successful at its appearance, it is nowadays virtually forgotten.

Critics
see panel below

Croatian National Opera
The company was organized in its present form by Ivan Zajc in 1870. Performances are given at the National Theatre (cap 850) in Zagreb, which opened in 1895. Musical directors have included Gotovac, Milan Sachs, Lovro von Matačić and Vjekoslav Sutej.

Croatian opera composers
see BARANOVIĆ; GOTOVAC; ZAJC

Other national opera composers include Blagoje Bersa (1873–1934), Antun Dubronić (1878–1955), Josip Hatze (1879–1959), Vatroslav Lisinski (1819–54), whose *Love and Malice* (*Ljubav i Zloba*, 1845) was the first opera written to a Croatian libretto, Boris Papandopulo (1906–91) and Stjepan Šulek (1914–86).

Crociato in Egitto, Il (*The Crusader in Egypt*)
Opera in two acts by Meyerbeer. 1st perf Venice, 7 March 1824; libr by Gaetano Rossi. Principal roles: Armando (mezzo), Palmide (sop), Adriano (ten), Felicia (mezzo), Aladino (bass). Meyerbeer's first major success, written in imitation of Rossini's style, it contains in Armando the last significant role to be written for a castrato. Enormously popular in the 19th century, it is nowadays only very rarely performed.
Plot: Damietta (Egypt) during the Sixth Crusade. Armando d'Orville, a knight of Rhodes, has been left for dead in Egypt. Assuming a false name, he becomes an adviser to the Sultan Aladino, whose daughter Palmide he secretly marries and converts to Christianity. His uncle Adriano arrives to seek peace, and Armando's real identity is discovered. This leads to a battle and to the Christians being condemned to death. Armando saves Aladino's life during

· *Critics* ·

Opera critics are nearly as old as opera itself and have always played an important and occasionally crucial role in its development. The term is perhaps an unfortunate one, as the best critics do a great deal more than simply criticize: they are constructive in nurturing new talent and encouraging high artistic standards. Some, of course, have been merely destructive or reactionary: one critic has gone down in operatic history by saying of *Die Lustige Witwe* 'this isn't music'! Both singers and composers have had their tussles with the critics, but the avidity with which they still read them (and usually respect their views) is indication enough of their importance. Several composers have themselves been notable critics, particularly Berlioz, Serov and Thomson.

Below are listed the nine critics with entries in this dictionary. Their nationalities are given in brackets afterwards.

Chorley, Henry F. (Br)	Kerman, Joseph (US)	Porter, Andrew (Br)
Hanslick, Eduard (Ger)	Milnes, Rodney (Br)	Rosenthal, Harold (Br)
Jacobs, Arthur (Br)	Newman, Ernest (Br)	Stasov, Vladimir (Russ)

a coup attempt by the Grand Vizier, after which Aladino reunites Armando and Palmide and signs a peace treaty. [R]

Cross, Joan (1900–93)
British soprano, particularly associated with Sadler's Wells Opera and with the English Opera Group, of which she was a founder member. Possessing a lovely voice and having a good stage presence, she had a wide repertory but was especially associated with Mozart and Britten roles. She created the title-role in Gerhard's *The Duenna*, roles in Collingwood's *Macbeth* and Benjamin's *The Devil Take Her* and, for Britten, Ellen Orford in *Peter Grimes*, the Female Chorus in *The Rape of Lucretia*, Lady Billows in *Albert Herring*, Elizabeth I in *Gloriana* and Mrs Grose in *The Turn of the Screw*. She also produced a number of operas, was administrator of Sadler's Wells Opera and was a co-founder of the London Opera Centre.

Crosse, Gordon (b 1937)
British composer. He has written four operas. The powerful one-act *Purgatory* (Cheltenham, 7 July 1966; libr after William Butler Yeats) [R] was followed by the comedy *The Grace of Todd* (Aldeburgh, 7 June 1969; libr David Rudkin), *The Story of Vasco* (London, 13 Mar 1974; libr Ted Hughes, after Georges Schehadé) and the children's opera *Potter Thompson* (London, 9 Jan 1975; libr Alan Garner).

Crown Diamonds, The
see DIAMANTS DE LA COURONNE, LES

Crozier, Eric (1914–94)
British librettist and producer. He wrote the libretti for Berkeley's *Ruth* and Britten's *Albert Herring*, *The Little Sweep* and *Billy Budd* (the last in collaboration with E.M. Forster). He produced a number of Britten operas, including the first performances of *Peter Grimes* and *The Rape of Lucretia*, and was a co-founder of both the Aldeburgh Festival and the English Opera Group. His wife **Nancy Evans** (*b* 1915) was a successful mezzo, who created Nancy in *Albert Herring* and the Poet in Williamson's *The Growing Castle*.

Crucible, The
Opera in four acts by Ward. 1st perf New York, 26 Oct 1961; libr by Bernard Stambler, after Arthur Miller's play. Principal roles: Samuel Parris (ten), John Hale (bar), Thomas Putnam (bass), Betsy (sop), Tituba (mezzo). Ward's most successful opera, which has been widely performed, it is a conservative but theatrically highly effective setting of Miller's play about the witchcraft trials in 1692 in Salem, Massachusetts. [R]

Cruda funesta
Baritone aria for Enrico in Act I of Donizetti's *Lucia di Lammermoor*, in which he expresses his anger at reports that Lucia has been meeting his enemy Edgardo.

Cruda sorte
Mezzo aria for Isabella in Act I of Rossini's *L'Italiana in Algieri*, in which she laments her separation from Lindoro.

Crudel, perchè finora
Soprano/baritone duet for Susanna and Count Almaviva in Act III of Mozart's *Le Nozze di Figaro*, in which he persuades her to make an assignation in the garden.

Cruz-Romo, Gilda (b 1940)
Mexican soprano, particularly associated with the Italian repertory, especially Verdi. A lirico-spinto soprano of style and refinement, she possesses a beautiful voice of considerable power and has a sympathetic stage presence.

Csárdás
A Hungarian dance, divided into slow and fast sections. Much the most famous operatic example is Rosalinde's 'Klänge der Heimat' in J. Strauss's *Die Fledermaus*.

Csárdásfürstin, Die (*The Gypsy Princess*)
Operetta in three acts by Kálmán. 1st perf Vienna, 13 Nov 1915; libr by Leo Stein and Béla Jenbach. Principal roles: Sylvia (sop), Edwin (ten), Boni (ten), Stasi (sop), Feri (ten), Prince (bar). Arguably Kálmán's most successful work, it is still regularly performed.
Plot: Early-20th-century Budapest and Vienna. The café singer Sylvia Varescu is loved by Prince Edwin, despite their social disparity and his childhood understanding with Countess Stasi. Sylvia's manager

Count Boni pretends to be her husband, so that the family of his friend Edwin will find her acceptable. However, he manages to fall in love with Stasi. After much intrigue, Edwin's father discovers that his own wife had been on the stage prior to their marriage. He is thus in no position to offer any further objection to his son's marriage with Sylvia. At the same time, Boni weds Stasi. [R]

Cuban opera composers
These include José Mauri Estévez (1856–1937), Laureano Fuentes y Matons (1825–98), whose *La Hija de Jefté* (Santiago de Cuba, 16 May 1875; libr Antonio Arnao) was the first Cuban opera, Alejandro García-Caturla (1906–40), Amadeo Roldán (1900–39), Eduardo Sánchez de Fuentes (1874–1944), Guillermo Tomás (1868–1933) and Gaspar Villate (1851–91).

Cuénod, Hughes (b 1902)
Swiss tenor, particularly associated with character roles, especially in early and 20th-century operas. Beginning as a nightclub singer, he possessed a highly invidual voice and stage manner and was an artist of outstanding intelligence and musicianship. He created Sellem in *The Rake's Progress* and a role in Martin's *Le Mystère de la Nativité*. He enjoyed one of the longest careers in operatic history, making his debut at the Metropolitan Opera, New York, at the age of 85 and continuing to sing for a while afterwards.

Cui, César (1835–1918)
Russian composer and soldier. A number of his operas met with considerable success in their time, but virtually none of them are remembered today. As well as four children's operas, his stage works are *The Captive of the Caucasus* (St Petersburg, 16 Feb 1883, begun 1857; libr Viktor Krylov, after Alexander Pushkin), *The Mandarin's Son* (St Petersburg, 19 Dec 1878, composed 1859; libr Krylov), WILLIAM RATCLIFF, his finest work, his contribution to the collective opera-ballet MLADA, *Angelo* (St Petersburg, 13 Feb 1876; libr Viktor Burenin, after Victor Hugo's *Angélo Tyran de Padoue*), *Le Filibustier* (Paris, 22 Jan 1894; libr Jean Richepin), *The Saracen* (St Petersburg, 14 Nov 1899; libr after Alexandre Dumas's *Charles VII Chez ses Grands Vassaux*), *A Feast in Time of Plague* (Moscow, 11 Nov 1901; libr after Pushkin), *Mam'selle Fifi* (Moscow, 15 Dec 1903; libr composer, after Guy de Maupassant), *Matteo Falcone* (Moscow, 27 Dec 1907; libr Vasily Zhukovsky, after Prosper Mérimée's *Mosaïque*) and *The Captain's Daughter* (St Petersburg, 27 Feb 1911; libr composer, after Pushkin).

With Balakierev, Cui was the co-founder of the Russian nationalist school of composers known as the MIGHTY HANDFUL. If he was its musically least talented member, he made up for this lack by his tireless championing of his contemporaries' music, and helped to complete Moussorgsky's *Sorochintsy Fair* and Dargomijsky's *The Stone Guest*. Like his contemporaries, he was a self-taught amateur, being a soldier by profession. A gifted military engineer, he rose to the rank of full general and wrote a standard textbook on military fortifications.

Cunning Little Vixen, The (*Příhody Lišky Bystroušky*)
Opera in three acts by Janáček. 1st perf Brno, 6 Nov 1924; libr by the composer, after Rudolf Těsnohlídek's verses for drawings by Stanislav Lolek. Principal roles: Vixen (sop), Forester (bar), Fox (sop), Harašta (b-bar), Schoolteacher (ten), Parson (bass), Forester's Wife (mezzo), Badger (bass), Cock (mezzo). One of Janáček's greatest works, its story allowed him to celebrate his love of nature and his fascination with the musical qualities of its sounds. The human and animal worlds are beautifully balanced and interwoven, and the overall effect is enchanting and moving without ever being cloying. Initially slow to make its way, it has been widely performed in recent years and has become one of the most popular of all Czech operas.
Plot: Early-20th-century Moravia. The Forester captures the vixen Sharpears and tries to domesticate her. She escapes by fomenting a revolt amongst the hens, takes over the Badger's home and marries the Fox. After raising a family, she is shot by the poacher Harašta. Seeing a vixen cub in the forest, the Forester dreams of the endless renewal of nature. [R]

Cunning Peasant, The (*Šelma Sedlák*)
Comic opera in two acts by Dvořák. (Op

37). 1st perf Prague, 27 Jan 1878; libr by Josef Otakar Veselý. Principal roles: Martin (bass), Bětuška (sop), Prince (bar), Princess (sop), Veruna (mezzo), Václav (ten), Jeník (ten). Dvořák's first major success, it is still sometimes performed in the Czech lands, but is almost unknown elsewhere. [R]

Cuno
Bass role in Weber's *Der Freischütz*. Agathe's father, he is the head forester.

Curlew River
Opera in one act by Britten (Op 71). 1st perf Orford, 13 June 1964; libr by William Plomer, after Juro Motomasa's Japanese Noh play *The Sumida River*. Principal roles: Madwoman (ten), Ferryman (bar), Traveller (bar), Abbot (bass). The first of Britten's *Three Church Parables*, it is a highly stylized mystery play of great musical concentration, requiring an orchestra of only seven players. The action is transposed from Japan to the English Fenlands and is given a Christian interpretation.
Plot: Medieval East Anglia. A Traveller joins a group of pilgrims waiting to cross the river. A Madwoman arrives and asks the Ferryman to be taken on board as she is seeking her lost son. During the crossing, the Ferryman tells how a year ago a boy was left to die in the area by a cruel heathen master and that miracles have been reported at his grave. The Madwoman realizes that the boy was her son and receives comfort at his grave. [R]

Curtin, Phyllis (b Smith) (b 1922)
American soprano, particularly associated with Mozart roles and with 20th century works. A fine singing-actress, she created three roles in Einem's *Der Prozess*, Rosina in Milhaud's *La Mère Coupable* and, for Floyd, the title-role in *Susannah* and Cathy in *Wuthering Heights*.

Curzio, Don
Tenor COMPRIMARIO role in Mozart's *Le Nozze di Figaro*. He is a stammering lawyer.

Cuts
The shortening of operas by the removal of some of the music is a depressingly frequent practice in major opera houses, those who sanction them having the presumption of considering that they know better than the composer the length required. In Italian opera, cuts usually take the form of lopping a verse off a CABALETTA, but sometimes extend to whole numbers or even entire scenes; almost a quarter of *Lucia di Lammermoor* is often cut when performed at Covent Garden. Such disfigurement of major works cannot be in any way condoned.

Cuzzoni, Francesca (c 1700–70)
Italian soprano, noted for her singing of soulful and lachrymose music. One of the greatest singers of her age, she created, for Händel, Teofane in *Ottone*, Emilia in *Flavio*, Antigone in *Admeto*, Cleopatra in *Giulio Cesare*, Asteria in *Tamerlano*, the title-role in *Rodelinda* and Lisaura in *Alessandro*. Her rivalry with FAUSTINA BORDONI led to the famous incident in 1727 when the two fell to fighting on stage during Bononcini's *Astianatte*. Despite the huge fees she was paid, she was imprisoned for a while in Holland for debt, and eventually returned to Italy, becoming a button-maker and dying in extreme poverty.

Cyrano de Bergerac
Opera in four acts by Damrosch. 1st perf New York, 27 Feb 1913; libr by William James Henderson, after Edmond Rostand's play. Principal roles: Cyrano (bar), Roxane (sop), Christian (ten). Damrosch's most successful opera, it is nowadays forgotten.

Cyrano de Bergerac
Opera in four acts by Alfano. 1st perf Rome, 22 Jan 1936; libr by Henri Cain, after Edmond Rostand's play. Principal roles: Cyrano (ten), Roxane (sop), Christian (ten), de Guiche (bar). Reasonably successful in its time, it is nowadays only very rarely performed.
Plot: Paris and Arras, *c* 1640. Cyrano, a noble knight with a large nose, is secretly in love with his cousin Roxane. She, however, loves the soldier Christian. She discovers too late that Christian's passionate love letters were actually written by Cyrano.

Czech opera composers
see BENATZKY; BENDA; BENDL; BLODEK; BURIAN; DVOŘÁK; FIBICH; FOERSTER; GASSMANN; HÁBA; HANUŠ; JANÁČEK; JEREMIÁŠ; JIRKO; JÍROVEC; KAREL; KOVAŘOVIC; KRÁSA; KREJČÍ; KUBELÍK; MARTINŮ; MYSLIVEČEK; NOVÁK; OSTRČIL; PAUER; ŠKROUP; SMETANA; STAMITZ; ULLMANN; WEINBERGER

Other national opera composers include Osvald Chlubna (1895–1971), Ján Fischer (*b* 1921), Karel Horký (1909–88), Ilja Hurník (*b* 1922), Ivo Jirásek (*b* 1920), Jaroslav Křička (1882–1969), Josef Rozkošný (1833–1913), Karel Šebor (1843–1905), Zbyněk Vostřák (1920–85) and Otakar Zich (1879–1934). *See also* SLOVAKIAN OPERA COMPOSERS

Czech Republic
see BRNO OPERA; OLOMOUC OPERA; OSTRAVA OPERA; PLZEŇ OPERA; PRAGUE NATIONAL THEATRE

Czerwenka, Oskar (b 1924)
Austrian bass, particularly associated with German comic roles. A rich-voiced singer with a fine stage presence, he was one of the finest Germanic BUFFOS of the post-war period. He created the title-role in Klebe's *Jakobowsky und der Oberst* and two roles in Einem's *Der Prozess.*

Czipra
Mezzo role in J. Strauss's *Der Zigeunerbaron.* Saffi's foster-mother, she is a gypsy fortune-teller.

D

D', Da
Names containing these prefixes are listed under the letter of the main surname. For example, Vincent d'Indy is listed under I and Lorenzo da Ponte is listed under P.

Da capo (Italian for 'from the head')
An aria in an 18th-century OPERA SERIA, with the structure A–B–A decorated. The second A was often not written out, the singer being given the instruction 'da capo'; in other words, back to the beginning. The best known da capo arias are in Händel's operas. A variant form is the DAL SEGNO aria, in which only a specified part of the first section is repeated.

Dafne
Opera in prologue and six scenes by Peri. 1st perf Florence, 1597; libr by Ottavio Rinuccini, after Ovid's *Metamorphoses.* Usually regarded as the first ever opera, the music is lost.

Dafne
Opera by Caccini. Composed *c* 1597; libr by Ottavio Rinuccini, after Ovid's *Metamorphorses.* The second opera to be composed, it was possibly never performed and its music is lost.

Dafne
Opera-ballet in prologue and six scenes by Gagliano. 1st perf Mantua, Jan 1608; libr by Ottavio Rinuccini, after Ovid's *Metamorphoses.* Principal roles: Dafne (sop), Apollo (ten), Love (sop), Tirsi (ten), Ovid (ten), Venus (sop). One of the earliest operas to have survived, it is written largely in madrigal style.
Plot: Legendary Greece. Apollo pursues the Python and shoots it to death with arrows, and is then himself wounded by the arrows of Cupid. He pursues the nymph Daphne, but she – through the machinations of Cupid – is turned into a laurel tree just before he can catch her. Her loss is lamented by Apollo and Tirsi. [R]

Dafne
Opera in prologue and five acts by Schütz. 1st perf Torgau, 23 April 1627; libr by Martin Optiz, after Ottavio Rinuccini's libretto for Peri, itself based on Ovid's *Metamorphoses.* The earliest German opera, the music is lost.

Dagl' immortali vertici
Baritone aria for Ezio in Act II of Verdi's *Attila*, in which he laments the decline of Roman power.

Dai campi
Tenor aria for Faust in Act I of Boito's *Mefistofele*, in which he hails the calm brought on by the night.

Dal
Names containing this prefix are listed under the letter of the main surname. For example, Toti dal Monte is listed under M.

Daland
Bass role in Wagner's *Der Fliegende Holländer.* Senta's father, he is a Norwegian sea captain.

Dalayrac, Nicolas (1753–1809)
French composer. He wrote 61 stage works, most of them light comedies and all of them now forgotten. His operas include *L'Éclipse Totale* (Paris, 7 Mar 1782; libr A.E.X. Poisson de la Chabeaussière, after Jean de la Fontaine), *Nina ou la Folle par Amour* (Paris, 15 May 1786; libr Benoît Joseph Marsollier), his most successful work, and *Tout Pour l'Amour* (Paris, 7 July 1796; libr J.M. Boutet de Monvel, after Shakespeare's *Romeo and Juliet*).

Dalibor
Opera in three acts by Smetana. 1st perf Prague, 16 May 1868; libr by Josef Wenzig and Ervín Špindler. Principal roles: Dalibor (ten), Milada (sop), Vladislav (bar), Beneš (bass), Budivoj (bar), Jitka (sop), Vítek (ten). Arguably Smetana's

masterpiece, it is one of the finest of all RESCUE OPERAS, and is sometimes referred to as the Czech *Fidelio*. Richly melodic with a powerful dramatic sweep, it has always had strong associations with Czech consciousness and aspirations, and its intense nationalism has perhaps been the reason why this noble and magnificent work is only seldom performed outside the Czech lands.
Plot: Late-15th-century Prague. The knight Dalibor has killed a burgrave in revenge for the killing of his friend Zdeněk. King Vladislav sentences him to life imprisonment. His main accuser, the burgrave's daughter Milada, is moved to pity and then to love by his noble bearing. She disguises herself as a boy and works as an assistant to the jailer Beneš at Dalibor's prison. She and Dalibor meet, fall in love and plan an escape. They are discovered, however, and after much hesitation the King alters Dalibor's sentence to immediate death. His supporters, led by Jitka and Vítek, wait outside to attack. Dalibor brings in Milada, who has been wounded and who dies in his arms. Dalibor stabs himself just before the captain of the guard Budivoj arrives with his troops. [R]

Dalila
Mezzo role in Saint-Saëns's *Samson et Dalila*. She is a beautiful Philistine who tempts Samson.

Dal labbro
Tenor aria for Fenton in Act III of Verdi's *Falstaff*, in which he hopes that his song will be echoed from his beloved's lips.

Dallapiccola, Luigi (1904–75)
Italian composer and pianist. Arguably the leading post-war Italian composer, his music presents a mixture of serial and more traditional and lyrical techniques. His first opera VOLO DI NOTTE was followed by the powerful IL PRIGIONIERO, his masterpiece, the dramatic oratorio JOB and ULISSE. His writings on opera include *Parole e' Musica* (1980).

Dallas Civic Opera
Founded in Nov 1957 by Lawrence Kelly (*d* 1974), it gives annual seasons in the Spring and again in November and December with top international casts at the Fair Park Music Hall (cap 3,420). The repertory tends to be conservative, with a preponderance of Italian works. Musical directors have included Nicola Rescigno and Graeme Jenkins.

Dalla sua pace
Tenor aria for Don Ottavio in Act I of Mozart's *Don Giovanni*, in which he says that his own future depends upon that of Donna Anna.

Dal segno (Italian for 'from the sign')
A modification of a DA CAPO aria, in which only a part of the first section (from a point indicated by a sign in the score) is repeated.

Dam, José van (b Joseph van Damme) (b 1940)
Belgian baritone, particularly associated with Mozart, the French repertory and 20th-century works. One of the finest contemporary operatic artists, he has an incisive voice which is used with outstanding intelligence and musicianship, and he is a powerful and committed singing-actor. His vocal range is wide enough to allow him to sing a number of bass roles, such as King Philip. He created the title-role in Messiaen's *Saint François d'Assise*, Pisandro in Dallapiccola's *Ulisse* and a role in Milhaud's *La Mère Coupable*.

Dama Boba, La (*The Confused Lady*)
Comic opera in three acts by Wolf-Ferrari. 1st perf Milan, 1 Feb 1939; libr by Mario Ghisalberti, after Félix Lope de Vega's play. It tells of a silly girl who, becoming sensible when she falls in love, has to pretend still to be silly to get her own way. Reasonably successful at its appearance, nowadays only the charming overture is at all remembered.

Dame Blanche, La (*The White Lady*)
Opera in three acts by Boïeldieu. 1st perf Paris, 10 Dec 1825; libr by Eugène Scribe, after Sir Walter Scott's *Guy Mannering, The Abbot* and *The Monastery*. Principal roles: George (ten), Anna (sop), Dickson (bar), Gaveston (b-bar), Jenny (sop), Marguerite (mezzo). Boïeldieu's finest and most enduring work, which contains some traditional Scottish melodies, it was

enormously popular throughout the 19th century: it reached its 1,000th performance at the Opéra-Comique, Paris, in 1864. It still receives an occasional performance.
Plot: Scotland, 1759. In a castle on the estate of the late Count Avenel is a mysterious White Lady, who the farmer Dickson has promised to serve. He tells the story to George Brown, a young English officer, who offers to answer a summons from the White Lady in place of Dickson. She turns out to be Anna, ward of the Count's steward Gaveston, whom she is determined to prevent from acquiring the estate. Relying on money to be provided by the 'ghost' from hidden family treasure, Brown – following the White Lady's instructions – outbids Gaveston at the auction for the estate. Anna reveals both her identity and the fact that Brown is actually the long-lost Avenel heir. [R]

Damnation de Faust, La
Dramatic legend in four parts by Berlioz (Op 24). 1st perf Paris, 6 Dec 1846; 1st stage perf Monte Carlo, 18 Feb 1893; libr by the composer and Almire Gandonnière, after Gérard de Nerval's version of Johann von Goethe's *Faust.* Principal roles: Faust (ten), Marguerite (mezzo), Méphistophélès (b-bar), Brander (bass). Despite its elements of strong theatricality, Berlioz never intended the work to be an opera. It is, however, frequently staged.
Plot: 16th-century Hungary and Germany. Faust trades his soul with Méphistophélès in exchange for youth, and embarks on a life of debauchery and military glory. He seduces and then abandons the beautiful Marguerite, and is finally transported to Hell, whilst Marguerite is redeemed. [R]

Damrosch, Walter (1862–1950)
German-born American conductor and composer. A leading interpreter of the German repertory, he introduced many of Wagner's operas to the United States and formed his own company, the Damrosch Opera Company, which performed Wagner with top casts between 1894 and 1899. He also wrote four operas: *The Scarlet Letter* (Boston, 11 Feb 1896; libr George Parsons Latrop, after Nathaniel Hawthorne), *The Dove of Peace* (Philadelphia, 15 Oct 1912; libr Wallace Irwin), CYRANO DE BERGERAC and *The Man Without a Country* (New York, 12 May 1937; libr Arthur Guiterman, after Edward Everett Hale). His autobiography, *My Musical Life*, was published in 1923. His father **Leopold** (1832–85) was also a leading conductor of the German repertory.

Danaïdes, Les
Opera in five acts by Salieri. 1st perf Paris, 26 April 1784; libr by Marie François Bailly Leblanc du Roullet and Baron Louis Théodore de Tchudy, partly after Ranieri de' Calzabigi's *Ippermestra.* Principal roles: Hypermnestre (sop), Danaüs (bass), Lyncée (ten), Plancippe (sop), Pélagus (bar). Originally thought to have been written by Gluck, and written under the influence of Gluck's reform ideas, it is one of Salieri's finest and most powerful operas. Very successful in its time, it is nowadays only rarely performed.
Plot: Legendary Greece. To end the feud between their families, the 50 daughters of Danaus are to wed the 50 sons of Aegyptus, and Danaus's eldest daughter Hypermnestra looks forward to future happiness with Lynceus, her beloved. Danaus tells his daughters that the reconciliation is a sham on Aegyptus's part, and he orders his daughters to kill their husbands on the wedding night. All obey except Hypermnestra, torn between love and filial duty. Danaus curses her. At Pelagus's signal, the women murder their husbands, but Lynceus escapes. As a force under Lynceus attacks the palace, Danaus has Hypermnestra led out for sacrifice, but he is killed by Pelagus before he can carry out the deed. Lightning strikes and destroys the palace. In the underworld, Danaus is chained to a rock with his entrails being eaten by a vulture and his daughters suffer the torments of the Furies. [R]

Dancairo
Baritone role in Bizet's *Carmen*. He is a smuggler.

Dance
see BALLET

Dance of the Apprentices
Dance in Act III of Wagner's *Die Meistersinger von Nürnberg.*

Dance of the Blessed Spirits
Dance in Act II of Gluck's *Orfeo ed Euridice.*

Dance of the Comedians
Dance in Act III of Smetana's *The Bartered Bride.*

Dance of the Hours
Ballet music in Act III of Ponchielli's *La Gioconda.*

Dance of the Seven Veils
Salome's dance for Herod in Strauss's *Salome.*

Dance of the Tumblers
Dance in: **1** Act III of Rimsky-Korsakov's *The Snow Maiden.* **2** Act I of Tchaikovsky's *The Enchantress.*

Dance types
see BOLERO; CAN-CAN; CSÁRDÁS; FURIANT; GALOP; GAVOTTE; GOPAK; HABAÑERA; HORNPIPE; JOTA; POLKA; POLONAISE; TARANTELLA

Danco, Suzanne (b 1911)
Belgian soprano, particularly associated with Mozart roles and with 20th-century operas. She possessed a clear and cool voice, which she used with fine musicianship and great versatility.

Dandini
Baritone role in Rossini's *La Cenerentola.* He is Don Ramiro's valet.

Daniel, Paul (b 1959)
British conductor, whose wide-ranging repertory encompasses Monteverdi to Reimann. A fine interpreter of 20th-century opera, he conducted the first performance of Michael Berkeley's *Baa Baa Black Sheep.* He was musical director of Opera Factory (1987–90) and Opera North (1990–). His wife **Joan Rodgers** (*b* 1956) is a successful Mozartian soprano.

Danish opera composers
see ENNA; GADE; HEISE; KLENAU; KUHLAU; NIELSEN; WEYSE

Other national opera composers include Niels Bentzon (*b* 1919), Hakon Børresen (1876–1954), Asger Hamerik (1843–1923), his son Ebbe (1898–1951), Johann Ernest Hartmann (1726–93), his grandson Johann Peter Emilius (1808–1900), Finn Høffding (*b* 1899), Vagn Holmboe (*b* 1909), Christian Horneman (1840–1906), Friedrich Ludwig Kunzen (1761–1817), Peter Lange-Müller (1850–1926), Per Nørgård (*b* 1932) and Knudåge Riisager (1897–1974).

Dankevich, Konstantin (1905–84)
Ukrainian composer. He wrote three operas: *Tragic Night* (*Trahediina Nich,* Odessa, 1935; libr composer and V. Ivanovich, after O. Bezymensky), *Bogdan Khmelnitsky* (Moscow, 15 June 1951; libr V. Vasylevska, after Olexander Korniychuk) [R], perhaps the most successful post-war Ukrainian opera, and *Nazar Stodolya* (Kharkov, 28 May 1960; libr L. Predslavich, after T.H. Shevchenko).

Danon, Oskar (b 1913)
Serbian conductor, particularly associated with the Russian repertory. One of the finest interpreters of Russian opera of the immediate post-war period, he was musical director of the Belgrade Opera (1945–63).

Dansker
Bass role in Britten's *Billy Budd.* He is an old sailor.

Dante
see panel on page 139

Dantons Tod (*Danton's Death*)
Opera in two parts by Einem (Op 6). 1st perf Salzburg, 6 Aug 1947; libr by the composer and Boris Blacher, after Georg Büchner's play. Principal roles: Danton (bar), Robspierre (ten), Camille and Lucille Desmoulins (ten and sop). Dealing with the last days of the French revolutionary leader Georges Jacques Danton (1759–94), it is Einem's first opera and one of his most successful works, and has been widely performed.
Plot: Paris, 1794. Disillusioned by the course taken by the Revolution, Danton delivers fiery speeches of public denunciation. He is arrested on the orders of Robspierre, tried by a revolutionary

· Dante ·

The Italian poet Dante Alighieri (1265–1321) himself appears as an operatic character in Rachmaninov's *Francesca da Rimini*, Godard's *Dante et Béatrice* and in operas by four minor composers. His trilogy *La Divina Commedia* has inspired some 25 operas, most of them based on the Francesca da Rimini episode in *L'Inferno*. Below are listed those operas by composers with entries in this dictionary.

Mercadante	*Francesca da Rimini*	1828
Generali	*Francesca da Rimini*	1829
Morlacchi	*Francesca da Rimini*	1836
Götz	*Francesca von Rimini*	1877 (U)
Cagnoni	*Francesca da Rimini*	1878
Thomas	*Françoise de Rimini*	1882
Nápravník	*Francesca da Rimini*	1902
Rachmaninov	*Francesca da Rimini*	1906
Mancinelli	*Paolo e Francesca*	1907
Ábrányi	*Paolo és Francesca*	1912
Zandonai	*Francesca da Rimini*	1914
Leoni	*Francesca da Rimini*	1914
Puccini	*Gianni Schicchi*	1918

tribunal and condemned to death. At his execution, the mob hails his death with singing and dancing. [R]

Dapertutto
Baritone role in Offenbach's *Les Contes d'Hoffmann*. He is a sinister magician in the Giulietta Act.

Daphne
Opera in one act by Strauss (Op 82). 1st perf Dresden, 15 Oct 1938; libr by Josef Gregor, partly after Ovid's *Metamorphoses*. Principal roles: Daphne (sop), Apollo (ten), Leukippos (ten), Gaea (mezzo), Peneios (bass). Described as a 'bucolic comedy', it contains some glorious music (notably in the final transformation scene), but has never been one of Strauss's more popular operas and is only infrequently performed.
Plot: Legendary Thessaly. Daphne, daughter of the fisherman Peneios, prefers nature to men. She rejects the shepherd Leukippos, for which her mother Gaea berates her. Enchanted by her beauty, Apollo appears in human form, but his ardour frightens and bewilders her. Apollo kills Leukippos in jealousy, but when he perceives Daphne's despair, he pleads with Zeus to change her into one of the trees she so loves. Gradually, she is transformed into a laurel tree. [R]

Dara, Enzo (b 1938)
Italian bass, particularly associated with comic Italian roles, especially Rossini. One of the leading contemporary BUFFOS, he has a good stage presence, although his voice is far from outstanding.

Darclée, Hariclea (b Hiracly Hartulary) (1860–1939)
Romanian soprano, particularly associated with the Italian and French repertories. Considered by Italians to have had a voice very similar to that of Lilli Lehmann, she created the title-roles in *Tosca*, *La Wally* and *Iris* and Luisa in Mascagni's *I Rantzau*. Her son **Ion Hartulary-Darclée** (1886–1969) was a conductor who also composed nine operas.

Dardanus
Opera in prologue and five acts by Rameau. 1st perf Paris, 19 Nov 1739; libr by Charles-Antoine Leclerc de la Bruyère. Principal roles: Dardanus (ten), Iphise (mezzo), Isménor (bar), Vénus (mezzo), Anténor (bar), Teucer (bass). One of

Rameau's finest operas, it is still performed from time to time.
Plot: Legendary Phrygia. Iphise loves Dardanus, the son of Jupiter. Her father King Teucer wishes her to marry Anténor. After a number of fantastical episodes, including much magic and a monster, Anténor renounces his claim to Iphise and she is united with Dardanus. [R]

Dargomijsky, Alexander (1813–69)
Russian composer. Like many 19th-century Russian composers, he was largely an amateur; Tchaikovsky described him as the 'supreme example of the dilettante in music'. His first opera *Esmeralda* (Moscow, 17 Dec 1847, composed 1840; libr composer, after Victor Hugo's *Notre-Dame de Paris*) is in French grand opera style and was fairly well received. Its successor, the opera-ballet *The Triumph of Bacchus* (*Torzhestvo Vakha*, Moscow, 11 Jan 1867, composed 1848; libr after Alexander Pushkin), was a failure. Of far greater substance was RUSALKA, which displays considerable wit and powers of characterization. His last opera was the unfinished THE STONE GUEST (completed by Cui and Rimsky-Korsakov), which is an experimental work, being a verbatim setting of an existing play and employing melodic recitative throughout. It exerted considerable influence on subsequent Russian composers, particularly Moussorgsky.

Darmstadt Opera
The Grosses Haus (cap 956) in this German town in Hesse-Darmstadt opened in 1972, replacing the previous theatre which opened in 1819 but which was destroyed by bombs in 1944. Musical directors have included Karl Böhm, Michael Balling and Gerd Albrecht.

Das
Titles beginning with this form of the German definite article are listed under the letter of the first main word. For example, *Das Rheingold* is listed under R.

Daughter of the Regiment, The
see FILLE DU RÉGIMENT, LA

Dauvergne, Antoine (1713–97)
French composer. He wrote a number of operas which met with some success in their time but which are nowadays largely forgotten. The most significant include the historically important LES TROQUEURS, which was the first French opera modelled on the Italian INTERMEZZO style, *La Coquette Trompée* (Fontainebleau, 13 Nov 1753; libr Charles-Simon Favart) [R], *Énée et Lavinie* (Paris, 14 Feb 1758; libr Bernard de Fontenelle, after Virgil), *Hercule Mourant* (Paris, 3 Apr 1761; libr Jean-François Marmontel) and *Pyrhhus et Polyxène* (Paris, 11 Jan 1763; libr N.-R. Joliveau).

David
Opera in five acts by Milhaud (Op 320). 1st perf (in concert) Jerusalem, 1 June 1954; 1st stage perf Milan, 2 Jan 1955; libr by Armand Lunel, after the Book of Samuel in the Old Testament. Principal roles: David (bar), Saul (bass), Bathsheba (sop), Jesse (bass), Goliath (bass), Samuel (bass). Written to commemorate the 3,000th anniversary of the founding of Jerusalem, it contains some fine music but is almost never performed.

David
1 Tenor role in Wagner's *Die Meistersinger von Nürnberg*. He is Hans Sachs's apprentice. **2** Baritone role in Mascagni's *L'Amico Fritz*. He is a rabbi. 3 Tenor role in Nielsen's *Saul og David* and counter-tenor role in Händel's *Saul*. He is Jonathan's friend. **4** Baritone role in Milhaud's *David*.

David, Félicien-César (1810–76)
French composer. His travels in the East inspired the oriental subjects of his operas and started the fashion for exotic orientalism in French opera continued by Delibes, Bizet, Gounod and Rabaud. His graceful and melodic operas enjoyed great success in their time but are nowadays largely forgotten. The most important are *La Perle du Brésil* (Paris, 22 Nov 1851; libr J. Gabriel and S. Saint-Étienne), *Herculanum* (Paris, 4 Mar 1859; libr François Joseph Méry and T. Hadot), *Lalla Roukh* (Paris, 12 May 1862; libr H. Lucas and Michel Carré, after Thomas Moore) and *Le Saphir* (Paris, 8 Mar 1865; libr Carré, Hadot and Adolphe de Leuven, after Shakespeare's *All's Well That Ends Well*).

Davide, Giovanni (1790–1864)
Italian tenor. Regarded by Stendhal as the finest tenor of his generation, he had an extraordinary range of b♭ to b♭ above high c. For Rossini he created the title-role in *Otello*, Don Narciso in *Il Turco in Italia*, Ilo in *Zelmira*, Ricciardo in *Ricciardo e Zoraide*, Oreste in *Ermione* and Giacomo in *La Donna del Lago*. After his voice failed in 1841, he taught in Naples and then became opera manager in St Petersburg. His father **Giacomo** (1750–1830) was also a successful tenor, and his daughter **Giuseppina** (1821–1907) was a soprano.

David et Jonathas
Opera in prologue and five acts by M.-A. Charpentier, 1st perf Paris, 28 Feb 1688; libr by Père François Bretonneau, after the Book of Samuel in the Old Testament. Principal roles: David (c-ten), Jonathan (sop), Saul (bass), Joabel (ten), Achish (bass), Prophetess (c-ten), Ghost of Samuel (bass). Charpentier's penultimate opera, it is a magnificent work containing some fine musical characterization, and is the finest example of the musico-religious dramas sponsored at that time by the Jesuits. After nearly 300 years of neglect, it has recently received a number of performances. [R]

Davies, Peter Maxwell
see MAXWELL DAVIES, SIR PETER

Davies, Ryland (b 1943)
British tenor, particularly associated with Mozart and lighter Italian and French roles. He possesses a small but pleasant and well-schooled voice and is an accomplished singing-actor, especially in comedy. Married for a time to the mezzo ANNE HOWELLS; his second wife, **Deborah Rees** is a soprano.

Davis, Andrew (b 1944)
British conductor, particularly associated with Strauss, Janáček and other 20th-century operas. One of the finest of the younger generation of British conductors, his operatic appearances were infrequent until the late 1980s. Musical director of the Glyndebourne Festival (1988–). His wife **Gianna Rolandi** (*b* 1952) is a successful COLORATURA soprano.

Davis, Anthony (b 1951)
American composer. One of the most significant contemporary black composers, his stage works employ a variety of musical styles, ranging from atonality to jazz and rap. His operas include X: THE LIFE AND TIMES OF MALCOLM X, *Under the Double Moon* (St Louis, 15 June 1989; libr Deborah Atherton) and *Tania* (Philadelphia, June 1992), which is about Patti Hearst.

Davis, Sir Colin (b 1927)
British conductor, particularly associated with Mozart, Stravinsky, post-war British operas and, especially, Berlioz, of whose music he is often regarded as the greatest living interpreter. One of the outstanding post-war British opera conductors, he co-founded the Chelsea Opera Group and was musical director of Sadler's Wells Opera (1961–5) and Covent Garden (1971–86). He conducted the first performances of *The Knot Garden*, *The Ice Break* and Bennett's *The Mines of Sulphur*, and in 1977 became the first British conductor to appear at the Bayreuth Festival. His first wife **April Cantelo** (*b* 1928) was a successful soprano, who created Helena in *A Midsummer Night's Dream* and, for Williamson, Beatrice in *Our Man in Havana*, the Swallow in *The Happy Prince*, Ann in *Julius Caesar Jones* and Berthe in *The Violins of St Jacques*.

De
Names containing this prefix are listed under the letter of the main surname. For example, Victoria de los Angeles is listed under A.

Death
Death appears as a character in a number of operas, including: **1** Baritone role in Holst's *Sāvitri*. **2** Contralto role in Stravinsky's *The Nightingale*. **3** Bass-baritone role in Ullmann's *Der Kaiser von Atlantis*. **4** Counter-tenor role in Alan Ridout's *The Pardoner's Tale*. **5** Bass role in Balassa's *The Man Outside*. **6** Counter-tenor role in Penderecki's *Paradise Lost*.

Death in Venice
Opera in two acts by Britten (Op 88). 1st

perf Snape, 16 June 1973; libr by Myfanwy Piper, after Thomas Mann's *Der Tod in Venedig*. Principal roles: Aschenbach (ten), Traveller (bar; multiple role), Voice of Apollo (c-ten), Tadzio (dancer). Britten's last opera, it is notable for the prominent place ascribed within the drama to dance.
Plot: Munich and Venice, 1911. The writer Gustav von Aschenbach, despairing of his creative paralysis, travels south to the sun. He finds himself attracted to the young boy Tadzio, whom he has seen with his family on the beach. The two never actually meet, but Aschenbach acknowledges to himself with mixed feelings that he loves the boy. Subsumed by fantasies about Tadzio's beauty, he ignores warnings of a cholera outbreak and falls a victim to it. He dies on the beach whilst watching Tadzio at play. [R]

Death of Klinghoffer, The
Opera in prologue and two acts by Adams. 1st perf Brussels, 19 March 1991; libr by Alice Goodman. Principal roles: Leon and Marilyn Klinghoffer (bar and mezzo), Captain (bar), First Officer (bass), Mamoud (bar), Omar (mezzo), Molqi (ten). The second of Adam's two MINIMALIST operas, it deals with the seizure by Middle Eastern terrorists of the Italian cruise liner *Achille Lauro* on 7 Oct 1985. [R]

Dèbora e Jaéle (*Deborah and Jael*)
Opera in three acts by Pizzetti. 1st perf Milan, 16 Dec 1922; libr by the composer, after the Book of Judges in the Old Testament. Principal roles: Dèbora (mezzo), Jaéle (sop), Sisera (ten), Blind Man (bass). Reasonably successful at its appearance, it is nowadays virtually forgotten.
Plot: Israel, *c* 1100 BC. When the Hebrews accuse Jael of friendship with their enemy Sisera, Deborah promises them victory and persuades Jael to murder Sisera. Jael goes to the enemy camp to carry out the deed, but when it comes to the point she is unable to go through with it. The Hebrews attack their enemy and win, and Sisera takes refuge with Deborah. She kills him to save him from torture at the hands of his captors.

Debussy, Claude (1862–1918)
French composer. One of the greatest and most original and influential composers of his age, his operatic fame rests on PELLÉAS ET MÉLISANDE, his only completed opera. Unique in style, its blending of a Wagnerian use of the orchestra with Impressionist music and complex symbolism has made it a seminal work in the history of opera. Debussy planned a number of other operas, but only two progressed beyond the stage of initial sketches. RODRIGUE ET CHIMÈNE contains nearly two hours of unorchestrated music. It has recently been completed by the Russian composer Edison Denisov. Debussy also completed just over half of LA CHÛTE DE LA MAISON USHER, orchestrating sufficient for the work to be stageable. Several different performing editions have been prepared.

Decembrists, The (*Dekabristy*)
Opera in four acts by Shaporin. 1st perf Moscow, 23 June 1953; libr by Vsevolod Rozhdestvensky, after Alexei N. Tolstoy and P.E. Shchogolev's poems. Principal roles: Ryleyev (bar), Bestuzhev (bass), Prince Dmitri (ten), Elena (sop), Pestel (bass), Kakhovsky (ten), Shchepin-Rostovsky (ten), Stesha (mezzo), Nicholas I (bass). Perhaps the most important and successful opera written in 'orthodox Soviet' style, it is a patriotic work in a strongly lyrical vein. Shaporin's only opera, two scenes were written much earlier and performed in Leningrad in 1925 as *Paulina Goebbel*.
Plot: Russia, 1825–6. Prevented by his mother Stesha from marrying Elena, Dmitri leaves the estate, well known for its tyranny over the peasants, and goes to join Ryleyev, a revolutionary leader. The Decembrist uprising takes place and, to celebrate its suppression, a courtier gives a masked ball. Elena attends and is pursued by a reveller whom she recognizes as the Tsar. She begs to be allowed to share Dmitri's fate and joins the revolutionaries on their way to Siberian exile. The revolution has failed, but Bestuzhev tells the people that 'from a spark rises a flame'. [R]

Decoration
The art of embellishing the vocal line, as

in the DA CAPO section of an 18th-century OPERA SERIA aria or in the CABALETTA of an aria in a 19th-century Italian opera.

Deh! tu di una umile preghiera
Soprano aria for Mary in Act III of Donizetti's *Maria Stuarda*. It is Mary's prayer before her execution.

Deh, vieni
Soprano aria for Susanna in Act IV of Mozart's *Le Nozze di Figaro*, in which she expresses her love for Figaro.

Deh vieni alla finestra
Baritone aria (the Serenade) for the Don in Act II of Mozart's *Don Giovanni*, in which he serenades Donna Elvira's maid.

Deidamia
Opera in three acts by Händel. 1st perf London, 10 Jan 1740; libr by Paolo Antonio Rolli. Principal roles: Deidamia (sop), Ulisse (mezzo), Acille (sop), Licomede (bass), Fenice (bass), Neraea (sop). Händel's last Italian opera, it was unsuccessful at its appearance and is nowadays only rarely performed.
Plot: Legendary Skyros. The young Achilles is living disguised as a girl at the court of King Licomedes. He is unmasked by Ulysses and Phoenix (Fenice) and is summoned to the Trojan War. Before departing, he marries Licomedes's daughter Deidamia, who has fallen in love with him.

Dein ist mein ganzes Herz
Tenor aria for Prince Sou-chong in Act II of Lehár's *Das Land des Lächelns*, in which he sings of his love for Lisa.

Del
Names containing this prefix are listed under the letter of the main surname. For example, Marie del Monaco is listed under M.

Delibes, Léo (1836–91)
French composer. He wrote his first stage work, *Deux Sous de Charbon* (Paris, 9 Feb 1856; libr Jules Moineaux), at the age of 19, going on to write a number of lighter pieces such as *Maître Griffard* (Paris, 3 Oct 1857; libr Mestépès), some of which enjoyed success in their time. After a successful period as a ballet composer, he turned to opera with the comedy LE ROI L'A DIT. This was followed by *Jean de Nivelle* (Paris, 8 Mar 1880; libr Edmond Gondinet and Philippe Gille) and LAKMÉ, his most successful and enduring opera. His last work, the grand opera *Kassya* (Paris, 24 Mar 1893; libr Gille and Henri Meilhac, after L. von Sacher-Masoch's *Frinko Balaban*), was left unfinished at his death and was completed by Massenet. His stage works are notable for their graceful and charming melodies and for their colourful orchestration, particularly when dealing with the oriental subjects so popular in France at that time.

Delius, Frederick (1862–1934)
British composer. His six operas, largely dating from the early period of his career, are notable for their richly orchestrated scores in Impressionist-late-romantic style. IRMELIN was followed by THE MAGIC FOUNTAIN, KOANGA, A VILLAGE ROMEO AND JULIET, his most successful opera, the quasi-VERISMO MARGOT LA ROUGE and FENNIMORE AND GERDA. Despite their beautiful music and the ardent advocacy of them by Sir Thomas Beecham and others, none of his operas has won a regular place in the repertory.

Della
Names containing this prefix are listed under the letter of the main surname. For example, Lisa della Casa is listed under C.

Deller, Alfred (1912–79)
British counter-tenor and conductor. The first important modern counter-tenor, he was particularly associated with Purcell and other baroque roles. A singer of style and outstanding musicianship, he created Oberon in *A Midsummer Night's Dream* and Death in Alan Ridout's *The Pardoner's Tale*. With his ensemble the Deller Consort, which he founded in 1948, he directed many notable performances and recordings of early operas. His son **Mark** (*b* 1938) is also a counter-tenor.

Demetrio e Polibio
Opera in two acts by Rossini. 1st perf Rome, 18 May 1812 (composed 1807); libr by Vincenza Vigarnò-Mombelli, after Pietro Metastasio's *Demetrio*. Principal

roles: Demetrio (ten), Polibio (bass), Siveno (mezzo), Lisinga (sop). Rossini's first opera, written at the age of 15, it is only very rarely performed.

Demetrius
Baritone role in Britten's *A Midsummer Night's Dream*. He is one of the four lovers.

De' miei bollenti spiriti
Tenor aria for Alfredo Germont in Act II of Verdi's *La Traviata*, in which he tells of his happiness living with Violetta.

Demon, The
Opera in prologue and three acts by Rubinstein. 1st perf St Peterburg, 25 Jan 1875; libr by Pavel Alexandrovich Viskovatov, after Mikhail Lermontov's poem. Principal roles: Demon (bar), Tamara (sop), Sinodal (ten), Gudal (bass), Angel (mezzo). Richly romantic, it is Rubinstein's finest and most successful work, and his only opera which is still performed in Russia.
Plot: Legendary Grusia (Caucasus). Tamara, daughter of Prince Gudal, is betrothed to Prince Sinodal, but is desired by the Demon. The Demon has Sinodal murdered and pursues Tamara into a convent. There, Sinodal – now an angel – mediates to release her from her fate through death. [R]

Denise
Soprano role in Tippett's *The Knot Garden*. She is a political activist.

Denmark
see JUTLAND OPERA; ROYAL DANISH OPERA

Dens, Michel (b 1915)
French baritone, particularly associated with lyrical French and Italian roles. Possessing a high, light voice and having a fine stage presence, especially in comedy, his long career – almost exclusively in France – included many operetta performances, in which he often sang tenor roles. He created Rodolphe in Bondeville's *Madame Bovary*.

Dent, Edward J. (1876–1957)
British musicologist and translator. A man of vast learning, his contribution to the improvement of operatic standards in Britain was enormous. Largely responsible for the British reappraisal of Mozart in the early years of the century, he was a champion of opera in English, and his translations of the Mozart operas set a new standard and remained in use for 50 years. He wrote major books on Mozart, Busoni and Scarlatti.

Denza, Luigi (1846–1922)
Italian composer. Although best known as a song composer, he also wrote one opera, the unsuccessful *Wallenstein* (Naples, 13 May 1876; libr A. Bruner, after Friedrich von Schiller).

Depuis le jour
Soprano aria for: **1** Louise in Act III of Charpentier's *Louise*, in which she recalls the day on which she first yielded to Julien's love. **2** Zélide in Adam's *Si J'Étais Roi*.

Der
Titles beginning with this form of the German definite article are listed under the letter of the first main word. For example, *Der Freischütz* is listed under F.

Dermota, Anton (1910–89)
Slovenian tenor, particularly associated with Mozart roles. Largely resident at the Vienna State Opera, where he latterly undertook character roles, he was one of the most stylish Mozartians of the immediate post-war period. He created Ferdinand in Martin's *Der Sturm* and was also later a distinguished teacher.

Dernesch, Helga (b 1939)
Austrian soprano and later mezzo, particularly associated with the German repertory. As a soprano, she was especially noted for her Wagnerian performances, in which her personal beauty, fine stage presence and warm singing compensated for some lack of the necessary weight. In 1973, she turned successfully to mezzo roles, especially those of Strauss. She created the title-role in Fortner's *Elisabeth Tudor* and, for Reimann, Goneril in *Lear* and Hecuba in *Troades*. Her husband **Werner Krenn** (*b* 1942) is a successful Mozartian tenor.

Des
Titles beginning with this form of the

German definite article are listed under the letter of the first main word. For example, *Des Teufels Lustschloss* is listed under T.

Desdemona
Soprano role in Verdi's and Rossini's *Otello*. She is Otello's wife.

Desderi, Claudio (b 1943)
Italian baritone, particularly associated with Mozart and Rossini roles. One of the leading contemporary BUFFOS, he possesses a good if not first-rate voice, has exemplary diction and is an outstanding singing-actor. He has had considerable success as a producer and has also conducted some Mozart operas.

Designers
see APPIA, ADOLPHE; BEATON, SIR CECIL; BENOIS, ALEXANDRE; CHAGALL, MARC; HOCKNEY, DAVID; KOKOSCHKA, OSKAR; KOLTAI, RALPH; LANCASTER, SIR OSBERT; LAZARIDIS, STEFANOS; MESSEL, OLIVER; NEHER, CASPAR; PIPER, JOHN; QUAGLIO FAMILY; SVOBODA, JOSEF

Désmorière, Roger (1898–1963)
French conductor, particularly associated with the French repertory and with contemporary operas. He was musical director of the Opéra-Comique, Paris (1944–6) and conducted the first performances of Roussel's *La Testament de la Tante Caroline*, Milhaud's *Esther de Carpentras* and Sauget's *La Gageure Imprévue*. He also orchestrated Satie's *Geneviève de Brabant*.

Despina
Soprano role in Mozart's *Così fan Tutte*. She is maid to Fiordiligi and Dorabella.

Dessau, Paul (1894–1979)
German composer and conductor. His first opera was the unfinished *Giuditta* (1912; libr M. May), but it was his post-war works which established him as a leading member of the German avant-garde. DIE VERURTEILUNG DES LUKULLUS, perhaps his most successful opera, was followed by *Puntila* (Berlin, 15 Nov 1966; libr Peter Palitzch and Manfred Wekwerth, after Bertolt Brecht's *Herr Puntila und sein Necht Marti*) [R], *Lanzelot* (Berlin, 19 Dec 1969; libr Heiner Müller and Ginka Cholakowa, after Yevgeni Schwartz's *Der Drache*), *Einstein* (Berlin, 16 Feb 1974; libr K. Mickel) and *Leonce und Lena* (Berlin, 24 Nov 1979; libr T. Körner, after Georg Büchner). His wife **Ruth Berghaus** (*b* 1927) is a noted avant-garde producer, whose extraordinary production of *Don Giovanni* for the Welsh National Opera raised many eyebrows.

Dessau Opernhaus
The theatre (cap 1,245) in this German city in Anhalt opened in 1885. It was rebuilt in 1938 and again in 1949. It has a strong Wagner tradition. Musical directors have included Hans Knappertsbusch, Heinz Röttger and Daniel Lipton.

Dessus (French for 'top')
A French term referring to the highest part in a vocal or instrumental ensemble, it was used in France from the 17th to the early 19th century to describe the highest soprano role in an opera. It was occasionally subdivided into *premier dessus* (with a range of c to b''') and *second dessus* (with a range of b to g'').

Destinn, Emmy (b Emilie Pavlína Kittlová; later known as Ema Destinnová) (1878–1930)
Czech soprano, particularly associated with Puccini and Wagner roles. One of the leading dramatic sopranos of her time, she was an outstanding singing-actress with a voice of highly individual timbre. She created Minnie in *La Fanciulla del West*. She also wrote a play, *Rahel*, as well as poetry and novels.

Destouches, André (b Cardinal) (1672–1749)
French composer. The historical link between Lully and Rameau, he wrote ten operas, notable for their elegant melodies, many of which were successful but which are now all largely forgotten. His operas are *Issé* (Fontainebleau, 7 Oct 1697; libr Antoine Houdard de la Motte), *Amadis de Grèce* (Fontainebleau, 26 Mar 1699; libr la Motte), *Mathésie* (Fontainebleau, 11 Oct 1699; libr la Motte), *Omphale* (Paris, 10 Nov 1701; libr la Motte), *Callirhoé* (Paris, 27 Dec 1712; libr Pierre Charles Roy), *Télémaque et Calypse* (Paris, 15 Nov 1714;

libr Abbé Simon de Pellegrin), *Sémiramis* (Paris, 4 Dec 1718; libr Roy), *Les Éléments* (Paris, 22 Dec 1721; libr Roy) and *Les Stratagèmes de l'Amour* (Paris, 19 Mar 1726; libr Roy).

Deus ex machina (Latin for 'god from the machine')
A theatrical device, dating back to the days of classical Greek drama, in which a god is lowered from above the stage to intervene and resolve the dramatic action. By extension, the term also refers to any arbitrary solution to a tangled plot. The convention was much used in early-18th-century OPERA SERIA.

Deutekom, Cristina (b Stientje Engel) (b 1932)
Dutch soprano, particularly associated with Italian BEL CANTO roles and with Mozart, especially the Queen of the Night in *Die Zauberflöte*. One of the leading COLORATURAS of the 1970s, she had a voice of remarkable agility, used with a fine technique, although her tone was sometimes a little white and hard.

Deutsche Oper, Berlin
Previously called the Städtische Oper, the theatre (cap 1,900) opened on 12 Nov 1912. Destroyed by bombs in 1944, it reopened in 1961. One of Germany's leading houses, it is noted for its adventurous repertory policy. The annual season runs from September to March. Musical directors have included Bruno Walter, Fritz Stiedry, Hans Schmidt-Isserstedt, Leopold Ludwig, Ferenc Fricsay, Lorin Maazel, Jesús López-Cobos, Giuseppe Sinopoli and Rafael Frühbeck de Burgos.

Deutsche Oper am Rhein
One of Germany's leading opera companies, it was formed in 1956 and performs in the North Rhine-Westphalian cities of Düsseldorf and Duisburg. Performances are given at the Düsseldorf Opernhaus (cap 1,344), which opened in 1875 and was rebuilt in 1956, and at the Duisburg Stadttheater (cap 1,200), which opened in 1912 and was rebuilt in 1950. The repertory is notable for its 20th-century works and for its complete cycles of works by major opera composers. The annual season runs from September to July. Musical directors have included Heinrich Hollreiser, Alberto Erede, Günther Wich, Lawrence Foster and Hans Wallat.

Deux Aveugles, Les (*The Two Blind Men*)
Operetta in one act by Offenbach. 1st perf Paris, 5 July 1855; libr by Jules Moinaux. Principal roles: Patachon (ten), Giraffier (bar). Offenbach's first real operetta, it still receives an occasional performance.
Plot: 19th-century Paris. Pretending blindness, Patachon begs on a bridge and makes calamitous attempts to play the trombone. He is joined by the mandolinist Giraffier, who also feigns blindness. After attempting to outplay and outsing each other, they decide to gamble for the begging place. Unaware that the other is not really blind, they both cheat and so recognize their rival of the previous day on a different bridge and in a different guise.

Deux Journées, Les (*The Two Days*) or **Le Porteur d'Eau** (*The Water Carrier*, by which name it is usually known in English)
Opera in three acts by Cherubini. 1st perf Paris, 16 Jan 1800; libr by Jean Nicolas Bouilly. Principal roles: Armand (ten), Mikéli (bar), Constance (sop). One of the most famous RESCUE OPERAS, it was both successful and influential in its time, but is nowadays only infrequently performed.
Plot: Paris, 1647. Count Armand has fallen into disfavour with Cardinal Mazarin. He arranges with the water carrier Mikéli to escape from Paris in a barrel. He and his wife Constance are captured, but Mikéli brings news of their pardon.

Devil
As well as in his guise as MEPHISTOPHELES, the Devil appears as a character in a number of operas, including: **1** Baritone role in Weinberger's *Shvanda the Bagpiper*. **2** Bass role in Dvořák's *The Devil and Kate*. **3** Bass role in Smetana's *The Devil's Wall*. **4** Baritone role in Massenet's *Grisélidis*. **5** Baritone role in Tchaikovsky's *Vakula the Blacksmith*. **6** Tenor role in Rimsky-Korsakov's *Christmas Eve*. **7** Bass role in Franchetti's *Asrael*. **8** Tenor role in Martin's *Le Mystère de la Nativité*. **9** Baritone role in Martinů's *The Miracle of*

Our Lady. **10** Bass role in Moore's *The Devil and Daniel Webster*. **11** Bass role in Sullivan's *The Beauty Stone*. **12** Tenor role in Ibert's *Angélique*. **13** Baritone role in Penderecki's *Paradise Lost*.

Devil and Daniel Webster, The
Opera in one act by Moore. 1st perf New York, 18 May 1939; libr by the composer, after Stephen Vincent Benét's story. Principal roles: Daniel Webster (bar), Jabez Stone (ten), Scratch (bass), Mary (sop). A work of almost folk-tale simplicity and strength, it is perhaps Moore's finest opera and has been widely performed.
Plot: New Hampshire, 1840s. The farmer Jabez Stone has sold his soul to the Devil in return for ten prosperous years. Disguised as Scratch the lawyer, the Devil appears at Stone's wedding to Mary and demands payment of his debt. Daniel Webster comes to the aid of Stone, demanding a trial and agreeing to a jury of dead men – provided that they are American. The jury are all notorious villains from America's past, and Webster secures an acquittal. [R]

Devil and Kate, The (*Čert a Káča*)
Comic opera in three acts by Dvořák (Op 112). 1st perf Prague, 23 Nov 1899; libr by Adolf Wenig, after Božena Němcová's *Fairy Tales*. Principal roles: Káča (mezzo), Jirka (ten), Marbuel (bass), Princess (sop), Lucifer (bass). One of Dvořák's most delightful works, it is still very popular in the Czech lands but is unaccountably only occasionally performed elsewhere.
Plot: Legendary Bohemia. Nobody wants to dance with the unattractive and talkative Kate, so she offers to dance 'with the Devil'. The fiend Marbuel appears and takes her down to Hell. The shepherd Jirka volunteers to rescue her, a task which does not prove too difficult as Lucifer is only too happy to be rid of her garrulity. Jirka's services are also enlisted by the Princess when she hears that the Devil is coming for her. In return for her abolishing serfdom, Jirka frightens Marbuel away from the castle by bringing Kate to it. [R]

Devils of Loudun, The (*Diabły z Loudun*)
Opera in three acts by Penderecki. 1st perf Hamburg, 20 June 1969; libr by the composer, after John Whiting's *The Devils*, itself based on Aldous Huxley's history. Principal roles: Jeanne des Anges (sop), Grandier (bar), Fr Barré (bass), Commissioner (ten), Mannoury (bar), Adam (ten), Fr Ambroise (bass). Penderecki's first opera, it tells of an historical case of the alleged demonic possession of a group of Ursuline nuns through the agency of a priest who was executed on 18 Aug 1634. One of the most powerful and disturbing of post-war operas, it has been widely performed, and is a harrowing indictment of inhumanity and intolerance.
Plot: Loudun (France), 1634. The prioress Jeanne des Anges and her Ursuline nuns claim to be possessed by the Devil. They accuse the worldly priest Urbain Grandier of engendering their possession. Grandier refuses to confess, is tortured and is finally burnt at the stake. [R]

Devil's Wall, The (*Čertova Stěna*)
Opera in three acts by Smetana. 1st perf Prague, 29 Oct 1882; libr by Eliška Krásnohorská. Principal roles: Vok (bar), Hedvika (sop), Jarek (ten), Devil/Beneš (bass), Michálek (ten), Záviš (mezzo), Katuška (sop). Smetana's last opera, it is a richly scored romantic comedy. Despite its magnificent music, it is hardly ever performed outside the Czech lands.
Plot: Mid-13th century Bohemia. The Devil overhears Jarek vow that he will not marry Katuška until his master Vok Vítkovic, the marshal of Bohemia, is himself married. Disguising himself as the disreputable hermit Beneš, the Devil causes vast confusion and nearly succeeds in preventing Vok's marriage to Hedvika by damming the River Vltava, which threatens to engulf Vok in the abbey in which he has taken refuge. [R]

Devin du Village, Le (*The Village Soothsayer*)
Comic opera in one act by Rousseau. 1st perf Fontainebleau, 18 Oct 1752; libr by the composer. Principal roles: Colette (sop), Colin (ten), Soothsayer (bar). Rousseau's only stage work still to be remembered, it was written in emulation of Pergolesi's *La Serva Padrona* and was part of his contribution to the GUERRE DES BOUFFONS. It had a wide influence and was frequently parodied or adapted, as in

Mozart's *Bastien und Bastienne*.
Plot: 18th-century France. Colette, fearing that Colin no longer loves her, seeks the aid of the Soothsayer to help her win him back. He advises her to feign indifference towards Colin. At the same time, he tells Colin that Colette is no longer interested in him. The ruse succeeds: Colin woos Colette with renewed ardour and all ends happily. [R]

Dexter, John (1925–90)
British producer. One of the most talented, exciting and controversial post-war British stage directors, he was mainly associated with the Hamburg State Opera and with the Metropolitan Opera, New York, where he was director of productions (1974–81). His most notable productions included a much-travelled *Les Vêpres Siciliennes* and the English National Opera's *The Devils of Loudun* in 1973. His autobiography, *The Honourable Beast*, was published in 1993.

Di
Names containing this prefix are listed under the letter of the main surname. For example, Giuseppe di Stefano is listed under S.

Dì all'azzurro spazio, Un
Tenor aria (the Improvviso) for Chénier in Act I of Giordano's *Andrea Chénier*, in which he denounces the selfishness of the ruling classes.

Dialogues des Carmélites
Opera in three acts by Poulenc. 1st perf Milan, 26 Jan 1957; libr by Ernest Lavery, after Georges Bernanos's play, itself based on Gertrude von le Forte's *Die Letzte am Scafott*. Principal roles: Blanche (sop), Madame Lidoine (sop), Madame de Croissy (mezzo), Constance (sop), Marie (mezzo), Marquis and Chevalier de la Force (bar and ten). One of the finest of all post-war operas, it is written in Poulenc's most lyrical and tender vein and has a powerful impact in the theatre.
Plot: Compiègne and Paris, 1789–94. The emotionally fragile Blanche de la Force enters a Carmelite convent in search of tranquility, but is horrified when the simple Sister Constance tells her of her premonition that the two will die together. Her fears are aggravated by the anguish of the dying prioress Madame de Croissy. The convent is attacked by the mob and the sisters, now led by Madame Lidoine, decide to accept martyrdom. Blanche flees but, watching the nuns go serenely singing to the guillotine, she emerges from the crowd and joins them. [R]

Diamants de la Couronne, Les
(*The Crown Diamonds*)
Opera in three acts by Auber. 1st perf Paris, 6 March 1841; libr by Eugène Scribe and Jules-Henri Vernoy de Saint-Georges. Principal roles: Catarina (sop), Don Henrique (ten), Diana (sop), Rebelledo (bass). One of Auber's most attractive scores, it was enormously successful in its time, but nowadays only the sparkling overture is still remembered.
Plot: Portugal, 1777. The beautiful young queen plans to replenish the nation's depleted treasury by selling the crown jewels and replacing them with imitations. To do so, she masquerades as La Catarina, queen of the brigands. The young nobleman Don Henrique falls in love with her and, with the help of his former fiancée Diana, saves her from capture.

Diamond Aria
Baritone aria ('Scintille diamant') for Dapertutto in the Giulietta Act of Offenbach's *Les Contes d'Hoffmann*, in which he addresses a huge diamond intended to captivate Giulietta. It was inserted from Offenbach's earlier *Le Voyage dans la Lune*.

Diana
The Graeco-Roman goddess of the chase appears in many operas, including: **1** Mezzo role in Cavalli's *La Calisto*. **2** Mezzo role in Offenbach's *Orphée aux Enfers*. **3** Soprano role in Bliss's *The Olympians*. **4** Soprano role in M.-A. Charpentier's *Actéon*. **5** Mezzo role in Gluck's *Iphigénie en Tauride*. **6** Mezzo role in Haydn's *La Fedeltà Premiata*. **7** Soprano role in Rameau's *Hippolyte et Aricie*.

Díaz, Justino (b 1940)
Puerto Rican bass, particularly associated with the Italian and French repertories. A fine singing-actor, he has a rich if somewhat

woolly voice of considerable range which enables him to sing some baritone roles such as Scarpia in *Tosca.* He created Antony in Barber's *Antony and Cleopatra* and Francesco in Ginastera's *Beatrix Cenci*, and played Iago in Zeffirelli's film of *Otello.*

Dibdin, Charles (1745–1814)
British composer, writer and theatre manager. He wrote an enormous number of stage works in various forms, the most important including *Lionel and Clarissa* (London, 25 Feb 1768; libr Isaac Bickerstaffe), *The Padlock* (London, 3 Nov 1768; libr Bickerstaffe, after Miguel Cervantes's *El Celoso Extremeño*); and *The Ephesian Matron* (London, 12 May 1769; libr Bickerstaffe, after Petronius) [R].

Dibuk, Il (*The Dybbuk*)
Opera in prologue and three acts by Rocca. 1st perf Milan, 24 March 1934; libr by Renato Simoni, after Shelomeh An-Ski's *Tzvishen Tzvei Velter*. Principal roles: Hanan (ten), Leah (mezzo), Sender (bar), Ezriel (bass). Rocca's most successful opera, it tells of a man's attempts to discover the secrets of the Qabala.

Dich, teure Halle
Soprano aria for Elisabeth in Act II of Wagner's *Tannhäuser*, in which she greets the Hall of Song.

Dickens, Charles
see panel below

Dickie, Murray (b 1924)
British tenor, particularly associated with German character roles. Largely resident at the Vienna State Opera, he had a light and pleasant voice and an engaging stage presence which also allowed him to achieve success in operetta. He created the Curé in Bliss's *The Olympians* and Trinculo in Martin's *Der Sturm*, and also produced a number of operas and operettas. His brother **William** (1914–84) was a baritone, and his son **John** is also a tenor.

Diction
Referring to the clarity of a singer's enunciation, it is a term which sadly does not feature in the vocabulary of many singers. There is no excuse for bad diction, which is symptomatic of an imperfect technique. Recent singers whose

· Charles Dickens ·

The British novelist Charles Dickens (1812–70) wrote one opera libretto himself, that for John Hullah's now long-forgotten *The Village Cocquettes* (1836). His novels have inspired some 25 operas. Below are listed, by work, those operas by composers with entries in this dictionary.

A Christmas Carol		
Herrmann	*A Christmas Carol*	1954
Cikker	*Mr Scrooge*	1958
Musgrave	*A Christmas Carol*	1979
The Cricket on the Hearth		
Goldmark	*Das Heimchen am Herd*	1896
Zandonai	*Il Grillo del Facolare*	1908
Mackenzie	*The Cricket on the Hearth*	1914
Great Expectations		
Argento	*Miss Havisham's Wedding Night*	1978
Argento	*Miss Havisham's Fire*	1979
The Pickwick Papers		
Coates	*Pickwick*	1936
A Tale of Two Cities		
Benjamin	*A Tale of Two Cities*	1953

diction has been an object lesson to their colleagues include Alfredo Kraus, Derek Hammond-Stroud, Valerie Masterson, Sesto Bruscantini and Norman Bailey.

Dido
Mezzo role in Berlioz's *Les Troyens* and Purcell's *Dido and Aeneas*. She is the Queen of Carthage.

Dido and Aeneas
Opera in prologue and three acts by Purcell. 1st perf Chelsea, Dec 1689; libr by Nahum Tate, after Virgil's *The Aeneid*. Principal roles: Dido (mezzo), Aeneas (bar), Belinda (sop), Witch (mezzo), Sailor (ten). A masterpiece in miniature, it is Purcell's finest stage work and one of the greatest of all British operas. Unperformed from 1704 until 1895, it is now regularly staged. Many different editions and realizations have been made, including one by Britten. The opera originally had an allegorical prologue, but the music is lost. **Plot**: Legendary Carthage. Belinda urges her sister Queen Dido to admit to her love for the Trojan prince Aeneas. The witches plot the downfall of Dido and of Carthage, agreeing to raise a storm so that the lovers, when they are out hunting, will be forced to seek shelter in a cave. This takes place and one of the witches, disguised as Mercury, reminds Aeneas of his destiny to go on to Italy. Heeding the summons, Aeneas prepares to depart. Dido brushes aside his explanations and makes ready for her death, after which she is mourned by Cupids. [R]

Die
Titles beginning with this form of the German definite article are listed under the letter of the first main word. For example, *Die Fledermaus* is listed under F.

Dies Bildnis ist bezaubernd schön
Tenor aria (the Portrait Aria) for Tamino in Act I of Mozart's *Die Zauberflöte*, in which he praises the beauty revealed in Pamina's portrait.

Dì felice, Un
Soprano/tenor duet for Violetta and Alfredo Germont in Act I of Verdi's *La Traviata*, in which he tells her of the happy day when he first saw her.

Dikoj
Bass role in Janáček's *Káťa Kabanová*. A wealthy merchant, he is Boris's uncle.

Dimitri
Tenor role in Moussorgsky's *Boris Godunov*. In reality the monk Grigori Ostrepyev, he is the false pretender.

Dimitrij
Opera in four acts by Dvořák (Op 64). 1st perf Prague, 8 Oct 1882; libr by Marie Červinková-Riegrová, after Friedrich von Schiller's *Demetrius* and Ferdinand Mikevec's *Dimitr Ivanovič*. Revised version 1st perf Prague, 7 Nov 1894. Principal roles: Dimitrij (ten), Marfa (mezzo), Marina (sop), Xenie (sop), Šujskij (bar), Jov (bass), Petr Basmanov (bass). Dvořák's most heroic opera, containing some splendid choral writing, it is hardly ever performed outside the Czech lands. The story begins at the point at which Moussorgsky's *Boris Godunov* ends. **Plots**: Moscow, 1605–6. Dimitri and his wife Marina arrive with Polish troops. Dimitri wins the hearts of the people, and even gains the endorsement of his supposed mother Marfa, Ivan the Terrible's widow. He foils a plot by Prince Vassili Shuisky, but forgives him after the intercession of Boris Godunov's daughter Xenia. The jealousy of Marina – exacerbated by growing Russo-Polish tension – is confirmed when she overhears Dimitri propose to Xenia. Marina renounces him as a pretender. Marfa is asked to swear before the patriarch Iov that he is not a pretender, but when Dimitri stops her he is shot dead by Shuisky. [R]

Dimitrova, Ghena (b 1941)
Bulgarian soprano, particularly associated with heavier dramatic Italian roles, especially Turandot and Lady Macbeth. She possesses a fine voice of great power and with a range that permits her to sing some dramatic mezzo roles such as Amneris. She has a strong if somewhat generalized stage presence.

Dinner Engagement, A
Comic opera in one act by Berkeley (Op 45). 1st perf Aldeburgh, 17 June 1954; libr by Paul Dehn. Principal roles:

Susan (sop), Philippe (ten), Earl Dunmow (bass), Countess (mezzo), Kneebone (sop), Boy (ten). Berkeley's most successful opera, it is an entertaining comedy of manners.
Plots: Mid-20th-century London. The newly impoverished Lord and Lady Dunmow attempt to marry their daughter Susan to Prince Philippe. The young couple do eventually fall in love, but for reasons very different from those envisaged by the Dunmows.

Dinorah or *Le Pardon de Ploërmel*
Opera in three acts by Meyerbeer. 1st perf Paris, 4 April 1859; libr by the composer, Jules Barbier and Michel Carré, after the last's *Les Chercheurs de Trésor*. Principal roles: Dinorah (sop), Hoël (bar), Corentin (ten), Goatherd (mezzo). Meyerbeer's lightest opera in style, it is a pastoral piece which was enormously popular throughout the 19th century but which is nowadays almost never performed.
Plots: Early-19th-century Brittany. A wizard reveals to the goatherd Hoël the location of a buried treasure trove, but warns that the first person to touch it will die. Hoël goes in search of the trove, but his betrothed Dinorah, believing him to have abandoned her, goes mad. Hoël saves her from drowning, and on seeing him she regains her sanity. Hoël promises to abandon his search for the treasure. [R]

Dio, che nell'alma infondere
Tenor/baritone duet for Carlos and Posa in Act II of Verdi's *Don Carlos*, in which they swear eternal frienship.

Dio di Giuda
Baritone aria for Nabucco in Act IV of Verdi's *Nabucco*, in which he prays to the god of the Hebrews for forgiveness.

Dio, mi potevi
Tenor monologue for Otello in Act III of Verdi's *Otello*, in which he says that the loss of all his glory would be easier than his fears of Desdemona's unchastity.

Di Provenza
Baritone aria for Giorgio Germont in Act II of Verdi's *La Traviata*, in which he urges Alfredo to return to his family.

Di quella pira
Tenor CABALETTA for Manrico in Act III of Verdi's *Il Trovatore*, in which he vows to save Azucena from being burnt at the stake. Perhaps the most famous (or infamous) cabaletta in all opera, the notorious high Cs at the end are *not* in the original score.

Di rigori armato il seno
Tenor aria for the Italian Tenor in Act I of Strauss's *Der Rosenkavalier*, sung during the Marschallin's levée.

Dis-moi, Vénus
Soprano aria for Helen in Act II of Offenbach's *La Belle Hélène*, in which she asks her mother Venus why she was born so beautiful.

Di tanti palpiti
Mezzo aria for Tancredi in Act I of Rossini's *Tancredi*, in which he looks forward to seeing his beloved Amenaida once more.

Dite alla giovine
Soprano/baritone duet for Violetta and Giorgio Germont in Act II of Verdi's *La Traviata*, in which she tells him to inform his daughter of her sacrifice in giving up Alfredo.

Dittersdorf, Karl Ditters von (1739–99)
Austrian composer. His 15 Italian OPERA SERIAS are of little significance. Of more importance are his 29 SINGSPIELS, whose liveliness and tunefulness helped shape the development of German comic opera. They include *Die Lustigen Weiber von Windsor* (Oels, 25 June 1797; libr composer, after Shakespeare's *The Merry Wives of Windsor*) and DOKTOR UND APOTHEKER, his only work still to be remembered.

Divertissement (French for 'amusement')
A term used in France in the 17th and 18th centuries to describe a danced stage work. It is used of some of the opera-ballets of Lully and Rameau.

Divinités du Styx
Soprano aria for Alceste in Act I of Gluck's *Alceste*, in which she rails against the powers of the underworld.

Divisions
An obsolete term for long vocal runs, as in many fast Handelian arias.

Djamileh
Comic opera in one act by Bizet. 1st perf Paris, 22 May 1872; libr by Louis Gallet after Alfred de Musset's *Namouna*. Principal roles: Djamileh (mezzo), Haroun (ten), Splendiano (bar). It was a failure at its appearance and is still only very rarely performed, despite its charming score.
Plot: 19th-century Cairo. Each month, Splendiano buys a new slave girl for his master Haroun. At the end of her month, Djamileh has fallen in love with Haroun and plots with Splendiano to disguise and reintroduce her. The plan succeeds and Haroun falls in love with her. [R]

Dobbs, Mattiwilda (b 1925)
American soprano, particularly associated with Italian COLORATURA roles. Her pleasant voice was used with an assured technique and she had an appealing stage presence. She was effectively the first black singer to enjoy a major international career in opera.

Dobrowen, Issay (b Barabeychik) (1891–1953)
Russian conductor, composer and producer. Resident in Stockholm from 1941, he was arguably the finest interpreter of the 19th-century Russian repertory in the immediate post-war period. He conducted the first performance of Sutermeister's *Raskolnikoff* and also composed one opera, *A Thousand and One Nights* (Moscow, 1922).

Dobson, John (b 1930)
British tenor, particularly associated with character roles. The best-known British COMPRIMARIO artist of the post-war period, he was long resident at Covent Garden, giving over 1,900 performances there. His voice, although far from outstanding, was intelligently used and he was a fine singing-actor, whose performances ranged from a grotesquely funny Spalanzani in Offenbach's *Les Contes d'Hoffman* to a fiercely bigoted Bob Boles in Britten's *Peter Grimes*. He created Paris in *King Priam*, Luke in *The Ice Break* and the Archangel Gabriel in Maxwell Davies's *Taverner*.

Docteur Miracle, Le
Operetta in one act by **1** Lecocq and **2** Bizet. 1st perf Paris, 8 and 9 April 1857; libr by Léon Battu and Ludovic Halévy. Principal roles: Laurette (sop), Pasquin (ten), Mayor (bass), Véronique (mezzo). In 1857, Offenbach organized a competition in which composers were provided with the libretto for a one-act OPÉRA-COMIQUE with four characters and lasting three-quarters of an hour. The jury (Auber, Halévy, Thomas, Gounod and Eugène Scribe) awarded the first prize jointly to Bizet and Lecocq. Both versions still receive an occasional performance.
Plot: Early-19th-century Padua. Capt Pasquin disguises himself as the charlatan doctor Miracle so as to make contact with his beloved Laurette, whose father the Mayor has forbidden her to consort with soldiers. After a series of escapades the lovers are united. [R]

Dogheads, The (*Psohlavci*)
Opera in three acts by Kovařovic. 1st perf Prague, 24 April 1898; libr by Karel Šípek, after Alois Jirásek's novel. Principal roles: Kozina (ten), Hančí (sop) Jiskra (bar), Laminger (bar), Mother Kozina (mezzo), Adam Ecl (ten). Kovařovic's most successful opera, dealing with the 17th-century Chod uprisings in southern Bohemia, it is still occasionally performed in the Czech lands but is virtually unknown elsewhere.
Plot: Újezd (Bohemia), 1695–6. The farmer Jan Kozina smarts under the reproaches of his mother that he is too friendly with the authorities, and turns to leading the Chod resistance. Count Laminger acquires and destroys the charters dealing with Chod freedoms, and Kozina is hanged for sedition. At a hunting party, Laminger brags about his victory over the Chods, but he suffers a stroke at the height of his boasting, and the ghost of Kozina summons him to the grave. [R Exc]

Dohnányi, Christoph von (b 1929)
German conductor, grandson of the composer ERNÖ VON DOHNÁNYI. Particularly associated with Mozart, Wagner and Strauss operas and with 20th-century works, he was musical director of

the Lübeck Opera (1957–63), the Kassel Staatstheater (1963–6), the Frankfurt Opera (1968–75) and the Hamburg State Opera (1975–84). He conducted the first performances of Cerha's *Baal*, Henze's *Der Junge Lord* and *The Bassarids* and Einem's *Kabale und Liebe*. Married to the soprano ANJA SILJA, his son **Oliver** is also a conductor.

Dohnányi, Ernö von (1877–1960)
Hungarian composer and pianist, grandfather of the conductor CHRISTOPH VON DOHNÁNYI. Although best known as a composer of piano music, he also wrote three operas: *Tante Simona* (Dresden, 23 Jan 1912; libr Viktor Heindl), *The Vaivode's Tower* (*A Vajda Tornya*, Budapest, 19 Mar 1922; libr Viktor Lányi, after Hanns Heinz Ewers and Marc Henry) and the comedy *Der Tenor* (Budapest, 9 Feb 1929; libr Ernö Goth, after Carl Sternheim's *Bürger Schippel*), his most successful work.

Doktor Faust
Opera in two prologues, interlude and three scenes by Busoni. 1st perf Dresden, 21 May 1925; libr by the composer, after Christopher Marlowe's *Dr Faustus*. Principal roles: Faust (bar), Mephistopheles (ten), Duke and Duchess of Parma (ten and sop), Brother (bar), Wagner (bar). Busoni's last opera, it was left unfinished at his death and was completed by his pupil Philipp Jarnach. Recently, a new edition – more complete and more faithful to Busoni's intentions – has been prepared by Anthony Beaumont. Busoni's stage masterpiece, it is an austere and vocally demanding work which has always been much admired by musicians but which is only infrequently performed.
Plot: 16th-century Wittenburg and Parma. Having made his pact with Mephistopheles, Faust seduces the Duchess of Parma soon after her wedding to the Duke, and elopes with her. She dies, but pursues him after death and attempts three times to give him the corpse of their child. He finally accepts the corpse and attempts to revive it by magical powers. When he falls dead, a young man arises from the corpse of the child who will accomplish all that Faust failed to do. [R]

Doktor und Apotheker (*Doctor and Apothecary*)
Comic opera in two acts by Dittersdorf. 1st perf Vienna, 11 July 1786; libr by Gottlieb Stephanie, after Le Comte N.'s *L'Apothicaire de Murcie*. Principal roles: Leonore (sop), Rosalia (sop), Sturmwald (ten), Stössel (bass), Gotthold (ten), Claudia (mezzo), Krautmann (bar), Sichel (ten). Arguably Dittersdorf's masterpiece, it is his only opera still to be in any way remembered.
Plot: 18th-century Germany. Gotthold and Leonore are in love but are unable to marry because of the rivalry between their fathers, the doctor Krautmann and the apothecary Stössel, who wishes Leonore to wed the invalid soldier Sturnwald. Leonore's cousin Rosalia and her beloved Sichel aid the pair by disguising Sturnwald as a notary and getting a wedding contract signed. Krautmann and Stössel are furious, but the intervention of the latter's wife Claudia leads them to accept the lovers' marriage. [R]

Dollarprinzessin, Die (*The Dollar Princess*)
Operetta in three acts by Fall. 1st perf Vienna, 2 Nov 1907; libr by Fritz Grünbaum and Alfred Maria Willner. Principal roles: Alice (sop), Fredy Wehrburg (ten), Olga Labinska (sop), John Couder (bar), Daisy Gray (sop). One of Fall's most successful works, it is still regularly performed in German-speaking countries. [R Exc]

Domgraf-Fassbaender, Willi (1897–1978)
German baritone, particularly associated with Mozart roles. One of the leading lyric baritones of the inter-war period, he had a beautiful voice used with fine musicianship and he was an accomplished SINGING-ACTOR. He was resident producer at the Nürnberg Stadttheater (1953–62). His daughter is the mezzo BRIGITTE FASSBAENDER.

Domingo, Plácido (b 1941)
Spanish tenor and conductor. Often regarded as the leading lyrico-dramatic tenor of the post-war era, he is especially associated with the Italian and French repertories, particularly the title-role in

Verdi's *Otello* and Don José in *Carmen* (both of which he has filmed). He has recently also sung Wagner with success and has sung some contemporary roles: he created the title-roles in Torroba's *El Poeta* and Menotti's *Goya.* His voice, both beautiful and heroic, is used with unfailing musicianship and he is a singing-actor of some stature. In recent years, he has also enjoyed success as a conductor. His autobiography, *My First Forty Years*, was published in 1983, and he has starred in a film about Puccini. Artistic director of the Washington Opera (1995–).

Dominik, Count
Baritone role in Strauss's *Arabella.* He is one of Arabella's suitors.

Domino Noir, Le (*The Black Domino*)
Opera in three acts by Auber. 1st perf Paris, 2 Dec 1837; libr by Eugène Scribe. Principal roles: Angèle (mezzo), Horace (ten), Brigitte (sop), Juliane (bass). Very successful in its time, nowadays only the delightful overture is remembered.
Plot: Early-19th-century Madrid. Angèle is to become an abbess. Dressed as a domino, she attends a masked ball with her companion Brigitte, where she is noted by Horace de Massarena, who had fallen in love with her at a similar ball a year previously. Returning unescorted, she chances upon the house of Horace's friend Juliano, where – still in disguise – she charms everyone. She manages to get back to her convent unrecognized. On the day of her installation as abbess, Horace comes to ask the abbess to be released from a loveless marriage contract with one of the sisters. He recognizes the new abbess as his beautiful domino, and she returns his love. She is released from her vows and the two are united. [R]

Dom Sébastien, Roi de Portugal (*Don Sebastian, King of Portugal*)
Opera in five acts by Donizetti. 1st perf Paris, 13 Nov 1843; libr by Eugène Scribe, after Paul-Henri Foucher's *Dom Sébastien de Portugal.* Principal roles: Sébastien (ten), Zaïda (mezzo), Camoëns (bar), Dom Juan (bass), Inquisitor (bass). Donizetti's penultimate and longest opera, written in French grand opera style, it was only moderately successful at its appearance and is nowadays only very rarely performed.
Plot: Lisbon and Fez, 1578. King Sébastien of Portugal releases the beautiful Moslem Zaïda from the Inquisition. He leaves for a crusade against the Moors in North Africa accompanied by Camoëns, whilst Dom Juan de Silva, head of the council, plots against him. Sébastien's forces are nearly annihilated, he himself being severely injured and tended by Zaïda. Returning home, he finds his throne usurped by Dom Antonio, his uncle the regent. Camoëns recognizes him and persuades him to reveal himself to the crowd at his supposed funeral. Sébastien and Zaïda are arrested, and are offered their lives if Sébastien will recognize the Spanish claim to Portugal. He refuses and the two are condemned to death. Camoëns engineers an escape, but they are observed descending by rope from their tower. Dom Juan orders his troops to fire, and Sébastien and Zaïda are killed.

Don, Donna
Operatic characters whose names begin with this title are listed under the letter of the main name. For example, Don Ottavio is listed under O. Operas containing this title (such as *Don Carlos*) are, however, listed under D.

Doña Francisquita
ZARZUELA in three acts by Vives. 1st perf Madrid, 17 Oct 1923; libr by Federico Romero and Guillermo Fernández Shaw, after Félix Lope de Vega's *La Discreta Enamorada.* Principal roles: Frasquita (sop), Fernando (ten), Matías (b-bar), Aurora (mezzo), Cardona (ten). Musically one of the finest of all zarzuelas, it is a story of complex amorous intrigue set in mid-19th-century Madrid. [R]

Donath, Helen (b 1940)
American soprano, particularly associated with Mozart roles and with the lighter German and Italian repertories. She possesses a beautiful and agile voice, used with a fine technique and outstanding musicianship, and has a delightful stage presence. Her husband **Karl** is a conductor.

Don Carlos
Opera in four (originally five) acts by Verdi. 1st perf Paris, 11 March 1867; libr by François Joseph Méry and Camille du Locle, after Friedrich von Schiller's *Don Carlos, Infant von Spanien* and Eugène Cormon's *Philippe II Roi d'Espagne*. Revised version 1st perf Milan, 10 Jan 1884. Principal roles: Don Carlos (ten), Elisabeth (sop), King Philip II (bass), Rodrigo (bar), Eboli (mezzo), Grand Inquisitor (bass), Monk/Charles V (bass), Tebaldo (mezzo). Once described as the 'thinking-man's grand opera', it is Verdi's longest and most complex work, dealing with two of his favourite themes: the relationship between Church and state and the way in which individual destinies can affect those of millions. One of Verdi's greatest, and nowadays one of his most popular operas, it contains not only fine arias and ensembles, but also much music in Verdi's dark late style: the tremendous confrontation between Philip and the Inquisitor (for two basses and a 'dark' orchestra) is one of the most remarkable musico-dramatic scenes in all opera. Verdi's sure-fire insight into character is strongly evident with the Inquisitor and Eboli, and still more so with King Philip, often regarded as the greatest bass role in the repertory. A number of different performing versions exist; most productions use the revised four-act version preceded by the original first act. A few modern productions have been given in the original French, and some have restored music that Verdi was forced to cut before the first performance; this includes a duet for Philip and Carlos following the death of Posa which Verdi later reworked as the Lachrymosa in his *Requiem*.
Plot: Fontainebleau and Spain, 1559–60. To mark the end of the Franco-Spanish war, the Infante Don Carlos is to marry Elisabeth, daughter of the King of France. They meet and fall in love, but it is then announced that King Philip has decided to marry Elisabeth himself. For the sake of peace, Elisabeth sorrowfully accepts. At the monastery to which the Emperor Charles V retired, Carlos is urged by his friend Rodrigo, the liberal Marquis of Posa, to aid the oppressed people of Spanish-ruled Flanders. Posa pleads with Philip for a less repressive regime and is appointed to the king's personal service but warned to beware the Grand Inquisitor. Philip confides to Posa his suspicions of Elisabeth and Carlos. At a masked ball, Elisabeth and Princess Eboli, who loves Carlos, exchange costumes. Carlos mistakes Eboli for Elisabeth and pours out his love before realizing his error. Rejected, Eboli threatens to reveal all to the king, but is constrained by Posa. At a grand auto-da-fé, Carlos openly defies his father on behalf of Flanders and is arrested. Alarmed at the growth of liberalism, the Grand Inquisitor demands of Philip the life of Posa, and Philip is forced to yield. Philip accuses Elisabeth of adultery, but it is revealed that the false charges were laid by Eboli, herself formerly seduced by the king. Visiting Carlos in prison, Posa is shot by agents of the Inquisition. A popular uprising on behalf of Carlos is quelled by terror at the appearance of the Inquisitor. In the confusion, however, Eboli helps Carlos to escape to the monastery. There he takes leave of Elisabeth, intending to go to Flanders. Philip and the Inquisitor arrive to arrest him, but the gates of the emperor's tomb open, and the Monk drags Carlos inside. [R]

Don Giovanni or **Il Convitato di Pietra** (*The Stone Guest*)
Comic opera in one act by Gazzaniga. 1st perf Venice, 5 Feb 1787; libr by Giovanni Bertati. Principal roles: Giovanni (ten), Donna Anna (sop), Donna Elvira (sop), Donna Ximena (sop), Pasquariello (bass), Duke Ottavio (ten), Maturina (sop), Biagio (bass), Commendatore (bass). Gazzaniga's only opera to be in any way remembered, and that largely because it had a slight influence on Mozart's version, which it preceded by nine months. [R]

Don Giovanni or **Il Dissoluto Punito** (*The Rake Punished*)
Opera in two acts by Mozart (K 527). 1st perf Prague, 29 Oct 1787; libr by Lorenzo da Ponte, partly after Giovanni Bertati's libretto for Gazzaniga. Principal roles: Giovanni (b-bar), Leporello (b-bar), Donna Anna (sop), Donna Elvira (sop), Don Ottavio (ten), Zerlina (sop), Masetto (b-bar), Commendatore (bass). Arguably Mozart's

operatic masterpiece and one of the greatest of all music-dramas, it has remained since its appearance one of the most popular of all operas. In its final scene, Mozart completely breaks through the operatic conventions of the period, producing a single sweep of action which for its musical complexity and dramatic power and insight is at least 70 years ahead of its time.
Plot: 17th-century Seville. The libertine Don Giovanni, aided by his servant Leporello, attempts to seduce Donna Anna, but is disturbed by her father the Commendatore, whom he kills in a duel. Anna and her fiancé Don Ottavio swear vengeance. Giovanni's attempts to seduce the peasant girl Zerlina, engaged to Masetto, are foiled by Donna Elvira, whom Giovanni has seduced and abandoned. All turn against Giovanni at a party at his villa, but he escapes and finds himself in a churchyard where the statue of the Commendatore speaks. Lightheartedly, Giovanni orders Leporello to invite the statue to supper. The statue arrives and drags the unrepentant Giovanni down to Hell. [R]

Donizetti, Gaetano (1797–1848)
Italian composer. A musician of great talent and facility, he wrote 69 operas. They are notable for their melodic beauty, their simple but deft orchestration, and for their superb vocal lines – few composers ever wrote better (if highly demandingly) for the voice, especially the tenor. Content to work largely within the rigid operatic structure of his day, Donizetti wrote too much too quickly, and many of his operas exhibit an over-reliance on formulae. What distinguishes him from his contemporaries Bellini, Mercadante and Pacini is the greater power and considerable, if intermittent, dramatic insight displayed in his best works. His operas went through a long period of neglect and critical disdain, but with the re-emergence of singers capable of doing justice to his music, they have been completely re-evaluated in the last 30 years, and several are now firmly re-established in the repertory. For some of his comedies, Donizetti wrote his own libretti and demonstrated a considerable talent for well-turned doggerel.

Donizetti's first 32 operas are pleasant but unremarkable, being heavily influenced by Rossini. The best of them are comedies, a genre in which he was to become one of the finest ever Italian exponents. L'AIO NELL'IMBARAZZO, the hilarious LE CONVENIENZE ED INCONVENIENZE TEATRALI and *Il Giovedì Grasso* (Naples, 26 Dec 1829; libr Domenico Gilardoni) are still performed from time to time. Of his earlier serious works, the most significant are *Emilia di Liwerpool* (Naples, 28 July 1824; libr Giuseppe Checcherini, after Stefano Scatizzi; revised version *L'Ermitaggio di Liwerpool*, Naples 8 Mar 1828) [R both versions] and *Il Castello di Kenilworth* (Naples, 6 July 1829; libr Andrea Leone Tottola, after Sir Walter Scott's *Kenilworth*).

The turning-point in Donizetti's career came in 1830, with the triumphant success of ANNA BOLENA, which placed him at the forefront of European opera composers. The most important of his mature works, some of which had a considerable influence on the young Verdi, are *Fausta* (Naples, 12 Jan 1832; libr composer, Gilardoni and Tottola), UGO CONTE DI PARIGI, the ever-popular L'ELISIR D'AMORE, *Il Furioso* (Rome, 2 Jan 1833; libr Jacopo Ferretti), PARISINA D'ESTE, TORQUATO TASSO, LUCREZIA BORGIA, his most frequently performed work in the 19th century, *Rosmonda d'Inghilterra* (Florence, 27 Feb 1834; libr Felice Romani, after *Fair Rosamund*), GEMMA DI VERGY, MARIA STUARDA, MARINO FALIERO, the hugely successful LUCIA DI LAMMERMOOR, the archetypal romantic opera and perhaps his best-known work, BELISARIO, the delightful IL CAMPANELLO, BETLY, L'ASSEDIO DI CALAIS, PIA DE' TOLOMEI, ROBERTO DEVEREUX, MARIA DE RUDENZ, POLIUTO (later revised as *Les Martyrs*), LA FILLE DU RÉGIMENT, LA FAVORITE, RITA, MARIA PADILLA, LINDA DI CHAMOUNIX, DON PASQUALE, one of the greatest of all OPERA BUFFAS, MARIA DI ROHAN, DOM SÉBASTIEN, CATERINA CORNARO and the unfinished LE DUC D'ALBE. A previously unknown opera, *Elisabetta* (*c* 1840), has recently been discovered in the Covent Garden archives.

Donna del Lago, La (*The Lady of the Lake*)
Opera in two acts by Rossini. 1st perf

Naples, 24 Sept 1819; libr by Andrea Leone Tottola, after Sir Walter Scott's poem. Principal roles: Elena (sop), Malcolm (mezzo), Giacomo (ten), Rodrigo (ten), Douglas (bass). Very popular until the mid-19th century, it suffered a long period of neglect, but has received a number of performances in the last 20 years. It is one of Rossini's most florid but at the same time most romantic scores. **Plot**: Early-16th-century Scotland. Elena, the 'lady of the lake', is in love with Malcolm, but has been promised by her father, Douglas of Angus, to Rodrigo. She is also loved by Uberto, in reality King James V (Giacomo) who, after Rodrigo is killed in a rebellion against him, pardons the banished Douglas and allows her to marry Malcom. [R]

Donna Diana
Comic opera in three acts by Rezniček. 1st perf Prague, 16 Dec 1894; libr by the composer, after A. Moreto y Cavaña's *El Lindo Don Diego*. Principal roles: Diana (sop), Cesar (ten), Perrin (bar), Diego (bass). Rezniček's most successful opera, it is nowadays almost never performed, although its sparkling overture is still popular.
Plot: 17th-century Barcelona. Don Cesar, Prince of Urgel, is staying at Don Diego's palace. His love for Diego's daughter Diana is met by her with indifference. The clown Perrin advises Cesar to return coldness for coldness. Cesar adopts this tactic, and after many intrigues and complications, Diana admits that she loves him.

Donna di quindici anni, Una
Soprano aria for Despina in Act II of Mozart's *Cosi fan Tutte*, in which she says that she knows everything about ensnaring a lover.

Donna è mobile, La
1 Tenor aria for the Duke of Mantua in Act III of Verdi's *Rigoletto*, in which he sings of the fickleness of women. Perhaps the most famous aria in all opera. **2** The title of a comic opera by R. Malipiero (1954).

Donna Juanita
Operetta in three acts by Suppé. 1st perf Vienna, 21 Feb 1880; libr by F. Zell (Camillo Walzel) and Richard Genée. Set in Spain during the British occupation in 1796, it tells of a French army cadet who disguises himself as a flirtatious girl to help the French capture San Sebastián. It is still occasionally performed in German-speaking countries.

Donna non vidi mai
Tenor aria for des Grieux in Act I of Puccini's *Manon Lescaut*, in which he expresses his joy on first beholding Manon.

Donne Curiose, Le (*The Inquisitive Women*)
Comic opera in three acts by Wolf-Ferrari. 1st perf Munich, 27 Nov 1903; libr by Luigi Sugana, after Carlo Goldoni's play. Principal roles: Ottavio (bass), Florindo (ten), Pantelone (bar), Lelio (bar), Beatrice (mezzo), Rosaura (sop), Eleonora (sop), Arlecchino (bar), Columbina (sop). Wolf-Ferrari's first major success, and one of the finest of his neo-classical comedies, it is a delightful work which is still occasionally performed.
Plot: 18th-century Venice. Their suspicions aroused, Eleonora, Rosaura and Beatrice decide to spy upon their menfolk at their all-male club, at which they fear that the men indulge in orgies. They contrive a series of subterfuges to gain entry to the club, only to discover that the men are harmlessly enjoying gourmet meals there. The men are initially horrified, but eventually share with the woman the secret password: 'friendship'.

Donner
Baritone role in Wagner's *Das Rheingold*. He is the god of thunder.

Donnerstag aus Licht
see LICHT

Don Pasquale
Comic opera in three acts by Donizetti. 1st perf Paris, 3 Jan 1843; libr by the composer and Giovanni Ruffini, after Angelo Anelli's libretto for Pavesi's *Ser Marc' Antonio*. Principal roles: Pasquale (bass), Norina (sop), Dr Malatesta (bar), Ernesto (ten). An eternally fresh if slightly bittersweet comedy, it is one of Donizetti's most technically assured works. An

immediate success, it has always remained one of the most popular of all OPERA BUFFAS.
Plot: Early-19th-century Rome. The elderly and wealthy bachelor Don Pasquale has decided to marry so as to disinherit his nephew Ernesto, who refuses to marry the woman his uncle has chosen for him because he is in love with the flighty widow Norina. The family doctor Malatesta aids the young lovers: he arranges a mock marriage between Pasquale and Norina, the latter disguised as Malatesta's demure sister 'Sofronia', a convent girl. No sooner has the ceremony taken place than Norina/Sofronia leads Pasquale such a dance that the old fellow is utterly miserable and is quite put off the whole idea of marriage. To get rid of 'Sofronia', he readily agrees to Malatesta's suggestion that he allow Ernesto and Norina to wed. When he discovers the deception practised on him, he generously forgives everyone and blesses the lovers' union. [R]

Don Procopio
Comic opera in two acts by Bizet. 1st perf Monte Carlo, 10 March 1906 (composed 1859); libr by Carlo Cambiaggio, after Luigi Prividali's libretto for Mosca's *I Pretendenti Delusi*. Principal roles: Procopio (b-bar), Odoardo (ten), Bettina (sop), Ernesto (bar), Andronico (bar), Pasquino (bar), Eufemia (mezzo). Bizet's second completed opera, it is a tuneful and entertaining little piece written in Italian OPERA BUFFA style. It is still occasionally performed.
Plot: Spain, *c* 1800. To the displeasure of his wife Eufemia and son Ernesto, Andronico plans to marry his daughter Bettina to the rich old Don Procopio. Bettina, however, loves the soldier Odoardo. Bettina pretends to be a virago and leads the old miser such a dance that he withdraws from the marriage. Andronico finally agrees that Bettina may wed Odoardo.

Don Quichotte
Opera in five acts by Massenet. 1st perf Monte Carlo, 19 Feb 1910; libr by Henri Cain, after Miguel de Cervantes Saavedra's *Don Quixote* and Jacques le Lorraine's *Le Chevalier de la Longue Figure*. Principal roles: Quichotte (bass), Sancho Panza (bar), Dulcinée (mezzo). Massenet's last fully successful opera, it is a gentle, melancholy and autumnal work, whose title-role has attracted many of the greatest basses. The story contains a number of episodes from Cervantes, but Dulcinea is changed from an aristocrat into a seductive courtesan. After a long period of neglect, it has had a number of performances in recent years.
Plot: Medieval Spain. Don Quichotte serenades the courtesan Dulcinée. Amused by his attentions, she agrees to become the 'Lady of his Thoughts' if he will restore a necklace stolen by brigands. Accompanied by Sancho Panza, Quichotte sets out, tilts at a windmill, and is captured by the brigands. Impressed by his courage, the brigands release him and give him the necklace, which he restores to Dulcinée. He proposes marriage, but she laughs at the idea. Later, Quichotte dies, telling Sancho that he has given him the 'Island of Dreams'. [R]

Don Rodrigo
Opera in three acts by Ginastera (Op 31). 1st perf Buenos Aires, 24 July 1964; libr by Alejandro Casona. Principal roles: Rodrigo (ten), Florinda (sop), Don Julián (bar), Teudiselo (bass), Fortunata (mezzo). Ginastera's first major success, written in a mixture of atonal and TWELVE-TONE styles, it sets a fine libretto which combines Christian, Arabic and Mozarabic traditions of the last Visigoth King of Spain (*d* AD 711).
Plot: Early-8th-century Spain. Rodrigo, having defeated his rivals for the throne, meets Florinda, daughter of his supporter Don Julián. At his coronation, the crown slips from Florinda's hand. This ill omen is reinforced when Rodrigo opens the iron chest of the Cave of Toledo to discover an Islamic prophecy of doom to the chest's violator. Lusting for Florinda, Rodrigo rapes her. She appeals to her father for vengeance and he orders the Arab invasion of Spain. Now a wandering beggar, Rodrigo is full of remorse and dies in Florinda's arms.

Don Sanche or **Le Château d'Amour** (*The Castle of Love*)
Opera in one act by Liszt. 1st perf Paris, 17 Oct 1825; libr by Émmanuel Guillaume Théaulon de Lambert and de Rancé, after

Jean-Pierre-Claris de Florian's story. Principal roles: Sanche (ten), Elzire (mezzo), Alidor (bar), Zélis (mezzo). Liszt's only opera, written at the age of 13 with the help of his teacher Paer, it is only very rarely performed.
Plot: The knight Don Sanche is refused admittance to the Castle of Love, where only couples may enter, because his beloved Princess Elzire does not return his affections. With the aid of the castle's ruler, the magician Alidor, Sanche contrives to bring Elzire and her maid Zélis to the castle. An evil knight also arrives and attempts to force Elzire to marry him. Sanche's defence of her honour awakens Elzire's love for him, and the two are united. [R]

Donzelli, Domenico (1790–1873)
Italian tenor, particularly associated with the Italian repertory. Sometimes regarded as the first dramatic tenor, he was famous for being able to sing a high A from the chest. Said to have been a fine singing-actor, he created Pollione in *Norma*, Claudio in Mercadante's *Elisa e Claudio*, Torvaldo in Rossini's *Torvaldo e Dorliska*, a role in Halévy's *Clari*, Belfiore in *Il Viaggio a Reims*, Don Ruiz in Donizetti's *Maria Padilla* and the title-roles in Winter's *Moametto*, Mercadante's *Il Bravo* and Donizetti's *Ugo Conte di Parigi*.

Dorabella
Mezzo role in Mozart's *Così fan Tutte*. Fiordiligi's sister, she is in love with Ferrando.

Doráti, Antal (1906–88)
Hungarian conductor and composer, particularly associated with the German repertory, especially Haydn, all of whose mature operas he recorded. Best known as a symphonic conductor, his operatic appearances were rare in his later years. He was musical director of the Münster Opera (1929–33) and also composed an opera about Elijah. His autobiography, *Notes of Seven Decades*, was published in 1979.

Dorothy
Operetta in three acts by Cellier. 1st perf (as *Nell Gwynne*) Manchester, 16 Oct 1876; libr by H.B. Farnie, after W.G.T. Montcrieff's *Rochester*. Revised version 1st perf London, 25 Sept 1886; libr by Benjamin Charles Stephenson, after Aphra Behn's *The City Heiress*. Cellier's best known work, set in Kent in 1740, it was sensationally successful at its appearance but is nowadays virtually forgotten.

Dortmund Stadttheater
The opera house (cap 1,160) in this German city in North Westphalia opened in 1966, replacing the previous theatre destroyed by bombs in 1943. Musical directors have included Wilhelm Schüchter, Marek Janowski, Hans Wallat and Klaus Weise.

Dosifei
Bass role in Moussorgsky's *Khovanschina*. He is the leader of the Old Believers.

Dostoyevsky, Fyodor
see panel on page 160

Dove sei, amato ben?
Mezzo aria for Bertarido in Act I of Händel's *Rodelinda*, in which he expresses his anguish at being away from his beloved.

Dove sono?
Soprano aria for Countess Almaviva in Act III of Mozart's *Le Nozze di Figaro*, in which she laments the loss of the Count's love.

Downes, Sir Edward (b 1926)
British conductor, particularly associated with Wagner, the Russian repertory (of which he has made several translations) and especially Verdi, of whose operas he is one of the outstanding contemporary interpreters. Closely associated with Covent Garden, where he was associate musical director from 1991, he was also musical director of the Australian Opera (1972–6). Also a champion of modern composers, he conducted the first performances of Maxwell Davies's *Taverner*, Bennett's *Victory*, Tavener's *Thérèse* and Prokofiev's *Maddalena*, which he edited and prepared for performance.

Down in the Valley
Opera in one act by Weill. 1st perf Bloomington (Indiana), 15 July 1948; libr by Arnold Sundgaard. Principal roles:

· Fyodor Dostoyevsky ·

The works of the Russian writer Fyodor Dostoyevsky (1821–81) have inspired some 25 operas. Below are listed, by work, those operas by composers with entries in this dictionary.

The Brothers Karamazov		
Jeremiáš	*The Brothers Karamazov*	1928
Blacher	*Der Grossinquisitor*	1948
Rossellini	*La Leggenda del Ritorno*	1966
Crime and Punishment		
Pedrollo	*Delitto e Castigo*	1926
Sutermeister	*Raskolnikoff*	1948
Petrovics	*Crime and Punishment*	1969
The Gambler		
Prokofiev	*The Gambler*	1929
The Idiot		
Chailly	*L'Idiota*	1970
Eaton	*Myshkin*	1973
Memoirs From the House of the Dead		
Janáček	*From the House of the Dead*	1930
Uncle's Dream		
Krása	*Verlobung im Traum*	1933

Brack Weaver (ten), Jennie Parsons (sop), Thomas Bouché (bass). Based on American folk song, it tells in a series of flashbacks the story of a man awaiting execution for having killed, in self-defence, his rival in love. [R]

D'Oyly Carte Opera Company
A British company founded in 1876 by Richard d'Oyly Carte to perform the Gilbert and Sullivan operettas. Long based at the Savoy Theatre in London, it also toured extensively in Britain and North America. It held a monopoly on professional performances of the Savoy Operas until the expiry of the copyright in 1961. Thereafter, comparison with other productions showed the company to be increasingly hidebound by tradition. It ceased operations in 1982, following the Arts Council's refusal of financial assistance, but was re-founded on non-traditional lines in 1988. Musical directors have included Isidore Godfrey, James Walker, Royston Nash, Alexander Faris, Bramwell Tovey, John Pryce-Jones and John Owen Edwards.

Draghi, Antonio (c 1634–1700)
Italian composer and librettist, resident in Vienna from 1658. Possibly the most prolific 17th-century opera composer, he wrote some 175 stage works, both small SERENATAS and full-scale operas. Usually attracted to heroic subjects suitable for the court of his patron Emperor Leopold I (who himself composed some additional parts for Draghi's operas), his works include *La Mascherata* (Vienna, 4 Mar 1666; libr composer), *Gundeberga* (Vienna, 12 July 1672; libr Nicolò Minato), one of the first operas to be based on a German historical subject, *Turia Lucrezia* (Vienna, 18 Nov 1675; libr Minato) and *La Magnanimità di Marco Fabrizio* (Vienna, 22 Nov 1695; libr Donato Cupeda). As well as those for some of his own earlier operas, he provided libretti for Abbatini, Ziani, Tricarico and others. His son **Carlo** (1669–1711) was also a composer.

Dragons de Villars, Les (*The Dragoons of Villars*)
Opera in three acts by Maillart. 1st perf Paris, 19 Sept 1856; libr by Joseph

Philippe Lockroy and Eugène Cormon. Principal roles: Rose (mezzo), Sylvain (ten), Thibaut (bar). Maillart's most successful opera, it was long popular, but nowadays only the overture is at all remembered.
Plots: Esterel, 1704. The determined peasant girl Rose Friquet is falsely accused of revealing the whereabouts of a group of Protestant refugees to the officer of the troops of Villars. However, the refugees manage to cross the border whilst the troops, notorious for their womanizing, are carousing. Rose, meanwhile saves the farmer Thibaut from a disastrous marriage and is eventually united with her sweetheart Sylvain.

Dramaturg
A German term which has no exact English equivalent. The dramaturg is a member of the staff of a German or Austrian opera house whose duties include adapting libretti, editing programmes, handling the press and sometimes also producing or acting.

Dramma eroicomico (Italian for 'comic-heroic drama')
A type of Italian comic opera which was developed in the late 18th century, largely by the playwright and librettist Giovanni Battista Casti (1724–1803), in which a famous historical or literary personage is placed in a ludicrous light. Haydn's *Orlando Paladino* is so described.

Dramma giocoso (Italian for 'humorous drama')
A term used in the late 18th century to describe a comic work which also contains some serious elements. Much the most famous example is Mozart's *Don Giovanni*.

Dramma per musica (Italian for 'drama through music')
A term used in the 17th century for a dramatic text, intended to be set to music, on a serious subject.

Dreaming About Thérèse (*Drömmen on Thérèse*)
Opera in two acts by Werle. 1st perf Stockholm, 26 May 1964; libr by Lars Runtsen, after Émile Zola's *Pour une Nuit d'Amour*. Principal roles: Thérèse (sop), Julien (bar), Colombel (ten). Designed for performance 'in the round', with the orchestra behind the audience, it makes use of both speech and melodrama.
Plot: Thérèse accidentally kills Colombel. Her price to Julien for a night of love is the disposal of Colombel's body. Julien throws the body into the river and then throws himself in afterwards. [R Exc]

Dreigroschenoper, Die (*The Threepenny Opera*)
Opera in prologue and eight scenes by Weill. 1st perf Berlin, 31 Aug 1928; libr by Bertolt Brecht, after John Gay's *The Beggar's Opera*. Adaptation by Blitzstein 1st perf Waltham (Mass), 14 June 1952. Principal roles: Polly (sop), Mack the Knife (bar), Jenny (sop), Peachum (bar), Lucy (sop), Tiger Brown (bar). A modern reworking of Gay's play with music in popular style, it was an immediate success and has always remained one of Weill's best-known works. Weill's chamber work *Kleine Dreigroschenmusik* is drawn from music from the opera.
Plot: Early-19th-century Soho. Mack the Knife marries Polly, daughter of the underworld leader Peachum. Betrayed by his in-laws and by the prostitute Jenny, he escapes from jail with the aid of Lucy, daughter of the corrupt police chief Tiger Brown. Recaptured, Mack is about to be hanged when he is pardoned by Queen Victoria on her coronation day. [R]

Drei Pintos, Die (*The Three Pintos*)
Comic opera in two acts by Weber. 1st perf Leipzig, 20 Jan 1888 (begun 1821); libr by Theodor Hell, after Carl Ludwig Seidl's *Der Brautkampf*. Principal roles: Don Pinto (bass), Don Gaston (ten), Clarissa (sop), Ambrosio (bar), Don Gomez (ten), Don Pantaleone (bar). Weber abandoned the piece halfway through, and it was completed by Mahler, who orchestrated it and filled in the gaps by using other music by Weber. It still receives an occasional performance as a musical curiosity.
Plot: Early-19th-century Madrid. Don Pinto is journeying to marry Clarissa, when a rival for her affections, Ambrosio, makes him drunk, seizes the marriage papers and masquerades as Pinto. Discovering that Clarissa loves Don Gomez, he passes the papers to him, and Gomez becomes the

third Pinto. After a complex series of muddles, all ends happily. [R]

Dresden State Opera
The present Schauspielhaus (cap 1,131) opened in 1948, replacing the Semper Opernhaus, which opened in 1841 but which was destroyed by bombs in Feb 1945. It has been one of Germany's most important operatic centres from earliest times, and has a particularly strong Wagner and Strauss tradition. The annual season runs from September to June. Musical directors have included Weber, Wagner, Ernst von Schuch, Fritz Reiner, Fritz Busch, Karl Böhm, Karl Elmendorff, Joseph Keilberth, Rudolf Kempe, Franz Konwitschny, Lovro von Matačić, Kurt Sanderling, Otmar Suitner and Siegfried Kurz.

Dress rehearsal
The final rehearsal of an opera production, consisting of a complete run-through in full costume, hopefully uninterrupted, at which the singers normally 'sing out'. At an 'open' dress rehearsal, an invited audience is present. It is called *Generalprobe* in Germany, *répétition génerale* in France and *prova generale* in Italy.

Drottningholm Castle Theatre
(*Drottningholms Slottsteater* in Swedish)
The opera house (cap 454) in the Palace of Drottningholm near Stockholm was designed by Carl Fredrik Adelcrantz in 1766, replacing the previous theatre of 1754, built by Frederick the Great's sister, which was destroyed by fire in 1762. It was restored in 1922 after a long period of neglect, and much of the original wooden scenery and stage machinery is still in use. Since 1948, it has given summer opera seasons with a repertory consisting predominantly of 18th-century works. Artistic directors have included Gustaf Hilleström, Charles Farncombe, Arnold Östman and Elisabeth Söderström.

Dublin Grand Opera Society
The company was formed in 1941 and gives two short seasons a year at the Gaiety Theatre (cap 1,075), which was built in 1871. The repertory is predominantly Italian and French, and the orchestra is the Radio Telefis Eireann Symphony.

Dubrovsky
Opera in four acts by Nápravník (Op 58). 1st perf St Petersburg, 15 Jan 1895; libr by Modest Tchaikovsky, after Alexander Pushkin's novella. Principal roles: Vladimir (ten), Masha (sop), Troekurov (bar), Count Vereisky (bass). Nápravník's most successful opera, it is still occasionally performed in Russia, but is virtually unknown elsewhere.
Plot: 18th-century Russia. Gen Troekurov brings an action and takes possession of the Dubrovsky estate, causing Vladimir's father to die of grief. In revenge, Vladimir burns down the estate. Troekurov's daughter Masha is sympathetic to the position of her childhood playmate Vladimir, and the latter disguises himself as a Frenchman and gains access to the Troekurov household as a tutor. Masha and Vladimir fall in love, but Troekurov insists that Masha marry the old Count Vereisky. At a ball to celebrate the betrothal, the police appear and tell Troekurov the real identity of the tutor. Vladimir is shot whilst attempting to flee and dies in Masha's arms. [R]

Duc d'Albe, Le (*The Duke of Alba*)
Opera in four acts by Donizetti. 1st perf Rome, 22 March 1882 (begun 1839); libr by Eugène Scribe and Charles Duvéyrier. Principal roles: Hélène (sop), Alba (bar), Henri (ten), Sandoval (bass). Left unfinished by Donizetti, it was completed by Matteo Salvi. It is only very rarely performed.
Plot: Brussels, 1573. Egmont's daughter Hélène is in love with Henri, who turns out to be the missing son of the Duke of Alba, the oppressive Spanish ruler of Flanders. In an attempt to murder the Duke, Hélène accidentally kills Henri, who intervenes to save his father. Dying, Henri begs Alba to forgive Hélène.

Due Foscari, I (*The Two Foscari*)
Opera in three acts by Verdi. 1st perf Rome, 3 Nov 1844; libr by Francesco Maria Piave, after Lord Byron's play. Principal roles: Francesco (bar), Lucrezia (sop), Jacopo (ten), Loredano (bass). Dealing with the historical Doge of

Venice Francesco Foscari (reigned 1423–57), it is a dark and sombre work which contains some striking prefigurements of Verdi's mature style. One of Verdi's finest early operas, it has been more admired by musicians than audiences and is not performed as often as its merits deserve.
Plot: Venice, 1457. The Doge Francesco Foscari accepts with resignation a decision by the Council of Ten to extend the exile of his son Jacopo, falsely accused of murder. Loredano, leader of the opposition, is unmoved by the pleas of Jacopo's wife Lucrezia, and Jacopo dies of a broken heart as his ship sails for Crete. Loredano persuades the Council to force Francesco to resign. The Doge (who twice in the past had wished to resign but was begged to remain until death) dies disgraced as the bells announce his successor. [R]

Due Illustri Rivali, Le (*The Two Illustrious Rivals*)
Opera in three acts by Mercadante. 1st perf Venice, 10 March 1838; libr by Gaetano Rossi. Principal roles: Elvira (sop), Bianca (sop), Armando (ten). It tells of the rivalry between the Queen of Navarre and a noblewoman for the love of a cavalier. One of Mercadante's best operas, it was highly successful in its time but is nowadays only very rarely performed.

Duenna, The or **Betrothal in a Monastery** (*Obrucheniye v Monastyre*)
Comic opera in four acts by Prokofiev (Op 86). 1st perf Leningrad, 3 Nov 1946 (composed 1940); libr by the composer and Mira Mendelson-Prokofieva, after Richard Brindsley Sheridan's play. Principal roles: Duenna (mezzo), Jerome (ten), Louisa (sop), Mendoza (bass), Ferdinand (bar), Clara (mezzo), Antonio (ten), Carlos (bass). Despite its delightful, witty and colourful score, it is only occasionally performed.
Plot: 18th-century Seville. The nobleman Don Jerome wishes his daughter Louisa to marry the elderly Don Mendoza, but she is in love with Antonio. By deceiving her father, Louisa succeeds in marrying Antonio, whilst Mendoza is tricked into marrying the Duenna. [R]

Duenna, The
Comic opera in three acts by Gerhard. 1st perf BBC Radio, 23 Feb 1949; 1st stage perf Madrid, 21 Jan 1992; libr by the composer and Christopher Hassall, after Richard Brindsley Sheridan's play. Principal roles: Duenna (mezzo), Jeronimo (bass), Isaac (bar), Antonio (ten), Louisa (sop), Fernando (bar). Gerhard's only opera, it is a brilliant setting which is unaccountably hardly ever performed. [R]

Duet
In opera, a musical number for two solo singers, in which the musical content is divided equally between both soloists.

Duettino (Italian for 'little duet')
A short duet in simple style, often lacking a strict formal structure.

Dugazon, Louise (b Lefèbvre) (1755–1821)
French soprano. One of the most popular singers of her age, she excelled in OPÉRA-COMIQUE. She created over 60 roles, including Zémaïde in *Le Calife de Bagdad* and Marguerite in *Richard Coeur de Lion*, in operas by Grétry, Isouard, Boïeldieu, Dalayrac and others. She gave her name to a type of French soprano voice, which is divided into four subcategories: *jeune Dugazon*, *première Dugazon*, *forte première Dugazon* and *mère Dugazon*. Her son **Gustave** (1782–1826) was a composer who wrote five operas.

Duisburg
see DEUTSCHE OPER AM RHEIN

Dukas, Paul (1865–1935)
French composer. He wrote only one opera, the ambitious symbolist ARIANE ET BARBE-BLEUE. He also helped to complete Guiraud's unfinished *Frédégonde* and edited a number of Rameau's operas.

Duke Bluebeard's Castle (*A Kékszakállú Herceg Vára*)
Opera in one act by Bartók (Op 16). 1st perf Budapest, 24 May 1918 (composed 1911); libr by Béla Balázs. Principal roles: Bluebeard (b-bar), Judith (mezzo). Bartók's only opera, it is a darkly symbolic work in which the rich, sensuous and superlatively

orchestrated score is tightly constructed to lead up to and then down from the climactic opening of the fifth door. Although never especially popular with audiences, it is regularly performed and ranks as one of the greatest of all 20th-century operas.
Plot: Bluebeard brings his new wife Judith home to his castle, which has seven doors and no windows. Wishing to dispel the darkness, Judith demands the keys to the doors. Bluebeard reluctantly yields the keys, and behind the doors Judith discovers a torture chamber, an armoury, a treasury, a rose garden, a vision of Bluebeard's domains and a lake of tears. All are defiled with blood. Behind the seventh door, Judith finds Bluebeard's three previous wives who were similarly curious. Judith must join them, leaving Bluebeard once more in darkness and solitude. [R]

Duke of Mantua
Tenor role in Verdi's *Rigoletto*. He is Rigoletto's libertine employer.

Dulcamara, Dr
Bass-baritone role in Donizetti's *L'Elisir d'Amore*. He is an itinerant quack.

Dumas, Alexandre
see panel on page 165

Duni, Egidio (1709–75)
Italian composer. Largely resident in France, he was a principal founder of the OPÉRA-COMIQUE form. He wrote some 30 operas, many of which enjoyed great success in their day but which are all now forgotten. His most important works include *La Buona Figliuola* (Parma, 26 Dec 1756; libr Carlo Goldoni, after Samuel Richardson's *Pamela*), *La Fille Mal Gardée* (Paris, 14 Mar 1758; libr Charles-Simon Favart). *La Fée Urgèle* (Fontainebleau, 26 Oct 1765; libr Favart, after Voltaire's *Ce Qui Plaît aux Dames*), *La Clochette* (Paris, 24 July 1766; libr Louis Anseaume), *Les Moissonneurs* (Paris, 27 Jan 1768; libr Favart, after the Book of Ruth in the Old Testament) and *Les Sabots* (Paris, 26 Oct 1768; libr Jean-Marie Sedaine, after J. Cazotte).

Dunque io son
Mezzo/baritone duet for Rosina and Figaro in Act I of Rossini's *Il Barbiere di Siviglia*, in which she says that she knew all along that she was the object of 'Lindoro's' attentions.

Duphol, Baron
Baritone COMPRIMARIO role in Verdi's *La Traviata*. He is Violetta's protector.

Duprez, Gilbert (1806–96)
French tenor and composer. One of the leading tenors of the first half of the 19th century, he created the title-role in *Benvenuto Cellini*, Gaston in Verdi's *Jérusalem*, roles in Meyerbeer's *L'Étole du Nord* and Auber's *Le Lac des Fées*, and, for Donizetti, Edgardo in *Lucia di Lammermoor*, Ugo in *Parisina d'Este*, the title-role in *Dom Sébastien*, Polyeucte in *Les Martyrs* and Fernand in *La Favorite*. He also composed eight operas and was a noted teacher, whose pupils included Emma Albani and Marie Miolan-Carvalho. His autobiography, *Souvenirs d'un Chanteur*, was published in 1880. His wife **Alexandrine Duperron** (*d* 1872) was a successful soprano; their daughter **Caroline** (1832–75) was also a soprano.

Durchkomponiert (German for 'continously composed')
The term is used in Germany to describe an opera with no spoken dialogue and in which the musical numbers merge without a break.

Düsseldorf
see DEUTSCHE OPER AM RHEIN

Dutch opera composers
see PIJPER
Other national opera composers include Hendrik Franciscus Andriessen (1892–1981), his son Louis (*b* 1939), Henk Badings (1907–87), Jan Brandts-Buys (1868–1933), Cornelius Dopper (1870–1939), Otto Ketting (*b* 1935), Willem Landré (1874–1948), his son Guillaume (1905–68), Kees Olthuis (*b* 1940), Peter Schat (*b* 1935) and Johan Wagenaar (1862–1941).

Dutoit, Charles (b 1936)
Swiss conductor, particularly associated with the French repertory, especially Berlioz, and with 20th-century works. Best

· Alexandre Dumas ·

The French novelist Alexandre Dumas (1802–70) was himself co-author of two opera libretti, those for Monpou's *Piquillo* and Thomas's *Le Roman d'Elvire*. He also appears as a character in Giordano's *Andrea Chénier*. Some 40 operas have been based on his novels. Below are listed, by work, those operas by composers with entries in this dictionary.

Benvenuto Cellini		
Saint-Saëns	*Ascanio*	1890
Charles VII Chez ses Grands Vassaux		
Donizetti	*Gemma di Vergy*	1834
Cui	*The Saracen*	1899
Le Chevalier d'Harmental		
Messager	*Le Chevalier d'Harmental*	1896
Les Demoiselles de St Cyr		
Humperdinck	*Die Heirat wider Willen*	1905
Don Juan de Maraña		
Pacini	*Carmelita*	1863
Enna	*Don Juan de Maraña*	1925
Gloria Arséna		
Enna	*Gloria Arséna*	1917
Henri III et sa Cour		
Coccia	*Caterina di Guisa*	1833
Flotow	*Le Comte de Saint-Mégrin*	1838
Joseph Balsame		
Litolff	*La Mandragore*	1876
The Man in the Iron Mask		
Thomas	*Raymond*	1851
Les Trois Mousquetaires		
Lara	*Les Trois Mousquetaires*	1921
Benatzky	*Die Drei Musketiere*	1929
Le Tulipe Noir		
Flotow	*Il Fiore d'Arlem*	1876

His son **Alexandre** (1824–95) was also a writer, whose *La Dame aux Camélias* was the source for Verdi's *La Traviata*. In addition, his *Les Danicheff* was the source for Gomes's *Lo Schiavo* and Catălani's *Edmea*.

known as a symphonic conductor, his operatic appearances have been intermittent. Married for a time to the pianist **Martha Argerich**.

Duval, Denise (b 1921)
French soprano, particularly associated with the French repertory, especially Poulenc. She was a fine singing-actress of great charm and personal beauty with a voice of highly individual timbre. She created Thérèse in *Les Mamelles de Tirésias*, Elle in *La Voix Humaine* and Francesca in Hahn's *Le Oui des Jeunes Filles*.

Dvořák, Antonín (1841–1904)
Czech composer, father-in-law of the composer Josef Suk. One of the most consistently underrated stage composers, he wrote 10 operas, notable for their fine

orchestration, their abundant melody and their often sharp sense of characterization. Many are still very popular in the Czech lands but are unaccountably seldom performed elsewhere. His operas are *Alfred* (Olomouc, 10 Dec 1938, composed 1870; libr Karl Theodor Körner), *King and Collier* (*Král a Uhlíř*, Prague, 24 Nov 1874; libr Bernard Guldener), *The Pigheaded Lovers* (*Tvrdé Palice*, Prague, 2 Oct 1881, composed 1874; libr I. Josef Štolba), the historical VANDA, THE CUNNING PEASANT, the heroic DIMITRIJ, the fine JAKOBÍN, the delightful comedy THE DEVIL AND KATE, RUSALKA, his finest opera and his only one to be well known internationally, and ARMIDA. His great-grandson is the violinist **Joseph Suk**.

Dvořáková, Ludmila (b 1923)
Czech soprano, particularly associated with Wagnerian roles and with the Czech repertory. A fine SINGING-ACTRESS with an exciting if not technically perfect voice, she was one of the leading Brünnhildes of the 1960s. Later in her career she turned to mezzo roles. Her husband **Rudolf Vašata** (1911–82) was a conductor, who was musical director of the Ostrava Opera (1949–56).

Dvorský, Peter (b 1951)
Slovakian tenor, particularly associated with the Italian and Czech repertories. One of the leading contemporary Slavic tenors, he has a fine and intelligently used lyric voice, but can sometimes be a little dull on stage.

Dyck, Ernest van (1861–1923)
Belgian tenor, particularly associated with Wagnerian roles, especially Lohengrin and Parsifal. Despite his odd appearance, his vanity and his reportedly ludicrous acting, he was one of the leading HELDENTENORS of the late 19th century. He created the title-role in *Werther*.

Dyer's Wife
Soprano role in Strauss's *Die Frau ohne Schatten*. She is Barak's wife.

Dzerzhinsky, Ivan (1909–78)
Russian composer. His operas – harmonically simple, lyrical and easily accessible – are representative of 'orthodox Soviet' (government approved) music. His musical abilities were strictly limited: he often had to have his orchestration done by other people. His first opera QUIET FLOWS THE DON was hugely successful and was hailed by Stalin as a model of 'socialist realism'. None of his 11 other operas recaptured this initial success. His later works include *Virgin Soil Upturned* (Leningrad, 23 Oct 1937; libr Leonid Dzerzhinsky, after Mikhail Sholokhov), *Winter Night* (Leningrad, 24 Nov 1946; libr Dzerzhinsky, after Alexander Pushkin's *The Snowstorm*), *The Fate of Man* (Moscow, 17 Oct 1961; libr Dzerzhinsky, after Sholokhov) and *Grigori Melekhov* (Leningrad, 4 Nov 1967; libr composer, after Sholokhov). With the collapse of the communist system in Russia, his music is likely to fall into oblivion.

E

Eames, Emma (1865–1962)
American soprano, particularly associated with the French repertory. One of the most popular sopranos of her time and famed for her personal beauty, she created Colombe in Saint-Saëns's *Ascanio*. Her autobiography, *Some Memories and Reflections*, was published in 1927.

Easter Hymn
Chorus with soprano solo ('Regina coeli') in Mascagni's *Cavalleria Rusticana*.

Easton, Florence (1884–1955)
British soprano, long resident at the Metropolitan Opera, New York. One of the most versatile sopranos of the inter-war period, her large repertory ranged from Brünnhilde to Cio-Cio-San (in *Madama Butterfly*), and she was able to learn a new role within 12 hours. She created Lauretta in *Gianni Schicchi*, Aelfrida in Taylor's *The King's Henchman* and Mother Tyl in Wolff's *L'Oiseau Bleu*. Her husband **Francis Maclennan** was a tenor.

Eaton, John (b 1935)
American composer, who has employed both microtonal techniques and electronic music. His operas include *Heracles* (Bloomington, 15 Apr 1972, composed 1964; libr M. Fried, after Sophocles's *Women of Thracis*), *Myshkin* (PBS TV, 23 Apr 1973; libr P. Creagh, after Fyodor Dostoyevsky's *The Idiot*), *Danton and Robspierre* (Bloomington, 21 Apr 1978; libr Creagh), *The Cry of Clytaemnestra* (Bloomington, 1 Mar 1980; libr Creagh, after Aeschylus's *Agamemnon*), *The Tempest* (Santa Fe, 27 July 1985; libr Andrew Porter, after Shakespeare), his most successful opera, and *The Reverend Jim Jones* (1989; libr J. Reston).

Ebert, Carl (1887–1980)
German producer and administrator. One of the most influential opera producers of the mid-20th century, particularly successful with Mozart and Verdi, he was general director of the Darmstadt Opera and the Berlin State Opera. He was also a co-founder of the Glyndebourne Festival and organized the Turkish National Theatre and Opera. His son **Peter** (*b* 1918) is also a producer and administrator. He was director of productions for Scottish Opera (1963–75), the Augsburg Stadttheater (1968–73) and the Wiesbaden Opera (1975–77) and was general administrator of Scottish Opera (1977–80).

Eboli, Princess
Mezzo role in Verdi's *Don Carlos*. King Philip's ex-mistress, she is the historical Ana de Mendoza y la Cerda (1540–92).

Ecco il mondo
Bass aria for Mefistofele in Act II of Boito's *Mefistofele*, in which he scorns the unbelief of evil mankind.

Ecco l'orrido campo
Soprano aria for Amelia in Act II of Verdi's *Un Ballo in Maschera*, in which she picks the magic herb from beneath the gallows.

Ecco ridente
Tenor aria for Count Almaviva in Act I of Rossini's *Il Barbiere di Siviglia*, in which he serenades Rosina beneath her window.

Écho et Narcisse (*Echo and Narcissus*)
Opera in prologue and three acts by Gluck. 1st perf Paris, 24 Sept 1779; libr by Baron Louis Théodore de Tchudy, after Ovid's *Metamorphoses*. Revised version 1st perf Paris, 8 Aug 1780. Principal roles: Écho (sop), Narcisse (ten), Cynire (ten), Amour (mezzo). Gluck's last opera, it was a failure despite its delicate and charming music. It is nowadays only rarely performed.
Plot: Legendary Thessaly. Narcissus is in love with his own reflection, thinking that it is a goddess. Echo, who loves him, can only imitate what others speak and so cannot draw Narcissus away from his self-love. Love, who instigated Echo's feelings, and Echo's relative Cynire are powerless

to help. Echo sees her only release in death, and Narcissus – realizing his fault – feels that he must join her. Love, however, refuses to allow them to die and ensures a happy ending. [R]

Ecuadorean opera composers
These include Luis H. Salgado (*b* 1903) and Pedro Pablo Traversari (1874–1956).

Éda-Pierre, Christiane (b 1932)
Martiniquan soprano, particularly associated with Mozart roles and with the French repertory. Possessing a rich, beautiful and remarkably agile voice, used with a fine technique, she created the Angel in Messiaen's *Saint François d'Assise* and the title-role in Chaynes's *Erzsebet*.

Edelmann, Otto (b 1917)
Austrian bass, particularly associated with Mozart and Wagner roles and with Baron Ochs. One of the leading Germanic basses of the immediate post-war period, he had a rich and large voice and was equally at home in serious or comic roles.

Edgar
Opera in three (originally four) acts by Puccini. 1st perf Milan, 21 April 1889; libr by Ferdinando Fontana, after Alfred de Musset's *La Coupe et les Lèvres*. Revised version 1st perf Ferrara, 28 Feb 1892. Principal roles: Edgar (ten), Fidelia (sop), Tigrana (mezzo), Frank (bar). Puccini's second opera, it is his least successful work and is only rarely performed.
Plot: Flanders, 1302. Edgar deserts his beloved Fidelia for the seductive Moorish girl Tigrana. His brother Frank, who also loves Tigrana, challenges him to a duel and is wounded. In remorse, Edgar leaves Tigrana and joins the army where he and Frank are reconciled. Later, Edgar is believed to have died and, at a requiem for him, a monk recites his crimes and then reveals himself as Edgar. Fidelia rushes to his arms but is murdered by Tigrana. [R]

Edgardo
Tenor role in Donizetti's *Lucia di Lammermoor*. The dispossessed master of Ravenswood, he is in love with Lucia.

Edinburgh Festival
An annual arts festival in Scotland, of which opera is a central feature, it was founded in 1947 by Audrey Mildmay and Sir Rudolf Bing. In the early days, opera was provided by Glyndebourne, but since 1956 it has been provided by visiting companies from around the world and by Scottish Opera. Ranking as one of the most important European summer festivals, artistic directors have been Bing, Ian Hunter, the Earl of Harewood, Peter Diamand, John Drummond, Frank Dunlop and Brian McMaster.

Edipo Rè (*Oedipus the King*)
Opera in one act by Leoncavallo. 1st perf Chicago, 13 Dec 1920; libr by the composer and Giovacchino Forzano, after Sophocles's play. Principal roles: Edipo (bar), Giocasta (sop), Creonte (ten), Tiresia (bass), Corinthian (bass), Shepherd (ten). Leoncavallo's most ambitious and most seriously considered opera, it is a work of considerable grandeur and dramatic scope which places enormous demands on the baritone protagonist. Arguably Leoncavallo's finest opera, it deserves more than the very occasional airing which it currently receives. For plot see *Oedipus Rex*.

Éducation Manquée, Une (*A Defective Education*)
Comic opera in one act by Chabrier. 1st perf Paris, 1 May 1879; libr by Eugène Leterrier and Albert Vanloo. Principal roles: Gontran (sop), Hélène (mezzo), Pausanias (b-bar). A delightful little work, it is still occasionally performed.
Plot: 18th-century France. The young Gontran de Boismassif has married his equally young cousin Hélène, and the two are ignorant of the facts of life. Gontran's tutor Pausanias has vast book learning, but is unable to help in this practical matter, and is sent off to make enquiries. A violent storm frightens Hélène, who seeks comfort in Gontran's bed. When Pausanias returns, he discovers that the youngsters have learnt the facts of life for themselves! [R]

Egisto, L' (*Aegisthus*)
Opera in prologue and three acts by Cavalli. 1st perf Venice, 1643; libr by Giovanni Battista Faustini. Principal roles: Egisto (ten), Clori (sop), Climene (mezzo), Hipparco (ten), Lidio (bass),

Dema (mezzo), Amor (sop). After nearly 300 years of neglect, it has had a number of performances in recent years.
Plot: Legendary Zante (Ionian Sea). Egisto and his beloved Clori were kidnapped by pirates and separated. The same fate also befell Lidio and his beloved Climene. The four, along with Climene's brother Hipparco, now find themselves together on an island. There, Lidio and Clori fall in love, and emotional tensions are aggravated by Hipparco's love for Clori. Egisto is driven to distraction until Amor eventually intervenes and restores everyone to their rightful partner. [R]

Egk, Werner (1901–83)
German composer and conductor. Influenced by Stravinsky, he wrote eight operas, whose theatrical flair and readily accessible melodies have won them considerable popularity in German-speaking countries; elsewhere they are very seldom performed. His operas are *Columbus* (Munich Radio, 13 July 1933; libr composer), DIE ZAUBERGEIGE, PEER GYNT, *Circe* (Berlin, 18 Dec 1948; libr composer, after Pedro Calderón de la Barca's *El Mayor Encanto Amor*), IRISCHE LEGEND, DER REVISOR, DIE VERLOBUNG IN SAN DOMINGO and *Siebzehn Tage und Vier Minuten* (Stuttgart, 2 June 1966), which is a revision of *Circe*. He also wrote the libretto for Blacher's *Abstrakte Oper No 1*.

Eglantine
Soprano role in Weber's *Euryanthe*. She is in love with Adolar.

Ehrling, Sixten (b 1918)
Swedish conductor, particularly associated with the German repertory. He was musical director of the Royal Opera, Stockholm (1953–60) and conducted the first performances of Blomdahl's *Aniara* and Atterberg's *Stormen*.

Ein, Eine
Titles beginning with the German indefinite article are listed under the letter of the first main word. For example, *Eine Nacht in Venedig* is listed under N.

Einem, Gottfried von (b 1918)
Austrian composer. One of the most successful post-war opera composers, his stage works are theatrically highly effective and are eclectic in musical style. His seven operas are DANTONS TOD, DER PROZESS, *Der Zerrissene* (*The Confused*, Hamburg, 17 Sept 1964; libr Boris Blacher, after Johann Nepomuk Nestroy), the highly successful DER BESUCH DER ALTEN DAME, *Kabale und Liebe* (Vienna, 17 Dec 1976; libr Blacher and Lotte Ingrisch, after Friedrich von Schiller), the controversial *Jesu Hochzeit* (Vienna, 18 May 1980; libr Ingrisch) and *Der Tulifant* (Vienna, 30 Oct 1990; libr Ingrisch).

Einsam in trüben Tagen
Soprano aria for Elsa (usually referred to as 'Elsa's Dream') in Act I of Wagner's *Lohengrin*, in which she describes her dream of a knight to champion her.

Eire
see DUBLIN GRAND OPERA SOCIETY; WEXFORD FESTIVAL

Eisenstein, Gabriel von
Tenor role in J. Strauss's *Die Fledermaus*. He is Rosalinde's philandering husband. The role is often sung by a baritone.

Eisler, Hanns (1898–1962)
German composer. He wrote a considerable number of musical plays, many in collboration with Bertolt Brecht, which reflect his strong Marxist views. The most important is *Die Mutter* (Berlin, 1931; libr Brecht, after Maxim Gorky). His one fully operatic project, *Faust*, was abandoned when he had written only the libretto.

Eisslinger, Ulrich
Tenor COMPRIMARIO role in Wagner's *Die Meistersinger von Nürnberg*. A grocer, he is one of the masters.

El
Titles beginning with the Spanish definite article are listed under the letter of the first main word. For example, *El Barberillo de Lavapiés* is listed under B.

È la solita storia
Tenor aria for Federico in Act II of Cilea's *L'Arlesiana*, in which he compares the shepherd's solitary song with his own feelings.

Elda
see LORELEY (Catalani)

Elder, Mark (b 1947)
British conductor, particularly associated with Verdi, Rossini and Janáček operas and with 20th-century works. An outstanding Verdian, he is perhaps the finest British opera conductor of the younger generation. He was musical director of the English National Opera (1980–93) and conducted the first performances of Blake's *Toussaint* and Harvey's *Inquest of Love*.

Éléazar
Tenor role in Halévy's *La Juive*. He is a Jewish goldsmith.

Electra
Soprano role in Mozart's *Idomeneo*. She is an Argive princess in love with Idamante.

Elegie für Junge Liebende (*Elegy for Young Lovers*)
Opera in three acts by Henze. 1st perf Schwetzingen, 20 May 1961; libr by W.H. Auden and Chester Kallman. Principal roles: Mittenhofer (bar), Hilda Mack (sop), Toni and Dr Reischmann (ten and bass), Elisabeth Zimmer (sop), Carolina (mezzo). One of Henze's finest operas, it has been widely performed.
Plot: Austrian Alps, 1910. The egocentric and narcissistic poet Gregor Mittenhofer goes to the Alps annually to seek inspiration for his work from the hallucinations of Hilda Mack, permanently waiting for the return of her husband who disappeared on their honeymoon 40 years previously. When Mack's body is recovered from a glacier, Mittenhofer has to find inspiration elsewhere and fastens upon the young lovers Elisabeth and Toni. He sends them out on to the Hammerhorn to collect edelweiss and allows them to die there. This inspires his greatest poem 'Elegy for Young Lovers'. [R Exc]

Elektra
Opera in one act by Strauss (Op 58). 1st perf Dresden, 25 Jan 1909; libr by Hugo von Hofmannsthal, after Sophocles's play. Principal roles: Elektra (sop), Chrysothemis (sop), Klytemnästra (mezzo), Orest (bar), Aegisth (ten). The first fruit of the Strauss/Hofmannsthal partnership and often regarded as Strauss's greatest opera, it is a powerful, harsh and frenzied setting of Sophocles's great tragedy. The title-role is one of the most vocally demanding in all opera.
Plot: Legendary Mycenae. Elektra, daughter of Clytemnestra and the murdered Agamemnon, lives in degradation, dreaming of the return of her brother Orestes to avenge the crime committed by Clytemnestra, who is wracked with remorse and guilt. Strangers arrive with news that Orestes is dead, and Elektra unsuccessfully tries to persuade her gentle sister Chrysothemis to help her. As she starts to dig up the axe which killed Agamemnon, she is interrupted by one of the strangers who, she gradually realizes, is Orestes. He enters the palace and kills Clytemnestra. When Clytemnestra's lover Aegisthus returns, Elektra joyously lights his way inside to his own death. The achievement of her long-dreamt vengeance is too much for Elektra: whilst dancing in half-crazed triumph, she falls dead. [R]

Elemer, Count
Tenor role in Strauss's *Arabella*. He is one of Arabella's suitors.

Elena
Soprano role in: **1** Boito's *Mefistofele*. She is Helen of Troy. **2** Rossini's *La Donna del Lago*. Douglas's daughter, she is in love with Malcolm. **3** Shaporin's *The Decembrists*. She is in love with Dmitri. **4** Donizetti's *Marino Faliero*. She is Faliero's wife. **5** Rota's *Il Cappello di Paglia di Firenze*. She is Fadinard's fiancée.

Elgar, Sir Edward (1857–1934)
British composer. Best known as an orchestral and choral composer, he began one opera, *The Spanish Lady* (Cambridge, 24 Nov 1994, composed *c* 1930; libr composer and Barry Jackson, after Ben Jonson's *The Devil is an Ass*), which did not progress beyond sketches. An orchestral suite was arranged from the music by Percy M. Young, who also subsequently prepared a performing edition.

Elias, Rosalind (b 1931)
American mezzo, particularly associated with the Italian and French repertories. A

rich-voiced singer of fine musicianship, she created, for Barber, Erika in *Vanessa* and Charmian in *Antony and Cleopatra*. She has also produced a number of operas.

Élisa or **Le Voyage aux Glaciers du Mont-Saint Bernard** (*The Journey to the Glaciers of Mount St Bernard*)
Opera in two acts by Cherubini. 1st perf Paris, 13 Dec 1794; libr by Jacques-Antoine Reveroni de Saint-Cyr. Principal roles: Élisa (sop), Florindo (ten), Germano (bar), Prior (bass), Laura (mezzo). An historically important work in that its avalanche scene introduced the fashion for *musique d'effet* into opera, it was long popular but is nowadays only very rarely performed.
Plot: Swiss Alps, 18th century. Florindo arrives at a monastic hospice to wait for news from his beloved Élisa, whom he cannot wed because of her father Germano's disapproval. A forged letter arrives informing him that Élisa has eloped with another man. Florindo is foiled in a suicide attempt, and Élisa arrives in search of him following the death of her father. Florindo is swept away in an avalanche, but the monks revive him and he is united with Élisa.

Elisabeth
Soprano role in: **1** Wagner's *Tannhäuser*. She is the Landrave Hermann's daughter. **2** Verdi's *Don Carlos*. She is the historical Élisabeth de Valois (1546–68), wife of Philip II. **3** Henze's *Elegie für Junge Liebende*. She is in love with Toni Reischmann.

Elisabetta Regina d'Inghilterra (*Elizabeth, Queen of England*)
Opera in two acts by Rossini. 1st perf Naples, 4 Oct 1815; libr by Giovanni Federico Schmidt, after Carlo Federici's play, itself based on Sophie Lee's *The Recess*. Principal roles: Elisabetta (sop), Leicester (ten), Mathilde (sop), Duke of Norfolk (ten). An important opera historically in that, for the first time, Rossini wrote out the vocal decorations himself, and also provided orchestral accompaniment for the recitatives. For it, Rossini reused the overture and finale from his earlier *Aureliano in Palmira*. The overture turns up again in *Il Barbiere di Siviglia*, where Rosina's first aria is not entirely dissimilar from Elisabetta's. Successful in its time, it suffered a long period of complete neglect, but has received a number of performances in the last 20 years.
Plot: Late-16th-century England. Elizabeth I is furious to discover from the Duke of Norfolk that her favourite the Earl of Leicester has secretly married Mathilde. Leicester refuses to give up Mathilde, so Elizabeth has him imprisoned under sentence of death. Norfolk's machinations are eventually unmasked, and Elizabeth forgives Leicester and Mathilde. [R]

Elisetta
Soprano role in Cimarosa's *Il Matrimonio Segreto*. She is Geronimo's daughter.

Elisir d'Amore, L' (*The Love Potion*)
Comic opera in two acts by Donizetti. 1st perf Milan, 12 May 1832; libr by Felice Romani, after Eugène Scribe's libretto for Auber's *Le Philtre*. Principal roles: Nemorino (ten), Adina (sop), Dulcamara (b-bar), Belcore (bar), Giannetta (sop). Always one of Donizetti's best-loved works, it is almost an OPERA SEMISERIA rather than a true OPERA BUFFA, as it contains both moments of real pathos and – in Dulcamara – one of the greatest of all BUFFO roles.
Plot: Early-19th-century Tuscany. Nemorino is distracted by his inability to win the heart of the capricious landowner Adina, and is further put out when she agrees (partly to spite him) to marry the bumptious sergeant Belcore. The ambulent quack Dr Dulcamara arrives proclaiming his miraculous nostroms. In desperation, Nemorino asks him for a love potion, and Dulcamara sells him a bottle of Bordeaux with a hastily affixed label. Nemorino's subsequent inebriated behaviour annoys Adina, who agrees to marry Belcore forthwith. Nemorino urgently needs a second bottle to provide immediate amatory effect, but he has no money. He enlists with Belcore and buys another bottle with his pay. Meanwhile, Giannetta discovers that Nemorino's uncle has died and left him a fortune. She and the other girls suddenly discover how handsome he is. Nemorino, ignorant of his uncle's death, puts their attentions down to the

effect of the potion. Adina, miffed by his new indifference, purchases his release from the army and finally admits that she loves him. The two are united and Dulcamara, claiming all the credit, does a roaring trade in love potions. [R]

Ella giammai m'amò
Bass monologue for King Philip in Act IV of Verdi's *Don Carlos*, in which he laments his loveless marriage.

Elle a fuit
Soprano aria for Antonia in the Antonia Act of Offenbach's *Les Contes d'Hoffmann*, sung as she accompanies herself at the piano.

Ellen Orford
Soprano role in Britten's *Peter Grimes*. She is the widowed village schoolmistress.

Elmendorff, Karl (1891–1962)
German conductor, particularly associated with the German repertory, especially Wagner. He was musical director of the Wiesbaden Opera (1932–6 and 1952–6), the Mannheim Opera (1936–42), the Dresden State Opera (1942–5) and the Kassel Staatstheater (1948–51). He conducted the first performances of Haas's *Die Hochzeit des Jobs* and Malipiero's *Torneo Notturno*.

Elsa
Soprano role in Wagner's *Lohengrin*. She is the falsely accused daughter of the Duke of Brabant.

Elsner, Józef (1769–1854)
Polish composer. The first Polish opera composer of significance, he wrote 32 stage works of various kinds, all of them now largely forgotten. The most successful include *Andromeda* (Warsaw, 14 Jan 1807; libr Ludwik Osiński), *The Echo in the Wood* (*Echo w Lesie*, Warsaw, 22 Apr 1807; libr W. Pekalski) [R], *Leszek the White* (*Leszek Biały*, Warsaw, 2 Dec 1809; libr L. Dmuszewski) and *King Lokietek* (*Krol Łokietek*, Warsaw, 3 Apr 1818; libr Dmuszewski) [R]. He was also a noted teacher, whose pupils included Chopin.

È lucevan le stelle
Tenor aria for Mario Cavaradossi in Act III of Puccini's *Tosca*, in which he thinks of his love for Tosca whilst he awaits his execution.

Elvino
Tenor role in Bellini's *La Sonnambula*. He is a young Swiss farmer engaged to Amina.

Elvira
Soprano role in: **1** Mozart's and Gazzaniga's *Don Giovanni*. She is a lady of Burgos, seduced and deserted by Giovanni. **2** Verdi's *Ernani*. She is in love with Ernani. **3** Bellini's *I Puritani*. Gualtiero Walton's daughter, she loves Arturo. **4** Rossini's *L'Italiana in Algieri*. She is Mustafà's wife.

Emerald Isle, The or **The Caves of Carig-Cleena**
Operetta in two acts by Sullivan. 1st perf London, 27 April 1901; libr by Basil Hood. Principal roles: Terence O'Brian (ten), Lady Rosie Pippin (sop), Pat Murphy (bar), Molly O'Grady (mezzo), Prof Bunn (bar), Earl of Newton (bass). Sullivan's last stage work, it was left unfinished at his death and was completed by German. Reasonably successful at its appearance, it is nowadays only very rarely performed.
Plot: Early-19th-century Ireland. The young rebel Terence O'Brian, scion of the local aristocracy, loves Rosie, daughter of the Viceroy Earl Newton. Through the treachery of the elocutionist Prof Bunn and from the activities of the supposedly blind fiddler Pat Murphy and his beloved Molly, the Viceroy learns of the revolutionary society, the Clan-na-Gael, based at the caves of Carig-Cleena. However, the revelation that O'Brian is in fact an aristocrat persuades the Viceroy to allow him to wed Rosie.

Emilia
Mezzo role in Verdi's and Rossini's *Otello*. Iago's wife, she is Desdemona's companion.

Emperor
1 Tenor role in Strauss's *Die Frau ohne Schatten*. **2** Baritone role in Stravinsky's *The Nightingale*. **3** Mezzo trouser role in Henze's *We Come to the River*.

Emperor Jones, The
Opera in prologue and two acts by

Gruenberg (Op 36). 1st perf New York, 7 Jan 1933; libr by Kathleen de Jaffa, after Eugene O'Neill's play. Principal roles: Brutus Jones (bar), Harry Smithers (ten), Old Nature Witch (sop). Gruenberg's finest opera, it met with considerable success at its appearance but is nowadays virtually forgotten.
Plot: A Caribbean island, early 20th century. Brutus Jones, ex-porter, crap shooter and murderer, has fled from American justice to the island, which he rules as a royal despot. Warned by Smithers that his subjects are about to rise against him, he flees through the jungle, tormented by his victims who come to him in hallucinations. Finally, he kills himself with a silver bullet – his last.

Empress
Soprano role in Strauss's *Die Frau ohne Schatten*. She is the childless woman without a shadow.

Enchantress, The (*Charoydeka*)
Opera in four acts by Tchaikovsky. 1st perf St Petersburg, 1 Nov 1887; libr by Ippolit Vassilevich Shpazhinsky, after his own play. Principal roles: Kuma (sop), Yuri (ten), Nikita (bar), Eupraksia (mezzo), Mamirov (bass). The least successful of Tchaikovsky's mature operas, it contains much fine music but is very rarely performed, even in Russia.
Plot: 15th-century Russia. Yuri visits the inn run by Kuma, who falls in love with him. Yuri's father Prince Nikita arrives on an inspection and is charmed by Kuma, who mocks his puritanical old clerk Mamirov. Nikita's frequent visits to Kuma arouse the anger of his wife, Princess Eupraksia, and Yuri vows to avenge his mother by killing Kuma. Kuma rejects Nikita's advances and wins over Yuri, who finally returns her love. They elope together. In a forest, a disguised Eupraksia gives Kuma poison and Nikita kills Yuri in anger and jealousy. [R]

Encore (French for 'again')
A word shouted by British audiences to demand a repeat; thus also meaning the repeat itself. In Italy and France *bis* is shouted. Originating in the 17th century, encores are a controversial business. Standard in operetta (particularly in Gilbert and Sullivan), they are frowned upon in opera except in Italy, where Toscanini had frequent rows with audiences for refusing to allow them. They are virtually unknown in Britain; the only encores in Covent Garden's post-war history have been Maria Callas and Ebe Stignani in *Norma* and the BUFFO duet in *Don Pasquale* (a standard encore). The longest encore in operatic history was the premiere of *Il Matrimonio Segreto*: Emperor Leopold II was so delighted with it that he ordered supper to be served to the company and then the entire opera to be repeated.

Enescu, George (1881–1955)
Romanian composer, violinist and conductor. Best known as an orchestral composer, he also wrote one opera, the magnificent and unjustly neglected OEDIPE, one of the finest of all 20th-century operas. He was musical director of the Bucharest Opera (1921–2).

Enfant et les Sortilèges, L' (*The Child and the Toys*)
Opera in two parts by Ravel. 1st perf Monte Carlo, 21 March 1925; libr by Colette. Principal roles: Child (mezzo), Mother (cont), Fire (sop), Arithmetic (ten), Tree (bass), Grandfather Clock (bar), Princess (sop), Squirrel (mezzo), Teapot (ten), Cats (mezzo and bar). A delightful work of great wit and orchestral virtuosity, it was an immediate success and has remained popular ever since.
Plot: Normandy. Bored with his homework and tired of good behaviour, the Child sticks his tongue out at his Mother and is confined to his room. In a fit of temper, he does all the damage he can, abusing and destroying furniture, crockery and books, pulling the Cat's tail and sticking his pen into his pet Squirrel. These objects and animals all come to upbraid him, and when he calls out for his Mother they attack him. In the ensuing fracas, a baby squirrel is hurt. The Child tends its injuries, thereby winning the forgiveness of the animals. [R]

England
see GREAT BRITAIN

English Bach Festival
An annual British music festival, largely

based in London, founded in 1963 by the harpsichordist Lina Lalandi. It has given a number of illuminating performances of baroque operas, especially Rameau, in productions recreating the costumes and acting and dancing styles of the period.

English Cat, The
Comic opera in two acts by Henze. 1st perf Schwetzingen, 2 June 1983; libr by Edward Bond, after Anne-Honoré de Balzac's *Peines de Coeur d'une Chatte Anglaise*. Principal roles: Minette (sop), Lord Puff (ten), Tom (bar), Babette (mezzo), Louise (sop), Mr Jones (bar), Plunkett (bar). A biting social satire, written from Henze's customary left-wing viewpoint, in which cats behave in the manner of their class-conscious owners, it has met with considerable success and has been widely performed. [R]

English Music Theatre
Founded in 1975 as a reorganization of the ENGLISH OPERA GROUP, it toured Britain with a repertory of small- and medium-scale works in productions which laid strong emphasis on the dramatic side. The director of productions was Colin Graham and the musical director was Steuart Bedford. A reduction in government subsidy led to its closure in 1979.

English National Opera
Founded by Lilian Baylis as Sadler's Wells Opera, the company began operations in Jan 1931 and was based at Sadler's Wells Theatre in north London and also toured extensively. In 1958, the company incorporated most of the membership of the Carl Rosa Opera Company, enabling it to undertake larger-scale works. In Aug 1968, the company moved to the London Coliseum (cap 2,354), adopting its present name from 3 Aug 1974. The annual season runs from August to June.

Perhaps the most exciting and innovative of British opera companies, it performs in English with predominantly British and Commonwealth artists. Since its move to the Coliseum, it has developed one of the most enterprising repertories of any major opera company, and a production style that places great emphasis on the dramatic aspect of the works. Productions, whilst sometimes highly controversial, are always thought-provoking. In recent years, the company has been especially noted for its 20th-century repertory and for its Janáček and Wagner productions, particularly the English-language *Ring*. Administrators have included Joan Cross, Norman Tucker, Stephen Arlen, the Earl of Harewood, Peter Jonas and Dennis Marks. The post-war musical directors have been Lawrence Collingwood, James Robertson, Sir Alexander Gibson, Sir Colin Davis, Sir Charles Mackerras, Sir Charles Groves, Mark Elder and Sian Edwards.

English Opera Group
A chamber opera company founded in 1946 by Britten, Eric Crozier and John Piper, for the performance of new operas. Based at Aldeburgh, the company also toured widely in Britain and abroad. Always maintaining high artistic standards, it gave the first performances of many important post-war British operas as well as reviving earlier British works. In 1975, it was reorganized as the ENGLISH MUSIC THEATRE.

Enna, August (1860–1939)
Danish composer. He wrote some 15 operas in late romantic style, all of which are now largely forgotten. His first opera *Agleia* (Copenhagen, 1884; libr T. Andersen) was followed by *The Witch* (*Heksen*, Copenhagen, 24 June 1892; libr A. Ipsen, after Fitger), by far his most successful work. His later operas include *Kleopatra* (Copenhagen, 7 Feb 1894; libr E. Christiansen, after H. Rider Haggard), *Aucassin og Nicolette* (Copenhagen, 2 Feb 1896; libr S. Michaëlis), *The Little Match Girl* (*Pigen Med Svovlstikkerne*, Copenhagen, 13 Nov 1897; libr composer, after Hans Christian Andersen), *Lamia* (Antwerp, 3 Oct 1899; libr H. Rode, after P. Mariager), *The Princess and the Pea* (*Prinsessen på Aerten*, Århus, 15 Sept 1901; libr P.A. Rosenberg, after Andersen), *Young Love* (*Ung Elskov*, Weimar, 6 Dec 1904; libr Rosenberg, after K. Mikszath), *The Nightingale* (*Nattergalen*, Copenhagen, 10 Nov 1912; libr K. Friis-Møller, after Andersen's *The Emperor and the Nightingale*), *Gloria Arséna* (Copenhagen, 15 Apr 1917; libr O. Hansen, after Alexandre Dumas) and *The Comedians*

(*Komedianter*, Copenhagen, 8 Apr 1920; libr E. and O. Hansen, after Victor Hugo's *L'Homme Qui Rit*).

Enrichetta
Mezzo role in Bellini's *I Puritani*. She is Queen Henrietta Maria (1609–69), widow of Charles I.

Enrico
1 Baritone role in Donizetti's *Lucia di Lammermoor*. He is Lucia's brother. **2** Bass role in Donizetti's *Anna Bolena*. He is King Henry VIII. **3** Tenor role in Donizetti's *Rosmonda d'Inghilterra*. He is King Henry II. **4** Baritone role in Donizetti's *Il Campanello*. He is Serafina's rejected suitor. **5** Tenor role in Donizetti's *Maria de Rudenz*. He is Corrado's brother. **6** Baritone role in Donizetti's *Maria di Rohan*. He is secretly married to Maria. **7** Baritone role in Haydn's *L'Isola Disabitata*. He is loved by Silvia. **8** Tenor role in Donizetti's *L'Aio nell' Imbarazzo*. Don Giulio's son, he is secretly married to Gilda. **9** Tenor role in Respighi's *La Campana Sommersa*. Magda's husband, he is a bell-founder. **10** Tenor COMPRIMARIO role in Verdi's *Aroldo*. He is Mina's cousin.

Ensemble (French for 'together')
The term has two meanings in opera: **1** A group or company of performers, and thus also their musical unanimity. **2** A concerted operatic number for several soloists, with or without chorus.

Ente autonomo (Italian for 'autonomous entity')
The name given to the independent and self-governing bodies which run the principal Italian opera houses, such as the Teatro San Carlo, Naples, and La Scala, Milan.

Entführung aus dem Serail, Die (*The Abduction from the Seraglio*)
Comic opera in three acts by Mozart (K 384). 1st perf Vienna, 16 July 1782; libr by Gottlieb Stephanie, after Christoph Friedrich Bretzner's libretto for Johann André's *Belmont und Constanze*, itself based on Isaac Bickerstaffe's *The Captive*. Principal roles: Constanze (sop), Belmonte (ten), Osmin (bass), Blönchen (or Blonde) (sop), Pedrillo (ten), Pasha Selim (speaker). Mozart's first major success, it contains some of his finest arias, much music in the then-popular *alla turca* (Turkish) style, and – in Osmin – one of the greatest comic roles in all opera.
Plot: Mid-16th-century Turkey. The Spanish nobleman Belmonte comes to the palace of Pasha Selim, where his betrothed Constanze and her English maid Blönchen, as well as his valet Pedrillo, have been enslaved since their capture by pirates. Constanze has refused the advances of the Pasha, as has Blönchen those (less politely offered) of the harem-keeper Osmin. Engaged by the Pasha as an architect, Belmonte and Pedrillo plan an escape, but they are caught by Osmin. The Pasha learns that Belmonte is the son of his greatest enemy, but as an act of magnanimity he allows all his prisoners to go free. [R]

Entr'acte (French for 'between act')
A short orchestral piece played between two acts or scenes of an opera.

Entrée (French for 'entry')
The term has two meanings in opera: **1** A term used to describe the individual acts of an early-18th-century French opera in which each act has a seperate and unrelated plot, as in Rameau's *Les Indes Galantes* and Campra's *L'Europe Galante*. **2** A short, march-like orchestral piece played for the entry of an important character in a late-17th-century French opera.

Enzo
Tenor role in Ponchielli's *La Gioconda*. He is a Genoese nobleman in love with Laura.

Equivoci, Gli (*The Doubles*)
Comic opera in two acts by Storace. 1st perf Vienna, 27 Dec 1786; libr by Lorenzo da Ponte, after William Shakespeare's *The Comedy of Errors*. Principal roles: Adriana (sop), two Euphemios (tens), Lesbia (sop), two Dromios (basses). Arguably Storace's finest opera, parts of which he later reused in other works, it enjoyed considerable success in its time but is nowadays only very rarely performed.

Era la notte
Baritone aria for Iago in Act II of Verdi's *Otello*, in which he relates to Otello his imaginary overhearing of Cassio talking in his sleep of his love for Desdemona.

Erb, Karl (1877–1958)
German tenor, particularly associated with Mozart roles. One of the leading lyric tenors of the inter-war period, he created the title-role in Pfitzner's *Palestrina* and was the inspiration for the character Erbe in Thomas Mann's *Dr Faustus*. Married for a time to the soprano MARIA IVOGÜN.

Ercole Amante (*Hercules in Love*)
Opera in prologue and five acts by Cavalli. 1st perf Paris, 7 Feb 1662; libr by Francesco Buti, after Ovid's *Metamorphoses*. Principal roles: Ercole (bass), Jole (sop), Hyllus (ten), Dejanira (mezzo), Juno (mezzo), Venus (sop). Written to celebrate the marriage of Louis XIV and Maria-Theresa of Austria, it has recently received a number of performances after nearly 300 years of total neglect. [R]

Erda
Contralto role in Wagner's *Das Rheingold* and *Siegfried*. She is the primeval Earth Mother.

Erede, Alberto (b 1908)
Italian conductor, particularly associated with the Italian repertory and with Wagner. A rock-solid Italian maestro of the old school, he was musical director of the Deutsche Oper am Rhein (1958–61) and conducted the first performance of Menotti's *The Old Maid and the Thief*.

Erik
Tenor role in: **1** Wagner's *Der Fliegende Holländer*. He is a huntsman in love with Senta. **2** Delius's *Fennimore and Gerda*. He is a painter engaged to Fennimore.

Erismena, L'
Opera in prologue and three acts by Cavalli. 1st perf Venice, 30 Dec 1655; libr by Aurelio Aureli. Revised version 1st perf Venice, 1670. Principal roles: Erismena (sop), Erimante (bass), Orimeno (c-ten), Aldimira (sop), Argippo (ten), Diarte (bass). It has recently received a few performances after 300 years of complete neglect. [R]

Eri tu
Baritone aria for Ankerström in Act III of Verdi's *Un Ballo in Maschera*, in which he resolves to punish Gustavus rather than his wife.

Erkel, Ferenc (1810–93)
Hungarian composer and conductor. The founder of the nationalist school of Hungarian opera, his stage works make considerable use of traditional Hungarian material. The first of his eight operas was the successful *Bátori Mária* (Budapest, 8 Aug 1840; libr Béni Egressy, after András Dugonics). It was followed by LÁSZLÓ HUNYADI and BÁNK BÁN, by far his best-known works. Their successors were *Sarolta* (Budapest, 26 Jan 1862; libr József Czanyuga), *Dózsa György* (Budapest, 6 Apr 1867; libr Ede Szigligeti, after Maurus Jókai), the nationalist *Brankovics György* (Budapest, 20 May 1874; libr Odri Lehel and Ferenc Ormai, after Károly Obernyik), *Unknown Heroes* (*Névtelen Hosök*, Budapest, 30 Nov 1880; libr Ede Tóth) and *King Stephen* (*István Király*, Budapest, 14 Mar 1885; libr Antal Váradi, after Lajos Dobra), most of which is by his son **Guala**. Erkel also developed a Hungarian equivalent of the English ballad opera, known as *népszínmü*, which incorporated both original songs and traditional ballads. The most successful example was *Two Pistols* (*Két Pisztoly*, 1844; libr Szigligeti). He was musical director of the Budapest State Opera (1838–74).

Erlanger, Baron Frédéric d' (1868–1943)
French-born British banker and composer. A long-time director and patron of Covent Garden, he wrote four operas. They are *Jehan de Saintré* (Aix-les-Bains, 1 Aug 1893; libr Jules Barbier), *Inès Mendo* (London, 10 July 1897; libr P. Decourcelle and A. Liorat, after Prosper Mérimée), *Tess* (Naples, 10 Apr 1906; libr Luigi Illica, after Thomas Hardy's *Tess of the d'Ubervilles*), which enjoyed some success in its time, and *Noël* (Paris, 28 Dec 1910; libr J. and P. Ferrier).

Ermione
Opera in two acts by Rossini. 1st perf Naples, 27 March 1819; libr by Andrea Leone Tottola, after Jean Baptiste Racine's *Andromaque*. Principal roles: Ermione (sop), Andromaca (mezzo), Oreste (ten), Pirro (ten), Fenicio (bass), Pilade (ten). Unsuccessful at its appearance, despite containing some of Rossini's finest serious

music, it is only in the last decade that it has been performed.
Plot: Legendary Epirus. King Pirrus, son of Achilles, is betrothed to Menelaus's daughter Hermione, but has fallen in love with Hector's widow Andromache. Orestes, in love with Hermione, arrives as Greek envoy, demanding the death of Andromache's young son so as to ensure that the Trojan War can never recommence. Pirrus rejects the demand, and Andromache agrees to wed him if he will swear to save her son. As the bridal procession approaches, the furious Hermione tells Orestes to kill Pirrus. She is filled with remorse, but cannot prevent Orestes from carrying out the murder. [R]

Ermler, Mark (b 1932)
Russian conductor, particularly associated with the Russian and Italian repertories, especially Tchaikovsky and Puccini. Long associated with the Bolshoi Opera, he is one of the finest contemporary Russian opera conductors.

Ernani
Opera in four acts by Verdi. 1st perf Venice, 9 March 1844; libr by Francesco Maria Piave, after Victor Hugo's *Hernani*. Principal roles: Ernani (ten), Elvira (sop), Carlo (bar), da Silva (bass). Verdi's fifth opera, it was the work which established his European reputation. It is notable for its full-blooded melodies as well as for being the first opera in which Verdi fully exploited the musico-dramatic potential of the baritone voice.
Plot: Aragon and Aix-la-Chapelle, 1519. Elvira is betrothed to the grandee Silva, but is in love with the banished nobleman-turned-outlaw known as Ernani. She is also loved by Carlo, the King of Spain. Carlo takes Elvira away, ostensibly for her safety, whilst Ernani is challenged to a duel by Silva. Allowing Silva's right to seek vengeance, Ernani asks that it be postponed so that he may first avenge himself on Carlo. He gives Silva a horn and promises that if he hears Silva use it he will take his life. A group of conspirators including Ernani and Silva plot to assassinate Carlo, but news arrives of Carlo's election as Holy Roman Emperor. At Elvira's request, he forgives the conspirators, restores Ernani's estates and blesses his marriage with Elvira. After a ball to celebrate the wedding, the horn is heard. Silva offers Ernani the choice of poison or the dagger, and Ernani stabs himself. [R]

Ernani involami
Soprano aria for Elvira in Act I of Verdi's *Ernani*, in which she prays that Ernani will rescue her from her forthcoming marriage.

Ernesto
1 Tenor role in Donizetti's *Don Pasquale*. Pasquale's nephew, he is in love with Norina. **2** Baritone role in Bellini's *Il Pirata*. He is Imogene's husband. **3** Mezzo trouser role in Haydn's *Il Mondo della Luna*. He is loved by Flaminia. **4** Soprano trouser role in Bononcini's *Griselda*. He is loved by Almirena. **5** Tenor role in Paer's *Agnese di Fitzhenry*. He is Agnese's lover.

Ernst II (Duke of Saxe-Coburg-Gotha) (1818–93)
German statesman and composer, brother of Queen Victoria's husband Prince Albert. One of the more talented of the many royal musical dilettantes, his opera *Diana von Solange* (Coburg, 5 Dec 1858; libr Otto Prechtler) achieved a production at the Metropolitan Opera, New York, in 1891.

Ero the Joker (*Ero s Onoga Svijeta*, which strictly means *Ero from the Other World)*
Comic opera in three acts by Gotovac. 1st perf Zagreb, 2 Nov 1935; libr by Milan Begović, after a Dalmatian folk tale. Principal roles: Mića (ten), Sima (bar), Doma (mezzo), Marko (bar), Djula (sop). Gotovac's most successful opera, it is the most popular of all Serbo-Croat operas and is the only one to have enjoyed international success. It is a delightful and tuneful folk-inspired work written in predominantly Italian style.
Plot: Dinura Mountains (Dalmatia). Mića drops out of a hayloft into a group of girls including Djula, claiming to be Ero and to have come to earth because heaven is boring. Djula's stepmother Doma tries to get rid of him, but he tells her that her mother is in a bad way in heaven, so Doma gives money for her. Mića and Djula run away together with the aid of the miller Sima. They return at the next village fair and Mića reveals that he is not

poor but is the son of a wealthy farmer and had wished to test Djula's love. Her father Marko blesses their union. [R]

Erwartung (*Expectation*)
Opera in one act by Schönberg (Op 17). 1st perf Prague, 6 June 1924 (composed 1909); libr by Marie Pappenheim. Principal role: Woman (sop). Schönberg's first stage work, it is a powerfully expressionist MONODRAMA written in atonal style.
Plot: A semi-deranged Woman is searching in a forest at night for her lover. Hearing weeping, she mistakes a log for her lover's body, is convinced that she is being watched and believes herself pursued by the moon. Arriving at her rival's house, she discovers that she has murdered her lover. She covers the body with hysterical kisses and departs. [R]

Escamillo
Baritone role in Bizet's *Carmen*. He is a toreador.

Esclarmonde
Opera in prologue, four acts and epilogue by Massenet. 1st perf Paris, 14 May 1889; libr by Alfred Blau and Louis de Gramont, after the medieval romance *Parthenopoeus de Blois*. Principal roles: Esclarmonde (sop), Roland (ten), Parséïs (mezzo), Bishop of Blois (bar), Phorcas (bass), Enéas (ten). An exotic and richly scored work in grand opera style, there is some evidence in it of Wagner's influence in Massenet's use of LEITMOTIVS. It is only rarely performed.
Plot: Medieval Byzantium and Blois. The sorceress Esclarmonde, daughter of Phorcas, wins the knight Roland de Blois through her powers of enchantment. She is subsequently forced to give him up in order to retain her kingdom and her magical powers. Later, in a tournament, Roland wins the hand of a veiled princess, who turns out to be Esclarmonde. [R]

È sogno?
Baritone aria (the Jealousy Monologue) for Ford in Act II of Verdi's *Falstaff*, in which Verdi parodies his own baritone style.

Essen Opera
Opera in this German city in North Rhine-Westphalia is given at the Städtische Bühnen (cap 637), which opened on 16 Sept 1892. Damaged in World War II, it was rebuilt in 1950. It has an adventurous repertory policy and stages many 20th-century operas. Musical directors have included Heinz Wallberg, Guido Ajmone-Marsan and Wolf-Dieter Hauschild.

Essex, Earl of
Robert Devereux (1566–1601), the favourite of Queen Elizabeth I, appears in a number of operas, including: **1** Tenor role in Donizetti's *Roberto Devereux*. **2** Baritone role in German's *Merrie England*. **3** Tenor role in Britten's *Gloriana*.

Esswood, Paul (b 1942)
British counter-tenor, particularly associated with Händel and other baroque roles. One of the most stylish and musicianly contemporary counter-tenors, he created the title-role in Glass's *Akhnaten* and Death in Penderecki's *Paradise Lost*.

Esterháza
A castle near Fertöd in Hungary, where the Prince Esterházy maintained an opera house in the 18th century. Haydn was musical director for a lengthy period and all of his mature operas were first performed there.

Estes, Simon (b 1938)
American bass, particularly associated with Wagnerian roles, especially the Dutchman in Wagner's *Der Fliegende Holländer*. One of the few male black singers to have enjoyed a major international career, he possesses a dark, rich and powerful voice and has a remarkable upper register which allows him to sing high baritone roles such as the title-role in Verdi's *Macbeth*. He has a strong stage presence, but can sometimes seem a little uncommitted. He created Carter Jones in Schuller's *The Visitation* and Martin Luther King in the musical *King*.

Estonian opera composers
see TUBIN
Other national opera composers include Evald Aav (1900–39), whose *The Vikings* (*Vikerlased*, 1928) was the first real Estonian opera, Gustav Ernesaks (*b* 1908),

Eugen Kapp (*b* 1908), his cousin Villem (1913–64), Artur Lemba (1885–1963), Leo Normet (*b* 1922), Eino Tamberg (*b* 1930), Veljo Tormis (*b* 1930) and Adolf Vedro (1890–1944).

Esultate!
Otello's entry line in Act I of Verdi's *Otello*. Perhaps the most musically thrilling entry of any operatic character.

Étoile, L' (*The Star*)
Comic opera in three acts by Chabrier. 1st perf Paris, 28 Nov 1877; libr by Eugène Leterrier and Albert Vanloo. Principal roles: Lazuli (mezzo), King Ouf (ten), Laoula (sop), Hérisson (bar), Siroco (bar), Aloés (sop), Tapioca (ten). Chabrier's first completed stage work, it is a delightful and amusing piece, well enough summed up by Stravinsky's description: 'a little masterpiece'.
Plot: The birthday of King Ouf I is customarily celebrated by a display of capital punishment as a diversion for the people. This year, the victim is to be the young peddlar Lazuli, who has slapped the king without knowing who he was. As Lazuli is about to be executed, the astrologer Siroco tells the king that his own fate is linked to that of Lazuli. Henceforth, Ouf's sole concern becomes the jealous guarding of Lazuli's life. After a series of adventures, Lazuli ends up marrying Princess Laoula, Ouf's supposed fiancée. [R]

Étoile du Nord, L' (*The Star of the North*)
Opera in three acts by Meyerbeer. 1st perf (as *Ein Feldlager in Schlesien*) Berlin, 7 Dec 1844; libr by Ludwig Rellstab. Revised version 1st perf (as *Vielka*) Vienna, 18 Feb 1847. Final version 1st perf Paris, 16 Feb 1854; libr revised by Eugène Scribe. Principal roles: Catherine (sop), Peters (bass), Danilowitz (ten), Prascovia (sop), Gritzenko (bar), Georges (ten), Ismailoff (ten), Nathalie (sop). Based on an incident in the life of Frederick the Great, but with the action transferred to Russia, it was enormously popular throughout the 19th century but is nowadays only very rarely performed.
Plot: Late-17th-century Russia. Tsar Peter, disguised as a carpenter, woos Catherine, who takes the place of her brother Georges in the Russian army. She is mistaken for a conspirator, ordered to be executed, and is wounded whilst escaping. Having lost her mind, she is brought to the Tsar's palace. She regains her sanity on seeing Peter, who makes her his Tsarina.

Et toi, Palerme
Bass aria for Procida in Act II of Verdi's *Les Vêpres Siciliennes*, in which he greets Sicily on his return from exile.

Eugene Onegin (*Yevgeny Onyegin*)
Opera in three acts by Tchaikovsky (Op 24). 1st perf Moscow, 29 March 1879; libr by the composer and Konstantin Shilovsky, after Alexander Pushkin's poem. Principal roles: Onegin (bar), Tatyana (sop), Lensky (ten), Gremin (bass), Olga (mezzo), Madame Larina (mezzo), Filipyevna (mezzo), M. Triquet (ten), Zaretsky (bass). Described as 'lyric scenes', it is Tchaikovsky's most popular opera and is usually regarded as his stage masterpiece.
Plot: Late-18th-century Russia. The sophisticated and blasé aristocrat Onegin is visiting in the country with his friend the poet Vladimir Lensky. They visit the house of Madame Larina, whose elder daughter Olga is Lensky's fiancée. There, Onegin meets Olga's sister Tatyana, an intense and bookish romantic, who falls in love with him at first sight. When Tatyana pours out her feelings in a letter to him, Onegin responds by saying that he can only offer friendship and advises her to exercise more self-restraint. At Tatyana's name-day party, Onegin – bored by the event's provincialism – amuses himself by flirting with Olga. The outraged Lensky challenges him to a duel. Both are reluctant to fight, but neither withdraws, and Lensky is killed. Some years later, returned from travelling, Onegin encounters Tatyana at a fashionable ball and learns that she is happily married to his elderly relative Prince Gremin, who adores her. He expresses his remorse for his past behaviour, and tells Tatyana that he loves her. She, however, is adamant that she will not leave Gremin. Rejected and despised, Onegin is left alone. [R]

Euridice
Opera in prologue and six scenes by Peri

(with contributions by Caccini). 1st perf Florence, 6 Oct 1600; libr by Ottavio Rinuccini. Principal roles: Euridice (sop), Orfeo (ten), Arcetro (bass), Dafne (mezzo), Persephone (mezzo). The earliest opera of which the music has survived, it has been regularly performed in recent years in a number of different realizations. [R]

Euridice
Opera in prologue and six scenes by Caccini. 1st perf Florence, 5 Dec 1602; libr by Ottavio Rinuccini. Principal roles: Euridice (mezzo), Orfeo (ten), Dafne (sop), Tragedy (mezzo), Charon (bass). One of the earliest operas whose music survives, it was the first to be published.

Euripides
see panel on page 181

Europe Galante, L' (*European Gallantry*)
Opera-ballet in prologue and four acts by Campra. 1st perf Paris, 24 Oct 1697; libr by Antoine Houdart de la Motte. Principal roles: Vénus (sop), Zaïde (sop), Céphise (sop), Pedro (c-ten). The most successful of Campra's opera-ballets, its four entrées describe the differing romantic attitudes of France, Spain, Italy and Turkey. [R]

Euryanthe
Opera in three acts by Weber (J 291). 1st perf Vienna, 25 Oct 1823; libr by Helmina von Chézy, after the 13th-century French romance *L'Histoire du Très-noble et Chevalereux Prince Gérard, Comte de Nevers.* Principal roles: Euryanthe (sop), Adolar (ten), Eglantine (sop), Lysiart (bar), King Louis VI (bass). The ludicrous and undramatic libretto has prevented the work from receiving anything more than an occasional performance, despite the fact that it contains some of the finest music in any German romantic opera. Musically, it is Weber's masterpiece.
Plot: Préméry and Nevers (France), 1110. Lysiart takes a wager with Adolar that he can seduce Adolar's beloved Euryanthe. Euryanthe confides to Eglantine, who also loves Adolar, the secret of the suicide of Adolar's sister. Eglantine passes this information to Lysiart, who uses it to make a false proclamation of Euryanthe's infidelity. Adolar takes Euryanthe into the desert, intending to kill her; but when she saves him from a serpent, he merely abandons her. She is rescued by King Louis, who is convinced of her innocence. Eglantine, who is about to marry Lysiart, reveals her treachery. Lysiart is arrested, and the lovers are reunited. [R]

Eurydice
The wife of the mythical Greek musician Orpheus appears in innumerable operas, including: **1** Soprano role in Gluck's *Orfeo ed Euridice.* **2** Soprano role in Milhaud's *Les Malheurs d'Orphée.* **3** Mezzo role in Birtwistle's *The Mask of Orpheus.* **4** Soprano role in Peri's *Euridice.* **5** Soprano role in Offenbach's *Orphée aux Enfers.* **6** Soprano role in Monteverdi's *La Favola d'Orfeo.* **7** Soprano role in Rossi's *Orfeo.* **8** Mezzo role in Caccini's *Euridice.*

Eva
Soprano role in Wagner's *Die Meistersinger von Nürnberg.* Pogner's daughter, she is loved by Walther.

Eva
Opera in three acts by Foerster (Op 50). 1st perf Prague, 1 Jan 1899; libr by the composer, after Gabriela Priessová's *The Innkeeper's Maid.* Principal roles: Eva (sop), Mánek (ten), Mešjanovka (sop), Samko (bar), Zuzka (mezzo), Rubač (bass). Foerster's most successful opera, it is almost unknown outside the Czech lands.
Plot: Late-19th-century Slovakia. The poor seamstress Eva loves Mánek, son of a wealthy farmer, but agrees to marry the tailor Samko, by whom she has a child which dies. Although now married to Zuzka, Mánek still loves Eva, and the two decide to run away together. Mánek's mother Mešjanovka reports that the authorities are angry about the relationship. Mánek is totally unconcerned, but Eva – after seeing a vision of her dead parents and child – throws herself into the Danube. [R]

Evangelimann, Der (*The Evangelist*)
Opera in two acts by Kienzl (Op 45). 1st perf Berlin, 4 May 1895; libr by the composer, after Leopold Florian Meissner's story. Principal roles: Mathias (ten), Martha (sop), Magdalene (mezzo), Johannes (bar), Engel (bass). Kienzl's most successful opera,

· Euripides ·

The tragedies of the Greek dramatist Euripides (480 – *c* 406 BC) have inspired some 60 operas. Below are listed, by play, those operas by composers with entries in this dictionary.

Alkestis		
Lully	*Alceste*	1674
Gluck	*Alceste*	1767/76
Portugal	*Alceste*	1798
Boughton	*Alkestis*	1922
Wellesz	*Alkestis*	1924
The Bacchae		
Wellesz	*Die Bakchantinnen*	1931
Ghedini	*I Baccanti*	1948
Henze	*The Bassarids*	1966
Buller	*The Bacchae*	1992
Xenakis	*The Bacchae*	1993
Hecuba		
Malipiero	*Ecuba*	1941
Helen in Egypt		
Strauss	*Die Ägyptische Helena*	1928/33
Hippolytus		
Rameau	*Hippolyte et Aricie*	1733
Traetta	*Ippolito ed Aricia*	1759
Pizzetti	*Fedra*	1915
Iphigenia in Aulis		
D. Scarlatti	*Ifigenia in Aulide*	1713
Caldara	*Ifigenia in Aulide*	1718
Graun	*Iphigenia in Aulide*	1748
Jommelli	*Ifigenia in Aulide*	1751
Gluck	*Iphigénie en Aulide*	1774
Zingarelli	*Ifigenia in Aulide*	1787
Cherubini	*Ifigenia in Aulide*	1788
Iphigenia in Tauris		
Campra	*Iphigénie en Tauride*	1704
D. Scarlatti	*Ifigenia in Tauri*	1713
Vinci	*Ifigenia in Tauride*	1725
Traetta	*Ifigenia in Tauride*	1763
Jommelli	*Ifigenia in Tauride*	1771
Gluck	*Iphigénie en Tauride*	1779
Piccinni	*Iphigénie en Tauride*	1781
Medea		
Mayr	*Medea in Corinto*	1813
Milhaud	*Médée*	1939
Orestes		
Křenek	*Leben des Orest*	1930
The Trojan Women		
Prodromidès	*Les Troyennes*	1963
Reimann	*Troades*	1985
Osborne	*Sarajevo*	1994

it applies Wagnerian techniques to a VERISMO style. Enormously popular at its appearance (with over 5,000 performances in 40 years), it is still occasionally performed in German-speaking countries. **Plot**: St Othmar (Austria), 1820–50. Johannes is wracked with jealousy for Martha's love for his brother Mathias, a monk. He has Mathias expelled from his monastery and arrested on a trumpted-up arson charge. After many years in prison, Mathias is released, becomes a street preacher and forgives Johannes. [R]

Evans, Anne (b 1939)
British soprano, particularly associated with Strauss and Wagner roles, especially Isolde and Brünnhilde. She possesses a warm and strong voice used with fine musicianship and has a sympathetic stage presence.

Evans, Sir Geraint (1922–92)
British baritone, particularly associated with Mozart and Britten roles and with Falstaff, Beckmesser and Wozzeck. One of the finest British singers of the post-war era, and the first to enjoy a major international career, he had a fine voice and excellent diction and was an outstanding singing-actor, especially in comedy. He created Mr Flint in *Billy Budd*, Lord Mountjoy in *Gloriana*, the Herald in *The Pilgrim's Progress*, Antenor in *Troilus and Cressida* and, for Hoddinott, Trader Case in *The Beach at Falesá* and the title-role in *Murder the Magician*. He also produced a number of operas. His autobiography, *A Knight at the Opera*, was published in 1984.

Everding, August (b 1928)
German producer and administrator. One of the leading post-war German producers, particularly noted for his Wagner stagings, he was administrator of the Munich Chamber Opera (1963–73), the Hamburg State Opera (1972–7) and the Bavarian State Opera (1977–).

Evirato (from the Italian *evirare*, 'to emasculate')
An alternative term used occasionally for CASTRATO.

Ewing, Maria (b 1950)
American mezzo and later soprano, particularly associated with dramatic roles such as the title-roles in *Carmen*, *Tosca* and *Salome*. She is an intense, committed and compelling singing-actress with a voice of highly individual timbre. Married for a time to the producer SIR PETER HALL.

Excursions of Mr Brouček, The (*Výlety Páně Broučkovy*)
Comic opera in two parts by Janáček. 1st perf Prague, 23 April 1920; libr by the composer, Viktor Dyk and František Procházka, after Svatopluk Čech's novels. The two parts (originally conceived separately) are *Mr Brouček's Excursion to the Moon* (*Výlet Pana Broučka do Měsíce*), composed 1915, and *Mr Brouček's Excursion to the 15th Century* (*Výlet Pana Broučka do XV Století*), composed 1917. Principal roles: Brouček (ten), Mazal (ten), Málinka (sop), Mr Würfl (bar), Sacristan (bar), Svatopluk Čech (ten), Potboy (sop). The two adventures of the bourgeois Mr Brouček provided Janáček with an opportunity to parody artistic pretentiousness and bogus patriotism. A delightful work of sardonic wit and great musical brilliance, it is the least frequently performed of Janáček's mature operas. **Plot**: Prague, late 19th century and 1420. The landlord Matěj Brouček has two dreams. Firstly, he is transported to the Moon, where he encounters an outlandish world inhabited by an over-refined artistic community. Secondly, he goes back in time to the 15th century and behaves in a cowardly fashion during the Hussite revolt. He is finally returned to the present, as narrow-minded and bourgeois as ever. [R]

Ezio
Baritone role in Verdi's *Attila*. He is a Roman general.

Ezio
Opera in three acts by Händel. 1st perf London, 26 Jan 1732; libr by Pietro Metastasio. Principal roles: Ezio (c-ten), Fulvia (sop), Massimo (ten), Varo (bass), Onoria (mezzo), Valentiniano (c-ten). Telling of events during the reign of the Roman Emperor Valentinian III (reigned 425–55), it has never been one of Händel's more popular operas and is only very rarely performed despite containing some magnificent music.

F

Faber
Baritone role in Tippett's *The Knot Garden*. He is Thea's husband.

Fabritiis, Oliviero de (1902–82)
Italian conductor, particularly associated with the Italian repertory. One of the finest and most reliable Italian conductors of the post-war era, he instigated the presentation of opera at the Caracalla Baths in Rome and conducted the first performances of Rossellini's *La Guerra* and operas by Mascagni, Pizzetti and Zafred.

Faccio, Franco (1840–91)
Italian conductor and composer. A close friend of Boito and one of the greatest conductors of his age, he was musical director of La Scala, Milan (1871–90). He conducted the first performances of Verdi's *Otello*, the revised versions of *Simon Boccanegra* and *Don Carlos*, Ponchielli's *I Lituani*, *La Gioconda* and *Il Figliuol Prodigo*, Catalani's *Dejanice* and *Edmea* and Puccini's *Edgar* and the revised *Le Villi*, as well as introducing Wagner's later works to Italy. He also composed two operas, both now forgotten: *I Profughi Fiamminghi* (Milan, 11 Nov 1863; libr Emilio Praga) and *Amleto* (Genoa, 30 May 1865; libr Arrigo Boito, after Shakespeare's *Hamlet*). He was also a noted teacher, whose pupils included Smareglia.

Fach (German for 'speciality')
In opera, the term describes the vocal category into which a singer falls, such as BASSO-BUFFO, COLORATURA mezzo, VERDI BARITONE or HELDENTENOR.

Fafner
Bass role in Wagner's *Das Rheingold* and *Siegfried*. One of the two giants, he is transformed into a dragon in *Siegfried*.

Fairy Queen, The
Opera in prologue and five acts by Purcell. 1st perf London, 2 May 1692; libr possibly by Elkanah Settle, after William Shakespeare's *A Midsummer Night's Dream*. Perhaps more accurately described as incidental music or a series of masques rather than a true opera, the score was lost by 1701 and was not rediscovered until 1901. Since then it has been regularly performed in a number of different realizations and editions, including one by Britten. [R]

Falcon, Marie Cornélie (1812–97)
French soprano. Her career lasted for only six years, but she was regarded as one of the leading dramatic sopranos of her age. She created Valentine in *Les Huguenots*, Rachel in *La Juive*, Morgiane in Cherubini's *Ali Baba* and Amélie in Auber's *Gustave III*. She gave her name to a type of French soprano voice, with a range of roughly b♭ to c'''.

Falke, Dr
Baritone role in J. Strauss's *Die Fledermaus*. A friend of von Eisenstein, he arranges the 'revenge of the bat'.

Fall, Leo (1873–1925)
Austrian composer. After unsuccessful attempts at opera, he turned to operetta, in which field he enjoyed enormous success. His many Viennese operettas include *Der Fidele Bauer* (Mannheim, 25 July 1907; libr Viktor Léon) [R Exc], DIE DOLLARPRINZESSIN, *Die Geschiedene Frau* (Vienna, 23 Dec 1908; libr Léon), *Eternal Waltz* (London, 22 Dec 1911; libr A. Hurgon), *Der Lieber Augustin* (Berlin, 3 Feb 1912; libr Rudolf Bernauer and E. Welisch), a revision of *Der Rebel* of 1905, *Die Rose von Stamboul* (Vienna, 2 Dec 1916; libr Julius Brammer and Alfred Grünwald), MADAME POMPADOUR, his most enduring work, and *Jugend im Mai* (Dresden, 22 Oct 1926; libr Welisch and Robert Schanzer). His brother **Richard** (1882–*c* 1944) was also a composer: he died in Auschwitz.

Falla, Manuel de (1876–1946)
Spanish composer. Arguably his country's greatest composer, his stage works make extensive use of traditional Spanish material. In his youth, he composed five ZARZUELAS, of which only *Los Amores de la Inés* (Madrid, 12 Apr 1902; libr Emilio Dugi), written in collaboration with Vives, has ever been performed. His first opera LA VIDA BREVE was the winner of a Madrid competition, and has become the most popular of all Spanish operas. His next work was a comedy based on the music of Chopin, *Fuego Fatuo* (*Will o' the Wisp*, 1918; libr Gregorio Martínez Sierra), which has never been published or performed, although a suite has been arranged from the music by the conductor Antonio Ros-Marbá. Its successor, the marionette opera EL RETABLO DE MAESE PEDRO, is a refined example of his mature style. His last stage work, the ambitious scenic oratorio L'ATLÁNTIDA, was left unfinished at his death and was completed by Ernesto Halffter.

Falsetto (Italian for 'false')
It indicates a male voice singing in a register higher than the voice's natural range. It is the type of vocal production employed by modern counter-tenors, and is also used occasionally by basses or baritones for comic effect.

Falstaff or **Le Tre Burle** (*The Three Jokes*)
Comic opera in two acts by Salieri. 1st perf Vienna, 3 Jan 1799; libr by Carlo Prospero Defrancheschi, after William Shakespeare's *The Merry Wives of Windsor*. Principal roles: Falstaff (bass), Mistress Ford (sop), Ford (ten), Slender (bar), Mrs Slender (mezzo), Bardolf (bar), Betty (sop). Demonstrating Salieri's considerable gift for comedy, it was successful in its time but is nowadays virtually forgotten. [R]

Falstaff
Comic opera in three acts by Verdi. 1st perf Milan, 9 Feb 1893; libr by Arrigo Boito, after William Shakespeare's *The Merry Wives of Windsor* and *King Henry IV*. Principal roles: Falstaff (bar), Ford (bar), Alice (sop), Mistress Quickly (mezzo), Nannetta (sop), Fenton (ten), Meg Page (mezzo), Dr Caius (ten), Pistol (bass), Bardolf (ten). Verdi's last and greatest masterpiece, and his first comedy for 50 years, it remains one of the miracles of operatic music. Boito's brilliant text is arguably the finest libretto which any composer has ever been given. Technically, the music is far more advanced even than *Otello*, with the structure seamless and the orchestra almost the principal character. The wit, warmth and wisdom of the score mark the natural culmination of Verdi's long creative career, and that a man of almost 80 could have produced a work of such strength and youthfulness and of such breathtaking pace is not the least of its glories. Perhaps the one perfect opera.
Plot: 15th-century Windsor. The fat and bibulous Sir John Falstaff sends identical amorous letters to Alice, wife of the wealthy merchant Ford, and to Meg Page. These two, with Mistress Quickly and Alice's daughter Nannetta, decide to accept Falstaff's advances and teach him a sharp lesson. Ford finds out about Falstaff's designs from the latter's henchmen Pistol and Bardolf and from the pedant Dr Caius, to whom he has promised Nannetta, despite her love for young Fenton. Ford also decides to punish Falstaff and calls on him in disguise, offering him money to help him to seduce Alice. Falstaff's assignation with Alice is interrupted by Ford's appearance and, hidden in a laundry basket, he is pitched into the Thames. Nonetheless, the old reprobate accepts a second invitation to meet Alice, this time at Herne's Oak in Windsor Forest. There, he is given a sound thrashing by the merry wives disguised as goblins and fairies. Ford discovers that in the confusion he has accidentally given Nannetta to Fenton in marriage, whilst Caius has been married to Bardolf! Ford accepts with good grace, and Falstaff points out that all the world is a joke. [R]

Falstaff, Sir John
The fat knight of Shakespeare's *The Merry Wives of Windsor* and *King Henry IV* appears in several operas, including: **1** Bass role in Nicolaï's *Die Lustigen Weiber von Windsor*. **2** Baritone role in Verdi's *Falstaff*. **3** Baritone role in Vaughan Williams's *Sir John in Love*. **4** Bass role in Salieri's *Falstaff*. **5** Bass role in Holst's *At the Boar's Head*. **6** Role in Thomas's *Le*

Songe d'une Nuit d'Été. **7** Mezzo trouser role in Balfe's *Falstaff*.

Fanciulla del West, La (known in English as *The Girl of the Golden West*)
Opera in three acts by Puccini. 1st perf New York, 10 Dec 1910; libr by Carlo Zangarini and Guelfo Civinini, after David Belasco's play. Principal roles: Minnie (sop), Dick Johnson (ten), Jack Rance (bar), Jake Wallace (bass), Sonora (bar), Ashby (bass), Nick (ten). One of Puccini's most modernistic scores, displaying a strong influence of Debussy, it is still regularly performed.
Plot: California, 1850. Minnie, keeper of the Polka Saloon and friend and confidante to the gold miners, falls in love with the stranger Dick Johnson, whom she discovers is the wanted bandit Ramírez. When Dick is wounded by the guns of a posse, she hides him at her cabin, but the sheriff Jack Rance, who loves Minnie, discovers him there. Minnie and Rance agree to a game of poker to decide Johnson's fate, which Minnie wins by cheating. Rance leaves, but Johnson is later captured by the miners and is about to be hanged. Minnie begs them to spare the man she loves and they release him. The lovers ride off to begin a new life together. [R]

Fanget an!
Tenor aria for Walther von Stolzing in Act I of Wagner's *Die Meistersinger von Nürnberg*. It is Walther's trial song.

Faninal
Baritone role in Strauss's *Der Rosenkavalier*. He is Sophie's recently ennobled father.

Fanu, Nicola le
see under MACONCHY, DAME ELIZABETH

Faramondo
Opera in three acts by Händel. 1st perf London, 7 Jan 1738; libr after Apostolo Zeno. Principal roles: Faramondo (c-ten), Clotilde (sop), Gustavo (bass), Adolfo (sop), Rosimonda (mezzo), Gernando (mezzo), Teobaldo (bass). Its extraordinarily complex plot deals with the planned vengeance of Faramondo for the supposed murder of his son by King Gustavo of the Cimbrians. Unsuccessful at its appearance, it is nowadays only very rarely performed.

Farinelli (b Carlo Broschi) (1705–82)
Italian CASTRATO. Sometime regarded as the greatest of all the castrati, he possessed a voice of extraordinary agility with a range up to high D. His London appearances caused women to faint, and in 1737 he was hired by King Philip V of Spain to assuage his melancholia. This he is reputed to have achieved by singing the same four songs every night for ten years! He is the subject of Barnett's *Farinelli*, Auber's *La Part du Diable* and Bretón's *Farinelli*.

Farncombe, Charles (b 1919)
British conductor (and also a qualified civil engineer), particularly associated with Händel and other baroque operas. He was musical director of the Drottningholm Castle Theatre (1970–79) and of the Handel Opera Society for the duration of its existence.

Farrar, Geraldine (1882–1967)
American soprano, particularly associated with the Italian and French repertories. Based at the Metropolitan Opera, New York, she combined a glorious voice with fine musicianship and great personal beauty. Her popularity was enhanced by appearances in some dozen films, and her young female admirers acquired the nickname of 'Gerry-flappers'. She created the Goose-girl in Humperdinck's *Die Königskinder*, Louise in Charpentier's *Julien* and the title-roles in Puccini's *Suor Angelica*, Giordano's *Madame Sans-Gêne* and Mascagni's *Amica*. Her autobiography, *Such Sweet Compulsion*, was published in 1938.

Farrell, Eileen (b 1920)
American soprano, particularly associated with dramatic Italian roles. She possessed a large and powerful voice and a keen dramatic sense and was vocally well suited for Wagner, which she sang frequently in the concert hall but never on stage.

Farsa (Italian for 'farce')
A term describing an early 19th-century

Italian comic opera in light style, usually in one act and without a chorus. An example is Rossini's *Il Signor Bruschino*.

Fasano, Renato (1902–79)
Italian conductor and musicologist, particularly associated with the 18th-century Italian repertory. As founder in 1947 of the chamber ensemble I Virtuosi di Roma and in 1957 of the Piccolo Teatro Musicale Italiano, he was responsible for important revivals of many works in performances throughout Europe.

Fasolt
Bass role in Wagner's *Das Rheingold*. He is one of the two giants.

Fassbaender, Brigitte (b 1939)
German mezzo, daughter of the baritone WILLI DOMGRAF-FASSBAENDER. Particularly associated with Mozart, Strauss and Wagner roles, she was a rich-voiced singer of outstanding musicianship. A fine singing-actress, she had especial success in trouser roles, notably Octavian in *Der Rosenkavalier*, Prince Orlofsky in *Die Fledermaus* and Countess Geschwitz in *Lulu*. She created Lady Milford in Einem's *Kabale und Liebe* and has also produced a number of operas.

Fatal mia donna
Soprano/baritone duet for Lady Macbeth and Macbeth in Act I of Verdi's *Macbeth*, in which they discuss the murder of Duncan.

Fata Morgana
Soprano role in Prokofiev's *The Love of Three Oranges*. She is a witch.

Fate (*Osud*)
Opera in three acts by Janáček. 1st perf Brno Radio, 18 Sept 1934 (composed 1904); 1st stage perf Brno, 25 Oct 1958; libr by the composer and Fedora Bartošová. Principal roles: Živný (ten), Míla (sop), Míla's Mother (mezzo), Dr Suda (ten), Lhotský (bar). Much the least known of Janáček's mature operas, it has been slow to make its way, even in the Czech lands, despite its magnificent music. A semi-autobiographical work, it was long thought to be virtually unstageable, a myth exploded by the English National Opera's award-winning production in 1983.
Plot: Luhačovice (Moravia), *c* 1890. Under pressure from her Mother, Míla has been obliged to stop meeting the composer Živný. They meet again and decide to live together. During a furious altercation, the Mother throws herself from a high staircase, also dragging Míla (who tries to save her) to her death. On the eve of its performance, students parody Živný's new opera. Živný explains it to them, and they realize that it is Živný's confession and autobiography. [R]

Fatinitza
Operetta in three acts by Suppé. 1st perf Vienna, 5 Jan 1876; libr by F. Zell (Camillo Walzel) and Richard Genée, after Eugène Scribe's libretto for Auber's *La Circassienne*. Principal roles: Wladimir (mezzo), Kantschukoff (bass), Lydia (sop). Suppé's first full-length work, it met with great initial success and is still occasionally performed in German-speaking countries.
Plot: Southern Russia, 1850s. During the Crimean War, the Russian Gen Kantschukoff falls for a girl called Fatinitza, who is in fact the young lieutenant Wladimir who is masquerading as a woman so that his beloved Lydia, Kantschukoff's niece, can elude her uncle's watchfulness. Wladimir is captured and taken to a Turkish harem, before Kantschukoff acknowledges that Fatinitza does not exist. He finally allows Wladimir and Lydia to marry.

Fauré, Gabriel (1845–1924)
French composer. He wrote two operas, both heavily influenced by Wagner. *Prométhée* (Béziers, 24 Aug 1900; libr Jean Lorrain and André-Ferdinand Hérold, after Aeschylus's *Prometheus*) is a vast work, designed for open-air performance, which is now forgotten. Far more successful was PÉNÉLOPE, which contains some of his most beautiful music.

Faure, Jean-Baptiste (1830–1914)
French baritone, particularly associated with the French repertory. Long resident at the Opéra-Comique, Paris, he created Nélusko in *L'Africaine*, Hoël in *Dinorah*, Posa in *Don Carlos*, the title-role in Thomas's *Hamlet* and, for Massé, Pygmalion in *Galathée* and Pédro in *La*

Mule de Pédro. He was also a noted teacher, publishing two books on singing. His wife **Caroline Lefèbvre** (1828–1905) was a successful soprano.

Faust
An itinerant German conjuror (*c* 1488–1541) who, in legend, is said to have sold his soul to the Devil in return for a period of renewed youth. He appears in several operas, including: **1** Tenor role in Gounod's *Faust*. **2** Tenor role in Berlioz's *La Damnation de Faust*. **3** Baritone role in Spohr's *Faust*. **4** Tenor role in Boito's *Mefistofele*. **5** Baritone role in Busoni's *Doktor Faust*. **6** Bass role in Prokofiev's *The Fiery Angel*. **7** Bass role in Egk's *Irische Legende*.

Faust
Opera in two acts by Spohr (Op 60). 1st perf Dresden, 1 Sept 1816; libr by Joseph Carl Bernard, after Maximilian von Klinger's *Fausts Leben, Thaten und Höllenfahrt*. Principal roles: Faust (bar), Mephistofeles (bass), Kunigunde (sop), Count Hugo (ten), Röschen (mezzo), Sir Gulf (bass). One of Spohr's finest operas, it was very successful in its time but is nowadays hardly ever performed.
Plot: 16th-century Strasbourg and Aachen. Faust gains power through a pact with Mephistofeles hoping thereby to do good, but his passions are too strong. He is torn between his love for the pure Röschen and his lust for Countess Kunigunde, who he rescues from the robber knight Gulf. At Kunigunde's wedding to her beloved Count Hugo, Faust seduces Kunigunde by means of a magic potion and subsequently kills Hugo in a duel. Röschen drowns herself, and Faust is dragged off to hell by Mephistofeles's denizens. [R]

Faust
Opera in five acts by Gounod. 1st perf Paris, 19 March 1859; libr by Jules Barbier and Michel Carré, after Johann von Goethe's play. Principal roles: Faust (ten), Marguerite (sop), Méphistophélès (bass), Valentin (bar), Siebel (mezzo), Dame Marthe (mezzo). Gounod's greatest success, notable for its wealth of melody, it was perhaps the most popular of all operas in the second half of the 19th century, and it is still regularly performed. In Germany, where it is not unjustifiably viewed as a travesty of Goethe, the title is usually given as *Marguerite*.
Plot: 16th-century Germany. The aging philosopher Faust sells his soul to Méphistophélès in return for renewed youth and the love of Marguerite. Méphistophélès frustrates the attentions of Siebel, Marguerite's faithful young admirer who has been charged with protecting her by her brother Valentin, and introduces her to Faust, with whom she falls in love. Valentin returns from the wars to find her compromised, and challenges Faust to a duel. Valentin is killed and Faust abandons Marguerite. She bears Faust's child and is condemned to death for killing it in shame. The repentant Faust tries to rescue her from prison where she is now deranged, but she recognizes him as evil and dies renouncing her love for him. Méphistophélès declares her condemned, but angels announce her salvation and raise her to heaven, whilst Méphistophélès forces Faust down to Hell. [R]

Favart, Charles-Simon (1710–92)
French librettist. The finest comic librettist of his time, he wrote the texts of over 150 operas. His libretti were set by Dauvergne, Duni, Gluck, Grétry, Monsigny, Philidor, Uttini and many others. His wife **Marie** (1727–72) was a successful soprano, who created Florise in Dauvergne's *La Coquette Trompée*. She is the subject of Offenbach's *Madame Favart*.

Favero, Mafalda (1903–81)
Italian soprano, particularly associated with the Italian repertory, especially the title-role in Puccini's *Manon Lescaut*. Largely based at La Scala, Milan, she created the title-role in Mascagni's *Pinotta*, Laura in Zandonai's *La Farsa Amorosa*, Madelon in Lattuada's *Le Preziose Ridicole* and, for Wolf-Ferrari, Gasparina in *Il Campiello* and Finea in *La Dama Boba*. Her husband **Alessandro Ziliani** (1907–77) was a successful tenor, who created Baldo in *Pinotta* and Bosco Nero in Wolf-Ferrari's *La Vedova Scaltra*.

Favola d'Orfeo, La (*The Fable of Orpheus*)
Opera in prologue and five acts by Monteverdi. 1st perf Mantua, Feb 1607;

libr by Alessandro Striggio. Principal roles: Orfeo (ten), Messenger (mezzo), Euridice (sop), Caronte (bass), Plutone (bass), Proserpina (sop), Apollo (ten), Music (sop). Unperformed from its premiere until the early 20th century, it is now established as the first great operatic masterpiece, and is the earliest opera which is nowadays regularly performed. Many different realizations and performing editions have been made.
Plot: Legendary Greece. The Messenger interrupts the celebrations of the forthcoming marriage between Eurydice and the singer Orpheus with the news of Eurydice's death. Orpheus determines to seek her in Hades, and persuades Charon to ferry him over the River Styx. Pluto and his wife Proserpina agree to his request to take Eurydice back to earth, on condition that he does not look at her until their journey is over. As they near their journey's end, however, Orpheus can no longer resist and turns and looks at Eurydice. She sinks back into Hades, leaving Orpheus grief-stricken. Apollo comforts him with the promise that in eternity he will be able to gaze upon Eurydice for ever. [R]

Favola per musica (Italian for 'fable with music')
A term used in the early 17th century to describe a musical setting of a mythological or legendary subject, such as the Orpheus myth.

Favorite, La
Opera in four acts by Donizetti. 1st perf Paris, 2 Dec 1840; libr by Alphonse Royer and Gustave Vaëz, after François-Thomas de Baculard d'Arnaud's *Le Comte de Comminges*. Principal roles: Léonor (mezzo), Fernand (ten), Alphonse (bar), Balthazar (bass), Inès (sop). Incorporating much music from his unfinished *L'Ange de Nisida*, it is one of Donizetti's finest works, still regularly performed, and arguably his most 'Verdian' in musico-dramatic style. It is nearly always given in an Italian translation.
Plot: Castile, 1340. Leonora di Gusmann returns the love of the novice Fernando, but conceals her identity because she is the illicit mistress of King Alfonso XI. She uses her influence to secure Fernando a military appointment, and he saves Alfonso's life in battle. He asks for Leonora's hand as a reward. Under the threat of excommunication because of his adulterous relationship with Leonora, Alfonso agrees, but Leonora is unable to tell Fernando the truth before their wedding takes place. When he learns of Leonora's past, Fernando returns to his monastery, which is ruled by Baldassarre (Balthazar). Before he takes his final vows, Leonora comes to beg his forgiveness. His passion is reawakened, but Leonora collapses and dies in his arms. [R]

Fedeltà Premiata, La (*Fidelity Rewarded*)
Opera in three acts by Haydn. 1st perf Esterháza, 25 Feb 1781; libr after Giovanni Battista Lorenzi's *L'Infedelità Fedele*. Principal roles: Celia (mezzo), Fileno (ten), Amaranta (mezzo), Perrucchetto (bar), Melibeo (bass), Nerina (sop), Lindoro (ten), Diana (sop). After a long period of complete neglect, it has received a number of performances in the last 20 years.
Plot: Legendary Cumae (Italy). The temple of Diana, run by the priest Melibeo, is cursed: a pair of faithful lovers must be sacrificed to a monster until 'an heroic soul shall offer his own life'. Around the love of Celia and Fileno revolve the intrigues and amorous complications of Amaranta, her brother Lindoro, his abandoned love Nerina and Count Perrucchetto. Despairing, because of the intrigues, of ever being united with Celia, Fileno offers to make the sacrifice. However, Diana intervenes to declare the curse lifted, and the lovers are united. [R]

Federica
Mezzo role in Verdi's *Luisa Miller*. The Duchess of Ostheim, she is Count Walther's niece.

Federico
1 Bass role in Verdi's *La Battaglia di Legnano*. He is the Emperor Frederick Barbarossa (*c* 1122–90). **2** Tenor role in Cilea's *L'Arlesiana*. He loves the girl from Arles. **3** Tenor role in Donizetti's *Emilia di Liverpool*. He is Don Romualdo's secretary. **4** Tenor COMPRIMARIO role in Verdi's *Stiffelio*. He is Lina's cousin.

Fedora
Opera in three acts by Giordano. 1st perf Milan, 17 Nov 1898; libr by Arturo Colautti, after Victorien Sardou's *Fédora*. Principal roles: Fedora (sop), Loris (ten), Jean de Siriex (bar), Olga (sop). A vulgar piece of VERISMO, it is Giordano's only opera apart from *Andrea Chénier* to have survived.
Plot: Late-19th-century St Petersburg, Paris and Switzerland. The nihilist Loris Ipanov kills the intended husband of Fedora Romazoff, because his wife had had an affair with the victim. Fedora sets out to extract vengeance, but falls in love with Loris when she discovers the reason for his crime. Meanwhile, members of Loris's family suffer, and he vows revenge, knowing only that an unknown woman is responsible. Fedora, realizing that the truth will soon come out, poisons herself, leaving Loris to understand only when it is too late. [R]

Fedra
Opera in three acts by Pizzetti. 1st perf Milan, 20 March 1915; libr by Gabriele d'Annunzio, after Euripides's *Hippolytus*. Principal roles: Fedra (mezzo), Ippolito (ten), Teseo (bass). Pizzetti's first opera to be performed, it is an austere but strong setting of the famous myth. Successful at its appearance, it is nowadays almost forgotten.
Plot: Legendary Athens. Phaedra, wife of King Theseus, conceives an uncontrollable passion for her stepson Hippolytus. When he spurns her advances, she hangs herself, leaving behind her a letter which falsely accuses Hippolytus of having dishonoured her.

Feen, Die (*The Fairies*)
Opera in three acts by Wagner. 1st perf Munich, 29 June 1888 (composed 1834); libr by the composer, after Carlo Gozzi's *La Donna Serpente*. Principal roles: Ada (sop), Arindal (ten), Günther (ten), Gernot (bass), Lora (sop), Drolla (sop), Morald (bar), Fairy King (bass). Wagner's first completed opera, which bears little resemblance to his mature works, it is only very rarely performed.
Plot: King Arindal of Tramond has married the fairy Ada, whom he is fated to lose if he should ever curse her under the strain of some misfortune of which she appears to be the cause. This, unfortunately, he does, and Ada is turned to stone. However, so great is his grief that the spell is broken and he is allowed to enter fairyland as Ada's husband. [R]

Feldlager in Schlesien, Ein
see ÉTOILE DU NORD, L'

Felsenstein, Walter (1901–75)
Austrian producer. One of the most brilliant post-war opera directors, his period as Intendant of the Komische Oper in the then East Berlin (1947–75) established that theatre's reputation for innovative, dramatically consistent and often controversial productions. His most famous productions there included *The Cunning Little Vixen*, *Barbe-Bleue*, *Carmen* and *Les Contes d'Hoffmann*.

Femmine d'Italia, Le
Bass aria for Ali in Act II of Rossini's *L'Italiana in Algieri*, in which he reflects on the trickery of Italian women.

Fenella
Mute role in Auber's *La Muette de Portici*. Masaniello's sister, she is the dumb girl of the opera's title. In the 19th century, the role was often played by a famous ballerina.

Fenena
Mezzo role in Verdi's *Nabucco*. She is Nabucco's younger but legitimate daughter. The role is sometimes sung by a soprano.

Fennimore and Gerda
Opera in 11 scenes by Delius. 1st perf Frankfurt, 21 Oct 1919 (composed 1910); libr by the composer, after Jens Peter Jacobsen's *Niels Lyhne*. Principal roles: Niels (bar), Erik (ten), Fennimore (sop), Gerda (sop). Delius's last opera, it is only rarely performed, despite containing much beautiful music, particularly in the orchestral interludes which connect the scenes.
Plot: 19th-century Denmark. Fennimore is engaged to the painter Erik, whose friend Niels also loves her. Niels leaves for Erik's sake, but the marriage is unsuccessful. Erik spends all his time with friends and Fennimore, feeling neglected, asks Niels to

help. Niels suggests that Erik travel to reawaken his inspiration, and Erik goes to a fair. Niels swears eternal fidelity to Fennimore, and their old love is rekindled. Whilst awaiting Niels, Fennimore receives a telegram saying that Erik has been killed in an accident. Full of remorse, she blames both herself and Niels. Subsequently, Niels settles down with the pretty young Gerda. [R]

Fenton
The young gentleman of Shakespeare's *The Merry Wives of Windsor* appears as a tenor role in: **1** Verdi's *Falstaff.* **2** Nicolaï's *Die Lustigen Weiber von Windsor.* **3** Vaughan Williams's *Sir John in Love.*

Feo, Francesco (c 1685–1761)
Italian composer. One of the leading early composers of Neapolitan opera, he wrote many OPERA SERIAS. A number of them were very successful in their day but are all now forgotten. They include *Siface* (Naples, 13 May 1723; libr Pietro Metastasio, after D. David's *La Forza della Virtù*) and *Ipermestra* (Rome, Jan 1728; libr Antonio Salvi).

Ferencsik, János (1907–84)
Hungarian conductor, particularly associated with the German and Hungarian repertories. He was musical director of the Budapest State Opera (1957–73 and 1978–84) and conducted the first performance of Jenö Zádor's *Asra.*

Fermata (Italian for 'stop')
A term describing a pause on a held note, written as the musical symbol 𝄐. In Italy, the term CORONA is used.

Fernand Cortez or **La Conquête du Mexique** (*The Conquest of Mexico*)
Opera in three acts by Spontini. 1st perf Paris, 28 Nov 1809; libr by Victor Joseph Étienne de Jouy and Joseph Alphonse d'Esménard, after Alexis Piron's play. Revised version 1st perf Paris, 28 May 1817. Principal roles: Cortez (ten), Amazily (sop), Montézuma (bass), Télasco (ten), Alvar (ten), High Priest (bass). One of Spontini's finest and most spectacular operas (the original version included a cavalry charge), it was enormously successful in its time but is nowadays only rarely performed.
Plot: Mexico, 1519. The conquistador Hernán Cortés loves Amazily, daughter of the Aztec King Montezuma, and hopes by their marriage to bring about peace. After putting down a mutiny by his troops, he burns his boats and with the help of Amazily (now a Christian), he rescues his brother Alvaro from being sacrificed to the Aztec gods by the High Priest. Montezuma finally agrees to his marriage with Amazily.

Fernández Caballero, Manuel
see CABALLERO, MANUEL FERNÁNDEZ

Fernando
Opera in one act by Schubert (D 220). 1st perf Magdeburg, 18 Aug 1918 (composed 1815); libr by Albert Stadler. Principal roles: Fernando (ten), Eleonore (sop), Philipp (sop). One of Schubert's earliest SINGSPIELS, it is almost never performed.
Plot: After killing the brother of his wife Eleonore, Fernando de la Porte lives as a hermit in a deep forest. The authorities pardon him, and Eleonore and their young son Philipp go in search of him. They become lost in the forest and seek shelter with the hermit. Gradually, husband and wife recognize one another and are reconciled. [R]

Ferne Klang, Der (*The Distant Sound*)
Opera in three acts by Schreker. 1st perf Frankfurt, 18 Aug 1912 (composed 1909); libr by the composer. Principal roles: Fritz (ten), Grete (sop), Dr Vigelius (bar), Mr and Mrs Graumann (bass and mezzo). Schreker's most successful opera, still occassionally performed, it is a lush Impressionist piece in late-romantic style.
Plot: Early-20th-century Germany and Venice. The composer Fritz declines to marry his beloved Grete until he has discovered a 'lost chord'. After ten years as queen of the demi-monde, Grete decides to marry whichever of her admirers can best move her with a song. The winner is a stranger, who she realizes is Fritz. However, he abandons her when he learns of her reputation. The ending of Fritz's new opera is a fiasco at its premiere, but Grete – now a prostitute – is touched by it. Fritz realizes that he has ruined Grete's life and when she comes to see him they fall into each other's arms. Finally hearing

his 'lost chord', Fritz rewrites the end of his opera, but immediately dies in Grete's arms. [R]

Ferrando
1 Tenor role in Mozart's *Così fan Tutte*. He is an officer in love with Dorabella. **2** Bass role in Verdi's *Il Trovatore*. He is the captain of di Luna's guard.

Ferrari-Trecate, Luigi (1884–1964)
Italian composer. He wrote 12 operas, some of which met with some success in Italy but which are unknown elsewhere. They include *Regina Ester* (Faenza, 1900; libr A. Montanari), the marionette opera *Ciotollino* (Rome, 8 Feb 1922; libr Giovacchino Forzano). *La Bella e il Mostro* (Milan, 20 Mar 1926; libr F. Salvatori), *L'Austuzie di Bertoldo* (Genoa, 10 Jan 1934; libr Carlo Zangarini and O. Lucarini), *Ghirlino* (Milan, 4 Feb 1940; libr E. Ancheschi), *L'Orso Rè* (Milan, 8 Feb 1950; libr Ancheschi and M. Corradi-Cervi) and *La Capanna del Zio Tom* (Parma, 17 Jan 1953; libr Ancheschi, after Harriet Beecher Stowe's *Uncle Tom's Cabin*).

Ferrero, Lorenzo (b 1951)
Italian composer, whose style mixes classical forms and traditional operatic devices with popular and electronic idioms. Perhaps the most successful Italian opera composer of the younger generation, his stage works include *Rimbaud* (Avignon, 24 July 1978; libr L.-F. Claude), *Marilyn* (Rome, 23 Feb 1980; libr composer and F. Bossi), which is about Marilyn Monroe, the children's opera *La Figlia del Mago* (Montepulciano, 31 July 1981; libr Marco Ravasini), the OPERA BUFFA *Mare Nostro* (Alessandria, 11 Sept 1985; libr Ravasini), *Night* (Munich, 8 Nov 1985; libr composer, after F.L. von Hardenberg's *Hymnen an die Nacht*), *Salvatore Giuliano* (Rome, 25 Jan 1986; libr Giuseppe di Leva), *Charlotte Corday* (Rome, 21 Feb 1989; libr Leva) and the marionette opera *Le Bleu-Blanc-Rouge et le Noir* (Paris, 11 Dec 1989). Artistic director of the Verona Arena (1991–).

Ferretti, Jacopo (1784–1852)
Italian librettist. A cut above most of his contemporary Italian colleagues, he was particularly noted for his comic texts with their elegant verses and subtle social comment. Writing his first libretto in 1810, he went on to produce over 60 more. He provided texts for Carafa, Coccia, Donizetti (*L'Aio nell' Imbarazzo*, *Torquato Tasso*, *Olivio e Pasquale* and *Il Furioso*), Fioravanti (*Didone Abbandonata*), Mayr, Mercadante, Morlacchi, Pacini (*Il Corsaro*), Portugal, L. and F. Ricci, Rossi, Rossini (*La Cenerentola* and *Matilde di Shabran*) and Zingarelli (*Baldovino* and *Berenice*) amongst others.

Ferrier, Kathleen (1912–53)
British contralto. One of the best-loved British singers of the 20th century and sometimes regarded as the greatest voice that Britain has ever produced, her tragically early death from cancer robbed music of a voice of exceptional beauty, nobility and compassion, well-nigh unparalleled in modern times. Well established as a concert artist, she turned to opera in 1946, singing only two roles: the title-role in *The Rape of Lucretia* (which she created) and Orpheus in *Orfeo ed Euridice*, with which role her name is indissolubly linked. The Kathleen Ferrier Memorial Prize, Britain's most prestigious vocal competition, was established in her memory.

Ferro, Gabriele
Italian conductor, particularly associated with Rossini and with revivals of neglected 19th-century Italian operas. One of the finest contemporary Rossini interpreters, he is noted for his crisp tempi and his attention to detail. Musical director of the Stuttgart Opera (1991–).

Fervaal
Opera in prologue and three acts by d'Indy (Op 40). 1st perf Brussels, 12 March 1897; libr by the composer, after Isaïas Tégner's *Axel*. Principal roles: Fervaal (ten), Guilhen (mezzo), Arfagard (bar), Kaito (mezzo). The most important of d'Indy's operas, heavily influenced by Wagner, it is nowadays only very rarely performed.
Plot: 8th-century France. Wounded in battle against the invading Saracens, the Celtic chief Fervaal is nursed back to health by the Saracen sorceress Guilhen, and the two fall in love. Deceived by the

Druid Arfagard into believing Fervaal unfaithful, Guilhen encompasses the destruction of the Celts.

Festa teatrale (Italian for 'theatrical festival')
A name used in the late 17th and early 18th centuries for the sumptuous operatic works provided for public and state occasions, such as royal weddings. An example is Händel's *Atalanta.*

Festival of Two Worlds, Spoleto
An annual festival in Umbria (Italy), founded by Menotti in 1958. Using young American and European artists, the festival specializes in contemporary works and in revivals of 19th-century Italian BEL CANTO operas. Performances are given at the Teatro Nuovo (cap 900), which opened in Aug 1864. Musical directors have included Thomas Schippers, Christopher Keene and Christian Badea. The festival has an American branch in Charleston (South Carolina).

Festivals
Although a few annual opera festivals (such as Bayreuth, Glyndebourne and Salzburg) date back further, the summer opera festival, sometimes in the open air, is essentially a post-war phenomenon. Some, such as Bayreuth and Halle, are devoted to the works of one composer; others, such as Salzburg and Bregenz, present the standard repertory with star-studded casts. Perhaps the most rewarding are those such as Wexford which specialize in the revival of long-neglected operas.

See AIX-EN-PROVENCE FESTIVAL; ALDEBURGH FESTIVAL; BAYREUTH FESTIVAL; BREGENZ FESTIVAL; BUXTON FESTIVAL; CAMDEN FESTIVAL; CARAMOOR FESTIVAL; EDINBURGH FESTIVAL; ENGLISH BACH FESTIVAL; FESTIVAL OF TWO WORLDS, SPOLETO; GLYNDEBOURNE FESTIVAL; GÖTTINGENER HÄNDELFESTSPIELE; HÄNDEL FESTIVAL, HALLE; MAGGIO MUSICALE FIORENTINO; ORANGE FESTIVAL; PESARO FESTIVAL; SALZBURG EASTER FESTIVAL; SALZBURG FESTIVAL; SAVONLINNA FESTIVAL; VERONA ARENA; WEXFORD FESTIVAL

Feuersnot (Fire Famine)
Opera in one act by Strauss (Op 50). 1st perf Dresden, 21 Nov 1901; libr by Baron Ernst von Wolzogen, after *The Quenched Fires of Oudenaarde* in Julius Wolff's *Sagas of the Netherlands.* Principal roles: Kunrad (bar), Diemut (sop). Strauss's second opera, only infrequently performed, it is a thinly veiled satirical attack on those who rejected first Wagner and then his disciple – Strauss himself.
Plot: 12th-century Munich. On St John's Eve, Kunrad causes all the fires in the city to go out. He allows them to burn again only when Diemut, whom he loves and who has publicly humiliated him for his passion, admits that she reciprocates his feelings. [R]

Février, Henri (1875–1957)
French composer. He wrote three operettas and six operas, the latter influenced by Massenet and the Italian VERISMO school. His operas are *Le Roi Aveugle* (Paris, 8 May 1906; libr H. le Roux), MONNA VANNA, by far his most successful work, *Carmosine* (Paris, 24 Feb 1913; libr Louis Payen and Henri Cain, after Giovanni Boccaccio), *Gismonda* (Chicago, 14 Jan 1919; libr Payen and Cain, after Victorien Sardou), *La Damnation de Blanche-Fleur* (Monte Carlo, 13 Mar 1920; libr Maurice Léna) and *La Femme Nue* (Monte Carlo, 22 Mar 1929; libr Payen, after Henri Batallie). He also wrote a biography of his friend and teacher Messager.

Fiakermilli
Soprano role in Strauss's *Arabella.* She is the regimental mascot.

Fiamma, La (*The Flame*)
Opera in three acts by Respighi. 1st perf Rome, 23 Jan 1934; libr by Claudio Guastalla, after Hans Wiers-Jenssen's *Anne Pedersdotter, the Witch.* Principal roles: Silvana (sop), Donello (ten), Basilio (bar), Eudossia (mezzo). Respighi's penultimate and most successful opera, it is still occasionally performed.
Plot: Late-7th-century Ravenna. The witch Agnese di Cervia is lynched and her daughter Silvana (second wife of Basilio, the Exharch of Ravenna) is unable to prevent it. Agnese curses Basilio's family, including Silvana, for whom she predicts a fate similar to her own. Silvana falls in

love with her stepson Donello and confesses her adultery to the ailing Basilio, who falls dead at the news. Silvana is accused of having killed Basilio by witchcraft, is arraigned before the bishop and, failing to defend herself, is condemned. [R]

Fibich, Zdeněk (1850–1910)
Czech composer. Influenced by Schumann and, more especially, by Wagner, he wrote seven operas, some of which deserve to have had more success outside the Czech lands than has come their way. His first two operas, *Bukovín* (Prague, 16 Apr 1874; libr Karel Sabina) and *Blaník* (Prague, 25 Nov 1881; libr Eliška Krásnohorská), are immature, but his powerful musical imagination is fully apparent in THE BRIDE OF MESSINA and THE TEMPEST. At this point, Fibich formed a liaison with the poetess **Anežka Schulzová** (1868–1905), for whom he left his family. She wrote the libretti for his last three operas, all of which are marked by considerable erotic fervour in the music. *Hedy* (Prague, 12 Feb 1896; libr after Lord Byron's *Don Juan*) was followed by ŠÁRKA, his masterpiece, and the ambitious *The Fall of Arkun* (*Pád Arkuna*, Prague, 9 Nov 1900).

In addition to his operas, Fibich also wrote the melodrama trilogy *Hippodamie* (libr Jaroslav Vrchlický). It comprises *The Wooing of Pelops* (*Námluvy Pelopovy*, Prague, 21 Feb 1890), *The Atonement of Tantalus* (*Smir Tantalův*, Prague, 2 June 1891) and *The Death of Hippodamia* (*Smirt Hippodamie*, Prague, 8 Nov 1891).

Fidalma
Mezzo role in Cimarosa's *Il Matrimonio Segreto*. She is Carolina's aunt.

Fidelio or **Die Eheliche Liebe** (*Wedded Love*)
Opera in two (originally three) acts by Beethoven (Op 72). 1st perf (as *Leonore*) Vienna, 20 Nov 1805; libr by Josef Sonnleithner, after Jean-Nicolas Bouilly's libretto for Gaveaux's *Léonore ou l'Amour Conjugal*. Revised version 1st perf Vienna, 29 March 1806; libr revised by Stefan von Breuning. Final version 1st perf Vienna, 23 May 1814; libr revised by Georg Friedrich Treitschke. Principal roles: Leonore (sop), Florestan (ten), Rocco (bass), Don Pizarro (bar), Marzelline (sop), Jacquino (ten), Don Fernando (b-bar). Beethoven's only opera, it is the most famous of all RESCUE OPERAS. Suffused with Beethoven's deep humanity and burning passion for human freedom, the music totally transcends the SINGSPIEL structure in which the opera is cast. One of the greatest of all operas, it occupies a unique position in the repertory. There are four different overtures to the opera: 'Leonora No 1' (composed for a projected Prague performance), 'Leonora No 2' (the first to be written and played at the premiere), the magnificent 'Leonora No 3' (which is occasionally inserted between the two final scenes) and 'Fidelio' (which now begins the work). The original version of the opera is still sometimes performed.
Plot: 18th-century Seville. The nobleman Florestan has been imprisoned for political reasons. His wife Leonore has disguised herself as the boy Fidelio and entered the service of the jailer Rocco. Rocco's daughter Marzelline has fallen in love with Fidelio, to the displeasure of her admirer Jacquino, the gatekeeper. Leonore discovers that Florestan is in the deepest dungeon and that the evil prison governor Don Pizarro plans to kill him before an imminent ministerial inspection. Rocco and Fidelio dig his grave in the dungeon and Pizarro attempts to murder Florestan, but is prevented from doing so by Leonore, who reveals herself as Florestan's wife. The arrival of the minister Don Fernando, a friend of Florestan's, puts paid to the murder attempt. Pizarro is arrested and Fernando allows Leonore herself to remove her husband's chains. [R both versions].

Fidès
Mezzo role in Meyerbeer's *Le Prophète*. She is Jean de Leyden's mother.

Fieramosca
Baritone role in Berlioz's *Benvenuto Cellini*. He is a sculptor in love with Teresa.

Fierrabras
Opera in three acts by Schubert (D 796). 1st perf (in concert) Vienna, 9 Feb 1858 (composed 1823); 1st stage perf Karlsruhe, 9 Feb 1897; libr by Josef Kupelwieser, after Friedrich Heinrich Carl

de la Motte Fouqué's *Eginhard und Emma*, a story in J.G.G. Büsching and F.H. von der Hagen's *Buch der Liebe* and Pedro Calderón de la Barca's *La Puente de Mantible*. Principal roles: Fierrabras (ten), Florinda (sop), Roland (bar), King Karl (bass), Emma (sop), Maragond (mezzo), Eginhard (ten), Boland (bar). Schubert's most structurally advanced opera, it contains some of his most dramatically effective music but is unaccountably only very rarely performed.
Plot: Southern France and Spain, late 8th century. Charlemagne's daughter Emma loves the knight Eginhard. Charlemagne returns victorious, bringing the Moorish prince Fierrabras, captured by Roland, as prisoner. Fierrabras is secretly in love with Emma, and Roland loves Fierrabras's sister Florinda. Eginhard and Roland are captured by Fierrabras's father Boland, but Eginhard escapes. Fierrabras aids the Christians in defeating the Moors. Peace is established, Roland is rescued and weds Florinda, Eginhard and Emma are united, but Fierrabras remains alone. [R]

Fiery Angel, The (*Ognenny Angel*)
Opera in five acts by Prokofiev (Op 37). 1st perf (in concert) Paris, 25 Nov 1954 (composed 1927); 1st stage perf Venice, 14 Sept 1955; libr by the composer, after Valery Bryusov's novel. Principal roles: Renata (sop), Ruprecht (bar), Inquisitor (bass), Mephistopheles (ten), Agrippa (ten), Faust (bass). A terrifying story of sorcery and demonic possession, it is one of Prokofiev's greatest works, but it has only been much performed in the last decade, and was not performed in Prokofiev's lifetime. He used some of the music in his third symphony.
Plot: North Germany, 1543. The knight Ruprecht meets Renata, who believes that a Count Heinrich is the incarnation of an angel which visited her when she was a child. She at first mistakes Ruprecht for Heinrich and he, having fallen in love with her, accompanies her to Cologne to help her search for Heinrich. When they finally find him, and he rejects her, she persuades Ruprecht to duel with him. Ruprecht is injured but wins Renata's affection. Later, however, in an increasing state of derangement, she accuses him of being possessed by the Devil. Eventually, Renata enters a convent where she seems to unleash evil spirits, and is ordered by the Inquisitor to be tortured and burnt. [R]

Fiesco, Jacopo
Bass role in Verdi's *Simon Boccanegra*. He is a stoical old patrician who has brought up Amelia.

Figaro
The barber of Beaumarchais's plays appears as: **1** Baritone role in Rossini's and Paisiello's *Il Barbiere di Siviglia*. **2** Bass-baritone role in Mozart's *Le Nozze di Figaro*. **3** Baritone role in Corigliano's *The Ghosts of Versailles*.

Figlia di Iorio, La (*Jorio's Daughter*)
Opera in three acts by Franchetti. 1st perf Milan, 29 March 1906; a word-for-word setting of Gabriele d'Annunzio's play. Principal roles: Mila (sop), Aligi (ten), Lazzaro (bar). Sometimes regarded as the finest of Franchetti's VERISMO operas, it is nowadays almost forgotten.

Figlia di Iorio, La (*Jorio's Daughter*)
Opera in three acts by Pizzetti. 1st perf Naples, 4 Dec 1954; a word-for-word setting of Gabrielle d'Annunzio's play. Principal roles: Mila (sop), Aligi (ten), Lazzaro (bar). Although it is one of Pizzetti's finest operas, it is hardly ever performed.
Plot: Legendary Abruzzi. Pursued by peasants who believe her to be a witch, Mila is saved by Aligi, who falls in love with her even though she is already engaged. They are discovered in a mountain cave by Aligi's father Lazzaro, who has his son beaten and tied up. Aligi escapes and kills Lazzaro, who is about to rape Mila. Mila accuses herself of Lazzaro's murder and the mob have her burnt.

Figner, Medea (b Mei) (1858–1952)
Italian-born Russian mezzo and later soprano, particularly associated with the Russian and French repertories. Possessing a beautiful voice used with a superb technique, she created Lisa in *The Queen of Spades* and the title-roles in Tchaikovsky's *Iolanta* and Nápravník's *Francesca da Rimini*. Her autobiography, *My Memoirs*, was published in 1912. Her husband **Nikolai** (1857–1918) was a successful

tenor, who created Herman in *The Queen of Spades*, Vaudémont in *Iolanta* and Vladimir in Nápravník's *Dubrovsky*.

Fila di voce (Italian for 'spinning of the voice')
It is an instruction to a singer to hold a soft, sustained note without either expanding or diminishing the tone. A famous example is the final note of Violetta's 'Addio del passato' in Verdi's *La Traviata*.

Fille de Madame Angot, La (*Mrs Angot's Daughter*)
Operetta in three acts by Lecocq. 1st perf Brussels, 4 Dec 1872; libr by Paul Siraudin, Louis François Clairville and Victor Koning, after A.F. Eve Maillot's *Madame Angot ou la Poissarde Parvenue*. Principal roles: Clairette (sop), Ange Pitou (bar), Pomponnet (ten), Mlle Lange (sop). By far Lecocq's most successful work, it enjoyed an initial run of 500 performances, and is still regularly performed. The ballet *Mam'zelle Angot* is derived from music from the operetta.
Plot: 18th-century Paris. Clairette, daughter of the late Madame Angot, is engaged to the hairdresser Pomponnet but loves the satirist Ange Pitou. She tries to release herself from her engagement, but ends up still planning to marry Pomponnet. [R]

Fille du Régiment, La (*The Daughter of the Regiment*)
Comic opera in two acts by Donizetti. 1st perf Paris, 11 Feb 1840; libr by Jules-Henri Vernoy de Saint-Georges and Jean François Alfred Bayard. Principal roles: Marie (sop), Tonie (ten), Sulpice (bass), Marquise (mezzo). Donizetti's first opera in French and one of his most delightful comedies (which Mendelssohn said that he wished he'd written), it was an immediate success and has remained popular ever since. It is written in OPÉRA-COMIQUE style, but when it is performed in Italy RECITATIVES replace the spoken dialogue.
Plot: Swiss Tyrol, *c* 1810. The orphan girl Marie has been raised as a 'daughter' by the 21st regiment, a section of which is led by Sgt Sulpice. She loves the young Tyrolean Tonie who had once saved her life. Tonie enlists in the regiment in order to marry her, but she is claimed as a long-lost niece by the Marquise de Berkenfeld. At her château, the Marquise, aided and abetted by Sulpice, attempts to teach Marie the social graces. She is bored, however, and the arrival of Tonie and the regiment rescues her from an arranged marriage. The Marquise confesses that Marie is actually her illegitimate daughter, and gives her blessing to Marie's marriage with Tonie. [R]

Fille du Tambour-Major, La
(*The Drum-Major's Daughter*)
Operetta in three acts by Offenbach. 1st perf Paris, 13 Dec 1879; libr by Henri Charles Chivot and Alfred Duru. Principal roles: Stella (sop), Robert (bar), Claudine (sop), Griolet (ten), Monthabor (bar). Offenbach's last substantial operetta, it has never ranked as one of his most popular works but it is still performed from time to time.
Plot: Milan, 1806. Stella, believed to be the daughter of the Duke della Volta, is to be married to the ludicrous Marquis Bambini. French troops arrive, and the drum-major Monthabor is billetted on the Duke. He recognizes the Duchess as his ex-wife by whom he had a daughter – Stella. Stella, full of revolutionary fervour, joins the French ranks and marries the handsome Lt Robert. [R]

Films
see OPERATIC FILMS

Filosofo di Campagna, Il (*The Country Philosopher*)
Comic opera in three acts by Galuppi. 1st perf Venice, 26 Oct 1764; libr by Carlo Goldoni. Principal roles: Don Tritemio (bar), Eugenia (sop), Lesbina (sop), Nardo (bar), Rinaldo (ten). Galuppi's most enduring work, and one of the finest of all 18th-century OPERA BUFFAS, it is still occasionally performed.
Plot: 18th-century Italy. Don Tritemio, who lives in the country with his daughter Eugenia, is in love with her companion Lesbina. Tritemio wishes Eugenia to marry the rich farmer Nardo, but she is in love with Rinaldo. To assist Eugenia, Lesbina disguises herself as Eugenia and succeeds in arousing Rinaldo's jealousy, but he then falls in love with Lesbina. [R]

Finale (Italian for 'end')
The final part of an operatic act. In the 18th and early 19th centuries, this usually consisted of an extended ensemble.

Finch' han dal vino
Baritone aria (the so-called Champagne Aria) for the Don in Act I of Mozart's *Don Giovanni*, in which he tells Leporello that by the end of the night there will be another dozen conquests to add to his list.

Finland
see FINNISH NATIONAL OPERA; SAVONLINNA FESTIVAL

Finnish National Opera (*Suomalainen Oopera* in Finnish)
The company was formed in 1914 by Aïno Ackté and others and in recent years has won international acclaim for its performances, especially of contemporary Finnish operas. Based in Helsinki, it performs at the opera house (cap 1,364) which opened on 30 Nov 1993. Musical directors have included Armas Järnefelt, Jussi Jalas, Leif Segerstam, Ulf Söderblom, Ádám Fischer and Miguel Gómez-Martínez. There is also a chamber company (*Suomen Kansallisooppera*), which performs at the Russky Theatre (cap 669) in Helsinki.

Finnish opera composers
see KOKKONEN; MADETOJA; MERIKANTO, A.; MERIKANTO, O. ; RAUTAVAARA; SALLINEN; SIBELIUS
Other national opera composers include Kalevi Aho (*b* 1949), Erik Bergman (*b* 1910), Paavo Heininen (*b* 1938), Ilkka Kuusisto (*b* 1933), Erkki Merlartin (1875–1937), Frederik Pacius (1809–91), whose *The Hunt of King Charles* (*Kung Karls Jakt*, Helsinki, 24 Mar 1852; libr Zacharias Topelius) [R] is usually regarded as the first Finnish opera, Tauno Pylkkänen (1918–80) and Väinö Raitio (1891–1945).

Finta Giardiniera, La (*The Pretended Gardening Girl*)
Comic opera in three acts by Mozart (K 196). 1st perf Munich, 13 Jan 1775; libr by Marco Coltellini, after Ranieri de' Calzabigi's libretto for Anfossi. Revised SINGSPIEL version *Die Gärtnerin aus Liebe* 1st perf Augsburg, 1 May 1780. Principal roles: Sandrina (sop), Arminda (sop), Ramiro (mezzo), Belfiore (ten), Nardo (bar), Serpetta (sop), Don Anchise (ten). An assured and attractive work, it is the earliest of Mozart's operas which is still regularly performed.
Plot: Mid-18th-century Italy. Countess Violante is believed to have died as a result of a violent quarrel with her lover Count Belfiore, who has disappeared. Disguised as the gardener Sandrina, the Countess, who is not dead, searches for Belfiore, who she has forgiven. She is employed by the mayor Don Anchise, whose daughter Arminda is being courted by Belfiore, and who sets his own sights on 'Sandrina'. After much amorous intrigue and a string of complications, everything is satisfactorily sorted out, and everyone except Don Anchise gets married. [R both versions]

Finta Semplice, La (*The Pretended Simpleton*)
Comic opera in three acts by Mozart (K 51). 1st perf Salzburg, 1 May 1769; libr by Marco Coltellini, after Carlo Goldoni's libretto for Perillo. Principal roles: Rosina (sop), Giacinta (sop), Ninetta (sop), Fracasso (ten), Polidoro (ten), Cassandro (bass), Simone (bass). Mozart's first opera to be publicly performed, it is still occasionally revived.
Plot: 18th-century Cremona. The Hungarian baroness Rosina exercises her charms, whilst pretending to be a simpleton, on the infatuated brothers Cassandro and Polidoro, so that they will allow her own brother Fracasso to marry their sister Giacinta. She is successful and herself marries Cassandro, whilst Fracasso's lieutenant Simone weds Giacinta's maid Ninetta. [R]

Finto Stanislao, Il
see GIORNO DI REGNO, UN; JÍROVEC

Fiora
Soprano role in Montemezzi's *L'Amore dei Tre Re*. Married to Manfredo, she is in love with Avito.

Fioravanti, Valentino (1764–1837)
Italian composer who excelled in OPERA BUFFA. He wrote 77 operas, including *I Virtuosi Ambulante* (Paris, 26 Sept 1807;

libr Luigi Balocchi) and *Ogni Eccesso e Vivioso* (Naples 1824; libr Andrea Leone Tottola), but only LE CANTATRICI VILLANE is in any way remembered today. His son **Vincenzo** (1799–1877) was also a composer of opera buffas, some of which met with success in Naples. Of his 35 operas, the most successful was *Il Ritorno di Pulcinella dagli Studi di Padova* (Naples, 28 Dec 1837; libr A. Passaro).

Fiordiligi
Soprano role in Mozart's *Così fan Tutte.* Dorabella's sister, she is in love with Guglielmo.

Fiorilla
Soprano role in Rossini's *Il Turco in Italia.* She is married to Don Geronio.

Fioritura (Italian for 'flowering')
A florid decoration of the vocal line. It is also known, not quite accurately, as COLORATURA.

Firenze è come un albero fiorito
Tenor aria for Rinuccio in Puccini's *Gianni Schicchi*, in which he salutes the glory of Florence.

Fischer, Ádám (b 1949)
Hungarian conductor, particularly associated with the German and Hungarian repertories. He was musical director of the Finnish National Opera (1974–7), the Freiburg Opera (1981–4) and the Karlsruhe Staatstheater (1987–9) and conducted the first performance of Tal's *Der Sturm.* His brother **Iván** (*b* 1951) is also a conductor, and is noted for his Mozart performances. He was musical director of Kent Opera at the very end of its life.

Fischer–Dieskau, Dietrich (b 1925)
German baritone, particularly associated with Mozart, Strauss, Wagner and Verdi roles and with the 20th-century German repertory. One of the greatest singers of the 20th century, he was equally renowned for his lieder singing as for his operatic interpretations. A fine singing-actor of outstanding intelligence and musicianship, he enjoyed a remarkably long career, singing into his late 60s. A champion of modern composers, he created Mittenhofer in Henze's *Elegie für Junge Liebende* and the title-role in Reimann's *Lear.* One of the most recorded singers in history, he has also had some success as a conductor. His writings include *Wagner und Nietzsche: der Mystagoge und sein Abtrunniger*, a biography of Schubert and his autobiography, *Echoes of a Lifetime*, which was published in 1986. He is married to the soprano JULIA VARADY, and his son **Martin** is a conductor.

Fisher, Sylvia (b 1910)
Australian soprano, particularly associated with Wagner and Britten roles. A fine dramatic soprano with a strong stage presence, she created Miss Wingrave in *Owen Wingrave.*

Flagello, Ezio (b 1931)
American bass, particularly associated with the Italian repertory and with Mozart roles, especially Leporello. He possessed a dark and very rich voice with a remarkable upper register extending to high a, and was a fine singing-actor, particularly in comedy. He created Enobarbus in Barber's *Antony and Cleopatra.*

Flagstad, Kirsten (1895–1962)
Norwegian soprano, particularly associated with Wagnerian roles, especially Isolde. One of the greatest dramatic sopranos of the 20th century, she possessed a radiant voice of remarkable power which she used with unfailing musicianship. She faced some hostility after the war because of her husband's association with the Quislings, but this was soon overcome and she remained a great favourite with audiences everywhere until her retirement in 1954. She was director of the Norwegian Opera (1959–60) and her autobiography, *The Flagstad Manuscript* (written with Louis Biancolli), was published in 1965.

Flammand
Tenor role in Strauss's *Capriccio.* He is a musician in love with Countess Madeleine.

Flat
Written as the musical symbol ♭, flat is the opposite of SHARP: it is a reduction in the

pitch by a semitone (or by a full tone if marked double flat). The term is also used to describe an unintentional and indeterminate lowering of the pitch. This second meaning is used to refer to the all-too-frequent tendency of singers to sing under the note.

Flavio, Rè di Longobardi (*Flavius, King of the Lombards*)
Opera in three acts by Händel. 1st perf London, 14 May 1723; libr by Nicola Francesco Haym, after Matteo Noris's *Il Flavio Cuniberto*, itself based on Pierre Corneille's *Le Cid* and S. Ghigi's libretto for Antonio Pollarolo's *Flavio Pertarido*. Principal roles: Flavio (c-ten), Emilia (sop), Guido (c-ten), Teodata (mezzo), Vitige (sop), Ugone (ten), Lotario (bass). Never one of Händel's more successful operas, it is only infrequently performed. **Plot**: Legendary Lombardy. Guido, son of King Flavio's counsellor Ugone, is betrothed to Emilia, daughter of his other counsellor Lotario. Ugone's daughter Teodata is secretly in love with Flavio's adjutant Vitige. Ugone and Lotario quarrel, and Guido – fighting a duel on behalf of his aged father – is killed by his new father-in-law. The various claims of duty and vengeance are complicated by Flavio's infatuation with Teodata. Eventually, Flavio resolves the conflicts with wisdom and forebearance. [R]

Fledermaus, Die (*The Bat*)
Operetta in three acts by J. Strauss II. 1st perf Vienna, 5 April 1874; libr by Carl Haffner and Richard Genée, after Henri Meilhac and Ludovic Halévy's *Le Réveillon*, itself based on Roderich Benedix's *Das Gefängnis*. Principal roles: Rosalinde (sop), Eisenstein (ten), Adele (sop), Dr Falke (bar), Alfred (ten), Col Frank (b-bar), Orlofsky (mezzo), Frosch (speaker), Dr Blind (ten). The quintessential Viennese operetta, and one of the greatest of all musical comedies, it is the only operetta to have established itself in the repertory of all major opera houses. There is a long tradition, especially in Vienna, of performing the work on New Year's Eve with guest stars appearing in Act II to give their party pieces. **Plot**: 19th-century Vienna. Dr Falke plans to take revenge on his friend Gabriel von Eisenstein for a humiliating practical joke of which he was the butt. Before leaving to serve a brief prison sentence, Eisenstein accepts Falke's invitation to a party. His wife Rosalinde is expecting a visit from an old flame, the opera singer Alfred. She gives her maid Adele the night off and she and Alfred sit down to a domestic evening. The prison governor Col Frank, on his way to the party, comes to escort Eisenstein to jail. Alfred, wearing Eisenstein's dressing-gown, allows himself to be arrested rather than compromise Rosalinde. At Prince Orlofsky's party, all the characters play the parts assigned to them in Falke's plot: Eisenstein, disguised as the Marquis de Renard, flirts with a disguised Adele, makes friends with Frank (disguised as the Chevalier Chagrin) and then provides Rosalinde with evidence of his infidelity by wooing her in her disguise as an Hungarian countess. Even the blasé young Orlofsky is amused. At the prison, Frosch presides boozily until the arrival of Frank, distinctly the worse for wear. Eisenstein, arriving to serve his sentence, discovers who was arrested in his stead and why, but Rosalinde has evidence of his own peccadillos. Falke irons everything out and claims his revenge, and all agree to blame everything on the champagne. [R]

Flemish opera composers
see BLOCKX
Other Flemish opera composers include Pierre Benoît (1834–1901), whose *The Village in the Mountains* (*Het Dorp in 't Gebergte*, 1856) was the first opera written to a Flemish libretto, August de Boeck (1865–1937), Paul Gilson (1865–1942) and Joseph Mertens (1834–1901). *See also* BELGIAN OPERA COMPOSERS

Fleur que tu m'avais jetée, La
Tenor aria (the Flower Song) for Don José in Act II of Bizet's *Carmen*, in which he tells Carmen that whilst he was in prison he kept the flower which she had thrown to him.

Fliegende Holländer, Der (*The Flying Dutchman*)
Opera in three acts (originally one act) by Wagner. 1st perf Dresden, 2 Jan 1843; libr by the composer, after Heinrich Heine's *Aus den Memorien des Herren von*

Schnabelewopski. Principal roles: Dutchman (b-bar), Senta (sop), Daland (bass), Erik (ten), Mary (mezzo), Steersman (ten). Wagner's first 'canonical' opera, it is a highly atmospheric setting, notable for its lusty choruses and for its remarkable characterization of the doomed sea captain. Most modern productions revert to Wagner's original one-act structure.
Plot: 18th-century Norway. The Dutchman, as a punishment for having uttered a blasphemy, has been condemned to sail the seas forever unless redeemed by the love of a woman faithful unto death. Allowed to come ashore once every seven years in search of such a woman, he lands and meets the old sea captain Daland, who – seduced by the Dutchman's wealth – suggests marriage to his daughter Senta. Senta, loved by the huntsman Erik, has long been obsessed with the legend of the Dutchman, and falls in love with him immediately. The Dutchman overhears her begging Erik to understand her feelings, mistakenly thinks her unfaithful and immediately sails away distraught. Senta throws herself off a cliff, calling to him that she has been faithful unto death. Her death is his redemption: his ghostly ship sinks, and he and Senta are seen ascending to heaven. [R]

Flight of the Bumble Bee
Orchestral excerpt, very popular in the concert hall, from Act III of Rimsky-Korsakov's *The Tale of Tsar Saltan*. It describes Gvidon's journey, transformed into a bee, to find the Tsar.

Flint, Mr
Bass role in Britten's *Billy Budd*. He is the Sailing Master of H.M.S. Indomitable.

Flora
1 Soprano role in Britten's *The Turn of the Screw*. She is one of the two children in the Governess's charge. **2** Soprano role in Tippett's *The Knot Garden*. She is the ward of Faber and Thea. **3** Mezzo role in Menotti's *The Medium*. She is a fake medium. **4** Mezzo role in Verdi's *La Traviata*. She is Violetta's friend Flora Bervoix.

Florence
see FLORENTINE CAMERATA; MAGGIO MUSICALE FIORENTINO; TEATRO COMUNALE, FLORENCE

Florence Pike
Mezzo role in Britten's *Albert Herring*. She is Lady Billow's housekeeper.

Florentine Camerata
An academy of musicians and writers founded in Florence at the end of the 16th century, whose aim was the recreation of the ideals of classical Greek tragedy, and who took as their point of departure Aristotle's description of drama as 'words sweetened by music'. They developed a declamatory style of singing called *recitar cantando*, which they applied to dramatic texts. They may thus be viewed as the inventors of opera. The leading members of the academy, which met at the home of Count Giovanni Bardi (1534–1612), included the poet OTTAVIO RINUCCINI, who wrote the earliest opera libretti, and the musicians CACCINI, DE CAVALIERI, PERI and Vincenzo Galilei (*c* 1520–91), the father of the astronomer.

Florentinische Tragödie, Eine
(*A Florentine Tragedy*)
Opera in one act by Zemlinsky (Op 16). 1st perf Stuttgart, 30 Jan 1917; libr by Max Meyerfeld, after Oscar Wilde's play. Principal roles: Simone (bar), Bianca (mezzo), Guido (ten). An orchestrally lush work in late romantic style, it suffered a long period of neglect but has recently received a number of performances.
Plot: Renaissance Florence. Through the arousal of his jealousy, the merchant Simone abandons his role of passive cuckold and murders Guido, the lover of his wife Bianca. [R]

Florestan
1 Tenor role in Beethoven's *Fidelio*. Leonore's husband, he is a political prisoner. **2** Tenor role in Messager's *Véronique*. He is a viscount engaged to Hélène. **3** Baritone role in Lully's *Amadis*. He is the king of Gaul's natural son.

Florid
A style of singing in which the vocal line is heavily ornamented, as for example in many arias by Händel or Rossini or in an ARIA DI BRAVURA in an OPERA SERIA.

Floridante
Opera in three acts by Händel. 1st perf London, 9 Dec 1721; libr by Paolo Antonio Rolli, after Francesco Silvani's libretto for Pietro Ziani's *La Costanza in Trionfo*. Principal roles: Floridante (c-ten), Elmira (mezzo), Rossane (sop), Timante (sop), Oronte (bass), Coralbo (bass). Never one of Händel's more successful operas, it is only infrequently performed. **Plot**: Legendary Persia. Oronte has usurped the throne. He has two daughters, Rossane and Elmira, but the latter is adopted and is in fact the daughter of the previous king. The Thracian Prince Floridante gains a naval victory and claims Elmira's hand, as agreed by Oronte. Oronte, however, refuses Floridante's reward, dismisses him and replaces him with Coralbo. Amongst Floridante's prisoners is the Tyrian Prince Timante, once engaged to Rossane. Oronte tells Elmira her real parentage and seeks to wed her, but she rejects him. She reveals her rank to Coralbo, who – aided by Floridante, Timante and Rosanne – has Oronte arrested. Elmira ascends the throne with Floridante as her husband, pardons Oronte and sends Timante and Rosanne to rule in Tyre. [R]

Flosshilde
Mezzo role in Wagner's *Das Rheingold* and *Götterdämmerung*. She is one of the three Rhinemaidens.

Flotow, Friedrich von (1812–83)
German composer. He wrote 18 operas in a light and sentimental style, which mixed German SINGSPIEL and French OPÉRA-COMIQUE elements with Italian lyricism. His operas are tuneful and engaging but are largely innocent of any dramatic or musical originality. Nowadays, only MARTHA, by far his most successful work, and ALESSANDRO STRADELLA are still remembered. Of his other operas, those which achieved some success in their day include *Le Naufrage de la Méduse* (Paris, 31 May 1839; libr Hippolyte and Théodore Cogniard), *La Veuve Grapin* (Paris, 21 Sept 1859; libr P.A.A. Pittaud de Forges), *Zilda* (Paris, 28 May 1866; libr Jules-Henri Vernoy de Saint-Georges, Henri Charles Chivot and Alfred Duru) and *L'Ombre* (Paris, 7 July 1870; libr Saint-Georges and Adolphe de Leuven).

Flower Duet
Soprano/mezzo duet for: **1** Cio-Cio-San and Suzuki ('Scuoti quella fronda di ciliego') in Act II of Puccini's *Madama Butterfly*, in which they deck the house with flowers in the hope of Pinkerton's return. **2** Lakmé and Mallika ('Dôme épais') in Act I of Delibes's *Lakmé*.

Flowermaidens
The seductive inhabitants of Klingsor's magic garden in Wagner's *Parsifal*.

Flower Song
Tenor aria ('La fleur que tu m'avais jetée') for Don José in Act II of Bizet's *Carmen*, in which he tells Carmen that whilst he was in prison he kept the flower which she had thrown to him.

Floyd, Carlisle (b 1926)
American composer. One of the leading contemporary American opera composers, he has written seven operas (for all of which he wrote his own libretti), most of which have had considerable success in the United States but which are largely unknown elsewhere. SUSANNAH established his reputation, which was upheld by *Wuthering Heights* (Santa Fe, 16 July 1958; libr after Emily Brontë) and *The Passion of Jonathan Wade* (New York, 12 Nov 1962; revised version Houston, 18 Jan 1991). His subsequent operas are *Markheim* (New Orleans, 31 Mar 1966; libr after Robert Louis Stevenson), *Of Mice and Men* (Seattle, 20 Jan 1970; libr after John Steinbeck), *Bilby's Doll* (Houston, 29 Feb 1976; libr after E. Forbes's *A Mirror for Witches*) and *Willie Stark* (Houston, 24 Apr 1981; libr after R.P. Warren's *All the King's Men*).

Flute
Tenor role in Britten's *A Midsummer Night's Dream*. A bellows mender, he is one of the mechanicals.

Fluth
Roles in Nicolaï's *Die Lustigen Weiber von Windsor*: Herr Fluth (bar), a wealthy merchant, and his wife Frau Fluth (sop).

Flying Dutchman, The
see FLIEGENDE HOLLÄNDER, DER

Foco insolito, Un
Bass aria for Pasquale in Act I of Donizetti's *Don Pasquale*, in which he dreams of the large family he will have after his wedding.

Foerster, Josef Bohuslav (1859–1951)
Czech composer. He wrote six operas, the first three of which are in traditional Czech style. *Debora* (Prague, 27 Jan 1893; libr Jaroslav Kvapil, after Salomon Mosenthal) was unsuccessful, but its successor EVA remains his best-known opera. It was followed by *Jessika* (Prague, 16 Apr 1905; libr Jaroslav Vrchlický, after Shakespeare's *The Merchant of Venice*). In his final three operas, for each of which he wrote his own libretto, his interests became increasingly spiritual and symbolic. They are *The Invincibles* (*Nepřemožení*, Prague, 19 Dec 1919), *The Heart* (*Srdce*, Prague, 15 Nov 1923) and *The Simpleton* (*Bloud*, Prague, 28 Feb 1936; libr after Tolstoy's *The Two Old Men*) and were largely unsuccessful. His three-volume autobiography, *The Pilgrim*, was published between 1932 and 1947. His wife **Berta Foestrová-Lautererová** (1869–1936) was a successful soprano, who created, for Dvořák, Julie in *Jakobín* and Xenie in *Dimitrij*.

Foltz, Hans
Bass COMPRIMARIO role in Wagner's *Die Meistersinger von Nürnberg*. A coppersmith, he is one of the masters.

Fomin, Yevstigeny (1761–1800)
Russian composer. Perhaps the most talented of the pre-Glinka Russian opera composers, his stage works include the opera-ballet *Boyeslav* (St Petersburg, 27 Nov 1786; libr Catherine the Great), LES COCHERS AU RELAIS, *The Americans* (*Amerikantsy*, St Petersburg, 8 Feb 1800; libr I.A. Krylov and A.I. Klushin) and *The Golden Apple* (*Zolotoye Yabloko*, St Petersburg, 15 Apr 1803; libr I. Ivanov).

Fontana, Ferdinando (1850–1919)
Italian playwright and librettist. He provided texts for Franchetti (*Asrael* and *Il Signor di Pourceaugnac*), Lattuada (*Sandha*) and Puccini (*Edgar* and *Le Villi*) amongst others.

Foppa, Giuseppe Maria (1760–1845)
Italian librettist. He wrote over 80 libretti, the best being comedies. He provided texts for Coccia, Fioravanti, Generali, Mayr (11 operas), Paer (*Sargino*), Portugal, Rossini (*L'Inganno Felice, La Scala di Seta, Sigismondo* and *Il Signor Bruschino*), Spontini, Zingarelli (*La Notte dell'Amicizia* and *Giulietta e Romeo*) and others.

Force of Destiny, The
see FORZA DEL DESTINO, LA

Ford
The wealthy merchant of Shakespeare's *The Merry Wives of Windsor* appears as: **1** Baritone role in Verdi's *Falstaff*. **2** Bass role in Vaughan Williams's *Sir John in Love*. **3** Tenor role in Salieri's *Falstaff*.

Ford, Bruce (b 1956)
American tenor, particularly associated with Rossini roles. Perhaps the finest Rossini tenor of the post-war era, he possesses an agile and strong-toned voice, used with musicianship and an outstanding technique, and he has a good stage presence. He created a role in Floyd's *Willie Stark*.

Forester
Baritone role in Janáček's *The Cunning Little Vixen*. He is the vixen's captor.

Forest Murmurs
Orchestral excerpt in Act II of Wagner's *Siegfried*, in which Siegfried listens to the sounds of nature.

Foresto
Tenor role in Verdi's *Attila*. He is an Aquilean knight in love with Odabella.

Forrester, Maureen (b 1930)
Canadian mezzo, particularly associated with Wagner and Händel roles. She possessed a rich voice of great range which she used with unfailing musicianship, and she was also an accomplished singing-actress, especially in comedy.

Forsell, John (b Carl Johan Jacob) (1868–1941)
Swedish baritone, particularly associated with Mozart roles, especially Don

Giovanni. He created Francesco in Schillings's *Mona Lisa* and was administrator of the Royal Opera, Stockholm (1923–39). He was also a noted teacher, whose pupils included Jussi Björling and Set Svanholm.

Fortner, Wolfgang (1907–87)
German composer. He wrote seven operas whose musical style attempts to reconcile diatonic and serial systems. Some of them have met with considerable success in Germany but are little known elsewhere. *Cress Ertrinkt* (1930; libr A. Zeitler) was written for performance by schools, and was followed by the radio opera *Der Wald* (*The Forest*, Hesse Radio, 25 June 1953; libr Enrique Beck, after Federico García Lorca). His reputation was established with DIE BLUTHOCHZEIT. His other operas are the comedy *Corinna* (Berlin, 3 Oct 1958; libr H. Schmidt, after Gérard de Nerval), *In Seinem Garten Liebt Don Perlimplin Belisa* (Schwetzingen, 10 May 1962; libr Beck, after Lorca's *Amor de Don Perlimplín con Belisa en su Jardín*), *Elisabeth Tudor* (Berlin, 23 Oct 1972; libr M. Braun) and the scenic cantata *Darnals* (Baden-Baden, 24 Apr 1977).

Fortunio
Operetta in three acts by Messager. 1st perf Paris, 5 June 1907; libr by Gaston de Caillavet and Roger de Flers, after Alfred de Musset's *Le Chandelier*. Principal roles: Fortunio (ten), Jacqueline (mezzo), Clavaroche (bass), Maître André (bar). One of Messager's most successful works, it is still occasionally performed.
Plot: 18th-century France. In search of amorous adventure, Capt Clavaroche falls for the pretty Jacqueline, wife of the old notary Maître André. To discourage this, André suggests that Jacqueline enjoy a platonic friendship with his young clerk Fortunio, who sighs with love for her. There is soon a chance for him to prove his promise that he would die for her, because André has heard of nocturnal visits to Jacqueline's room, and Clavaroche persuades Fortunio to take his place the next night. Jacqueline hides him so well, however, that André is unable to find him. After he has left, Jacqueline and Fortunio fall into each other's arms. [R]

Forza del Destino, La (*The Force of Destiny*)
Opera in four acts by Verdi. 1st perf St Petersburg, 10 Nov 1862; libr by Francesco Maria Piave, after Angel de Saavedra Ramírez de Baquedano, Duke of Rivas's *Don Alvaro ó la Fuerza del Sino* and a scene from Friedrich von Schiller's *Wallensteins Lager*. Revised version 1st perf Milan, 27 Feb 1869; libr revised by Antonio Ghislanzoni. Principal roles: Don Alvaro (ten), Leonora (sop), Don Carlo (bar), Padre Guardiano (bass), Fra Melitone (bar), Preziosilla (mezzo), Marquis of Calatrava (bass), Trabuco (ten). One of Verdi's richest 'middle-period' scores, with one of the greatest of all operatic overtures, it was for long either heavily cut or grossly reorganized on account of its sprawling plot. Recently it has been realized that the piece is most effective when performed as Verdi wrote it: the 'genre' scene is as integral to the drama as the private tragedy of the Calatrava family. It is also notable for containing, in Melitone, Verdi's only wholly comic character before *Falstaff*.
Plot: Mid-18th-century Spain and Italy. Don Alvaro and his beloved Leonora are about to elope when they are disturbed by her father, the Marquis of Calatrava. In an ensuing confrontation, Alvaro accidentally kills the Marquis, and the lovers flee. Circumstances separate them, and Leonora seeks refuge at the monastery ruled by Padre Guardiano, who allows her to become a hermit by way of penance. Alvaro joins a regiment under an assumed name and saves the life of a comrade who he has befriended. Alvaro is subsequently injured, and entrusts to this friend the destruction of a box containing private documents. Unbeknownst to him, his friend is Leonora's brother Carlo, also serving incognito, who has sworn to avenge his father's death and his sister's dishonour. His suspicions aroused, Carlo opens the box, discovers Leonora's portrait, and realizes that his comrade is his enemy. He challenges Alvaro to a duel, which is interrupted, and Alvaro seeks refuge at the monastery. Carlo tracks him down, resumes the duel, and is mortally wounded. Alvaro seeks absolution for him from the hermit, who is revealed to be Leonora, and the dying Carlo stabs his

sister to death. (In the original version, Alvaro throws himself from a cliff, uttering a curse against Destiny.) [R]

Forzano, Giovacchino (1883–1970)
Italian librettist and producer. After a short period as a baritone, he turned to writing and production. He wrote many libretti, including texts for Ferrari-Trecate (*Ciotollino*), Franchetti (*La Notte di Leggenda* and *Glauco*), Giordano (*Il Rè*), Leoncavallo (*La Reginetta delle Rose, La Candidata* and *Edipo Rè*), Marinuzzi (*Palla de' Mozzi*), Mascagni (*Lodoletta* and *Il Piccolo Marat*), Pedrollo (*Delitto e Castigo*), Puccini (*Suor Angelica* and *Gianni Schicchi*), Vittadini (*Fiametta e l'Avaro*) and Wolf-Ferrari (*Gli Amanti Sposi* and *Sly*). He produced the first performances of *Turandot*, Boito's *Nerone*, Giordano's *La Cena delle Beffe* and Zandonai's *I Cavalieri di Ekebù*. His autobiography, *Come li ho Conosciuti*, was published in 1957.

Fosca
Opera in four acts by Gomes. 1st perf Milan, 16 March 1873; libr by Antonio Ghislanzoni, after Luigi Capranica's *La Festa delle Mary*. Revised version 1st perf Milan, 7 Feb 1878. Principal roles: Fosca (sop), Paolo (ten), Cambro (bar), Gajolo (ten), Delia (sop), Giotta (bass). Gomes's most Italianate opera, and his finest apart from *Il Guarany*, it was very successful in its revised version but is nowadays hardly ever performed.
Plot: 10th-century Venice and Istria. Pirates under Gajolo are planning the kidnap of a wealthy bride. Gajolo's sister Fosca loves Paolo, captured by the pirates, but he does not return her love as he is engaged to Delia. He is ransomed by his father Senator Giotta. Gajolo's slave Cambro loves Fosca and offers to bring Paolo back if Fosca will marry him. At the wedding of Paolo and Delia, Cambro abducts bride and groom, but Gajolo is captured. He agrees with the Senate to rescue Paolo and Delia in exchange for his freedom. He succeeds, killing Cambro, and Fosca takes poison.

Foss, Lukas (b Fuchs) (b 1922)
German-born American composer. He has written three operas, which have met with some success in the United States but which are unknown elsewhere. They are *The Jumping Frog of Calaveras County* (Bloomington, 18 May 1950; libr Jean Karsavina, after Mark Twain), the television opera *Griffelkin* (NBC, 6 Nov 1955; libr Alastair Reid) and the nine-minute mini-opera *Introductions and Goodbyes* (New York, 6 May 1960; libr Gian-Carlo Menotti).

Four Saints in Three Acts
Opera in four acts by Thomson. 1st perf Ann Arbor, 20 May 1933; libr by Gertrude Stein. Principal roles: St Teresa I and II (sop and mezzo), St Settlement (sop), St Ignatius (bar). One of the finest and most successful American operas, Thomson's lyrical score contrasts with the surreal and almost plotless libretto. Thomson hoped for (and productions have often had) an all-black cast.
Plot: 16th-century Spain. Framed by processions and tableaux, the daily life of a religious community is depicted, ranging from beatific visions to a garden party, as two saints and their followers help one another to achieve salvation. [R]

Fox, Carol (1926–81)
American administrator. She was a co-founder of the Chicago Lyric Opera in 1952 and was subsequently its general manager (1956–80).

Fra Diavolo (*Brother Devil*) or **L'Hôtellerie de Terracine** (*The Inn of Terracina*)
Opera in three acts by Auber. 1st perf Paris, 28 Jan 1830; libr by Eugène Scribe. Principal roles: Fra Diavolo (ten), Zerlina (sop), Lord Cockburn (bar), Lady Pamela (mezzo), Lorenzo (ten), Mathés (bass). Auber's only opera still to be regularly performed, it is a delightful and tuneful OPÉRA-COMIQUE based on the historical Fra Diavolo (*d* 1806), who was an Italian brigand and renegade monk.
Plot: Late-18th-century Naples. The notorious bandit Fra Diavolo, disguised as a marquis, institutes a series of elaborate plans to relieve the travelling Englishman Lord Cockburn and his wife Pamela of their gold. In the course of his machinations, he compromises the honour of Zerlina, daughter of the innkeeper Mathés and loved by the soldier Lorenzo, and also of Lady Pamela. His schemes are

to no avail, however, and he is eventually captured by Lorenzo. The honour of the innocent ladies is restored and Lorenzo gets the reward offered by Lord Cockburn for Diavolo's capture. [R]

Fra Gherardo (*Brother Gerard*)
Opera in three acts by Pizzetti. 1st perf Milan, 16 May 1928; libr by the composer, after the 13th-century *Chronicles of Salimbene da Parma*. Principal roles: Gherardo (ten), Mariola (sop). Written in ARIOSO form, it was successful at its appearance but is nowadays almost never performed.
Plot: Parma, 1260. The wealthy weaver Gherardo leaves the city after having had an affair with the orphan girl Mariola, and joins an order of friars. He returns to lead a peasant uprising against the corrupt authorities, is arrested and charged with heresy, and is burnt at the stake. Mariola, meanwhile, meets her death at the hands of a mad woman.

Françaix, Jean (b 1912)
French composer. He has written five operas, some of which have met with a modicum of success in France. They are *Le Diable Boîteux* (*The Limping Devil*, Paris, 30 June 1938; libr composer, after Alain René le Sage) [R], the comedy *L'Apostrophe* (Amsterdam, 1 July 1951, composed 1942; libr composer, after Anne-Honoré de Balzac), *Le Main de Gloire* (Bordeaux, 18 May 1951; libr composer, after Gérard de Nerval), *Paris à Nous Deux* (Fontainebleau, 7 Aug 1954; libr composer and France Roche) [R] and *La Princesse de Clèves* (Rouen, 11 Dec 1965; libr composer and M. Lanjean, after Madame de la Fayette).

France
see AIX-EN-PROVENCE FESTIVAL; ARTS FLORISSANTS, LES; GRAND THÉÂTRE, MARSEILLES; GRAND THÉÂTRE GRASLIN, NANTES; GRAND THÉÂTRE MUNICIPAL, BORDEAUX; MONTE CARLO OPERA; OPÉRA BASTILLE, PARIS; OPÉRA-COMIQUE, PARIS; OPÉRA DE LYON; OPÉRA DU RHIN; ORANGE FESTIVAL; PARIS OPÉRA; SALLE DE L'OPÉRA, VERSAILLES, THÉÂTRE BOUFFES-PARISIENS; THÉÂTRE DE L'OPÉRA, NICE; THÉÂTRE DES ARTS, ROUEN; THÉÂTRE DES CHAMPS-ÉLYSÉES, PARIS; THÉÂTRE MUNICIPAL, NANCY; TOULOUSE CAPITOLE

Francesca da Rimini
Opera in prologue, two scenes and epilogue by Rachmaninov (Op 25). 1st perf Moscow, 24 Jan 1906; libr by Modest Tchaikovsky, after *L'Inferno* in Dante Alighieri's *La Divina Commedia*. Principal roles: Lanzeotto (b-bar), Francesca (sop), Paolo (ten), Virgil (bass), Dante (ten). Containing some of Rachmaninov's most powerful music, it is still occasionally performed (usually in concert), but it is hampered by its weak libretto.
Plot: Late-13th-century Rimini. The ghost of Virgil tells Dante that the souls in the Inferno are those who have overindulged sexually, and cites the story of Paolo and Francesca. Lanzeotto Malatesta suspects his wife Francesca of loving his younger brother Paolo, who conducted Lanzeotto's courtship by proxy and led Francesca to believe that she was to marry him. Fancesca asks to enter a convent whilst Lanzeotto is away at the wars, but he appoints Paolo to look after her. Francesca gives in to Paolo's passionate urgings and Lanzeotto, returning, kills them both. [R]

Francesca da Rimini
Opera in four acts by Zandonai. 1st perf Turin, 19 Feb 1914; libr by Tito Ricordi, after Gabriele d'Annunzio's play, itself based on *L'Inferno* in Dante Alighieri's *La Divina Commedia*. Principal roles: Francesca (sop), Paolo (ten), Gianciotto (bar), Malatestino (ten). Zandonai's most successful and enduring opera, it is still quite often performed in Italy.
Plot: Late-13th-century Ravenna and Rimini. The hideous Gianciotto, wishing to marry Francesca, tricks her into a betrothal by sending his handsome young brother Paolo to escort her to him. Paolo and Francesca fall instantly in love, and matters are further complicated when a third brother, Malatestino, becomes violently infatuated with her. When Francesca rejects Malatestino, he betrays her and Paolo to Gianciotto, who is thus provoked into murdering them both. [R]

Francesco
1 Baritone role in Verdi's *I Due Foscari*. He is the historical Francesco Foscari (*d* 1457), Doge of Venice. **2** Baritone role in Verdi's *I Masnadieri*. He is Massamiliano's evil son. **3** Tenor

COMPRIMARIO role in Auber's *Fra Diavolo.* **4** Tenor comprimario role in Berlioz's *Benvenuto Cellini.* He is Cellini's foreman.

Franchetti, Alberto (1860–1942)
Italian composer. His considerable personal wealth allowed him to ensure the best performances for his works and to indulge his taste for the spectacular. In style, his operas are a kind of VERISMO Meyerbeer. He wrote nine operas, a number of them enjoying considerable success in their time. They are *Asrael* (Reggio Emilia, 11 Feb 1888; libr Ferdinando Fontana, after Thomas Moore's *Loves of the Angels*), CRISTOFORO COLOMBO, *Fior d'Alpe* (Milan, 15 Mar 1894; libr L. di Castelnuovo), *Il Signor di Pourceaugnac* (Milan, 10 Apr 1897; libr Fontana, after Molière's *Monsieur de Pourceaugnac*), the successful GERMANIA, LA FIGLIA DI IORIO, sometimes regarded as his finest opera, *Notte di Leggenda* (Milan, 14 Jan 1915; libr Giovacchino Forzano), *Giove di Pompei* (Rome, 5 July 1921; libr Luigi Illica and Ettore Romagnoli), written in collaboration with Giordano, and *Glauco* (Naples, 8 Apr 1922; libr Forzano, after Ercole Morselli). His son **Arnold** (*b* 1909) is also a composer, who has written 12 operas.

Franci, Carlo (b 1927)
Argentinian conductor and composer, particularly associated with Rossini and with 20th-century operas. He conducted the first performances of Rota's *La Lampada di Aladino* and operas by Henze, Lualdi and Tosatti, and has himself composed one opera, *L'Imperatore* (Bergamo, 1958). His father **Benvenuto** (1891–1985) was a successful baritone, who created Neri in Giordano's *La Cena delle Beffe*, Cristiano in Zandonai's *I Cavalieri di Ekebù* and the Carpenter in Mascagni's *Il Piccolo Marat.*

Franck, César (1822–90)
Belgian composer. He wrote three operas, none of them remembered today. They are the OPÉRA-COMIQUE *Valet de Ferme* (1852; libr Gustave Vaëz and Alphonse Royer), which has never been performed, HULDA and the unfinished *Ghisèle* (Monte Carlo, 5 Apr 1896; libr Gilbert-Augustin Thierry), which was completed by five of his pupils including d'Indy and Chausson.

Frank, Col
Bass-baritone role in J. Strauss's *Die Fledermaus.* He is the prison governor.

Frankfurt Opera
One of Germany's leading companies, the opera house in Frankfurt-am-Main in Hesse originally opened in 1880, but was destroyed by bombs in 1943. The rebuilt Schauspielhaus (cap 1,430) reopened in 1951. The annual season runs from October to June. Musical directors have included Clemens Krauss, Wilhelm Steinberg, Franz Konwitschny, Sir Georg Solti, Lovro von Matačić, Christoph von Dohnányi, Michael Gielen, Gary Bertini and Sylvain Cambreling.

Franklin, David (1908–73)
British bass, particularly associated with Mozart roles and with Rocco in *Fidelio.* A fine singing-actor with a rich voice, he created Mars in Bliss's *The Olympians.* An operation for throat cancer ended his singing career in 1951, but he later enjoyed great success as a radio and television personality. He wrote the libretto for Phyllis Tate's *The Lodger* and his autobiography, *Basso Cantante*, which was published in 1969.

Frantz, Ferdinand (1906–59)
German bass-baritone, particularly associated with Wagnerian roles, especially Wotan and Hans Sachs. Apart from Hans Hotter, he was the finest Wagnerian Heldenbariton (*see* BARITONE) of the immediate post-war period. His wife **Helena Braun** (1903–90) was a successful Wagnerian soprano.

Franz
Tenor role in Offenbach's *Les Contes d'Hoffmann.* He is Crespel's deaf servant.

Fra poco a me
Tenor aria for Edgardo in Act III of Donizetti's *Lucia di Lammermoor*, in which he laments the sorrows which fate has brought him. Its CABALETTA 'Tu che a Dio' is the final scene of the opera.

Fraschini, Gaetano (1816–87)
Italian tenor. One of the leading lyric tenors of the mid-19th century, he created Gerardo in Donizetti's *Caterina Cornaro*, six

roles for Pacini including Faone in *Saffo* and, for Verdi, Foresto in *Attila*, Zamoro in *Alzira*, Corrado in *Il Corsaro*, Arrigo in *La Battaglia di Legnano*, the title-role in *Stiffelio* and Gustavus in *Un Ballo in Maschera*. He was known as the '*tenore della maledizione*' (the cursing tenor) from the force with which he delivered Edgardo's curse in *Lucia di Lammermoor*. The Teatro Fraschini in Pavia is named after him.

Frasquita
Operetta in three acts by Lehár. 1st perf Vienna, 12 May 1922; libr by Heinrich Reichert and Alfred Maria Willner, after Pierre Louÿ's *La Femme et le Pantin*. Principal roles: Frasquita (sop), Armand (ten), Aimée (sop), Aristide (bar), Hippolyte (ten). Set in Barcelona, it has never been one of Lehár's most popular works but it is still occasionally performed in German-speaking countries. [R Exc]

Frasquita
Soprano role in: **1** Bizet's *Carmen*. She is a gypsy friend of Carmen's. **2** Wolf's *Der Corregidor*. She is the miller's wife. **3** Lehár's *Frasquita*. She is a gypsy dancer.

Frate 'Nnamorato, Lo (*The Lovestricken Brother*)
Comic opera in three acts by Pergolesi. 1st perf Naples, 27 Sept 1732; libr by Gennarantonio Federico. Principal roles: Ascanio (sop), Nena (sop), Nina (mezzo), Marcaniello (bar), Don Pietro (b-bar), Carlo (ten), Vannella (mezzo), Cardella (mezzo), Luggrezia (sop). Pergolesi's only full-length comedy, it still receives an occasional performance.
Plot: 18th-century Capodimonte (Italy). The young Ascanio is loved by the twin sisters Nina and Nena and also by Luggrezia, sister of Don Pietro and daughter of Marcaniello. After much amorous intrigue and confusion, Ascanio is discovered to be the twins' brother and Luggrezia is able to marry him. [R]

Frau ohne Schatten, Die (*The Woman Without a Shadow*)
Opera in three acts by Strauss (Op 65). 1st perf Vienna, 10 Oct 1919; libr by Hugo von Hofmannsthal, after his own story. Principal roles: Empress (sop), Dyer's Wife (sop), Emperor (ten), Barak (bar), Nurse (mezzo), Spirit Messenger (b-bar), Barak's brothers (ten, bar and bass). The most ambitious (and, some would say, the most pretentious) work of the Strauss/ Hofmannsthal partnership, it is an exotically scored and vocally highly demanding symbolic fairy tale. Despite Strauss's description of it as his *Die Zauberflöte*, it is heavily Wagnerian.
Plot: The Emperor is married to a supernatural being, whose father has stipulated that if the marriage remains childless (a condition symbolized by the Empress's inability to cast a shadow), she must return whence she came whilst her husband will be turned to stone. With her Nurse, the Empress goes in search of a shadow and comes to the hut of the humble dyer Barak. Barak's complaining wife has no children, but she does have a shadow. She agrees to sell her prospects of motherhood for the riches which the Nurse offers her. Seeing Barak's anguish when his wife tells him of his plan, the Empress refuses to take the shadow. Later, she sees Barak and his wife undergoing supernatural punishment and then witnesses the Emperor being nearly turned to stone. However, she still refuses to accept a shadow at someone else's expense. In this moment of supreme unselfishness, the Empress is granted a shadow, thus releasing everyone from their sufferings. [R]

Frazzi, Vito (1888–1975)
Italian composer. His operas, most of them on an ambitious scale, include *Rè Lear* (Florence, 29 Apr 1939; libr G. Papini, after Shakespeare's *King Lear*), *L'Ottava Moglie di Barbablù* (Florence, 1940; libr D. Cincelli) and *Don Chisciotte* (Florence, 27 Apr 1952; libr composer, after Miguel Cervantes's *Don Quixote*). He was also a noted editor of early Italian operas.

Freddo ed immobile
The ensemble which ends Act I of Rossini's *Il Barbiere di Siviglia*, in which all say that they are frozen stiff by surprise at the turn of events.

Frederick the Great (Friedrich II, King of Prussia) (1712–86)
German statesman, soldier, writer, flautist

and composer. Much the most accomplished of the various royal musical dilettantes, he was one of the greatest flautists of his age, and wrote much music for flute and orchestra. He also composed four arias for inclusion in Graun's *Demofoonte* (1746) and contributed the overture and two arias to *Il Rè Pastore* (Lietzenburg, Aug 1747; libr Pietro Metastasio), written jointly with Graun, Quantz and Christoph Nichelmann. He also wrote the libretti for Graun's *Montezuma, Silla, I Fratelli Nemici* and *Merope*. He appears as a character in d'Albert's *Flauto Solo*.

Freeman, David (b 1952)
Australian producer. He founded Opera Factory in Sydney in 1973, in Zürich in 1976 and in London in 1981. His productions, often highly controversial but always thought-provoking, lay great stress on the dramatic side. He has also been associated with the English National Opera and directed a notable *The Fiery Angel* for the Kirov Opera. He also wrote the libretto for Osborne's *Hell's Angels*. His wife **Marie Angel** (*b* 1953) is a soprano who created, for Birtwistle, Hannah in *Yan Tan Tethera*, the Oracle of the Dead in *The Mask of Orpheus* and Morgan le Fay in *Gawain*.

Freia
Soprano role in Wagner's *Das Rheingold*. She is the goddess of youth.

Freiburg Opera
Opera in this German town in Baden-Württemberg is given at the Grosses Haus, which opened in 1910. Destroyed by bombs in 1944, it reopened (cap 1,133) in 1949. Musical directors have included Franz Konwinschny, Leopold Hager, Marek Janowski, Ádám Fischer, Donald Runnicles and Johannes Fritzsche.

Freischütz, Der (*The Free-Shooter*)
Opera in three acts by Weber (J 277). 1st perf Berlin, 18 June 1821; libr by Johann Friedrich Kind, after Johann Apel and Friedrich Laun's *Gespentsterbuch*. Principal roles: Agathe (sop), Max (ten), Ännchen (sop), Caspar (bass), Ottakar (bar), Cuno (bass), Hermit (bass), Kilian (bar), Samiel (speaker). Weber's most successful and enduring opera, it tells the legend of the free-firing bullets: six will unerringly reach their target, but the seventh belongs to the Devil. The premiere was one of the most sensationally successful in operatic history, and the piece has had an enormous influence on the subsequent development of opera. The famous Wolf's Glen scene has probably never been surpassed as a musical depiction of the macabre.
Plot: 17th-century Bohemia. The head forester Cuno intends to hold a shooting contest to decide the hand of his daughter Agathe. Max, who loves her, is off-form and in desperation accepts the offer of Caspar (who has sold his soul to the Devil) to obtain the free-firing bullets for him. In spite of warnings by Agathe and her cousin Ännchen, Max goes to the haunted Wolf's Glen, where Caspar invokes Samiel and casts the bullets. At the contest, held before Prince Ottakar, five bullets have been used and Caspar secretly fires the sixth; the seventh is thus at Samiel's disposal. Max fires and both Agathe and Caspar fall. A Hermit restores Agathe to life, whilst Samiel claims Caspar. Max is set to undergo a year's probation to prove himself worthy of Agathe. [R]

Fremstad, Olive (b Olivia Rundquist) (1871–1951)
Swedish-born American soprano. Beginning as a mezzo, she turned to soprano roles in 1903 and became one of the greatest Wagnerian sopranos of the early 20th century. She had a rich and sumptuous voice and a powerful dramatic sense. She was the inspiration for the principal character in Willa Cather's novel *The Song of the Lark*.

French opera composers
see ADAM; AUBER; AUDRAN; AURIC; BARRAUD; BÉCAUD; BERLIOZ; BIZET; BLAVET; BOÏELDIEU; BONDEVILLE; BRUNEAU; CAMBERT; CAMPRA; CANTELOUBE; CHABRIER; CHARPENTIER, G.; CHARPENTIER, M.-A.; CHAUSSON; CHAYNES; CHRISTINÉ; DALAYRAC; DAUVERGNE; DAVID; DEBUSSY; DELIBES; DESTOUCHES; DUKAS; FAURÉ; FÉVRIER; FRANÇAIX; GANNÉ; GAVEAUX; GODARD; GOUNOD; GUIRAUD; HALÉVY; HÉROLD; HERVÉ; IBERT; D'INDY; JOLIVET; KREUTZER, R.; LALO; LANDOWSKI; LAPPARA; LECLAIR; LECOCQ; LEROUX; LESUEUR; LESUR; LULLY; MAGNARD; MAILLART; MARAIS;

· French royalty in opera ·

French kings and queens who appear as operatic characters include:

- Charles Martel in Offenbach's *Geneviève de Brabant.*
- Charlemagne in Schubert's *Fierrabras.*
- Louis V in Donizetti's *Ugo Conte di Parigi.*
- Louis VI in Weber's *Euryanthe.*
- Philip II in Spontini's *Agnes von Hohenstaufen* and Donizetti's *Gabriella di Vergy.*
- Louis IX in Milhaud's *Saint Louis.*
- Charles VI in Halévy's *Charles VI.*
- Charles VII in Verdi's *Giovanna d'Arco* and Tchaikovsky's *The Maid of Orleans.*
- Louis XII in Messager's *La Basoche.*
- Henri III in Chabrier's *Le Roi Malgré Lui.*
- Henri IV in Méhul's *La Chasse du Jeune Henri*, Pucitta's *La Caccia di Enrico IV* and Hiller's *Die Jagd.*
- Louis XVI and Marie-Antoinette in Corigliano's *The Ghosts of Versailles.*
- Napoleon I in Giordano's *Madame Sans-Gêne*, Blake's *Toussaint*, Prokofiev's *War and Peace* and Kodály's *Háry János.*
- Josephine in Kálmán's *Kaiserin Josephine.*

MASSÉ; MASSENET; MÉHUL; MESSAGER; MESSIAEN; MEYERBEER; MILHAUD; MONDONVILLE; MONPOU; MONSIGNY; MONTÉCLAIR; MOURET; NOUGUÈS; OFFENBACH; PHILIDOR; PIERNÉ; PLANQUETTE; POULENC; PRODROMIDÈS; RABAUD; RAMEAU; RAVEL; REBEL; REYER; ROUSSEL; SAINT-SAËNS; SATIE; SAUGET; TERRASSE; THOMAS; TOMASI; VARNEY; VIARDOT-GARCÍA; WIDOR

Freni, Mirella (b Fregni) (b 1935)
Italian soprano, particularly associated with the Italian and French repertories. Combining an outstanding voice used with fine musicianship with a charming stage presence (enhanced by her personal beauty), she began as a soubrette, but subsequently turned successfully to more dramatic roles. Married to the bass NICOLAI GHIAUROV.

Freunde von Salamanka, Die (*The Friends of Salamanca*)
Opera in two acts by Schubert (D 326). 1st perf Vienna, 19 Dec 1875 (composed 1815); libr by Johann Mayrhofer. Principal roles: Olivia (sop), Alonso (ten), Fidelio (bar), Mayor (bass). Like all of Schubert's early SINGSPIELS, it contains some charming music but is almost never performed.
Plot: 18th-century Spain. Countess Olivia is wooed by Alonso, one of three close friends, and by Count Tormes, who – having never met her – is mainly interested in her money. To impress her, Alonso and his friends carry out a mock abduction and rescue Olivia in the forest. Alonso confesses the deception and is forgiven by Olivia, who falls in love with him. The attempts of the Count to win Olivia are thwarted by a legal deception, and the lovers are united. [R]

Frezzolini, Erminia (1818–84)
Italian soprano. One of the leading lyric sopranos of mid-19th century, she created Giselda in *I Lombardi*, the title-role in *Giovanna d'Arco* and Camilla in Mercadante's *Orazi e Curiazi*. Her husband **Antonio Poggi** (1806–75) was a successful tenor who treated Carlo in *Giovanna d'Arco*. Her father **Giuseppe** (1789–1861) was a leading BUFFO, who created Dr Dulcamara in *L'Elisir d'Amore* and roles in Pacini's *Il Talismano* and Donizetti's *Olivio e Pasquale* and *Alina Regina di Golconda.*

Frick, Gottlob (1906–94)
German bass, particularly associated with Wagnerian roles, especially Hagen, and with Rocco and Osmin. One of the finest

Wagnerian basses of the post-war era, with a black and powerful voice, he enjoyed a remarkably long career, singing into his 70s. He created Caliban in Sutermeister's *Die Zauberinsel*, the Carpenter in Haas's *Die Hochzeit des Jobs* and a role in Egk's *Irische Legende*.

Fricka
Mezzo role in Wagner's *Das Rheingold* and *Die Walküre*. Wotan's consort, she is the goddess of wedlock.

Fricsay, Ferenc (1914–63)
Hungarian conductor, particularly associated with Mozart operas. One of the finest opera conductors of the immediate post-war period, he was musical director of the Budapest State Opera (1939–45), the Berlin State Opera (1951–2) and the Bavarian State Opera (1956–8). He conducted the first performances of Martin's *Le Vin Herbé*, Orff's *Antigonae* and Einem's *Dantons Tod*.

Friedenstag (*Peace Day*)
Opera in one act by Strauss (Op 81). 1st perf Munich, 24 July 1938; libr by Josef Gregor, after Pedro Calderón de la Barca's *La Rendención de Breda*. Principal roles: Maria (sop), Commandant (bar), Bürgermeister (ten), Holsteiner (ten), Rifleman (ten). An anti-militarist tract and a plea for peace, it is one of Strauss's least successful operas and is only rarely performed.
Plot: A Catholic German town, 24 Oct 1648. On the last day of the Thirty Years' War, the Catholic Commandant of the town plans to blow up the citadel rather than surrender to the besieging Lutheran commander. However, his wife Maria persuades him to accept the Peace of Westphalia. [R]

Friederike
Operetta in three acts by Lehár. 1st perf Berlin, 4 Oct 1928; libr by Ludwig Herzer and Fritz Löhner. Principal roles: Friederike (sop), Goethe (ten), Salomea (sop), Lenz (ten). Dealing with an episode from the life of Goethe concerning Friederike Brion, it was successful at its appearance and is still quite often performed in German-speaking countries.
Plot: Sesenheim and Strasbourg, 1771. Freiderike and her sister Salomea await the arrival of Goethe and his fellow students. Friederike loves Goethe but has never been kissed by him, because a girl who had once kissed him placed a curse on anyone else who should do so. Despite the curse, Goethe does finally kiss her. Goethe is offered a post at Weimar open only to bachelors. Friederike is persuaded by the poet's friend Lenz to place no obstructions in the way of his career. She therefore flirts with other students. Goethe, who had been about to refuse the post, is deeply hurt and leaves for Weimar without a word. [R]

Friedrich, Götz (b 1930)
German producer and administrator. A brilliant but controversial producer of left-wing political views, he was closely associated with the Komische Oper, Berlin and with Covent Garden, where he was director of productions (1976–81) and produced two separate *Ring* cycles. Administrator of the Deutsche Oper, Berlin (1981–). He wrote a biography of his teacher Walter Felsenstein and was co-author of the libretto of Matthus's *Der Letzte Schuss*. His wife **Karan Armstrong** (*b* 1941) is a successful dramatic soprano, who created the title-role in Sinopoli's *Lou Salomé* and a role in Berio's *Un Rè in Ascolto*.

Friml, Rudolf (1879–1972)
Czech-born American composer. A highly successful operetta composer, the most enduring of his 24 stage works are *The Firefly* (New York, 2 Dec 1912; libr Otto Harbach), *High Jinks* (New York, 10 Dec 1913), *Rose Marie* (New York, 2 Sept 1924; libr Harbach and Oscar Hammerstein II) and *The Vagabond King* (New York, 21 Sept 1925; libr W.H. Post and Brian Hooker, after Justin Huntly McCarthy's *If I Were King*).

Frist ist um, Die
Bass-baritone monologue for the Dutchman in Act I of Wagner's *Der Fliegende Holländer*, in which he tell how he was doomed to sail the seas for ever.

Fritz
1 Tenor role in Offenbach's *La Grande-Duchesse de Gérolstein*. He is a soldier in love with Wanda. **2** Tenor role in Mascagni's *L'Amico Fritz*. He is a wealthy

landowner. **3** Tenor role in Schreker's *Der Ferne Klang*. He is a composer. **4** Baritone role in Korngold's *Die Tote Stadt*.

Froh
Tenor role in Wagner's *Das Rheingold*. He is the god of spring.

From the House of the Dead (*Z Mrtvého Domu*)
Opera in three acts by Janáček. 1st perf Brno, 12 April 1930; libr by the composer, after Fyodor Dostoyevsky's *Memoirs from the House of the Dead*. Principal roles: Šiškov (bar), Skuratov (ten), Luka Kuzmič (ten), Gorjančikov (bar), Aljeja (sop), Šapkin (ten), Čekunov (bar), Commandant (b-bar), Čerevin (ten). Janáček's last and most overwhelmingly powerful opera, it is a harrowing but ultimately hopeful work, which he had not entirely completed at his death. It was prepared for performance by Břetislav Bakala and Osvald Chlubna. Initially slow to make its way, it has been widely performed in the last quarter century.
Plot: A Siberian prison camp, *c* 1860. The arrival and release of the political prisoner Alexander Petrovich Gorianchikov frame scenes from prison life where the inmates relate their past histories, go about their daily prison life and enact two playlets. [R]

Frosch
Speaking role in J. Strauss's *Die Fledermaus*. He is the tipsy jailer who presides over the proceedings in Act III. The role is often taken by a star actor: recent British Froschs have included Frankie Howerd, Bernard Breslaw, Clive Dunn and Griff Rhys-Jones.

Frühbeck de Burgos, Rafael (b 1933)
Spanish conductor, particularly associated with the German and Spanish repertories. Best known as a choral and symphonic conductor, his operatic appearances have been intermittent, but have included some notable ZARZUELA performances. Musical director of the Deutsche Oper, Berlin (1993–).

Frumerie, Gunnar de (1908–87)
Swedish composer and pianist. He wrote one opera, the successful *Singoalla* (Stockholm, 16 Mar 1940; libr Ella Byström-Baeckström, after Victor Rydberg) [R].

Fugère, Lucien (1848–1935)
French baritone, particularly associated with the French repertory and with Mozart roles. Based largely at the Opéra-Comique in Paris, he enjoyed an exceptionally long career, singing into his early 80s. An outstanding singing-actor, he created over 30 roles, including the Father in *Louise*, Henri de Valois in Chabrier's *Le Roi Malgré Lui*, for Massenet Pandolfe in *Cendrillon*, the Devil in *Grisélidis* and des Grieux in *Le Portrait de Manon* and, for Messager, Maître André in *Fortunio* and the Duc de Longueville in *La Basoche*. His brother **Paul** (1851–*c* 1910) was also a baritone. A leading exponent of French operetta, he created Paillasse in Ganné's *Les Saltimbanques*, a role in Planquette's *Mam'zelle Quat'sous* and Maxim in Audran's *La Poupée*.

Fugue
A contrapuntal piece of music for a given number of voices or instruments, in which each participant enters successively in imitation of the others. The most famous operatic example is the great comic fugue 'Tutto nel mondo è burla' which ends Verdi's *Falstaff*.

Full score (or orchestral score)
The complete printed music of an opera, showing all the vocal and orchestral parts.

Fundación para Arte Lirica
Peru's opera company, it was founded in 1981 by Luigi Alva, who is its artistic director. It gives a short annual season at the Teatro Municipal in Lima.

Fuor del mar
Tenor aria for Idomeneo in Act II of Mozart's *Idomeneo*, in which he says that the fury of the sea matches the storm of anger and doubt raging inside himself. Probably the most fearsomely demanding Aria di Bravura in any major opera, Mozart provided an alternative, somewhat less murderous version.

Furiant
A fast Czech dance with rapidly changing rhythms. There is a famous operatic example in Smetana's *The Bartered Bride*.

Furtiva lagrima, Una
Tenor aria for Nemorino in Act II of Donizetti's *L'Elisir d'Amore*, in which he realizes that the tear in Adina's eye betrays her love for him. One of the best-loved of all tenor arias.

Furtwängler, Wilhelm (1886–1954)
German conductor, particularly associated with Wagner operas and with *Fidelio*. One of the greatest 20th-century interpreters of the German repertory, he was musical director of the Lübeck Opera (1911–15), the Mannheim Opera (1915–20) and the Berlin State Opera. His equivocal relationship with the Nazis caused him difficulties after the war, and he was not allowed to conduct in the United States.

Fux, Johann Joseph (1660–1741)
Austrian composer. Best known as a composer of church music and as the author of a famous treaty on counterpoint, he also wrote 19 operas. The most successful include *Angelica Vincatrice di Alcina* (Vienna, 14 Sept 1716; libr Pietro Pariati, after Lodovico Ariosto's *Orlando Furioso*), *Elisa* (Laxenburg, 28 Aug 1719; libr Pariati) and *Costanza e Fortezza* (Prague, 28 Apr 1723; libr Pariati), his finest opera.

Fyodor
Mezzo trouser role in Moussorgsky's *Boris Godunov*. He is the Tsarevich. The role is occasionally sung by a treble.

G

Gabriele
1 Tenor role in Verdi's *Simon Boccanegra*. The patrician Gabriele Adorno, he is in love with Amelia. **2** Soprano role in Offenbach's *La Vie Parisienne*. She is a glove-maker. **3** Soprano role in J. Strauss's *Wiener Blut*. She is Count Zedlau's wife.

Gade, Niels (1817–90)
Danish composer. His stage works include the SINGSPIEL *Mariotta* (Copenhagen, 17 Jan 1850; libr Carl Borgaard, after Eugène Scribe) and the opera-ballet *Fairy Spell* (1854) [R].

Gagliano, Marco da (1582–1643)
Italian composer. One of the earliest opera composers, he was – like Gluck 150 years later – a reformer anxious to banish the excesses of singers and to achieve dramatic naturalness. These aims he expressed in the preface to his LA DAFNE. He wrote two other operas, both in collaboration with Peri: *Lo Sposalizio di Medoro e Angelica* (Florence, 25 Sept 1619; libr Andrea Salvadori, after Lodovico Ariosto's *Orlando Furioso*), which is lost, and *La Flora* (Florence, 14 Oct 1628; libr Salvadori).

Gaito, Constantino (1878–1945)
Argentinian composer. Perhaps the most important Argentinian nationalist composer, his 11 operas include *Shafras* (Buenos Aires, 29 Oct 1907; libr F. Scubla), *Caio Petronio* (Buenos Aires, 2 Sept 1919; libr H. Romanelli), *Fior de Neve* (Buenos Aires, 3 Aug 1922; libr G. Colelli), *Ollantay* (Buenos Aires, 23 July 1926; libr V. Mercante, after a Quechua legend), *Lázaro* (Buenos Aires, 19 Nov 1929; libr Mercante), which marked the first appearance in opera of the tango, and *La Sangre de las Guitarras* (Buenos Aires, 17 Aug 1932; libr V.G. Retta and C.M. Viale, after H. Blomberg), his most successful work which incorporates regional *gaucho* dances.

Galeffi, Carlo (1882–1961)
Italian baritone, particularly associated with the Italian repertory, especially Verdi. One of the finest Italian baritones of the inter-war period, he created Manfredo in Montemezzi's *L'Amore dei Tre Re*, Fanuèl in Boito's *Nerone* and, for Mascagni, Raimondo in *Isabeau*, Nicolò d'Este in *Parisina* and a role in *Amica*.

Galitsky, Prince
Bass role in Borodin's *Prince Igor*. He is Igor's brother-in-law.

Gallet, Louis (1835–95)
French librettist. One of the most prolific French librettists of the second half of the 19th century, he provided texts for Audran (*Photis*), Bizet (*Djamileh* and the unfinished *La Coupe du Roi de Thulé* and *Don Rodrigue*), Bruneau (*L'Attaque du Moulin* and *Le Rêve*), Godard (*Les Guelfes*), Gounod (*Cinq-Mars* and the unfinished *Maître Pierre*), Guiraud (*Frédégonde* and *Le Kobold*), Lara (*Moïna*), Massenet (*Le Roi de Lahore*, *Le Cid*, *Marie-Magdeleine* and *Thaïs*) and Saint-Saëns (*La Princesse Jaune*, *Étienne Marcel*, *Proserpine* and *Déjanire*) amongst others. His autobiography, *Notes d'un Librettiste*, was published in 1891.

Galli, Filippo (1783–1853)
Italian tenor and later bass. After ten years as a successful tenor, an illness changed his voice and he became one of the greatest basses of the early 19th century and was said to have been a fine singing-actor. He created Henry VIII in *Anna Bolena*, Dandini in Pavesi's *Agatina*, Zopiro in Winter's *Maometto* and, for Rossini, Mustafà in *L'Italiana in Algieri*, Fernando in *La Gazza Ladra*, the title-role in *Maometto Secondo*, Macrobio in *La Pietra del Paragone*, Assur in *Semiramide*, Selim in *Il Turco in Italia*, the Duke of Ordow in *Torvaldo e Dorliska* and Tarabotto in *L'Inganno Felice*. His brother **Vincenzo** (1798–1858) was a successful BUFFO.

Galli-Curci, Amelita (1882–1963)
Italian soprano, particularly associated with lighter Italian roles. The leading COLORATURA soprano of the early 20th century, she possessed a voice of extraordinary agility, but tended always to sing slightly sharp.

Galli-Marié, Celestine (b Marié de l'Isle) (1840–1905)
French mezzo, particularly associated with the French repertory. An outstanding singing-actress, with excellent diction and a fine voice, she created the title-roles in *Carmen* and Thomas's *Mignon*, Man Friday in Offenbach's *Robinson Crusoé* and Lazarillo in Massenet's *Don César de Bazan*, as well as roles in operas by Guiraud, Maillart and Massé. Of her Carmen, Tchaikovsky said that she 'managed to combine with the display of unbridled passion an element of mystical fatalism'. Her father **Félix Mécène Marié de l'Isle** (1811–82) was a successful tenor, who created Tonie in *La Fille du Régiment*.

Galop
A fast ballroom dance in 2/4 time. Originally deriving from Germany, where it was called *Hopser* ('hopper'), it first appeared under its present name in Paris in 1829. There is a fine operatic example in Balfe's *The Bohemian Girl*.

Galuppi, Baldassarre (1706–85)
Italian composer. He wrote 91 operas, enjoying particular success in comedy, especially with the 13 works written in collaboration with Carlo Goldoni. His comedies include *L'Arcadia in Brenta* (Venice, 14 May 1749; libr Goldoni), *Il Mondo della Luna* (Venice, 29 Jan 1750; libr Goldoni), *Il Mondo alla Roversa* (Venice, 14 Nov 1750; libr Goldoni), *Le Virtuose Ridicole* (Venice, 1752; libr Goldoni, after Molière's *Les Précieuses Ridicules*) and IL FILOSOFO DI CAMPAGNA, his only work which is still remembered. He occupies an important place in operatic history as a pioneer of the ensemble-type finale.

Gambler, The (*Igrok*)
Opera in four acts by Prokofiev (Op 24). 1st perf Brussels, 29 April 1929 (composed 1917); libr by the composer, after Fyodor Dostoyevsky's novella. Principal roles: Alexei (ten), Pauline (sop), General (bass), Grandmother (mezzo), Marquis (ten), Blanche (mezzo), Mr Astley (bar). Written in Prokofiev's most aggressively expressionist style, it is a powerful depiction of greed and obsession. Initially slow to make its way, it is nowadays quite often performed.
Plot: A German spa town, 1860s. The General is in love with the penniless coquette Blanche, but has gambled away his money and is in debt to the Marquis. He anxiously awaits the death of his wealthy old aunt whose fortune he is to inherit, but she arrives at the spa bursting with health and loses every penny at the gaming tables. Meanwhile, Alexei – tutor to the General's children – loves Pauline, his employer's stepdaughter. To prevent Pauline from having to marry the Marquis to salve the General's debts, Alexei – who has already lost money lent by Pauline at gambling – tries his luck again. This time he wins a fortune, but when he gives the money to Pauline she throws it back in his face. [R]

Gamblers, The (*Igroki*)
Unfinished opera in three acts by Shostakovich. 1st perf (in concert) Leningrad, 18 Sept 1978 (composed 1942); 1st stage perf Moscow, 24 Jan 1990; completion by Krzysztof Meyer 1st perf Wuppertal, 12 June 1983; a word-for-word setting of Nikolai's Gogol's play. Principal roles: Ikharyov (ten), Gavryushka (bass), Alexei (bass), Krugel (ten), Shvokhnev (bass), Uteshitelny (bass). Written in a similar style to *The Nose*, Shostakovich abandoned the work after completing some 50 minutes of music, roughly one-third of the opera. [R]

Ganné, Louis (1862–1923)
French composer. He wrote a number of operettas, of which the most important are LES SALTIMBANQUES, by far his most successful work, and *Hans le Joueur de Flûte* (Monte Carlo, 14 Apr 1906; libr Maurice Vaucaire and Georges Mitchell) [R Exc]. He also completed Planquette's unfinished *Le Paradis de Mahomet*.

García, Manuel (I) (1775–1832)
Spanish tenor and composer. One of the

leading lyric tenors of the early 19th century, he created Count Almavia in *Il Barbiere di Siviglia*, the Duke of Norfolk in *Elisabetta Regina d'Inghilterra*, Achille in Manfroce's *Ecuba* and, for Mayr, Rolla in *Cora* and Egeo in *Medea in Corinto*. He also composed 43 light operas in Italian, Spanish and French which were admired by Rossini but which are all now forgotten. In 1825, he founded an opera company in New York, which toured the United States and Mexico, where he lost all his money to bandits. He was also a noted teacher, whose pupils included Adolphe Nourrit, Henriette Méric-Lalande and his own famous children. His second wife **María Joaquina Sithces** (1780–1854) was a successful mezzo, who created Ismene in *Medea in Corinto*. Their children included MARÍA MALIBRAN, MANUEL GARCÍA (II) and PAULINE VIARDOT-GARCÍA.

García, Manuel (II) (1805–1906)
Spanish baritone and teacher, son of MANUEL GARCÍA I and brother of PAULINE VIARDOT-GARCÍA and MARÍA MALIBRAN. His singing career lasted only five years, after which he retired because of vocal problems and devoted himself to teaching, becoming one of the greatest singing teachers in history. The first person to make a scientific study of vocal production, he invented the laryngoscope in 1855 and was a professor at the Royal Academy of Music in London (1848–95). His theoretical writings include *Mémoires sur la Voix Humaine* (1840), *Traîté Complet de l'Art du Chant* (1847) and *Hints on Singing* (1894); the second is often regarded as the finest treatise on singing ever written, and is still in widespread use. His most famous pupils included Jenny Lind, Erminia Frezzolini, Hans Hermann Nissen and Sir Charles Santley. His first wife **Eugénie Mayer** (1815–80) was a successful soprano; their son **Gustave** (1837–1925) was a baritone.

Gardelli, Lamberto (b 1915)
Italian conductor and composer, particularly associated with the Italian repertory, especially Verdi, all of whose early operas he recorded. Based for long periods at the Royal Opera, Stockholm, and the Budapest State Opera, he was one of the outstanding Verdi interpreters of the post-war era. He also composed four operas, including *Alba Novella* (1933; libr A. Chiodo) and *Il Sogno* (1942; libr Claudio Guastalla).

Garden, Mary (1874–1967)
British soprano, particularly associated with the French repertory. One of the finest lyric sopranos of the early 20th century, she had a lovely voice used with great intelligence and was an outstanding singing-actress, especially as Salome. She created Mélisande in *Pelléas et Mélisande*, Queen Orlanda in Leroux's *La Reine Fiammette* and the title-roles in Massenet's *Chérubin*, Herbert's *Natoma* and Saint-Saëns's *Hélène*. Later resident in the United States, she was director of the Chicago Opera (1919–20). Her autobiography, *The Mary Garden Story*, was published in 1951.

Gardiner, John Eliot (b 1943)
British conductor, particularly associated with Gluck, Händel, Purcell, Monteverdi and Mozart operas and with the French repertory. Founder in 1968 of the original instrument Monteverdi Orchestra (later English Baroque Soloists), he is one of the finest contemporary exponents of the baroque repertory. He conducted the first performance of Rameau's *Les Boréades*, which he prepared and edited. He was musical director of the Göttingener Händelfestspiele (1981–90) and the Opéra de Lyon (1983–88).

Gardner, John (b 1917)
British composer. He has written four operas: *The Moon and Sixpence* (London, 24 May 1957; libr Patrick Terry, after W. Somerset Maugham), *The Visitors* (Aldeburgh, 7 June 1972; libr John Ormerod Greenwood), the children's opera *Bel and the Dragon* (London, 15 Dec 1973; libr T. Kraemer) and *Tobermory* (London, 26 Oct 1977; libr G. Ewart, after Saki).

Gasdia, Cecilia (b 1960)
Italian soprano, particularly associated with Rossini, Bellini and Donizetti roles. Possessing a beautiful and agile voice used with a fine technique, she is one of the finest exponents of the BEL CANTO repertory to have come to the fore in recent years.

Gasparini, Francesco (1668–1727)
Italian composer. He wrote 61 operas, all of them now long forgotten, of which the most successful was *Ambleto* (Venice, Jan 1706; libr Apostolo Zeno and Pietro Pariati), which is not based on Shakespeare.

Gasparone
Operetta in three acts by Millöcker. 1st perf Vienna, 26 Jan 1884; libr by F. Zell (Camillo Walzel) and Richard Genée. Principal roles: Stranger (bar), Carlotta (sop), Sora (sop), Nasoni (bass), Benozzo (ten). Millöcker's last work to enjoy significant success, it is a tuneful piece which is still performed in German-speaking countries.
Plot: Sicily, 1820. The Stranger reads an announcement by the mayor Nasoni about the notorious bandit Gasparone. He is suspicious of the motives of Nasoni, who plans to marry his son to the Countess Carlotta, who the Stranger himself loves. The wedding is halted by the abduction of Nasoni's son, and a vast ransom demand signed by Gasparone is received. After much intrigue, it is revealed that the 'abduction' was staged by the Stranger, who is in fact the Governor, investigating Nasoni's activities incognito. He reveals that Gasparone has been safely in jail for months, and that Nasoni was using the fear of him to aid his illegal business ventures. Nasoni is discomfited and the Stranger is united with Carlotta. [R]

Gassmann, Florian (1729–74)
Bohemian composer. He wrote 25 operas, many of which enjoyed considerable success in their time but which are nowadays all virtually forgotten. He was especially successful with comedy, in which genre his most important operas are *L'Amore Artigano* (Vienna, 26 Apr 1767; libr Carlo Goldoni), *La Notte Critica* (Vienna, 5 Jan 1768; libr Goldoni) and *La Contessina* (Mährisch-Neustadt, 3 Sept 1770; libr Marco Coltellini, after Goldoni).

Gatti-Casazza, Giulio (1869–1940)
Italian administrator. He was administrator of La Scala, Milan (1898–1908) and of the Metropolitan Opera, New York (1908–35), and was responsible for a vast improvement in the standard and prestige of both houses. Married for a time to the soprano FRANCES ALDA. His autobiography, *Memories of Opera*, was published posthumously in 1941.

Gatty, Nicholas Comyn (1874–1946)
British composer. He wrote six operas in a direct and readily accessible style which enjoyed some success in their time but which are all now forgotten. They are *Greysteel* (Sheffield, 1 Mar 1906; libr Reginald Gatty, after the Icelandic saga *Gisli the Outlaw*), *Duke or Devil* (Manchester, 16 Dec 1909; libr Ivor Gatty), *Prince Ferelon* (London, 21 May 1921; libr composer), *The Tempest* (London, 17 Apr 1920; libr after Shakespeare), the unperformed *Macbeth* (1920; libr after Shakespeare) and *King Alfred and the Cakes* (London, Dec 1930; libr R. Gatty).

Gavazzeni, Gianandrea (b 1909)
Italian conductor, composer and musicologist. Particularly associated with the 19th-century and contemporary Italian repertory, he conducted the first performances of Pizzetti's *L'Assassinio nella Cattedrale* and *La Figlia di Iorio*. A rock-solid and sometimes inspiring Italian maestro of the old school, he was artistic director of La Scala, Milan (1965–8). He wrote books on Donizetti, Moussorgsky, Pizzetti and Wagner, and also composed one opera, *Paolo e Virginia* (Bergamo, 1935; libr after Bernadin de Saint-Pierre). His wife **Denia Mazzola** is a successful soprano.

Gaveaux, Pierre (1761–1825)
French composer. He wrote some 30 operas, all now long forgotten, of which the most important (for historical rather than musical reasons) is LÉONORE, the first setting of the *Fidelio* story.

Gavotte
An old dance in 4/4 time which begins on the third beat of the bar. There is a famous operatic example in Sullivan's *The Gondoliers*.

Gawain
Opera in two acts by Birtwistle. 1st perf London, 30 May 1991; libr by David Harsent, after the anonymous 14th-century

Sir Gawayne and the Grene Knyght. Principal roles: Gawain (bar), Morgan le Fay (sop), Green Knight/Bertilak (bass), Lady de Hautdesert (mezzo), King Arthur (ten), Guinevere (sop), Fool (bar), Bishop Baldwin (c-ten). Birtwistle's longest and most ambitious opera, it is a compelling work of considerable imaginative scope and of great orchestral power and complexity.
Plot: Legendary Britain. The Green Knight comes to the decaying court of King Arthur and challenges a knight to behead him. Gawain accepts the challenge and the Green Knight rides away carrying his severed head. During a masque, *The Turning of the Seasons*, Gawain undergoes purification for the trials ahead of him. Gawain travels to the castle of Bertilak de Hautdesert, whose wife – manipulated by the sorceress Morgan le Fay – attempts to seduce him. Gawain breaks faith with his host, revealed as the Green Knight himself, and escapes from the challenge he had accepted by means of a deceit. Although Gawain is given a hero's welcome on his return, Morgan le Fay knows that she has morally subverted Arthur's court.

Gay, John (1685–1732)
British poet, playwright and librettist. He wrote the texts for Pepusch's *The Beggar's Opera* and *Polly* and (in part) Händel's *Acis and Galatea.* He also built the first theatre at Covent Garden.

Gayarré, Julián (1844–90)
Spanish tenor, particularly associated with the Italian and French repertories. During his finest period, from 1876 to 1886, he was regarded by many as the greatest tenor of his age. He created Enzo in *La Gioconda* and Henri in Donizetti's *Le Duc d'Albe.*

Gayer, Catherine (b Ashkenasi) (b 1937)
American soprano, particularly associated with COLORATURA roles and with contemporary operas. A fine singing-actress with an agile and intelligently-used voice, she created the Companion in Nono's *Intolleranza*, Nausikaa in Dallapiccola's *Ulisse*, the title-role in Reimann's *Melusine*, Christina in Orr's *Hermiston*, the Woman in Tal's *Der Versuchung* and Lady Astor in Siebert's *Untergang der Titanic.*

Gayle
Soprano role in Tippett's *The Ice Break.* She is Yuri's girlfriend.

Gaztambide y Garbayo, Joaquín (1792–1870)
Spanish composer. He wrote 44 ZARZUELAS, of which the first, *La Mensajera* (Madrid, 24 Dec 1849; libr L. Olona), helped to revive the popularity of the genre after its long period of decline. Of his other works, the most successful was *La Catalina* (Madrid, 23 Oct 1854; libr Olana, after Eugène Scribe's libretto for Meyerbeer's *L'Étoile du Nord*).

Gazza Ladra, La (*The Thieving Magpie*)
Opera in two acts by Rossini. 1st perf Milan, 31 May 1817; libr by Giovanni Gherardini, after Jean-Marie-Théodore Bauduin d'Aubigny and Louis-Charles Caigniez's *La Pie Voleuse.* Principal roles: Ninetta (sop), Podestà (bass), Giannetto (ten), Fernando (bass), Pippo (mezzo), Fabrizio (bar), Lucia (mezzo), Isaac (ten). Beginning with one of the most famous of all operatic overtures, it is one of Rossini's finest works and is an outstanding example of OPERA SEMISERIA. It is still quite often performed, but not as frequently as its merits deserve.
Plot: Early-19th-century Italy. Fabrizio's daughter Ninetta is engaged to Giannetto, the son of the farmer Fernando, in whose house she is employed as a maid. She is suspected of having stolen and sold some of Fernando's silverware, and the Podestà presses charges against her, largely because she has rebuffed his advances. She is found guilty and condemned to death. However, when she is on her way to execution, the real thief is discovered – a magpie. [R]

Gazzaniga, Giuseppe (1743–1818)
Italian composer. He wrote some 50 operas, virtually all of them nowadays forgotten, achieving his best successes in comedy. His only opera still to be in any way remembered is DON GIOVANNI, which had a slight influence on Mozart's version which it preceded by nine months.

Gebet
The German term for a PREGHIERA.

Geburstag der Infantin, Der (*The Birthday of the Infanta*) or **Der Zwerg** (*The Dwarf*) Opera in one act by Zemlinsky (Op 17). 1st perf Cologne, 28 May 1922; libr by Georg Klaren, after Oscar Wilde's short story. Principal roles: Dwarf (ten), Infanta (sop), Ghita (sop), Estóban (bass). Zemlinsky's finest opera, whose principal role offers a great dramatic challenge, it suffered a long period of neglect but has recently been widely performed.
Plot: Spain. As a birthday present, the spoilt Infanta Donna Clara is given an ugly dwarf. The dwarf falls in love with her, even though she treats him like a toy. When, for the first time, the dwarf sees himself in a mirror, he dies of a broken heart. The Infanta is merely annoyed that her toy no longer works. [R]

Gedda, Nicolaï (b Ustinoff) (b 1925)
Swedish tenor, particularly associated with lyrical French, German, Italian and Russian roles and with Mozart and Viennese operetta. One of the greatest singers of the 20th century, and an outstanding linguist fluent in six languages, he possessed a voice of great beauty which he used with style, elegance, good taste and a superb technique. Although not large, his projection was so good that he was able to sing a number of heroic roles, such as Arnold in Rossini's *Guillaume Tell*. He created the Husband in Orff's *Trionfo d'Afrodite*, a role in Sutermeister's *Der Rote Stiefel* and Anatol in Barber's *Vanessa*. He enjoyed a long career, singing into his late 60s, and made more operatic recordings than any other singer in history.

Gedge, Mr
Baritone role in Britten's *Albert Herring*. He is the vicar.

Geduldige Socrates, Der (*Patient Socrates*)
Comic opera in three acts by Telemann. 1st perf Hamburg, 28 Jan 1721; libr by Johann Ulrich von König, after Nicolò Minato's *La Pazienza di Socrate*. Principal roles: Socrates (bar), Xantippe (sop), Amitta (sop), Aristophanes (ten), Melito (ten), Nicia (bass), Rodisette (sop), Edronica (sop). An entertaining piece about the domestic trials of the Greek philosopher Socrates (469–399 BC), it still receives an occasional performance. [R]

Gelsenkirchen Stadttheater
The original opera house in this German town in North Rhine Westphalia opened in 1935, but was destroyed by bombs in Jan 1945. The new house (cap 1,050) opened on 3 Dec 1959. In conjunction with the Bochum Opera, it forms the Musiktheater im Revier. Musical directors have included Ljubomir Romansky, Uwe Mund, Johannes Kalitzke and Neil Varon.

Gemma di Vergy
Opera in two acts by Donizetti. 1st perf Milan, 26 Dec 1834; libr by Giovanni Emanuele Bidera, after Alexandre Dumas's *Charles VII Chez ses Grands Vassaux*. Principal roles: Gemma (sop), Conte di Vergy (bar), Guido (bass), Tamas (ten), Ida (mezzo). An uneven work containing some fine moments, it suffered a long period of complete neglect but has recently received a number of performances.
Plot: Berry (France), 1428. The Count of Vergy plans to divorce his barren wife Gemma and has already chosen a successor. Gemma's Arab slave Tamas, who is in love with her, kills the Count's esquire, but is offered a pardon if he will confess to planning to kill the Count. Gemma intervenes on Tamas's behalf and a reconciliation with her husband seems possible until the new wife Ida appears. Gemma, with a knife at Ida's throat, forces the Count to confess his love for Ida, but she is disarmed by Tamas. At the wedding, Gemma begs Tamas to kill her, but instead he stabs the Count before killing himself. [R]

Gencer, Leyla (b 1924)
Turkish soprano, particularly associated with Donizetti and Verdi roles and with the revival of a number of long-forgotten Italian BEL CANTO operas. A highly dramatic singing-actress, she had a fine and agile if occasionally slightly wayward voice. She created Madame Lidoine in Poulenc's *Dialogues des Carmélites* and the First Woman of Canterbury in Pizzetti's *L'Assassinio nella Cattedrale*.

Gendarmes' Duet
Baritone/bass duet ('Protéger le repos des villes') in Act II of Offenbach's *Geneviève de Brabant*. One of the most famous of all comic duets.

Genée, Richard (1823–95)
German librettist and composer. One of the best librettists of the Viennese school of operetta, he often wrote in collaboration with F. Zell (Camillo Walzel). He provided texts for Millöcker (*Der Bettelstudent* and *Gasparone*), Offenbach (*Der Schwarze Korsar*), J. Strauss (*Die Fledermaus*, *Cagliostro in Wien*, *Eine Nacht in Venedig* and *Das Spitzentuch der Königin*), Suppé (*Fatinitza*, *Donna Juanita* and *Boccaccio*) and Ziehrer (*Ein Deutschmeister*). He also composed several operettas, including *Der Geiger aus Tirol* (*The Fiddler from Tyrol*, Danzig, Mar 1857; libr Rudolf Genée), *Der Seekadett* (*The Naval Cadet*, Vienna, 24 Oct 1876; libr F. Zell) and *Nanon* (Vienna, 10 Mar 1877; libr composer and Zell, after Émmanuel Guillaume Théaulon and F.V.A. d'Artois).

Generali, Pietro (b Mercandetti) (1773–1832)
Italian composer. He wrote some 50 operas, a number of which were successful in their day. He was soon eclipsed by Rossini, and nowadays none of his works are remembered. Perhaps his most successful opera was *Pamela Nubile* (Venice, 12 Apr 1804; libr Gaetano Rossi, after Samuel Richardson's *Pamela*).

Generalmusikdirektor
The title of the musical director of a German or Austrian opera house.

Generalprobe (German for 'principal rehearsal')
The dress rehearsal of an opera in a German or Austrian opera house. The final preceding rehearsal, and the last at which any adjustments may still be made, is called Hauptprobe.

Género chico (Spanish for 'little type')
A type of ZARZUELA, also known as zarzuelita, which is in one act and is always on a comic subject.

Geneva
see GRAND THÉÂTRE, GENEVA

Geneviève
Mezzo role in Debussy's *Pelléas et Mélisande*. She is Golaud's mother.

Gennaro
Tenor role in: **1** Donizetti's *Lucrezia Borgia*. Maffio Orsini's friend, he turns out to be Lucrezia's son. **2** Wolf-Ferrari's *I Gioielli della Madonna*. He is a blacksmith. **3** Prokofiev's *Maddalena*. An artist, he is Maddalena's husband.

Genoa
see TEATRO CARLO FELICE, GENOA

Genoveva
Opera in four acts by Schumann (Op 81). 1st perf Leipzig, 25 June 1850; libr by the composer and Robert Reinick, after Christian Friedrich Hebbel's play and Johann Ludwig Tieck's *Leben und Tod der Heiligen Genoveva*. Principal roles: Genoveva (sop), Golo (ten), Siegfried (bar), Drago (bass), Margareta (sop). Schumann's only completed opera, it contains some fine music but is dramatically very weak. It is only rarely performed, although the overture is well known.
Plot: Trier and Strasbourg, *c* 730. During the absence of her husband Siegfried, who has gone on the Crusades, Genoveva rebuffs the advances made to her by Golo. Embittered, Golo has her tried for betraying her husband with the chaplain Drago. In spite of the evil intrigues of the witch Margareta, the returning Siegfried saves his wife from the executioner. [R]

Gentele, Göran (1917–72)
Swedish producer and administrator. His many notable productions, mainly in Sweden, included the controversial *Un Ballo in Maschera*, in which Gustavus III was portrayed as a homosexual, as he was in history. He was director of the Royal Opera, Stockholm (1963–71) and was appointed general manager of the Metropolitan Opera, New York, but was killed in a car crash a few weeks before taking up the appointment.

Georgia
see TBILSI OPERA AND BALLET THEATRE

Georgian opera composers
see PALIASHVILI; TAKTAKISHVILI
Other national opera composers include Dmitry Arakishvili (1873–1953), Andrey Balanchivadze (*b* 1906), brother of the choreographer George Balanchine, Victor Dolidze (1890–1933), Grigory Kiladze (1902–62), Shalva Mshevelidze (1904–84) and Iona Tuskiya (1901–63).

Gérald
Tenor role in Delibes's *Lakmé*. He is a British army officer.

Gérard, Carlo
Baritone role in Giordano's *Andrea Chénier*. He is a servant in the Coigny household who becomes a revolutionary leader.

Gerechter Gott
Soprano aria for Adriano in Act III of Wagner's *Rienzi*, in which he prays for the strength to mediate between Rienzi and the Roman nobility.

Gergiev, Valery (b 1953)
Russian conductor, particularly associated with the Russian repertory. Perhaps the finest Russian conductor of the younger generation, his performances are noted for their scrupulous preparation and attention to detail and for their sometimes broad tempi. Artistic director of the Kirov Opera (1988–).

Gerhard, Roberto (1896–1970)
Spanish composer, resident in Britain from 1939. His only opera is the brilliant and unjustly neglected THE DUENNA.

Gerhilde
Soprano role in Wagner's *Die Walküre*. She is one of the Valkyries.

German, Sir Edward (b Jones) (1862–1936)
British composer. His first stage work, *The Two Poets* (London, July 1886; libr W.H. Scott), is insignificant, but the enormous success of MERRIE ENGLAND led to his being hailed as Sullivan's successor. However, although his operettas are tuneful and solidly written, they are not on the same level as Sullivan's and are nowadays hardly ever performed. His later works are *A Princess of Kensington* (London, 22 Jan 1903; libr Basil Hood), the highly successful TOM JONES, perhaps his finest work, and *Fallen Fairies* (London, 15 Dec 1909; libr W.S. Gilbert). He also completed Sullivan's unfinished THE EMERALD ISLE.

Germania (*Germany*)
Opera in prologue, two acts and epilogue by Franchetti. 1st perf Milan, 11 March 1902; libr by Luigi Illica. Principal roles: Ricke (sop), Loewe (ten), Worms (bar). One of the most successful and most grandiose of Franchetti's VERISMO operas, it is nowadays hardly ever performed.
Plot: Königsberg and Leipzig, 1806–13. Ricke, married to Loewe, has been seduced before her marriage by Loewe's friend Carlo Worms. The two men fight alongside the students opposed to the Napoleonic invasion of Germany. Both are eventually killed, and the dying Loewe begs Ricke to forgive Worms.

German opera composers
see AGRICOLA; D'ALBERT; BACH, J.C.; BEETHOVEN; BLACHER; BRUCH; CORNELIUS; DESSAU; EGK; EISLER; ERNST II OF SAXE-COBURG; FLOTOW; FORTNER; FREDERICK THE GREAT; GERSTER; GLUCK; GOLDSCHMIDT; GÖTZ; GRAUN; HAEFFNER; HÄNDEL; HARTMANN; HASSE; HENZE; HILLER; HINDEMITH; HOFFMANN; KEISER; KLEBE; KRAUS; KREUTZER, K.; KÜNNEKE; LACHNER; LOEWE; LORTZING; MARSCHNER; MATTHESON; MATTHUS; MENDELSSOHN; NAUMANN; NESSLER; NICOLAÏ; ORFF; PFITZNER; POISSL; REIMANN; REINECKE; RIHM; RIOTTE; SCHILLINGS; SCHREKER; SCHUMANN; SCHÜTZ; SPOHR; STOCKHAUSEN; STRAUSS, R.; SUDER; TELEMANN; WAGNER; WAGNER, S.; WAGNER-RÉGENY; WEBER; WEILL; WERZLAU; WINTER; WOLF; ZIMMERMANN; ZIMMERMANN, U.

Germany
see AACHEN OPERA; AUGSBURG STADTTHEATER; BAVARIAN STATE OPERA; BAYREUTH FESTIVAL; BERLIN STATE OPERA; BIELEFELD STADTTHEATER; BONN STADTTHEATER; BREMEN OPERA; BRUNSWICK STAATSTHEATER; COLOGNE OPERA; DARMSTADT OPERA; DESSAU OPERNHAUS; DEUTSCHE OPER, BERLIN; DEUTSCHE OPER AM RHEIN; DORTMUND STADTTHEATER; DRESDEN STATE OPERA; ESSEN OPERA;

FRANKFURT OPERA; FREIBURG OPERA; GELSENKIRCHEN STADTTHEATER; GÖTTINGENER HÄNDELFESTSPIELE; HAGEN OPERA; HANDEL FESTIVAL, HALLE; HAMBURG STATE OPERA; HANOVER OPERA; KAISERSLAUTERN OPERA; KARSLRUHE STAATSTHEATER; KASSEL STAATSTHEATER; KIEL STADTTHEATER; KOMISCHE OPER, BERLIN; LEIPZIG OPERA; LÜBECK OPERA; MAINZ OPERA; MANNHEIM OPERA; NÜRNBERG STADTTHEATER; SAARBRÜCKEN OPERA; STUTTGART OPERA; WEIMAR OPERA; WIESBADEN OPERA; WUPPERTAL OPERA

Germont
Roles in Verdi's *La Traviata*: Alfredo Germont (ten), Violetta's lover, and his father Giorgio (bar).

Geronimo
Bass-baritone role in Cimarosa's *Il Matrimonio Segreto*. He is Carolina's father.

Geronio, Don
Bass role in Rossini's *Il Turco in Italia*. He is Fiorilla's husband.

Gershwin, George (1898–1937)
American composer whose early death from a brain tumour cut short a brilliant career. His many stage works include 16 musical comedies, of which two may be considered operatic. *Blue Monday Blues* (New York, 28 Aug 1922; libr de Sylva), later called *135th Street*, was an unsuccessful piece employing jazz-style recitative as a link to popular songs. His operatic fame rests on his masterpiece, the all-black PORGY AND BESS.

Gerster, Ottmar (1897–1969)
German composer. The most successful of his six operas were *Enoch Arden* (Düsseldorf, 15 Nov 1936; libr K.M. von Livetzov, after Alfred Lord Tennyson) and *Die Hexe von Passau* (Düsseldorf, 11 Oct 1941; libr R. Billinger).

Gertrude
1 Soprano role in Humperdinck's *Hänsel und Gretel*. She is the children's mother. **2** Mezzo role in Gounod's *Roméo et Juliette*. She is Juliet's nurse. **3** Mezzo role in Thomas's and Searle's *Hamlet*. The Queen of Denmark, she is Hamlet's mother.

Gesamtkunstwerk (German for 'unified artwork')
A term much used by Wagner to describe a form of drama in which all aspects of the arts (music, poetry, drama, design etc) combine to form a single unified work of art.

Geschwitz, Countess
Mezzo role in Berg's *Lulu*. She is Lulu's lesbian lover.

Gesler
Bass role in Rossini's *Guillaume Tell*. He is the tyrannical Austrian governor of Switzerland.

Gespenstersonate, Die (*The Ghost Sonata*)
Opera in three scenes by Reimann. 1st perf Berlin, 25 Sept 1984; libr by the composer and Uwe Schendel, after August Strindberg's *Spöksonaten*. Principal roles: Hummel (bar), Arkenholz (ten), Mummy (mezzo), Girl (sop), Colonel (ten), Bengtsson (bass), Johansson (ten). One of the most successful modern chamber operas, written for an orchestra of 12 players, it has been widely performed.
Plot: The student Arkenholz is befriended by Hummel, an old man in a wheelchair. Through the window of a house they see a beautiful girl, Hummel's illegitimate daughter, whom Hummel says Arkenholz can meet. In the house, the mistress is the girl's mother, known as the Mummy, who sits in a cupboard and talks like a parrot. Hummel accuses those in the house of various crimes which he threatens to expose, but the Mummy threatens in turn to expose a murder he committed in the past. Hummel crawls into the Mummy's cupboard and hangs himself. Arkenholz declares his love for the girl, but she is tainted like everybody else in the house and dies.

Gezeichneten, Die (*The Signified*)
Opera in three acts by Schreker. 1st perf Frankfurt, 25 April 1918; libr by the composer. Principal roles: Duke Adorno (bass), Tamare (bar), Carlotta (mezzo), Nardi (bass), Alviano (ten). One of Schreker's most richly scored works, it met with considerable success at its appearance but is nowadays only infrequently performed.

Plot: 16th-century Genoa. The nobleman Alviano Salvago thinks that he can overcome his ugliness by letting young nobles use his island of Elysium as an erotic paradise. To conceal the murder of several young girls, he gives the island to the people. He is in love with Carlotta, daughter of the mayor Lodovico Nardi, but she is loved by the young Count Andrae Tamare. During the celebrations for the island's handover, Carlotta appears to have been raped in the same way as the previous girls. Alviano is accused of murdering her, but he leads the crowd to a cave, where the dying Carlotta declares that she has voluntarily given herself to Tamare in rejection of Alviano. [R]

Ghedini, Giorgio (1892–1965)
Italian composer. Several of his eight operas met with considerable success in Italy, but are virtually unknown elsewhere. They include *Maria d'Alessandria* (Bergamo, 9 Sept 1937; libr Cesare Meano), *Rè Hassan* (Venice, 26 Jan 1939; libr Tullio Pinelli), *La Pulce d'Oro* (Genoa, 15 Feb 1940; libr Pinelli), *Le Baccanti* (Milan, 22 Feb 1948; libr Pinelli, after Euripides's *The Bacchae*), *Billy Budd* (Venice, 8 Sept 1949; libr S. Quasimodo, after Herman Melville's *Billy Budd, Sailor*) and *Lord Inferno* (later called *L'Ipocrita Felice*, RAI, 22 Oct 1952; libr Franco Antonicelli, after Max Beerbohm's *The Happy Hypocrite*).

Ghent
see ROYAL OPERA, GHENT

Ghiaurov, Nicolai (b 1929)
Bulgarian bass, particularly associated with the Italian and Russian repertories, especially Boris and King Philip. One of the outstanding basses of the post-war era, he possessed a large, rich and beautiful voice, which he used with fine musicianship. He was an accomplished singing-actor with a commanding stage presence, equally at home in serious or comic roles. Married to the soprano MIRELLA FRENI.

Ghislanzoni, Antonio (1824–93)
Italian librettist and baritone. After a short singing career, he turned to writing, providing some 85 libretti. He wrote texts for Catalani (*Edmea*), Cagnoni (*Rè Lear*, *Papà Martin* and *Francesca da Rimini*), Gomes (*Fosca* and *Salvator Rosa*), Petrella (*I Promessi Sposi*), Ponchielli (*I Lituani*) and Verdi (*Aida* and the revised *La Forza del Destino*) amongst others. His autobiography, *Reminiscenze Artistichi*, was published in 1869.

Ghiuselev, Nicola (b 1936)
Bulgarian bass, particularly associated with the Russian and Italian repertories. An often underrated singer, he possesses a rich and powerful voice, used with considerable intelligence, and he has a good stage presence. Also a champion of Bulgarian composers, he created the title-role in Goleminov's *Zahari Zograf*, Padre Gavril in Iliev's *Master of Boyan* and Krumov in Pipkov's *Antigonae 43*.

Ghosts
see SUPERNATURAL IN OPERA

Ghost Sonata, The
see GESPENSTERSONATE, DIE

Giacomini, Giuseppe (b 1940)
Italian tenor, particularly associated with heavier Italian roles. He possesses a fine and incisive voice, tastefully used, and has a forthright stage presence. He created Nanni in Tutino's *La Lupa*.

Giacomo
1 Baritone role in Verdi's *Giovanna d'Arco*. He is Joan of Arc's father. **2** Tenor role in Rossini's *La Donna del Lago*. He is King James V of Scotland.

Giacosa, Giuseppe
see under ILLICA, LUIGI

Già d'insolito ardore
Bass aria for Mustafà in Act I of Rossini's *L'Italiana in Algieri*, in which he tells of his excited state at the thought of meeting an Italian girl.

Già i sacerdoti
Mezzo/tenor duet for Amneris and Radamès in Act IV of Verdi's *Aida*, in which she offers to save him from the judgement of the priests.

Già nella notte
Soprano/tenor duet for Desdemona and

Otello in Act I of Verdi's *Otello*. It is the love duet.

Giannetto
Tenor role in Rossini's *La Gazza Ladra*. Fernando's son, he is engaged to Ninetta.

Giannini, Vittorio (1903–66)
American composer. He wrote six operas: *Lucidia* (Munich, 20 Oct 1934; libr Karl Flaster), *The Scarlet Letter* (Hamburg, 2 June 1938; libr Flaster, after Nathaniel Hawthorne), *The Taming of the Shrew* (Cincinnati, 31 Jan 1953; libr composer and Dorothy Fee, after Shakespeare) [R], his most successful opera, *The Harvest* (Chicago, 25 Nov 1961; libr Flaster), *Rehearsal Call* (New York, 15 Feb 1962; libr F. Swann), and *The Servant of Two Masters* (New York, 9 Mar 1967; libr Bernard Stambler, after Carlo Goldoni). His father **Ferruccio** (1868–1948) was a successful tenor, and his sister **Dusolina** (1900–86) was a dramatic soprano, who created Hester in his *The Scarlet Letter*.

Gianni Schicchi
Comic opera in one act by Puccini. 1st perf New York, 14 Dec 1918; libr by Giovacchino Forzano, after Canto XXX of *L'Inferno* in Dante Alighieri's *La Divina Commedia*. Principal roles: Schicchi (bar), Lauretta (sop), Rinuccio (ten), Simone (bass), Zita (mezzo). The third panel of *Il Trittico*, it is Puccini's only comedy and is an entertaining piece of great technical brilliance.
Plot: Florence, 1299. The greedy relatives gathered at the deathbed of the deceased Buoso, led by Simone and Zita, are horrified to discover that Buoso has left his entire fortune to a monastery. They ask the wily Gianni Schicchi, whose daughter Lauretta loves Zita's nephew Rinuccio, to help them to make a new will. They give him detailed instructions as to how everything is to be bestowed. After warning them of the dire penalties for forging a will, Schicchi dresses up as Buoso and gets into his bed. When the notary arrives, Schicchi dictates a will which – apart from the house, which he leaves to the lovers – bequeaths everything to his 'good friend Gianni Schicchi'. [R]

Giasone (*Jason*)
Opera in prologue and three acts by Cavalli. 1st perf Venice, 6 Jan 1649; libr by Giacinto Andrea Cicognini, after Apollonius of Rhodes's *Argonautica*. Principal roles: Giasone (c-ten), Medea (mezzo), Isifile (sop), Egeo (ten), Oreste (bass). Telling of Jason's quest for the Golden Fleece and of his embroilment with the sorceress Medea, it was the most popular of Cavalli's operas in his own lifetime. After 300 years of total neglect, it has received several performances in the last decade. [R]

Gibson, Sir Alexander (1926–95)
British conductor with a wide-ranging repertory. He was musical director of Sadler's Wells Opera (1957–9) and Scottish Opera (1962–87), of which he was the founder. He conducted the first performances of Gardner's *The Moon and Sixpence*, John Purser's *The Undertaker*, Orr's *Hermiston* and *Full Circle* and Hamilton's *The Catiline Conspiracy*.

Gielen, Michael (b 1927)
German conductor, particularly associated with 20th-century operas, especially Schönberg. He was musical director of the Royal Opera, Stockholm (1960–5), the Netherlands Opera (1973–7) and the Frankfurt Opera (1977–87). He conducted the first performances of Zimmermann's *Die Soldaten*, Hauer's *Die Schwarze Spinne* and Reimann's *Ein Traumspiel*.

Gigli, Beniamino (1890–1957)
Italian tenor, particularly associated with the Italian repertory. One of the greatest tenors of the 20th century, despite his virtual inability to act and his occasional paucity of taste, he possessed a beautiful, honeyed voice used with passion and a superb technique. His *Memoirs* were published in 1957. His daughter **Rina** (*b* 1916) was a successful soprano.

Gil, Count
Baritone role in Wolf-Ferrari's *Il Segreto di Susanna*. He is Susanna's jealous and anti-smoking husband.

Gilbert, Sir William Schwenk (1836–1911)
British poet, playwright, librettist and producer. His collaboration with Sullivan

on the 14 Savoy Operas was one of the most remarkable artistic partnerships in history, producing *Thespis*, *Trial By Jury*, *The Sorcerer*, *H.M.S. Pinafore*, *The Pirates of Penzance*, *Patience*, *Iolanthe*, *Princess Ida*, *The Mikado*, *Ruddigore*, *The Yeomen of the Guard*, *The Gondoliers*, *Utopia Limited* and *The Grand Duke*. Whatever their settings, his texts for Sullivan are parodies of all the institutions and ideals which the British hold most sacred, and are marked by his especial brand of topsy-turvy humour, pithy dialogue and a brilliance of versification (especially in the patter songs) which has seldom, if ever, been equalled. He also wrote the libretti for Cellier's *The Mountebanks* and German's *Fallen Fairies*. A brilliant wit and a theatrical martinet, he also acted as producer for the Savoy Operas.

Gilbert and Sullivan
see CARTE, RICHARD D'OYLY; D'OYLY CARTE OPERA COMPANY; GILBERT, SIR WILLIAM SCHWENK; SAVOY OPERAS; SULLIVAN, SIR ARTHUR

Gilda
Soprano role in: **1** Verdi's *Rigoletto*. She is Rigoletto's daughter. **2** Donizetti's *L'Aio nell' Imbarazzo*. She is Enrico's wife.

Giménez y Bellido, Gerónimo (b Jiménez) (1854–1923)
Spanish composer and conductor. Musical director of the Teatro Apolo and then of the Teatro de la Zarzuela in Madrid, he wrote many ZARZUELAS, mainly in GÉNERO CHICO form, which are notable for their use of traditional gypsy music. His most successful works include *Tannhauser el Estanquero* (Madrid, 26 Apr 1890; libr E. Gonzalvo), *Trafalgar* (Barcelona, Jan 1891; libr J. de Burgos), *La Boda de Luis Alonso* (Madrid, 27 Jan 1897; libr Burgos), *La Tempranica* (Madrid, 19 Sept 1900; libr Julián Romea) [R], his most successful work which is about the famous popular dancer, *El Barbero de Sevilla* (Madrid, Feb 1901; libr Miguel de Palacios), *Los Viajes de Gulliver* (Madrid, 21 Feb 1911; libr Antonio Paso and Joaquím Abiati, after Jonathan Swift's *Gulliver's Travels*), which was written in collaboration with Vives, and *Tras Tristán* (Madrid, 1918; libr José Ramos Martín).

Ginastera, Alberto (1916–83)
Argentinian composer, writing mainly in TWELVE-TONE style. The leading modern South American composer, his observation that 'sex, violence and hallucination are three of the basic elements from which grand opera can be constructed' was put into practice in his stage works. His four operas, which have been widely performed, are DON RODRIGO, BOMARZO, BEATRIX CENCI and the unfinished *Barabbas* (1977; libr after Michel de Ghelderode).

Gioconda, La (*The Joyful Girl*)
Opera in four acts by Ponchielli. 1st perf Milan, 8 April 1876; libr by Arrigo Boito (under the pen-name of Tobia Gorria), after Victor Hugo's *Angélo, Tyran de Padoue*. Principal roles: Gioconda (sop), Enzo (ten), Barnaba (bar), Laura (mezzo), Alvise (bass), La Cieca (cont). By far Ponchielli's most successful work and his only opera still to be performed. The ballet music (the 'Dance of the Hours') has become a popular concert item.
Plot: 17th-century Venice. The banished nobleman Enzo Grimaldo has returned disguised as a sailor. He is loved by the street singer Gioconda, but is himself in love with Laura, wife of the councillor Alvise Badoero. The spy Barnaba, who lusts after Gioconda, denounces Enzo to the council. Enzo has a secret meeting with Laura on his ship, where Gioconda comes to confront him. Recognizing Laura as the woman who saved her blind mother La Cieca from the mob when she had been accused of witchcraft by Barnaba, she warns her that Alvise is coming to arrest Enzo. Laura escapes and Enzo sets fire to his ship and flees with Gioconda. Finding out about her affair with Enzo, Alvise orders Laura to take poison, but Gioconda substitutes a sleeping potion and contrives to have Laura's 'corpse' taken to her home, where Enzo will fetch her. To win Enzo's freedom, she promises herself to Barnaba, but after Enzo and Laura have been reunited and have left, she takes Laura's poison herself. As she falls at the furious Barnaba's feet, he tells her that he has strangled La Cieca. [R]

Gioielli della Madonna, I (*The Jewels of the Madonna*)
Opera in three acts by Wolf-Ferrari. 1st

perf Berlin, 23 Dec 1911; libr by Enrico Golisciani and Carlo Zangarini. Principal roles: Maliella (sop), Raffaele (bar), Gennaro (ten). Wolf-Ferrari's one excursion into the VERISMO field, it is still performed from time to time, and the orchestral suite arranged from the opera has given the music wider currency.
Plot: Early-20th-century Naples. Raffaele, a leader of the Camorra (the Neapolitan Mafia), tells Maliella that he loves her so much that he would dare to steal the jewels from the statue of the Madonna. The blacksmith Gennaro, himself in love with Maliella, overhears her considering the offer, and commits the theft himself. Maliella accepts Gennaro but then confesses to Raffaele, who rejects her. She throws the jewels at Gennaro's feet and then drowns herself. Gennaro returns the jewels to the statue and then stabs himself in despair.

Giordano, Umberto (1867–1948)
Italian composer. He wrote 12 operas in VERISMO style, notable for their violent passions and for their skilful use of the tried and trusted Mascagnian clichés of the genre. Several are theatrically effective, but they have only limited musical qualities and are largely innocent of any genuine dramatic insight. His operas are the unperformed *Mariana* (1889; libr Enrico Golisciani), *Mala Vita* (Rome, 21 Feb 1892; libr Nicola Daspuro, after Salvatore di Giacomo; revised version *Il Voto*, Milan, 10 Nov 1897), *Regina Diaz* (Naples, 5 Mar 1894; libr Giovanni Targioni-Tozzetti and Guido Menasci, after Édouard Lockroy's *Un Duel Sous le Cardinal de Richelieu*), ANDREA CHÉNIER, by far his most enduring work, the successful FEDORA, SIBERIA, *Marcella* (Milan, 9 Nov 1907; libr L. Stecchetti, after Henri Cain and Jules Adenis), *Mese Mariano* (Palermo, 17 Mar 1910; libr di Giacomo), MADAME SANS-GÊNE, *Giove di Pompei* (Rome, 5 July 1921; libr Ettore Romagnoli and Luigi Illica), which was written in collaboration with Franchetti, LA CENA DELLE BEFFE and *Il Rè* (Milan, 12 Jan 1929; libr Giovacchino Forzano).

Giorgetta
Soprano role in Puccini's *Il Tabarro*. Michele's wife, she is loved by Luigi.

Giorgio
Bass role in Bellini's *I Puritani*. The Puritan Lord George Walton, he is Elvira's uncle.

Giorno di Regno, Un (*A One-Day Reign*) or **Il Finto Stanislao** (*The False Stanislaus*)
Comic opera in two acts by Verdi. 1st perf Milan, 5 Sept 1840; libr by Felice Romani, after Alexandre Vincent Pineu-Duval's *Le Faux Stanislas*. Principal roles: Belfiore (bar), Marchesa (sop), Giulietta (mezzo), Edoardo (ten), Baron Kelbar (b-bar), Treasurer (b-bar). Very loosely based on an incident in the War of the Polish Succession, it is Verdi's only OPERA BUFFA. It was a total failure at its appearance and is still only rarely performed despite its enjoyable if not particularly sophisticated melodies.
Plot: Brest, 1733. The Parisian officer Belfiore poses as Stanislaus, King of Poland, so as to act as a decoy whilst the real Stanislaus attempts to secure his throne. In his capacity as 'King', Belfiore visits Baron Kelbar's castle and helps the Baron's daughter Giulietta to be united with her true love Edoardo by removing her unwanted betrothed, the Treasurer, from the proceedings. At the same time, he effects a reconciliation with his own beloved, the Marchesa del Poggio, who thought that he had abandoned her. [R]

Giovanna
1 Mezzo role in Donizetti's *Anna Bolena*. She is the historical Jane Seymour (*c* 1509–37), third wife of Henry VIII. **2** Soprano role in Verdi's *Giovanna d'Arco*. She is Joan of Arc. **3** Mezzo COMPRIMARIO role in Verdi's *Rigoletto*. She is Gilda's maid. **4** Mezzo comprimario role in Verdi's *Ernani*. She is Elvira's companion.

Giovanna d'Arco (*Joan of Arc*)
Opera in prologue and three acts by Verdi. 1st perf Milan, 15 Feb 1845; libr by Temistocle Solera, after Friedrich von Schiller's *Die Jungfrau von Orleans*. Principal roles: Giovanna (sop), Carlo (ten), Giacomo (bar). Like many of Verdi's early operas, it is an uneven work containing some beautiful and original music side-by-side with passages of rumbustious claptrap. After a long period of neglect, it has received a number of performances in recent years.

Plot: France, 1429. King Charles VII of France is considering surrender to the English, but is inspired to fight on by the peasant Giovanna, who has heard celestial voices urging her to come to the aid of her country. After inspiring the French troops to victory, Giovanna tells the King that she returns his affection but that she cannot yield to it, because her voices have forbidden her mortal love Her father Giacomo, fearing that she is a witch, denounces her and she is captured by the English. Learning the truth, Giacomo contrives her escape, but she is mortally wounded whilst leading the French to another victory. [R]

Gira la cotte
Chorus in Act I of Puccini's *Turandot*, in which they tell how the executioner is never idle. It leads into the Hymn to the Moon.

Girl of the Golden West, The
see FANCIULLA DEL WEST, LA

Giselda
Soprano role in Verdi's *I Lombardi*. Arvino's daughter, she loves Oronte.

Giudici ad Anna
Anna's great phrase at the end of Act I of Donizetti's *Anna Bolena*, when she is told that she is to be tried.

Giuditta (*Judith*)
Opera in three acts by Lehár. 1st perf Vienna, 20 Jan 1934; libr by Paul Knepler and Fritz Löhner. Principal roles: Giuditta (sop), Octavio (ten), Manuelle (bar), Antonio (bass), Anita (sop), Pierrino (ten), Sebastiano (ten). Lehár's last stage work and his one successful opera, it is still regularly performed in German-speaking countries.
Plot: Italy and North Africa, 1920s. Giuditta deserts her husband and goes to Africa with the army officer Octavio, who has seduced her. After Octavio's regiment has departed, Giuditta becomes a dancer. Octavio deserts from the army and takes a job as a pianist in a restaurant, where he again meets Giuditta, who is dining with a new lover. Giuditta leaves with her admirer, and Octavio continues to play as the restaurant lights are turned out. [R]

Giulia
Soprano role in Spontini's *La Vestale*. She is a vestal virgin loved by Licinio.

Giulietta
1 Soprano role in Offenbach's *Les Contes d'Hoffmann*. A Venetian courtesan, she is the third of Hoffmann's loves. The role is sometimes sung by a mezzo. **2** Soprano role in Bellini's *I Capuleti e i Montecchi*. Capelio's daughter, she is loved by Romeo. **3** Mezzo role in Verdi's *Un Giorno di Regno*. Baron Kelbar's daughter, she is in love with Edoardo.

Giulietta e Romeo
Opera in two acts by Vaccai. 1st perf Milan, 31 Oct 1825; libr by Felice Romani, after William Shakespeare's *Romeo and Juliet*. Principal roles: Giulietta (sop), Romeo (mezzo). Vaccai's most successful opera, which was long popular, it is nowadays virtually forgotten. In the 19th century part of the final scene was often incorporated into Bellini's *I Capuleti e i Montecchi*.

Giulietta e Romeo
Opera in three acts by Zandonai. 1st perf Rome, 14 Feb 1922; libr by Arturo Rossato, after Matteo Bandello's novel, itself based on William Shakespeare's *Romeo and Juliet*. Principal roles: Giulietta (sop), Romeo (ten), Tebaldo (bar). One of Zandonai's most successful operas, it is still occasionally performed in Italy. For plot see *Roméo et Juliette*. [R]

Giulini, Carlo Maria (b 1914)
Italian conductor, particularly associated with Mozart, Rossini and Verdi operas, especially *Don Carlos*. One of the outstanding conductors of the post-war era, his operatic appearances were extensive early in his career, especially during his period as musical director of Italian Radio (1946–51). He abandoned opera in the late 1960s, returning to it only for a few recordings and for a single production of *Falstaff* in 1982.

Giulio Cesare in Egitto (*Julius Caesar in Egypt*)
Opera in three acts by Händel. 1st perf London, 20 Feb 1724; libr by Nicola Francesco Haym, after Giacomo Francesco

Bussani's libretto for Antonio Sartorio. Principal roles: Cesare (c-ten), Cleopatra (sop), Tolomeo (c-ten), Sesto (mezzo), Cornelia (mezzo), Achillas (bass). It is one of Händel's greatest and nowadays most frequently performed operas.
Plot: Egypt, 48–47 BC. Caesar has arrived in pursuit of Pompey, who has been murdered by Ptolemy. Hearing of Caesar's wrath, Ptolemy (Tolomeo) plans to murder him as well and imprisons Pompey's widow Cornelia and son Sextus (Sesto). Ptolemy's sister Cleopatra attempts to charm Caesar into helping her against her brother, whilst Ptolemy's attempts on Cornelia's virtue are thwarted by Sextus. The dalliance of Caesar and Cleopatra is interrupted by a mob calling for Caesar's blood. Although defeated by Ptolemy, Caesar swims to safety, finds a secret way into the place and kills Ptolemy. He crowns Cleopatra sole ruler of Egypt. [R]

Giunto sul passo estremo
Tenor aria for Faust in the epilogue of Boito's *Mefistofele*, in which he reflects on his life as his death approaches.

Giuramento, Il (*The Oath*)
Opera in three acts by Mercadante. 1st perf Milan, 11 March 1837; libr by Gaetano Rossi, after Victor Hugo's *Angélo Tyran de Padoue*. Principal roles: Elaisa (sop), Viscardo (ten), Bianca (mezzo), Manfredo (bar), Brunoro (bass). Mercadante's finest and most successful opera, it is still occasionally performed.
Plot: 14th-century Syracuse. Viscardo di Benevento loves Bianca, the wife of Manfredo, Count of Syracuse. Elaisa, who also loves Viscardo, has sworn eternal friendship with an unknown benefactress who once saved her father's life and who has given her a medallion. The benefactress turns out to be Bianca, who is threatened with death by Manfredo because the traitrous Brunoro has sent him a note making him believe her unfaithful. True to her vow, Elaisa contrives to save Bianca's life, but is killed by Viscardo who wrongly believes that she has poisoned Bianca.

Giustino (*Justin*)
Opera in three acts by Händel. 1st perf London, 16 Feb 1737; libr after Nicolò Beregan. Principal roles: Giustino (c-ten), Anastasio (sop), Vitaliano (ten), Arianna (sop), Leocasta (mezzo), Fortuna (sop), Polidarte (bass), Amanzio (mezzo). It tells a largely fictitious story of events surrounding the accession of the Eastern Emperor Anastasius (reigned AD 491–518). Although never one of Händel's more popular operas, it still receives an occasional performance.
Plot: Constantinople, AD 491. The celebration of Ariadne's crowning of Anastasius is interrupted by Amantius's news of an advance by the rebel Vitalian, who seeks to wed Ariadne and succeeds in capturing her. Justin saves Leocasta from a bear and is asked to rescue Ariadne, who, having rejected Vitalian's love, has been exposed to a sea monster. Justin kills the monster, rescues Ariadne and captures Vitalian. The jealous Amantius intrigues against Justin and Ariadne, and has Anastasius banish them. However, it is revealed that Justin and Vitalian are brothers, and the two unite to expose Amantius's machinations. Amantius is arrested, Ariadne and Anastasius are reunited and Justin weds Leocasta. [R]

Glanville-Hicks, Peggy (1912–90)
Australian composer. One of the few women opera composers of any significance, her operas include *The Transposed Heads* (Louisville, 3 Apr 1954; libr composer, after Thomas Mann's *Die Vertauschten Köpfe*), *The Glittering Gate* (New York, 15 May 1959; libr composer, after Lord Dunsany), *Nausicaa* (Athens, 19 Aug 1961; libr A. Reid, after Robert Graves's *Homer's Daughter*), which reflects her study of ancient Greek demotic music, and the unperformed *Sappho* (1965; libr after Lawrence Durrell).

Glasgow
see SCOTTISH OPERA

Glass, Philip (b 1937)
American composer. The leading member of the MINIMALIST school of composition, he has written five full-length stage works, which have enjoyed a remarkable degree of success. They are *Einstein on the Beach* (Avignon, 26 July 1976; libr Robert Wilson) [R], *Satyagraha* (Rotterdam, 5 Sept 1980; libr Constance de Jong, after the *Bhagavad Gita*) [R], the hugely successful

AKHNATEN, *The Making of the Representative for Planet 8* (Houston, 8 July 1988; libr Doris Lessing, after her novel) and *The Voyage* (New York, 12 Oct 1992; libr David Henry Hwang). He has also written three chamber operas: *The Photographer* (Amsterdam, 30 May 1982), *The Juniper Tree* (Cambridge, Mass, 6 Dec 1985) and *The Fall of the House of Usher* (Cambridge, 18 May 1988; libr Arthur Yorinx, after Edgar Allan Poe). His writings include *Opera on the Beach* (1988).

Glazunov, Alexander (1865–1936)
Russian composer. Best known as an orchestral composer, he wrote no operas himself, but helped to complete Borodin's unfinished *Prince Igor*.

Gli
Titles beginning with this form of the Italian definite article are listed under the letter of the first main word. For example, *Gli Equivoci* is listed under E.

Glière, Reinhold (1875–1956)
Russian composer. He wrote several operas, all now largely forgotten, of which the most significant is *Shah-Senem* (Baku, 17 Mar 1927; libr Jabarla and Halperin), which is rooted in Azerbaijani folk music.

Glinka, Mikhail (1804–57)
Russian composer. The founder of the Russian nationalist school of opera and the first Russian composer to win international recognition, he created Russian opera virtually single-handedly. Largely self-taught, his only two completed operas are A LIFE FOR THE TSAR (known in Russia during the Soviet period as *Ivan Susanin*) and RUSLAN AND LUDMILA. His use of folk polyphony, of regional dances and, in *Ruslan*, his choice of a colourful Russian fairy tale all had an incalculable influence on the development of Russian music, especially when combined with his brilliant and colourful orchestration and his fine vocal writing. He occupies a seminal position in the history of music, and the infrequency of performance of his operas in the West is utterly inexplicable.

Gloire immortelle
Soldiers' chorus in Act IV of Gounod's *Faust*.

Gloria all' Egitto
The chorus which opens the Triumph Scene in Act II of Verdi's *Aida*.

Gloriana
Opera in three acts by Britten (Op 53). 1st perf London, 8 June 1953; libr by William Plomer, after Lytton Strachey's *Elizabeth and Essex*. Principal roles: Elizabeth I (sop), Earl of Essex (ten), Lord Mountjoy (bar), Lady Penelope Rich (sop), Sir Walter Ralegh (bass), Cecil (bar), Henry Cuffe (bar), Frances (mezzo), Spirit of the Masque (ten), Blind Ballad Singer (b-bar), Recorder of Norwich (bass). Commissioned to celebrate the coronation of Queen Elizabeth II, it was a failure at its appearance but has subsequently been revived with great success and its merits totally re-evalued. A pageant of Tudor scenes, it concentrates on events in the later part of Elizabeth I's reign, particularly the conflicting demands made upon her by her duty and her love for Essex. [R]

Glossop, Peter (b 1928)
British baritone, particularly associated with Verdi roles, especially Rigoletto and Iago (which he filmed). One of the finest Verdi baritones of the post-war era, he had a rich voice of considerable power and with an exciting upper register and he had a strong stage presence. His first wife **Joyce Blackham** (*b* 1935) was a successful mezzo.

Glover, Jane (b 1949)
British conductor and musicologist, particularly associated with Cavalli, about whom she wrote the definitive biography as well as preparing critical editions of his *Rosinda* and *L'Eritrea*. The first British woman conductor of importance, she has had particular success with Mozart, and was musical director of Glyndebourne Touring Opera (1981–5) and artistic director of the Buxton Festival (1993).

Gluck, Alma (b Reba Fiersohn) (1884–1938)
Romanian-born American soprano, particularly associated with lighter French and Italian roles. A singer of outstanding musicianship, her operatic career lasted only four years, as she devoted herself exclusively to the concert platform from

1913. She was married to the violinist Efrem Zimbalist, and her daughter was the novelist Marcia Davenport who, in addition to her fictional works, wrote biographies of Mozart and Toscanini.

Gluck, Christoph Willibald von (1714–87)
German composer. One of the most important figures in the history of opera, and sometimes regarded as its second founder, he wrote 46 operas. His early works are unremarkable essays in established forms, mainly Metastasian OPERA SERIA. Those to texts by Pietro Metastasio include *Artaserse* (Milan, 26 Dec 1741), his first opera, *La Clemenza di Tito* (Naples, 4 Nov 1752) and the serenade LE CINESI. He then composed a series of French OPÉRA-COMIQUES in which his sense of characterization begins to emerge. Of these L'IVROGNE CORRIGÉ and LE CADI DUPÉ still receive an occassional performance.

The turning-point in Gluck's career came in 1762 with ORFEO ED EURIDICE, his most famous work. Six conventional operas followed, of which only LA RENCONTRE IMPRÉVUE and TELEMACO are of much significance, before he began his great reform of opera in collaboration with the poet RANIERI DE' CALZABIGI. The apperance of ALCESTE marked the birth of modern music-drama. In his famous preface to the musical score, Gluck set out his reform aims: to strive for simplicity and total clarity, to banish the excesses and abuses of singers, and to 'restrict music to its true office by means of expression and by following the situations of the story'. In effect, Gluck was returning to the principles of the original founders of opera who had desired to recreate the simplicity and drama of Greek tragedy. This is reflected in his choice of subjects for his later operas, all but one of which are derived from Greek mythology. Following PARIDE ED ELENA, he moved to Paris, where he produced IPHIGÉNIE EN AULIDE as well as major French revisions of *Orfeo ed Euridice* and *Alceste*. These sparked off the famous feud between his supporters and those of Piccinni. ARMIDE was followed by IPHIGÉNIE EN TAURIDE, his masterpiece and one of the greatest of all music-dramas. In his last opera ÉCHO ET NARCISSE he returned unsuccessfully to a simpler pastoral form.

Glückliche Hand, Die (*The Lucky Hand*)
Opera in one act by Schönberg (Op 18). 1st perf Vienna, 14 Oct 1924 (composed 1917); libr by the composer. Principal role: Man (bar). Telling of a man's search for artistic fulfilment and for his own identity, it is an attempted synthesis of music, movement and the 'orchestration' or 'colour modulation' of lighting. [R]

Glyndebourne Festival
An annual summer opera festival held near Lewes in Sussex in southern England, which opened on 28 May 1934. The opera house was built in 1934 by JOHN CHRISTIE and his wife AUDREY MILDMAY in the grounds of the former's estate. It has been enlarged three times, reopening (cap 1,150) in 1994 after a complete rebuilding. The annual season runs from May to August, and its aim is the presentation of opera in ideal surroundings in productions of rigorous musical and dramatic preparation. Particularly noted for its Mozart productions, it also has a strong Rossini and Strauss tradition and has played an important part in the recent revival of interest in Monteverdi and Cavalli. Performances are given in the original language with international casts, and the festival has an enviable reputation for presenting many great singers before they become famous. The resident orchestra is the London Philharmonic, and the musical directors have been Fritz Busch, Vittorio Gui, Sir John Pritchard, Bernard Haitink and Andrew Davis.

Glyndebourne Touring Opera
A company founded in 1968 to tour throughout England with young, predominantly British and Commonwealth singers. It usually performs the Glyndebourne Festival's productions, but has also mounted a few of its own productions. The musical directors have been Myer Fredman, Kenneth Montgomery, Nicholas Braithwaite, Jane Glover, Graeme Jenkins and Ivor Bolton.

Gnecchi, Vittorio (1876–1954)
Italian composer. A number of his operas enjoyed success in their time, but all of them are now forgotten. The most important include *Cassandra* (Bologna, 5 Dec 1905; libr Luigi Illica, after Homer's *The Iliad*), which Strauss was accused of plagiarizing in *Elektra* because of the remarkable similarity of some of the motifs, and *La Rosiera* (Gera, 12 Feb 1927; libr composer and Carlo Zangarini, after Alfred de Musset), which contains one of the earliest uses of quarter-tones.

Goat's Trill
An alternative name for BLEAT. It is called *chevrotement* in France, *trillo caprino* in Italy, *Bockstriller* in Germany and *trino de cabra* in Spain.

Gobatti, Stefano (1852–1913)
Italian composer. His first opera *I Goti* (Bologna, 30 Nov 1873; libr S. Interdonato) was sensationally successful at its appearance and he was hailed as a second Verdi. The popularity soon waned, however, and Verdi himself – not normally given to being rude about other composers – described the opera as 'the most monstrous musical abortion ever created'. Its successors, *Luce* (Bologna, 25 Nov 1875; libr Interdonato) and *Cordelia* (Bologna, 6 Dec 1881; libr Carlo d'Omerville, after Shakespeare's *King Lear*), were failures, and *Masias* (1900; libr E. Sanfelice) was never performed. Accused of having the evil eye, he developed persecution mania, retreated to a monastery and finally died in a lunatic asylum.

Gobbi, Tito (1913–84)
Italian baritone, particularly associated with the Italian repertory, especially Boccanegra, Iago, Falstaff, Scarpia and Gianni Schicchi. One of the greatest singing-actors in operatic history, he possessed a fine voice used with great intelligence and extraordinary tonal variety: each of his 100 roles had its own vocal colour. An actor of outstanding ability and insight and a master of make-up, he set – particularly when in partnership with Maria Callas – entirely new standards of dramatic performance in opera. Equally at home in serious or comic roles, he created Teperlov in Rocca's *Monte Ivnor*, Ulysses in Malipiero's *Ecuba*, Albafiorita in Persico's *La Locandiera*, Ahmed in Lualdi's *Le Nozze di Huara*, the Storyteller in Napoli's *Il Tesoro* and the title-role in Ghedini's *Lord Inferno*. He also appeared in 26 films, notably *Glass Mountain* and *Pagliacci* (with Gina Lollobrigida), and later in his career produced a number of operas. He also established a school for the advanced training of young singers at the Villa Schifanoia in Italy. His autobiography, *My Life*, was published in 1979.

Godard, Benjamin (1849–95)
French composer. His eight operas include *Les Guelfes* (Rouen, 17 Jan 1902, composed 1882; libr Louis Gallet), *Pedro de Zalaméa* (Antwerp, 31 Jan 1884; libr Léonce Détroyat and Armand Silvestre, after Pedro Calderón de la Barca), the once-popular JOCELYN, *Dante et Béatrice* (Paris, 31 May 1890; libr Édouard Blau) and the successful *La Vivandière* (Paris, 11 Apr 1895; libr Henri Cain). His facile style and early success did not always endear him to his contemporaries: when he said to Chabrier that it was a pity that he had turned to opera so late, the latter retorted 'what a pity you started so soon'!

God of battle, The
Bass aria for Hercules in Act I of Händel's *Hercules*, in which he says that he has come home to domesticity after his adventures.

Goehr, Alexander (b 1932)
British composer. He has written five stage works: the black comedy ARDEN MUST DIE, the 'dramatic madrigal' *Naboth's Vineyard* (London, 1968; libr composer), *Shadow Play* (London, 1970; libr K. Cavender, after Plato's *Republic*), *Behold the Sun* (Duisburg, 19 Apr 1985; libr composer and John McGrath) and *Arianna* (London, Sept 1995). His father **Walter** (1903–60) was a conductor and composer. He wrote the first opera for radio, *Malpopita* (1930), and as a conductor was particularly associated with early and baroque operas.

Goethe, Johann Wolfgang von
see panel on page 230

· *Goethe* ·

The German playwright and poet Johann Wolfgang von Goethe (1749–1832) was himself interested in opera. He wrote a number of SINGSPIEL texts, and as director of the Weimar Theatre included many operas in the repertory. He appears as a character in Lehár's *Friederike*. Some 120 operas have been based on his works. Below are listed, by work, those operas by composers with entries in this dictionary.

Die Braut von Korinth		
Chabrier	*Briséïs*	1899 (U)
Claudine von Villa Bella		
Schubert	*Claudine von Villa Bella*	1815
Coccia	*Claudine in Torino*	1817
Erwin und Elmire		
Schoeck	*Erwin und Elmire*	1916
Faust		
Berlioz	*La Damnation de Faust*	1846
Gounod	*Faust*	1859
Boito	*Mefistofele*	1868/75
Brian	*Faust*	1956
Der Gott und die Bajadere		
Auber	*Le Dieu et la Bayadère*	1830
Götz von Berlichingen		
Goldmark	*Götz von Berlichingen*	1902
Jery und Bätely		
Winter	*Jery und Bätely*	1790
K. Kreutzer	*Jery und Bätely*	1810
Adam	*Le Châlet*	1834
Donizetti	*Betly*	1836
Die Leiden des Jungen Werthers		
K. Kreutzer	*Charlotte et Werther*	1792
Coccia	*Carlotta e Werther*	1814
Massenet	*Werther*	1892
Märchen		
Klebe	*Das Märchen von der Schönen Lilie*	1969
Pandora		
Gerster	*Das Verzauberte Ich*	1949
Scherz, List und Rache		
Winter	*Scherz, List und Rache*	1790
Hoffman	*Scherz, List und Rache*	1801
Bruch	*Scherz, List und Rache*	1858
Wellesz	*Scherz, List und Rache*	1928
Tasso		
Donizetti	*Torquato Tasso*	1833
Wilhelm Meisters Lehrjahre		
Thomas	*Mignon*	1866

· Nikolai Gogol ·

The works of the Russian writer Nikolai Vasilievich Gogol (1809–52) have inspired some 60 operas, mostly by Russian composers. Below are listed, by work, those operas by composers with entries in this dictionary.

Christmas Eve		
Tchaikovsky	*Vakula the Blacksmith/The Little Slippers*	1874/85
Lysenko	*Christmas Eve*	1874
Rimsky-Korsakov	*Christmas Eve*	1895
Dead Souls		
Shchedrin	*Dead Souls*	1976
The Diary of a Madman		
Searle	*The Diary of a Madman*	1958
The Gamblers		
Shostakovich	*The Gamblers*	1942 (U)
The Inspector-General		
Chukhadjian	*Arif*	1872
Egk	*Der Revisor*	1957
May Night		
Serov	*May Night*	1853
Rimsky-Korsakov	*May Night*	1879
Lysenko	*The Drowned Woman*	1885
The Nose		
Shostakovich	*The Nose*	1930
Sorochintsy Fair		
Moussorgsky	*Sorochintsy Fair*	1874 (U)
Taras Bulba		
Lysenko	*Taras Bulba*	1890
Beruti	*Taras Bulba*	1895
The Wedding		
Moussorgsky	*The Marriage*	1868 (U)
Martinů	*The Marriage*	1953

Goetz
see GÖTZ

Gogol, Nikolai
see panel above

Golaud
Baritone role in Debussy's *Pelléas et Mélisande*. Geneviève's son, he is Pelléas's half-brother.

Golden Cockerel, The (*Zolotoy Petuschok;* sometimes incorrectly called *Le Coq d'Or*) Opera in three acts by Rimsky-Korsakov. 1st perf Moscow, 7 Oct 1909; libr by Vladimir Ivanovich Belsky, after Alexander Pushkin's poem. Principal roles: King Dodon (bass), Queen of Shemakha (sop), Astrologer (ten), Prince Polkan (bar), Amelfa (mezzo), Prince Afron (bar), Cockerel (sop). Rimsky's last opera, and his best-known in the West, it is a fairy-tale work which ran into censorship problems at its appearance because of its alleged satire on Nicholas II's handling of the Russo-Japanese War. It is notable for its brilliant and colourful orchestration and for containing, in the Astrologer, possibly the highest tenor role ever written. The orchestral suite arranged from the opera has given the music a wider currency.
Plot: Legendary Russia. The Astrologer gives the doddery old King Dodon a

golden cockerel which will crow if Dodon is threatened with danger. The delighted Dodon offers the Astrologer whatever he desires in exchange for the magic bird, but the Astrologer defers his choice. The cockerel crows and the King goes off to war. He meets and marries the beautiful Queen of Shemakha and brings her back to his kingdom where the Astrologer, claiming his promised payment, asks to be given the Queen. Dodon kills the Astrologer for his impertinence, whereupon the cockerel pecks Dodon on the head. He falls dead and the Queen disappears. [R]

Goldmark, Karl (b Károly) (1830–1915)
Hungarian composer. He wrote seven operas in eclectic style, being particularly influenced by Mendelssohn and Wagner. His greatest success was his first opera DIE KÖNIGIN VON SABA, his only stage work which is still remembered. Its successors were *Merlin* (Vienna, 19 Nov 1886; libr Siegfried Lipiner), *Das Heimchen am Herd* (Vienna, 21 Mar 1896; libr Alfred Maria Willner, after Charles Dickens's *The Cricket on the Hearth*), *Die Kriegsgefangene* (*The Prisoner of War*, Vienna, 17 Jan 1899; libr A. Formey), *Götz von Berlichingen* (Budapest, 16 Dec 1902; libr Willner, after Goethe) and *Ein Wintermärchen* (Vienna, 2 Jan 1908; libr Willner, after Shakespeare's *A Winter's Tale*). His two volumes of autobiography, *Erinnerungen aus meinen Leben*, were published in 1922 and 1929.

Goldoni, Carlo (1707–93)
Italian playwright and librettist. His comedies were set by many composers, including Anfossi, Duni, Galuppi (13 including *Il Filosofo di Campagna*), Gassmann (*L'Amore Artigiano*), Paisiello, Piccinni (*La Buona Figliuola*), Sarti, Traetta and Vivaldi. In the 20th century, his plays have inspired operas by Giannini, Malipiero, Martinů and, particularly, Wolf-Ferrari.

Goldovsky, Boris (b 1908)
Russian conductor and producer, long resident in the United States. He was head of opera at the New England Conservatory in Boston (1942–64) and of the Berkshire Music Center at Tanglewood (1946–62), where he presented the US premieres of many important operas. He founded the New England Opera Theater in 1946, and was also director of the Goldovsky Opera Theater, which toured the USA until 1984 and nurtured many leading American singers. His autobiography, *My Road to Opera*, was published in 1979.

Goldschmidt, Berthold (b 1903)
German composer and conductor, resident in Britain since fleeing the Nazis. He wrote two operas: *Der Gewaltige Hahnrei* (Mannheim, 14 Feb 1932; libr after Fernand Crommelynck's *Le Cocu Magnifique*) [R] and *Beatrice Cenci* (London, 16 Apr 1988, composed 1951; libr Martin Esslin, after Percy Bysshe Shelley's *The Cenci*) [R], which was a joint winner of the Festival of Britain competition. After a long period of total neglect, there has recently been a major revival of interest in his music.

Golitsin, Prince
Tenor role in Moussorgsky's *Khovanschina*. He is loved by the regent Sophia.

Goltz, Christel (b 1912)
German soprano, particularly associated with Strauss roles and with post-war German operas. An intense singing-actress with a clear, well-projected and powerful voice of great range, she created the title-roles in Orff's *Antigonae* and Liebermann's *Penelope*.

Gomes, António Carlos (1836–96)
Brazilian composer. The finest Latin American opera composer, and the only one before Ginastera to win international recognition, he wrote eight operas in a predominantly Italian style, many of which enjoyed great success. *A Noite do Castelo* (Rio de Janeiro, 4 Sept 1861; libr António José Fernandes dos Reis, after António Feliciano de Castilho) was followed by *Joanna de Flandres* (Rio de Janeiro, 15 Sept 1863; libr Salvador de Mendonça), his masterpiece IL GUARANY, the fine FOSCA, *Salvator Rosa* (Genoa, 12 Mar 1874; libr Antonio Ghislanzoni, after Eugène de Méricourt's *Masaniello*), *Maria Tudor* (Milan, 27 Mar 1879; libr Emilio Praga, after Victor Hugo's *Marie Tudor*), the successful *Lo Schiavo* (Rio de Janeiro, 27 Sept 1889; libr Rodolfo Paravicini, after

Alexandre Dumas fils' *Les Danicheff*), which incorporates native Brazilian Indian instruments, and *Côndor* (Milan, 21 Sept 1891; libr Mario Canti). After a long period of neglect outside Brazil, there has recently been a minor revival of interest in his operas.

Gomez, Jill (b 1942)
Guyanese-born British soprano, particularly associated with Mozart roles and with the British and Spanish repertories. She possesses a pure and silvery voice used with fine musicianship and has an affecting stage presence. She created Flora in *The Knot Garden* and the Countess in Musgrave's *The Voice of Ariadne*.

Gondoliers, The or **The King of Barataria**
Operetta in two acts by Sullivan. 1st perf London, 7 Dec 1889; libr by W.S. Gilbert. Principal roles: Don Alhambra (b-bar), Marco and Giuseppe Palmieri (ten and bar), Duke and Duchess of Plaza-Toro (bar and mezzo), Gianetta (sop), Tessa (mezzo), Casilda (sop), Luiz (ten or bar), Antonio (bar), Inez (cont). One of the finest and most popular of all the Savoy Operas, it enjoyed an initial run of over 550 performances. It contains some of Sullivan's freshest and most delightful music, which is married to a brilliant text satirizing republican ideas.
Plot: Venice and the imaginary kingdom of Barataria, 1750. To prevent the spread of Wesleyan Methodism, the Grand Inquisitor Don Alhambra del Bolero abducted the son of the King of Barataria and entrusted him to the care of a Venetian gondolier. Over the years, the latter grew unable to remember who was the prince and who was his own son. The two boys have now grown up to be the gondoliers Marco and Giuseppe, who marry Gianetta and Tessa. The Duke and Duchess of Plaza-Toro arrive and inform their daughter Casilda (who is in love with their attendant Luiz) that she was married in infancy to the prince of Barataria, and that as his father is dead she is now queen. Don Alhambra arranges for Marco and Giuseppe to reign jointly until the real king is revealed, and the two remodel the monarchy on republican principles, with everyone ranking equal. The king's foster-mother Inez, who is Luiz's mother, is found and reveals that when the Inquisition came to take the prince she substituted her own son. Luiz is thus the real king and is united with Casilda. [R]

Gondromark
Roles in Offenbach's *La Vie Parisienne*: the Swedish baron (bar) and his wife the baroness (mezzo).

Gonzalve
Tenor role in Ravel's *L'Heure Espagnole*. He is one of Concepción's admirers.

Goodall, Sir Reginald (1901–90)
British conductor, particularly associated with Wagner operas. After conducting the first performance of Britten's *Peter Grimes*, he was a member of the music staff at Covent Garden from 1946, initially conducting a wide repertory but soon becoming almost completely ignored. It was not until he was approaching his 70s that his stature as a Wagnerian was appreciated, first with the Sadler's Wells *Die Meistersinger von Nürnberg* in 1968 and still more with the English National Opera's *Ring*, which established him alongside Wilhelm Furtwängler as one of the greatest Wagnerians of the post-war era. His appearances were infrequent, largely because of the extraordinarily long preparation and rehearsal time which he demanded.

Good Friday Music (*Karfreitagzauber*)
The music in Act III Scene I of Wagner's *Parsifal*, during which Parsifal is anointed before entering the castle of the Grail.

Goossens, Sir Eugène (1893–1962)
British composer and conductor. He wrote two operas: the successful JUDITH and *Don Juan de Mañara* (London, 24 June 1937; libr Arnold Bennett, after Prosper Mérimée's *Les Âmes du Purgatoire*). He conducted the first performance of Holst's *The Perfect Fool* and was also a distinguished director of the New South Wales Conservatory (1947–56). His autobiography, *Overture and Beginners*, was published in 1951. His brother Leon was a celebrated oboist and his sisters Sidonie and Marie were both harpists. Their father **Eugène** (1867–1958) was a conductor,

who was musical director of the Carl Rosa Opera Company (1899–1915) and who conducted the first performance of Stanford's *The Critic*.

Gopak
A fast Russian folk dance in 2/4 time. There is a famous operatic example in Tchaikovsky's *Mazeppa*.

Gorgheggio (Italian for 'warbling')
A form of decorative vocalization which consists of rapid and numerous rising and falling notes. It was much used in the 18th and 19th centuries by singers to show off their virtuosity.

Gorchakova, Galina (b 1962)
Russian soprano, particularly associated with the Russian repertory, especially Tatyana in *Eugene Onegin* and Renata in *The Fiery Angel*. Possessing a warm, radiant and seemingly tireless voice, used with excellent musicianship, she is one of the finest singers to have come to the fore in recent years.

Goro
Tenor role in Puccini's *Madama Butterfly*. He is a marriage broker.

Gorr, Rita (b Marguerite Geirnaert) (b 1926)
Belgian mezzo, particularly associated with the French repertory and with Wagnerian roles. She possessed a large and rich-toned voice, used with intelligence and fine musicianship, and was an intense singing-actress, especially successful in dramatic roles such as Kundry in *Parsifal* and Amneris in *Aida*. She enjoyed a remarkably long career, singing into her late 60s.

Gossec, François (b Gossé) (1734–1829)
Belgian composer. An admirer of Gluck, he wrote some 20 operas, all of them now forgotten, of which the comedies were the most successful. His most important operas include *Les Pêcheurs* (Paris, 23 Apr 1766; libr Adrien Nicolas de la Salle d'Offémont), *Toinon et Toinette* (Paris, 20 June 1767; libr Jean Auguste Julien des Boulmiers), the TRAGÉDIE-LYRIQUE *Sabinus* (Versailles, 4 Dec 1773; libr Michel Paul Guy de Chabanon de Maugris), which contains some anticipations of Spontini's style, and *Thésée* (Paris, 1 Mar 1782; libr Étienne Morel de Chéfdeville, after Philippe Quinault's libretto for Lully).

Göteborg Opera
Opera in this town in Sweden is given at the Stora Theatre (cap 605), which opened in Sept 1859. Musical directors have included Tullio Voghera, Sixten Ehrling, Gunnar Staern and Nicholas Braithwaite.

Gothenburg
see GÖTEBORG OPERA

Gotovac, Jakov (1895–1982)
Croatian composer and conductor. His eight stage works are *Morana* (Brno, 29 Nov 1930; libr A. Muradbegović), ERO THE JOKER, the only Serbo-Croat opera to have achieved international success, *Kamenik* (Zagreb, 17 Dec 1946; libr R. Nikolić), *Mila Gojsalića* (Zagreb 18 May 1952; libr D. Andelinović), the SINGSPIEL *Derdan* (Zagreb, 29 Nov 1955; libr composer and C. Jakelić), *Stanac* (Zagreb, 6 Dec 1959; libr Martia Držić and V. Radaban), *Dalmaro* (Zagreb, 20 Dec 1964; libr R.L. Petelinova) and the unperformed opera-oratorio *Petar Svačić* (1969; libr Z. Tomičić). Also a distinguished conductor, he was musical director of the Croatian National Opera (1923–57).

Götterdämmerung (*Twilight of the Gods*)
Opera in three acts by Wagner; part 4 of DER RING DES NIBELUNGEN. 1st perf Bayreuth, 17 Aug 1876 (composed 1874); libr by the composer, after the *Nibelungenlied*. Principal roles: Brünnhilde (sop), Siegfried (ten), Hagen (bass), Günther (bar), Gutrune (sop), Waltraute (mezzo), Alberich (bar), Norns (sop, mezzo and cont), Woglinde (sop), Wellgunde (mezzo), Flosshilde (mezzo). For plot see *Der Ring des Nibelungen*. [R]

Göttingener Händelfestspiele
An annual summer festival in the German town of Göttingen in Lower Saxony, it is devoted to Händel's works. The inaugural production of *Rodelinda* under Oskar Hagen on 26 June 1920 may be said to mark the beginning of the modern Händel revival. Performances are given at the Stadttheater (cap 740), which opened in 1890. Musical directors have included John Eliot Gardiner and Nicholas McGegan.

· Carlo Gozzi ·

The works of the Italian comic playwright Carlo Gozzi (1720–1806) have inspired some 20 operas. Below are listed, by play, those operas by composers with entries in this dictionary.

L'Amore Delle Tre Melerance		
Prokofiev	*The Love of Three Oranges*	1921
La Donna Serpente		
Wagner	*Die Feen*	1834
Casella	*La Donna Serpente*	1932
Il Rè Cervo		
Henze	*König Hirsch*	1956/63
Turandot		
Busoni	*Turandot*	1917
Puccini	*Turandot*	1926 (U)
Brian	*Turandot*	1950

Götz, Hermann (1840–76)
German composer. He is chiefly remembered for the Shakespearian DER WIDERSPÄNSTIGEN ZÄHMUNG, whose quasi-Mozartian elegance makes it one of the finest German comic operas of the period. His second opera *Francesca von Rimini* (Mannheim, 30 Sept 1877; libr composer, after *L'Inferno* in Dante Alighieri's *La Divina Commedia*) was left unfinished at his death and was completed by Ernst Frank.

Gounod, Charles (1818–93)
French composer. One of the most successful of all 19th-century opera composers, he wrote 13 stage works. They are notable for their wealth of appealing melodies, their graceful vocal writing and their deft orchestration. It must, however, be admitted that for all the immense popularity of his best works (a popularity that has waned somewhat in recent years), his operas cannot be considered great music-dramas. Rather, they are pleasant confections which need not be taken too seriously. In addition, the sanctimonious and quasi-religious side of his nature, coupled with his taste for the grandiose, often stifled his simple but genuine gifts of musical characterization.

His first opera SAPHO was a success, but it was followed by a failure, the melodramatic *La Nonne Sanglante* (Paris, 18 Oct 1854; libr Eugène Scribe and Germain Delavigne, after Matthew Gregory Lewis's *The Monk*). He displayed a considerable gift for comedy in LE MÉDECIN MALGRÉ LUI, which was followed by the sensationally successful FAUST, which placed him at the forefront of European composers. The successful PHILÉMON ET BAUCIS was followed by *La Colombe* (Baden-Baden, 3 Aug 1860; libr Jules Barbier and Michel Carré, after Jean de la Fontaine's *Le Faucon*), LA REINE DE SABA, the beautiful Provençal MIREILLE, the highly successful ROMÉO ET JULIETTE, CINQ-MARS, the unfinished *Maître Pierre* (1877; libr Louis Gallet), *Polyeucte* (Paris, 7 Oct 1878; libr Barbier and Carré, after Pierre Corneille) and *Le Tribut de Zamora* (Paris, 1 Apr 1881; libr Adolphe Philippe d'Ennery and Jules Brésil).

Goyescas
Opera in three scenes by Granados. 1st perf New York, 28 Jan 1916; libr by Fernando Periquet y Zuaznabar. Principal roles: Rosario (sop), Fernando (ten), Paquiro (bar), Pepa (mezzo). Inspired by paintings by Francisco Goya, it is Granados's only stage work which is still remembered, and was arranged from his earlier piano pieces of the same name.
Plot: Madrid, *c* 1800. The high-born Rosario arouses the jealousy of her lover Fernando by accepting the attentions of the bull-fighter Paquiro, whose own beloved Pepa is also outraged. Fernando escorts Rosario to a ball, where Paquiro challenges him to a duel. After a garden meeting with Rosario, Fernando is killed in the duel. [R]

Gozzi, Carlo
see panel above

Grace note
A vocal ornament consisting of one or more notes inserted by a singer as an embellishment or decoration of the vocal line, as in an APPOGGIATURA.

Graf, Herbert (1904–73)
Austrian producer. Son of the Viennese critic Max Graf, he was one of the leading opera producers of the mid-20th century. His productions were traditional in the best sense of the word, and he was dedicated to the encouragement of young talent. He was director of productions at the Metropolitan Opera, New York (1936–60), the Zürich Opernhaus (1960–63) and the Grand Théâtre, Geneva (1965–73). His writings include *Opera for the People* (1951) and *Producing Opera for America* (1961).

Gräfin Mariza (*Countess Maritza*)
Operatta in three acts by Kálmán. 1st perf Vienna, 28 Feb 1924; libr by Julius Brammer and Alfred Grünwald. Principal roles: Mariza (sop), Tassilo (ten), Zsupán (ten), Lisa (sop), Manja (mezzo), Bozena (mezzo). An immediate success, it has remained ever since one of Kálmán's most popular works.
Plot: Early-20th-century Hungary. To get rid of her importunate admirers, Countess Maritza enters into a none-too-serious engagement with Zsupán. Her estate manager, the impoverished Count Tassilo, falls in love with her, and she is drawn to him. However, she becomes jealous of the attentions paid by Tassilo to the pretty Lisa. Maritza is unaware that Lisa is Tassilo's sister, and when this misunderstanding is cleared up the lovers are united. [R]

Graf von Luxemburg, Der (*The Count of Luxembourg*)
Operetta in three acts by Lehár. 1st perf Vienna, 12 Nov 1909; libr by Robert Bodanzky and Alfred Maria Willner. Principal roles: René (ten), Angèle (sop), Juliette (sop), Brissard (ten), Basil (bass). One of Lehár's earliest successes, it is still regularly performed.
Plot: 19th-century Paris. The famous singer Angèle Didier is due to marry the Russian Prince Basil. However, she must first marry another nobleman and then divorce him, so that she will come to Basil already ennobled. René, the penniless Count of Luxembourg, agrees to a short marriage in exchange for a suitable remuneration. He is not to meet or see Angèle, but at the ceremony their hands touch through the curtain screen and they feel drawn to one another. Eventually, Basil's heart is drawn elsewhere, so that René and Angèle are able to remain married. [R]

Graham, Colin (b 1931)
British producer. One of the leading post-war British opera producers, his uncontroversial productions are notable for their elucidation of character and for their handling of crowd scenes (particularly so in Sadler's Wells Opera's *War and Peace*). He was director of productions of the English Opera Group (1963–75), the English Music Theatre (1975–8) and the English National Opera (1978–80) and artistic director of the Opera Theater of St Louis (1978–). He also wrote the libretto for Bennett's *A Penny for a Song*.

Gramophone
see OPERA RECORDINGS

Gramm, Donald (b Grambsch) (1927–83)
American bass-baritone, particularly associated with Mozart roles and with 20th-century operas. He possessed a powerful and incisive voice of considerable range, which he used with great intelligence, and he was an outstanding singing-actor, equally at home in serious or comic roles. He created a role in Martinů's *The Marriage*.

Granados y Campiña, Enrique (1867–1916)
Spanish composer. His first stage work, the ZARZUELA *María del Carmen* (Madrid, 12 Nov 1898; libr José Felíu y Codina), was a success, but his five following zarzuelas are forgotten. They are the unperformed *Petrarca* (1900; libr Apeles Mestres), *Picarol* (Barcelona, 25 Feb 1901; libr Mestres, after Victor Hugo's *Notre Dame de Paris*), *Follet* (Barcelona, 4 Apr 1903; libr Mestres), *Gaziel* (Barcelona, 27 Oct 1906; libr Mestres) and *Liliana* (Barcelona, 9 July 1911; libr Mestres). Success returned, however, with his last work, the opera GOYESCAS, his stage masterpiece. He died

when the ship on which he was returning from America was sunk by a torpedo. His son **Edoardo** (1894–1928) was also a composer, and wrote 13 zarzuelas. The most successful were *Bufón y Hastelero* and *La Ciudad Eterna*.

Grand Duke, The or **The Statutory Duel**
Operetta in two acts by Sullivan. 1st perf London, 7 March 1896; libr by W.S. Gilbert. Principal roles: Ludwig (b-bar), Julia (sop), Rudolph (bar), Ernest (ten), Dr Tannhäuser (bar), Baroness (mezzo), Lisa (mezzo), Prince and Princess of Monte Carlo (bass and sop), Herald (bar). The last and least successful of the Savoy Operas, it is a complex and over-laboured piece, redeemed in places by flashes of Sullivan's old genius. It is only rarely performed.
Plot: The imaginary German duchy of Pfennig Halbfennig, 1750. An old law banning duelling lays down that instead contestants will each draw a card, and that the one drawing the lowest will become technically and legally dead, with all his rank and obligations being assumed by the winner. Ludwig, the leading actor of Ernest Dummkopf's theatrical troupe, challenges the miserly Grand Duke Rudolph to such a duel and wins, thus taking over the reins of government. There are soon many claimants to Ludwig's hand: his own fiancée the soubrette Lisa, the leading lady Julia Jellicoe, the aging Baroness von Krakenfeldt who had been about to wed Rudolph, and the Princess of Monte Carlo, engaged to Rudolph in infancy. Eventually, all is resolved when the notary Dr Tannhäuser discovers that the law states that the ace which Ludwig drew in the duel always counts low. Thus Ludwig never was Grand Duke, and the couples sort themselves out to their mutual satisfaction. [R]

Grande-Duchesse de Gérolstein, La
Operetta in three acts by Offenbach. 1st perf Paris, 12 April 1867; libr by Henri Meilhac and Ludovic Halévy. Principal roles: Grand-Duchess (mezzo), Fritz (ten), Wanda (sop), Gen Boum (b-bar), Prince Paul (ten), Baron Puck (ten). One of Offenbach's most brilliant musical and political satires, Bismarck said of its portrayal of petty German princedoms, 'C'est tout à fait ça.' An instant and triumphant success, it has remained popular ever since.
Plot: The imaginary German duchy of Gerolstein. The Prime Minister Baron Puck wishes his amorous Grand-Duchess to wed the wimpish Prince Paul, but she has an eye for the military. That eye lights upon Fritz, whose sweetheart Wanda is desired by the bombastic military commander Gen Boum. She promotes Fritz through the ranks from private to commander-in-chief in the space of five minutes, to the fury of Boum. Fritz wins a bloodless battle, but refuses the Duchess's love because of Wanda. The piqued Duchess joins a conspiracy by Boum, Puck and Paul to remove Fritz. Persuaded to marry Paul, she allows Fritz to be tricked and humiliated, and then demotes him with the same rapidity with which she promoted him. Fritz and Wanda are reunited, Boum is reinstated and the Duchess, although lumbered with Paul, soon notices another handsome soldier. [R]

Grandi, Margerita (b Marguerite Garde) (b 1894)
Australian (Tasmanian) soprano, particularly associated with dramatic Italian roles. She possessed a powerful voice and was a forceful singing-actress in the grand manner. She created the title-role in Massenet's *Amadis* and Diana in Bliss's *The Olympians*.

Grandier
Baritone role in Penderecki's *The Devils of Loudun*. He is the historical Urbain Grandier (1590–1634), a worldly Catholic priest.

Grand Inquisitor
Bass role in Verdi's *Don Carlos*. He is the blind, 90-year-old Hernando Valdés, Cardinal-Archbishop of Seville.

Grand Macabre, Le
Opera in two acts by Ligeti. 1st perf Stockholm, 12 April 1978; libr by the composer and Michael Meschke, after Michel de Ghelderode's *La Balade du Grand Macabre*. Principal roles: Nekrotzar (b-bar), Piet the Pot (ten), Astradamors (bass), Spermando (sop), Clitoria (sop), Mescalina (mezzo), Prince Go-Go (c-ten),

Secret Police Chief (sop). Ligeti's only opera, it is a black comedy revolving around sex, politics, drink and death. Written in aggressively avant-garde style and employing some strange instruments such as motor horns and outsize mallets, it has been widely performed, even though its language and subject-matter have shocked the easily offended.
Plot: The imaginary dictatorship of Breugheland. Human activity has been reduced to its lowest levels: the populist politician Piet the Pot is permanently drunk; Spermando and Clitoria spend their entire time in ceaseless copulation; the marriage of Mescalina and Astradamors is kept alive only through the lavish employment of sex-aids and sadomasochism; Prince Go-Go is surrounded by sycophantic politicians; and the proclamations of the Secret Police Chief are COLORATURA gibberish. Nekrotzar claims to be Death, but when he announces the End of the World even his powers are seemingly weakened by overindulgence. [R]

Grand opera
A vague term which can have a number of meanings, including: **1** In Britain, an opera on a serious subject with no spoken dialogue. Sullivan's *Ivanhoe*, for example, is described as a grand opera. **2** Very loosely, a large-scale spectacular opera, such as *Aida* or *Rienzi*. **3** Most accurately, the type of opera (frequently with libretti by Eugène Scribe) produced at the Paris Opéra in the first half of the 19th century. These are in four, or more usually five acts, are on heroic subjects requiring magnificent scenic effects and had to include a ballet. Pioneered by Spontini, they are epitomized by Halévy's *La Juive* and the mature operas of Meyerbeer, and also include Berlioz's *Les Troyens* and Massenet's *Le Cid*. The works written by Italians for the Opéra also fall into this category: Rossini's *Guillaume Tell*, Donizetti's *La Favorite* and *Dom Sébastien* and Verdi's *Les Vêpres Siciliennes* and *Don Carlos*.

Grand Théâtre, Geneva
The opera house (cap 1,488) in this Swiss city opened in Dec 1952, replacing the previous theatre of the same name which had opened in Oct 1879 but which burnt down in 1951. It has enjoyed a high reputation in recent times, particularly when Herbert Graf was director of productions, and it has an enterprising repertory policy. The annual season runs from September to June. Musical directors have included Ernest Ansermet, and the resident orchestra is the Suisse Romande.

Grand Théâtre, Liège
The opera house (cap 1,246) in this city in Belgium opened in 1820. The home of the Opéra Royale de Wallonie from 1967 to 1974, it is now the base of the Centre Lyrique de Wallonie. Musical directors have included Edgar Doneux.

Grand Théâtre, Marseilles
The opera house (cap 1,786) in this French city in Provence opened in 1924. It gives an annual season from October to May with a predominantly Italian and French repertory. Musical directors have included Reynaldo Giovanninetti and Diego Masson.

Grand Théâtre, Nancy
The opera house (cap 1,310) in this French city in Vosges opened on 14 Oct 1919.

Grand Théâtre Graslin, Nantes
The opera house in this town in Loire-Atlantique (France) opened on 23 Mar 1788; it burnt down in 1796, reopened after rebuilding on 3 May 1813 and was renovated (cap 980) in 1968. The home since 1973 of the Opéra de Nantes et des Pays de la Loire, it shares productions with Avignon, Rouen and Tours. Musical directors have included Jésus Etcheverry.

Grand Théâtre Municipal, Bordeaux
The opera house (cap 1,205) in this French city in the Gironde was designed by Victor Louis and opened in 1780 and was rebuilt in 1977. The annual season runs from October to May, and productions are shared with the Toulouse Capitole.

Grane
The name of Brünnhilde's horse in Wagner's *Der Ring des Nibelungen*.

Graun, Carl Heinrich (c 1704–59)
German composer, largely resident in Berlin, brother of the composer **Johann Gottlieb Graun**. Court composer to Frederick the Great of Prussia (who wrote the libretti for four of his operas), he was one of the leading exponents in Germany of the OPERA SERIA style. His 33 operas include *Cleopatra e Cesare* (Berlin, 7 Dec 1742; libr Giovanni Gualberto Bottarelli, after Pierre Corneille's *La Mort de Pompée*), MONTEZUMA and *Merope* (Berlin, 27 Mar 1756; libr Frederick the Great). After a long period of complete neglect, there has recently been a minor revival of interest in his operas.

Graz Opernhaus
The present opera house (cap 1,400) in this town in Styria (Austria) opened in 1899. Musical directors have included Franz Schalk and Berislav Klobučar.

Great Britain
see ALDEBURGH FESTIVAL; BEECHAM OPERA COMPANY; BRITISH BROADCASTING CORPORATION; BRITISH NATIONAL OPERA COMPANY; BUXTON FESTIVAL; CAMDEN FESTIVAL; CARL ROSA OPERA COMPANY; CHELSEA OPERA GROUP; D'OYLY CARTE OPERA COMPANY; EDINBURGH FESTIVAL; ENGLISH BACH FESTIVAL; ENGLISH MUSIC THEATRE; ENGLISH NATIONAL OPERA; ENGLISH OPERA GROUP; GLYNDEBOURNE FESTIVAL; GLYNDEBOURNE TOURING OPERA; HANDEL OPERA SOCIETY; KENT OPERA; LONDON OPERA CENTRE; NATIONAL OPERA STUDIO; NEW OPERA COMPANY; NEW SADLER'S WELLS OPERA; OPERA FACTORY; OPERA NORTH; OPERA NORTHERN IRELAND; OPERA RARA; ROYAL OPERA HOUSE, COVENT GARDEN; SCOTTISH OPERA; WELSH NATIONAL OPERA

Greece
see GREEK NATIONAL OPERA

Greek drama
The originators of opera in the late 16th century developed the form as an attempt to recreate classical Greek tragedy, taking as their cue Aristotle's description of drama as 'words sweetened by music'. Classical Athenian drama was indeed chanted to an orchestral accompaniment and involved both dance and choral singing. The earliest opera composers all took their subject matter from Graeco-Roman mythology, as did Gluck for his reform operas. The Greek tragedies have been important source material for 18th-century OPERA SERIA and also in the later 20th century (Buller's *The Bacchae* sets Euripides's original Greek almost verbatim). Well over 250 operas have been based directly on the plays of the Athenian tragedians AESCHYLUS, SOPHOCLES and EURIPIDES. In addition, a few operas have been based on Aristophanes's comedies.

Greek National Opera (*Ethniki Lyriki Skini* in Greek)
The company was founded in 1939 and achieved its present form in 1944. Based at the Olympia Theatre (cap 1,000) in Athens, it also visits Salonika and sometimes gives open-air performances in the classical amphitheatre at Epidauros. The annual season runs from November to May. Artistic directors have included Kostas Paskalis.

Greek opera composers
see KALOMIRIS; XENAKIS; XYNDAS

Other national opera composers include Dionysios Lavrangas (1864–1951), Andreas Nezeritis (1897–1980), Spiros Samaras (1863–1917) and Marios Varvoglis (1885–1967).

Greek Passion, The (*Řecké Pašije*)
Opera in four acts by Martinů. 1st perf Zürich, 9 June 1961; libr by the composer, after Nikos Kazantzakis's *Christ Recrucified*. Principal roles: Grigoris (bass), Michelis (ten), Kostandis (bar), Yannakos (ten), Catherine (sop), Manolios (ten), Panait (ten), Lenio (sop), Fotis (b-bar). One of Martinů's finest operas, sadly only infrequently performed, it is notable for its superb choral writing, based on the composer's study of Orthodox church music.
Plot: Early-20th-century Greece. The inhabitants of a village are to put on a passion play, and the various local actors begin to take on the characteristics of the individuals they are to portray. The rich farmer's son Manolios, who is to play Jesus, begs for compassion for a group of refugees and is supported by the local

whore Catherine, who is to play Mary Magdalene, and by the three apostles (Michelis, Kostandis and Yannakos). The priest Grigoris denies shelter to the refugees and excommunicates Manolios who he feels is undermining his authority. Manolios is then killed by Panait, who is to play Judas Iscariot. [R]

Gregor, Albert
Tenor role in Janáček's *The Macropolus Case*. He is a disputant in the Gregor vs Prus case.

Greindl, Josef (1912–93)
German bass, particularly associated with Wagnerian roles, especially Gurnemanz in *Parsifal*. One of the finest Germanic basses of the immediate post-war period, he had a rich voice used with outstanding artistry. He created, for Orff, the Chorus Leader in *De Temporum Fine Comoedia* and a role in *Antigonae*.

Gremin, Prince
Bass role in Tchaikovsky's *Eugene Onegin*. He is Tatyana's elderly husband.

Gretel
Soprano role in Humperdinck's *Hänsel und Gretel*. She is Hänsel's sister.

Grétry, André-Modeste (1741–1813)
Belgian composer. He wrote over 50 operas, achieving his greatest successes in OPÉRA-COMIQUE style. His operas are notable for their grace and elegance and for their charming melodies, but his self-confessed paucity in harmony tends after a while to lead to a feeling of sameness. The most important of his operas are LE HURON, his first major success and an early operatic example of the theme of Rousseau's 'noble savage', *Lucile* (Paris, 5 Jan 1769; libr Jean-François Marmontel) [R], *Le Tableau Parlant* (Paris, 20 Sept 1769; libr Louis Anseaume), ZÉMIRE ET AZOR, his most successful and enduring work, *Le Magnifique* (Paris, 4 Mar 1773; libr Jean-Marie Sedaine, after Jean de la Fontaine), *Le Jugement de Midas* (Paris, 28 Mar 1778; libr Thomas d'Hèle) [R], *L'Amant Jaloux* (Versailles, 20 Nov 1778; libr d'Hèle, after S. Centlivre's *The Wonder: a Woman Keeps a Secret*) [R], *La Caravane du Caire* (Fontainebleau, 30 Oct 1783; libr Étienne Morel de Chédeville) [R], RICHARD COEUR DE LION, his finest and most ambitious opera, and the once-popular *Guillaume Tell* (Paris, 9 Apr 1791; libr Sedaine, after Antoine Marin Lemierre).

Grieg, Edvard (1843–1907)
Norwegian composer. Best known as a composer of piano music, he also wrote one opera, the unfinished OLAV TRYGVASON.

Grieux, Chevalier des
The lover of Manon appears as a tenor role in: **1** Massenet's *Manon*. **2** Puccini's and Auber's *Manon Lescaut*. **3** Henze's *Boulevard Solitude*.

Grieux, Comte des
Bass role in Massenet's *Manon*. He is the Chevalier des Grieux's father.

Grigori
1 Tenor role in Moussorgsky's *Boris Godunov*. A young monk, he becomes the false pretender Dimitri. **2** Baritone role in Rimsky-Korsakov's *The Tsar's Bride*. He is in love with Marfa.

Grimgerde
Mezzo role in Wagner's *Die Walküre*. She is one of the Valkyries.

Griselda
Opera in three acts by Bononcini. 1st perf London, 22 Feb 1722; libr by Paolo Antonio Rolli, after Apostolo Zeno's libretto for Antonio Pollarolo. Principal roles: Griselda (mezzo), Ernesto (sop), Gualtiero (mezzo), Almirena (sop), Rambaldo (bass). One of Bononcini's most successful operas, it is nowadays virtually forgotten.
Plot: Palermo. King Gualtiero of Sicily has married the poor but beautiful Griselda, who has borne him a daughter. Inspired by the general Rambaldo, who loves Griselda, Gualtiero's subjects protest at his lowly marriage. To pacify them, Gualtiero has the child sent away, and she is believed lost at sea. Later, after further troubles, Gualtiero says that he will renounce Griselda and wed a princess – Almirena, brought up by the Prince of Puglia. She, accompanied by the prince's brother Ernesto whom she loves, arrives in

Sicily. Gualtiero recognizes her as his daughter, Rambaldo's intrigues are laid bare and Gualtiero acknowledges Griselda as his queen. [R Exc]

Griselda, La
Opera in three acts by A. Scarlatti. 1st perf Rome, Jan 1721; libr possibly by Prince Francesco Maria Ruspoli, after Apostolo Zeno's libretto for Antonio Pollarolo. Principal roles: Griselda (sop), Gualtiero (b-bar), Roberto (ten), Corrado (ten), Ottone (b-bar), Costanza (sop). Scarlatti's last extant opera, it is a fine work which deserves more than the very occasional airing which it currently receives.

Grisélidis
Opera in prologue and three acts by Massenet. 1st perf Paris, 20 Nov 1901; libr by Armande Silvestre and Eugène Morand, after Giovanni Boccaccio's *Decameron*. Principal roles: Grisélidis (sop), Devil (bar), Alain (ten), Marquis (bar), Fiamina (mezzo). Telling the same story as the 'the pleasant comedy of patient Griselidis' in Geoffrey Chaucer's *The Canterbury Tales*, it was reasonably successful at its appearance but is nowadays only very rarely performed. **Plot**: Medieval Provence. Grisélidis, wife of the Marquis de Saluces, is loved by the Shepherd Alain. The Devil, aided by his wife Fiamina, attempts to persuade her to accept Alain, maintaining that the Marquis is unfaithful. She refuses, and the Devil abducts her child. However, the Marquis succeeds in rescuing the child. [R]

Grisi, Giuditta (1805–40)
Italian mezzo. One of the outstanding mezzos of the first half of the 19th century, she created Romeo in Bellini's *I Capuleti e i Montecchi* and the title-role in L. Ricci's *Chiara di Rosembergh*. She tended to be overshadowed by her younger sister GUILIA GRISI and by her cousin, the great ballerina **Carlotta Grisi**.

Grisi, Giulia (1811–69)
Italian soprano, sister of the mezzo GIUDITTA GRISI and cousin of the ballerina **Carlotta Grisi**. Regarded as one of the greatest of all 19th-century sopranos, she possessed a rich and flexible voice, suitable for both dramatic and lyrical roles. She created the title-role in Coccia's *Rosmonda*, Adalgisa in *Norma*, Elvira in *I Puritani* and, for Donizetti, Adelia in *Ugo Conte di Parigi*, Norina in *Don Pasquale* and Elena in *Marino Faliero*. She retired in 1861 and her attempted comeback in 1866 as Lucrezia Borgia was a disaster. She lived for many years with the tenor GIOVANNI MARIO.

Grist, Reri (b 1932)
American soprano, particularly associated with Mozart roles and with COLORATURA roles such as Zerbinetta in Strauss's *Ariadne auf Naxos* and Oscar in Verdi's *Un Ballo in Maschera*. She possessed a sweet and agile voice, used with fine musicianship, and she had a most appealing stage presence.

Grossmächtige Prinzessin
Soprano aria for Zerbinetta in Strauss's *Ariadne auf Naxos*, in which she tries to persuade Ariadne to take a more light-hearted view of love. Described by Strauss as 'the grand COLORATURA aria with all the tricks'.

Groves, Sir Charles (1915–92)
British conductor, particularly associated with the Italian and British repertories. One of the most popular post-war British conductors, more successful in the concert hall than in the opera house, he was musical director of the Welsh National Opera (1961–3) and the English National Opera (1977–9). He conducted the first performance of Crosse's *The Story of Vasco*.

Gruberová, Edita (b 1946)
Slovakian soprano, particularly associated with Mozart roles and with COLORATURA roles, especially Zerbinetta in Strauss's *Ariadne auf Naxos* and the title-role in Donizetti's *Lucia di Lammermoor*. Her voice, if sometimes a little white, is of considerable size and of remarkable agility and is used with musicianship and an excellent technique. She has a good stage presence.

Gruenberg, Louis Theodore (1884–1964)
Polish-born American composer. His operas include THE EMPEROR JONES, by far his most successful work, *Jack and the Beanstalk* (New York, 31 Nov 1930; libr John Erskine) and the radio opera *Green*

Mansions (CBS, 17 Oct 1937; libr after W.H. Hudson).

Grümmer, Elisabeth (1911–86)
German soprano, particularly associated with Mozart and Strauss roles. She possessed a beautiful voice used with a fine technique and was an accomplished and affecting singing-actress.

Guadagni, Gaetano (c 1725–92)
Italian CASTRATO. Possessor of a superb voice and said to have been unrivalled as an operatic actor (he studied with David Garrick), he created, for Gluck, Orpheus in *Orfeo ed Euridice* and the title-role in *Telemaco*.

Guarany, Il
Opera in four acts by Gomes. 1st perf Milan, 19 March 1870; libr by Antonio Scalvini and Carlo d'Ormeville, after José Martiniano de Alençar's novel. Principal roles: Pery (ten), Cecilia (sop), Antonio (bass), Don Alvaro (ten), Gonzales (bar), Ruy-Bento (ten), Alonso (bass), Pedro (bass). Gomes's masterpiece, it was enormously successful at its appearance and is still occasionally performed. The *Symphonia do Guarany*, added in 1872, has become a second unofficial Brazilian national anthem.
Plot: Brazil, 1560. The Guarani prince Pery rescues his beloved Cecilia from the Spaniards Alonso, Ruy-Bento and Gonzales, who had planned to hand her over to the enemy Aymara tribe. Cecilia's father Don Antonio de Mariz rescues them from hostile Indians. Pery and Cecilia reach safety and freedom, but Antonio is killed when a dynamite charge explodes in his castle, also killing the Spanish villains. [R]

Guarnieri, Antonio (1880–1952)
Italian conductor and composer, particularly associated with the Italian repertory. Mainly based at La Scala, Milan, he was one of the finest Italian conductors of the inter-war period and conducted the first performances of Respighi's *Belfagor* and Casella's *Il Deserto Tentato*. He also composed two operas. His sons **Arrigo** (1910–75) and **Ferdinando** (*b* 1936) were also both conductors.

Guatemalan opera composers
These include José Escolástico Andrino and Jesús Castillo (1877–1946).

Gueden, Hilde (1917–88)
Austrian soprano, particularly associated with Mozart and Strauss roles. She had a beautiful silvery voice which was able to encompass lyrical, SOUBRETTE and COLORATURA roles. She also sang a number of Italian roles and enjoyed considerable success in Viennese operetta.

Guelfi, Giangiacomo (b 1924)
Italian baritone, particularly associated with Verdi and Puccini roles. He had a large, powerful and exciting voice and was an extrovert stage performer. He created Lazzaro in Pizzetti's *La Figlia di Iorio*, a Priest in Dallapiccola's *Il Prigioniero* and roles in Castro's *Proserpina y el Extranjero*, Napoli's *Masaniello* and Mortari's *La Figlia del Diavolo*.

Guercoeur
Opera in three acts (five tableaux) by Magnard (Op 12). 1st perf Paris, 24 April 1931 (composed 1900); libr by the composer. Principal roles: Guercoeur (bar), Vérité (sop), Heurtal (ten), Giselle (mezzo). Magnard's finest opera, the orchestral parts of two acts were destroyed in 1914 when advancing Germans burnt down Magnard's house, killing him; they were reconstructed by his friend Guy Ropartz. An austere and powerful work in Wagnerian style, it is only very rarely performed.
Plot: In a paradise ruled by the supreme deity Truth, Guercoeur, dead for two years, misses his earthly existence. Truth restores him to life. Despite her oath of fidelity, his wife Giselle has a new lover, Heurtal. His people, who he had freed from tyranny, are discontented and riven by faction, and Heurtal plans to seize power. The crowd repudiates Guercoeur's mediation attempts and puts him to death before turning on each other and then acclaiming Heurtal as dictator. Returned to Truth's domain, Guercoeur acknowledges that his dream of peace, love and freedom will not become reality until far into the future. [R]

Guerre des Bouffons (French for 'war of the comic actors'; also known as *Querelle des Bouffons*)
The name given to one of the most extraordinary episodes in operatic history, when all of Paris was divided from 1752 to 1754 between the supporters of traditional French serious opera as exemplified by Lully and Rameau, and those of the new Italian OPERA BUFFA, epitomized by Pergolesi's *La Serva Padrona.* The traditionalists included Louis XV, Madame de Pompadour, the court and the aristocracy; on the other hand, the Queen and the intellectuals (particularly Diderot, Rousseau and d'Alembert) supported the Italians for breathing new life into a moribund and stiflingly conventional form. Rousseau's contribution (in addition to composing operas in the Italian style, notably LE DEVIN DU VILLAGE) was his famous *Lettre sur la Musique Française* of 1753.

Guerrero y Torres, Jacinto (1895–1951)
Spanish composer. He wrote some 50 ZARZUELAS, of which the most successful included *La Alsaciana* (Barcelona, 12 Nov 1921; libr José Ramos Martín) [R], *La Montería* (Zaragoza, 24 Nov 1922; libr Ramos Martín) [R], *Los Gavilanes* (Madrid, 7 Dec 1923; libr Ramos Martín) [R] and *El Huésped del Sevillano* (Madrid, 3 Dec 1926; libr Enrique Reoyo and Juan Ignacio Luca de Tena, after Miguel Cervantes's *La Ilustre Fregona)* [R].

Guglielmi, Pietro Alessandro (1728–1804)
Italian composer. He wrote 103 operas, all of them now forgotten, achieving his greatest success with comedy, where his innovations were admired by Rossini. In his serious operas, such as *Tito Manlio* (Rome, 8 Jan 1763; libr G. Roccaforte), he considerably expanded the role of the chorus. His son **Pietro Carlo** (*c* 1763–1817) was also a composer. His most successful opera was *Paolo e Virginia* (Naples, 2 Jan 1817; libr Giuseppe Maria Diodati, after Bernadin de Saint-Pierre).

Guglielmo
Baritone role in Mozart's *Così fan Tutte.* He is an officer in love with Fiordiligi.

Guglielmo Ratcliff (*William Ratcliff*)
Opera in four acts by Mascagni. 1st perf Milan, 16 Feb 1895; libr by Count Andrea Maffei, after Heinrich Heine's *Wilhelm Ratcliff.* Principal roles: Guglielmo (ten), Maria (sop), Count Douglas (bar), MacGregor (bass), Margherita (mezzo). Reasonably successful at its appearance, it is nowadays only very rarely performed.
Plot: 17th-century Scotland. Ratcliff (Guglielmo) falls in love with Maria and vows to kill anyone who tries to marry her. Count Douglas becomes engaged to Maria and Ratcliff challenges him to a duel, in which Douglas spares his life. Maria learns from her nurse Margherita that Ratcliff's father and her mother had once hoped to marry but were prevented from doing so, that her mother married her father MacGregor instead, and that MacGregor had killed Ratcliff's father. The injured Ratcliff bursts in, kills Maria and dies. On discovering the two corpses, Douglas commits suicide.

Gui, Vittorio (1885–1975)
Italian conductor and composer, particularly associated with Rossini and Mozart operas. One of the outstanding conductors of the inter-war period, he was a co-founder of the Maggio Musicale Fiorentino in 1933 and was musical director of the Glyndebourne Festival (1952–63). He conducted the first performance of Lualdi's *Il Diavolo nel Campanile* and also composed several operas, including *Fata Malerba* (Turin, 15 May 1927; libr Fausto Salvatori).

Guillard, Nicolas François (1752–1814)
French librettist. Less prolific than most of his contemporaries, but producing work of a far higher standard, he wrote some dozen libretti, including texts for Grétry, Lesueur (*La Mort d'Adam*), Paisiello, Sacchini (three, including *Oedipe à Colone*), Salieri (*Les Horaces*) and Gluck (*Iphigénie en Tauride*). This last was described by Alfred Einstein as 'the best book that ever came into Gluck's hands'.

Guillaume Tell (*William Tell*)
Opera in four acts by Rossini. 1st perf Paris, 3 Aug 1829; libr by Victor Joseph Étienne de Jouy, Florent Bis and Armand

Marrast, after Friedrich von Schiller's *Wilhelm Tell*. Principal roles: Tell (bar), Arnold (ten), Mathilde (sop), Walter (bass), Edwige (mezzo), Melcthal (bass), Jemmy (sop), Gesler (bass), Roudi (ten). Rossini's last, longest, most serious and most ambitious opera, it is hampered by its appalling libretto and has suffered from disfiguring cuts almost from its inception. It is an uneven work, but in the scenes which fired his imagination Rossini wrote some of his greatest and noblest music, as well as providing the work with perhaps the most famous of all operatic overtures. The great scene of the summoning of the cantons was highly praised by Wagner and Berlioz and prompted Donizetti to remark 'Acts I and III may have been written by Rossini, but Act II was written by God.' It has had a considerably increased number of productions in the last decade, but it is still not performed as often as its merits deserve.

Plot: Uri (Switzerland), 1307. The Swiss patriot Tell helps a fugitive to escape from the occupying Austrians, who arrest Melcthal, the father of Arnold, who is in love with the Habsburg princess Mathilde. She wishes Arnold to join the Austrians and marry her, but he joins the patriots when he learns that the Austrians have executed his father. He witnesses the oath of the cantons to resist the Austrians, which is led by Tell and Walter Furst. Tell and his young son Jemmy refuse to pay homage to the tyrannical Austrian governor Gesler, and Tell is forced to shoot an apple placed on Jemmy's head. Stating that if he had failed he would have shot a second arrow at Gesler, he is arrested. However, Mathilde – having rescued Jemmy – gives herself as a hostage for Tell to the patriots. Jemmy sets fire to the house of Tell and his wife Edwige as the signal for the revolt led by Arnold. During a storm Tell escapes from the boat taking him to captivity, kills Gesler and joins the patriots in a victory over the Austrians. [R]

Guillot de Morfontaine

Tenor role in Massenet's *Manon*. He is an ageing roué.

Guiraud, Ernest (1837–92)

French composer. He wrote eight operas, all of them now forgotten, including *Le Kobold* (Paris, 2 July 1870; libr Charles Nuitter and Louis Gallet), *Madame Turlupin* (Paris, 23 Nov 1872; libr Eugène Cormon and C. Grandvallet), *Piccolino* (Paris, 11 Apr 1876; libr Nuitter, after Victorien Sardou) and *Frédégonde* (Paris, 18 Dec 1895; libr Gallet), which was left unfinished at his death and which was completed by Saint-Saëns and Dukas. Nowadays he is largely remembered for having completed Offenbach's *Les Contes d'Hoffmann* and for having provided recitatives for *Carmen*. He was also a noted teacher, whose pupils included Debussy, and his *Traité d'Instrumentation* (1895) was one of the earliest analyses of Wagner.

Günther

Baritone role in Wagner's *Götterdämmerung*. Gutrune's brother, he is the leader of the Gibichungs.

Guntram

Opera in three acts by Strauss (Op 25). 1st perf Weimar, 10 May 1894; libr by the composer. Principal roles: Guntram (ten), Freihild (sop), Friedhold (bass), Duke Robert (bar), Jester (ten). Strauss's first opera, it was dedicated to Verdi but is written in imitation of Wagner. A failure at its appearance, it is nowadays only very rarely performed.

Plot: 13th-century Germany. Wishing to free the populace from Duke Robert's tyrannical rule, Guntram kills Robert in a duel. Subsequently, because he feels guilty for having loved Robert's wife Freihild, he gives her up to embark upon a life of solitude. [R]

Guridi y Bidaolo, Jesús (1886–1961)

Spanish composer. One of the leading 20th-century Basque composers, his stage works include the operas *Mirentxu* (Bilbao, 31 May 1910; libr A. Echave) and *Amaya* (Bilbao, 23 May 1920; libr J.M. Arroita Jáuregui) and a number of ZARZUELAS, of which *El Caserío* (Madrid, 11 Nov 1926; libr Federico Romero and Carlos Fernández Shaw) [R] was highly successful.

Gurnemanz

Bass role in Wagner's *Parsifal*. He is an old knight of the Grail.

Gustafson, Nancy (b 1956)
American soprano, particularly associated with the Italian and Czech repertories. She possesses a rich and beautiful voice used with artistry and great intelligence and she is a committed and highly affecting singing-actress. One of the finest artists to have come to prominence in recent years. Her husband **Brian Dickie** (*b* 1941) is an administrator, who was artistic director of the Wexford Festival (1967–73), general administrator of the Glyndebourne Festival (1980–88) and general director of the Canadian Opera Company (1989–93).

Gustave III or *Le Bal Masqué (The Masked Ball)*
Opera in five acts by Auber. 1st perf Paris, 27 Feb 1833; libr by Eugène Scribe. Principal roles: Gustave (ten), Amélie (sop), Ankastrom (bar), Oscar (sop), Arvedson (mezzo), Ribbing (bass), Dehorn (bass). One of Auber's finest operas, it was very successful at its appearance but is nowadays hardly ever performed and is only remembered as the source for Verdi's *Un Ballo in Maschera*.

Gustavo
1 Tenor role in Verdi's *Un Ballo in Maschera*. He is King Gustavus III of Sweden. **2** Bass role in Händel's *Faramondo*. He is King of the Cimbrians.

Guthrie, Sir Tyrone (1900–71)
British producer, particularly associated with Sadler's Wells Opera. One of the leading British theatre producers of the immediate post-war era, his productions were noted for their dramatic naturalness and for their vivid handling of the chorus. His autobiography, *A Life in the Theatre*, was published in 1960.

Gutrune
Soprano role in Wagner's *Götterdämmerung*. She is Günther's sister.

Gwendoline
Opera in two acts by Chabrier. 1st perf Brussels, 10 April 1886; libr by Catulle Mendès. Principal roles: Gwendoline (sop), Armel (ten), Harald (bar). Chabrier's only completed serious opera, it is heavily influenced by Wagner. It is nowadays hardly ever performed, although the fine overture is still remembered.
Plot: 8th-century Britain. Gwendoline, daughter of the captured Saxon chieftain Armel, is handed over as bride to the Viking leader Harald, with orders to kill Harald on their wedding night. Gwendoline, however, falls in love with Harald. Their attempted escape from a Saxon attack is foiled and the two perish together at the stake.

Gypsy Baron, The
see ZIGEUNERBARON, DER

Gypsy Princess, The
see CSÁRDÁSFÜRSTIN, DIE

Gyrowetz, Adalbert
see JÍROVEC, VOJTĚCH

H

Hába, Alois (1893–1973)
Czech composer. The leading exponent of microtonal music, his first opera **THE MOTHER** is the most important **QUARTER-TONE OPERA**. His second opera, the unperformed *New Earth* (*Nová Země*, 1936; libr Fedor Gladkov and Ferdinand Půjman), is in the traditional semitonal system, but his last opera, the also unperformed *Thy Kingdom Come* (*Přijd Království Tvé*, 1942; libr composer, after Půjman), employs sixth-tones. Hába's interest in quarter-tone music derived from its use by Moravian folk singers, who employ microtonal inflections to darken or brighten the mood of the music they are singing. Despite the respect and interest which his operas aroused, they have been little performed, partly, no doubt, because of the obvious practical difficulty for singers to pitch microtones accurately. His brother **Karel** (1898–1972) was also a composer. His three operas are *Jánošík* (Prague, 23 Feb 1934; libr Antonín Klášterský), *Ancient History* (*Stará Historie*, Prague Radio, 25 Sept 1940) and the children's opera *Smolíček* (Prague Radio, 28 Sept 1950; libr V. Čtvrtek).

Habañera
A Spanish song and dance in 2/4 time. Its origins are Cuban, deriving from the dancing of the *ñañigos*, the black inhabitants of a district of Havana (Habana in Spanish). The best-known operatic example is 'L'Amour est un oiseau rebelle' in Bizet's *Carmen*, which is adapted from the song 'El Arregilito' by the Spanish composer Sebastián Yradier (1809–65).

Hab' mir's gelobt
Soprano/soprano/mezzo trio for Sophie, the Marschallin and Octavian in Act III of Strauss's *Der Rosenkavalier*, in which the Marschallin resigns herself to Octavian's love for a girl of his own age.

Habunek, Vlado (1906–94)
Croatian producer. Internationally respected for both theatre and opera direction, his productions were traditional in the best sense of the word. Based largely at the Croatian National Theatre, he also worked widely in Britain and the United States. His most successful productions included several Britten operas as well as his work at Covent Garden (Moussorgsky's *Khovanschina* and Shostakovich's *Katerina Ismailova*) and the New York City Opera (the first performance of Weisgall's *Nine Rivers From Jordan*).

Haddon Hall
Operetta in two acts by Sullivan. 1st perf London, 24 Sept 1892; libr by Sydney Grundy. Principal roles: Dorothy (sop), John (ten), Dorcas (mezzo), Rupert (bass), Sir George (b-bar), Lady Vernon (mezzo), Oswald (ten). Successful at its appearance, it is nowadays hardly ever performed.
Plot: England, 1660. Dorothy, daughter of the Royalist Sir George Vernon, is betrothed to her cousin, the Puritan Rupert, but she loves the Royalist John Manners and rejects Rupert. With the aid of her maid Dorcas, she elopes with John. Cheated of his bride, Rupert dispossesses Sir George of his estate. However, news arrives of the restoration of Charles II, so that all ends happily – except for Rupert.

Hadjibeyov, Uzeir (1885–1948)
Azerbaijani composer. Founder of the first Azerbaijani school of music in 1922, he wrote seven operas in addition to a number of successful musical comedies. His operas are *Leila and Medjun* (Baku, 25 Jan 1908; libr composer, after Mohammed Fizuli), *Sheikh Senan* (Baku, 1909; libr composer), *Rustam and Sohrab* (Baku, 1910; libr composer, after Firdousi), *Asli and Kerem* (Baku, 1912; libr composer), *Shah Abbas and Hurshidbanu* (Baku, 1912; libr composer), the unperformed *Harun and Leila* (1915) and the epic *Kyor-Oly* (Moscow, 30 Apr 1937; libr M. Ordubadi [R], his most successful

opera. His brother **Zulfugar** (1884–1950) was also a composer who wrote one opera, *Ashug Garib* (Baku, 13 May 1916; libr composer).

Hadley, Henry (1871–1937)
American composer. He wrote six operas, some of which enjoyed success in their time but which are nowadays all forgotten. They are *Nancy Brown* (New York, 1903; libr F. Ranken), *Safié* (Mainz, 4 Apr 1909; libr E. Oxenford), *Azora, Daughter of Montezuma* (Chicago, 26 Dec 1917; libr David Stevens), *Bianca* (New York, 18 Oct 1918; libr G. Stewart, after Carlo Goldoni's *La Locandiera*), *Cleopatra's Night* (New York, 31 Jan 1920; libr Alice Leal Pollock, after Théophile Gautier's *Une Nuit de Cléopâtre*) and the radio opera *A Night in Old Paris* (NBC, 20 Jan 1930; libr F. Truesdell, after G. McDonough).

Hadley, Jerry (b 1952)
American tenor, particularly associated with Mozart and with lighter Italian and French roles. Possessing a pleasant lyric voice and having a good stage presence, he has also enjoyed great success in musical comedies.

Haeffner, Johann Christian (1759–1833)
German composer, resident in Sweden from 1781. Best known as a choral composer, he also wrote one opera, the fine *Electra* (Drottningholm, 22 July 1787; libr Adolf Fredrik Ristell and Nicolas-François Guillard, after Sophocles) [R].

Häfliger, Ernst (b 1919)
Swiss tenor, particularly associated with Mozart roles and with 20th-century operas. A stylish singer of fine musicianship, he created Tiresias in Orff's *Antigonae*, roles in Blacher's *Zweihunderttausand Taler* and *Zwischenfälle bei einer Notlandung* and roles in operas by Frank Martin. His son **Andreas** is a pianist.

Hagegård, Håkan (b 1945)
Swedish baritone, particularly associated with Mozart roles, especially Papageno in *Die Zauberflöte*, which he played in Ingmar Bergman's film. He has a warm and easily-produced voice, used with intelligence and musicianship, and has a most engaging stage personality. He created Crispin in Werle's *Tintomara*, Beaumarchais in Corigliano's *The Ghosts of Versailles* and the Officer in Lidholm's *A Dream Play*. His wife **Barbara Bonney** (*b* 1956) is a successful lyric soprano, and his cousin **Erland** (*b* 1944) is a tenor.

Hagen
Bass role in Wagner's *Götterdämmerung*. Alberich's son, he is Günther's evil half-brother.

Hagen Opera
The opera house in this German city in North-Rhine Westphalia opened in 1911. Damaged by bombs in 1944, it was rebuilt (cap 940) in 1949. Musical directors have included Martin Fischer-Dieskau.

Hager, Leopold (b 1935)
Austrian conductor, particularly associated with Mozart, all of whose early operas he has recorded with the Salzburg Mozarteum. He was musical director of the Freiburg Opera (1965–9).

Hahn, Reynaldo (1875–1947)
Venezuelan composer and conductor, largely resident in France. He wrote many stage works, both operas and operettas, much the most successful being CIBOULETTE. His other works include *Mozart* (Paris, 2 Dec 1925; libr Sacha Guitry) and *Le Marchand de Venise* (Paris, 25 Mar 1935; libr Miguel Zamacoïs, after Shakespeare's *The Merchant of Venice*). He was director of the Paris Opéra (1945–6).

Haitink, Bernard (b 1929)
Dutch conductor, particularly associated with Mozart, Strauss and Wagner operas. Quickly establishing himself as one of the outstanding post-war symphonic conductors, his operative appearances were rare until 1976. He was musical director of the Glyndebourne Festival (1978–88) and Covent Garden (1988–).

Haken, Eduard (b 1910)
Czech bass, particularly associated with the Czech repertory, especially Kecal in Smetana's *The Bartered Bride* and the Watersprite in Dvořák's *Rusalka*. He had a rich and powerful voice and was a fine singing-actor, equally at home in serious or comic roles.

Halévy, Fromental (b Elias Lévy) (1799–1862)
French composer, father-in-law of Bizet and uncle of the librettist LUDOVIC HALÉVY. He wrote 37 operas and, along with Meyerbeer, may be regarded as the archetypal composer of the mid-19th-century French grand opera tradition. His most successful operas include *Clari* (Paris, 9 Dec 1829; libr Pietro Giannone), LA JUIVE, his masterpiece and his only opera which is still remembered, the comedy *L'Éclair* (Paris, 16 Dec 1835; libr Jules-Henri Vernoy de Saint-Georges and François-Antoine-Eugène de Planard), *La Reine de Chypre* (Paris, 22 Dec 1841; libr Saint-Georges), *La Tempestà* (London, 8 June 1850; libr Giannone and Eugène Scribe, after Shakespeare's *The Tempest*), *La Dame de Pique* (Paris, 28 Dec 1850; libr Scribe, after Prosper Mérimée's translation of Alexander Pushkin's *The Queen of Spades*) and the unfinished *Noé* (Karlsruhe, 5 Apr 1885; libr Saint-Georges), which was completed by Bizet. He also completed Hérold's unfinished *Ludovic*. He was a noted teacher, whose pupils included Gounod, Lecocq, Massé, Saint-Saëns and Bizet.

Halévy, Ludovic (1834–1908)
French playwright and librettist, nephew of the composer FROMENTAL HALÉVY. One of the finest of all French librettists, he is best known for his texts (often written in collaboration with HENRI MEILHAC) for Offenbach, with their biting satire on Second Empire society. He provided libretti for Bizet (*Carmen* and *Le Docteur Miracle*), Delibes, Flotow (*Naida*), Lecocq (six, including *Le Petit Duc* and *Le Docteur Miracle*) and Offenbach (*Barbe-Bleue, La Belle Hélène, Les Brigands, La Chanson de Fortunio, La Grande-Duchesse de Gérolstein, Monsieur Choufleuri Restera Chez-Lui, Orphée aux Enfers, La Périchole, Pomme d'Api* and *La Vie Parisienne*). His play *Le Réveillon* is the source for *Die Fledermaus*.

Halka (*Helen*)
Opera is four (originally two) acts by Moniuszko. 1st perf Wilno, 11 Jan 1848; libr by Włodzimierz Wolski, after Kazimierz Władysław Wójcicki's *Góralka*. Revised version 1st perf Wilno, 28 Feb 1854. Principal roles: Halka (sop), Jontek (ten), Stolnik (bass), Janusz (bar), Zofia (mezzo). Moniuszko's most successful work and perhaps the most popular of all Polish operas, it is unaccountably only rarely performed outside Poland.
Plot: Late-18th-century Cracow and Tatras. Halka loves the nobleman Janusz, by whom she is pregnant, but he has become engaged to Zofia. He sends Halka back to her village, where the inhabitants become enraged at her treatment. Halka drowns herself in the river, news of which arrives as Janusz and Zofia are being married. The ceremony is aborted, and the peasantry drive them from the village. [R]

Hall, Sir Peter (b 1930)
British producer. Director of the National Theatre (1973–87), he has had a long association with opera, which he treats as total music theatre. He worked first at Covent Garden, most notably producing Schönberg's *Moses und Aron* and Wagner's *Tristan und Isolde*, but did not take up his post as co-director in 1971 because of artistic disagreements. Since then he has worked largely at Glyndebourne, where he was artistic director (1984–90), winning particular acclaim for his Mozart productions. He also produced the *Ring* at Bayreuth in 1983. Married for a time to the mezzo MARIA EWING, his autobiography, *Making an Exhibition of Myself*, was published in 1993.

Halle
see HÄNDEL FESTIVAL, HALLE

Hallé, Sir Charles (b Carl Halle) (1819–95)
German-born British conductor. Although best known as a symphonic conductor and as the founder of the Manchester orchestra which bears his name, he also conducted a number of operas in the early part of his career.

Hallén, Andreas (1846–1925)
Swedish composer and conductor. His three operas, heavily influenced by Wagner, are *Harald der Wiking* (Leipzig, 16 Oct 1881; libr Hans Herrig, after Adam Oehlenschläger's *Hagbarth and Signe*) [R Exc], which enjoyed considerable success, *Häxfällan* (Stockholm, 16 Mar

1896; libr Frans Hedberg; revised as *Valborgmässan*, Stockholm, 15 Mar 1902; libr revised E. von Enzberg) and *Valdemar's Treasure* (*Waldemarskatten*, Stockholm, 8 Apr 1899; libr A. Klinckowström).

Hallström, Ivar (1826–1901)
Swedish composer. He wrote a large number of operas and operettas, many of them inspired by Swedish folk legend. Several enjoyed considerable success in their time but are nowadays mostly forgotten. His most successful works include the operetta *The Enchanted Cat* (*Den Förtrollade Katten*, Stockholm, 20 Apr 1869; libr Frans Hedberg), *The Miller-Wolf* (*Mjölnarvargen*, Stockholm 18 Feb 1871; libr after Michel Carré and Eugène Cormon's *Le Diable au Moulin*), *The Bewitched* (*Den Bergtagna*, Stockholm, 24 May 1874; libr Hedberg), his finest work which is still occasionally revived in Sweden, *The Vikings* (*Vikingarna*, Stockholm, 6 June 1877; libr Hedberg), *The Silver Ring* (*Silverringen*, Stockholm, 13 Dec 1880; libr after Léon Battu and Jules Barbier), the operetta *Neaga* (Stockholm, 24 Feb 1885; libr Queen Carmen Sylva of Romania) and *The Devil's Snares* (*Den Ondes Snaror*, Göteborg, 7 Mar 1900; libr H. Christiernson).

Hamburg State Opera
The present opera house (cap 1,674) was designed by Gerhard Weber and opened in 1874. Bombed in 1943, it reopened in 1955. One of Germany's leading houses, it has had a long tradition of presenting 20th-century works, particularly when Rolf Liebermann was administrator (1959–72). The annual season runs from August to June. Musical directors have included Hans von Bülow, Mahler, Felix Weingartner, Egon Pollack, Karl Böhm, Eugen Jochum, Leopold Ludwig, Horst Stein, Christoph von Dohnányi and Gerd Albrecht.

Hamilton, Iain (b 1922)
British composer, writing first in serial style and later in a more tonal form. His stage works, some of which have met with success in Britain, are all written to his own libretti. They include the unperformed *Agamemnon* (1969; libr after Aeschylus), THE ROYAL HUNT OF THE SUN, THE CATILINE CONSPIRACY, *Tamburline* (BBC Radio, 14 Mar 1977; libr after Christopher Marlowe), *Anna Karenina* (London, 7 May 1981; libr after Leo Tolstoy) and *Lancelot* (Arundel, 24 Aug 1985; libr after Thomas Malory's *Morte d'Arthur*).

Hamlet
Opera in five acts by Thomas. 1st perf Paris, 9 March 1868; libr by Jules Barbier and Michel Carré, after William Shakespeare's play. Principal roles: Hamlet (bar), Ophélie (sop), Laërte (ten), Gertrude (mezzo), Claudius (bass), Ghost (bass). Thomas's only opera apart from *Mignon* to have survived, it was enormously popular in the 19th century and still receives an occasional performance.
Plot: 14th-century Elsinore (Denmark). Prince Hamlet vows vengeance when he learns from his father's ghost that his father was killed by his brother Claudius who has usurped the throne. Hamlet feigns insanity, which causes his beloved Ophelia to lose her reason and commit suicide. Claudius poisons Hamlet's drink, but it is drunk instead by Queen Gertrude, who dies. Claudius engineers a duel between Hamlet and Ophelia's brother Laertes, in which both are mortally wounded. The dying Hamlet succeeds in stabbing Claudius. [R]

Hamlet
Opera in three acts by Searle (Op 48). 1st perf Hamburg, 6 March 1968; libr by the composer, after William Shakespeare's play. Principal roles: Hamlet (bar), Ophelia (mezzo), Claudius (ten), Gertrude (mezzo), Polonius (bass), Laertes (ten), Player King and Queen (bass and sop). Searle's most successful opera, the plot follows Shakespeare closely.

Hammond, Dame Joan (b 1912)
New Zealand soprano, particularly associated with the Italian repertory, especially Puccini. A greatly loved singer, she had a rich and beautiful lyric soprano which was, sadly, heard only intermittently in the opera house. Her autobiography, *A Voice, A Life*, was published in 1970.

Hammond-Stroud, Derek (b 1929)
British baritone, particularly associated

with the roles of Alberich in three of the *Ring* operas, Bunthorne in *Patience*, Melitone in Verdi's *La Forza del Destino*, Faninal in *Der Rosenkavalier* and Beckmesser in *Die Meistersinger von Nürnberg*. Possessor of a fine voice and phenomenal diction, he was an outstanding singing-actor, equally at home in serious or comic roles. He created the Old Fisherman in Williamson's *The Violins of St Jacques*.

Hampson, Thomas (b 1955)
American baritone, particularly associated with Mozart and with lyrical French and Italian roles. He possesses a warm and beautiful voice used with outstanding musicianship and is a fine singing-actor with a handsome stage presence. Equally distinguished in lieder as in opera, he has also enjoyed great success in a number of musicals. One of the finest artists to have come to the fore in recent years, he created Valmont in Conrad Susa's *Les Liaisons Dangereuses*.

Händel, Georg Friedrich (1685–1759)
German composer, largely resident in Britain. Apart from the masque ACIS AND GALATEA, his stage works fall into two categories: firstly, Italian OPERA SERIAS written between 1705 and 1741, and secondly dramatic oratorios, both sacred and secular, mostly written after 1743. Into the stiflingly formal structure of opera seria Händel poured magnificent and often highly dramatic music, and he may be regarded as the finest exponent of the genre. His early operas enjoyed great success, but owing to changes in public taste (epitomized by the success of *The Beggar's Opera* and its satire on the excesses of opera seria), they met with increasing disfavour. Turning to dramatic oratorios, a form which allowed him to use a chorus, Händel once again achieved great success.

His first opera ALMIRA was followed by *Nero* (Hamburg, 25 Feb 1705; libr Friedrich Christian Feustking), the music of which is lost, RODRIGO, AGRIPPINA and RINALDO, his first opera for London. His subsequent operas are II PASTOR FIDO, TESEO, SILLA, AMADIGI DI GAULA, RADAMISTO, *Muzio Scevola* (London, 15 Apr 1721; libr Paolo Antonio Rolli, after Silvio Stampiglia), which has an act each by Filippo Mattei, Händel and his great rival Bononcini, FLORIDANTE, OTTONE, FLAVIO, GIULIO CESARE, TAMERLANO, RODELINDA, SCIPIONE, ALESSANDRO, ADMETO, RICCARDO PRIMO, SIROE, TOLOMEO, LOTARIO, PARTENOPE, PORO, EZIO, SOSARME, ORLANDO, ARIANNA IN CRETA, ARIODANTE, ALCINA, ATALANTA, ARMINIO, GIUSTINO, BERENICE, FARAMONDO, SERSE, IMENEO and DEIDAMIA. His first dramatic oratorio was SAMSON. Originally performed in concert, they nonetheless conform to virtually all accepted notions of what constitutes an opera and they have been frequently staged in the 20th century. The most successful include SEMELE, HERCULES, SAUL, ATHALIA, BELSHAZZAR and JEPHTHA.

By the late 18th century, Händel operas had fallen into complete neglect. The 20th-century revival of interest in his stage works began in Germany in the 1920s. Since World War II, the revival has spread to Britain (pioneered by the work of the Handel Opera Society) and to the United States. Currently, Händel's stock stands higher than ever, with nearly all major opera companies including him in their regular repertories.

Händel Festival, Halle
An annual German festival in Saxony devoted to the operas of Händel, it was founded in 1953. Performances are given at the Theater des Friedens (cap 1,035), which originally opened in 1886.

Handel Opera Society
A British company founded in 1955 at the instigation of Edward J. Dent to revive public interest in Händel's stage works. Until its demise in 1985, it staged over 30 of Händel's operas and dramatic oratorios. The musical director was Charles Farncombe. There is also a Handel Opera Society in the United States.

Hand of Bridge, A
Mini-opera in one act by Barber (Op 35). 1st perf Spoleto, 17 June 1959; libr by Gian-Carlo Menotti. Principal roles: Sally (mezzo), Bill (ten), Geraldine (sop), David (bar). Lasting for just nine minutes, it is written in classical style with mild jazz overtones.
Plot: Two couples, bored with their mates, meet for their usual evening of bridge and

indulge in mental fantasies. Bill dreams of an extramarital affair, while his rebuffed wife Sally thinks of new clothes. Geraldine, estranged both from her husband David and from Bill with whom she had had a brief flirtation, is concerned about her dying mother. David rages at his job and dreams of erotic escape from the tedium of existence. [R]

Hannah
1 Mezzo role in Tippett's *The Ice Break*. A nurse, she is Gayle's black friend.
2 Soprano role in Birtwistle's *Yan Tan Tethera*. She is Alan's wife.

Hanover Opera
The present Niedersächsiches Staatstheater (cap 1,207) in this German city in Lower Saxony opened on 30 Nov 1950, replacing the previous Royal Opera House, which opened on 1 Sept 1852 but which was destroyed in World War II. Musical directors have included Marschner, Ludwig Fisher, Hans von Bülow, Arno Grau, Emil Ábrányi, Rudolf Krasselt, Franz Konwitschny, Johannes Schüler, Günther Wich, Georg Alexander Albrecht and Christoph Perick.

Hänsel und Gretel
Opera in three acts by Humperdinck. 1st perf Weimar, 23 Dec 1893; libr by Adelheid Wette, after Jacob and Wilhelm Grimm's *Fairy Tales*. Principal roles: Gretel (sop), Hänsel (mezzo), Peter (bar), Witch (mezzo), Gertrude (sop), Sandman (sop), Dew Fairy (sop). Humperdinck's greatest success and one of the most popular of all operas, it is an expansion in Wagnerian style of his earlier nursery music written for a children's play by his sister.
Plot: Legendary Harz Mountains. Gertrude scolds her children Hänsel and Gretel for playing instead of doing the household chores, and sends them off into the wood to pick strawberries. When their father Peter comes home, he is alarmed for the children's safety: a Witch lives in the wood and bakes children in her oven. The children lose their way in the wood and the Sandman sends them asleep and 14 angels to guard them. Roused by the Dew Fairy, they find a house made of sweets and surrounded by gingerbread children. Starting to eat, they are captured by the Witch. However, the children outwit the Witch, push her into her own oven and break her spell. Gretel releases the gingerbread children and when Peter and Gertrude, who have been searching for them, arrive, all join in a hymn of thanks. [R]

Hans Heiling
Opera in prologue and three acts by Marschner (Op 80). 1st perf Berlin, 24 May 1833; libr by Eduard Devrient, after Karl Theodor Körner. Principal roles: Heiling (bar), Anna (sop), Spirit Queen (sop), Konrad (ten). Marshner's finest and most successful opera, it is still occasionally performed.
Plot: 14th-century Harz Mountains. Hans Heiling, the son of a mortal father and the Spirit Queen, assumes human form and falls in love with Anna. She rejects him when she discovers who he really is and marries Konrad. Heiling's attempts to kill Konrad are thwarted by his mother, who takes him back to the spirit world. [R]

Hanslick, Eduard (1825–1904)
Austrian critic. An advocate of non-representational music, a theory he expounded in *Vom Musikalisch-Schönen* (1854), he came into conflict with the new ideas of Liszt and, even more so, of Wagner. Largely because of Wagner's merciless caricature of him as Beckmesser in *Die Meistersinger von Nürnberg*, he has gone down in history as the archetypal rigid, conservative and reactionary critic. In fact, he was far more generous, cultured and intelligent than his detractors would admit.

Hanson, Howard (1896–1982)
American composer. Best known as a symphonic composer, he also wrote one opera: *Merry Mount* (New York, 10 Feb 1934; libr Richard L. Stokes, after Nathaniel Hawthorne's *The May-Pole Lovers of Merry Mount*).

Hanuš, Ján (b 1915)
Czech composer. He wrote five operas: *The Flames* (*Plameny*, Plzeň, 8 Dec 1956; libr J. Pokorný), *The Servant of Two Masters* (*Sluha Dvou Pánů*, Plzeň, 18 Apr 1959; libr Pokorný, after Carlo Goldoni), *The Torch*

of Prometheus (*Pocodeň Prométheova*, Prague 30 Apr 1965; libr Pokorný, after Aeschylus), the unperformed *The Tale of One Night* (*Pohádka Jedné Noci*, 1968; libr Pokorný, after *The Thousand and One Nights*) and *A Dispute Over the Goddess* (*Spor o Bohyni*, Czech TV, 13 July 1986; libr composer, J.F. Fischer and A. Moskalyk, after Aristophanes).

Harašta
Baritone role in Janáček's *The Cunning Little Vixen*. He is a poacher.

Harewood, Earl of (b George Henry Hubert Lascelles) (b 1923)
British critic and administrator, first cousin of Queen Elizabeth II. He was controller of opera planning at Covent Garden (1953–60), artistic director of the Leeds Festival (1958–74) and of the Edinburgh Festival (1961–5) and managing director of the English National Opera (1972–86). He founded *Opera* magazine in 1950 and was its editor until 1953, and he edited and was a contributor to the revised *Kobbé's Complete Opera Book*.

Harlequin
The traditional COMMEDIA DELL'ARTE character appears in a number of operas, including: **1** Baritone role in Strauss's *Ariadne auf Naxos*. **2** Speaking role in Busoni's *Arlecchino*. **3** Tenor role in Cowie's *Commedia*. **4** Baritone role in Wolf-Ferrari's *Le Donne Curiose*. **5** Tenor role in Mascagni's *Le Maschere*.

Harmonie der Welt, Die (*The Harmony of the World*)
Opera in five scenes by Hindemith. 1st perf Munich, 11 Aug 1957; libr by the composer. Principal roles: Kepler (bar), Wallenstein (ten), Katharina (mezzo), Susanna (sop), Ferdinand II (bass), Tansur (bass), Grüsser (ten). Set during the Thirty Years' War, it deals with the life of the astronomer Johannes Kepler (1571–1630) and his musical theories of planetary motion, and is a study of the relationship between the artist and the social and political currents of his time. The music, in Hindemith's fully tonal late style, is best known through the symphony of the same name which employs themes from the opera.

Harnoncourt, Nikolaus (b 1929)
Austrian conductor and cellist, particularly associated with Mozart operas and with the baroque repertory. He has directed many outstanding operatic performances and recordings on original instruments, mainly with the Vienna Concentus Musicus, which he founded in 1953.

Harper, Heather (b 1930)
British soprano, particularly associated with Mozart, Strauss and Wagner roles and with post-war British operas. She had a beautiful voice used with intelligence and fine musicianship and she had a sympathetic stage presence. She created Mrs Coyle in *Owen Wingrave*, Nadia in *The Ice Break* and, for Benjamin, Luisita in *Mañana* and Lucie Manette in *A Tale of Two Cities*.

Harriet, Lady
Soprano role in Flotow's *Martha*. She is a maid of honour to Queen Anne.

Harris, Sir Augustus (1852–96)
British administrator. As administrator of Covent Garden (1888–96), he presided over one of its most brilliant periods. He insisted that operas be performed in their original language, built up a roster of many of the world's greatest singers, and introduced Wagner's later works and the early VERISMO operas to London. His father **Augustus** was stage manager at Covent Garden for 27 years, and was co-author of the libretti for Balfe's *The Rose of Castille* and *Satanella*, Wallace's *The Desert Flower* and Lara's *Amy Robsart*.

Hartmann, Karl Amadeus (1905–63)
German composer. His chamber opera *Der Simplicius Simplicissimus Jugend* (Cologne, 10 Oct 1949, composed 1935; revised version Mannheim, 9 July 1957; libr composer, Hermann Scherchen and Wolfgang Petzet, after Hans Jakob Christoffel von Grimmelhausen) met with considerable success in Germany.

Hartmann, Rudolf (1900–88)
German producer, particularly associated with Wagner and Strauss, for whom he staged the first performances of *Friedenstag*, *Die Liebe der Danae* and *Capriccio*. A producer in the traditional

mould, he was administrator of the Bavarian State Opera (1953–67).

Harvey, Jonathan (b 1939)
British composer who employs synthesized music. His stage works include the church opera *Passion and Resurrection* (Winchester, 1981) and *Inquest of Love* (London, 5 June 1993; libr composer and David Rudkin).

Harwood, Elizabeth (1938–90)
British soprano, particularly associated with Mozart and Händel roles and with COLORATURA roles. She had a beautiful, silvery voice capable of wonderfully poised pianissimi, and her lovely appearance and fine stage presence made her a most appealing singing-actress in both serious and comic roles. Sadly, the cancer from which she died caused her voice to deteriorate severely at an early age.

Háry János
Opera in prologue, five parts and epilogue by Kodály (Op 15). 1st perf Budapest, 16 Oct 1926; libr by Béla Paulini and Zsolt Harsányi, after János Garay's *The Veteran*. Principal roles: Háry (bass), Örzse (mezzo), Marie-Louise (sop), Empress (sop), Bombazine (bass), Napoleon (bar), Marczi (bar). Kodály's best-known opera, which contains long stretches of spoken dialogue, it tells of the great liar of Hungarian folklore and his love for Napoleon's second wife. The music has gained extra popularity from the orchestral suite, which comprises six numbers from the opera. [R]

Hasse, Johann (1699–1783)
German composer. He wrote some 100 operas and may be regarded as the archetypal German composer of OPERA SERIA. He set virtually every one of Pietro Metastasio's texts (56 operas and 13 INTERMEZZI) with music which at its best is rich and elegant, but which was already outdated at the end of his own life. The most successful of his operas include *Il Sesostrate* (Naples, 13 May 1726; libr Angelo Caresale, after Apostolo Zeno and Pietro Pariati), *Artaserse* (Venice, Feb 1730; libr Domenico Lalli, after Metastasio), *Cleofide* (Dresden, 13 Sept 1731; libr Michelangelo Boccardo, after Metastasio) [R] and *Attilio Regolo* (Dresden, 12 Jan 1750; libr Metastasio). Married to the soprano FAUSTINA BORDONI.

Háta
Mezzo role in Smetana's *The Bartered Bride*. She is Tobiaš Mícha's wife.

Hat man nicht
Bass aria (the Gold Aria) for Rocco in Act I of Beethoven's *Fidelio*, in which he says that life holds no happiness if one lacks money.

Haugland, Aage (b 1944)
Danish bass, particularly associated with Wagner and Moussorgsky roles and with Baron Ochs in *Der Rosenkavalier*. He has a dark and powerful (if not always perfectly focused) voice, and has a strong stage presence which is enhanced by his powerful physique.

Hauk, Minnie (b Mignon Hauck) (1851–1929)
American soprano, particularly associated with the French repertory, especially Carmen, which she sang over 500 times. She made her debut at the age of 14 and enjoyed a brilliant career, including forming her own company, but unexpectedly retired at the height of her powers. Her autobiography, *Memoirs of a Singer*, was published in 1925.

Haunted Manor, The (*Straszny Dwór*)
Opera in four acts by Moniuszko. 1st perf Warsaw, 28 Sept 1865; libr by Jan Checkiński, after a story in Kazimierz Wł adysław Wójcicki's *Legends and Pictures*. Principal roles: Hanna (sop), Jadwiga (mezzo), Damazy (ten), Stefan (ten), Miecznik (bar), Zbigniew (bass), Cześnikowa (mezzo). One of Moniuszko's finest operas, it remains very popular in Poland but is hardly ever performed elsewhere.
Plot: Mid-18th-century Poland. So as to be ready to serve their country at any time, two soldier brothers Stefan and Zbigniew have vowed to remain single. Their aunt Cześnikowa wishes them to marry two local girls, and dislikes their visits to the mansion of the nobleman Miecznik, who has two pretty daughters, Hanna and Jadwiga. She tells the brothers that the mansion is cursed, and

tells the girls that the brothers are timorous and superstitious. The girls, with whom the brothers have fallen in love despite their vow, plan to frighten them with a mock haunting. After much confusion, Miecznik accepts the brothers as sons-in-law. [R]

Hauptprobe (German for 'chief rehearsal') The last rehearsal of an opera production prior to the dress rehearsal in a German or Austrian opera house, and the last at which any changes may still be made.

Häusliche Krieg, Der
see VERSCHWORENEN, DIE

Haute-contre (French for 'high-counter') The term used in France in the 18th century to describe a high tenor (not singing falsetto). The voice's range was roughly d to b'.

Ha! welch' ein Augenblick'
Baritone aria for Don Pizarro in Act I of Beethoven's *Fidelio*, in which he resolves to murder Florestan.

Ha wie will ich triumphieren
Bass aria for Osmin in Act III of Mozart's *Die Entführung aus dem Serail*, in which he expresses his glee at the prospect of his prisoners being strung up.

Haydn, Joseph (1732–1809)
Austrian composer. In addition to five marionette operas, of which only *Philemon und Baucis* (Esterháza, 2 Sept 1773; libr Gottlieb Konrad Pfeffel) [R] survives, he wrote 20 operas, both serious and comic. His mature operas, all but the last of which were written for the Esterháza ensemble, are notable for their fine orchestration, their blending of serious and comic elements in the same work, their fine ensemble writing and their freeing of the formal aria structure. His first opera was *Der Krumme Teufel* (*The Limping Devil*, Vienna, 29 May 1753; libr Johann Kurz, after Alain René le Sage's *Le Diable Boîteux*); its music is lost, as also is the music for his next four operas. His first surviving work is *Acide e Galatea* (Esterháza, 11 Jan 1763; libr Giannambrogio Migliavacca, after Ovid's *Metamorphoses*). Its successors were *La Canterina* (Pressburg, 16 Feb 1767), LO SPEZIALE, *Le Pescatrici* (Esterháza, 16 Sept 1770; libr Carlo Goldoni), L'INFEDELTÀ DELUSA, L'INCONTRO IMPROVVISO, IL MONDO DELLA LUNA, his most frequently performed opera in recent years, LA VERA COSTANZA, L'ISOLA DISABITATA, LA FEDELTÀ PREMIATA, the fine ORLANDO PALADINO, ARMIDA and *L'Anima del Filosofo*, usually known as ORFEO ED EURIDICE.

Although Haydn did not possess the dramatic insight of either Gluck or Mozart, the musical qualities of his operas are such that the oblivion into which they fell was wholly unjustified. In the last 20 years, there has been a major revival of interest in his operas: all the mature ones have been recorded and performances are becoming quite frequent. His younger brother was the composer MICHAEL HAYDN and Suppé's *Joseph Haydn* (1887) is based on incidents in his life.

Haydn, Michael (1737–1806)
Austrian composer, younger brother of Joseph Haydn. He wrote a number of SINGSPIELS and operas, including *Andromeda e Perseo* (Salzburg, 14 Mar 1787; libr Giovanni Battista Varesco), all of which are now forgotten. His wife **Maria Magdalena Lipp** (1745–1827) was a successful soprano, who created Rosina in Mozart's *La Finta Semplice*.

Haymon, Cynthia (b 1958)
American soprano, particularly associated with lighter Puccini roles and with Bess in *Porgy and Bess* and Micaëla in *Carmen*. She possesses a beautiful voice used with taste and musicianship and has a most affecting stage presence which is enhanced by her personal beauty. She created the title-role in Musgrave's *Harriet, a Woman Called Moses* and Mrs Martin Luther King in the musical *King*. Her husband **Barrington Coleman** is a tenor.

Head Voice (often referred to by its Italian equivalent, *voce di testa*)
The highest register of the voice, so named because it gives the singer the sensation of vibration at the top of the head. It is the brightest and most brilliant register in tone.

Hebrew National Opera
Founded by the soprano Edis de Philippe (*d* 1978), the company gave its first performance on 29 Nov 1947. Reorganized in 1985 as the New Israeli Opera, it is based at the Noga Hall (cap 830) in Tel-Aviv and also performs in Jerusalem and Haifa. Apart from the Russian repertory, nearly all performances are sung in Hebrew. The operas of Wagner and Strauss are banned because of their alleged Nazi associations.

Hector
The Trojan hero appears in a number of operas, including: **1** Baritone role in Tippett's *King Priam.* **2** Bass role in Berlioz's *Les Troyens*, in which he is a ghost.

Heger, Robert (1886–1978)
German conductor and composer, particularly associated with the German repertory. He was musical director of the Ulm Stadttheater (1908–9), the Kassel Staatstheater (1935–44) and the Berlin State Opera (1944–50). He conducted the first performances of Haas's *Tobias Wunderlich* and Klenau's *Elisabeth von England.* He also composed five operas, including *Der Bettler Namenlos* (Munich, 8 Apr 1932; libr composer) and *Lady Hamilton* (Nürnberg, 11 Feb 1951; libr composer).

Heinrich
1 Bass role in Wagner's *Lohengrin.* He is Henry the Fowler (*d* 936), King of Saxony. **2** Tenor role in Wagner's *Tannhäuser.* He is a minstrel-knight.

Heise, Peter (1830–79)
Danish composer. His two operas are *The Pasha's Daughter* (*Paschaens Datter*, Copenhagen, 30 Sept 1869; libr Henrik Hertz) and the fine KING AND MARSHAL, which is one of the most popular of all Danish operas.

Heldenbariton
see under BARITONE

Heldentenor (German for 'heroic tenor')
A tenor with the power and stamina required to sing the heavier roles in the German repertory, particularly many of those by Wagner. It is the German equivalent of the Italian TENORE DI FORZA.

Helena
Soprano role in Britten's *A Midsummer Night's Dream.* She is one of the four lovers.

Hélène
1 Soprano role in Verdi's *Les Vêpres Siciliennes.* She is the sister of Duke Frederick of Austria. **2** Mezzo role in Prokofiev's *War and Peace.* She is Prince Anatol's sister. **3** Mezzo role in Chabrier's *Une Éducation Manquée.* She is Gontran's young wife. **4** Mezzo role in Offenbach's *La Belle Hélène.* She is Helen of Troy. **5** Soprano role in Messager's *Véronique.* She is betrothed to Florestan. **6** Soprano role in O. Straus's *Ein Walzertraum.* She is a princess married to Niki. **7** Soprano role in Donizetti's *Le Duc d'Albe.* She is Egmont's daughter. **8** Soprano role in Verdi's *Jérusalem.* She is the Count of Toulouse's daughter.

Helen of Troy
The wife of Menelaus appears in many operas, including: **1** Soprano role in Strauss's *Die Ägyptische Helena.* **2** Mezzo role in Tippett's *King Priam.* **3** Mezzo role in Offenbach's *La Belle Hélène.* **4** Soprano role in Boito's *Mefistofele.* **5** Soprano role in Gluck's *Paride ed Elena.* **6** Soprano role in Saint-Saëns's *Hélène.*

Helmwige
Soprano role in Wagner's *Die Walküre.* She is one of the Valkyries.

Helsinki
see FINNISH NATIONAL OPERA

Hempel, Frieda (1885–1955)
German soprano, particularly associated with the German repertory. One of the finest sopranos of the early 20th century, she possessed a technically impeccable voice and a fine stage presence. Her versatility was such that she could sing the Queen of the Night in *Die Zauberflöte* and Rosina in Rossini's *Il Barbiere di Siviglia* as well as Eva in *Die Meistersinger von Nürnberg* and the Marschallin in *Der Rosenkavalier.* Her autobiography, *Mein Leben dem Gesang*, was published in 1955.

Hemsley, Thomas (b 1927)
British baritone, particularly associated with 20th-century roles and with Beckmesser. His rather dry-toned voice was not outstanding, but it was used with great intelligence and musicianship and he was an accomplished singing-actor with excellent diction. He created Demetrius in *A Midsummer Night's Dream*, Mangus in *The Knot Garden*, Smirnov in Walton's *The Bear* and Caesar in Hamilton's *The Catiline Conspiracy*.

Hendricks, Barbara (b 1948)
American soprano, particularly associated with Mozart and with lyrical French and Italian roles. She possesses one of the loveliest voices to have come to the fore in recent years, which she uses with musicianship and great intelligence. She also has a charming stage presence. She played Mimì in Luigi Comencini's film of *La Bohème* and created a role in Thomson's *Lord Byron*. She is also an ambassador for the United Nations High Commission for Refugees.

Henri
Tenor role in: **1** Verdi's *Les Vêpres Siciliennes*. Guy de Montfort's son, he loves Hélène. **2** Donizetti's *Le Duc d'Albe*. He is the Duke of Alba's son. **3** Bizet's *La Jolie Fille de Perth*. He is an armourer in love with Catharine.

Henri VIII
Opera in four acts by Saint-Saëns. 1st perf Paris, 5 March 1883; libr by Pierre Léonce Détroyat and Paul Armande Silvestre. Principal roles: Henri (bar), Anne (mezzo), Gomez (ten), Catherine (sop), Campeggio (bass). Saint-Saëns's most successful opera apart from *Samson et Dalila*, it is nowadays only very rarely performed.
Plot: England, 1530. King Henry VIII has tired of his Queen, Katherine of Aragon, and has fallen in love with Anne Boleyn. She, however, loves the Spanish Ambassador Gomez. Nevertheless, Henry divorces Katherine and weds Anne in the face of papal disapproval, expressed by Cardinal Campeggio.

Henze, Hans Werner (b 1926)
German composer. One of the most prolific and successful contemporary opera composers, his operas are written in a variety of forms and styles, but all tend to reflect his left-wing political views, and his interest in the artist as an individual and in his relationship with society. His first opera was *Das Wundertheater* (Heidelberg, 7 May 1949; libr A. Graf von Scheck, after Miguel Cervantes). It was followed by the radio opera *Ein Landarzt* (Hamburg, 19 Nov 1951; libr after Franz Kafka) and BOULEVARD SOLITUDE, his first major success. The radio opera *Das Ender einer Welt* (Hamburg, 4 Dec 1953; libr W. Hildesheimer) was followed by the controversial KÖNIG HIRSCH, in which his penchant for lyrical fantasy is first apparent. His later operas are DER PRINZ VON HOMBERG, the highly successful ELEGIE FÜR JUNGE LIEBENDE, the satirical DER JUNGE LORD, the powerful THE BASSARIDS, perhaps his finest opera, *Rachel la Cubana* (New York, 4 Mar 1974; libr Hans Magnus Enzensberger, after Miguel Barnet) [R], the vast and pretentious WE COME TO THE RIVER, the satirical THE ENGLISH CAT and *Das Verratene Meer* (Berlin, 5 May 1990; libr Hans-Ulrich Treichel, after Yukio Mishima's *The Sailor Who Fell From Grace With the Sea*). He has also made realizations, so drastic as to amount virtually to new works, of Paisiello's *Don Chisciotte* (Montepulciano, 1 Aug 1976) and Monterverdi's *Il Ritorno d'Ulisse in Patria* (Salzburg, 16 Aug 1985).

Herbert, Victor (1859–1924)
Irish-born American composer. He is best known as a composer of operettas, of which he wrote 35. The most successful were *Naughty Marietta* (New York, 24 Oct 1910; libr Rida Johnson Young) and *Eileen* (New York, 19 Mar 1917; libr Henry Blossom). He also wrote two long-forgotten operas: *Natoma* (New York, 25 Feb 1911; libr Joseph Deighn Redding) and *Madeleine* (New York, 24 Jan 1914; libr Grant Stewart, after A. Decourcelle and L. Thibaut's *Je Dîne Chez Ma Mère*). His wife **Therese Foerster** (1861–1927) was a successful soprano.

Hercules
Secular oratorio in three acts by Händel. 1st perf London, 5 Jan 1745; libr by Thomas Broughton, after Sophocles's

Women of Thracis. Principal roles: Hercules (bass), Dejanira (mezzo), Iole (sop), Hyllus (ten), Lichas (sop). Although it is not strictly speaking an opera, it is quite often staged. [R]

Herincx, Raimund (b 1927)
British baritone, particularly associated with 20th-century operas, although his enormous repertory also included Wagner and many Italian and French roles. A fine singing-actor with a powerful and incisive voice, he created Faber in *The Knot Garden*, the White Abbot in Maxwell Davies's *Taverner*, Segura in Williamson's *Our Man in Havana*, the Old Man in Crosse's *Purgatory* and the Governor in Henze's *We Come to the River*.

Hermia
Mezzo role in Britten's *A Midsummer Night's Dream*. She is one of the four lovers.

Héro
Soprano role in Berlioz's *Béatrice et Bénédict*. She is in love with Claudio.

Herod
The Tetrarch of Judea (*c* 74–4 BC) appears as: **1** Tenor role in Strauss's *Salome*. **2** Baritone role in Massenet's *Hérodiade*.

Hérodiade
Opera in four acts by Massenet. 1st perf Brussels, 19 Dec 1881; libr by Paul Milliet and Georges Hartmann, after Gustave Flaubert's *Hérodias*. Principal roles: Salomé (sop), Hérode (ten), Jean (ten), Hérodiade (mezzo), Phanuel (bass), Vitellius (bar). One of Massenet's richest and most powerful scores, it is still performed from time to time.
Plot: Jerusalem, *c* AD 30. The orphan Salome has been brought up by John the Baptist, whose violent denunciations of her infuriate Herodias, wife of the Tetrarch Herod. The mage Phanuel urges Herod to lead the resistance to Rome, but Herod is powerless before the Roman general Vitellius, whose justice wins over the people. Herod is besotted with Salome, but she rejects him, as she is in love with John. John admits that he loves her, but Herod – at the urging of Herodias – has John killed. Salome stabs herself. [R Exc]

Herodias
Mezzo role in Strauss's *Salome*. Salome's mother, she is married to Herod.

Herman
1 Tenor role in Tchaikovsky's *The Queen of Spades*. He is a young officer in love with Lisa. **2** Baritone role in Catalani's *Loreley*. He is Walther's friend.

Hérold, Ferdinand (1791–1833)
French composer, whose early death cut short a career of great promise. His first opera, *La Gioventù di Enrico V* (Naples, 5 Jan 1815; libr Landriani, after Shakespeare's *King Henry IV*), was a success, and was followed by *Charles de France* (Paris, 18 June 1816), written in collaboration with Boïeldieu, and *Les Rosières* (Paris, 27 Jan 1817; libr Émmanuel Guillaume Théaulon), his first major work. There followed 14 further operas (including one written in collaboration with Auber) before ZAMPA, his masterpiece, and the fine LE PRÉ AUX CLERCS. His last opera *Ludovic* (Paris, 16 May 1833; libr Jules-Henri Vernoy de Saint-Georges) was left unfinished at his death and was completed by Halévy. His operas are notable for their delightful melodies, their fine orchestration and their sometimes ambitious structure.

Herrmann, Bernard (1911–75)
American composer. Best known as a highly successful composer of film music, he also wrote three operas. They are WUTHERING HEIGHTS and two short television operas: *A Christmas Carol* (CBS, 23 Dec 1954; libr M. Anderson, after Charles Dickens) and *A Child is Born* (CBS, 25 Dec 1955; libr Stephen Vincent Benét).

Hervé (b Florimond Ronger) (1825–92)
French composer and singer. He wrote over 100 operettas, for many of which he provided his own libretti. The most successful included *Chilpéric* (Paris, 24 Oct 1868; libr composer), *Le Petit Faust* (Paris, 28 Apr 1869; libr Adolphe Jaime and Héctor Crémieux), a send-up of Gounod's opera, and MAM'ZELLE NITOUCHE, his most enduring work.

Herz, Joachim (b 1924)
German producer and administrator. A

disciple of Walter Felsenstein, his powerful productions are conceived as total music-theatre. He was director of the Leipzig Opera (1957–77) and the Komishce Oper, Berlin (1977–81). He has also worked in Britain with the English National Opera (*Salome* and *Fidelio*) and the Welsh National Opera (*Madama Butterfly*).

Herzeleide
Soprano monologue for Kundry in Act II of Wagner's *Parsifal*, in which she tells Parsifal about his mother.

Heuberger, Richard (1850–1914)
Austrian composer. He wrote four operas, including *Manuel Venegas* (Leipzig, 27 Mar 1889; libr J.V. Wildmann, after Pedro de Alarcón's *El Niño de la Bola*), but is best known for his operettas. The most successful of his six works in this genre were DER OPERNBALL and *Don Quichotte* (Vienna, 1 Dec 1910; libr Heinrich Reichert and Franz Grünbaum, after Miguel Cervantes).

Heure Espagnole, L' (*Spanish Time*)
Comic opera in one act by Ravel. 1st perf Paris, 19 May 1911; libr by Franc-Nohain (Maurice Legrand), after his own play. Principal roles: Concepción (mezzo), Ramiro (bar), Gonzalve (ten), Don Iñigo (bass), Torquemada (ten). A witty, elegant and brilliantly orchestrated work, it was an immediate success and has remained popular ever since.
Plot: 18th-century Toledo. The clockmaker Torquemada has to spend a day away servicing the town's public clocks. This leaves the coast clear for his wife Concepción to pursue her love affairs, but Torquemada makes problems by allowing a customer, the muleteer Ramiro, to wait in his shop until he returns. Concepción's admirers, Gonzalve and the banker Don Iñigo Gómez, arrive and successively hide inside large clocks. After a good deal of complication and clock-changing, Concepción decides to give her favours to Ramiro. [R]

Hidalgo, Elvira de (1892–1980)
Spanish soprano, particularly associated with Italian COLORATURA roles. One of the leading lyric sopranos of the early 20th century, she was also a noted teacher, whose pupils included Maria Callas.

Hiller, Johann Adam (b Hüller) (1728–1804)
German composer. Usually regarded as the founder of SINGSPIEL, he wrote 12 works in this genre. The most important are *Der Teufel ist Los* (Leipzig, 28 May 1766; libr Christian Felix Weise, after Charles Coffey and John Mottley's *The Devil to Pay*), *Lottchen am Hofe* (Leipzig, 24 Apr 1767; libr Weise, after Carlo Goldoni's *Bertoldo*), the enormously successful DIE JAGD and *Der Dorfbarbier* (*The Village Barber*, Leipzig, 18 Apr 1771; libr Weise, after Jean-Marie Sedaine's *Blaise le Savetier*). His son **Friedrich** (*c* 1767–1812) was also a composer, who wrote three singspiels.

Hindemith, Paul (1895–1963)
German composer, resident in the United States after he was banned by the Nazis as 'musically degenerate'. One of the most influential 20th-century German composers, he was the inventor of what came to be known as *Gebrauchsmusik* ('utility music'). His early stage works verge on atonality, but he later reverted to an advanced tonal idiom which he explained in much theoretical writing. His first three operas, all in one act, are largely forgotten. They are MÖRDER, HOFFNUNG DER FRAUEN, the MARIONETTE OPERA *Das Nusch-Nuschi* (Stuttgart, 4 June 1921; libr Franz Blei) [R], which is based on a Burmese story, and *Sancta Susanna* (Frankfurt, 26 Mar 1922; libr August Stramm) [R]. His next opera CARDILLAC remains his best-known stage work. It was followed by HIN UND ZURÜCK, the satirical NEUES VOM TAGE, which so displeased Dr Goebbels, the children's opera *Wir Bauen eine Stadt* (Berlin, 21 June 1930; libr R. Seitz), the fine MATHIS DER MALER, which was banned by the Nazis, DIE HARMONIE DER WELT and *Das Lange Weihnachtsmahl* (Mannheim, 17 Dec 1961; libr after Thornton Wilder's *The Long Christmas Dinner*).

Hines, Jerome (b Heinz) (b 1921)
American bass (and mathematician), particularly associated with Verdi and Wagner roles and with the title-role in *Boris Godunov*. Resident at the

Metropolitan Opera, New York, for over 40 years, he possessed a good, if not absolutely outstanding voice of huge size. A fine singing-actor, his imposing stage presence was aided by his great height. He also composed an opera, *I Am the Way* (Philadelphia, 1969), about the life of Jesus. His writings include a book of interviews with 40 leading singers about the art of singing and his autobiography, *This is My Story, This is My Song*, which was published in 1968.

Hin und Zurück (*There and Back*)
Opera in one act by Hindemith (Op 45a). 1st perf Baden-Baden, 17 July 1927; libr by Marcellus Schiffer, after an English revue sketch. Principal roles: Robert (ten), Helene (sop), Wise Man (ten). A clever little piece, it is nowadays only very rarely performed.
Plot: Helene is unfaithful to her husband Robert. The action reaches a climax with a pistol shot, after which the supernatural Wise Man intervenes to re-enact the story in reverse until the point at which it started is reached. [R]

Hippolyte et Aricie (*Hippolytus and Aricia*)
Opera in prologue and five acts by Rameau. 1st perf Paris, 1 Oct 1733; libr by Abbé Simon Joseph de Pellegrin, after Jean Baptiste Racine's *Phèdre*, Euripides's *Hippolytus* and Seneca's *Phaedra*. Principal roles: Phèdre (mezzo), Thésée (bar), Hippolyte (ten), Aricie (sop), Pluton (bass), Diane (mezzo), Tisiphone (ten), Neptune (bass), High Priestess (sop). Rameau's first full-length opera and often regarded as his stage masterpiece, it is his best-known work and has been regularly performed in recent years.
Plot: Legendary Greece. Hippolytus, the illegitimate son of Theseus, loves Aricia. His step-mother Phedra, regent in Theseus's absence, unsuccessfully opposes the match and finally reveals to Hippolytus that she herself loves him. Hippolytus is horrified and calls down divine retribution upon her. Rejected, Phedra begs Hippolytus to kill her. As he struggles to disarm her, Theseus – released by Pluto from Hades – returns and misinterprets the situation, believing that Hippolytus was threatening Phedra. Hippolytus is exiled. The dying Phedra reveals the truth to a remorse-stricken Theseus, and Diana intervenes to appoint Hippolytus king, with Aricia as his consort. [R]

Hislop, Joseph (1884–1977)
British tenor, largely resident in Sweden. Particularly associated with the French repertory and with Verdi and Puccini roles, he possessed a strong voice which he used with style and musicianship. He was also a noted teacher, whose pupils included Jussi Björling, Birgit Nilsson and Peter Glossop.

History of Dioclesian, The
see PROPHETESS, THE

H.M.S. Pinafore or **The Lass That Loved a Sailor**
Operetta in two acts by Sullivan. 1st perf London, 25 May 1878; libr by W.S. Gilbert. Principal roles: Sir Joseph (bar), Josephine (sop), Capt Corcoran (bar), Ralph (ten), Little Buttercup (mezzo), Dick Deadeye (bass), Bill Bobstay (bar), Hebe (mezzo). One of the most enduringly popular of all the Savoy Operas, which enjoyed an initial run of over 700 performances, it is a satire on class levels and the traditions of the British Navy. Sir Joseph is a thinly disguised portrait of the newspaper tycoon W.H. Smith, who rose from office boy to First Lord of the Admiralty.
Plot: 19th-century Portsmouth. Sir Joseph Porter, former office boy and now First Lord of the Admiralty, seeks the hand of Capt Corcoran's daughter Josephine. She loves the common sailor Ralph Rackstraw, but cannot bring herself to admit it to him because of their social disparity. Sir Joseph, thinking her dazzled by his rank, propounds the theory that love is a platform upon which all ranks meet – thus neatly pleading Ralph's case. Ralph and Josephine plan to elope, but they are betrayed to the Captain by Dick Deadeye. However, the bumboat woman Little Buttercup reveals that when younger she was a baby-farmer and mixed up two children: Ralph and the Captain. So the Captain (socially) is really Ralph, and Ralph is really the Captain and can wed Josephine. The Captain married Buttercup, whilst Sir Joseph contents himself with his cousin Hebe. [R]

Hobson, Jim
Bass role in Britten's *Peter Grimes*. He is the town carter.

Hochzeit des Camacho, Die
(*The Marriage of Camacho*)
Comic opera in two acts by Mendelssohn (Op 10). 1st perf Berlin, 29 April 1827; libr by Karl Klingemann, after Miguel de Cervantes Saavedra's *Don Quixote*. Principal roles: Camacho (ten), Quiteria (sop), Don Quixote (bass), Sancho Panza (bass), Carrasco (bar), Basilio (ten), Lucinda (sop), Vivaldo (ten). The most substantial of Mendelssohn's early SINGSPIELS, it is a charming and tuneful piece which deserves more than the very occasional performance which it currently receives. [R]

Hockney, David (b 1937)
British painter and designer. One of the most successful contemporary British artists, his operatic designs have included *The Rake's Progress* and *Die Zauberflöte* for Glyndebourne, *Tristan und Isolde* for the Los Angeles Music Center Opera and *The Nightingale*, *L'Enfant et les Sortilèges* and *Die Frau ohne Schatten* for Covent Garden.

Hoddinott, Alun (b 1929)
British composer. He has written five operas: *The Beach at Falesá* (Cardiff, 26 Mar 1974; libr Glyn Jones, after Robert Louis Stevenson), *Murder the Magician* (Welsh TV, 11 Feb 1976; libr J. Morgan), *What the Old Man Does is Always Right* (Fishguard, 27 July 1977; libr Myfanwy Piper, after Hans Christian Andersen), *The Rajah's Diamond* (Welsh TV, 24 Nov 1979; libr Piper, after Stevenson) and *The Trumpet Major* (Manchester, 1 Apr 1981; libr Piper, after Thomas Hardy).

Hodgson, Alfreda (1940–92)
British mezzo, particularly associated with the British and French repertories. She possessed a rich and beautiful voice which she used with intelligence and outstanding musicianship. Best known as a concert artist, her operatic appearances were sadly infrequent.

Höffgen, Marga (b 1921)
German mezzo, particularly associated with Wagnerian roles, especially Erda. A rich-toned and highly musical singer, she was best known as an oratorio artist and sadly only appeared intermittently in opera.

Hoffman, Grace (b Goldie) (b 1925)
American mezzo, particularly associated with Verdi and Wagner roles. She possessed a rich and beautiful voice used with fine musicianship and she had a good stage presence.

Hoffmann, E.T.A.
see panel on page 261

Hoffmann, Peter (b 1944)
German tenor, particularly associated with Wagnerian roles, especially Siegmund and Parsifal. One of the leading Wagnerian tenors of the 1980s, he was not really a true HELDENTENOR. His voice deteriorated sharply following a motor accident, and it had not earlier been helped by his appearances as a rock singer.

Hofmannsthal, Hugo von (1874–1929)
Austrian poet, playwright and librettist. One of the greatest of all operatic librettists, his collaboration with Strauss produced *Elektra*, *Der Rosenkavalier*, *Ariadne auf Naxos*, *Die Frau ohne Schatten*, *Die Ägyptische Helena* and *Arabella*. The workings of their partnership may be studied in their joint correspondence, first published in English in 1961. He also wrote the libretti for Wellesz's *Alkestis* and Varèse's lost *Oedipus und der Sphinx*.

Hofoper (German for 'court opera')
The title in the 18th and 19th centuries of a German or Austrian opera house which was under the direct control of an imperial or princely court.

Ho! Jolly Jenkins
Baritone aria for Friar Tuck in Act II of Sullivan's *Ivanhoe*. It is Tuck's drinking song.

Ho-jo-to-ho!
Brünnhilde's war cry in Act II of Wagner's *Die Walküre*.

Holbrooke, Josef (1878–1958)
British composer. He wrote five operas, much the most important being the

· E.T.A. Hoffmann ·

The German writer, composer, critic and conductor Ernst Theodor Amadeus Hoffmann (1776–1822) occupies an important place in operatic history, both as a composer and as the literary source of several later operas. One of the most influential figures in the German romantic movement, he directed theatre companies in Bamberg, Leipzig and Dresden and, in addition to his writing, composed 12 SINGSPIELS. His operas are: *Die Maske* (Berlin 1799; libr composer), *Scherz, List und Rache* (Posen 1801; libr composer, after Goethe), *Der Renegat* (1804), *Faustina* (1804), *Die Lustigen Musikanten* (Warsaw, 6 Apr 1805; libr Clemens von Brentane) [R Exc], the lost *Der Kanonikus von Mailand* (1805; libr Rohrmann, after Alexandre Duval's *Le Souper Imprévue*), *Liebe und Eifersucht* (1808; libr composer, after Pedro Calderón de la Barca's *La Banda y la Flor*), *Der Trank der Unsterblichkeit* (1808; libr J. von Soden), *Dirna* (Bamberg, 11 Oct 1809; libr Soden), *Saul* (Bamberg, 29 June 1811; libr J. Seyfried, after Louis-Charles Caignez's *Le Triomphe de David*), *Aurora* (Bamberg, 5 Nov 1933, composed 1812; libr Franz von Holbein) and the fine UNDINE, his most important composition, parts of which anticipate the later German romantic operas of Weber, Marschner and Lortzing.

Hoffmann revised the libretto of Spontini's *Olympie*, and he appears as a character in Offenbach's *Les Contes d'Hoffmann* and in three other operas by minor composers. Some 30 operas have been based on his writings. Below are listed, by story, those operas by composers with entries in this dictionary.

Die Bergwerke von Falun		
Stanford	*The Miner of Falun*	1888 (U)
Wagner-Régeny	*Das Bergwerk zu Falun*	1961
Die Brautwahl		
Busoni	*Die Brautwahl*	1912
Doge und Dogaresse		
Rezniček	*Der Gondoliere des Dogen*	1931
Das Fraulein von Scuderi		
Offenbach	*Der Goldschmied von Toledo* (pastice)	1919
Hindemith	*Cardillac*	1926/52
Geschichte vom Verlorenen Spiegelbilde		
Offenbach	*Les Contes d'Hoffmann* (Giulietta Act)	1881
Die Königsbraut		
Offenbach	*Le Roi Carotte*	1872
Meister Martin		
Blockx	*Maître Martin*	1892
Prinzessin Brambilla		
Malipiero	*I Capricci di Callot*	1942
Rat Krespel		
Offenbach	*Les Contes d'Hoffmann* (Antonia Act)	1881
Der Sandmann		
Adam	*La Poupée de Nuremberg*	1852
Offenbach	*Les Contes d'Hoffmann* (Olympia Act)	1881
Audran	*La Poupée*	1896

Wagnerian trilogy THE CAULDRON OF ANNWN, which comprises *Dylan, Son of the Wave, The Children of Don* and *Bronwen*. His other works are *Pierrot and Pierrette* (London, 11 Nov 1909; libr Walter E. Grogan; revised version *The Stranger*, Liverpool, Oct 1924), the opera-ballet *The Enchanter* (Chicago, 1915; libr D. Malloch, after M. Rabinoff) and the unperformed comedy *The Snob* (libr G.K. Chesterton, C. McEvoy and H.H. Ryan).

Holland
see NETHERLANDS OPERA

Hölle Rache, Die
Soprano aria for the Queen of the Night in Act II of Mozart's *Die Zauberflöte*, in which she orders Pamina to kill Sarastro.

Holm, Richard (1912–88)
German tenor, particularly associated with Mozart roles. He had a small but well-schooled voice, used with fine musicianship, and he had a good stage presence. He created Kent in Reimann's *Lear*, Wallenstein in Hindemith's *Die Harmonie der Welt* and Black in Egk's *Die Verlobung in San Domingo*.

Holst, Gustav (1874–1934)
British composer. His first four operas, only the first of which has ever been performed, are pale imitations of Sullivan and are forgotten. They are *Landsdown Castle* (Cheltenham, 7 Feb 1893; libr A.C. Cunningham), *The Revoke* (1895; libr Fritz Hart), *The Idea* (1898; libr Hart) and *The Youth's Choice* (1902; libr composer). Also forgotten is his next opera, the unperformed *Sita* (1906; libr composer, after the *Ramayana*), which Holst later dismissed as 'good old Wagnerian bawling'. His operatic maturity dates from the beautiful Sanskrit SĀVITRI, possibly the finest British opera since *Dido and Aeneas* and the founding work of modern British chamber opera. It was followed by THE PERFECT FOOL, the Shakespearian AT THE BOAR'S HEAD and THE WANDERING SCHOLAR. His daughter **Imogen** (1907–84) was a conductor, composer and musicologist who wrote the standard work on her father's music.

Holzbauer, Ignaz (1711–83)
Austrian composer. His most successful opera, *Günther von Schwarzburg* (Mannheim, 5 Jan 1777; libr Anton Klein), which was much admired by Mozart, is historically important in that it was the first full-length opera on a German subject with RECITATIVE replacing the dialogue of SINGSPIEL.

Homer, Louise (b Dilworth Beatty) (1871–1947)
American mezzo, particularly associated with Wagnerian roles. One of the finest mezzos of the early 20th century, she created the Witch in *Die Königskinder* and roles in Converse's *The Pipe of Desire* and Parker's *Mona*. Her nephew was the composer SAMUEL BARBER.

Home, Sweet Home
Aria from Bishop's *Clari*. As well as being a great concert favourite in the 19th century (Adelina Patti sometimes sang it in the lesson scene in *Il Barbiere di Siviglia*), it has also been used in altered form by a number of other composers, most notably by Donizetti in 'Al dolce guidami' in *Anna Bolena*, which led Bishop to bring an unsuccessful action for 'piracy and breach of copyright'.

Honegger, Arthur (1892–1955)
Swiss composer. A member of the group LES SIX, he wrote 13 stage works in a variety of forms. His first work, the dramatic psalm LE ROI DAVID, immediately placed him in the forefront of contemporary composers. It was followed by ANTIGONE, JUDITH, the operetta *Les Aventures du Roi Pausole* (Paris, 12 Dec 1930; libr Albert Willemetz, after Pierre Louÿs) [R], the melodrama *Amphion* (Paris, 23 June 1931; libr Paul Valéry) and the dramatic oratorio JEANNE D'ARC AU BÛCHER, perhaps his best-known work. His later operas are L'AIGLON and *Gonzague* (Paris, 17 Dec 1931; libr R. Kerdyck, after Pierre Veber), both written in collaboration with Ibert, *Les Milles et Une Nuit* (Paris, 1937; libr after *The Thousand and One Nights*), the operetta *Les Petites Cardinal* (Paris, 13 Feb 1938; libr Willemetz and P. Brach, after Ludovic Halévy), also written with Ibert, the dramatic legend *Nicolas de Flue* (Neuchâtel, 31 May 1941;

libr Denis de Rougemont) [R] and *Charles le Téméraire* (Mézières, May 1944; libr René Morax). Married to the pianist Andrée Vaurabourg.

Höngen, Elisabeth (b 1906)
German mezzo, particularly associated with Wagner and Strauss roles and with Lady Macbeth in Verdi's *Macbeth*. She had a fine, rich and well-projected voice and was an impressive singing-actress. She created Bebett in Erbse's *Julietta*.

Honour and arms
Bass aria for Harapha in Act I of Händel's *Samson*, in which he brags that he could slay Samson with a single blow.

Honour Monologue
Baritone aria ('L'onore! Ladri!') for Falstaff in Act I of Verdi's *Falstaff*, in which he harangues Pistol and Bardolf about the worthlessness of honour.

Hopf, Hans (1916–93)
German tenor, particularly associated with dramatic German roles, especially Wagner. One of the leading HELDENTENORS of the immediate post-war period, he enjoyed a long career, latterly undertaking character roles.

Hopkins, Antony (b Reynolds) (b 1921)
British composer and conductor. His stage works include *Lady Rohesia* (London, 17 Mar 1948; libr composer, after Richard Harris Barham's *Ingoldsby Legends*), *The Man From Tuscany* (Canterbury, 20 July 1951; libr Christopher Hassell) and *Three's Company* (Crewe, 10 Nov 1953; libr Michael Flanders) [R]. He was musical director of Intimate Opera (1952–63) and also enjoyed a highly successful broadcasting career as a commentator on music.

Horche, die Lerche singt
Tenor aria for Fenton in Act II of Nicolai's *Die Lustigen Weiber von Windsor*, in which he serenades Anne.

Horn, Count
Bass role in Verdi's *Un Ballo in Maschera*. Tom in the Boston setting, he is one of the two conspirators.

Horne, Marilyn (b 1934)
American mezzo, particularly associated with Rossini and other BEL CANTO roles. One of the greatest singers of the 20th century, she first came to prominence dubbing the singing for Dorothy Dandridge in the 1954 film of *Carmen Jones*. She possesses a large, rich and dark-toned voice of extraordinary agility and with a phenomenal range of over three octaves, which is used with outstanding musicianship and a matchless technique. Although best known as one of the greatest ever exponents of the bel canto repertory, she has also sung Wagner, Verdi, Berg, Händel and the French repertory with equal success. She created Samira in Corigliano's *The Ghosts of Versailles* and Laura in Giannini's *The Harvest*. She has a good stage presence, especially in comedy. Her autobiography, *My Life*, was published in 1984. Her first husband **Henry Lewis** (*b* 1932) is a successful black conductor; her second husband is the bass NICOLA ZACCARIA.

Hornpipe
A lively British sailor's dance originally with three, but more recently with two beats in the bar. It is so named because it was originally accompanied by a pipe which was made from animal horn. The best known operatic example is in Sullivan's *Ruddigore*.

Horseman, The (*Ratsumies*)
Opera in three acts by Sallinen. 1st perf Savonlinna, 17 July 1975; libr by Paavo Haavikko. Principal roles: Antti (bass), Anna (sop), Merchant of Novgorod and Wife (ten and sop). Sallinen's first opera, it is one of the finest operas of the 1970s and has been widely performed.
Plot: 17th-century Novgorod and Finland. After the Merchant has seduced his wife Anna, the horseman Antti burns down his house, killing the Merchant and his wife. The dying Merchant foretells that Antti will become a great king at whose coronation many candles will be lighted. Antti and Anna flee to Finland. There, Antti reluctantly takes command of a rebellion, but the plot is betrayed and he and his men are killed. As Anna laments over Antti, soldiers wishing to see more clearly light many candles. [R]

Hosenrolle
The German term for trouser role.

Hotter, Hans (b 1909)
German bass-baritone, particularly associated with Wagnerian roles, especially Wotan, of which he is often regarded as the greatest 20th-century exponent. He possessed a large, rich and finely-projected voice and was a singing-actor of exceptional intelligence and insight. Also a distinguished interpreter of other German roles, he created Olivier in *Capriccio*, the Commandant in *Friedenstag* and the Schoolteacher in Einem's *Der Besuch der Alten Dame*. He enjoyed an exceptionally long career, continuing to appear as the Speaker in *Die Zauberflöte* and Schigolch in *Lulu* into his early 80s. He also produced a number of operas, notably the *Ring* at Covent Garden.

Houston Grand Opera Association
Founded in 1956, the company gives an annual season at the John and Alice Wortham Theater (cap 2,176), which opened in Oct 1987. Operas are given in both English and the original language, and the company has encouraged American operas and young American artists. Musical directors have included Walter Herbert, John de Main and Vjekoslav Sutej.

Howarth, Elgar (b 1935)
British conductor and trumpeter, particularly associated with contemporary operas. One of the leading interpreters of modern music, he conducted the first performances of Ligeti's *Le Grand Macabre*, Birtwistle's *The Mask of Orpheus, The Second Mrs Kong, Gawain* and *Yan Tan Tethera* and Chaynes's *Erzsebet*.

Howell, Gwynne (b 1938)
British bass, particularly associated with Verdi and Wagner roles. He possesses a rich and warm voice of great beauty, although his acting abilities are somewhat limited. He created Richard Taverner in Maxwell Davies's *Taverner*.

Howells, Anne (b 1941)
British mezzo, particularly associated with the French repertory and with Mozart roles and contemporary works. A fine singing-actress, especially in comedy, with a warm and intelligently-used voice, she created Lena in Bennett's *Victory*, Cathleen in Maw's *The Rising of the Moon* and Régine in Liebermann's *La Forêt*. Her first husband was the tenor RYLAND DAVIES; her second husband **Stafford Dean** (*b* 1942) is a successful bass noted for his Mozart performances.

Hughes, Arwel (1909–88)
British composer and conductor. One of the most important composers to set Welsh texts, his two operas are *Menna* (Cardiff, 9 Nov 1953; libr Wyn Griffith) and *Love the Doctor* (*Serch yw'r Doctor*, Cardiff, 1 Aug 1960; libr Saunders Lewis, after Molière's *L'Amour Médecin*). His son **Owain Arwel** (*b* 1942) is a conductor.

Hugh the Drover or **Love in the Stocks**
Opera in two acts by Vaughan Williams. 1st perf London, 14 July 1924 (composed 1914); libr by Harold Child. Principal roles: Hugh (ten), Mary (sop), John (bar), Constable (bass), Aunt Jane (mezzo). Described as a ballad opera, it incorporates traditional folk material into the operatic structure. Successful at its appearance, it is nowadays only very rarely performed.
Plot: Cotswolds, 1812. Jane's niece Mary, daughter of the Constable, is engaged against her will to John the Butcher. She meets and falls in love with the drover Hugh, who accepts a challenge to meet John in a boxing fight and wins. He is subsequently accused by John of spying for the French and is put into the village stocks. Mary releases him, and the sergeant of an arriving army detachment clears Hugh of John's false allegations. Hugh and Mary are united, whilst John is forcibly enlisted. [R]

Hugo, Victor
see panel on page 265

Huguenots, Les
Opera in five acts by Meyerbeer. 1st perf Paris, 29 Feb 1836; libr by Eugène Scribe and Émile Deschamps. Principal roles: Raoul (ten), Valentine (sop), Marguerite (sop), St Bris (bar), Nevers (bar), Marcel (bass), Urbain (mezzo). Meyerbeer's best-known opera, it is the archetypal French

· Victor Hugo ·

The French playwright, novelist and poet Victor Hugo (1802–85) himself wrote one opera libretto, an adaptation of his own *Notre-Dame de Paris* for Bertin's long-forgotten *Esmeralda* (1836). His plays and novels have inspired some 75 operas. Below are listed, by work, those operas by composers with entries in this dictionary.

Angélo, Tyran de Padoue		
Mercadante	*Il Giuramento*	1837
Cui	*Angelo*	1876
Ponchielli	*La Gioconda*	1876
d'Albert	*Der Improvisator*	1902
Bruneau	*Angélo, Tyran de Padoue*	1928
Antoine et Cléopâtre		
(translation of Shakespeare's *Antony and Cleopatra*)		
Bondeville	*Antoine et Cléopâtre*	1972
Han d'Islande		
Moussorgsky	*Han d'Islande*	1856 (U)
Hernani		
Bellini	*Ernani*	1830 (U)
Verdi	*Ernani*	1844
L'Homme qui Rit		
Enna	*The Comedians*	1920
Pedrollo	*L'Uomo Che Ride*	1920
La Légende des Siècles		
Mancinelli	*Isora di Provenza*	1884
Lucrèce Borgia		
Donizetti	*Lucrezia Borgia*	1833
Marie Tudor		
Pacini	*Maria Tudor*	1843
Balfe	*The Armourer of Nantes*	1863
Gomes	*Maria Tudor*	1879
Wagner-Régeny	*Der Günstling*	1935
Marion Délorme		
Bottesini	*Marion Delorme*	1862
Pedrotti	*Marion Delorme*	1865
Ponchielli	*Marion Delorme*	1885
Notre-Dame de Paris		
Dargomijsky	*Esmeralda*	1847
Poniatowski	*Esmeralda*	1847
Pedrell	*Quasimodo*	1875
A.G. Thomas	*Esmeralda*	1883
Granados	*Picarol*	1901
Schmidt	*Notre-Dame*	1914
Quatre-Vingt-Treize		
Chapí	*Las Hijas del Batallón*	1898
Le Roi s'Amuse		
Verdi	*Rigoletto*	1851
Ruy Blas		
Poniatowski	*Ruy Blas*	1843
Marchetti	*Ruy Blas*	1869
Godard	*Ruy Blas*	1891
Torquemada		
Rota	*Torquemada*	1943

grand opera. Dealing with events surrounding the Massacre of St Bartholemew on 24 Aug 1572, it was for nearly a century one of the most popular of all operas. Nowadays it is only intermittently performed. Performances are often known as the 'Night of the Seven Stars' because of the seven great voices which it requires.
Plot: Touraine and Paris, Aug 1572. To mark a truce between the warring Catholic and Huguenot factions, the Protestant nobleman Raoul de Nangis is engaged to marry Valentine, daughter of the Catholic Count of St Bris. Raoul and his retainer Marcel dine with the Catholics, and Raoul is summoned before Queen Marguerite de Valois, who expresses her hopes for religious reconciliation. Raoul meets Valentine and recognizes her as someone whose life he had once saved, and also as someone he has seen visiting the Catholic Count of Nevers at night. Unaware that the reason for her visit was to break off a previous engagement to Nevers, Raoul believes her unfaithful and cancels the planned marriage. The outraged Catholics plan to kill Raoul, but Valentine – now married to Nevers – warns him via Marcel. Coming to thank her, Raoul overhears the Catholics plotting the massacre of the Huguenots. Valentine confesses her love for him and, when Nevers is killed, they exchange vows of fidelity before they are both killed along with Marcel in the massacre. [R]

Hulda
Opera in prologue, three acts and epilogue by Franck. 1st perf (abridged) Monte Carlo, 8 March 1894 (composed 1885); 1st complete perf London, 15 March 1994; libr by Charles Grandmougin, after Bjørnstjerne Bjørnson's play. Principal roles: Hulda (mezzo), Eiolf (ten), Swanhilde (sop), Gudrun (mezzo), Aslak (bass), Gudleik (bar), Thordis (sop). Franck's most important opera, it is a heavily Wagnerian piece which is hardly ever performed.
Plot: 11th-century Norway. Hulda swears vengeance after her kin are killed by Aslak and his followers in a tribal clash. She is betrothed to her captor, Aslak's son Gudleik, but he is killed by Eiolf, the royal emissary. Eiolf pays court to Hulda, but then returns to his first love, Swanhilde. Hulda incites Aslak's other sons to kill Eiolf, and having achieved her revenge she throws herself into a fjord.

Hummel, Johann Nepomuk (1778–1837)
Austrian composer. Although best known as an orchestral composer, he also wrote a number of operas and SINGSPIELS, of which the most successful was *Mathilde von Guise* (Vienna, 26 Mar 1810; libr after L.E.F.C. Mercier-Dupary).

Humming
see BOCCA CHIUSA

Humming Chorus
Chorus in Act II of Puccini's *Madama Butterfly*, sung as Cio-Cio-San and Suzuki await Pinkerton's arrival.

Humperdinck, Engelbert (1854–1921)
German composer. A disciple of Wagner, he assisted in the preparation of *Parsifal*, even composing eight bars of it (which were later removed). His first opera HÄNSEL UND GRETEL was by far his most successful, and its formula of presenting children's fairy tales with simple melodies woven into a Wagnerian orchestral structure was followed in many of his later works. His subsequent operas are *Die Sieben Geslein* (Berlin, 19 Dec 1895; libr Adelheid Wette, after the Grimm brothers' *Fairy Tales*), *Dornröschen* (Frankfurt, 12 Nov 1902; libr E. Ebeling and B. Filhès, after Charles Perrault), *Die Heirat Wider Willen* (Berlin, 14 Apr 1905; libr Hedwig Humperdinck, after Alexandre Dumas's *Les Demoiselles de St Cyr*), DIE KÖNIGSKINDER, his only other work to have survived, *Die Marketenderin* (Cologne, 10 May 1914; libr Robert Misch) and *Gaudeamus* (Darmstadt, 18 Mar 1919; libr Misch).

Hunding
Bass role in Wagner's *Die Walküre*. He is Sieglinde's husband.

Hungarian opera composers
see ÁBRÁNYI; BALASSA; BARTÓK; DOHNÁNYI; ERKEL; GOLDMARK; KACSÓH; KÁLMÁN; KODÁLY; LEHÁR; LIGETI; LISZT; PETROVICS; SZOKOLAY

Other national opera composers include Sigismund Bachrich (1841–1913), András Bartay (1799–1854), Attila Bozay (*b* 1939),

Ferenc Doppler (1821–83), Ferenc Farkas (*b* 1905), Ödön Farkas (1851–1912), Pál Kadosa (1903–83), Ödön Mihalovich (1842–1929), Mihály Mosonyi (1815–70), József Ruzitska (1758–1823), Albert Siklós (1878–1942), János Vajda (*b* 1949), Jenö Zádor (1894–1977) and Géza Zichy (1849–1924).

Hungary
see BUDAPEST STATE OPERA; ESTERHÁZA

Hunter, Rita (b 1933)
British soprano, particularly associated with Verdi and Wagner roles, especially Brünnhilde. One of the finest lyrico-dramatic British sopranos of the post-war period, she had a strong, pure and surprisingly agile voice, heard at its best as Leonora in *Il Trovatore*. Her technique was such that she was able to sing Brünnhilde and the title-role in Bellini's *Norma* in the same season at the Metropolitan Opera, New York. She had an appealing stage presence, but her very substantial physique was a serious handicap. Her autobiography, *Wait Till the Sun Shines, Nellie*, was published in 1986.

Huon, Sir
Tenor role in Weber's *Oberon*. A knight, he is the Duke of Guienne.

Huron, Le
Opera in two acts by Grétry. 1st perf Paris, 20 Aug 1768; libr by Jean-François Marmontel, after Voltaire's *L'Ingénu*. Principal roles: Huron (bar), Mlle Saint-Yves (sop), Gilotin (ten), Kerkabon (bass), Saint-Yves (bass). Grétry's first major success and an early operatic example of the theme of Rousseau's 'noble savage', it is nowadays virtually forgotten.
Plot: 17th-century Britanny. Saint-Yves's daughter does not wish to go through with her arranged marriage with Gilotin because she has fallen in love with a Huron Indian. The Huron is recognized by Abbot Kerkabon and his sister as the son of their brother, who died on a mission to the Hurons, and they attempt to instil the social graces into him. Saint-Yves decides to send his daughter to a convent rather than permit her to make a socially unsuitable marriage, but he eventually relents and the lovers are united.

Hvorostovsky, Dmitri (b 1962)
Russian baritone, particularly associated with lyrical Italian and Russian roles, especially Prince Yeletsky in Tchaikovsky's *The Queen of Spades*. He possesses a beautiful if not overlarge voice, which is used with style and musicianship. A good singing-actor with a handsome stage presence.

Hylas
Tenor role in Berlioz's *Les Troyens*. He is a homesick sailor.

Hymn to the Sun
1 Soprano aria for the Queen of Shemakha in Act II of Rimsky-Korsakov's *The Golden Cockerel*. **2** Chorus ('Son io! Son io la vita') in Act I of Mascagni's *Iris*. **3** Baritone aria ('Soleil, on a détruit tes superbes asiles') for Huascar in Act II of Rameau's *Les Indes Galantes*.

Hynninen, Jorma (b 1941)
Finnish baritone, particularly associated with Mozart and Verdi roles and with the Finnish repertory. A singer of style and musicianship and a fine singing-actor, he has been especially noted for his performances in modern Finnish operas, creating the title-roles in Rautavaara's *Thomas* and *Vincent* and, for Sallinen, Topi in *The Red Line*, the King in *The King Goes Forth to France* and the title-role in *Kullervo*. He was artistic director of the Finnish National Opera (1984–92) and the Savonlinna Festival (1992–).

Hytner, Nicholas (b 1956)
British producer. One of the most talented of the younger generation of opera directors, his productions are original and challenging without ever betraying or twisting the composer's intentions. He was associated first with Kent Opera and later with the English National Opera, where his most notable productions have been *Rienzi*, *Serse* and *Die Zauberflöte*.

I

I
Titles beginning with this plural form of the Italian definite article are listed under the letter of the first main word. For example, *I Masnadieri* is listed under M.

Iago
Otello's ensign, he appears as: **1** Baritone role in Verdi's *Otello*. **2** Tenor role in Rossini's *Otello*.

Ibert, Jacques (1890–1962)
French composer. He wrote seven operas in a light classical style. *Persée et Andromède* (Paris, 15 May 1929, composed 1921; libr Nino, after Jules Laforgue's *Moralités Légendaires*) was followed by the comedy ANGÉLIQUE, his most successful work, and *Le Roi d'Yvetot* (Paris, 15 Jan 1930; libr Jean Limozin and André de la Tourrasse, after Pierre-Jean Béranger). Next came three operas written in collaboration with Honegger: *Gonzague* (Paris, 17 Dec 1931; libr R. Kerdyck, after Pierre Veber), L'AIGLON and the operetta *Les Petites Cardinal* (Paris, 12 Feb 1938; libr Albert Willemetz and P. Brach, after Ludovic Halévy). His last work was *Barbe-Bleue* (Lausanne Radio, 10 Oct 1943; libr W. Aguet).

Ice Break, The
Opera in three acts by Tippett. 1st perf London, 7 July 1977; libr by the composer. Principal roles: Lev (bar), Nadia (sop), Hannah (mezzo), Yuri (bar), Gayle (sop), Olympion (ten), Luke (ten), Astron (mezzo and c-ten). Discussing contemporary issues such as race relations and political imprisonment, it deals with the submerging of personality and the need for rebirth.
Plot: An American airport, late 20th century. Lev arrives home after 20 years in a prison camp to join his wife Nadia and their son Yuri. Also at the airport is the fan club of the black champion Olympion, led by Yuri's girlfriend Gayle and her black friend, the nurse Hannah. Violent tensions develop in the crowd, and between individuals, and a race riot breaks out in which Olympion and Gayle are killed and Yuri is seriously injured. After treatment by the doctor Luke, Yuri – released from his plasters – is reconciled with Lev in the wake of Nadia's death. [R]

Ich baue ganz
Tenor aria for Belmonte in Act III of Mozart's *Die Entführung aus dem Serail*, which he sings as a cover for the placing of escape ladders at the seraglio windows.

Icelandic opera composers
These include Jón Ásgeirsson, Karólína Eiríksdóttir (*b* 1951) and Atli Heimir Sveinsson (*b* 1938).

Iceland Opera
Founded in 1979 by the tenor Gardar Cortes, the company has performed since 9 Jan 1982 at a converted cinema, Gamla Bíó (cap 505), in Reykjavík. It mounts three productions a year, some of them sung in Icelandic.

Idamante
Soprano trouser role in Mozart's *Idomeneo*. He is Idomeneo's son. The role is often sung by either a tenor or a mezzo.

Idoménée
Opera in prologue and five acts by Campra. 1st perf Paris, 12 Jan 1712; libr by Antoine Danchet, after Claude Prosper Jolyot de Crébillon's play. Principal roles: Idoménée (bass), Ilione (sop), Electre (sop), Idamante (ten), Neptune (bass), Vénus (sop). A work of considerable dramatic power, which contains some magnificent music, it has recently received a few performances after a long period of total neglect. [R]

Idomeneo, Rè di Creta (*Idomeneus, King of Crete*) or **Ilia ed Idamante**
Opera in three acts by Mozart (K 366).

1st perf Munich, 29 Jan 1781; libr by Giambattista Varesco, after Antoine Danchet's libretto for Campra's *Idoménée*. Principal roles: Idomeneo (ten), Idamante (sop), Ilia (sop), Elettra (sop), Arbace (ten), Voice of Neptune (bass), High Priest (bar). Mozart's first undisputed masterpiece, it remained virtually unperformed for many years, but in recent decades has become the earliest of his operas to win a permanent place in the repertory. Despite its static nature as an OPERA SERIA, it is intensely dramatic and contains some of Mozart's greatest music. **Plot**: Legendary Crete. While returning home from the Trojan War, Idomeneo is threatened by a storm at sea and, in exchange for his safety, promises Neptune that he will sacrifice to him the first person he meets on landing. This turns out to be his son Idamante, who is in love with the Trojan captive Ilia. The appalled Idomeneo attempts to circumvent his vow by accepting the advice of his counsellor Arbace that Idamante should escort the princess Elettra home to Argos. Another storm delays their departure and a sea-monster ravages the coasts. Idamante kills the monster and, learning of his father's vow, offers himself for sacrifice. The voice of Neptune is heard, however, decreeing that Idamante shall reign in Idomeneo's place with Ilia as his bride. Elettra, who loves Idamante, collapses distraught. [R]

I dreamt that I dwelt in marble halls
Soprano aria for Arline in Act II of Balfe's *The Bohemian Girl*, in which she tells of her dim memories of her aristocratic childhood.

I got plenty o' nuttin'
Bass aria for Porgy in Act I of Gershwin's *Porgy and Bess*, in which he tells of his contentment despite his abject poverty.

I have attained the highest power
Bass aria for Boris in Act II of Moussorgsky's *Boris Godunov*, in which he reflects on the cares which the crown has brought him.

Il
Titles beginning with the masculine form of the Italian definite article are listed under the letter of the first main word. For example, *Il Trovatore* is listed under T.

Ilia
Soprano role in Mozart's *Idomeneo*. The daughter of Priam, she is a captive Trojan princess loved by Idamante.

Illica, Luigi (1857–1919)
Italian playwright and librettist. He wrote 88 libretti, often in collaboration with Giuseppe Giacosa (1847–1906) and others. He provided texts for Alfano (*La Fonte di Enschir* and *Il Principe Zilah*), Catalani (*La Wally*), d'Erlanger (*Tess*), Franchetti (*Cristoforo Colombo* and *Germania*), Giordano (*Andrea Chénier* and *Siberia*), Gnecchi (*Cassandra* and *Giuditta*), Mascagni (*Le Maschere*, *Iris* and *Isabeau*), Mascheroni (*Lorenza* and *La Perugina*), Montemezzi (*Héllera*), Panizza (*Aurora*), Puccini (*La Bohème*, *Manon Lescaut*, *Madama Butterfly* and *Tosca*), Smareglia (*Il Vassallo di Szigeth*, *Cornil Schut* and *Nozze Istriane*) and Vittadini (*Il Mare di Tiberiade*) amongst others.

Ilosfalvy, Róbert (b 1927)
Hungarian tenor, particularly associated with the German and Italian repertories. Possessing a well-schooled and tastefully and intelligently-used voice, he began by singing lyrical Italian roles but later turned successfully to heavier roles such as Walther von Stolzing in *Die Meistersinger von Nürnberg*.

Imeneo (*Hymen*)
Opera in three acts by Händel. 1st perf London, 22 Nov 1740; libr after Silvio Stampiglia's libretto for Porpora. Principal roles: Imeneo (bass), Tirinto (mezzo), Rosmene (sop), Clomiri (sop), Argenio (bass). Händel's penultimate Italian opera, it was a failure at its appearance and is nowadays only very rarely performed. **Plot**: Legendary Athens. Rosmene and Clomiris are captured by pirates but are rescued by Hymen, who claims Rosmene's hand in reward. His claim is supported by Clomiris's father Argenius, but Rosmene's fiancé Tirinthus is desolated. Rosmene is torn between love and gratitude and the situation is complicated when Clomiris falls in love with Hymen. Rosmene eventually choses Hymen.

Immolation Scene
The final part of Act III of Wagner's *Götterdämmerung*, in which Brünnhilde lights Siegfried's funeral pyre and the old order is destroyed by fire.

Immortal Hour, The
Opera in two acts by Boughton. 1st perf Glastonbury, 26 Aug 1914; libr by the composer, after Fiona Mcleod (William Sharp)'s play. Principal roles: Etain (sop), Midir (ten), Eochaidh (bar), Dalua (bass), Manus (bass), Maive (mezzo). Boughton's finest opera, written in Wagnerian style, it was sensationally successful at its appearance but is nowadays unaccountably almost never performed.
Plot: Dalua, the Lord of Shadow, allows the mortal Eochaidh, High King of Eiré, to marry the fairy princess Etain. A year later, the fairy Prince Midir comes to claim Etain and she accompanies him to the Land of Heart's Desire. Eochaidh falls dead at Dalua's touch. [R]

Imogene
Soprano role in Bellini's *Il Pirata*. Married to Ernesto, she loves the pirate Gualtiero.

Impresario, The
see SCHAUSPIELDIREKTOR, DER

Impresario in Anguistie, L' (*The Anguished Impresario*)
Comic opera in one act by Cimarosa. 1st perf Naples, Oct 1786; libr by Giuseppe Maria Diodati. Principal roles: Don Grisobalo (bass), Fiordispina (sop), Don Perinzonio (bar), Gelindo (ten), Merlina (sop), Doralba (mezzo), Strabinio (bass). Dealing with backstage operatic politics, it was one of Cimarosa's most successful short works and still receives an occasional performance in Italy.

Inaffia l'ugola
Baritone aria (the Drinking Song) for Iago in Act I of Verdi's *Otello*, in which – with Roderigo's assistance – he gets Cassio drunk.

In alt (Italian for 'in the high')
A term describing the octave above the top line of the treble stave. The octave higher is called *in altissimo*.

Inbal, Eliahu (b 1936)
Israeli conductor, particularly associated with the Italian repertory. Long based at the Teatro la Fenice, Venice, he has been responsible for the revival of a number of forgotten 19th-century Italian operas.

Incontro Improvviso, L' (*The Unexpected Meeting*)
Comic opera in three acts by Haydn. 1st perf Esterháza, 29 Aug 1775; libr by Karl Friberth, after Alain René le Sage's *Les Pèlerins de la Mecque*. Principal roles: Ali (ten), Rezia (sop), Balkis (sop), Dardane (mezzo), Osmin (bass), Calandro (bar). A typical example of the musical craze of the period for all things '*alla turca*', it is nowadays hardly ever performed.
Plot: 17th-century Cairo. King Ali had eloped with the King of Persia's daughter Rezia, but their ship was captured by pirates and they were seperated. Ali arrives penniless in Egypt where, unknown to him, Rezia is the favourite slave of the Sultan. Aided by his gluttonous servant Osmin and by the dervish Calandro, Ali enters the palace and the lovers escape. The reward offered by the Sultan leads Calandro to betray them, but the magnanimous Sultan forgives and releases them. [R]

Incoronazione di Poppea, L'
(*The Coronation of Poppea*)
Opera in prologue and three acts by Monteverdi. 1st perf Venice, autumn 1643; libr by Gian Francesco Busenello, after Tacitus's *Annals*. Principal roles: Poppea (mezzo), Nero (ten), Ottavia (mezzo), Ottone (bar), Seneca (bass), Drusilla (sop), Arnalta (mezzo), Valletto (ten). Monteverdi's last and arguably greatest stage work, it was the first opera written on an historical rather than a mythological subject. Unperformed for nearly 300 years, it has won a permanent place in the repertory in recent decades. Many different realizations have been made, that by Raymond Leppard being the most frequently used.
Plot: Rome, AD 65. Returning home to his mistress Poppea, Ottone discovers that she has been appropriated by Nero. Nero's mortified wife Ottavia bemoans her fate and is offered solace by the philosopher Seneca. Although the goddess of wisdom

has forewarned Seneca that he may die if he interferes, he counsels Nero against his plans to divorce Ottavia, and is subsequently ordered by Nero to take his own life. When Ottone's attempts at reconciliation with Poppea are rejected, he transfers his affections to her lady-in-waiting Drusilla, who loves him. Ottavia orders Ottone, under threat of exposure to Nero, to murder Poppea in her bed. Disguised as Drusilla, he makes the attempt, but Poppea awakens and Drusilla is charged with the attempted crime. She is condemned to death, whereupon Ottone confesses and they are both exiled. Nero banishes Ottavia and Poppea is crowned empress. [R]

Indes Galantes, Les (*The Gallant Indies*)
Opera-ballet in prologue and four (originally three) acts by Rameau. 1st perf Paris, 23 Aug 1735; libr by Louis Fuzelier. Principal roles: Hébé (sop), Émilie (sop), Huascar (bar), Phani (mezzo), Zaïre (sop), Tacmas (ten), Zima (sop), Adario (ten). One of Rameau's greatest successes, still quite often performed, it tells four love stories from different parts of the world. The four self-contained *entrées* are: **1** *Le Turc Genereux* (*The Generous Turk*); **2** *Les Incas de Pérou* (*The Incas of Peru*), much the finest of the four; **3** *Les Fleurs* (*The Flowers*); **4** *Les Sauvages* (*The Savages*), which was added in 1736.
Plot: As Europe forsakes love, Hébé decides to emigrate and witness true love in the Indies. **1** Turkey. Émilie is a prisoner of Osman Pasha, who loves her. Her lover Valère is thrown ashore after a storm. In thanks for a former good deed, Osman releases the lovers. **2** Peru. The Inca princess Phani loves the conquistador Carlos. The high priest Huascar also loves her. Having failed to thwart the lovers' union by using his priestly powers, Huascar throws himself into a volcano. **3** Persia. Prince Tacmas comes to the garden of his friend Ali to spy upon the latter's slave Zaïre, who he loves. She, however, loves Tacmas's slave Fatime. Tacmas mistakes a disguised Fatime for a rival, but all is eventually resolved satisfactorily. **4** Illinois. The Indian Zima is courted by the French and Spanish officers Damon and Alvar. However, she prefers the warrior Adario and rejects Europe in favour of her native land. [R]

In des Lebens Frühlingstagen
Tenor aria for Florestan in Act II of Beethoven's *Fidelio*, in which he reflects that chains are his reward for having championed the truth.

Indian Queen, The
Masque in five acts by Purcell. 1st perf London, autumn 1695; libr after John Dryden and Sir Robert Howard's play. Really more of a play with music rather than a real opera. The music for Act V is by Purcell's brother Daniel. [R]

In diesen heil'gen Hallen
Bass aria for Sarastro in Act II of Mozart's *Die Zauberflöte*, in which he tells Pamina that no ideas of violence can find a home within their community.

Indy, Vincent d' (1851–1931)
French composer. He wrote six stage works, all of them now largely forgotten. They are the OPÉRA-COMIQUE *Attendez-Moi Sous l'Orme* (*Wait for Me Under the Oak*, Paris, 11 Feb 1882; libr Jules Prével and Robert de Bonnières, after J.F. Régnard), the Wagnerian *La Chant de la Cloche* (Brussels, 21 Nov 1912, composed 1886; libr composer, after Friedrich von Schiller's *Das Lied von der Glocke*), FERVAAL, his most successful opera, *L'Étranger* (Brussels, 7 Jan 1903; libr composer), *La Légende de St Christophe* (Paris, 9 June 1920; libr composer, after J. de Voragine's *Legenda Aurea*) and the operetta *La Rêve de Cinyras* (Paris, 10 June 1927, composed 1923; libr Xavier de Courville). He also helped to complete the unfinished *Ghisèle* by his teacher, Franck.

In einem Waschkert
Baritone/bass duet for Herr Fluth and Falstaff in Act II of Nicolaï's *Die Lustigen Weiber von Windsor*. One of the finest of all BUFFO duets.

Infedeltà Delusa, L' (*Infidelity Deluded*)
Comic opera in two acts by Haydn. 1st perf Esterháza, 26 July 1773; libr by Marco Coltellini. Principal roles: Sandrina (sop), Filippo (ten), Vespina (sop), Nanni (bar), Nencio (ten). After a long period of neglect it has received a number of performances in the last decade.
Plot: 18th-century Tuscany. Filippo wishes

his daughter Sandrina to wed the wealthy young Nencio, but she loves the peasant Nanni. Nanni's sister Vespina loves and is loved by Nencio. However, for social advantage, Nencio is prepared to marry Sandrina, and Vespina sets out to put a stop to it. Disguising herself in turn as a nagging old harridan, a drunken German flunkey, a notary and a nobleman, she causes total confusion and finally manages to transpose the names on the wedding contract so that the true lovers are united. [R]

Infelice, e tu credevi
Bass aria for da Silva in Act I of Verdi's *Ernani*, in which he expresses his distress on discovering that Elvira loves Ernani.

In fernam Land
Tenor aria (the *Gralserzählung*) for Lohengrin in Act III of Wagner's *Lohengrin*, in which he discloses his identity and tells of the Holy Grail.

Inganno Felice, L' (*The Happy Deceit*)
Comic opera in one act by Rossini. 1st perf Venice, 8 Jan 1812; libr by Giuseppe Maria Foppa, after Giovanni Palomba's libretto for Paisiello. Principal roles: Isabella (sop), Batone (bass), Bertrando (ten), Ormondo (bass), Tarabotto (bar). One of Rossini's early little farces, it is still occasionally performed.
Plot: Duke Bertrando's wife Isabella refused the advances of Ormondo, who – with the aid of his henchman Batone – set her adrift in a boat. Bertrando believes her dead, but she survived and is under the protection of Tarabotto. They encounter the Duke who is reunited with his wife and who, at Isabella's request, is merciful to Ormondo and Batone. [R]

Inghilleri, Giovanni (1894–1959)
Italian baritone and composer, particularly associated with the Italian repertory. One of the leading Italian baritones of the inter-war period, he created the title-role in Malipiero's *Giulio Cesare* and a role in Casella's *La Donna Serpente*. He also composed one opera, *La Burla*.

Iñigo Gómez, Don
Bass role in Ravel's *L'Heure Espagnole*. He is a banker in love with Concepción.

In mia man
Soprano/tenor duet for Norma and Pollione in Act II of Bellini's *Norma*, in which she threatens him with the death of their children.

Innsbruck
see TIROLESE LANDESTHEATER, INNSBRUCK

In quegli anni
Tenor aria for Don Basilio in Act IV of Mozart's *Le Nozze di Figaro*. An idealized self-portrait, it is frequently cut.

In quelle trine morbide
Soprano aria for Manon in Act II of Puccini's *Manon Lescaut*, in which she laments the emptiness of the splendour in which she lives.

In questa reggia
Soprano aria for Turandot in Act II of Puccini's *Turandot*, in which she tells now the rape of her ancestress Lo-u-Ling has made her resolved to be avenged upon men through her riddles.

Intendant
The title of the administrator of a German or Austrian opera house.

Interlude
In opera, an orchestral piece between two scenes, such as the Storm Interlude in Britten's *Peter Grimes*.

Intermezzo
The term has two meanings in opera:
1 A short, self-contained and usually comic work placed between the acts of an 18th-century Italian OPERA SERIA. Usually for two singers and one mute character, much the most famous example is Pergolesi's *La Serva Padrona*. The earliest known intermezzo is Francesco Silvani's *Bleso e Lesba*, given in 1700 between the acts of *L'Oracolo in Sogno*. Some short 20th-century comic operas are imitations of the form, notably Wolf-Ferrari's *Il Segreto di Susanna* and Menotti's *The Telephone*. It has also been used occasionally for specific dramatic purposes, as, for example, in Henze's *The Bassarids*. **2** A short orchestral piece played between two scenes. Mascagni wrote famous examples in *Cavalleria Rusticana* and *L'Amico Fritz*.

Intermezzo
Opera in two acts by Strauss (Op 72). 1st perf Dresden, 4 Nov 1924; libr by the composer. Principal roles: Christine (sop), Robert (bar), Baron Lummer (ten), Anna (sop), Stroh (ten), Kammersänger (bass). Described as a 'bourgeois comedy with symphonic interludes', it is based on incidents in Strauss's own married life. It is only infrequently performed.
Plot: Vienna and Grundlsee, 1920s. The composer Robert Storch is permanently castigated by his shrewish wife Christine because he is too mild to stand up to her. She flirts with the young Baron Lummer but threatens divorce when she opens a passionate love letter accidentally addressed to her husband. The misunderstanding is cleared up, but Christine is appeased only when Robert is finally driven to upbraid her. [R]

In the Well (*V Studni*)
Comic opera in one act by Blodek. 1st perf Prague, 17 Nov 1867; libr by Karel Sabina. Principal roles: Lidunka (sop), Vojtěk (ten), Jánek (bass), Veruna (mezzo). The most successful of all Czech comic operas apart from *The Bartered Bride*, it is a charming and tuneful little piece. Still very popular in the Czech lands, it is virtually unknown elsewhere.
Plot: 19th-century Bohemia. Lidunka loves Vojtěk, but her mother wants her to wed the rich old farmer Jánek. She consults the local witch Veruna, who tells her that she will see the face of her lover in a nearby well on St John's Eve. Jánek overhears this and climbs a tree overlooking the well, but falls into it. During his attempts to get out he startles Lidunka and is publicly disgraced, leaving Lidunka able to marry Vojtěk. [R]

Intolleranza (*Intolerance*)
Opera in two acts by Nono. 1st perf (as *Intolleranza 1960*) Venice, 13 April 1961; libr by the composer, after Angelo Maria Ripellino and other sources. Revised version 1st perf Florence, 1974; libr revised by J. Karsunke. Principal roles: Emigrant (ten), Companion (sop), Tortured Man (bass). Nono's first opera, which has exercised a considerable influence on the younger generation of Italian composers, it is a condemnation – written from Nono's customary extreme left-wing political viewpoint – of the indifference and intolerance of the modern world. Its stormy premiere was one of the most notorious in modern operatic history, provoking a major political riot orchestrated by the neo-fascist group Ordine Nuovo.
Plot: Unsympathetic towards her lover's homesickness, a woman becomes estranged from her him, a refugee miner. He becomes accidentally embroiled in a political demonstration and is sent to a prison camp. Despite the appalling conditions, he experiences love and humanity. A purifying flood covers the lands to symbolize a new understanding amongst mankind.

Intonation
A term describing whether or not a singer remains at the correct pitch, neither sharp nor flat; in other words, stays in tune.

Intrusive H
A vocal fault usually appearing in long runs on a single syllable. An effect of 'ha-ha-ha' rather than 'a-a-a' is produced because the singer has started each note with an unvocalized breath.

In uomini
Soprano aria for Despina in Act I of Mozart's *Così fan Tutte*, in which she ridicules the idea that men would ever be faithful.

Invano, Alvaro
Tenor/baritone duet for Don Alvaro and Don Carlo in Act IV of Verdi's *La Forza del Destino*, in which Alvaro attempts to dissuade Carlo from fighting a duel.

Invisible City of Kitezh, The
Full title: **The Legend of the Invisible City of Kitezh and the Maiden Fevronia**
(*Skazaniye o Nevidimon Grade Kitezhe i Devie Fevronie*)
Opera in four acts by Rimsky-Korsakov. 1st perf St Petersburg, 20 Feb 1907; libr by Vladimir Ivanovich Belsky, after Pavel Ivanovich Melnikov's *In the Wood*, I.S. Meledin's *Kitezh Chronicle* and other sources. Principal roles: Prince Vsevelod (ten), Fevronia (sop), Grishka (ten), Prince Yuri (bass), Poyarok (bar). One of Rimsky's finest operas, notable both for its

superb orchestration and for its characterization of the drunken Grishka, it combines two traditional Russian legends: those of St Fevronia and of the rescue of Kitezh from a Tartar attack. Apart from the orchestral suite, it is virtually unknown outside Russia.
Plot: Legendary Russia. Whilst hunting, Prince Vsevelod meets and falls in love with the woodcutter's sister Fevronia. At first unaware of his identity, she agrees to wed him. In Kitezh the Less, the marriage preparations are halted by the Tartar sack of the city. Only Fevronia and the drunken Grishka Kuterma escape. At Great Kitezh, Vsevelod and all his troops are killed by the Tartars and the city vanishes. Grishka and Fevronia are journeying through a forest when Fevronia collapses with exhaustion. She receives a dying vision of Vsevelod beckoning her to a rebuilt city. In another world, Kitezh stands once more and its inhabitants celebrate Fevronia's marriage to Vsevelod. [R]

Iolanta
Opera in nine scenes by Tchaikovsky (Op 69). 1st perf St Petersburg, 18 Dec 1892; libr by Modest Tchaikovsky, after Henrik Hertz's *Kong Renés Datter*. Principal roles: Iolanta (sop), Vaudémont (ten), Robert (bar), King René (bass), Ibn Hakia (bar), Martha (mezzo). Tchaikovsky's last opera, it has never been one of his more popular works, despite its beautiful music, and is only infrequently performed outside Russia.
Plot: 15th-century Provence. King René's daughter Iolanta is unaware that she is blind. The doctor Ibn Hakia tells René that she can be cured only if she is conscious of her blindness and wants to see, but René will not have her told. Vaudémont, to whom she was engaged as a child, arrives and falls in love with her. He describes to her the beauties of the world. René threatens him with death, but her sight is restored and the couple are betrothed. [R]

Iolanthe or **The Peer and the Peri**
Operetta in two acts by Sullivan. 1st perf London, 25 Nov 1882; libr by W.S. Gilbert. Principal roles: Lord Chancellor (bar), Phyllis (sop), Fairy Queen (cont), Mountarrarat (b-bar), Tolloller (ten), Strephon (bar), Iolanthe (mezzo), Pvte Willis (bass), Celia (sop), Leila (sop). One of the best-loved of the Savoy Operas, enjoying an initial run of almost 400 performances, it is a satire on the House of Lords and also contains some of Sullivan's finest music.
Plot: 19th-century Arcadia and Westminster. Strephon, son of a mortal father and the fairy Iolanthe, loves the shepherdess Phyllis, a ward of court. Iolanthe, exiled for her marriage with a mortal, is pardoned by the Fairy Queen, who promises Strephon her protection. The entire House of Lords wishes to marry Phyllis, and the Lord Chancellor forbids Strephon to see her. Phyllis overhears Strephon talking to Iolanthe and thinks him unfaithful – nobody believes that the young-looking woman is his mother. Strephon calls upon the Fairy Queen for aid, and it is decided that he will enter Parliament, where – because of his fairy powers – the members will vote as he wishes on all measures, including throwing the peerage open to competitive examination. Phyllis, having turned to Earls Mountarrarat and Tolloller, is wretched, and forgives Strephon when she learns the truth that he is only half a mortal. Iolanthe pleads Strephon's case to the Lord Chancellor, who is unmoved until she reveals that she is the wife he thought long dead. All objection to Strephon and Phyllis marrying is thus removed and fairy law is changed so that it is death not to marry a mortal. To save herself, the Fairy Queen marries the guardsman Private Willis. [R]

Io la vidi
Tenor aria for Carlos in Act 1 of Verdi's *Don Carlos*, in which he tells of the love that awoke in him when he first saw Elisabeth.

Io morrò
Baritone aria for Rodrigo in Act IV of Verdi's *Don Carlos*, in which he says that he dies in happiness knowing that Carlos will try to liberate Flanders.

Iopas
Tenor role in Berlioz's *Les Troyens*. He is Dido's court poet.

Io son l'umile ancella
Soprano aria for Adriana in Act I of Cilea's *Adriana Lecouvreur*, in which she states that she is the humble servant of her art.

Io son rico
Soprano/bass duet (the Barcarolle) for Adina and Dr Dulcamara in Act II of Donizetti's *L'Elisir d'Amore*, sung to entertain the wedding guests.

Iphigénie en Aulide (*Iphigenia in Aulis*)
Opera in three acts by Gluck. 1st perf Paris, 19 April 1774; libr by François Bailly Leblanc du Roullet, after Jean Baptiste Racine's play, itself based on Euripides's play. Principal roles: Iphigénie (sop), Agamemnon (bar), Achille (ten), Clytemnestre (mezzo), Patrocle (bass), Calchas (b-bar). One of Gluck's finest works, even if a little below the level of his other *Iphigénie*, it is still performed from time to time, sometimes in the edition prepared by Wagner in 1846.
Plot: Legendary Aulis (Euboea). Having vowed to sacrifice his daughter Iphigenia in return for a favourable wind to Troy, Agamemnon is beset by remorse. When Iphigenia and her mother Clytemnestra arrive (believing that the girl has come to wed Achilles), he attempts to circumvent the sacrifice demanded by the high priest Calchas. Meanwhile Achilles, enraged at the proposed killing of his betrothed, leads an attack on the Greeks, but Calchas announces that the gods have decided to grant a fair wind without the sacrifice. [R original and Wagner versions]

Iphigénie en Tauride (*Iphigenia in Tauris*)
Opera in four acts by Gluck. 1st perf Paris, 18 May 1779; libr by Nicolas François Guillard, after Euripides's play. Principal roles: Iphigénie (mezzo), Oreste (bar), Pylade (ten), Thoas (b-bar), Diane (mezzo). Gluck's finest work and one of the greatest of all operas, it is still quite frequently performed, but not as often as its outstanding musico-dramatic merits deserve.
Plot: Legendary Tauris (Scythia). After the Trojan War, Iphigenia has become a priestess of Diana and is unaware of her father's murder by her mother and the revenge taken by her brother Orestes. Orestes and his companion Pylades arrive incognito and are captured. The Scythian King Thoas orders them to be sacrificed. Orestes gives Iphigenia the news of her parents' death, but also says that Orestes is dead. Iphigenia wishes to save him, but he – pursued by the Furies – persuades her to save Pylades instead. Just as the sacrifice is about to take place, brother and sister recognize each other and Diana intervenes with a pardon for Orestes. [R]

Iphigénie en Tauride (*Iphigenia in Tauris*)
Opera in four acts by Piccinni. 1st perf Paris, 23 Jan 1781; libr by Alphonse du Congé Dubreuil, after Claude Guymond de la Touche's play, itself based on Euripides's play. Principal roles: Iphigénie (mezzo), Oreste (bass), Pylade (ten), Thoas (bar), Diane (sop). As a result of the famous feud between the supporters of Piccinni and Gluck, an enterprising impresario had them both set the same story. Piccinni's version contains some fine music, but both the contemporary public and history decided in favour of Gluck.

Ippolitov-Ivanov, Mikhail (1859–1935)
Russian composer and conductor. He wrote seven operas, all of them now forgotten. They include *Ruth* (Tiflis, 23 Jan 1887; libr after the Old Testament), *Azra* (Tiflis, 22 Nov 1890; libr composer, after Adam Mickiewicz), *Asya* (Moscow, 28 Sept 1900; libr N. Manykin-Nevstruyev, after Ivan Turgenev), *Treachery* (*Izmena*, Moscow, 4 Dec 1910; libr after I.A. Sumbatov), *Ole the Norseman* (Moscow, 8 Nov 1916; libr composer, after M. Jersen) and the unperformed *The Last Barricade* (1933; libr after N.A. Krasheninnikov). He also prepared Moussorgsky's unfinished *The Marriage* for performance (1931) and conducted the first performances of Rimsky-Korsakov's *The Tale of Tsar Saltan*, *Kashchey the Immortal* and *The Tsar's Bride*.

Ireland
see DUBLIN GRAND OPERA SOCIETY; OPERA NORTHERN IRELAND; WEXFORD FESTIVAL

Irene
1 Soprano role in Wagner's *Rienzi*. She is Rienzi's sister. **2** Mezzo role in Donizetti's

Belisario. She is Belisario's daughter. **3** Mezzo role in Händel's *Tamerlano*. She is a princess betrothed to Tamburlaine. **4** Mezzo role in Händel's *Atalanta*. Nicandro's daughter, she loves Aminta.

Iris
Opera in three acts by Mascagni. 1st perf Rome, 22 Nov 1898; libr by Luigi Illica. Principal roles: Iris (sop), Osaka (ten), Kyoto (bar), Il Cieco (bass). A brutal and unpleasant piece of VERISMO, it met with considerable success at its appearance and is still occasionally performed.
Plot: Legendary Japan. When the pure Iris, whom Osaka loves, cannot be persuaded to reciprocate his feelings, he arranges for the brothel-keeper Kyoto to abduct her and hold her captive in the brothel. Il Cieco, her blind father, believes that she has gone there voluntarily and curses her, flinging mud at her. In despair, Iris throws herself down a laundry chute and drowns in a sewer. [R]

Irische Legende (*Irish Legend*)
Opera in five scenes by Egk. 1st perf Salzburg, 17 Aug 1955; libr by the composer, after William Butler Yeats's *The Countess Cathleen* and *Cathleen O'Shea*. Principal roles: Cathleen (sop), Aleel (bass), Oona (mezzo). It has met with some success in German-speaking countries but is little known elsewhere.
Plot: Ireland in the future. The Devil has brought about a famine and people sell their souls to him in exchange for food. The poet Aleel is abducted by demons and his lover Countess Cathleen offers to sell her soul to redeem him. However, she is saved and rises to heaven.

Irish opera composers
see BALFE; STANFORD; WALLACE
Other national opera composers include Denis Aplvor (*b* 1916), Augusta Holmès (1847–1903), Robert O'Dwyer, whose *Eithne* (Dublin, 16 May 1910; libr Thomas O'Kelly) was the first opera written to an Erse libretto, Gerard Victory (*b* 1921) and James Wilson (*b* 1922).

Irmelin
Opera in three acts by Delius. 1st perf Oxford, 4 May 1953 (composed 1892); libr by the composer. Principal roles: Irmelin (sop), Nils (ten), King (bass), Rolf (bar). Delius's first opera, it is only very rarely performed.
Plot: Medieval Europe. The Princess Irmelin seeks true love and rejects several suitors proposed by her father, the King. Prince Nils, disguised as a swineherd, is in search of the ideal woman and is told that he will find her at the end of a silver stream. He goes there, discovers Irmelin, and the two fall in love. [R]

Isabeau
Opera in three acts by Mascagni. 1st perf Buenos Aires, 2 June 1911; libr by Luigi Illica. Principal roles: Isabeau (sop), Folco (ten), Raimondo (bar), Cornelio (bass), Giglietta (mezzo). Moderately successful in its time, this version of the Lady Godiva story is nowadays only very rarely performed.
Plot: Medieval Italy. As a punishment for refusing to choose a husband, King Raimondo orders his daughter Isabeau to ride naked through the streets at noon. The people pass a law that anybody daring to look at her shall be put to death. The law is disobeyed by the young woodsman Folco. Isabeau, now in love with him, tries to prevent his being lynched by the mob and then kills herself over his dying body. [R Exc]

Isabella
1 Mezzo role in Rossini's *L'Italiana in Algieri*. Lindoro's beloved, she is the Italian girl of the opera's title. **2** Soprano role in Suppé's *Boccaccio*. She is Lotteringhi's wife. **3** Soprano role in Wagner's *Das Liebesverbot*. She is a novice. **4** Soprano role in Meyerbeer's *Robert le Diable*. She is a Sicilian princess loved by Robert. **5** Soprano role in Rossini's *L'Inganno Felice*. She is Bertrando's long-lost wife. **6** Soprano role in Donizetti's *L'Assedio di Calais*. She is the wife of King Edward III. **7** Mezzo role in Fibich's *The Bride of Messina*. She is the widowed princess of Messina.

Isabella, Queen
Queen Isabella I of Spain (1451–1504) appears in a number of operas, including: **1** Soprano role in Milhaud's *Christophe Colomb*. **2** Soprano role in de Falla's *L'Atlántida*. **3** Mezzo role in Offenbach's

Christopher Columbus. **4** Soprano role in Egk's *Columbus*. **5** Soprano role in Franchetti's *Cristoforo Colombo*. **6** Mezzo role in Škroup's *Columbus*. **7** Mezzo role in Glass's *The Voyage*. **8** Soprano role in Martín y Soler's *Una Cosa Rara*.

Ishmael
Tenor role in Verdi's *Nabucco*. He is an Israelite in love with Nabucco's daughter Fenena.

Isola Disabitata, L' (*The Uninhabited Island*)
Opera in two acts by Haydn. 1st perf Esterháza, 6 Dec 1779; libr by Pietro Metastasio. Principal roles: Costanza (mezzo), Gernando (ten), Silvia (sop), Enrico (bar). Despite some fine music, it is almost never performed.
Plot: Gernando, his wife Costanza and her sister Silvia are shipwrecked on an island and Gernando is captured by pirates. After 13 years, Costanza is convinced that Gernando has deserted her and teaches Silvia that all men are hateful. Freed at last, Gernando arrives with his friend Enrico, whom Silvia observes in wonder. Gernando believes Costanza is dead and is comforted by Enrico, but Silvia – now in love with Enrico – reports that she is alive. Costanza and Gernando finally meet, and, after some suspicions, Costanza is assured of his fidelity. [R]

Isolde
Soprano role in Wagner's *Tristan und Isolde*. She is an Irish princess betrothed to King Marke of Cornwall.

Isolier
Mezzo trouser role in Rossini's *Le Comte Ory*. He is Ory's page.

Isouard, Nicolò (sometimes known simply as Nicolò) **(1775–1818)**
Maltese composer. He wrote some 40 operas, a number of which enjoyed considerable success in their time but which are all now forgotten. They include *Artaserse* (Livorno, Sept 1794; libr Pietro Metastasio), *Le Tonnelier* (Paris, 17 May 1801; libr E.J.B. Delrieu and François Antoine Quêtant), *Cendrillon* (Paris, 22 Feb 1810; libr Charles-Guillaume Étienne, after Charles Perrault), *Joconde* (Paris, 28 Feb 1814; libr Étienne) and *Jeannot et Colin* (Paris, 17 Oct 1714; libr Étienne), his finest opera.

Israel
see HEBREW NATIONAL OPERA

Israeli opera composers
see TAL
Other national opera composers include Menachem Avidom (*b* 1908), Mark Kopytman (*b* 1929), Marc Lavry (1903–67) and Ami Maayani (*b* 1936).

It ain't necessarily so
Tenor aria for Sportin' Life in Act II of Gershwin's *Porgy and Bess*, in which he casts doubts upon some biblical stories.

Italiana in Algieri, L' (*The Italian Girl in Algiers*)
Comic opera in two acts by Rossini. 1st perf Venice, 22 May 1813; libr by Angelo Anelli. Principal roles: Isabella (mezzo), Lindoro (ten), Mustafà (bass), Taddeo (bar), Ali (bass), Elvira (sop), Zulma (mezzo). Rossini's first great comic success, it remains one of the finest and most popular of all OPERA BUFFAS, rich in humour, melody and florid arias.
Plot: Algiers, *c* 1800. The Bey Mustafà is bored with his wife Elvira and orders Ali, the captain of his corsairs, to find him a European wife. The Italian Isabella, searching for her beloved Lindoro who is held captive by Mustafà, is shipwrecked along with her ever-hopeful elderly admirer Taddeo, and is brought to Mustafà. He is captivated by her, and Isabella devises a plan to gain everyone's freedom. She flirts with Mustafà, and Lindoro and Taddeo initiate him into the brotherhood of the 'Papatachi', who must eat and remain silent. Isabella, Lindoro and Taddeo escape in a ship from under Mustafà's nose, while he believes that this is just a test of his fidelity to his 'Papatachi' vow. When he realizes that he has been duped he returns to the arms of Elvira, having had enough of European women. [R]

Italianate
A term used to describe singing which is in the lyrical and full-bodied style usually associated with Italian operas. It is used

mainly in reference to non-Italian works and to non-Italian singers where such singing is unusual and comes as a welcome surprise. An example is Alberto Remedios's singing of the title-role of *Siegfried*.

Italian opera composers
see ABBATINI; ALBINONI; ALFANO; ANFOSSI; APOLLONI; ARDITI; BANFIELD; BELLINI; BERIO; BOCCHERINI; BOITO; BONONCINI; BONTEMPI; BOTTESINI; BUSONI; BUSOTTI; CACCINI; CAGNONI; CALDARA; CARAFA; CASELLA; CASTELNUOVO-TEDESCO; CATALANI; CAVALIERI, DE; CAVALLI; CESTI; CHAILLY; CHERUBINI; CILEA; CIMAROSA; COCCIA; DALLAPICCOLA; DENZA; DONIZETTI: DRAGHI; DUNI; FACCIO; FEO; FERRARI-TRECATE; FERRERO; FIORAVANTI; FRANCHETTI; FRAZZI; GAGLIANO; GALUPPI; GASPARINI; GAZZANIGA; GENERALI; GHEDINI; GIORDANO; GNECCHI; GOBATTI; GUGLIELMI; JOMMELLI; LANDI; LATTUADA; LEO; LEONCAVALLO; LEONI; LOTTI; LUALDI; MADERNA; MALIPIERO; MANCINELLI; MANFROCE; MARAZZOLI; MARCHETTI; MASCAGNI; MAYR; MERCADANTE; MONTEMEZZI; MONTEVERDI; MORLACCHI; MORTARI; MOSCA; NAPOLI; NICOLINI; NONO; OREFICE; PACINI; PAER; PAISIELLO; PAVESI; PEDROLLO; PEDROTTI; PERGOLESI; PERI; PETRASSI; PETRELLA; PICCINNI; PICK-MANGIAGALLI; PIZZETTI; PONCHIELLI; PORPORA; PUCCINI; REEICE; RESPIGHI; RICCI, F.; RICCI, L.; RINALDO DA CAPUA; ROCCA; ROSSELLINI; ROSSI, LAURO; ROSSI, LUIGI; ROSSINI; ROTA; SACCHINI; SALIERI; SARTI; SCARLATTI, A.; SCARLATTI, D.; SMAREGLIA; SPONTINI; STEFFANI; STRADELLA; TOSATTI; TRAETTA; UTTINI; VACCAI; VECCHI; VERACINI; VERDI; VERETTI; VINCI; VIOZZI; VITTADINI; VIVALDI; WOLF-FERRARI; ZAFRED; ZANDONAI; ZIANI; ZINGARELLI

Italian Straw Hat, The
see CAPPELLO DI PAGLIA DI FIRENZE, IL

Italian Tenor
Tenor role in: **1** Strauss's *Der Rosenkavalier*. **2** Strauss's *Capriccio*.

Italy
see FESTIVAL OF TWO WORLDS, SPOLETO; FLORENTINE CAMERATA; MAGGIO MUSICALE FIORENTINO; PESARO FESTIVAL; PICCOLA SCALA, LA; TEATRO ALLA SCALA, MILAN; TEATRO CARLO FELICE, GENOA; TEATRO COMUNALE, BOLOGNA; TEATRO COMUNALE, FLORENCE; TEATRO COMUNALE GIUSEPPE VERDI, TRIESTE; TEATRO DELL'OPERA, ROME; TEATRO DONIZETTI, BERGAMO; TEATRO LA FENICE, VENICE; TEATRO MASSIMO, PALERMO; TEATRO MASSIMO BELLINI, CATANIA; TEATRO MUNICIPALE, REGGIO EMILIA; TEATRO PETRUZZELLI, BARI; TEATRO REGIO, PARMA; TEATRO REGIO, TURIN; TEATRO SAN CARLO, NAPLES; VERONA ARENA

Ite sul colle
Bass aria for Oroveso in Act I of Bellini's *Norma*, in which he summons the Druids for the cutting of the sacred mistletoe.

Ivan IV
Opera in five acts by Bizet. 1st perf Tübingen, 1946 (composed 1862); libr by François-Hippolyte Leroy and Henri Trianon. Principal roles: Ivan (bar), Marie (sop), Igor (ten), Temrouk (bass), Yorloff (bass), Young Bulgarian (ten). Bizet's only grand opera, telling of events in the reign of Ivan the Terrible of Russia (1547–84), the last act was never quite completed and Bizet incorporated some of the music into later works. Although it contains some fine moments, it is only very rarely performed. [R Exc]

Ivanhoe
Opera in four acts by Sullivan. 1st perf London, 31 Jan 1891; libr by Julian Russell Sturgis, after Sir Walter Scott's novel. Principal roles: Ivanhoe (ten), Bois-Guilbert (bar), Rowena (sop), Rebecca (sop), Richard I (bass), Friar Tuck (bar), Ulrica (cont), Cedric (bar). Sullivan's only opera, it contains some fine music and intermittent moments of dramatic power, but the overall effect is cold and unconvincing. Reasonably successful at its appearance (it enjoyed an initial run of 160 consecutive performances), it is nowadays only very rarely performed.
Plot: Britain, 1190s. Ivanhoe and King Richard I return in disguise from the Third Crusade to rescue England from misrule. At a tournament, Ivanhoe defeats the templar Brian de Bois-Guilbert. The templar abducts Rowena, daughter of the Saxon Cedric, and makes an attempt upon the honour of Rebecca, daughter of Isaac of York. Rebecca escapes and nurses a

wounded Ivanhoe back to health whilst Richard leads Friar Tuck and the men of Sherwood against the templar and burns his castle. Richard persuades Cedric to consent to Rowena's marriage to Ivanhoe. Ivanhoe fights the templar for the hand of Rowena (who has been unjustly accused of witchcraft) and kills him.

Ivan Susanin
see LIFE FOR THE TSAR, A

Ivan the Terrible
see MAID OF PSKOV, THE

Ivogün, Maria (b Ilse Kempner) (1891–1987)
Hungarian soprano, particularly associated with COLORATURA roles, especially Zerbinetta in Strauss's *Ariadne auf Naxos*. She created Ighino in Pfitzner's *Palestrina* and was later a noted teacher, whose pupils included Elisabeth Schwarzkopf, Renate Holm and Rita Streich. Marriaed first to the tenor KARL ERB and later to the pianist **Michael Raucheisen**.

Ivrogne Corrigé, L' (*The Reformed Drunkard*) or **Le Mariage du Diable** (*The Devil's Wedding*)
Comic opera in two acts by Gluck. 1st perf Vienna, April 1760; libr by Louis Anseaume and Jean-Baptiste Lourdet de Santerre, after Jean de la Fontaine's *L'Ivrogne en Enfer*. Principal roles: Colette (sop), Cléon (ten), Mathurin (ten), Lucas (bass), Mathurine (sop). It is one of the few of Gluck's earlier works in OPÉRA-COMIQUE style which still receives an occasional performance.
Plot: France, *c* 1760. Mathurin wishes his niece Colette to marry his old friend Lucas, but she is in love with Cléon. When Mathurin and Lucas are heavily in their cups, Colette and Cléon simulate a scene from hell which so frightens Mathurin that he agrees to Colette's marriage with Cléon and also vows to forswear alcohol. [R]

J

Jack
Tenor role in Tippett's *The Midsummer Marriage*. He is Bella's boyfriend.

Jacobs, Arthur (b 1922)
British critic and musicologist. One of the most perceptive and scholarly of contemporary British critics, his writings include the *Penguin Dictionary of Music* and a biography of Sullivan. A champion of opera in English, he has made some 20 translations and also wrote the libretto for Maw's *One Man Show*.

Jacobs, René (b 1946)
Belgian counter-tenor and conductor, particularly associated with Händel and other baroque roles and with early operas. Founder of the Concerto Vocale, he is a male alto of fine style and musicianship, and has also enjoyed considerable success as a conductor, being closely associated with La Petite Bande and with Il Complesso Barocco.

Jacquino
Tenor role in Beethoven's *Fidelio*. The assistant jailer, he is in love with Marzelline.

Jagd, Die (*The Hunt*)
Opera in three acts by Hiller. 1st perf Leipzig, 29 Jan 1770; libr by Christian Felix Weisse, after Charles Collé's *La Partie de Chasse de Henri IV* and Jean-Marie Sedaine's *Le Roi et le Fermier*. Principal roles: King (bass), Röschen (sop), Michel (ten), Christel (ten), Hannchen (sop), Töffel (bass), Marthe (sop), Schmetterling (speaker). Hiller's finest work and the archetypal early SINGSPIEL, it was one of the most popular of all operas in Germany in the late 18th and early 19th centuries. It is nowadays virtually forgotten.
Plot: Late-16th-century France. The local judge Michel and his wife Marthe await the arrival of the King's hunting party. Their daughter Röschen cannot wed her beloved Töffel until her elder brother Christel is married. His betrothed Hannchen has been abducted by the evil Count von Schmetterling, but she escapes and Christel is convinced of her fidelity. A storm separates the King from his retinue and he arrives at Michel's house incognito and learns of Schmetterling's misdeeds. When Schmetterling appears, the King reveals himself, exiles Schmetterling and gives the two pairs of lovers a generous dowry.

J'ai des yeux
Bass aria for Coppélius in the Olympia Act of Offenbach's *Les Contes d'Hoffmann*, in which he tells Hoffmann of the magical eyes which he has for sale.

Jakobín (*The Jacobin*)
Opera in three acts by Dvořák (Op 84). 1st perf Prague, 12 Feb 1889; libr by Marie Červinková-Riegrová. Principal roles: Jiří (ten), Terinka (sop), Bohuš (bar), Benda (ten), Filip (bass), Julie (sop), Vilém (bass), Adolf (bar). One of Dvořák's most attractive scores, notable for its delightful characterization of the schoolmaster Benda, it is unaccountably only infrequently performed outside the Czech lands.
Plot: Bohemia, 1793. Bohuš, the son of Count Vilém, returns from France with his wife Julie and learns that he is about to be replaced as heir by his cousin Adolf. Bohuš is arrested for his Jacobin sympathies, but Julie – with the help of the schoolmaster Benda, his daughter Terinka and the young gamekeeper Jiří – succeeds in persuading the Count to change his mind. [R]

Jakob Lenz
Opera in 12 scenes by Rihm. 1st perf Karlsruhe, 6 March 1980; libr by Michael Fröhling, after Georg Büchner's *Lenz*. Principal roles: Lenz (bar), Oberlin (bass), Kaufmann (ten). A study in madness, it deals with events in the life of the German poet Jakob Michael Lenz (1751–92), who went insane and died in Moscow as a

beggar. Written in atonal style, it has proved one of the most successful contemporary chamber operas and has been widely performed. [R]

Janáček, Leoš (1854–1928)
Czech (Moravian) composer. His nine operas, which inhabit a sound world unlike that of any other composer, contain much of his greatest music and most date from his remarkable late creative flowering which occurred in his 70s. Born in Brno and spending most of his life there, he lived and worked outside the mainstream of European music, whose developments influenced him hardly at all. Long considered a minor provincial composer, he was unknown outside Brno until 1916, when the Prague production of *Jenůfa* made him famous in the country at large; his international fame and status date only from recent decades. His operas are characterized by a strong humanism, a deep feeling for nature and the musical qualities of its sounds, an almost total disregard for traditional dramatic values, a vocal line largely dictated by the nuances of Czech speech rhythms, intense lyricism, and harmonies and orchestration which might best be described as 'spikey'.

His first opera ŠÁRKA gives sporadic indications of what was to come, but its successor, THE BEGINNING OF A ROMANCE, is in traditional Czech style. It is in JENŮFA, the most popular and immediately accessible of his mature operas, that he found his true voice. His later operas, for each of which he wrote his own libretto, are the semi-autobiographical FATE (*Osud*), the historico-surrealist comedy THE EXCURSIONS OF MR BROUČEK, the Ostrovskian KÁŤA KABANOVÁ, the delightful nature-inspired THE CUNNING LITTLE VIXEN, the compelling THE MACROPOLUS CASE and his last and overwhelmingly powerful masterpiece, the Dostoyevskian FROM THE HOUSE OF THE DEAD, which was produced posthumously.

For many years, *Jenůfa* was Janáček's only opera to be regularly performed internationally, but in the last 25 years all of his mature operas have won a permanent place in the repertory. This has been especially the case in Britain, where he has now become one of the most frequently performed of all opera composers. This has arisen as a result of the initially almost single-handed championship of his works by Sir Charles Mackerras, the finest contemporary interpreter of his music.

Jánek
1 Tenor role in Janáček's *The Macropolus Case*. Jaroslav Prus's son, he is in love with Kristina. **2** Bass role in Blodek's *In the Well*. He is a rich old farmer.

Janků, Hana
see SVOBODOVÁ-JANKŮ, HANA

Janowitz, Gundula (b 1937)
German soprano, particularly associated with Mozart and Strauss roles. She was an intelligent singer with a rich and creamy voice used with fine musicianship, but sometimes appeared a little cool and distant on stage. She was director of the Graz Opernhaus (1990–91).

Janowski, Marek (b 1940)
Polish conductor, particularly associated with the German repertory, especially Wagner. He was musical director of the Freiburg Opera (1973–4) and the Dortmund Stadttheater (1975–9).

Japan
see NIKIKAI OPERA COMPANY; TOKYO CHAMBER OPERA GROUP

Japanese opera composers
These include Yasushi Akutagawa (1925–89), Sadao Bekku (*b* 1922), Ikuma Dan (*b* 1924), Hikaru Hayashi (*b* 1931), Yoshirō Irino (1921–80), Saburo Takata (*b* 1913), Kunio Todo (*b* 1915) and Kōsaku Yamada (1886–1965).

Järnefelt, Armas (1869–1958)
Finnish conductor and composer, brother-in-law of Sibelius. Particularly associated with Wagner operas, he was musical director of the Royal Opera, Stockholm, and artistic director of the Finnish National Opera (1932–6). His first wife **Maikki Pakarinen** (1871–1929) was a soprano; his second wife **Liva Edström** (1876–1971) was a successful mezzo.

Järvi, Neeme (b 1927)
Estonian conductor, particularly associated

with the Russian and Scandinavian repertories. He was musical director of the Estonian Opera Theatre from 1966 until he defected from the then Soviet Union in 1980. Nowadays best known as a symphonic conductor, his recent operatic appearances have been sporadic. His son **Paavo** (*b* 1962) is also a conductor.

Jasager, Der (*The Yes-Sayer*)
Opera in two acts by Weill. 1st perf Berlin Radio, 23 June 1930; libr by Bertolt Brecht, after Arthur Waley's translation of the 15th-century Japanese Noh play *Taniko*. Principal roles: Student (treble), Mother (mezzo), Teacher (bar). Written specifically for student performance, it is a strongly didactic piece which is still performed from time to time. **Plot**: Whilst on a mountain journey to obtain medicine for his Mother, the Student becomes ill and endangers the rest of the party. In accordance with ancient tradition, he allows himself to be thrown into the valley, but only with the proviso that the Teacher will deliver the medicine. [R]

Jason
The mythical Greek hero appears in a number of operas, including: **1** Tenor role in Cherubini's and M.-A. Charpentier's *Médée*. **2** Tenor role in Mayr's *Medea in Corinto*. **3** Baritone role in Křenek's *Der Goldene Bock*. **4** Counter-tenor role in Cavalli's *Giasone*.

Jealousy Monologue
Baritone aria ('È sogno?') for Ford in Act II of Verdi's *Falstaff*, in which he rails against women's untrustworthiness. In it, Verdi parodies his own baritone writing.

Jean
Tenor role in Massenet's *Le Jongleur de Notre-Dame*. He is the juggler of the opera's title. The role has occasionally been sung by a soprano.

Jean de Leyden
Tenor role in Meyerbeer's *Le Prophète*. Fidès's son, he is the leader of the Anabaptists. In history, he was Jan Beuckelzoon (1509–36).

Jean de Paris (*John of Paris*)
Opera in two acts by Boïeldieu. 1st perf Paris, 4 April 1812; libr by Claude Godard d'Aucour de Saint-Just. Principal roles: Jean (ten), Princess (sop), Seneschal (bar), Lorenza (mezzo), Olivier (ten), Pedrigo (sop). One of Boïeldieu's most successful operas, it is nowadays virtually forgotten. **Plot**: 17th-century Pyrenees. The widowed Princess of Navarre is betrothed to the French crown prince. Preparations for her arrival at an inn are interrupted by the appearance of the Prince, disguised as Jean de Paris, together with his entourage. Despite the protests of the Princess's Seneschal, they take over the inn, but Jean says that the Princess may stay there. The Princess arrives and recognizes Jean, but plays along with his disguise and, during a dance, tells him that she has already chosen her husband. All is revealed and the two are united.

Jeanne
Soprano role in Penderecki's *The Devils of Loudun*. The historical Jeanne des Anges (1605–65), she is the prioress of an Ursuline convent.

Jeanne d'Arc au Bûcher (*Joan of Arc at the Stake*)
Dramatic oratorio in prologue and ten scenes by Honegger. 1st perf Basel, 12 May 1938; libr by Paul Claudel. Principal roles: Joan (speaker), Friar Dominic (speaker), Virgin Mary (sop), Archbishop Cauchon (ten). Described as a lyric mystery play, it is Honegger's most frequently performed stage work. Tied to the stake, Joan relives her life and trial at the moment of her death. [R]

Je crois entendre encore
Tenor aria for Nadir in Act I of Bizet's *Les Pêcheurs de Perles*, in which he sings of his love for Leïla.

Je dis que rien
Soprano aria for Micaëla in Act III of Bizet's *Carmen*, in which she prays for aid in overcoming her fears travelling in the mountains.

Jemmy
Soprano trouser role in Rossini's *Guillaume Tell*. He is Tell's young son.

Jenifer
Soprano role in Tippett's *The Midsummer Marriage*. King Fisher's daughter, she is in love with Mark.

Jeník
Tenor role in: **1** Smetana's *The Bartered Bride*. He turns out to be Tobiaš Mícha's elder son. **2** Dvořák's *The Cunning Peasant*. He is a poor country lad.

Jenůfa Official title: **Her Foster-Daughter** (*Její Pastorkyňa*)
Opera in three acts by Janáček. 1st perf Brno, 21 Jan 1904; libr by the composer, after Gabriela Priessová's play. Principal roles: Jenůfa (sop), Kostelnička (sop), Laca (ten), Števa (ten), Foreman of the Mill (b-bar), Karolka (mezzo), Mayor (bass), Grandmother Buryjovka (mezzo). Notable for its rich lyricism and for its remarkable portrayal of the guilt-ridden Kostelnička, it was Janáček's first major success and remains one of the most frequently performed of all Czech operas.
Plot: Late-19th-century Moravia. Jenůfa, pregnant by the drunken layabout Števa Buryja, fears that he will join the army rather than marry her. Števa's stepbrother Laca Klemeň also loves Jenůfa and is jealous. Jenůfa's formidable foster-mother, the Kostelnička (or sexton's wife), is unaware of Jenůfa's condition and rules that there can be no wedding until Števa has stayed sober for a year. Laca makes advances to Jenůfa, who rebuffs him. In a jealous fury, he scars her face with his knife, but is immediately overwhelmed with remorse. Kostelnička hides Jenůfa until after the birth of her baby, but Števa – now engaged to the Mayor's daughter Karolka – promises nothing beyond financial help. Realizing that Laca loves Jenůfa but that the baby stands in the way, Kostelnička drugs Jenůfa and throws the baby into the millstream, telling Jenůfa that it died whilst she was delirious. Jenůfa agrees to marry Laca, but on their wedding day a child's body is found under the melting ice, and Jenůfa recognizes it as hers. She is accused of murder, but the penitent Kostelnička confesses. She is forgiven by Jenůfa, who also offers Laca his freedom. Loving her truly, however, he stands by her. [R]

Jephtha
Oratorio in three parts by Händel. 1st perf London, 26 Feb 1752; libr by Thomas Morell, after the Book of Judges in the Old Testament. Principal roles: Jephtha (ten), Isis (sop), Zebul (bass), Storge (mezzo), Hamor (c-ten). Händel's last oratorio, it is not strictly speaking an opera, but it is sometimes staged. [R]

Jeremiáš, Otakar (1892–1962)
Czech composer and conductor. His operas, written in post-Janáček style, include *The Brothers Karamazov* (*Bratři Karamazovi*, Prague, 8 Oct 1928; libr composer and Jaroslav Maria, after Fyodor Dostoyevsky) and *Owlglass* (*Enšpígl*, Prague, 13 May 1949; libr Jiří Mařánek, after Charles de Coster), a setting of the Till Eulenspiegel legend, about a 14th-century figure renowned for playing practical jokes. He was musical director of the Prague National Theatre (1945–7 and 1948–51). His brother **Jaroslav** (1889–1919) was also a composer, who wrote one opera: *The Old King* (*Starý Král*, Prague, 13 Apr 1919; libr Remy de Gourmont).

Jerger, Alfred (1889–1976)
Austrian baritone, particularly associated with Mozart and Strauss roles. Based largely in Vienna, he began as a conductor, later becoming one of the finest Mozartians of the inter-war period. He created Mandryka in *Arabella* and the Man in Schönberg's *Die Glückliche Hand*. He later produced a number of operas and was also a noted teacher, whose pupils included Leonie Rysanek.

Jeritza, Maria (b Mizzi Jedlitzková) (1887–1982)
Czech soprano, particularly associated with Strauss roles and with the title-roles of *Tosca*, *Thaïs* and *Carmen*. One of the finest singing-actresses of the inter-war period, she created the Empress in *Die Frau ohne Schatten*, the title-role in both versions of *Ariadne auf Naxos* and Marietta in *Die Tote Stadt*. Her autobiography, *Sunlight and Song*, was published in 1924.

Jerum! Jerum!
Baritone aria (the Cobbling Song) for Hans Sachs in Act II of Wagner's *Die Meistersinger von Nürnberg*.

Jérusalem
see LOMBARDI, I

Jerusalem, Siegfried (b 1940)
German tenor (originally a bassoonist), particularly associated with the German repertory. He began by making his name in lyric roles such as Tamino in *Die Zauberflöte*, but has recently turned successfully to Wagnerian roles, including Siegfried, although he is by no means a natural HELDENTENOR.

Jessel, Miss
Soprano role in Britten's *The Turn of the Screw*. She is the former governess whose ghost attempts to corrupt Flora.

Jessonda
Opera in three acts by Spohr (Op 63). 1st perf Kassel, 28 July 1823; libr by Eduard Heinrich Gehe, after Antoine-Marin Lemièrre's *La Veuve de Malabar*. Principal roles: Jessonda (sop), Nadori (ten), Amazili (sop), Tristan d'Acunha (bar), Dandau (bass). Spohr's most successful opera, it is nowadays only very rarely performed.
Plot: Early-16th-century India. Custom decrees that the Rajah's widow Jessonda must die on her husband's funeral pyre. The young Brahmin priest Nadori, who must tell her this, falls in love with her sister Amazili and agrees to help save Jessonda. Meanwhile, Jessonda is recognized by her former lover, the Portuguese general Tristan d'Acunha, who is besieging Goa. He is unable to attack and rescue her because of a truce, but when he learns that the priest Dandau has broken the truce, he enters the temple by a secret passage and saves Jessonda. [R]

Je suis Brésilien
Tenor aria for the Brazilian in Act I of Offenbach's *La Vie Parisienne*, in which he says that he intends to spend his millions on having a good time. It contains some of operetta's fastest patter.

Je vais mourir
Mezzo aria for Dido in Act V of Berlioz's *Les Troyens*, in which she says that she will die of grief as a result of Aeneas's departure.

Je veux vivre
Soprano aria for Juliet in Act I of Gounod's *Roméo et Juliette*, in which she says that she wishes to live life to the full whilst she is young.

Jewels of the Madonna, The
see GIOIELLI DELLA MADONNA, I

Jewel Song
Soprano aria ('Ah, je ris') for Marguerite in Act III of Gounod's *Faust*, sung as she tries on the jewels she finds in the casket left by Méphistophélès.

Ježibaba
Mezzo role in Dvořák's *Rusalka*. She is a witch.

Jiménez, Jerónimo
see GIMÉNEZ, GERÓNIMO

Jírko, Ivan (1926–78)
Czech composer and critic (and also a practising psychiatrist). He wrote four operas which met with some success in the Czech lands but which are unknown elsewhere. They are *Twelfth Night* (*Večer Tříkrálový*, Liberec, 25 Feb 1967; libr composer, after Shakespeare), *The Strange Adventure of Arthur Rowe* (*Podivuhodné Dobrodružství Arthura Rowa*, Liberec, 25 Oct 1969; libr composer, after Graham Greene's *The Ministry of Fear*; revised version *The Return*, Prague, 11 Oct 1979), *The Strumpet* (*Děvka*, Olomouc, 23 June 1974; libr composer, after Cesare Zavattini) and *The Millionairess* (*Milionářka*, Brno, 28 Apr 1977; libr composer, after Zavattini).

Jírovec, Vojtěch (sometimes Germanized as Adalbert Gyrowetz) **(1763–1850)**
Bohemian composer. He wrote 30 operas and SINGSPIELS, none of them remembered nowadays. The most important include *Agnes Sorel* (Vienna, 4 Dec 1806; libr Josef Sonnleithner), his most successful work, *Der Augenarzt* (*The Optician*, Vienna, 1 Oct 1811; libr Johann Emanuel Veith), *Il Finto Stanislao* (Milan, 5 July 1818; libr Felice Romani, after Alexandre Vincent Pineu-Duval's *Le Faux Stanislas*) and *Hans Sachs im Vorgerückten* (Dresden, 1834).

Joan of Arc
see GIOVANNA D'ARCO; JEANNE D'ARC AU BÛCHER; MAID OF ORLEANS, THE

Job
Dramatic oratorio by Dallapiccola. 1st perf Rome, 30 Oct 1950; libr by the composer, after the Old Testament. Principal roles: Job (b-bar), Elifàz (sop), Baldad (mezzo), Zofàr (ten). It comprises a series of tableaux introduced and linked by a narrator.

Jobin, Raoul (1906–74)
Canadian tenor, particularly associated with the French repertory. He created Luca in Menotti's *The Island God*, Miguel in Tomasi's *Don Juan de Mañara* and Fabrice in Sauget's *La Chartreuse de Parme*. His son **André** (*b* 1933) is also a tenor.

Jocasta
Oedipus's mother and wife appears in a number of operas, including: **1** Mezzo role in Stravinsky's *Oedipus Rex*. **2** Soprano role in Orff's *Oedipus der Tyrann*. **3** Mezzo role in Enescu's *Oedipe*. **4** Soprano role in Leoncavallo's *Edipo Rè*.

Jocelyn
Opera in four acts by Godard (Op 100). 1st perf Brussels, 25 Feb 1888; libr by Paul Armand Silvestre and V. Capone, after Alphonse de Lamartine's poem. Godard's most successful opera, telling of a brother at a seminary tempted by earthly love, it is nowadays remembered solely for the tenor's *Berceuse*.

Jochum, Eugen (1902–87)
German conductor, particularly associated with the German repertory, especially Wagner. One of the finest 20th-century interpreters of the German romantic repertory, he was musical director of the Duisburg Opera (1930–32) and the Hamburg State Opera (1934–45). His brother **Georg** (1909–70) was also a conductor, who was musical director of the Linz Opera (1940–45).

Johnson, Dick
Tenor role in Puccini's *La Fanciulla del West*. He is the wanted bandit Ramírez.

Johnson, Edward (1878–1959)
Canadian tenor and administrator, particularly associated with heavier Italian and German roles. One of the leading lyrico-dramatic tenors of the inter-war period, he created Ippolito in Pizzetti's *Fedra*, Sir Gower in Hanson's *Merry Mount*, roles in Alfano's *L'Ombra di Don Giovanni* and Montemezzi's *La Nave* and, for Taylor, the title-role in *Peter Ibbetson* and Aethelwold in *The King's Henchman*. He was general manager of the Metropolitan Opera, New York (1935–50).

Jo ho hoe
Soprano aria (Senta's Ballad) for Senta in Act II of Wagner's *Der Fliegende Holländer*, in which she recounts the legend of the Dutchman.

Jokanaan
Baritone role in Strauss's *Salome*. He is John the Baptist.

Jolie Fille de Perth, La (*The Fair Maid of Perth*)
Opera in four acts by Bizet. 1st perf Paris, 26 Dec 1867; libr by Jules-Henri Vernoy de Saint-Georges and Jules Adenis, after Sir Walter Scott's novel. Principal roles: Catharine (sop), Henri (ten), Ralph (bar), Duc de Rothsay (bar), Simon (b-bar), Mab (mezzo). A work of great melodic charm, if dramatically rather creaky, it is only rarely performed, although the orchestral suite has given the music a wider currency.
Plot: 16th-century Perth. The armourer Henry Smith loves Catharine Glover. He gives shelter to the gypsy Mab and is then visited by Catharine, her father Simon, and Ralph, who also loves Catharine. The Duke of Rothsay invites Catharine to his castle and asks Mab, his former mistress, to help abduct her. Mab pretends to agree, but foils the Duke's machinations and engineers a reconciliation between Catharine and Henry. [R]

Jolivet, André (1905–74)
French composer. A member of the Jeune France group (founded in Paris in 1936 in opposition to the neo-classical musical style of the time), he wrote one opera, the comedy *Dolorès ou Le Miracle de la Femme Laide* (French Radio, 1947, composed 1942; libr Henri Ghéon).

Jommelli, Niccolò (1714–74)
Italian composer. He wrote 82 operas, of which 29 are lost. They include *L'Errore*

Amoroso (Naples, 1737; libr A. Palombo), *Ricimero* (Rome, 16 Jan 1740; libr Apostolo Zeno and Pietro Pariati), *Astianatte* (Rome, 4 Feb 1741; libr Antonio Salvi), *Ezio* (Bologna, 29 Apr 1741; libr Pietro Metastasio), *Merope* (Venice, 26 Dec 1741; libr Zeno), *Semiramide* (Venice, 26 Dec 1742; libr Francesco Silvani), ARTASERSE, *La Clemenza di Tito* (Stuttgart, 30 Aug 1753; libr Metastasio) and *Armida Abbandonata* (Naples, 30 May 1770; libr F. Saverio de' Rogati, after Torquato Tasso's *Gerusalemme Liberata*) [R]. In his later operas, he made a number of innovations in OPERA SERIA, notably by loosening the DA CAPO aria structure, by providing accompanied RECITATIVE and by introducing the chorus. None of his operas are remembered today. His nephew **Gaetano Andreozzi** (1755–1826) was also a composer, whose most successful opera was *La Principessa Filosofa* (Venice, 6 Oct 1794; libr Antonio Sografi, after A. Moreto's *Donna Diana*). His wife **Anna dei Santi** was a successful soprano.

Jonathan
The biblical friend of David and son of King Saul appears in a number of operas, including: **1** Tenor role in Händel's *Saul*. **2** Tenor role in Nielsen's *Saul og David*. **3** Soprano trouser role in M.-A. Charpentier's *David et Jonathas*.

Jones, Della (b 1946)
British mezzo, particularly associated with Rossini, Händel and Mozart roles. The finest Rossini mezzo to have emerged in Britain in the post-war period, she possesses a rich voice of considerable range and remarkable agility and has a fine stage presence, especially in comedy. She created Dolly in Hamilton's *Anna Karenina*.

Jones, Dame Gwyneth (b 1936)
British soprano, particularly associated with Wagner and Strauss roles and with *Turandot* and (earlier in her career) with Verdi. Probably the finest British dramatic soprano of the post-war era, she has a radiant and powerful voice of seemingly limitless resources. Her voice was afflicted with a serious beat (*see* VIBRATO) in her middle career, but this was later largely eradicated. She is an intense and deeply committed singing-actress with a handsome stage presence.

Jongleur de Notre-Dame, Le (*Our Lady's Juggler*)
Opera in three acts by Massenet. 1st perf Monte Carlo, 18 Feb 1902; libr by Maurice Léna, after Anatole France's *L'Étui de Nacre*. Principal roles: Jean (ten), Boniface (b-bar), Prior (bass). One of Massenet's finest operas, whose title-role presents a wonderful challenge to an actor-tenor, it was very successful at its appearance but is nowadays only rarely performed.
Plot: 14th-century Cluny. The juggler Jean becomes a novice in an order of monks who utilize their various talents in praise of the Virgin Mary. Jean pays his homage to her in the only way he can: he puts on his costume and does his juggling routine in front of the altar. Apart from the kindly Boniface, the brothers are scandalized, but the statue of the Virgin smiles and blesses him, accepting his offering. [R]

Jonny Spielt Auf (*Johnny Strikes Up*)
Opera in two parts by Křenek (Op 45). 1st perf Leipzig, 10 Feb 1927; libr by the composer. Principal roles: Jonny (bar), Anita (sop), Max (ten), Daniello (bass), Yvonne (sop). A jazz-inspired piece, it is Křenek's most successful and enduring opera and provides a marvellous vehicle for a black baritone.
Plot: Central Europe, mid-1920s. The lives of four musicians intertwine: the opera singer Anita, the jazz-band leader Jonny, the composer Max and the violin virtuoso Daniello. Jonny steals Daniello's violin and becomes the world's greatest living player, setting all the world dancing the Charleston with his performance from the North Pole. [R]

Joplin, Scott (c 1868–1917)
American composer. He wrote two ragtime operas: *A Guest of Honour* (St Louis, Apr 1903; libr composer), which is lost, and TREEMONISHA.

José, Don
1 Tenor role in Bizet's *Carmen*. He is a soldier in love with Carmen. **2** Bass role in Delius's *Koanga*. He is a plantation owner. **3** Baritone role in Goossens's *Don*

Juan de Mañara. **4** Baritone role in Wallace's *Maritana*. He is the King of Spain's adviser.

Joseph Full title: **La Légende de Joseph en Égypte** (*The Legend of Joseph in Egypt*) Opera in three acts by Méhul. 1st perf Paris, 17 Feb 1807; libr by Alexandre Duval after the Book of Genesis in the Old Testament. Principal roles: Joseph (ten), Jacob (bar), Siméon (bass), Benjamin (sop), Ruben (ten). Méhul's finest and most successful opera, it is nowadays unaccountably only very rarely performed. **Plot**: Legendary Memphis. Joseph, under the assumed name of Cleophas, has saved Egypt from famine. His brothers and his blind father Jacob arrive seeking food, but do not recognize Joseph. Joseph subsequently reveals his identity, pardons his brothers for having sold him into slavery and begs Jacob to do the same.

Jota
An exhilarating Spanish dance in 3/4 time, native especially to Navarre and Aragon. Its origins go back to the 12th century, and it is believed to be named after a Moor, Aben Jot. There are a number of examples in ZARZUELA and Spanish opera, the finest being in Bretón's *La Dolores*.

Joubert, John (b 1927)
South African composer. He has written seven operas: the radio opera *Antigone* (BBC, 21 July 1954; libr Rachel Trickett, after Sophocles), *In the Drought* (Johannesburg, 20 Oct 1956; libr A. Wood), *Silas Marner* (Cape Town, 20 May 1961; libr Trickett, after George Eliot), the children's opera *The Quarry* (London, 25 Mar 1965; libr D. Holbrook), *Under Western Eyes* (London, 29 May 1969; libr Cedric Cliffe, after Josef Conrad) and the children's operas *The Prisoner* (Barnet, 16 May 1973; libr Stephen Tunnicliffe, after Leo Tolstoy) and *The Wayfarers* (Huntingdon, 4 Apr 1984; libr Tunnicliffe, after Geoffrey Chaucer's *The Canterbury Tales*).

Jour et nuit
Tenor aria for Franz in the Antonia Act of Offenbach's *Les Contes d'Hoffmann*, in which he demonstrates that he has missed his vocation as a singer and dancer.

Journet, Marcel (1867–1933)
French bass with a remarkable range which also enabled him to sing high baritone roles. Particularly associated with the German and French repertories, especially Hans Sachs and Méphistophélès, he was one of the finest basses of the inter-war period. He created Simon Mago in Boito's *Nerone*.

Jouy, Victor Joseph Étienne de (1764–1846)
French playwright and librettist. As resident librettist at the Paris Opéra, he specialized in spectacular subjects and situations, sometimes providing verses of considerable quality. His most fruitful collaboration was with Spontini, for whom he wrote the libretti for *Milton, La Vestale* and *Fernand Cortez*. He also provided texts for Boïeldieu, Cherubini (*Les Abencérages*), Dalayrac, García, Méhul and Rossini (*Moïse et Pharaon* and *Guillaume Tell*).

Judgement Scene
A name often given to Act IV Scene I of Verdi's *Aida*, in which Radamès silently faces his judges offstage whilst Amneris curses the priests' lust for blood. One of opera's most powerful scenes.

Judith
Mezzo role in Bartók's *Duke Bluebeard's Castle*. She is Bluebeard's new wife. The role is sometimes sung by a soprano.

Judith (*Yudif*)
Opera in five acts by Serov. 1st perf St Petersburg, 28 May 1863; libr by the composer, Apollon Maykov and others, after Paolo Giacometti's *Giuditta*, itself based on the Apocrypha. Principal roles: Judith (sop), Holofernes (bass), Bagoas (ten), Avra (mezzo), Achior (ten), Ozias (bass). Serov's first and finest opera, it is still occasionally performed in Russia but is virtually unknown elsewhere. [R]

Judith
Opera in three acts by Honegger. 1st perf Monte Carlo, 13 Feb 1926; libr by René Morax, after the Apocrypha. Principal roles: Judith (mezzo), Holopherne (bar), Ozias (bass), Bagoas (ten). One of Honegger's finest works, it is nowadays only very rarely performed. [R]

Judith
Opera in one act by Goossens (Op 46). 1st perf London, 25 June 1929; libr by Arnold Bennett, after the Apocrypha. Principal roles: Judith (sop), Holofernes (bar), Bagoas (ten), Achior (bar), Haggith (mezzo). Goossens's finest opera, it deserves to be better known.
Plot: Legendary Palestine. Achior warns the Assyrian general Holofernes to beware the power of Israel's god and to avoid the city of Bethulia. Holofernes is angered and has Achior tied up, but he is released by Judith and her servant Haggith. Judith goes to Holofernes's camp and, despite the warnings of his chief eunuch Bagoas, the general insists on seeing her. He is soon utterly bewitched by Judith's beauty, offering to forsake his religion and marry her. She inflames his passion and asks him to kiss her. As he does so she cuts off his head. [R]

Judith
Opera in two acts by Matthus. 1st perf Berlin, 28 Sept 1985; libr by the composer, after Christian Friedrich Hebbel's play, itself based on the Apocrypha. Principal roles: Judith (sop), Holofernes (b-bar), Achior (bar), Osias (bass), Ammon (bar), Ephraim (ten), Daniel (ten), Mirza (mezzo). It is one of the finest modern operas from the former East Germany. [R]

Juha
Opera in three acts by A. Merikanto. 1st perf Helsinki Radio, 3 Dec 1958 (composed 1922); 1st stage perf Lahti, 28 Oct 1963; libr by Aïno Ackté, after Juhani Aho's novel. Principal roles: Juha (b-bar), Marja (sop), Shemeikka (ten), Anja (sop). One of the finest of all Finnish operas, it is little known outside Finland.
Plot: Finland, 1880. The decent but simple farmer Juha lives in the remote north-west, where the drab monotony of their lives makes his wife Marja restless. They are visited by the trader Shemeikka, who seduces Marja. Pregnant by Shemeikka she visits him at his home in the east, only to discover that he has a harem of similar women. Nonetheless, Marja decides to stay with Shemeikka, and Juha throws himself into a river and is drowned. [R]

Juive, La (*The Jewess*)
Opera in five acts by Halévy. 1st perf Paris, 23 Feb 1835; libr by Eugène Scribe. Principal roles: Éléazar (ten), Rachel (sop), Léopold (ten), Eudoxie (sop), Cardinal de Brogni (bass). Halévy's masterpiece, it was hugely popular throughout the 19th century, but is nowadays only infrequently performed, partly, no doubt, because of the difficulty of finding a tenor equal to the enormous demands of Éléazar.
Plot: Constance, 1414. Rachel, believed to be the daughter of the Jewish goldsmith Éléazar, discovers that her lover, whom she knows as Samuel, is actually Prince Léopold, who is married to Princess Eudoxie. Rachel exposes the relationship to the court, and Cardinal de Brogni condemns her, Léopold and Éléazar to death. Léopold's sentence is commuted to banishment, and Brogni offers to spare Rachel if Éléazar will accept Christianity. When he refuses, Rachel is thrown into a vat of boiling oil as Éléazar reveals that she was in fact the Cardinal's own long-lost daughter. [R]

Julien or **La Vie du Poète** (*The Poet's Life*)
Opera in prologue and four acts by Charpentier. 1st perf Paris, 4 June 1913; libr by the composer. Principal roles: Julien (ten), Ghost of Louise (sop). Incorporating music from his earlier dramatic symphony *La Vie du Poète*, it is Charpentier's unsuccessful attempt to provide a follow-up to *Louise*. It is nowadays totally forgotten.

Julietta or **The Dream Book** (*Snář*)
Opera in three acts by Martinů. 1st perf Prague, 16 March 1938; libr by the composer, after Georges Neveux's *Juliette ou La Clé des Songes*. Principal roles: Michel (ten), Julietta (sop). Martinů's most frequently performed opera, it is a surrealist dream fantasy.
Plot: France. The travelling bookseller Michel has returned to a small coastal town haunted by the memory of a girl singing at a window. The inhabitants have all lost their memories. Michel, ignorant of this fact, finds their behaviour inexplicable and comes to question his own reality and finds his meetings with Julietta unsatisfactory. Michel is unable to return to Paris because the railway station has

disappeared. He finds himself in a 'Dream Office' where he thinks that he hears Julietta calling to him. However – as he is shown – there is no one at all there. [R]

Julius Caesar
see GIULIO CESARE

Jullien, Louis (1812–60)
French conductor and composer, largely resident in Britain. A flamboyant personality in London's mid-19th-century musical scene, he was an operatic conductor of some stature, and also composed one opera, the unsuccessful *Pietro il Grande* (London, 17 Aug 1852; libr Desmond Ryan), which he financed himself.

Junge Lord, Der (*The Young Lord*)
Comic opera in two acts by Henze. 1st perf Berlin, 7 Aug 1965; libr by Ingeborg Bachmann, after Wilhelm Hauff's *Der Scheik von Alexandria und seine Sklaven.* Principal roles; Lord Barrat (ten), Secretary (bar), Luise (sop), Wilhelm (ten), Baroness Grünwiesel (mezzo), Sir Edgar (mime). One of Henze's most successful operas, it is a biting satire on bourgeois manners and has been widely performed. **Plot**: Hülsdorf-Gotha (Germany), 1830. The rich Englishman Sir Edgar, who has rented a house on the town square, antagonizes the local notables by his superior and distant manner. However, when he introduces his nephew Lord Barrat to the community, they sycophantically condone his wildly eccentric and outrageous behaviour until it is revealed that he is a circus ape dressed in human clothes. [R]

Jungwirth, Manfred (b 1919)
Austrian bass, particularly associated with Strauss roles, especially Baron Ochs in *Der Rosenkavalier* and Count Waldner in *Arabella.* He had a dark and rich voice and was a highly accomplished singing-actor, excelling in comic roles. He created the Priest in Einem's *Der Besuch der Alten Dame* and enjoyed a remarkably long career, singing into his early 70s.

Junius
Baritone role in Britten's *The Rape of Lucretia.* He is a Roman general.

Juno
The wife of Jupiter, the Graeco-Roman goddess appears in many operas, including: **1** Mezzo role in Händel's *Semele.* **2** Soprano role in Cavalli's *La Calisto.* **3** Mezzo role in Offenbach's *Orphée aux Enfers.* **4** Mezzo role in Cavalli's *Ercole Amante.* **5** Mezzo role in Monteverdi's *Il Ritorno d'Ulisse in Patria.* **6** Mezzo role in M.-A. Charpentier's *Actéon.* **7** Soprano role in Rameau's *Platée.* **8** Soprano role in Bontempi's *Il Paride.* **9** Mezzo role in Händel's *Agrippina.*

Jupiter
The Graeco-Roman supreme god appears in many operas, including: **1** Tenor role in Händel's *Semele.* **2** Bass role in Cavalli's *La Calisto.* **3** Tenor role in Monteverdi's *Il Ritorno d'Ulisse in Patria.* **4** Baritone role in Rameau's *Platée.* **5** Baritone role in Rameau's *Naïs.* **6** Baritone role in Offenbach's *Orphée aux Enfers.* **7** Baritone role in Strauss's *Die Liebe der Danae.* **8** Bass role in Klebe's *Alkmene.* **9** Baritone role in Bliss's *The Olympians.* **10** Baritone role in Gounod's *Philémon et Baucis.* **11** Bass role in Bontempi's *Il Paride.* **12** Tenor role in Rossi's *Orfeo.*

Jurinac, Sena (b Srebrenka) (b 1921)
Croatian soprano, particularly associated with Mozart and Strauss roles, especially Ilia in *Idomeneo* and Octavian in *Der Rosenkavalier.* She possessed one of the loveliest voices of the immediate post-war period, which she used with outstanding artistry and intelligence. She was also an affecting singing-actress. Married for a time to the baritone SESTO BRUSCANTINI.

Jutland Opera (*Den Jyske Opera* in Danish)
Denmark's second most important opera company, it was founded in 1947. It is based at the Musikhuset (cap 1,477) in Århus and also tours throughout the country.

K

Kabaiwanska, Raina (b 1934)
Bulgarian soprano, particularly associated with Verdi and Puccini roles and with the VERISMO repertory. She possessed a beautiful and creamy voice, used with intelligence and musicianship, and she was a singing-actress of considerable ability.

Kabalevsky, Dimitri (1904–87)
Russian composer. He wrote five operas, of which much the best known is THE CRAFTSMAN OF CLAMECY (sometimes incorrectly called *Colas Breugnon* after its famous overture). His other operas are *Under Fire* (*Vogne*, Moscow, 19 Sept 1943; libr S. Solodar), *The Family of Taras* (*Semya Tarasa*, Moscow, 2 Nov 1947; libr Sergei Alexandrovich Tsenin, after Boris Gorbatov's *The Unvanquished*; revised version Leningrad, 7 Nov 1950) [R], *Nikita Vershinin* (Moscow, 26 Nov 1955; libr Tsenin, after V. Ivanov's *Armoured Train*) and the operetta *The Sisters* (Perm, 31 May 1969; libr S. Bogomazov, after I. Lazrov's *Encounter With a Miracle*).

Kabanicha
Mezzo role in Janáček's *Káťa Kabanová*. A merchant's widow, she is the formidable head of the Kabanov household. The role is sometimes sung by a soprano.

Kacsóh, Pongrác (1873–1923)
Hungarian composer. He wrote three operettas, of which much the most successful was *János Vitéz* (*John the Hero*, Budapest, 18 Nov 1904; libr Sándor Petőfi) [R], which is the Hungarian national operetta.

Kaiserslautern Opera
The first opera house in this German city in the Rhineland-Palatinate opened in 1862, but burnt down five years later. A second theatre opened in 1897, but was destroyed by bombs in 1944. The present house (cap 750) opened in 1950. Musical directors have included Rudolf Moralt, Herbert Albert, Otmar Suitner, Erich Riede and Wilfried Emmert.

Kaiser von Atlantis, Der (*The Emperor of Atlantis*) or **Die Tod Dank Ab** (*Death Abdicates*)
Opera in four scenes by Ullmann. 1st perf Amsterdam, 16 Dec 1975 (composed 1943 in Theresienstadt concentration camp); libr by Peter Kien. Principal roles: Emperor Überall (bar), Death (bass), Pierrot (ten), Drummer (mezzo), Soldier (ten), Girl (sop). Written in a mixture of musical styles, it is a powerful defiance of the Nazi system by both composer and librettist – both of whom were murdered in Auschwitz. Prepared for performance by the conductor Kerry Woodward, it has been widely performed in the last decade and is a powerful work rendered even more compelling and harrowing by the appalling circumstances of its composition. [R]

Kálmán, Emmerich (b Imre) (1882–1953)
Hungarian composer. His first stage work was *The Gay Hussars* (*Tártájárás*, Budapest, 22 Feb 1908; libr K. von Bakonyi and A. Gábor). Of his many Viennese operettas, the most successful include DIE CSÁRDÁSFÜRSTIN, *Die Faschingsfee* (*The Carnival Fairy*, Vienna, 21 Sept 1917; libr R. Österreicher and Alfred Maria Willner), *Das Hollandweibchen* (Vienna, 30 Jan 1920; libr Leo Stein and Béla Jenbach), GRÄFIN MARIZA, his most enduring work, DIE ZIRKUSPRINZESSIN, *Die Herzogin von Chicago* (Vienna, 5 Apr 1928; libr Julius Brammer and Alfred Grünwald), *Das Veilchen von Montmartre* (Vienna, 21 Mar 1930; libr Brammer and Grünwald) [R] and *Kaiserin Josephine* (Zürich, 18 Jan 1936; libr G. Herczeg and Paul Knepler). His last work, *Arizona Lady* (Munich Radio, 1 Jan 1954; libr Grünwald and G. Beer), was left unfinished at his death and was completed by his son **Charles** (*b* 1929), who also composed operettas.

Kalomiris, Manolis (1883–1962)
Greek composer. The most important Greek opera composer, he wrote five

operas. *The Master Mason* (*O Protomastoros*, Athens, 11 Mar 1916; libr N. Poriotis and Y. Stefopoulos, after Nikos Kazantzakis) was followed by *The Mother's Ring* (*To Dakhtiliditis Manas*, Athens, 8 Dec 1917; libr Stefopoulos, after J. Kambyssis; revised version Berlin, 10 Feb 1940) [R], his most successful work, *Sunrise* (*Anatoli*, Athens, 18 Dec 1945; libr composer, after Kambyssis), *The Shadowy Waters* (*Ta Xotika Nera*, Athens, 4 Jan 1951; libr composer, after William Butler Yeats) and *Konstantinos o Palaeologos* (Athens, 12 Aug 1962; libr after Kazantzakis).

Kammersänger (German for 'chamber singer')
A distinguished honorific title bestowed upon individual singers by the Austrian and German governments.

Kanawa, Dame Kiri Te (b 1944)
New Zealand soprano, particularly associated with Mozart and lyrical Strauss and Verdi roles, especially Countess Almaviva in *Le Nozze di Figaro*, Donna Elvira in *Don Giovanni*, the title-role in *Arabella* and Desdemona in Verdi's *Otello*. Her rich, alluring and creamy voice, combined with her beautiful stage appearance, has made her one of the best-loved singers of modern times. She can be a most affecting singing-actress, but needs a strong producer.

Kansas City Lyric Theater
Founded by Russell Patterson and Morton Walker, the company gave its first performance in Sept 1958. Based at the Lyric Theater (cap 1,659), it presents opera in English and uses young American artists. Its repertory is notable for its large number of American operas.

Kapellmeister
see MAESTRO DI CAPPELLA

Karajan, Herbert von (1908–89)
Austrian conductor and producer, particularly associated with Wagner, Verdi, Mozart and Strauss operas. One of the most famous conductors of the 20th century, if sometimes dictatorial and controversial in his attitude to music making, he was musical director of the Ulm Stadttheater (1928–34), the Aachen Opera (1934–8), the Vienna State Opera (1958–64) and the Salzburg Festival (1958–60 and 1964–88), where he founded the Salzburg Easter Festival in 1967. At Salzburg, he nearly always acted as his own producer, being especially interested in the technical side. He conducted and directed a film of Verdi's *Otello* and conducted the first performances of Orff's *Trionfo d'Afrodite* and *De Temporum Fine Comoedia*.

Karel, Rudolf (1890–1945)
Czech composer. He completed two operas and began two others. His first opera *Ilsea's Heart* (*Ilseino Srdce*, Prague, 11 Oct 1924, composed 1909; libr K.H. Hilar and A. Kropáček) was followed by *Godmother Death* (*Smrt Kmotřička*, Brno, 3 Feb 1933; libr S. Lom), a fairy-tale work which is still occasionally performed in the Czech lands. Work on *The Taming of the Shrew* (*Zkrocení zlé Ženy*; libr after Shakespeare) was interrupted by his arrest by the Nazis. *Three Hairs of an Old Wise Man* (*Tři Vlasy děda Vševěda*, Prague, 28 Oct 1948; libr composer) was sketched in prison and was completed by his pupil Zbyněk Vostřák. He died in Terezín concentration camp.

Karetnikov, Nikolai (1930–94)
Russian composer. He wrote two operas: the fine *Till Eulenspiegel* (1993, composed 1985; libr composer and Pavel Lounguin, after Charles de Coster) [R] and the unperformed opera-oratorio *The Mystery of St Paul* (*Misteriya Apostola Pavla*, 1987).

Karlsruhe Staatstheater
Opera in this German town in Baden-Württemberg is given at the theatre built in 1851, destroyed in World War II, and rebuilt (cap 1,055) in 1954. Musical directors have included Hermann Levi, Felix Mottl, Josef Krips, Joseph Keilberth, Otto Matzerath, Alexander Krannhals and Günter Neuhold.

Karolka
Mezzo role in Janáček's *Jenůfa*. The Mayor's daughter, she is Števa's fiancée.

Kashchey the Immortal (*Kashchey Bessmertnij*)
Opera in three scenes by Rimsky-Korsakov. 1st perf Moscow, 12 Dec 1902;

libr by the composer, after a synopsis by Yevgeny Maximovich Petrovsky. Principal roles: Kashchey (ten), Princess (sop), Kashcheyevna (mezzo), Storm Knight (bass), Ivan (bar). Notable for the chromatic daring of its depiction of the supernatural, it is one of Rimsky's most powerful operas, but is virtually unknown outside Russia.
Plot: Legendary Russia. By his use of magic, the evil Kashchey has attained immortality. His death is contained in the tears of his daughter Kashcheyevna: so long as she does not weep, he will never die. Kashchey holds captive the Princess, betrothed to the knight Ivan Korolevich, who is ensnared by Kashcheyevna. Ivan escapes her enchantments and forces the Storm Knight to take him to Kashchey's realm. Ivan and the Princess prepare to escape, but Kashcheyevna – who has fallen in love with Ivan – appears and bars their way. The Princess, pitying Kashcheyevna's misery, kisses her on the forehead. Transformed, Kashcheyevna weeps and changes into a weeping willow. Kashchey thus dies and the Storm Knight opens the gates for the lovers to leave. [R]

Kašlík, Václav (1917–89)
Czech producer, conductor and composer. One of the leading – and most controversial – post-war producers, he was noted for his application of experimental visual techniques to opera, often working in collaboration with the designer JOSEF SVOBODA. He described his rule for production as being 'to present contemporary problems and feelings amusingly, even in a form which is so often so stiff as opera'. He was musical director of the Brno Opera (1943–5) and wrote four operas, including *Krakatit* (Czech TV, 5 Mar 1961; libr O. Vávra, after Karel Čapek), which employs jazz and popular elements, and *La Strada* (Prague, 13 Jan 1982; libr composer, after Federico Fellini).

Kassel Staatstheater
The Hoftheater in this German city in Hesse was opened in Feb 1814 but was destroyed by bombs in 1943. The present opera house (cap 1,010) opened in Sept 1959. Musical directors have included Spohr, Mahler, Ernst Legal, Robert Heger, Karl Elmendorff, Christoph von Dohnányi, Gerd Albrecht, James Lockhart and Ádám Fischer.

Káťa Kabanová
Opera in three acts by Janáček. 1st perf Brno, 23 Nov 1921; libr by the composer, after Alexander Nikolayevich Ostrovsky's *The Storm*. Principal roles: Káťa (sop), Kabanicha (mezzo), Boris (ten), Tichon (ten), Dikoj (bass), Váňa Kudrjáš (ten), Varvara (mezzo), Kuligin (bar). One of Janáček's finest operas, notable for its lyrical love music and for its portrayal of the formidable Kabanicha, it was initially slow to make its way but is now firmly established in the repertory.
Plot: Kalinov (Russia), 1860s. Katya lives with her husband Tichon and her intimidating mother-in-law Kabanicha, who loathes her. Unable to suppress her secret passion for Boris, nephew of the merchant Dikoj, Katya yields to temptation and meets him during Tichon's absence on business. At the height of a violent thunderstorm, she confesses the situation to Tichon and Kabanicha and runs away. She meets Boris one last time and then drowns herself in the Volga. [R]

Kate and the Devil
see DEVIL AND KATE, THE

Katerina Ismailova
see LADY MACBETH OF THE MTSENSK DISTRICT, THE

Kauer, Ferdinand (1751–1831)
Austrian composer. He wrote a large number of stage works in various styles, several of which enjoyed great success in their time, but which are all now forgotten. His most important work is *Das Donauweibchen* (*The Danube Spirit*, Vienna, 11 Jan 1798; libr Karl Friedrich Hensler), which was one of the most popular of all operas in Central Europe in the early 19th century.

Kay, Ulysses (b 1917)
American composer, son of the jazzman King Oliver. One of the few black composers to have turned to opera, his stage works include *The Boor* (Lexington, 12 Apr 1968, composed 1955; libr composer, after Anton Chekhov's *The Bear*),

The Juggler of Our Lady (New Orleans, 23 Feb 1962, composed 1956; libr Alexander King), *The Capitoline Venus* (Urbana, Illinois, 12 Mar 1971; libr Judith Dvorkin, after Mark Twain), *Jubilee* (Jackson, 20 Nov 1976; libr Donald Dorr, after M. Walker) and *Frederick Douglass* (Newark, 14 Apr 1991; libr Dorr).

Kecal
Bass role in Smetana's *The Bartered Bride.* He is a marriage broker.

Keene, Ned
Baritone role in Britten's *Peter Grimes.* He is an apothecary.

Keilberth, Joseph (1908–68)
German conductor, particularly associated with Strauss and Wagner operas. He was musical director of the Karlsruhe Staatstheater (1933–40) and the Bavarian State Opera (1959–68). He once said that his wish was to die as Felix Mottl had done: whilst conducting *Tristan und Isolde*; his wish was granted at Bayreuth.

Keiser, Reinhard (1674–1739)
German composer. Based predominantly in Hamburg, he wrote over 100 operas, some with polyglot libretti, many of which were successful in their time but which are nowadays largely forgotten. His most important operas include *Störtebecker und Jöedje Michel* (Hamburg, 1701), *Die Edelmüthige Octavia* (Hamburg, 5 Aug 1705; libr Barthold Feind), *Masagnello* (Hamburg, June 1706; libr Feind), *Die Grossmütige Tomyris* (Hamburg, July 1717; libr Johann Joachim Hoë) [R], *Der Lächerliche Printz Jodelet* (Hamburg, 1726; libr Johann Peter Praetorius) and *Croesus* (Hamburg, 1730; libr Luca von Bostel, after Nicolò Minato) [R Exc].

Kéléman, Zoltán (1926–79)
Hungarian baritone, particularly associated with Wagnerian roles, especially Alberich. The outstanding Alberich of the 1970s, he had a powerful and incisive voice and was a fine singing-actor.

Kellog, Clara Louise (1842–1916)
American soprano, particularly associated with the French and Italian repertories. One of the earliest American singers to win fame in Europe, in 1872 she formed the Lucca-Kellog Company in partnership with the soprano Pauline Lucca (1841–1908), which toured the USA until 1874. She then formed her own English Opera Company, supervising every aspect of performance. Her autobiography, *Memoirs of an American Prima Donna*, was published in 1913.

Kelly, Michael (1762–1826)
Irish tenor and composer. One of the leading singing-actors of his time, he enjoyed a long career in Italy, Vienna and England. A friend of Mozart, he created Don Basilio and Don Curzio in *Le Nozze di Figaro* and Corrado in Martín y Soler's *Una Cosa Rasa.* His two-volume autobiography, *Reminiscences of Michael Kelly of the King's Theatre*, was published in 1826 and is a principal source of details of operatic life at that time. He also composed a number of light operas, including *Blue Beard* (London, 16 Jan 1798; libr George Colman), and he completed Storace's unfinished *Mahmoud.*

Kempe, Rudolf (1910–76)
German conductor, particularly associated with Wagner and Strauss operas. One of the finest and most highly respected interpreters of the German repertory in the post-war era, he was musical director of the Dresden State Opera (1949–52) and the Bavarian State Opera (1952–4). His wife **Elisabeth Lindermeier** (*b* 1925) was a successful soprano.

Kent Opera
Founded in 1969 by Norman Platt (*b* 1920), it was based in Canterbury and Tunbridge Wells and visited most towns in southern England. It quickly developed remarkably high artistic standards, with many fine productions by Jonathan Miller, and was particularly noted for its Mozart and Monteverdi performances. All operas were sung in English, and the musical directors were Roger Norrington and Iván Fischer. A shameful withdrawal of government subsidy led to its demise in 1989. The company was refounded on a small-scale basis in 1994.

Kerman, Joseph (b 1924)
American musicologist and critic. His

Opera as Drama (1956) is one of the most influential, as well as controversial, operatic books of the post-war period. His thesis is that only Mozart and Verdi achieved true music-drama, whilst Wagner, Monteverdi, Beethoven, Gluck, Debussy and Berg fell only just short. The book is famous for its diatribes against Strauss and Puccini, particularly his description of *Tosca* as 'that shabby little shocker'.

Kertesz, István (1929–73)
Hungarian conductor, particularly associated with Mozart operas. He was musical director of the Augsburg Stadttheater (1958–63) and the Cologne Opera (1964–73). His death in a boating accident cut short a brilliant career. His wife **Edith Kertesz-Gabry** (*b* Gáncs) (*b* 1927) was a successful lyric soprano, who created Marie in Zimmermann's *Die Soldaten*.

Khaikin, Boris (1904–78)
Russian conductor, particularly associated with the Russian repertory. He was musical director of the Kirov Opera (1936–54) and conducted the first performances of Prokofiev's *The Story of a Real Man* and *The Duenna* and Kabalevsky's *The Craftsman of Clamecy*.

Khovanschina
Opera in five acts by Moussorgsky. 1st perf St Petersburg, 21 Feb 1886 (composed 1873); libr by the composer and Vladimir Stasov. Principal roles: Dosifei (bass), Ivan Khovansky (bass), Marfa (mezzo), Prince Golitsin (ten), Shaklovity (b-bar), Andrei (ten), Scribe (ten), Emma (sop). A gloomy but powerful musico-dramatic work, which incorporates the one completed scene from Moussorgsky's earlier *The Landless Peasant*, it was left unfinished and was completed and orchestrated by Rimsky-Korsakov. Some productions use the version prepared by Shostakovich in 1960. **Plot**: Moscow, 1682–89. A time of strife ensues between various factions when Peter the Great becomes Tsar. The party led by Prince Ivan Khovansky finds common cause with the Old Believers, led by Dosifei, against Peter's adherents, who are led by Prince Golitsin. Ivan's son Andrei is reunited with his former love Marfa, an Old Believer and prophetess. Peter and his followers emerge triumphant, and Ivan is murdered by the treacherous boyar Shaklovity. Rather than submit to religious reform, the Old Believers – with Marfa and Andrei – immolate themselves in their forest refuge. [R]

Khrennikov, Tichon (b 1913)
Russian composer. As secretary of the Union of Soviet Composers from 1948, he exercised a baleful influence on Russian music, playing a prominent part in the Stalin-inspired denunciations of Prokofiev and Shostakovich. He wrote seven operas in 'orthodox Soviet' style, which have not been performed outside Russia. They are *Into the Storm* (*V Buryu*, Moscow, 10 Oct 1939; libr Alexei Faiko, after Nikolai Virta's *Solitude*) [R], *Frol Skobeyev* (Moscow, 24 Feb 1950; libr Sergei Alexandrovich Tsenin, after D. Averkiyev), *The Mother* (Moscow, 26 Oct 1957; libr Faiko, after Maxim Gorky) [R Exc], *Much Ado About Hearts* (Moscow, 11 Mar 1972; libr Boris Pokrovsky, after Shakespeare's *Much Ado About Nothing*), *Doroteya* (Moscow, 26 May 1983; libr Y. Khaletsky, after Richard Brindsley Sheridan's *The Duenna*), *The Golden Calf* (*Zolotoy Telyonok*, Moscow, 9 Mar 1985; libr H. Khaletsky and I. Sharoyev, after E. Petrov) [R] and *The Naked King* (Leningrad, May 1988; libr R. Rozhdestvensky and Sharoyev, after E. Schvarts). He also wrote two operettas and a children's opera.

Kiel Stadttheater
The present opera house (cap 866) in this German city in Schleswig-Holstein opened in 1953, replacing the previous theatre of 1841 which was destroyed by bombs in 1944. Musical directors have included Georg Winkler, Peter Ronnefeld, Klaus Tennstedt, Hans Zender and Klaus-Peter Seibel.

Kienzl, Wilhelm (1857–1941)
Austrian composer. He wrote ten operas in Wagnerian style, including *Urvasi* (Dresden, 20 Feb 1886; libr A. Gödel, after Kalidasa), *Heilmar der Narr* (Munich, 8 Mar 1892; libr composer's father), DER EVANGELIMANN, by far his most successful work and his only opera still to be

remembered, and *Der Kuhreigen* (Vienna, 2 Nov 1911; libr Richard Batka, after R.H. Bartsch).

Kiev Opera
The opera house in the capital of Ukraine opened in 1851 as the Gorodski Theatre. It was rebuilt in 1901 as the Liebknecht Opera Theatre, and is now called the Shevchenko Opera and Ballet Theatre. Most performances are sung in Ukrainian.

King, James (b 1925)
American tenor, particularly associated with heavier German roles, especially Florestan and Siegmund. Beginning as a baritone, he turned to tenor roles in 1961 and enjoyed a remarkably long career. His voice was powerful and incisive, if not intrinsically beautiful, and he had a good stage presence.

King and Marshal (*Drot og Marsk*)
Opera in four acts by Heise. 1st perf Copenhagen, 25 Sept 1878; libr by Christian Richardt. Principal roles: Erik (ten), Stig (b-bar), Ingeborg (mezzo), Åse (sop), Rane (ten). Telling of events surrounding the murder of King Erik V of Denmark on 22 Nov 1286, it is one of the finest and most popular of all Danish operas but is almost unknown outside Denmark.
Plot: Jutland, 1286. The womanizing King Erik seduces both the poor Åse and the virtuous Lady Ingeborg, the wife of his Lord Marshal Stig Andersen. Stig joins with disaffected elements in a conspiracy against the King, and with the assistance of Erik's treacherous valet Rane Jonsen they kill him. [R]

King Arthur or **The British Worthy**
Opera in prologue, five acts and epilogue by Purcell. 1st perf London, June 1691; libr by John Dryden. It is really more of a play with music rather than a true opera. [R]

King Fisher
Baritone role in Tippett's *The Midsummer Marriage*. Jenifer's father, he is a business tycoon.

King Goes Forth to France, The
(*Kuningas Lähte Ranskaan*)
Opera in three acts by Sallinen. 1st perf Savonlinna, 7 July 1984; libr by Paavo Haavikko. Principal roles: King (bar), Prime Minister (bass), Nice Caroline (sop), Caroline with the Mane (mezzo), Anne who Steals (sop), Anne who Strips (mezzo), English Archer (bar), Guide (ten), Froissart (speaker). Although it is a fine work, it has proved rather less successful than Sallinen's other operas.
Plot: England and France in the future. As England is being overwhelmed by a new Ice Age, the Prime Minister urges the young King to marry, introducing to him the two Carolines and the two Annes. However, the King resolves to assume power, abandon England and lead his people across the Channel to France. The Prime Minister, fearful of the King's adventurist policies, observes that their route is following that of Edward III. The Hundred Years' War is re-enacted, including the Battle of Crécy and the incident of the six burghers at the siege of Calais, and the King marches on Paris.

King Priam
Opera in three acts by Tippett. 1st perf Coventry, 29 May 1962; libr by the composer, after Homer's *The Iliad*. Principal roles: Priam (bass), Paris (ten), Achilles (ten), Hector (bar), Helen (mezzo), Andromache (mezzo), Hecuba (sop), Old Man (bass), Hermes (ten), Young Guard (ten), Nurse (mezzo), Patroclus (bar). One of the finest 20th-century British operas, it views the events of the Trojan War from the Trojan standpoint and deals with what Tippett describes as 'the mysterious nature of human choice'.
Plot: Legendary Troy and Sparta. The main characters each make choices and suffer the consequences: Priam in supposedly killing the infant Paris and later restoring his son's patrimony; Paris himself in having abducted Helen; Hector in killing Patroclus, and Achilles in killing Hector in revenge; and, finally, Priam's choice of death as the price of dishonour when he realizes that he has no choices remaining. [R]

King Roger (*Król Roger*)
Opera in three acts by Szymanowski (Op 46). 1st perf Warsaw, 19 June 1926; libr by Jarosław Iwaszkiewicz. Principal

roles: Roger (bar), Roxane (sop), Shepherd (ten), Edrisi (ten), Archbishop of Palermo (bass), Abbess (mezzo). Szymanowski's masterpiece and virtually the only Polish opera to be performed internationally, it deals with supposed events in the reign of Roger II of Sicily (*c* 1095–1154). Following to some extent the ideas and plot of Euripides's *The Bacchae*, it is notable for its choral writing and for its superbly rich orchestration.
Plot: 12th-century Sicily. A shepherd prophet from India arrives at the court of King Roger, whose wife Roxane falls in love with him. He is denounced as a heretic by the Archbishop, but eventually he converts Roger from Christianity to his own Dionysian cult, and a bacchanal is celebrated in a Greek temple. [R]

King's Henchman, The
Opera in three acts by Taylor (Op 19). 1st perf New York, 17 Feb 1927; libr by Edna St Vincent Millay. Principal roles: Eadgar (bar), Aethelwold (ten), Aelfrida (sop), Ase (mezzo). Taylor's finest opera, it was very successful at its appearance but is nowadays virtually forgotten.
Plot: 10th-century Britain. King Eadgar has heard rumour of the beauty of the Princess Aelfrida of Devon. He sends his closest associate Aethelwold to Devon to woo her on his behalf, but Aethelwold and Aelfrida fall in love. Aethelwold marries her, sending word to Eadgar that Aelfrida is ugly and unworthy of his attention. However, Eadgar himself arrives, discovers the falsehood and kills Aethelwold.

Kipnis, Alexander (1891–1978)
Ukrainian bass, particularly associated with the German repertory and with the title-role in *Boris Godunov*. One of the greatest basses of the inter-war period, he had a rich, majestic and smoothly-produced voice, a fine technique and outstanding interpretative abilities. His son is the harpsichordist **Igor Kipnis**.

Kirov Opera
The company is based at the Maryinsky Theatre (cap 1,780) in St Petersburg (formerly Leningrad), which was designed by Alberto Cavos and opened in 1860. It became the State Academic Theatre in 1919 and was renamed the Kirov Opera in 1935, being named after the Politbureau member Sergei Kirov, who was assassinated in the city in 1934. Since 1991, the company has been known as either the Maryinsky or the Kirov interchangeably. For long Russia's principal opera house, it ranked second to the Bolshoi during the Soviet period, but is now regaining its pre-eminence. Its repertory and stagings tend to be a little conservative, but its musical standards are very high. Musical directors have included Eduard Nápravník, Albert Coates, Boris Khaikin, Yuri Temirkanov and Valery Gergiev.

Kirsten, Dorothy (1917–92)
American soprano, particularly associated with the French and Italian repertories, especially Puccini. An accomplished singing-actress of great personal beauty, she had a fine lyric soprano voice and appeared in a number of films, including *The Great Caruso*. Her autobiography, *A Time To Sing*, was published in 1982.

Kiss, The (*Hubička*)
Comic opera in three acts by Smetana. 1st perf Prague, 7 Nov 1876; libr by Eliška Krásnohorská, after Karolina Světlá's short story. Principal roles: Vendulka (sop), Lukáš (ten), Martinka (mezzo), Paloucký (bass), Matouš (bass). A slight but delightful love story, it was the first work which Smetana composed after becoming deaf. Still very popular in the Czech lands, it is only rarely performed elsewhere.
Plot: 19th-century Bohemia. The widower Lukáš wishes to marry his old love Vendulka. She is delighted but – believing the superstition that a kiss given to a widower before his remarriage causes grief to the deceased wife – refuses to let him kiss her. This causes a lovers' tiff and Vendulka flees to the mountains with her aunt Martinka, who engages in border smuggling. Lukáš follows her, begs forgiveness, and reconciliation follows. [R]

Klänge der Heimat
Soprano aria (the Csárdás) for Rosalinde in Act II of J. Strauss's *Die Fledermaus*, sung to lend verisimilitude to her disguise as a Hungarian countess.

Klebe, Giselher Wolfgang (b 1925)
German composer. He has written 12

operas, for all of which he wrote his own libretti. A number have met with success in Germany but are virtually unknown elsewhere. They are *Die Räuber* (Düsseldorf, 3 June 1957; libr after Friedrich von Schiller), *Die Ermordrung Cäsars* (Essen, 20 Sept 1959; libr after Shakespeare's *Julius Caesar*), *Die Tödlichen Wünsche* (*The Deathly Wishes*, Düsseldorf, 14 June 1959; libr after Anne-Honoré de Balzac's *La Peau de Chagrin*), ALKMENE, his most successful opera, *Figaro lässt sich Scheinen* (*Figaro Seeks a Divorce*, Hamburg, 28 June 1963; libr after Ödön von Horváth), *Jakobowsky und der Oberst* (Hamburg, 2 Nov 1965; libr after Franz Werfel), *Das Märchen von der Schönen Lilie* (Schwetzingen, 15 May 1969; libr after Goethe's *Märchen*), *Ein Wahrer Held* (*A True Hero*, Zürich, 18 Jan 1975; libr after John Millington Synge's *The Playboy of the Western World*), *Das Mädchen von Domrémy* (Stuttgart, 19 June 1976; libr after Schiller's *Die Jungfrau von Orleans*), *Das Rendez-vous* (Hanover, 7 Oct 1977; libr after M. Soschtschenko), *Der Jüngste Tag* (Mannheim, 12 July 1980; libr after Horváth) and *Die Fastnachtsbeichte* (Darmstadt, 20 Dec 1983; libr after Carl Zuckmayer).

Kleiber, Carlos (b 1930)
German-born Argentinian conductor, son of the conductor ERICH KLEIBER. Particularly associated with the German repertory and with Verdi's *Otello*, he is one of the outstanding contemporary opera conductors. His appearances are intermittent, as he is a perfectionist who demands very long rehearsal periods. His repertory is small.

Kleiber, Erich (1890–1956)
Austrian conductor, particularly associated with Mozart operas and with the German repertory. One of the greatest operatic conductors of the 20th century, he was musical director of the Mannheim Opera (1922–3) and the Berlin State Opera (1923–34). He conducted the first performances of *Wozzeck*, Schreker's *Der Singende Teufel* and Milhaud's *Christophe Colomb*. His son is the conductor CARLOS KLEIBER.

Klemperer, Otto (1885–1973)
German conductor and composer, particularly associated with Mozart and Wagner operas and with *Fidelio* (which he also produced at Covent Garden). He was regarded as one of the greatest conductors of all time, and his performances were noted for their majestic breadth, becoming progressively slower as he got older. He was musical director of the Strasbourg Opera (1914–17), the Cologne Opera (1917–24), the Wiesbaden Opera (1924–7) and the Berlin State Opera (1927–33). He conducted the first performances of Korngold's *Die Tote Stadt*, Schreker's *Irrelhoe*, Hindemith's *Neues vom Tage* and Zemlinsky's *Der Geburstag der Infantin*. He also composed one opera, *Das Ziel* (Berlin, 1931, composed 1915). His autobiography, *Minor Recollections*, was published in 1964.

Klenau, Paul von (1883–1946)
Danish composer and conductor. He wrote six operas, some of them successful in their time but all of them now forgotten. They are *Sulamith* (Munich, 16 Nov 1913), *Kjartan und Gudrun* (Mannheim, 4 Apr 1918; libr composer; revised version *Gudrun auf Island*, Hagen, 27 Nov 1924), *Die Lästerschule* (Frankfurt, 25 Dec 1926; libr R.S. Hoffmann, after Richard Brindsley Sheridan's *The School for Scandal*), *Michael Kohlaas* (Stuttgart, 4 Nov 1933; libr composer, after Heinrich Wilhelm von Kleist), *Rembrandt van Rijn* (Berlin, 23 Jan 1937; libr composer) and *Elisabeth von England* (Kassel, 29 Mar 1939; libr composer).

Klingsor
Bass-baritone role in Wagner's *Parsifal*. He is an evil sorcerer who had been expelled from the brotherhood of the Grail.

Klose, Margarete (1902–68)
German mezzo, particularly associated with Wagner and Verdi roles. One of the finest German mezzos of the inter-war period, she was a versatile artist with a fine voice and a good stage presence. She created Oona in Egk's *Irische Legende*.

Kluge, Die (*The Clever Girl*)
Comic opera in six scenes by Orff. 1st perf Frankfurt, 20 Feb 1943; libr by the composer, after *Die Kluge Bauerntochter* in Jacob and Wilhelm Grimm's *Fairy Tales*. Principal roles: Girl (sop), King (bar), Peasant (bass), Donkey Man (ten), Muleteer (bass), Tramps (ten, bar and

bass). Orff's best known and most accessible opera, which has sometimes been performed with marionettes, it is still quite often performed.
Plot: The King is bored with the cleverness and wise sayings of the Girl he married after she had answered his riddles. He sends her packing and says that she may have anything in the palace that she wants as a parting gift. When she tells him that it is the King himself she wants, he relents upon the condition that she stops being clever. [R]

Knaifel, Alexander (b 1943)
Russian composer. He has written one opera, *The Canterville Ghost* (*Kentervilskoye Privedeniye*, Leningrad, 26 Feb 1974, composed 1966; libr T. Kramarova, after Oscar Wilde) [R].

Knappertsbusch, Hans (1888–1965)
German conductor, particularly associated with Wagner and Strauss operas. One of the finest 20th-century Wagnerian interpreters, he was musical director of the Dessau Opera (1920–22) and the Bavarian State Opera (1922–35). He conducted the first performances of Coates's *Samuel Pepys* and Pfitzner's *Das Herz*.

Kniplová, Naděžda (b Pokorná) (b 1932)
Czech soprano, particularly associated with the Czech repertory and with Wagnerian roles. One of the finest Czech dramatic sopranos of the post-war era, she had a powerful voice and a keen dramatic sense.

Knot Garden, The
Opera in three acts by Tippett. 1st perf London, 2 Dec 1970; libr by the composer. Principal roles: Faber (bar), Thea (mezzo), Denise (sop), Dov (ten), Mel (bar), Flora (sop), Mangus (bar). A complex metaphysical drama with human relationships discussed through a comparison with characters in Shakespeare's *The Tempest*, its structure is defined by the titles of its three acts: Confrontation, Labyrinth and Charade. The tenor song cycle *Songs For Dov* is derived from music from the opera.
Plot: The psychoanalyst Mangus and the physically scarred revolutionary activist Denise act as catalysts to explore the emotional entanglements of two couples: Faber, whose marriage to Thea has grown stale and who lusts for his ward Flora and the musician Dov and his black lover, the poet Mel. [R]

Knussen, Oliver (b 1952)
British composer and conductor. His two operas, which have met with very considerable success, are *Where the Wild Things Are* (Brussels, 28 Nov 1980; libr Maurice Sendak) [R] and *Higglety-Pigglety Pop!* (Glyndebourne, 8 May 1985; libr Sendak). A fine interpreter of contemporary music, he conducted the first performance of Holloway's *Clarissa*. He has been artistic director of the Aldeburgh Festival since 1983.

Koanga
Opera in prologue, three acts and epilogue by Delius. 1st perf Elberfeld, 30 March 1904; libr by Charles Francis Keary, after George Washington Cable's *The Grandissimes*. Principal roles: Koanga (bar), Palmyra (sop), Don José (bass), Pérez (ten), Clotida (mezzo), Uncle Joe (bass). One of Delius's finest operas, it is unaccountably only very rarely performed.
Plot: Late-18th-century Mississippi. The mulatto Palmyra repulses the plantation overseer Simón Pérez and falls in love with a newly arrived slave, the former African chieftan Koanga. The plantation owner Don José agrees to their marriage, but Pérez abducts Palmyra at the wedding. Koanga escapes into the forest and causes a plague by means of voodoo. Koanga kills Pérez, but he is himself captured and killed, and Palmyra stabs herself. [R]

Kobbé, Gustav (1857–1918)
American musicologist and critic. His *Complete Opera Book* (1919) is one of the classic operatic reference works. It was revised and updated by the Earl of Harewood in 1976.

Kodály, Zoltán (1882–1967)
Hungarian composer. He wrote three operas on nationalist themes, all of which make use of Hungarian folk material and which all contain long passages of spoken dialogue. The highly successful HÁRY JÁNOS was followed by THE SPINNING ROOM and *Czinka Panna* (Budapest, 15 Mar 1948; libr Béla Balázs).

Kokkonen, Joonas (b 1921)
Finnish composer. His sole opera THE LAST TEMPTATIONS has proved to be one of the finest and most successful contemporary operas.

Kokoschka, Oskar (1886–1980)
German painter, designer and playwright. Famous for his use of greens, he undertook a number of operatic designs, notably *Die Zauberflöte* in Geneva in 1965. He also wrote the libretti for Hindemith's *Mörder, Hoffnung der Frauen* and Křenek's *Orpheus und Eurydike*.

Kolenatý, Dr
Baritone role in Janáček's *The Macropolus Case*. He is a lawyer.

Kollo, René (b Kollodzievski) (b 1937)
German tenor, particularly associated with Wagnerian roles, especially Lohengrin and Siegfried. He was the leading Wagnerian tenor of the 1970s and 1980s, although he was not a true HELDENTENOR. He also achieved success in operetta, and has recently produced a number of operas. His grandfather **Walter** (1878–1940) was an operetta composer.

Köln
see COLOGNE OPERA

Koltai, Ralph (b 1924)
Hungarian-born British designer. Often working in collaboration with the producer Michael Geliot (*b* 1933), his modernistic sets make extensive use of scaffolding and tubular effects. He has worked extensively for Scottish Opera and for the English National Opera, where he designed the famous English-language *Ring*.

Komische Oper, Berlin
Formerly the Metropol-Theater, this opera house (cap 1,120) in the former East Berlin opened on 23 Dec 1947. Under the administration of WALTER FELSENSTEIN it soon became one of the most innovative, controversial and stimulating companies in Europe. The annual season runs from September to July, and musical directors have included Kurt Masur, Zdeněk Košler, Rolf Reuter and Yakov Kreizberg.

Konchak
Bass role in Borodin's *Prince Igor*. He is the Polovtsian Khan.

Konchakovna
Mezzo role in Borodin's *Prince Igor*. She is Konchak's daughter.

Kondrashin, Kiril (1914–81)
Russian conductor, particularly associated with the Russian repertory. Best known as a symphonic conductor, he conducted much opera in the early part of his career, but subsequently his operatic appearances were rare. He defected from the then USSR in 1978.

Konetzni, Hilde (b Konerczny) (1905–80)
Austrian soprano, particularly associated with Wagnerian roles, especially Sieglinde. Based largely at the Vienna State Opera, she possessed a voice of great beauty which she used with fine style. She created the title-role in Sutermeister's *Niobe* and Elvira in Stolz's *Trauminsel*. Her sister **Anny** (1902–68) was also a soprano, noted for her Strauss and Wagner roles.

König Hirsch (*King Stag*)
Opera in three acts by Henze. 1st perf Berlin, 23 Sept 1956; libr by Heinz von Cramer, after Carlo Gozzi's *Rè Cervo*. Revised version *Il Rè Cervo*, 1st perf Kassel, 10 March 1963. Principal roles: Leandro (ten), Costanza (sop), Tartaglia (b-bar), Checco (ten), Coltellino (ten), Scollatella (sop). One of Henze's most successful operas, it is a melodic and almost neo-classical fairy-tale piece. Henze's orchestral work *La Selva Incantata* is drawn from music from the opera.
Plot: Legendary Venice. King Leandro, abandoned in the forest as a child by the evil governor Tartaglia, has been nurtured by wild animals. He returns to claim his crown and to choose his bride, but the machinations of Tartaglia lead to his renouncing the throne and returning to the forest. He enters the body of a stag, whilst Tartaglia assumes his form and initiates a cruel dictatorship. Unable to sublimate his human longings, Leandro once more returns to the city, where Tartaglia is murdered by his own assassins. Leandro recovers his human form and weds the faithful Costanza.

Königin von Saba, Die (*The Queen of Sheba*)
Opera in four acts by Goldmark (Op 27). 1st perf Vienna, 10 March 1875; libr by Salomon Hermann Mosenthal, after the First Book of Kings in the Old Testament. Principal roles: Assad (ten), Solomon (bar), Sulamith (sop), Queen of Sheba (mezzo), High Priest (bass). By far Goldmark's most successful opera, it is an exotic work of great lyrical beauty which still receives an occasional performance.
Plot: Jerusalem, *c* 950 BC. Although engaged to Sulamith, daughter of the High Priest, Solomon's favourite Assad has fallen in love with the Queen of Sheba. Solomon insists, however, that the planned marriage must take place. Assad commits a sacrilege and is imprisoned. When he is freed, he searches for Sulamith in the desert, finds her, and dies in her arms. [R]

Königskinder, Die (*The Royal Children*)
Opera in three acts by Humperdinck. 1st perf New York, 28 Dec 1910 (composed 1897 and later revised); libr by Else Bernstein-Porges under the pen-name of Ernst Rosmer, after her own play. Principal roles: Goose-girl (sop), Prince (ten), Fiddler (bar), Witch (mezzo). Humperdinck's only opera apart from *Hänsel und Gretel* to have survived, it was originally written as pitched speech over music – the first appearance in opera of SPRECHSTIMME.
Plot: Legendary Germany. The Goose-girl, who is in reality a princess placed under a spell by the Witch, falls in love with the Prince. With the aid of the Fiddler, she takes flight and joins the Prince. The people reject her, however, and she and the Prince, poisoned by the Witch, die together in the snow. [R]

Konwitschny, Franz (1901–62)
German conductor, particularly associated with Wagner operas. He was musical director of the Freiburg Opera (1933–7), the Frankfurt Opera (1937–45), the Hanover State Opera (1945–9) and the Berlin State Opera (1955–62). His brother **Peter** was a producer.

Kónya, Sándor (b 1923)
Hungarian tenor, particularly associated with the Italian and German repertories. A fine artist with an incisive and intelligently-used voice, he was able to sing both lyrical roles and heroic roles such as Calaf and Lohengrin. He created Leandro in Henze's *König Hirsch*.

Korngold, Erich (1897–1957)
Austrian composer, writing in a lush, late-romantic style. His five operas are *Der Ring des Polykrates* (Munich, 28 Mar 1916; libr after Heinrich Teweles), VIOLANTA, DIE TOTE STADT, his most successful opera, *Das Wunder der Heliane* (Hamburg, 10 Oct 1927; libr Hans Müller, after Hans Kaltneker's *Die Heilige*) [R] and *Die Kathrin* (Stockholm, 7 Oct 1939; libr composer). He also enjoyed a highly successful career writing film music. One of his film scores, *Give Us This Night* (1936), contains a mini-opera *Romeo and Juliet.* He also prepared an edition of J. Strauss's *Eine Nacht in Venedig* in 1923.

Korrepetitor
The title of the RÉPÉTITEUR in a German or Austrian opera house.

Košler, Zdeněk (b 1928)
Czech conductor, particularly associated with the Czech repertory, contemporary works and with Prokofiev operas. He was musical director of the Olomouc Opera (1958–62), the Ostrava Opera (1962–6), the Komische Oper, Berlin (1966–8), the Bratislava Opera (1971–6) and the Prague National Theatre (1980–85 and 1989–91).

Kostelnička
Soprano role in Janáček's *Jenůfa*. The sexton's wife, she is Jenůfa's formidable foster-mother. The role is sometimes sung by a mezzo.

Köth, Erika (1927–89)
German soprano, particularly associated with COLORATURA roles, especially Zerbinetta in *Ariadne auf Naxos* and the title-role in Donizetti's *Lucia di Lammermoor*. She possessed a smallish voice of great agility with a range extending remarkably high. She also enjoyed success as an operetta artist.

Kothner, Fritz
Baritone role in Wagner's *Die Meistersinger von Nürnberg*. A baker, he is one of the masters.

Koussevitsky, Serge (1874–1951)
Russian conductor, particularly associated with the Russian repertory. Best known as a symphonic conductor, his operatic appearances were rare. In 1942, he founded the Koussevitsky Music Foundation (since 1950 permanently endowed as the Serge Koussevitsky Foundation in the Library of Congress), which has commissioned many important new works, including *Peter Grimes*. He also founded the Berkshire Music Festival in 1937.

Kovalyov
Baritone role in Shostakovich's *The Nose*. He is the unfortunate owner of the nose which detatches itself and begins to lead an independent life.

Kovařovic, Karel (1862–1920)
Czech composer and conductor. He completed five operas, most of them written in nationalist style. They are *The Bridegrooms* (*Ženichové*, Prague, 15 May 1884; libr composer, after K.Š. Macháček), *The Way Through the Window* (*Cesta Oknem*, Prague, 11 Feb 1886; libr Emanuel Züngl, after Eugène Scribe and Gustave Lemoine), *Noc Šimona a Judy* (Prague, 5 Nov 1892; libr Karel Šípek, after Pedro de Alarcón's *El Sombrero de Tres Picos*), THE DOGHEADS, his most successful opera, and *The Old Bleaching House* (*Na Starem Bělidle*, Prague, 22 Nov 1901; libr Šípek, after Božena Němcova's *Babička*). He also wrote the operatic parody *Oedipus the King* (*Edip Král*, Prague, 19 Mar 1894; libr A.V. Nevšsímal, after Sophocles). He was musical director of the Prague National Theatre (1900–20) and conducted the first performances of *Rusalka* and operas by Ostrčil, Foerster and Novák.

Kowalski, Jochen (b 1954)
German counter-tenor, particularly associated with Händel and other baroque roles and with Orfeo in Gluck's *Orfeo ed Euridice*. A male alto of considerable range and flexibility, his voice is more powerful than most counter-tenors, and is used with intelligence, musicianship and a fine technique. An impressive singing-actor, he has also successfully undertaken roles such as Fyodor in *Boris Gudonov* and Prince Orlofsky in J. Strauss's *Die Fledermaus*.

Kozlovsky, Ivan (1900–93)
Ukrainian tenor, particularly associated with the Russian and French repertories, especially Lensky. One of the leading Russian lyric tenors of the inter-war period, he founded an opera company of his own which functioned from 1938 to 1941, for which he also acted as producer. Based largely at the Bolshoi Opera, he enjoyed a remarkably long career, singing into his 70s, and came out of retirement to sing Monsieur Triquet in *Eugene Onegin* on his 90th birthday.

Krása, Hans (1899–1944)
Czech composer. He wrote two operas: *Verlobung im Traum* (Prague, 18 May 1933; libr Rudolf Fuchs and Rudolf Thomas, after Fyodor Dostoyevsky's *Uncle's Dream*) and the highly successful children's opera *Brundibár* (Terezín, 23 Sept 1943; libr Adolf Hoffmeister) [R], which is still quite frequently performed. He was murdered by the Nazis in Auschwitz.

Krásnohorská, Eliška (1847–1926)
Czech poetess and librettist. She provided texts for Bendl (*Lejla*, *Břetislav*, *The Child of Tabor* and *Karel Škretá*), Fibich (*Blaník*) and Smetana (*The Kiss, The Secret, The Devil's Wall* and the unfinished *Viola*).

Kraus, Alfredo (b 1927)
Spanish tenor, particularly associated with lyrical Italian and French roles, especially Nemorino, the Duke of Mantua, Edgardo, Alfredo Germont and Werther, which last was one of the most remarkable operatic interpretations of modern times. His beautiful voice, his innate musicianship, his flawless technique, his thrilling upper register, his dapper stage presence, his impeccable diction and his scrupulous good taste combined to make him one of the greatest of all 20th-century exponents of the BEL CANTO repertory. He was also a successful exponent of ZARZUELA. He enjoyed a remarkably long career, still singing superbly in his mid-60s.

Kraus, Joseph Martin (1756–92)
German composer, largely resident in Sweden. His SINGSPIELS include *Proserpin* (Stockholm, 1 June 1781; libr Johan Henrik Kellgren, after Gustavus III) [R] and

Soliman II (Stockholm, 22 Sept 1789; libr Johan Gabriel Oxenstierna, after Charles-Simon Favart) [R], his most successful work. His most ambitious opera *Aeneas at Carthage* (*Aeneas i Cartago*, Stockholm, 18 Nov 1799; libr Kellgren, after Jean-Jacques le Franc's *Didon*) was produced posthumously.

Kraus, Otakar (1909–80)
Czech baritone, long resident at Covent Garden. A fine singing-actor with an incisive voice, he was particularly associated with the role of Wagner's Alberich. He created Tarquinius in *The Rape of Lucretia*, Nick Shadow in *The Rake's Progress*, Diomede in *Troilus and Cressida* and King Fisher in *The Midsummer Marriage*. He was also a noted teacher, whose pupils included Robert Lloyd, Jonathan Summers, Elizabeth Connell, Gwynne Howell, Christian du Plessis and Clifford Grant.

Krause, Tom (b 1934)
Finnish baritone, particularly associated with Mozart roles. He had a beautiful lyrical voice, used with style and fine musicianship, and he had a good stage presence. He created Jason in Křenek's *Der Goldene Bock*, Herr von Lipps in Einem's *Der Zerrissene*, a role in Sallinen's *The Palace* and the title-role in Searle's *Hamlet*.

Krauss, Clemens (1893–1954)
Austrian conductor, particularly associated with the German repertory, especially Strauss. He was musical director of the Bavarian State Opera (1937–43) and conducted the first performances of *Arabella*, *Friedenstag*, *Capriccio* (of which he was co-author of the libretto), *Die Liebe der Danae* and Orff's *Die Kluge*. Married to the soprano VIORICA URSULEAC.

Krejčí, Iša (1904–68)
Czech composer and conductor, son of the philosopher František Krejčí. The leading member of the Czech neo-classical school, his most important opera is *The Tumult at Ephesus* (*Pozdvižení v Efesu*, Prague, 8 Sept 1946; libr J. Bachtík, after Shakespeare's *The Comedy of Errors*), which has had considerable success in the Czech lands. He was musical director of the Olomouc Opera (1945–58).

Křenek, Ernst (1900–91)
Austrian composer, who wrote in traditional, jazz and serial (see TWELVE-TONE OPERAS) styles. His 16 stage works are *Die Zwingburg* (Berlin, 21 Oct 1924; libr Franz Werfel, after F. Demuth), *Der Sprung über den Schatten* (*The Jump Over the Shadow*, Frankfurt, 9 June 1924; libr composer), *Orpheus und Eurydike* (Kassel, 27 Nov 1926; libr Oskar Kokoschka), the jazz-inspired JONNY SPIELT AUF, his most successful opera, the three ZIETOPERN *Der Diktator*, *Das Geheime Königreich* and *Schwergewicht* (Weisbaden, 6 May 1928; libr composer), *Leben des Orest* (Leipzig, 19 Jan 1930; libr composer, after Euripides's *Orestes*), *Cefalo e Procri* (Venice, 15 Sept 1934; libr R. Küfferle), the fine *Karl V* (Prague, 22 June 1938, composed 1934; libr composer), which was banned by the Nazis, *Tarquin* (Cologne, 16 July 1950, composed 1940; libr Emmet Lovey), *What Price Confidence?* (Saarbrücken, 23 May 1962, composed 1946; libr composer), *Pallas Athene Weint* (Hamburg, 17 Oct 1955; libr composer), *Der Goldene Bock* (Hamburg, 16 June 1964; libr composer), the television opera *Der Zauberspiegel* (*The Magic Mirror*, Munich, 23 Dec 1968; libr composer) and *Das Kommt Davon* (Hamburg, 27 June 1970; libr composer). His autobiography, *Horizons Circled*, was published in 1974. Married first to Mahler's daughter **Anna** and later to the composer **Gladys Nordenstrom**.

Kreutzer, Konradin (1780–1849)
German composer. His most important operas are *Konradin von Schwaben* (Stuttgart, 30 Mar 1812; libr K.R. Weitzmann), *Feodora* (Stuttgart, 1812; libr August von Kotzebue), *Libusse* (Vienna, 4 Dec 1922; libr J.K. Bernard) and DAS NACHTLAGER VON GRANADA, by far his most successful work.

Kreutzer, Rodolphe (1766–1831)
French violinist, composer and conductor. Best known as the dedicatee of Beethoven's 'Kreutzer' violin sonata, he was also a successful opera composer. His 40 operas, all now long forgotten, include *Paul et Virginie* (Paris, 15 Jan 1791; libr E.G.F. de Favières, after Bernadin de Saint-Pierre), *Lodoïska* (Paris, 1 Aug 1791;

libr J.C.B. Dejaure), *Imogène* (Paris, 27 Apr 1796; libr Dejaure, after Shakespeare's *Cymbeline*), *Astyanax* (Paris, 12 Apr 1801; libr Dejaure), *Aristippe* (Paris, 24 May 1808; libr P.F. Giraud and M.T. Leclercq) and *Abel* (Paris, 23 Mar 1810; libr François Benoît Hoffman). His last opera *Matilde* (1827) was never performed. He conducted the first performances of Spontini's *Olympie* and Liszt's *Don Sanche*.

Krips, Josef (1902–74)
Austrian conductor, particularly associated with Mozart operas and with *Fidelio*. One of the finest opera conductors of the 20th century, he was musical director of the Karlsruhe Staatstheater (1926–33) and the Vienna State Opera (1945–50). His brother **Henry** (1912–87) was also a conductor, noted for his performances of Viennese operetta.

Kristina
Soprano role in Janáček's *The Macropolus Case*. Vítek's daughter, she is a young singer.

Krombholc, Jaroslav (1918–83)
Czech conductor, particularly associated with the Czech repertory, especially Smetana. One of the finest Czech conductors of the post-war era, he was musical director of the Prague National Theatre (1963–83) and conducted the first performances of Cikker's *Resurrection* and Bořkovec's *Satyr*. His wife **Marie Tauberová** (*b* 1911) was a successful soprano.

Kubelík, Rafael (b 1914)
Czech conductor and composer, son of the composer Jan Kubelík. Particularly associated with the Czech and German repertories, he was musical director of the Brno Opera (1931–41), Covent Garden (1955–8) and the Metropolitan Opera, New York (1973–4). He also wrote five operas, of which the most important is *Cornelia Faroli* (Augsburg, 1972; libr Dalibor Faltis). Married to the soprano ELSIE MORISON.

Kubiak, Teresa (b 1937)
Polish soprano, particularly associated with the Italian and Russian repertories. A lyrico-dramatic soprano with a voice of considerable power and beauty, she also had an affecting stage presence. She created Herodiade in Twardowski's *Tragedy of John and Herod*.

Kuhlau, Friedrich (1786–1832)
Danish composer and flautist. He wrote a number of operas, some highly successful in their time, but nowadays little remembered outside Denmark. The most important are *Lulu* (Copenhagen, 29 Oct 1824; libr Carl Christian Frederik Güntelberg, after A.J. Liebeskind) [R] and *The Elf's Hill* (*Elverhøj*, Copenhagen, 6 Nov 1828, libr J.L. Heiberg) [R].

Kullervo
Opera in two acts and epilogue by Sallinen. 1st perf Los Angeles, 25 Feb 1992 (composed 1988); libr by the composer, after the *Kalevala* and Aleksis Kivi's *Kullervo*. Principal roles: Kullervo (bar), Mother (mezzo), Kalervo (bass), Kimmo (ten), Sister (sop), Untamo (bar). Sallinen's fourth opera and arguably his masterpiece, it is based on Finnish mythology and confirms his position as one of the world's finest living opera composers. [R]

Kundry
Soprano role in Wagner's *Parsifal*. She is an enchantress enslaved by Klingsor. The role is often sung by a mezzo.

Künneke, Eduard (1885–1953)
German composer. He wrote over 30 operettas, of which the most successful were *Der Vetter aus Dingsda* (Berlin, 15 Apr 1921; libr F. Oliven and H. Haller) [R], his best known work, *Lady Hamilton* (Breslau, 25 Sept 1926; libr R. Bars and Leopold Jacobson) and *Die Grosse Sünderin* (Berlin, 31 Dec 1935; libr Katharina Stoll and Hermann Roemmer) [R Exc].

Kunz, Erich (b 1909)
Austrian bass-baritone, particularly associated with the German repertory, especially Papageno in *Die Zauberflöte* and Beckmesser in *Die Meistersinger von Nürnberg*. A fine singing-actor with a superb and almost irrepressible sense of comedy, he also enjoyed great success as an operetta artist.

Kupfer, Harry (b 1935)
German producer and designer. One of the leading contemporary German opera directors, his 'deconstructionist' productions were epitomized by his *Ring* and *Der Fliegende Holländer* at Bayreuth. He was director of the Weimar Opera (1967–72) and director of productions for the Dresden State Opera (1972–81) and the Komische Oper, Berlin (1981–), where his most notable productions have included *Orfeo ed Euridice* and the premiere of Matthus's *Judith*. He was co-author of the libretto for Penderecki's *Die Schwarze Maske*.

Kupper, Annelies (1906–88)
German soprano, particularly associated with Mozart roles, especially Countess Almaviva in *Le Nozze di Figaro*. A warm-voiced and musicianly singer, she created the title-role in Strauss's *Die Liebe der Danae*.

Kurka, Robert (1921–57)
American composer, whose early death from leukaemia robbed music of a considerable talent. Influenced by Weill and by jazz, he wrote one opera, *The Good Soldier Schweik* (New York, 23 Apr 1958; libr Lewis Allan, after Jaroslav Hašek), which enjoyed considerable success, especially in the orchestral suite arranged from the opera.

Kurwenal
Baritone role in Wagner's *Tristan und Isolde*. He is Tristan's retainer.

Kurz, Selma (1874–1933)
Austrian soprano, particularly associated with French and Italian COLORATURA roles. Renowned for her phenomenal trill, she was arguably the finest coloratura of the inter-war period and was also an affecting singing-actress. She created Zerbinetta in *Ariadne auf Naxos* and the Princess in Zemlinsky's *Es War Einmal*.

Kusche, Benno (b 1916)
German bass-baritone, particularly associated with German character roles. A fine singing-actor, equally at home in opera and operetta, he created a role in Orff's *Antigonae*. His wife **Christine Görner** was a soprano.

Kutuzov, Marshal
Bass-baritone role in Prokofiev's *War and Peace*. He is the historical Russian commander during the Napoleonic invasion.

Kuznetsova, Maria (1880–1966)
Russian soprano, daughter of the painter Nikolai Kuznetsov. Particularly associated with the Russian and French repertories, she was the leading Russian soprano of the immediate pre-revolutionary period. She created Fevronia in Rimsky-Korsakov's *The Invisible City of Kitezh* and, for Massenet, Fausta in *Roma* and the title-role in *Cléopâtre*. She escaped from Russia in 1918, allegedly disguised as a boy and hidden in a trunk on a Swedish ship. Later, influenced by Isadora Duncan, she gave dance recitals and appeared in the first performance of Strauss's ballet *Josephslegende*. She also directed her own touring opera company in the 1920s and 1930s.

Kyoto
Baritone role in Mascagni's *Iris*. He is a brothel-keeper.

L

La
Titles beginning with the feminine form of the Italian, French and Spanish definite article are listed under the letter of the first main word. For example, *La Vida Breve* is listed under V.

Lablache, Luigi (1794–1858)
Italian bass. A fine singing-actor with a huge physique, he was one of the greatest basses of the first half of the 19th century. He created Massamiliano in *I Masnadieri*, Caliban in Halévy's *La Tempestà*, Sulemano in Mayerbeer's *L'Esule di Granata*, Claudio in Mercadante's *Amleto*, eight roles for Donizetti including the title-roles in *Marino Faliero* and *Don Pasquale* and, for Bellini, Filippo in *Bianca e Fernando*, Orosmane in *Zaira* and Giorgio in *I Puritani*. He was also a noted teacher, whose pupils included Queen Victoria, and he published a method of singing. His son **Federico** was also a bass and his son-in-law was the pianist Sigismond Thalberg.

Laca Klemeň
Tenor role in Janáček's *Jenůfa*. He is Števa Buryja's stepbrother.

Lacerato spirito, Il
Bass aria for Jacopo Fiesco in the prologue of Verdi's *Simon Boccanegra*, in which he laments the death of his daughter.

Lachner, Franz (1803–90)
German composer and conductor. His four operas, all now long forgotten, are *Die Bürgschaft* (Budapest, 30 Oct 1828; libr K. von Biedenfeld, after Friedrich von Schiller), *Alidia* (Munich, 12 Apr 1839; libr Otto Prechtler, after Edward Bulwer-Lytton's *The Last Days of Pompei*), *Caterina Cornaro* (Munich, 3 Dec 1841; libr after Jules-Henri Vernoy de Saint-Georges's *La Reine de Chypre*) and *Benvenuto Cellini* (Munich, 7 Oct 1849; libr Auguste Barbier and Léon de Wailly). He was musical director of the Munich Opera (1852–68). His brother **Ignaz** (1807–95) was also a composer, whose operas include *Die Geistersturm* (Stuttgart, 14 Apr 1837; libr K. Hanisch), *Die Regenbrüder* (Stuttgart, 20 May 1839; libr E. Möricke and H. Kuz) and *Loreley* (Munich, 6 Sept 1846; libr Wendling and E.W. Molitor).

Là ci darem la mano
Soprano/baritone duet for Zerlina and Giovanni in Act I of Mozart's *Don Giovanni*, in which the Don woos the initially reluctant Zerlina.

Lady Macbeth
Soprano role in Verdi's and Bloch's *Macbeth*. She is Macbeth's ambitious wife. The Verdi is occasionally sung by a mezzo.

Lady Macbeth of the Mtsensk District, The (*Ledi Makbet Mtsenskovo Uyezda*)
Opera in four acts by Shostakovich (Op 29/114). 1st perf Leningrad, 22 Jan 1934; libr by the composer and Alexander Preis, after Nikolai Leskov's short story. Revised version *Katerina Ismailova*, 1st perf Moscow, 26 Dec 1962. Principal roles: Katerina (sop), Sergei (ten), Boris (bass), Zinovy (ten), Sonyetka (mezzo), Aksinya (sop). One of the greatest operas of the 20th century, it was successful at its premiere but provoked the famous anti-formalism attack in *Pravda* on 28 Jan 1936, entitled 'Chaos instead of music'. The opera then disappeared in Russia until the production of the toned-down revised version. This second version initially made the work known in the West, but nowadays the original version is nearly always preferred.
Plot: Russia, 1865. Katerina is bored and frustrated by life with her ineffectual husband, the merchant Zinovy Ismailov. During Zinovy's absence on business, she falls in love with Sergei, a new and handsome employee on the family farm, and commences an illicit affair with him. When Katerina's brutish and autocratic father-in-law Boris realizes the situation, she feeds him mushrooms laced with rat

poison and he dies a horrible death. On Zinovy's return, she strangles him with the help of Sergei and hides his body in the cellar. During the celebrations of the subsequent wedding of Katerina and Sergei, the police arrive, find Zinovy's corpse and arrest the couple. Exiled to Siberia, they are on a long march through the snow when Sergei, grown tired of Katerina, takes up with the prisoner Sonyetka and publicly humiliates his wife. As the convicts cross a bridge, Katerina seizes Sonyetka and jumps with her into the icy river below. [R both versions]

Lakmé
Opera in three acts by Delibes. 1st perf Paris, 14 April 1883; libr by Philippe Gille and Edmond Gondinet, after Pierre Loti's *Rarahu ou Le Mariage de Loti*. Principal roles: Lakmé (sop), Gérald (ten), Nilakantha (bar), Mallika (mezzo), Frédéric (bass). By far Delibes's most successful opera, notable for its lush orientalism, it is still quite often performed.
Plot: Mid-19th-century India. The British officer Gérald loves and is loved by Lakmé, daughter of the Brahmin priest Nilakantha. Swearing to take revenge on the violator of his temple, Nilakantha forces Lakmé to sing at the bazaar so as to identify him. When Gérald appears, Lakmé faints and so gives him away. Nilakantha stabs Gérald, but Lakmé nurses him back to health at a secret hideout in the forest where he is eventually found by his brother officer Frédéric, who persuades him to return to his duty as a soldier. When Lakmé returns, she senses the change in Gérald, and kills herself by eating the poisonous datura leaf. [R]

Lalo, Édouard (1823–92)
French composer. His first opera *Fiesque* (Paris, 1873, composed 1866; libr Charles Beauquier, after Friedrich von Schiller's *Die Verschwörung des Fiesco zu Genua*) made little impression; only a section of it has ever been performed. This failure discouraged Lalo, and it was 20 years before he turned to opera again with the highly successful LE ROI D'YS. His last opera was the unfinished *La Jacquerie* (Monte Carlo, 8 Mar 1895; libr Édouard Blau and Simone Arnaud), of which he completed only one act; the remaining four acts were written by Arthur Coquard.

Lamento (Italian for 'lament')
A tragic aria, often placed just before the climax of the plot in an early-17th-century Italian opera. The most famous example is 'Lasciatemi morire' in Monteverdi's *Arianna*.

Lamoral, Count
Bass role in Strauss's *Arabella*. He is one of Arabella's suitors.

Lamoureux, Charles (1834–99)
French conductor and violinist who, in 1881, founded the Paris orchestra which bore his name. The leading French conductor of his time, he was one of the earliest champions of Wagner.

Lancaster, Sir Osbert (1908–86)
British cartoonist and designer. A famous lampooner of the foibles of the British upper classes, he turned to opera design in 1952, and was closely associated with Glyndebourne. Always wittily executed and with a superb eye for ludicrous detail, his most notable designs included *The Rake's Progress* and *L'Heure Espagnole* for Glyndebourne and *The Sorcerer* for the D'Oyly Carte Opera Company.

Land des Lächelns, Das (*The Land of Smiles*)
Operetta in three acts by Lehár. 1st perf Berlin, 10 Oct 1929; libr by Ludwig Herzer and Fritz Löhner. Principal roles: Prince Sou-chong (ten), Lisa (sop), Mi (sop), Gustl (bar). A revision of his unsuccessful *Die Gelbe Jacke* of 1923, it was an immediate success and has always remained one of Lehár's most popular works.
Plot: Vienna and Peking, 1912. At a party given at her father's home, Lisa tells her suitor, the hussar Gustl, that she loves the Chinese diplomat Prince Sou-chong. News arrives that Sou-chong has been appointed President and must return to China. Lisa decides to go with him, and the two are married. Sou-chong's sister Mi is European-minded – to the displeasure of the Mandarin Uncle Tschang – and meets Gustl (now Austrian military attaché) at a tennis party. Gustl's home news makes Lisa homesick, but Sou-chong refuses her permission to visit her home for fear of

losing her. They quarrel and Lisa is confined to her quarters. With the aid of Gustl and Mi, she escapes but runs straight into Sou-chong. Realizing that he cannot restrain her, he allows Lisa to leave with his blessing. [R]

Landgrave
Bass role in Wagner's *Tannhäuser*. He is Hermann, Landgrave of Thuringia, father of Elisabeth.

Landi, Stefano (1587–1639)
Italian composer. An important operatic innovator, he introduced choral scenes, developed ensemble writing, introduced comic episodes into serious works, provided orchestral introductions to the acts in a prefigurement of the overture, and used the STILE RAPPRESENTATIVO in a more flexible dramatic way, foreshadowing the division between RECITATIVE and aria. His *La Morte d'Orfeo* (1619; libr composer) was the first opera to be performed in Rome, and was followed by *Il Sant' Alessio* (Rome, 18 Feb 1632; libr Giulio Rospigliosi).

Landowski, Marcel (b 1915)
French composer. His operas include *Le Fou* (Nancy, 1 Feb 1956; libr composer) [R], *Le Ventriloque* (Paris, 6 Feb 1956; libr composer and Paul Arnold) [R], *Les Adieux* (Paris, 8 Oct 1960; libr composer), *L'Opéra de Poussière* (Avignon, 25 Oct 1962; libr composer and G. Caillet), *Montségur* (Toulouse, 1 Feb 1985; libr composer, Gérard Caillet and Guy Patrick Saindérichin, after Duc de Lévis-Mirepoix) and *L'Opéra de la Bastille* (Paris, 12 Dec 1989).

Langdon, Michael (b Frank Birtles) (1920–91)
British bass, particularly associated with the British and German repertories, especially Baron Ochs in *Der Rosenkavalier*. One of the leading post-war British basses, he had a large and rich voice and was a fine singing-actor, especially in comedy. He created the He-Ancient in *The Midsummer Marriage*, Apollyon in *The Pilgrim's Progress*, Mr Ratcliffe in *Billy Budd*, the Recorder of Norwich in *Gloriana*, the Doctor in Henze's *We Come to the River* and the title-role in Orr's *Hermiston*. He was the first director of the National Opera Studio (1978–86). His autobiography, *Notes From a Low Singer*, was published in 1982.

Langridge, Philip (b 1939)
British tenor, particularly associated with Britten, Mozart, Stravinsky and Janáček roles, especially Aschenbach, Idomeneo and Živný in *Fate*. A singer of outstanding intelligence and musicianship, with a voice of highly individual timbre, he is also a compelling singing-actor of great insight. A superb exponent of 20th-century opera, he created for Birtwistle, the title-role in *The Mask of Orpheus*, Kong in *The Second Mrs Kong* and roles in Penderecki's *Paradise Lost* and Thomas Wilson's *Confessions of a Justified Sinner*. Married to the mezzo ANN MURRAY.

Lantern, The (*Lucerna*)
Opera in four acts by Novák (Op 56). 1st perf Prague, 13 May 1923; libr by Hanuš Jelínek, after Alois Jirásek's play. Principal roles: Miller (bar), Hanička (sop), Countess (sop), Bailiff (bass), Zajíček (ten), Klásková (mezzo). Described as a musical fairy tale, it is Novák's most successful opera. Still sometimes performed in the Czech lands, it is virtually unknown elsewhere. [R]

Laparra, Raoul (1876–1943)
French composer, whose works make considerable use of Basque and Spanish traditional music. He wrote a number of operas, of which the most successful was *La Habañera* (Paris, 26 Feb 1908; libr composer). He was killed in an air raid.

Lara, Isidore de (b Cohen) (1858–1935)
British composer, who wrote in a style influenced by Saint-Saëns and Massenet. He wrote several operas which enjoyed some success in their day but which are all now forgotten. They include *The Light of Asia* (London, 11 June 1892), a revision of an earlier cantata, *Amy Robsart* (London, 20 July 1893; libr Augustus Harris and Frederick Wheatherly, after Sir Walter Scott's *Kenilworth*), *Moïna* (Monte Carlo, 11 Mar 1897; libr Louis Gallet), *Messaline* (Monte Carlo, 21 Mar 1899; libr Paul Armand Silvestre and Eugène Morand) and *Les Trois Mousquetaires* (Cannes, 3 Mar 1921; libr Henri Cain and Louis Payen, after Alexandre Dumas).

Largo (Italian for 'broad')
A musical notation meaning slow. In opera, the term is best known as the name often given to 'Ombra mai fù' in Händel's *Serse* – even though it is marked larghetto in the score.

Largo al factotum
Baritone aria for Figaro in Act I of Rossini's *Il Barbiere di Siviglia*, in which he introduces himself as an invaluable and versatile inhabitant of the town.

Là rivedrà nell'estasi
Tenor aria for Gustavus in Act I of Verdi's *Un Ballo in Maschera*, in which he sings of his joy at the prospect of seeing Amelia at the ball.

Lascia ch'io pianga
Soprano aria for Almirena in Act II of Händel's *Rinaldo*, in which she expresses the grief which her captivity has brought her.

Lasciatemi morire
The lament from the final scene of Monteverdi's *Arianna*. It is the only substantial piece of music from the opera which survives.

Last rose of summer, The
A traditional Irish air (originally called 'The Groves of Blarney') for which new words were written by poet Thomas Moore (1779–1852). It was used in this form by Flotow for Lady Harriet's 'Die letzte Rose' in Act II of *Martha*.

Last Savage, The
Opera in three acts by Menotti. 1st perf Paris, 21 Oct 1963; libr by the composer. Principal roles: Kodanda (ten), Kitty (sop), Abdul (bar), Sardula (sop). One of the stronger of Menotti's later operas, it satirizes modern civilization.
Plot: Mid-20th-century India and Chicago. Wishing to marry off his daughter, the American college girl Kitty, to the Indian prince Kodanda, her father devises a complicated scheme to prepare her for this. He arranges for her to capture and tame a 'prehistoric man', Abdul (hired to play the part), but his plans miscarry: Kitty falls in love with Abdul, and Kodanda marries the servant girl Sardula.

Last Temptations, The (*Viimeiset Kiusaukset*)
Opera in two acts by Kokkonen. 1st perf Helsinki, 2 Sept 1975; libr by Lauri Kokkonen, after his own play. Principal roles: Paavo (bass), Riitta (sop), Juhana (ten), Blacksmith (bar). Kokkonen's only opera, it tells of the historical religious revivalist Paavo Routsalinen (1777–1852), with his life being recalled in a series of flashbacks as he lies on his deathbed. It has proved to be one of the finest and most dramatically effective modern operas and has been widely performed. [R]

László, Magda (b 1919)
Hungarian soprano, particularly associated with 20th-century operas. A fine singing-actress, she created Cressida in *Troilus and Cressida* and the Mother in Dallapiccola's *Il Prigioniero*.

László Hunyadi
Opera in four acts by Erkel. 1st perf Budapest, 27 Jan 1844; libr by Béni Egressy, after Lörnic Tóth's *The Two Lászlós*. Principal roles: László (ten), Mária (sop), King (bar), Erzsébet (sop), Miklós (bar), Cilley (bar). One of Erkel's finest works, and the piece which may be said to mark the foundation of Hungarian opera, it is strongly nationalist and employs traditional Hungarian material. Still very popular in Hungary, it is hardly ever performed elsewhere.
Plot: Hungary, 1456–57. László Hunyadi becomes aware of the treacherous plans of Cilley, uncle of King László V, and kills him. The King, who has fallen in love with Hunyadi's fiancée Mária, promises Hunyadi's mother Erzsébet that he will not seek vengeance for Cilley's death. However, the Palatine Miklós Gara promises the King Mária's hand if Hunyadi is executed. The wedding of Hunyadi and Mária is interrupted, and Hunyadi is imprisoned. Believing the King's promise, Hunyadi refuses Mária's offer of aid for an escape and is executed. [R]

Lattuada, Felice (1882–1962)
Italian composer. He wrote six operas, mainly in VERISMO style. Some enjoyed considerable success in their time but are nowadays largely forgotten, and his close association with the fascists has not helped

his posthumous reputation. His operas are *La Tempestà* (Milan, 23 Nov 1922; libr Arturo Rossato, after Shakespeare's *The Tempest*), *Sandha* (Genoa, 21 Feb 1924; libr Ferdinando Fontana), the comedy LE PREZIOSE RIDICOLE, *Don Giovanni* (Naples, 18 May 1929; libr Rossato, after José Zorilla y Moral's *Don Giovanni Tenorio*), *La Caverna di Salamanca* (Genoa, 1 Mar 1938; libr Valentino Piccoli, after Miguel Cervantes) and *Caino* (Milan, 10 Jan 1957; libr composer and G. Zambianchi, after Lord Byron's *Cain*). His autobiography, *La Passione Dominante*, was published in 1951. His son **Alberto** is a producer and film director.

Latvian opera composers
These include Alfrēds Kalninš (1879–1951), whose *Banjuta* (Riga, 29 May 1920; libr A. Krūnš) was the first real Latvian opera, his son Jānis (*b* 1904), Jānis Medinš (1890–1966), his brother Jāzeps (1877–1947), Margers Zarinš (*b* 1910) and Arvīds Žilinskis (*b* 1905).

Laughing Song
Soprano aria ('Mein Herr Marquis') for Adele in Act II of J. Strauss's *Die Fledermaus*, in which she tells Eisenstein that he has committed a faux-pas in saying that she looks like his parlourmaid.

Laura
1 Mezzo role in Ponchielli's *La Gioconda*. She is Alvise's wife. **2** Soprano role in Weber's *Die Drei Pintos*. **3** Soprano role in Millöcker's *Der Bettelstudent*. She is in love with Simon. **4** Mezzo role in Dargomijsky's *The Stone Guest*. She is Don Carlos's lover. **5** Mezzo COMPRIMARIO role in Verdi's *Luisa Miller*. She is a village girl.

Lauretta
Soprano role in Puccini's *Gianni Schicchi*. Schicchi's daughter, she loves Rinuccio.

Lauri-Volpi, Giacomo (1892–1979)
Italian tenor, particularly associated with the Italian repertory. One of the greatest tenors of the inter-war period, his ringing voice and outstanding technique made him especially famous in dramatic roles such as Calaf in *Turandot*, although he had equal success in lyrical roles. He enjoyed an exceptionally long career, singing into his early 70s. He wrote five books, including *Voci Parallale* (1955) and *Misteri della Voce Umana* (1957). His wife **Maria Ros** (1895–1970) was a successful soprano.

Lawrance, Marjorie (1909–79)
Australian soprano (who also sang some mezzo roles), particularly associated with the German and French repertories. A distinguished Wagnerian, she was striken by poliomyelitis in 1941 but managed to continue her career even though she was never again able to walk unaided. She created Keltis in Canteloube's *Vercingétorix*. Her autobiography, *Interrupted Melody*, was published in 1949.

Lazaridis, Stefanos (b 1944)
Greek-born British designer, principally associated with the English National Opera, where his most notable designs have included *Hänsel und Gretel*, *Il Trovatore*, *The Mikado* and *Lady Macbeth of Mtsensk*.

Lazzari, Virgilio (1887–1953)
Italian bass, particularly associated with the Italian repertory, especially Archibaldo in *L'Amore dei Tre Re*. Although his voice was not absolutely outstanding, his intelligence and his excellent dramatic abilities made him one of the leading basses of the inter-war period. He was largely resident at the Metropolitan Opera, New York, from 1933.

Le
Titles beginning with the masculine singular form of the French definite article are listed under the letter of the first main word. For example, *Le Roi d'Ys* is listed under R.

Lear
Opera in two acts by Reimann. 1st perf Munich, 9 July 1978; libr by Claus H. Hanneberg, after William Shakespeare's *King Lear*. Principal roles: Lear (bar), Cordelia (sop), Goneril (sop), Regan (sop), Edgar (c-ten), Gloucester (b-bar), Kent (ten), Edmund (ten), Fool (speaker), French King (bass). Reimann's best-known work and one of the most widely performed contemporary operas, it is a powerful and often violent setting which follows Shakespeare closely. [R]

Lear, Evelyn (b Schulman) (b 1926)
American soprano, particularly associated with Strauss, Mozart and Berg roles. A singer of outstanding intelligence and artistry, she created the title-role in Klebe's *Alkmene*, Jeanne in Egk's *Die Verlobung in San Domingo*, Lavinia in Levy's *Mourning Becomes Electra*, Magda in Ward's *Minutes Till Midnight*, Ranyevska in Kelterborn's *Kirschgarten* and Arkadina in Pasatieri's *The Seagull*. Married to the baritone THOMAS STEWART.

Leave me loathsome light
Bass aria for Somnus in Act III of Händel's *Semele*, in which he complains about the light which stops him sleeping.

Leclair, Jean-Marie (1697–1764)
French composer. Best known as a composer of chamber music, he also wrote one opera, the fine SCYLLA ET GLAUCUS. He was perhaps the only composer to be murdered.

Lecocq, Charles (1832–1918)
French composer. He wrote over 50 operettas, notable for their graceful melodies, many of which found great favour. His most successful works include LE DOCTEUR MIRACLE, *Fleure-de-Thé* (Paris, 11 Apr 1868; libr Henri Charles Chivot and Alfred Duru), *Les Cents Vièrges* (Brussels, 16 Mar 1872; libr Chivot, Duru and Louis François Clairville), LA FILLE DE MADAME ANGOTR, his most enduring work, *Girolfé-Girofla* (Brussels, 21 Mar 1874; libr Eugène Letterier and Albert Vanloo), *La Petite Mariée* (Paris, 21 Dec 1875; libr Letterier and Vanloo), LE PETIT DUC, *Le Coeur et le Main* (Paris, 19 Oct 1883; libr Charles Nuitter and A. Beaumont), *Ali-Baba* (Brussels, 11 Nov 1888; libr Vanloo and William Busnach) and *La Belle au Bois Dormant* (Paris, 19 Feb 1900; libr Vanloo and G. Duval). His only more serious work, *Plutus* (Paris, 31 May 1886; libr Jollivet and Albert Millaud), was a failure.

Legato (Italian for 'bound together')
It denotes singing smoothly. Its opposite is STACCATO.

Légende de Joseph en Égypte, La
see JOSEPH

Légende de Kleinzach, La
Tenor aria for Hoffmann in the prologue of Offenbach's *Les Contes d'Hoffmann*. Sung to entertain the students, it is a song about a strange dwarf.

Legend of the Invisible City of Kitezh and the Maiden Fevronia, The
see INVISIBLE CITY OF KITEZH, THE

Leggero (originally spelt *leggiero*) (Italian for 'light')
In opera, the term describes a type of Italian soprano suited to lighter lyrical roles such as Gilda in Verdi's *Rigoletto* and Nannetta in *Falstaff*.

Lehár, Franz (b Ferenc) (1870–1948)
Hungarian composer. His first stage work was an unsuccessful opera, *Kakuška* (Leipzig, 27 Nov 1896; libr F. Falzari), but it was as an operetta composer that he achieved outstanding success. His first work in this genre was *Wiener Frauen* (Vienna, 21 Nov 1902; libr O. Tann-Bergler and E. Norini). It was followed by *Tatyana* (Brünn, 21 Feb 1905; libr M. Kalbeck), a revision of *Kakuška*, and his masterpiece DIE LUSTIGE WITWE, which immediately made him world famous. There followed *Der Mann mit den drei Frauen* (Vienna, 21 Jan 1908; libr Julius Bauer), DER GRAF VON LUXEMBURG, *Das Fürstenkind* (Vienna, 7 Oct 1909; libr Viktor Léon), ZIGEUNERLIEBE, *Eva* (Vienna, 24 Nov 1911; libr Robert Bodanzky, Alfred Maria Willner and E. Spero) [R Exc], *Endlich Allein* (Vienna, 10 Feb 1914; libr Willner and Bodanzky), *Der Sterngucker* (*The Astronomer*, Vienna, 14 Jan 1916; libr Willner and Fritz Löhner), *Wo die Lerche Singt* (Budapest, 1 Jan 1918; libr Willner and Heinrich Reichert, after Ferenc Martos), *Die Blaue Mazur* (Vienna, 28 May 1920; libr Leo Stein and Béla Jenbach), FRASQUITA, *Die Gelbe Jacke* (Vienna, 9 Feb 1923; libr Léon) and *Clo-Clo* (Vienna, 8 Mar 1924; libr Jenbach). Many of the later works were unsuccessful but, partly because of their championship by Richard Tauber, his next works re-established his popularity. PAGANINI was followed by DER ZAREWITSCH, FRIEDERIKE, the highly successful DAS LAND DES LÄCHELNS (a revision of *Die Gelbe Jacke*) and *Schön ist die Welt* (Berlin, 3 Dec 1930; libr Löhner

and Ludwig Herzer) [R Exc], a revision of *Endlich Allein*. For his last work he returned to opera, this time successfully, with GIUDITTA.

Lehmann, Lilli (1848–1929)
German soprano, particularly associated with Mozart and Wagner roles. One of the most famous singers of the 19th century, she had an enormous repertory of 170 roles, and created Woglinde in *Götterdämmerung* and the Woodbird in *Siegfried*. She was artistic director of the Salzburg Festival, as well as a noted teacher, whose pupils included Geraldine Farrar and Olive Fremstad. Her autobiography, *Mein Weg*, was published in 1913, and she also translated Victor Maurel's autobiography into German. Her sister **Marie** (1851–1931) was also a successful soprano, who created Wellgunde in *Götterdämmerung*, and her husband **Paul Kalisch** (1855–1946) was a noted heroic tenor.

Lehmann, Lotte (1888–1976)
German soprano, particularly associated with Strauss roles, especially the Marschallin. One of the greatest and best-loved singers of the 20th century, her glorious voice, superlative artistry and aristocratic stage presence made her one of the finest artists in operatic history. She created the Composer in *Ariadne auf Naxos*, the Dyer's Wife in *Die Frau ohne Schatten* and Christine in *Intermezzo*. She wrote novels, poetry and her autobiography, *On Wings of Song*, which was published in 1937. She was also a distinguished teacher, whose pupils included Mattiwilda Dobbs, Grace Bumbry and Judith Beckmann.

Leibowitz, René (1913–72)
Polish-born French conductor, composer and musicologist. He was a noted interpreter of the Russian and French repertories and also composed five operas, of which the most significant was *Les Espagnoles à Venise* (Grenoble, 27 Jan 1970; libr G. Limbour).

Leicester, Earl of
The historical Robert Dudley, Earl of Leicester (1533–88) appears in a number of operas, including tenor roles in: **1** Donizetti's *Maria Stuarda*. **2** Rossini's *Elisabetta Regina d'Inghilterra*. **3** Donizetti's *Il Castello di Kenilworth*. **4** Auber's *Leicester*.

Leider, Frida (1888–1975)
German soprano, particularly associated with Wagnerian roles. Her rich voice and powerful dramatic sense made her arguably the finest of all inter-war Wagnerian sopranos. Her autobiography, *Das war mein Teil*, was published in 1959.

Leiferkus, Sergei (b 1946)
Russian baritone, particularly associated with the Italian and Russian repertories, especially Eugene Onegin and Iago. One of the finest contemporary baritones, he possesses a bright, beautiful and smoothly-produced voice used with outstanding musicianship and he has a good stage presence. He was the first Soviet singer to appear with a regional British opera company.

Leïla
Soprano role in Bizet's *Les Pêcheurs de Perles*. She is a Brahmin priestess loved by Zurga and Nadir.

Leinsdorf, Erich (b Landauer) (1912–93)
Austrian conductor, particularly associated with Wagner, Verdi, Strauss and Puccini operas. Resident in the United States since 1937, he was musical director of the New York City Opera (1956–7), but was principally associated with the Metropolitan Opera. His autobiography, *Cadenza: a Musical Career*, was published in 1976.

Leipzig Opera
The present opera house (cap 1,682) opened on 8 Oct 1960, replacing the previous theatre which had been destroyed by bombs in 1943. One of Germany's leading houses its orchestra is the famous Leipzig Gewandhaus. Musical directors have included Artur Nikisch, Gustav Brecher, Helmut Seidelmann, Paul Schmitz, Václav Neumann, Rolf Reuter and Lothar Zagrosek.

Leise, leise
Soprano aria for Agathe in Act II of

Weber's *Der Freischütz*, in which she prays that Max may be given divine protection.

Leitmetzerin, Marianne
Soprano role in Strauss's *Der Rosenkavalier*. She is Sophie's duenna.

Leitmotiv (German for 'leading motif')
A musical fragment – melodic, harmonic or rhythmic – which is associated with a particular character, object or idea and which serves as a musical identification tag. Although it had previously been used embryonically (most notably in Grétry's *Richard Coeur de Lion*), it was with Wagner that the concept reached its fullest development, especially in *Der Ring des Nibelungen*, with motifs combining and metamorphosing as an integral part of the symphonic structure.

Leitner, Ferdinand (b 1912)
German conductor, particularly associated with the German repertory. He was musical director of the Munich Opera (1946–7), the Stuttgart Opera (1950–69) and the Zürich Opernhaus (1969–84). He conducted the first performances of Orff's *Oedipus der Tyrann* and *Prometheus* and Klebe's *Ein Wahrer Held*.

Lemeshev, Sergei (1902–77)
Russian tenor, particularly associated with lyrical French, Russian and Italian roles. Possessor of a beautiful and luscious voice used with fine musicianship and a superb technique, he was also a noted teacher and producer. His writings include *The Path to Art* (1968).

Lemnitz, Tiana (1897–1994)
German soprano, particularly associated with the German and Italian repertories, especially Octavian in *Der Rosenkavalier* and Pamina in *Die Zauberflöte*. Noted for her pianissimo singing, she was a versatile singer with a voice of great beauty and was one of the finest lyric sopranos of the inter-war period.

Leningrad
see SAINT PETERSBURG

Lensky, Vladimir
Tenor role in Tchaikovsky's *Eugene Onegin*. He is a poet engaged to Olga.

Lenya, Lotte (b Karoline Wilhelmine Blamauer) (1898–1981)
Austrian singer and actress. Following her marriage to Kurt Weill in 1926, she became one of the leading exponents of his music, creating Jenny in *Die Dreigroschenoper* and Anna in *Die Sieben Todsünden*. As a straight actress she appeared in a number of films, including *From Russia With Love*.

Leo, Leonardo (1694–1744)
Italian composer. He wrote over 70 operas, all now long forgotten, but a number of which (particularly the comedies) were successful in their time. He was the first composer to introduce the chorus into Neapolitan opera, in *L'Olimpiade* (Naples, 19 Dec 1737; libr Pietro Metastasio). He was also a noted teacher, whose pupils included Jommelli and Piccinni.

Leoncavallo, Ruggero (1857–1919)
Italian composer. Although his name is inevitably coupled with that of Mascagni, he was a far more talented and sophisticated artist. His choice of subjects and styles (from vast Wagnerian music-drama to fatuous operettas) often led to failure, but in the field of moderate VERISMO he was a composer of considerable dramatic effectiveness. His stage works, for several of which he wrote his own libretti, are *I Medici* (Milan, 9 Nov 1893, composed 1889; libr composer), the first part of a projected Wagnerian trilogy dealing with Renaissance Italy, PAGLIACCI, which made him world-famous and on which his reputation chiefly rests, *Chatterton* (Rome, 10 Mar 1896; libr composer, after Alfred de Vigny), the unjustly neglected LA BOHÈME, the successful ZAZÀ, *Der Roland* (Berlin, 13 Dec 1904; libr composer, after Willibald Alexis), *Maià* (Rome, 15 Jan 1910; libr Angelo Nessi, after Paul de Choudens), *Malbruk* (Rome, 19 Jan 1910; libr Nessi, after Giovanni Boccaccio), *La Reginetta delle Rose* (Rome, 24 June 1912; libr Giovacchino Forzano), *Zingari* (London, 16 Sept 1912; libr E. Cavacchioli and G. Emanuel, after Alexander Pushkin's *The Gypsies*), *Are You There?* (London, 1 Nov 1913; libr E. Wallace and A. de Courville), *La Candidata* (Rome, 6 Feb 1915; libr Forzano), *Goffredo Mameli* (Genoa, 27 Apr

1916; libr composer and G. Belvederi), *Prestammi Tua Moglie* (Montecatini, 2 Sept 1916; libr E. Corradi), the operetta *A Chi la Giarettiera?* (Rome, 16 Oct 1919), the ambitious and unjustly forgotten EDIPO RÈ, the operetta *Il Primo Bacio* (Montecatini, 29 Apr 1923; libr L. Bonelli) and the unfinished *La Maschera Nuda* (Naples, 26 June 1925; libr Bonelli and F. Paolieri), which was completed by Salvatore Allegra. He also wrote the libretto for Augusto Machado's *Mario Wetter*.

Leoni, Franco (1864–1949)
Italian composer. His nine VERISMO operas, all the-palest-of-pale imitations of Puccini and Mascagni, are *Raggio di Luna* (Milan, 5 June 1890), *Rip van Winkle* (London, 4 Sept 1897; libr after Washington Irving), *Ib and Little Christina* (London, 14 Nov 1901; libr after Hans Christian Andersen), the once-popular L'ORACOLO, *Tzigana* (Genoa, 3 Feb 1910; libr E. Moschini), *Francesca da Rimini* (Paris 1914; libr M. Crawford, after Dante's *La Divina Commedia*), *La Baruffe Chiozzotte* (Milan, 2 Jan 1920; libr after Carlo Goldoni), *La Terra del Sogno* (Milan, 10 Jan 1920) and *Falene* (Milan, 1920; libr C. Linati).

Leonora
1 Soprano role in Verdi's *La Forza del Destino*. Don Carlo's sister, she loves Don Alvaro. **2** Soprano role in Verdi's *Il Trovatore*. A lady-in-waiting to the queen, she loves Manrico. **3** Soprano role in Verdi's *Oberto*. She is Oberto's daughter. **4** Soprano role in Paer's *Leonora*. She is Florestano's wife. **5** Mezzo role in Cimarosa's *Le Astuzie Femminili*. She is Romualdo's fiancée. **6** Soprano role in Nielsen's *Maskarade*. She is Leonard's daughter. **7** Soprano role in Donizetti's *Rosmonda d'Inghilterra*. **8** Soprano role in Berio's *La Vera Storia*.

Leonora or **L'Amore Conjugale** (*Wedded Love*)
Opera in two acts by Paer. 1st perf Dresden, 3 Oct 1804; libr by Giovanni Federico Schmidt, after Jean Nicolas Bouilly's libretto for Gaveaux's *Léonore*. Principal roles: Leonora (sop), Florestano (ten), Don Pizzarro (ten), Rocco (bass), Giacchino (bar), Marcellina (sop), Fernando (ten). Arguably Paer's finest opera, it contains some excellent music but is nowadays virtually forgotten. For plot see FIDELIO. [R]

Leonore
see FIDELIO

Leonore
1 Soprano role in Beethoven's *Fidelio*. She is Florestan's wife. **2** Mezzo role in Donizetti's *La Favorite*. She is the historical Leonor di Guzmán, Alfonso of Castile's mistress. **3** Soprano role in Dittersdorf's *Doktor und Apotheker*. She is Stössel's daughter. **4** Soprano role in Flotow's *Alessandro Stradella*. She is Bassi's ward. **5** Soprano role in Grétry's *L'Amant Jaloux*. She is Lopez's daughter.

Léonore or **L'Amour Conjugal** (*Wedded Love*)
Opera in two acts by Gaveaux. 1st perf Paris, 19 Feb 1798; libr by Jean Nicolas Bouilly. Gaveaux's only opera to be in any way remembered, and that solely because it is the work which provided Beethoven with the story of *Fidelio*.

Leonore 40/45
Opera in two acts by Liebermann. 1st perf Basel, 26 March 1952; libr by Heinrich Strobel. Principal roles: Huguette (sop), Alfred (ten), Emile (bar). Liebermann's most successful opera.
Plot: Paris, 1940s. The French girl Huguette meets the German soldier Alfred at a concert during the Nazi occupation. Alfred deserts and is held as a prisoner of war, but the two are reunited after the war through the intervention of Huguette's guardian angel Emile.

Léonor viens
Baritone aria for Alphonse in Act II of Donizetti's *La Favorite*, in which he says that he would lay his crown at his mistress's feet.

Léopold, Prince
Tenor role in Halévy's *La Juive*. Eudoxie's husband, he loves Rachel.

Leporello
Bass-baritone role in Mozart's *Don Giovanni* and Dargomijsky's *The Stone Guest*. He is Don Juan's servant.

Leppard, Raymond (b 1927)
British conductor and musicologist, particularly associated with Händel and other baroque composers and with 17th-century Italian composers. One of the first British champions of early opera, he has made somewhat controversial realizations of Monteverdi's *L'Incoronazione di Poppea* and *Il Ritorno d'Ulisse in Patria* and Cavalli's *La Calisto*, *L'Egisto*, *L'Ormindo* and *Orione*. He conducted the first performance of Maw's *The Rising of the Moon*.

Leroux, Xavier (1863–1919)
French composer. He wrote a number of operas in the style of his teacher Massenet, all of which are now forgotten. They include *Astarté* (Paris, 15 Feb 1901; libr Louis de Gramont), *La Reine Fiammette* (Paris, 23 Dec 1903; libr Catulle Mendès), *Le Chemineau* (Paris, 6 Nov 1907; libr Jean Richepin) and *Le Carillonneur* (Paris, 20 Mar 1913; libr Richepin, after Georges Rodenbach).

Les
Titles beginning with the plural form of the French definite article are listed under the letter of the first main word. For example, *Les Huguenots* is listed under H.

Lescaut
Manon's brother, he appears as a baritone role in: **1** Massenet's *Manon*. **2** Puccini's and Auber's *Manon Lescaut*. **3** Henze's *Boulevard Solitude*.

Lesson scenes
A popular device in 18th- and 19th-century comic opera. The two most famous examples are singing lessons: for Rosina in Rossini's *Il Barbiere di Siviglia* and for Marie in Donizetti's *La Fille du Régiment*.

Lesueur, Jean-François (1760–1837)
French composer. An important forerunner of French grand opera and of continuous non-NUMBER OPERAS, he ranked during the Napoleonic period as one of the three leading opera composers with Cherubini and Méhul. His operas, many of them on a large scale, are nowadays largely forgotten. They are *La Caverne* (Paris, 15 Feb 1793; libr Palat-Dercy, after Alain René le Sage's *Gil Blas de Santillane*), *Paulin et Virginie* (Paris, 13 Jan 1794; libr Alphonse du Congé Dubreuil, after Bernardin de Saint-Pierre), *Télémaque* (Paris, 11 May 1896; libr Palat-Dercy), OSSIAN, his most successful work, *Le Triomphe de Trajan* (Paris, 23 Oct 1807; libr Joseph Alphonse d'Esménard), the ambitious LA MORT D'ADAM and the unperformed *Alexandre à Babylon* (1815; libr Baour-Lormain). He was also a noted teacher, whose pupils included Berlioz, Thomas and Gounod.

Lesur, Daniel (b 1908)
French composer. A member of the Jeune France group (founded in Paris in 1936 in opposition to the neo-classical musical style of the time), his operas are *Andrea del Sarto* (Marseilles, 24 Jan 1969; libr composer, after Alfred de Musset) [R] and *Ondine* (1982).

Let's Make an Opera
see LITTLE SWEEP, THE

Letter Duet
Soprano/soprano duet ('Sull'aria') for Susanna and Countess Almaviva in Act III of Mozart's *Le Nozze di Figaro*, in which the Countess dictates a note of assignation to the Count.

Letter scene
A popular device in 18th- and early-19th-century operas, in which a character reads (not sings) a letter brought to him. Nowadays, however, the name is usually used to refer to Tatyana's scene in Act I of Tchaikovsky's *Eugene Onegin*, in which she writes a love letter to Onegin.

Let the bright seraphim
Soprano aria for the Israelite Woman in Act III of Händel's *Samson*.

Letzte Rose, Die
see LAST ROSE OF SUMMER, THE

Lev
Baritone role in Tippett's *The Ice Break*. Nadia's husband and Yuri's father, he is a released political prisoner.

Levi, Hermann (1839–1900)
German conductor, particularly associated with Wagner operas. One of the first great

Wagnerian interpreters, admired by Wagner despite being Jewish, he was musical director of the Karlsruhe Staatstheater (1867–72) and the Munich Opera (1872–96) and conducted the first performance of *Parsifal*.

Levine, James (b 1943)
American conductor, particularly associated with the Italian and German repertories, especially Verdi and Wagner. His interpretations are carefully prepared and finely balanced and nuanced, if occasionally rather hard-driven. Musical director of the Metropolitan Opera, New York, from 1975 and artistic director since 1986, he conducted the first performance of Corigliano's *The Ghosts of Versailles*. He is also an accomplished pianist.

Levy, Martin David (b 1932)
American composer. His operas, in a mildly dissonant style, include *The Tower* (Santa Fe, 2 Aug 1957; libr T. Brewster), *Escorial* (New York, 4 May 1958); libr composer and L. Abel, after Michel de Ghelderode) and *Mourning Becomes Electra* (New York, 16 Mar 1967; libr Henry Butler, after Eugene O'Neill), his finest work.

Lewis, Sir Anthony (1915–83)
British conductor, composer and musicologist, particularly associated with Händel and other baroque composers. A distinguished principal of the Royal Academy of Music (1968–82), his operatic appearances were infrequent.

Lewis, Richard (1914–90)
British tenor, particularly associated with Mozart roles and with 20th-century operas, especially the title-roles in Mozart's *Idomeneo, Rè di Creta* and Achilles in Tippett's *King Priam*. A versatile artist of outstanding musicianship, he enjoyed a long career, singing into his late 60s. He created Troilus in *Troilus and Cressida*, Mark in *The Midsummer Marriage*, Achilles in *King Priam*, Gwyn in Hughes's *Menna* and Amphitryon in Klebe's *Alkmene*.

Libiamo, libiamo
Soprano/tenor duet (the Brindisi) for Violetta and Alfredo Germont in Act I of Verdi's *La Traviata*.

Librettists
see panel on page 316. See also COMPOSER-LIBRETTISTS; WRITERS AS LIBRETTISTS

Libretto (Italian for 'little book')
The term now almost universally used to describe the words of an opera or operetta. It is called *livret* in France.

Libuše
Opera in three acts by Smetana. 1st perf Prague, 11 June 1881 (composed 1872); libr by Josef Wenzig and Ervín Špindler. Principal roles: Libuše (sop), Přemysl (bar), Chrudoš (bass), Šťáhlav (ten), Krasava (sop). An intensely nationalistic work, written for the inauguration of the Prague National Theatre, its ending with Libuše's prophecy of the history of the Czech nation has ensured that it is always the work performed on special national occasions. Its nationalism is the reason why it is only very seldom performed outside the Czech lands, despite its magnificent music.
Plot: Legendary Bohemia. The Czech ruler Princess Libuše mediates in a dispute over patrimony between the brothers Chrudoš and Šťáhlav. When Chrudoš denigrates her integrity and suitability to rule, Libuše chooses the wise and strong peasant Přemysl as her husband and abdicates her power to him. He becomes the founder of the Přemyslide dynasty. [R]

Licht (*Light*)
Operatic cycle by Stockhausen. A vast project intended to comprise seven works (one representing each day of the week), four have so far been produced: *Donnerstag* (Milan, 15 Mar 1981) [R], *Samstag* (Milan, 25 May 1984) [R], *Montag* (Milan, 7 May 1988) and *Dienstag* (Lisbon, 10 May 1992).

Lidholm, Ingvar (b 1921)
Swedish composer. He has written one opera, *A Dream Play* (*Ett Drömspel*, Stockholm, 12 Sept 1992; libr composer, after August Strindberg) [R].

Liebe der Danae, Die (*The Love of Danae*)
Opera in three acts by Strauss (Op 83). 1st perf Salzburg, 14 Aug 1952 (composed 1940); libr by Josef Gregor. Principal roles: Danae (sop), Midas (ten),

· Librettists ·

Sadly, few major writers have turned their hands to the fashioning of opera libretti, perhaps because the librettist is always overshadowed by the composer, however good the libretto might be. There have, of course, been some important exceptions: Maurice Maeterlinck wrote the libretto for Dukas's *Ariane et Barbe-Bleue*, Arnold Bennett that for Goossen's *Judith*, E.M. Forster that for Britten's *Billy Budd*, W.H. Auden those for Henze's *Elegie für Junge Liebende* and *The Bassarids*, Colette that for Ravel's *L'Enfant et les Sortilèges*, J.B. Priestley that for Bliss's *The Olympians*, and in earlier times both Voltaire and Carlo Goldoni wrote operatic libretti. By and large, however, the purveyors of libretti (particularly in 19th-century Italy and France) were all too often minor playwrights – such as Eugène Scribe – or journalists and plain literary hacks such as Andrea Leone Tottola, accustomed to churning out words at a moment's notice. A few, such as Felice Romani, were of a considerably higher calibre, but they were exceptional. The overall literary quality of operatic libretti is thus poor; few composers enjoyed the good fortune of Verdi, Mozart, Strauss and Sullivan of collaborating regularly with artists of the stature of Boito, da Ponte, Hofmannsthal and Gilbert.

Unusual or surprising operatic librettists have included Catherine the Great of Russia (three operas by Pashkevich), Frederick the Great of Prussia (four operas by Graun), the director Franco Zeffirelli (Barber's *Antony and Cleopatra*), the poet Ted Hughes (Crosse's *The Story of Vasco*), Hans Christian Andersen (four Danish operas), the film director Ingmar Bergman (Börtz's *The Bacchae*), the comedian Michael Flanders (Hopkins's *Three's Company*), the painter Oskar Kokoschka (Hindemith's *Mörder, Hoffnung der Frauen* and Křenek's *Orpheus und Eurydike*), Charles Dickens (Hullah's *The Village Coquettes*), the conductor Clemens Krauss (Strauss's *Capriccio*) and the singers David Franklin (Phyllis Tate's *The Lodger*) and Aïno Ackté (Merikanto's *Juha*).

Several composers (particularly Berlioz, Janáček, Leoncavallo, Lortzing, Moussorgsky, Pizzetti, Menotti, Tippett and Wagner) usually or always preferred to write their own libretti, and some (Blacher, Boito, Egk and Menotti) have provided libretti for other composers.

Below are listed the 57 librettists with entries in this dictionary. Their nationalities are given in brackets afterwards.

Adami, Giuseppe (It)
Anelli, Angelo (It)
Auden, W.H. (Br)
Barbier, Jules (Fr)
Bertati, Giovanni (It)
Boito, Arrigo (It)
Bouilly, Jean Nicolas (Fr)
Brecht, Bertolt (Ger)
Cain, Henri (Fr)
Calzabigi, Ranieri de' (It)
Cammarano, Salvatore (It)
Carré, Michel (Fr)
Claudel, Paul (Fr)
Cocteau, Jean (Fr)
Coltellini, Marco (It)
Crozier, Eric (Br)
Favart, Charles Simon (Fr)
Ferretti, Jacopo (It)
Fontana, Ferdinando (It)
Foppa, Giuseppe Maria (It)
Forzano, Giovacchino (It)
Gallet, Louis (Fr)
Gay, John (Br)
Genée, Richard (Ger)
Ghislanzoni, Antonio (It)
Gilbert, W.S. (Br)
Guillard, Nicolas François (Fr)
Halévy, Ludovic (Fr)
Hofmannsthal, Hugo von (Aus)
Illica, Luigi (It)
Jouy, Victor Joseph Étienne de (Fr)
Krásnohorská, Eliška (Cz)
Marmontel, Jean-François (Fr)
Meilhac, Henri (Fr)
Mélesville, Anne-Honoré Joseph de (Fr)
Mendès, Catulle (Fr)
Merelli, Bartolomeo (It)
Metastasio, Pietro (It)
Neher, Caspar (Ger)
Piave, Francesco Maria (It)
Ponte, Lorenzo da (It)
Quinault, Philippe (Fr)
Rinuccini, Ottavio (It)
Romani, Felice (It)
Rospigliosi, Giulio (It)
Rossato, Arturo (It)
Rossi, Gaetano (It)
Sabina, Karel (Cz)
Saint-Georges, Jules-Henri Vernoy de (Fr)
Schikaneder, Emanuel (Aus)
Scribe, Eugène (Fr)
Tchaikovsky, Modest (Russ)
Tottola, Andrea Leone (It)
Vrlichký, Jaroslav (Cz)
Willner, Alfred Maria (Aus)
Zell, F. (Aus)
Zeno, Apostolo (It)

Jupiter (bar), Mercury (ten), Pollux (ten), Xanthe (mezzo). A semi-comic mixture of classical legends, it has never been one of Strauss's more popular works and is only infrequently performed.
Plot: Legendary Eos. Jupiter is in love with Danae, daughter of King Pollux, and assumes the form of Midas, who also loves her, in order to win her. Danae prefers Midas, so Jupiter deprives him of his divinity and his golden touch. Midas and Danae live an ordinary mortal existence, and when Jupiter again offers Danae wealth and position she again refuses. Jupiter is impressed by such loyalty and gives the couple his blessing. [R]

Liebermann, Rolf (b 1910)
Swiss composer and administrator. He has written five operas, all of which have met with a degree of success, in styles ranging from jazz to TWELVE-TONE. LEONORE 40/45 was followed by PENELOPE, *Die Schule der Frauen* (Louiseville, 3 Dec 1955; libr Elisabeth Montagu, after Molière's *L'École des Femmes*; revised version Salzburg, 17 Aug 1957; libr revised Heinrich Strobel), *La Forêt* (Geneva, 11 Apr 1987; libr H. Vidal, after Alexander Nikolayevich Ostrovsky) and *Medea* (Hamburg, 1995). He was administrator of the Hamburg Opera (1959–73) and of the Paris Opéra (1973–80), where he re-established the house's international position. His autobiography, *Actes et Entractes*, was published in 1976.

Liebestod (German for 'love-death')
The name always given to Isolde's final monologue ('Mild und leise') in Act III of Wagner's *Tristan und Isolde*. Wagner himself used the term to describe the love duet in Act II.

Liebesverbot, Das (*The Ban on Love*) or **Die Novize von Palermo** (*The Novice of Palermo*)
Opera in two acts by Wagner. 1st perf Magdeburg, 29 March 1836; libr by the composer, after William Shakespeare's *Measure for Measure*. Principal roles: Friedrich (bass), Isabella (sop), Luzio (ten), Brighella (bass), Mariana (sop), Dorella (sop), Claudio (ten). Wagner's second completed opera and his first to be staged, it bears little resemblance to his mature works and is only very rarely performed.
Plot: 16th-century Palermo. Friedrich, the hypocritical governor of Sicily, has issued a ban on love-making under penalty of death. Claudio is falsely condemned and his sister, the novice Isabella, intercedes for him. Friedrich agrees to reprieve Claudio in return for Isabella's favours. Isabella sends Friedrich's estranged wife Mariana to the rendezvous in disguise. Friedrich is humiliated and is forced to revoke his decree, whilst Isabella marries Claudio's friend Luzio.

Lied (German for 'song')
A term used in 19th-century German opera to describe a solo number in a simpler style than a formal aria.

Liederspiel (German for 'song play')
A German dramatic form, consisting of dialogue interspersed with songs, which developed from SINGSPIEL. Few important composers have used the form, an example of which is Mendelssohn's *Die Heimkehr aus der Fremde*.

Liège
see GRAND THÉÂTRE, LIÈGE

Lieto fine (Italian for 'happy end')
The term was first used in the mid-17th century by Cavalli's librettist Giacinto Andrea Cicognini to describe a last-minute twist in the plot which ensured a happy ending to the opera. It became an established convention in 18th-century OPERA SERIA, despite the fact that it almost invariably involved an arbitrary and sometimes ridiculous divine intervention which nearly always altered the whole nature of the myths on which the operas were based. Famous operatic examples of Greek myths provided with happy endings include Gluck's *Orfeo ed Euridice* and *Écho et Narcisse* and Mozart's *Idomeneo*.

Life for the Tsar, A (*Zhizn'za Tsarya*)
Opera in four acts by Glinka. 1st perf St Petersburg, 9 Dec 1836; libr by Baron Gyorgy Fyodorovich Rosen and others. Principal roles: Susanin (bass), Sobinin (ten), Antonida (sop), Vanya (mezzo). Glinka's first opera, it may be said to mark the foundation of the Russian nationalist opera school and is a work of crucial historical importance. Notable for its fine orchestration and for its magnificent

choruses, it is still regularly performed in Russia and Eastern Europe, but unaccountably only seldom in the West. Originally entitled *Ivan Susanin*, the title was changed before the first performance; the original title was used in Russia during the Soviet period.
Plot: Russia and Poland, 1613. An invading Polish army is attempting to capture the recently-elected Tsar, who is a student at a monastery. The patriotic Russian peasant Ivan Susanin accepts a Polish bribe to lead them to their quarry but, in reality, he leads them astray in the forest whilst his son-in-law Sobinin, married to Antonida, takes a group of men to warn the Tsar. When the Poles discover what Ivan has done they kill him, but the Tsar is safe. [R]

Life With an Idiot (*Zhizn s Idiotom*)
Opera in two acts by Schnittke. 1st perf Amsterdam, 13 April 1992; libr by Victor Erofeyev, after his own novella. Principal roles: I (bar), Wife (sop), Vova (ten), Marcel Proust (ten), Guard (bass). Schnittke's first opera, dealing with themes that were taboo under the old Soviet system, it has proved one of the most controversial operas of recent years.
Plot: Moscow, 1980. As a punishment, a husband and wife are forced to accept an idiot into their lives. They choose Vova (Lenin's nickname), who undermines and destroys their lives. As a result of his depraved sexual practices and his murderous proclivities Vova eventually drives the pair to insanity and death. [R]

Ligendza, Catarina (b Katarina Beyron) (b 1937)
Swedish soprano, particularly associated with Wagnerian roles, especially Brünnhilde. She had a beautiful and even-toned voice with a gleaming upper register, and had a fine stage presence. Her father **Einar Beyron** (1901–79) was a successful heroic tenor, especially noted for his Tristan.

Ligeti, György (b 1923)
Hungarian composer. His one opera, the controversial black comedy LE GRAND MACABRE, has met with considerable success and has been widely performed.

Lighthouse, The
Opera in prologue and one act by Maxwell Davies. 1st perf Edinburgh, 2 Sept 1980; libr by the composer. Principal roles: Sandy (ten), Blazes (bar), Arthur (bar). Arguably Maxwell Davies's finest opera, it has been widely performed and is a powerful and claustrophobic work based on a true story of the disappearance of three lighthouse keepers.
Plot: Flannan Isle (Hebrides), Dec 1900. The characters of the three lighthouse keepers Arthur, Blazes and Sandy are explored, along with their interrelationships. Tension between them mounts until they (along with the audience) are blinded by mysterious lights. The ending is deliberately ambiguous regarding their fate: either they were mad, or they were ghosts, or they were destroyed by a sea beast. [R]

Lily of Killarney, The
Opera in three acts by Benedict. 1st perf London, 10 Feb 1862; libr by John Oxenford and Dion Boucicault, after the latter's *Colleen Bawn or The Brides of Garryowen*. Principal roles: Hardress (ten), Eily (sop), Danny Man (bar), Myles (ten), Mrs Cregan (mezzo). Benedict's most successful work, it was enormously popular in the second half of the 19th century but is nowadays almost never performed.
Plot: 19th-century Ireland. Hardress is urged by his mother Mrs Cregan to wed an heiress, but he is already secretly married to the peasant Eily O'Connor. Eily refuses to return her marriage certificate to Hardress. The family retainer Danny throws Eily into a lake when she continues to refuse. The peasant Myles, mistaking Danny for an otter (*sic*), shoots him and rescues Eily. Hardress is accused of the supposed murder of Eily, but the dying Danny confesses, and Myles admits to the shooting of Danny. Eily and Hardress are reunited.

Lima
see FUNDACIÓN PARA ARTE LIRICA

Lima, Luis (b 1948)
Argentinian tenor, particularly associated with lyrical Verdi, Donizetti and Puccini roles. He possesses a warm voice with an exciting upper register and has a rather better stage presence than most Italianate tenors.

Lincoln Center for the Performing Arts
An arts complex in New York which houses, amongst other bodies, the New York City Opera, the Metropolitan Opera and the Julliard School of Music.

Lind, Jenny (b Johanna) (1820–87)
Swedish soprano, particularly associated with Italian and French COLORATURA roles, especially Lucia, Amina and Catherine in *L'Étoile du Nord*. Known as the 'Swedish Nightingale', she was one of the greatest and most popular singers of the 19th century, possessing a well-focused, limpid and agile voice of great purity. She had an affecting stage presence, particularly in roles requiring pathos. She created Amalia in *I Masnadieri* and a role in Berwald's *I Enter a Monastery*.

Linda di Chamounix
Opera in three acts by Donizetti. 1st perf Vienna, 19 May 1842; libr by Gaetano Rossi, after Adolphe Philippe d'Ennery and Gustave Lemoine's *La Grâce de Dieu*. Principal roles: Linda (sop), Carlo (ten), Antonio (bar), Pierotto (mezzo), Preffeto (bass), Marchese (bar), Maddalena (mezzo). Once described as '*Lucia di Lammermoor* with a happy ending', it is one of the finest examples of OPERA SEMISERIA. Enormously popular throughout the 19th century, it is still quite often performed.
Plot: Haute-Savoie and Paris, *c* 1760. To save their daughter Linda from the attentions of the Marchese de Boisfleury, Antonio and Maddalena send her to Paris. There she falls in love with Carlo, who she knows as a poor painter but who is in fact the Marchese's nephew. Although her honour is not compromised, Linda lives in an apartment owned by Carlo. Believing her to be Carlo's mistress, Antonio curses her. Hearing that Carlo is to marry someone else, Linda loses her reason. Returning home, her senses are restored when she discovers that Carlo has refused the marriage planned by his family. The two are united. [R]

Lindholm, Berit (b Jonsson) (b 1934)
Swedish soprano, particularly associated with Wagner and Strauss roles, especially Brünnhilde. Possessing a vibrant and incisive voice and a good stage presence, she was one of the leading Wagnerian sopranos of the 1970s. She created Divana in Goehr's *Behold the Sun* and Alpha in Börtz's *The Bacchae*.

Lindorf, Councillor
Bass role in Offenbach's *Les Contes d'Hoffmann*. Hoffmann's evil genius, he appears in the three tales in the guises of Coppélius, Dr Miracle and Dapertutto.

Lindoro
Tenor role in: **1** Rossini's *L'Italiana in Algieri*. He is in love with Isabella. **2** Haydn's *La Fedeltà Premiata*. He is Amaranta's brother. **3** Paisiello's *Nina*. He is Nina's beloved.

Linley, Thomas (1733–95)
British composer. He wrote many stage works, of which only *The Duenna* (London, 21 Nov 1775), a setting of his son-in-law Richard Brindsley Sheridan's play, is still in any way remembered. It was written in collaboration with his son **Thomas** (1756–78), who was also a composer. The latter's youthful death from drowning cut short a potentially brilliant career. His only opera was *The Cady* (London, 19 Feb 1778; libr Abraham Portal).

Linz Landestheater
The opera house (cap 756) in this Austrian city was designed by Clemens Holzmeister and opened in 1958. Musical directors have included Theodor Gaschbauer and Manfred Mayrhofer.

Lionel
1 Tenor role in Flotow's *Martha*. He loves Lady Harriet. **2** Baritone role in Tchaikovsky's *The Maid of Orleans*. He is a Burgundian allied to the English.

Lisa
Soprano role in: **1** Tchaikovsky's *The Queen of Spades*. She is Prince Yeletsky's fiancée. **2** Kálmán's *Gräfin Mariza*. She is Count Tassilo's sister. **3** Bellini's *La Sonnambula*. She is the innkeeper. **4** Lehár's *Das Land des Lächelns*. She marries Prince Sou-chong.

Lisbon
see TEATRO SÃO CARLOS, LISBON

Lisette
Soprano role in Puccini's *La Rondine*. She is Magda's maid.

Lisitsian, Pavel (b Pogos) (b 1911)
Armenian baritone, particularly associated with the Russian and Italian repertories. One of the finest baritones of the immediate post-war period, he possessed a glorious, bright-toned voice used with an outstanding technique. He created Napoleon in *War and Peace* and in 1960 became the first Soviet singer to appear at the Metropolitan Opera, New York.

Liszt, Franz (b Ferenc) (1811–86)
Hungarian composer, pianist and conductor. Although he wrote only one opera, the youthful DON SANCHE, he made a considerable contribution to opera, largely through his friendship with and championing of Wagner, whose father-in-làw he eventually became. He was musical director of the Weimar Opera (1848–59), where he conducted the first performances of *Lohengrin*, Cornelius's *Der Barbier von Bagdad*, Rubinstein's *The Siberian Huntsman* and Schubert's *Alfonso und Estrella*. He also produced many transcriptions of operatic melodies for the piano, mainly of the Italian and German repertories.

Lithuanian opera composers
These include Vitolis Baumilas (*b* 1928), Balis Dvarionas (1904–72), Benjaminas Gorbulskis (1925–86), Julius Juzeliūnas (*b* 1916), Jurgis Karnavičius (1884–1941), Abel Klenickis (*b* 1904), Vytautas Klova (*b* 1926), Vytautas Laurušas (*b* 1930), Mikas Petrauskas (1873–1937), whose *Birute* (Vilnius, 1906) was the first Lithuanian opera, Antanas Račiūnas (1905–84) and Stasas Šimkus (1887–1943).

Litolff, Henry Charles (1818–91)
British composer. Although best known as an orchestral composer, he also wrote a number of operas, none of which are remembered today. They include *La Mandragore* (Brussels, 29 Jan 1876; libr Jules Brésil, after Alexandre Dumas's *Joseph Balsamo*) and *Les Templiers* (Brussels, 25 Jan 1886; libr Jules Adenis, Paul Armand Silvestre and L. Bonnemère).

Little Slippers, The
see VAKULA THE BLACKSMITH

Little Sweep, The
Children's opera in one act by Britten (Op 45). 1st perf Aldeburgh, 14 June 1949; libr by Eric Crozier, forming the second half of his play *Let's Make an Opera*. Principal roles: Sammy (treble), Black Bob (bass), Clem (ten), Mrs Baggot (mezzo), Rowan (sop). A charming and educational introduction to opera for younger children, the audience itself takes part in four numbers. In the first half, preparations for the opera are discussed, and in the opera itself – set in 1810 – the story of a family's rescue of a little sweep's boy is enacted. [R]

Lituani, I (*The Lithuanians*)
Opera in prologue and three acts by Ponchielli. 1st perf Milan, 7 March 1874; libr by Antonio Ghislanzoni, after Adam Mickiewicz's *Konrad Wallenrod*. Principal roles: Walter (ten), Aldona (sop), Arnolda (sop), Arnoldo (bar), Vitoldo (bass), Albano (bass). Ponchielli's most ambitious opera, notable for its massive ensembles, it is nowadays virtually never performed.
Plot: Late-14th-century Marienburg. The Lithuanians are attempting to repel the invading Teutonic knights, but are betrayed by Vitoldo. Their leader Walter, with his retainer Albano, infiltrates the enemy camp, leaving his wife Aldona in the care of her brother Arnoldo. After ten years, Walter (disguised as Corrado) has led the Germans to many victories and is appointed Grand Master of the Teutonic Order. At a feast, two prisoners are revealed as Aldona and Arnoldo. Walter and Aldona are reunited after an insurrection in which the Germans are defeated. However, Walter is condemned to death for treason by the Vehmgericht. He takes poison and dies in Aldona's arms.

Litvinne, Félia (b Françoise Jeanne Schütz) (1860–1936)
Russian-born French soprano, particularly associated with Wagnerian roles and with Alceste. She possessed a brilliant, flexible and resonant voice and had a powerful stage presence. Her autobiography, *Ma Vie et Mon Art*, was published in 1933.

Liù
Soprano role in Puccini's *Turandot.* She is a slave girl attending Timur.

Lizzie Borden
Opera in three acts by Beeson. 1st perf New York, 25 March 1965; libr by Kenward Elmslie, after Richard Plant's scenario. Principal roles: Elizabeth, Andrew, Abigail and Margret Borden (mezzo, b-bar, sop and sop), Rev Harrington (ten), Capt MacFarlane (bar). Beeson's most successful opera, described as a 'family portrait', it is virtually unknown outside the United States. [R]

Lloyd, George (b 1913)
British composer. His three operas, written in a strongly melodic vein, are *Iernin* (Penzance, 6 Nov 1934; libr William Lloyd) [R], *The Serf* (London, 20 Oct 1938; libr Lloyd) and *John Socman* (Bristol, 15 May 1951; libr Lloyd) [R Exc].

Lloyd, Robert (b 1940)
British bass, particularly associated with Mozart and Wagner roles, the Italian repertory and with *Boris Godunov.* Arguably the finest British bass of the post-war era, he possesses a voice of great beauty and richness and considerable power and has a good stage presence. He created Mikulin in Joubert's *Under Western Eyes.*

Lloyd Jones, David (b 1934)
British conductor and musicologist, particularly associated with the Russian repertory. He produced the critical edition, now in almost universal use, of the original version of *Boris Godunov*, and was musical director of Opera North (1977–89). He conducted the first performances of Hamilton's *The Royal Hunt of the Sun* and Wilfred Joseph's *Rebecca.*

Lo
Titles beginning with this form of the Italian definite article are listed under the letter of the first main word. For example, *Lo Speziale* is listed under S.

Locke, Matthew (c 1630–77)
British composer. His stage works include the masque *Cupid and Death* (London, 26 Mar 1653), written in collaboration with Christopher Gibbons, the opera *The Siege of Rhodes* (London, 1656), written with other composers, and *The Tempest* (London, 1674; libr Thomas Shadwell, after Shakespeare) [R].

Lockhart, James (b 1930)
British conductor with a wide-ranging repertory. He was musical director of the Welsh National Opera (1968–72), the Kassel Staatstheater (1972–81) – the first British conductor to be musical director of a German opera house – and the Koblenz Opera (1981–). He conducted the first performances of Walton's *The Bear* and Edlin's *The Fisherman.*

Lockit
Bass role in Pepusch's *The Beggar's Opera.* He is the jailer.

Lodoïska
Opera in three acts by Cherubini. 1st perf Paris, 18 July 1791; libr by Claude-François Fillette-Loraux, after Jean-Baptiste Louvet de Couvrai's *Les Amours du Chevalier de Faublas.* Principal roles: Lodoïska (sop), Dourlinski (bar), Floreski (ten), Titzikan (bar), Varbel (bar). An important early example of a rescue opera, it was both popular and influential in its time but is nowadays only very rarely performed.
Plot: Poland, 1600. Dourlinski wishes to marry Lodoïska and keeps her incarcerated in his border castle. She, however, loves Floreski, who (with the aid of his servant Varbel) is able to rescue her when the castle is attacked and destroyed by the Tartars led by Titzikan. [R]

Lodoletta
Opera in three acts by Mascagni. 1st perf Rome, 30 April 1917; libr by Giovacchino Forzano, after Ouida's *Bebè or The Two Little Wooden Shoes.* Principal roles: Lodoletta (sop), Flammen (ten), Gianetto (bar), Antonio (bass). Reasonably successful at its appearance, it is nowadays only rarely performed.
Plot: Mid-19th-century Holland and Paris. Antonio loves Lodoletta and gives her a pair of red shoes. After his death, Lodoletta falls in love with the artist Flammen, and goes to Paris to seek him. Afraid to enter his house because she can hear a party in progress, she waits outside

and freezes to death in the snow, where Flammen finds her. [R]

Lodovico
Bass role in Verdi's *Otello*. He is the Venetian envoy.

Loewe, Carl Gottfried (1796–1869)
German composer. Although best known as a song composer, he also wrote a number of operas, none of which are remembered today. They include *Malekadhel* (Stettin, 1832; libr C. Pichler, after Sir Walter Scott's *The Talisman*) and *Emmy* (1842; libr Melzer and Hauser, after Scott's *Kenilworth*).

Loge
Tenor role in Wagner's *Das Rheingold*. He is the god of fire.

Lohengrin
Opera in three acts by Wagner. 1st perf Weimar, 28 Aug 1850; libr by the composer, after an anonymous 13th-century German epic. Principal roles: Lohengrin (ten), Elsa von Brabant (sop), Ortrud (sop), Telramund (bar), Heinrich (bass), Herald (bar). Wagner's last 'traditional' opera, it is notable for its lyric beauty and for its fine characterization of Ortrud. It is probably Wagner's most frequently performed opera.
Plot: Early-10th-century Antwerp. King Henry (Heinrich) the Fowler of Saxony arrives to find a dispute in progress concerning the succession to the Dukedom of Brabant. Friedrich of Telramund claims the title, accusing Elsa of having murdered the true heir, her brother Gottfried. Heinrich decrees single combat between Telramund and Elsa's champion to decide the issue. The Herald calls for the champion but nobody comes forward, and Elsa describes her dream of a shining knight. Lohengrin, drawn by a swan, then appears and agrees to champion and marry her provided that she never asks his name or origin. Lohengrin defeats Telramund, who is outlawed as a traitor. Telramund conspires with his wife Ortrud to undermine Elsa's faith in Lohengrin. During the wedding ceremony, they publicly accuse Lohengrin of using sorcery. Later, the now troubled Elsa is unable to restrain herself and asks Lohengrin's identity. Telramund breaks in but is killed by Lohengrin, who tells everyone the answer to Elsa's question: he is Lohengrin, a knight of the Holy Grail, permitted to live amongst men only so long as his identity is unknown. He bids farewell to Elsa and his swan is revealed as the bewitched Gottfried, the rightful heir, now returned to human form. [R]

Lola
Mezzo role in Mascagni's *Cavalleria Rusticana*. She is Alfio's wife and Turiddù's mistress.

Lombard, Alain (b 1940)
French conductor, particularly associated with the French repertory. A sensitive and often exciting interpreter of his native repertory, he began his career as a child prodigy. He was musical director of the Opéra du Rhin (1974–80), the Paris Opéra (1981–3) and the Opéra-Comique, Paris (1983).

Lombardi alla Prima Crociata, I
(*The Lombards at the First Crusade*)
Opera in four acts by Verdi. 1st perf Milan, 11 Feb 1843; libr by Temistocle Solera, after Tomasso Grossi's narrative poem. Revised version *Jérusalem*, 1st perf Paris, 26 Nov 1847; libr revised by Alphonse Reyer and Gustave Vaëz. Principal roles (with *I Lombardi* first): Giselda/Hélène (sop), Pagano/Roger (bass/bar), Oronte/Gaston (ten), Arvino/Comte de Toulouse (ten/bass). Verdi's fourth opera, it is a typical example of his vigorous early style and has been regularly performed in recent years. The original version is nearly always preferred.
Plot: Milan and Palestine, 1096–97. Pagano returns from an exile imposed for an attempt to kill his brother Arvino. He bungles a second attempt at the crime, accidentally killing his father. Exiled again, he becomes a hermit living near Antioch. Arvino's daughter Giselda is captured by the Moslems and falls in love with Oronte, their leader's son. Arvino, leading the Crusaders, is disowned by Giselda when Oronte is killed by the Lombard forces. In sight of Jerusalem, the now saintly Pagano is mortally wounded and is granted forgiveness by Arvino and Giselda, now reconciled with her father. [R]

London
see CAMDEN FESTIVAL; ENGLISH NATIONAL OPERA; LONDON OPERA CENTRE; NATIONAL OPERA STUDIO; NEW SADLER'S WELLS OPERA; ROYAL OPERA HOUSE, COVENT GARDEN

London, George (b Burnstein) (1919–85)
Canadian-born American baritone, producer and administrator. Making his name as a member of the Bel Canto Trio with Mario Lanza and Frances Yeend, he became particularly associated with the German and Italian repertories and with Boris Godunov, in which role he became the first American singer ever to appear at the Bolshoi Opera. A superb singing-actor with a magnificent and powerful dark-toned voice, he was one of the finest operatic artists of the post-war era. He was responsible for a number of notable productions in the United States, and was administrator of the Opera Society of Washington (1975–80), the Los Angeles Opera Association and the Kennedy Center, Washington (1968–71).

London Coliseum
see ENGLISH NATIONAL OPERA

London Opera Centre
Britain's principal school of advanced operatic study until 1977, when it was superceded by the NATIONAL OPERA STUDIO. Musical directors included James Robertson.

Loose, Emmy (1914–87)
Czech-born Austrian soprano, particularly associated with Mozart roles. She possessed an appealingly silvery voice used with a fine technique, and had an attractive stage presence.

López-Cobos, Jesús (b 1940)
Spanish conductor, particularly associated with the Italian repertory and with *Carmen*. A scholarly and sensitive interpreter of the BEL CANTO repertory, he was musical director of the Deutsche Oper, Berlin (1981–90).

Lorca, Federico García
see panel below

Lord Byron
Opera in three acts by Thomson. 1st perf New York, 20 April 1972; libr by Jack

· *Federico García Lorca* ·

The works of the Spanish playwright Federico García Lorca (1898–1936) have inspired some 20 operas, more than almost any other literary source in the post-war period. Below are listed, by play, those operas by composers with entries in this dictionary.

Amor de Don Perlimplín con Belisa en su Jardín		
Fortner	*In Seinem Garten Liebt Don Perlimplin Belisa*	1962
Maderna	*Don Perlimplin*	1962
Bodas de Sangre		
Castro	*Bodas de Sangre*	1956
Fortner	*Die Bluthochzeit*	1957
Szokolay	*Blood Wedding*	1964
Chaynes	*Noces de Sang*	1988
Le Fanu	*Blood Wedding*	1992
Yerma		
Villa-Lobos	*Yerma*	1956
La Zapatiera Prodigosa		
Castro	*La Zapatiera Prodigosa*	1949
Zimmermann	*Die Wundersame Schusterfrau*	1982

Larson. Principal roles: Byron (ten), Lady Byron (mezzo), Thomas Moore (bar), Augusta Leigh (sop), Countess Guiccioli (sop), John Hobhouse (bass), Lady Caroline Lamb (sop), Dean Ireland (bass). Originally commissioned by the Metropolitan Opera, New York, but never performed there, it is Thomson's last opera. Hardly ever performed, it is a fine work whose merits have never been fully appreciated. [R]

Loreley
Opera in three acts by Catalani. 1st perf (as *Elda*) Turin, 31 Jan 1880; libr by Carlo d'Ormeville. Revised version 1st perf Turin, 16 Feb 1890; libr revised by Angelo Zanardini. Principal roles: Loreley (sop), Walther (ten), Hermann (bar), Rudolfo (bass), Anna (sop). Catalani's only opera apart from *La Wally* to have survived, it is still occasionally performed in Italy.
Plot: Rhineland, *c* 1300. The orphan girl Loreley is in love with Walther, who rejects her in favour of Anna, who is also loved by Walther's friend Hermann. Loreley promises herself to Alberich, King of the Rhine, if he will transform her into an irresistible enchantress. At the wedding of Walther and Anna, Loreley appears in her new guise and Walther falls in love with her, abandoning Anna. However, Loreley now belongs to the river, into which Walther throws himself.

Loreley, Die
Opera in four acts by Bruch (Op 16). 1st perf Mannheim, 14 April 1863; libr by Emmanuel Geibel. Principal roles: Lenore (sop), Otto (ten), Bertha (sop), Hubert (bar), Reinald (bass). Telling of the water siren of Central European legend, it is Bruch's finest opera but is nowadays virtually never performed.

Lorengar, Pilar (b Lorenza García) (b 1928)
Spanish soprano, particularly associated with Mozart and lyrical Italian roles. She had a beautiful silvery voice, used with fine musicianship, and had a warmly sympathetic stage presence. Earlier in her career she was also a successful exponent of ZARZUELA.

Lorenz, Max (1901–75)
German tenor, particularly associated with Wagnerian roles and with the title-role of Verdi's *Otello*. Possibly the finest HELDENTENOR of the inter-war period, he created Joseph K in Einem's *Der Prozess*, the Podestà in Liebermann's *Penelope* and a role in Wagner-Régeny's *Das Bergwerk zu Falun*.

Lorenzo
1 Bass role in Bellini's *I Capuleti e i Montecchi*. He is the Capulet doctor. **2** Tenor role in Auber's *Fra Diavolo*. He is a soldier in love with Zerlina. **3** Tenor COMPRIMARIO role in Auber's *La Muette de Portici*.

Loris
Tenor role in Giordano's *Fedora*. He is Count Loris Ipanov, a Russian nihilist.

Lortzing, Albert (1801–51)
German composer. He wrote 16 operas, notable for their sparkling melodies, which developed SINGSPIEL into a more sophisticated form. Many of his operas (for all of which he wrote his own libretti) are still popular in Germany, especially the comedies, but are unaccountably hardly ever performed elsewhere. His first opera *Ali Pascha von Janina* (Münster, 1 Feb 1828, composed 1824) was followed by *Der Pole und sein Kind* (Osnabrück, 11 Oct 1832), *Andreas Hofer* (Mainz, 14 Apr 1887, composed 1832; libr after K. Immermann), the comedy *Die Beiden Schützen* (Leipzig, 20 Feb 1837; libr after Joseph Patrat) and ZAR UND ZIMMERMANN, which established his reputation and which remains his most popular work. His subsequent operas are *Caramo* (Leipzig, 20 Sept 1839; libr after A. Vilain de Saint-Hilaire and Paul Duport's *Cosimo*), *Hans Sachs* (Leipzig, 23 June 1840; libr composer, Philipp J. Düringer and Philipp Reger, after Johann Ludwig Deinhardtstein), *Casanova* (Leipzig, 31 Dec 1841; libr after A. Lebrun), the highly successful DER WILDSCHÜTZ, UNDINE, the still-popular DER WAFFENSCHMIED, *Zum Grossadmiral* (Leipzig, 13 Dec 1847; libr after A.W. Iffland's *Heinrich des Fünften Jugenjahre*), the pro-revolutionary *Regina* (Berlin, 21 Mar 1899, composed 1848), which lost him his job, *Rolands Knappen*

(Leipzig, 25 May 1899; libr after Johann Karl August Musäus) and the comedy **DIE OPERNPROBE**. In addition, the early opera *Die Schatzkammer des Ynkas* (1836; libr Robert Blum) is lost and *Szenen aus Mozarts Leben* (1832) is a pastiche.

Los Angeles Music Center Opera
Many opera companies have been formed in Los Angeles, but none lasted for more than a few years. The present company was formed in 1986 and gives an annual season from September to March. Performances are given at the Dorothy Chandler Pavilion (cap 3,098), which opened in 1965.

Lotario
Opera in three acts by Händel. 1st perf London, 2 Dec 1729; libr after Antonio Salvi's *Adelaide*. Principal roles: Lotario (c-ten), Adelaida (sop), Berengario (ten), Idelberto (mezzo), Clodomiro (bass), Matilda (mezzo). Telling of supposed events following the murder of King Lothair II in 950, it has never been one of Händel's more successful operas and is only very rarely performed.
Plot: Mid-10th-century Pavia. Duke Berengario of Spoleto has usurped the throne and wishes to force the murdered king's widow Adelaida to marry his son Idelberto. Despite pressure from Berengario's wife Matilda and from the general Clodomiro, Adelaida refuses any connection with Berengario's family. An army under the German King Lotario rescues Adelaida, who marries Lotario.

Lott, Felicity (b 1947)
British soprano, particularly associated with Mozart and lyrical Strauss roles and with the French repertory. Her beautiful, creamy (although literally bottomless) voice is used with outstanding musicianship and intelligence. She has fine diction and is a singing-actress of considerable accomplishment.

Lotti, Antonio (c 1667–1740)
Italian composer. Beginning with *Il Trionfo dell'Innocenza* (Venice, 1693; libr R. Cialli), he wrote 28 operas, many of them much admired in their day. They include *Isacio Tiranno* (Venice, 24 Nov 1710; libr Francesco Briani), *Alessandro Severo* (Venice, 26 Dec 1716; libr Apostolo Zeno), *Ascanio* (Dresden, Feb 1718; libr Antonio Maria Luchini) and *Teofane* (Dresden, 13 Sept 1719; libr Stefano Benedetto Pallavicino). He was also a noted teacher, whose pupils included Galuppi, Gasparini and Marcello.

Loughran, James (b 1931)
British conductor. Best known as a symphonic conductor, his recent operatic appearances have been rare. He conducted the first performances of Williamson's *Our Man in Havana*, Thomas Wilson's *The Charcoal Burner* and Musgrave's *The Abbot of Drimock*.

Louise
Opera in four acts by Charpentier. 1st perf Paris, 2 Feb 1900; libr by the composer. Principal roles: Louise (sop), Julien (ten), Father (bar), Mother (mezzo). Charpentier's only work to have survived, it is a **VERISMO** piece with socialist overtones. Sensationally successful at its appearance, it clocked up over 1,000 performances in Paris alone during the composer's lifetime. Charpentier's follow-up to the story, **JULIEN**, was a complete failure.
Plot: Montmartre (Paris), *c* 1900. Not permitted by her parents to marry the painter Julien, the working-class girl Louise leaves home and goes to live with him. When her mother informs her that her father is seriously ill and wishes to see her, Louise agrees to go home on the condition that she will be free to return to Julien. However, when her father has recovered, her parents will not allow her to leave. Eventually, a violent quarrel erupts and Louise is expelled from the house, leaving her father to curse Paris, which has stolen so much from him. [R]

Love of Three Oranges, The
(*Lyubov k Tryom Apelsinam*)
Comic opera in four acts by Prokofiev (Op 33). 1st perf Chicago, 30 Dec 1921; libr by the composer, after Carlo Gozzi's *L'Amore delle Tre Melarance*. Principal roles: Prince (ten), Truffaldino (ten), Clarissa (mezzo), King of Clubs (bass), Leander (bar), Fata Morgana (sop), Ninetta (sop), Pantaloon (bar), Chelio (bass), Smeraldina (mezzo), Cook (bass). Partly

constructed as an opera within an opera, it is a delightful satirical comedy based on the COMMEDIA DELL'ARTE tradition, and is the most frequently performed of Prokofiev's operas in the West. The orchestral suite arranged by the composer has given the music wider currency.
Plot: The King of Clubs fears that his ailing son the Prince will die, and is told that only laughter can cure him. Various amusing diversions are provided by Truffaldino, but all are in vain until the witch Fata Morgana accidentally succeeds by falling flat on her back and showing her knickers. She prophesies that the Prince will fall in love with three oranges, and he leaves in search of them. In the desert, he discovers three enormous oranges, all of which contain a princess, and cuts them open. Two of the princesses die of thirst, but the third, Ninetta, survives and eventually goes home with the Prince. [R]

Lualdi, Adriano (1885–1971)
Italian composer and conductor. His operas, written in neo-classical style and for all of which he wrote his own libretti, include *Le Furie di Arlecchino* (Milan, 7 May 1915), the MARIONETTE OPERA *Guerrin Meschino* (Rome, 1920), *La Figlia del Rè* (Turin, 18 Mar 1922), *Il Diavolo del Campanile* (Milan, 22 Apr 1925; libr after Edgar Allan Poe's *The Devil in the Belfry*), *La Grançeola* (Venice, 10 Sept 1932; libr after Riccardo Bacchelli) and *La Luna dei Caraibi* (Rome, 29 Jan 1953; libr after Eugene O'Neill's *The Moon of the Caribbees*).

Lübeck Opera
The opera house (cap 1,012) in this German city in Schleswig-Holstein opened in 1908. Musical directors have included Hermann Abendroth, Wilhelm Furtwängler, Berthold Lehmann, Christoph von Dohnányi, Gerd Albrecht, Bernhard Klee and Martin Fischer-Dieskau.

Luca, Giuseppe de (1876–1950)
Italian baritone, particularly associated with the Italian repertory. One of the greatest baritones of the 20th century, possessing a beautiful voice used with a matchless technique, he enjoyed an unusually long career, singing into his 70s. He created Michonnet in *Adriana Lecouvreur*, Sharpless in *Madama Butterfly*, the title-role in *Gianni Schicchi*, Paquiro in Granados's *Goyescas* and Gleby in Giordano's *Siberia*.

Luce langue, La
Soprano aria for Lady Macbeth in Act II of Verdi's *Macbeth*, in which she welcomes night's darkness as a cover for Duncan's murder. It was newly composed for the 1865 revised version.

Lucerne
see LUZERN STADTTHEATER

Luchetti, Veriano (b 1939)
Italian tenor, particularly associated with the Italian repertory. An accomplished and sometimes underrated singer, he has a fine voice used with a good technique but is a little dull on stage. His wife **Mietta Sighele** is a soprano.

Lucia
1 Mezzo role in Mascagni's *Cavalleria Rusticana*. She is Turiddù's mother.
2 Soprano role in Donizetti's *Lucia di Lammermoor*. Enrico's sister, she loves Edgardo. **3** Mezzo role in Rossini's *La Gazza Ladra*. She is Fabrizio's wife.
4 Soprano role in Britten's *The Rape of Lucretia*. She is Lucretia's attendant.

Lucia, Fernando de (1860–1925)
Italian tenor, particularly associated with Italian BEL CANTO roles and with Verdi. Possessor of a beautiful voice used with a flawless technique, he was also an accomplished singing-actor. He created, for Mascagni, the title-roles in *L'Amico Fritz* and *Silvano*, Osaka in *Iris* and Giorgio in *I Rantzau*. He was also a distinguished teacher, whose pupils included Georges Thill.

Lucia di Lammermoor
Opera in three acts by Donizetti. 1st perf Naples, 26 Sept 1835; libr by Salvatore Cammarano, after Sir Walter Scott's *The Bride of Lammermoor*. Principal roles: Lucia (sop), Edgardo (ten), Enrico (bar), Raimondo (bass), Arturo (ten), Alisa (mezzo). The quintessential romantic opera, it was sensationally successful at its appearance and remains Donizetti's most popular serious work. Whilst the famous

Mad Scene provides a spectacular vehicle for a singing-actress, the work's greatest musico-dramatic strengths are to be found in the tenor's final scene and in the great sextet, the epitome of operatic ensemble writing.
Plot: Late-17th-century Scotland. Lucia loves Edgardo, the dispossessed master of Ravenswood and an enemy of her family. The couple exchange rings and vows before Edgardo leaves on a mission. Lucia's brother Enrico is outraged to learn of this. He wishes her to make a politically advantageous marriage to Lord Arthur Bucklaw (Arturo), and shows her a forged letter supposedly written by Edgardo which seems to prove his infidelity. In the light of this, and urged on by the chaplain Raimondo, she unwillingly accepts the marriage. Edgardo returns, breaks in on the wedding celebrations, curses Lucia and flings her ring at her. Enrico goes to Edgardo's hide-out at the Wolf's Crag and challenges him to a duel. The strain placed upon her proves too great for Lucia, who loses her reason, murders Arthur and hallucinates about a marriage with Edgardo. Arriving for the duel, Edgardo is told by Raimondo that Lucia is dead. In anguish, Edgardo stabs himself. [R]

Lucio Silla
Opera in three acts by Mozart (K 135). 1st perf Milan, 26 Dec 1772; libr by Giovanni de Gamerra and Pietro Metastasio. Principal roles: Lucio (ten), Cecilio (sop), Giunia (sop), Cinna (sop), Celia (sop), Aufidio (ten). Usually regarded as the finest of Mozart's youthful operas, it is an astonishingly assured work with an impressive overture. Telling of an incident in the life of the Roman dictator Lucius Cornelius Sulla (138–78 BC), it is still quite often performed.
Plot: Rome, 79 BC. Lucio Silla wishes to marry Giunia and has her exiled lover Cecilio condemned to death for plotting against him. Giunia retaliates by censuring him before the Senate, an act which moves Lucio to mercy. Cecilio and Giunia are reunited. [R]

Lucky Peter's Journey
Opera in three acts by Williamson. 1st perf London, 18 Dec 1969; libr by Edmund Tracey, after August Strindberg's *Lycko-Pers Resa*. Principal roles: Peter (bar), Lisa (mezzo). It tells of a quest hero who finds both himself and true love after rejecting the false attractions of worldly success. It is virtually never performed.

Lucrezia
Opera in one act by Respighi. 1st perf Milan, 24 Feb 1937; libr by Claudio Guastalla, partly after Livy and André Obey's *Le Viol de Lucrèce*. Principal roles: Lucrezia (sop), Tarquinio (bar), Voice (mezzo), Collatino (ten). Respighi's last opera, it was not quite finished at his death and was completed by his wife Elsa. A fine work, it is written in the style of a 17th-century opera, but is based on contemporary melodic style and is richly orchestrated. For plot see *The Rape of Lucretia*. [R]

Lucrezia Borgia
Opera in prologue and two acts by Donizetti. 1st perf Milan, 26 Dec 1833; libr by Felice Romani, after Victor Hugo's *Lucrèce Borgia*. Principal roles: Lucrezia (sop), Gennaro (ten), Alfonso (bass), Maffio Orsini (mezzo). Telling a largely fictitious story about Pope Alexander VI's daughter Lucrezia Borgia (1480–1519), it was the most frequently performed of all Donizetti's operas throughout the 19th century. Arguably Donizetti's finest tragic opera, it marked the appearance in Italian opera of full-blooded romantic melodrama and had a considerable influence on other composers.
Plot: Early-16th-century Venice and Ferrara. During the Venetian carnival, Gennaro is drawn to an unknown woman, until Maffio Orsini and his other friends reveal her as the infamous Lucrezia Borgia. Lucrezia's husband, Duke Alfonso d'Este of Ferrara, is jealous of his wife's interest in Gennaro, and Gennaro – to prove that he has no feelings for Lucrezia – defaces the Borgia crest in front of his friends. Lucrezia demands of Alfonso the death penalty for the offender, but is horrified when she discovers that the offender is Gennaro who, unbeknownst to all but herself, is her son. Alfonso makes her give Gennaro the poisoned Borgia wine, but after his departure she persuades Gennaro to drink an antidote. Gennaro joins Maffio and his friends at a banquet, where

Lucrezia – in revenge for her treatment in Venice – has poisoned the wine. Appalled to discover Gennaro amongst the guests, Lucrezia reveals that she is his mother and begs him to take the antidote again. Shocked to learn his true parentage, however, Gennaro prefers to die with his friends. [R]

Ludmila
1 Mezzo role in Smetana's *The Bartered Bride*. She is Krušina's wife. **2** Soprano role in Glinka's *Ruslan and Ludmila*. She is Svyetozar's daughter.

Ludwig, Christa (b 1928)
German mezzo, particularly associated with Mozart, Strauss and Wagner roles. One of the outstanding mezzos of the post-war era, she had a rich voice used with fine musicianship and great intelligence. Her range and technique were such that she was also able to sing a number of soprano roles, notably Leonore in *Fidelio*. A fine singing-actress, she created Miranda in Martin's *Der Sturm*, Claire in Einem's *Der Besuch der Alten Dame* and a role in Orff's *De Temporum Fine Comoedia*. Married for a time to the baritone WALTER BERRY.

Ludwig, Leopold (1908–79)
Austrian conductor, particularly associated with the German repertory. He was musical director of the Hamburg State Opera (1951–71) and conducted the first performances of Křenek's *Pallas Athene Weint* and Henze's *Der Prinz von Homberg*.

Luigi
Tenor role in Puccini's *Il Tabarro*. He is a bargehand in love with Giorgetta.

Luisa Fernanda
ZARZUELA in three acts by Torroba. 1st perf Madrid, 26 March 1932; libr by Federico Romero and Guillermo Fernández Shaw. Principal roles: Luisa (mezzo), Javier (ten), Vidal (bar), Carolina (sop). Set during the time of political upheaval during the reign of Isabella II, it is perhaps the most successful of all 20th-century zarzuelas.
Plot: Mid-19th-century Spain. Luisa loves the womanizing young royalist colonel Javier, and is also being wooed by the wealthy landowner Vidal, who joins the republicans so as to oppose Javier. When Javier turns his attention to the duchess Carolina, Luisa accepts Vidal. Javier is captured by the republicans, but Luisa interceeds for him. News arrives of the collapse of the royalist cause, and a chastened Javier offers Luisa his love. She accepts him and Vidal sadly gives his consent. [R]

Luisa Miller
Opera in three acts by Verdi. 1st perf Naples, 8 Dec 1849; libr by Salvatore Cammarano, after Friedrich von Schiller's *Kabale und Liebe*. Principal roles: Luisa (sop), Rodolfo (ten), Miller (bar), Count Walther (bass), Wurm (bass), Federica (mezzo). The work which marks the transition between Verdi's early and middle periods (with Act III entirely inhabiting the second), it has won a permanent place in the repertory in recent years.
Plot: Early-17th-century Tyrol. Luisa, daughter of the old soldier Miller, loves Rodolfo, who she believes to be a commoner but who is in fact the son of Count Walther. Walther wishes Rodolfo to marry Federica, Duchess of Ostheim, and plots with his evil steward Wurm to separate him from Luisa. Walther has Miller arrested and, to obtain his freedom, Luisa is forced by Wurm to write a letter saying that she never loved Rodolfo but actually loves Wurm. Luisa and Miller plan to go into exile together, but Rodolfo arrives and he and Luisa drink wine that he has poisoned. Realizing that she is dying, Luisa tells him the truth, and the dying Rodolfo kills Wurm. [R]

Lully, Jean-Baptiste (b Giovanni Battista Lulli) (1632–87)
Italian-born French composer. Court composer to Louis XIV, Lully may be regarded – through his collaborations with Molière and PHILIPPE QUINAULT – as the effective founder of French opera. With Molière, he produced a number of comedy-ballets, of which the most successful was LE BOURGEOIS GENTILHOMME. His first true opera was *Les Fêtes de l'Amour et de Bacchus* (Paris, 15 Nov 1672), which was followed by *Cadmus et Hermione* (Paris, 27 Apr 1673), the first of his TRAGÉDIE-LYRIQUES written

with Quinault. These are marked by a clarity of declamation and the first appearance in opera of the modern orchestra with its solid string foundation. To modern ears and eyes, these works can seem extremely stiff and formal, but nevertheless they often exhibit considerable dramatic power. His other operas are ALCESTE, perhaps his finest stage work, *Thésée* (St Germain, 12 Jan 1675) [R Exc], ATYS, *Isis* (Paris, 5 Jan 1677) [R Exc], *Psyché* (Paris, 19 Apr 1678; libr after Molière), *Bellérophon* (Paris, 31 Jan 1679), *Proserpine* (St Germain, 3 Feb 1680), *Persée* (Paris, 18 Apr 1682; libr after Pierre Corneille's *Andromède*), PHAËTON, AMADIS, *Roland* (Versailles, 18 Jan 1685; libr after Lodovico Ariosto's *Orlando Furioso*) ARMIDE ET RENAUD, *Acis et Galathée* (Anet, 6 Sept 1686; libr Jean-Galbert de Campistron) and the unfinished *Achille et Polyxène* (Paris, 7 Nov 1687; libr Campistron), which was completed by his pupil Pascal Colasse. There has recently been a considerable revival of interest in Lully's stage works, and performances are becoming more frequent.

Lully appears as a character in Grétry's *Les Trois Âges de l'Opéra* and in Isouard's *Lully et Quinault*. Lully may be said to be the only composer whose profession caused his death: he hit his foot with the pole used to beat time and died of gangrene. His son **Louis** (1664–1734) was also a composer, who wrote a number of operas, some of them in collaboration with Marais.

Lulu

Opera in three acts by Berg. 1st perf (Acts I and II only) Zürich, 2 June 1937; 1st complete perf (edited by Friedrich Cerha) Paris, 24 Feb 1979; libr by the composer, after Frank Wedekind's *Erdgeist* and *Die Büchse der Pandora*. Principal roles: Lulu (sop), Alwa (ten), Dr Schön (bar), Schigolch (b-bar), Countess Geschwitz (mezzo), Painter (ten), Acrobat (bass), Schoolboy (mezzo), Marquis (ten), Animal Tamer (bar), Banker (bass), Prince (ten). One of the finest and most compelling of 20th-century operas, its title-role is one of the most musico-dramatically challenging in the repertory. The world had to wait for over 40 years after Berg's death to hear the opera complete because of his widow's refusal to release the material of Act III.

Plot: Late-19th-century Germany, Paris and London. The Animal Tamer introduces his menagerie, the star turn of which is the femme fatale Lulu, mistress of the newspaper editor Dr Schön. She destroys all her admirers and lovers, and finally kills Schön whom she has manipulated into marrying her. She escapes from prison with the aid of her lesbian lover Countess Geschwitz. She visits Paris and then settles in London, where she supports herself, Geschwitz, Schön's son Alwa and the old swindler Schigolch (who might have been her father) by prostitution. She and Geschwitz are killed by her last customer, Jack the Ripper. [R]

Luna, Conte di

Baritone role in Verdi's *Il Trovatore*. In reality Manrico's brother, he is in love with Leonora.

Luna y Carné, Pablo (1880–1942)

Spanish composer. He wrote many successful zarzuelas, of which the most enduring include *Los Molinos de Viento* (*The Windmills*, Seville, 2 Dec 1910; libr Luis Pascual Frutos) [R], *Los Cadetes de la Reina* (Madrid, 18 Jan 1913; libr J. Moyrón) [R], *El Asombro de Damasco* (Madrid, 20 Dec 1916; libr Antonio Paso and Joaquín Abati) [R], *El Niño Judío* (Madrid, 5 Feb 1918; libr Paso and García Álvarez) [R] and *La Pícara Molinera* (Saragossa, 28 Oct 1928; libr A. Torres del Alama, after A. Camín's *La Carmona*).

Lustigen Weiber von Windsor, Die

(*The Merry Wives of Windsor*)

Comic opera in three acts by Nicolaï. 1st perf Berlin, 9 March 1849; libr by Salomon Hermann Mosenthal, after William Shakespeare's play. Principal roles: Falstaff (bass), Frau and Herr Fluth (sop and bar), Anne Reich (sop), Fenton (ten), Frau and Herr Reich (mezzo and bass). Arguably the finest of all German comic operas, notable for its wealth of melody, it is Nicolaï's only work to have survived. An instant success, it remains enormously popular in German-speaking countries but quite unaccountably is only seldom performed elsewhere, although the sparkling overture is very well known.

Plot: 15th-century Windsor. Falstaff sends identical love letters to Frau Fluth and

Frau Reich, who determine to teach him a lesson. Herr Fluth wishes his daughter Anne to marry Slender and repels her admirer Fenton. Falstaff, arriving for his assignation with Frau Fluth, is dumped into the Thames in a laundry basket. The disguised Fluth visits Falstaff at the Garter Inn whilst Anne is serenaded in her garden by her admirers. Fluth institutes a search for his wife's supposed lover, and Falstaff is smuggled out, disguised as a deaf old woman. In Windsor Forest, Falstaff is discomfited by the merry wives disguised as fairies, but all ends happily without malice. [R]

Lustige Witwe, Die (*The Merry Widow*)
Operetta in three acts by Lehár. 1st perf Vienna, 30 Dec 1905; libr by Viktor Léon and Leo Stein, after Henri Meilhac's *L'Attaché de l'Ambassade*. Principal roles: Hanna Glawari (sop), Danilo (ten), Valencienne (sop), Camille (ten), Baron Mirko (bar), Cascada (ten), St Brioche (bar). The work which established Lehár's reputation, it was sensationally successful at its appearance, remaining ever since one of the most enduringly popular of all operettas.
Plot: Early-19th-century Paris. Hanna, widow of the banker Glawari, has been left a vast fortune. It is essential to the finances of Pontevedro that she marries a Pontevedrian rather than a foreigner. The Pontevedrian Ambassador Baron Mirko Zita – whose 'highly respectable' wife Valencienne is persued by Camille de Rossilon – orders his high-living attaché Count Danilo to serve his fatherland for a change and marry Hanna. The two had been in love in the past, but Danilo has vowed that he will never say 'I love you' to Hanna. It takes much intrigue and all Hanna's wiles to get him to give in so that all can end happily and Pontevedro be saved from bankruptcy. [R]

Lutyens, Elisabeth (1906–83)
British composer. Her operas, written in TWELVE-TONE style, include *The Pit* (London, 18 May 1947; libr W.R. Rodgers), *Infidelio* (London, 17 Apr 1973, composed 1954; libr composer), the unperformed *The Numbered* (1967; libr M. Volonakis, after Elias Canetti's *Die Befristeten*), *Time Off? Not a Ghost of a Chance* (London, 1 Mar 1972; libr composer) and *Isis and Osiris* (London, 26 Nov 1976; libr composer, after Plutarch). Her autobiography, *A Goldfish Bowl*, was published in 1972.

Luxon, Benjamin (b 1937)
British baritone, particularly associated with Mozart and Britten roles and with the title-role in Tchaikovsky's *Eugene Onegin*. An intelligent and warm-voiced singer and a fine singing-actor, he created the title-role in *Owen Wingrave*, a role in Williamson's *The Growing Castle*, Jean in Alwyn's *Miss Julie* and the Jester in Maxwell Davies's *Taverner*.

Luzern Stadttheater
The opera house in this town in Switzerland was designed by Luis Pfuffler von Wyer and opened on 17 Nov 1879. It burnt down in 1924, was rebuilt to the same design in 1926 and was enlarged (cap 564) in 1929. Musical directors have included Ernest Hans Baar, Ulrich Mayer, Roderick Brydon and Marcello Viotti.

Lyons
see OPÉRA DE LYON

Lyric
Strictly meaning a vocal performance accompanied by the lyre, the term has come to mean anything that is sung. Hence the frequent description of opera as lyric drama and of its stage as the lyric theatre.

Lysander
Tenor role in Britten's *A Midsummer Night's Dream*. He is one of the four lovers.

Lysenko, Mykola (1842–1912)
Ukrainian composer. He wrote a number of operas and operettas, many of them locally successful, but his aversion to having his works translated into Russian prevented them from becoming more widely known. His most successful operas include *Christmas Eve* (Kharkov, 27 Jan 1883, composed 1873; libr M. Starytsky, after Nikolai Gogol), *Natalka Poltavka* (Odessa, 12 Nov 1889; libr Starytsky, after I. Koltayrevsky) [R] and *Taras Bulba* (Kharkov, 4 Oct 1924, composed 1890; libr Starytsky, after Gogol) [R].

· Bulwer Lytton ·

The works of the British writer and statesman Edward Bulwer Lytton (later Baron Lytton) (1803–73) have inspired some 20 operas. Below are listed, by novel, those operas by composers with entries in this dictionary.

The Lady of Lyons		
Cowen	*Pauline*	1876
Millöcker	*Der Bettelstudent*	1882
The Last Days of Pompeii		
Pacini	*L'Ultimo Giorno di Pompei*	1825
Lachner	*Alidia*	1839
Petrella	*Jone*	1858
Leila		
Apolloni	*L'Ebreo*	1855
Bendl	*Lejla*	1868
Rienzi		
Wagner	*Rienzi*	1842

Lysiart
Baritone role in Weber's *Euryanthe*. The Count of Forest, he is the knight who wagers that he can prove Euryanthe unfaithful.

Lytton, Edward Bulwer
see panel above

Lytton, Sir Henry (1865–1936)
British baritone, particularly associated with Sullivan roles. Perhaps the most famous of all Savoyards, he played the comic leads with the D'Oyly Carte Opera Company for some 40 years. His singing voice was nothing special, but he amply compensated for this with his comic talents and his outstanding diction. He created roles in German's *Merrie England* and *A Princess of Kensington* and, for Sullivan, Simon Limal in *The Beauty Stone* and Sultan Mahmoud in *The Rose of Persia*. His autobiography, *The Secrets of a Savoyard*, was published in 1922.

M

Maag, Peter (b 1919)
Swiss conductor, particularly associated with Mozart operas. He has been responsible for the revival of a number of neglected 18th- and early-19th-century operas, and often also acts as producer. He was musical director of the Bonn Stadttheater (1955–9), the Teatro Regio, Parma (1972) and the Teatro Regio, Turin (1974–6).

Maazel, Lorin (b 1930)
American conductor, particularly associated with Wagner, Verdi and Puccini operas. One of the leading contemporary American conductors, who first appeared as a child prodigy, he is a technically brilliant but sometimes controversial interpreter, whose readings can be highly idiosyncratic. He was musical director of the Deutsche Oper, Berlin (1965–71) and the Vienna State Opera (1982–4) and in 1960 he became the first American conductor to appear at the Bayreuth Festival. He conducted the first performances of Dallapiccola's *Ulisse* and Berio's *Un Rè in Ascolto*. He is also an accomplished violinist.

Macbeth
Opera in four acts by Verdi. 1st perf Florence, 14 March 1847; libr by the composer and Francesco Maria Piave, after William Shakespeare's play. Revised version 1st perf Paris, 21 April 1865; libr revised by Count Andrea Maffei. Principal roles: Macbeth (bar), Lady Macbeth (sop), Banquo (bass), Macduff (ten), Malcolm (ten). Verdi's first Shakespearean opera, and much the greatest of his early works, he revised it at the height of his powers. Despite occasional unevenness, it is a dark and powerful setting which follows the play reasonably closely but makes Lady Macbeth even more the dominant partner. It suffered a long period of neglect but is nowadays firmly re-established in the repertory, the revised version nearly always being preferred.

Plot: Mid-11th-century Scotland. The generals Macbeth and Banquo are met by the witches who foretell that Macbeth will reign but that Banquo's issue will reign after him. Macbeth's ambitious wife persuades him to murder King Duncan during his visit to their castle. Macbeth gains the crown and has Banquo murdered. The pair's consciences give them no rest: the witches reiterate to Macbeth that Banquo's line will rule, and Lady Macbeth, walking in her sleep, is obsessed by the image of Duncan's blood and eventually dies. Rebels led by Macduff invade from England and Macbeth is defeated and killed by Macduff himself. Duncan's son Malcolm is proclaimed king. [R]

Macbeth
Opera in three acts by Bloch. 1st perf Paris, 30 Nov 1910; libr by Edmond Fleg, after William Shakespeare's play. Principal roles: Macbeth (bar), Lady Macbeth (sop), Banquo (ten), Macduff (bass), Three Witches (sop, mezzo and cont), Duncan (ten). Bloch's only completed opera, it is a powerful and imaginative setting, which concentrates heavily on Macbeth himself. The opera's almost total neglect is unjust and unaccountable.

Macchia, Una
Soprano aria (the Sleepwalking Scene) for Lady Macbeth in Act III of Verdi's *Macbeth*.

MacCunn, Hamish (1868–1916)
British composer and conductor. Influenced by Wagner, he was a leading advocate of a native Scottish musical school. Much the most successful of his operas was *Jeanie Deans* (Edinburgh, 15 Nov 1894; libr Joseph Bennett, after Sir Walter Scott's *The Heart of Midlothian*). Of his other works, only *Diarmid* (London, 23 Oct 1897; libr Duke of Argyl) met with any success.

Macduff
A Scottish nobleman, he appears as:
1 Tenor role in Verdi's *Macbeth*. **2** Bass role in Bloch's *Macbeth*.

MacFarren, Sir George (1813–87)
British composer. He wrote seven operas, all now long forgotten, including *The Devil's Opera* (London, 13 Aug 1838; libr composer's father), *An Adventure of Don Quixote* (London, 3 Feb 1846; libr composer, after Miguel Cervantes), *King Charles II* (London, 24 Oct 1849; libr M.D. Ryan, after J.H. Payne), *Robin Hood* (London, 2 Nov 1863; libr John Oxenford) and *Helvellyn* (London, 3 Nov 1864; libr Oxenford, after Salomon Hermann Mosenthal's *Der Sonnenwendhof*). He also completed Balfe's unfinished *Il Talismano*. His wife **Natalia** (*b* Clarina Andrae) (1827–1916) was a contralto who also made many fine opera translations for the music publisher Novello.

MacHeath
Baritone role in Pepusch's *The Beggar's Opera*. He is a highwayman loved by Lucy and Polly.

Mackerras, Sir Charles (b 1925)
Australian conductor, particularly associated with Händel, Gluck, Mozart, Verdi and Sullivan operas and, especially, with the Czech repertory: he is widely regarded as the greatest living interpreter of Janáček, and the immense current popularity of Janáček in Britain is due almost exclusively to his initial and tireless advocacy. His wide tastes, his exciting and dynamic style and his outstanding scholarship and musicianship have combined to make him one of the foremost contemporary opera conductors. He was musical director of the English National Opera (1970–77) and the Welsh National Opera (1987–92). He conducted the first performances of Britten's *Noye's Fludde*, Goehr's *Arden Must Die* and Berkeley's *Ruth*. He also arranged the popular ballets *Pineapple Poll* and *The Lady and the Fool* from the operatic music of Sullivan and early Verdi.

MacNeil, Cornell (b 1922)
American baritone, particularly associated with Verdi roles, especially Rigoletto. One of the finest Verdi baritones of the 1960s, he had a strong and rich voice but at times could seem a little uncommitted on stage. He created John Sorel in Menotti's *The Consul*. His son **Walter** (*b* 1949) is a tenor.

Maconchy, Dame Elizabeth (1907–94)
British composer. She wrote six operas: *The Sofa* (London, 13 Dec 1959; libr Ursula Vaughan Williams, after Claude Prosper Jolyot de Crébillon), *The Departure* (London, 16 Dec 1962; libr Anne Ridler), *The Birds* (Bishop's Stortford, 5 June 1968; libr composer, after Aristophanes), *The Three Strangers* (Bishop's Stortford, 5 June 1968; libr composer, after Thomas Hardy), *The Jesse Tree* (Dorchester, 7 Oct 1970; libr Ridler) and *The King of the Golden River* (Oxford, 29 Oct 1975; libr composer, after John Ruskin). Her daughter **Nicola le Fanu** (*b* 1947) is also a composer, whose operas include *Downpath* (London, 29 Sept 1977; libr composer) and *Blood Wedding* (London, 26 Oct 1992; libr Deborah Levy, after Federico García Lorca's *Bodas de Sangre*).

Macropolus Case, The (*Věc Makropulos*)
Opera in three acts by Janáček. 1st perf Brno, 18 Dec 1926; libr by the composer, after Karel Čapek's play. Principal roles: Emilia Marty (sop), Jaroslav Prus (bar), Albert Gregor (ten), Dr Kolenatý (bar), Vítek (ten), Kristina (sop), Jánek (ten), Hauk Šendorf (ten). One of Janáček's greatest operas, the central figure of the 300-year-old woman provides a magnificent challenge to a great singing-actress. Initially slow to make its way, it has been widely performed in recent years.
Plot: Prague, 1922. As a result of having been forced to test an elixir of life invented by her alchemist father, Elena Macropolus has lived in various guises for over 300 years. She is currently assuming the name of Emilia Marty and is a famous opera singer. Afraid that the strength of the elixir is fading, she goes to great lengths to procure the original formula which is amongst the papers which form part of an estate which has been the subject of a long-running law suit between the families of Albert Gregor and Jaroslav Prus. After giving herself to Prus, who declares her totally cold, she gains the formula but realizes that she is tired of life, incapable of emotion and wishes to die. Expiring, she gives the formula to the young singer Kristina, who loves Prus's son Jánek, who immediately burns it. [R]

Madama Butterfly
Opera in three (originally two) acts by Puccini. 1st perf Milan, 17 Feb 1904; libr by Giuseppe Giacosa and Luigi Illica, after David Belasco's play, itself based on John Luther Long's story. Revised version 1st perf Brescia, 28 May 1904. Principal roles: Cio-Cio-San (sop), Pinkerton (ten), Sharpless (bar), Suzuki (mezzo), Goro (ten), Bonze (bass), Yamadori (bar), Kate (mezzo). Although it was a fiasco at its first performance, it soon established itself as one of the best-loved of all operas.
Plot: Nagasaki, early 1900s. The American naval officer Lt B.F. Pinkerton has arranged through the marriage broker Goro to wed the 15-year-old Cio-Cio-San, known as Butterfly – an arrangement which he does not take seriously. Despite the warnings of her uncle the Bonze, she renounces both family and religion and marries Pinkerton, to whom she gives her heart and soul. He returns to America and, although three years pass with no word from him, she remains faithful to him, living with her devoted companion Suzuki and the child that she has borne to Pinkerton in his absence. She rejects the offers of Prince Yamadori and other suitors. The American Consul Sharpless breaks the news to her, as gently as he can, that Pinkerton is returning with an American wife. She refuses to listen, however, and undertakes an all-night vigil with Suzuki, eagerly waiting for his arrival. The next day, as Pinkerton arrives with his new wife Kate, Cio-Cio-San has to face reality. Giving her child an American flag to play with, she commits harakiri. [R]

Madame Pompadour
Operetta in three acts by Fall. 1st perf Berlin, 9 Sept 1922; libr by Robert Schanzer and E. Welisch. An immediate success, it has always been one of Fall's most popular works and is still regularly performed in German-speaking countries.

Madame Sans-Gêne (*Madam Free-and-Easy*)
Opera in three acts by Giordano. 1st perf New York, 25 Jan 1915; libr by Renato Simoni, after Émile Moreau and Victorien Sardou's play. Principal roles: Madame Sans-Gêne (sop), Napoleon (bar), Lefèbvre (ten). A romantic comedy and rather different from Giordano's normal VERISMO style, it was reasonably successful at its appearance but is nowadays only very rarely performed.
Plot: Paris and Compiègne, 1792 and 1811. The laundress Caterina Hubscher, who later became the Duchess of Danzig, twice during the revolutionary period saves the life of Lefèbvre, Count of Neipperg. As Duchess, she takes pleasure in presenting the Emperor Napoleon with an unpaid laundry bill dating from the time when he was a young army lieutenant.

Madamina
Bass-baritone aria (the Catalogue Aria) for Leporello in Act I of Mozart's *Don Giovanni*, in which he shows Donna Elvira his book containing the names of all the Don's conquests.

Mädchen oder Weibchen, Ein
Baritone aria for Papageno in Act II of Mozart's *Die Zauberflöte*, in which he uses his magic bells to attract the women.

Maddalena
Mezzo role in: **1** Verdi's *Rigoletto*. She is Sparafucile's sister. **2** Donizetti's *Linda di Chamounix*. Antonio's wife, she is Linda's mother. **3** Rossini's *Il Viaggio a Reims*. She is the housekeeper of the Golden Lily inn.

Maddalena
Opera in one act by Prokofiev (Op 13). 1st perf (in concert) Manchester, 22 Dec 1978 (composed 1911); 1st stage perf Graz, 28 Nov 1981; libr by the composer, after Magda Gustavovna Liven-Orlova's play. Principal roles: Maddalena (sop), Genaro (ten), Stenio (bar). Prokofiev's first mature opera, it was edited and prepared for performance by Sir Edward Downes.
Plot: Early-15th-century Venice. Maddalena is married to the artist Genaro, who she professes to love passionately. The alchemist Stenio visits his friend Genaro, telling him that he is in torment over the lover whom he has had for three months and who will not reveal her name. He recognizes Maddalena as his unknown lover, and the two men fight and kill each other. [R]

Madeleine
Soprano role in Giordano's *Andrea Chénier.* The Countess of Coigny's daughter, she loves Chénier.

Maderna, Bruno (1920–73)
Italian composer and conductor. His operas, some of which employ electronic music, include *Don Perlimplin* (RAI, 12 Aug 1962; libr composer, after Federico García Lorca's *Amor de Don Perlimplín con Belisa en su Jardín*), *Hyperion* (Venice, 6 Oct 1964; libr composer and Virginia Puechner, after Friedrich Hölderlin) and *Satyricon* (Scheveningen, 16 Mar 1973; libr composer and Ian Strasfogel, after Petronius). As a conductor, he specilized in early and modern operas and conducted the first performance of Nono's *Intolleranza.*

Madetoja, Leevi (1887–1947)
Finnish composer. He wrote two fine operas, successful in Finland but virtually unknown elsewhere. They are *The Ostrobothnians* (*Pohjalaisia*, Helsinki, 25 Oct 1924; libr composer, after Artturi Järviluoma) [R] and *Juha* (Helsinki, 17 Feb 1935; libr composer and Aïno Ackté, after Juhani Aho) [R].

Madre, pietosa vergine
Soprano aria for Leonora in Act II of Verdi's *La Forza del Destino*, in which she begs heaven for forgiveness as she arrives at the monastery.

Madrid
see TEATRO DE LA ZARZUELA, MADRID

Madrigal
A contrapuntal composition for several voices which originated in Italy in the 16th century and soon afterwards became very popular in England. A number of early operas are written in madrigal style, notably Gagliano's *La Dafne*. The madrigals in 19th-century British stage works, such as 'Sing a merry madrigal' in Sullivan's *The Mikado*, are not true madrigals in the original sense in that they have independent instrumental parts which the 16th-century madrigal did not. Menotti's *The Unicorn, the Gorgon and the Manticore* is a 20th-century operatic usage of madrigal style.

Mad scenes
An enormously popular device in 19th-century Italian and French romantic opera, it provided an opportunity for exciting and demanding vocal writing for great singers. Much the most famous example is in *Lucia di Lammermoor*, but there are also well-known scenes in *I Puritani*, *Anna Bolena* and Thomas's *Hamlet.* They are nearly always for soprano, although Donizetti also wrote mad scenes for tenor (in *Maria Padilla*) and for baritone (in *Torquato Tasso* and *Il Furioso*). Modern 20th-century sophisticates tend to sneer at the convention, but it should be remembered that in the early 19th-century madness was widely regarded as a romantic rather than a clinical state of mind. The convention is gloriously parodied by Gilbert and Sullivan with Mad Margaret in *Ruddigore.*

Maestro (Italian for 'master')
A courtesy title by which composers and conductors are often referred to and addressed as.

Maestro di cappella (Italian for 'chapel master')
A term used to describe the 18th-century official who was in charge of the music at a royal or princely court, as for example Haydn was at Esterháza. He was called *Kapellmeister* in Germany and *Maître de Chapelle* in France.

Maestro di Cappella, Il (*The Chapel Master*; often given in English as *The Music Master*)
Comic intermezzo in one act by Cimarosa. 1st perf *c* 1790. Principal role: Maestro (b-bar). A highly amusing little monodrama, it concerns a pompous maestro rehearsing an orchestra and often imitating the sounds of the instruments. Always popular with great BUFFOS, it is still regularly performed. [R]

Maestro di Musica, Il (*The Music Master*)
Comic opera in two acts attributed to Pergolesi. 1st perf Paris, 19 Sept 1752; librettist unknown. Principal roles: Lauretta (sop), Lamberto (bar), Colagianni (ten). Long believed to have been written by Pergolesi, the work's authorship and exact date of composition are unknown, and it

may be the work of several composers including Sammartini, Pietro Auletta and (conceivably) Pergolesi himself. A delightful little work, it still receives an occasional performance.
Plot: 18th-century Italy. The pretty young singer Lauretta is a pupil of the maestro Lamberto, who loves her. The impresario Colagianni arrives in search of talent and immediately falls for Lauretta. By inflaming the two men's passion and by arousing their jealousy, Lauretta ensures the advancement of her career. [R]

Maeterlinck, Maurice (1862–1949)
Belgian symbolist playwright. He wrote the libretto for Dukas's *Ariane et Barbe-Bleue*, and Debussy's *Pelléas et Mélisande* is a word-for-word setting of his play. His *Monna Vanna* was set by Février, Ábrányi and Rachmaninov, his *Soeur Béatrice* and *L'Oiseau Bleu* were set by Wolff, and his *La Mort de Tintagiles* was set by Collingwood and Nougués.

Magda
Soprano role in: **1** Puccini's *La Rondine*. She is Rambaldo's mistress. **2** Menotti's *The Consul*. She is John Sorel's wife. **3** Respighi's *La Campana Sommersa*. She is Enrico's wife.

Magdalene
Mezzo role in: **1** Wagner's *Die Meistersinger von Nürnberg*. She is Eva's nurse. **2** Keinzl's *Der Evangelimann*. She is Martha's friend.

Maggio Musicale Fiorentino (Italian for Florence May Festival)
The festival was founded by Vittorio Gui in 1933. Originally biannual, it became an annual event in 1938. Performances are given at the TEATRO COMUNALE, the Teatro Pergola (cap 1,000) and the Boboli Gardens. The repertory is mainly Italian, with an emphasis on Verdi, early-19th-century works and contemporary operas. Artistic directors have included Igor Markevich, Riccardo Muti, Bruno Bartoletti and Luciano Berio.

Magic Fire Music
The ending of Act III of Wagner's *Die Walküre* as Wotan calls on Loge to surround Brünnhilde's rock with flames.

Magic Flute, The
see ZAUBERFLÖTE, DIE

Magic Fountain, The
Opera in three acts by Delius. 1st perf BBC Radio, 20 Nov 1977 (composed 1893); libr by the composer. Principal roles: Solana (ten), Watawa (mezzo), Wapanacki (bar), Talum Madjo (bass). Delius's second opera, it has never been staged.
Plot: Early-16th-century Florida. The Spanish nobleman Solano has sailed to the Americas in search of a spring of eternal youth: a 'fountain ready for those prepared'. Shipwrecked, he is tended by the local natives led by Wapanacki, and falls in love with the Indian girl Watawa. The seer Talum Hadjo, who has drunk from the spring, warns Solano against doing so himself: for him it will be poisoned. Regardless, the lovers drink and die together. [R]

Magnard, Albéric (1865–1914)
French composer. Influenced by Wagner, he composed three operas in a dramatic but austere style, for all of which he wrote his own libretti. They are *Yolande* (Brussels, 27 Dec 1892), the fine GUERCOEUR and *Bérénice* (Paris, 15 Dec 1911; libr after Jean Baptiste Racine). He was killed whilst defying German soldiers who were advancing across his land.

Magnifico, Don
Bass role in Rossini's *La Cenerentola*. He is Cenerentola's stepfather.

Mahagonny Songspiel
Opera in one act by Weill. 1st perf Baden-Baden, 18 July 1927; libr by Bertolt Brecht. Principal roles: Jessie (sop), Billy (ten), Bessie (mezzo), Johnnie (ten), Jimmy (bass). The short work from which Brecht and Weill developed AUFSTIEG UND FALL DER STADT MAHAGONNY. [R]

Mahler, Gustav (1860–1911)
Austrian composer and conductor. He wrote three youthful operas, all to his own libretti: *Herzog Ernst von Schwaben* (*c* 1878; libr after Uhland), which he destroyed, *Die Argonauten* (*c* 1880), also

destroyed, and *Rübezahl* (*c* 1882), which is lost. He also completed Weber's unfinished DIE DREI PINTOS.

Mahler's operatic importance rests on his reputation as one of the greatest conductors of his age. He was musical director of the Kassel Staatstheater (1884), the Budapest State Opera (1888–91), the Hamburg State Opera (1891–97) and the Vienna State Opera (1897–1907), where his performances became legendary, both for their musical and dramatic qualities. He conducted the first performance of Zemlinsky's *Es War Einmal*.

Maiden in the Tower, The (*Jungfruburen*)
Opera in one act by Sibelius. 1st perf Helsinki, 7 Nov 1896; libr by Rafael Hertzberg. Principal roles: Maiden (sop), Lover (ten), Bailiff (bar), Chatelaine (mezzo). Sibelius's only opera, he withdrew it after its premiere and always refused requests for subsequent performances. Although it is an early work and is dramatically rather creaky, it contains some fine music. It has received a few performances in the last decade.
Plot: The Maiden and the Lover, retainers of the castle, wish to marry. She rejects the love of the Bailiff, who has her shut up in the castle's tower. The Lover comes to rescue her, but the Bailiff threatens to throw him into the dungeon The two take up arms, but the Chatelaine intervenes to set things right. The Bailiff is arrested and the lovers are united. [R]

Maid of Orleans, The (*Orleanskaya Deva*)
Opera in four acts by Tchaikovsky. 1st perf St Petersburg, 25 Feb 1881; libr by the composer, after Vasily Zhukovsky's translation of Friedrich von Schiller's *Die Jungfrau von Orleans*. Principal roles: Johanna (mezzo), Charles (ten), Lionel (bar), Thibault (bass), Dunois (bar), Raimond (ten), Agnès (sop), Archbishop (bass). Telling of Joan of Arc, it is written in French grand opera style and is only infrequently performed outside Russia despite its fine music.
Plot: France, 1430–31. Johanna feels called to take up arms and predicts a French victory over the English. She recognizes King Charles, whom she has never seen, and is entrusted with the command of the army. Johanna encounters the Burgundian knight Lionel and experiences stirrings of love. At Charles's coronation, her father Thibault, believing her to be in league with the devil, denounces her in public. Because of her feelings of guilt over her love for Lionel, she is unable to reply. She goes into hiding and is joined by Lionel. The English launch a surprise attack in which Lionel is killed and Johanna is captured and is condemned to be burnt at the stake. [R]

Maid of Pskov, The (*Pskovityanka*)
Opera in four acts by Rimsky-Korsakov. 1st perf St Petersburg, 13 Jan 1873; libr by the composer, after Lev Alexandrovich Mey's play. Revised version composed 1877 but never performed; its prologue was later revised as the one-act *Boyarinya Vera Sheloga*, 1st perf Moscow, 27 Dec 1898; final version *Ivan the Terrible*, 1st perf St Petersburg, 18 April 1895. Principal roles: Olga (sop), Ivan (bass), Mikhail (ten), Yuri (bass), Nikita (ten). Rimsky's first opera, it is almost unknown outside Russia.
Plot: Pskov, 1570. Ivan IV has destroyed Novgorod and is approaching Pskov. There, Princess Olga loves Mikhail Tucha, but has been promised by her presumed father Prince Yuri Tokmakov to Nikita Matuta. Ivan enters Pskov and meets Olga. He grants clemency to the city and takes Olga with him, later revealing that she is his own daughter. Tucha attempts to rescue Olga, but she is accidentally shot dead. [R *Maid of Pskov* and *Boyarinya Vera Sheloga*]

Maillart, Aimé (1817–71)
French composer. He wrote six operas, nowadays all virtually forgotten. They are *Gastibelza* (Paris, 15 Nov 1847; libr Adolphe Philippe d'Ennery and Eugène Cormon), *Le Moulin de Tilleuls* (Paris, 9 Nov 1849; libr Cormon and J. de Maillan), *La Croix de Marie* (Paris, 19 July 1852; libr d'Ennery and Jean Philippe Lockroy), LES DRAGONS DE VILLARS, by far his most successful work, *Les Pêcheurs de Catane* (Paris, 19 Dec 1860; libr Cormon and Michel Carré) and *Lara* (Paris, 21 Mar 1864; libr Cormon and Carré, after Lord Byron).

Mainz Opera
The present opera house (cap 1,100) in this German city in the Rhineland-Palatinate opened in 1951, replacing the previous theatre of 1813 which was destroyed by bombs in 1942. Musical directors have included Karl Maria Zwisler, Helmut Wessell-Therhorn and Peter Erckens.

Maître de Chapelle, Le (*The Chapel Master*; often given in English as *The Music Master*)
Comic opera in two acts by Paer. 1st perf Paris, 29 March 1821; libr by Sophie Gay, after Alexandre Duval's *Le Souper Imprévu ou Le Chanoine de Milan*. Principal roles: Bernabé (bar), Célénie (sop), Gertrude (sop), Benetto (ten). Paer's most successful opera, still occasionally performed, it tells of a fashionable opera composer's attempts to be up-to-date, and contains some digs at opera's then rising star Rossini. [R]

Makropulos Affair, The
see MACROPOLUS CASE, THE

Malas, Spiro (b 1933)
American bass, particularly associated with the Italian repertory. Possessing a rich and warm if not over-large voice, his extensive repertory ranged from baroque to contemporary American operas. A fine singing-actor, especially in comedy, he created King Alcinous in Glanville-Hicks's *Nausicaa*.

Malatesta, Dr
Baritone role in Donizetti's *Don Pasquale*. He is Ernesto's friend and Pasquale's physician. The name means 'Dr Headache'.

Malfitano, Catherine (b 1948)
American soprano, particularly associated with the Italian and French repertories and with Mozart. Originally singing SOUBRETTE and COLORATURA roles, she has recently turned successfully to heavier Verdi and Puccini roles, notably Cio-Cio-San and Tosca. She possesses a rich and agile voice of individual timbre and is a fine singing-actress. She created Doll in Floyd's *Bilby's Doll*, Catherine Sloper in Pasatieri's *Washington Square* and a role in William Bolcom's *McTeague*.

Malgoire, Jean-Claude (b 1940)
French conductor and oboist, particularly associated with Monteverdi and with baroque operas, especially Rameau, Lully and Händel. With his original instrument orchestra La Grande Écurie et la Chambre du Roy, which he founded in 1966, he has been responsible for performances and recordings of many long-neglected works. Musical director of the Atelier Lyrique de Tourcoing (1982–).

Malheurs d'Orphée, Les (*The Sorrows of Orpheus*)
Opera in three acts by Milhaud (Op 85). 1st perf Brussels, 7 May 1926; libr by Armand Lunel. Principal roles: Orphée (bar), Eurydice (mezzo), Blacksmith (ten), Wheelwright (bass), Weaver (bass). A retelling of the Orpheus myth in a contemporary setting, it is arguably Milhaud's most successful opera and still receives an occasional performance.
Plot: 20th-century Camargue. The chemist Orpheus, who treats animals, falls in love with the gypsy Eurydice. The two live in the forest, where the animals protect them. When Eurydice becomes ill, neither Orpheus's skills nor the sympathy of the animals can save her. Eurydice's sisters the Furies accuse Orpheus of letting her die and kill him. He does not resist, as in death he will be reunited with Eurydice. [R]

Malibran, María (b García) (1808–36)
Spanish mezzo, daughter of MANUEL GARCÍA I and sister of PAULINE VIARDOT-GARCÍA and MANUEL GARCÍA II. One of the most famous singers of the first half of the 19th century, she was essentially a contralto with a soprano register added; the dead patch in between she was apparently able to conceal with great skill. Said to have had an exciting stage presence, she created the title-roles in *Maria Stuarda* and Balfe's *The Maid of Artois*. She died as a result of injuries sustained in a riding accident. Alfred de Musset's *Stances* is a tribute to her, and she is the subject of an opera by a minor composer, Robert R. Bennett.

Malipiero, Gian Francesco (1882–1973)
Italian composer. A currently much underrated composer, he wrote over 30 operas in contemporary style but strongly

influenced by his love and knowledge of early music. His operas, for nearly all of which he wrote his own libretti, include the triptych L'ORFEIDE, *Giulio Cesare* (Genoa, 8 Feb 1936; libr after Shakespeare's *Julius Caesar*), *Antonio e Cleopatra* (Florence, 4 June 1938; libr after Shakespeare), *Ecuba* (Rome, 11 Jan 1941; libr after Euripides), *I Capricci di Callot* (Rome, 24 Oct 1942; libr after E.T.A. Hoffmann's *Fantasiestücke*), *Il Figliuolo Prodigo* (RAI, 25 Jan 1953; libr P. Castellano Castellani) and *Venere Prigioniera* (Florence, 14 May 1957; libr after Emmanuel Gonzales's *Giangurgolo*). He also helped to produce complete critical editions of the works of Montevedi and Vivaldi. His nephew **Riccardo** (*b* 1914) is also a composer. His three operas are the 12-tone *Minnie la Candida* (Parma, 19 Nov 1942; libr composer, after Massimo Bontempelli), the comedy *La Donna è Mobile* (Milan, 22 Feb 1957; libr G. Zucconi, after Bontempelli's *Nostra Dea*) and the television opera *Battone alla Porta* (RAI, 12 Feb 1962; libr Dino Buzzati).

Mal per me
Baritone aria for Macbeth in Act IV of the original 1847 version of Verdi's *Macbeth*, in which he curses the crown which has brought him only tragedy. Macbeth's death aria, it was cut in the revised version but a number of modern productions have reinstated it.

Maltese opera composers
see ISOUARD
Other national opera composers include Girolamo Abos (1715–60) and Carmelo Pace.

Mamelles de Tirésias, Les (*The Breasts of Tirésias*)
Comic opera in two acts by Poulenc. 1st perf Paris, 3 June 1947; libr by Guillaume Apollinaire. Principal roles: Thérèse (sop), Husband (ten), Gendarme (bar), Director (bar), Lacouf (ten), Presto (bass), Reporter (ten). An outrageously funny surrealist piece, it was an immediate success and is still regularly performed.
Plot: The imaginary town of Zanzibar on the French Riviera, 1910. Thérèse is converted to feminism and to demonstrate her emancipation she undoes her blouse so as to lose her sinful breasts (symbolically shown as balloons which she explodes). Now to be called Tirésias, she defies her husband, informing him that from now on he must undertake all the duties of a housewife, including bearing children. This last he achieves in spectacular fashion, producing 40,000 in a single day. After appearing as a fortune teller to recommend frequent procreation, Thérèse eventually resumes her normal role and rejoins her relieved husband. [R]

Mamma morta, La
Soprano aria for Madeleine de Coigny in Act III of Giordano's *Andrea Chénier*, in which she says that she brings misfortune upon all who love her.

Mam'zelle Nitouche
Operetta in three acts by Hervé. 1st perf Paris, 26 Jan 1883; libr by Henri Meilhac, Albert Millaud and Ernest Blum. Principal roles: Denise (sop), Célestin (ten), Fernand (ten), Loriet (bar). Hervé's most successful work, it is still sometimes performed in France. [R Exc]

Manaus
see TEATRO AMAZONES, MANAUS

Manca un foglio
Bass aria for Dr Bartolo in Act I of Rossini's *Il Barbiere di Siviglia*. A less demanding alternative to the aria 'A un dottor', it was composed by Pietro Romani (1791–1877). Nowadays, Rossini's original aria is almost invariably performed.

Mancinelli, Luigi (1848–1921)
Italian composer and conductor. He wrote four operas, all of them now forgotten. They are *Isora di Provenza* (Bologna, 2 Oct 1884; libr Angelo Zanardini, after Victor Muge's *La Légende des Siècles*), *Ero e Leandro* (Norwich, 8 Oct 1896; libr Arrigo Boito), *Paolo e Francesca* (Bologna, 11 Nov 1897; libr Arturo Colautti, after Dante's *La Divina Commedia*) and the unperformed *Il Sogno di una Notte d'Estato* (1917; libr Fausto Salvatori, after Shakespeare's *A Midsummer Night's Dream*). One of the leading conductors of his time, he was musical director of the Teatro Real, Madrid (1888–95) and was also closely associated with Covent Garden, the Teatro Comunale,

Bologna and the Metropolitan Opera, New York. He conducted the first performances of Stanford's *Much Ado About Nothing* and Franchetti's *Cristoforo Colombo*.

Mandryka
Baritone role in Strauss's *Arabella*. Arabella's suitor, he is a wealthy landowner.

Manfredo
Baritone role in: **1** Montemezzi's *L'Amore dei Tre Re*. Archibaldo's son, he is married to Fiora. **2** Mercadante's *Il Giuramento*. The Count of Syracuse, he is Bianca's husband.

Manfroce, Nicola Antonio (1791–1813)
Italian composer whose early promise was never fully developed, as he died young, of tuberculosis. He wrote two operas: *Alzira* (Rome, 10 Sept 1810; libr Gaetano Rossi, after Voltaire) and the highly successful *Ecuba* (Naples, 20 Dec 1812; libr Giovanni Federico Schmidt, after M. Milcent).

Mangus
Baritone role in Tippett's *The Knot Garden*. He is a pyschoanalyst.

Manners, Charles (b Southcote Mansergh) (1857–1935)
Irish bass and administrator. A popular British singer of the late 19th century, he created Private Willis in *Iolanthe*. His wife **Fanny Moody** (1866–1945) was a successful soprano. In 1898, they jointly formed the Moody-Manners Opera Company, which toured Britain until May 1916.

Mannheim Opera
Opera in this German city in Baden-Württemberg is given at the Nationaltheater (cap 1,200), which opened in Jan 1957, replacing the previous theatre of the same name which was destroyed by bombs in 1943. Musical directors have included Rezniček, Vincenz Lachner, Felix Weingartner, Artur Bodansky, Wilhelm Furtwängler, Erich Kleiber, Karl Elmendorff, Horst Stein, Hans Wallat, Friedemann Layer, Peter Schneider, Wolfgang Rennert and Miguel Gómez-Martínez.

Manon
Opera in five acts by Massenet. 1st perf Paris, 19 Jan 1884; libr by Henri Meilhac and Philippe Gille, after the Abbé Antoine-François Prévost's *L'Histoire du Chevalier des Grieux et de Manon Lescaut*. Principal roles: Manon (sop), des Grieux (ten), Lescaut (bar), Comte des Grieux (bass), Guillot (ten), de Brétigny (bar). An immediate success, it has always been one of the most popular of French operas, although Sir Thomas Beecham's famous remark that he would give all six of Bach's Brandenburg Concerti for it would seem to be pushing its merits a little far. Massenet's follow-up to the story, *Le Portrait de Manon* (Paris, 8 May 1894; libr Georges Boyer), was unsuccessful.
Plot: Amiens and Paris, 1721. The high-spirited Manon arrives at an inn to meet her cousin Lescaut, who is charged with escorting her to a convent. She encounters the Chevalier des Grieux, with whom she falls in love, and they run away together to Paris. Lescaut disapproves of the liaision and des Grieux assures him of his honourable intentions. However, his father Comte des Grieux also disapproves and has his son abducted. Manon allows herself to be tempted by a life of luxury with the tax farmer de Brétigny, but when she learns that des Grieux has entered a seminary she rushes to him and wins him back. Des Grieux is accused of cheating in a gaming-house row, and he and Manon are arrested. Des Grieux is released after his father's intercession, but Manon is condemned to deportation as a prostitute. On the road to Le Havre, des Grieux attempts to rescue her, but her strength fails and she dies in his arms. [R]

Manon Lescaut
Opera in three acts by Auber. 1st perf Paris, 23 Feb 1856; libr by Eugène Scribe, after the Abbé Antoine-François Prévost's *L'Histoire du Chevalier des Grieux et de Manon Lescaut*. Principal roles: Manon (sop), des Grieux (ten), Marqis d'Hérigny (b-bar), Lescaut (bar). One of Auber's best operas, with a wealth of melody, it was very successful at its appearance. After a long period of complete neglect, it has received a few performances in the last decade. [R]

Manon Lescaut
Opera in four acts by Puccini. 1st perf Turin, 1 Feb 1893; libr by Luigi Illica, Giuseppe Giacosa, Giulio Ricordi, Marco Praga and Domenico Oliva, after the Abbé Antoine-François Prévost's *L'Histoire du Chevalier des Grieux et de Manon Lescaut.* Principal roles: Manon (sop), des Grieux (ten), Lescaut (bar), Geronte (bass), Edmondo (ten). Puccini's third opera and the work which established his reputation, it is still regularly performed.
Plot: Early-18th-century France and America. Manon, accompanied by her brother Lescaut, is on her way to a convent. She meets and falls in love with the Chevalier des Grieux. With the help of the student Edmondo, they take the coach of the elderly Geronte (who had himself hoped to use it to abduct Manon) and go to Paris. After a while, Manon is seduced by the wealth offered by Geronte and leaves des Grieux. They are later reunited and decide to go away together. Before leaving, Manon stops to pick up her jewellery, the gift of Geronte. This delay leads to their arrest by agents hired by Geronte, and Manon is sentenced to deportation to New Orleans. Des Grieux gains permission to accompany her, helps her to escape when they reach America, and takes her in search of an English colony. However, the now failing Manon loses all strength and dies in the wilderness. [R]

Manrico
Tenor role in Verdi's *Il Trovatore*. The troubador of the opera's title, he is believed to be Azucena's son.

Manru
Opera in three acts by Paderewski (Op 20). 1st perf Dresden, 29 May 1901; libr by Alfred Nossig, after Josef Ignacy Krazewski's *The Cabin Behind the Wood.* Principal roles: Manru (ten), Ulana (sop), Asa (sop), Oros (bar). Paderewski's only opera, it met with considerable success at its appearance but is nowadays virtually forgotten outside Poland.
Plot: 19th-century Galicia. Ulana has married the gypsy Manru against her mother's wishes and Manru has proved inconstant. Ulana rekindles his passion with the aid of a love potion, but he is drawn back to his own people by the gypsy girl Asa. Ulana drowns herself in despair. Now leader of the gypsy tribe, Manru is killed by Oros, who also loves Asa, and who Manru had deposed for the leadership.

Manuguerra, Matteo (b 1924)
Tunisian-born French baritone, particularly associated with the French and Italian repertories, especially Verdi. Possessing a rich and firm voice of considerable power, he did not begin singing until the age of 35, but became one of the leading Verdi baritones of the 1970s and enjoyed a remarkably long career, singing into his early 70s.

Maometto Secondo (*Mahomet II*)
Opera in two acts by Rossini. 1st perf Naples, 3 Dec 1820; libr by Cesare della Valle, after his own *Anna Erizo* and Voltaire's *Mahomet.* Principal roles: Anna (sop), Maometto (bass), Erisso (ten), Calbo (mezzo). Revised version LE SIÈGE DE CORINTHE. After a long period of neglect, this fine original version has received a number of performances in the last few years.
Plot: Mid-15th-century Negroponte (Greece). The Venetian colony is besieged by the Turks under Maometto. The young general Calbo leads a vow to fight until death. The governor Paolo Erisso wishes his daughter Anna to wed Calbo, but she has fallen in love with an unknown young man she has met in Corinth. The Turks capture Calbo and Erisso, and Anna recognizes Maometto as the man she met. Maometto offers Anna a life of luxury if she will stay with him, but instead she answers the call of duty. She tricks Maometto into giving her the imperial seal, by the use of which the Turks are defeated. She is married to Calbo and then stabs herself as Maometto and his troops rush in seeking vengeance. [R]

Mapleson, James Henry (1830–1901)
British impresario. Originally a singer and violinist, he was manager of Her Majesty's Theatre, London (1862–7 and 1877–81), the Theatre Royal, Drury Lane (1868 and 1871–6), Covent Garden (1885) and the Academy of Music, New York (1878–97). He gave many British and US premieres

and organized several financially questionable coast-to-coast US tours. Always calling himself, with no justification, 'Colonel', his entertaining if sometimes tendentious autobiography, *The Mapleson Memoirs*, was published in 1888. He appears as a character in Beeson's *Captain Jinks of the Horse Marines*. His nephew **Lionel** (1865–1937) was a violinist, who was librarian of the Metropolitan Opera, New York, for nearly half a century.

M'appari
see ACH SO FROMM

Mar, Norman del (1919–94)
British conductor and musicologist, particularly associated with Strauss and with 20th-century works. Best known as an orchestral conductor, his operatic appearances were infrequent. His three-volume study of Strauss is a seminal work, and he conducted the first performances of Delius's *The Magic Fountain* and *Margot la Rouge*, Maw's *One Man Show*, Thomas Wilson's *Confessions of a Justified Sinner*, Bliss's *Tobias and the Angel* and Britten's *The Little Sweep*.

Marais, Marin (1656–1728)
French composer. He is best known as the greatest viola da gamba virtuoso of his age and as a composer for that instrument. He also wrote four operas: *Alcide* (Paris, 3 Feb 1693; libr Jean-Galbert de Campistron), composed jointly with Lully's son Louis, *Ariane et Bacchus* (Paris, 8 Mar 1696; libr Saint-Jean), *Alcyone* (Paris, 18 Feb 1706; libr Antoine Houdart de la Motte) [R], his finest opera and long famous for its storm music, and *Sémélé* (Paris, 9 Apr 1709; libr la Motte).

Marazzoli, Marco (c 1605–62)
Italian composer, singer and harpist. His first opera *Chi Soffre, Speri* or *Il Falcone* (Rome, 27 Feb 1639; libr Giulio Rospigliosi), written in collaboration with Virgilio Mazzochi, is the first comic opera and contains some of the earliest use of RECITATIVO SECCO. His subsequent operas include the lost *Gli Amori di Giasone e d'Issifile* (Venice, 22 Feb 1642; libr Orazio Persiani), *Le Pretensioni del Tebro e del Po* (Ferrara, 4 Mar 1642; libr Pio di Savoia), *Il Capriccio* (Paris, Feb 1645; libr Francesco Buti) and the comedy *Dal Male il Bene* (Rome, 12 Feb 1654; libr Rospigliosi, after Sigler de Huerta's *No Ay Bien*), written with Abbatini, which makes pioneering use of ensemble.

Marcellina
Mezzo role in Mozart's *Le Nozze di Figaro*. She is Dr Bartolo's housekeeper.

Marcello
A Parisian painter in love with Musetta, he appears as: **1** Baritone role in Puccini's *La Bohème*. **2** Tenor role in Leoncavallo's *La Bohème*.

Marchesi de Castrone, Mathilde (b Graumann) (1821–1913)
German teacher and mezzo. One of the most famous singing teachers of the 19th century, her pupils included Emma Calvé, Emma Eames, Mary Garden, Selma Kurz, Sibyl Sanderson and Dame Nellie Melba. She wrote a method of singing and her autobiography, *Marchesi and Music*, which was published in 1897. Her husband **Salvatore** (Cavalieri de Castrone, Marchese della Raiata) (1822–1908) was a successful baritone who also translated French and German operas into Italian. Their daughter **Blanche** (1863–1940) was a Wagnerian soprano and later a noted teacher. Her autobiography, *Singer's Pilgrimage*, was published in 1923.

Marchetti, Filippo (1831–1902)
Italian composer. He wrote seven operas, all of them now forgotten. They are *Gentile de Varano* (Turin, Feb 1856; libr Raffaele Marchetti), *La Demente* (Turin, 29 Nov 1856; libr G. Checchetelli), the unperformed *Il Paria* (1859; libr Checchetelli), *Romeo e Giulietta* (Trieste, 25 Oct 1865; libr Marcelliano Marcello, after Shakespeare), *Ruy Blas* (Milan, 3 Apr 1869; libr Carlo d'Ormeville, after Victor Hugo), by far his most successful work which was widely performed, *Gustavo Wasa* (Milan, 7 Feb 1875; libr d'Ormeville) and *Don Giovanni d'Austria* (Turin, 11 Mar 1880; libr d'Ormeville).

Marcoux, Vanni (b Jean Émile Diogène) (1877–1962)
French bass-baritone, particularly

associated with the French and Italian repertories. His huge repertory of 240 roles ranged from Scarpia in *Tosca* to Arkel in *Pelléas et Mélisande* and the title-role in *Boris Godunov* and he was an outstanding singing-actor. He created Uin-Sci in Leoni's *L'Oracolo*, Colonna in Février's *Monna Vanna*, the title-role in Massenet's *Panurge* and Flambeau in Honegger and Ibert's *L'Aiglon*. He was director of the Grand Théâtre, Bordeaux (1948–51).

Mařenka
Soprano role in Smetana's *The Bartered Bride*. She is Jeník's beloved.

Marfa
Mezzo role in: **1** Moussorgsky's *Khovanschina*. She is Prince Andrei's former lover. **2** Dvořák's *Dimitrij*. She is Ivan the Terrible's widow.

Margot la Rouge (*Margot the Red*)
Opera in one act by Delius. 1st perf BBC Radio, 9 Oct 1981 (composed 1902); 1st stage perf St Louis, 8 June 1983; libr by Berthe Gaston-Danville. Principal roles: Margot (sop), Thibault (ten), Artist (b-bar), Lili (sop), Poigne (bar), Patronne (mezzo). A taut, quasi-VERISMO piece, it is only very rarely performed.
Plot: 19th-century Paris. Soldiers discuss Margot's latest affair, and their sergeant Thibault realizes that they are talking about his own former lover. Margot arrives and their mutual passion is rekindled. When her current lover appears, he tries to stab her, but Thibault takes the blow and is killed. Margot runs her lover through with Thibault's bayonet. [R]

Marguerite
1 Soprano role in Gounod's *Faust* and mezzo role in Berlioz's *La Damnation de Faust*. She is the girl seduced by Faust. **2** Soprano role in Meyerbeer's *Les Huguenots*. She is Queen Marguerite de Valois of Navarre (1553–1615). **3** Soprano role in Grétry's *Richard Coeur de Lion*. She is the Countess of Flanders and Artois.

Maria
1 Soprano role in Tchaikovsky's *Mazeppa*. She is Kochubei's daughter. **2** Mezzo role in Gershwin's *Porgy and Bess*. **3** Soprano role in Mascagni's *Guglielmo Ratcliff*. MacGregor's daughter, she is loved by Ratcliff. **4** Mezzo role in Prokofiev's *War and Peace*. She is Prince Bolkonsky's daughter. **5** Soprano role in Strauss's *Friedenstag*. She is the Commandant's wife. **6** Soprano role in Erkel's *Lászlo Hunyadi*. She is Hunyadi's fiancée. **7** Soprano role in Tchaikovsky's *The Voyevoda*. She is loved by Bastryukov. **8** Soprano role in Egk's *Der Revisor*. She is Anna's daughter.

Maria de Rudenz
Opera in three acts by Donizetti. 1st perf Venice, 30 Jan 1838; libr by Salvatore Cammarano, after Eugène Anicet-Bourgeois, J.-G.-A. Cuvelier and J. de Mallian's *La Nonne Sanglante*, itself based on Matthew Lewis's *The Monk*. Principal roles: Maria (sop), Corrado (bar), Enrico (ten), Matilde (mezzo), Rambaldo (bass). A strongly melodramatic piece, it has received a few performances in recent years after a long period of total neglect.
Plot: 15th-century Switzerland. In his youth, Corrado had eloped with Maria and then abandoned her in the catacombs. He now wishes to marry Matilde di Wolff, heiress of the late Comte de Rudenz now that the Count's daughter Maria is presumed dead. Corrado's brother Enrico also loves Matilde. Maria returns secretly to Rudenz and, hearing of Corrado's intentions, determines on vengeance. She interrupts the wedding and hints to Enrico that Corrado is not his brother. She shows Corrado the proof that he is the son of an assassin, but – in spite of everything – offers him her love if he will give up Matilde. He refuses and Maria opens a trapdoor, saying that it leads to Matilde's grave. Corrado injures her with a knife stroke, and Enrico challenges Corrado to a duel and is killed. Maria stabs Matilde, confesses her crime and dies. [R]

Maria di Rohan
Opera in three acts by Donizetti. 1st perf Vienna, 5 June 1843; libr by Salvatore Cammarano, after Édouard Lockroy's *Un Duel Sous le Cardinal de Richelieu*. Principal roles: Maria (sop), Riccardo (ten), Enrico (bar), Armando di Gondi (mezzo), de Fiesque (bass). Highly successful at its appearance, it still receives an occasional performance.

Plot: Early-17th-century France. Enrico di Chevreuse, secretly married to Maria, has been arrested for killing Cardinal Richelieu's nephew. Maria falls in love with Riccardo, Comte de Chalais, with whom she intercedes on Enrico's behalf. Enrico challenges Riccardo to a duel and kills him. Maria herself wishes to die, but Enrico insists that she must suffer a life of disgrace.

Maria Egiziaca (*Mary of Egypt*)
Opera in one act (three episodes) by Respighi. 1st perf (in concert) New York, 16 March 1932; 1st stage perf Venice, 10 Aug 1933; libr by Claudio Guastalla, after Fra Domenico Cavalca's *The Lives of Holy Fathers*. Principal roles: Maria (sop), Zosimo (bar), Leper (ten), Blind Woman (sop), Sailor (ten). Almost an opera-oratorio, the vocal writing resembles the 16th-century monodic style, whilst the orchestral interludes are in lush, late-romantic form. It is only rarely performed.
Plot: 4th-century Alexandria and Palestine. After spending 17 years as a prostitute, Mary takes ship with a group of pilgrims bound for Jerusalem, where she experiences conversion. She retires to the desert as a solitary, living alone for 40 years until, as she is dying, the monk Zosimus encounters her. They bless one another and a lion digs her grave. [R]

Maria Golovin
Opera in three acts by Menotti. 1st perf Brussels, 20 Aug 1958; libr by the composer. Revised version 1st perf Washington, 22 Jan 1965. Principal roles: Maria (sop), Donato (bar), Mother (mezzo), Agata (sop), Prisoner (bar), Zuckertanz (ten). One of the more successful of Menotti's full-length works, it has slightly more musical substance than most of them.
Plot: Central Europe, late 1940s. The blind Donato lives with his mother and her maid Agata. A floor of their house is rented to Maria Golovin, who is awaiting the release of her husband from the nearby prisoner-of-war camp. Accompanied by her young son and his Swiss tutor Dr Zuckertanz, she moves in and she and Donato fall in love. Donato becomes obsessive, but Maria refuses to leave her husband for him. He pulls out a gun and asks his mother to guide his sightless aim at Maria. Telling him to kill her, the mother motions Maria out of the way and Donato fires into space and is led away. [R]

Mariani, Angelo (1821–73)
Italian conductor, particularly associated with Verdi operas. The first of the great modern-style Italian conductors, he was musical director of the Teatro Carlo Felice, Genoa (1852–73) and the Teatro Comunale, Bologna (1860–73). His performances of Verdi's patriotic early operas were so exciting that he was threatened with imprisonment for inciting revolution. He conducted the first performance of Verdi's *Aroldo* and was the first Italian conductor to champion Wagner's works.

Maria Padilla
Opera in three acts by Donizetti. 1st perf Milan, 26 Dec 1841; libr by Gaetano Rossi, after François Ancelot's play. Principal roles: Maria (sop), Don Pedro (bar), Don Ruiz (ten), Ines (mezzo). Notable for containing a tenor mad scene, it contains some fine music but has never been one of Donizetti's more popular operas and is only very rarely performed.
Plot: Mid-14th-century Castile. Maria tells her sister Ines that she has had visions of a throne, which she connects with the attentions of 'Mendez', a friend of Prince Pedro. She learns that Mendez is actually Pedro himself, and she makes him swear to marry her. Pedro becomes king and duly marries Maria, although she has sworn to keep the marriage a secret and live as his mistress. Her father Don Ruiz, believing her dishonoured, insults Pedro in public and is ordered to be beaten with rods. This causes him to lose his mind. The court, ignorant of Pedro's marriage, wishes him to wed a French princess, and Pedro has to agree. At the ceremony, Maria breaks in, snatches the crown and places it on her own head. Pedro, conscience-striken by his treatment of Maria and Don Ruiz, relents and openly acknowledges her as queen. [R]

Maria Stuarda (*Mary Stuart*)
Opera in three acts by Donizetti. 1st perf (as *Buondelmonte*) Naples, 18 Oct 1834;

1st perf in original form Milan, 30 Dec 1835; libr by Giuseppe Bardari, after Friedrich von Schiller's *Maria Stuart.* Principal roles: Maria (sop), Elisabetta (sop) Leicester (ten), Talbot (b-bar), Cecil (bar). Censorship problems caused the music to be hastily adapted to a new libretto by Pietro Salatino. One of Donizetti's finest operas, it is notable for the richly-wrought Confession Scene and for the tremendous (albeit fictitious) confrontation between the two queens. Unsuccessful at its appearance, it remained totally unperformed for over a century, but in the last 20 years it has firmly established itself in the repertory.
Plot: London and Fotheringhay, 1587. Elizabeth I loves the Earl of Leicester, but he loves the imprisoned Mary Queen of Scots. He promises Mary's sympathetic jailer George Talbot that he will do all in his power to secure Mary's release, and persuades Elizabeth – against her better judgement – to meet Mary. On Leicester's advice, Mary humbles herself before Elizabeth and begs for mercy. Elizabeth so taunts her that Mary's patience finally snaps and she roundly insults Elizabeth, calling her 'vile bastard'. Despite Leicester's pleas, Elizabeth – urged on by her counsellor Cecil – signs Mary's death warrant and names Leicester as witness at the execution. Mary confesses to Talbot (revealed as a secret Catholic priest) and prays with the crowd for peace in England. Forgiving Elizabeth, she is led to execution. [R]

Marie
Soprano role in: **1** Donizetti's *La Fille du Régiment.* She is the regimental 'daughter' loved by Tonie. **2** Berg's *Wozzeck.* She is Wozzeck's common-law wife. **3** Poulenc's *Dialogues des Carmélites.* She is a nun. **4** Bizet's *Ivan IV.* She is Prince Temrouk's daughter. **5** Korngold's *Die Tote Stadt.* She is Paul's dead wife. **6** Lortzing's *Der Waffenschmied.* She is Stadinger's daughter. **7** Lortzing's *Zar und Zimmermann.* The Bourgomaster's daughter, she is loved by Peter Ivanov. **8** Varney's *Les Mousquetaires au Couvent.* She is the Governor of Touraine's niece.

Marina Mniszek
Mezzo role in Moussorgsky's *Boris Godunov.* The daughter of a Sandomir noble, she is wooed by the false Dimitri.

Marino Faliero
Opera in three acts by Donizetti. 1st perf Paris, 12 March 1835; libr by Giovanni Emanuele Bidera, after Casimir Delavigne's play and Lord Byron's play. Principal roles: Marino (bass), Elena (sop), Israele (bar), Fernando (ten), Steno (bass). Successful at its appearance, it is nowadays only rarely performed.
Plot: Venice, 1355. The young patrician Michele Steno has angered the Doge Faliero by impugning the chastity of his young wife Elena. Steno publicly insults the captain of the arsenal Israele Bertucci, who enlists the Doge's support in a plot against the Council. Elena is in love with the Doge's nephew Fernando, but breaks off the liaison, giving him a scarf as a token. Steno insults Elena at a ball, and Fernando challenges him to a duel. Fernando is killed, and while the Doge is telling Elena, Israele's conspiracy is unmasked and the Doge is arrested. Condemned, Faliero begs Elena to have the scarf cover his face when he is dead and buried in the same tomb as Fernando. Elena confesses her adultery with Fernando and the Doge eventually forgives her. Faliero is led to execution and Elena collapses when she hears the axe descend.

Marinuzzi, Gino (b Giuseppe) (1882–1945)
Italian conductor and composer, particularly associated with Wagner operas and with 20th-century Italian works. He was musical director of the Chicago Opera (1919–21) and the Rome Opera (1928–34) and conducted the first performances of *La Rondine*, Wolf-Ferrari's *Il Campiello* and *La Vedova Scaltra*, Respighi's *Lucrezia* and Pizzetti's *Fedra.* He also composed three operas: *Barberina* (Palermo, 1903), *Jacquerie* (Buenos Aires, 11 Aug 1918; libr Alberto Donaudy) and *Palla de' Mozzi* (Milan, 5 Apr 1932; libr Giovacchino Forzano). His son **Gino** (*b* 1920) is also a composer and conductor.

Mario, Giovanni (b Giovanni Matteo, Cavaliere di Candia) (1810–83)
Italian tenor, particularly associated with Donizetti roles. Regarded as one of the

greatest lyric tenors of the first half of the 19th century, he combined a beautiful and stylish voice with acting ability and a handsome stage presence. He created Ernesto in *Don Pasquale* and a role in Halévy's *Le Drapier*. He was for many years the companion of the soprano GIULIA GRISI, but they were unable to marry.

Marionette operas
The earliest known opera written for performance with marionettes is Francesco Pistocchi's *Leandro* (Venice, 1679). In the 18th century, a puppet theatre was maintained at Esterháza, for which Haydn wrote five marionette operas, of which the only one extant is *Philemon und Baucis*. Marionette operas of the 20th-century include de Falla's *El Retablo de Maese Pedro*, Castelnuovo-Tedesco's *Aucassin et Nicolette*, Hindemith's *Das Nusch-Nuschi* and several by Lualdi. The two main European marionette companies are the Teatro dei Piccoli in Rome and the Salzburg Marionettentheater, which specializes in Mozart operas.

Maritana
Opera in three acts by Wallace. 1st perf London, 15 Nov 1845; libr by Edward Fitzball, after Adolphe Philippe d'Ennery and Philippe François Pinel Dumanoir's *Don César de Bazan*. Principal roles: Maritana (sop), Don José (bar), Charles II (bass) Don César (ten), Lazarillo (mezzo). Built around a character from Victor Hugo's *Ruy Blas*, it is by far Wallace's most successful opera and was very popular for half a century. It is nowadays virtually never performed.
Plot: 17th-century Madrid. A disguised King Charles II is in love with the gypsy street singer Maritana. His adviser Don José de Santarem loves the Queen and sees an opportunity to compromise the King and further his own ends. For fighting a duel on behalf of the apprentice Lazarillo, the nobleman Don César de Bazan is condemned to hang. In return for the privilege of being shot instead, José persuades César to marry Maritana, hoping that a noble's widow could be presented at court. The execution takes place, but Lazarillo has succeeded in removing the bullets. César meets and falls in love with his new wife, who reveals José's plots to the King. Charles returns to his forgiving wife.

Mark
Tenor role in Tippett's *The Midsummer Marriage*. He is in love with Jenifer.

Marke
Bass role in Wagner's *Tristan und Isolde*. The King of Cornwall, he is Tristan's uncle.

Markevich, Igor (1912–83)
Russian conductor and composer, particularly associated with the Russian and French repertories. Best known as a symphonic conductor, his operatic appearances were infrequent. He was artistic director of the Maggio Musicale Fiorentino (1944).

Marmontel, Jean-Francois (1723–99)
French playwright and librettist. Author of the entry on opera in the *Grand Encyclopédie* and a supporter of Piccinni in the famous controversy with Gluck, he wrote a large number of libretti. He provided texts for Cherubini (*Démophoon*), Dauvergne, Grétry (*Le Huron*, *Lucile* and *Zémire et Azor*), Philidor (*Persée*), Piccinni (*Roland* and *Atys*), Rameau (*Acanthe et Céphise*) and Zingarelli (*Antigone*) amongst others.

Mârouf, Savetier du Caire (*Mârouf, Cobbler of Cairo*)
Comic opera in four acts by Rabaud. 1st perf Paris, 15 May 1914; libr by Lucien Népoty, after *The Thousand and One Nights*. Principal roles: Mârouf (ten), Sultan (bass), Princess (sop), Vizier (bass). By far Rabaud's most successful opera, it is still occasionally performed in France.
Plot: Legendary Cairo and Khaitan. The cobbler Mârouf goes to sea to escape his cruel wife. After being shipwrecked, he is introducted to the Sultan as a wealthy merchant, and marries the potentate's daughter. He plunders the royal treasury, eternally promising that his caravans of valuable goods are on their way. Eventually he tells his wife the truth. She continues to love him despite his chicanery, and together they decamp. A magic ring provides Mârouf with money

and a palace and, when the furious Sultan finally catches up with him, the evidence of his son-in-law's wealth earns the Sultan's forgiveness. [R]

Marquise de Berkenfeld
Mezzo role in Donizetti's *La Fille du Régiment.* She turns out to be Marie's mother.

Marquise de Brinvilliers, La
Opera in three acts by Auber, Désiré Batton, Henri-Montan Berton, Felice Blangini, Boïeldieu, Carafa, Cherubini, Hérold and Paer. 1st perf Paris, 31 Oct 1831; libr by Eugène Scribe and François Castil-Blaze. Telling of a woman executed in 1675 for poisoning her father and two brothers to gain an inheritance, it was the most successful of the many collectively-written operas popular in Paris in the first half of the 19th century. It is nowadays totally forgotten.

Marriner, Sir Neville (b 1924)
British conductor and violinist, particularly associated with Mozart and with the baroque repertory. Founder in 1959 of the Academy of St Martin-in-the-Fields, his operatic appearances (mainly Mozart and Rossini) have been very rare. His son **Andrew** is a clarinettist.

Marschallin (or Feldmarschallin)
Soprano role in Strauss's *Der Rosenkavalier.* She is the Princess von Werdenberg, in love with Octavian.

Marriage, The or **The Matchmaker** (*Zhenitba*)
Unfinished opera in four acts by Moussorgsky. 1st perf (Act I only) St Petersburg, 1 April 1908 (composed 1864); a word-for-word setting of Nikolai Gogol's play. Principal roles: Podkolesin (bar), Fyokla (mezzo), Kochkaryov (ten), Stepan (bass). Moussorgsky completed only the first act and the work is usually performed as a torso. There is, however, a completed version, with the remaining three acts written by Ippolitov-Ivanov (1931). It is an historically important work in that it applies Dargomijsky's ideas of melodic RECITATIVE (as shown in his opera *The Stone Guest*) to a prose text, and also marks the first use in Russian opera of LEITMOTIV.

Plot: St Petersburg, 1830. The clerk Podkolesin is undecided about marrying a merchant's daughter but is urged by the marriage broker Fyokla not to delay. Kochkaryov, whose own marriage was arranged by Fyokla and which turned out to be a disaster, extols the blessings of married life. [R original and Ippolitov-Ivanov versions]

Marriage of Figaro, The
see NOZZE DI FIGARO, LE

Marschner, Heinrich (1795–1861)
German composer. One of the most important figures in German romantic opera, and often regarded as the link between Weber and Wagner, his best works are notable for their complex harmonies, their rich orchestration and their delineation of character, especially figures combining both good and evil elements. He was musical director of the Dresden Opera (1824–6), the Leipzig Opera (1827–31) and the Hanover Opera. His operas are *Saidir und Zulima* (Pressburg, 26 Nov 1818; libr A.G. Hornbostel), *Heinrich IV* (Dresden, 19 July 1820; libr Hornbostel), *Der Holzdieb* (Dresden, 22 Feb 1825; libr Friedrich Kind), *Lukretia* (Danzig, 17 Jan 1827; libr August Eckschlager, after Livy), DER VAMPYR, his first major success, the fine DER TEMPLER UND DIE JÜDIN, *Des Falkners Braut* (Leipzig, 10 Mar 1832; libr Wilhelm August Wohlbrück, after Karl Spindler), HANS HEILING, his finest and most enduring opera, *Das Schloss am Ätna* (Leipzig, 29 Jan 1836; libr August Klingermann), *Der Bäbu* (Hanover, 19 Feb 1838; libr Wohlbrück), his only comedy, *Kaiser Adolf von Nassau* (Dresden, 5 Jan 1845; libr Heribert Rau), *Austin* (Hanover, 25 Jan 1852; libr Marianne Marschner) and *Sangeskönig Hiarne* (Frankfurt, 13 Sept 1863; libr Wilhelm Grote, after Isaïas Tegnér). A currently much underrated composer, a few of his operas are still occasionally performed in Germany but elsewhere are virtually ignored.

Marseilles
see GRAND THÉÂTRE, MARSEILLES

Marten aller Arten
Soprano aria for Constanze in Act II of

Mozart's *Die Entführung aus dem Serail*, in which she declares that neither torture nor death will make her yield to the Pasha.

Martha or **Der Markt zu Richmond** (*The Fair at Richmond*)
Opera in four acts by Flotow. 1st perf Vienna, 25 Nov 1847; libr by Friedrich Wilhelm Riese, after Jules-Henri Vernoy de Saint-Georges's ballet-pantomine *Lady Henriette ou la Servante de Greenwich*. Principal roles: Lady Harriet (sop), Lionel (ten), Nancy (mezzo), Plunkett (b-bar), Sir Tristram (b-bar). By far Flotow's most successful opera, it is still regularly performed.
Plot: Richmond, *c* 1710. Lady Harriet, a lady-in-waiting to Queen Anne, and her maid Nancy disguise themselves as peasant girls and go to Richmond Fair. They hire themselves out as domestic servants to the young farmers Plunkett and Lionel. Despite the women's inability to cook or sew, the two farmers fall in love with them. The women depart and Lionel is left heartbroken. Returned to court, Harriet realises that she loves Lionel and, when he discovers that he is the lost heir to the earldom of Derby, the couple are reunited. [R]

Marthe, Dame
Mezzo role in Gounod's *Faust*. She is Marguerite's companion.

Martin, Frank (1890–1974)
Swiss composer. He wrote four stage works, which have not received the recognition which their merits deserve. The dramatic oratorio LE VIN HERBÉ was followed by the Shakespearean opera DER STURM, the scenic oratorio *Le Mystère de la Nativité* (Geneva, 23 Dec 1959) and the comedy *Monsieur de Pourceaugnac* (Geneva, 23 Apr 1963; libr composer, after Molière).

Martin, Janis (b 1939)
American soprano, particularly associated with Wagnerian roles and with 20th-century operas, especially Marie in *Wozzeck*. Beginning as a mezzo, she turned to soprano roles in 1971. She has a powerful and incisive voice and is an outstanding singing-actress.

Martin, Jean-Blaise (1768–1837)
French baritone, long resident at the Opéra-Comique, Paris. He created 14 roles in operas by Boïeldieu, Dalayrac, Halévy, Isouard and Méhul. Specializing in comic servant roles, he possessed a voice of extraordinary range and has given his name to a type of very high French baritone who sings roles such as Pelléas. He also composed one light opera, *Les Oiseaux de Mer* (Paris, 1796).

Martinelli, Giovanni (1885–1969)
Italian tenor, particularly associated with the Italian repertory. One of the most famous tenors of the 20th century, he had a bright and silvery voice used with style and an impeccable technique. Although the voice was not large, his projection was so good that he was able to sing heroic roles such as Calaf and Tristan. He created Fernando in Granados's *Goyescas*, Pantagruel in Massenet's *Panurge* and Lefèbvre in Giordano's *Madame Sans-Gêne*. He enjoyed a remarkably long career, giving his final performance (as Emperor Altoum in *Turandot*) at the age of 82.

Martinů, Bohuslav (1890–1959)
Czech composer who wrote in a wide variety of styles and whose operas deserve a wider currency than they have so far achieved. His stage works are the comedy *The Soldier and the Dancer* (*Voják a Tanečnice*, Brno, 5 May 1928; libr Jan Löwenbach-Budín, after Plautus's *Pseudolus*), the jazz-inspired *Les Larmes du Couteau* (Brno, 22 Oct 1969, composed 1928; libr Georges Ribemont-Dessaignes), the Dadaist *Les Trois Souhaits* (Brno, 16 June 1971, composed 1929; libr Ribemont-Dessaignes), the unfinished operatic film *La Semaine de Bonté* (1929; libr Ribemont-Dessaignes, after I. Erenburg), the beautiful mystery cycle THE MIRACLE OF OUR LADY, the radio opera *The Voice of the Forest* (*Hlas Lesa*, Czech Radio, 6 Oct 1935; libr Vitězslav Nezval), *The Suburban Theatre* (*Divadlo za Bránou*, Brno, 20 Sept 1936; libr composer), the comedy *Alexandre Bis* (Mannheim, 18 Mar 1964, composed 1937; libr André Wurmser) [R], the surrealist JULIETTA, his most successful opera, the brilliant radio opera COMEDY ON THE BRIDGE, the two

television operas *What Men Live By* (*Čím Člověk Žije*, New York, May 1953; libr composer, after Tolstoy) and *The Marriage* (*Ženitba*, NBC, 7 Feb 1953; libr composer, after Nikolai Gogol), the unfinished *La Plaint Contre Inconnu* (1953; libr composer, after Georges Neveux), the comedy *Mirandolina* (Prague, 17 May 1959; libr composer, after Carlo Goldoni's *La Locandiera*), the powerful THE GREEK PASSION and the neo-classical ARIANE, inspired by Maria Callas.

Martín y Soler, Vicente (1754–1806)
Spanish composer. His vivacious and tuneful comedies met with great success in their day, first in Vienna (where he collaborated with Lorenzo da Ponte) and later in St Petersburg, where two of his operas had libretti by Catherine the Great. His only opera still to be remembered is UNA COSA RARA.

Marton, Éva (b Heinrich) (b 1943)
Hungarian soprano, particularly associated with dramatic Italian and German roles, especially Turandot, Tosca, Brünnhilde and Elektra. One of the leading contemporary dramatic sopranos, she possesses a powerful and exciting voice and has a strong stage presence.

Marty, Emilia
Soprano role in Janáček's *The Macropolus Case*. She is the woman who has lived for over 300 years.

Martyrdom of St Magnus, The
Opera in nine scenes by Maxwell Davies. 1st perf Kirkwall (Orkneys), 18 June 1977; libr by the composer, after George Mackay Brown's *Magnus*. Principal roles: Magnus (ten), Blind Mary (mezzo), Tempter (bar), Bishop of Orkney (bass). Set in the 12th century and dealing with the Viking pacifist Earl Magnus, subsequently the patron saint of the Orkney Islands, it is a chamber work written for an orchestra of 11 players. [R]

Martyrs, Les
see POLIUTO

Marullo
Baritone COMPRIMARIO role in Verdi's *Rigoletto*. He is a courtier.

Mary
Mezzo role in Wagner's *Der Fliegende Holländer*. She is Senta's companion.

Maryinsky Theatre, St Petersburg
see KIROV OPERA

Mary Queen of Scots
Opera in three acts by Musgrave. 1st perf Edinburgh, 6 Sept 1977; libr by the composer, after Amalia Elguera's *Moray*. Principal roles: Mary (sop), James Stewart (bar), Lord Darnley (ten), Earl of Bothwell (ten), David Riccio (bass), Earl of Ruthven (ten), Earl of Morton (bar), Cardinal Beaton (bar). Telling of events during Mary's time in Scotland, it is a rich historical pageant which has proved to be one of the most successful modern British operas and which has been widely performed. [R]

Mary Stuart
see MARIA STUARDA

Marzelline
Soprano role in Beethoven's *Fidelio*. Rocco's daughter, she is loved by Jacquino.

Masaniello
Tenor role in Auber's *La Muette de Portici*. He is the historical Thomas Aniello (1622–47), who led the Neapolitan revolt against Spanish rule. The opera itself is sometimes referred to by this name.

Mascagni, Pietro (1863–1945)
Italian composer. He wrote 16 operas, his fame resting largely on the first: CAVALLERIA RUSTICANA, the winner of a competition for a one-act opera, which introduced the vogue for VERISMO into Italian opera. His subsequent operas are the pastoral L'AMICO FRITZ, the heavily melodramatic *I Rantzau* (Florence, 10 Nov 1892; libr Giovanni Targioni-Tozzetti and Guido Menasci, after Émile Erckmann and Alexandre Chatrian's *Les Deux Frères*), GUGLIELMO RATCLIFF, *Silvano* (Milan, 25 Mar 1895; libr Targioni-Tozzetti, after Alphonse Karr's *Romano*), ZANETTO, the successful IRIS, the COMMEDIA DELL'ARTE LE MASCHERE, *Amica* (Monte Carlo, 16 Mar 1905; libr Paul Choudens), ISABEAU, PARISINA, LODOLETTA, the operetta *Sì* (Rome, 13 Dec 1919; libr Carlo Lombardo

and Arturo Franci, after Granichstädten's *Mäjestat Mimì*), the unjustly neglected IL PICCOLO MARAT, arguably his finest opera, *Pinotta* (San Remo, 23 Mar 1932; libr Targioni-Tozzetti) and the pretentious NERONE, written in praise of Mussolini. The use made of him by the Fascists as their musical mouthpiece led to a boycott of his works by most Italian musicians and he spent his last years in virtual disgrace. Musically coarse, vulgar and bombastic and displaying almost no dramatic insight, Mascagni is perhaps the most overrated of all opera composers.

Maschere, Le (*The Masks*)
Opera in prologue and three acts by Mascagni. 1st perf Milan, Rome, Venice, Turin, Verona and Genoa simultaneously, 17 Jan 1901; libr by Luigi Illica. Principal roles: Colombina (sop), Florindo (ten), Arlecchino (ten), Rosaura (mezzo), Tartaglia (bass), Spavento (bar). Its premiere was one of the most famous fiascos in operatic history: only in Rome, where Mascagni conducted, did it have any success; elsewhere it was roundly hissed and the Genoese audience did not even allow it to be finished. A COMMEDIA DELL'ARTE story, nowadays only its neo-classical overture is in any way remembered.

Mascheroni, Edoardo (1852–1941)
Italian conductor and composer. One of the leading Verdi and Wagner interpreters of his time, he conducted the first performances of *Falstaff* and Catalani's *Loreley* and *La Wally*. He also composed two operas: *Lorenza* (Rome, 13 Apr 1901; libr Luigi Illica) and *La Perugina* (Naples, 24 Apr 1909; libr Illica). His brother **Angelo** (1855–95) was also a conductor.

Mascotte, La
Operetta in three acts by Audran. 1st perf Paris, 28 Dec 1880; libr by Alfred Duru and Henri Charles Chivot. Principal roles: Bettina (sop), Pippo (ten), Laurent (bar), Rocco (ten), Fiametta (mezzo). By far Audran's most successful and enduring work, it was an immediate success and had clocked up over 1,700 performances in Paris alone within 20 years. It is still quite often performed in France.
Plot: 17th-century Piombino. The farmer Rocco is plagued by ill-luck, and his brother sends him as a mascot the goose-girl Bettina, loved by Rocco's shepherd Pippo. The unlucky Prince Laurent persuades Bettina to come to his castle. Knowing that her power as a mascot depends on her continuing virginity, Laurent keeps Pippo away from her by pretending to be about to marry her himself. Pippo turns to Laurent's sister Fiametta, but his love returns to Bettina before the wedding and the two escape together. After a war in which Laurent is defeated and Pippo covers himself in glory, all is sorted out and forgiven. Pippo and Bettina marry, hoping that her good luck will prove hereditary. [R]

Ma se m'è forza perditi
Tenor aria for Gustavus in Act III of Verdi's *Un Ballo in Maschera*, in which he agonizes over the possibility of losing Amelia.

Masetto
Bass-baritone role in Mozart's *Don Giovanni*. He is Zerlina's peasant fiancé.

Maskarade
Comic opera in three acts by Nielsen (Op 39). 1st perf Copenhagen, 11 Nov 1906; libr by Vilhelm Andersen, after Ludvig Holberg's play. Principal roles: Leander (ten), Leonora (sop), Jeronimus (bass), Arv (ten), Magdelone (mezzo), Henrik (bar). A brilliant and delightful work, still very popular in Denmark (where it is the national opera), it is inexplicably only very seldom performed elsewhere.
Plot: Copenhagen, 1723. Jeronimus, the husband of Magdelone, wishes his son Leander to wed the daughter of his friend Leonard, but the young man resists the idea of marrying a girl he has never met. Leonard's daughter Leonora is equally opposed to the scheme. She wishes instead to marry the young man with whom she fell in love at a masked ball. After much intrigue and complication, and to the joy of all concerned, it transpires that the young man at the ball was Leander. [R]

Masked Ball, A
see BALLO IN MASCHERA, UN

Masnadieri, I (*The Robbers*)
Opera in four acts by Verdi. 1st perf London, 22 July 1847; libr by Count Andrea Maffei, after Friedrich von Schiller's *Die Räuber*. Principal roles: Carlo (ten), Amalia (sop), Francesco (bar), Massamiliano (bass), Arminio (ten), Pastor Moser (bass). One of the most consistent of Verdi's early operas, it is notable for containing in Francesco Verdi's first serious study of evil. After a long period of neglect, it has received a number of performances in recent years.
Plot: Early-18th-century Germany. Carlo has been banished from the home of his father Count Massamiliano Moor through the intrigues of his jealous younger brother Francesco, who wishes to usurp his position. Carlo becomes the leader of a robber band. Francesco brings false evidence of Carlo's death, but Carlo's beloved Amalia continues to repulse his advances. After Carlo has burnt down a city to rescue a captured comrade, he is reunited with Amalia and rescues his father, who Francesco has imprisoned and who is starving to death. He contrives Francesco's death but his men refuse to release him from his oath of loyalty to them. He kills Amalia in their presence. [R]

Masque
A 16th- and 17th-century court entertainment which originated in Italy and France and soon reached Britain. Usually treating mythological subjects, it combined music, poetry, dancing and elaborate costumes and scenery. It was superseded by opera proper, but for a while the two forms existed together, and it is almost impossible to draw a strict distinction between them in works such as Purcell's *The Fairy Queen*, Blow's *Venus and Adonis* and Arne's *Comus*.

Massamiliano
Bass role in Verdi's *I Masnadieri*. Count Moor, he is the father of Francesco and Carlo.

Massard, Robert (b 1925)
French baritone, particularly associated with the French and Italian repertories. One of the very few really outstanding French singers of the post-war era, his rich and beautiful voice was used with fine musicianship, and he had a good stage presence. He created the Harpist in Barraud's *Numance*.

Massé, Victor (b Félix Marie) (1822–84)
French composer. He wrote over 20 operettas, of which the most successful included LES NOCES DE JEANETTE, his best-known work, *La Reine Topaze* (Paris, 27 Dec 1856; libr Jean Philippe Lockroy and Léon Battu) and *Paul et Virginie* (Paris, 15 Nov 1876; libr Jules Barbier and Michel Carré, after Bernardin de Saint-Pierre). He was chorus master of the Paris Opéra (1860–76).

Massenet, Jules (1842–1912)
French composer. His 28 operas begin with *La Grande-Tante* (Paris, 3 Apr 1867; libr Jules Adénis and Charles Granvallet), *Don César de Bazan* (Paris, 30 Nov 1872; libr Adolphe Philippe d'Ennery, Philippe Dumanoir and Jules Chantepie) and the operetta *L'Adorable Bel-Boule* (1874; libr Louis Gallet), which he later destroyed, as also he did *Bérengère et Anatole* (Paris, 1876; libr Henri Meilhac and Paul Poirson). His first major success was LE ROI DE LAHORE. It was followed by HÉRODIADE, MANON, perhaps his most popular opera, LE CID, ESCLARMONDE, *Le Mage* (Paris, 16 Mar 1891; libr Jean Richepin), his masterpiece WERTHER, the exotic THAÏS, *Le Portrait de Manon* (Paris, 8 May 1894; libr Georges Boyer), an unsuccessful follow-up to *Manon*, the VERISMO LA NAVARRAISE, SAPHO, CENDRILLON, GRISÉLIDIS, LE JONGLEUR DE NOTRE-DAME, *Amadis* (Monte Carlo, 1 Apr 1922, composed 1902; libr Jules Clarétie, after García Rodríguez de Montalvo's *Amadís de Gaula*), *Maria-Magdeleine* (Nice, 9 Feb 1903; libr Gallet), a revision of his oratorio of 1873, CHÉRUBIN, *Ariane* (Paris, 31 Oct 1906; libr Catulle Mendès), THÉRÈSE, *Bacchus* (Paris, 5 May 1909; libr Mendès), DON QUICHOTTE, *Roma* (Monte Carlo, 17 Feb 1912; libr Henri Cain, after Alexandre Parodi's *Rome Vaincue*), *Panurge* (Paris, 25 Apr 1913; libr Georges Spitzmüller, after Françoise Rabelais's *Pantagruel*) and CLÉOPÂTRE.

Massenet's operas are notable for their grace and charm, their fine sense of theatre and their elegant orchestration. What d'Indy described as the 'discreet and semi-religious eroticism' of his music, particularly in works such as *Thaïs*, can both attract and repel; in Britain the second has often been the case. After a period of neglect and denigration, his stage works have returned to favour in recent years and performances have become far more frequent. Massenet also completed Delibes's unfinished *Kassya*, and was a distinguished teacher, whose pupils included Bruneau, Charpentier, Chausson, Enescu, Leroux, Pierné and Rabaud.

Massimilla Doni
Opera in four acts by Schoeck (Op 50). 1st perf Dresden, 2 March 1937; libr by Armin Rüger, after Anne-Honoré de Balzac's novel. Principal roles: Massimilla (sop), Emilio (ten), Cattaneo (ten), Tinti (sop), Genovese (ten), Capraja (bass). One of Schoeck's finest works, but only very rarely performed.
Plot: Venice, 1830s. The elderly eccentrics Duke Cattaneo and his friend Capraja are opera mad, and are patrons respectively of the soprano Tinti and the tenor Genovese. Cattaneo ignores his fiancée Massimilla, who is anyway in love with the young Emilio Memmi. Emilio is seduced by Tinti, and much ingenuity is required of Massimilla before she can win Emilio back. Tinti has to content herself with Genovese. [R]

Master Peter's Puppet Show
see RETABLO DE MAESE PEDRO, EL

Mastersingers of Nuremburg, The
see MEISTERSINGER VON NÜRNBERG, DIE

Masterson, Valerie (b 1937)
British soprano, particularly associated with Mozart, Sullivan and Händel roles and, especially, with the French repertory, of which she was one of the finest modern exponents. Her beautiful and agile voice and her exemplary diction, combined with her handsome and most affecting stage presence, made her one of the most popular British artists of recent times. She created Wife of Soldier 2 in Henze's *We Come to the River*.

Mastilović, Danica (b 1933)
Serbian soprano, particularly associated with Strauss and Wagner and with heavier Italian roles. She possessed a large and bright-toned, if sometimes slightly unwieldy voice, which she used to exciting effect, and she had a strong stage presence.

Masur, Kurt (b 1927)
German conductor, particularly associated with the German repertory, especially *Fidelio*. One of the finest contemporary interpreters of 19th-century German music, he is best known as a symphonic conductor. He conducted much opera earlier in his career, but his recent operatic appearances have sadly been infrequent. He was musical director of the Mecklenburg Staatstheater (1958–60) and the Komische Oper, Berlin (1960–64). His wife **Tomoko Sakurai** is a soprano.

Matačić, Lovro von (1899–1985)
Slovenian conductor, particularly associated with the German repertory. He was musical director of the Belgrade Opera (1926–32), the Croatian National Opera (1932–38), the Dresden State Opera (1956–8) and the Frankfurt Opera (1961–6). He also produced a number of operas.

Matchmaker, The
see MARRIAGE, THE

Mathis, Edith (b 1938)
Swiss soprano, particularly associated with Mozart roles and with Sophie in *Der Rosenkavalier*. A highly intelligent and musical singer with a beautiful voice and a delightful stage presence, she created Luise in Henze's *Der Junge Lord*, Queen Mary in Sutermeister's *Le Roi Bérenger* and Kathi in Einem's *Der Zerrissene*. Her husband **Bernhard Klee** (*b* 1936) is a successful conductor.

Mathis der Maler (*Matthias the Painter*)
Opera in seven scenes by Hindemith. 1st perf Zürich, 28 May 1938 (composed 1934); libr by the composer. Principal roles: Mathis (bar), Albrecht (ten), Ursula (mezzo), Regina (sop), Riedinger (bass), Schwalb (ten). Telling of the painter Matthias Grünewald (*c* 1480–1528), creator of the Isenheim altarpiece, and his involvement in the Peasants' War of 1524, its 1934 premiere in Berlin was banned by the Nazis. One of Hindemith's finest

works, it is still occasionally performed, but it is best known through the symphony which Hindemith arranged from music from the opera.
Plot: Mainz, 1524. Through their leader Hans Schwalb and his daughter Regina, the painter Matthias becomes involved in the Peasants' War. His patron Archbishop Albrecht decides to renounce the world and become a hermit. Matthias is tempted to give up painting and espouse the peasants' cause, but in a dream sequence (recreating two of his paintings) he comes to see that his best way of serving mankind is through his art. Regina dies and Matthias returns to his painting with fresh inspiration. [R]

Mathilde
Soprano role in Rossini's *Guillaume Tell*. She is a Habsburg princess in love with Arnold.

Matilde de Shabran or **Bellezza e Cuor di Ferro** (*Beauty and Heart of Iron*)
Opera in two acts by Rossini. 1st perf Rome, 24 Feb 1821; libr by Jacopo Ferretti, after J.M. Boutet de Monvel's *Mathilde* and François Benoît Hoffman's libretto for Méhul's *Euphrosine ou le Tyran Corrigé*. Principal roles: Matilde (sop), Corradino (ten), Isidoro (bar), Edoardo (mezzo), Aliprando (b-bar). Never one of Rossini's more successful works, it is an OPERA SEMISERIA which is only very rarely performed despite its fine music.
Plot: 18th-century Spain. The minx Matilde charms and outwits the loutish Corradino, aided and abetted by the wandering poet Isidoro and by Edoardo, the son of Corradino's arch-enemy. She foils the machinations of a countess to displace her, secures the freedom of the captive Edoardo and finally escapes Corradino's plans to have her thrown from a cliff into a raging torrent.

Matrimonio Segreto, Il (*The Secret Marriage*)
Comic opera in two acts by Cimarosa. 1st perf Vienna, 7 Feb 1792; libr by Giovanni Bertati, after George Colman and David Garrick's *The Clandestine Marriage*. Principal roles: Geronimo (bass), Elisetta (sop), Count Robinson (bar), Carolina (sop), Paolino (ten), Fidalma (mezzo). Cimarosa's only opera still to be regularly performed, it is arguably the greatest 18th-century OPERA BUFFA apart from those by Mozart. Its premiere was the occasion of the longest encore in operatic history: Emperor Leopold II was so delighted that he ordered supper served to the company and the entire opera repeated immediately.
Plot: Late-18th-century Bologna. The lawyer Paolino has secretly married Geronimo's daughter Carolina. Their situation is complicated by Carolina's aunt Fidalma, who is in love with Paolino, and by the arrival of the Englishman Count Robinson who, although betrothed to Geronimo's other daughter Elisetta, falls in love with Carolina. After much scheming and amorous intrigue, the truth about the marriage is revealed and all ends happily. [R]

Matteo
1 Tenor role in Strauss's *Arabella*. Arabella's former suitor, he is loved by Zdenka. **2** Bass role in Busoni's *Arlecchino*. A tailor, he is Annunziata's husband.

Mattheson, Johann (1681–1764)
German composer and theorist. His operas, many of which enjoyed great success in their day, include *Die Plejades* (Hamburg, 1699; libr F.C. Bressand), *Der Edelmüthige Porsenna* (Hamburg, 1702; libr Bressand), *Die Unglückselige Cleopatra* (Hamburg, 20 Oct 1704; libr Friedrich Christian Feustking), *Boris Goudenow* (Hamburg, 1710; libr composer) and *Die Geheimen Begebenheiten Henrico IV* (Hamburg, 9 Feb 1711; libr Johann Joachim Hoë). An important musical theorist, his writings include *Der Vollkommene Capellmeister* (1739) and *Grundlage einer Ehrenpforte* (1740).

Matthus, Siegfried (b 1934)
German composer. One of the most important contemporary opera composers from the former East Germany, his operas include *Lazarillo von Tormes* (Karl-Marx-Stadt, 23 May 1964; libr Horst Seeger), *Der Letzte Schuss* (Berlin, 5 Nov 1967; libr composer and Götz Friedrich, after Boris Lawrenjow's *Der Einundvierzigste*), *Der Barbier von Berlin* (Berlin, 7 June 1970; libr M. Vogler), *Herr Ohnezeit* (Berlin,

15 Dec 1970; libr G. Branstner), *Noch einen Löffel Gift* (Berlin, 16 Apr 1972; libr Peter Hacks, after Saul O'Hara's *Heiraten ist immer ein Risiko*), *Omphale* (Weimar, 7 Sept 1976; libr Hacks), *Die Weise von Liebe und Tod* (Dresden, 16 Feb 1985; libr composer, after Rainer Maria Rilke), the impressive JUDITH, *Graf Mirabeau* (Berlin and Karlsruhe simultaneously, 14 July 1989; libr composer) and *Desdemona und ihre Schwestern* (Schwetzingen, 12 May 1992; libr composer, after Christine Brückner).

Mauceri, John (b 1945)
American conductor, particularly associated with the American and Italian repertories, especially Verdi and Puccini. A scholarly and often exciting conductor, he has also had success with lighter stage works, such as those of Bernstein and Weill. He was musical director of the Opera Society of Washington (1980–82) and Scottish Opera (1987–93) and conducted the first performance of Menotti's *Tamu-Tamu*.

Maurel, Victor (1848–1923)
French baritone, particularly associated with the Italian repertory, especially Verdi. Although his voice was not outstanding, he was a singing-actor of exceptional ability – he sometimes appeared as a straight actor – and is often regarded as the leading baritone of his age. He created Tonio in *Pagliacci*, for Gomes Gonzales in *Il Guarany* and Cambro in *Fosca* and, for Verdi, Iago in *Otello*, the title-roles in *Falstaff* and the revised *Simon Boccanegra* and (whilst still a student) a Flemish Deputy in *Don Carlos*. He was also a painter of some ability and designed *Mireille* in 1919 for the Metropolitan Opera, New York. He wrote three books on singing and his autobiography, *Dix Ans de Carrière*, which was published in 1897 and which was later translated into German by Lilli Lehmann.

Maurizio
1 Tenor role in Cilea's *Adriana Lecouvreur*. The historical Maurice, Count of Saxony, he loves Adriana. **2** Bass role in Wolf-Ferrari's *I Quatro Rusteghi*. He is Filipeto's father.

Mavra
Comic opera in one act by Stravinsky. 1st perf Paris, 3 June 1922; libr by Boris Kechno, after Alexander Pushkin's *The Little House at Kolomna*. Principal roles: Vasili (ten), Parasha (sop), Mother (mezzo), Sosedka (mezzo). A witty little piece, written in a blend of Russian and Italian styles, it is still quite often performed.
Plot: 17th-century Russia. Parasha's mother sends her to look for a replacement for their deceased cook. Parasha dresses her boyfriend, the hussar Vasili, as a woman and introduces him to the house as the maid Mavra. Unfortunately, her mother catches 'Mavra' shaving and he is forced to make a precipitate exit through a window. [R]

Maw, Nicholas (b 1935)
British composer. He has written two operas: the comedy *One Man Show* (London, 12 Nov 1964; libr Arthur Jacobs, after Saki's *The Background*) and *The Rising of the Moon* (Glyndebourne, 19 July 1970; libr Beverley Cross).

Max
Tenor role in: **1** Weber's *Der Freischütz*. He is a forester in love with Agathe. **2** Křenek's *Jonny Spielt Auf*. He is a composer.

Maximilien
Opera in three acts by Milhaud (Op 110). 1st perf Paris, 4 Jan 1932; libr by Armand Lunel, after Rudolf Stephen Hoffmann's play, itself based on Franz Werfel's *Jaurez und Maximilian*. Part of Milhaud's 'New World Trilogy' (along with *Bolivar* and *Christophe Colomb*), it tells of the ill-fated establishment of the Habsburg Archduke Ferdinand Maximilian (1832–67) as Emperor of Mexico in 1864. Unsuccessful at its appearance, it is nowadays virtually forgotten.

Maxwell Davies, Sir Peter (b 1934)
British composer and conductor. One of the most original and successful contemporary British composers, and founder of both the Fires of London ensemble and the Kirkwall Festival in the Orkney Islands, he has written six operas. The historical TAVERNER was followed by

the chamber opera THE MARTRYDOM OF SAINT MAGNUS, the children's opera *The Two Fiddlers* (Kirkwall, 16 June 1978; libr composer), the powerful and claustrophobic THE LIGHTHOUSE, *Resurrection* (Darmstadt, 18 Sept 1988) and *The Doctors of Myddfai* (Cardiff, 1996; libr David Pountney).

May Night (*Mayskaya Noch*)
Opera in three acts by Rimsky–Korsakov. 1st perf St Petersburg, 21 Jan 1880; libr by the composer, after Nikolai Gogol's story. Principal roles: Levko (ten), Hanna (mezzo), Pannochka (sop), Mayor (bass), Kalenik (bass), Distiller (ten). The first of Rimsky's fairy-tale operas, it contains some delightful music but is only infrequently performed outside Russia.
Plot: Legendary Ukraine. The Mayor disapproves of his son Levko's love for Hanna. Levko tells the story of Pannochka: to escape her stepmother she drowned herself and became a water-nymph; the stepmother also drowned and cannot now be distinguished from the good spirits. After catching his father serenading Hanna, Levko goes to the lake and the water-nymphs appear. In return for being able to identify the step-mother, Pannochka aids Levko in outwitting the Mayor and marrying Hanna. [R]

Mayr, Richard (1877–1935)
Austrian bass, particularly associated with Wagner and Strauss roles, especially Baron Ochs in *Der Rosenkavalier*, a role of which he is usually regarded as the greatest ever interpreter. A fine singing-actor with a rich and powerful voice, he created Barak in *Die Frau ohne Schatten* and Quasimodo in Schmidt's *Notre-Dame*.

Mayr, Simone (b Johannes Simon) (1763–1845)
German-born Italian composer. A crucial figure in the development of Italian opera, he introduced the full symphony orchestra into Italy from Germany, himself made major advances in orchestration which influenced composers throughout Europe, and developed the range and fluency of both serious and comic Italian opera. His first opera *Saffo* (Venice, 17 Feb 1794; libr Antonio Sografi) was a success and was followed by 61 others. The most important include *Che Originali* (Venice, 18 Oct 1798; libr Gaetano Rossi), which established his European reputation, *Ginevra di Scozia* (Trieste, 21 Apr 1801; libr Rossi, after Lodovico Ariosto's *Orlando Furioso*), *L'Amor Conjugale* (Padua, 26 July 1805; libr Rossi, after Jean Nicolas Bouilly's libretto for Gaveaux's *Léonore*), *La Rosa Bianca e la Rosa Rossa* (Genoa, 21 Feb 1813; libr Felice Romani, after René–Charles Guilbert de Pixérécourt), which began the Italian craze for operas on historical British subjects, the magnificent MEDEA IN CORINTO, his masterpiece, *Cora* (Naples, 27 Mar 1815; libr Francesco Berio di Salsa, after Jean-François Marmontel's *Les Incas*), and *Fedra* (Milan, 26 Dec 1820; libr Luigi Romanelli, after Jean Baptiste Racine's *Phèdre*). He founded the Bergamo Conservatory in 1805, where his pupils included Donizetti, who he taught free for ten years. For long Mayr was merely a name in the history books, but recent years have witnessed a revival of interest in his music.

Mazeppa
Opera in three acts by Tchaikovsky. 1st perf Moscow, 15 Feb 1884; libr by the composer and Viktor Burenin, after Alexander Pushkin's *Poltava*. Principal roles: Mazeppa (bar), Kochubei (bass), Maria (sop), Andrei (ten), Liubov (mezzo), Iskra (ten), Orlik (bar). Telling of the historical hetman of the Dnieper Cossacks, Ivan Stepanovich Mazeppa (1645–1709), it is Tchaikovsky's most 'nationalist' opera in style. Although it contains some magnificent music, it is only infrequently performed outside Russia.
Plot: Early-18th-century Ukraine. Having been refused the hand of Vassili Kochubei's daughter Maria, Mazeppa abducts her. Andrei, who loves Maria, takes revenge by informing the authorities that Mazeppa is in league with the invading Swedes. The Tsar believes Mazeppa rather than Andrei, however, and has Kochubei executed. Mazeppa shoots Andrei, and Maria goes insane. [R]

Mazurok, Yuri (b 1931)
Russian baritone, particularly associated with Verdi and Tchaikovsky roles, especially the title-role in *Eugene Onegin*.

One of the finest Russian baritones of the post-war era, he possessed a beautiful, bright-toned and finely projected voice which he used with outstanding musicianship. On stage, he sometimes appeared a little uncommitted.

McCormack, Count John (1884–1945)
Irish tenor, particularly associated with the Italian repertory. His operatic career was short: he retired because of his self-confessed lack of acting ability. He had a beautiful, limpid voice and outstanding diction, and his elegant phrasing and remarkable breath control remain an object lesson to all singers. He created Paul Merrill in Herbert's *Natoma.* His autobiography, *John McCormack: His Life Story*, was published in 1918.

McCracken, James (1926–88)
American tenor, particularly associated with dramatic roles, especially the title-role in Verdi's *Otello.* An exciting heroic tenor, he had a powerful physique and a thrilling stage presence which distracted attention from some quite serious vocal shortcomings. His wife **Sandra Warfield** (*b* 1929) was a mezzo. Their joint autobiography, *A Star in the Family*, was published in 1971.

McIntyre, Sir Donald (b 1934)
New Zealand bass-baritone, particularly associated with Wagnerian roles, especially Wotan and the Dutchman in *Der Fliegende Holländer.* One of the leading HELDENBARITONS of the 1970s, he had a powerful and incisive if not intrinsically beautiful voice and a strong if sometimes rather generalized stage presence. He created Axel Heyst in Bennett's *Victory.*

McLaughlin, Marie (b 1954)
British soprano, particularly associated with Mozart and with lighter Italian and German roles. She possesses a beautiful and agile voice used with fine musicianship and has a delightful stage presence, especially in comedy.

McNair, Sylvia (b 1956)
American soprano, particularly associated with Mozart roles. One of the outstanding Mozartians of the younger generation, she possesses a warm and creamy voice used with outstanding artistry and a fine technique. She has an affecting stage presence.

Meco all'altar di Venere
Tenor aria for Pollione in Act I of Bellini's *Norma*, in which he tells of his premonition of Norma's revenge for his infidelity.

Medea
see MÉDÉE

Medea in Corinto
Opera in two acts by Mayr. 1st perf Naples, 28 Nov 1813; libr by Felice Romani, partly after Euripides's *Medea.* Principal roles: Medea (sop), Giasone (ten), Creusa (sop), Egeo (ten), Creonte (bass), Ismene (mezzo). Mayr's masterpiece, it is a work of considerable dramatic power and the delineation of the title-role presents a wonderful challenge to a great singing-actress, especially in the remarkable Invocation Scene. Enormously popular until the mid-19th century, it was long forgotten, but has received a number of performances in recent years.
Plot: Legendary Corinth. Jason returns victorious to his fiancée, Creon's daughter Creusa. Medea arrives and upbraids Jason for abandoning her. He is unrepentant and she swears vengeance. Medea overturns the altar at the wedding ceremony and attempts to abduct Creusa with the help of the latter's rejected suitor Egeo. Medea invokes the aid of the Furies and prepares a poisoned robe for Creusa, which burns her to death when she puts it on. To complete her vengeance, Medea murders her two children by Jason and then escapes in her dragon-drawn chariot. [R]

Médecin Malgré Lui, Le (*The Doctor Despite Himself*)
Comic opera in three acts by Gounod. 1st perf Paris, 15 Jan 1858; libr by Jules Barbier and Michel Carré, after Molière's play. Principal roles: Lucinde (sop), Léandre (ten), Géronte (bass), Sganarelle (bar), Jacqueline (mezzo). Gounod's first major success, it is nowadays only rarely performed despite its charming music.
Plot: 17th-century France. Lucinde, daughter of the wealthy Géronte, is pretending to be dumb so as to avoid

having to marry a rich suitor, because she is in love with Léandre. The doctor Sganarelle is called to attend her and decides to aid the young lovers. He introduces Léandre as his apothecary, and Lucinde is cured. The two elope together, and when he discovers that Léandre has just inherited a fortune, Géronte gives his blessing to their union.

Médée (*Medea*)
Opera in prologue and five acts by M.-A. Charpentier. 1st perf Paris, 4 Dec 1693; libr by Thomas Corneille. Principal roles: Médée (sop), Jason (ten), Créon (bass), Nérine (sop), Oronte (bass), Créuse (sop). Charpentier's last and greatest stage work, it has received a number of performances in recent years. [R]

Médée (*Medea*)
Opera in three acts by Cherubini. 1st perf Paris, 13 March 1797; libr by François Benoît Hoffman, after Thomas Corneille's libretto for Charpentier. Principal roles: Médée (sop), Jason (ten), Dircé (sop), Créon (bass), Néris (mezzo). Cherubini's best-known and most enduring opera, notable for its powerful final act, it has been regularly performed since its first modern revival in 1953 for Maria Callas. Most performances are given in Italian, using the recitatives composed by Franz Lachner in 1855.
Plot: Legendary Corinth. Medea, abandoned by Jason, arrives at the court of Creon in a vain attempt to win him back from Dircé. Despite the people's fear of her as an enchantress, she obtains Creon's permission to remain for a further day. Taking revenge, she contrives a horrible death for Dircé and, with her own hands, kills her two children by Jason. [R]

Méditation
Orchestral intermezzo with solo violin in Act II of Massenet's *Thaïs*.

Medium, The
Opera in two acts by Menotti. 1st perf New York, 8 May 1946; libr by the composer. Principal roles: Madame Flora (mezzo), Monica (sop), Toby (mute), Mr and Mrs Gobineau (bar and mezzo). Often regarded as Menotti's finest opera and still regularly performed, it is a powerfully atmospheric piece of theatre.
Plot: America, 1940s. Assisted by her daughter Monica and by the dumb boy Toby, who loves Monica, the fake medium Madame Flora puts gullible clients in touch with their dead children. During a séance, she has the sensation of a hand around her threat, and confesses her fraudulence to her clients, the Gobineaus. They refuse to believe her, but she dismisses them and beats and evicts Toby. The boy returns to look for Monica, and hides in a cupboard. Madame Flora takes him for a ghost and shoots him. [R]

Mefistofele
Opera in prologue, four acts and epilogue by Boito. 1st perf Milan, 5 March 1868; libr by the composer, after Johann von Goethe's *Faust*. Revised version 1st perf Bologna, 4 Oct 1875. Principal roles: Mefistofele (bass), Faust (ten), Margherita (sop), Elena (sop), Marta (mezzo). The work on which Boito's reputation as a composer rests, its disastrous premiere led to a virtual pitched battle between its admirers and detractors. The revised version was an immediate success and it has been regularly performed ever since, especially in Italy and the United States. Drawing on both parts of Goethe's work, and notable for its magnificient choral writing, it has always been a controversial opera, with opinions sharply divided as to its merits. It is certainly the most high-minded Italian opera since those of Gluck, and the title-role remains one of the greatest roles ever written for a bass.
Plot: Heaven, 16th-century Frankfurt and legendary Greece. Mefistofele visits the Empyrean and wagers that he can win the soul of Faust. Faust accepts his offer of service and renewed youth in return for his soul after death. Faust meets and seduces Margherita but then abandons her. Margherita, having killed the child she bore to Faust, dies insane in prison. Mefistofele shows Faust his power at the Witches' Sabbath and then transports him back to classical Greece, where Faust dallies with Helen of Troy. Finding his youth gone once again, the dying Faust repents and the heavenly host announces his salvation. Mefistofele has lost his wager and yells his defiance at heaven. [R]

Meg Page
Mezzo role in Verdi's *Falstaff*. She is one of the merry wives.

Mehta, Zubin (b 1936)
Indian conductor, particularly associated with Verdi, Wagner and Puccini operas. One of the foremost contemporary conductors, more frequently heard in the concert hall than the opera house, he conducted the first performance of Levy's *Mourning Becomes Electra*.

Méhul, Étienne-Nicolas (1763–1817)
French composer. Inspired by Gluck, his operas are notable for their lofty and austere style, for their originality of orchestration and for their blending of classical and romantic elements. Not only successful but also highly respected in his day, he had a crucial influence on the development of both German romantic opera and of French grand opera. His first performed opera was *Euphrosine* (Paris, 4 Sept 1790; libr François Benoît Hoffman). It was followed by 24 others, of which the most successful included ARIODANT, his own favourite of his works, *Les Deux Aveugles de Tolède* (Paris, 28 Jan 1806; libr Benoît Joseph Marsollier), the Ossianic UTHAL and his masterpiece JOSEPH, which was popular for a century. A fine and historically significant composer who is currently unjustly neglected.

Meier, Waltraud (b 1956)
German mezzo (who also sings a few soprano roles), particularly associated with Wagnerian roles, especially Kundry. Possessing a rich voice of great beauty and considerable power, used with fine musicianship, as well as a strong and handsome stage presence, she is one of the finest singers to have come to the fore in recent years.

Meilhac, Henri (1831–97)
French playwright and librettist. One of the finest French librettists of the 19th century and an outstanding satirist, he wrote a large number of libretti, many in collaboration with LUDOVIC HALÉVY. He provided texts for Bizet (*Carmen*), Delibes (*Kassya*), Hervé (*Mam'zelle Nitouche*), Lecocq (four including *Le Petit Duc*), Massenet (*Bérengère et Anatole* and *Manon*), Offenbach (*Barbe-Bleue*, *La Belle Hélène*, *Les Brigands*, *La Grande-Duchesse de Gérolstein*, *La Périchole*, *Vert–Vert*, *Château à Toto*, *La Diva*, *La Boulangère*, *La Créole* and *La Vie Parisienne*) and Planquette (*Rip*). Of his plays, *L'Attaché de l'Ambassade* was the source for *Die Lustige Witwe* and *Le Réveillon* for *Die Fledermaus*.

Mein Herr Marquis
Soprano aria (the Laughing Song) for Adele in Act II of J. Strauss's *Die Fledermaus*, in which she teases Einsenstein for his gaffe in believing she looks like his parlourmaid.

Meistersinger von Nürnberg, Die (*The Mastersingers of Nuremburg*)
Comic opera in three acts by Wagner. 1st perf Munich, 21 June 1868; libr by the composer. Principal roles: Hans Sachs (bar), Walther (ten), Eva (sop), Pogner (bass), Beckmesser (bar), David (ten), Magdalene (mezzo), Fritz Kothner (bar), Night Watchman (b-bar). Wagner's only mature comedy and his only opera to deal with ordinary historical figures, it concerns the cobbler-poet Hans Sachs (1494–1576) and the Guild of the Mastersingers. Beckmesser is a merciless caricature of the critic EDUARD HANSLICK.
Plot: Mid-16th-century Nuremburg. The Franconian knight Walther von Stolzing is in love with Eva, daughter of the wealthy goldsmith Veit Pogner, who has decided that her hand will be given to the winner of a singing contest. Walther wishes to enter the contest but is ignorant of the strict and complex rules of the guild of mastersingers. They are explained to him by David, apprentice to the cobbler-poet Hans Sachs. With the aid of Sachs and in the face of the bitter opposition of the pedantic town clerk Sixtus Beckmesser, who also aspires to marry Eva, Walther wins the contest with his Prize Song and is given Eva's hand. [R]

Mel
Baritone role in Tippett's *The Knot Garden*. A poet, he is Dov's black lover.

Melba, Dame Nellie (b Helen Porter Mitchell) (1861–1931)
Australian soprano, particularly associated

with the Italian and French repertories. One of the most famous singers in operatic history, she began as a high COLORATURA but later moved to the lyric repertory. She had a fresh, pure and beautiful voice of remarkable agility with a range up to f''', which she used with a matchless technique. Long resident at Covent Garden, where her word was law, she created the title-roles in Saint-Saëns's *Hélène* and Bemberg's *Elaine*. She retired to Australia in 1926 as director of the Melbourne Conservatory. Her autobiography, *Melodies and Memoirs*, was published in 1925. Both the famous toast and an ice cream dish were named in her honour and a film of her life, starring Patrice Munsel, was made in 1953.

Melchoir, Lauritz (b Lebrecht Hommel) (1890–1973)
Danish tenor, particularly associated with Wagnerian roles, especially Tristan. One of the greatest of all HELDENTENORS, he began as a baritone, turning to tenor roles in 1918. He had a large, ringing voice which he used to thrilling effect and he seemed tireless. He gave more Wagner performances than possibly any other singer in history, singing Tristan alone over 200 times. He took part in the first ever operatic radio broadcast in 1920, and also appeared in a number of Hollywood films, including *Luxury Liner* (1947) and *The Stars are Singing* (1952).

Melcthal
Bass role in Rossini's *Guillaume Tell*. He is Arnold's father.

Mélesville, Anne-Honoré Joseph de (b Duvéyrier) (1787–1865)
French playwright and librettist. A prolific writer, he provided texts for Adam (*Le Châlet* and *Lambert Simnel*), Auber (*Leicester* and *Le Lac des Fées*), Carafa (*Le Valet de Chambre*), Cherubini (*Ali Baba*), García, Hérold (*Zampa*), Offenbach (*La Chatte Metamorphosée*) and others. Many were written in collaboration with EUGÈNE SCRIBE.

Mélisande
Soprano role in: **1** Debussy's *Pelléas et Mélisande*. She is a girl discovered in the forest by Golaud. The role in occasionally sung by a mezzo. **2** Dukas's *Ariane et Barbe–Bleue*. She is one of Bluebeard's former wives.

Melismata (from the plural of the Greek *Melisma*, 'song')
A group of notes sung to a single syllable. The term is also used loosely to describe any florid passage of CADENZA style.

Melitone, Fra
Baritone role in Verdi's *La Forza del Destino*. A grumbling monk, he is Verdi's only wholly comic character before *Falstaff*.

Melodrama
A spoken text accompanied by instrumental music. If it is for a single actor it is sometimes called monodrama, if for two duodrama. Developing in the mid-18th century, the first full-scale melodrama was Rousseau's *Pygmalion* and the finest examples were written by Benda. The form has been used more recently by Fibich. A number of early-19th-century operas contain melodrama scenes, the most famous being the Wolf's Glen Scene in Weber's *Der Freischütz* and the grave-digging scene in Beethoven's *Fidelio*.

Melodramma (Italian for 'melodic drama')
Not to be confused with melodrama (see above), the term simply means a sung drama, in other words an opera.

Melot
Tenor role in Wagner's *Tristan und Isolde*. He is Tristan's jealous friend. The role is sometimes sung by a baritone.

Mendelssohn-Bartholdy, Felix (1809–47)
German composer and conductor. He wrote seven, mainly small-scale operas early in his career, none of which achieved any lasting success. They are *Die Soldatenliebschaft* (Wittenberg, 28 Apr 1962, composed 1820; libr Johann Ludwig Casper), *Die Beiden Pädagogen* (Berlin, 27 May 1962, composed 1821; libr Casper, after Eugène Scribe's *Les Deux Précepteurs*) [R], *Die Wandernden Komödianten* (Berlin, 1822; libr Casper), *Der Onkel aus Boston* (Berlin, 3 Feb 1824; libr Casper), DIE HOCHZEIT DAS CAMACHO

and *Die Heimkehr aus der Fremde* (*The Return from Abroad*, sometimes known in Britain as *Son and Stranger*, Leipzig, 10 Apr 1851, composed 1829; libr Klingemann) [R]. The only opera of his maturity is the unfinished *Loreley* (Birmingham, 8 Sept 1852, composed 1847; libr Emmanuel Geibel).

Mendès, Catulle (1841–1909)
French poet and librettist. A member of the Parnassiens, a school of poets noted for their emphasis on form and repression of emotion in their works, and a disciple of Wagner (about whom he wrote a book), he wrote a number of opera libretti. He provided texts for Chabrier (*Gwendoline* and *Briséïs*), Debussy (the unfinished *Rodrigue et Chimène*), Hahn (*La Carmélite*), Leroux (*La Reine Fiamette*), Massenet (*Ariane* and *Bacchus*) and Messager (*Isoline*). He was killed in a railway accident.

Menelaus
The husband of Helen of Troy appears in a number of operas, including tenor role in: **1** Offenbach's *La Belle Hélène*. **2** Strauss's *Die Ägyptische Helena*.

Menotti, Gian-Carlo (b 1911)
Italian-born American composer, librettist and producer. One of the most successful and prolific post-war opera composers, he shows considerable theatrical flair, although his music, in a readily accessible post-Puccinian style, is thought by some to be shallow, inconsequential and devoid of any dramatic insight. His first surviving opera is the successful satire AMELIA AL BALLO. It was followed by the quasi-verismo THE OLD MAID AND THE THIEF, *The Island God* (New York, 20 Feb 1942), the powerfully theatrical THE MEDIUM, the comic duodrama THE TELEPHONE, written in the style of an 18th-century INTERMEZZO, the highly successful THE CONSUL, the popular AMAHL AND THE NIGHT VISITORS, the first opera written specifically for television, the verismo THE SAINT OF BLEECKER STREET, the satirical *The Unicorn, the Gorgon and the Manticore* (Washington, 21 Oct 1956) [R], which is written in madrigal style, and MARIA GOLOVIN. His more recent operas are the television opera *Labyrinth* (NBC, 3 May 1963), the satirical THE LAST SAVAGE, the science-fiction fantasy *Help! Help! The Globolinks* (Hamburg, 18 Dec 1968), described as written for 'children and those who like children', *The Most Important Man in the World* (New York, 12 Mar 1971), *Tamu-Tamu* (Chicago, 5 Sept 1973), *The Hero* (Philadelphia, 1 June 1976), *La Loca* (San Diego, 3 June 1979), *A Bride From Pluto* (Washington, 12 Apr 1982), *The Boy Who Grew Too Fast* (Wilmington, 24 Sept 1982) [R], *Goya* (Washington, 11 Nov 1986), *The Wedding* (Seoul, 16 Sept 1988) and *The Singing Child* (Charleston, 31 May 1993).

In addition to writing the libretti for all of his own operas, Menotti also wrote those for Barber's *Vanessa*, *A Hand of Bridge* and the revised *Antony and Cleopatra* and Foss's *Introductions and Goodbyes*. He founded the Festival of Two Worlds, Spoleto, in 1958, where he often acted as producer.

Mephistopheles
The Devil appears in this guise in a number of operas, including: **1** Bass role in Gounod's *Faust*. **2** Bass role in Boito's *Mefistofele*. **3** Bass-baritone role in Berlioz's *La Damnation de Faust*. **4** Tenor role in Busoni's *Doktor Faust*. **5** Bass role in Spohr's *Faust*. **6** Tenor role in Prokofiev's *The Fiery Angel*.

Mercadante, Saverio (1795–1870)
Italian composer. One of the most prolific and successful Italian composers of his day, his career spanned Rossini's peak, Donizetti's whole career and Verdi's early and middle periods. He played an important role in the development of Italian opera by enriching the orchestration and by pioneering a freer dramatic form in a way which influenced Verdi. His first major success was his seventh opera *Elisa e Claudio* (Milan, 30 Oct 1821; libr Luigi Romanelli, after Filippo Casari's *Rosella*). The most successful of the more than 50 operas which followed included *Donna Caritea* (Venice, 21 Feb 1826; libr Paolo Pola), *Zaira* (Naples, 31 Aug 1831; libr Felice Romani, after Voltaire's *Zaïre*), *I Normanni a Parigi* (Turin, 7 Feb 1832; libr Romani), *I Briganti* (Paris, 22 Mar 1836; libr Jacopo Crescini, after Friedrich von Schiller's *Die Räuber*), IL GIURAMENTO,

arguably his finest opera, LE DUE ILLUSTRI RIVALI, IL BRAVO, the once popular LA VESTALE, IL REGGENTE, the highly successful ORAZI E CURIAZI and *Virginia* (Naples, 7 Apr 1866, composed 1851; libr Salvatore Cammarano, after Vittorio Alfieri). After a long period of complete neglect, there has recently been a revival of interest in his works and performances are becoming more frequent. He was a respected director of the Naples Conservatory from 1840.

Mercédès
Mezzo role in Bizet's *Carmen*. She is a gypsy friend of Carmen's.

Mercury
The Graeco-Roman messenger of the gods appears in many operas, including: **1** Baritone role in Cavalli's *La Calisto*. **2** Tenor role in Offenbach's *Orphée aux Enfers*. **3** Tenor role in Rameau's *Platée*. **4** Baritone role in Oliver's *Tom Jones*. **5** Baritone role in Klebe's *Alkmene*. **6** Bass role in Händel's *Atalanta*. **7** Tenor role in Rameau's *Hippolyte et Aricie*. **8** Bass role in D. Purcell's *The Judgement of Paris*. **9** Tenor role in Bontempi's *Il Paride*. **10** Tenor role in Strauss's *Die Liebe der Danae*. **11** Bass COMPRIMARIO role in Berlioz's *Les Troyens*.

Merelli, Bartolomeo (1794–1879)
Italian administrator and librettist. One of the great 19th-century Italian impresarios, he was manager of La Scala, Milan (1836–46 and 1861–3) and the Kärntnertortheater in Vienna (1836–48 and 1853–5). One of the first to encourage Verdi, he also wrote a number of libretti, providing texts for his fellow student Donizetti (*Enrico di Borgogna* and *Zoraide di Granata*), Mayr, Morlacchi and Vaccai (*Il Lupo d'Ostenda*).

Méric-Lalande, Henriette (1798–1867)
French soprano. One of the leading lyric sopranos of the early 19th century, she created Palmide in Meyerbeer's *Il Crociato in Egitto* and, for Bellini, Bianca in *Bianca e Fernando*, Imogene in *Il Pirata*, Alaide in *La Straniera* and the title-role in *Zaira*. When past her prime, she also created (unsuccessfully) the title-role in *Lucrezia Borgia*, causing Donizetti much trouble: she refused to make her first entry masked (on the grounds that her adoring public might not recognize her) and stood on her prerogative as prima donna in demanding a brilliant final aria, despite its dramatic unsuitability. Donizetti was forced to give way, but looking at the fearsome difficulty of 'Era desso il figlio mio' it is clear that he exacted a subtle and terrible revenge which contributed substantially to her débâcle.

Merikanto, Aarre (1893–1958)
Finnish composer, son of the composer OSKAR MERIKANTO. His two operas are the youthful *Helene* (Helsinki, 16 Mar 1912; libr Jalmari Finne) and JUHA, which is one of the finest of all Finnish operas.

Merikanto, Oskar (1868–1924)
Finnish composer. He wrote three operas, all of them unknown outside Finland. They are *The Maid of the North* (*Pohjan Neiti*, Viipuri, 18 June 1908, composed 1898; libr Antti Rytkönen, after the *Kalevala*), which was the first opera written to a Finnish libretto, *Elina's Death* (*Elinan Surma*, Helsinki, 17 Nov 1910; libr Jalmari Finne, after Gustaf Adolf von Numers) and *Regina von Emmeritz* (Helsinki, 30 Jan 1920; libr Väinö Sola, after Zachris Topelius). His son was the composer AARRE MERIKANTO.

Mérimée, Prosper
see panel on page 362

Merli, Francesco (1887–1976)
Italian tenor, particularly associated with heavier Italian roles, especially Calaf in Puccini's *Turandot*. One of the leading lyrico-dramatic tenors of the inter-war period, he created Baldo in Respighi's *Belfagor* and Fausto in Favara's *Urania*.

Merrie England
Operetta in two acts by German. 1st perf London, 2 April 1902; libr by Basil Hood. Principal roles: Bessie (sop), Ralegh (ten), Elizabeth I (mezzo), Earl of Essex (bar), Jill-All-Alone (mezzo), Walter Wilkins (bass). German's best-known stage work, it was sensationally successful at its appearance and still receives an occasional performance.
Plot: Late-16th-century England. Sir Walter Ralegh and the Earl of Essex vie for the

· Prosper Mérimée ·

The works of the French writer Prosper Mérimée (1803–70) have inspired some 30 operas. Below are listed, by work, those operas by composers with entries in this dictionary.

Les Âmes du Purgatoire		
Alfano	*Don Juan de Mañara/L'Ombra di Don Giovanni*	1914/41
Goossens	*Don Juan de Mañara*	1937
Carmen		
Bizet	*Carmen*	1875
La Carrosse du Saint-Sacrement		
Offenbach	*La Périchole*	1868
Berners	*La Carrosse du Saint–Sacrement*	1924
Chronique du Règne de Charles IX		
Hérold	*Le Pré aux Clercs*	1832
Le Ciel et l'Enfer		
Malipiero	*Donna Urraca*	1954
Colomba		
Pacini	*La Fidanzata Corsa*	1842
La Dame du Pique		
(translation of Alexander Pushkin's *The Queen of Spades*)		
Halévy	*La Dame du Pique*	1850
Inès Mendo		
d'Erlanger	*Inès Mendo*	1897
Mosaïque		
Cui	*Matteo Falcone*	1907
La Vénus d'Ille		
Schoeck	*Venus*	1919

favours of Queen Elizabeth. She discovers that Ralegh is secretly in love with Bessie Throckmorton, but her attempts to have Bessie killed are thwarted by a plot of Essex's. [R]

Merrill, Nathaniel (b 1927)
American producer, resident at the Metropolitan Opera, New York, from 1960. His productions, often in collaboration with the designer Robert O'Hearn (*b* 1921), are in traditional style.

Merrill, Robert (b 1917)
American baritone, particularly associated with the Italian repertory, especially Verdi. One of the finest Verdi baritones of the post-war era, he had a rich and beautiful voice used with fine musicianship but was a little dull on stage. He also appeared in a number of films, and his autobiography, *Once More From the Beginning*, was published in 1965. Married for a time to the soprano ROBERTA PETERS.

Merriman, Nan (b Katherine-Ann) (b 1920)
American mezzo, particularly associated with the Italian repertory. She had a rich, warm and characterful voice and was an accomplished singing-actress, especially in comedy.

Merritt, Chris (b 1952)
American tenor, particularly associated with Rossini roles, especially Arnold, and with heavier French roles. The leading contemporary exponent of Rossini's heroic tenor roles, he has a strong and flexible voice with an exciting upper register

extending to high d. He can be a little dull on stage.

Merry Widow, The
see LUSTIGE WITWE, DIE

Merry Wives of Windsor, The
see FALSTAFF; LUSTIGEN WEIBER VON WINDSOR, DIE; SIR JOHN IN LOVE

Mes amis, écoutez l'histoire
Tenor aria for Chapelou in Act I of Adam's *Le Postillon de Longjumeau*, in which he tells the story of a handsome postillion.

Mesplé, Mady (b 1931)
French soprano, particularly associated with the French repertory, both opera and operetta. She had an appealing stage presence and her voice, if rather small and sometimes a little brittle, was intelligently used and was remarkably agile. She created Kitty in Menotti's *The Last Savage*, the title-role in Tomasi's *Princesse Pauline* and the Voice in Ohana's *Syllabaire pour Phèdre*.

Messa di voce (Italian for 'placing of voice')
The art of increasing and diminishing the tone on a single note, it is an important indication of a singer's technique and control. It is called *Schwelton* in Germany and *son filé* in France.

Messager, André (1853–1929)
French composer and conductor. He wrote 17 stage works, mostly operettas, which are notable for their elegant and delightful melodies, their deft orchestration and their sure theatrical sense. His most successful works include LA BASOCHE, *Madame Chrysanthème* (Paris, 26 Jan 1893; libr Georges Hartmann and André Alexandre, after Pierre Loti), *Mirette* (London, 3 July 1894; libr Michel Carré), *Les P'tites Michu* (Paris, 16 Nov 1897; libr Georges Duval and Albert Vanloo) [R Exc], FORTUNIO, VÉRONIQUE, his most enduring work, and MONSIEUR BEAUCAIRE. One of the finest conductors of the early 20th century, he was musical director of the Opéra-Comique, Paris (1898–1903 and 1919–20), Covent Garden (1901–7) and the Paris Opéra (1907–14). A champion of Wagner and of the French and Russian repertories, he conducted the first performances of *Pelléas et Mélisande*, *Louise*, Leoni's *L'Oracolo*, Leroux's *La Reine Fiamette* and Massenet's *Grisélidis*.

Messel, Oliver (1904–78)
British designer. One of the most successful and fanciful designers of the immediate post-war period, he worked mainly at Glyndebourne (on Mozart and Rossini), Covent Garden (notably *Die Zauberflöte*) and the Metropolitan Opera, New York (*Le Nozze di Figaro* and *Ariadne auf Naxos*).

Messiaen, Olivier (1908–92)
French composer and organist, notable for his musical use of bird song. A member of the Jeune France group (started in Paris in 1936, and opposed to the neo-classical musical style of the time), he wrote one opera, the vast and compelling SAINT FRANÇOIS D'ASSISE.

Metaphor Aria
An aria, very popular in 18th-century OPERA SERIA, in which a character takes a metaphor or simile to illustrate his or her dramatic or emotional situation. A famous example is Fiordiligi's 'Come scoglio' in Mozart's *Così fan Tutte*.

Metastasio, Pietro (b Trapassi) (1698–1782)
Italian poet and librettist. The leading librettist of Italian OPERA SERIA, most of his texts were written in Vienna, where he succeeded APOSTOLO ZENO as court poet in 1729. Aiming to elevate and purify Italian opera, his dramas (mostly derived from Roman history or Greek mythology) usually involve complex amorous relationships entwined around a central conflict between love and duty. His verses are elegant and frequently vivid in their imagery, but to 20th-century audiences their plots often appear artificial and dramatically disjointed. He wrote some 50 texts in all, including INTERMEZZI and religious pieces. The 29 opera seria texts are *Achille in Sciro*, *Adriano in Siria*, *Alessandro nell'Indie*, *Antigono*, *Artaserse*, *Attilio Regolo*, *Catone in Utica*, *Ciro Riconosciuto*, *La Clemenza di Tito*, *Demetrio*, *Demofoonte*, *Didone Abbandonata*, *L'Eroe*

Cinese, *Ezio*, *L'Impresario delle Canarie*, *Ipermestra*, *L'Isola Disabitata*, *Issipile*, *Nitteti*, *L'Olimpiade*, *Il Rè Pastore*, *Romola ed Ersilia*, *Ruggiero*, *Semiramide*, *Siface*, *Siroe*, *Temistocle*, *Il Trionfo di Clelia* and *Zenobia*. They were set innumerable times (there are at least 50 settings of *Artaserse*), until well into the 19th century. Amongst the many composers who set Metastasian texts are Agricola, Anfossi, Arne, J.C. Bach, Bononcini, Bortnyansky, Caldara, Cherubini, Cimarosa, Duni, Feo, Gluck, Graun, Händel, Hasse (56 settings), Haydn, Isouard, Jommelli, Leo, Mayr, Mercadante, Mozart, Mysliveček, Naumann, Pacini, Paer, Paisiello, Pergolesi, Piccinni, Porpora, Portugal, Sacchini, Salieri, D. Scarlatti, Traetta, Uttini, Vinci, Vivaldi, Winter and Zingarelli.

Métella
Soprano role in Offenbach's *La Vie Parisienne*. She is loved by Raoul and Bobinet.

Metropolitan Opera, New York
The leading opera house in the United States, the original theatre on Broadway opened on 22 Oct 1883. The present house (cap 3,500) in the Lincoln Center for the Performing Arts opened on 16 Sept 1966. In the post-war period, administrators have been Edward Johnson, Sir Rudolf Bing, Anthony Bliss, Bruce Crawford and Hugh Southern, and musical directors Rafael Kubelík and James Levine. The repertory tends to be conservative and productions are traditional. The annual season runs from September to April.

The Metropolitan Opera Guild, founded in 1935 and with a membership of over 200,000, does outstanding work in sponsorship and in encouraging educational activities. The weekly radio programme, Metropolitan Opera Auditions of the Air, begun in 1936, was one of the world's most prestigious vocal competitions and was responsible for discovering most of the leading American singers. Sadly, the broadcasts were discontinued.

Mexican opera composers
These include Gustavo Campo (1863–1934), Julián Carrillo (1875–1965), Ricardo Castro (1864–1907), Daniel Catán (*b* 1949), Carlos Chávez (1899–1978), Frederico Ibarra (*b* 1946), Miguel Bernal Jiménez (1910–56), Melesio Morales (1838–1908), Aniceto Ortega (1823–75), Cenobio Paniagua (1821–82) and Manuel de Zumaya (*c* 1678–1756), whose *La Parténope* (Mexico City, 1 May 1711; libr Silvio Stampiglia) is probably the first Latin American opera by a native composer.

Mexico
see PALACIO DE LAS BELLAS ARTES, MEXICO CITY

Meyer, Kerstin (b 1928)
Swedish mezzo, particularly associated with Strauss roles, especially Clytemnestra, and with contemporary operas. An outstanding singing-actress of great intelligence and musicianship, she created Agave in Henze's *The Bassarids*, Elisabeth in Maw's *The Rising of the Moon*, Alice in Goehr's *Arden Must Die*, Gertrude in Searle's *Hamlet*, Spermando in Ligeti's *Le Grand Macabre* and Mrs Clairborne in Schuller's *The Visitation*.

Meyerbeer, Giacomo (b Jakob Liebmann Beer) (1791–1864)
German-born French composer. His first two operas *Jephthas Gelübde* (Munich, 23 Dec 1812; libr Alois Schreiber) and the comedy *Wird und Gast* (Stuttgart, 6 Jan 1813; libr Johann Gottfried Wohlbrück) were failures, and it was only when he moved to Italy and wrote in imitation of Rossini that he met with success. His Italian operas are *Romilda e Costanza* (Padua, 19 July 1817; libr Gaetano Rossi), *Semiramide* (Turin, 3 Feb 1819; libr Rossi, after Pietro Metastasio), *Emma di Resburgo* (Venice, 26 June 1819; libr Felice Romani, after René-Charles Guilbert de Pixérécourt), *L'Esule di Granata* (Milan, 12 Mar 1822; libr Romani) and IL CROCIATO IN EGITTO, his first opera of real significance. It was, however, in France that he achieved his greatest successes, becoming the leading purveyor of French grand opera. The premiere of ROBERT LE DIABLE was one of the most sensationally successful in operatic history, and LES HUGUENOTS placed him at the forefront of European composers. *Ein Feldlager in Schlesien* (Berlin, 7 Dec 1844; libr Ludwig Rellstab) was less successful, but

triumphed in its second revised form as L'ÉTOILE DU NORD. His last three operas, all highly successful, were LE PROPHÈTE, arguably his masterpiece, the more pastoral DINORAH and the vast L'AFRICAINE, which was produced posthumously.

Few composers have ever enjoyed a more inflated reputation. In his lifetime, Meyerbeer stood pre-eminent in his field, and for 50 years his operas were performed more often than those of almost any other composer. History (and changing tastes) have subsequently come to view him very differently. His vast and spectacular works, with their marches, ballets, scenic splendours and all the other paraphernalia – described by Wagner as 'effects without causes' – are now perceived to have cloaked a strictly limited musical talent. He did possess a very considerable ability as an orchestrator, but his melodies are short-winded and show virtually no insight into character or dramatic situation. As one critic has so aptly observed: 'the inflated form leads to inflated music'. His influence on other composers (notably Donizetti, Verdi, the later French school and early Wagner) has been overestimated: it was one of style and presentation rather than of music.

Mezza voce (Italian for 'half voice')
Singing at half-power, in other words quietly and unemotionally.

Mezzo-contralto
A term which is occasionally used to denote a dark-hued mezzo-soprano whose voice is nearer in range and tonal colour to a true contralto than to a soprano.

Mezzo-soprano
see panel on page 366. See also ALTO; COLORATURA MEZZO; CONTRALTO

Mia letizia, La
Tenor aria for Oronte in Act II of Verdi's *I Lombardi*, in which he tells his mother of his love for Giselda.

Miami
see OPERA GUILD OF GREATER MIAMI

Micaëla
Soprano role in Bizet's *Carmen*. She is a country girl in love with Don José.

Mícha, Tobiaš
Bass role in Smetana's *The Bartered Bride*. A landowner, he is Vašek's and – as it turns out – Jeník's father.

Micheau, Janine (1914–76)
French soprano, particularly associated with lyrical French roles. Her voice, if occasionally slightly tremulous, was pleasingly silvery and used with fine musicianship, and she had an appealing stage presence. She created, for Milhaud, Créuse in *Médée* and Manuela in *Bolivar*.

Michele
Baritone role in Puccini's *Il Tabarro*. He is a bargee married to Giorgetta.

Mi chiamono Mimì
Soprano aria for Mimì in Act I of Puccini's *La Bohème*, in which she tells Rodolfo about herself.

Michonnet
Baritone role in Cilea's *Adriana Lecouvreur*. He is the stage manager of the Comédie-Française.

Midsummer Marriage, The
Opera in three acts by Tippett. 1st perf London, 27 Jan 1955; libr by the composer. Principal roles: Mark (ten), Jenifer (sop), King Fisher (bar), Bella (sop), Jack (ten), He- and She-Ancients (bass and mezzo), Sosostris (cont). Tippett's first and most frequently performed opera, it is an orchestrally lush symbolic work telling of two couples' quests for sexual and spiritual fulfilment.
Plot: 20th-century England, Midsummer Day. Mark is engaged to Jenifer, daughter of the business tycoon King Fisher, but she feels the need to seek and find a greater understanding of herself before she can go through with the wedding ceremony. The two enter, separately, a cave in a mysterious clearing in the woods, and are followed by King Fisher, his secretary Bella and her boyfriend Jack. After a series of rituals and dances held under the auspices of the two Ancients, which involves the death of King Fisher, the couple emerge, having found new understanding, both of themselves and of each other, and are now ready to marry. [R]

· Mezzo-Soprano ·

Mezzo-soprano is the middle female vocal range, between soprano and contralto, and is often referred to simply as mezzo. The voice's range, of roughly g to b''', is similar to that of soprano minus the very top notes, but the voice is heavier and the tone is darker. There is no hard and fast distinction between mezzo and contralto; nowadays, mezzo is usually used to describe virtually all non-sopranos, with contralto reserved for exceptionally low and dark voices such as Kathleen Ferrier and Dame Clara Butt. The term mezzo-contralto is occasionally used to denote a mezzo nearer in range and tonal colour to a true contralto than to a soprano. The term COLORATURA MEZZO is also sometimes encountered, mainly in reference to Rossini roles such as the title-role in *La Cenerentola*.

Below are listed the 72 mezzos and contraltos with entries in this dictionary. Their nationalities are given in brackets afterwards.

Alboni, Marietta (It)
Anderson, Marian (US)
Arkhipova, Irina (Russ)
Baker, Dame Janet (Br)
Baltsa, Agnes (Gk)
Barbieri, Fedora (It)
Bartoli, Cecilia (It)
Berbié, Jane (Fr)
Berganza, Teresa (Sp)
Brambilla, Marietta (It)
Bumbry, Grace (US)
Burmeister, Annelies (Ger)
Butt, Dame Clara (Br)
Coates, Edith (Br)
Cossotto, Fiorenza (It)
Dernesch, Helga (Aus)
Elias, Rosalind (US)
Ewing, Maria (US)
Fassbaender, Brigitte (Ger)
Ferrier, Kathleen (Br)
Forrester, Maureen (Can)
Galli-Marié, Celestine (Fr)
Gorr, Rita (Belg)
Grisi, Giuditta (It)
Hodgson, Alfreda (Br)
Höffgen, Marga (Ger)
Hoffman, Grace (US)
Homer, Louise (US)
Höngen, Elisabeth (Ger)
Horne, Marilyn (US)
Howells, Anne (Br)
Jones, Della (Br)
Klose, Margarete (Ger)
Ludwig, Christa (Ger)
Malibran, María (Sp)
Meier, Waltraud (Ger)
Merriman, Nan (US)
Meyer, Kerstin (Swe)
Minton, Yvonne (Aust)
Murray, Ann (Br)
Obraztsova, Elena (Russ)
Onegin, Sigrid (Swe)
Otter, Anne Sofie van (Swe)
Palmer, Felicity (Br)
Parr, Gladys (Br)
Pollak, Anna (Br)
Quivar, Florence (US)
Randová, Eva (Cz)
Resnik, Regina (US)
Schumann-Heink, Ernestine (Cz)
Simionato, Giulietta (It)
Sinclair, Monica (Br)
Stade, Frederica von (US)
Stevens, Risë (US)
Stignani, Ebe (It)
Supervia, Conchita (Sp)
Tassinari, Pia (It)
Thebom, Blanche (US)
Toczyska, Stefania (Pol)
Tourangeau, Huguette (Can)
Tourel, Jennie (Can)
Troyanos, Tatiana (US)
Unger, Caroline (Hung)
Valentini-Terrani, Lucia (It)
Veasey, Josephine (Br)
Verrett, Shirley (US)
Viardot-García, Pauline (Fr)
Walker, Edith (US)
Walker, Sarah (Br)
Watts, Helen (Br)
Zareska, Eugenia (Ukr)
Zimmermann, Margarita (Arg)

Midsummer Night's Dream, A
Opera in three acts by Britten (Op 64). 1st perf Aldeburgh, 11 June 1960; libr by the composer and Peter Pears, after William Shakespeare's play. Principal roles: Oberon (c-ten), Titania (sop), Bottom (bass), Lysander (ten), Demetrius (bar), Hermia (mezzo), Helena (sop), Puck (speaker), Peter Quince (bass), Flute (ten), Theseus (bass), Hippolyta (mezzo), Snout (ten), Snug (bass), Starveling (bar). One of Britten's finest operas, it is an ingenious and faithful setting of the play, and is notable for its brilliant and witty orchestration, for containing in Oberon the first operatic role written for a modern

counter-tenor, and for its operatic parody in the Pyramus and Thisbe scene – Flute has a mad scene. An immediate success, it is still regularly performed. [R]

Migenes-Johnson, Julia (b 1945)
American soprano who began as a SOUBRETTE but who has recently undertaken more dramatic roles. A powerful and at times flamboyant singing-actress of great intensity, who has a voice of highly individual timbre, she came to international prominence in 1984 playing Carmen in Franco Rosi's film. She created Toinette in Wolpert's *Der Eingebildete Kranke* and has also had considerable success as a television personality.

Mighty Handful, The or **The Mighty Five**
A translation of the Russian term *Moguchaya Kuchka*, it was coined by the critic VLADIMIR STASOV and was applied to the five great Russian nationalist composers: Balakirev, Borodin, Cui, Moussorgsky and Rimsky-Korsakov.

Mignon
Opera in three acts by Thomas. 1st perf Paris, 17 Nov 1866; libr by Jules Barbier and Michel Carré, after Johann von Goethe's *Wilhelm Meisters Lehrjahre*. Principal roles: Mignon (mezzo), Wilhelm (ten), Lothario (bass), Frédéric (mezzo), Philine (sop). Thomas's best and most enduring opera, notable for its fine overture.
Plot: Late-18th-century Germany and Italy. Wilhelm Meister purchases Mignon from a gypsy band which had abducted her as a child, in order to save her from the ill-treatment meted out to her. She serves him as a page, grows to love him and is jealous of his feelings for the actress Philine. Mignon has befriended the elderly and deranged minstrel Lothario (in fact her father, who has been searching for her). He overhears her wishing that a castle in which Philine is acting would catch fire. He sets it alight, unaware that Mignon has entered it. Wilhelm rescues her from the fire and realizes that he loves her. [R]

Mikado, The or **The Town of Titipu**
Operetta in two acts by Sullivan. 1st perf London, 14 March 1885; libr by W.S. Gilbert. Principal roles: Ko-Ko (bar), Nanki-Poo (ten), Yum-Yum (sop), Pooh-Bah (b-bar), Katisha (mezzo), Pish-Tush (bar), Mikado (bass), Pitti-Sing (mezzo), Peep-Bo (sop). An instant success, which enjoyed an initial run of 672 performances, it has remained ever since the most enduringly popular of all the Savoy Operas. Despite its Japanese setting, the butts of its satire are, of course, all very English.
Plot: The imaginary city of Titipu (Japan). Under the Mikado's law, the cheap tailor Ko-Ko was condemned to death for flirting but was reprieved at the last moment and appointed Lord High Executioner. He is due to marry Yum-Yum, one of his three wards, but she has fallen in love with the strolling musician Nanki-Poo. Nanki-Poo reveals to Yum-Yum that he is in fact the Mikado's son, who fled from court to escape the attentions of the elderly Katisha. The Mikado sends word that he is displeased that no executions have taken place recently and requires the situation to be rectified within a month. Nanki-Poo, in despair because he cannot have Yum-Yum, agrees to be executed in a month rather than commit suicide, provided that he can marry Yum-Yum in the meantime. Ko-Ko agrees, but just after the wedding the Mikado is seen approaching and Ko-Ko cannot bring himself to execute anyone. He makes a false affidavit of execution, but Katisha sees Nanki-Poo's name on it. The Mikado – although 'not a bit angry' – condemns Ko-Ko to death for compassing the death of the heir apparent. Ko-Ko persuades Katisha to love him and she pleads successfully with the Mikado for mercy. [R]

Milan
see PICCOLA SCALA, LA; TEATRO ALLA SCALA, MILAN

Milanov, Zinka (b Kunc) (1906–89)
Croatian soprano, particularly associated with heavier Verdi roles, especially Leonora in *Il Trovatore*. Largely resident first at the Zagreb Opera and then from 1938 at the Metropolitan Opera, New York, she was one of the outstanding Verdi sopranos of the immediate post-war period, possessing a voice of great beauty and sensitivity.

Mildmay, Audrey (1900–53)
British soprano, particularly associated with Mozart roles. Her marriage to JOHN CHRISTIE inspired the foundation of the Glyndebourne Festival, and she was also a co-founder of the Edinburgh Festival.

Mild und leise
Soprano aria (the *Liebestod*) for Isolde in Act III of Wagner's *Tristan und Isolde*. Sung over Tristan's body, it is the final scene of the opera.

Miles
Treble role in Britten's *The Turn of the Screw*. He is the boy corrupted by the ghost of a former manservant.

Milhaud, Darius (1892–1974)
French composer. A member of the group LES SIX and one of the most prolific 20th-century French composers, he wrote many stage works in a variety of styles and forms. They include *La Brebis Égarée* (Paris, 10 Dec 1923, composed 1915; libr Francis Jammes), *Esther de Carpentras* (Paris Radio, May 1937, composed 1925; libr Armand Lunel), LES MALHEURS D'ORPHÉE, perhaps his most successful opera, LE PAUVRE MATELOT, CHRISTOPHE COLOMB, MAXIMILIEN, *Médée* (Angers, 7 Oct 1939; libr Madeleine Milhaud, after Euripides's *Medea*), BOLIVAR, LES CHOËPHORES, DAVID, *Fiesta* (Berlin, 3 Oct 1958; libr Boris Vian), *La Mère Coupable* (Geneva, 13 June 1966; libr M. Milhaud, after Pierre Augustin Caron de Beaumarchais) and *Saint Louis* (RAI, 18 Mar 1972; libr Paul Claudel). He also wrote the three OPÉRAS-MINUTES as well as three children's operas. His autobiography, *Ma Vie Heureuse*, was published in 1974.

Miller
Baritone role in Verdi's *Luisa Miller*. Luisa's father, he is an old soldier.

Miller, Jonathan (b 1934)
British producer (and also a qualified doctor), associated first with Kent Opera and later with the English National Opera. His productions are notable for their striking innovativeness and originality of setting, as shown in his 'Mafia' *Rigoletto*, set in New York in the 1950s, and in his 1920s *The Mikado*. His strong feel for character interplay was demonstrated in his deeply disturbing production of *The Turn of the Screw*.

Millo, Aprile (b 1958)
American soprano, particularly associated with the Italian repertory, especially Verdi and Puccini. Possessing a good stage presence and an excellent voice used with an assured technique, she is one of the finest *lirico spinto* sopranos to have come to the fore in recent years.

Millöcker, Karl (1842–99)
Austrian composer. He wrote many Viennese operettas, of which the most successful were *Gräfin Dubarry* (Vienna, 31 Oct 1879; libr F. Zell and Richard Genée), DER BETTELSTUDENT, his most famous work, GASPARONE and *Der Arme Jonathan* (Vienna, 4 Jan 1890; libr H. Wittmann and Julius Bauer). *Die Dubarry* (1931) [R Exc] is a pastiche of his music arranged by Theo Mackeben.

Milnes, Rodney (b Blumer) (b 1936)
British critic. One of the most discerning, constructive, lively and witty of contemporary British opera critics, he has written for *The Spectator*, *The Evening Standard* and *The Times* and became editor of *Opera* in 1986. He has also made several successful opera translations.

Milnes, Sherrill (b 1935)
American baritone, particularly associated with the Italian repertory, especially Verdi. His incisive and intelligently-used voice had a firm line and thrilling high notes, but he was not really a true Verdi baritone. He had a strong if somewhat generalized stage presence. He created Adam Brandt in Levy's *Mourning Becomes Electra*. His wife **Nancy Stokes** was a soprano.

Milton
Opera in one act by Spontini. 1st perf Paris, 27 Nov 1804; libr by Victor Joseph Étienne de Jouy. Principal roles: Milton (bass), Emma (sop), Davenant (ten), Godwin (bass), Carlotta (mezzo). Based on the life of the English poet John Milton (1608–74), it was Spontini's first major success. A fine work, it is nowadays all but forgotten. A revised version, *Das Verlorence Paradies*, was left unfinished at Spontini's death.

Plot: Mid-17th-century Horton (Buckinghamshire). Milton, sought as a rebel by the authorities, has taken refuge at the home of the Quaker Godwin. His daughter Emma and Godwin's niece Carlotta both love Milton's reader Arthur, who returns Emma's love. Arthur is revealed as Lord Davenant and produces a royal pardon for the poet, secured by Davenant. He asks for Emma's hand and Milton gladly agrees.

Mime
Tenor role in Wagner's *Das Rheingold* and *Siegfried*. A Nibelung dwarf, he is Alberich's brother.

Mimì
Soprano role in Puccini's and Leoncavallo's *La Bohème*. She is a poor seamstress.

Mines of Sulphur, The
Opera in three acts by Bennett. 1st perf London, 24 Feb 1965; libr by Beverley Cross. Principal roles: Jenny (sop), Boconnion (ten), Rosalind (mezzo), Tovey (bar), Braxton (b-bar), Leda (mezzo), Fenney (ten), Sherrin (b-bar). Bennett's most successful opera, it is written in serial style, but much of the vocal writing is nonetheless lyrical and readily accessible. It tells of the murder by a deserter and his gypsy girlfriend of the 18th-century owner of a manor house, for which the arrival of a group of strolling players acts as catalyst.

Minimalism
A form of musical composition pioneered by Glass (and given its name by Michael Nyman), in which the same musical figure is repeated many times before modulating to another figure only very slightly different; this figure is in turn repeated many times, and so on indefinitely. The most successful minimalist operas have been Glass's AKHNATEN and Adams's NIXON IN CHINA.

Minnie
Soprano role in Puccini's *La Fanciulla del West*. She is the miners' Bible teacher.

Minton, Yvonne (b 1938)
Australian mezzo, particularly associated with Mozart, Strauss, Wagner and Berlioz roles. One of the leading mezzos of the 1970s, she possessed a rich and beautiful voice used with unfailing musicianship, and she had a strong stage presence. She created Thea in *The Knot Garden*, Maggie Dempster in Maw's *One Man Show* and Countess Geschwitz in the three-act version of *Lulu*.

Miolan-Carvalho, Marie (b Caroline Félix) (1827–95)
French soprano, particularly associated with the French repertory. The leading French lyric soprano of the mid-19th century, she created, for Gounod, Marguerite in *Faust*, Baucis in *Philémon et Baucis*, Juliette in *Roméo et Juliette* and the title-role in *Mireille*. Married to the administrator LÉON CARVALHO.

Mio tesoro, Il
Tenor aria for Don Ottavio in Act II of Mozart's *Don Giovanni*, in which he sings of his love for Donna Anna.

Mira, o Norma
Soprano/soprano duet for Norma and Adalgisa in Act II of Bellini's *Norma*, in which Adalgisa begs Norma not to renounce her children.

Miracle, Dr
Bass role in Offenbach's *Les Contes d'Hoffmann*. He is a sinister quack who treats Antonia by remote control.

Miracle of Our Lady, The (*Hry o Marii*)
Opera in four parts by Martinů. 1st perf Brno, 23 Feb 1935; libr by the composer, Henri Ghéon and Vítězslav Nezval, after Flemish and Moravian folk tales. Principal roles: Mariken (sop), Devil (bar), Archangel Gabriel (cont), Foolish Virgin (mezzo), Mary (sop), Paskalina (sop), Marta (mezzo). It is a cycle of four mystery plays: **1** *Wise Virgins and Foolish Virgins* (*Panny Moudré a Panny Pošetilé*), **2** *Mariken of Nimègue*, **3** *The Nativity* (*Narození Páně*) and **4** *Sister Pasqualina* (*Sestra Paskalina*). Although it contains some beautiful music, it is only very rarely performed. [R]

Mireille
Opera in three (originally five) acts by

Gounod. 1st perf Paris, 19 March 1864; libr by Michel Carré, after Frédéric Mistral's *Mirèio*. Revised version 1st perf Paris, 15 Dec 1864. Principal roles: Mireille (sop), Vincent (ten), Ourrias (bar), Taven (mezzo) Maître Ramon (bass). Containing some of Gounod's most beautiful music, it is still quite often performed in France but only infrequently elsewhere.
Plot: 19th-century Arles. Mireille loves Vincent, but her father Maître Ramon wishes her to marry the bull-tender Ourrias. Mireille and Vincent agree to meet at a certain place of sanctuary if they are in trouble. Ourrias attempts to kill Vincent but fails. The lovers meet at their sanctuary and Maître Ramon finally blesses their union. (In the original version, Vincent is killed by Ourrias who then drowns, and Mireille dies of exhaustion attempting to reach the sanctuary.) [R]

Mir ist die Ehre Widerfahren
The Presentation of the Rose in Act II of Strauss's *Der Rosenkavalier*.

Mir is so wunderbar
Soprano/soprano/tenor/bass quartet for Marzelline, Leonore, Jacquino and Rocco in Act I of Beethoven's *Fidelio*. It is the canon in which the four express outwardly similar feelings of wonder for inwardly dissimilar reasons.

Misail
Tenor role in Moussorgsky's *Boris Godunov*. He is an itinerant monk.

Miserere
Soprano aria for Leonora in Act IV of Verdi's *Il Trovatore*, in which off-stage monks chant whilst Leonora sings beneath the tower in which Manrico is being held. The words are the opening of Psalm 51.

Miserly Knight, The
see COVETOUS KNIGHT, THE

Miss Julie
Opera in two acts by Alwyn. 1st perf BBC Radio, 17 Feb 1977; libr by the composer, after August Strindberg's play. Principal roles: Miss Julie (sop), Jean (bar), Kristin (mezzo), Ulrik (ten). Alwyn's finest opera, which deserves to be better known.
Plot: Sweden, 1895. After flirting with the cook Kristin, the Count's valet Jean plays up to Miss Julie. She responds to his advances, but they are interrupted by the drunken gamekeeper Ulrik. She hides, but Ulrik insinuates that he is aware of what is going on. Julie agrees to elope with Jean, but after a night spent together she regrets her behaviour. However, she agrees to pack and steal the Count's money. Kristin and Ulrik see her ready for travel and, after a violent scene involving the killing of her dog on Jean's orders, the Count is heard returning. Jean points to a razor blade, telling her that the only remedy for her compromised honour is to follow her mother's example and commit suicide. [R]

Mitchell, Leona (b 1949)
American soprano, particularly associated with the Italian and French repertories. She possesses a rich and creamy voice used with fine musicianship, and she has an affecting stage presence.

Mitchinson, John (b 1932)
British tenor, particularly associated with heavier German and Czech roles. Long established as a concert artist, he turned to opera only much later in his career, successfully undertaking roles such as Tristan and Dalibor. An often underrated singer, he displayed great musicianship and sensitivity and was possibly the finest lyrico-heroic British tenor of the post-war era. He created Solano in Delius's *The Magic Fountain* and the Poet in Tal's *Masada 967*. His wife **Maureen Guy** was a successful mezzo.

Mitridate, Rè di Ponto (*Mithridates, King of Pontus*)
Opera in three acts by Mozart (K 87). 1st perf Milan, 26 Dec 1770; libr by Vittorio Amadeo Cigna-Santi, after Jean Baptiste Racine's *Mithridate*. Principal roles: Mitridate (ten), Aspasia (sop), Sifare (mezzo), Farnace (c-ten), Ismene (sop), Arbate (mezzo), Marzio (ten). Telling of Mithridates Eupator (*c* 132–63 BC), it is Mozart's first full-length serious opera, written at the age of 14. A work of astonishing musical fluency and assurance, it has received a number of performances in the last decade.
Plot: Nymphaeum, 63 BC. Mitridate and

his two sons Farnace and Sifare – each of a different and former marriage – vie for the affections of Aspasia. Farnace, betrothed to Ismene, is also in alliance with Mitridate's enemies, the Romans. He redeems his honour by avenging his father's defeat by the Romans, and the dying Mitridate, having taken poison, gives him his blessing. [R]

Mitropoulos, Dmitri (1896–1960)
Greek conductor and composer. One of the outstanding conductors of the mid-20th century, at his best in complex works such as Berg's *Wozzeck*, his operatic appearances were sadly infrequent. He conducted the first performance of Barber's *Vanessa*, and himself wrote one opera, *Soeur Béatrice* (Athens, 1920; libr after Maurice Maeterlinck). The Dmitri Mitropoulos Prize, established in his memory in 1961, is one of the world's most prestigious conducting competitions.

Mittenhofer, Gregor
Baritone role in Henze's *Elegie für Junge Liebende*. He is an egotistical poet.

Miura, Tamaki (1884–1946)
Japanese soprano, particularly associated with the Italian and French repertories, especially Cio-Cio-San in *Madama Butterfly*. She was the first oriental artist to enjoy a major career in Western music.

Mlada
Unfinished opera-ballet in four acts by Borodin, Cui, Moussorgsky and Rimsky-Korsakov. Begun 1872; libr by Viktor Krylov. Abandoned because of expense, little of the work was actually written, Borodin's final dance being the only substantial portion which survives. Rimsky later set the whole work (see below).

Mlada
Opera in four acts by Rimsky-Korsakov. 1st perf St Petersburg, 1 Nov 1892; libr by the composer, after Viktor Krylov's libretto for the unfinished collective opera-ballet (see above). Principal roles: Voislava (sop), Jaromir (ten), Mstivoi (bass), Lumir (mezzo), Morena (mezzo), High Priest (bar), Mlada (dancer). A loosely-knit historical pageant, it is only very rarely performed, even in Russia, despite its colourful and exciting music.
Plot: 10th-century Pomerania. To remove her rival for the affections of Jaromir, Voislava poisons Mlada. Morena, the queen of the underworld, causes Jaromir to love Voislava, but Mlada's spirit appears and tells him what happened. The High Priest advises Jaromir to interrogate the spirits sent by Morena to haunt him, and they affirm Voislava's guilt. When Voislava is condemned to death, Morena raises a great storm which kills Jaromir, which unites him with Mlada for ever. [R]

Mödl, Martha (b 1912)
German soprano and later mezzo, particularly associated with Wagnerian roles. Beginning as a mezzo, she turned to dramatic soprano roles, becoming one of the leading Brünnhildes of the 1950s. A warm-voiced dramatic singer of great intelligence, she returned to the mezzo repertory in the 1960s, latterly singing character roles such as the Countess in *The Queen of Spades*. She created Abbot Lambert in Wilfried Hiller's *Der Rattenfänger*, the Mother in Cerha's *Baal*, roles in Einem's *Kabale und Liebe* and Fortner's *Elisabeth Tudor* and, for Reimann, the Mummy in *Die Gespenstersonate* and a role in *Melusine*. She enjoyed an exceptionally long career, singing up to the age of 80.

Moffo, Anna (b 1935)
American soprano, particularly associated with lighter Italian and French roles. She had a seductive and agile voice and was an appealing singing-actress of great personal beauty. Her charms – both vocal and physical – were not always wisely deployed, however, and her voice deteriorated severely at an early age. Her attempted comeback in the early 1970s was unsuccessful.

Moïse et Pharaon
see MOSÈ IN EGITTO

Moldavian opera composers
These include David Herschfeld (*b* 1911), whose *Grozovan* (1956) was the first national Moldavian opera, Yevgeny Koka (1893–1954), Mark Kopitman (*b* 1929), Edward Lazarev (*b* 1935), Solomon Lobel (1910–81) and Zlata Tkach (*b* 1928).

· Molière ·

The French playwright and actor Molière (*b* Jean-Baptiste Poquelin) (1622–73) himself assisted in laying the foundations of French opera through his collaborations with Lully and M.-A. Charpentier. They produced a number of comedy-ballets, of which the most famous is *Le Bourgeois Gentilhomme*. Molière's works have inspired over 80 operas. Below are listed, by play, those operas by composers with entries in this dictionary.

Les Amants Magnifiques		
Lully	*Les Amants Magnifiques*	1670
L'Amour Médecin		
Lully	*L'Amour Médecin*	1675
Wolf-Ferrari	*L'Amore Medico*	1913
Hughes	*Love the Doctor*	1960
L'Avare		
Pashkevich	*The Miser*	1782
Le Bourgeois Gentilhomme		
Lully	*Le Bourgeois Gentilhomme*	1670
Hasse	*Larinda e Vanesio*	1726
Strauss	*Ariadne auf Naxos* (prologue only)	1916
L'École des Femmes		
Liebermann	*The School for Wives*	1955
Mortari	*La Scoula delle Moglie*	1959
L'École des Maris		
Bondeville	*L'École des Maris*	1936
Georges Dandin		
Lully	*Georges Dandin*	1668
Le Malade Imaginaire		
Charpentier	*Le Malade Imaginaire*	1673
Napoli	*Il Malato Immaginario*	1939
Pauer	*The Hypochondriac*	1970
Le Mariage Forcé		
Lully	*Le Mariage Forcé*	1664
Le Médecin Malgré Lui		
Gounod	*Le Médecin Malgré Lui*	1858
Le Médecin Volant		
Veretti	*Il Medico Volante*	1927
Le Misanthrope		
Caldara	*I Disingannati*	1729
Monsieur de Pourceaugnac		
Lully	*Monsieur de Pourceaugnac*	1669
Franchetti	*Il Signor di Pourceaugnac*	1897
Martin	*Monsieur de Pourceaugnac*	1963
Les Précieuses Ridicules		
Galuppi	*Le Virtuose Ridicole*	1752
Lattuada	*Le Preziose Ridicole*	1929
Bush	*If the Cap Fits*	1956

La Princesse d'Élide		
Galuppi	*Alcimena*	1749
Psyché		
Lully	*Psyché*	1678
Uttini	*Psyché*	1766
Sganarelle		
Wagner-Régeny	*Sganarelle*	1929
Pasatieri	*Il Signor Deluso*	1974
Le Sicilien		
Lully	*Le Sicilien*	1667
Dibdin	*The Metamorphoses*	1776
Dauvergne	*Le Sicilien*	1780
Tartuffe		
Benjamin	*Tartuffe*	1964 (U)
Malipiero	*Don Tartufo Bacchetone*	1970

Molière
see panel above

Molinara, La (*The Maid of the Mill*) or **L'Amor Contrastate** (*Doubtful Love*)
Comic opera in three acts by Paisiello. 1st perf Naples, autumn 1788; libr by Giovanni Palomba. Principal roles: Rachelina (sop), Caloandro (ten), Pistofolo (b-bar), Rospolone (bass). One of Paisiello's best works, which was long popular, it is nowadays largely remembered for containing the famous 'Nel cor più'.
Plot: 18th-century Italy. The pretty mill-owner Rachelina is courted by the young Coloandro, the lawyer Pistofolo and the elderly governor Rospolone. In an attempt to outmanoeuvre Rospolone, Coloandro disguises himself as a gardener and Pistofolo pretends to be a miller. Rachelina choses Pistofolo, whereupon Coloandro goes mad and attempts to kill Pistofolo. The rejected Rospolone successfully intimates to Rachelina that Pistofolo is also insane. Rather than marry a madman, Rachelina decides to stay single.

Molinari-Pradelli, Francesco (b 1911)
Italian conductor, particularly associated with the Italian repertory. Appearing mainly at La Scala, Milan, and the Metropolitan Opera, New York, he was rock-solid and reliable if not always particularly inspiring.

Moll, Kurt (b 1938)
German bass, particularly associated with Wagner, Mozart and Strauss roles. One of the finest contemporary Germanic basses, he possesses a large, rich and beautiful voice which he uses with intelligence and fine musicianship. He is an accomplished singing-actor, equally at home in serious or comic roles. He created the King in Bialas's *Der Gestiefelte Kater*.

Monaco
see MONTE CARLO OPERA

Monaco, Mario del (1915–82)
Italian tenor, particularly associated with heavier Italian roles, especially the title-role in Verdi's *Otello*. The leading TENORE DI FORZA of the 1950s and one of the greatest post-war Otellos, he possessed a thrilling voice of considerable range and great power which he used to strong dramatic effect. His autobiography, *La Mia Vita e i Miei Successi*, was published in 1982. His wife **Rina Solveni** (1918–91) was a soprano; their son **Giancarlo** (*b* 1943) is a successful producer.

Mona Lisa
Opera in prologue, two acts and epilogue by Schillings. 1st perf Stuttgart, 26 Sept 1915; libr by Beatrice Dovsky. Principal roles: Wife/Mona Lisa (sop), Lay Brother/Giovanni (ten), Husband/Giocondo (bar). Schillings's most successful opera, which is still occasionally performed, it is a gruesome piece of VERISMO.
Plot: Florence, the present and 1492. In the prologue, a honeymooning couple visit

a Carthusian monastery, where a lay brother recounts the tale of Mona Lisa. Her elderly husband Francesco del Giocondo shut her lover Giovanni del Salviati into a cupboard to suffocate. When Giocondo opened the cupboard, Mona Lisa pushed him in and locked it. In the epilogue, the three characters are shown to be the modern counterparts of those in the story.

Monckton, Lionel (1861–1924)
British composer and critic. He wrote a number of operettas and musical comedies. Nowadays he is largely remembered for the sensationally successful THE ARCADIANS, written in collaboration with Talbot, and for *The Quaker Girl* (London, 5 Nov 1910; libr James T. Tanner, Adrian Ross and Percy Greenbank).

Mon coeur s'ouvre à ta voix (often known in English as 'Softly awakes my heart') Mezzo aria for Dalila in Act II of Saint-Saëns's *Samson et Dalila*, in which she nearly succeeds in extracting from Samson the secret of his strength.

Mond, Der: ein kleines Welttheater (*The Moon: a Little World Theatre*)
Opera in three acts by Orff. 1st perf Munich, 5 Feb 1939; libr by the composer, after Jacob and Wilhelm Grimm's *Fairy Tales*. Principal roles: Narrator (ten), four Boys (ten, bar, bar and bass), St Peter (b-bar). One of Orff's most successful operas, it is still quite often performed in Germany.
Plot: Four boys steal the Moon, each taking a quarter of it to their graves. As the world darkens, the boys put the pieces back together and raise up the Moon as a lamp. This causes all the dead to awaken with such an uproar that St Peter hears it in Heaven, descends to the nether regions, takes the Moon and puts it in the heavens as a star. [R]

Mondo della Luna, Il (*The World on the Moon*)
Comic opera in three acts by Haydn. 1st perf Esterháza, 3 Aug 1777; libr by P.F. Pastor, after Carlo Goldoni's play. Principal roles: Ecclitico (ten), Buonafede (bar), Lisetta (mezzo), Clarice (sop), Flaminia (sop), Ernesto (mezzo), Cecco (ten). A delightful work, it is Haydn's most frequently performed opera.
Plot: 18th-century Venice. The wealthy merchant Buonafede opposes his daughter Flaminia's wish to marry Ernesto. The pseudo-astrologer Ecclitico, who loves Buonafede's other daughter Clarice, deceives the merchant into believing that he can travel through the heavens. Ecclitico gives Buonafede a drugged potion and disguises his garden as a moonscape. There, Buonafede is tricked into allowing the lovers to marry the mates of their choice. When the deception is revealed, he eventually forgives everyone. [R]

Mondonville, Jean-Joseph Cassanéa de (1711–72)
French composer and violinist, chosen as the representative of the traditional French school in the GUERRE DES BOUFFONS. His operas and opera-ballets, now largely forgotten, are *Isbé* (Paris, 10 Apr 1742; libr Marquis H.-F. de la Rivière), *Bacchus et Erigone* (Versailles, 1747; libr C.A. le Clerc de la Bruère), *Le Carnaval du Parnasse* (Paris, 23 Sept 1749; libr Louis Fuzelier), *Vénus et Adonis* (Paris, 27 Apr 1752; libr J.B. Collet de Messine), *Titon et l'Aurore* (Paris, 9 Jan 1753; libr C.-H. de F. de Voisenon and Abbé de la Marre) [R], *Daphnis et Alcimadure* (Fontainebleau, 29 Oct 1754; libr composer), *Les Fêtes de Paphos* (Paris, 9 May 1758; libr Voisenon, la Bruère and Charles Collé), *Thésée* (Fontainebleau, 7 Nov 1765; libr Philippe Quinault) and *Les Projects de l'Amour* (Paris, 29 May 1771; libr Voisenon).

Moniuszko, Stanisław (1819–72)
Polish composer. Poland's most important opera composer, and a crucial figure in the development of Polish national music, be began as an operetta composer. His first opera HALKA was an immediate success and remains his best-known work. His other operas include THE RAFTSMAN, *The Countess* (*Hrabina*, Warsaw, 7 Feb 1860; libr Włodzimierz Wolski, after J. Dierzowski) [R Exc], *Verum Nobile* (Warsaw, 1 Jan 1861; libr Jan Checiński) [R], the highly successful THE HAUNTED MANOR and *Paria* (Warsaw, 11 Dec 1869; libr Checiński, after Casimir Delavigne). He was musical director of the Warsaw National Opera.

Monna Vanna
Opera in four acts by Février. 1st perf Paris, 10 Jan 1909; a word-for-word setting of Maurice Maeterlinck's play. Principal roles: Monna Vanna (sop), Prinzivalle (ten), Colonna (bar). Février's most successful opera, it is nowadays virtually forgotten.
Plot: Late-15th-century Pisa. The Florentine commander Prinzivalle offers to lift his forces' siege of the city if Monna Vanna, married to the Pisan leader Guido Colonna, will come to him. Colonna refuses the offer, but Monna is prepared to make the sacrifice to save the city. Prinzivalle recognizes her as a childhood friend and respects her honour, whilst also lifting the siege. Colonna refuses to believe that his wife has not been compromised and has Prinzivalle jailed. This causes Monna to turn against her husband: she obtains the prison key, tells Prinzivalle that she loves him, and the two escape together.

Monodrama
The term has two meanings in opera: **1** Strictly speaking, a MELODRAMA with one actor. **2** More generally, the term is used of any work with a single character, such as Schönberg's *Erwartung*, Poulenc's *La Voix Humaine* and Weisgall's *The Stronger*.

Monostatos
Tenor role in Mozart's *Die Zauberflöte*. He is Sarastro's Moorish slave.

Monpou, Hippolyte (1804–41)
French composer. He wrote a number of comic operas which enjoyed some success in their day but which are all now forgotten. They include *Les Deux Reines* (Paris, 6 Aug 1835; libr Arnould and F. Soulié), *Le Luthier de Vienne* (Paris, 30 June 1836; libr Adolphe de Leuven and Jules-Henri Vernoy de Saint-Georges), *Le Piquillo* (Paris, 31 Oct 1837; libr Alexandre Dumas père), *Le Planteur* (Paris, 1 Mar 1839; libr Saint-Georges) and the unfinished *Lambert Simnel* (Paris, 14 Sept 1843; libr Eugène Scribe and Anne-Honoré Joseph de Mélesville), which was completed by Adam.

Monsieur Beaucaire
Operetta in prologue and three acts by Messager. 1st perf Birmingham, 7 April 1919; libr by André Rivoir and Pierre Veber, after Booth Tarkington's novel. Principal roles: Beaucaire (bar), Mary (sop), Lucy (mezzo), Molyneux (ten). One of Messager's most successful works, set in the time of the dandy Beau Nash, it still receives an occasional performance.
Plot: Late-18th-century Bath. Philip Molyneux tells his beloved, the coquettish Lady Lucy, that the fashionable French barber Beaucaire has fallen for Lady Mary Carlisle. Through an aristocratic friend, he is introduced to her as the Duke of Châteaurien. When his lowly status is revealed, Mary decides that she loves him all the same. The French Ambassador arrives with a royal order ending the exile and the incognito of the supposed barber, who is none other than Louis Philippe, Duke of Orleans, the future French King. [R Exc]

Monsigny, Pierre-Alexandre (1729–1817)
French composer. He was a prolific composer of OPÉRA-COMIQUES, whose form he was responsible for deepening and enriching. The most important of his operas, which are notable for their great melodic charm, are *Le Cadi Dupé* (Paris, 4 Feb 1761; libr Pierre René Lemonnier, after *The Arabian Nights*), *Le Roi et le Fermier* (Paris, 22 Nov 1762; libr Jean-Marie Sedaine, after Robert Dodsley's *The King and the Miller of Mansfield*), *Rose et Colas* (Paris, 8 Mar 1764; libr Sedaine), *Aline Reine de Golconde* (Paris, 15 Apr 1766; libr Sedaine, after Jean Stanislas de Boufflers), *Le Déserteur* (Paris, 6 Mar 1769; libr Sedaine), his finest opera, *La Belle Arsène* (Fontainebleau, 6 Nov 1773; libr Charles–Simon Favart, after Voltaire's *La Bégueule*) and *Félix* (Fontainebleau, 10 Nov 1777; libr Sedaine). Nowadays, his operas are all virtually forgotten.

Montano
Bass COMPRIMARIO role in Verdi's *Otello*. He is Otello's predecessor as governor of Cyprus.

Montarsolo, Paolo (b 1925)
Italian bass, particularly associated with Italian BUFFO roles, especially Rossini. One of the leading buffos of the post-war era,

he enjoyed a remarkably long career and was a fine comic actor with a good, if not outstanding, voice. He created the title-role in Rota's *Notte di un Nevrastenico* and Marcopulos in Tosatti's *Fiera delle Maravaglie* and has also produced many operas.

Monte, Toti dal (b Antonietta Meneghel) (1893–1975)
Italian soprano, particularly associated with lighter Italian roles. The outstanding *soprano leggiero* of the inter-war period, her voice, although small and sometimes inclined to whiteness, was pure and extraordinarily agile. She created Rosalina in Giordano's *Il Rè* and her autobiography, *Una Voce nel Mondo*, was published in 1962.

Monte Carlo Opera
The Grand Théâtre (cap 600), designed by Jean-Louis-Charles Garnier, opened on 25 Jan 1879. Its greatest period was under the management of Raoul Gunsbourg (1859–1955) from 1893 to 1951, especially the first 20 years of the century, when many operas by leading French and Italian composers received their first performances. For a time, admission was free, as it was subsidized by the casino. The annual season runs from January to April and the repertory tends to be conservative. Artistic directors have included Henri Tomasi and Renzo Rossellini.

Montéclair, Michel Pignolet de (1667–1737)
French composer and double bass player. His two stage works are the opera-ballet *Les Festes de l'Été* (Paris, 12 June 1716; libr Abbé Joseph Simon Pellegrin) and the fine TRAGÉDIE-LYRIQUE *Jephté* (Paris, 28 Feb 1732; libr Pellegrin) [R], one of the earliest operas to be based on a biblical subject and notable for its choral writing.

Montemezzi, Italo (1875–1952)
Italian composer. Largely self-taught and writing in an eclectic late romantic style, his operas stand outside the mainstream of Italian music of his time. His first opera, the unperformed *Bianca* (*c* 1900; libr Z. Strani), was followed by *Giovanni Gallurese* (Turin, 28 Jan 1905; libr Francesco d'Angelantonio), *Héllera* (Turin, 17 Mar 1909; libr Luigi Illica, after Benjamin Constant's *Adolphe*) and the magnificent L'AMORE DEI TRE RE, his masterpiece. Its successors were the once-popular *La Nave* (Milan, 3 Nov 1918; libr Tito Ricordi, after Gabriele d'Annunzio), *La Notte di Zoraima* (Milan, 31 Jan 1931; libr Mario Ghisalberti) and the radio opera *L'Incantesino* (NBC, 1943; libr Sem Benelli).

Monterone, Count
Bass-baritone role in Verdi's *Rigoletto*. He is an old nobleman whose daughter has been seduced by the Duke.

Monteux, Pierre (1876–1964)
French conductor, particularly associated with the French repertory. Although best known as a symphonic conductor, he also gave many fine opera performances in the United States and France. A consummate musician, he was a greatly loved artist with a delightful sense of humour: when he took over the London Symphony Orchestra at the age of 86, he insisted on a 25-year contact! He conducted the first performance of Stravinsky's *The Nightingale*.

Monteverdi, Claudio (1567–1643)
Italian composer. The first major figure in the history of opera, and one of the greatest of all opera composers, only a wretched portion of his stage works has survived. His first work for the stage, which combines the existing vocal and orchestral traditions with the new dramatic ideas of the FLORENTINE CAMERATA, is LA FAVOLA D'ORFEO, opera's earliest masterpiece. He wrote some works for a festival in Mantua in 1608, of which the opera-ballet IL BALLO DELLE INGRATE survives, as do fragments of the opera ARIANNA. Of the works which he wrote for Venice, Parma and Mantua in the 1620s only IL COMBATTIMENTO DI TANCREDI E CLORINDA is extant; at least 12 others are lost, including a comedy *La Finta Pazza* (1627; libr Giulio Strozzi). In his old age, he returned to opera with three final works: *Le Nozze d'Enea con Lavinia* (Venice, 1641; libr Giacomo Badoaro), which is lost, IL RITORNO D'ULISSE IN PATRIA and the magnificent L'INCORONAZIONE DI POPPEA.

Monteverdi was the first composer to grasp the essentials of music-drama and to execute them in music of beauty, subtlety and fluidity which illuminates and heightens emotional and dramatic situations. The first great musical delineator of character, both serious and comic, he was also the first (and is still one of the very few) composers to achieve true music-drama. For nearly 300 years his operas were all but forgotten, but nowadays he is acknowledged as the first opera composer of genius, and his works are firmly established in the repertory.

Montezuma
Opera in three acts by Graun. 1st perf Berlin, 6 Jan 1755; libr by Frederick the Great. Principal roles: Montezuma (mezzo), Eupaforice (sop), Tezeuco (ten), Pilpatoè (sop), Erissena (sop), Cortes (mezzo), Navrès (sop). Dealing with supposed events in the life of Montezuma II (1466–1520), the last Aztec ruler of Mexico, it is one of Graun's finest operas and still receives a very occasional performance.
Plot: Mexico, 1519–20. King Montezuma intends to wed Princess Eupaforice. His general Pilpatoè tells him of the barbarity of the newly-arrived Spaniards, but Montezuma extends them his hospitality. Ferdinando Cortes and his captain Navrès despise the heathen Aztecs, and Cortes decides to wed Eupaforice himself. His troops seize the city, slaughter the inhabitants and capture Montezuma. Cortes offers to spare Montezuma if Eupaforice will renounce her religion and marry him. She refuses and stabs herself as Montezuma is led to execution. [R]

Montezuma
Opera in three acts by Sessions. 1st perf Berlin, 19 April 1964; libr by Giuseppe Antonio Borgese, after Bernal Díaz del Castillo. Principal roles: Montezuma (ten), Díaz (bass), Malinche (sop), Córtez (bar), Alvarado (ten), Coanhutemoc (bar). Sessions' finest work, it is a lush historical pageant.
Plot: Early-16th-century Mexico. Through the eyes of the chronicler Bernal Díaz, are shown the Spanish landing in Mexico, the love of Fernand Córtez for Malinche, the controversy amongst the Spanish over how to treat the Aztecs, and the killing of Montezuma by his own people.

Montfort, Guy de
Baritone role in Verdi's *Les Vêpres Siciliennes*. Henri's father, he is the French governor of Sicily.

Montreal
see OPÉRA DE MONTRÉAL

Moore, Douglas (1893–1969)
American composer. Written in a lyrical and romantic style, his stage works are readily accessible, with a strong foundation in American folk music, and have met with considerable success in the United States. His operas include the chamber work *White Wings* (Hartford, 9 Feb 1949; libr Philip Barry), the fine THE DEVIL AND DANIEL WEBSTER, *Giants in the Earth* (New York, 28 Mar 1951; libr Arnold Sundgaard, after O.E. Rölvaag), THE BALLAD OF BABY DOE, one of the most successful of all American operas, and CARRY NATION.

Moore, Grace (1901–47)
American soprano, largely resident at the Metropolitan Opera, New York. After singing in musical comedy, she turned to opera, becoming particularly associated with the Italian and French repertories, especially the title-role in Charpentier's *Louise* (the film of which she starred in). A fine actress of great personal beauty, she was a great favourite with audiences, even if some maintained that her talents were predominantly plastic rather than vocal. She also enjoyed great success in the cinema, with films such as *New Moon*, *Love Me For Ever* and *One Night of Love*. Her autobiography, *You're Only Human Once*, was published in 1944. She was killed in an air crash.

Moravia
see BRNO OPERA; OLOMOUC OPERA; OSTRAVA OPERA

Mörder, Hoffnung der Frauen (*Murder, Hope of Women*)
Opera in one act by Hindemith (Op 12). 1st perf Stuttgart, 4 June 1921; libr by Oskar Kokoschka. Principal roles: Man (bar), Woman (sop). Hindemith's first

opera, it is written in his early expressionist style and represents a metaphor of the dualism between man and woman according to psychological theories current at the time. It is only very rarely performed. [R]

Moreno Torroba, Federico
see TORROBA, FEDERICO MORENO

Morgenlich leuchtend'
Tenor aria (the Prize Song) for Walther von Stolzing in Act III of Wagner's *Die Meistersinger von Nürnberg*.

Morison, Elsie (b 1924)
Australian soprano, particularly associated with Mozart roles. An expressive and musical singer with a good stage presence, she created the title-role in Hughes's *Menna*. Married to the conductor RAFAEL KUBELÍK.

Morlacchi, Francesco (1784–1841)
Italian composer. He wrote many operas which, although notable for their abundant melody, fine vocal writing and adventurous orchestration, are all now forgotten. His most successful operas include *Il Corradino* (Parma, 25 Feb 1808; libr Antonio Sografi), *Le Danaidi* (Rome, 11 Feb 1810; libr Stefano Scatizzi, after Pietro Metastasio's *Ipermestra*), *Il Barbiere di Siviglia* (Dresden, Apr 1816; libr Giuseppe Petrosellini, after Pierre Augustin Caron de Beaumarchais's *Le Barbier de Séville*) and *Tebaldo ed Isolina* (Venice, 4 Feb 1822; libr Gaetano Rossi). He was Kapellmeister (see MAESTRO DI CAPPELLA) in Dresden (1810–32), where he had a bitter rivalry with Weber, who said of him 'the fellow has little musical knowledge, but he has talent, a flow of ideas, and especially a fund of good comic stuff in him'.

Morris, James (b 1947)
American bass-baritone, particularly associated with Wagnerian roles, especially Wotan and the Dutchman in *Der Fliegende Holländer*. Often regarded as the leading contemporary Wotan, his voice is powerful and incisive, if not intrinsically beautiful. Although he has a strong (but somewhat generalized) stage presence, he can often seem uncommitted.

Morrò, ma prima in grazia
Soprano aria for Amelia in Act III of Verdi's *Un Ballo in Maschera*, in which she begs Ankerström to let her say farewell to their child before he kills her.

Mortari, Virgilio (1902–93)
Italian composer. His operas, in neo-classical style, include *La Scuola delle Mogli* (1930; libr Cesare Lodovici, after Molière's *L'École des Femmes*), *La Figlia del Diavolo* (Milan, 24 Mar 1954; libr Corrado Pavolini) and *Il Contratto* (RAI, 1962; libr G. Marotta and B. Randone). He was also a noted editor of the music of 17th- and 18th-century Italian composers, and made a new edition of Mozart's unfinished *L'Oca del Cairo* in 1936. He was administrator of the Teatro la Fenice, Venice (1955–9).

Mort d'Adam, La (*The Death of Adam*)
Opera in three acts by Lesueur. 1st perf Paris, 21 March 1809; libr by Nicolas François Guillard, after Friedrich Klopstock's *Der Tod Adams* and also drawing on John Milton's *Paradise Lost* and the Book of Genesis in the Old Testament. Principal roles: Adam (bass), Cain (ten), Seth (ten). One of the most ambitious operas ever written (calling for the entire population of heaven and hell), it has intermittent power and grandeur but fails overall to match its conception. It is notable for its complex early use of LEITMOTIF, Adam's death scene employing a dozen earlier themes.
Plot: Feeling the approach of death, Adam fears that his sons Cain and Seth will have to suffer for his own sins. Cain curses Adam, but his father forgives him. The Devil arrives to carry Adam to hell, but is defeated by the power of prayer, and Adam is raised up to heaven.

Mosca, Luigi (1775–1824)
Italian composer. His many operas, all nowadays forgotten, include *Gli Sposi in Cimenti* (Naples, Jan 1800; libr Saverio Zini) and *L'Italiana in Algieri* (Milan, 16 Aug 1808; libr Angelo Anelli), his most successful work which was soon eclipsed by Rossini's version. His brother **Giuseppe** (1772–1839) was also a composer. His more than 40 operas include *I Pretendenti Delusi* (Milan, 14 Apr 1811; libr Luigi Prividali), from which he claimed that

Rossini had stolen his use of the crescendo, and *Le Bestie in Uomini* (Milan, 17 Aug 1812; libr Anelli, after Lodovico Ariosto's *Orlando Furioso*).

Moscow
see BOLSHOI OPERA; MOSCOW CHAMBER OPERA

Moscow Chamber Opera
Founded in 1972 by the producer Boris Pokrovsky (*b* 1912), it specializes in the 18th-century repertory and in 20th-century Russian operas. Based at 71 Leningradsky Prospekt, the annual season runs for 11 months of the year. Its most famous production has been Shostakovich's *The Nose*, and it has pioneered the revival of pre-Glinka Russian operas. Musical directors have been Vladimir Delman, Gennadi Rozhdestvensky and Lev Ossovsky.

Mosè in Egitto (*Moses in Egypt*)
Opera in four (originally three) acts by Rossini. 1st perf Naples, 5 March 1818; libr by Andrea Leone Tottola, after Francesco Ringhieri's *L'Osiride*. Revised version *Moïse et Pharaon*, 1st perf Paris, 26 March 1827; libr revised by Luigi Balocchi and Victor-Joseph Étienne de Jouy. Principal roles (with *Moïse* second): Mosè/Moïse (bass), Elcia/Anaide (sop), Osiride/Oziride (ten/bass), Faraone/Pharaon (bar), Aronne/Eliser (ten), Amaltea/Sinaide (mezzo), Amenosi/Aménofis (mezzo/ten). One of the finest of Rossini's serious works, still quite often performed, it is notable for its grave and noble delineation of Moses and for its fine choruses. Most performances are given in a conflation of the two versions.
Plot: Legendary Egypt. Pharaoh has failed to keep his promise to release the Hebrews and Egypt is plunged into darkness. The dark is dispelled by Moses when Pharaoh relents. Fearful of losing the Hebrew Elcia, who he loves, Pharoah's son Osiride attempts to thwart the Hebrew's departure. His machinations are ultimately unsuccessful, and when he orders Moses's execution he is struck down by lightning. The Hebrews flee, and Moses parts the waters of the Red Sea for them to cross. Pharaoh and his pursuing army are overwhelmed. [R]

Moser, Augustin
Tenor COMPRIMARIO role in Wagner's *Die Meistersinger von Nürnberg*. A tailor, he is one of the masters.

Moses und Aron
Unfinished opera in three acts by Schönberg. 1st perf (in concert) Darmstadt, 2 July 1951 (composed 1932); 1st stage perf Zürich, 6 June 1957; libr by the composer, after the Book of Exodus in the Old Testament. Principal roles: Aron (ten), Moses (speaker or b-bar), Ephraimite (bar). Schönberg's last and greatest opera, the final act remained unset at his death. The work is usually performed in two acts, although some productions have included Act III with the text spoken.
Plot: Legendary Sinai. The inspired but inarticulate Moses cannot communicate to the Hebrews his revelation of God's word. He therefore allows his brother Aron to explain by miracles and other familiar images. Descending from Mount Sinai, Moses discovers the people worshipping the Golden Calf. He shatters the idol, but despairs of being able to put across his message without the help of a distorting intermediary such as Aron. [R]

Moshinsky, Elijah (b 1946)
Australian producer, particularly associated with Verdi operas. One of Britain's leading contemporary theatre directors, his opera productions are notable for their delineation of character and for their fine handling of crowd scenes, and are traditional in the best sense of the word. Associate producer at Covent Garden (1988–), his most successful productions there have included *Peter Grimes*, *Lohengrin* and *Stiffelio*.

Mother, The (*Matka*)
Opera in ten scenes by Hába (Op 35). 1st perf Munich, 19 May 1931; libr by the composer. Principal roles: Křen (ten), Maruša (sop), Sister-in-law (mezzo), Brother-in-law (bass). Hába's best-known work, it was the first (and remains the most important) QUARTER-TONE OPERA. It is only infrequently performed, partly because of its great technical difficulties.
Plot: Early-20th-century Moravia. The farmer Křen has worried his first wife to

death and has remarried. His new wife Maruša does not content herself with the traditional role of subservience to male will and passion. By her spiritual conception of conjugal love and motherhood, she eventually succeeds in breaking Křen's defiant nature. She bears children and educates them according to the image of her soul, and becomes the fellow-agent of life, for ever regenerating itself. [R]

Mother of Us All, The
Opera in three acts by Thomson. 1st perf New York, 7 May 1947; libr by Gertrude Stein. Principal roles: Susan Anthony (mezzo), Jo the Loiterer (ten), Anne (sop), Daniel Webster (bar). One of the finest of all American operas, it tells of the 19th-century American feminist leader Susan Brownell Anthony (1820–1906). [R]

Motif
see LEITMOTIF

Mottl, Felix (1856–1911)
Austrian conductor and composer, particularly associated with Wagner operas, all of whose vocal scores he edited. He was musical director of the Karlsruhe Staatstheater (1881–1903) and conducted the first performances of Part I of *Les Troyens*, Pfitzner's *Das Christelflein*, Schillings's *Ingwelde* and Wolf-Ferrari's *Il Segreto di Susanna* and *I Quatro Rusteghi*. He also composed three operas, including *Agnes Bernauer* (Weimar, 28 Mar 1880; libr composer). He died whilst conducting *Tristan und Isolde* in Munich. His wife **Zdenka Fassbender** (1879–1954) was a successful dramatic soprano.

Mouret, Jean-Joseph (1682–1738)
French composer. Director of the Paris Opéra (1714–18), his stage works include *Les Amours de Ragonde* (Sceaux, Dec 1714; libr Néricault Destouches) [R], one of the earliest French comic operas, and the TRAGÉDIE-LYRIQUE *Ariane* (Paris, 6 Apr 1717; libr F.-J. de Lagrange and Pierre Charles Roy).

Mousquetaires au Couvent, Les (*The Musketeers at the Convent*).
Operetta in three acts by Varney. 1st perf Paris, 16 March 1880; libr by Paul Ferrier and Jules Prével. Principal roles: Marie (sop), Gontran (ten), Louise (sop), Brissac (bar), Simone (mezzo), Bridaine (bass). Varney's most successful work, it is a delightful and amusing piece which is still sometimes performed in France.
Plot: Early-17th-century Vouvray (France). Gontran loves Marie, niece of the Governor of Touraine and a border at an Ursuline convent. For political reasons, the Governor wishes Marie and her sister Louise to take the veil immediately. With the aid of his friend the musketeer Capt Brissac and of Father Bridaine, Gontran enters the convent. After many vicissitudes, they are able, with the help of the innkeeper Simone, to thwart the Governor's plans. Marie and Gontran are united. [R]

Moussorgsky, Modest (1839–81)
Russian composer. A member of the MIGHTY HANDFUL, he was largely without formal musical training. He completed only one opera, but nonetheless ranks as one of the greatest of all opera composers. His first three operatic projects amounted to little more than sketches: *Han d'Islande* (1856; libr after Victor Hugo), *Oedipus in Athens* (1858; libr after V.A. Ozerov), which was incorporated into later works, and *St John's Eve* (1858; libr after Nikolai Gogol). Much more was written of his next opera SALAMMBÔ, but he completed only one act of THE MARRIAGE, an important work in that it sets Gogol's text verbatim and marks the first use of LEITMOTIF in Russian music. Next came his one completed work, his masterpiece BORIS GODUNOV, not only a seminal work in the development of Russian music, but also one of the finest music-dramas ever written. Only one scene of *The Landless Peasant* (1870; libr after F. Spielhagen's *Hans und Grete*) was completed, and the collective opera-ballet MLADA, written with Borodin, Cui and Rimsky-Korsakov, was abandoned. Much nearer to completion was the dark and magnificient KHOVANSCHINA, which was followed by the unfinished comedy SOROCHINTSY FAIR. His last project, *Pugachevschina* (1877; libr after Alexander Pushkin), amounts to little more than sketches.

Moussorgsky's genius and startling originality lie in his musical use of the inflections and speech rhythms of the Russian language, his unerring dramatic insight, his superb musical delineation of both serious and comic characters, his brilliant if highly unorthodox orchestration, and his nationalism and identification with the Russian people. One of the very few true musical dramatists, his influence on the subsequent history of music, not just in Russia, has been enormous.

Mozart, Wolfgang Amadeus (1756–91)
Austrian composer, son of the composer Leopold Mozart. A child prodigy, his first stage work, the sacred musical play DIE SCHULDIGKEIT DES ERSTEN GEBOTES, was written at the age of 11. His early operas, all of which display astonishing musical assurance, are the Latin comedy APOLLO ET HYACINTHUS, the OPERA BUFFA LA FINTA SEMPLICE, the little SINGSPIEL BASTIEN UND BASTIENNE, the OPERA SERIA MITRIDATE RÈ DI PONTO, ASCANIO IN ALBA, IL SOGNO DI SCIPIONE, the fine opera seria LUCIO SILLA and LA FINTA GIARDINIERA, his first work of real significance. It was followed by the pastoral IL RÈ PASTORE, the unfinished singspiel ZAÏDE and his first masterpiece, IDOMENEO. The highly successful DIE ENTFÜHRUNG AUS DEM SERAIL was followed by the two unfinished comedies, L'OCA DEL CAIRO and LO SPOSO DELUSO, and the theatrical satire DER SCHAUSPIELDIREKTOR before the full glories of his last five operas: LE NOZZE DI FIGARO, DON GIOVANNI, COSÌ FAN TUTTE, the Masonic DIE ZAUBERFLÖTE and the opera seria LA CLEMENZA DI TITO.

In his three great Italian works, written in collaboration with Lorenzo da Ponte, Mozart broke through the rigid structures of opera, presenting music-drama of great fluidity and remarkable human insight. His mastery of extended ensemble, his blending of serious and comic elements, his dramatic insight and his loosening of the musico-dramatic structures all had an incalculable influence on the subsequent development of opera. Mozart appears as a character in Hahn's *Mozart*, Rimsky-Korsakov's *Mozart and Salieri*, Flotow's *Die Musikanten* and the Lortzing pastiche *Szenen aus Mozarts Leben.*

Mozart and Salieri
Opera in two acts by Rimsky-Korsakov (Op 48). 1st perf Moscow, 7 Dec 1898; a virtual word-for-word setting of Alexander Pushkin's play. Principal roles: Salieri (bass), Mozart (ten). Dealing with the jealousy of mere talent for the unpredictability of genius, it perpetuates the myth that Salieri poisoned Mozart. It is still performed from time to time. [R]

Much Ado About Nothing
Opera in four acts by Standford (Op 76a). 1st perf London, 30 May 1901; libr by Julian Russell Sturgis, after William Shakespeare's play. Principal roles: Beatrice (mezzo), Benedict (bar), Hero (sop), Don John (bass), Claudio (ten), Don Pedro (bar), Borachio (ten), Leonato (bass). It is nowadays virtually forgotten.

Muck, Karl (1859–1940)
German conductor, particularly associated with the German repertory. Widely regarded as the finest Wagnerian conductor of his time, he was musical director of the Berlin State Opera (1908–12) and conducted the first performances of Kienzl's *Der Evangelimann* and Smyth's *The Forest.*

Muette de Portici, La (*The Dumb Girl of Portici*) (also known as *Masaniello*)
Opera in five acts by Auber. 1st perf Paris, 29 Feb 1828; libr by Eugène Scribe and Germain Delavigne. Principal roles: Masaniello (ten), Elvire (sop), Alphonse (ten), Pietro (bar), Fenella (mute). Telling of the Neapolitan fisherman Thomas Aniello (1622–47), who led an anti-Spanish revolt, it is arguably Auber's greatest opera, but is currently unjustly neglected. During a performance of the work in Brussels on 25 Aug 1830, the great patriotic duet 'Amour sacré de la patrie' caused a riot which sparked off the revolution which led to Belgian independence.
Plot: Naples, 1647. The fisherman Masaniello is moved by the oppression of his people by the Spanish. When the viceroy Alphonse betrays his dumb sister Fenella, he leads a revolt against Spanish rule. The revolt is initially successful but is subsequently crushed. Masaniello is killed and Fenella commits suicide by jumping into the erupting mouth of Mount Vesuvius. [R]

Mugnone, Leopoldo (1858–1941)
Italian conductor and composer, particularly associated with the Italian repertory. One of the most admired operatic conductors of his time, he conducted the first performances of *Cavalleria Rusticana*, *Tosca*, Franchetti's *La Figlia di Iorio* and Giordano's *Mese Mariano*. He also composed five operas.

Mulhouse
see OPÉRA DU RHIN

Müller, Wenzel (b Václav) (1767–1835)
Austrian composer. One of the most successful and prolific composers of SINGSPIELS, he wrote over 200 stage works, all of them now forgotten. The most successful included *Kaspar der Fagottist* (Vienna, 8 June 1791; libr J. Perinet), *Das Neue Sonntagskind* (Vienna, 10 Oct 1793; libr Perinet, after P. Hafner's *Der Furchtsame*) and *Die Teufelsmuhle am Wienerberg* (Vienna, 12 Nov 1799; libr K.F. Hensler).

Mullings, Frank (1881–1953)
British tenor, particularly associated with Wagnerian roles and with the title-role in Verdi's *Otello*. The only true British HELDENTENOR, he had a powerful voice and physique and was an imposing singing-actor. He created a role in Stanford's *The Critic* and, for Boughton, Apollo in *Alkestis* and Herod in *Bethlehem*.

Munich
see BAVARIAN STATE OPERA

Murray, Ann (b 1949)
British mezzo, particularly associated with Mozart, Händel, Rossini and Strauss roles and with the French repertory. Arguably the finest contemporary British mezzo, she is an outstanding singing-actress who possesses a beautiful voice of considerable range and great agility which is used with unfailing intelligence and musicianship. Married to the tenor PHILIP LANGRIDGE.

Musetta
Marcello's old flame, she appears as:
1 Soprano role in Puccini's *La Bohème*.
2 Mezzo role in Leoncavallo's *La Bohème*.

Musgrave, Thea (b 1928)
British composer. One of the most successful contemporary British opera composers, she has an assured sense of theatre and has written eight operas in lyrical serial style. They are *The Abbot of Drimock* (London, 19 Dec 1962, composed 1955; libr Maurice Lindsay), *The Decision* (London, 30 Nov 1967; libr Lindsay, after Ken Taylor's *The Devil and John Brown*), THE VOICE OF ARIADNE, MARY QUEEN OF SCOTS, A CHRISTMAS CAROL, *An Occurrence at Owl Creek* (BBC Radio, 14 Sept 1982; libr composer, after Ambrose Bierce), *Harriet, the Woman Called Moses* (Norfolk, 1 Mar 1985; libr composer) and *Simón Bolívar* (Norfolk, 20 Jan 1995; libr composer). Her husband **Peter Mark** (*b* 1940) is a conductor who is musical director of the Virginia Opera Association.

Music drama
A term used to describe an opera in which the musical and dramatic elements are intended to be totally fused. The term first came into prominence with Wagner who used it in his theoretical writings and to describe his later operas.

Musico (Italian for 'musician')
Originally applied (often in a slightly derogatory sense) to CASTRATI, the term was subsequently used in Italy in the first half of the 19th century to describe a young man's role sung by a mezzo or a contralto. Examples include Maffio Orsini in *Lucrezia Borgia*, Romeo in *I Capuleti e i Montecchi* and Smeton in *Anna Bolena*.

Musorgsky, Modeste
see MOUSSORGSKY, MODEST

Mustafà
Bass role in Rossini's *L'Italiana in Algieri*. The Bey of Algiers, he is married to Elvira.

Muti, Riccardo (b 1941)
Italian conductor, particularly associated with Mozart and with the Italian repertory, especially Verdi. One of the most brilliant and exciting of the younger generation of conductors, who has also championed lesser known composers such as Cherubini and Pergolesi, his performances

are noted for their intensity, their thorough preparation and their scrupulous regard for the composer's intentions. He was musical director of the Maggio Musicale Fiorentino (1977–80) and La Scala, Milan (1987–).

Muzio, Claudia (1889–1936)
Italian soprano, particularly associated with the Italian repertory. One of the leading lyric sopranos of the inter-war period, she possessed a beautiful voice and a warm stage presence. She created Giorgetta in *Il Tabarro*, Mariela in Smareglia's *L'Abiso* and the title-roles in Zandonai's *Melonis* and Refice's *Cecilia*.

Mysliveček, Joseph (1737–81)
Bohemian composer, largely resident in Italy, were he was known as 'il divino Boemo'. He wrote over 30 OPERA SERIAS, many to Metastasian texts. Perhaps his finest opera is *Il Bellerofonte* (Naples, 20 Jan 1767; libr Giuseppe Bonechi) [R]. Widely praised in his day, his operas are nowadays largely forgotten.

N

Nabokov, Nicolas (b Nikolai) (1903–78)
Russian-born American composer. He wrote two operas, both of which met with some success. They are *The Holy Devil* (Louisville, 16 Apr 1958; libr Stephen Spender; revised version *Der Tod der Grigori Rasputin*, Cologne, 27 Nov 1959) and *Love's Labour's Lost* (Brussels, 7 Feb 1973; libr W.H. Auden and Chester Kallman, after Shakespeare). He was secretary-general of the anti-communist Congress for Cultural Freedom.

Nabucco
Official title: **Nabucodonosor** (*Nebuchadnezzar*)
Opera in four acts by Verdi. 1st perf Milan, 9 March 1842; libr by Temistocle Solera, after Eugène Anicet-Bourgeois and Francis Cornu's play. Principal roles: Nabucco (bar), Abigaille (sop), Zaccaria (bass), Ishmael (ten), Fenena (mezzo), High Priest (bass). Verdi's third opera, it was an immediate and triumphant success and was the work which established his reputation. One of the most popular of Verdi's early operas, it is notable for its fine choruses and for the powerful characterization of the vengeful Abigaille.
Plot: Jerusalem and Babylon, 587 BC. The prophet Zaccaria comforts the Hebrews as the attacking Assyrian forces close in. The Hebrew Ishmael loves Fenena, younger daughter of the Assyrian King Nabucco, and rejects the love of Abigaille, Nabucco's elder but illegitimate child. Nabucco arrives in triumph and Zaccaria threatens to kill Fenena if the Temple is profaned. To the horror of his compatriots (who are unaware that Fenena is a secret convert), Ishmael releases Fenena and Nabucco orders the destruction of Jerusalem. In Nabucco's absence, Abigaille discovers the document proving her illegitimacy, and when the High Priest of Bel tells her that Fenena is releasing the Hebrews, she vows to seize the throne. Nabucco returns and quells the revolt. He proclaims himself god, whereupon a lightning bolt strikes him down and he loses his reason. Abigaille seizes the crown which falls from his head and later tricks the demented Nabucco into signing the death warrant of all the Hebrews (and of Fenena). However, Nabucco's senses are restored after he prays to the god of the Hebrews, and he regains control. The dying Abigaille repents and Zaccaria crowns Nabucco King of Kings. [R]

Nachtigal, Konrad
Baritone COMPRIMARIO role in Wagner's *Die Meistersinger von Nürnberg*. A tinsmith, he is one of the masters.

Nacht in Venedig, Eine (*A Night in Venice*)
Operetta in three acts by J. Strauss II. 1st perf Berlin, 3 Oct 1883; libr by F. Zell (Camillo Walzel) and Richard Genée, after Eugène Cormon and Michel Carré's *Château Trompette*. Principal roles: Duke of Urbino (ten), Annina (sop), Caramello (ten), Ciboletta (mezzo), Pappacoda (bar), Delaquà (bar), Agricola (mezzo). One of Strauss's most successful works, it is still regularly performed, sometimes in the version prepared by Korngold and Hubert Marischka (Vienna, 21 June 1923).
Plot: 18th-century Venice. During Carnival, the libidinous Duke of Urbino is entertaining the senators. Amongst them, Delaquà has a young and pretty wife and is concerned about the Duke's intentions. He sends her away and plans to take his cook Ciboletta to the ball instead. His plans are overheard by the Duke's barber Caramello, who takes the place of the gondolier for the journey to the Duke's palace, but does not know that Delaquà's wife has arranged for a friend to take her place. Caramello discovers that the girl he has brought to the Duke is his own sweetheart Annina. After much amorous intrigue and misunderstanding, everyone is finally restored to their rightful lover and all join in the fun of Carnival. [R]

Nachtlager von Granada, Das (*The Night Camp in Granada*)
Opera in two acts by K. Kreutzer. 1st perf Vienna, 13 Jan 1834; libr by Karl Johann Braun von Braunthal, after Johann Friedrich Kind's play. Principal roles: Infante (bar), Gabriele (sop), Gómez (ten), Vasco (bass), Ambrosio (bass). By far Kreutzer's most successful opera, it still receives an occasional performance in German-speaking countries.
Plot: Mid-16th-century Granada. The Infante of Spain is disguised as a huntsman and seeks shelter for the night from a group of shepherds. They agree, but when they catch him flirting with Gabriele, who is loved by Gómez, they decide to kill him and relieve him of his possessions. Gabriele, who returns Gómez's love, is also pursued by Vasco, and she asks the huntsman for help. The latter promises to intercede on her behalf with the Infante. Meeting the Infante's followers, Gabriele and Gómez learn the huntsman's true identity, and reveal the plans against his life. The Infante ensures their betrothal. [R]

Nadia
Soprano role in Tippett's *The Ice Break*. Lev's wife, she is Yuri's mother.

Nadir
Tenor role in: **1** Bizet's *Les Pêcheurs de Perles*. A fisherman, he is Zurga's friend and rival for Leïla's love. **2** Cherubini's *Ali Baba*. He loves Morgiane.

Nancy
see THÉÂTRE MUNICIPAL, NANCY

Nancy
Mezzo role in: **1** Flotow's *Martha*. She is Lady Harriet's maid. **2** Britten's *Albert Herring*. She is Sid's girlfriend.

Nannetta
Soprano role in Verdi's *Falstaff*. Ford's and Alice's daughter, she loves Fenton.

Nantes
see GRAND THÉÂTRE GRASLIN, NANTES

Naples
see TEATRO SAN CARLO, NAPLES

Napoleon
Emperor Napoleon I of France (1768–1821) appears in a number of operas, including: **1** Baritone role in Prokofiev's *War and Peace*. **2** Baritone role in Giordano's *Madame Sans-Gêne*. **3** Bass role in Kodály's *Háry János*. **4** Baritone role in Blake's *Toussaint*.

Napoli, Jacopo (1911–94)
Italian composer. His comic operas, often incorporating Neapolitan songs, met with some success in Italy but are unknown elsewhere. His operas are *Il Malato Immaginario* (Naples, 2 Feb 1939; libr Mario Ghisalberti, after Molière's *Le Malade Imaginaire*), *Miseria e Nobilità* (Naples, 24 Mar 1946; libr Vittorio Viviani, after E. Scarpetta), *Un Curioso Accidente* (Bergamo, 19 Sept 1950; libr Ghisalberti, after Carlo Goldoni), *Masaniello* (Milan, 25 Mar 1953; libr Viviani), *I Pescatori* (Naples, 26 Mar 1954; libr Viviani), *Il Tesoro* (Rome, 26 Mar 1958; libr Viviani), *Il Rosario* (Brescia, 5 Mar 1962; libr Viviani, after F. de Roberto), *Il Povero Diavolo* (Trieste, 23 Nov 1963; libr Viviani), *Il Barone Avaro* (Naples, 18 Mar 1970; libr M. Pasi, after Alexander Pushkin's *The Covetous Knight*), *Dubrovski II* (Naples, 4 Mar 1973; libr Pasi, after Pushkin), *Palinuro* (Naples, 13 May 1978; libr E. Cetrangelo) and *A San Francisco* (Naples, 1982; libr Viviani, after Salvatore di Giacomo).

Nápravník, Eduard (1839–1916)
Czech-born Russian composer and conductor. He wrote four operas which met with some success in their time but which are nowadays little remembered. They are *Nizhegorodtsy* (St Petersburg, 8 Jan 1868; libr Pyotor Ivanovich Kalashnikov, after Mikhail Zagoskin's *Yuri Miloslavsky*), *Harold* (St Petersburg, 23 Nov 1886; libr P.I. Veynberg, after E. von Wildenbruch), DUBROVSKY, his most successful work, and *Francesca da Rimini* (St Petersburg, 9 Dec 1902; libr O.O. Palaček and E.P. Ponomarev, after Dante's *La Divina Commedia*). As musical director of the Maryinsky Theatre, St Petersburg, he was a tireless champion both of higher standards and of young Russian composers. He conducted the first performances of over 80 operas, including *The Stone Guest*, the revised *Boris Godunov*,

Tchaikovsky's *The Oprichnik*, *Vakula the Blacksmith*, *The Maid of Orleans*, *The Queen of Spades*, *The Enchantress* and *Iolanta*, Rimsky-Korsakov's *May Night*, *The Maid of Pskov*, *Christmas Eve*, *Mlada* and *The Snow Maiden*, Rubinstein's *The Demon*, Serov's *The Power of Evil* and Cui's *William Ratcliff*, *Angelo* and *The Captive of the Caucasus*.

Narbal
Bass role in Berlioz's *Les Troyens*. He is Dido's minister.

Narciso, Don
Tenor role in Rossini's *Il Turco in Italia*. He is Fiorilla's lover.

Narraboth
Tenor role in Strauss's *Salome*. He is the captain of the palace guard.

Nash, Heddle (1894–1961)
British tenor, particularly associated with Mozart roles and with David in *Die Meistersinger*. One of the most stylish and elegant British Mozartians, he created Dr Manette in Benjamin's *A Tale of Two Cities*. His son **John Heddle Nash** (1928–94) was a baritone.

Natasha
Soprano role in: **1** Prokofiev's *War and Peace*. Count Rostov's daughter, she loves Prince Andrei. **2** Tchaikovsky's *The Oprichnik*. She loves Andrei.

National Opera Studio
The British centre for advanced operatic training, it opened in 1978 as the successor to the LONDON OPERA CENTRE. Situated in London, its directors have been Michael Langdon and Richard Van Allan.

Naumann, Johann Gottlieb (1741–1801)
German composer. He wrote some 25 operas, all of them now virtually forgotten, for Italy, Germany, Sweden and Denmark, where his *Orpheus og Euridice* (Copenhagen, 31 Jan 1786; libr Charlotte Dorothea Biehl, after Ranieri de' Calzabigi) was the first major opera written to a Danish libretto. His most successful works were *Gustaf Wasa* (Stockholm, Jan 1786; libr Johan Henrik Kellgren) and the comedy *La Dama Soldata* (Dresden, 30 Mar 1791; libr Caterino Mazzolà).

Navarini, Francesco (1853–1923)
Italian bass, particularly associated with the Italian and French repertories. One of the leading basses of the late 19th century, he had a powerful voice and a strong stage presence which was aided by his great height (6′ 6″). He created Lodovico in Verdi's *Otello*.

Navarraise, La (*The Girl from Navarre*)
Opera in two acts by Massenet. 1st perf London, 20 June 1894; libr by Jules Clarétie and Henri Cain, after the former's *La Cigarette*. Principal roles: Anita (sop), Araquil (ten), Garrido (bar), Remigio (bass). Massenet's one excursion into the VERISMO field, it was successful at its appearance and is still occasionally performed.
Plot: Near Bilbao, 1874. The orphan girl Anita loves the sergeant Araquil, whose father Remigio opposes the match because she lacks a dowry. Learning that Gen Garrido is offering a large reward for the death of a rebel, Anita decides to do the deed. She crosses enemy lines and is followed by Araquil, who wishes to discover if she is a spy, as rumour reports. Anita kills the rebel and is given the reward by Garrido, but Araquil has been mortally wounded and accuses her of selling herself to Garrido. Anita loses her reason and, thinking that distant bells signal her wedding with Araquil, falls dead on top of his corpse. [R]

Neapolitan opera
A loose term which describes the 18th-century school of Italian opera composers, many of whom (but by no means all) were based in Naples. The leading figures were Cimarosa, Jommelli, Paisiello, Pergolesi, Piccinni, Sacchini, A. Scarlatti and Traetta. Although the term is usually used to describe a style of OPERA SERIA, many Neapolitan composers were also masters of OPERA BUFFA, which in this school is marked by great vivacity.

Neblett, Carol (b 1946)
American soprano, particularly associated with Puccini roles, especially Minnie in *La Fanciulla del West*. She possesses a rich and powerful if not absolutely outstanding voice, and is a compelling singing-actress.

Nedbal, Oskar (1874–1930)
Slovakian composer and conductor. With the exception of *Jacob the Farmer* (*Sedlák Jakub*, Brno, 13 Oct 1922; libr L. Novák, after Félix Lope de Vega), all of his stage works are operettas, a few of which are still occasionally performed. They include *Die Keusche Barbora* (Vienna, 7 Oct 1911; libr Robert Bernauer and Leopold Jacobson), *Polenblut* (Vienna, 25 Oct 1913; libr Leo Stein) [R Exc], *Die Winzerbraut* (Vienna, 11 Feb 1916; libr Stein and J. Wilhelm), *Die Schöne Saskia* (Vienna, 16 Nov 1917; libr Alfred Maria Willner and Heinrich Reichert), *Mamzel Napoleon* (Vienna, 21 Jan 1918; libr E. and A. Golz) and *Donna Gloria* (Vienna, 30 Dec 1925; libr Reichert and Victor Léon). He was musical director of the Bratislava Opera from 1923, and played a crucial role in the promotion of Slovak music.

Nedda
Soprano role in Leoncavallo's *Pagliacci*. She is Canio's wife.

Neher, Caspar (1897–1962)
German designer and librettist. One of the leading operatic designers of the inter-war period, he also wrote a number of libretti, providing texts for Einem (*Agamemnon*), Wagner-Régeny (*Persiche Episode*, *Der Günstling*, *Die Bürger von Calais* and *Johanna Balk*) and Weill (*Die Bürgschaft*).

Neidlinger, Gustav (1912–91)
German baritone, particularly associated with Wagnerian roles, especially Alberich. A fine singing-actor with a powerful and incisive voice, he was the leading Alberich of the 1950s and 1960s, and was one of the few who really sang the role rather than barking or shouting it. He created King Klaus in Schultze's *Schwarze Peter*.

Nel cor più
Originally a soprano/tenor duet for Rachelina and Caloandro in Act II of Paisiello's *La Molinara*, in an altered form it has become one of the most popular of all ARIE ANTICHE.

Nel giardin del bello
Mezzo aria (the Veil Song) for Eboli in Act II of Verdi's *Don Carlos*, in which she sings about a Saracen beauty.

Nélusko
Baritone role in Meyerbeer's *L'Africaine*. He is a captured African slave.

Nè mai dunque
Soprano aria for Wally in Act III of Catalani's *La Wally*, in which she laments that her love for Hagenbach has destroyed the easy simplicity of her life.

Németh, Mária (1897–1967)
Hungarian soprano, particularly associated with the Italian repertory. One of the leading dramatic sopranos of the inter-war period, her remarkable technique enabled her to sing roles as diverse as the Queen of the Night in *Die Zauberflöte* and the title-role in *Turandot*.

Nemico della patria
Baritone aria for Carlo Gérard in Act III of Giordano's *Andrea Chénier*, in which he muses on the anti-revolutionary charges laid against Chénier.

Nemirovich-Danchenko, Vladimir (1858–1943)
Russian producer. A co-founder in 1898 with the actor-director Konstantin Stanislavsky (1863–1938) of the Moscow Arts Theatre, his revolutionary stage methods had a vast influence on opera performance both in Russia and elsewhere. He founded a Musical Studio in 1919, which in 1926 became the Nemirovich-Danchenko Musical Theatre and merged with the Stanislavsky Opera Theatre in 1941. He rejected conventional stagings in favour of abstract and stylized productions and freely altered libretti, as in his famous Bizet staging *Carmencita and the Soldier* (1924). He also wrote the libretto for Rachmaninov's *Aleko*.

Nemorino
Tenor role in Donizetti's *L'Elisir d'Amore*. He is a country lad in love with Adina.

Neri, Giulio (1909–58)
Italian bass, particularly associated with the Italian repertory, especially the Grand Inquisitor, Don Basilio and Mefistofele. He had a dark, powerful and cavernous voice and a strong stage presence.

Néris
Mezzo role in Cherubini's *Médée*. She is Medea's servant.

Nero
The Roman Emperor Nero (AD 37–68) appears in a number of operas, including: **1** Tenor role in Monteverdi's *L'Incoronazione di Poppea*. **2** Tenor role in Boito's *Nerone*. **3** Tenor role in Rubinstein's *Nero*. **4** Counter-tenor role in Händel's *Agrippina*. **5** Tenor role in Mascagni's *Nerone*.

Nerone (*Nero*)
Opera in four acts by Boito. 1st perf Milan, 1 May 1924; libr by the composer. Principal roles: Nerone (ten), Simon Mago (b-bar), Fanuèl (bar), Asteria (sop), Rubria (mezzo), Tigellino (bass), Gobrias (ten). Boito's second opera, on which he worked intermittently for some 40 years, it was left unfinished at his death and was prepared for performance by Toscanini and Vincenzo Tommasini. The libretto for a fifth act was written, but the music was never composed. Dealing with the confrontation between the decadent Roman Empire and the new Christianity, it was greeted at its appearance with respect rather than enthusiasm, and is nowadays only very rarely performed.
Plot: Rome, *c* AD 60. Simon Mago, who has been unmasked by Nero as a fake magician, betrays the Christians to the Emperor, who condemns them to die in the circus. Simon and his followers set Rome on fire. Many of Nero's intended victims escape, but Rubria is mortally wounded and dies in the arms of the Christian leader Fanuèl. [R]

Nerone (*Nero*)
Opera in three acts by Mascagni. 1st perf Milan, 16 Jan 1935; libr by Giovanni Targioni-Tozzetti, after Pietro Cossa's play. Principal roles: Nerone (ten), Atte (sop), Ègloge (sop), Menècrate (bar), Clivio Rufo (bass), Faònte (ten). Mascagni's last opera, written in honour of Mussolini, it is a pretentious piece which is nowadays justifiably forgotten.
Plot: Rome, AD 68. Nero is upbraided by his mistress Atte for his drunken carousing, for his ignoring state affairs and for his pursuit of the Greek dancer Ègloge. Nonetheless, Nero installs Ègloge in the palace and saves her from an attempt on her life by Atte. However, Atte later succeeds in poisoning Ègologe at a banquet. The plebians revolt and slaughter the praetorian guard, but Nero and Atte escape. The freed slave Phaontis brings Nero the news that the Senate has deposed him. Atte stabs herself, and Nero is stabbed to death by Phaontis.

Nessi, Giuseppe (1887–1961)
Italian tenor, particularly associated with Italian character roles. The leading Italian COMPRIMARIO artist of the inter-war period, he was a master of make-up and was an accomplished comic actor. He created Pang in *Turandot*, Malatestino in Zandonai's *Francesca da Rimini*, Gobrias in Boito's *Nerone*, Donna Pasqua in Wolf-Ferrari's *Il Campiello* and a role in Pizzetti's *Fra Gherardo*.

Nessler, Viktor (1841–90)
German composer and conductor. He wrote ten operas, of which the most successful were *Der Rattenfänger von Hameln* (*The Ratcatcher of Hamelin*, Leipzig, 19 Mar 1879; libr Friedrich Hofmann, after Julius Wolff) and DER TROMPETER VON SÄCKINGEN, his only opera still to be remembered.

Nessun dorma
Tenor aria for Calaf in Act III of Puccini's *Turandot*, in which he reflects on the people's all-night search to discover his name.

Nesterenko, Yevgeny (b 1938)
Russian bass, particularly associated with the Russian and Italian repertories. One of the outstanding basses of the post-war era, he possesses a magnificently rich and powerful voice used with unfailing musicianship and intelligence and is an accomplished singing-actor, equally at home in serious or comic roles.

Netherlands Opera (*De Nederlandsche Opera*)
Holland's principal opera company, which is based at the Town Hall Music Theatre (cap 1,594) in Amsterdam, it was founded in 1946. It became the *Nieuwe Nederlandsche Opera* in 1965 on its

reorganization, and an associated opera studio (for chamber works) was founded in 1974. Also performing in Rotterdam and other cities, musical directors have included Charles Bruck, Michael Gielen, Edo de Waart and Hartmut Haenchen.

Neues vom Tage (*News of the Day*)
Opera in three acts by Hindemith. 1st perf Berlin, 8 June 1929; libr by Marcellus Schiffer. Principal roles: Laura (sop), Edward (bar), Press Chief (bass), Agency Employees (mezzo and ten). A comedy, with serious undertones, about the way in which the gutter press goes about getting its stories, it is still occasionally performed in Germany. Like many of Hindemith's operas, it fell foul of the Nazis: Dr Goebbels objected to the scene in which the young wife lies in the bath and extols the joys of constant hot water.
Plot: Germany, late 1920s. The recently married Laura and Edward have a violent quarrel and decide to get divorced. So slow is the legal machinery that they go to an agency in an attempt to speed up the process. However, the agency's methods so infuriate them that they become reconciled. The agency persuades them to enact their story in their own theatre, which enables them to be exploited by the tabloid press. [R]

Neumann, František (1874–1929)
Czech conductor and composer. Particularly associated with the Czech repertory, he was musical director of the Brno Opera (1919–29), where he conducted the first performances of Novák's *The Grandfather's Heritage*, Ostrčil's *The Legend of Erin* and Janáček's *Kátă Kabanová, Sărka, The Cunning Little Vixen* and *The Macropolus Case*. He also composed eight operas, including *Liebelei* (Frankfurt, 18 Sept 1910; libr after Arthur Schnitzler) and *Beatrice Caracci* (Brno, 29 Apr 1922; libr composer, after Ludwig Hunn).

Neumann, Václav (b 1920)
Czech conductor (originally a viola player), particularly associated with the German and Czech repertories. He was musical director of the Leipzig Opera (1964–68), the Stuttgart Opera (1969–73) and the Prague National Theatre. He conducted the first performance of Cikker's *The Play of Love and Death*.

Nevers, Comte de
Baritone role in Meyerbeer's *Les Huguenots*. He is betrothed to Valentine.

Neway, Patricia (b 1919)
American soprano, particularly associated with 20th-century operas. An intense singing-actress with a powerful and steely voice, she created Geraldine in Barber's *A Hand of Bridge*, Leah in David Tamkin's *The Dybbuk* and, for Menotti, Magda Sorel in *The Consul* and the Mother in *Maria Golovin*.

Newman, Ernest (b William Roberts) (1868–1959)
British critic and musicologist. One of the most influential 20th-century British critics, he is principally remembered for his analyses of Wagner. His *Wagner Nights* (1949), *Wagner as Man and Artist* (1914) and the four-volume *Life of Richard Wagner* (1933–47) remain seminal studies. His writings also include *Gluck and the Opera* (1895), *Opera Nights* (1943) and books on Wolf, Liszt and Strauss.

New Opera Company
A British company founded in 1957 to promote 20th-century operas. Often working in collaboration with Sadler's Wells Opera, the company gave eight world premieres as well as some 20 British premieres. The musical director was Leon Lovett.

New Orleans Opera House Association
New Orleans has a long operatic tradition, and – partly because of Louisiana's historical background as a French colony – has always been particularly associated with the French repertory. The present company was formed in 1943 and performs at the New Orleans Theater of the Performing Arts (cap 2,317), which opened in 1973. The annual season runs from October to March. Musical directors have included Walter Herbert, Renato Cellini, Knud Anderson and Arthur Cosenza.

New Sadler's Wells Opera
Based at Sadler's Wells Theatre (cap

1,499) in London and also touring Britain, the company was formed in 1980 and its repertory consisted largely of operetta. Financial difficulties forced it into liquidation in 1989. The musical director was Barry Wordsworth.

New World Trilogy
A title often given to Milhaud's three otherwise unconnected operas on Latin American subjects: CHRISTOPHE COLOMB, MAXIMILIEN and BOLIVAR.

New Year
Opera in three acts by Tippett. 1st perf Houston, 27 Oct 1989; libr by the composer. Principal roles: Jo Ann (sop), Pelegrin (ten), Donny (bar), Regan (sop), Merlin (bar), Nan (mezzo). Tippett's last opera, it deals with the dreams and fantasies of two sets of characters (three from Somewhere Today and three from Nowhere Tomorrow). Its orchestration includes electric guitars, saxophones and specially-created electronic ingredients. **Plot**: Jo Ann, fostered by Nan, dares not venture out into Terror Town, and the delinquent behaviour of her black foster-brother Donny further scares her. The computer of the techno-wizard Merlin malfunctions: instead of images of the future – where Regan wishes them to go – it shows only the past. An image of Jo Ann fascinates Pelegrin, who directs their spaceship to it. The crowd enact New Year rituals, identifying Donny as the sacrificial scapegoat. Pelegrin puts Jo Ann through a ritual which enables her to forget her past traumas. After Pelegrin's departure, she is able to venture into the city and join humanity.

New York
see AMERICAN OPERA SOCIETY; LINCOLN CENTER FOR THE PERFORMING ARTS; METROPOLITAN OPERA, NEW YORK; NEW YORK CITY OPERA

New York City Opera
Standing in a relationship to the Metropolitan Opera somewhat similar to that of the English National Opera to Covent Garden, the company was formed in Feb 1944. Since 22 Feb 1966, it has been based at the New York State Theater (cap 2,779) in the Lincoln Center for the Performing Arts. One of the most exciting opera companies in the United States, it pursues a highly adventurous repertory policy, encourages American opera and has nurtured many of the finest modern American singers. Musical directors have been László Halász, Joseph Rosenstock, Erich Leinsdorf, Julius Rudel, Christopher Keene and Sergiu Comissiona, and general directors have included Beverly Sills.

New Zealand Opera Company
The company was founded in 1954 by the singer David Munrow and gives an annual season at venues throughout the country with a largely conservative repertory. Musical directors have included James Robertson and László Heltay.

Nice
see THÉÂTRE DE L'OPÉRA, NICE

Nice dilemma, A
Soprano/tenor/baritone/baritone quartet for the Plaintiff, the Defendant, Counsel for Plaintiff and the Judge in Sullivan's *Trial By Jury*, in which they reflect on the complexity of the situation. One of Sullivan's finest pieces of musical satire, it is based on the quintet 'D'un pensiero' in Act I of Bellini's *La Sonnambula.*

Nicklausse
Mezzo trouser role in Offenbach's *Les Contes d'Hoffmann*. Hoffmann's young companion, he is the physical embodiment of the Muse of Poetry.

Nicolaï, Otto (1810–49)
German composer and conductor. His first opera *Enrico II* (Trieste, 26 Nov 1839; libr Felice Romani) was a failure, but its successor *Il Templario* (Turin, 11 Feb 1840; libr Girolamo Maria Marini, after Sir Walter Scott's *Ivanhoe*) established his reputation. *Gildippe ed Odoardo* (Genoa, 26 Dec 1840; libr Temistocle Solera, after Torquato Tasso) and *Il Proscritto* (Milan, 13 Mar 1841; libr Gaetano Rossi) were unsuccessful, but his last opera DIE LUSTIGEN WEIBER VON WINDSOR remains one of the finest and most popular of all German comic operas. A distinguished conductor, he was musical director of the Berlin Opera and was the effective founder of the Vienna Philharmonic Orchestra.

Nicolini (b Nicolò Grimaldi) (1673–1732)
Italian CASTRATO. One of the most famous singers of the 18th century, also highly regarded as an actor, he sang in Italy and then in London, where he created the title-roles in Händel's *Rinaldo* and *Amadigi di Gaula*. The critic Joseph Addison described him as 'the greatest performer in dramatic music that is now living, or that ever appeared on a stage'.

Nicolini, Giuseppe (1762–1842)
Italian composer. He wrote some 40 operas, many of which enjoyed great success in their day, but which soon came to be regarded as old-fashioned. None of his operas are remembered today. His works include *I Baccanali di Roma* (Milan, 21 Jan 1801; libr Luigi Romanelli) and *Trajano in Dacia* (Rome, 3 Feb 1807; libr Michelangelo Prunetti).

Nicolò
see ISOUARD, NICOLÒ

Nielsen, Carl (1865–1931)
Danish composer. His two operas, the magnificent SAUL OG DAVID and the comedy MASKARADE (which is the Danish national opera), both remain very popular in Denmark and are amongst the greatest works of Scandinavian music, but for quite unaccountable reasons have failed to establish themselves in the international repertory where they belong. His early autobiography, *My Childhood on Fünen*, which was published in 1927, is regarded as one of the classics of Danish literature.

Nightingale, The (*Solovey*; sometimes incorrectly called *Le Rossignol*)
Opera in three acts by Stravinsky. 1st perf Paris, 26 May 1914; libr by the composer and Stepan Nikolayevich Mitusov, after Hans Christian Andersen's *The Emperor and the Nightingale*. Principal roles: Nightingale (sop), Emperor (bar), Fisherman (ten), Kitchenmaid (mezzo), Bonze (bass), Chamberlain (bass), Death (cont). Written over two different periods, the music is stylistically a little disjointed but nevertheless offers a delightful setting of Andersen's fairy tale. The symphonic poem *Le Chant du Rossignol* is drawn from music from the opera.

Plot: Legendary China. The Nightingale sings in the forest for the Fisherman. Although she knows that her voice will be less sweet there, she agrees to sing at the palace, where the Emperor is moved to tears by the beauty of her song. Three Japanese envoys arrive bearing a mechanical nightingale as a gift for the Emperor. The real bird leaves sadly, which causes offence to the Emperor, who banishes it. However, when Death stands at the Emperor's bedside, the real bird returns to restore his life with her song. [R]

Night in Venice, A
see NACHT IN VENEDIG, EINE

Night on Bare Mountain, A (More correctly *St John's Night on the Bare Mountain*)
A work by Moussorgsky, based on the witches' sabbath scene in Nikolai Gogol's *St John's Eve*. Originally written as a symphonic poem in 1867, it was rewritten (as *Night on Mount Triglav*) for orchestra and chorus as part of the abortive OPERA-BALLET *Mlada*, written with Borodin, Cui and Rimsky-Korsakov. An elaborated version of this second arrangement was used as an INTERMEZZO before Act III of *Sorochintsy Fair*. This final version, arranged by Rimsky-Korsakov for orchestra alone, is the work so popular in the concert hall.

Nikikai Opera Company
Japan's leading opera company, it was founded in 1952 by Mutsumu Shibata. It gives an annual season at the Nissei Theatre (cap 1,350) in Tokyo, which opened in 1964.

Nikisch, Artur (1855–1922)
Hungarian conductor, particularly associated with the German repertory. One of the leading conductors of his age, he was musical director of the Leipzig Opera (1879–99) and the Budapest State Opera (1893–5). He conducted the first performances of Nessler's *Der Trompeter von Säckingen*, Holbrooke's *Dylan Son of the Wave*, Smyth's *The Wreckers* and Hallén's *Harald der Wiking*. His son **Mitja** was a pianist.

Nilakantha
Baritone role in Delibes's *Lakmé*. Lakmé's father, he is a Brahmin priest.

Nile Scene
A title often given to Act III of Verdi's *Aida*, which is set on the banks of the Nile.

Nilsson, Birgit (b Svennsson) (b 1918)
Swedish soprano, particularly associated with Wagner, Strauss and heavier Verdi roles and with the title-role in *Turandot*. One of the greatest dramatic sopranos of all time, she possessed an enormous, steely voice of truly awesome power and incisiveness, which she used with a fine technique and with unfailing musicianship. She had a keen dramatic sense but could occasionally seem a little cool and distant, although this never diminished the overwhelming impact of her singing. Her Isolde and Elektra are unlikely ever to be equalled, let alone surpassed.

Nilsson, Christine (b Kristina Törnerhjelm) (1843–1921)
Swedish soprano, particularly associated with the French and Italian repertories. One of the leading lyric sopranos of the mid-19th century, she created Ophélie in Thomas's *Hamlet* and Edith in Balfe's *Il Talismano*. Björn Hallman's opera *Solitaire* is based on incidents in her life.

Nimsgern, Siegmund (b 1940)
German baritone, particularly associated with the German repertory, especially Strauss and Wagner and 20th-century works. One of the leading contemporary German baritones, he has a rich voice of considerable power which is used with fine intelligence and musicianship. A versatile singer with a good stage presence, he has also had success in the Italian repertory, notably in Rossini roles.

Nina or **La Pazza per Amore** (*The Girl Sent Mad by Love*)
Comic opera in two acts by Paisiello. 1st perf Naples, 25 June 1789; libr by Giovanni Battista Lorenzi and Giuseppe Carpani, after Benoît Joseph Marsollier des Vivetière's libretto for Dalayrac's *Nina ou la Folle par Amour*. Principal roles: Nina (sop), Lindoro (ten), Count (bass), Elisa (sop), Giorgio (bar). More of an OPERA SEMISERA than a true comedy, it is one of Paisiello's finest works and is still given an occasional performance.
Plot: 18th-century Italy. Nina's nurse Elisa tells Giorgio, servant to Nina's father the Count, about her mistress: the Count first promised her to her beloved Lindoro but then preferred a nobler match. Lindoro is believed dead, following a duel with his rival, and Nina has lost her wits. Giorgio discovers that Lindoro is still alive. The Count receives Lindoro kindly and tells him of Nina's condition. At first, Nina fails to recognize Lindoro, but her mind gradually clears, and when the Count consents to her marriage with Lindoro her joy is complete. [R]

Ninetta
Soprano role in: **1** Rossini's *La Gazza Ladra*. She is the girl falsely accused of stealing. **2** Prokofiev's *The Love of Three Oranges*. She is a princess found in an orange.

Nissen, Hans-Hermann (1893–1980)
German bass-baritone, particularly associated with Wagnerian roles. Possessing a rich and sonorous voice and a good stage presence, he was one of the finest interpreters of Wotan and Hans Sachs of the inter-war period.

Niun mi tema
Tenor monologue for Otello in Act IV of Verdi's *Otello*. The final scene of the opera, in which Otello says that none but himself is at risk from the weapon he is carrying.

Nixon in China
Opera in three acts by Adams. 1st perf Houston, 22 Oct 1987; libr by Alice Goodman. Principal roles: Nixon (bar), Mao Tse-Tung (ten), Henry Kissinger (bass), Chiang Ch'ing (sop), Chou En-Lai (bar), Pat Nixon (sop), Nancy T'ang (mezzo). Adam's first opera, written in MINIMALIST style, it deals with President Richard Nixon's visit to China in Feb 1972. One of the most successful operas of the 1980s, it has been widely performed. [R]

Noble, Dennis (1899–1966)
British baritone, particularly associated with the Italian repertory. The leading British baritone of the inter-war period, he

created Sam Weller in Coates's *Pickwick*, a role in Lloyd's *The Serf* and, for Goossens, Achior in *Judith* and Don José in *Don Juan de Mañara*.

Noble, John (b 1931)
British baritone. One of the most underrated British singers of the post-war era, he possessed a warm and beautiful voice used with outstanding intelligence and musicianship. Best known as a concert artist, his operatic appearances were infrequent, but he was particularly associated with the title-role in Vaughan Williams's *The Pilgrim's Progress*.

Nobles seigneurs
Mezzo aria for Urbain in Act I of Meyerbeer's *Les Huguenots*, in which she delivers Queen Marguerite's invitation to Raoul.

Noces de Jeanette, Les *(Jeannette's Wedding)*
Operetta in one act by Massé. 1st perf Paris, 4 Feb 1853; libr by Jules Barbier and Michel Carré. Principal roles: Jeannette (sop), Jean (bar). Massé's most successful work, famous for the COLORATURA 'Air du Rossignol', it is still quite often performed in France.
Plot 19th-century France. Jeannette is engaged to the boorish rustic Jean, but Jean absconds in fear on the wedding day. Jeannette follows him to his home, saying that she does not wish to wed him if he has changed his mind, but that she must protect her reputation. Jean agrees to her suggestion that they sign a marriage contract and that she then publicly denounce him and destroy the contract. As soon as Jean signs, Jeannette insists that he honour the contract. Jean smashes the furniture in fury and finally falls asleep. He wakens to discover that Jeannette has tidied everything up for him, and he decides to marry her after all. [R]

Nonet
In opera, a musical number for nine solo singers, with or without chorus. There is a fine example in Act I Scene II of Verdi's *Falstaff*.

Noni, Alda (b 1916)
Italian soprano. One of the leading SOUBRETTES of the immediate post-war period, she was an accomplished singing-actress with a tremendous sense of humour and was particularly associated with the roles of Norina in Donizetti's *Don Pasquale*, Despina in Mozart's *Così fan Tutte* and Zerbinetta in Strauss's *Ariadne auf Naxos*.

Non mi dir
Soprano aria for Donna Anna in Act II of Mozart's *Don Giovanni*, in which she tells Don Ottavio not to think of marriage so soon after her father's murder.

Nono, Luigi (1924–90)
Italian composer, son-in-law of Schönberg. A leading exponent of the extreme avant-garde in Italy, his intensely left-wing political views – always paraded in his music – tended to obscure his considerable musical abilities. His first opera INTOLLERANZA is one of the most controversial post-war operas and provoked a serious political riot at its first performance. His two other stage works are *Al Gran Sole Carico d'Amore* (Milan, 4 Apr 1975; libr composer and Yuri Lyubimov) and *Prometeo* (Venice, 1984; libr Massimo Cacciari).

Non pianger
Soprano aria for Elisabeth in Act II of Verdi's *Don Carlos*, in which she comforts a companion who has been dismissed by King Philip.

Non più andrai
Bass-baritone aria for Figaro in Act I of Mozart's *Le Nozze di Figaro*, in which he tells Cherubino that his philandering days are over now that he is to be a soldier. Mozart quotes it in the Supper Scene in *Don Giovanni*.

Non più di fiori
Soprano aria for Vitellia in Act II of Mozart's *La Clemenza di Tito*, in which she reflects that the hoped-for god of marriage must now yield to death. The OBBLIGATO instrument is a basset-horn.

Non più mesta
Mezzo aria for Angelina in Act II of Rossini's *La Cenerentola*, in which she expresses her joy at her change of circumstances. The final scene of the opera.

Non so più
Soprano aria for Cherubino in Act I of Mozart's *Le Nozze di Figaro*, in which he tells of his bewilderment at the new sensation of sexual desire.

Non temer, amato bene
Soprano aria for Idamante in Act II of Mozart's *Idomeneo*, in which he comforts Ilia.

No! pazzo son!
Tenor aria for des Grieux in Act III of Puccini's *Manon Lescaut*, in which he begs the captain to allow him to take ship with Manon.

Nordica, Lillian (b Norton) (1857–1914)
American soprano. Originally noted for her performances in the French and Italian repertories, she later turned with equal success to Wagner. Her technique was so assured that she was able to sing Brünnhilde and Violetta on consecutive nights. She created Zelika in Stanford's *The Veiled Prophet of Khorassan.*

Norina
Soprano role in Donizetti's *Don Pasquale.* She is a flighty young widow loved by Ernesto.

Norma
Opera in two acts by Bellini. 1st perf Milan, 26 Dec 1831; libr by Felice Romani, after Louis Alexandre Soumet's play. Principal roles: Norma (sop), Adalgisa (sop), Pollione (ten), Oroveso (bass). Bellini's masterpiece and one of the finest of all BEL CANTO operas, the title-role is one of the most musico-dramatically demanding in the entire repertory.
Plot: 1st-century Gaul. Norma is the daughter of the Druid high priest Oroveso, and is herself their high priestess. Oroveso desires war against the Romans, but Norma, leading the temple rituals, seeks to avoid it because she loves the Roman Proconsul Pollione, to whom she has secretly borne two children. Pollione, however, has left her for another woman whose identity she does not know. Her rival is, in fact, her best friend Adalgisa, a young priestess, who agrees to join Pollione in Rome, and comes to Norma to confess her betrayal of her chastity and her religion. During their meeting, Pollione appears, and the women learn that he is the lover of both of them. Norma resolves to renounce Pollione in favour of Adalgisa, on the understanding that the latter will care for her children, but Adalgisa is incapable of such betrayal and pleads with Pollione to return to Norma. He refuses, inflaming Norma to call for war just as Pollione is arrested for breaking into the temple in an attempt to abduct Adalgisa. His deed carries the death penalty, but Norma – realizing that she still loves him – offers her tribe a substitute: a defiled virgin of the priesthood. She confesses her sins, gives her children to Oroveso, and mounts the pyre that has been prepared for her. Pollione, moved to renewed love by her self-sacrifice, joins her in the flames. [R]

Norman, Jessye (b 1945)
American soprano who also sings some mezzo roles. One of the best-loved singers of modern times and possessor of one of the richest and loveliest voices of the 20th century, she is particularly associated with Wagner and Strauss roles and with the French repertory. An artist of outstanding sensitivity and musicianship, her operatic appearances have sadly been intermittent, and her substantial physique means that her roles have to be selected with care.

Norns
Soprano, mezzo and contralto roles in Wagner's *Götterdämmerung.* Daughters of Erda, they are the three fates.

Norrington, Roger (b 1934)
British conductor, particularly associated with Mozart, early and baroque operas and with the French repertory. Originally a tenor, he was musical director of Kent Opera (1969–85) and has prepared many scholarly editions of early operas. His recent operatic appearances have been infrequent.

Norwegian Opera
Norway's first full-time opera company (*Norsk Operaselskap*) was founded in 1951. It acquired its present form (as *Den Norske Opera*) in Nov 1957, with Kirsten

Flagstad as administrator. Based in Oslo, it also visits Bergen and other towns. The annual season runs from August to June. Musical directors have included Oivin Fjelstad, Martin Turnovský, Heinz Fricke, Antonio Pappano and Paavo Järvi.

Norwegian opera composers
see GRIEG; SINDING

Other national opera composers include Sigvardt Apestrand (1856–1941), Antonio Bibalo (*b* 1922), Edvard Fliflet Braein (1924–76), Bjarne Brustad (1895–1978), Arne Eggen (1881–1955), Catharinus Elling (1858–1942), Johannes Haarklou (1847–1925), Alfred Janson (*b* 1937), Ludvig Paul Irgens Jensen (1894–1969), Ole Olsen (1850–1927), Gerhard Schjelderup (1859–1933), Waldemar Thrane (1790–1828), whose *A Mountain Adventure* (*Fjeldeventyret*, Oslo, 9 Feb 1925; libr H.A. Bjerregaard) was the first opera written to a Norwegian libretto, and Geirr Tveitt (1908–81).

Nose, The (*Nos*)
Comic opera in three acts by Shostakovich (Op 15). 1st perf Leningrad, 12 Jan 1930; libr by the composer, Alexander Preis, Yevgeny Zamyatin and Georgy Yonin, after Nikolai Gogol's story. Principal roles: Kovalyov (bar), Police Inspector (ten), Ivan (ten), Doctor (bass), Nose (ten), Countess (mezzo). A merciless skit on philistinism and Soviet officialdom, it is one of Shostakovich's most complex scores. Not surprisingly, it proved unacceptable in the 'anti-formalist' Stalin period, but more recently it has been successfully reintroduced in Russia. It has also met with success elsewhere – officialdom, after all, being much the same the world over. It contains in the Police Inspector possibly the highest tenor role ever written.
Plot: St Petersburg, 1830s. The civil servant Kovalyov wakes up one morning to discover that his nose is missing, a condition confirmed by his servant Ivan. Having detached itself, the nose leads an independent existence, turning up in all sorts of bizarre places, including Kazan Cathedral, where Kovalyov encounters it at its devotions dressed as a high official. Kovalyov tries to put an advertisement in the 'missing' columns of the press, but the newspaper editor refuses to accept the advert. Finally, the nose is returned to him by the Police Inspector, but the Doctor is unable to replace it in its proper state and suggests pickling it in vodka. Eventually, however, the nose returns to a relieved Kovalyov of its own free will. [R]

Notary
Notaries are stock figures in comic opera, and in a tradition going back at least as far as Pergolesi, they often stammer – as do, for example, Dr Blind in *Die Fledermaus* and Don Curzio in *Le Nozze di Figaro*.

Nothung! Nothung!
Tenor aria (the Forging Song) for Siegfried in Act I of Wagner's *Siegfried*. Nothung (German for 'needful') is the name of Siegfried's sword.

Notre-Dame
Opera in two acts by Schmidt. 1st perf Vienna, 1 Apr 1914; libr by the composer and Leopold Wilk, after Victor Hugo's *Notre-Dame de Paris*. Principal roles: Quasimodo (bar), Esmeralda (sop), Phoebus (ten), Archdeacon (bar), Pierre (ten). Much the finer of Schmidt's two operas, it is still occasionally performed.
Plot: Medieval Paris. The Captain of the Guard Phoebus loves the gypsy Esmeralda, who is married to the jealous former poet Pierre Gringoire, but who returns his love. Catching the lovers together, Pierre stabs Phoebus. Esmeralda is sentenced to death, despite her pleas to the Archdeacon that she is innocent. The hunchbacked bell-ringer Quasimodo interrupts the execution and drags Esmeralda to safety inside the cathedral. The Archdeacon obtains an edict nullifying the right of sanctuary, and Esmeralda is dragged off to execution. Quasimodo, who had loved Esmeralda as a daughter, attacks the Archdeacon and throws him off the platform between the two towers of the cathedral. [R]

Notte e giorno
Leporello's opening words at the beginning of Act I of Mozart's *Don Giovanni*, in which he complains about always having to serve whilst his master enjoys himself. They are quoted by Nicklausse in the prologue of Offenbach's *Les Contes d'Hoffmann*.

Nouguès, Jean-Charles (1875–1932)
French composer. Largely self-taught, he wrote some 20 operas, a few of which achieved some success in their day but which are all now forgotten. His operas include *La Mort de Tintagiles* (Paris, 28 Dec 1905; libr after Maurice Maeterlinck), *Quo Vadis?* (Nice, 10 Feb 1909; libr Henri Cain, after Henryk Sienkiewicz), his most successful work, and *La Danseuse de Pompéï* (Paris, 29 Oct 1912; libr Cain and H. Ferrare, after J. Bertheroy).

Nourabad
Bass role in Bizet's *Les Pêcheurs de Perles*. He is the high priest.

Nourrit, Adolphe (1802–39)
French tenor. One of the outstanding tenors of the first half of the 19th century, he was principally associated with the Paris Opéra. His replacement there in 1837 by GILBERT DUPREZ caused him to suffer from severe melancholia which led to his committing suicide. He created the title-roles in *Robert le Diable*, Auber's *Gustave III* and Liszt's *Don Sanche*, Raoul de Nangis in *Les Huguenots*, Éléazar in *La Juive*, Masaniello in *La Muette de Portici*, Nadir in Cherubini's *Ali Baba* and, for Rossini, Néoclès in *Le Siège de Corinthe*, the title-role in *Le Comte Ory*, Aménofis in *Moïse et Pharaon* and Arnold in *Guillaume Tell*. His father **Louis** (1780–1831) was also a successful tenor, who created Seth in Lesueur's *La Mort d'Adam*, Cassandre in Spontini's *Olympie* and Almansor in Cherubini's *Les Abencérages*.

Novák, Vítězslav (1870–1949)
Czech composer. His four operas, all on nationalist subjects, have had considerable success in the Czech lands but have made little headway elsewhere. The comedy *The Imp of Zvíkov* (*Zvíkovský Rarášek*, Prague, 10 Oct 1915; libr Ladislav Stroupežnický) was followed by the patriotic *Karlštejn* (Prague, 18 Nov 1916; libr Otakar Fischer, after Jaroslav Vrchlický), THE LANTERN, his most successful opera, and *The Grandfather's Heritage* (*Dědů Odkaz*, Brno, 16 Jan 1926; libr Antonín Klášterský, after Adolf Heyduk). He was also a noted teacher, whose pupils included Cikker, Jeremiáš, Krejčí and Suchoň.

Novotná, Jarmila (1907–94)
Czech soprano, particularly associated with Mozart and Strauss roles and with the Czech repertory. One of the most stylish and aristocratic sopranos of the inter-war period, she was also a fine singing-actress. Also a successful exponent of operetta, she created the title-role in Lehár's *Giuditta*.

Now the Great Bear
Tenor aria for Grimes in Act I of Britten's *Peter Grimes*, in which he compares the weather with the storms of human suffering.

Noye's Fludde (*Noah's Flood*)
Church opera in one act by Britten (Op 59). 1st perf Orford, 18 June 1958; a setting of part of a Chester miracle play. Principal roles: Noye (bass), Mrs Noye (mezzo), Voice of God (speaker). Telling the biblical story of the Flood, the score calls for a children's orchestra and chorus and for audience participation in hymn singing. [R]

Nozze di Figaro, Le (*The Marriage of Figaro*)
Opera in four acts by Mozart (K 492). 1st perf Vienna, 1 May 1786; libr by Lorenzo da Ponte, after Pierre Augustin Caron de Beaumarchais's *La Folle Journée ou Le Mariage de Figaro*. Principal roles: Figaro (b-bar), Susanna (sop), Count and Countess Almaviva (bar and sop), Cherubino (sop), Dr Bartolo (bass), Don Basilio (ten), Marcellina (mezzo), Barbarina (sop), Antonio (bass), Don Curzio (ten). One of the greatest, most human and most popular of all operas, it is the earliest of Mozart's mature masterpieces, and is notable for its depth of characterization and for the plasticity of its kaleidoscopic ensembles.
Plot: Mid-18th-century Andalusia. Count Almaviva's valet Figaro is to be married to the Countess's maid Susanna, and the Count is regretting having abolished the old custom of first rights to the lord of the manor. The Count keeps attempting to thwart or postpone the wedding – and the activities of the lovesick adolescent pageboy Cherubino nearly give him grounds by seeming to compromise the Countess and Susanna. However, he is always outwitted

by his servants with the aid of the Countess. After much intrigue and disguise and many complications, everything is sorted out. The wedding can finally take place, and a chastened Count begs for and receives the Countess's forgiveness. [R]

Nucci, Leo (b 1942)
Italian baritone, particularly associated with the Italian repertory, especially Verdi. A true Verdi baritone, he possesses a rich and bright-toned voice with a thrilling upper register and has a good stage presence.

Nuit d'ivresse
Mezzo/tenor duet for Dido and Aeneas in Act IV of Berlioz's *Les Troyens*. The love duet.

Number opera
A loose term meaning an opera in which the scenes are composed of self-contained individual musical numbers (arias, duets, choruses etc), rather than an opera in which each scene is a single, unbroken piece of music.

Nürnberg Stadttheater
The present opera house (cap 1,082) in this German city in Bavaria was designed by Heinrich Seeling and opened on 1 Oct 1905. The annual season runs from September to July. Musical directors have included Robert Heger, Hans Gierster and Christian Thielemann.

Nurse
Mezzo role in: **1** Strauss's *Die Frau ohne Schatten*. **2** Moussorgsky's *Boris Godunov*. **3** Dukas's *Ariane et Barbe-Bleue*. **4** Tippett's *King Priam*. **5** Sutermeister's *Romeo und Julia*. **6** Rossi's *Orfeo*.

Nyman, Michael (b 1944)
British composer, writing in MINIMALIST style. The coiner of the term minimalism, he has written five stage works, of which the most successful has been the chamber opera *The Man Who Mistook His Wife for a Hat* (London, 27 Oct 1986; libr Christopher Rawlence, after Oliver Sacks) [R]. He also wrote the libretto for Birtwistle's *Down by the Greenwood Side*.

O

Obbligato (Italian for 'obligatory')
Strictly speaking, it refers to a substantial part for a solo instrument that cannot be omitted. Confusingly, however, it is also occasionally used to mean a part that may be omitted. In opera, it is easiest to regard it as a term referring to a major instrumental solo in an aria or ensemble, as for example the flute in the Mad Scene in *Lucia di Lammermoor* or the basset-horn in 'Non più di fiori' in *La Clemenza di Tito*. An extended aria with an obbligato instrument was a regular feature of 18th-century OPERA SERIA.

Ô beau pays de la Touraine
Soprano aria for Queen Marguerite in Act II of Meyerbeer's *Les Huguenots*, in which she expresses her love for the beauty of Touraine.

Oberon or the **Elf King's Oath**
Opera in three acts by Weber (J 306). 1st perf London, 12 April 1826; libr by James Robinson Planché, after William Sotheby's translation of Christoph Martin Wieland's poem, itself based on *Huon de Bordeaux* in the 13th-century *La Bibliothèque Bleue*. Principal roles: Reiza (sop), Sir Huon (ten), Sherasmin (bar), Fatima (mezzo), Oberon (ten), Puck (sop). Weber's last opera, it contains some of his greatest music. The ludicrous libretto has prevented it from taking the regular place in the repertory which its musical merits deserve. Many attempts have been made to revise or 'improve' the libretto, but these have nearly always succeeded only in making matters worse.
Plot: Early-9th-century France, Baghdad and Tunis. Oberon has quarrelled with his wife and decides not to see her again until a pair of faithful lovers can be found. He chooses Sir Huon (aided by his esquire Sherasmin) to rescue Reiza and her attendant Fatima from Baghdad. Through the connivance of Oberon and Puck, the foursome undergo shipwreck, capture by pirates, slavery and sentence of death before Oberon intervenes to save them and transport them to the court of Charlemagne, having accepted them as examples of fidelity. [R]

Oberon
Counter-tenor role in Britten's *A Midsummer Night's Dream*. Titania's husband, he is the king of the fairies. It was the first role written specifically for the modern counter-tenor voice.

Oberspielleiter (German for 'senior producer')
The title of the principal resident producer in a German or Austrian opera house.

Oberto, Conte di San Bonifacio
(*Oberto, Count of St Boniface*)
Opera in two acts by Verdi. 1st perf Milan, 17 Nov 1839; libr by Antonio Piazza and Temistocle Solera. Principal roles: Oberto (bass), Leonora (sop), Riccardo (ten), Cuniza (mezzo). Verdi's first extant opera, it may include material from his earlier unperformed and lost *Rocester*. A strongly melodic work with hints of Verdi's later development, it still receives an occasional performance.
Plot: Bassano (Italy), 1228. Riccardo, Count of Salinguerra, has seduced Leonora, the daughter of Count Oberto, but now intends to marry Cuniza. With the aid of Cuniza, Leonora and her father challenge Riccardo with his faithlessness, and he agrees to return to Leonora. Even so, the outraged Oberto insists on fighting a duel with Riccardo in which he losses his life. [R]

Obraztsova, Elena (b 1939)
Russian mezzo, particularly associated with the Italian and Russian repertories. An exciting dramatic mezzo in the grand tradition, she possesses a rich and powerful voice (even if the registers are not always fully knit together) and she has a strong stage presence. Her husband **Algis Zhuraitis** is a conductor.

Oca del Cairo, L' (*The Goose of Cairo*)
Unfinished comic opera in two acts by Mozart (K 422). 1st perf Paris, 6 June 1867 (composed 1783); libr by Giovanni Battista Varesco. Principal roles: Don Pippo (bar), Celidora (sop), Lavina (sop), Biondello (ten), Calandrino (ten), Auretta (sop), Chichibio (bass). Mozart abandoned the piece because of difficulties with the libretto, the surviving music consisting of seven numbers in various states of completion. A number of realizations have been made, including editions by Mortari (1936) and Oliver (1991). The work's title derives from a mechanical Egyptian goose which was intended to appear in Act II as a kind of *deus ex machina*.
Plot: 18th-century Italy. Celidora loves Biondello, but has been promised elsewhere by her father Don Pippo. Pippo has shut her up in a castle with her companion Lavina. In an attempt to rescue her, Biondello builds a bridge, but is discovered before he can complete it. [R]

Occasione Fa il Ladro, L' (*The Occasion Makes the Thief*) or **Il Cambio della Vaglia** (*The Change of Luggage*)
Comic opera in one act by Rossini. 1st perf Venice, 24 Nov 1812; libr by Luigi Prividali, after Eugène Scribe's *Le Prétendu par Hasard ou L'Occasion Fait le Non.* Principal roles: Don Eusebio (ten), Berenice (sop), Alberto (ten), Don Parmenione (bar), Martino (bass), Ernestina (mezzo). One of Rossini's early little farces, it is an entertaining piece which still receives an occasional performance.
Plot: Early-19th-century Naples. Sheltering from a violent storm, Count Alberto encounters the adventurer Parmenione at an inn, and tells him of his forthcoming marriage to Don Eusebio's daughter Berenice, whom he has yet to meet. When the storm passes, he leaves, unaware that his sleepy servant Martino has picked up Parmenione's luggage instead of his. Finding a passport and Berenice's picture in Alberto's luggage, Parmenione decides to masquerade as Alberto and wed her himself. Berenice, meanwhile, is unhappy about marrying a man she does not know, so she persuades her maid Ernestina to change places with her. Parmenione duly falls for the wrong woman, and when Alberto arrives he is attracted to the 'maid'. Eventually, Parmenione's skulduggery is unmasked and Alberto and Berenice are united. [R]

Ochs von Lerchenau, Baron
Bass role in Strauss's *Der Rosenkavalier*. He is the Marschallin's boorish country cousin.

Octavian
Mezzo trouser role in Strauss's *Der Rosenkavalier*. The young Count Rofrano, he is the Rose Cavalier of the opera's title.

Octet
In opera, a musical number for eight solo singers, with or without chorus. There is a fine example in Strauss's *Capriccio*.

Odabella
Soprano role in Verdi's *Attila*. The daughter of the Lord of Aquileia, she loves Foresto.

O del mio dolce ardor
Tenor aria for Paris in Act I of Gluck's *Paride ed Elena*, in which he expresses his tender feelings at the prospect of meeting Helen.

O don fatale
Mezzo aria for Eboli in Act IV of Verdi's *Don Carlos*, in which she curses the fatal gift of beauty which has caused so much unhappiness.

O du mein holder Abendstern (often known in English as 'Star of eve')
Baritone aria for Wolfram von Eschenbach in Act III of Wagner's *Tannhäuser*, in which he serenades the evening star.

Oedipe
Opera in four acts by Enescu (Op 23). 1st perf Paris, 13 March 1936; libr by Edmond Fleg, after Sophocles's *Oedipus the King* and *Oedipus at Colonus*. Principal roles: Oedipe (bar), Jocaste (mezzo), Antigone (sop), Tiresias (b-bar), Thésée (bar), Sphinx (cont), Shepherd (ten), Laïos (ten), Mérope (mezzo), High Priest (bass), Créon (bar), Watchman (bass). Enescu's only opera, it is an extraordinary work of sustained imagination and of great musical power and complexity. It is especially

notable for its choral writing, for its remarkable orchestration, and for containing one of the most demanding baritone roles ever written. Its total neglect by opera companies is utterly inexplicable as it is one of the greatest operas of the 20th century.
Plot: Legendary Thebes, Corinth and Attica. The High Priest blesses the infant son of Jocasta and Laius, but the seer Tiresias foretells that he will kill his father and marry his mother. Laius gives the baby to the Shepherd with orders to expose it. However, he survives and believes himself to be the son of Merope and Polybus of Corinth. When the Delphic oracle tells him his fate he flees Corinth. Approaching Thebes, he kills an old man, unaware that he is Laius, and defeats the Sphinx which has ravaged the area by answering its riddle. He is acclaimed king and marries the widowed Jocasta. Thebes is visited by plague and Creon reports that the oracle has stated that it will end only when Laius's murder is avenged. From Tiresias and the Shepherd Oedipus learns the appalling truth. Jocasta commits suicide and Oedipus puts out his eyes. He departs for exile accompanied by his daughter Antigone. After long wanderings, Oedipus is offered his throne back by Creon if he will defend Thebes. Oedipus refuses and Creon takes Antigone hostage, but she is saved by Theseus. The Athenians absolve Oedipus and drive Creon away. Finally at peace, Oedipus's sight is restored and he dies in a blaze of light. [R]

Oedipus
The mythical Greek king of Thebes who kills his father and marries his mother appears in a number of operas, including: **1** Tenor role in Stravinsky's *Oedipus Rex*. **2** Baritone role in Enescu's *Oedipe*. **3** Tenor role in Orff's *Oedipus der Tyrann*. **4** Baritone role in Leoncavallo's *Edipo Rè*. **5** Bass role in Sacchini's *Oedipe à Colone*.

Oedipus der Tyrann (*Oedipus the King*)
Opera in three acts by Orff. 1st perf Stuttgart, 11 Dec 1959; a word-for-word setting of Friedrich Hölderlin's translation of Sophocles's play. Principal roles: Oedipus (ten), Jokasta (sop), Kreon (bass), Tiresias (ten), Shepherd (ten), Priest (bar). An austere and powerful setting, consisting largely of heightened declamation over a predominantly percussive accompaniment, it is only infrequently performed. For plot see *Oedipus Rex*. [R]

Oedipus Rex
Opera-oratorio in two acts by Stravinsky. 1st perf Paris, 30 May 1927; libr by Jean Cocteau, after Sophocles's *Oedipus the King*, translated into Latin by Jean Daniélou. Principal roles: Oedipus (ten), Jocasta (mezzo), Creon (bar), Messenger (bar), Tiresias (bass), Shepherd (ten), Narrator (speaker). Deliberately written in a dead language so as to lend a timeless quality to the drama (although a narrator describes events in contemporary language), the action is restricted to a minimum: the characters are masked, and move only their heads and arms, so as to give 'the impression of living statues'. One of Stravinsky's greatest works, notable for its choral writing, it is still regularly performed, more often in the concert hall than the opera house.
Plot: Legendary Thebes. Creon, sent by Oedipus to Delphi to discover from the oracle why the city has been visited by plague, returns with the message that the murderer of Oedipus's father is living in the city and must be punished. Oedipus forces the seer Tiresias to reveal that the murderer is a king. Queen Jocasta is adamant that oracles should be disregarded – had they not wrongly foretold that the former king, her husband, would be killed by his own son, whereas he had been killed by robbers at a crossroad? The truth begins to emerge: Oedipus knows that he himself killed an old man at a crossroad, and the Shepherd reveals that the parents who raised him had in fact adopted him. Jocasta, realizing that she has married her son, hangs herself and Oepidus puts out his eyes with her golden pin. The people gently drive Oedipus into exile. [R]

Oestvig, Karl (1889–1968)
Norwegian tenor, particularly associated with heroic German roles. One of the leading HELDENTENORS of the inter-war period, he created the Emperor in *Die Frau ohne Schatten* and Giovanni in Schillings's

Mona Lisa. His wife **Maria Rajdl** (1900–72) was a successful soprano.

Offenbach, Jacques (b Jakob Eberst) (1819–80)
German-born French composer and cellist, described by Rossini as 'the little Mozart of the Champs-Élysées'. His operettas, particularly those written in collaboration with HENRI MEILHAC and LUDOVIC HALÉVY, are irreverent and merciless satires on the society and morals of the Second Empire and often simultaneously debunk famous mythological stories. Offenbach also satirized famous composers, often by quoting their music in absurd situations or by setting it to ludicrous words. His own music is unfailingly tuneful, with tangy and sparkling orchestration, and is often marked by his exuberant high spirits. After the Franco-Prussian War and the fall of the Second Empire, the mood of Paris was less receptive to Offenbach's outrageous frivolity, and his later works are often of a more lyrical and sentimental character.

Beginning with LES DEUX AVEUGLES in 1855, he wrote nearly 100 stage works, first for his THÉÂTRE BOUFFES-PARISIENS and later for larger theatres. The most successful include *Le Mariage aux Lanternes* (Paris, 10 Oct 1857; libr Léon Battu and Michel Carré), the immortal ORPHÉE AUX ENFERS, *Mesdames de la Halle* (Paris, 3 Mar 1858; libr Armand Lapointe) [R], *Geneviève de Brabant* (Paris, 19 Nov 1859; libr Adolphe Jaime and Étienne Tréfue), *La Chanson de Fortunio* (Paris, 5 Jan 1861; libr Héctor Crémieux and Ludovic Halévy, after Alfred de Musset's *Le Chandelier*), *Monsieur Choufleuri Restera Chez-Lui* (Paris, 14 Sept 1861; libr Crémieux and Halévy) [R], *Les Bavards* (Paris, 20 Feb 1863; libr Charles Nuitter, after Miguel Cervantes's *Los Habladores*) [R], the ever-popular LA BELLE HÉLÈNE, BARBE-BLEUE, LA VIE PARISIENNE, the sensationally successful LA GRANDE-DUCHESSE DE GÉROLSTEIN, ROBINSON CRUSOÉ, the more sentimental LA PÉRICHOLE, LES BRIGANDS, POMME D'API, *Madame Favart* (Paris, 28 Dec 1878; libr Henri Charles Chivot and Alfred Duru) and LA FILLE DU TAMBOUR-MAJOR. In a very different vein are his two operas: the unsuccessful *Die Rheinnixen* (Vienna, 14 Feb 1864; libr August von Wolzogen, after Nuitter and Tréfue) and his masterpiece LES CONTES D'HOFFMANN, which was not quite completed at his death. The popular ballet *Gaîté Parisienne* was arranged by Manuel Rosenthal in 1938 from music from his operettas, and the operetta CHRISTOPHER COLUMBUS is the finest of a number of pastiches arranged from his forgotten stage works.

Ognivstev, Alexander (b 1920)
Russian bass, particularly associated with the Russian repertory. One of the finest Russian basses of the post-war era, he possessed a rich and velvety voice of considerable power and range and was an outstanding singing-actor, equally at home in serious or comic roles. He created Nicholas I in Shaporin's *The Decembrists* and the Leader in Kholminov's *An Optimistic Tragedy.*

Oiseaux dans la charmille, Les
Soprano aria (the Doll's Song) for Olympia in the Olympia Act of Offenbach's *Les Contes d'Hoffmann.*

O Isis und Osiris
Bass aria for Sarastro in Act II of Mozart's *Die Zauberflöte*, in which he prays to the Egyptian gods.

Olav Trygvason
Unfinished opera by Grieg (Op 50). 1st perf Christiania, 19 Oct 1889 (composed 1873); libr by Bjørnstjerne Bjørnson. Principal roles: Sibyl (mezzo), High Priest (bar). Grieg completed only three scenes of his sole operatic project, dealing with the first Christian king of Norway (reigned 995–1000). The scenes are sometimes performed in concert as a CANTATA. [R]

Old Maid and the Thief, The
Opera in one act by Menotti. 1st perf NBC Radio, 22 April 1939; 1st stage perf Philadelphia, 11 Feb 1941; libr by the composer. Principal roles: Bob (bar), Miss Todd (mezzo), Laetitia (sop), Miss Pinkerton (sop). A quasi-VERISMO piece, it is Menotti's second opera and is still occasionally performed.
Plot: Mid-20th-century Westchester (Pennsylvania). The vagabond Bob is befriended by the respectable Miss Todd, and is waited on by her maid Laetitia. Both

women connive at and commit robbery to aid him and delay his departure. Hearing that a notorious criminal is at large, the women assume him to be Bob. He denies it, but when he refuses Miss Todd's offer to elope, she goes for the police. While she is out, Bob and Laetitia steal her silver and run away together. [R]

Olga
1 Mezzo role in Tchaikovsky's *Eugene Onegin*. Tatyana's sister, she is engaged to Lensky. **2** Soprano role in Prokofiev's *The Story of a Real Man*. She loves Alexei. **3** Soprano role in Rimsky-Korsakov's *The Maid of Pskov*. She is Ivan the Terrible's daughter. **4** Soprano role in Dargomijsky's *Rusalka*. She is an orphan girl. **5** Soprano role in Giordano's *Fedora*. She is a Russian countess.

Olimpiade, L' (*The Olympiad*)
Opera in three acts by Vivaldi. 1st perf Venice, 17 Feb 1734; libr by Pietro Metastasio. Principal roles: Clistene (bass), Aristea (mezzo), Argene (sop), Licidia (bar), Megacle (ten), Aminta (ten), Alcandro (bass). One of the best settings of this frequently used Metastasian text, it deals with the historical Clysthenes (reigned *c* 600–*c* 570 BC), tyrant of Sicyon. It is hardly ever performed.
Plot: Greece, early-6th-century BC. Lycidas has asked his friend Megacles to represent him at the Olympic Games, where the victor will win the hand of King Clysthenes's daughter Aristea. However, Megacles is himself in love with Aristea. Clysthenes banishes Lycidas for his betrayal of Argene, to whom he had sworn fidelity. Lycidas attempts to kill Clysthenes and is sentenced to death. Argene offers to take his place, but it is revealed that Lycidas is Clysthenes's son, cast adrift as a child after an oracle had foretold that he would attempt to kill his father. Lycidas is forgiven and reconciled with Argene, whilst Megacles and Aristea are united. [R]

Oliver, Stephen (1948–92)
British composer, who wrote in a fluent and readily accessible if somewhat shallow style. He wrote some 50 musical theatre pieces, ranging from short one-acters for small forces to full-scale operas. They include *The Duchess of Malfi* (Oxford, 23 Nov 1971; libr composer, after John Webster), *The Donkey* (Stirling, 20 Sept 1973; libr David Poutney), *Tom Jones* (Snape, 6 Apr 1976; libr composer, after Henry Fielding), *The Garden* (Batignano, 27 July 1977; libr composer), the duodrama *A Man of Feeling* (London, 17 Nov 1980; libr composer, after Arthur Schnitzler's *Der Empfindsame*), *Sasha* (Banff, 7 Apr 1983; libr composer, after Alexander Nikolayevich Ostrovsky's *Artists and Admirers*), *Beauty and the Beast* (Batignano, 26 July 1984; libr composer, after Jean Marie le Prince de Beaumont), *Mario and the Magician* (Batignano, 5 Aug 1988; libr composer, after Thomas Mann) and *Timon of Athens* (London, 17 May 1991; libr composer, after Shakespeare). He also produced editions – so radical as to amount almost to new works – of Peri's *Euridice* (London, 4 Mar 1981) and Mozart's *L'Oca del Cairo* (Batignano, 28 July 1991). He died of AIDS.

Olivero, Magda (b Maria Maddalena) (b 1912)
Italian soprano, particularly associated with the Italian repertory, especially Tosca and Adriana Lecouvreur. An outstanding singing-actress, she enjoyed two careers: she retired in 1941, but returned to the stage in 1951 and enjoyed a remarkably long career, making her debut at the Metropolitan Opera, New York, at the age of 63. She created Maria in Rossellini's *La Guerra* and Melibea in Testi's *Celestina*.

Olivier
Baritone role in Strauss's *Capriccio*. He is a poet in love with the Countess.

Olomouc Opera
(Olmütz when it was part of Austria-Hungary). Opera in this Czech town in Moravia is given at the Oldřich Stibor Theatre (cap 750). Musical directors have included Iša Krejčí and Zdeněk Košler.

O luce di quest' anima
Soprano aria for Linda in Act I of Donizetti's *Linda di Chamounix*, in which she sings of her love for Carlo.

Olympia
Soprano role in Offenbach's *Les Contes d'Hoffmann*. The first of Hoffmann's loves,

she is a mechanical doll invented by Spalanzani.

Olympians, The
Opera in three acts by Bliss. 1st perf London, 29 Sept 1949; libr by J.B. Priestley. Principal roles: Diana (sop), Madeleine (sop), Héctor (ten), Bardeau (mezzo), Lavatte (bass), Jupiter (bar), Bacchus (ten), Mars (bass), Curé (ten). The first of Bliss's two operas, it was a failure at its appearance and is nowadays almost never performed.
Plot: Provence, Midsummer Day 1836. The ancient gods are reduced to travelling the world as a group of destitute strolling players, and are staying at Bardeau's inn. Once a century, on Midsummer's Night, they regain their former powers. They use these powers to aid the love of Madeleine and the playwright Héctor de Florac and to humiliate Madeleine's miserly father Lavatte.

Olympie
Opera in three acts by Spontini. 1st perf Paris, 22 Dec 1819; libr by Michel Dieulafoy and Charles Brifaut, after Voltaire's play. Revised version 1st perf Berlin, 14 May 1821; libr revised by E.T.A. Hoffmann. Principal roles: Olympie (sop), Statire (mezzo), Cassandre (ten), Antigone (b-bar), Hiérophante (bass). Although it is one of Spontini's finest operas, it is only very rarely performed.
Plot: Ephesus, 332 BC. Alexander the Great's successors Cassandre and Antigone vie for the hand of his daughter Olympie. She prefers Cassandre, but her choice is opposed by Alexander's widow Statire (disguised as a priestess), who believes that Cassandre poisoned her husband. Antigone is mortally wounded in battle with Cassandre's forces and confesses to the poisoning. The way is thus clear for the lovers to be united, and Statire is installed as supreme ruler. [R]

Olympion
Tenor role in Tippett's *The Ice Break*. He is a black 'champion'.

Ô ma lyre immortelle
Mezzo aria for Sapho in Act III of Gounod's *Sapho*, in which she says that her art can no longer soothe her inner pain. The final scene of the opera.

Ombra mai fù
Mezzo aria for Xerxes in Act I of Händel's *Serse*, in which he praises the tree which provides him with shade. It is nearly always referred to as 'Handel's Largo', even though it is marked larghetto in the score.

Ombre légère
Soprano aria (the Shadow Song) for Dinorah in Act II of Meyerbeer's *Dinorah*, in which she expresses her love for the shadows cast by the moonlight.

O mio babbino caro
Soprano aria for Lauretta in Puccini's *Gianni Schicchi*, in which she begs her father to let her marry Rinuccio.

Ô mon Fernand
Mezzo aria for Léonor in Act III of Donizetti's *La Favorite*, in which she expresses her love for Fernand.

O monumento
Baritone aria for Barnaba in Act I of Ponchielli's *La Gioconda*, in which he contemplates the dogal palace and reflects on the joys and sorrows which it represents.

O namenlose Freude
Soprano/tenor duet for Leonore and Florestan in Act II of Beethoven's *Fidelio*, in which they express their joy at finally being reunited.

Ô Nature
Tenor aria for Werther in Act I of Massenet's *Werther*, in which he rhapsodizes over the beauties of nature.

Oncina, Juan (b 1925)
Spanish tenor, particularly associated with Rossini and lighter Donizetti roles. One of the leading tenore di grazias of the 1950s, he later – unwisely and unsuccessfully – undertook heavier roles. His wife **Tatiana Menotti** (*b* 1910) was a successful soprano.

Onegin, Sigrid (b Hoffmann) (1889–1943)
Swedish mezzo, particularly associated with Wagnerian roles and with Amneris in Verdi's *Aida*. One of the leading mezzos of

the inter-war period, she possessed a rich and beautiful voice of great range and had a regal stage presence. She created Dryad in *Ariadne auf Naxos*.

O'Neill, Dennis (b 1948)
British tenor, particularly associated with the Italian repertory, especially Verdi. One of the few British tenors of the post-war period to produce a real Italianate sound, he has a fine and intelligently-used voice and a good stage presence. His sister **Patricia** is a soprano; her husband **Patrick Wheatley** is a baritone.

Onore! ladri!, L'
Baritone aria (the Honour Monologue) for Falstaff in Act I of Verdi's *Falstaff*, in which he lectures Pistol and Bardolf on the worthlessness of honour.

Ô Paradis
Tenor aria for Vasco da Gama in Act IV of Meyerbeer's *L'Africaine*, in which he salutes the island of Madagascar.

O patria mia
Soprano aria for Aida in Act III of Verdi's *Aida*, in which she laments that she cannot see her homeland.

Open-air performances
The earliest open-air opera performances were probably those of a number of Lully's works in the gardens of Versailles. Nowadays, open-air performances are a frequent feature of the European summer festival scene. The most notable are at Bregenz in Austria, Aix-en-Provence and Orange in France, Savonlinna in Finland and Verona in Italy.

Opera (Italian for 'work')
A shortening of the term *opera in musica*, it means a dramatic text which is sung by one or more singers to an instrumental accompaniment. It originated in Italy in the last decade of the 16th century with the endeavours of the FLORENTINE CAMERATA to recreate the conditions of Greek drama. Many varieties of opera have subsequently evolved, which are described in this dictionary under their various titles. *see* AZIONE SACRA; AZIONE TEATRALE; BALLAD OPERA; BALLET-HÉROÏQUE; BURLETTA; CANTATA; CHAMBER OPERA; COMIC OPERA; DIVERTISSEMENT; DRAMMA EROICOMICO; DRAMMA GIOCOSO; DRAMMA PER MUSICA; FARSA; FAVOLA PER MUSICA; FESTA TEATRALE; GÉNERO CHICO; GRAND OPERA; INTERMEZZO; LIEDERSPIEL; MARIONETTE OPERAS; MASQUE; MELODRAMA; MELODRAMMA; MONODRAMA; MUSIC-DRAMA; NEAPOLITAN OPERA; NUMBER OPERA; OPERA-BALLET; OPÉRA-BOUFFE; OPERA BUFFA; OPÉRA-COMIQUE; OPÉRA-LYRIQUE; OPERA-ORATORIO; OPERA SEMISERIA; OPERA SERIA; OPERETTA; PASTORALE HÉROÏQUE; QUARTER-TONE OPERAS; RESCUE OPERA; SAINETE; SECULAR ORATORIO; SINGSPIEL; SPIELOPER; TONADILLA; TRAGÉDIE-LYRIQUE; TWELVE-TONE OPERAS; VERISMO; ZARZUELA; ZAUBEROPER; ZIETOPER; ZWISCHENSPIEL

Opera
A monthly British magazine, founded by the Earl of Harewood in 1950, it deals with both the national and international opera scenes. Its editors have been Lord Harewood, Harold Rosenthal and Rodney Milnes.

Opéra, Paris
see PARIS OPÉRA

Opera-ballet
A theatrical form which flourished in France in the late 17th and early 18th centuries and which refers to a work which combines dance with a sung dramatic text. Many of Lully's stage works fall into this category, and Rameau used the term to describe several of his works, such as *Les Fêtes d'Hébé* and *Les Indes Galantes*.

Opéra-Bastille, Paris
Designed by Carlos Ott, the theatre (cap 2,716) opened on 13 July 1989. Now the principal operatic venue in Paris, Daniel Barenboim was appointed its first musical director, but was dismissed in Jan 1989 over artistic and financial differences and was replaced by Myung-Whun Chung, who was also subsequently dismissed. Plagued by technical and political problems since its opening, it is already being used less and less often.

Opéra-bouffe (French for 'comic opera')
The term derives from the Italian OPERA

BUFFA, although its meaning is not quite the same. It describes a comic work (either opera or operetta) with spoken dialogue, and is the term used by Offenbach to describe many of his stage works.

Opera buffa (Italian for 'comic work') An Italian opera on a comic subject. Developing as a form in its own right from the early 18th-century INTERMEZZI, the term should strictly speaking be used to describe works of the period 1750–1850, in other words from Galuppi, through Paisiello, Cimarosa and Rossini to Donizetti.

Opéra-comique (French for 'comic opera') A slightly vague and misleading term. It refers to a French opera that contains spoken dialogue. The term was used from about 1790 to 1880 to refer to any piece, whether serious or comic, which was not THROUGH-COMPOSED. It is applied to operas as diverse as *Médée*, *Carmen*, *Fra Diavolo* and *Les Contes d'Hoffmann*.

Opéra-Comique, Paris
Often referred to as the Salle Favart after its location in the Rue Favart, the present theatre (cap 1,750) opened on 7 Dec 1898, replacing the previous theatre of the same name which opened in 1783 but which was destroyed by fire in 1887 with the loss of 131 lives. Paris's second house, it was originally the home of those works named after it which could not be produced at the Opéra because of the latter's ban on spoken dialogue. The annual season runs from September to July. Musical directors have included Messager, Jean Fournet, André Cluytens, Roger Désmorière and Alain Lombard.

Opera Company of Boston
Founded in 1957 by the conductor Sarah Caldwell, who is its artistic and musical director, it pursues an enterprising repertory policy, having given many US premieres. The annual season runs from December to May. Since 1979, performances have been given at the Opera House (formerly the Keith Memorial Theater) (cap 2,605).

Opéra de Lyon
The opera company in this city in the Rhône (France) performs at the Grand Théâtre (cap 3,000), which opened in 1831 and which was enlarged in 1842. The annual season runs from October to June, and the company has been noted in recent years for its adventurous repertory, particularly of 20th-century works. Musical directors have included André Cluytens, Theodor Guschlbauer, Serge Baudo, John Eliot Gardiner and Kent Nagano.

Opéra de Montréal
Founded in 1980 to replace the defunct Opéra du Québec, which had operated from 1971 to 1975, this Canadian company gives four productions a year at the Salle Wilfrid Pelletier (cap 2,874), which opened in 1967. The artistic director is Jean-Paul Jeannotte.

Opéra du Rhin
Formed in 1972, the company is based at the Théâtre Municipal (cap 1,000) in Strasbourg, and also gives performances at the Théâtre Municipal (cap 750) in Colmar and the Théâtre Municipal (cap 867) in Mulhouse. The annual season runs from September to July. Musical directors have included Alain Lombard, Theodor Guschlbauer and Alain Housset.

Opera Factory
A chamber company formed by the producer DAVID FREEMAN in Sydney in 1973, in Zürich in 1976 and in London in 1981. It gives small-scale and sometimes highly controversial productions which place great stress on the dramatic side. Musical directors have been Paul Daniel and Mark Wigglesworth.

Opera films
Operatic films are nearly as old as the cinema itself, many being made even in the silent days; the first was *Faust* in 1903. The first sound film of an opera was an Italian *Pagliacci* in 1928, since when a large number have been made, especially in Italy and Russia. Some have been content to reproduce a theatrical performance on the large screen, whilst others have adopted a large-scale, often open-air approach, removing the work entirely from its theatrical setting. Among the most successful of earlier operatic films are *Louise* with Grace Moore and

Georges Thill, *Pagliacci* with Tito Gobbi and Gina Lollobrigida, the Thomas Beecham/Robert Helpmann *The Tales of Hoffmann* and Stroyeva's *Boris Godunov*. More recently, Franco Zeffirelli's *La Traviata* and Josef Losey's *Don Giovanni* have met with considerable success, as have Ingmar Bergman's *The Magic Flute* and Franco Rosi's *Carmen*. More controversial was Zeffirelli's *Otello*. No operas have been written specifically for the cinema, but mention may be made of Korngold's *Romeo and Juliet*, a mini-opera written for the film *Give Us This Night* (1936). *See also* VIDEO RECORDINGS

Opera Guild of Greater Miami
Founded in 1941 by the tenor Arturo di Filippi, it gives performances at the Miami Beach Auditorium (cap 3,700) and at the Dade County Auditorium (cap 2,500). The repertory tends to be conservative. The musical director is Emerson Buckley.

Opéra-lyrique (French for 'lyric opera')
The term was used in France in the second half of the 19th century to describe an opera slightly lighter and less formal in style than grand opera but more serious than OPÉRA-COMIQUE. It was used to define many of the operas by Gounod, Thomas and Massenet.

Opera North
Originally called English National Opera North, the company began operations on 15 Nov 1978 as an offshoot of the English National Opera, but is now completely autonomous. Noted for its highly adventurous repertory policy, it is based at the Grand Theatre, Leeds (cap 1,534) and also visits other towns in northern and central England. Musical directors have been David Lloyd-Jones and Paul Daniel.

Opera Northern Ireland
The company was formed in 1984 and gives two short annual seasons at the Grand Opera House in Belfast, which was designed by Frank Matcham. The orchestra is the Ulster Orchestra, and musical directors have included Alun Francis, Kenneth Montgomery and Stephen Barlow.

Opera-oratorio
A term describing a work which partakes of the qualities of both opera and oratorio, being of a largely static nature but setting a dramatic text and intended to be staged. Much the best-known example is Stravinsky's *Oedipus Rex*.

Opera Rara
A British company founded to promote the revival of long-forgotten operas, mainly of the early 19th century. Originally devoted to giving staged or concert performances, it has recently concentrated on recordings, particularly of Donizetti. The artistic director is Patric Schmid.

Opera recordings
The gramophone has, from its earliest days, played an important part in operatic life, as indeed opera and opera singers have played an important part in the gramophone's life: it was well observed that 'Caruso made the gramophone and the gramophone made Caruso'. The earliest operatic recordings were of extracts made on cylinders in the mid-1890s, but these were soon superseded by those made on Emile Berliner's shellac plate, the familiar flat disc. The first 'complete' opera recording was a heavily abridged *Il Trovatore* made between 1903 and 1906; very soon afterwards Leoncavallo conducted a virtually uncut recording of *Pagliacci*. The advent of electrical, as opposed to the earlier acoustic, recordings in the 1920s marked a great improvement in sound quality, but the gramophone did not fully come into its own until the appearance of the long-playing record in 1950 made complete opera recordings a far more practical proposition. Sound quality and facility of storage were both improved in the 1980s with the advent of the compact disc. In the last 40 years, the gramophone has made a vast contribution to the expansion of the repertory – nearly 1,100 different operas, operettas and ZARZUELAS have been commercially recorded – and to making opera more widely accessible.

Against the great benefits to opera brought by the gramophone must be set some drawbacks and dangers. The major record companies are now so important and powerful that their plans are sometimes allowed to dictate both repertory and casting to opera houses;

they have been largely responsible for the evils of the 'star system', which has come near to destroying the ideal of ensemble performance. Also, modern technology is now so far advanced that the finished product can often sound clinical, artificial and devoid of any drama or spontaneity. In addition, recording techniques are such that artists can be (and often are) made to sound a great deal better than they actually are. Finally, it must be acknowledged that the hype with which the recording companies surround their young stars is not only rather vulgar, but is also potentially damaging to the artists themselves. *See Appendix 1 for a listing of all commercially recorded operas, operettas and zarzuelas.*

Opera semiseria (Italian for 'half-serious work')
The term originated in the mid-18th century with Piccinni's *La Buona Figliuola* to describe an opera largely of a light character but also containing some serious elements. Famous 19th-century examples include *La Gazza Ladra* and *Linda di Chamounix*.

Opera seria (Italian for 'serious work')
The principal operatic form of the 18th century, it describes an opera on a serious subject with certain fixed conventions, such as formalized emotions, elaborate DA CAPO arias and plots involving characters from mythology or ancient history. The drama usually revolves around a conflict between love and duty, as epitomized by the texts of Apostolo Zeno and Pietro Metastasio, the two most important opera seria librettists. Flourishing particularly in Italy, Germany and England, the form's main composers were Händel, Hasse, A. Scarlatti, Vivaldi, Bononcini and Graun. The form soon developed a rigid formality which was both highly artificial and dramatically suffocating. The SINGSPIEL in Germany and OPERA BUFFA in Italy developed in reaction to this.

Opéras-minutes
Three mini-operas in one act by Milhaud (Op 94, 98 and 99). Comprising *L'Enlèvement de l'Europe* (*The Abduction of Europa*), 1st perf Baden-Baden, 17 Aug 1927, *L'Abandon d'Ariane* (*The Desertion of Ariadne*), 1st perf Wiesbaden, 20 Apr 1928 and *La Déliverance de Thésée* (*The Rescue of Theseus*), 1st perf Wiesbaden, 20 Apr 1928; libr by Henri Hoppenot. All drawn from Greek mythology, the works last between eight and twelve minutes each. [R]

Opera Society of Washington
Founded in 1956, the company now performs at the Kennedy Center for the Performing Arts (cap 2,200), which opened in Sept 1971. It pursues one of the most enterprising repertory policies of any American company. Artistic directors have included George London and Plácido Domingo, and musical directors Paul Calloway and Heinz Fricke.

Operetta (Italian for 'little work')
There is no exact definition of the term operetta. It describes a musical stage work in lighter operatic style, usually with spoken dialogue and nearly always of a comic nature. A great deal of musical snobbery exists on the subject of operetta: many people (but seldom professional musicians) fall into the error of equating lightness of style and subject with lightness of quality. By any criteria, the four major exponents of the genre (Offenbach, Sullivan, J. Strauss II and Lehár) were master composers, and the finest operettas are of vastly superior musical quality to, for example, the works of the minor Italian VERISMO composers.

Although virtually every country (except perhaps Italy) has its own operetta tradition, there are four principal schools. Viennese operetta is exemplified by Lehár, J. Strauss, Suppé, Millöcker, Kálmán and Zeller; French operetta is dominated by Offenbach, the considerable contribution of Planquette, Lecocq, Audran and especially Messager often being overlooked; English operetta is synonymous with Sullivan, as virtually no other composers' works have survived; in Spain, ZARZUELA has had many fine exponents, particularly Barbieri, Bretón, Giménez, Serrano and Vives. Most opera companies carry a few operettas in their repertories and some (such as the Vienna Volksoper, the D'Oyly Carte Opera Company and New Sadler's Wells Opera) have specialized in it. *See also* OPÉRA-BOUFFE; TONADILLA; ZARZUELA.

· Operatic deaths ·

Many operatic characters meet their ends – invariably untimely ones – during the course of the story. Some of these come by their deaths in the most bizarre and extraordinary fashion. Below are listed some of the more recherché deaths to be found in operatic plots.

- Fenella in Auber's *La Muette de Portici* jumps from the royal palace of Naples into the erupting mouth of Mount Vesuvius.
- Rachel in Halévy's *La Juive* is thrown into a vat of boiling oil on the orders of her father (who is a Roman Catholic cardinal).
- Iris in Mascagni's *Iris* throws herself down a laundry chute into a sewer.
- Adriana in Cilea's *Adriana Lecouvreur* dies from smelling a bunch of poisoned violets.
- Sélika in Meyerbeer's *L'Africaine* dies from inhaling the poisonous scent of the Manchineel tree.
- Lakmé in Delibes's *Lakmé* dies from eating the poisonous datura leaf.
- Manfredo and Avito in Montemezzi's *L'Amore dei Tre Re* die from kissing the poison-smeared lips of a dead woman.
- Fredegundis in Schmidt's *Fredegundis* dies after a falling coffin traps her by the hair.
- Creusa in Mayr's *Medea in Corinto* dies from wearing a poisoned wedding robe.
- Wally and Hagenbach in Catalani's *La Wally* are killed in an avalanche.
- Owen in Britten's *Owen Wingrave* dies from sleeping in a haunted room.
- Antonia in Offenbach's *Les Contes d'Hoffmann* sings herself to death.
- Danny Man in Benedict's *The Lily of Killarney* is shot when he is mistaken for an otter.
- Zampa in Hérold's *Zampa* is drowned by the hand of a statue.
- Cio-Cio-San in Puccini's *Madama Butterfly* commits harakiri (mercifully offstage).
- The Archdeacon in Schmidt's *Notre Dame* is thrown off the platform linking the two towers of Notre-Dame Cathedral.
- Boris in Shostakovich's *Lady Macbeth of Mtsensk* dies from rat poison administered by his daughter-in-law in a dish of mushrooms.
- Aida and Radamès in Verdi's *Aida* are buried alive.
- Huascar in Rameau's *Les Indes Galantes* throws himself into a volcano.
- Giovanni in Schillings's *Mona Lisa* suffocates in a cupboard after being locked in by his wife.
- Baron Scarpia in Puccini's *Tosca* is stabbed by an opera singer.
- Billy in Britten's *Billy Budd* is hung from the yard-arm.
- Vrenchen and Sali in Delius's *A Village Romeo and Juliet* commit suicide by sinking the barge in which they are floating.
- Marietta in Korngold's *Die Tote Stadt* is strangled with her own hair.
- Gueniėvre in Chausson's *Le Roi Arthus* strangles herself with her own hair.
- Chim-Fen in Leoni's *L'Oracolo* is strangled with his own pigtail.
- Gherardo in Pizzetti's *Fra Gherardo* is burnt at the stake.
- Robbins in Gershwin's *Porgy and Bess* is killed with a cotton hook.
- Leonora in Verdi's *Il Trovatore* dies from poison sucked from a ring.
- Barbara in Tubin's *Barbara von Tisenhusen* is pushed through a hole in an ice floe by her brothers.
- Pentheus in Henze's *The Bassarids* is torn to pieces by a group of women (including his mother).
- Magda Sorel in Menotti's *The Consul* commits suicide by gassing herself.
- King Dodon in Rimsky-Korsakov's *The Golden Cockerel* dies from being pecked on the head by a bird.
- The forty thieves in Cherubini's *Ali Baba* are burnt alive whilst sown into coffee sacks.
- Most of the cast in Poulenc's *Dialogues des Carmélites* are guillotined.

Opernball, Der (*The Opera Ball*)
Operetta in three acts by Heuberger (Op 40). 1st perf Vienna, 5 Jan 1898; libr by Heinrich von Waldeberg and Viktor Léon, after Alfred Delacour and Alfred Hennequin's *Les Dominos Roses*. Principal roles: Angèle (sop), Marguérite (sop), Georges Duméail (ten), Hortense (sop), Henri (mezzo). By far Heuberger's most successful work, still quite frequently performed in German-speaking countries, it tells of a ball at the Paris Opéra to which two philandering husbands take two pretty women who turn out to be each other's wives. [R Exc]

Opernprobe, Die (*The Opera Rehearsal*) or **Die Vornehmen Dilettanten** (*The Aristocratic Amateurs*)
Comic opera in one act by Lortzing. 1st perf Frankfurt, 20 Jan 1851; libr by the composer, after Johann Friedrich Jünger's *Die Komödie aus dem Stegreif*. Principal roles: Hannchen (sop), Adolph (ten), Johann (b-bar), Count (bar), Countess (mezzo), Louise (sop). Lortzing's last opera, it is an amusing little piece which is still occasionally performed in Germany. [R]

Ô Prêtres de Baal
Mezzo aria for Fidès in Act V of Meyerbeer's *Le Prophète*, in which she prays for her son despite his rejection of her.

Oprichnik, The
Opera in two acts by Tchaikovsky. 1st perf St Petersburg, 24 April 1874; libr by the composer, after Ivan Ivanovich Lazhechnikov's play. Principal roles: Andrei (ten), Natasha (sop), Mitkov (bass), Morozova (mezzo). Tchaikovsky's first opera to be publicly performed, it incorporates music from the discarded *The Voyevoda*. A powerful work, it is hardly ever performed outside Russia.
Plot: 16th-century Russia. Andrei Morozov has joined the dreaded Oprichniks, Ivan the Terrible's ruthless guard. He has done this to revenge himself on a nobleman who robbed him and his mother Morozova of their estate, and who forced his daughter Natasha – who loves Andrei – to become engaged to another man. It is announced that the Tsar will release Andrei from his oath of loyalty so that he can marry Natasha. Natasha is summoned to the Tsar and Andrei, although assured that this is merely a final test of his loyalty, refuses to let her go. For this disobedience, Andrei is dragged off to execution, and Morozova is forced to watch. [R]

O quante volte
Soprano aria for Giulietta in Act I of Bellini's *I Capuleti e i Montecchi*, in which she expresses her longing for Romeo. Bellini adapted the music from an aria in his earlier *Adelson e Salvini*.

Oracolo, L' (*The Oracle*)
Opera in one act by Leoni. 1st perf London, 28 June 1905; libr by Camillo Zanoni, after Chester Bailey Fernald's *The Cat and the Cherub*. Principal roles: Uin-Sci (bass), Ah-Yoe (sop), Chim-Fen (bar), San-Lui (ten), Hu-Tsin (bass), Hua-Qui (mezzo). Leoni's only work still to be in any way remembered, its lurid story of murder, madness and mayhem in San Francisco's Chinatown ensured it an initial success and disguised its banal musical qualities. It is nowadays only very rarely performed.
Plot: 19th-century San Francisco. The evil opium dealer Chim-Fen abducts the child of the rich merchant Hu-Tsin and offers to 'find' the child in return for marriage to his niece Ah-Yoe. Chim-Fen murders Ah-Yoe's beloved San-Lui, thus causing Ah-Yoe to go insane. San-Lui's father Uin-Sci (the oracle of the opera's title) kills Chim-Fen by strangling him with his own pigtail and then props him up against a lamppost and talks to him whilst a policeman walks by. [R]

Ora di morte
Soprano/baritone duet for Lady Macbeth and Macbeth in Act III of Verdi's *Macbeth*, in which they vow to spill more blood so as to secure the throne. Written for the revised version, it replaces Macbeth's cabaletta 'Vada in fiamme'.

Ora e per sempre addio
Tenor monologue for Otello in Act II of Verdi's *Otello*, in which he bids farewell to his past glories.

Orange Festival
An annual open-air summer festival in

Provence (France), which was founded in 1971 by Jacques Bourgeois and Jean Darnel. Performances – usually of 'spectacular' operas such as *Aida* – are given at the Roman amphitheatre (cap 9,000). Top international casts are engaged and the setting is majestic, although the Mistral presents an occasional and unpredictable acoustical hazard.

Orazi e Curiazi (*Horatii and Curiatii*)
Opera in three acts by Mercadante. 1st perf Naples, 10 Nov 1846; libr by Salvatore Cammarano, after Pierre Corneille's *Horace*. Principal roles: Camilla (sop), Orazio (bar), Curiazio (ten), Il Vecchio (bass), High Priest (ten). One of Mercadante's most successful operas, it is nowadays hardly ever performed. [R]

Orazi e i Curiazi, Gli (*The Horatii and the Curiatii*)
Opera in two acts by Cimarosa. 1st perf Venice, 26 Dec 1796; libr by Antonio Simone Sografi, after Pierre Corneille's *Horace*. Principal roles: Curiazio (sop), Orazia (mezzo), Marco Orazio (ten), High Priest (bass), Sabina (sop), Publio Orazio (ten). Often regarded as the finest of Cimarosa's serious operas, it is the only one which still receives an occasional performance.
Plot: Rome, 7th century BC. The Romans led by the Horatii are at war with the Alba Longans led by the Curiatii, and Sabina Curiatius is torn between her people and her husband Publius Horatius's son Marcus. To mark a truce, Horatia is wedded to Curiatius, and it is decided that the final outcome of the war will be determined by a combat between three Horatii and three Curiatii. In this combat, Curiatius is killed by Marcus. The distraught Orazia curses both Rome and her brother Marcus, who stabs her to death.

Orchestration
The art of writing for the orchestra. The fathers of modern operatic orchestration are usually regarded as Mayr and Berlioz. Subsequent masters of orchestration have included Strauss, Chabrier, Rimsky-Korsakov, Verdi in his later works, and Ravel.

Or co' dadi
Soldiers' chorus in Act II of Verdi's *Il Trovatore*.

Orefice, Giacomo (1865–1922)
Italian composer. He wrote a number of operas in VERISMO style, of which the most successful included *Chopin* (Milan, 25 Nov 1901; libr A. Orvieto) and *Il Mosè* (Genoa, 18 Feb 1905; libr Orvieto). He was also a leading advocate and editor of early music.

Oresteia
Operatic trilogy by Taneyev. 1st perf St Petersburg, 29 Oct 1895; libr by Alexei Venkstern, after Aeschylus's Oresteian Trilogy. Principal roles: Agamemnon (bass), Clytemnestra (mezzo), Aegisthus (bar), Cassandra (sop), Elektra (sop), Orestes (ten), Apollo (bar), Pallas Athene (sop). Taneyev's only operatic work, it is more a three-act opera rather than a real trilogy. Although it contains some fine music, it is virtually unknown outside Russia. [R]

Orestes
The son of Agamemnon and Clytemnestra appears in several operas, including:
1 Baritone role in Strauss's *Elektra*.
2 Baritone role in Gluck's *Iphigénie en Tauride*. **3** Mezzo trouser role in Offenbach's *La Belle Hélène*. **4** Baritone role in Milhaud's *Les Choëphores*. **5** Tenor role in Taneyev's *Oresteia*. **6** Tenor role in Rossini's *Ermione*. **7** Baritone role in Křenek's *Leben des Orest*.

Orfeide, L'
Operatic triptych by Malipiero, comprising *La Morte delle Maschere* (*The Death of the Masks*), *Sette Canzoni* (*Seven Songs*) and *Orfeo, ovvero l'Ottavo Canzone* (*Orpheus, or the Eighth Song*). 1st perf (Part II only) Paris, 10 July 1920; 1st complete perf Düsseldorf, 31 Oct 1925; libr by the composer, after Angelo Poliziano and other sources. Malipiero's finest stage work.

Orfeo (*Orpheus*)
Opera in prologue and three acts by Rossi. 1st perf Paris, 2 March 1647; libr by Francesco Buti. Principal roles: Orfeo (sop), Euridice (sop), Aristeo (sop), Jupiter (ten), Endimione (bass), Venere (sop), Satyr (bass), Nurse (mezzo), Augur

(bass), Momus (bar). The second of Rossi's two operas and the first opera to be performed in France, it is described as a 'tragicomédie en musique' and is notable for its portrayal of Jupiter disguised as an old woman. [R]

Orfeo, L'
see FAVOLA D'ORFEO, LA

Orfeo ed Euridice (*Orpheus and Eurydice*)
Opera in three acts by Gluck. 1st perf Vienna, 5 Oct 1762; libr by Ranieri de' Calzabigi. Revised version *Orphée et Eurydice*, 1st perf Paris, 2 Aug 1774; libr revised by Pierre-Louis Moline. Principal roles: Orfeo (c-ten or mezzo or ten), Euridice (sop), Amor (sop). Gluck's most famous work and his first reform opera.
Plot: Legendary Greece. The musician Orpheus laments the death of his beloved wife Eurydice. Amor tells him that Zeus will permit him to go to the underworld to plead for her return, but that if she is released he must not look back on her until they have returned to the living world. Orpheus charms the Furies with the beauty of his singing and finds Eurydice amongst the blessed spirits. He leads her away, but his seeming indifference in not looking at her makes Eurydice threaten to go back to Hades. Her distress moves Orpheus to look at her, and she immediately sinks back into the shadows. Orpheus laments her loss and Amor, taking pity on him, once again brings Eurydice back to life. [R both versions]

Orfeo ed Euridice (*Orpheus and Eurydice*) or **L'Anima del Filosofo** (*The Spirit of the Philosopher*)
Opera in four acts by Haydn. 1st perf Florence, 10 June 1951 (composed 1791); libr by Carlo Francesco Badini. Principal roles: Orfeo (ten), Euridice (sop), Creonte (bass), Genio (sop). Haydn's last opera, intended for performance in London, it contains some of his greatest stage music but is unaccountably only very rarely performed.
Plot: Legendary Greece. Eurydice has left the kingdom of her father Creon to avoid marrying a man she despises. She is threatened by monsters, but is saved by Orpheus, who calms them with the beauty of his singing. Creon agrees to their union. Whilst fleeing from an agent of her rejected suitor, Eurydice treads on a snake and is fatally bitten. Orpheus descends to Hades in search of her and is permitted to take her back provided that he does not look at her until they return to the living world. Unaware of this condition, Eurydice steps in front of Orpheus, who is thus forced to look at her. She is lost to him for ever and he renounces the world and takes poison. [R]

Orff, Carl (1895–1982)
German composer. His stage works were intended to free opera from what he regarded as late-19th-century excesses, and are heavily dependant on simple rhythms and on traditional folk melodies. His operas are DER MOND, DIE KLUGE, his most successful opera, the play with songs DIE BERNAUERIN, ANTIGONAE, TRIONFO D'AFRODITE, OEDIPUS DER TYRANN, *Ludus de Nato Infante Mirificus* (Stuttgart, 11 Dec 1960; libr composer) [R], *Prometheus* (Stuttgart, 24 Mar 1968; libr composer, after Aeschylus) and *De Temporum Fine Comoedia* (Salzburg, 20 Aug 1973; libr composer) [R].

Orlando (*Roland*)
Opera in three acts by Händel. 1st perf London, 23 Jan 1733; libr by Grazio Braccioli, after Carlo Sigismondo Capeci's libretto for D. Scarlatti's *L'Orlando*, itself based on Lodovico Ariosto's *Orlando Furioso*. Principal roles: Orlando (c-ten), Angelica (sop), Dorinda (sop), Zoroastro (bass), Medoro (ten). One of Händel's finest operas, it has been quite frequently performed in recent years.
Plot: Despite the magician Zoroastro's urgings that he turn to military glory, Orlando sighs for Queen Angelica of Cathay, although she loves the prince Medoro, who is loved by the shepherdess Dorinda. Dorinda gets Angelica to admit that she and Medoro are betrothed and is given a piece of jewellery by Angelica. This is recognized by Orlando, who had given it to Angelica. The furious Orlando pursues Angelica and Medoro, but Zoroastro intervenes and Angelica is spirited away. Orlando loses his reason, but his mind is restored by Zoroastro, and he gives his blessing to Angelica's union with Medoro. [R]

Orlando Furioso (*Mad Roland*)
Opera in three acts by Vivaldi. 1st perf Venice, autumn 1727; libr by Grazio Braccioli, after Lodovico Ariosto's epic poem. Principal roles: Orlando (mezzo), Angelica (sop), Alcina (mezzo), Ruggiero (bass), Bradamante (mezzo), Medoro (ten), Astolfo (bass). Vivaldi's second setting of the Orlando story, notable for its remarkable mad scene, it was long totally forgotten but has received a number of performances in the last decade, many as a vehicle for Marilyn Horne. [R]

Orlando Paladino (*Roland the Paladin*)
Opera in three acts by Haydn. 1st perf Esterháza, 6 Dec 1782; libr by Nunziato Porta, after Lodovico Ariosto's *Orlando Furioso*. Principal roles: Orlando (ten), Angelica (sop), Alcina (mezzo), Medoro (ten), Pasquale (bar), Rodomonte (bar), Eurilla (sop), Charon (bass). Described as a 'dramma eroicomico', it combines serious and comic elements in one of Haydn's finest operas. After a long period of total neglect, it has received a number of performances in the last decade.
Plot: Rodomonte, King of Barbary, seeking the deranged Orlando, learns that Queen Angelica of Cathay and her lover Medoro are in a nearby castle. Angelica fears that Orlando will kill Medoro and seeks the aid of the sorceress Alcina. Rodomonte challenges Orlando, but they are told by the shepherdess Eurilla that Angelica and Medoro are attempting to escape by sea. Orlando thwarts that escape and is taken by Alcina to the River Lethe to cure his madness. At Alcina's command, Charon's spell of madness is lifted and Orlando and Rodomonte are reconciled. Angelica and Medoro are now able to marry, and Eurilla marries Orlando's squire Pasquale. [R]

Orlofsky, Prince
Mezzo trouser role in J. Strauss's *Die Fledermaus*. He is an easily-bored young Russian prince.

Ormandy, Eugene (b Jenö Blau) (1899–1985)
Hungarian conductor and violinist, long resident in the United States. Best known as a symphonic conductor, his operatic appearances were very rare.

Ormindo, L'
Opera in three acts by Cavalli. 1st perf Venice, spring 1644; libr by Giovanni Battista Faustini. Principal roles: Ormindo (ten), Erisbe (mezzo), Ariadeno (bass), Osmano (bass), Erice (ten), Sicle (sop). After more than 300 years of complete neglect, it has received several performances in recent years, usually in the edition prepared by Raymond Leppard.
Plot: Legendary North Africa. Queen Erisbe of Mauritania elopes with the Tunisian prince Ormindo. Erisbe's husband Ariadeno orders the pair to be poisoned, but his captain Osmano substitutes a sleeping draught. When the lovers waken, the repentant Ariadeno gives up both his throne and his wife to Ormindo. [R]

Ornamentation
The art of embellishing the vocal line. *See* APPOGGIATURA; COLORATURA; FIORITURA

Oronte
1 Tenor role in Verdi's *I Lombardi*. The son of the ruler of Antioch, he loves Giselda. **2** Bass role in Händel's *Floridante*. He is Rossane's father. **3** Soprano trouser role in Vivaldi's *L'Incoronazione di Dario*. He is a Persian nobleman in love with Statira.

Orontea
Opera in prologue and three acts by Cesti. 1st perf Innsbruck, 19 Feb 1656; libr by Giacinto Andrea Cicognini and Giovanni Filippo Apolloni. Principal roles: Orontea (sop), Alidoro (ten), Silandra (sop), Corindo (c-ten), Giacinta (mezzo), Aristea (mezzo), Tibrino (sop), Creonte (bass). One of Cesti's most successful operas, it is set in ancient Egypt and still receives an occasional performance. [R]

Oroveso
Bass role in Bellini's *Norma*. Norma's father, he is the Druid high priest.

Orphée aux Enfers (*Orpheus in the Underworld*)
Operetta in four (originally two) acts by Offenbach. 1st perf Paris, 21 Oct 1858; libr by Héctor Crémieux and Ludovic Halévy. Revised version 1st perf Paris, 7 Feb 1874. Principal roles: Eurydice

(sop), Orphée (ten), Pluton (ten), Jupiter (bar), Public Opinion/Calliope (mezzo), John Styx (ten), Diane (mezzo), Cupidon (sop), Junon (mezzo), Vénus (sop), Mercure (ten), Mars (bass). Perhaps the most enduringly popular of all French operettas, it is an hilarious burlesque of Greek mythology as well as a satire on Second Empire society.
Plot: Legendary Greece. Eurydice is bored to death with her husband Orpheus and his everlasting fiddle playing, and has been having an affair with the shepherd Aristeus. She is bitten by a snake and when Aristeus reveals himself as Pluto she is delighted to accompany him to the underworld. Orpheus, in any event carrying on with a shepherdess, is only too happy to see the back of her, but Public Opinion insists that he try to claim her back. Jupiter's attempts to instil some moral decorum into the other deities are thwarted first by their reminding him of his own innumerable amorous adventures and then by the arrival of Orpheus, who pleads – most unwillingly – to have Eurydice back. Jupiter decides to investigate the affair personally, and descends to Hades with the rest of the gods who are fed up with Mount Olympos and want a holiday. Eurydice, kept in seclusion and guarded by the dim-witted former King of Boeotia John Styx, is bored and accepts the advances of Jupiter, who disguises himself as a fly to gain entry into her room via the keyhole. Orpheus arrives and Jupiter allows him to have Eurydice back provided that he does not turn and look at her. To make sure that he does just that, Jupiter hurls a thunderbolt at the departing Orpheus's feet. Eurydice decides to become a Bacchante, and all join in the famous can-can. [R]

Orr, Robin (b Robert Kemsley) (b 1909)
British composer. He wrote three operas: *Full Circle* (Perth, 10 Apr 1968; libr Sydney Goodsir Smith), *Hermiston* (Edinburgh, 27 Aug 1975; libr Bill Bryden, after Robert Louis Stevenson's *Weir of Hermiston*) and *On the Razzle* (Glasgow, 27 June 1988; libr composer, after Tom Stoppard's adaptation of Johann Nepomuk Nestroy's *Einen Jux will er sich Machen*).

Or sai chi l'onore
Soprano aria for Donna Anna in Act I of Mozart's *Don Giovanni*, in which she demands that Don Ottavio help her in securing vengeance for her father's murder.

Orsini, Maffio
Mezzo trouser role in Donizetti's *Lucrezia Borgia*. He is Genaro's young friend.

Ortel, Hermann
Baritone COMPRIMARIO role in Wagner's *Die Meistersinger von Nürnberg*. A soap boiler, he is one of the masters.

Ortlinde
Soprano role in Wagner's *Die Walküre*. She is one of the Valkyries.

Ortrud
Soprano role in Wagner's *Lohengrin*. She is Telramund's wife. The role is often sung by a mezzo.

Osborne, Nigel (b 1948)
British composer. His four operas are *Hell's Angels* (London, 6 Jan 1986; libr David Freeman, after Oskar Panizza's *Liebeskonzil*), *The Electrification of the Soviet Union* (Glyndebourne, 5 Oct 1987; libr Craig Raine, after Boris Pasternak's *The Last Summer*), *Terrible Mouth* (London, 10 July 1992; libr Howard Barker), which is about Goya, and *Sarajevo* (London, 23 Aug 1994; libr Raine, partly after Euripides's *The Trojan Women*).

Oscar
Soprano trouser role in Verdi's *Un Ballo in Maschera* and Auber's *Gustave III*. He is Gustavus's page.

O silver moon
Soprano aria for Rusalka in Act I of Dvořak's *Rusalka*, in which she begs the moon to reveal her lover to her.

Oslo
see NORWEGIAN OPERA

Osmin
Bass role in: **1** Mozart's *Die Entführung aus dem Serail*. He is the harem-keeper.
2 Haydn's *L'Incontro Improvviso*. He is Ali's

gluttonous servant. **3** Mozart's *Zaïde*. He is the captain of the Sultan's guard.

O soave fanciulla
Soprano/tenor duet for Mimì and Rodolfo in Act I of Puccini's *La Bohème*, in which they declare their love for each other.

Ô souverain
Tenor aria for Rodrigue in Act II of Massenet's *Le Cid*. It is the Cid's prayer.

Ossian
An almost certainly mythical 3rd-century Gaelic bard. The 'rediscovery' of his works in the 1760s caused a sensation, which their exposure as the work of James Macpherson did little to abate. They began the fashion for romantic subjects set in Scotland and had a considerable influence on the romantic movement as a whole. The most important Ossianic operas are Méhul's UTHAL, Lesueur's OSSIAN and Winter's *Colmal*.

Ossian or **Les Bardes** (*The Bards*)
Opera in five acts by Lesueur. 1st perf Paris, 10 July 1804; libr by Palet-Dercy and Jacques-Marie Deschamps, after James Macpherson's poems. Principal roles: Ossian (ten), Rosmala (sop), Duntalmo (bass), Mornal (ten), Rozmor (bass). Lesueur's most successful work which was long popular (it was Napoleon's favourite opera), it is perhaps the most important 'Ossianic' opera and was an influential forerunner of French grand opera. It is nowadays virtually forgotten.
Plot: Legendary Scotland. Rosmala is to marry Mornal, son of Duntalmo, leader of the Scandinavians, who have overrun Caledonia. However, she is in love with the Caledonian warrior Ossian. Ossian, Rosmala and her father Rozmor are captured after a revolt and are about to be sacrified to Odin. Ossian dreams of the bards and heroes of the past, and the three are rescued by the Caledonians. Ossian and Rosmala are wedded.

Östman, Arnold (b 1939)
Swedish conductor, particularly associated with Mozart and other 18th-century operas. One of the leading contemporary advocates of original instrument performances, he was musical director of the Drottningholm Castle Theatre (1979–91).

Ostrava Opera
(Ostrau when it was part of Austria-Hungary). Opera in this Czech town in Moravia is given at the Antonín Dvořák Theatre, which originally opened in 1908 and which was reconstructed in 1942 and enlarged (cap 874) in 1971. Musical directors have included Jaroslav Vogel, Zdeněk Chalabala, Rudolf Vašata, Bohumil Gregor and Zdeněk Košler.

Ostrčil, Otakar (1879–1935)
Czech composer and conductor. He wrote eight operas, influenced by the styles of Fibich and Mahler. They are the unfinished *The Fishermen* (*Rybáň*, 1893; libr J. Prušák), *Jan Zhořelecký* (Prague, 7 Mar 1939, composed 1898; libr A. Šetelík), the unfinished *Cymbelin* (1899; libr F. Zakrejs, after Shakespeare), *The Death of Vlasta* (*Vlasty Skon*, Prague, 14 Dec 1904; libr Karel Pippich), *Kunál's Eyes* (*Kunálovy Oči*, Prague, 25 Nov 1908; libr K. Mašek, after Julius Zeyer), *The Bud* (*Poupě*, Prague, 25 Jan 1912; libr F.X. Svoboda), *The Legend of Erin* (*Legenda z Erinu*, Brno, 16 June 1921; libr Zeyer) and *Johnny's Kingdom* (*Honzovo Království*, Brno, 26 May 1934; libr Jiří Mařánek, after Tolstoy's *The Tale of Ivan the Jester*), by far his most successful work. He was musical director of the Prague National Theatre (1920–35) and conducted the first performances of Janáček's *The Excursions of Mr Brouček*, Weinberger's *Shvanda the Bagpiper*, Foerster's *Debora*, Jeremiáš's *The Brothers Karamazov*, Hába's *Jánošík* and Karel's *Ilsa's Heart*.

Ostrovsky, A.N.
see panel on page 415

Osud
see FATE

Otello or **Il Moro di Venezia** (*The Moor of Venice*)
Opera in three acts by Rossini. 1st perf Naples, 4 Dec 1816; libr by Marchese Francesco Maria Berio di Salsa, after William Shakespeare's play. Principal roles: Otello (ten), Desdemona (sop), Iago (ten), Rodrigo (ten), Elmiro (bass), Emilia (mezzo). Although it is a travesty of Shakespeare, it contains some of Rossini's finest and most beautiful

· A.N. Ostrovsky ·

The works of the Russian playwright Alexander Nikolayevich Ostrovsky (1823–86) have inspired some 30 operas. Below are listed, by play, those operas by composers with entries in this dictionary.

Artists and Admirers		
Oliver	*Sasha*	1983
A Dream on the Volga		
Tchaikovsky	*The Voyevoda*	1869
Arensky	*A Dream on the Volga*	1890
The Forest		
Liebermann	*La Forêt*	1987
Live Not the Way You'd Like		
Serov	*The Power of Evil*	1871
Poverty No Crime		
Tcherepnin	*The Matchmaker*	1937
The Snow Maiden		
Rimsky-Korsakov	*The Snow Maiden*	1882
The Storm		
Janáček	*Káťa Kabanová*	1921
Rocca	*L'Uragano*	1952
Dzerzhinsky	*The Storm*	1956

serious music, particularly in the last act. Enormously popular throughout the 19th century, it still receives an occasional performance.
Plot: 15th-century Venice. Otello is in love with Desdemona, but she has been promised to Rodrigo. Otello interrupts the wedding ceremony, and Desdemona is locked away by her father Elmiro. Iago contrives to persuade Otello that Desdemona is unfaithful to him with Rodrigo, and Otello challenges Rodrigo to a duel. Otello is banished but secretly returns and kills Desdemona. He and Iago both kill themselves in remorse. [R]

Otello
Opera in four acts by Verdi. 1st perf Milan, 5 Feb 1887; libr by Arrigo Boito, after William Shakespeare's play. Principal roles: Otello (ten), Desdemona (sop), Iago (bar), Emilia (mezzo), Cassio (ten), Lodovico (bass). Verdi's last and finest tragic opera, it has been acknowledged from its appearance as one of the greatest of all music-dramas. It is faithful to Shakespeare's plot, except that the Venetian act is omitted and that Iago is largely stripped of all motivation, acting solely because it is his nature to be evil. The title-role is usually regarded as the most demanding ever written for a dramatic tenor.
Plot: 15th-century Cyprus. The Moorish governor Otello returns through a storm, having conquered the Turkish infidels. His evil ensign Iago is jealous of Otello's favour towards Cassio, and through a series of cunning manoeuvres makes it appear to Otello that Cassio is having an affair with his wife Desdemona. Iago's insidious and poisonous innuendos arouse Otello's jealousy and when he is told by Lodovico of his recall to Venice and replacement by Cassio, he strangles Desdemona in her bed. Iago's wife Emilia reveals her husband's treachery and Otello stabs himself. [R]

O terra addio
Soprano/tenor duet for Aida and Radamès in Act IV of Verdi's *Aida*, in which they bid farewell to life. The final scene of the opera.

Ottakar
1 Baritone role in Weber's *Der Freischütz*. He is the local prince. **2** Tenor role in J. Strauss's *Der Zigeunerbaron*. He is Mirabella's son.

Ottavia
Mezzo role in Monteverdi's *L'Incoronazione di Poppea*. She is Nero's wife.

Ottavio, Don
Tenor role in Mozart's *Don Giovanni*. He is Donna Anna's fiancé.

Otter, Anne Sofie von (b 1955)
Swedish mezzo, particularly associated with Gluck, Rossini and Mozart roles, especially Cherubino. Her beautiful, creamy and agile voice is used with outstanding intelligence and musicianship, and she is a singing-actress of considerable ability. One of the finest singers to have come to the fore in recent years.

Ottone
Baritone role in Monteverdi's *L'Incoronazione di Poppea*. He is in love with Poppea.

Ottone, Rè di Germania (*Otho, King of Germany*)
Opera in three acts by Händel. 1st perf London, 12 Jan 1723; libr by Nicola Francesco Haym, after Stefano Benedetto Pallavicino's libretto for Lotti's *Teofane*. Principal roles: Ottone (c-ten), Teofane (sop), Adelberto (c-ten), Gismonda (sop), Emireno (bass), Matilda (mezzo). Never one of Händel's more popular operas, it is only infrequently performed.
Plot: 10th-century Rome. Thanks to the scheming of his mother Gismonda, Adelberto – betrothed to Ottone's cousin Matilda – is to become King of Italy. His claim is disputed by Ottone, who is to wed the princess Teofane, who has never met him. Gismonda persuades Adelberto to woo Teofane as Ottone, but Ottone arrives and has Adelberto imprisoned. With the aid of Matilda and the pirate Emireno, Adelberto escapes and has Teofane abducted. However, Emireno is revealed as a disguised Byzantine prince and he realizes that he is Teofane's brother. He frees Teofane, who is united with Ottone, who magnanimously forgives everybody. [R]

O tu che in seno
Tenor aria for Don Alvaro in Act III of Verdi's *La Forza del Destino*, in which he remembers Leonora, who he believes to be dead.

Our Man in Havana
Opera in three acts by Williamson. 1st perf London, 2 July 1963; libr by Sidney Gilliat, after Graham Greene's novel. Principal roles: Bramble (ten), Milly (sop), Beatrice (sop), Segura (bar), Dr Hasselbacher (bass). Williamson's first major opera, it is a melodrama with satirical overtones. Williamson arranged an orchestral suite from the opera's music in 1966.

Où va la jeune Hindoue?
Soprano aria (the Bell Song) for Lakmé in Act II of Delibes's *Lakmé*.

Overture (from the French *ouverture*, 'opening')
The instrumental music which is played before the start of an opera. It was originally simply a short prelude, but was developed by Lully into a longer piece with a slow section in dotted rhythm followed by a faster section. The Italian overture, developed by A. Scarlatti, was in three sections: fast-slow-fast. In the 19th century the overture became more complex, often being developed symphonically and usually employing thematic material from the opera itself. A number of famous operatic overtures, such as *Ruslan and Ludmila*, *Zampa*, *La Forza del Destino*, *Rienzi* and many by Rossini, are regularly played in the concert hall, and some composers – such as Auber and Suppé – are nowadays remembered almost solely for their overtures. The overture is called *sinfonia* in Italy and *Ouvertüre* in Germany.

O welche lust
1 Prisoners' chorus in Act I of Beethoven's *Fidelio*, in which they praise freedom and the sun as they emerge from their cells. **2** Baritone aria for Sir Ruthven in Act I of Marschner's *Der Vampyr*, in which he expresses his craving for blood.

Owen Wingrave
Opera in two acts by Britten (Op 85). 1st perf BBC TV, 24 May 1971; 1st stage perf London, 10 May 1973; libr by Myfanwy Piper, after Henry James's *Owen Wyngrave*. Principal roles: Owen (bar), Kate Julian (mezzo), Mr and Mrs Coyle (bar and sop), Miss Wingrave (sop), Mrs Julian (mezzo), Sir Philip (ten), Lechmere (ten). Perhaps the most important opera written specifically for television, it gave Britten the opportunity to preach his long-held views on pacifism.
Plot: Late-19th-century England. Owen and Lechmere study with the military cram Coyle, but Owen is a pacifist and wants nothing to do with war. He returns to his country seat, where his family, with their long military tradition, are horrified when he tells them of his refusal to join the army. He is disinherited by his uncle, the old general Sir Philip. His fiancée, Mrs Julian's daughter Kate, accuses him of cowardice and dares him to sleep in the haunted room. He does so, and is found dead by Lechmere. [R]

Ozawa, Seiji (b 1935)
Japanese conductor. Best known as a symphonic conductor, his operatic appearances were infrequent until recently. He conducted the first performance of Messiaen's *Saint François d'Assise*.

Ozean, zu Ungeheuer! (often known in English as 'Ocean thou mighty monster')
Soprano aria for Reiza in Act II of Weber's *Oberon* in which she reflects on the power of the sea and then hails the ship she believes to be coming to rescue her.

O zitt're nicht
Soprano aria for the Queen of the Night in Act I of Mozart's *Die Zauberflöte*, in which she charges Tamino with rescuing her daughter.

P

Pace, pace
Soprano aria for Leonora in Act IV of Verdi's *La Forza del Destino*, in which she prays for death as the only way of finding peace.

Pacini, Giovanni (1796–1867)
Italian composer. One of the most prolific and successful Italian composers of his day, he wrote over 70 operas, virtually all of them now forgotten. Known as '*il maestro della cabaletta*', his melodies are strong and eminently singable and he made some advances in harmony and orchestration. However, his operas lack any real dramatic insight, and are not on the same level as those of Donizetti, Bellini and Mercadante. His most important operas include *Adelaide e Comingio* (Milan, 30 Dec 1817; libr Gaetano Rossi), *Alessandro nell'Indie* (Naples, 29 Sept 1824; libr Andrea Leone Tottola, after Pietro Metastasio), *L'Ultimo Giorno di Pompei* (Naples, 19 Nov 1825; libr Tottola, after Edward Bulwer Lytton's *The Last Days of Pompei*), *Niobe* (Naples, 19 Nov 1826; libr Tottola), *Il Talismano* (Milan, 10 June 1829; libr G. Barbieri, after Sir Walter Scott's *The Talisman*), *Ivanhoe* (Venice, 19 Mar 1832; libr Rossi, after Scott), SAFFO, his finest opera, *La Fidanzata Corsa* (Naples, 10 Dec 1842; libr Salvatore Cammarano, after Prosper Mérimée's *Colomba*), *Maria Tudor* (Palermo, 11 Feb 1843; libr Leopoldo Tarantini, after Victor Hugo's *Marie Tudor*), *Medea* (Palermo, 28 Nov 1843; libr Benedetto Castiglia) and *Lorenzino de' Medici* (Venice, 4 Mar 1845; libr Francesco Maria Piave). His autobiography, *Le Mie Memorie Artistiche*, was published in 1865.

Paderewski, Ignacy (1860–1941)
Polish pianist, composer and statesman. One of the greatest pianists of his age (and the first Prime Minister of the recreated state of Poland in 1919), he also wrote one opera, the successful MANRU.

Padmâvatî
Opera-ballet in two acts by Roussel (Op 18). 1st perf Paris, 1 June 1923 (composed 1914); libr by Louis Laloy. Principal roles: Padmâvatî (mezzo), Alaouddin (bar), Ratan-sen (ten), Nakamti (mezzo), Brahmin (ten). Roussel's most successful stage work, it is notable for the prominent place given to dance.
Plot: Tchitor (India), 1303. Ratan-sen, King of Tchitor, is offered an alliance by the Mogul sultan Alaouddin, who demands Ratan-sen's wife Padmâvatî as a pledge. Ratan-sen reluctantly agrees, but when a Brahmin arrives to ask that she be handed over, the mob riots and he is torn to pieces. Ratan-sen's troops are defeated by Alaouddin. Rather than have the betrayal of her on his conscience, Padmâvatî stabs Ratan-sen. By custom, she must therefore die on his funeral pyre. [R]

Padre Guardiano
Bass role in Verdi's *La Forza del Destino*. He is the abbot of the monastery.

Paer, Ferdinando (1771–1839)
Italian composer, resident in France from 1807. He wrote some 40 operas, achieving his greatest successes in OPERA SEMISERIA. His most important operas include *Griselda* (Parma, Jan 1798; libr Angelo Anelli), *Camilla* (Venice, 28 Feb 1799; libr Giuseppe Carpani, after Benoît Joseph Marsollier des Vivetières), *Achille* (Vienna, 6 June 1801; libr Giovanni de Gamerra, after Homer), *Sargino* (Dresden, 26 May 1803; libr Giuseppe Maria Foppa, after J.M. Monvel), the fine LEONORA, *Sofonisba* (Bologna, 19 May 1805; libr Domenico Rossetti), *Agnese di Fitzhenry* (Parma, 20 Oct 1809; libr Luigi Buonavoglia, after Filippo Casari's *Agnese*) and LE MAÎTRE DE CHAPELLE, his most enduring work. He was also a distinguished teacher, whose pupils included Liszt, whose youthful DON SANCHE he helped to complete.

Paganini
Operetta in three acts by Lehár. 1st perf Vienna, 30 Oct 1925; libr by Paul Knepler and Béla Jenbach. Principal roles: Paganini (ten), Maria Anna (sop), Prince Felice (ten), Bella (mezzo), Beppo (bar). Loosely based on the life of the violinist and composer Niccolò Paganini (1782–1840), it is still regularly performed in German-speaking countries.
Plot: Lucca, 1809. Paganini attracts the attention of Princess Anna, who is feeling neglected by her husband Prince Felice. She persuades Felice, who is involved with the opera singer Bella Giretti, to allow Paganini to perform at court. His liaison with the Princess causes a scandal, and she aids his escape from the court to avoid arrest. Feeling called to a higher cause, Paganini renounces amorous adventures to devote himself to his art. [R]

Pagano
Bass role in Verdi's *I Lombardi*. He is Arvino's brother.

Pagliacci (*Clowns*)
Opera in prologue and two acts by Leoncavallo. 1st perf Milan, 21 May 1892; libr by the composer. Principal roles: Canio (ten), Nedda (sop), Tonio (bar), Silvio (bar), Beppe (ten). Leoncavallo's masterpiece, it is based on a genuine incident which he learnt of from his magistrate father. Almost invariably coupled with Mascagni's *Cavalleria Rusticana*, it is one of the finest of all VERISMO operas, and the 'play within a play' is handled with great theatrical skill.
Plot: Calabria, late 1860s. Tonio tells the audience that they are to witness a piece of true life. A theatrical troupe led by Canio arrives in the village, and the hunchbacked clown Tonio makes advances to Canio's wife Nedda, who repulses him with a whip. Tonio overhears Nedda planning to elope with her lover, the farmer Silvio, and tells the jealous Canio. During the evening's COMMEDIA DELL'ARTE performance, Canio is struck by the similarities of the play and his own situation. He demands the name of Nedda's lover and stabs her when she refuses to tell him. Silvio hastens to her aid and is also stabbed by Canio. [R]

Pagliughi, Lina (1907–80)
Italian soprano, particularly associated with lighter Italian roles, especially Gilda. She possessed a beautiful, limpid voice which she used with an outstanding technique, but she was rather dull on stage. Her husband **Primo Montanari** (1895–1972) was a successful tenor.

Paisiello, Giovanni (1740–1816)
Italian composer. Arguably the finest Italian composer of the late 18th century, he wrote at least 83 operas in various styles, achieving his greatest successes in comedy. His operas are notable for their elegant and charming melodies, for their deft orchestration and for their sharp and sometimes sensitive delineation of character. His most important operas include *L'Idolo Cinese* (Naples, 1767; libr Giovanni Battista Lorenzi), the enormously successful IL BARBIERE DI SIVIGLIA, IL RÈ TEODORO IN VENEZIA, LA MOLINARA, *Fedra* (Naples, 1 Jan 1788; libr L.B. Salvioni, after C.I. Frugoni), the fine NINA and *Elfrida* (Naples, 4 Nov 1792; libr Ranieri de' Calzabigi).

Palacio de las Bellas Artes, Mexico City
The theatre (cap 2,000) opened in 1934, and is the home of Mexico's Opera Nacional, which was founded in 1943 by the mezzo Fanny Anitúa (1887–1968). The annual season runs from September to June.

Palacios, Ernesto (b 1946)
Peruvian tenor, particularly associated with Rossini and Mozart roles. He possesses a small but well-projected voice of considerable range and remarkable agility and accuracy, which is used with an outstanding technique. One of the finest contemporary TENORE DI GRAZIAS.

Paladins, Les
Opera in three acts by Rameau. 1st perf Paris, 10 Feb 1760; libr by Duplat de Monticourt. Principal roles: Argie (sop), Nérine (sop), Orcan (bar), Atis (ten), Anselme (bass), Manto (ten). Rameau's last completed stage work, it still receives an occasional performance. [R]

Palermo
see TEATRO MASSIMO, PALERMO

Palestrina
Opera in three acts by Pfitzner. 1st perf Munich, 12 June 1917; libr by the composer. Principal roles: Palestrina (ten), Borromeo (bar), Ighino (sop), Silla (mezzo), Cardinals Morone, Navagerio and Madruscht (bar, ten and bass), Count Luna (bar), Pope Pius IV (bass). Pfitzner's masterpiece, it tells of the Italian composer Giovanni Pierluigi da Palestrina (1525–94) and his saving of the art of contrapuntal music at the time of the Counter-Reformation through the composition of his *Missa Papae Marcelli*. Notable for its detailed depiction of the Council of Trent and for its remarkable portrayal of Cardinal Borromeo, its infrequency of performance outside Germany is utterly inexplicable.
Plot: Rome and Trent, Nov–Dec 1563. The Council of Trent is preparing to ban polyphonic music. The retired composer Palestrina resists the blandishments of Cardinal Borromeo to compose an exemplary new-style mass. The spirits of past masters encourage the tired and uncertain Palestrina, and eventually his great mass is completed and acclaimed. His son Ighino, however, is drawn to the new music and joins the Florentine Camerata. [R]

Paliashvili, Zakhary (1871–1933)
Georgian composer. Perhaps the most important Georgian composer, his three operas are the magnificent ABSALOM AND ETERY, which incorporates traditional Georgian music, TWILIGHT and *Latavra* (Tbilsi, 16 Mar 1928).

Palma, Piero de (b 1916)
Italian tenor, particularly associated with Italian character roles. Perhaps the finest and most famous of all post-war COMPRIMARIO artists, he had a fine voice, excellent diction and a good stage presence. He enjoyed a remarkably long career, singing into his mid-70s.

Palmer, Felicity (b 1944)
British soprano and later mezzo. Beginning as a soprano, she achieved considerable success in Mozart and Händel roles. Turning to mezzo roles, she has excelled in the German and Russian repertories. She has a strong and incisive, if occasionally slightly harsh voice, and is an outstanding singing-actress of great intelligence, equally at home in serious or comic roles. She created a role in Testi's *Riccardo III*.

Pamina
Soprano role in Mozart's *Die Zauberflöte*. She is the daughter of the Queen of the Night.

Panerai, Rolando (b 1924)
Italian baritone, particularly associated with the Italian repertory and with Mozart roles. A fine singing-actor with a rich and beautiful voice, he enjoyed a remarkably long career, firstly as a Verdi baritone (especially notable as Ford in *Falstaff*) and subsequently as a BUFFO. He created the title-role in Turchi's *Il Buon Soldato Svejk*, Palletta in Tosatti's *Partita a Pugni* and, for Rossellini, the Comandante in *La Campane* and Zio in *Il Linguaggio dei Fiori*.

Pang
Tenor role in Puccini's *Turandot*. The General Purveyor, he is one of the three courtiers.

Panizza, Ettore (b Héctor) (1875–1967)
Argentinian composer and conductor. He wrote four operas: *Il Fidanzato del Mare* (Milan, 1897; libr R. Carugati), *Medioevo Latino* (Genoa, 1900; libr Luigi Illica), *Aurora* (Buenos Aires, 5 Sept 1908; libr Illica and Héctor Quesada), his most successful work, and *Bisanzio* (Buenos Aires, 1939; libr G. Macchi, after Auguste Bailly's *Théodore et Bizance*). One of the leading conductors of the early 20th century, he was closely associated with La Scala, Milan, Covent Garden, the Metropolitan Opera, New York, and the Teatro Colón, Buenos Aires. He conducted the first performances of Zandonai's *Conchita* and *Francesca da Rimini*, Seymour's *In the Pasha's Garden*, Wolf-Ferrari's *Sly* and Menotti's *The Island God*. His autobiography, *Medio Siglo de Vida Musical*, was published in 1952.

Pantomime (from the Greek παντόμιμος, 'imitation of everything')
A dramatic form in which the artists express themselves in dumb show. Many operas, particularly the 18th-century

INTERMEZZI, include a pantomine character. Examples include Vespone in *La Serva Padrona* and Sante in *Il Segreto di Susanna*.

Paolino
Tenor role in Cimarosa's *Il Matrimonio Segreto*. A young lawyer, he is secretly married to Carolina.

Paolis, Alessio de (1893–1964)
Italian tenor, particularly associated with Italian character roles. He abandoned principal roles in 1932 and became one of the outstanding COMPRIMARIO artists of the 20th century. He was resident at the Metropolitan Opera, New York, from 1938 and sang there until his death. He created Le Bleau in Wolf-Ferrari's *La Vedova Scaltra*.

Paolo
1 Baritone role in Verdi's *Simon Boccanegra*. He is the goldsmith Paolo Albiani. **2** Bass role in Wagner's *Rienzi*. He is the conspirator Paolo Orsini. **3** Tenor role in Rachmaninov's and Zandonai's *Francesca da Rimini*. He is Francesca's lover. **4** Tenor role in Gomes's *Fosca*. Giotta's son, he is engaged to Delia.

Papagena
Soprano role in Mozart's *Die Zauberflöte*. She is the girl reserved by Sarastro to be Papageno's wife.

Papageno
Baritone role in Mozart's *Die Zauberflöte*. He is a bird-catcher.

Pariati, Pietro
see under ZENO, APOSTOLO

Paride ed Elena (*Paris and Helen*)
Opera in five acts by Gluck. 1st perf Vienna, 3 Nov 1770; libr by Ranieri de' Calzabigi, after Ovid. Principal roles: Elena (sop), Paride (ten), Erasto (sop), Athene (sop). Never one of the more successful of Gluck's operas, it is more soft and tender than his other mature works, and lacks their dramatic power. Gluck incorporated parts of it into several later works. It is nowadays only rarely performed.
Plot: Legendary Sparta. Paris arrives to collect his reward of the most beautiful woman in the world, promised him for having picked Venus in the Judgement of Paris. His wooing of Helen is initially unsuccessful and he is ordered to depart. As he leaves, Helen confesses that she loves him, and they elope together. They are pursued by the wrath of Athene but are succoured by Erasto (Cupid in disguise). [R]

Parigi o cara
Soprano/tenor duet for Violetta and Alfredo Germont in Act III of Verdi's *La Traviata*, in which they agree to resume their life together away from Paris.

Paris
see OPÉRA-BASTILLE, PARIS; OPÉRA-COMIQUE, PARIS; PARIS OPÉRA; THÉÂTRE BOUFFES-PARISIENS; THÉÂTRE DES CHAMPS-ÉLYSÉES, PARIS

Paris
The legendary Trojan prince who steals Helen appears in a number of operas, including tenor roles in: **1** Tippett's *King Priam*. **2** Offenbach's *La Belle Hélène*. **3** Gluck's *Paride ed Elena*. **4** Bontempi's *Il Paride*. **5** Cesti's *Il Pomo d'Oro*.

Pari siamo
Baritone monologue for Rigoletto in Act I of Verdi's *Rigoletto*, in which he compares his profession with that of Sparafucile.

Parisina
Opera in four acts by Mascagni. 1st perf Milan, 15 Dec 1913; libr by Gabriele d'Annunzio. Principal roles: Parisina (sop), Ugo (ten), Nicolò (bar), Stella (mezzo), Aldobrandino (bass). One of Mascagni's most pretentious operas, it is nowadays virtually forgotten.
Plot: Ferrara, 1425. Ugo is the bastard son of Nicolò d'Este and Stella dell'Assassino, who hates Nicolò's new wife Parisina Malatesta. Ugo does not share his mother's feelings and comes to love Parisina. Eventually, he confesses his love to Parisina and she returns it. They engage in a secret affair, until Nicolò returns unexpectedly one day and discovers Ugo in Parisina's chamber. Outraged at this double betrayal, Nicolò has both of them executed.

Parisina d'Este
Opera in three acts by Donizetti. 1st perf Florence, 17 March 1833; libr by Felice Romani, after Lord Byron's poem. Principal roles: Parisina (sop), Ugo (ten), Azzo (bar), Ernesto (bass). Very successful at its appearance, it still receives an occasional performance and is notable for its richly wrought final scene.
Plot: Early-15th-century Ferrara. Azzo has married Parisina Malatesta. Ugo, Azzo's son by his first wife, lives with them, and he and Parisina fall in love. After a year's secret affair they are discovered and Azzo sentences them both to death. After Ugo's execution, Azzo sends his still-warm heart to Parisina, who collapses and dies.

Paris Opéra
The present opera house (cap 2,131), which has the largest stage in the world, opened on 5 Jan 1875, replacing the previous theatre which opened in 1822 and which burnt down in 1873. It is often referred to as the Salle Garnier after its designer Jean-Louis-Charles Garnier (1825–98). Its greatest period was in the mid-19th century, when grand opera as epitomized by Meyerbeer reigned supreme. It drew all the great composers like a magnet, even those – such as Verdi and Wagner – who despised its conventions; Verdi called it '*la grande boutique*'. In the post-war era, its artistic standards fell alarmingly until they were dramatically revived during Rolf Liebermann's administration (1971–80). Nowadays, the theatre is used largely for ballet, with opera mainly being given at the OPÉRA-BASTILLE. Musical directors included Messager, Pierre Dervaux, Georges Prêtre, Serge Baudo, Alain Lombard, Silvio Varviso and Lothar Zagrosek.

Parlando (Italian for 'speaking')
An instruction to allow the vocal tone to approximate to that of ordinary speech.

Parma
see TEATRO REGIO, PARMA

Parmi veder le lagrime
Tenor aria for the Duke of Mantua in Act II of Verdi's *Rigoletto*, in which he laments the disappearance of Gilda.

Parr, Gladys (1892–1988)
British mezzo, particularly associated with Wagner and Britten roles. The leading British mezzo of the inter-war period, she possessed a finely projected if not overlarge voice, had excellent diction and was a good singing-actress. She created, for Britten, Florence Pike in *Albert Herring*, Miss Baggott in *The Little Sweep* and Mrs Noye in *Noye's Fludde*. Later in her career she turned to straight acting.

Parry, Sir Hubert (1848–1918)
British composer. Although best known as a choral composer, he also wrote one opera, the unorchestrated and unperformed *Guinevere* (1886; libr Una Taylor).

Parry, Joseph (1841–1903)
British composer. He wrote six operas, of which *Blodwen* (Swansea, 20 June 1878; libr R. Davies) [R Exc] was the first opera written to a Welsh libretto. His son **Joseph Haydn** (1864–94) was also a composer, who wrote three operas.

Parsifal
Opera in three acts by Wagner. 1st perf Bayreuth, 26 July 1882; libr by the composer, after Wolfram von Eschenbach's *Parzival*. Principal roles: Parsifal (ten), Kundry (sop), Gurnemanz (bass), Amfortas (bar), Klingsor (b-bar), Titurel (bass). Wagner's last opera, he described it as *Buhnenweihfestspiel* (German for 'stage consecration festival play'). The most expansive of all Wagner's music-dramas, its copyright forbade performances outside Bayreuth until the end of 1913, although this was occasionally infringed.
Plot: Montsalvat (Spain), early Middle Ages. Many years previously, the vessel of the Holy Grail was given into the keeping of Titurel and his knights, as was the Sacred Spear, and they are guarded in a fortified castle. Nearby lives the evil sorcerer Klingsor – a fallen knight – and the beautiful enchantress Kundry, enemies of the knights. When Titurel grew old, he handed over his rule to his son Amfortas who, determined to kill Klingsor, entered Klingsor's magic garden. There, he fell prey to Kundry's charms and lost the Spear to Klingsor. Badly wounded by the Spear, he continues to suffer – only the

touch of the Spear will close the gash it made. A prophecy from the Grail sanctuary has told Amfortas that only a 'holy fool', unaware of sin, will be able to resist Kundry and regain the Spear. The guileless youth Parsifal is brought to the venerable knight Gurnemanz charged with killing a holy swan. When it becomes clear that the lad is an innocent and entirely ignorant of the world, he is selected to rescue the Spear. He eventually triumphs, heals Amfortas, and is annointed King of the Grail by Gurnemanz. As Amfortas and the knights kneel to Parsifal, he baptizes Kundry, who finds at last the redemption of peaceful death. [R]

Partagez-vous mes fleurs
Soprano aria (the Mad Scene) for Ophélie in Act IV of Thomas's *Hamlet*.

Partenope
Opera in three acts by Händel. 1st perf London, 24 Feb 1730; libr by Silvio Stampiglia. Principal roles: Partenope (sop), Rosmira (mezzo), Emilio (ten), Arsace (c-ten), Armindo (sop), Ormonte (bass). Written in a slightly lighter and more whimsical style, it is still performed from time to time.
Plot: Legendary Naples. Queen Partenope is courted by three suitors. With the first, Emilio Prince of Cumae, she is at war. Emilio is defeated and captured, but Partenope releases him and offers friendship but not love. She prefers Prince Arsace of Corinth, unaware that he has just jilted his fiancée Rosmira, Princess of Cyprus. Rosmira, disguised as an Armenian prince, arrives and humbles Arsace. Partenope eventually gives her love to the faithful Armindo, Prince of Rhodes. [R]

Parto, parto
Mezzo aria for Sextus in Act I of Mozart's *La Clemenza di Tito*, in which he tells Vitellia that he will always love and serve her.

Pasatieri, Thomas (b 1945)
American composer. His 17 operas, which have met with some success in the United States, are written in an accessible neo-romantic style. They include *Calvary* (Seattle, 7 Apr 1971; libr after William Butler Yeats), *The Trial of May Lincoln* (New York TV, 14 Feb 1972; libr Anne Bailey), *Black Widow* (Seattle, 2 Mar 1972; libr composer, after Miguel de Unamuno's *Dos Madres*), *The Seagull* (Houston, 5 Mar 1974; libr Kenward Elmslie, after Anton Chekhov), his finest opera, *Ines de Castro* (Baltimore, 1 Apr 1976; libr Bernard Stambler), *Washington Square* (Detroit, 1 Oct 1976; libr Elmslie, after Henry James), *Three Sisters* (Columbus, 13 Mar 1986, composed 1979; libr Elmslie, after Chekhov) and *Maria Elena* (Tuscon, 6 Apr 1983; libr composer).

Pasero, Tancredi (1893–1983)
Italian bass, particularly associated with the Italian repertory. Largely resident at La Scala, Milan, he was one of the finest basses of the inter-war period. He created the title-role in Pizzetti's *Orsèolo*, the Miller in Giordano's *Il Rè*, the Father in Refice's *Margherita da Cortona*, the title-role in Ghedini's *Rè Hassan* and Babilio in Mascagni's *Nerone*.

Pashkevich, Vasily (1742–97)
Russian composer. One of the most significant forerunners of the Russian nationalist school, his operas employ traditional folk material and make use of natural speech rhythms. The most important of his works include *Misfortune from a Carriage* (*Neschastye ot Karoty*, St Petersburg, 7 Nov 1779; libr Yakov Borisovich Knyazhnin), *The Miser* (*Skupoy*, St Petersburg, 1782; libr Knyazhnin, after Molière's *L'Avare*) [R], *Fevey* (Moscow, 19 Apr 1786; libr Catherine the Great) and *Fedul and his Children* (*Fedul s Det'mi*, Moscow, 16 Jan 1791; libr Catherine and A.V. Khrapovitsky), which was written in collaboration with Martín y Soler.

Paskalis, Kostas (b 1929)
Greek baritone, particularly associated with Verdi roles, especially Macbeth. An intense singing-actor with a rich and powerful voice, he created Pentheus in Henze's *The Bassarids* and the Youth in Banfield's *Alissa*. Director of the Greek National Opera (1988–). His wife **Marina Krilovici** (*b* 1942) is a successful soprano.

Pasta, Giuditta (b Negri) (1797–1865)
Italian soprano. One of the greatest singers

of the first half of the 19th century, she had a voice of great range with a powerful lower register, even if it was not always of even quality. Her real greatness lay in her reputation as the outstanding singing-actress of her time. She created Amina in *La Sonnambula*, Bianca in Donizetti's *Ugo Conte di Parigi*, the title-roles in *Anna Bolena*, *Norma*, *Beatrice di Tenda* Coccia's *Maria Stuart* and Pacini's *Niobe* and Corinna in Rossini's *Il Viaggio a Reims*.

Pasticcio (Italian for 'pie')
Known in Britain by its French translation, pastiche, it is an opera or operetta put together from parts of already written works by one or more composers. Very popular in the 18th century, they have more recently been restricted largely to operetta: two famous Offenbach examples are CHRISTOPHER COLUMBUS and *Der Goldschmied von Toledo* (Mannheim, 7 Feb 1919; libr Zwerenz, after E.T.A. Hoffmann's *Das Fräulein von Scuderi*), which was arranged by Zamara and Stern.

Pastorale héroïque (French for 'heroic-pastoral')
A term used in France in the 18th century to describe an opera or opera-ballet on a heroic subject. Mondonville's *Titon et l'Aurore* is so described.

Pastor Fido, Il (*The Faithful Shepherd*)
Opera in three acts by Händel. 1st perf London, 22 Nov 1712; libr by Giacomo Rossi, after Giovanni Battista Guarini's play. Revised version 1st perf London, 18 May 1734. Principal roles: Mirtillo (sop), Amarilli (sop), Silvio (mezzo), Dorinda (sop), Eurilla (sop). Händel's second opera written for London and his most pastoral in style, it is still occasionally performed.
Plot: Legendary Arcadia. Amarilli loves Mirtillo but is betrothed against her will to Silvio. Silvio, loved by Dorinda, cares only for hunting. Eurilla, also in love with Mirtillo, traps Amarilli in a compromising situation for which the punishment is death. Whilst hunting, Silvio shoots Dorinda in mistake for an animal and falls in love with her. By the orders of the goddess Diana, Amarilli is reprieved and united with Mirtillo and Silvio is united with Dorinda. [R]

Patanè, Giuseppe (1932–89)
Italian conductor, particularly associated with the Italian repertory. Always conducting from memory, he was a fine and often underrated interpreter of Verdi and Puccini. He died whilst conducting *Il Barbiere di Siviglia* in Munich. His father **Franco** (1908–68) was also a successful conductor, and his brother **Vittorio** (1934–92) was a producer.

Patience or **Bunthorne's Bride**
Operetta in two acts by Sullivan. 1st perf London, 25 April 1881; libr by W.S. Gilbert, after *The Rival Curates* in his *Bab Ballads*. Principal roles: Bunthorne (bar), Patience (sop), Grosvenor (bar), Col Calverley (b-bar), Lady Jane (mezzo), Duke of Dunstable (ten), Angela (mezzo), Maj Murgatroyd (bar), Saphir (mezzo), Ella (sop). A brilliant satire on the aesthetic movement, with send-ups of Oscar Wilde and Whistler, it was an immediate success, enjoying an initial run of over 550 performances.
Plot: 19th-century England. The rapturous maidens had been engaged to officers of the Dragoon Guards, but have become aesthetic under the influence of the fleshly poet Reginald Bunthorne, with whom they are all in love. Bunthorne loves the village milkmaid Patience. When her childhood sweetheart Archibald Grosvenor, now an idyllic poet, arrives, she feels unable to respond to him, much as she loves him, because Lady Angela has explained to her that true love must be utterly unselfish. She therefore offers herself to the morose Bunthorne, and all the other ladies (except the middle-aged Lady Jane) immediately transfer their affection to Grosvenor. Grosvenor hates their attentions and Bunthorne cannot live without admiration, so they come to an arrangement: Grosvenor agrees to become an ordinary young man, which allows Patience to love him. Bunthorne's hopes of a bride are frustrated, however: at great personal inconvenience, the Dragoons, led by Col Calverley, have adopted aestheticism to show how much they love the ladies. The ladies are won over and the Duke decides to marry Lady Jane. [R]

Patineurs, Les
Ballet music (the Skaters' Waltz) in Act III of Meyerbeer's *Le Prophète*.

Patter
Music in which an enormous number of words are fitted into the shortest possible period of time. Developed in Italian opera in the mid-18th century, it has since had an important place in both OPERA BUFFA and operetta. Its finest exponents have been Mozart, Rossini, Donizetti, Offenbach and Sullivan. It is usually found in an aria (*see* ARIA DI CATALOGO) or in a duet (such as 'Cheti, cheti' in *Don Pasquale*), but is sometimes for more voices, as in the trio 'My eyes are fully open' in Sullivan's *Ruddigore*.

Patti, Adelina (1843–1919)
Italian soprano, particularly associated with Italian and French lyric roles. Largely based at Covent Garden, she was the reigning COLORATURA soprano of the second half of the 19th century. She had a voice of great range and remarkable agility, said to have been outstandingly pure and beautiful. The highest paid singer of her day, she insisted on contracts excusing her from rehearsal, and dictated the size in which her name was to appear on posters. She purchased a castle at Craig-y-Nos in South Wales, and in 1891 built a beautiful private opera house in it. The second of her three husbands **Ernest Nicolini** (*b* Nicolas) (1834–98) was a successful tenor.

Patzak, Julius (1898–1974)
Austrian tenor, particularly associated with heavier German roles, especially the title-role in Pfitzner's *Palestrina* and Florestan in Beethoven's *Fidelio*. Although his voice was not outstanding, he is ranked amongst the greatest tenors of the 20th century on account of his great intelligence and musicianship, his fine diction and his almost total identification with the role he was performing. He created the Rifleman in Strauss's *Friedenstag*, the Narrator in Orff's *Der Mond*, Desmoulins in Einem's *Dantons Tod*, Tristan in Martin's *Le Vin Herbé* and a role in Pfitzner's *Das Herz*.

Pauer, Jiří (b 1919)
Czech composer. One of the most successful post-war Czech composers, his five operas are *The Garrolous Slug* (*Žvanivý Slimejš*, Prague, 5 Apr 1958; libr M. Mellanová, after J. Hloucha), ZUZANA VOJÍŘOVÁ, his finest work, *Little Red Riding Hood* (*Červená Karkulka*, Olomouc, 22 Oct 1960; libr Mellanová), the comedy *Matrimonial Counterpoints* (*Manželské Kontrpunkty*, Ostrava, 22 Feb 1962; libr composer, after S. Grodzieńská) and *The Hypochondriac* (*Zdravý Nemocný*, Prague, 22 May 1970; libr composer, after Molière's *Le Malade Imaginaire*) [R Exc]. He was general director of the Prague National Theatre (1979–89).

Paul Bunyan
Operetta in prologue and two acts by Britten (Op 17). 1st perf New York, 5 May 1941; libr by W.H. Auden. Revised version 1st perf BBC Radio, 1 Feb 1976. Principal roles: Narrator (bar), Tiny (sop), Johnny Inkslinger (ten), Hot Biscuit Slim (ten), Sam Sharkey (ten), Ben Benny (bass). Britten's first stage work, based on American folk legend, it was soon withdrawn and did not reappear until Britten revised it. Since then, it has enjoyed a number of successful productions. [R]

Pauly, Rosa (b Rose Pollak) (1894–1975)
Hungarian soprano, particularly associated with Strauss roles, especially the title-role in *Elektra*. One of the leading dramatic sopranos of the inter-war period, she was an outstanding singing-actress. She created Agave in Wellesz's *Die Bakchantinnen*.

Pauvre Matelot, Le (*The Poor Sailor*)
Opera in three acts by Milhaud (Op 92). 1st perf Paris, 16 Dec 1927; libr by Jean Cocteau. Principal roles: Sailor (ten), Wife (sop), Friend (bar), Father (bass). A strange story, although based on an actual event, Milhaud set it with deliberately light and banal music. It is only very rarely performed.
Plot: Early-20th-century France. The Sailor has been away at sea for 15 years. His Wife remains faithful, ignoring the Father's suggestions that she should find another man and repulsing the advances of the Friend. The Sailor returns home, telling his Wife (who does not recognize him) that he is a rich friend of her husband's, and attempts to seduce her. She kills him and steals his money to help her husband return. [R]

Pavarotti, Luciano (b 1935)
Italian tenor, particularly associated with the Italian repertory, especially Verdi, Donizetti and Puccini. Arguably the most popular and certainly the most hyped singer of recent decades, he is one of the greatest tenors of the 20th century. He has a voice of great beauty and richness, with thrilling high notes, which is used with an outstanding technique, and he has exemplary diction. However, his very substantial physique makes it difficult for some to take him seriously on stage. He starred in the film *Yes Giorgio*, and his autobiography, *My Own Story*, was published in 1981.

Pavesi, Stefano (1779–1850)
Italian composer. One of the most prolific Italian composers, he wrote some 70 operas, all of them now long forgotten. They include *Elisabetta d'Inghilterra* (Turin, 26 Dec 1809; libr Giovanni Federico Schmidt), *Ser Marcantonio* (Milan, 26 Dec 1810; libr Angelo Anelli), *Agatina* (Milan, 10 Apr 1814; libr Francesco Fiorini, after Charles Perrault's *Cendrillon*) and *Fenella* (Venice, 5 Feb 1831; libr Gaetano Rossi, after Eugène Scribe's libretto for Auber's *La Muette de Portici*).

Peachum
Roles in Pepusch's *The Beggar's Opera*: Peachum (bass), a receiver, his wife Mrs Peachum (mezzo) and their daughter Polly (sop).

Pearl Fishers, The
see PÊCHEURS DE PERLES, LES

Pears, Sir Peter (1910–86)
British tenor, particularly associated with Britten and other English roles. One of the outstanding post-war British operatic artists, he was a musician of great intelligence and artistry with a beautiful voice of highly individual timbre and had excellent diction. A singing-actor of subtlety and insight, he was Britten's constant companion, and with him founded both the English Opera Group and the Aldeburgh Festival. Much of Britten's music was written specifically for him, and he created the title-roles in *Peter Grimes* and *Albert Herring*, the Male Chorus in *The Rape of Lucretia*, Capt Vere in *Billy Budd*, the Earl of Essex in *Gloriana*, Peter Quint in *The Turn of the Screw*, Flute in *A Midsummer Night's Dream*, the Madwoman in *Curlew River*, Nebuchadnezzar in *The Burning Fiery Furnace*, the Tempter in *The Prodigal Son*, Sir Philip in *Owen Wingrave* and Aschenbach in *Death in Venice*. He also created Pandarus in *Troilus and Cressida*, Ferdinand in Gerhard's *The Duenna* and, for Berkeley, the title-role in *Nelson* and Boaz in *Ruth*.

Pêcheurs de Perles, Les (*The Pearl Fishers*)
Opera in three acts by Bizet. 1st perf Paris, 30 Sept 1863; libr by Eugène Cormon and Michel Carré. Principal roles: Leïla (sop), Zurga (bar), Nadir (ten), Nourabad (bass). Bizet's most successful opera apart from *Carmen*, it is notable for its colourful and exotic orchestration and for the great friendship duet, one of the most famous numbers in all opera.
Plot: Legendary Sri Lanka. The local fishermen elect Zurga as their leader. Nadir returns to the village, and he and Zurga recall how their friendship was once threatened when they both fell in love with an unknown priestess. They swear eternal friendship. The priestess Leïla arrives for a vigil of prayer for the safety of the fishermen, and Nadir recognizes her as the woman he and Zurga had loved. He goes to her and they acknowledge their love, but they are discovered by the high priest Nourabad. Leïla is condemned to death for breaking her vow of chastity and Nadir is condemned with her. Zurga discovers that in the past Leïla had saved his life, and sets fire to the village to allow the lovers to escape. He remains to face the villagers' wrath. [R]

Pedrell, Felipe (1841–1922)
Spanish composer. A champion of Spanish national music, he is regarded as the father of Spanish music-drama and is sometimes called the 'Spanish Wagner'. After writing some youthful ZARZUELAS, he turned to opera, taking his inspiration from folk music. His operas include *El Último Abencerraje* (Barcelona, 14 Apr 1874; libr J.B. Altés y Alabert and F. Fors de Casamayor), *Quasimodo* (Barcelona, 20

Apr 1875; libr J. Barret, after Victor Hugo's *Notre-Dame de Paris*), the unperformed *Cléopâtre* (1878; libr A. de Lauzières de Thémines), *Tasse à Ferrare* (Madrid, 1881; libr Lauzières) and *Los Pirineos* (Barcelona, 4 Jan 1902; libr V. Baleguer). Whilst they contain some fine music, his operas are considered too academic and studious to have won popular acceptance. He exercised most influence as a teacher, whose pupils included Albéniz, de Falla, Gerhard and Granados.

Pedrillo
Tenor role in Mozart's *Die Entführung aus dem Serail*. He is Belmonte's servant.

Pedro
1 Tenor role in d'Albert's *Tiefland*. He is a shepherd married to Marta. **2** Baritone role in Donizetti's *Maria Padilla*. He is Pedro the Cruel, King of Castile (*d* 1369). **3** Bass role in Meyerbeer's *L'Africaine*. He is married to Inès. **4** Bass role in Berlioz's *Béatrice et Bénédict*. He is general of the Sicilian army. **5** Tenor role in Offenbach's *La Périchole*. He is the governor of Lima. **6** Tenor role in Vittadini's *Anima Allegra*. He loves Consuela. **7** Baritone role in Albéniz's *Pepita Jiménez*. A farmer, he is Luis's father.

Pedrollo, Arrigo (1878–1964)
Italian composer. He wrote ten operas, all now forgotten, of which the most important are *Juana* (Vicenza, 3 Feb 1914; libr C. de Carli), *La Veglia* (Milan, 2 Jan 1920; libr C. Linati, after John Millington Synge's *The Shadow of the Glen*), *L'Uomo che Ride* (Rome, 6 Mar 1920; libr A. Lega, after Victor Hugo's *L'Homme Qui Rit*), *Delitto e Castigo* (Milan, 16 Nov 1926; libr Giovacchino Forzano, after Fyodor Dostoyevsky's *Crime and Punishment*) and *L'Amante in Trappola* (Vicenza, 22 Sept 1936; libr G. Franceschini).

Pedrotti, Carlo (1817–93)
Italian composer and conductor. He wrote many operas, achieving most success in comedy or OPERA SEMISERIA. Many of his operas were admired in their day, but they are all now forgotten. They include *Lina* (Verona, 2 May 1840; libr Marco Marcello), *Fiorina* (Verona, 22 Nov 1851; libr L. Serenelli Honorati), *Tutti in Maschera* (Verona, 4 Nov 1856; libr Marcello, after Carlo Goldoni's *L'Impresario delle Smirne*), *Mazeppa* (Bologna, 3 Dec 1861; libr A. de Lauzières de Thémines, after Alexander Pushkin's *Poltava*) and *Marion Delorme* (Trieste, 16 Nov 1865; libr Marcello, after Victor Hugo). He was artistic director of the Teatro Regio, Turin (1868–82).

Peerce, Jan (b Jacob Pincus Perlemuth) (1904–84)
American tenor, particularly associated with the Italian and French repertories. An artistic and musical singer with a fine technique, he enjoyed a remarkably long career, singing into his early 70s. In 1956, he became the first American tenor to appear at the Bolshoi Opera since World War II. He also appeared in a number of films. His brother-in-law was the tenor RICHARD TUCKER.

Peer Gynt
Opera in prologue and three acts by Egk. 1st perf Berlin, 24 Nov 1938; libr by the composer, after Henrik Ibsen's play. Principal roles: Peer Gynt (bar), Solveig (sop), Aase (mezzo), Ingrid (sop), Mads (ten), Old Man (ten). One of Egk's most successful operas, it is still sometimes performed in Germany. [R]

Pèlerins de la Mecque, Les
see RENCONTRE IMPRÉVUE, LA

Pelléas et Mélisande
Opera in five acts by Debussy. 1st perf Paris, 30 April 1902; a virtual word-for-word setting of Maurice Maeterlinck's play. Principal roles: Mélisande (sop), Pelléas (ten), Golaud (bar), Arkel (bass), Geneviève (mezzo), Yniold (sop). Debussy's only completed opera, it is a symbolic work of haunting beauty and expressiveness, notable for its remarkable orchestration and for having a vocal line determined by the speech rhythms of the text. Unique in style, it is one of the seminal works of 20th-century music.
Plot: The imaginary kingdom of Allemonde. Golaud discovers the distraught Mélisande in the forest, persuades her to follow him and later marries her. He brings her to the home of

his grandfather King Arkel, where she meets Golaud's mother Geneviève and his young half-brother Pelléas, to whom she is attracted. Her loss of her wedding ring arouses Golaud's suspicions, and he sets his little son Yniold to spy on the pair. The two finally admit their love for each other, and Golaud murders Pelléas. Mélisande flees, is discovered and brought back to the castle dying. She tells Golaud that she has done nothing to be ashamed of. [R]

Penderecki, Krzysztof (b 1933)
Polish composer and conductor. One of the most important contemporary composers, he has written four operas, all of which demonstrate his strong theatrical flair. They are the powerful and disturbing THE DEVILS OF LOUDUN, *Paradise Lost* (Chicago, 29 Nov 1978; libr Christopher Fry, after John Milton), *Die Schwarze Maske* (Salzburg, 15 Aug 1986; libr composer and Harry Kupfer, after Gerhart Hauptmann) and *Ubu Rex* (Munich, 6 July 1991; libr composer and J. Jarocki, after Alfred Jarry's *Roi Ubu*).

Penella, Manuel (1880–1939)
Spanish composer. He wrote some 80 ZARZUELAS, some of them near to opera in style and weight. The most successful were *El Gato Montés* (*The Mountain Cat*, Valencia, 1916; libr composer) [R] and *Don Gil de Alcalá* (Barcelona, 1932; libr composer).

Penelope
Opera in two parts by Liebermann. 1st perf Salzburg, 17 Aug 1954; libr by Heinrich Strobel. Principal roles: Penelope (sop), Odysseus (bar), Telemachus (sop), Ercole (ten). An updating of the Greek legend of Penelope and Odysseus, it is based on an actual incident in World War II. It is only very rarely performed. [R]

Pénélope
Opera in three acts by Fauré. 1st perf Monte Carlo, 4 March 1913; libr by René Fauchois, after Homer's *The Odyssey*. Principal roles: Pénélope (sop), Ulysse (ten), Eurimaque (bar), Eumée (bar), Euryclée (mezzo), Antinoüs (bass), Alkandre (mezzo), Phylo (sop). Containing some of Fauré's most refined and beautiful music, it is unaccountably only rarely performed.
Plot: Legendary Ithaca. Ulysses returns after his adventures to his faithful wife Penelope. He is recognized by the swineherd Eumaeus and with the help of his son Telemachus he drives away Penelope's arrogant suitors, led by Antinous. [R]

Pensa alla patria
Mezzo aria for Isabella in Act II of Rossini's *L'Italiana in Algieri*, in which she extols patriotism as a source of inner strength.

Penthesilea
Opera in one act and epilogue by Schoeck (Op 39). 1st perf Dresden, 8 Jan 1927; libr by the composer, after Heinrich Wilhelm von Kleist's play. Principal roles: Penthesilea (mezzo), Achilles (bar), Prothoe (sop), Diomedes (ten), High Priestess (mezzo). Telling of the Amazon queen who fought against the Greeks in the Trojan War, it is often regarded as Schoeck's finest opera but is only very rarely performed. [R]

Pepita Jiménez
Opera in three acts by Albéniz. 1st perf Barcelona, 5 Jan 1896; libr by Francis Burdett Money-Coutts, after Juan Valera's novel. Principal roles: Pepita (sop), Luis (ten), Don Pedro (bar), Antoñona (mezzo), Vicario (bass). Albéniz's most successful stage work, it is still sometimes performed in Spain, usually in the edition prepared by Pablo Sorazábal in 1958.
Plot: Mid-19th-century Andalusia. The wealthy young widow Pepita is courted by the farmer Don Pedro de Vargas, but she falls in love with his son Luis, who is a seminarian. Don Pedro and Pepita's maid Antoñona encourage Pepita's feelings, but Luis determines to follow his calling. Only when he fears that she is about to kill herself does Luis give in to his own feelings for Pepita. [R]

Pepusch, John Christopher (b Johann Christoph) (1667–1752)
German-born British composer. He composed a number of MASQUES, but is best known for his arrangements of other composers' music in the ballad operas THE

BEGGAR'S OPERA and POLLY. His wife **Margherita de l'Épine** (*c* 1683–1746) was a successful soprano, who created, for Händel, Agilea in *Teseo* and Eurilla in *Il Pastor Fido*.

Perchè non ho
Soprano aria for Rosmonda in Act I of Donizetti's *Rosmonda d'Inghilterra*. In the 19th century it was often substituted for 'Regnava nel silenzio' in Act I of *Lucia di Lammermoor*.

Percy, Riccardo
Tenor role in Donizetti's *Anna Bolena*. He is Anna's former lover.

Perfect Fool, The
Comic opera in one act by Holst (Op 39). 1st perf London, 14 May 1923; libr by the composer. Principal roles: Princess (sop), Troubador (ten), Traveller (bass), Fool (speaker), Wizard (bar), Mother (mezzo). An allegory in Elizabethan style, which contains parodies of Verdi and Wagner, it tells of a Princess wooed by a Wagnerian Traveller and a Verdian Troubador, who is finally won by a Fool who is not interested in her. Reasonably successful at its appearance, it is nowadays almost never performed, although the ballet music is occasionally given in the concert hall.

Pergolesi, Giovanni Battista (1710–36)
Italian composer, whose early death cut short a brilliant talent. Sometimes regarded as the father of comic opera, his works are notable for their sharp rhythms, for their delightful melodies and for their witty and characterful vocal writing. His first opera *Salustia* (Naples, Jan 1732; libr after Apostolo Zeno's *Alessandro Severo*) was a failure and its music is lost, but the full-length comedy LO FRATE 'NNAMORATO was a success. The OPERA SERIA *Il Prigionier Superbo* (Naples, 5 Sept 1733; libr after Francesco Silvani's *La Fede Tradita e Vendicata*) is notable largely for having the most famous of all INTERMEZZI: LA SERVA PADRONA, and much the same may be said for *Adriano in Siria* (Naples, 25 Oct 1734; libr Pietro Metastasio) with its successful intermezzo *La Contadina Astuta* (libr Tommaso Mariani) [R]. *L'Olimpiade* (Rome, 8 Jan 1735; libr Metastasio) was a failure, but his last opera *Il Flaminio* (Naples, 1735; libr Gennarantonio Federico) was his most successful serious opera and is still occasionally revived. After his death, he was claimed to be the author of several other intermezzi, notably IL MAESTRO DI MUSICA and *Il Geloso Schernito* [R], but it is now certain that he did not write them.

Peri, Jacopo (1561–1633)
Italian composer. A leading member of the FLORENTINE CAMERATA, his DAFNE of 1597 is usually regarded as the first opera, and his EURIDICE is the earliest opera of which the music survives. His other operas are the unperformed *Tetide* (1608; libr F. Cini), the lost *Il Medoro* (Florence, 25 Sept 1619; libr Andrea Salvadori, after Lodovico Ariosto's *Orlando Furioso*), written in collaboration with Gagliano, the unperformed *Adone* (1620; libr J. Cicognini) and *La Flora* (Florence, 14 Oct 1628; libr Salvadori), also written with Gagliano.

Périchole, La
Operetta in three (originally two) acts by Offenbach. 1st perf Paris, 6 Oct 1868; libr by Henri Meilhac and Ludovic Halévy, after Prosper Mérimée's *La Carrosse du Saint Sacrement*. Revised version 1st perf Paris, 25 Apr 1874. Principal roles: Périchole (mezzo), Piquillo (ten), Don Andrès (bar), Don Pédro (ten), Count Panatellas (bar). One of Offenbach's most popular works, it is in a more lyrical and romantic style than most of his other operettas. It tells of the historical Peruvian street singer Michaela Villegas, whose house may still be seen in Lima.
Plot: Mid-18th-century Lima. The impoverished street singers Périchole and her lover Piquillo cannot even afford a wedding service. The Viceroy Don Andrès del Ribeira, during an incognito tour of the city, falls for Périchole and offers her a position at court, which she accepts, leaving a remorseful letter for Piquillo. Etiquette does not allow unmarried women to live within the palace, so a husband has to be found for Périchole. By chance, the Viceroy's men choose Piquillo, getting him too drunk to recognize the bride. When he appreciates what has happened, he denounces Périchole and is imprisoned.

The two finally escape, happily reconciled, and Don Andrès forgives them. [R]

Perlea, Jonel (b Ionel) (1900–70)
Romanian conductor, particularly associated with the Italian and German repertories. A fine and often underrated conductor, he was musical director of the Bucharest Opera (1929–30 and 1934–6). Following a heart attack and a stroke in 1957, he learnt to conduct with his left arm only.

Per pietà
Soprano aria for Fiordiligi in Act II of Mozart's *Così fan Tutte*, in which she laments her lessening resistance to Ferrando's advances.

Persiani, Fanny (b Tacchinardi) (1812–67)
Italian soprano. One of the leading lyric sopranos of the early 19th century, she was said to have possessed a small but extraordinarily agile voice of great range. She created, for Donizetti, the title-roles in *Lucia di Lammermoor*, *Rosmonda d'Inghilterra* and *Pia de' Tolomei*. Her father **Niccolò Tacchinardi** (1772–1850) was a successful tenor, despite being a virtual hunchback. Her husband **Giuseppe** (*c* 1800–69) was a composer, the most successful of whose operas was *Ines de Castro* (Naples, 28 Jan 1835; libr Salvatore Cammarano).

Pertichino (Italian for 'understudy')
A name given in Italy in the 18th and 19th centuries to a character who listens to another singer's narration during an aria, for example Inez during Leonora's 'Tacea la notte' in *Il Trovatore*.

Pertile, Aureliano (1885–1952)
Italian tenor, particularly associated with the Italian repertory. Although his voice was not especially beautiful, he was an intense and highly intelligent singing-actor with a bright-toned voice able to encompass roles as diverse as the title-role in Verdi's Otello and Edgardo in Donizetti's *Lucia di Lammermoor*. Toscanini's favourite tenor, and one of the finest Italian artists of the inter-war period, he created the title-roles in Wolf-Ferrari's *Sly* and both Boito's and Mascagni's *Nerone*.

Peru
see FUNDACIÓN PARA ARTE LIRICA

Peruvian opera composers
These include César Bolaños (*b* 1931), Reynaldo la Rosa (*c* 1852–1954) and José María del Valle Riestra (1859–1925), whose *Ollanta* (Lima, 14 Feb 1919; libr after the Quechuan poem *Ollantai*), is the principal Peruvian opera on a national subject.

Pesaro Festival
An Italian summer festival founded in 1980 and devoted to the operas of Rossini. Performances are given at the Teatro Comunale Gioacchino Rossini (cap 914), which opened (as the Teatro Nuovo) on 10 June 1818.

Peter
Baritone role in: **1** Lortzing's *Zar und Zimmermann*. He is Peter the Great of Russia. **2** Humperdinck's *Hänsel und Gretel*. He is the children's father.

Peter Grimes
Opera in three acts by Britten (Op 33). 1st perf London, 7 June 1945; libr by Montagu Slater, after George Crabbe's *The Borough*. Principal roles: Grimes (ten), Ellen Orford (sop), Balstrode (bar), Ned Keene (bar), Swallow (bass), Auntie (mezzo), Bob Boles (ten), Mrs Sedley (mezzo), Hobson (bass), Rector (ten). Britten's first opera and often regarded as his masterpiece, it deals with his favourite theme: the position of the outsider in society. Its premiere was one of the most important events in British musical history, as it marked not only the appearance of a composer of genius but also heralded the post-war British operatic renaissance. It is the only British opera which is firmly established in the international repertory.
Plot: East Suffolk, *c* 1830. Although the locals distrust his isolation and his temper, the fisherman Grimes is cleared of responsibility in the death of his young apprentice. Grimes is befriended by the widowed schoolteacher Ellen Orford, whom he hopes to marry, and who assists and supports him in finding him a new apprentice. The boy meets with a fatal accident and the frightened Grimes puts to sea just before a deputation of suspicious

townsfolk, led by the lawyer Swallow and the bigoted Methodist preacher Bob Boles, arrives at his hut. Grimes returns to shore in the fog, almost deranged by his experiences, and the retired sea captain Balstrode advises him to avoid the consequences of the boy's death by taking his boat out to sea and sinking it. [R]

Peter Ibbetson
Opera in three acts by Taylor (Op 20). 1st perf New York, 7 Feb 1931; libr by the composer and Constance Collier, after George du Maurier's novel. Principal roles: Peter (ten), Col Ibbetson (bar), Mary (sop), Mrs Deane (mezzo), Maj Dusquenois (bass). One of the most successful of all American operas at its appearance, it is nowadays almost never performed.
Plot: England and France, 1855–87. Peter, tyrannized by his cruel uncle Col Ibbetson, finds escape in dreams about his childhood. He returns to his birthplace and meets his childhood playmate Mary. He kills his uncle and is sentenced to life imprisonment. For over 40 years, he finds solace in dreams as Mary visits him. When he learns of her death he joins her.

Peter Schmoll und seine Nachbarn (*Peter Schmoll and His Neighbours*)
Comic opera in two acts by Weber (J 8). 1st perf Augsburg, March 1803; libr by Joseph Türk, after Carl Gottlob Cramer's novel. Principal roles: Peter and Martin Schmoll (bar and ten), Minette (sop), Karl Pirkner (ten), Hans Bast (bar). Weber's first opera of any significance, it is virtually never performed, and only the overture is nowadays at all remembered. [R]

Peters, Roberta (b 1930)
American soprano, particularly associated with Italian COLORATURA roles. One of the leading coloraturas of the 1950s, she possessed a bright-toned voice of great agility if a little lacking in individuality. Married for a time to the baritone ROBERT MERRILL.

Peter the Miner (*Piér li Houïeu*)
Opera in one act by Ysaÿe. 1st perf Liège, 4 March 1931; libr (in Walloon) by the composer. Ysaÿe's only opera, it is based on an incident during a miners' strike which he witnessed in his youth. Successful at its appearance, it is nowadays virtually forgotten.

Petit Duc, Le (*The Little Duke*)
Operetta in three acts by Lecocq. 1st perf Paris, 25 Jan 1878; libr by Henri Meilhac and Ludovic Halévy. Principal roles: Raoul (ten), Montlandry (bar), Diane (mezzo), Frimousse (ten). One of Lecocq's most successful works, it is still sometimes performed in France. [R]

Petrassi, Goffredo (b 1904)
Italian composer. He wrote two operas: the controversial *Il Cordovano* (Milan, 12 May 1949; libr Eugenio Montale, after Miguel Cervantes's *Entremes del Viejo Celoso*) and *Morte dell'Aria* (Rome, 24 Oct 1950; libr T. Scialoja). He was artistic director of the Teatro la Fenice, Venice (1937–40).

Petrella, Clara (1914–87)
Italian soprano, particularly associated with the Italian repertory. An outstanding singing-actress, she was nicknamed the 'Duse of Singers'. She created Anna in Rossellini's *Il Vortice*, the title-role in Pannain's *Madame Bovary*, Beatrice in Rossellini's *Uno Sguardo dal Ponte* and, for Pizzetti, Mila in *La Figlia di Iorio*, the title-role in *Clitennestra* and a role in *Cagliostro*.

Petrella, Errico (1813–77)
Italian composer. He wrote his first opera *Il Diavolo Color di Rosa* (Naples, July 1829; libr Andrea Leone Tottola) at the age of 15 and went on to write many more, a number of which enjoyed considerable success in their time but which are all now largely forgotten. The most important include *Le Precauzioni* (Naples, 12 May 1851; libr M. d'Arienzo), *Marco Visconti* (Naples, 9 Feb 1854; libr D. Bolognese), *Jone* (Milan, 26 Jan 1858; libr Giovanni Peruzzini, after Edward Bulwer Lytton's *The Last Days of Pompei*), perhaps his finest opera, and *I Promessi Sposi* (Lecco, 20 Oct 1869; libr Antonio Ghislanzoni, after Alessandro Manzoni).

Petrov, Andrei (b 1930)
Russian composer, writing in 'orthodox Soviet' style. His two operas are the epic *Peter I* (Leningrad, 14 June 1975; libr Natalia Kasatkina and Vladimir Vasilyov)

[R] and *Mayakovsky Comes Into Existence* (Leningrad, 13 Apr 1983; libr M. Rozovsky) [R].

Petrov, Ivan (b Hans Krause) (b 1920)
Russian bass, particularly associated with the Italian and Russian repertories, especially the male leads in *Boris Godunov* and Glinka's *Ruslan and Ludmila.* The leading Russian bass of the 1950s, he possessed a magnificent, rich and beautiful voice of considerable range and power which he used with outstanding artistry. He created Bestuzhev in Shaporin's *The Decembrists.*

Petrov, Osip (1806–78)
Russian bass, particularly associated with the Russian repertory. One of the greatest of all Russian singers, he had a magnificent voice of great range (B to f♯) and was an outstanding singing-actor fully in tune with the aims of the emerging nationalist school of composers, whose finest interpreter he became. He created Varlaam in *Boris Godunov*, Ivan in *A Life for the Tsar*, Ruslan in *Ruslan and Ludmila*, Ivan in Rimsky-Korsakov's *The Maid of Pskov*, the Mayor in Tchaikovsky's *Vakula the Blacksmith*, Prince Gudal in Rubinstein's *The Demon*, for Dargomijsky Leporello in *The Stone Guest* and the Miller in *Rusalka* and, for Serov, Oziya in *Judith* and Vladimir in *Rogneda.* His wife **Anna Yakovlevna Vorobyova** (1816–1901) was a successful mezzo, who created Vanya in *A Life for the Tsar.*

Petrovics, Emil (b 1930)
Hungarian composer. His three operas, written in atonal style, have met with considerable success. They are *C'Est la Guerre* (Budapest, 17 Aug 1962; libr Miklós Hubay) [R], *Lysistrate* (Budapest, 1962; libr Gábor Devecseri, after Aristophanes) [R] and *Crime and Punishment* (*Bün és Bünhödés*, Budapest, 26 Oct 1969; libr Gyula Maár, after Fyodor Dostoyevsky) [R]. He was artistic director of the Budapest State Opera (1986–90).

Pfitzner, Hans (1869–1949)
German composer and conductor. An ardent admirer of Wagner, his operas are traditional in style, in line with his dislike of modernism in music. His five operas are DER ARME HEINRICH, *Die Rose von Liebesgarten* (Elberfeld, 9 Nov 1901; libr James Grun), *Das Christelflein* (Munich, 11 Dec 1906; libr composer and Ilse von Stach; revised version Dresden, 11 Dec 1917), his masterpiece PALESTRINA and *Das Herz* (Munich, 12 Nov 1931; libr Hans Mahner-Mons) [R]. Although it has many ardent advocates, his music remains little performed. He was musical director of the Strasbourg Opera (1910–16) and also prepared a revised edition of Marschner's *Der Vampyr* in 1925.

Phaëton
Opera in prologue and five acts by Lully. 1st perf Versailles, 6 Jan 1683; libr by Philippe Quinault. Principal roles: Phaëton (ten), Clymène (sop), Théone (sop), Libye (sop), Epaphus (ten), Triton (ten), Mérops (bar), Saturne (bar). One of Lully's richest scores, it still receives an occasional performance. [R]

Philadelphia Opera Company
Formed in March 1975 by a merger of the Philadelphia Lyric Opera Company (founded in 1923) and the Philadelphia Grand Opera Company (founded in 1927), it is the latest of many companies which have existed in Philadelphia. The annual season runs from October to May and performances are given at the Academy of Music (cap 2,818).

Philémon et Baucis
Opera in two (originally three) acts by Gounod. 1st perf Paris, 18 Feb 1860; libr by Jules Barbier and Michel Carré, after Jean de la Fontaine's story, itself based on Ovid's *Metamorphoses.* Revised version 1st perf Paris, 16 May 1876. Principal roles: Baucis (sop), Philémon (ten), Jupiter (bar), Vulcain (bass). Successful in its time, it is nowadays only very rarely performed.
Plot: Legendary Phrygia. Jupiter and Vulcan are travelling in disguise and are shown great hospitality by the poor elderly couple Philemon and Baucis. As a reward for their kindness, the couple's youth is restored, whereupon Jupiter promptly falls in love with the now young and pretty Baucis.

Philidor, François-André (b Danican) (1726–95)
French composer. One of the most important early composers of OPÉRA-COMIQUE, he wrote over 30 operas, notable for their imaginitive orchestration and for their melodic and harmonic richness. His most successful operas include *Blaise le Savetier* (Paris, 9 Mar 1759; libr Jean-Marie Sedaine, after Jean de la Fontaine), *Le Sorcier* (Paris, 2 Jan 1764; libr Antoine Poinsinet), *Tom Jones* (Paris, 27 Feb 1765; libr Poinsinet, after Henry Fielding), arguably his finest work, and *Le Bon Fils* (Paris, 11 Jan 1773; libr F.A. Devaux). He was also an outstanding chess player, publishing a notable study of the game.

Philip
Bass role in Verdi's *Don Carlos*. Carlos's father, he is King Philip II of Spain (1527–98).

Phrasing
A phrase is a group of notes which constitute a melodic unit. Phrasing is thus a singer's ability correctly to observe a melody's division into these units. It can often give an indication of a singer's breath control: whether, for example, a baritone can produce the final section of Ford's Jealousy Monologue in Verdi's *Falstaff* without breaking the phrase.

Pia de' Tolomei
Opera in two acts by Donizetti. 1st perf Venice, 18 Feb 1837; libr by Salvatore Cammarano, after Bartolemeo Sestini's novella, itself based on the *Purgatorio* in Dante Alighieri's *La Divina Commedia*. Principal roles: Pia (sop), Nello (bar), Ghino (ten), Rodrigo (mezzo), Lamberto (bass). Very successful at its appearance, it is nowadays only rarely performed.
Plot: 13th-century Rome. Ghino desires his cousin Nello della Pietra's young wife Pia. When she refuses him, he accuses her of adultery with her young brother Rodrigo. A secret meeting between brother and sister is betrayed, and Rodrigo barely escapes before Nello appears and orders Pia to be incarcerated. Ghino offers Pia her freedom, but she replies that she is faithful and that the suspect meeting was merely with her brother. Nello gives orders that Pia is to be killed if he does not survive a forthcoming battle against the Guelphs under Rodrigo. Ghino is fatally injured and, dying, confesses that he had falsely accused Pia. Nello hurries to Pia, but too late: she has been given poison. She urges Nello and Rodrigo to compose their feud and expires.

Piangea cantando
Soprano aria (the Willow Song) for Desdemona in Act IV of Verdi's *Otello*.

Piave, Francesco Maria (1810–76)
Italian librettist. He wrote some 70 libretti in all, providing texts for Balfe (*Pittore e Duca*), Mercadante, Pacini (*Lorenzino de' Medici*) and F. and L. Ricci (*Crispino e la Comare*) amongst others, but he is best known for his texts for Verdi: *I Due Foscari, Ernani, Il Corsaro, Macbeth, Stiffelio, Rigoletto, La Traviata, Simon Boccanegra, Aroldo* and *La Forza del Destino*. His complaisance and willingness to take orders made him the type of librettist Verdi liked best: the kind he could bully. This has perhaps led to his work being rather underrated; some of his texts are a distinct cut above the contemporary average, and that for *Rigoletto* is theatrically superb. He was resident stage manager at the Teatro la Fenice, Venice (1843–67).

Piccaver, Alfred (b Peckover) (1884–1958)
British tenor, particularly associated with the Italian repertory. Largely resident at the Vienna State Opera, he possessed a beautiful and velvety lyric tenor, used with elegance and an outstanding technique.

Picchi, Mirto (1915–80)
Italian tenor, particularly associated with the Italian repertory and with 20th-century operas. One of the leading tenors of the immediate post-war period, he had a fine voice and was an admired singing-actor. He created Aligi in Pizzetti's *La Figlia di Iorio*, Quiroga in Castro's *Proserpina y el Extranjero* and roles in Testi's *La Celestina*, Bussotti's *Lorenzaccio* and Pizzetti's *Cagliostro*. His autobiography, *Un Trono Vicino al Sol*, was published in 1978.

Piccinni, Niccolò (1728–1800)
Italian composer. His first opera was *Le Donne Dispettose* (Naples, 1754; libr A. Palomba), which was followed by over 100 others. One of the last masters of the Neapolitan school, the greatest successes of his first (Italian) period were in comedy, particularly LA BUONA FIGLIUOLA, his only opera still to be remembered. His OPERA SERIAS, such as *L'Olimpiade* (Rome, 1768; libr Pietro Metastasio), were successful in their time but were soon forgotten. He moved to Paris in 1776, where his supporters became involved in an aesthetic disagreement with Gluck's supporters. Between the two composers there was no ill-feeling. The success of *Roland* (Paris, 27 Jan 1778; libr Jean-François Marmontel, after Philippe Quinault) fuelled the controversy, which came to a head when an enterprising impresario had both composers set IPHIGÉNIE EN TAURIDE. The popular verdict (and that of history) went in favour of Gluck, but even so, Piccinni's works continued to be performed in Paris long after his death, especially the fine *Didon* (Fontainebleau, 16 Oct 1783; libr Marmontel). His son **Luigi** (1766–1827) was also a composer who wrote several operas.

Piccola Scala, La
A chamber theatre (cap 600) within the building of the Teatro alla Scala in Milan, it opened in Dec 1955. It presents smaller-scale 18th- and 19th-century works as well as contemporary operas.

Piccolo Marat, Il (*The Little Marat*)
Opera in three acts by Mascagni. 1st perf Rome, 2 May 1921; libr by Giovacchino Forzano and Giovanni Targioni-Tozzetti, after Victor Martin's *Sous la Terreur*. Principal roles: Fleury (ten), Mariella (sop), L'Orco (bass), Carpenter (bar), Soldier (bar). Telling of the Terror in France which followed the murder of the revolutionary leader Jean-Paul Marat in 1793, it was successful at its appearance and is arguably Mascagni's finest opera. Its almost complete disappearance in recent years in unjustified.
Plot: Nantes, 1793. The young Prince Jean-Charles de Fleury insinuates himself into the favour of the President of the Council (known as L'Orco) to secure the release of his mother, who has been condemned to death by the Jacobins. His seeming revolutionary zeal earns him the soubriquet of 'the little Marat'. With the aid of his beloved Mariella and of the Carpenter, he captures L'Orco in a drunken sleep and forces him to sign his mother's release warrant. He is wounded, but all escape to freedom. [R]

Pick-Mangiagalli, Riccardo (1882–1949)
Czech-born Italian composer. He wrote three operas in a tuneful if derivative style which enjoyed some success in their day but which are now forgotten. They are *Basi e Bote* (Rome, 3 Mar 1927; libr Arrigo Boito), *L'Ospite Inatteso* (RAI, 25 Oct 1931; libr C. Veneziani) and *Notturno Romantico* (Rome, 25 Apr 1936; libr Arturo Rossato).

Pierné, Gabriel (1863–1937)
French composer and organist. He wrote eight operas, of which the most successful were *La Coupe Enchantée* (Royan, 24 Aug 1895; libr F. Matrat, after Jean de la Fontaine), *On Ne Badine Pas Avec l'Amour* (Paris, 20 May 1910; libr Gabriel Nigond and L. Leloir, after Alfred de Musset), *Sophie Arnould* (Paris, 21 Feb 1927; libr Nigond), which is based on the life of the 18th-century soprano, and *Fragonard* (Paris, 17 Oct 1934; libr A. Rivoire and R. Coolus).

Pietà, rispetto, amore
Baritone aria for Macbeth in Act IV of Verdi's *Macbeth*, in which he laments that infamy will be his only memorial.

Pietra del Paragone, La (roughly *The Touchstone*)
Comic opera in two acts by Rossini. 1st perf Milan, 26 Sept 1812; libr by Luigi Romanelli. Principal roles: Asdrubale (bar), Clarice (mezzo), Pacuvio (bar), Macrobio (bass), Giocondo (ten), Fulvia (sop). One of Rossini's first big successes, it is still quite often performed.
Plot: Early-19th-century Tuscany. So as to test the genuineness of his friends' affections, Count Asdrubale pretends to have been stripped of his riches by an African prince, whom he then proceeds to impersonate. All of his friends fail the test

dismally, except for the poet Giocondo and Marchesina Clarice, with whom Asdrubale is in love. [R]

Pietro
Bass COMPRIMARIO role in Verdi's *Simon Boccanegra*. He is Paolo's henchman.

Piff, paff
Bass aria for Marcel in Act I of Meyerbeer's *Les Huguenots*, in which he sings a Huguenot song in front of the Catholic leaders.

Pijper, Willem (1894–1947)
Dutch composer. His one completed opera *Halloween* (*Halewijn*, Amsterdam, 13 June 1933; libr Emmy van Lokhorst, after Martinus Nijhoff) [R] met with considerable success in Holland. His second opera *Merlijn* (Rotterdam, 7 June 1952; libr S. Vestdijk) was left unfinished.

Pilarczyk, Helga (b 1925)
German soprano, particularly associated with 20th-century operas, especially *Erwartung*. A singer of great intelligence and an outstanding singing-actress, she created Costanza in Henze's *König Hirsch* and roles in Křenek's *Pallas Athene Weint* and *Der Goldene Bock*.

Pilgrims' Chorus
Chorus of pilgrims in Acts I and III of Wagner's *Tannhäuser*.

Pilgrim's Progress, The
Opera in four acts by Vaughan Williams. 1st perf London, 26 April 1951; libr by the composer, after John Bunyan's allegory. Principal roles: Pilgrim (bar), Watchful (bar), Evangelist (bar), Lord Hate-Good (b-bar), Herald (bar), Apollyon (bass), Bunyan (bar), Mr and Mrs By-Ends (ten and mezzo), Lord Lechery (ten). Described as a 'morality', it is Vaughan Williams's last opera and incorporates his earlier Bunyan setting *The Shepherds of the Delectable Mountains* of 1922. Although its structure may not be conventionally operatic, it contains some of the finest music of any British opera (some of which found its way into his Fifth Symphony). Its failure deeply hurt the composer, and the work's relegation to almost total neglect is both unaccountable and quite unjust. [R]

Pimpinone
Comic opera in two parts by Albinoni. 1st perf Venice, autumn 1708; libr by Pietro Pariati. Principal roles: Pimpinone (b-bar), Vespetta (mezzo). An early example of the Italian INTERMEZZO, it was originally given between the acts of the OPERA SERIA *Astarto*. It is Albinoni's only opera still to be in any way remembered. [R]

Pimpinone or **Die Ungleiche Heyrath**
(*The Unequal Marriage*)
Comic opera in two parts by Telemann. 1st perf Hamburg, 27 Sept 1725; libr by Johann Peter Praetorius, after Pietro Pariati's libretto for Albinoni. Principal roles: Pimpinone (bar), Vespetta (sop). Telemann's best-known stage work, it is still quite often performed.
Plot: The maid Vespetta is looking for an easy life through marriage. She obtains a post with the rich but stingy merchant Pimpinone, and tricks him into wedding her. In return for her promise to be quiet and virtuous, he offers her a 10,000 thaler dowry. Once married, she forgets her promises and demands her pleasures. When Pimpinone tries to force her to obey him, she offers him a choice: concede her her rights or pay her the dowry. The infatuated old miser resigns himself to allowing Vespetta to do as she pleases. [R]

Pimyen
Bass role in Moussorgsky's *Boris Godunov*. He is an old monkish chronicler.

Ping
Baritone role in Puccini's *Turandot*. The Grand Chancellor, he is one of the three courtiers.

Pini-Corsi, Antonio (1858–1918)
Italian baritone, particularly associated with comic Italian roles. An outstanding BUFFO, he created Ford in *Falstaff*, Schaunard in *La Bohème*, Happy in *La Fanciulla del West*, the Innkeeper in *Die Königskinder*, Mishinsky in Giordano's *Siberia* and roles in Herbert's *Madeleine* and Franchetti's *La Figlia di Iorio*. His brother **Giacomo** (1860–*c* 1924) was a leading COMPRIMARIO tenor who created Goro in *Madama Butterfly*.

Pinkerton, Lt B.F.
Tenor role in Puccini's *Madama Butterfly*. He is an American naval officer who marries and then abandons Cio-Cio-San.

Pinza, Ezio (b Fortunato) (1892–1957)
Italian bass, particularly associated with the Italian and Russian repertories. Long resident at the Metropolitan Opera, New York, he was arguably the greatest bass of the inter-war period. He possessed a large, beautiful voice used with nobility and fine musicianship; he was also an outstanding singing-actor. He created Tigellino in Boito's *Nerone* and the Blind Man in Pizzetti's *Dèbora e Jaéle*. He appeared in a number of films, notably *South Pacific* (1949), and his autobiography, *Ezio Pinza*, was published in 1958. His daughter **Claudia** (*b* 1927) was a soprano.

Piper, John (1903–92)
British painter and designer. A founder member of the English Opera Group, his stage designs followed the same shaded and atmospheric style as his paintings. His most notable designs were for Britten premieres: *The Rape of Lucretia*, *Albert Herring*, *Billy Budd*, *Gloriana*, *The Turn of the Screw*, *Owen Wingrave* and, particularly, *A Midsummer Night's Dream* and *Death in Venice*. His wife **Myfanwy** (*b* Evans) (*b* 1911) is a librettist who provided texts for Britten (*The Turn of the Screw*, *Owen Wingrave* and *Death in Venice*) and Hoddinott (*What the Old Man Does is Always Right*, *The Trumpet Major* and *The Rajah's Diamond*).

Pique Dame
see QUEEN OF SPADES, THE

Piquillo
Tenor role in Offenbach's *La Périchole*. He is a poor street singer in love with Périchole.

Pirata, Il (*The Pirate*)
Opera in two acts by Bellini. 1st perf Milan, 27 Oct 1827; libr by Felice Romani, after Charles Maturin's *Bertram or the Castle of St Aldobrand*. Principal roles: Imogene (sop), Gualtiero (ten), Ernesto (bar), Goffredo (bass), Adele (mezzo). Bellini's third opera, and the work which established his reputation, it suffered a long period of neglect, but has received a number of performances in recent years.
Plot: 13th-century Sicily. After the Battle of Benevento, Gualtiero has been deprived of his estates and has turned to piracy. He returns to discover that his beloved Imogene has married his enemy Ernesto. Ernesto catches Imogene at a secret meeting with Gualtiero and challenges the latter to a duel. Ernesto is killed, Gualtiero is arrested and Imogene goes out of her mind. [R]

Pirates of Penzance, The or **The Slave of Duty**
Operetta in two acts by Sullivan. 1st perf Paignton and New York (virtually simultaneously), 30/31 Dec 1879; libr by W.S. Gilbert. Principal roles: Frederic (ten), Mabel (sop), Pirate King (b-bar), Maj-Gen Stanley (bar), Ruth (mezzo), Sgt of Police (bass), Edith (mezzo), Samuel (bar). A satire on the army and police which also contains some superb operatic send-ups, it was an immediate success which enjoyed an initial run of nearly 400 performances, and it has always been one of the most popular of the Savoy Operas.
Plot: 19th-century Cornwall. Because of an error by his nurse Ruth, Frederic has been apprenticed to the Pirate King and is out of his indentures, having reached his 21st birthday. He falls in love with Mabel, daughter of Maj-Gen Stanley, and decides that for the sake of society his former associates must be exterminated. As the police expedition against the pirates is about to set out, the Pirate King informs Frederic that he was born in leap year on 29 February and that his contract states that he is apprenticed until his 21st birthday, not his 21st year. Frederic feels honour-bound to rejoin the pirates, who defeat the policemen, but who submit when called upon to do so in Queen Victoria's name. Ruth reveals that the pirates are noblemen who have 'gone wrong', and the snobbish Gen Stanley orders them to be released and to resume their former positions. The pirates marry his large brood of daughters and Mabel and Frederic are united. [R]

Pistol
Falstaff's associate appears in a number of operas, including: **1** Bass role in Verdi's

Falstaff. **2** Baritone role in Holst's *At the Boar's Head.* **3** Bass role in Vaughan Williams's *Sir John in Love.*

Pizarro, Don
Baritone role in Beethoven's *Fidelio* and tenor role in Paer's *Leonora.* He is the evil prison governor.

Pizzetti, Ildebrando (1880–1968)
Italian composer. Perhaps the most important post-Puccinian Italian opera composer, he wrote three youthful one-act operas, including *Il Cid* (1902), and began work on several other projects, none of which he finished. The first of his 13 mature operas, mostly written in ARIOSO style and for nearly all of which he wrote his own libretti, was FEDRA. It was followed by the unpublished *Gigliola* (1915; libr after Gabriele d'Annunzio's *La Fiaccola sotto il Moggio*), DÈBORA E JAÉLE, FRA GHERARDO, *Lo Straniero* (Rome, 29 Apr 1930), *Orsèolo* (Florence, 4 May 1935), *L'Oro* (Milan, 2 Jan 1947, composed 1941), VANNA LUPA, the radio operas *Ifigenia* (RAI, 30 Oct 1950; libr composer and A. Perrini) and *Cagliostro* (RAI, 5 Nov 1952), LA FIGLIA DI IORIO, the successful L'ASSASSINIO NELLA CATTEDRALE, *Il Calzare d'Argento* (Milan, 23 Mar 1961; libr Riccardo Bacchelli) and *Clitennestra* (Milan, 1 Mar 1965).

Plançon, Pol (b Paul-Henri) (1854–1914)
French bass, particularly associated with the French repertory, especially Méphistophélès. A fine singing-actor, he possessed a beautiful and smooth voice of enormous range and remarkable flexibility. He created Francis in Saint-Saëns's *Ascanio*, a role in Bemberg's *Elaine*, Friar Francis in Stanford's *Much Ado About Nothing*, and, for Massenet, Don Gormas in *Le Cid* and Garrido in *La Navarraise.*

Planquette, Robert (1848–1903)
French composer. He wrote some 20 operettas, of which LES CLOCHES DE CORNEVILLE was much the most successful. Of the others, the most impression was made by *Rip* (London, 14 Oct 1882; libr H.B. Farnie, after Washington Irving's *Rip van Winkle*) [R Exc], *Nell Gwynne* (London, 7 Feb 1884; libr Farnie) and *Mam'zelle Quat'sous* (Paris, 5 Nov 1897; libr A. Mars and M. Desvallières).

Plasson, Michel (b 1933)
French conductor, particularly associated with the French repertory, especially Massenet and Offenbach. A persuasive interpreter of 19th-century French music, he was musical director of the Metz Opera (1965–71) and the Toulouse Capitole (1972–82). He conducted the first performance of Landowski's *Montségur.*

Platée or **Junon Jalouse** (*Jealous Juno*)
Opera-ballet in prologue and three acts by Rameau. 1st perf Versailles, 31 March 1745; libr by Adrien-Joseph le Valois d'Orville, after Jacques Autreau's play. Principal roles: Platée (ten), Cithéron (bar), Jupiter (bar), Mercure (ten), Folly (sop), Momus (ten), Thespis (ten), Junon (sop), Thalie (sop). One of the very earliest French comic operas, it tells a rather bitter and unpleasant story, but contains some delightful music. It is still performed from time to time.
Plot: Legendary Greece. Platée, the ugly goddess of swamps and frogs, thinks herself irresistible to men. To escape her attentions, King Cithéron, aided by Mercury, persuades her that Jupiter loves her and wishes to marry her after repudiating Juno. A mock marriage ceremony is arranged, presided over by Momus, to which Juno (unaware of the joke) comes incognito. As Jupiter begins to recite his vows, Juno bursts out in fury. However, when she discovers Platée beneath the bridal veil she sees the joke and is reconciled with Jupiter. [R]

Plebe! Patrizi!
Baritone aria for Boccanegra in the Council Chamber Scene of Verdi's *Simon Boccanegra*, in which he pleads for peace and love between the patricians and the plebians.

Pleurez mes yeux
Soprano aria for Chimène in Act III of Massenet's *Le Cid*, in which she expresses her sorrow over the conflicting demands upon her of love and filial duty.

Plishka, Paul (b 1941)
American bass, particularly associated with the Italian and French repertories. One of the leading contemporary American basses, he possesses a rich and smooth voice

which is used with fine musicianship, but he can sometimes be a little dull on stage.

Plowright, Rosalind (b 1949)
British soprano, particularly associated with the Italian repertory, especially Verdi. She is an exciting, rich-voiced singer with a voice of highly individual timbre, and has a good stage presence which is enhanced by her personal beauty.

Plunkett
Bass-baritone role in Flotow's *Martha*. He is a farmer who falls in love with Nancy.

Pluto
The Graeco-Roman god of the underworld appears in many operas, including: **1** Bass role in Rameau's *Hippolyte et Aricie*. **2** Bass role in Monteverdi's *Il Ballo delle Ingrate*. **3** Tenor role in Offenbach's *Orphée aux Enfers*. **4** Bass role in Monteverdi's *La Favola d'Orfeo*. **5** Bass role in Rameau's *Naïs*.

Plzeň Opera
(Pilsen when it was part of Austria–Hungary). Opera in this Czech town is given at the J.K. Tyl Theatre (cap 1,100), which opened in 1902. Musical directors have included Bohumír Liška.

Poe, Edgar Allan
see panel below

Pogner, Veit
Bass role in Wagner's *Die Meistersinger von Nürnberg*. A goldsmith, he is Eva's father.

Poisoned Kiss, The or **The Empress and the Necromancer**
Opera in three acts by Vaughan Williams. 1st perf Cambridge, 12 May 1936; libr by Evelyn Sharp (revised by Ursula Vaughan Williams), after Richard Garnett's *The Poison Maid* and Nathaniel Hawthorne's *Rapaccini's Daughter*. Principal roles: Tormentilla (sop), Amaryllus (ten), Dipsacus (bass), Persicaria (mezzo). A ludicrous story of rival magicians and their poisons and antidotes, it contains some delightful music in Vaughan Williams's lighter vein, but the dire libretto has ensured that the piece is almost never performed.

· *Edgar Allan Poe* ·

The works of the American writer and poet Edgar Allan Poe (1809–49) have inspired many composers, although the most important works (such as Rachmaninov's *The Bells*) are non-operatic. Poe's influence on opera was more general than simply providing source material: in his position as the leading exponent of the Gothic movement, he exerted a strong influence in Europe, especially in France, on composers such as Debussy. He is the subject of Argento's *The Voyage of Edgar Allan Poe*. Below are listed, by story, those operas based on his works by composers with entries in this dictionary.

The Devil in the Belfry		
Lualdi	*Il Diavolo nel Campanile*	1925
The Fall of the House of Usher		
Debussy	*La Chûte de la Maison Usher*	1915 (U)
Glass	*The Fall of the House of Usher*	1988
The Purloined Letter		
Blacher	*Das Geheimnis des Entwendeten Briefes*	1975
Some Words with a Mummy		
Viozzi	*Allamistakeo*	1954
The System of Dr Tarr and Prof Fether		
Tosatti	*Il Sistema della Dolcezza*	1950

Poissl, Johann Nepomuk von (1783–1865)
German composer. An historically important figure, he was the transitional German composer between Mozart and Weber (who admired his works). His operas show a move away from Italian and French models towards THROUGH-COMPOSED German opera. The most important of his operas, for many of which he wrote his own libretti, include *Antigonus* (Munich, 12 Feb 1808; libr composer), *Athalia* (Munich, 3 June 1814; libr G. Wöhlbruck, after Jean Baptiste Racine's *Athalie*), *Der Wettkampf zu Olympia* (Munich, 21 Apr 1815; libr composer, after Pietro Metastasio's *L'Olimpiade*), *Nittetis* (Darmstadt, 29 June 1817; libr composer, after Metastasio) and *Der Untersberg* (Munich, 30 Oct 1829; libr Eduard von Schenk). Nowadays, all of his operas are forgotten.

Poland
see POZNAŃ OPERA; WARSAW NATIONAL OPERA

Polish opera composers
see ELSNER; MONIUSZKO; PADEREWSKI; PENDERECKI; PONIATOWSKI; RUDZIŃSKI; SZYMANOWSKI; ZELEŃSKI

Other national opera composers include Tadeusz Baird (1928–81), József Damse (1789–1852), Maciej Kamieński (1734–1821), whose *Sorrow Turned to Joy* (*Nedza Uszczesliwiona*, Warsaw, 1778; libr Wojciech Bogusławski) was the first Polish opera, Karol Kurpiński (1785–1857), Feliks Nowowiejski (1877–1946), Ludomir Rózucki (1884–1953), Roman Statkowski (1860–1925), Tadeusz Szeligowski (1896–1963), Romuald Twardowski (*b* 1930) and Adam Wieniawski (1876–1950).

Poliuto
Opera in three acts by Donizetti. 1st perf Naples, 30 Nov 1848 (composed 1838); libr by Salvatore Cammarano, after Pierre Corneille's *Polyeucte*. Revised version *Les Martyrs*, 1st perf Paris, 10 April 1840; libr revised by Eugène Scribe. Principal roles (with *Les Martyrs* second): Poliuto/Polyeucte (ten), Paolina/Pauline (sop), Severo/Sévère (bar), Callistene/Callysthènes (bass), Nearco/Néarche (ten). One of Donizetti's best operas (with some unusual features such as a duet-finale and an overture with chorus), it is still quite often performed, usually in the original version.
Plot: Melitene (Armenia), AD 257. Poliuto, a secret convert to Christianity, is arrested and condemned to death. His wife Paolina, although still partly in love with her former betrothed the Roman pro-consul Severo, decides to share her husband's martyrdom. [R]

Polka
A Bohemian dance in 2/4 time which originated in the early 19th century. There is a famous operatic example in Weinberger's *Shvanda the Bagpiper*.

Pollak, Anna (b 1912)
Austrian-born British mezzo, long resident at Sadler's Wells Opera. A fine singing-actress, especially notable as the title-role in *Carmen* and Prince Orlofsky in J. Strauss's *Die Fledermaus*, she created Bianca in *The Rape of Lucretia*, Mrs Strickland in Gardner's *The Moon and Sixpence*, several roles in Williamson's *English Eccentrics* and, for Berkeley, Lady Nelson in *Nelson* and the title-role in *Ruth*.

Pollione
Tenor role in Bellini's *Norma*. A Roman pro-consul, he is Norma's former lover.

Polly
Ballad opera in three acts arranged by Pepusch and Samuel Arnold. 1st perf London, 19 June 1777 (composed 1729); libr by John Gay. Principal roles: Polly (sop), Macheath (ten). A much less successful follow-up to *The Beggar's Opera*, with the characters transported to the Caribbean, it was banned by the Lord Chamberlain and did not reach the stage for nearly 50 years, when Arnold's songs were added. It is only very rarely performed.

Polonaise (French for 'Polish')
A Polish ceremonial dance in 3/4 time. There are many fine operatic examples, including *Eugene Onegin* and *Boris Godunov*. It is called *polacca* in Italy.

Polovtsian Dances
Choral dances in Act II of Borodin's *Prince Igor*.

Pomme d'Api (*The Cherry*)
Operetta in one act by Offenbach. 1st perf Paris, 4 Sept 1873; libr by Ludovic Halévy and William Busnacht. Principal roles: Catherine (sop), Rabastens (bar), Gustave (ten). Written in Offenbach's more lyrical and sentimental later style, it is a delightful little piece which is still occasionally performed.
Plot: Paris, 1873. Rabastens disapproves of his nephew Gustave's liaison with a girl known as 'Pomme d'Api'. He is heavily smitten with his new maid Catherine, who – to the horror of Gustave, who has promised his uncle to give up his mistress – turns out to be 'Pomme d'Api'. Feeling abandoned by Gustave, she encourages Rabastens's attentions. However, when Gustave – although penniless – resolves to leave, she realizes that she still loves him. After an initial explosion of fury, Rabastens is persuaded to bless the young couple's union. [R]

Pomo d'Oro, Il (*The Golden Apple*)
Opera in prologue and five acts by Cesti. 1st perf Vienna, 12 and 14 July 1667; libr by Francesco Sbarra. Principal roles: Paride (ten), Momo (bass), Pallade (sop), Ennone (sop). Written to celebrate the wedding of Emperor Leopold I, its premiere was probably the most splendid and elaborate operatic performance in history, involving a specially built theatre and 21 separate stage sets. Based on the Greek legend of the Judgement of Paris, it is still occasionally performed, even though the music for Act V is lost.

Ponchielli, Amilcare (1834–86)
Italian composer. The last Italian romantic composer, he wrote nine operas. They are *I Promessi Sposi* (Cremona, 30 Aug 1856; libr after Alessandro Manzoni; revised version Milan, 4 Dec 1872; libr Emilio Praga), the unperformed *Bertrand dal Bormio* (1858), *La Savoiarda* (Cremona, 19 Jan 1861; libr F. Guidi; revised version *Lina*, Milan, 17 Nov 1877; libr Carlo d'Ormeville), *Roderico* (Piacenza, 26 Dec 1863; libr Guidi, after Robert Southey's *Roderick*), the ambitious I LITUANI, LA GIOCONDA, his masterpiece and his only opera still to be performed, *Il Figliuol Prodigo* (Milan, 26 Dec 1880; libr Angelo Zanardini) and *Marion Delorme* (Milan, 17 Mar 1885; libr Enrico Golisciani, after Victor Hugo). The unfinished *I Mori di Valenza* (Monte Carlo, 17 Mar 1914, begun 1874; libr Ghislanzoni, after Eugène Scribe's *Piquillo Alliaga*) was completed by Arturo Cadore. He was also a noted teacher, whose pupils include Puccini, Leoni and Mascagni. He was married to the soprano TERESINA BRAMBILLA.

Pong
Tenor role in Puccini's *Turandot*. The Chief Cook, he is one of the three courtiers.

Poniatowski, Józef (Prince of Monte Rotondo) (1816–73)
Polish composer, tenor and diplomat, great-nephew of King Stanisław August of Poland. He wrote 13 operas, all now largely forgotten, including *Giovanni di Procida* (Florence, 25 Nov 1839; libr composer, after G.N. Niccolini), *Ruy Blas* (Lucca, 2 Sept 1843; libr C. Zaccagnini, after Victor Hugo), *La Sposa d'Abido* (Venice, Feb 1845; libr G. Peruzzini, after Lord Byron's *The Bride of Abydos*), *Pierre de Médicis* (Paris, 9 Mar 1860; libr Jules-Henri Vernoy de Saint-Georges), *L'Aventurier* (Paris, 26 Jan 1865; libr Saint-Georges) and *Gelmina* (London, 4 June 1872; libr F. Rizzelli).

Ponnelle, Jean-Pierre (1932–88)
French producer and designer. An original and brilliantly inventive producer, especially in comedy (although he made his debut with *Tristan und Isolde*), and a designer of great talent, his productions were notable for their sharp precision and sense of ensemble and, occasionally, for their excess of detail and stage business. His most notable work included the Cologne Opera's Mozart cycle, Rossini operas at La Scala, *Don Pasquale* at Covent Garden and the Zürich Opera's Monteverdi cycle.

Pons, Lily (b Alice Joséphine) (1898–1976)
French-born American soprano, particularly associated with Italian and French COLORATURA roles. One of the few outstanding coloraturas of the inter-war period, she possessed a light and agile voice extending up to high f and had a charming stage presence. Based largely at

the Metropolitan Opera, New York, from 1931, she also appeared in a number of films. Married for a time to the conductor **André Kostelanetz** (1901–80).

Ponselle, Rosa (b Ponzillo) (1897–1981)
American soprano, particularly associated with the Italian repertory. Largely resident at the Metropolitan Opera, New York, she was possibly the finest lyrico-dramatic soprano of the inter-war period. She combined a gloriously rich and beautiful voice with great intelligence and considerable dramatic ability. She created Carmelita in Breil's *The Legend*. She was artistic director of the Baltimore Civic Opera from 1954, and was also a distinguished teacher, whose pupils included Sherrill Milnes and James Morris. Her sister **Carmelita** (1888–1977) was a successful mezzo.

Ponte, Lorenzo da (b Emmanuele Conegliano) (1749–1838)
Italian poet and librettist. He wrote 36 opera libretti, including texts for Gazzaniga, Martín y Soler (*Una Cosa Rara, L'Arbore di Diana* and *Il Burbero di Buon Cuore*), Paer (*Il Nuovo Figaro*), Salieri (*Il Ricco d'un Giorno, Il Talismano, Il Pastor Fido, Axur, Rè d'Ormus* and *La Cifra*), Storace (*Gli Equivoci*) and Winter (*Il Ratto di Proserpina*), but is best known for his collaboration with Mozart, for whom he wrote *Le Nozze di Figaro, Don Giovanni, Così fan Tutte* and (possibly) the unfinished *Lo Sposo Deluso*. He was later Professor of Italian at Columbia University and helped to establish opera in the United States. His libertine life may be studied in his four-volume *Memorie*, which was published between 1823 and 1827.

Popp, Lucia (1939–93)
Slovakian soprano, particularly associated with Mozart roles. Beginning as a SOUBRETTE, she subsequently turned with equal success to slightly heavier German and Italian roles. She had a beautiful, silvery voice, used with great intelligence and musicianship, and was a fine singing-actress with a delightful stage presence. Her first husband **György Fischer** (*b* 1935) is a conductor, especially known for his Mozart; her second husband **Peter Seiffert** (*b* 1954) is a successful tenor.

Porgi amor
Soprano aria for Countess Almaviva in Act II of Mozart's *Le Nozze di Figaro*, in which she laments her loss of the Count's love.

Porgy and Bess
Opera in three acts by Gershwin. 1st perf Boston, 30 Sept 1935; libr by Ira Gershwin and Du Bose Heyward, after Dorothy and Du Bose Heyward's *Porgy*. Principal roles: Porgy (bass), Bess (sop), Sportin' Life (ten), Crown (bar), Serena (mezzo), Jake (bass), Clara (sop), Maria (mezzo), Robbins (ten). Gershwin's stage masterpiece, it is notable both for its incorporation of Broadway musical idioms into opera and for its highly successful use of traditional Negro music such as spirituals. Gershwin's will stipulates that all stage performances must be given with an all-black cast.
Plot: Catfish Row (Charleston, South Carolina), 1920s. The pugnacious

· *Popes* ·

A number of pontiffs appear as operatic characters, including:

- St Peter (traditionally the first pope) in Orff's *Der Mond* and Nouguès's *Quo Vadis?*
- Leo I in Verdi's *Attila*.
- Alexander VI in Osborne's *Hell's Angels*.
- Pius IV in Pfitzner's *Palestrina*.
- Clement VII in Berlioz's *Benvenuto Cellini* and Křenek's *Karl V*.
- Leo X in Boehmer's *Docteur Faustus*.

see also ROSPIGLIOSI, GIULIO (later Pope Clement IX)

stevedore Crown kills Serena's husband Robbins in a gaming dispute and then vies with the crippled Porgy for the affections of Bess. Bess moves from Crown to Porgy, who eventually kills Crown. Lured by the gambler Sportin' Life, Bess leaves for New York and Porgy decides to follow her. [R]

Poro, Rè dell'Indie (*Porus, King of India*)
Opera in three acts by Händel. 1st perf London, 2 Feb 1731; libr by Samuel Humphries, after Pietro Metastasio's *Alessandro nell'Indie*. Principal roles: Poro (c-ten), Alessandro (ten), Cleofide (sop), Erissena (mezzo), Gandarte (c-ten), Timagene (bass). It deals with supposed events surrounding Alexander the Great's defeat of the Indian King Poros in 325 BC. Never one of Händel's more successful operas, it is only very rarely performed. [R]

Porpora, Nicola (1686–1768)
Italian composer and teacher. He wrote some 50 operas, mainly OPERA SERIAS to Metestasian texts, many of which enjoyed considerable success in their day but which are all now long forgotten. They include *Siface* (Milan, 26 Dec 1725; libr Pietro Metastasio), *Ezio* (Venice, 20 Nov 1728; libr Metastasio) and *Mitridate* (London, 24 Jan 1736; libr C. Cibber). He was also one of the most famous singing teachers of his age, whose pupils included Caffarelli and Farinelli.

Portamento (Italian for 'carrying')
The vocal technique of bridging the interval between two notes with no break in the sound and with a very slight anticipation of the second note.

Porter, Andrew (b 1928)
British critic and translator. One of the most perceptive, intelligent and constructive of contemporary British critics, he wrote largely for *The Financial Times* and later for *The New Yorker*. He won great acclaim for his magnificent translation of the *Ring* for the English National Opera, for whom he also made fine translations of *Rigoletto* and *Don Carlos* (the full original score of which he rediscovered in Paris). He wrote the libretto for Eaton's *The Tempest*.

Porterlied
Bass-baritone aria (the drinking song) for Plunkett in Act III of Flotow's *Martha*.

Portugal
see TEATRO SÃO CARLOS, LISBON

Portugal, Marcos António da Fonseca (b Ascenção; also known as Portogallo) (1762–1830)
Portuguese composer. He wrote 21 light comedies in Portuguese, including the popular *A Castanheira* (Lisbon, 1788; libr J.C. de Figueiredo), and 35 Italian operas. Many of the latter enjoyed great success in their day but are all now forgotten. They include *Alceste* (Venice, 26 Dec 1798; libr Antonio Simone Sografi) and *La Semiramide* (London, 13 Dec 1806; libr Giuseppe Caravita, after Voltaire's *Sémiramis*).

Portuguese opera composers
see ALMEIDA; PORTUGAL; SILVA

Other national opera composers include José d'Arneiro (1838–1903), Rui Coelho (1892–1986), Alfredo Keil (1850–1907), António Leal Moreira (1758–1819) and Francisco da Sá Noronha (1820–81).

Posa, Marquis of
Baritone role in Verdi's *Don Carlos*. He is Rodrigo, the liberal friend of Carlos.

Postillon de Longjumeau, Le
Opera in three acts by Adam. 1st perf Paris, 13 Oct 1836; libr by Adolphe de Leuven and Léon Lévy Brunswick. Principal roles: Chapelou (ten), Madame de Latour (sop), de Courcy (bar), Biju (bass). Adam's most successful opera and his only work which is still performed. **Plot**: France, 1766. The postillion Chapelou leaves his bride Madeleine on their wedding night, intending to become a great opera singer. Possessing a fine voice, he is engaged by the Marquis de Courcy, manager of the royal amusements, to sing at Fontainebleau, where he becomes a great star. He proposes to the wealthy Madame de Latour, who turns out to be none other than Madeleine. All thus ends happily. [R]

Postlude
The opposite of prelude, it means a final

piece of music. In opera, it usually refers to a short orchestral piece after an aria. A famous example is that to Fiesco's 'Il lacerato spirito' in Verdi's *Simon Boccanegra*.

Poulenc, Francis (1899–1963)
French composer. A member of the group LES SIX, he wrote four stage works. They are the operetta *Le Gendarme Incompris* (Paris, May 1921; libr Jean Cocteau), the surrealist comedy LES MAMELLES DE TIRÉSIAS, the magnificent DIALOGUES DES CARMÉLITES, his only full-length opera, and the MONODRAMA LA VOIX HUMAINE.

Pountney, David (b 1947)
British producer. One of the outstanding British opera producers of the younger generation, his productions are sometimes highly controversial, but are always powerfully theatrical and are always thought-provoking. He has had particular success with the Welsh National Opera and Scottish Opera Janáček cycle and with *Fate*, *Hänsel und Gretel*, *Doktor Faust*, *Macbeth* and *Christmas Eve* for the English National Opera. He was director of productions for Scottish Opera (1976–80) and for the English National Opera (1982–93). He wrote the libretti for Oliver's *The Donkey* and *The Three Wise Monkeys* and Maxwell Davies's *The Doctors of Mydffai*.

Poveri fiori
Soprano aria for Adriana in Act IV of Cilea's *Adriana Lecouvreur*, in which she contemplates the faded violets she had given to Maurizio.

Poznań Opera
(Posen when it was part of Prussia). The opera house (cap 950) in this Polish city opened on 2 June 1945, and in 1949 was named the Stanisław Moniuszko Opera House. The repertory is notable for its large number of Polish works, and its artistic standards have always been high. Musical directors have included Walerian Bierdiajew and Robert Satanowski.

Prague National Theatre
The present opera house (cap 1,598) in the Czech capital opened on 18 Nov 1883, replacing the previous theatre of the same name which opened on 11 June 1881 but which burnt down less than two months later. The leading Czech opera house, which maintains very high artistic standards, musical directors have included Adolf Čech, Karel Kovařovic, Otakar Ostrčil, Václav Talich, Otakar Jeremiáš, Zdeněk Chalabala, Jaroslav Krombholc, Václav Neumann, Zdeněk Košler and Oliver von Dohnányi. Also associated with the National Theatre complex are the Tyl Theatre (cap 1,129), which opened on 21 Apr 1783 and was enlarged in 1834, and the Smetana Theatre (originally called the Neues Deutches Theater) (cap 1,044), which opened in 1887 and whose musical directors included Angelo Neumann, Zemlinsky and George Széll.

Pré aux Clercs, Le (*The Clerks' Meadow*)
Opera in three acts by Hérold. 1st perf Paris, 15 Dec 1832; libr by François-Antoine-Eugène de Planard, after Prosper Mérimée's *Chronique du Règne de Charles IX*. Principal roles: Marguerite (sop), Isabelle (sop), Baron de Mergy (ten), Comte de Comminge (bar), Nicette (sop). Set at the time of the St Bartholemew Massacre, it is Hérold's last completed opera. It was sensationally successful at its appearance, clocking up 1,000 performances in Paris alone within 40 years, but for some peculiar reason it is nowadays almost never performed.
Plot: Mid-16th-century Paris. The Baron de Mergy and the Comte de Comminge are rivals for the love of Isabelle de Béarn, the ward of Queen Marguerite de Valois. The two men fight a duel at the field known as 'Pré aux Clercs' and Comminge is killed. Isabelle and de Mergy are united. [R Exc]

Preghiera (Italian for 'prayer')
An aria or chorus in which the characters pray for divine assistance, it was a highly popular ingredient of early-19th-century Italian opera. There are famous examples in Rossini's *Mosè in Egitto* and Donizetti's *Maria Stuarda*. It is called *Gebet* in Germany.

Prelude (from the Latin *praeludium*, 'before-game')
An orchestral introduction to the act of an opera, such as the openings to the third acts of *Parsifal* and *La Traviata*. Usually

shorter than an overture, it lacks the latter's formal structure. It is called *preludio* in Italy and *Vorspiel* in Germany.

Près des remparts de Séville
Mezzo aria (the Seguidilla) for Carmen in Act I of Bizet's *Carmen*, in which she sings to herself of the pleasures at Lilas Pastia's tavern.

Prêtre, Georges (b 1924)
French conductor and composer, particularly associated with the French and Italian repertories. One of the leading post-war interpreters of French opera, even if sometimes rather idiosyncratic, he was musical director of the Paris Opéra (1970–71) and conducted the first performances of Poulenc's *La Voix Humaine*, Rossellini's *La Reine Morte* and Bécaud's *Opéra d'Aran*. He also composed the operetta *Pour Toi* (1951).

Previn, André (b Andreas Priwin) (b 1929)
American conductor, composer and pianist, long resident in Britain. Best known as a symphonic conductor, his operatic appearances have been very rare indeed, being limited to an occasional concert performances. Married for a time to the actress Mia Farrow.

Previtali, Fernando (1907–85)
Italian conductor, particularly associated with the Italian repertory, especially Verdi and 20th-century operas. He was musical director of the Radio Italiana Orchestra (1936–53), with which he conducted the 1951 Verdi cycle, and was artistic director of the Teatro Regio, Turin, and the Teatro Carlo Felice, Genoa. He conducted the first performances of Dallapiccola's *Volo di Notte*, Ghedini's *Rè Hassan* and *Le Baccanti* and Napoli's *Dubrovski II*.

Prey, Hermann (b 1929)
German baritone, particularly associated with Mozart and Schubert roles and with Viennese operetta. One of the outstanding operatic artists (and lieder singers) of the post-war era, he possessed a warm and beautiful voice used with great intelligence and musicianship, and was a fine singing-actor, especially in comedy, who had a most engaging stage personality. He created Meton in Křenek's *Pallas Athene Weint*. His autobiography, *First Night Fever*, was published in 1986.

Preziose Ridicole, Le (*The Ridiculous Snobs*)
Comic opera in one act by Lattuada. 1st perf Milan, 9 Feb 1929; libr by Arturo Rossato, after Molière's *Les Précieuses Ridicules*. Principal roles: Madelon (sop), Cathos (mezzo), la Grange (ten), Croissy (bar), Gorgibus (bass), Jodelet (bar), Mascarille (ten). Arguably Lattuada's best opera, written in neo-classical style, it was successful at its appearance but is nowadays only very rarely performed.
Plot: Mid-17th-century Paris. Cathos and Madelon, daughter and niece of Gorgibus, consider vapid social affectation to be more important than genuine feelings, and reject the attentions of their noble-minded suitors la Grange and Croissy. The suitors take their revenge by sending their servants Mascarille and Jodelet to woo the ladies in an exaggeratedly artificial style.

Preziosilla
Mezzo role in Verdi's *La Forza del Destino*. She is a gypsy camp-follower.

Přibyl, Vilém (1925–90)
Czech tenor, particularly associated with heavier Czech, Italian and German roles especially Florestan and Dalibor. Possibly the finest Czech tenor of the post-war era, he had a strong and remarkably well-placed voice which he used with musicianship and great intelligence. He had a good stage presence, particularly in roles requiring nobility of bearing. He created roles in Karel Horký's *The Poison of Elsinore* and *Atlantida*.

Price, Leontyne (b 1927)
American soprano, particularly associated with Puccini and Verdi roles, especially the title-role in *Aida*. One of the outstanding lyrico-dramatic sopranos of the post-war era, she had a rich, warm and luscious voice of considerable power and range which she used with unfailing musicianship. Her fine and sympathetic stage presence was enhanced by her great personal beauty. She created Cleopatra in Barber's *Antony and Cleopatra*. Married for a time to the baritone **William Warfield** (*b* 1920).

Price, Dame Margaret (b 1941)
British soprano, particularly associated with Mozart and Verdi roles, especially Donna Anna in *Don Giovanni*, Countess Almaviva in *Le Nozze di Figaro* and Desdemona in *Otello*. One of the outstanding contemporary Mozartians, she possesses a rich and creamy voice, with considerable reserves of power, which she uses with fine musicianship and an assured technique.

Prigioniero, Il (*The Prisoner*)
Opera in prologue and one act by Dallapiccola. 1st perf RAI, 1 Dec 1949; 1st stage perf Florence, 20 May 1950; libr by the composer, after Count Philippe-Auguste Villiers de l'Isle Adam's *La Torture par l'Espérance* and Charles de Coster's *La Légende d'Ulenspiegel et de Lamme Goedzak*. Principal roles: Prisoner (bar), Mother (sop), Jailer/Grand Inquisitor (ten). Dallapiccola's masterpiece and arguably the finest post-war Italian opera, it is an intense and powerful work, notable for its impressive choral writing.
Plot: Late-16th-century Zaragoza. A Prisoner of the Inquisition finds new hope when the Jailer calls him 'friend'. He finds his prison door ajar, and makes his way past monks, who appear not to notice him, into a spring garden. There, however, he is enfolded in the arms of the Jailer, now revealed as the Grand Inquisitor. The Prisoner realizes that he has succumbed to the worst torture of all: that of hope. [R]

Prima, Primo (Italian for 'first')
A title given to the leading singer, as in *prima donna*, *primo uomo*, *primo tenore* etc. A reigning diva is sometimes called *prima donna assoluta*.

Prima Donna
Comic opera in one act by Benjamin. 1st perf London, 23 Feb 1949 (composed 1933); libr by Cedric Cliffe. Principal roles: Olimpia (sop), Fiametta (sop), Florindo (bar), Alcino (ten), Bellina (sop), Count (bass). Set in 18th-century Venice, it is a satire about the rivalry of two jealous singers. Reasonably successful at its appearance, it is nowadays virtually forgotten.

Prima la Musica e Poi le Parole (*First the Music and Then the Words*)
Comic opera in one act by Salieri. 1st perf Vienna, 7 Feb 1786; libr by Giovanni Battista Casti. Principal roles: Maestro (bass), Poet (bar), Eleonora (sop), Tonina (mezzo). Salieri's best-known opera, it was first performed together with Mozart's *Der Schauspieldirektor* as a kind of unofficial competition between the two composers. Discussing the relative importance of words and music in opera, it is still quite often performed.
Plot: Late-18th-century Vienna. The Maestro informs the Poet that he has accepted a commission to write an opera within four days. The Poet reluctantly agrees to co-operate, deploring that he must write words to already-written music. The two disagree over the casting of the principal role: the Maestro wants the prima donna Eleonora, whilst the Poet wants the SOUBRETTE Tonina. After both have given an example of their abilities, it is decided that the two will share the role between them. [R Exc]

Prince Igor (*Knyaz Igor*)
Opera in prologue and four acts by Borodin. 1st perf St Petersburg, 4 Nov 1890 (composed 1869); libr by the composer, after a scenario by Vladimir Stasov based on the 12th-century poem *The Song of Igor's Campaign*. Principal roles: Igor (bar), Konchak (bass), Vladimir (ten), Yaroslavna (sop), Konchakova (mezzo), Galitsky (bass), Ovlur (ten). Borodin's masterpiece, it was left unfinished at his death and was completed and orchestrated by Rimsky-Korsakov and Glazunov. A vast nationalist epic, it incorporates much traditional material, and few operas have depicted so successfully (or so excitingly) the clash of different cultures. It is especially notable for its characterization of Khan Konchak and for containing the famous Polovtsian Dances.
Plot: Russia, 1185. Igor departs to wage battle against the Tartar Polovtski tribe. In his absence, his wife Yaroslavna forces the governor Prince Galitsky, Igor's brother, to curb his feverish supporters. Igor is defeated by the Polovtski, and he and his son Vladimir are captured. Vladimir falls in love with Konchakovna, the daughter of the Polovtsian Khan Konchak, who treats

his captives with every consideration. Konchak offers Igor his freedom if he will cease hostilities against him, but Igor refuses and escapes. Holding Vladimir as a hostage and allowing him to marry Konchakovna so as to discourage escape attempts, Konchak decides to march against the Russians. Igor returns home to a warm welcome and resolves to raise new troops to meet the Polovtsian threat. [R]

Princess
Mezzo role in Puccini's *Suor Angelica*. She is Angelica's aunt.

Princess Ida or **Castle Adamant**
Operetta in three acts by Sullivan. 1st perf London, 5 Jan 1884; libr by W.S. Gilbert, partly after Alfred Lord Tennyson's *The Princess*. Principal roles: Ida (sop), Hilarion (ten), Cyril (ten), Florian (bar), King Hildebrand (b-bar), King Gama (bar), Arac (bass), Lady Blanche (mezzo), Lady Psyche (sop), Melissa (sop). Musically one of the finest of all the Savoy Operas (and the only one to be in three acts and to have dialogue in blank verse), it is a satire on women's emancipation and on the Darwinian theory of evolution.
Plot: King Gama's daughter Ida, married as a baby to King Hildebrand's son Hilarion, believes that man – being descended from apes – is an inferior species to woman. She has shut herself away in a university with her followers, all resolved to have nothing further to do with men. Hilarion, with his friends Cyril and Florian, secretly enter Ida's castle disguised as women undergraduates. Their identity is protected by the two lecturers, the embittered Lady Blanche and Florian's sister Lady Psyche, but they are unmasked when Cyril gets drunk. Hilarion is condemned to death and Hildebrand's forces besiege the castle. The issue is resolved in a combat in which Hilarion, Cyril and Florian defeat Gama's three stupid warrior sons led by Arac. Ida relents and accepts Hilarion when Hildebrand points out to her that without men there will be no posterity to praise her noble ideals. [R]

Prinz von Homberg, Der (*The Prince of Homberg*)
Opera in three acts by Henze. 1st perf Hamburg, 22 May 1960; libr by Ingeborg Backmann, after Heinrich Wilhem von Kleist's *Prinz Friedrich von Homberg*. Principal roles: Friedrich (bar), Natalie (sop), Elector (ten). One of Henze's earliest successes, it is still sometimes performed in Germany.
Plot: Fehrbellin (Germany), 1675. The military exploits of Prince Friedrich have been responsible for Brandenburg's military victory. Nonetheless, the Elector of Brandenburg condemns him to death for military disobedience. Friedrich accepts the sentence, but he is then pardoned and united with his beloved Natalie.

Prise de Troie, La (*The Capture of Troy*)
Part I (Acts I and II) of Berlioz's LES TROYENS.

Pritchard, Sir John (1921–89)
British conductor, particularly associated with Mozart operas and with the Italian repertory. One of the finest British opera conductors of the post-war era, he was musical director of the Glyndebourne Festival (1969–78), the Cologne Opera (1979–88), the Théâtre Royal de la Monnaie, Brussels (1981–6) and the San Francisco Opera Association (1986–9). He conducted the first performances of *Gloriana*, *King Priam* and *The Midsummer Marriage*.

Procida
Bass role in Verdi's *Les Vêpres Siciliennes*. He is the historical John of Procida (1210–*c* 98), a physician and Italian patriot. He is also the subject of Poniatowski's *Giovanni di Procida* (1839).

Prodigal Son, The
Church opera in one act by Britten (Op 81). 1st perf Orford, 10 June 1968; libr by William Plomer, after St Luke's Gospel. Principal roles: Tempter/Abbot (ten), Younger Son (ten), Elder Son (bar), Father (bass). The last of Britten's *Three Church Parables*, it is a taut and economical setting of the famous biblical story and is written for very small forces. [R]

Prodomidès, Jean (b 1927)
French composer. His stage works include the dramatic oratorio *Les Perses* (French TV, 1961; libr Jean Prat, after Aeschylus's *The Persians*) [R], *Les Troyennes* (Spoleto,

1963; libr after Euripides's *The Trojan Women*), *L'Amérique* (1965), *Marat-Sade* (Paris, 1966) and *H.H. Ulysse* (Strasbourg, 2 Mar 1984; libr Serge Ganzl, after Homer's *The Odyssey*) [R].

Producer
see panel below

Prokofiev, Sergei (1891–1953)
Russian composer. He wrote three youthful operas which he later destroyed, including *The Giant* (*Velikan*, 1901), written at the age of nine. His eight mature operas are MADDALENA, which was prepared for performance by Sir Edward Downes, the powerfully expressionist THE GAMBLER, his first major success, the satirical THE LOVE OF THREE ORANGES, his best-known opera in the West, the powerful and disturbing THE FIERY ANGEL, the nationalist SEMEON KOTKO, the comedy THE DUENNA

· *Producer* ·

The operatic producer (sometimes also called director) is essentially a 20th-century phenomenon. In the 17th century, the ballet master was in charge of stage movement, and in the 18th century either the stage manager or (in comedy) the principal BASSO-BUFFO was responsible. In the mid-19th century, composers began to realize the importance of the overall mis-en-scène, and a number – such as Weber, Verdi and Spohr – took an active part in production. The modern concept of the producer derives (as do virtually all developments in operatic performance) from Wagner, with his insistence on *Gesamtkunstwerk* ('unified work of art'). His ideas were quickly adopted by musicians elsewhere (especially by Mahler and Toscanini), and it was soon realized that they were best executed by producers from the theatre. The results of this last development have contributed greatly to the raising of dramatic standards in opera performances, but they have not always been happy. Some producers (especially in the post-war period) have used opera as a means of promoting their personal political views, often wilfully twisting the composer's intentions in the process. The producer is called *régisseur* in France, *Spielleiter* in Germany, *regista* in Italy and general stage director in the United States.

In recent years, a number of conductors have acted as their own producers, such as Herbert von Karajan, Otto Klemperer, Yuri Temirkanov and Peter Maag. Many singers have also acted as producers, the most successful including Tito Gobbi, Sir Geraint Evans, Graziella Sciutti, George London, Ragnar Ulfung, Hans Hotter and Regina Resnik.

Below are listed the 37 operatic producers with entries in this dictionary. Their nationalities are given in brackets afterwards.

Arundell, Dennis (Br)
Capobianco, Tito (Arg)
Chéreau, Patrice (Fr)
Copley, John (Br)
Cox, John (Br)
Dexter, John (Br)
Ebert, Carl (Ger)
Everding, August (Ger)
Felsenstein, Walter (Aus)
Freeman, David (Aus)
Friedrich, Götz (Ger)
Gentele, Göran (Swe)
Graf, Herbert (Aus)
Graham, Colin (Br)
Guthrie, Sir Tyrone (Br)
Habunek, Vlado (Cro)
Hall, Sir Peter (Br)
Hartmann, Rudolf (Ger)
Herz, Joachim (Ger)
Hytner, Nicholas (Br)
Kašlík, Václav (Cz)
Kupfer, Harry (Ger)
Merrill, Nathaniel (US)
Miller, Jonathan (Br)
Moshinsky, Elijah (Aust)
Nemirovich-Danchenko, Vladimir (Russ)
Ponelle, Jean-Pierre (Fr)
Pountney, David (Br)
Rennert, Günther (Ger)
Sellars, Peter (US)
Strehler, Giorgio (It)
Ustinov, Sir Peter (Br)
Vick, Graham (Br)
Visconti, Luchino (It)
Wagner, Wieland (Ger)
Wallmann, Margherita (Aus)
Zeffirelli, Franco (It)

(sometimes known as *Betrothal in a Monastery*), the vast and magnificent epic WAR AND PEACE and THE STORY OF A REAL MAN, which was written as a kind of apologia after his condemnation for 'formalism' by the Stalinists in 1948. His pungent, witty and sometimes grotesque and iconoclastic early style gave way in his later works (partly as a result of political circumstances) to a more lyrical, accessible and patriotic vein.

Prompter
He sits in a small box (called *buca* in Italy) and feeds the singers the words of nearly every line, and in Italy also relays the conductor's beat. The system, one of opera's worst features, is hardly conducive to a musico-dramatic performance – particularly when some prompters are so loud that an aria becomes a duet. Some companies, such as the English National Opera, have mercifully banished the prompt box from most performances. The prompter is called *maestro suggeritore* in Italy and *souffleur* in France and Germany.

Prophète, Le (*The Prophet*)
Opera in five acts by Meyerbeer. 1st perf Paris, 16 April 1849; libr by Eugène Scribe. Principal roles: Jean (ten), Fidès (mezzo), Berthe (sop), Count Oberthal (b-bar), Zacharias (bass), Jonas (ten), Mathisen (bar). Based on an historical incident during the 16th-century Anabaptist uprising when Jan Beuckelzoon (1509–36) had himself crowned in Münster, it is arguably Meyerbeer's finest opera. Enormously popular in the 19th century, it is nowadays only infrequently performed.
Plot: Early-16th-century Dordrecht and Münster. The wedding of Jean de Leyden and Berthe is frustrated by Count Oberthal, who desires Berthe for himself and orders her to his castle. To take revenge against Oberthal, Jean joins the rebellious Anabaptists, whose prophet he becomes, and leads them in the capture of Münster. His arbitrary power goes to his head: he develops a taste for cruelty, degrades his mother Fidès, drives Berthe to commit suicide and proclaims himself the son of god. At last, appreciating the extent of his depravity, he readily joins his revelling followers in a building which he knows will explode. Fidès joins him in the inferno. [R]

Prophetess, The or **The History of Dioclesian**
Opera by Purcell. 1st perf London, 1690; libr by Thomas Betterton, after Sir Francis Beaumont and John Fletcher's play. Really more of a play with music, only the central masque may be said to be truly operatic. [R]

Prosdocimo
Baritone role in Rossini's *Il Turco in Italia*. He is a poet.

Protagonist, Der
Opera in one act by Weill (Op 14). 1st perf Dresden, 27 March 1926; libr by Georg Kaiser, after his own play. Principal roles: Protagonist (ten), Catherine (sop), Major-Domo (ten). Weill's first opera, set in Shakespearean England, it is still occasionally performed.

Prova generale (Italian for 'general trial')
The title of the dress rehearsal in an Italian opera house.

Prozess, Der (*The Trial*)
Opera in two acts by Einem (Op 14). 1st perf Salzburg, 17 Aug 1953; libr by Boris Blacher and Heinz von Kramer, after Franz Kafka's novel. Principal role: Josef K. (ten). One of Einem's best operas, it has met with considerable success in German-speaking countries but is little known elsewhere.
Plot: Central Europe, 1911. The bank clerk Josef K. is unexpectedly told that he has been arrested. After a number of bizarre encounters and a court appearance at which he is denied cross-examination, he comes to realize that he can never find justice. He is informed that his case has gone against him, and he is led off to execution.

Prus, Jaroslav
Baritone role in Janáček's *The Macropolus Case*. Jánek's father, he is a disputant in the Gregor v Prus case.

Publius
Bass role in Mozart's *La Clemenza di Tito*. He is a Roman centurion.

Puccini, Giacomo (1858–1924)
Italian composer. Usually regarded as the master VERISMO composer, few of his operas are in fact truly verismo works in the mould set by Mascagni. More lyrical and eclectic in style than his contemporaries, he was influenced by Verdi and later by Wagner, Debussy and even Lehár and Stravinsky. His first opera LE VILLI was followed by the unsuccessful EDGAR. Its successor MANON LESCAUT was his first mature work and placed him at the forefront of contemporary opera composers. It was followed by his three most enduringly popular works: LA BOHÈME, TOSCA and the initially unsuccessful MADAMA BUTTERFLY. His later operas are LA FANCIULLA DEL WEST, the quasi-operetta LA RONDINE, *Il Trittico* (comprising IL TABARRO, SUOR ANGELICA and GIANNI SCHICCHI, his only comedy) and the unfinished TURANDOT.

George Bernard Shaw was quick off the mark to hail Puccini as Verdi's successor, but this is to push Puccini's merits too far. He was an accomplished musical craftsman, whose technique became ever more impressive, he had a happy gift for comedy and he possessed a sure theatrical sense. However, his music – for all its emotionalism and rich lyricism – is largely innocent of the true dramatic insight possessed by Verdi. His grandfather **Domenico** (1771–1815) was also a composer, who wrote five operas.

Punch and Judy
Opera in one act by Birtwistle. 1st perf Aldeburgh, 8 June 1968; libr by Stephen Pruslin. Principal roles: Punch (bar), Choregus (bar), Judy (mezzo), Lawyer (ten), Doctor (bass), Pretty Polly (sop). Birtwistle's first opera, it is a study of violence.
Plot: Under the direction of the Choregus, the traditional marionette characters enact a violent puppet play. Punch murders his wife Judy and their baby so that he can marry Pretty Polly, and subsequently murders all the other characters as well. [R]

Puppet operas
see MARIONETTE OPERAS

Purcell, Henry (c 1659–95)
British composer. He wrote only one true opera, DIDO AND AENEAS, a masterpiece in miniature which ranks him as the greatest British opera composer before Britten. He wrote many other stage works, mainly masques and incidental music to plays. Of these, THE FAIRY QUEEN, KING ARTHUR, THE PROPHETESS, THE TEMPEST and THE INDIAN QUEEN are quasi-operatic and are sometimes staged as operas. His brother **Daniel** (*c* 1663–1717) was also a composer who wrote many stage works, including *The Judgement of Paris* (London, 11 Apr 1701; libr William Congreve) and the last act of his brother's *The Indian Queen*.

Puritani di Scozia, I (*The Puritans of Scotland*)
Opera in three acts by Bellini. 1st perf Paris, 25 Jan 1835; libr by Carlo Pepoli, after Jacques-Arsène Ancelot and Joseph-Xavier Boniface Saintine's *Têtes Rondes et Cavaliers*, itself based on Sir Walter Scott's *Old Morality*. Principal roles: Elvira (sop), Arturo (ten), Ricardo (bar), Giorgio (bass), Enrichetta (mezzo), Gualtiero (bass). Bellini's last opera and one of his finest works, it was a triumphant success at its appearance and is still regularly performed.
Plot: Mid-17th-century Plymouth. The Puritan governor Gualtiero Walton has promised the hand of his daughter Elvira to Sir Richard Forth. However, Elvira loves the royalist Lord Arthur Talbot, and Gualtiero consents to the match. On the wedding day, Arthur is given a pass to leave the castle with his bride. He discovers that Charles I's widow Henrietta is held captive in the castle, and uses his pass to let her escape, wearing Elvira's bridal dress as a disguise. Sir Richard sees Arthur leaving with another woman, and the knowledge causes Elvira to go out of her mind. Returning later to see Elvira, Arthur is arrested and sentenced to death. However, news is brought of a Puritan victory and a general amnesty for all prisoners. Elvira regains her reason and is united with Arthur. [R]

Pushkin, Alexander
see panel on pages 450–1

· Alexander Pushkin ·

The works of the Russian writer and poet Alexander Sergeyevich Pushkin (1799–1837) have inspired some 110 operas, far more than any other Russian writer. He is also the subject of operas by two minor composers. Below are listed, by work, those operas based on his writings by composers with entries in this dictionary.

Boris Godunov		
Moussorgsky	*Boris Godunov*	1869/73
The Captain's Daughter		
Cui	*The Captain's Daughter*	1911
The Captive of the Caucasus		
Cui	*The Captive of the Caucasus*	1883
The Covetous Knight		
Rachmaninov	*The Covetous Knight*	1906
Napoli	*Il Barone Avaro*	1970
Dubrovsky		
Nápravník	*Dubrovsky*	1895
Napoli	*Dubrovski II*	1973
Eugene Onegin		
Tchaikovsky	*Eugene Onegin*	1879
A Feast in Time of Plague		
Cui	*A Feast in Time of Plague*	1901
The Golden Cockerel		
Rimsky-Korsakov	*The Golden Cockerel*	1909
The Gypsies		
Rachmaninov	*Aleko*	1893
Leoncavallo	*Zingari*	1912
The Little House at Kolomna		
Stravinsky	*Mavra*	1922
Mistress into Maid		
Zajc	*Lizinka*	1878
Mozart and Salieri		
Rimsky-Korsakov	*Mozart and Salieri*	1898
Poltava		
Pedrotti	*Mazeppa*	1861
Tchaikovsky	*Mazeppa*	1884
The Queen of Spades		
Halévy	*La Dame du Pique*	1850
Suppé	*Pique Dame*	1865
Tchaikovsky	*The Queen of Spades*	1890
Rusalka		
Alyabyev	*The Fisherman and the Water-Nymph*	1843
Dargomijsky	*Rusalka*	1856
Ruslan and Ludmila		
Glinka	*Ruslan and Ludmila*	1842
The Snowstorm		
Dzerzhinsky	*Winter Night*	1946

The Stone Guest		
Dargomijsky	*The Stone Guest*	1872 (U)
The Tale of Tsar Saltan		
Rimsky-Korsakov	*The Tale of Tsar Saltan*	1900
The Triumph of Bacchus		
Dargomijsky	*The Triumph of Bacchus*	1848

Pygmalion
Opera-ballet in one act by Rameau. 1st perf Paris, 27 Aug 1784; libr by Ballot de Sauvot, after Antoine Houdart de la Motte's *Le Triomphe des Arts*. Principal roles: Pygmalion (ten), Céphise (sop), Love (sop), Statue (sop). It is still occasionally performed.
Plot: Legendary Cyprus. The sculptor Pygmalion has fallen in love with a female statue which he has created. He rejects the love of Céphise, and Love brings the statue to life. Pygmalion takes her hand and she falls in love with him. Love summons the Graces, who instruct the statue in dancing. [R]

Pylade
Tenor role in Gluck's *Iphigénie en Tauride*. He is Oreste's companion.

Q

Quadri, Argeo (b 1911)
Italian conductor, particularly associated with the Italian and French repertories. Largely resident at the Vienna Volksoper for 1957, he was a reliable and rock-solid Italian maestro of the old school.

Quaglio family
A family of German designers of Italian extraction, descended from the fresco-painter Giulio Quaglio (1610–*c* 69). At least 15 members of the family worked in opera. The most important included:

1 **Giulio Quaglio** (*c* 1700–65), who worked in Vienna and designed the original *Orfeo ed Euridice*.
2 **Lorenzo Quaglio** (1730–1804), who worked mainly in Mannheim and Munich and who designed the original *Idomeneo*.
3 **Simon Quaglio** (1795–1878), who worked in Munich and who was one of the first designers to use built scenery. He designed over 100 productions, including a notable *Die Zauberflöte* in 1818.
4 **Angelo Quaglio** (1829–90), who worked in Munich and who designed in an illusionistic historical style. He assisted Wagner on the first performances of *Tristan und Isolde*, *Die Meistersinger von Nürnberg*, *Das Rheingold* and *Die Walküre*.
5 **Eugen Quaglio** (1857–1942), who worked mainly in Berlin and Prague.

Quand'ero paggio
Baritone ARIETTA for Falstaff in Act II of Verdi's *Falstaff*, in which he recalls his youthful sylph-like figure when he was page to the Duke of Norfolk.

Quand j'étais roi de Béotie
Tenor aria for John Styx in Act III of Offenbach's *Orphée aux Enfers*, in which he compares his greatness when alive with his miserable status in Hades.

Quand l'Helvétie
Tenor/baritone/bass trio for Arnold, Tell and Walter Furst in Act II of Rossini's *Guillaume Tell*, in which Arnold is urged to support the patriots. It is mercilessly parodied by Offenbach in the Patriotic Trio in Act III of *La Belle Hélène*.

Quando le sere al placido
Tenor aria for Rodolfo in Act II of Verdi's *Luisa Miller*, in which he grieves over Luisa's supposed betrayal of their love.

Quanto è bella
Tenor aria for Nemorino in Act I of Donizetti's *L'Elisir d'Amore*, in which he rhapsodizes over Adina's beauty.

Quarter-tone operas
A quarter-tone is half of a semitone, and is a musical interval which was not found in Western music until the 20th century, when its use still remained exceptional. Very few quarter-tone operas have been written, partly because of the obvious practical difficulty for singers to pitch a quarter-tone accurately. The most important quarter-tone opera is Hába's THE MOTHER.

Quartet
In opera, a musical number for four solo singers, with or without chorus. There are particularly fine examples in Verdi's *Rigoletto* and Beethoven's *Fidelio*.

Quatre Saisons, Les (*The Four Seasons*)
The title of the ballet music in Act III of Verdi's *Les Vêpres Siciliennes*.

Quatro Rusteghi, I (*The Four Curmudgeons*; usually given in Britain as *The School for Fathers*)
Comic opera in three acts by Wolf-Ferrari. 1st perf Munich, 19 March 1906; libr (in Venetian dialect) by Giuseppe Pizzolato, after Carlo Goldoni's *I Rusteghi*. Principal roles: Lunado (bass), Margarita (mezzo), Lucieta (sop), Simone (b-bar), Marina (sop), Maurizio (bass), Filipeto (ten), Cancian (bass), Felice (sop), Riccardo

(ten). Wolf-Ferrari's most successful full-length opera, it is still regularly performed. **Plot**: Late-18th-century Venice. Four curmudgeonly husbands – Lunado, Simone, Maurizio and Cancian – vainly attempt to keep their women in order. The women decide to teach their menfolk a lesson by allowing Lunado's daughter Lucieta to see Filipeto, the son of Maurizio, before their prearranged wedding, even though the men have expressly forbidden this. [R]

Queen of Cornwall, The
Opera in two acts by Boughton. 1st perf Glastonbury, 21 Aug 1924; a virtual word-for-word setting of Thomas Hardy's play. Boughton's penultimate opera and one of his finest works, it is a setting of the Tristan legend. Reasonably successful at its appearance, it is nowadays virtually forgotten.

Queen of Golconda, The (*Drottningen av Golconda*)
Comic opera in three acts by Berwald. 1st perf Stockholm, 3 April 1968 (composed 1864); libr by the composer, after Jean Vial and Étienne de Favières's libretto for Berton's *Aline Reine de Golconde*, itself based on Jean Stanislas de Bouffler's novel. Principal roles: Aline (sop), St Phar (bar), Zélie (mezzo), Nadir (ten), Sadomar (bass). Arguably Berwald's finest stage work, only the delightful overture is at all well known.

Queen of Sheba, The
see KÖNIGIN VON SABA, DIE; REINE DE SABA, LA

Queen of Shemakha
Soprano role in Rimsky-Korsakov's *The Golden Cockerel*. She marries King Dodon.

Queen of Spades, The (*Pikovaya Dama*; sometimes incorrectly called *Pique Dame*)
Opera in three acts by Tchaikovsky (Op 68). 1st perf St Petersburg, 19 Dec 1890; libr by the composer and Modest Tchaikovsky, after Alexander Pushkin's story. Principal roles: Herman (ten), Lisa (sop), Count Tomsky (bar), Countess (mezzo), Prince Yeletsky (bar), Pauline (mezzo), Surin (bass), Chekalitsky (ten). One of Tchaikovsky's finest and most powerful operas, it is notable for its strong delineation of the obsessed Herman and for its neo-Mozartian Pastorale.
Plot: Late-18th-century St Petersburg. The poor soldier Herman has fallen in love with a girl whom his friend Count Tomsky tells him is engaged to Prince Yeletsky. She is Lisa, granddaughter of the old Countess who was once known as the Queen of Spades because she possessed the secret of the 'three cards'. Lisa returns Herman's love and he becomes obsessed with learning the secret of winning at gambling so as to win money to marry Lisa. He demands the secret from the Countess, but she dies of fright without telling him. Lisa asks Herman to meet her by the river, where the ghost of the Countess reveals the secret to Herman and tells him to marry Lisa. When they meet, Herman confirms Lisa's fears that he now cares more about gambling than about her by rushing off to a gaming house. In despair, Lisa drowns herself in the river. Herman wins on his first two cards and stakes his all on the third, but loses to Yeletsky, who draws the Queen of Spades. Herman curses the Countess, whose ghost appears to him, and then kills himself. [R]

Queen of the Night
Soprano role in Mozart's *Die Zauberflöte*. She is Pamina's mother.

Queler, Eve (b Rabin) (b 1936)
American conductor, particularly associated with revivals of long-forgotten operas. One of the most talented American woman conductors, she founded the Opera Orchestra of New York in 1968, which gives concert performances of rare works with top international casts.

Quel sangue versato
Soprano CABALETTA for Elizabeth I in Act III of Donizetti's *Roberto Devereux*, in which she laments the execution of Essex. The final scene of the opera and one of Donizetti's finest slow cabalettas, it is unusual in form in that the two verses have different words.

Querelle des Bouffons
see GUERRE DES BOUFFONS

Questa o quella
Tenor aria for the Duke of Mantua in Act I

of Verdi's *Rigoletto*, in which he abjures constancy because all women attract him.

Questo è il bacio di Tosca ('This is the kiss of Tosca')
Tosca's famous cry as she stabs Baron Scarpia in Act II of Puccini's *Tosca*.

Quickly, Mistress
The gossip in Shakespeare's *The Merry Wives of Windsor* and *King Henry IV* appears in a number of operas, including: **1** Mezzo role in Verdi's *Falstaff*. **2** Soprano role in Holst's *At the Boar's Head*. **3** Mezzo role in Vaughan Williams's *Sir John in Love*.

Quiet Flows the Don (*Tikhiy Don*)
Opera in four acts by Dzerzhinsky. 1st perf Leningrad, 22 Oct 1935; libr by Leonid Ivanovich Dzerzhinsky, after Mikhail Sholokhov's novel. Principal roles: Grigory (ten), Natalya (sop), Aksinya (mezzo), Yevgeny (bar), Gen Listnitsky (bass). Much the most successful of Dzerzhinsky's operas, it was hailed by Stalin as a model of 'socialist realism', and was a landmark in the development of 'orthodox Soviet' music. It has met with no success outside Russia, and with the collapse of the communist system it is likely even there to fall into obscurity.
Plot: Russia, 1914–17. Grigory Melekhov's parents are forcing him into a marriage with Natalya. His beloved Aksinya appears at the wedding and the two elope together. Grigory goes to war and Aksinya works as a cook in the household of Gen Listnitsky. She hears (incorrectly) that Grigory has been killed, and is seduced by Listnitsky's son Yevgeny. On the Austrian front, Grigory foretells that the Tsar will be overthrown and the war concluded. Discovering Aksinya's infidelity, he kills Yevgeny before marching off with the revolutionary forces.

Quiet Place, A
Opera in three acts by Bernstein. 1st perf Houston, 17 June 1983; libr by Stephen Wadsworth. Revised version 1st perf Milan, 19 June 1984. Principal roles: Sam Jr (bar), Sam (bar), Dede (sop), François (ten). Bernstein's only full-length opera, it was originally written as a sequel to his TROUBLE IN TAHITI, but in the revised version the earlier opera was incorporated as two flashbacks. An attempt to write an 'all-American opera', it has not been successful. [R]

Qui la voce
Soprano aria (the Mad Scene) for Elvira in Act III of Bellini's *I Puritani*.

Quilico, Louis (b 1929)
Canadian baritone, particularly associated with the Italian and French repertories. He possessed a rich, warm and bright-toned voice with an exciting upper register and had a good stage presence. He created the Count in Milhaud's *La Mère Coupable*. His son **Gino** (*b* 1955) is also a successful baritone, who created Figaro in Corigliano's *The Ghosts of Versailles* and Gautier des Ormes in Landowski's *Montségur*.

Quilter, Roger (1877–1953)
British composer. Best known as a song composer, he also wrote one light opera, the unsuccessful *Julia* (London, 3 Dec 1936; libr J. Lambourne and R. Bennett).

Quinault, Philippe (1635–88)
French playwright and librettist. His long collaboration with Lully laid the foundations of French opera. Beginning with *Cadmus et Hermione*, he later provided the texts for *Alceste*, *Thésée*, *Atys*, *Isis*, *Proserpine*, *Persée*, *Phaëton*, *Amadis*, *Roland* and *Armide et Renaud*. A number of his texts were subsequently set by other composers, including Gluck, Mondonville, Piccinni and Uttini. He appears as a character in Isouard's *Lully et Quinault*.

Quince, Peter
Bass role in Britten's *A Midsummer Night's Dream*. A carpenter, he is the leader of the mechanicals.

Quint, Peter
Tenor role in Britten's *The Turn of the Screw*. He is the dead manservant whose ghost attempts to corrupt Miles.

Quintet
In opera, a musical number for five solo singers, with or without chorus. There is a

famous example in Wagner's *Die Meistersinger von Nürnberg.*

Quivar, Florence (b 1944)
American mezzo, particularly associated with the Italian and French repertories. She possesses a rich and beautiful voice used with fine musicianship. Best known as a concert artist, her operatic appearances to date have been sporadic.

Quixote, Don
The hero of Miguel Cervantes's novel appears in several operas, including: **1** Baritone role in de Falla's *El Retablo de Maese Pedro.* **2** Bass role in Massenet's *Don Quichotte.* **3** Bass role in Mendelssohn's *Die Hochzeit des Camacho.* **4** Tenor role in Paisiello's *Don Chisciotte.*

Quotations
see panel 455–6

· *Quotations* ·

Composers have often quoted other composers' music in their works. This takes three forms. Firstly, there is plagiarism or straight theft; for example, the introduction to the Ulrica scene in Verdi's *Un Ballo in Maschera* is lifted from the beginning of the Tower Scene in Donizetti's *Roberto Devereux*. Secondly, there is quotation for satirical purposes: the sending-up of a famous operatic number. Usually found in operetta, examples include the Patriotic Trio in *La Belle Hélène* (based on *Guillaume Tell*), the conspiracy scene in *La Grande-Duchesse de Gérolstein* (based on *Les Huguenots*), 'A nice dilemma' in *Trial By Jury* (based on *La Sonnambula*) and the courtiers' chorus in *La Périchole* (based on *La Favorite*). Finally, there is direct quotation for a specific purpose. Examples of music deliberately quoted include:

- Gluck's *Orfeo ed Euridice* in Offenbach's *Orphée aux Enfers.*
- Grétry's *Richard Coeur de Lion* in Tchaikovsky's *The Queen of Spades.*
- Martín y Soler's *Una Cosa Rara* in Mozart's *Don Giovanni.*
- Mozart's *Don Giovanni* in Offenbach's *Les Contes d'Hoffman*, Fibich's *Hedy* and Busoni's *Arlecchino.*
- Mozart's *Le Nozze di Figaro* in Mozart's *Don Giovanni* and Corigliano's *The Ghosts of Versailles.*
- Rossini's *Guillaume Tell* in Shostakovich's Symphony No 15.
- Rossini's *Otello* in Donizetti's *Il Campanello* and *Le Convenieze ed Inconvenienze Teatrali.*
- Mozart's *Requiem* in Rimsky-Korsakov's *Mozart and Salieri.*
- Wagner's *Tristan und Isolde* in Hindemith's *Das Nusch-Nuschi*, Britten's *Albert Herring* and Weisgall's *The Tenor.*
- Cherubini's *Faniska* in Lehár's *Paganini.*
- Mozart's *Die Zauberflöte* in Knussen's *Higglety! Pigglety! Pop!*
- Mozart's *Die Entführung aus dem Serail* in Henze's *Der Junge Lord.*
- Auber's *La Muette de Portici* in Offenbach's *Le Pont des Soupirs.*
- Halévy's *La Juive* in Offenbach's *L'Île de Tulipatan.*
- Wagner's *Das Rheingold* in Strauss's *Feuersnot.*
- Schönberg's *Moses und Aron* in Goehr's *The Death of Moses.*
- Sarti's *Fra Due Litiganti* in Mozart's *Don Giovanni.*
- Sullivan's *H.M.S. Pinafore* in Sullivan's *Utopia Limited.*
- Naumann's *Gustaf Wasa* in Ludwig Norman's Festive Overture.
- Donizetti's *Marino Faliero* in Donizetti's *Il Campanello.*
- Rossini's *Il Barbiere di Siviglia* in Corigliano's *The Ghosts of Versailles.*
- Monteverdi's *L'Incoronazione di Poppea* in Strauss's *Die Schweigsame Frau.*

- Wagner's *Die Walküre* in Holloway's *Clarissa.*
- Méhul's *Chant du Départ* in Offenbach's *La Fille du Tambour-Major.*
- Beethoven's Diabelli Variations in Henze's *The English Cat.*
- David's *Le Désert* in the ballet music in Verdi's *Otello.*
- Jommelli's *Demofoonte* in Argento's *Casanova's Homecoming.*
- Bellini's *Norma* in Beeson's *Captain Jinks of the Horse Marines.*
- Humperdinck's *Hänsel und Gretel* in Humperdinck's *Die Königskinder.*
- J. Strauss's *Die Fledermaus* in Stravinsky's ballet *Jeu de Cartes.*
- Sarti's *Giulio Sabino* in Salieri's *Prima la Musica e Poi le Parole.*
- Suk's Asrael Symphony in Ulmann's *Der Kaiser von Atlantis.*
- The 14th-century 'Lamento di Tristano' in Ginastera's *Bomarzo.*
- Sullivan's *The Yeomen of the Guard* in Tippett's 'Divertimento on Sellinger's Round'.
- Leoncavallo's *Pagliacci* in Sorozábal's *Black.*
- Verdi's *La Traviata* in Beeson's *Captain Jinks of the Horse Marines.*
- 'Greensleaves' in Petrov's *Peter I* and Vaughan Williams's *Sir John in Love.*
- Donizetti's *Lucia di Lammermoor* in Arrieta's *Marina.*

R

Rabaud, Henri (1873–1949)
French composer and conductor. He wrote six operas: *La Fille de Roland* (Paris, 16 Mar 1904; libr P. Ferrari, after H. de Bornier), MÂROUF, by far his most successful work, *L'Appel de la Mer* (Paris, 10 Apr 1924; libr composer, after John Millington Synge's *Riders to the Sea*), *Rolande et le Mauvais Garçon* (Paris, 28 May 1934; libr Lucien Népoty), *Martine* (Strasbourg, 26 Apr 1947; libr J.-J. Bernard) and the unfinished *Les Jeux de l'Amour et du Hasard* (Monte Carlo, 19 Nov 1954; libr after Pierre de Chamblain de Marivaux), which was completed by Henri Busser and Max d'Ollone. He was director of the Paris Opéra (1914–18) and of the Paris Conservatory (1922–41).

Rachel
Soprano role in Halévy's *La Juive*. Prince Léopold's lover, she turns out to be Cardinal de Brogni's daughter.

Rachel, quand du Seigneur
Tenor aria for Éléazar in Act IV of Halévy's *La Juive*, in which he agonizes over his dilemma concerning Rachel's fate.

Rachmaninov, Sergei (1873–1943)
Russian composer, pianist and conductor. He wrote four operas, which have never been ranked amongst his greatest works but whose neglect is unjustified. They are the student graduation work ALEKO, THE COVETOUS KNIGHT, FRANCESCA DA RIMINI and the unfinished *Monna Vanna* (Saratoga, 11 Aug 1984, composed 1906; libr Mikhail Slonov, after Maurice Maeterlinck) [R Exc], which was orchestrated by Igor Buketoff. He also played the piano in the first performance of Rimsky-Korsakov's *Mozart and Salieri*.

Racine, Jean Baptiste
see panel on page 458

Radamès
Tenor role in Verdi's *Aida*. He is an Egyptian general loved by Amneris and in love with Aida.

Radamisto
Opera in three acts by Händel. 1st perf London, 27 April 1720; libr possibly by Nicola Francesco Haym, after Domenico Lalli's *L'Amor Tirranico* and Matteo Noris's *Zenobia*. Principal roles: Radamisto (c-ten), Polissena (sop), Zenobia (mezzo), Tigrane (sop), Tiridate (ten), Farasmane (bass), Fraate (sop). Although never one of Händel's most popular operas, it is still performed from time to time.
Plot: Armenia, *c* AD 50. King Tiridate turns from his faithful wife Polissena to Zenobia, the wife of Polissena's brother Radamisto, the son of King Farasmane of Thrace. Tiridate captures Farasmane and lays siege to his city. The situation is further complicated by the love of Tiridate's ally, Tigrane Prince of Pontus, for Polissena. Zenobia is captured but defies Tiridate despite all his threats. Eventually, a rebellion of Tiridate's army, engineered by Tigrane, leads to Tiridate's overthrow. Farasmane is released and Radamisto and Zenobia are reunited. [R]

Radio
see BRITISH BROADCASTING CORPORATION

Raftsman, The (*Flis*)
Opera in one act by Moniuszko. 1st perf Warsaw, 24 Sept 1858; libr by Stanisław Bogusławski. Principal roles: Franek (ten), Zosia (sop), Jakub (bar), Antoni (bass), Szóstak (bass). One of Moniuszko's most successful operas, it is a work of great melodic charm, but is virtually unknown outside Poland.
Plot: 19th-century Poland. The farmer Antoni has promised his daughter Zosia to the Warsaw barber Jakub, but she loves the raftsman Franek. The old soldier Szóstak vainly tries to persuade Jakub to give up Zosia, and she and Franek are also unable to get Antoni to change his mind. In despair, Franek announces that he will

· Jean Baptiste Racine ·

Along with Philippe Quinault and Pierre Corneille, the French poet and playwright Jean Baptiste Racine (1633–99) exercised a considerable influence on opera in that his tragedies, with their theme of the conflict between love and duty and their concept of the benevolent despot, were the models upon which Apostolo Zeno and Pietro Metastasio based many of their OPERA SERIA libretti. Some 90 operas have been based directly on his plays. Below are listed, by play, those operas by composers with entries in this dictionary.

Andromaque		
Caldara	*Andromaca*	1724
Bononcini	*Astianatte*	1727
Feo	*Andromaca*	1730
Sacchini	*Andromaca*	1761
Grétry	*Andromaque*	1780
Martín y Soler	*Andromaca*	1780
Paisiello	*Andromaca*	1797
Rossini	*Ermione*	1814
Athalie		
Händel	*Athalia*	1733
Poissl	*Athalia*	1814
Weisgall	*Athaliah*	1964
Bajazet		
Vivaldi	*Bajazet*	1735
Generali	*Bajazetto*	1813
Hervé	*Les Turcs*	1869
Bérénice		
Caldara	*Tito e Berenice*	1714
Magnard	*Bérénice*	1911
Britannicus		
Porpora	*Agrippina*	1708
Graun	*Britannico*	1751
Iphigénie en Aulide		
Graun	*Iphigenia in Aulide*	1748
Gluck	*Iphigénie en Aulide*	1774
Cherubini	*Ifigenia in Aulide*	1788
Mayr	*Il Sacrifizio d'Ifigenia*	1811
Mithridate		
A. Scarlatti	*Il Mitridate Eupatore*	1707
Graun	*Mitridate*	1750
Mozart	*Mitridate, Rè di Ponto*	1774
Sacchini	*Mitridate*	1781
Zingarelli	*La Morte di Mitridate*	1797
Phèdre		
Rameau	*Hippolyte et Aricie*	1733
Gluck	*Ippolito*	1745
Mayr	*Fedra*	1820
Bussotti	*Fedra*	1988
La Thébaïde		
Graun	*I Fratelli Nemici*	1756

leave the village to seek his long-lost brother. Intrigued, Jakub questions Franek about his brother, and it transpires that the brother is Jakub himself. Delighted, Jakub gives up his claim to Zosia and she and Franek are united. [R]

Ragin, Derek Lee (b 1958)
American counter-tenor, particularly associated with Händel and other baroque roles and, especially, with Gluck's *Orfeo ed Euridice*. The first black counter-tenor of importance, he is a male soprano of remarkable range and agility, and his voice is used with outstanding musicianship and sensitivity.

Ragonde
Mezzo role in Rossini's *Le Comte Ory*. She is Countess Adèle's companion.

Raimbaud
Baritone role in Rossini's *Le Comte Ory*. He is Ory's friend.

Raimondi, Gianni (b 1923)
Italian tenor, particularly associated with Verdi, Donizetti and heavier Rossini roles. He had a pure, warm-timbred voice with a brilliant upper register which he used with style and great elegance of phrasing. He created a role in Pannain's *Madame Bovary*.

Raimondi, Ruggero (b 1941)
Italian bass, particularly associated with Verdi and Rossini roles and with Boris and Don Giovanni (which he played in Joseph Losey's film). Widely regarded as the leading contemporary Italian bass, he possesses a warm and beautiful basso cantante, which is used with fine musicianship and intelligence. The quasi-baritonal timbre of his upper register allows him to sing some baritone roles such as Scarpia. He is an outstanding singing-actor, equally at home in serious or comic roles.

Raimondo
Bass role in Donizetti's *Lucia di Lammermoor*. He is the Ravenswood chaplain.

Raisa, Rosa (b Rose Burchstein) (1893–1963)
Polish soprano. One of the greatest dramatic sopranos of the first half of the 20th century, she possessed an imposing voice of great power with a thrilling upper register, and was an admired singing-actress. She created Asteria in Boito's *Nerone* and the title-roles in *Turandot* and Romano Romani's *Fedra*. Her husband **Giacomo Rimini** (1888–1952) was a successful baritone, who created Pong in *Turandot*.

Rake's Progress, The
Opera in three acts and epilogue by Stravinsky. 1st perf Venice, 11 Sept 1951; libr by W.H. Auden and Chester Kallman, after engravings by William Hogarth. Principal roles: Tom Rakewell (ten), Anne Truelove (sop), Nick Shadow (bar), Baba the Turk (mezzo), Truelove (bass), Mother Goose (mezzo), Sellem (ten). The culmination of Stravinsky's neo-classical period, it ranks as one of the finest of all post-war operas.
Plot: 18th-century England. Tom Rakewell is engaged to Truelove's daughter Anne. The sinister Nick Shadow arrives to tell Tom that he has inherited a fortune from an unknown relative, and lures him to London for a life of vice and dubious business ventures. Shadow becomes his servant and Tom, rejecting the faithful Anne, marries the bearded Baba the Turk at Nick's suggestion. Nick then persuades him to invest all his money in an invention supposed to turn stones into bread. Tom is ruined, and the auctioneer Sellem disposes of his possessions. After a year, Shadow reveals himself as the Devil, and offers Tom a game of cards with Tom's life as the stake. Tom wins, but Shadow drives him insane. Confined to the lunatic asylum of Bedlam, Tom believes himself to be Adonis and thinks that the visiting Anne is Venus. When she leaves he dies of grief. [R]

Rakhmaninoff, Sergey
see RACHMANINOV, SERGEI

Rákoczy March
March in Part I of Berlioz's *La Damnation de Faust*. It is an arrangement of a Hungarian nationalist melody named after Prince Ferencz Rákócki, the leader of the anti-Austrian revolt of 1703–11.

Ralegh, Walter
The British explorer and statesman Sir Walter Ralegh (*c* 1552–1618) appears in a number of operas, including: **1** Bass role in Britten's *Gloriana*. **2** Tenor role in German's *Merrie England*. **3** Bass COMPRIMARIO role in Donizetti's *Roberto Devereux*.

Ralf, Torsten (1901–54)
Swedish tenor, particularly associated with Strauss and Wagner roles. One of the leading dramatic tenors of the inter-war period, he created Apollo in *Daphne* and a role in Sutermeister's *Die Zauberinsel*. His brother **Oscar** (1881–1964) was also a successful heroic tenor, who also translated some 40 operas into Swedish. His autobiography, *The Tenor Goes Into the Ring*, was published in 1953.

Rameau, Jean-Philippe (1683–1764)
French composer. His first real opera was the unperformed *Samson* (1733; libr Voltaire). It was followed, amongst others, by HIPPOLYTE ET ARICIE, possibly his best-known work, the fine opera-ballet LES INDES GALANTES, CASTOR ET POLLUX, DARDANUS, the opera-ballet *Les Fêtes d'Hébé* (Paris, 21 May 1739; libr Antoine Gautier de Montdorge) [R Exc], *Le Temple de la Gloire* (Versailles, 27 Nov 1745; libr Voltaire) [R], *La Princesse de Navarre* (Versailles, 23 Feb 1745; libr Voltaire) [R Exc], the comedy PLATÉE, ZAÏS, ZOROASTRE, *Naïs* (Paris, 22 Apr 1749; libr Louis de de Cahusac) [R], *La Guirlande* (Paris, 21 Sept 1751; libr Jean-François Marmontel) [R], *Acanthe et Céphise* (Paris, 18 Nov 1751; libr Marmontel), the opera-ballets ANACRÉON and PYMALION, LES PALADINS and the unfinished LES BORÉADES.

Building on Lully's groundwork, Rameau was one of the fathers of French opera. Whilst retaining Lully's classical formality, Rameau brought far greater flexibility and power to his work, and laid greater emphasis on the drama, both musically and structurally. He expanded the role of the orchestra whilst simultaneously curbing the excesses of singers, in a way which looks forward to (and indeed influenced) Gluck, who said of one of his operas 'it stinks of music'. The leading representative of the French traditionalists in the GUERRE DES BOUFFONS, Rameau was highly regarded by his contemporaries: Campra said of *Hippolyte et Aricie* that it had 'enough music for ten operas' and went on to predict – correctly – 'this man will drive us all from the stage'. Rameau's stature and historical importance have only recently been fully appreciated. His works suffered a long period of neglect, but in the last 20 years there has been a major revival of interest in his operas and performances are now quite frequent, especially in Britain and France through the advocacy of the English Bach Festival and Les Arts Florissants.

Ramey, Samuel (b 1942)
American bass, particularly associated with the Italian and French repertories, especially the title-roles in Verdi's *Attila*, Boito's *Mefistofele* and, above all, Rossini. Arguably the world's finest contemporary bass, he possesses a rich and magnificent voice of considerable power and remarkable agility which he uses with fine musicianship and an excellent technique. His impressive range enables him to encompass some baritone roles such as Scarpia in Puccini's *Tosca* and Dapertutto in Offenbach's *Les Contes d'Hoffman*. He has a strong (if somewhat generalized) stage presence which is enhanced by his powerful physique.

Ramiro
1 Tenor role in Rossini's *La Cenerentola*. He is the prince in search of a wife. **2** Baritone role in Ravel's *L'Heure Espagnole*. He is a muleteer. **3** Mezzo trouser role in Mozart's *La Finta Giardiniera*. He is Armida's rejected lover.

Ramphis
Bass role in Verdi's *Aida*. He is the High Priest of Egypt.

Rance, Jack
Baritone role in Puccini's *La Fanciulla del West*. He is the sheriff.

Randle, Thomas (b 1958)
American tenor, particularly associated with Mozart roles and with 20th-century operas. He possesses a beautiful, smoothly-produced and dark-toned voice of considerable range, used with musicianship and good taste, and he has

exemplary phrasing and diction. An impressive singing-actor with a handsome stage appearance, he is one of the most talented and versatile young artists to have come to the fore in recent years. He created Dionysus in Buller's *The Bacchae*, Rimbaud in Kevin Volan's *The Man Who Strides the Wind* and Bob in Schat's *Symposion*.

Randová, Eva (b 1936)
Czech mezzo, particularly associated with the Czech and German repertories, especially Kostelnička in Janáček's *Jenůfa* and Ortrud in Wagner's *Lohengrin*. An intense and powerful singing-actress with a rich and intelligently-used voice, she is a dramatic mezzo in the grand tradition. Director of the Brno Opera (1993–).

Rangoni
Baritone role in Moussorgsky's *Boris Godunov*. He is a Jesuit priest.

Rangström, Ture (1884–1947)
Swedish composer. He wrote three operas which met with some success in Sweden but which are unknown elsewhere. They are *The Crown Bride* (*Kronbruden*, Stuttgart, 21 Oct 1919, composed 1915; libr after August Strindberg), *In the Middle Ages* (*Middelalderlig*, Stockholm, 11 May 1921; libr H. Drachman) and the unfinished *Gilgamesj* (Stockholm, 20 Nov 1952, composed 1944; libr E. Linde, after *The Epic of Gilgamesh*), which was completed by John Fernström.

Rankl, Karl (1898–1968)
Austrian conductor and composer, particularly associated with the German repertory. He was musical director of Covent Garden (1946–51), where he helped to build up the new company, and of the Australian Opera (1958–60). He conducted the first performances of Křenek's *Karl V* and Bliss's *The Olympians*. He also composed one opera, the unperformed *Deidre of the Sorrows* (1951; libr after John Millington Synge), which was a joint winner of the Festival of Britain competition.

Raoul
Tenor role in: **1** Meyerbeer's *Les Huguenots*. He is the Huguenot soldier Raoul de Nangis, betrothed to Valentine. **2** Offenbach's *La Vie Parisienne*. He is a rake in love with Métella.

Rape of Lucretia, The
Opera in two acts by Britten (Op 37). 1st perf Glyndebourne, 12 July 1946; libr by Ronald Duncan, after André Obey's *Le Viol de Lucrèce*, itself based on Livy and William Shakespeare's *The Rape of Lucrece*. Principal roles: Lucretia (mezzo), Tarquinius (bar), Male and Female Chorus (ten and sop), Bianca (mezzo), Junius (bar), Collatinus (bass), Lucia (sop). Britten's second opera, it is a taut and powerful chamber work, written for an orchestra of 12, which interprets the classical legend from a Christian standpoint.
Plot: Rome, 510 BC. Collatinus's wife Lucretia is the only wife proved to have been faithful to her absent officer husband, when the men unexpectedly return home. Her fidelity inflames and challenges the proud prince Tarquinius, who rides from Rome and rapes her. Lucretia kills herself in shame. [R]

Rappresentazione di Anima e di Corpo, La (*The Representation of the Soul and the Body*)
Sacred dramatic oratorio in prologue and three acts by de Cavalieri. 1st perf Rome, Feb 1600; libr by Agostino Manni. Principal roles: Soul (mezzo), Body (bar), Intellect (ten), Counsel (bass), Time (bass), Pleasure (c-ten). An allegorical work, which includes solo as well as choral singing, marking one of the earliest uses of the monodic style in sacred music, the characters represent various human attributes as well as the soul and the body. Perhaps the most important proto-opera. [R]

Rataplan
A word used to describe the sound of a drum, and so often used in vocal music with a military flavour. There are operatic examples in Meyerbeer's *Les Huguenots*, Donizetti's *La Fille du Régiment* and Verdi's *La Forza del Destino*. Sullivan and Offenbach send it up in *Cox and Box* and *La Vie Parisienne*.

Rattle, Sir Simon (b 1955)
British conductor, particularly associated with Mozart and Janáček operas and with

Porgy and Bess. Perhaps the most talented and exciting of the younger generation of British conductors, his operatic appearances, mainly at Glyndebourne, have to date been sadly sporadic. He was married for a time to the soprano **Elise Ross** (*b* 1947).

Rautavaara, Einojuhani (b 1928)
Finnish composer. His operas, written in eclectic style, have met with considerable success in Finland. They include *The Mine* (*Kaivos*, Finnish TV, 10 Apr 1963; libr composer), *Apollo ja Marsyas* (Helsinki, 30 Aug 1973; libr composer, after B. V. Wall), *Thomas* (Joensuu, 21 June 1985; libr composer) [R] and *Vincent* (Helsinki, 17 May 1990; libr composer) [R], which is about van Gogh. His father **Eino** (1976–1939) was a baritone and his cousin **Aulikki** (1906–90) was a successful Mozartian soprano.

Ravel, Maurice (1875–1937)
French composer, notable for his witty and brilliantly orchestrated music. He wrote two highly successful one-act operas: L'HEURE ESPAGNOLE and L'ENFANT ET LES SORTILÈGES.

Reardon, John (1930–88)
American baritone, particularly associated with the Italian repertory and with 20th-century operas, especially American. A fine singing-actor with a warm voice and a wide-ranging repertory, he was also a successful film and television artist. He created Trigorin in Pasatieri's *The Seagull*, Orin in Levy's *Mourning Becomes Electra*, the 2nd Guest in Menotti's *The Saint of Bleecker Street*, Yehoyada in Weisgall's *Athaliah* and, for Moore, Miles Dunster in *Wings of the Dove* and Charles in *Carry Nation*.

Rebel, Jean-Féry (1666–1747)
French composer. Best known as an orchestral composer, he also wrote one opera, *Ulisse* (Paris, 23 Jan 1703; libr Henri Guichard). His son **François** (1701–75) was also a composer who wrote several operas.

Rè Cervo, Il
see KÖNIG HIRSCH

Recitative
Musical declamation, written in ordinary notation but in which some freedom of rhythm is allowed and which follows the patterns of ordinary speech rhythms, it is the term applied to the declamatory parts of an opera between the formal numbers. It is called *recitativo* in Italy and *Rezitativ* in Germany. There are two types:

1 *Secco* (Italian for 'dry'). Accompanied by the harpsichord (and sometimes also by a string bass), it is used for the rapid dialogue which carries forward the plot in 18th-century OPERA SERIA and in early-19th-century OPERA BUFFA. It had ceased to be used by the mid-19th century.

2 *Accompagnato* (Italian for 'accompanied'), also known as *Stromentato* (Italian for 'instrumented'). Possibly first employed in 1663 by the composer Gaetano Rovettino, it is a more elaborate accompaniment of the vocal line using the normal orchestra. It was used to accompany more emphatic phrases, such as the declamatory introduction to an aria. The dividing line between accompanied recitative and aria proper became increasingly blurred as the 19th century progressed.

Recondita armonia
Tenor aria for Mario Cavaradossi in Act I of Puccini's *Tosca*, in which he compares Tosca's beauty with that of the model for his painting of the Madonna.

Recorded opera
see OPERA RECORDINGS; VIDEO RECORDINGS
A checklist of all operas which have been commercially recorded will be found in Appendix 1.

Redburn, Mr
Baritone role in Britten's *Billy Budd*. He is the first lieutenant aboard H.M.S. Indomitable.

Rè dell'abisso
Mezzo aria for Ulrica in Act I of Verdi's *Un Ballo in Maschera* in which she invokes the spirits.

Red Line, The (*Punainen Viiva*)
Opera in two acts by Sallinen. 1st perf Helsinki, 30 Nov 1978; libr by the composer, after Ilmari Kianto's novel. Principal roles: Topi (bar), Riika (sop),

Puntarpää (bar), Simana (bass). Sallinen's second opera, it is a powerfully effective work which has been widely performed.
Plot: Kainuu (Finland), 1907. The poor crofter Topi and his wife Riika are troubled by a marauding bear. The revolutionary agitator Puntarpää urges the people to put a red line on their ballot papers in a forthcoming election so as to free themselves from oppression. The people's political aspirations are dashed, however, and Riika and Topi's two children die of malnutrition. The bear returns, and Topi is killed by it. Riika finds him with his throat slit in a red line. [R]

Red Whiskers
Tenor role in Britten's *Billy Budd*. He is an indentured sailor.

Reeves, Sims (b John) (1818–1900)
British tenor, particularly associated with the Italian and French repertories. The leading British tenor of the mid-19th century, he created Lyonnel in Balfe's *The Maid of Honour* and a role in MacFarren's *Robin Hood*. The later part of his career was devoted solely to oratorio. His autobiography, *My Jubilee or Fifty Years of Singing*, was published in 1889.

Refice, Licinio (1883–1954)
Italian composer and cleric. Most of his music was written for the church, but he also completed two operas: the successful AZIONE SACRA, CECILIA and *Margherita da Cortona* (Milan, 1 Jan 1938; libr Emidio Mucci). A third opera, *Il Mago* (libr Mucci, after Pedro Calderón de la Barca), was left unfinished. He died whilst conducting a performance of *Cecilia* in Rio de Janeiro.

Reggente, Il (*The Regent*)
Opera in three acts by Mercadante. 1st perf Turin, 2 Feb 1843; libr by Salvatore Cammarano, after Eugène Scribe's libretto for Auber's *Gustave III ou le Bal Masqué*. Principal roles: Count Murray (ten), Amelia (sop), Duke of Hamilton (bar), Oscar (mezzo), Meg (sop), Lord Howe (ten), Lord Kilkardy (bass). In this version, the action is transposed from Sweden to Scotland, and tells of the assassination of the Regent, James Stuart Murray on 21 Jan 1570. One of Mercadante's best operas, it was very successful in its time but is nowadays hardly ever performed.

Reggio Emilia
see TEATRO MUNICIPALE, REGGIO EMILIA

Regina
Opera in three acts by Blitzstein. 1st perf New Haven (Connecticut), 6 Oct 1949; libr by the composer, after Lillian Hellman's *The Little Foxes*. Principal roles: Regina (mezzo), Horace (bass), Alexandra (sop), Ben (bar), Oscar (bar), Leo (ten), Cal (bass), Birdie (sop). Blitzstein's most successful and most conventionally operatic stage work, it is still occasionally performed.
Plot: Bowden (Alabama), 1900. The cold and calculating Regina Giddens fails to persuade her frail husband Horace to enter into a business venture with her unscrupulous brothers Oscar and Ben. Horace suffers a heart attack and Regina withholds his medicine and calmly watches him die. She then proceeds to blackmail her brothers and ensures that she retains control of Horace's money. [R]

Regina coeli
Chorus (the Easter Hymn) in Mascagni's *Cavalleria Rusticana*.

Régisseur
The term used in France and Belgium for an opera producer.

Register
A part of the compass of the voice, which imparts its own distinctive sensation to the singer. The three registers are chest, middle and head.

Regnava nel silenzio
Soprano aria for Lucia in Act I of Donizetti's *Lucia di Lammermoor*, in which she tells Alisa the legend of the fountain by which they are sitting. In the 19th century, it was often replaced by 'Perchè non ho' from *Rosmonda d'Inghilterra*.

Reich, Günter (1921–89)
German baritone, particularly associated with 20th-century German roles, especially Schönberg and Dr Schön in *Lulu*. An outstanding interpreter of 20th-century music, his powerful and incisive voice was

used with great intelligence, and he had a strong stage presence. He created Stolzius in Zimmermann's *Die Soldaten*, Flavius Silva in Tal's *Masada 967*, Soroker in Blacher's *Zweihunderttausend Taler* and, for Penderecki, Satan in *Paradise Lost* and Löwel Perl in *Die Schwarze Maske*.

Reimann, Aribert (b 1936)
German composer and pianist. One of the most successful contemporary German opera composers, he has written six operas in atonal style. They are *Ein Traumspiel* (Kiel, 20 June 1965; libr Carla Henius, after August Strindberg's *A Dream Play*), *Melusine* (Schwetzingen, 29 Apr 1971; libr Claus H. Henneberg, after Iwan Goll), the powerful Shakespearean LEAR, the chamber opera DIE GESPENSTERSONATE, *Troades* (Munich, 7 July 1985; libr composer and Gerd Albrecht, after Euripides's *The Trojan Women*) [R] and *Das Schloss* (Berlin, 2 Sept 1992; libr composer, after Franz Kafka's *The Castle*).

Rè in Ascolto, Un (*A King Listens*)
Opera in one act by Berio. 1st perf Salzburg, 7 Aug 1984; libr by Italo Calvino. Principal roles: Prospero (bar), Regista (ten), Protagonista (sop). Discussing the relationship of the artist to his work by way of preparations for a production of Shakespeare's *The Tempest*, it has proved to be one of the finest and most successful operas of the 1980s and has been widely performed.

Reinecke, Carl (1824–1910)
German composer. Best known as a composer of piano music, he also wrote six long-forgotten operas in Wagnerian style. They are *Der Vierjährige Posten* (Barmen, 1855; libr after Theodor Körner), *König Manfred* (Weisbaden, 26 July 1867; libr Friedrich Röber, after Lord Byron's *Manfred*), his finest opera, *Ein Abenteuer Handels* (Schwerin, 18 Mar 1874; libr W. te Grove), the unperformed *Glückskind und Pechvogel* (1883), *Auf Hohen Befehl* (Hamburg, 1 Oct 1886; libr composer, after Riehl's *Ovidius at Court*) and *Der Gouverneur von Tours* (Schwerin, 22 Nov 1891; libr E. Bormann). Also a distinguished teacher, he was director of the Leipzig Conservatory from 1897.

Reine de Saba, La (*The Queen of Sheba*)
Opera in four acts by Gounod. 1st perf Paris, 28 Feb 1862; libr by Jules Barbier and Michel Carré, after *Les Nuits de Ramazan* in Gérard de Nerval's *Le Voyage en Orient*. Principal roles: Balkis (sop), Adoniram (ten), Solomon (bass). A richly exotic work, it was very successful in its time but is nowadays only rarely performed.
Plot: Jerusalem, *c* 950 BC. Queen Balkis, engaged to Solomon, arrives and is astounded by Solomon's Temple. She witnesses the strange powers possessed by its architect Adoniram, powers which disturb Solomon. Adoniram invokes his powers to assist in his mightiest work, but he is humbled before Solomon and Balkis because three disgruntled workers have sabotaged his foundry. Balkis realizes that she loves Adoniram, and he returns her love. They plan to flee together, but Adoniram is stabbed by the disaffected workers whilst he awaits her. She arrives in time for him to die in his arms, and she sees a vision of him ascending to the heavens as a demi-god.

Reiner, Fritz (1888–1963)
Hungarian conductor, particularly associated with Wagner and Strauss operas. He was musical director of the Dresden State Opera (1914–21) and from 1922 was resident in the United States, where he conducted the first performances of Menotti's *Amelia al Ballo* and Moore's *The Devil and Daniel Webster*.

Reinmar von Zweter
Bass role in Wagner's *Tannhäuser*. He is a minstrel-knight.

Reiza
Soprano role in Weber's *Oberon*. She is Haroun de Raschid's daughter.

Reizen, Mark (1895–1992)
Ukrainian bass, particularly associated with the Russian repertory. One of the finest basses of the inter-war period, with a voice of great beauty used with outstanding musicianship, he enjoyed an extraordinarily long career, singing Prince Gremin in Tchaikovsky's *Eugene Onegin* at the Bolshoi Opera on his 90th birthday.

Remedios, Alberto (b 1935)
British tenor, particularly associated with Wagnerian roles, especially Siegfried and Walther von Stolzing. A lyric tenor rather than a heldentenor, he also had success in the French and Italian repertories, and was one of the very few post-war Siegfrieds to have truly sung the role rather than shouted it. His voice was warm, Italianate and seemingly tireless. His brother **Ramon** (*b* 1940) is also a tenor.

Remendado
Tenor role in Bizet's *Carmen*. He is a smuggler.

Renard
Burlesque in two parts by Stravinsky. 1st perf Paris, 18 May 1922; libr by the composer and Charles Ferdinand Ramuz, after Alexander Afanasyev's *Russian Folktales*. Described as *histoire burlesque chantée et jouée*, it is played by dancers or acrobats whilst the soloists (two tenors and two basses) are placed in the orchestra pit.
Plot: By preaching to it, the fox persuades the cock down from its perch, but it is rescued by the tomcat and the ram. The fox tries again and very nearly succeeds, the cock being saved this time by suggestions to the fox that his wife is unfaithful. Eventually, the ram and the tomcat strangle the fox. [R]

Renato
Baritone role in Verdi's *Un Ballo in Maschera*. Ankerström in the Swedish setting, he is Amelia's husband.

Rencontre Imprévue, La (*The Unforseen Encounter*)
Comic opera in three acts by Gluck. 1st perf Vienna, 7 Jan 1764; libr by Louis Hurtaut Dancourt, after d'Orneval and Alain René le Sage's *Les Pèlerins de la Mecque*. Principal roles: Rezia (sop), Ali (ten), Vertigo (bass), Dardané (sop), Osmin (ten). Gluck's last comic work, it was long popular but is nowadays only rarely performed. For plot see *L'Incontro Improvviso*. [R]

Rennert, Günther (1911–78)
German producer and administrator. One of the leading post-war German producers, his stagings were notable for their handling of crowd scenes and for his deep insight into character motivation. He was administrator of the Hamburg Opera (1946–56), turning it into one of Germany's finest companies, and the Bavarian State Opera (1967–76). His brother **Wolfgang** (*b* 1922) is a successful conductor who was musical director of the Mannheim Opera (1980–85).

Rè Pastore, Il (*The Shepherd King*)
Opera in two acts by Mozart (K 208). 1st perf Salzburg, 23 April 1775; libr by Pietro Metastasio. Principal roles: Alessandro (ten), Amintas (sop), Elisa (sop), Tamiris (sop), Agenore (ten). A pastoral work of great charm, dealing with a supposed event in the life of Alexander the Great, it is still quite often performed.
Plot: Sidon, 332 BC. Alexander, having conquered Sidon, discovers that the poor shepherd Amintas is in fact the rightful heir to the throne. Alexander reinstates him and wishes him to marry Tamiris, the daughter of the late usurper, unaware that Tamiris is in love with his own counsellor Agenor. Rather than be separated from his beloved, the shepherdess Elisa, Amintas renounces the throne. Alexander gives in, appointing Amintas 'shepherd-king' with Elisa as his consort. [R]

Répétiteur (French for 'rehearser')
The title in France and Britain of that member of an opera house's music staff who coaches the singers in their roles. He is called *Korrepetitor* in Germany and *maestro collaboratore* in Italy.

Répétition générale (French for 'general repetition')
The final dress rehearsal in a French or Belgian opera house.

Rescigno, Nicola (b 1916)
American conductor, particularly associated with the Italian repertory. Reliable rather than inspiring and known as a good 'singers' conductor', he was musical director of the Chicago Lyric Opera (1954–6), of which he was a co-founder, and the Dallas Civic Opera (1957–90).

Rescue opera
A term which describes an opera in which the central feature of the plot is the rescue of one of the principal characters from a dangerous situation. The genre became very popular in France at the time of the Revolution, when the story often involved the rescue of an illegally held political prisoner. It was exemplified by Jean Nicolas Bouilly's libretto for Gaveaux's *Léonore ou l'Amour Conjugal* (said to have been based on a true incident), which provided Beethoven with the story of *Fidelio*. Other influential early examples were Cherubini's *Lodoïska* and *Les Deux Journées*, and a fine later example is Smetana's *Dalibor*.

Resnik, Regina (b 1922)
American soprano and later mezzo, particularly associated with Carmen and with Strauss roles, especially Clytemnestra in *Elektra*. An outstanding singing-actress with a rich and powerful voice, she created the Baroness in Barber's *Vanessa* and Delilah in Bernard Rogers's *The Warrior*. From 1971, she turned successfully to opera production.

Respighi, Ottorino (1879–1936)
Italian composer. He wrote nine operas in a late-romantic style which was also influenced by his interest in 17th-century music. The comedy *Rè Enzo* (Bologna, 12 Mar 1905; libr A. Donini) was followed by the unperformed *Marie-Victoire* (1909; libr E. Guiraud), *Semirâma* (Bologna, 20 Nov 1910; libr Alessandro Cerè) [R], the MARIONETTE OPERA *La Bella Addormentata nel Bosco* (Rome, 13 Apr 1922; libr Gian Bistolfi, after Charles Perrault) and the comedy BELFAGOR, his first significant opera. His later operas are LA CAMPANA SOMMERSA, MARIA EGIZIACA, the fine LA FIAMMA, his most successful opera, and the neo-classical LUCREZIA. A leading advocate of early Italian music, he prepared an edition of Monteverdi's *La Favola d'Orfeo* in 1935. His wife **Elsa** (*b* Olivieri–Sangiacomo) (*b* 1894) was also a composer who wrote two operas.

Reszke, Édouard de (b Edward) (1853–1917)
Polish bass, brother of the tenor JEAN DE RESZKE, particularly associated with Verdi and Wagner roles and with the French repertory, especially Méphistophélès. One of the greatest basses in operatic history, he had a rich voice of enormous proportions, an imposing stage presence (aided by his great height), and was an outstanding singing-actor. He created Don Diègue in *Le Cid*, Gilberto in Gomes's *Maria Tudor*, Ruben in Ponchielli's *Il Figliuol Prodigo*, the King in Catalani's *Elda*, a role in Bemberg's *Elaine* and Fiesco in the revised *Simon Boccanegra*. He retired to Poland where, after the outbreak of World War I, he lived for a time in great hardship, first in a cellar and then in a cave.

Reszke, Jean de (b Jan Mieczysław) (1850–1925)
Polish tenor, particularly associated with the French repertory. Regarded as one of the greatest tenors in history, he sang as a baritone for the first five years of his career. He had a voice of outstanding beauty used with an impeccable technique, and was a fine singing-actor. He created Rodrigue in *Le Cid* and a role in Bemberg's *Elaine*. He was also a distinguished teacher, whose pupils included Bidú Sayão, Dame Maggie Teyte and Steuart Wilson. His brother was the bass ÉDOUARD DE RESZKE; their sister **Joséphine** (*b* Józefina) (1855–91) was a successful soprano, who created Sita in Massenet's *Le Roi de Lahore*.

Retablo de Maese Pedro, El (*Master Peter's Puppet Show*)
MARIONETTE OPERA in one act by de Falla. 1st perf (in concert) Seville, 23 March 1923; 1st stage perf Paris, 25 June 1923; libr by the composer, partly after Miguel de Cervantes Saavedra's *Don Quixote*. Principal roles: Peter (ten), Don Quixote (bar), Narrator (treble or sop). The most famous of all marionette operas, it marks a change in de Falla's style to a more austere and medieval-influenced mode.
Plot: Medieval Spain. Peter's puppets perform the story of the rescue of Melisandra from the Moors in the stable of an inn. The audience includes Don Quixote, who views the marionettes as real humans in need of help and leaves his seat to do battle. He beheads the 'Moors' and thus ruins the performance. [R]

Rè Teodoro in Venezia, Il (*King Theodore in Venice*)
Comic opera in two acts by Paisiello. 1st perf Vienna, 23 Aug 1784; libr by Giovanni Battista Casti. Principal roles: Teodoro (bar), Lisetta (sop), Taddeo (bar), Sandrino (ten), Gafforio (ten), Acmet (bar), Belisa (sop). One of Paisiello's most successful works, described as a '*dramma eroicomico*', it still receives a very occasional performance.
Plot: Mid-18th-century Venice. To avoid both creditors and assassins, Teodoro, the deposed King of Corsica, accompanied by his chamberlain Gafforio, is staying incognito at an inn owned by the wealthy Taddeo. Teodoro loves Taddeo's daughter Lisetta, but is unsuccessful in his suit as she prefers her lover Sandrino. Thus unable to gain Taddeo's financial assistance, Teodoro ends up in the debtors' prison.

Rethberg, Elisabeth (b Lisbeth Sattler) (1894–1976)
German soprano, particularly associated with the German and Italian repertories, especially the title-role in *Aida*. One of the finest lyrico-dramatic sopranos of the inter-war period, with a voice of exceptional beauty, she created the title-role in Strauss's *Die Ägyptische Helena*. Her husband **George Cehanovsky** (1892–1986) was a distinguished COMPRIMARIO baritone, who sang for 40 seasons at the Metropolitan Opera, New York.

Revisor, Der (*The Inspector*)
Comic opera in five acts by Egk. 1st perf Schwetzingen, 9 May 1957; libr by the composer, after Nikolai Gogol's *The Inspector-General*. Principal roles: Clestakov (ten), Militia captain (bass), Anna (mezzo), Maria (sop). A fast-moving satire, it is one of Egk's most successful operas and has been widely performed.
Plot: Mid-19th-century Russia. A visit by a senior government inspector is expected. A mysterious stranger has been staying at the inn (without paying his bills), and the inhabitants are convinced that he is the inspector, working incognito, and that he has noticed the town's none-too-innocent goings-on. The local militia captain feels it safer to invite the stranger – in reality the destitute minor civil servant Clestakov – to stay at his own home. Clestakov takes full advantage of this, fleecing local officials, flirting with the captain's wife Anna and becoming engaged to his daughter Maria. Clestakov decamps and the truth is discovered when a letter from Clestakov to a friend, recounting his adventures, is intercepted. The locals' fury turns to terror as the arrival of the real inspector is announced.

Reykjavík
see ICELAND OPERA

Rezniček, Emil (1860–1945)
Austrian composer and conductor. His most important operas are *Die Jungfrau von Orleans* (Prague, 19 June 1887; libr composer, after Friedrich von Schiller), DONNA DIANA, by far his best-known work, *Till Eulenspiegel* (Karlsruhe, 12 Jan 1902; libr composer, after J. Fischart's *Eulenspiegel Reimensweiss*) and *Holofernes* (Berlin, 27 Oct 1923; libr composer, after Christian Friedrich Hebbel's *Judith*). He was musical director of the Mannheim Opera (1896–9).

Rheinberger, Josef (1839–1901)
Leichtensteinian composer and organist. Although best known as a composer of organ music, he also wrote two long-forgotten operas: *Die Sieben Raben* (Munich, 23 May 1869; libr F. Bonn and F. von Hoffnaass) and *Türmers Töchterlein* (Munich, 23 Apr 1873; libr M. Stahl). He also wrote some children's SINGSPIELS.

Rheingold, Das (*The Rhine Gold*)
Opera in one act by Wagner; the prologue or preliminary evening of DER RING DES NIBELUNGEN. 1st perf Munich, 22 Sept 1869 (composed 1854); libr by the composer, after the *Nibelungenlied*. Principal roles: Wotan (bar), Alberich (bar), Loge (ten), Fricka (mezzo), Fasolt (bass), Fafner (bass), Mime (ten), Erda (cont), Donner (bar), Freia (sop), Froh (ten), Woglinde (sop), Wellgunde (mezzo), Flosshilde (mezzo). For plot see *Der Ring des Nibelungen*. [R]

Ribbing, Count
Bass role in Verdi's *Un Ballo in Maschera*. Samuel in the Boston setting, he is one of the two conspirators.

Riccardo Primo, Rè d'Inghilterra (*Richard I, King of England*)
Opera in three acts by Händel. 1st perf London, 11 Nov 1727; libr by Paolo Antonio Rolli, after Francesco Briani's libretto for Lotti's *Isacio Tiranno*. Principal roles: Riccardo (c-ten), Pulcheria (mezzo), Costanza (sop), Oronte (c-ten), Isacio (bass), Berardo (bass). Never one of Händel's more successful operas, it is only very rarely performed.
Plot: Cyprus, 1191. Costanza, accompanied by Berardo, has arrived to wed Richard, whose fleet is wrecked in a storm but who manages to land safely. She is found by Isaac, the tyrannical ruler of the island, who falls in love with her. Wishing to keep Costanza and to increase his own power, he orders his daughter Pulcheria, betrothed to the Syrian prince Oronte, to masquerade as Costanza. She agrees through filial duty, but Oronte reveals the truth to Richard and allies with him. Their joint forces defeat those of Isaac. Richard is united with Costanza, magnanimously spares Isaac and appoints Oronte, now united with Pulcheria, as the island's new ruler.

· *Revolution* · · *and assassination* ·

A number of opera composers gave active support to revolutionary and nationalist movements. In the 1848 revolutions, Wagner was at the barricades in Dresden and Lortzing's pro-revolutionary *Regina* lost him his job in Leipzig. The ageing Rimsky-Korsakov joined students on the streets during the 1905 uprising in St Petersburg. The most important revolutionary contribution by a composer, however, was that of Verdi. Many of his early operas are overtly nationalistic and were deliberately intended to inflame enthusiasm for Italian unification. Audiences identified themselves with the great choruses 'Va, pensiero' in *Nabucco* and 'Patria oppressa' in *Macbeth*, and Verdi's setting of Ezio's line in *Attila*, 'Avrai tu l'universo, resti l'Italia a me', aroused frenzied cheering from audiences. The slogan 'Viva Verdi' – scrawled on walls all over Italy – was universally known to stand for 'Viva Vittorio Emanuele Rè d'Italia'. *La Battaglia di Legnano*, written when the Italians were attempting to eject the Austrians from Lombardy and telling of the Lombard League's great defeat of the Emperor Frederick Barbarossa, was Verdi's gift to the Risorgimento.

One important revolution actually began in an opera house. During a performance of Auber's *La Muette de Portici* in Brussels on 25 Aug 1830, the patriotic duet 'Amour sacré de la patrie' sparked off anti-Dutch rioting in the theatre which spread on to the streets and triggered the uprising which led to Belgian independence.

Opera houses have also been the scene of a number of political assassinations. For musicians, the most famous victim was Gustavus III of Sweden, who was assassinated in his own opera house on 16 March 1792 – an event which forms the basis of Verdi's *Un Ballo in Maschera*. The Duc de Berry, heir to Louis XVIII, was stabbed to death as he left the Paris Opéra on 13 Feb 1820. Napoleon III escaped the Italian revolutionary Felice Orsini's bomb attack as he arrived at the same theatre on 14 Jan 1858, but the attack killed eight and injured 156. In historical terms, the most significant victim was the Russian Prime Minister Peter Stolypin, assassinated at the Kiev Opera on 1 Sept 1911 as he bowed to Tsar Nicholas II during the interval of Rimsky-Korsakov's *The Tale of Tsar Saltan*. An opera house also witnessed one of the few occasions when an intended victim has retaliated: during a visit to the Vienna State Opera, a gunman took an inaccurate shot at King Zog of Albania; his majesty took refuge behind a potted plant and returned the fire!

Ricci, Federico (1809–77)
Italian composer, brother of the composer LUIGI RICCI. He wrote many operas in Donizettian style, achieving his greatest successes in comedy. His operas, all now forgotten, include *La Prigone di Edimburgo* (Trieste, 13 Mar 1838; libr Gaetano Rossi, after Sir Walter Scott's *The Heart of Midlothian*), *Un Duello Sotto Richelieu* (Milan, 17 Aug 1839; libr F. dall'Ongaro, after Édouard Lockroy's *Un Duel Sous le Cardinal de Richelieu*) and *Une Folie à Rome* (Paris, 30 Jan 1869; libr V. Wilder). In collaboration with his brother he also wrote four further operas, including CRISPINO E LA COMARE, the most successful mid-19th-century Italian comic opera.

Ricci, Luigi (1805–59)
Italian composer, brother of the composer FEDERICO RICCI. His operas, all now long forgotten, include *Chiara di Rosemberg* (Milan, 11 Oct 1831; libr Gaetano Rossi), *Un Avventura di Scaramuccio* (Milan, 8 Mar 1834; libr Felice Romani), *Le Nozze di Figaro* (Milan, 13 Feb 1838; libr Rossi, after Pierre Augustin Caron de Beaumarchais's *La Folle Journée*) and *La Festa di Piedigrotta* (Naples, 23 June 1852; libr M. d'Arienzo). He also wrote four operas in collaboration with his brother, including the highly successful CRISPINO E LA COMARE. His son **Luigino** (1852–1906) was also a composer, whose operas include *Frosina* (1870), *Cola di Rienzi* (1880; libr after Edward Bulwer Lytton) and *Don Chischiotte* (1887; libr after Miguel Cervantes).

Ricciarelli, Katia (b 1946)
Italian soprano, particularly associated with Bellini, Donizetti and Verdi roles, especially Luisa Miller. The leading contemporary Italian lyric soprano, she has a beautiful, agile, well-schooled and intelligently-used voice and an attractive and affecting stage personality. She appeared as Desdemona in Zeffirelli's film of *Otello*.

Richard Coeur de Lion (*Richard Lionheart*)
Opera in three acts by Grétry. 1st perf Paris, 21 Oct 1784; libr by Jean-Marie Sedaine. Principal roles: Richard (ten), Blondel (bar), Laurette (sop), Marguerite (sop), Williams (bass). Grétry's masterpiece, which is still occasionally performed, it is notable for the romance 'Une fièvre brûlante', which appears nine times in various musical transformations, and is one of the finest early uses of LIETMOTIV. Tchaikovsky quotes from the opera in *The Queen of Spades*.
Plot: Linz, 1193. Disguised as a blind troubador, Blondel, the minstrel of King Richard I of England, travels in search of his imprisoned master. With the aid of Marguerite of Flanders, he contacts Richard through the use of his song, and finally rescues him. [R]

Richter, Hans (1843–1916)
Hungarian conductor, particularly associated with Wagnerian operas. Considered to have been the leading interpreter of his age of the German repertory, he conducted the first performances of *Siegfried*, *Götterdämmerung* and Smareglia's *Il Vassallo di Szigeth*. He was musical director of the Vienna State Opera (1893–1900).

Ricordi
An Italian family music publishing company, specializing in opera. Founded in 1808 by Giovanni Ricordi (1785–1853), it is based in Milan and handles the operas of Bellini, Boito, Catalani, Donizetti, Menotti, Montemezzi, Pizzetti, Poulenc, Puccini, Respighi, Rossini, Verdi and Zandonai.

Ridderbusch, Karl (b 1932)
German bass, particularly associated with the German repertory, especially Wagner. One of the leading Wagnerian basses of the 1970s, he had a dark, powerful and incisive voice, intelligently used, and had a strong stage presence.

Ride of the Valkyries
The name usually given to the opening of Act III of Wagner's *Die Walküre*.

Riders to the Sea
Opera in one act by Vaughan Williams. 1st perf London, 30 Nov 1937; a virtual word-for-word setting of John Millington Synge's play. Principal roles: Maurya (mezzo), Bartley (bar), Cathleen (sop), Nora (sop). Vaughan Williams's operatic

masterpiece, and one of the finest of all British operas, it is a taut, powerful and intense work that can have an overwhelming impact in the theatre. Its infrequency of performance is utterly inexplicable.
Plot: West coast of Ireland, early 20th century. Maurya has already lost four sons and her husband to the sea. Her daughters Nora and Cathleen identify some clothing that has been washed up on the shore as belonging to a fifth son. When her last son Bartley is also claimed by the sea as he is taking horses to a fair, Maurya's anguish at last finds peace in resignation. [R]

Riegel, Kenneth (b 1938)
American tenor, particularly associated with German character roles, especially the Dwarf in Zemlinsky's *Der Geburstag der Infantin*. An outstanding singing-actor, his voice – although far from beautiful – is used with intelligence and musicianship. He created Alwa in the three-act version of *Lulu* and the Leper in Messiaen's *Saint François d'Assise*.

Rienzi Full title: **Cola Rienzi, der letzte der Tribunen** (*Cola Rienzi, the Last of the Tribunes*)
Opera in five acts by Wagner. 1st perf Dresden, 20 Oct 1842; libr by the composer, after Mary Russell Mitford's play and Edward Bulwer Lytton's novel. Principal roles: Rienzi (ten), Adriano (mezzo), Irene (sop), Paolo Orsini (bar), Stefano Colonna (bass), Cardinal Raimondo (bass). Wagner's third opera and his first major success, it is one of the longest operas ever written. Dealing with the historical Cola di Rienzo (1313–54), it was composed in the grandest and most spectacular style in an attempt to out-Meyerbeer Meyerbeer. It is still performed from time to time, usually in a cut version, and the rousing overture continues to be popular in the concert hall.
Plot: Mid-14th-century Rome. The patrician Paolo Orsini, endeavouring to abduct Irene, sister of the papal notary Rienzi, is disturbed in the act by Stefano Colonna, another patrician from a rival faction. A fight breaks out, attracting a crowd, which includes Adriano, Colonna's son who is in love with Irene, and the infuriated Rienzi himself. Spurred on by Cardinal Raimondo, Rienzi urges the crowd to stand up to the excesses of the patricians and, because of his feelings for Irene, Adriano supports him. The defeated nobles swear loyalty to Rienzi, but plot to murder him and are condemned to death. Adriano pleads their cause successfully, but when they later break their oath of allegiance the populace is aroused and kills them. Feelings turn, however, and Rienzi becomes the object of the people's hostility and the Cardinal's disfavour, and he is excommunicated. Adriano, warning Irene that her brother is in danger, begs her to flee with him, but she refuses and seeks Rienzi, who is praying in the capitol, and who also advises her to find safety with Adriano. The outraged mob appears and, ignoring Rienzi's appeals, stone him and set fire to the capitol. As Irene and Rienzi are about to perish, Adriano arrives and rushes headlong to join them in the flames. [R]

Rigoletto
Opera in three acts by Verdi. 1st perf Venice, 11 March 1851; libr by Francesco Maria Piave, after Victor Hugo's *Le Roi s'Amuse*. Principal roles: Rigoletto (bar), Gilda (sop), Duke of Mantua (ten), Sparafucile (bass), Maddalena (mezzo), Count Monterone (b-bar). Verdi's first 'middle-period' opera, it marks a turning-point in the history of Italian opera in that Verdi, for the first time, broke right through the restricting operatic conventions of the day. The finest Italian music-drama since those of Monteverdi, its title-role ('burnt into music by Verdi' as Vaughan Williams put it) is often regarded as the most musico-dramatically demanding ever written for a baritone. An immediate success, it has remained ever since one of the most enduringly popular of all operas.
Plot: 16th-century Mantua. The hunchbacked court jester Rigoletto laughs publicly at the grief of the aged Count Monterone, whose daughter has been seduced by the libertine Duke, and Monterone lays a father's curse on him. The courtiers, who hate Rigoletto, discover that he has a young girl hidden away. Unaware that she is his adored daughter Gilda, whom he has raised in convent-like seclusion, they assume her to be a mistress and abduct her for the Duke's

enjoyment, even tricking Rigoletto into helping them. Meanwhile, the Duke is already aware of Gilda: he visits her disguised as a poor student, and she falls in love with him. The courtiers show no pity towards Rigoletto, even when they discover who Gilda really is, and he vows vengeance on the Duke for having dishonoured her. He hires the assassin Sparafucile to kill the Duke, who is lured to a lonely inn by Sparafucile's sister Maddalena. Despite her dishonour, Gilda still loves the Duke, and when she realizes what is to happen she manoeuvres herself into taking his place and is fatally stabbed. Rigoletto gloats over the sack delivered to him, but at the height of his exultation he hears the Duke's voice in the distance. Ripping open the sack, he discovers the dying Gilda. As she expires in his arms, Rigoletto recalls Monterone's curse. [R]

Rihm, Wolfgang (b 1952)
German composer. One of the most successful contemporary avant-garde composers in Germany, his operas include the widely performed JAKOB LENZ, *Die Hamletmaschine* (Mannheim, 25 Mar 1987; libr composer, after Heinrich Müller) [R], *Die Eroberung von Mexiko* (Hamburg, 9 Feb 1992; libr composer, after Antonin Artaud) and *Oedipus* (Berlin, 22 Jan 1995).

Rimsky-Korsakov, Nikolai (1844–1908)
Russian composer (and also a senior naval officer). A member of the MIGHTY HANDFUL, his 15 operas are notable for their use of colourful Russian folk tales, for their brilliant orchestration and for their rich and often exotic harmonies. His first opera THE MAID OF PSKOV (later revised as *Ivan the Terrible*) was followed by MAY NIGHT, THE SNOW MAIDEN, the opera-ballet MLADA, CHRISTMAS EVE, the epic SADKO, the duodrama MOZART AND SALIERI, *Boyarinya Vera Sheloga* (Moscow, 27 Dec 1898) [R], derived from the prologue of the unperformed second version of *The Maid of Pskov*, THE TSAR'S BRIDE, THE TALE OF TSAR SALTAN, *Serviliya* (St Petersburg, 14 Oct 1902; libr composer, after Lev Alexandrovich Mey), KASHCHEY THE IMMORTAL, *Pan Voyevoda* (St Petersburg, 16 Oct 1904; libr Ilya Fyodorovich Tumenev) [R], THE INVISIBLE CITY OF KITEZH and THE GOLDEN COCKEREL, his best-known opera in the West.

An ardent advocate of the music of his nationalist contemporaries, he completed Dargomijsky's *The Stone Guest*, Moussorgsky's *Khovanschina* and Borodin's *Prince Igor*, as well as preparing a version of *Boris Godunov* which was in almost universal use for some 70 years. He was also a noted teacher, whose pupils included Arensky, Glazunov, Ippolitov-Ivanov, Lysenko, Prokofiev, Respighi, Stravinsky and Tcherepnin. Married to the pianist **Nadezhda Purgold**, his autobiography, *My Musical Life*, was published in 1909. His son **Andrei Nikolayevich** (1878–1940) was a noted critic and musicologist; his wife **Julia Lazarevna Weissberg** (1878–1942) was a composer.

Rinaldo
Opera in three acts by Händel. 1st perf London, 24 Feb 1711; libr by Giacomo Rossi, after Torquato Tasso's *Gerusalemme Liberata*. Principal roles: Rinaldo (c-ten), Goffredo (ten), Almirena (sop), Armida (sop), Argante (bass). Händel's first opera written for London, it was an immediate success and is still quite often performed.
Plot: Late-11th-century Palestine. The crusader Rinaldo, who is in love with Almirena, is fighting against the Saracens under Argante. Argante's mistress Armida uses her magical powers against Rinaldo, but ends up by falling in love with him. Eventually, Argante and Armida are defeated. [R]

Rinaldo da Capua (c 1710–c 80)
Italian composer. Reputed to have been the illegitimate son of a nobleman, very little is known about him. He wrote many stage works, beginning with OPERA SERIAS and later turning with great success to comedy. He is nowadays remembered solely for the charming intermezzo LA ZINGARA. Only a fraction of his music survives because his son sold off most of his collected works as waste paper.

Ring des Nibelungen, Der (*The Ring of the Nibelung*)
Operatic tetralogy by Wagner (described as 'stage festival play for three days and a preliminary evening'). 1st complete perf Bayreuth, 13, 14, 16 and 17 Aug 1876 (composed 1854–74); libr by the

composer, after the *Nibelungenlied*. An allegory of humanity and its search for power, it is the largest and most complex work in the history of opera, and is the music-drama which accords most closely with Wagner's artistic theories as propounded in his writings. Originally conceived as a single opera, *Siegfrieds Tod (The Death of Siegfried)*, Wagner was irresistibly drawn towards the earlier mythological aspects of the legend, and the figure of the suffering god Wotan came to dominate the final conception. The work's composition spanned over 20 years, as Wagner laid the project aside for a long period after completing the second act of *Siegfried*. The tetralogy comprises:

1 *Das Rheingold (The Rhine Gold)*. Opera in one act. 1st perf Munich, 22 Sept 1869 (composed 1854). Principal roles: Wotan (bar), Alberich (bar), Loge (ten), Fricka (mezzo), Fasolt (bass), Fafner (bass), Mime (ten), Erda (cont), Donner (bar), Freia (sop), Froh (ten), Woglinde (sop), Wellgunde (mezzo), Flosshilde (mezzo). The opera (about 2¾ hours) is played without a break.

Plot: The Rhinemaidens Woglinde, Wellgunde and Flosshilde guard a lump of magic gold. Anyone who renounces love and fashions a ring from it will become the master of the world. This they explain to Alberich, the leader of the Nibelung dwarfs, as they reject his advances. Alberich curses love and steals the gold. On Valhalla, the chief god Wotan has had his fortress built by the giants Fasolt and Fafner, the price for which has been agreed as Freia, the goddess whose golden apples keep the gods young and vigorous. Hearing of the vast wealth acquired by Alberich through the power of the Ring which he has forged from the stolen gold, the giants agree to accept gold as payment in place of Freia. With the aid of Loge, the god of fire, Wotan takes from Alberich by force both the Ring and the Tarnhelm, a magic helmet made by Alberich's brother Mime which can transform its wearer into any shape. Wotan ignores Alberich's curse of death, placed on all who possess the Ring. Freia must be hidden by gold before the giants will release her, and only the Ring will fill the final chink. After the earth-mother Erda has urged him to shun the Ring, Wotan reluctantly yields it to the giants. Fafner kills Fasolt and takes both Ring and Tarnhelm. Accompanied by his consort Fricka, Wotan enters Valhalla. [R]

2 *Die Walküre (The Valkyrie)*. Opera in three acts. 1st perf Munich, 26 June 1870 (composed 1856). Principal roles: Wotan (bar), Brünnhilde (sop), Siegmund (ten), Siegliende (sop), Fricka (mezzo), Hunding (bass), eight Valkyries (sop and mezzo).

Plot: In search of wisdom, Wotan has visited Erda, who has borne him nine daughters, the warrior-maidens the Valkyries. Knowing that his treaties forbid him to take action himself to recover the Ring, Wotan is attempting to bring forward a free agent who can do what he is powerless to accomplish. With a mortal woman he has begotten two children, Siegmund and Sieglinde. The two were seperated at birth and Sieglinde is unhappily married to Hunding. Exhausted after fighting, Siegmund arrives at Hunding's home, and he and Sieglinde are immediately attracted to one another. Drugging Hunding, they realize their kinship, declare their love and elope together. As the guardian of wedlock, Fricka is outraged at the love of a brother and sister, and Wotan is forced to agree that Siegmund must die. He explains his dilemma to Brünnhilde, the leader of the Valkyries, telling her that she must shield Hunding in the coming fight. Knowing that this goes against Wotan's innermost wishes, Brünnhilde rebels against him and shields Siegmund. However, Wotan intervenes and both contestants are killed. Brünnhilde realizes that Sieglinde is pregnant and is bearing the future hero who will redeem the gods. She aids Sieglinde's escape and gives her the shards of Siegmund's sword which had been made by Wotan. The furious Wotan deprives Brünnhilde of her godhead and puts her into a deep sleep on a rock surrounded by fire. He decrees that the man who braves both the flames and the power of his spear can claim her as bride. [R]

3 *Siegfried*. Opera in three acts. 1st perf Bayreuth, 16 Aug 1876 (composed 1869). Principal roles: Siegfried (ten), Wanderer/Wotan (bar), Brünnhilde (sop), Mime (ten), Alberich (bar), Fafner (bass), Erda (cont), Woodbird (sop).

Plot: Sieglinde has died during the birth of her son Siegfried, who has been raised by Alberich's brother Mime, who plans to use the boy to gain the Ring for himself. He knows that only the shards of Siegmund's sword will suffice to kill Fafner, but he is unable to reforge them. Wotan (disguised as the Wanderer) tells him that they will be forged only by one who has never learnt fear. The fearless Siegfried duly reforges the sword, naming it Nothung ('Needful'). Wishing to learn fear, he allows Mime to lead him to the lair of Fafner, transformed by the Tarnhelm into a mighty dragon. Siegfried kills Fafner, and the dragon's blood which he tastes allows him to understand the song of the Woodbird, which warns him of Mime's plans, tells him of Brünnhilde's rock and advises him to take the Ring and the Tarnhelm. Siegfried kills the treacherous Mime. In conversation with Erda, Wotan resolves that the younger generation must inherit his lordship, but the arrogant behaviour of Siegfried on his arrival forces him to bar the boy's way with his spear. Siegfried shatters the spear with Nothung, and Wotan allows him to pass through the flames unhindered. He discovers Brünnhilde, awakens her with a kiss and the two fall in love. [R]

4 *Götterdämmerung* (*Twilight of the Gods*). Opera in three acts. 1st perf Bayreuth, 17 Aug 1876 (composed 1874). Principal roles: Brünnhilde (sop), Siegfried (ten), Hagen (bass), Günther (bar), Gutrune (sop), Waltraute (mezzo), Alberich (bar), Norns (sop, mezzo and cont), Woglinde (sop), Wellgunde (mezzo), Flosshilde (mezzo).

Plot: Pledging his love to Brünnhilde by giving her the Ring, Siegfried travels down the Rhine and arrives at the hall of the Gibichungs, led by Günther and his half-brother Hagen (who is Alberich's son). Siegfried is given a drugged drink which makes him forget Brünnhilde and fall in love with Günther's sister Gutrune. In the meantime, Brünnhilde is visited by her sister Valkyrie Waltraute, who tells her of Wotan's anguish and fear and of the necessity for the Ring to be returned to the Rhine. Brünnhilde rejects Waltraute's pleas. Disguised as Günther by the power of the Tarnhelm, Siegfried drags Brünnhilde from her rock and delivers her as an unwilling wife for Günther, taking the Ring from her hand. Seeing the Ring on the drugged Siegfried's finger, Brünnhilde believes him unfaithful and plots with Hagen against him. Hagen stabs Siegfried in the back and in a dispute over the Ring kills Günther. When Hagen goes to take the Ring, the dead Siegfried's hand rises against him. Brünnhilde orders a vast funeral pyre to be built, which she lights and mounts. The flames destroy the hall and eventually also Valhalla and the entire old order. The Rhine overflows its banks, and the Rhinemaidens take back their gold. [R]

Rinuccini, Ottavio (1552–1621)
Italian poet and librettist. A member of the FLORENTINE CAMERATA, he was the earliest opera librettist. His *Dafne* was set by Peri, Caccini, Gagliano and (in translation) by Schütz, and his *Euridice* by Peri and Caccini. He also wrote the texts for Monteverdi's *Arianna* and *Il Ballo delle Ingrate*.

Rinuccio
Tenor role in Puccini's *Gianni Schicchi*. Zita's nephew, he loves Lauretta.

Rio de Janeiro
see TEATRO MUNICIPAL, RIO DE JANEIRO

Riotte, Philipp Jakob (1776–1856)
German composer. He wrote a number of operas and SINGSPIELS, all of them now long forgotten, of which the most successful included *Pietro und Elmira* (Magdeburg, 1806), *Nurredin, Prinz von Persien* (Vienna, 1 Feb 1825; libr F. Xavier Gewey) and the Weber parody *Staberl als Freischütz* (1826).

Risurrezione (*Resurrection*)
Opera in four acts by Alfano. 1st perf Turin, 30 Nov 1904; libr by Cesare Hanau, after Lev Nikolayevich Tolstoy's novel. Principal roles: Katusha (sop), Dimitri (ten), Simonson (bar), Matrena Pavlovna (mezzo). Written in VERISMO style, it is one of Alfano's best operas. Successful in its time, it is nowadays almost never performed.

Plot: Late-19th-century Russia. Prince Dimitri Nekludov seduces and then abandons his childhood friend Katusha

Mikailovna. She attempts but fails to meet him at a railway station. She is exiled to Siberia on a false charge, and when Dimitri comes to her there she proudly rejects him. He visits her a second time, now offering marriage, but although she still loves him, Katusha decides to marry her fellow prisoner Simonson.

Rita or **Le Mari Battu** (*The Beaten Husband*)
Comic opera in one act by Donizetti. 1st perf Paris, 7 May 1860 (composed 1841); libr by Gustave Vaëz. Principal roles: Rita (sop), Gasparo (bar), Beppe (ten). A delightful little piece, it is still quite often performed.
Plot: Early-19th-century Switzerland. Rita, the proprietress of an inn, henpecks her husband Gasparo. Gasparo meets Rita's former husband Beppe (who had been believed dead), and the two gamble for the privilege of losing her. Beppe loses, but Rita promises to mend her ways. [R]

Ritorna vincitor
Soprano aria for Aida in Act I of Verdi's *Aida*, in which she reflects that a victory by her beloved Radamès will mean a defeat for her fatherland.

Ritornello (Italian for 'little return')
An orchestral section added to the end of an aria in a 17th- or early-18th-century opera to summarize and encapsulate the emotional content of the piece.

Ritorno d'Ulisse in Patria, Il (*The Return of Ulysses to his Country*)
Opera in prologue and five acts by Monteverdi. 1st perf Venice, Feb 1641; libr by Giacomo Badoaro, after Homer's *The Odyssey*. Principal roles: Ulisse (ten), Penelope (mezzo), Minerva (sop), Ericlea (mezzo), Jove (ten), Telemaco (ten), Eumete (ten), Iro (ten), Eurimaco (ten), Anfimono (c-ten), Antinoo (bass), Melanto (mezzo), Neptune (bass). Unperformed for nearly 300 years, it has won a permanent place in the repertory in recent times, often being given in the edition prepared by Raymond Leppard.
Plot: Legendary Ithaca. Ulysses's faithful wife Penelope, surrounded by suitors, laments her husband's continued absence at the Trojan War. Ulysses is urged by Minerva to return to his home, which he does disguised as a beggar. Penelope announces that she will marry the suitor who is able to draw Ulysses's bow. None of them are able to do so, but the 'beggar' succeeds with ease. With the aid of his son Telemachus and the faithful swineherd Eumaeus, Ulysses kills the suitors and is reunited with Penelope. [R]

Ritual Dances
Choral dances in Act II of Tippett's *The Midsummer Marriage*. The four dances are 'The Earth in Autumn', 'The Waters in Winter', 'The Air in Spring' and 'Fire in Summer' and are often given in the concert hall.

Rizza, Gilda dalla (1892–1975)
Italian soprano, particularly associated with Italian VERISMO roles and with Verdi. She possessed an agile and intelligently-used voice and was an outstanding singing-actress. She created Magda in Puccini's *La Rondine*, Giulietta in Zandonai's *Giulietta e Romeo*, Mariella in Mascagni's *Il Piccolo Marat*, Consuela in Vittadini's *Anima Allegra* and a role in Marinuzzi's *Palla de' Mozzi*.

Rizzi, Carlo (b 1960)
Italian conductor, particularly associated with the Italian repertory, especially Rossini and Verdi. One of the most talented of the younger generation of Italian conductors, his performances are notable for their careful preparation and for the fizz of his Rossinian finales. Musical director of the Welsh National Opera (1992–).

Robert le Diable (*Robert the Devil*)
Opera in five acts by Meyerbeer. 1st perf Paris, 21 Nov 1831; libr by Eugène Scribe and Germain Delavigne. Principal roles: Robert (ten), Bertram (bass), Alice (sop), Isabella (sop). The work which established Meyerbeer's reputation in France, its premiere was one of the most sensationally successful in operatic history and it set the pattern for the style of French grand opera. It remained very popular throughout the 19th century, but is nowadays only rarely performed.
Plot: 13th-century Palermo. Robert Duke of Normandy is the son of a mortal woman and the Devil, who is masquerading as Bertram. In exchange for

his soul, Bertram offers Robert the love of Princess Isabella, but Robert is dissuaded by his foster-sister Alice. Renouncing the Devil, Robert is redeemed and marries Isabella, whilst Bertram returns to Hell.

Roberto Devereux or **Il Conte d'Essex**
(*The Count of Essex*)
Opera in three acts by Donizetti. 1st perf Naples, 29 Oct 1837; libr by Salvatore Commarano, after François Ancelot's *Élisabeth d'Angleterre*. Principal roles: Elisabetta (sop), Roberto (ten), Nottingham (bar), Sara (mezzo). An embroidered version of the story of the love of Elizabeth I and the Earl of Essex, it is an uneven work, but in its best passages it achieves an almost Verdian sweep and power. The overture contains an anachronism, in that it employs 'God Save the Queen', which was not written until long after Elizabeth's time. After a century's neglect, the opera has been regularly performed in recent years, and provides a magnificent vehicle for a singing-actress.
Plot: England, 1598. Elizabeth loves the Earl of Essex, who is secretly in love with Sarah, the wife of his staunch friend the Duke of Nottingham. Elizabeth has given Robert a ring, promising her help at any time it is presented to her. Robert gives the ring to Sarah, who gives him a scarf embroidered with her initials. Despite Nottingham's pleas, the Council sentences Robert to death for treason, and when he is searched the scarf is found. Nottingham realises that his wife has been unfaithful with his best friend, and a furious Elizabeth signs Robert's death warrant. Robert writes to Sarah asking her to deliver the ring to Elizabeth, but Nottingham intercepts the letter and deliberately holds up the ring's delivery until after Robert has been executed. The heartbroken Elizabeth has Nottingham arrested and makes ready to abdicate. [R]

Robin, Mado (1918–60)
French soprano, particularly associated with French and Italian COLORATURA roles. She possessed a small and sometimes rather tremulous voice of great agility and extraordinary range, and is said to have sung the highest note ever emitted by a singer: C above high C.

Robinson, Count
Baritone role in Cimarosa's *Il Matrimonio Segreto*. He is an English 'Milord'.

Robinson, Forbes (1926–87)
British bass, particularly associated with Mozart, Verdi, Händel and Britten roles. He possessed a superbly rich and powerful voice, and was an outstanding singing-actor, whose interpretations ranged from a terrifyingly malevolent Claggart to an outrageously funny Dulcamara. He created the title-role in *King Priam*, Theseus in *A Midsummer Night's Dream*, Horaste in *Troilus and Cressida* and Black Jack in Hoddinott's *The Beach at Falesá*.

Robinson Crusoé
Operetta in three acts by Offenbach. 1st perf Paris, 23 Nov 1867; libr by Eugène Cormon and Héctor Crémieux, after Daniel Defoe's novel. Principal roles: Crusoe (ten), Edwige (sop), Man Friday (mezzo), Suzanne (sop), Toby (ten), Jim Cocks (bar), Sir William Crusoe (bass), Deborah (mezzo). It contains some of Offenbach's most charming and entertaining music, but has been hampered by its weak libretto. Modern British performances have used an entirely new libretto written for Opera Rara by Don White. [R]

Rocca, Lodovico (1895–1986)
Italian composer. His operas, written in late VERISMO style, met with some success in Italy but are virtually unknown elsewhere. They are *La Morte di Frine* (Milan, 24 Apr 1937, composed 1920; libr C. Meano), *In Terra di Leggenda* (Bergamo, 1 Oct 1936, composed 1923; libr Meano), IL DIBUK, his most successful opera, *Monte Ivnor* (Rome, 23 Dec 1939; libr Meano, after Franz Werfel's *Die Vierzig Tage de Musa Dagh*) and *L'Uragano* (Milan, 7 Feb 1952; libr E. Possenti, after Alexander Nikolayevich Ostrovsky's *The Storm*). He was director of the Turin Conservatory (1950–66).

Rocco
Bass role in Beethoven's *Fidelio* and Paer's *Leonora*. Marzelline's father, he is the jailer.

Rodelinda, Regina de' Longobardi
(*Rodelinda, Queen of the Lombards*)
Opera in three acts by Händel. 1st perf

London, 13 Feb 1725; libr by Antonio Salvi and Nicola Francesco Haym, after Pierre Corneille's *Pertharite, Roi des Lombards*. Principal roles: Rodelinda (sop), Grimoaldo (ten), Bertarido (mezzo), Eduige (sop), Unulfo (mezzo), Garibaldo (bass). One of the most successful of all Händel's operas, it is still regularly performed.
Plot: 7th-century Milan. Bertarido, the rightful King of Lombardy, is believed to be dead. He returns home in secret to discover that Grimoaldo has usurped the throne and is trying to force his wife Rodelinda to marry him. Bertarido is arrested and imprisoned. He escapes and prevents Grimoaldo from being murdered by his own evil henchman Garibaldo. In gratitude, Grimoaldo gives up the throne and pays homage to Bertarido as his rightful ruler. [R]

Rodolfo
1 Tenor role in Puccini's and baritone role in Leoncavallo's *La Bohème*. He is a poor poet. **2** Tenor role in Verdi's *Luisa Miller*. He is Count Walther's son. **3** Bass role in Bellini's *La Sonnambula*. He is a Count recently returned to the village.

Rodrigo
Opera in three acts by Händel. 1st perf Florence, Nov 1707; libr after Francesco Silvani's libretto for Marc' Antonio Ziani's *Il Duello d'Amore e di Vendetta*. Principal roles: Rodrigo (c-ten), Esilena (sop), Florinda (sop), Giuliano (ten), Evanco (c-ten), Fernando (c-ten). One of Händel's earliest operas, telling of supposed events in the life of the last Visigoth King of Spain, it is only very rarely performed. Some of the recitative is lost, and Händel reused some of the music for his incidental music for Ben Jonson's *The Alchemist*.

Rodrigo
1 Baritone role in Verdi's *Don Carlos*. He is the liberal Marquis of Posa. **2** Tenor role in Rossini's *La Donna del Lago*. He is a rebel chief married to Elena. **3** Tenor role in Massenet's *Le Cid*. He is the Cid of the opera's title.

Rodrigue et Chimène
Unfinished opera in three acts by Debussy. 1st perf BBC Radio, 9 Nov 1968 (composed 1892); libr by Catulle Mendès, after Pierre Corneille's *Le Cid* and Guilhem de Castro's *La Jeunesse du Cid*. 1st full perf Lyon, 14 May 1993; libr completed by George Beck. Principal roles: Rodrigue (ten), Chimène (sop), Don Diègue (bass), Gomez (bar), Hernan (ten). It contains nearly two hours of unorchestrated music, Acts I and III being in short score and Act II being in full vocal score. Edited for performance with piano by Richard Langham Smith, it was subsequently completed and orchestrated by the Russian composer Edison Denisov. [R]

Rodríguez de Hita, Antonio (1724–87)
Spanish composer. The most important early ZARZUELA composer, his collaboration with the dramatist Ramón de la Cruz (1731–94) had an enormous influence on the subsequent development of the genre. Their most important works are the heroic *Briseida* (Madrid, 10 July 1768), *Las Segadoras de Vallecas* (Madrid, 13 Sept 1768), an impressive depiction of peasant life, and *Las Labradoras de Murcia* (Madrid, 16 Sept 1769), which is almost a slice of VERISMO over a century before its time.

Roi Arthus, Le (*King Arthur*)
Opera in three acts by Chausson (Op 23). 1st perf Brussels, 30 Nov 1903 (composed 1895); libr by the composer. Principal roles: Arthus (bar), Guinèvre (sop), Lancelot (ten), Mordred (bar), Merlin (bass). The only one of Chausson's operas ever to have been staged, it is a heavily Wagnerian setting of parts of the Arthurian cycle. It contains much fine music but is hardly ever performed.
Plot: Legendary Britain. Arthur, victorious over the Saxons, praises Lancelot. The jealous Mordred surprises Lancelot at a tryst with Arthur's queen Guinevere. Lancelot injures Mordred and flees. Mordred informs Arthur who, reluctant to believe the pair's guilt, summons Lancelot to court. Unwilling to perjure himself, Lancelot refuses the summons and elopes with Guinevere. Merlin's prediction that the kingdom will fall spurs Arthur to pursue Lancelot, who flees with Arthur's sword, Excalibur.

Guinevere upbraids Lancelot, who returns to fight, and then strangles herself in shame with her own hair. Arthur wounds Lancelot and then forgives him. A heavenly chariot descends to convey Arthur to a better world. [R]

Roi David, Le (*King David*)
Dramatic psalm in three parts by Honegger. 1st perf Mézières, 11 June 1921; libr by René Morax, after the Book of Samuel in the Old Testament. Principal roles: David (ten), Young David (mezzo), Michal (sop), Angel (sop). The work which established Honegger's reputation, it is still performed from time to time, usually in the concert hall. [R]

Roi de Lahore, Le (*The King of Lahore*)
Opera in five acts by Massenet. 1st perf Paris, 27 April 1877; libr by Louis Gallet, after the *Mahabharata*. Principal roles: Sita (sop), Alim (ten), Scindia (bar), Indra (bass), Kaled (mezzo), Timour (b-bar). Massenet's first major success, it is an exotically scored work which is nowadays only very rarely performed.
Plot: 11th-century India. The priestess Sita is loved by King Alim of Lahore and by his minister Scindia. Scindia kills Alim, but the Hindu god Indra permits Alim to return to earth as a beggar. Sita kills herself so as to be with Alim in paradise. [R]

Roi d'Ys, Le (*The King of Ys*)
Opera in three acts by Lalo. 1st perf Paris, 7 May 1888; libr by Édouard Blau, after a Breton legend. Principal roles: Rozenn (sop), Mylio (ten), Margared (mezzo), Karmac (bar), King (bass), St Corentin (bass). By far Lalo's most successful stage work, it is a powerful and finely orchestrated piece which deserves more than the occasional performance which it currently receives.
Plot: Legendary Brittany. The princess Margared loves the warrior Mylio, but he is engaged to Margared's sister Rozenn. On the night of the wedding, the jealous Margared opens the floodgates and allows the sea to drown the city of Ys. Only after Margared has confessed and thrown herself into the sea does the city's patron saint Corentin cause the waters to recede. [R]

Roi l'a Dit, Le (*The King Said It*)
Comic opera in three acts by Delibes. 1st perf Paris, 24 May 1873; libr by Edmond Gondinet. Principal roles: Moncontour (bar), Benoît (ten), Javotte (sop). A delightful little piece, it is Delibes's only opera apart from *Lakmé* still to be remembered.
Plot: 17th-century France. Having falsely maintained that he has fathered a son, the Marquis de Moncontour is forced by circumstances to enrol the peasant lad Benoît to play the part. Benoît immediately takes advantage of the situation, causing the Marquis acute embarrassment. The Marquis is forced to get rid of him and allow him to marry his sweetheart Javotte, but he is compensated for the loss of his 'son' with a dukedom.

Roi Malgré Lui, Le (*The King Despite Himself*)
Comic opera in three acts by Chabrier. 1st perf Paris, 18 May 1887; libr by Émile de Najac and Paul Burani (revised by the composer and Jean Richepin), after François Ancelot's play. Principal roles: Henri (bar), Minka (sop), de Nangis (ten), Fritelli (bar), Laski (bass), Alexina (sop). One of the Chabrier's most sparkling, entertaining and brilliantly orchestrated scores, containing the famous *Fête polonaise*, it is still performed from time to time, but not as often as its charm and merits deserve.
Plot: Cracow, 1574. Henri de Valois is about to be crowned King of France and is unwilling to accept his simultaneous election as King of Poland. He learns from the serf Minka that there is a plot afoot, led by Count Laski, to assassinate him. Disguising himself as his friend Comte de Nangis, Henri joins the conspirators. Nangis himself arrives at the conspirator's camp and is mistaken for Henri. The plot is foiled and both Henri and de Nangis escape unharmed. Henri agrees to accept the crowns of both France and Poland. [R]

Rolfe-Johnson, Anthony (b 1940)
British tenor, particularly associated with Mozart, Händel, Britten and Monteverdi roles. Possessing a beautiful voice used with intelligence and outstanding musicianship, he is one of the most stylish contemporary Mozartians and is a

· Roman Emperors · · in opera ·

Amongst the Roman Emperors who appear as operatic characters are:

- Augustus in Graun's *Cleopatra e Cesare* and Barber's *Antony and Cleopatra.*
- Claudius in Händel's *Agrippina.*
- Tiberius in Biber's *Arminio.*
- Caligula in Biber's *Arminio.*
- Nero in Monteverdi's *L'Incoronazione di Poppea*, Händel's lost *Nero*, Mascagni's *Nerone*, Rubinstein's *Nero*, Händel's *Agrippina*, Boito's *Nerone*, Biber's *Arminio* and Duni's *Nero.*
- Titus in Hasse's *La Clemenza di Tito*, Mozart's *La Clemenza di Tito* and Gluck's *La Clemenza di Tito.*
- Trajan in Lesueur's *Le Triomphe de Trajan* and Nicolini's *Trajano in Dacia.*
- Hadrian in Pergolesi's *Adriano in Siria* and J.C. Bach's *Adriano in Siria.*
- Marcus Aurelius in Steffani's *Marco Aurelio.*
- Elagabalus in Cavalli's *Eliogabolo.*
- Aurelian in Rossini's *Aureliano in Palmira.*
- Constantine in Donizetti's *Fausta*, Bononcini's *Crispo* and Massenet's *Roma.*
- Valentinian III in Händel's *Ezio.*

dignified and restrained stage performer. Recently he has also achieved some success as a conductor.

Romani, Felice (1788–1865)
Italian librettist. By far the most accomplished Italian librettist of his day, he wrote over 100 texts, notable for their elegant verses and for their illumination of a character's inner feelings. He provided libretti for Bellini (*Il Pirata*, *La Straniera*, *Zaira*, *I Capuleti e i Montecchi*, the unfinished *Ernani*, *La Sonnambula*, *Norma*, *Beatrice di Tenda* and the revised *Bianca e Fernando*), Coccia, Donizetti (ten, including *Anna Bolena*, *L'Elisir d'Amore*, *Ugo Conte di Parigi*, *Parisina d'Este*, *Lucrezia Borgia* and *Rosmonda d'Inghilterra*), Generali, Jírovec (*Il Finto Stanislao*), Mayr (*La Rosa Bianca e la Rosa Rossa* and *Medea in Corinto*), Mercadante (16, including *I Normanni a Parigi*), Meyerbeer (*L'Esule di Granata* and *Margherita d'Anjou*), Morlacchi, Nicolaï (*Enrico II*), L. Ricci, Rossi, Rossini (*Aureliano in Palmira*, *Bianca e Faliero* and *Il Turco in Italia*), Vaccai (*Giulietta e Romeo*), Verdi (*Un Giorno di Regno*) and Winter (*Maometto II*) amongst others.

Romania
see BUCHAREST OPERA

Romanian opera composers
see ENESCU
Other national opera composers include Mansi Barberis (1899–1986), Tiberiu Brediceano (1877–1969), Nicolae Bretan (1887–1968), Eduard Caudella (1841–1924), Paul Constantinescu (1909–63), Gheorghe Dima (1847–1925), Sabin Dragoi (1894–1968), Martian Negrea (1893–1973), Constantin Nottara (1890–1951), Ciprian Porombescu (1853–83), Anatol Vieru (*b* 1926) and Alexandru Zirra (1883–1946).

Romanza (Italian for 'romance')
The term has two meanings in opera:
1 A slow, single-movement aria in 19th-century Italian opera, such as 'Una furtiva lagrima' in Donizetti's *L'Elisir d'Amore.*
2 More generally, any song or aria of a lyrical and intimate nature.

Romberg, Sigmund (1877–1951)
Hungarian-born American composer. He wrote some 50 operettas and musical comedies of which the most successful included *Blossom Time* (New York, 29 Sept

1921; libr Dorothy Donnelley), THE STUDENT PRINCE, *The Desert Song* (New York, 30 Nov 1926; libr Otto Harbach and Oscar Hammerstein II) [R] and *The New Moon* (New York, 11 Sept 1928; libr Hammerstein and L. Schwab) [R].

Rome
see TEATRO DELL'OPERA, ROME

Romeo and Juliet
see CAPULETI E I MONTECCHI, I; GIULIETTA E ROMEO; ROMÉO ET JULIETTE; ROMEO UND JULIA

Roméo et Juliette
Opera in five acts by Gounod. 1st perf Paris, 27 April 1867; libr by Jules Barbier and Michel Carré, after William Shakespeare's *Romeo and Juliet*. Principal roles: Juliette (sop), Roméo (ten), Frère Laurent (bass), Mercutio (bar), Tybalt (ten), Capulet (bar), Gertrude (mezzo), Stephano (mezzo), Duke of Verona (bass). One of Gounod's most successful operas, still quite often performed, it contains some of his most beautiful and melodious music, even if the work as a whole is a travesty of Shakespeare.
Plot: 13th-century Verona. Juliet meets and falls in love with Romeo at a masked ball given by her father Capulet, unaware that he is a member of the rival Montagu family. Romeo escapes when recognized by Juliet's cousin Tybalt, but returns to serenade her under her balcony. The next day, Friar Lawrence, hoping for peace between the warring families, secretly marries them. Tybalt kills Romeo's friend Mercutio in a street brawl and Romeo kills Tybalt in revenge, for which he is banished. The lovers say farewell, and to avoid a marriage which Capulet has arranged, Friar Lawrence gives Juliet a sleeping draught which simulates death. Romeo, unaware of this, returns to find Juliet apparently dead and poisons himself in her tomb. When she wakes and the dying Romeo tells her that he has taken poison, Juliet stabs herself and the lovers die in each other's arms. [R]

Romeo und Julia
Opera in two acts by Sutermeister. 1st perf Dresden, 13 April 1940; libr by the composer, after William Shakespeare's *Romeo and Juliet*. Principal roles: Romeo (ten), Julia (sop), Pater Lorenzo (bass), Nurse (mezzo), Capulet (bass), Countess Capulet (mezzo), Balthasar (bar), Duke Escalus (bar). Sutermeister's most successful opera, it is a concise treatment, written in a readily accessible lyrical vein, which concentrates almost exclusively on the two lovers. [R]

Romerzählung
Tenor monologue for Tannhäuser in Act III of Wagner's *Tannhäuser*, in which he tells of his pilgrimage to Rome.

Ronconi, Giorgio (1810–90)
Italian baritone. One of the greatest baritones of the 19th century (more highly regarded than any other by Donizetti), he was also considered an outstanding actor. He created the title-role in *Nabucco* and, for Donizetti, Cardenio in *Il Furioso*, the title-role in *Torquato Tasso*, Nello della Pietra in *Pia de' Tolomei*, Enrico in *Il Campanello*, Corrado in *Maria de Rudenz*, Don Pedro in *Maria Padilla* and Enrico in *Maria di Rohan*. His brother **Sebastiano** (1814–1900) was also a baritone; their father **Domenico** (1772–1839) was a successful tenor and also a noted teacher.

Rondine, La (*The Swallow*)
Opera in three acts by Puccini. 1st perf Monte Carlo, 27 March 1917; libr by Giuseppe Adami, after Alfred Maria Willner and Heinrich Reichert's libretto. Principal roles: Magda (sop), Ruggero (ten), Prunier (ten), Lisette (sop), Rambaldo (bar). Originally planned as a Viennese operetta, it is Puccini's lightest work in style. Although never one of his more popular operas, it is still performed from time to time.
Plot: Mid-19th-century Paris and Nice. Magda is the mistress of the wealthy businessman Rambaldo. At one of their parties, she meets and falls in love with the young Ruggero. She meets him in disguise at a café and they decide to elope together. They set up house together and Ruggero wishes them to marry. However, rather than make Ruggero suffer his family's disapproval, she renounces him and returns to Rambaldo. [R]

Rosa, Carl
see CARL ROSA OPERA COMPANY

Rosalinde
Soprano role in J. Strauss's *Die Fledermaus*. She is von Eisenstein's wife.

Rosbaud, Hans (1895–1962)
Austrian conductor, particularly associated with 20th-century operas, especially those of Schönberg. He was musical director of the Münster Opera (1937–41), the Strasbourg Opera (1941–4) and the Aix-en-Provence Festival (1947–59). He conducted the first performance of *Moses und Aron*.

Rosenberg, Hilding (1892–1985)
Swedish composer and conductor. His operas have met with some success in Sweden but are unknown elsewhere. They include *Journey to America* (*Resan till Amerika*, Stockholm, 24 Nov 1932; libr A. Henriksson), *Marionettes* (Stockholm, 14 Feb 1939; libr after Jacinto Benavente's *Los Intereses Creados*), *The Island of Happiness* (*Lychsalighetens Ö*, Stockholm, 1 Feb 1945; libr P.D.A. Atterbom), the four-part opera-oratorio *Joseph and his Brothers* (*Josef och hans Bröder*, Swedish Radio 1946–8; libr after Thomas Mann) and *The House With Two Entrances* (*Hus Med Dubbel Ingång*, Stockholm, 24 May 1970; libr after Pedro Calderón de la Barca).

Rosenkavalier, Der (*The Rose Cavalier*)
Opera in three acts by Strauss (Op 59). 1st perf Dresden, 26 Jan 1911; libr by Hugo von Hofmannsthal. Principal roles: Marschallin (sop), Octavian (mezzo), Baron Ochs (bass), Sophie (sop), Faninal (bar), Valzacchi (ten), Annina (mezzo), Italian Tenor (ten), Marianne (sop). Possibly Strauss's most popular opera, it is his first work in neo-classical style.
Plot: Vienna, 1740s. The middle-aged Marschallin is having an affair with the young nobleman Octavian. Her boorish country cousin Baron Ochs von Lerchenau is engaged to Sophie, daughter of the recently ennobled businessman Faninal. He asks the Marschallin to recommend a suitable young man to make the traditional presentation of the Silver Rose to the intended bride, and Octavian is selected for the task. Octavian and Sophie are immediately attracted to one another, while Ochs's vulgarity revolts Sophie. Eventually, Ochs is discomfited, Sophie and Octavian are united, and the Marschallin resigns herself with dignity to the loss of her lover to a girl of his own age. [R]

Rosenthal, Harold (1917–87)
British critic. One of the most influential post-war British opera critics, he was editor of *Opera* and was ardent in encouraging and championing British artists, although this led him occasionally to overrate them. His autobiography, *My Mad World of Opera*, was published in 1982.

Rose of Persia, The or **The Story-Teller and the Slave**
Operetta in two acts by Sullivan. 1st perf London, 29 Nov 1899; libr by Basil Hood. Principal roles: Mahmoud (bar), Hassan (bar), Yussuf (ten), Zubeydeh (sop). Reasonably successful at its appearance, it is nowadays hardly ever performed.
Plot: Legendary Persia. The wealthy merchant Abu el Hassan enjoys entertaining the city's beggars. The Sultana Zubeydeh has been visiting his house disguised as a dancing girl, but is unmasked when Sultan Mahmoud sends the police to bring some of Hassan's guests to the palace for inspection. Mahmoud orders everyone involved to be put to death, but is dissuaded by Yussuf, a favourite slave. Instead, Mahmoud orders Hassan to tell a story by instalments with the penalty of death if the ending is sad. By persuading the Sultan that the ending could not possibly be happy if he were executed, he gains Mahmoud's pardon.

Rosina
Mezzo role in Rossini's and soprano role in Paisiello's *Il Barbiere di Siviglia*. She is Dr Bartolo's ward.

Rosina
Comic opera in two acts by Shield. 1st perf London, 31 Dec 1782; libr by Frances Moore Brooke, after Charles-Simon Favart's *Les Moissonneurs*. Principal roles: Rosina (sop), Phoebe (sop), William (mezzo), Mr Belville (ten), Capt Belville (ten). One of the most successful 18th-century British operas, it is a work of great melodic charm which still receives an occasional performance.
Plot: Northern England, 18th century. The orphan Rosina works on a farm, where Phoebe and her lover William are forever

squabbling. She is in love with the local squire Mr Belville, whose brother Capt Belville also desires her. She refuses the Captain's advances, so he has her abducted, but she is rescued by two labourers. The bashful Mr Belville, realizing that Rosina does not love his brother, finally wins her hand. [R]

Rospigliosi, Giulio (later Pope Clement IX) (1600–69)
Italian poet, librettist and cleric. A keen patron of letters and music, he provided libretti for Abbatini (*Dal Male il Bene* and *La Baltasara*), Landi (*Il Sant' Alessio*), Marazzoli (*Chi Soffre, Speri* and *Le Armi e gli Amori*) and Rossi (*Il Palazzo Incantato*) amongst others.

Rossato, Arturo (1882–1942)
Italian librettist. He provided texts for Alfano (*L'Ultimo Lord* and *Madonna Imperia*), Lattuada (*La Tempestà*, *Don Giovanni* and *Le Preziose Ridicole*), Pick-Mangiagalli (*Notturno Romantico*), Veretti (*Il Favorito del Rè*), Vittadini (*Caracciolo*) and Zandonai (*I Cavalieri di Ekebù*, *Giulietta e Romeo*, *Guiliano*, *Una Partita*, *La Farsa Amorasa* and *Il Bacio*) amongst others.

Rossellini, Renzo (1908–82)
Italian composer. His operas, some of which have met with considerable success in Italy, are written in late-romantic style. They are *La Guerra* (Naples, 25 Feb 1956; libr composer), *Il Vortice* (Naples, 8 Feb 1958; libr composer), *La Piovra* (Naples, 1958; libr composer), the television opera *La Campane* (RAI, 9 May 1959; libr composer), *Uno Sguardo dal Ponte* (Rome, 11 Mar 1961; libr composer, after Arthur Miller's *A View From the Bridge*), *Il Linguaggio dei Fiori* (Milan, 1963; libr composer, after Federico García Lorca), *La Leggenda del Ritorno* (Milan, 1966; libr D. Fabbri, after Fyodor Dostoyevsky's *The Brothers Karamazov*), *L'Avventuriero* (Milan, 1968; libr Fabbri, after Dostoyevsky), the successful *L'Annonce Faite à Marie* (Paris, 1970; libr Paul Claudel) and *La Reine Morte* (Monte Carlo, 1973; libr H. de Montherlant). He was artistic director of the Monte Carlo Opera (1972–6). His brother **Roberto** (1906–77) was a successful producer, also famous as a film director and one-time husband of the actress Ingrid Bergman.

Rossi, Gaetano (1774–1855)
Italian librettist. Official playwright of the Teatro la Fenice, Venice, he wrote over 120 libretti, providing texts for Carafa, Coccia, Donizetti (*Linda di Chamounix* and *Maria Padilla*), Generali, Manfroce (*Alzira*), Mayr, Mercadante (including *Le Due Illustri Rivali*, *Il Bravo* and *Il Giuramento*), Meyerbeer (*Il Crociato in Egitto*), Morlacchi, Nicolai (*Il Proscritto*), Pacini, Paer, Pavesi, Portugal, F. and L. Ricci, Rossini (*La Cambiale di Matrimonio*, *La Scala di Seta*, *Tancredi* and *Semiramide*), Vaccai (*Giovanna d'Arco*) and Winter amongst others.

Rossi, Lauro (1812–85)
Italian composer. He wrote 29 operas, all now long forgotten, achieving considerable success in comedy, in which field he was widely regarded in his time as Donizetti's successor. His operas include *La Villana Contessa* (Naples, 8 May 1831; libr A. Passaro), *La Casa Disabitata* (Milan, 11 Aug 1834; libr Jacopo Ferretti), his most successful work, *Giovanna Shore* (Mexico, 1836; libr Felice Romani) and *Biorn* (London, 17 Jan 1877; libr F. Marshall, after Shakespeare's *Macbeth*).

Rossi, Luigi (c 1597–1653)
Italian composer. His two operas are *Il Palazzo Incantato* (Rome, 22 Feb 1642; libr Giulio Rospigliosi, after Lodovico Ariosto's *Orlando Furioso*) and the fine ORFEO, which was the first opera to be performed in France.

Rossignol, Le
see NIGHTINGALE, THE

Rossi-Lemeni, Nicola (1920–91)
Italian bass, particularly associated with the Italian repertory (both classical and modern) and with Boris Godunov and Méphistophélès. One of the leading basses of the 1950s, his powerful voice was not perfectly knit together, but this was amply compensated for by his outstanding dramatic abilities. He created Thomas à Becket in Pizzetti's *L'Assassinio nella Cattedrale*, the title-role in Zafred's *Wallenstein* and roles in Napoli's *Dubrovski II* and Rossellini's *Uno Sguardo dal Ponte*

and *La Reine Morte*. He also produced a number of operas. Married to the soprano VIRGINIA ZEANI.

Rossini, Gioacchino (1792–1868)
Italian composer. One of the greatest of all composers of comic opera, and the founder of Italian romantic opera, his first opera, DEMETRIO E POLIBIO, was written at the age of 14. His first commissioned work, LA CAMBIALE DI MATRIMONIO, was followed by *L'Equivoco Stravagante* (Bologna, 26 Oct 1811; libr Gaetano Gasparri), L'INGANNO FELICE, CIRO IN BABILONIA, LA SCALA DI SETA, LA PIETRA DEL PARAGONE, L'OCCASIONE FA IL LADRO and IL SIGNOR BRUSCHINO. The triumphs of TANCREDI and L'ITALIANA IN ALGIERI placed him at the forefront of Italian composers. There followed AURELIANO IN PALMIRA, IL TURCO IN ITALIA, the unsuccessful *Sigismondo* (Venice, 26 Dec 1814; libr Giuseppe Maria Foppa) and the works written during his period as musical director in Naples (1815–23): ELISABETTA REGINA D'INGHILTERRA, TORVALDO E DORLISKA, the immortal IL BARBIERE DI SIVIGLIA, *La Gazzetta* (Naples, 26 Sept 1816; libr Giovanni Palomba, after Carlo Goldoni's *Il Matrimonio per Concorso*), OTELLO, the highly successful LA CENERENTOLA, LA GAZZA LADRA, ARMIDA, ADELAIDE DI BORGOGNA, MOSÈ IN EGITTO, *Adina* (Lisbon, 22 June 1826, composed 1818; libr Gherardo Bevilaqua-Albobrandini), *Ricciardo e Zoraide* (Naples, 3 Dec 1818; libr Francesco Berio di Salsa, after Nicolò Forteguerri's *Il Ricciardetto*), ERMIONE, *Edoardo e Cristina* (Venice, 24 Apr 1819; libr Giovanni Federico Schmidt and Andrea Leone Tottola), LA DONNA DEL LAGO, BIANCA E FALIERO, MAOMETTO SECONDO, MATILDE DI SHABRAN, ZELMIRA and the fine SEMIRAMIDE. He moved to Paris in 1824 as musical director of the Théâtre des Italiens, and there wrote the superb IL VIAGGIO A REIMS, LE SIÈGE DE CORINTHE (a revision of *Maometto Secondo*), *Moïse et Pharaon* (a revision of *Mosè in Egitto*), LE COMTE ORY and the grand opera GUILLAUME TELL, his finest serious work.

Rossini retired in 1830, writing virtually nothing for the rest of his life apart from the little vocal and instrumental pieces *The Sins of My Old Age*. His historical importance and influence can hardly be overstated; his works were the models for every subsequent Italian and many French composers. His brilliant orchestration, his introduction of accompanied RECITATIVE, his powers of comic characterization and his introduction of elements from OPERA BUFFA into serious works all began the process of freeing Italian opera from its suffocating conventions, which led through Donizetti to Verdi. His operas are regarded as some of the most florid ever written, but it is important to remember that Rossini was the first composer to write out his own decorations in an attempt to curb the extravagant excesses of singers. A legendary wit and notoriously indolent (he was the worst self-borrower in musical history), his first wife was the soprano ISABELLA COLBRAN. He later married Olimpe Pélissier, previously the mistress of the painter Horace Vernet. He appears as a character in Paumgartner's *Rossini in Neapel*.

Rostropovich, Mstislav (b 1927)
Russian conductor and cellist, particularly associated with the Russian repertory. An outstanding interpreter of Russian music, his operatic appearances have sadly been intermittent. Married to the soprano GALINA VISHNEVSKAYA, their support of the dissident author Alexander Solzhenitsyn led to their having to leave the then USSR in 1974 and they were stripped of their Soviet citizenship. He was artistic director of the Aldeburgh Festival and conducted the first performances of Schnittke's *Life With an Idiot* and *Gesualdo* and Shchedrin's *Lolita*.

Roswaenge, Helge (b Rosenvig le-Hansen) (1897–1972)
Danish tenor, particularly associated with heroic German and Italian roles. Widely regarded as the finest lyrico-dramatic tenor of the inter-war period, he had a thrilling voice of bite and brilliance. His autobiography, *Mach es besser, mein Sohn*, was published in 1945.

Rota, Nino (1911–79)
Italian composer. His operas, written in a tuneful and readily accessible style, are the unperformed student work *Il Principe Porcaro* (1925; libr composer, after Hans Christian Andersen's *The Prince and the Swineherd*), *Ariodante* (Parma, 18 Nov

1942; libr E. Trucchi, after Lodovico Ariosto's *Orlando Furioso*), *Torquemada* (Naples, 24 Jan 1976, composed 1943; libr Trucchi, after Victor Hugo), the radio opera *I Due Timidi* (RAI, 15 Nov 1950; libr S. Cecchi d'Amico), IL CAPPELLO DI PAGLIA DI FIRENZE, by far his most successful opera, *Lo Scoiattolo in Gamba* (Bari, 13 June 1973, composed 1959; libr Eduardo de Filippo), the radio opera *La Notte di un Nevrastenico* (RAI, 19 Nov 1959; libr Riccardo Bacchelli), *Aladino e la Lampada Magica* (Naples, 14 Jan 1968; libr V. Verginelli, after *The Thousand and One Nights*), *La Visita Meravigliosa* (Palermo, 6 Feb 1970; libr composer, after H.G. Wells's *The Wonderful Visit*) and *Napoli Milionaria* (Spoleto, 22 June 1977; libr de Filippo). He also achieved international fame as a composer of film music, especially for Federico Fellini.

Rothenberger, Anneliese (b 1924)
German soprano, particularly associated with lyrical German roles, Mozart, Viennese operetta and some modern dramatic roles such as the title-role in Berg's *Lulu*. She had a light and beautiful voice, used with intelligence and musicianship, and had a charming stage presence. She created Telemachus in Liebermann's *Penelope* and the title-role in Sutermeister's *Madame Bovary*.

Rothmüller, Marko (1908–93)
Croatian baritone, particularly associated with Verdi roles and with Wozzeck. One of the finest baritones of the immediate post-war period, he had a beautiful voice used with great intelligence and was a characterful singing-actor. He created Truchsess in Hindemith's *Mathis der Maler*. His writings include *Die Musik der Juden* (1951).

Rouen
see THÉÂTRE DES ARTS, ROUEN

Rouleau, Joseph (b 1929)
Canadian bass, particularly associated with the Italian and French repertories. He possessed a large and dark voice (occasionally inclined to woolliness) and had an impressive stage presence. He created Bishop Tâché in Somers's *Louis Reil* and Pranzini in Tavener's *Thérèse*.

Rousseau, Jean-Jacques (1712–78)
Swiss philosopher, composer and writer. His music is charming if simple, but has no great technical skill. His first opera *Les Muses Galantes* (Paris, 1742) was followed by the highly successful LE DEVIN DU VILLAGE, *Pygmalion* (Lyon, 1770), written in collaboration with Horace Coignet, which is an early operatic example of MELODRAMA, and the unfinished *Daphnis et Chloé*. He appears as a character in Dalayrac's *L'Enfance de Jean-Jacques Rousseau*.

Rousseau's operatic importance lies principally in his writings. Siding with the Italians, he was a central figure in the GUERRE DES BOUFFONS, advocating melody as a form of heightened speech and the use of emotion and personal sensibility as a guide, an advocacy which exercised a powerful influence on the early romantic composers. These beliefs were propounded in his famous *Lettre Sur La Musique Française* (1753) and expanded in his *Dictionnaire de Musique* (1768) and in his contributions on music to the *Grande Encyclopédie*.

Roussel, Albert (1869–1937)
French composer. He was deeply interested in Indian music, which provided the inspiration for his first and finest stage work, the opera-ballet PADMÂVATÎ. His two other operas are *La Naissance de la Lyre* (Paris, 11 July 1925; libr Théodore Reinach, after Sophocles's *Ichneutae*) and the comedy *La Testament de la Tante Caroline* (Olomouc, 14 Nov 1936; libr Nino).

Royal Danish Opera
The Theatre Royal (cap 1,300) in Copenhagen opened in 1874 and a second house, New Stage (cap 1,091), opened in 1931. The annual season runs from September to June. Musical directors have included Johan Svendsen, Nielsen, Georg Hoeberg, Johan Hye-Knudsen, Egisto Tango, John Frandsen and Michael Schønwandt.

Royal Flemish Opera (*Koninklijke Vlaamse Opera* in Flemish)
Formed in 1893 by the bass Hendrik Fontaine, the company performs at the Royal Opera House (cap 1,050) in

Antwerp. The adventurous repertory has included several operas by Flemish composers. All performances are sung in Flemish, and musical directors have included Fritz Célis, Rudolf Werthen and Stefan Soltesz. The Flemish Chamber Opera (*Vlaamse Kameropera*), based at the Ring Theatre in Antwerp, was formed in 1971 from an amalgamation of the Dutch Chamber Opera and the Antwerp Chamber Opera, which had been founded in 1960.

Royal Hunt of the Sun, The
Opera in two acts by Hamilton. 1st perf London, 2 Feb 1977 (composed 1969); libr by the composer, after Peter Shaffer's play. Principal roles: Pizarro (bar), Atahualpa (bar), Young Martin (ten), Villac Umu (bass), Old Martin (bass), Valverde (bass), Hernando de Soto (ten), Don Diego (ten). Set in 16th-century Peru, it is a powerfully theatrical work telling of the clash of cultures during the Spanish conquest of the Inca Empire.

Royal Opera, Ghent
Originally named the Théâtre Lyrique and acquiring its present name in 1921, the theatre opened in Aug 1840 and pursues the most adventurous repertory policy of any Belgian house. Artistic directors have included Vina Bovy.

Royal Opera, Stockholm
The present opera house (cap 1,264) in the Swedish capital opened in 1898, replacing the previous theatre built by Gustavus III (and in which he was assassinated), which had opened in 1782. One of Europe's leading houses, with a long Wagner tradition, the annual season runs from September to June. Artistic directors have included Armas Järnefelt, John Forsell, Harald André, Joel Berglund, Set Svanholm and Göran Gentele.

Royal Opera House, Covent Garden
Britain's principal international opera house, the present theatre (cap 2,250) is the third on the site. The first theatre was opened by John Rich on 7 Dec 1732 and was destroyed by fire on 19 Sept 1808. It was rebuilt in 1809 but burnt down in 1856. The present house, designed by Edward Barry, opened on 15 May 1858. Named the Royal Opera in 1892, it became the home of the present company in 1946. The annual season, given in tandem with that of the Royal Ballet, runs from mid-September to mid-July, and the wide-ranging repertory has been particularly notable for its Wagner, Strauss, Berlioz, Mozart and Tippett productions. Post-war general administrators have been Sir David Webster, Sir John Tooley and Jeremy Isaacs, and the musical directors have been Karl Rankl, Rafael Kubelík, Sir Georg Solti, Sir Colin Davis and Bernard Haitink.

Rozdestvensky, Gennady (b 1931)
Russian conductor, particularly associated with the Russian repertory. One of the most brilliant and exciting contemporary conductors, even if occasionally a little idiosyncratic, his operatic appearances outside Russia have sadly been intermittent. He was musical director of the Bolshoi Opera (1964–70) and the Moscow Chamber Opera (1974–90) and conducted the first performance of Shostakovich's *The Gamblers*. Married to the pianist **Victoria Postnikova**.

Rubato (Italian for 'robbed')
Short for *tempo rubato*, it means performing with a degree of freedom as regards time, so as to give greater expressiveness to the music. Usually used with reference to pianists, it can also be applied to singers.

Rubini, Giovanni Battista (1794–1854)
Italian tenor. One of the outstanding lyric tenors of the early 19th century, although said to have been a poor actor, he created eight roles for Donizetti, including Percy in *Anna Bolena* and Fernando in *Marino Faliero*, and, for Bellini, Fernando in *Bianca e Fernando*, Gualtiero in *Il Pirata*, Elvino in *La Sonnambula* and Arturo in *I Puritani*. His wife **Adelaide Chaumel** (*c* 1798–1874) was a successful soprano, who created Calbo in Rossini's *Maometto Secondo* and, for Donizetti, Matilde in *Gianni di Calais* and Nina in *Il Giovedì Grasso*.

Rubinstein, Anton (1830–94)
Russian composer and pianist, brother of the pianist Nikolai Rubinstein. His 15 operas and three opera-oratorios, all but one now largely forgotten, were modelled on

contemporary European composers and show only flashes of the nationalist sentiment which so absorbed his fellow Russian composers. His most successful operas include *Feramors* (Dresden, 24 Feb 1863; libr Julius Rodenberg, after Thomas Moore), THE DEMON, by far his most successful work, *Nero* (Hamburg, 1 Nov 1879; libr Jules Barbier), the more nationalist *Kalashnikov the Merchant* (St Petersburg, 22 Feb 1880; libr N.I. Kulikov, after Mikhail Lermentov) and *Sulamith* (Hamburg, 8 Nov 1883; libr Rodenberg).

Ruddigore or **The Witch's Curse**
Operetta in two acts by Sullivan. 1st perf (as *Ruddygore*) London, 22 Jan 1887; libr by W.S. Gilbert. Principal roles: Robin/Sir Ruthven (bar), Rose (sop), Richard (ten), Sir Despard (b-bar), Mad Margaret (mezzo), Dame Hannah (mezzo), Sir Roderic (bass), Old Adam (bass), Zorah (sop). A satire on the Victorian passion for Gothic melodrama, it contains some of Sullivan's finest music, particularly in the ghosts' scene.
Plot: Early-19th-century Cornwall. The Murgatroyd family, baronets of Ruddigore, are accursed: each baronet must commit a serious crime every day or perish in agony. To avoid inheriting the title, the meek and mild Ruthven has disguised himself as the farmer Robin Oakapple and is in love with Rose Maybud, but is too diffident to propose to her. His bumptious foster-brother, the sailor Richard Dauntless, offers to help him, but falls in love with Rose himself. Rose, however, decides that she prefers Robin and the disappointed Richard reveals Robin's true identity to the present baronet, Robin's brother Despard. Robin is forced to accept his inheritance and Despard returns to ordinary life, marrying Mad Margaret, one of his earlier victims. Robin's ancestors, led by Sir Roderic, are contemptuous of Robin's pathetic little crimes and order him to do something desperate or perish. He has his servant Old Adam carry off Rose's aunt Dame Hannah, who turns out to be Sir Roderic's former sweetheart. Robin realizes that refusal to commit a daily crime amounts to suicide, which is in itself a crime, and that Sir Roderic should thus never have died. Roderic feels at liberty to resume life and marry Dame Hannah, whilst Robin is now free to marry Rose. [R]

Rudel, Julius (b 1921)
Austrian conductor, long resident in the United States. Particularly associated with the Italian and French repertories, he was musical director of the New York City Opera (1957–79), the Caramoor Festival (1963–76) and the Kennedy Center, Washington (1971–6). He conducted the first performances of Ginastera's *Bomarzo*, Kurka's *The Good Soldier Schweik*, Moore's *Wings of the Dove*, Floyd's *The Passion of Jonathan Wade* and Giannini's *The Servant of Two Masters*.

Rudziński, Witold (b 1913)
Polish composer. His six operas in late-romantic style have met with considerable success in Poland, particularly *The Dismissal of the Greek Envoys* (*Odprawa Poslów Greckich*, Cracow, 6 Nov 1966; libr B. Ostromecki, after Jan Kochanowski) [R].

Ruffo, Titta (b Ruffo Cafiero Titta) (1877–1953)
Italian baritone, particularly associated with the Italian repertory, especially Verdi. One of the greatest baritones of the 20th century, he possessed a beautiful voice of great richness and remarkable power, described by Giuseppe de Luca as 'not a voice, but a miracle'. He created the title-role in Leoncavallo's *Edipo Rè*. His autobiography, *La Mia Parabola*, was published in 1937.

Ruggero
Tenor role in Puccini's *La Rondine*. He is a young aristocrat in love with Magda.

Rumania
see ROMANIA

Rusalka
Opera in four acts by Dargomijsky. 1st perf St Petersburg, 16 May 1856; libr by the composer, after Alexander Pushkin's dramatic poem. Principal roles: Natasha (sop), Miller (bass), Prince (ten), Princess (mezzo), Olga (sop). A richly melodic work, showing considerable powers of characterization, it is still quite often performed in Russia but is virtually unknown elsewhere.

Plot: Legendary Ukraine. The Prince seduces the Miller's daughter Natasha, and then abandons her after getting her pregnant. She dies and becomes the water-nymph Rusalka. The Miller goes mad with grief and finally throws the Prince into the River Dnieper. [R]

Rusalka

Opera in three acts by Dvořák (Op 114). 1st perf Prague, 31 March 1901; libr by Jaroslav Kvapil, after Friedrich de la Motte Fouqué's *Ondine* and parts of Hans Christian Andersen's *The Little Mermaid* and Gerhard Hauptmann's *Die Versunkene Glocke*. Principal roles: Rusalka (sop), Prince (ten), Watersprite (bass), Ježibaba (mezzo), Foreign Princess (sop), Forester (ten), Kitchen Boy (mezzo). Dvořák's finest and most successful opera, it is a richly orchestrated piece of great melodic charm and is his only stage work to be regularly performed outside the Czech lands.
Plot: The naiad Rusalka, daughter of the Watersprite, wishes to become human so as to win the love of the Prince. The witch Ježibaba agrees to arrange this provided that Rusalka remains dumb and the Prince remains faithful: if not, both will be damned. After a while, the Prince tires of the mute Rusalka and turns to the Foreign Princess. Repenting his treatment of her, the Prince frees Rusalka from Ježibaba's curse but dies himself. [R]

Ruslan and Ludmila

Opera in five acts by Glinka. 1st perf St Petersburg, 9 Dec 1842; libr by the composer, Valerian Fyodorovich Shirkov, Nestor Vasileyvich Kukolnik, K.A. Bakturin, Mikhail Alexandrovich Gedeonov and Nikolai Andreyevich Markevich, after Alexander Pushkin's poem. Principal roles: Ruslan (bass), Ludmila (sop), Svyetozar (bass), Farlaf (bass), Ratmir (mezzo), Gorislava (sop), Finn (ten), Naina (mezzo), Minstrel (ten). The second of Glinka's two operas, it is a vast, sprawling fairy-tale work containing much colourful and magnificent music. In its subject matter, structure and harmonic and orchestral aspects, it marks the foundation of the distinctively Russian nationalist school of opera. Quite unaccountably, it is almost never performed outside Russia, although the exhilarating overture remains very popular in the concert hall.
Plot: Legendary Ukraine. Ludmila is wooed by the poet-prince Ratmir, by the cowardly warrior Farlaf and by the knight Ruslan. She disappears at a feast and is promised by her father Svyetozar to whichever of the suitors can find her. The wizard Finn tells Ruslan that she has been stolen by an evil dwarf and warns him against Farlaf's helper, the wicked fairy Naina. Ruslan encounters a giant head whose breathing causes a storm. He calms it and finds a magical sword beneath it. With the sword, he kills the dwarf and rescues Ludmila,

· *Russian royalty* · · *in opera* ·

The Russian Tsars and Empresses who appear as operatic characters include:

- Ivan the Terrible in Bizet's *Ivan IV* and Rimsky-Korsakov's *The Maid of Pskov*.
- Boris Godunov in Moussorgsky's *Boris Godunov* and Mattheson's *Boris Goudenow*.
- Shuisky in Moussorgsky's *Boris Godunov* and Dvořák's *Dimitrij*.
- Peter the Great in Lortzing's *Zar und Zimmermann*, Donizetti's *Il Falegname di Livonia*, Meyerbeer's *L'Étoile du Nord*, Jullien's *Pietro il Grande*, Petrov's *Peter I*, Grétry's *Pierre le Grand* and Adam's *Pierre et Catherine*.
- Catherine the Great in Cui's *The Captain's Daughter*.
- Nicholas I in Shaporin's *The Decembrists*.
- Alexander III in Schat's *Symposion*.

awakening her from a magical sleep with a ring given to him by the Finn. He and Ludmila are united. [R]

Russia
see BOLSHOI OPERA; KIROV OPERA; MOSCOW CHAMBER OPERA
see also AZERBAIJAN; GEORGIA; UKRAINE

Russian opera composers
see ALYABYEV; ARENSKY; BORODIN; BORTNYANSKY; CUI; DARGOMIJSKY; DZERZHINSKY; FOMIN; GLAZUNOV; GLIÈRE; GLINKA; IPPOLITOV-IVANOV; KABALEVSKY; KARETNIKOV; KHRENNIKOV: KNAIFEL; MOUSSORGSKY; NÁPRAVNÍK; PASHKEVICH; PETROV; PROKOFIEV; RACHMANINOV; RIMSKY-KORSAKOV; RUBINSTEIN; SCHNITTKE; SEROV; SHAPORIN; SHCHEDRIN; SHEBALIN; SHOSTAKOVICH; SLONIMSKY; STRAVINSKY; TANEYEV; TCHAIKOVSKY; TCHEREPNIN; VERSTOVSKY
see also ARMENIAN OPERA COMPOSERS; AZERBAIJANI OPERA COMPOSERS; GEORGIAN OPERA COMPOSERS; MOLDAVIAN OPERA COMPOSERS; TARTAR OPERA COMPOSERS; UKRAINIAN OPERA COMPOSERS; UZBEK OPERA COMPOSERS

Other national opera composers include Alexander Abramsky (1898–1985), Fyodor Akimenko (1876–1945), Anatol Alexandrov (1888–1982), Boris Asafyev (1884–1949), Anatoly Bogatirev (*b* 1913), Edison Denisov (*b* 1929), Alexander Kholminov (*b* 1925), Vano Muradely (1907–70) and Alexei Nikolayev (*b* 1931).

Rysanek, Leonie (b 1926)
Austrian soprano, particularly associated with Wagner and Strauss roles. One of the finest Strauss interpreters of the immediate post-war period, she had a rich and beautiful voice with a strong upper register and was a committed singing-actress. She enjoyed a long career, singing into her late 60s, latterly as a dramatic mezzo. Her sister **Lotte** (*b* 1928) was a successful lyric soprano.

S

Saarbrücken Opera
Opera in this German city in the Saar is given at the Gautheater Saarpfalz (cap 1,132), which originally opened in 1938 and which was rebuilt in 1947 after being damaged in World War II. Musical directors have included Matthias Kuntsch and Jun Märkl.

Sabata, Victor de (1892–1967)
Italian conductor and composer. One of the outstanding operatic conductors of the mid-20th century, particularly admired for his Verdi and Wagner, his fiery and sometimes dynamically idiosyncratic readings were often compared to Toscanini's. He conducted the first performance of *L'Enfant et les Sortilèges* and was musical director of La Scala, Milan (1953–7). He also composed an opera, *Il Macigno* (Milan, 1917).

Sabina, Karel (1813–87)
Czech librettist, excelling in comedy. He provided texts for Bendl (*The Old Bridegroom*), Blodek (*In the Well* and the unfinished *Zítek*), Fibich (*Bukovín*), Rozkošný (*Mikuláš*), Šebor (*The Templars in Moravia*) and Smetana (*The Brandenburgers in Bohemia* and *The Bartered Bride*). He led a remarkable double life, writing in support of Czech nationalism whilst simultaneously acting as a spy for the Austro-Hungarian authorities. He died in poverty and disgrace following his exposure.

Sacchini, Antonio (1730–86)
Italian composer. He wrote many operas, much admired in their day but nowadays nearly all largely forgotten, for Italy, London, Germany and Paris. His most important operas are *La Contadina in Corte* (Barcelona, 1764), ARMIDA and his masterpiece *Oedipe à Colone* (Paris, 4 Jan 1786; libr Nicolas François Guillard, after Sophocles's *Oedipus at Colonus*), which was performed nearly 600 times at the Paris Opéra alone in 60 years. A fine and historically important composer who is currently unjustly neglected.

Sachs, Hans
Baritone role in Wagner's *Die Meistersinger von Nürnberg*. He is the historical cobbler-poet (1494–1576). He is also the subject of Jírovec's *Hans Sachs im Vorgerückten Alter* (1834) and Lortzing's *Hans Sachs* (1840).

Sacra la sceltra
Baritone aria for Miller in Act I of Verdi's *Luisa Miller*, in which he says that a father should not force a husband on his daughter.

Sadko
Opera in seven scenes (three or five acts) by Rimsky-Korsakov. 1st perf Moscow, 7 Jan 1898; libr by the composer and Vladimir Ivanovich Belsky. Principal roles: Sadko (ten), Volkova (sop), Lyubava (mezzo), Sea King (bass), Viking, Indian and Venetian Merchants (bass, ten and bar). One of the most colourful and successful of Rimsky's fairy-tale operas, it is still regularly performed in Russia but only infrequently elsewhere. Some of the music is drawn from Rimsky's earlier symphonic poem *Sadko* (1867).
Plot: Legendary Novgorod. The local merchants beg Sadko to find wealth for the city. He meets the sea princess Volkhova, who falls in love with him and encourages him to catch three golden fish in a lake. This he does and sets sail to bring back treasure. He is becalmed on his return because he failed to make an offering to the Sea King. The treasure is tipped overboard and Sadko is cast adrift on a plank. He sinks to the bottom of the ocean, where he is offered the hand of Volkhova. The energetic dancing at their wedding causes storms which sink shipping. The Sea King's reign is declared over and Sadko and his bride are carried off in a shell drawn by birds. The next day, Volkhova is transformed into a river and Sadko, having been conveyed back to

land by St Nicholas, is found by his wife Lyubava. [R]

Sadler's Wells
see ENGLISH NATIONAL OPERA; NEW SADLER'S WELLS OPERA

Saedén, Erik (b 1924)
Swedish baritone, particularly associated with Mozart and Wagner roles and with 20th-century operas. An outstanding singing-actor, he created the title-role in Dallapiccola's *Ulisse*, Julien in Werle's *Dreaming About Thérèse*, Anfelt in Lars Runsten's *Amorina*, Mimarobe in Blomdahl's *Aniara*, St Phar in Berwald's *The Queen of Golconda* and roles in Ligeti's *Le Grand Macabre* and Rosenberg's *The House With Two Entrances*.

Saffi
Soprano role in J. Strauss's *Der Zigeunerbaron*. A gypsy girl, she is Czipra's foster-daughter.

Saffo
Opera in three acts by Pacini. 1st perf Naples, 29 Nov 1840; libr by Salvatore Cammarano, after Pietro Beltrame's play. Principal roles: Saffo (sop), Faone (ten), Alcandro (bar), Climene (mezzo). Telling of the historical Greek poetess, it is Pacini's finest and most successful opera. It is nowadays only very rarely performed.
Plot: Lesbos, 6th century BC. Alcandro, the high priest of Apollo, disapproves of the love of Faone and the poetess Saffo. He separates them and marries Faone to his daughter Climene. Saffo learns of the wedding only at the ceremony itself and overturns the altar of Apollo in fury. She is condemned to death for sacrilege. Alcandro learns that Saffo is in fact his other daughter, whom he believed to be dead, but he is unable to have the sentence reversed. Saffo accepts her fate, blesses Climene's marriage to Faone and takes the Leukadian leap, drowning in the Aegean.

Sainete
A genre of Spanish comic opera which portrayed scenes of everyday life in the form of low comedy. Its principal exponents were Blas Laserna (1751–1816) and Antonio Soler (1729–83).

Saint François d'Assise (*Saint Francis of Assisi*)
Opera in three acts by Messiaen. 1st perf Paris, 28 Nov 1983; libr by the composer, after the 14th-century monkish books *Fioretti* and *Considérations Sur les Stigmates*. Principal roles: St Francis (bar), Angel (sop), Leper (ten), Frère Massé (ten), Frère Léon (bar), Frère Bernard (bass), Frère Élie (ten). Messiaen's only opera, it is a vast work of great orchestral beauty and complexity (built around his notations of bird songs), which charts the progress of grace in St Francis's soul.
Plot: Early-13th-century Italy. The eight tableaux or 'Franciscan scenes' are:
1 Francis explains the necessity to endure suffering. **2** Francis asks God to make him capable of loving a leper. **3** Francis kisses the Leper, who is cured. **4** The Angel discusses predestination with the monks. **5** The Angel gives Francis a foretaste of heavenly bliss. **6** Francis preaches his sermon to the birds. **7** Francis receives the Stigmata. **8** Francis dies and enters a new life. [R]

Saint-Georges, Jules-Henri Vernoy de (1799–1875)
French librettist. One of the most prolific 19th-century French librettists, he wrote (in whole or in part) over 80 texts, the best being comedies. He provided libretti for Adam (*Falstaff*), Auber (*Les Diamants de la Couronne* and *Zanetta*), Bizet (*La Jolie Fille de Perth*), Donizetti (*La Fille du Régiment* and the unfinished *Ne M'Oubliez Pas*), Flotow (*Zilda* and *L'Ombre*), Halévy (*La Reine de Chypre* and *Noé*), Hérold (*Ludovic*), Monpou and Poniatowski amongst others.

Saint of Bleecker Street, The
Opera in three acts by Menotti. 1st perf New York, 27 Dec 1954; libr by the composer. Principal roles: Annina (sop), Michele (ten), Desideria (mezzo), Maria (sop). A VERISMO piece, it met with some success at its appearance but is nowadays seldom performed.
Plot: New York's 'Little Italy', mid-20th century. The religious mystic Annina receives the Stigmata on her palms, arousing great awe amongst her Catholic neighbours. Her brother Michele is devoted to her, although he is an agnostic,

but his mistress Desideria is violently antagonistic. Desideria is killed in a quarrel and Michele runs away. He later returns and is captured. [R]

Saint Petersburg
see KIROV OPERA

Saint-Saëns, Camille (1835–1921)
French composer. His 12 operas, written in a lyrical and conservative style, are notable for their fine craftsmanship and for their sometimes striking orchestration, but show little dramatic flair. His first opera *La Princesse Jaune* (Paris, 12 June 1872; libr Louis Gallet) was followed by *Le Timbre d'Argent* (Paris, 23 Feb 1877; libr Jules Barbier and Michel Carré), SAMSON ET DALILA, by far his most successful and enduring opera, *Étienne Marcel* (Lyon, 8 Feb 1879; libr Gallet), the once-popular HENRI VIII, *Proserpine* (Paris, 14 Mar 1887; libr Gallet, after Auguste Vacquerie), *Ascanio* (Paris, 21 Mar 1890; libr Gallet, after Paul Meurice's *Benvenuto Cellini*), *Phryné* (Paris, 24 May 1893; libr L. Augé de Lassus), *Les Barbares* (Paris, 23 Oct 1901; libr P.B. Gheusi and Victorien Sardou), *Hélène* (Monte Carlo, 18 Feb 1904; libr composer), *L'Ancêtre* (Monte Carlo, 24 Feb 1906; libr de Lassus) and *Déjanire* (Monte Carlo, 14 Mar 1911; libr composer and Gallet, after Sophocles's *Women of Thracis*). He also helped to complete Guiraud's unfinished *Frédégonde*.

Sakùntala
Opera in three acts by Alfano. 1st perf (as *La Leggenda di Sakùntala*) Bologna, 10 Dec 1921; libr by the composer, after Kalidasa's play. Revised version 1st perf Rome, 9 Jan 1952. Principal roles: Sakùntala (sop), King (ten), Priyamvada (mezzo), Anùsuya (sop), Kanva (bass). Sometimes regarded as Alfano's finest opera, it is nowadays only very rarely performed.
Plot: Legendary India. The young King visits a hermitage and falls in love with Sakùntala, the adopted daughter of the house's leader Kanva. After initial hesitation, she returns his love and receives a ring from him. An old priest unjustly curses Sakùntala, saying that the King will forget her. Discovering his error, the priest – although unable to retract his curse – modifies it by saying that it can be circumvented by showing the King the ring. Sakùntala loses the ring, and the King fails to recognize her. A fisherman finds the ring and it is brought to the King, whose memory returns. The heartbroken Sakùntala, however, has vanished in a cloud of fire. Her voice is heard announcing the birth of her son, and holy men arrive and present the child to the King.

Salammbô
Unfinished opera in four acts by Moussorgsky. 1st perf Milan, 10 Nov 1980 (composed 1863); libr by the composer, after Gustave Flaubert's novel. Principal roles: Salammbô (mezzo), Mathô (bass), Spendius (bar). Moussorgsky abandoned the work halfway through and incorporated much of the music into other works, including *Boris Godunov*. It was edited and prepared for performance by the conductor Zoltán Peskó. [R]

Salammbô
Opera in five acts by Reyer. 1st perf Brussels, 10 Feb 1890; libr by Camille du Locle, after Gustave Flaubert's novel. Principal roles: Salammbô (sop), Mathô (ten), Hamilcar (bar). Set in an austere and static style, it met with considerable success at its appearance but is nowadays virtually never performed.
Plot: Carthage, 240 BC. Mathô, leader of the forces besieging the city, loves the Carthaginian priestess Salammbô, daughter of Hamilcar. He steals a sacred veil from the temple of Tanit and is condemned to die at Salammbô's hands. She kills herself in his place, and Mathô stabs himself in grief.

Salgo già il trono aurato
Soprano cabaletta for Abigaille in Act II of Verdi's *Nabucco*, in which she vows to seize the throne. One of the most splendid pieces of invective in all opera.

Salieri, Antonio (1750–1825)
Italian composer. His first opera *Le Donne Letterate* (Vienna, 10 Jan 1770; libr Giovanni Gastone Boccherini) was followed by 34 others, many of which enjoyed great success in their day. His serious works are finely constructed and

have a certain grandeur, even if they are somewhat stiff and formal; his comedies show a lively sense of characterization. His most important operas include *La Fiera di Venezia* (Vienna, 29 Jan 1772; libr Boccherini), *L'Europa Riconosciuta* (Milan, 3 Aug 1778; libr Mattia Verazi), written for the opening of La Scala, the comedy *La Grota di Trofonio* (Vienna, 12 Oct 1785; libr Giovanni Battista Casti), PRIMA LA MUSICA E POI LE PAROLE, his best-known work which was first performed together with Mozart's *Der Schauspieldirektor*, LES DANAÏDES (once thought to have been written by Gluck, and written under the influence of Gluck's reforms), *Les Horaces* (Paris, 7 Dec 1786; libr Nicolas François Guillard, after Voltaire's *Horace*), the sensationally successful TARARE, *Catilina* (Darmstadt, 16 Apr 1994, composed 1792; libr Casti) and the Shakespearian FALSTAFF.

In the early 19th century, a rumour spread that Salieri had poisoned Mozart out of jealousy, and he appears in this guise as a character in Rimsky-Korsakov's *Mozart and Salieri*, which is a setting of Alexander Pushkin's play. He has long been acquitted of this charge. He was a noted theorist and a respected teacher, whose pupils included Beethoven, Hummel, Liszt and Schubert. Perhaps partly as a result of the success of the play and film of Peter Shaffer's *Amadeus*, there has recently been a considerable revival of interest in Salieri's music.

Salle de l'Opéra, Versailles
Designed by Ange-Jacques Gabriel for Louis XV, the beautiful theatre (cap 600) opened on 16 May 1770. After being the seat of the National Assembly in the 1870s, it fell into disuse until 1952. Since then, it has been used as a venue for special performances.

Sallinen, Aulis (b 1935)
Finnish composer. His five operas, written in serial style but incorporating both tonal and folk-music elements, show a powerful musico-dramatic imagination which ranks him as one of the finest contemporary opera composers. THE HORSEMAN and THE RED LINE have both proved highly successful and have been widely performed. THE KING GOES FORTH TO FRANCE was followed by KULLERVO, arguably his masterpiece, and *The Palace* (Savonlinna, 26 July 1995).

Salminen, Matti (b 1945)
Finnish bass, particularly associated with Wagner and Mozart roles. He possesses a dark, rich and powerful voice, used with fine musicianship, and has a strong stage presence which is aided by his powerful physique. He created, for Sallinen, Antti in *The Horseman* and Kalervo in *Kullervo*.

Salome
Opera in one act by Strauss (Op 54). 1st perf Dresden, 9 Dec 1906; a setting of Hedwig Lachmann's translation of Oscar Wilde's play. Principal roles: Salome (sop), Herod (ten), Jokanaan (bar), Herodias (mezzo), Narraboth (ten), Page (mezzo). A work of great orchestral power and brilliance, in which Strauss carried harmonic audacity to new lengths, the unashamedly erotic nature of the music caused it to be condemned as obscene, and many early performances were banned. If the work has nowadays lost its capacity to shock, it has lost none of its power to thrill.
Plot: Galilee, *c* AD 30. Salome, daughter of Herodias and stepdaughter of the tetrarch Herod, is fascinated by the prophetic voice of Jokanaan (John the Baptist), which she hears emerging from the cistern in which Herod has imprisoned him. She demands to see him and becomes infatuated physically. He repulses her, but she has become obssessed with him and is quite unmoved when Narraboth, the captain of the guard who is in love with her, kills himself. The lascivious Herod, who lusts after his stepdaughter, asks Salome to dance for him. She refuses until he promises to grant her anything she should ask. She performs the Dance of the Seven Veils and, as her reward, demands the head of Jokanaan, much to the delight of Herodias, against whose marriage Jokanaan has preached. Herod prevaricates but eventually has to agree. Jokanaan's severed head is brought to Salome on a platter and she exults over it, finally kissing the dead lips. Overcome with revulsion, Herod orders her to be crushed to death by the shields of his guards. [R]

Saltimbanques, Les (*The Acrobats*)
Operetta in three acts by Ganné. 1st perf Paris, 30 Dec 1899; libr by Maurice Ordonneau. Principal roles: Suzanne (sop), André (ten), Paillasse (bar), Marion (sop), Malicorne (bar), Grand-Pingouin (bass). By far Ganné's most successful operetta, it is still popular in France.
Plot: 18th-century Versailles and Normandy. Suzanne, adopted daughter of the circus owner Malicorne, rejects the advances of the juggler Paillasse and of the Strong Man Grand-Pingouin. She meets and is loved by the lieutenant André de Langeac, but feels unworthy of so noble a match. To escape the maltreatment of Malicorne, the troupe flees to Normandy. Performing before Comte des Etiquettes, Suzanne sings a song of her childhood. The Count recognizes the words as his own and Suzanne as his long-lost daughter. She is thus able to wed André. [R]

Salud
Soprano role in de Falla's *La Vida Breve*. She is in love with Paco.

Salut à la France
Soprano aria for Marie in Act II of Donizetti's *La Fille du Régiment*, in which she sings the praises of France.

Salut, demeure
Tenor aria for Faust in Act II of Gounod's *Faust*, in which he hails Marguerite's house.

Salzburg Easter Festival
Founded in 1967 as an adjunct to the main summer festival, it is devoted largely to Wagner. Artistic directors have included Herbert von Karajan and Sir Georg Solti.

Salzburg Festival
An annual summer festival in Austria, which was founded in 1921. Opera performances are given at the Grosses Festpielhaus (cap 2,177), which opened in 1960. One of the most prestigious (and expensive) European festivals, opera is given with top international casts and the repertory consists principally of Mozart, Strauss, Verdi and contemporary works. Artistic directors have included Lilli Lehmann and Herbert von Karajan.

Samson
Dramatic oratorio in three parts by Händel. 1st perf London, 18 Feb 1743; libr by Newburgh Hamilton, after John Milton's *Samson Agonistes*. Principal roles: Samson (ten), Dalila (sop), Micah (mezzo), Harapha (bass), Manoah (bass), Israelite Woman (sop). One of Händel's greatest oratorios, it is not strictly speaking an opera, but it is frequently staged. [R]

Samson et Dalila
Opera in three acts by Saint-Saëns. 1st perf Weimar, 2 Dec 1877; libr by Ferdinand Lemaire, after the Book of Judges in the Old Testament. Principal roles: Samson (ten), Dalila (mezzo), High Priest (bar), Old Hebrew (bass), Abimélech (bass). Saint-Saëns's operatic masterpiece, it is notable for its superb choruses, for its lavish spectacle and for the sensuous beauty of Dalila's music.
Plot: Gaza, *c* 1150 BC. Samson leads a successful Hebrew revolt against their Philistine overlords, in which the satrap Abimélech is killed. Prompted by the High Priest of Dagon, the Philistine seductress Dalila renders Samson powerless by cutting off his hair, from which his great strength is derived. Finally, Samson's strength is restored to him through prayer, and he pulls down the temple of Dagon, killing his enemies and himself. [R]

Sanderson, Sibyl (1865–1903)
American soprano, particularly associated with the French repertory. Famed for her personal beauty and for her acting ability as much as for her wide-ranging voice, she created the title-roles in Massenet's *Esclarmonde* and *Thaïs* and Saint-Saëns's *Phryné*.

San Diego Opera Guild
Founded in 1964, the company performs at the Civic Auditorium (cap 2,992). The annual season runs from January to April, and the repertory has mixed standard works with a number of US premieres. Musical directors have included Walter Herbert.

San Francisco Opera Association
Founded in 1923, the company performs at the War Memorial Opera House (cap 3,176), which opened on 15 Oct 1932.

The annual season runs from September to December, and the repertory consists largely of standard Italian and German operas given with top international casts. Musical directors have included Gaetano Merola, Kurt Herbert Adler, Sir John Pritchard and Donald Runnicles.

Santa Fe Opera
Founded in 1956 by John Crosby, the company gives an annual summer season, notable for its highly adventurous repertory. The original outdoor theatre burnt down in 1967; the present modernistic replacement (cap 1,773) opened the following year.

Santi, Nello (b 1931)
Italian conductor, particularly associated with the Italian repertory. Considered a good 'singer's conductor', his performances can occasionally seem a little sluggish, but sometimes (such as his recording of *L'Amore dei Tre Re*), they can be thrilling.

Santiago
see TEATRO MUNICIPAL, SANTIAGO

Santini, Gabriele (1886–1964)
Italian conductor, particularly associated with the Italian repertory. A rock-solid Italian maestro of the old school, especially fine in Verdi, he was musical director of the Rome Opera (1945–7). He conducted the first performances of Giordano's *Il Rè*, Lattuada's *Le Preziose Ridicole* and Alfano's *Dottor Antonio*.

Santley, Sir Charles (1834–1922)
British baritone. The finest British baritone of the 19th century, his voice – whilst not intrinsically beautiful – was used with expressiveness and fine musicianship, and he was an effective dramatic performer. He sang the Dutchman (in *Der Fliegende Holländer*) in the first ever performance in Britain of a Wagner opera and created Danny Man in Benedict's *The Lily of Killarney*, the Rhine King in Wallace's *Lurline*, a role in MacFarren's *Robin Hood*, Claude Melnotte in Cowen's *Pauline* and, for Balfe, Clifford in *The Puritan's Daughter* and Fabio in *The Armourer of Nantes*. His writings include three books on singing and his autobiography, *Reminiscences of My Life*, which was published in 1909.

Santuzza
Soprano role in Mascagni's *Cavalleria Rusticana*. She is the girl seduced and abandoned by Turiddù. The role is often sung by a mezzo.

Sanzogno, Nino (1911–83)
Italian conductor, particularly associated with 20th-century operas and with 18th-century Italian works. Based largely at La Scala, Milan, he conducted the first performances of *Dialogues des Carmélites*, Milhaud's *David*, Malipiero's *L'Allegra Brigata*, Turchi's *Il Buon Soldato Svejk*, Petrassi's *Il Cordovano*, Tosatti's *Partita a Pugni* and Chailly's *Una Domanda di Matrimonio*.

Sapho
Opera in four (originally three) acts by Gounod. 1st perf Paris, 16 April 1851; libr by Émile Augier. Revised version 1st perf Paris, 2 April 1884. Principal roles: Sapho (mezzo), Phaon (ten), Glycère (sop), Pythéas (bar). Dealing with the historical Greek poetess, it contains some of Gounod's finest music but is only infrequently performed.
Plot: Lesbos, 6th century BC. Phaon, the lover of Glycère, falls in love with the poetess Sapho, who returns his love. Phaon conspires to overthrow the oppressive rule of the tyrant Pythéas. The jealous Glycère threatens to expose the plot if Sapho does not leave Phaon. Sapho agrees and Phaon returns to Glycère, who poisons his mind against Sapho. Heartbroken, Sapho throws herself into the sea from a clifftop. [R]

Sapho
Opera in five acts by Massenet. 1st perf Paris, 27 Nov 1897; libr by Henri Cain and Arthur Bernède, after Alphonse Daudet's novel. Principal roles: Fanny (sop), Jean (ten), Caoudal (bar). One of Massenet's most erotically-scented operas, it is only very rarely performed.
Plot: 19th-century France. At a fancy-dress party given by the sculptor Caoudal, the young Provençal Jean Gaussin meets the beautiful artists' model Fanny Legrand (known as Sapho), and the two fall in love. Rejecting the quiet life that he might have enjoyed with his family, Jean lives for a year with Fanny. From Caoudal and his

circle Jean learns that Fanny is not the angel of purity he believed her to be. The lovers part after a violent quarrel, and Jean returns to Provence. Fanny goes to him and nearly overcomes his coldness, but Jean's parents send her away. Realizing that he cannot live without her, Jean returns to her in Paris, but she knows that something between them has been lost. As Jean sleeps, she tiptoes out and leaves him for ever. [R]

Sara
Mezzo role in Donizetti's *Roberto Devereux*. The Duke of Nottingham's wife, she is in love with Robert.

Sarastro
Bass role in Mozart's *Die Zauberflöte*. He is the priest of Isis.

Sardou, Victorien
see panel below

Sargent, Sir Malcolm (1895–1967)
British conductor, particularly associated with the British repertory, especially Sullivan. He conducted much opera in the early part of his career (including the first performances of Walton's *Troilus and Cressida*, Holst's *At the Boar's Head* and Vaughan Williams's *Sir John in Love*, *Hugh the Drover* and *Riders to the Sea*), but later devoted himself largely to the concert hall. A great showman who always wore a carnation in his buttonhole – he was nicknamed 'Flash Harry' – he did invaluable work in making music more readily accessible to ordinary people.

Šárka
Opera in three acts by Janáček. 1st perf Brno, 11 Nov 1925 (composed 1887 and revised 1888 and 1918); libr by Julius Zeyer, after his own play. Principal roles: Šárka (sop), Ċtirad (ten), Přemysl (bass), Lumír (ten). Janácek's first opera, only very rarely performed, it is written in Czech romantic style but gives some indication of his future development.
Plot: Legendary Bohemia. When his wife Queen Libuše has died, Přemysl resolves

· *Victorien Sardou* ·

The French playwright Victorien Sardou (1831–1908) himself wrote a number of operatic libretti, including Offenbach's *Le Roi Carotte* and *Fantasio*, Saint-Saëns's *Les Barbares* and Bizet's unfinished *Grisélidis*. Some 25 operas have been based on his works. Below are listed, by play, those operas by composers with entries in this dictionary.

Fédora		
Giordano	*Fedora*	1898
Gismonda		
Février	*Gismonda*	1919
Madame Sans-Gêne		
Giordano	*Madame Sans-Gêne*	1915
Les Noces de Fernande		
Millöcker	*Der Bettelstudent*	1882
Patrie!		
Rossi	*La Contessa di Mons*	1874
Piccolino		
J. Strauss	*Der Karneval in Rom*	1873
Guiraud	*Piccolino*	1876
Les Prés St-Gervais		
Lecocq	*Les Prés St-Gervais*	1874
La Tosca		
Puccini	*Tosca*	1900

to disband her council of women. Under the leadership of Šárka, the women revolt. Šárka falls in love with the warrior-hero Ctirad, but nonetheless causes his death. She throws herself on to his funeral pyre. [R]

Šárka
Opera in three acts by Fibich (Op 51). 1st perf Prague, 28 Dec 1897; libr by Anežka Schulzová, after Jaroslav Vrchlický's play. Principal roles: Šárka (sop), Ctirad (ten), Přemysl (bar), Vlasta (mezzo). Fibich's finest and most successful opera, it is still regularly performed in the Czech lands but is little known elsewhere.
Plot: Legendary Bohemia. At the court of Přemysl, the women have lost their influence following the death of his wife Queen Libuše. Šárka challenges Ctirad, the leading opponent of the women, to a duel, which he contemptuously refuses. In the fighting which follows, Šárka tricks Ctirad into 'rescuing' her when he discovers her tied to a tree. However, instead of calling her troops, Šárka falls in love with him and warns him of the ambush. Ctirad, returning Šárka's love, refuses to escape and summons the women's troops himself. The women take him away injured, but Šárka tells Přemysl where he is being held and the men rescue him. The women are killed and Šárka leaps to her death. [R]

Sarti, Giuseppe (1729–1802)
Italian composer. He wrote some 75 operas, mostly for Denmark, Russia and Italy, some of which enjoyed great success in their day but which are all now forgotten. They include *Fra Due Litiganti* (Milan, 14 Sept 1782; libr after Carlo Goldoni's *Le Nozze*), containing an aria which Mozart quotes from in the Supper Scene of *Don Giovanni*, and *The First Government of Oleg* (St Petersburg, 26 Oct 1790; libr Catherine the Great), written in collaboration with Pashkevich, which is one of the earliest Russian operas.

Sass, Marie (b Sax) (1834–1907)
Belgian soprano, particularly associated with the Italian and French repertories. One of the leading sopranos of the mid-19th century, she possessed a strong and flexible FALCON voice and was noted for her temperamental behaviour. She created Élisabeth in *Don Carlos*, Sélika in *L'Africaine* and Elisabeth in the revised version of *Tannhäuser*. Her husband **Armand Castelmary** (1834–97) was a successful bass, who created Don Diego in *L'Africaine*, the Monk in *Don Carlos* and Horatio in Thomas's *Hamlet*.

Sass, Sylvia (b 1951)
Hungarian soprano, particularly associated with the Italian repertory, especially Verdi. Her exceptional vocal and dramatic talent prompted some to hail her as a second Maria Callas. However, partly as a result of taking on too much too young, her voice deteriorated sadly for a while, and it is only recently that she has once more been singing as she always should have. She created the Mother in Durko's *Moses*.

Satie, Érik (b Alfred Éric Leslie) (1866–1925)
French composer. Best known for his witty piano music, he also wrote a number of stage works, including the MARIONETTE OPERA *Geneviève de Brabant* (Paris, 17 May 1926, composed 1899; libr J.P. Contamine de Latour) [R], the operetta *Pousse l'Amour* (Paris, 22 Nov 1907), which is lost, *Le Piège de Méduse* (Paris, 1913; libr composer) [R] and the 'symphonic drama' *Socrate* (Paris, 14 Feb 1920; libr after Plato) [R].

Sauget, Henri (b Jean Pierre Poupard) (1901–89)
French composer, writing mainly in the smart, slick, metropolitan style influenced by the music of the group LES SIX. His seven operas are *Le Plumet de Colonel* (Paris, 27 Feb 1924; libr composer), *La Contrebasse* (Paris, 1930; libr Henri Troyat, after Anton Chekhov's *Romance With a Double Bass*), *La Voyante* (1932), which is a monodrama for soprano, *La Chartreuse de Parme* (Paris, 16 Mar 1939; libr Armand Lunel, after Stendahl), by far his most substantial work, *La Gageure Imprévue* (Paris, 4 July 1944; libr P. Bertin, after Jean-Marie Sedaine), *Les Caprices de Marianne* (Aix-en-Provence, 1954; libr J.P. Grédy, after Alfred de Musset) and *Le Pain des Autres* (1974; libr E. Kinds, after Ivan Turgenev's *The Bread of Others*). He also wrote the children's opera *Tistou les Pouces Verts* (Paris, 1980; libr Jean-Luc Tardieu, after Maurice Druon) [R].

Saul
Oratorio in three parts by Händel. 1st perf London, 16 Jan 1739; libr by Charles Jennens, after A. Cowley's *Davideis* and the Book of Samuel in the Old Testament. Principal roles: Saul (bass), David (c-ten), Jonathan (ten), Merab (sop), Michal (sop), Abner (bass). One of the greatest of all Händel's oratorios, it is not strictly speaking an opera but it is quite often staged. [R]

Saul og David
Opera in four acts by Nielsen (Op 25). 1st perf Copenhagen, 28 Nov 1902; libr by Einar Christiansen, after the Book of Samuel in the Old Testament. Principal roles: Saul (bass), David (ten), Mikal (sop), Jonathan (ten), Samuel (bass), Abner (bass), Witch of Endor (mezzo). One of the greatest works of Scandinavian music, it is notable for its magnificent choruses, for its vividly contrasting vocal writing and for its compelling dramatic sweep, which presents Saul as a tragic figure of considerable complexity. The opera's failure to have entered the international repertory is utterly explicable.
Plot: Israel, *c* 1000 BC. The elements of the biblical story covered in the opera are the summoning of the ghost of Samuel by the Witch of Endor, David's love for Saul's daughter Mikal, Jonathan's return with news of the victory over the Philistines, Saul's jealousy of David, and David's accession to the throne following the death of Saul. [R]

Sāvitri
Opera in one act by Holst (Op 25). 1st perf London, 5 Dec 1916; libr by the composer, after the *Mahabharata*. Principal roles: Sāvitri (mezzo), Satyavan (ten), Death (bar). Perhaps the finest British opera since Purcell's *Dido and Aeneas*, it is a highly stylized work drawn from Hindu mythology, whose refined and beautiful music is achieved with a remarkable economy of means.
Plot: Legendary India. Sāvitri hears the voice of Death. It has come for her husband Satyavan, who is approaching. Sāvitri promises Death anything which it demands except for Satyavan's life. Satyavan dies, although he has told Sāvitri that he is under the spell of Maya (illusion). So great is Sāvitri's love that Satyavan is restored to life. [R]

Savonlinna Festival
Originally founded in 1912, this annual summer festival in Finland – held in July in the courtyard of the medieval Olavinlinna Castle (cap 2,262) – was established on a regular basis in 1967. Its wide-ranging repertory has included notable productions of modern Finnish operas, and its very high artistic standards have established it as one of Europe's major summer festivals; a visiting critic was recently prompted to observe that 'opera is alive and well and living in Finland'. Artistic directors have included Martti Talvela, Walton Grönroos and Jorma Hynninen.

Savoy Operas
A collective title often given to the 14 Gilbert and Sullivan operettas, all but the first six of which were first performed at London's Savoy Theatre (cap 1,122) built by Richard D'Oyly Carte in 1881 and rebuilt in 1930. It was for long the London base of the D'Oyly Carte Opera Company.

Sawallisch, Wolfgang (b 1923)
German conductor and pianist, particularly associated with the German repertory, especially Strauss. One of the leading contemporary interpreters of 19th- and 20th-century German opera, he was musical director of the Aachen Opera (1953–8), the Wiesbaden Opera (1958–60), the Cologne Opera (1960–63) and the Bavarian State Opera (1971–92). He conducted the first performance of Einem's *Der Zerrissene*. His autobiography, *Im Interesse der Deutlichkeit*, was published in 1988.

Saxton, Robert (b 1953)
British composer. He has written one opera, *Caritas* (Huddersfield, 21 Nov 1991; libr Arnold Wesker, after his play) [R].

Sayão, Bidú (b Balduina de Oliveira) (b 1902)
Brazilian soprano, particularly associated with lighter French and Italian roles. She had a light, silvery and flexible voice used

with taste and style. As an actress, she was both a skilled comedienne and affectingly pathetic in tragic roles. Her second husband **Giuseppe Danise** (1883–1963) was a successful baritone.

Scala, La
see PICCOLA SCALA, LA; TEATRO ALLA SCALA, MILAN

Scala di Seta, La (*The Silken Ladder*)
Comic opera in one act by Rossini. 1st perf Venice, 9 May 1812; libr by Giuseppe Maria Foppa, after François-Antoine-Eugène de Planard's libretto for Gaveaux's *L'Échelle de Soie*. Principal roles: Giulia (sop), Dorvil (ten), Dormont (bass), Blansac (bar), Lucilla (mezzo), Germano (bass). One of Rossini's early farces, it is still quite often performed and its delightful overture is popular in the concert hall.
Plot: 18th-century France. Dorvil, secretly married to Giulia, climbs a silken ladder every night to reach her bedroom. She devises various schemes to keep her marriage a secret from her guardian Dormont, who is arranging a marriage for her, and to ward off the attentions of the servant Germano and of Dorvil's friend Blansac. When the secret marriage is revealed, all is satisfactorily resolved. [R]

Scaramuccio
Tenor role in Strauss's *Ariadne auf Naxos*. He is a member of the COMMEDIA DELL'ARTE troupe.

Scarlatti, Alessandro (1660–1725)
Italian composer, father of the composer DOMENICO SCARLATTI. One of the most important figures in the history of opera, he wrote 115 stage works, of which some 70 have survived. Regarded as the founder of classical opera, he gave to OPERA SERIA its established format: the so-called 'Italian' overture, the DA CAPO aria, the use of recitativo secco and also of accompanied recitative (which he used to powerful dramatic effect). The first great master of the Neapolitan school, his operas are nowadays only rarely revived and he is more widely regarded by musicologists than by opera-goers. His most important operas include *Il Pompeo* (Rome, 25 Jan 1683; libr Nicolò Minato), *Gli Equivoci in Amore* (Rome, Dec 1690; libr Giovanni Battista Lucini), *Il Mitridate Eupatore* (Venice, 5 Jan 1707; libr Girolamo Frigimelica Roberti, after Jean Baptiste Racine's *Mithridate*), often regarded as his masterpiece, IL TRIONFO DELL'ONORE, his one wholly comic opera, and LA GRISELDA.

Scarlatti, Domenico (1685–1757)
Italian composer, son of the composer ALESSANDRO SCARLATTI. Although best known as a keyboard composer, he also wrote seven operas, of which the most important are TETIDE IN SCIRO and *Ambleto* (Rome, 1715; libr Apostolo Zeno and Pietro Pariati) with its intermezzo *La Dirindina* (libr Girolamo Gigli). His nephew **Giuseppe** (*c* 1720–77) was also a composer, who wrote some 30 operas.

Scarpia, Baron Vitellio
Baritone role in Puccini's *Tosca*. He is the sadistic chief of police.

Scena (Italian for 'scene')
It is derived from the Greek σκηυη, meaning 'stage'. The term has two applications to opera: **1** A musical piece of predominantly dramatic purpose, usually for a solo singer, which is less formally constructed and less lyrical than an aria. A famous example is Leonore's 'Abscheulicher!' in Beethoven's *Fidelio*. **2** A part of an operatic act in which the scenery and/or the number of characters on the stage remains the same.

Scenario (Italian for 'scenery')
An outline libretto, giving indications of the plot, the characters and the number and type of scenes. The German term *Scenarium* refers to a complete libretto, including detailed indications of staging.

Schalk, Franz (1863–1931)
Austrian conductor, particularly associated with the German repertory, especially Wagner. A co-founder of the Salzburg Festival, he was musical director of the Vienna State Opera (1924–9). He conducted the first performances of *Die Frau ohne Schatten*, the revised *Ariadne auf Naxos* and Schmidt's *Notre-Dame*.

Schatzgräber, Der (*The Treasure Seeker*)
Opera in prologue, four acts and epilogue by Schreker. 1st perf Frankfurt, 21 Jan 1920; libr by the composer. Principal roles: Elis (ten), Els (sop), King (bass), Fool (ten), Bailiff (bar), Albi (ten). Schreker's only opera other than *Der Ferne Klang* still to be in any way remembered, it was highly successful in its time, being given in nearly 50 cities within a decade, but it is nowadays hardly ever performed. [R]

Schaunard
Baritone role in Puccini's and Leoncavallo's *La Bohème*. He is the musician of the four bohemians.

Schauspieldirektor, Der (*The Impresario*)
Comic opera in one act by Mozart (K 486). 1st perf Vienna, 7 Feb 1786; libr by Gottlieb Stephanie. Principal roles: Silberklang (sop), Herz (sop), Vogelsang (ten), Bu (bass). First given on the same evening as Salieri's *Prima la Musica e Poi le Parole*, it is often given with an altered libretto, sometimes making Mozart himself the impresario.
Plot: Late-18th-century Vienna. The put-upon impresario Bu has to cope with the rivalry between two prima donnas, Mesdames Silberklang and Herz. Each offers an example of their vocal accomplishments and quarrel over which of them should be paid more, until finally they attempt to out-sing each other in a trio with the tenor Vogelsang. [R]

Schenk, Johann Baptist (1753–1836)
Austrian composer. He wrote a large number of SINGSPIELS, all of them now forgotten. Much the most successful was *Der Dorfbarbier* (*The Village Barber*, Vienna, 30 Oct 1796; libr Josef and Paul Weidmann, after Jean-Marie Sedaine's *Blaise le Savetier*), which enjoyed wide popularity for quarter of a century.

Scherasmin
Baritone role in Weber's *Oberon*. He is Sir Huon's esquire.

Scherchen, Hermann (1891–1966)
German conductor, particularly associated with 20th-century operas. A tireless champion of contemporary composers, he conducted the first performances of Dallapiccola's *Il Prigioniero*, Hába's *The Mother*, Henze's *König Hirsch*, Dessau's *Die Verurteilung des Lukullus*, Milhaud's *Fiesta* and Searle's *The Diary of a Madman*.

Schigolch
Baritone role in Berg's *Lulu*. He is an asthmatic old swindler who might be Lulu's father.

Schikaneder, Emanuel (b Johann) (1751–1812)
Austrian actor, playwright, impresario and librettist. As manager of the Theater an der Weiden in Vienna, he presented seasons of ZAUBEROPER, and commissioned *Die Zauberflöte* from Mozart, writing the libretto and creating Papageno. In 1800, he opened the Theater an der Wien, which he managed until 1806. He also provided libretti for Beethoven (the sketched-only *Vestas Feuer*), Paisiello, Seyfried, Süssmayr (*Der Spiegel von Arkadien*) and Winter (*Das Labyrinth*, a follow-up to *Die Zauberflöte*).

Schiller, Friedrich von
see panel on page 499

Schillings, Max von (1868–1933)
German composer and conductor. He wrote four operas. *Ingwelde* (Karlsruhe, 13 Nov 1894; libr Ferdinand von Sporck, after *Svarfdälasaga*), *Der Pfeifertag* (Schwerin, 26 Nov 1899; libr Sporck; revised version Berlin, 26 Sept 1931) and *Moloch* (Dresden, 8 Dec 1906; libr Emil Gerhäuser, after Christian Friedrich Hebbel) were written under the influence of Wagner, but MONA LISA, by far his most successful opera, is an essay in VERISMO. He was musical director of the Stuttgart Opera (1911–18), where he conducted the first performance of Zemlinsky's *Eine Florentinische Tragödie*, and administrator of the Berlin State Opera (1919–25). His wife **Barbara Kemp** (1881–1951) was a successful Wagnerian soprano, who created the title-role in *Mona Lisa*.

Schipa, Tito (b Raffaele Attilio Amadeo) (1889–1965)
Italian tenor and composer, particularly associated with lighter Italian and French

· Friedrich von Schiller ·

The works of the German poet and playwright Friedrich von Schiller (1759–1805) have inspired some 60 operas. Below are listed, by play, those operas by composers with entries in this dictionary.

Die Braut von Messina		
Vaccai	*La Sposa di Messina*	1839
Fibich	*The Bride of Messina*	1884
Die Bürgschaft		
Schubert	*Die Bürgschaft*	1816 (U)
Lachner	*Die Bürgschaft*	1828
Demetrius		
Dvořák	*Dimitrij*	1882/94
Don Carlos		
Costa	*Don Carlo*	1844
Verdi	*Don Carlos*	1866/84
Der Gang nach dem Eisenhammer		
K. Kreutzer	*Fridolin*	1837
Die Jungfrau von Orleans		
Carafa	*Jeanne d'Arc à Orléans*	1821
Vaccai	*Giovanna d'Arco*	1827
Pacini	*Giovanna d'Arco*	1830
Balfe	*Joan of Arc*	1837
Verdi	*Giovanna d'Arco*	1845
Tchaikovsky	*The Maid of Orleans*	1881
Rezniček	*Die Jungfrau von Orleans*	1887
Klebe	*Das Mädchen von Domrémy*	1976
Kabale und Liebe		
Verdi	*Luisa Miller*	1849
Einem	*Kabale und Liebe*	1976
Das Lied von der Glocke		
d'Indy	*Le Chant de la Cloche*	1912
Maria Stuart		
Mercadante	*Maria Stuarda*	1821
Coccia	*Maria Stuarda*	1827
Donizetti	*Maria Stuarda*	1834
Die Räuber		
Mercadante	*I Briganti*	1836
Verdi	*I Masnadieri*	1847
Zajc	*Amelia*	1860
Klebe	*Die Räuber*	1957
Die Verschwörung des Fiesco zu Genua		
Lalo	*Fiesque*	1866
Wallenstein		
Verdi	*La Forza del Destino* (one scene only)	1865
Denza	*Wallenstein*	1876
Weinberger	*Wallenstein*	1937
Zafred	*Wallenstein*	1965
Wilhelm Tell		
Rossini	*Guillaume Tell*	1829

roles. One of the finest lyric tenors of the inter-war period, he had a small but elegant and beautiful voice used with a matchless technique, aristocratic phrasing and impeccable diction. His contemporary, Beniamino Gigli, said of him, 'When Schipa sang we all had to bow down to his greatness.' He created Ruggero in Puccini's *La Rondine* and also composed an operetta, *La Principessa Liana* (Rome, 2 June 1929; libr A. Santoro and E. Neri). His autobiography, *Si Confessa*, was published in 1961.

Schippers, Thomas (1930–77)
American conductor, whose tragically early death from cancer cut short a brilliant career. He was particularly associated with the German and Italian repertories, especially Verdi, for whom his vigorous and dynamic style was well suited. Also a champion of modern composers (especially American), he conducted the first performances of Copland's *The Tender Land*, de Falla's *L'Atlántida*, Barber's *Antony and Cleopatra* and Menotti's *The Saint of Bleecker Street, The Unicorn, the Gorgon and the Manticore* and *Amahl and the Night Visitors*.

Schlusnus, Heinrich (1888–1952)
German baritone, particularly associated with Verdi and Wagner roles. One of the finest German baritones of the inter-war period, he played an important part in the Verdi revival which began in Germany at that time.

Schmidt, Franz (1874–1939)
Austrian composer, writing in late-romantic style. The more important of his two operas is NOTRE-DAME. Its successor *Fredegundis* (Berlin, 29 Dec 1922; libr Bruno Wradatsch and Ignaz Welleminsky, after F. Dahn) was a failure.

Schmidt-Isserstedt, Hans (1900–73)
German conductor and composer. An outstanding Mozart interpreter, he was musical director of the Deutsche Oper, Berlin (1942–5). He also composed one opera, *Hassan Gewinnt* (Rostock, 1928). His son **Erik Smith** is a recording producer who has been responsible for a number of notable opera recordings for Philips.

Schneider, Hortense (1833–1920)
French soprano, particularly associated with Offenbach roles. The greatest operetta star of the 19th century, she combined a good voice with outstanding acting ability and an inimitable sense of comedy. For Offenbach, she created Boulotte in *Barbe-Bleue* and the title-roles in *La Périchole*, *La Belle Hélène* and *La Grande-Duchesse de Gérolstein*. Her bewitching performance in the last was the talk of Europe and made her sought after by many of its crowned heads. On arriving at the Paris International Exhibition at the entrance reserved for royalty, she announced, 'I am the Grand-Duchess of Gerolstein', and was immediately admitted!

Schnittke, Alfred (b 1934)
Russian composer. The leading contemporary Russian avant-garde composer, he has written three operas: LIFE WITH AN IDIOT, *Faust* (Hamburg, May 1995) and *Gesualdo* (Vienna, 26 May 1995).

Schock, Rudolf (1915–86)
German tenor, particularly associated with the German and Italian repertories, and also a highly successful exponent of operetta. The leading German lyric tenor of the immediate post-war period, he had a warm and smoothly-produced voice of sufficient power to enable him to sing some heavier roles such as Walther von Stolzing. He created Ercole in Liebermann's *Penelope*.

Schoeck, Othmar (1886–1957)
Swiss composer. His stage works include the comedy *Don Ranudo de Colibrados* (Zürich, 16 Apr 1919; libr Armin Rüger, after Ludvig af Holberg), *Venus* (Zürich, 10 May 1922; libr Rüger, after Prosper Mérimée's *La Vénus de l'Ille*) [R], PENTHESILEA, arguably his finest opera, VOM FISHCER UN SYNER FRU, the comedy MASSIMILLA DONI and *Das Schloss Dürande* (Berlin, 1 Apr 1943; libr H. Burte, after Joseph von Eichendorff). For long his works made little headway outside Switzerland, but recently there has been some increase of interest in his music.

Schöffler, Paul (1897–1977)
German baritone, particularly associated with Wagner and Strauss roles. Beginning

as a lyric baritone, he later successfully undertook heavier roles, notably Hans Sachs. A fine singing-actor, he created Jupiter in Strauss's *Die Liebe der Danae*, the Green One in Hauer's *Die Schwarze Spinne* and the title-role in Einem's *Dantons Tod*. He enjoyed a remarkably long career, singing well into his 70s.

Schön, Dr
Baritone role in Berg's *Lulu*. A newspaper editor, he is Alwa's father and Lulu's admirer.

Schönberg, Arnold (1874–1951)
Austrian composer, writer and painter. One of the most influential figures in 20th-century music, he began composing in late-romantic style, but then abandoned tonality and subsequently developed the TWELVE-TONE or serial system of composition. His four remarkable stage works are the atonal monodrama ERWARTUNG, the expressionistic DIE GLÜCKLICHE HAND, the comedy VON HEUTE AUF MORGEN, which was the first twelve-tone opera, and his unfinished masterpiece MOSES UND ARON. He was also a distinguished teacher, whose pupils included Berg, Blitzstein, Gerhard, Ullmann and Webern. He was the brother-in-law of Zemlinsky and the father-in-law of Nono.

Schöne Galatea, Die (*Beautiful Galatea*)
Operetta in one act by Suppé. 1st perf Berlin, 30 June 1865; libr by Leopold K. Dittmar Kohl von Kohlenegg. Principal roles: Galatea (sop), Pygmalion (ten), Gannymede (bass), Mydas (bar). One of Suppé's most successful works, it is still regularly performed in German-speaking countries.
Plot: Legendary Cyprus. The sculptor Pygmalion refuses to sell his statue Galatea to the pompous art dealer Mydas. In response to his prayers, the statue is brought to life. Galatea flirts with Pygmalion's lazy servant Gannymede, accepts a huge jewel from Mydas, and drinks too much. A distraught Pygmalion once again prays to the gods, and Galatea is returned to her petrified state. Pygmalion is now only too happy to sell her to Mydas. [R]

School for Fathers, The
see QUATRO RUSTEGHI, I

Schorr, Friedrich (1888–1953)
Hungarian bass-baritone, particularly associated with Wagnerian roles, especially Wotan and Hans Sachs. Regarded as the outstanding HELDENBARITON of the inter-war period, he had a warm and noble voice of considerable power, capable of great beauty in quiet passages, and his diction was exemplary.

Schreier, Peter (b 1935)
German tenor, particularly associated with Mozart and lyrical German roles. One of the most stylish Mozartians of the post-war era, his beautiful voice is used with innate style and outstanding musicianship. An accomplished singing-actor (and a renowned lieder singer), he created the Physicist in Dessau's *Einstein* and a role in Orff's *De Temporum Fine Comoedia*. Since 1970, he has also enjoyed considerable success as a conductor.

Schreker, Franz (1878–1934)
Austrian composer. He wrote eight operas (for all but the first of which he wrote his own libretti), first in late-romantic, then in avant-garde and lastly in neo-classical style. His first opera *Flammen* (Vienna, 24 April 1902; libr Dora Leen) [R] was followed by DER FERNE KLANG, his best-known opera, *Das Spielwerk und die Prinzessin* (Frankfurt, 5 Mar 1913), DIE GEZEICHNETEN, the once-popular DER SCHATZGRÄBER, *Irrelohe* (Cologne, 27 Mar 1924), *Christophorus* (Frieburg, 1 Oct 1978, composed 1927), *Der Singende Teufel* (Berlin, 10 Dec 1928) and *Der Schmied von Gent* (Berlin, 29 Oct 1932; libr after Charles de Coster's *Smetse Smee*). His wife **Maria Binder** was a soprano.

Schröder-Devrient, Wilhelmine (1804–60)
German soprano. She was the first great singing-actress in the modern sense. The outstanding dramatic soprano of her day, especially renowned as Leonore in *Fidelio*, her actual vocal technique was deficient, but the power of her acting overcame this problem, and her abilities opened up new musico-dramatic possibilities to composers. She was highly regarded by contemporary composers such as Weber and, particularly, Wagner. She created Adriano in *Rienzi*, Senta in *Der Fliegende*

Holländer, Venus in *Tannhäuser* and the title-role in Spohr's *Jessonda*. Wagner's *Über Schauspieler und Sänger* includes a detailed tribute to her and is dedicated to her memory. Her father **Friedrich Schröder** (1744–1816) was a successful bass.

Schubert, Franz (1797–1828)
Austrian composer. One of the greatest vocal composers in history, he was also one of history's most ill-fated opera composers. Only three of his 14 operas were performed in his lifetime, and many are seriously weakened by poor libretti. Their structural and dramatic weaknesses have sadly ensured that they are only very rarely performed, despite the magnificent music which many of them contain. His stage works are the unfinished *Der Spiegelritter* (Swiss Radio, 11 Dec 1949, composed 1812; libr August von Kotzebue) [R], DES TEUFELS LUSTSCHLOSS, DER VIERJÄHRIGE POSTEN, FERNANDO, CLAUDINE VON VILLA BELLA, of which two acts are lost, DIE FREUNDE VON SALAMANKA, the unfinished *Die Bürgschaft* (Vienna, 7 Mar 1908, composed 1816; libr after Friedrich von Schiller), DIE ZWILLINGSBRÜDER, the melodrama DIE ZAUBERHARFE, the unfinished *Sacontala* (Vienna, 12 June 1971, composed 1820; libr Johann Philip Neumann, after Kalidasa), the musically superb ALFONSO UND ESTRELLA, perhaps his finest opera, FIERRABRAS, his structurally most advanced stage work, the Aristophanic DIE VERSCHWORENEN (or *Der Häusliche Krieg*) and the unfinished *Der Graf von Gleichen* (Cincinnati, 11 Mar 1994, composed 1827; libr Eduard von Bauernfeld). The virtual oblivion into which Schubert's operas have fallen is one of the scandals of contemporary music.

Schuch, Ernst von (1846–1914)
Austrian conductor, particularly associated with the German repertory, especially Wagner. One of the greatest conductors of the late 19th century, he was musical director of the Dresden Opera (1882–1914). He conducted the first performances of 51 operas, including *Feuersnot*, *Salome*, *Elektra*, *Der Rosenkavalier*, Paderewski's *Manru*, Wolf-Ferrari's *L'Amore Medico*, Smareglia's *Cornil Schut*, Schillings's *Moloch* and Dohnányi's *Tante Simona*. His wife **Klementine Schuch-Proska** (*b* Clementine Procházka) (1850–1932) was a successful COLORATURA soprano; their daughter **Liesel** (1891–1990) was also a coloratura soprano.

Schuldigkeit des Ersten Gebotes, Die
(*The Obligation of the First Commandment*)
Sacred SINGSPIEL in one act by Mozart (K 35). 1st perf Salzburg, 12 March 1767; libr by Jacobus Antonius Wimmer. Principal roles: Worldliness (sop), Justice (sop), Mercy (sop), Christian Spirit (ten), Christian (ten). Mozart's first stage work, written at the age of 11, it forms the first part of a sacred trilogy. The other sections (by Michael Haydn and a local organist Anton Cajetan Adelgasser) are lost. A work of astonishing fluency, it still receives an occasional performance. [R]

Schuller, Gunther (b 1925)
American composer and conductor (originally a horn player). He has written two operas which have met with some success in the United States: *The Visitation* (Hamburg, 12 Oct 1966; libr composer, after Franz Kafka's *The Trial*) and the children's opera *The Fisherman and his Wife* (Boston, 8 May 1970; libr John Updike, after the brothers Grimm). An advocate of 'third stream' music, his works fuse traditional and jazz styles. He also orchestrated Joplin's *Treemonisha*.

Schuman, William (1910–92)
American composer. Although best known as a symphonic composer, he also wrote one opera, *The Mighty Casey* (Hartford, 4 May 1953; libr Jerome Gury, after Ernest L. Thayer's *Casey At the Bat*)[R], which is about baseball.

Schumann, Elisabeth (1885–1952)
German soprano, particularly associated with Mozart and Strauss roles, especially Sophie. She had a light and silvery voice of great beauty, used with superlative musicianship and allied to a stage personality of great warmth and charm. One of the greatest singers of the inter-war period, she was also an outstanding lieder singer and later a distinguished teacher.

The second of her three husbands, **Karl Alwin** (1891–1945), was a successful conductor.

Schumann, Robert (1810–56)
German composer. His one completed opera GENOVEVA contains some fine music, but betrays Schumann's basic lack of any dramatic talent. He toyed with a number of other operatic projects, of which fragments of the unfinished *Der Korsar* (1844; libr Owsald Marbach, after Lord Byron's *The Corsair*) have survived. He was married to the pianist **Clara Wieck**.

Schumann-Heink, Ernestine (b Tini Rössler) (1861–1936)
Czech contralto, particularly associated with Wagnerian roles. One of the greatest contraltos of all time, her enormous repertory of some 150 roles ranged from Amneris to Katisha in *The Mikado*. She had a rich and opulent voice of extraordinary flexibility and vast range (virtually three octaves), which she used with total technical assurance and innate musicianship. Her recording of the Brindisi from *Lucrezia Borgia* remains one of the most astonishing pieces of vocalization ever committed to disc. She created Clytemnestra in *Elektra*, a work which she described as 'a frightful racket'.

Schütz, Heinrich (1585–1672)
German composer. The leading 17th-century German composer of sacred music, he also wrote two stage works: DAFNE, which was the first German opera, and the opera-ballet *Orpheus und Eurydice* (1638; libr August Buchner). The music for both works is lost.

Schwarz, Hans
Bass COMPRIMARIO role in Wagner's *Die Meistersinger von Nürnberg*. A stocking-weaver, he is one of the masters.

Schwarzkopf, Dame Elisabeth (b 1915)
German soprano, particularly associated with Mozart roles and with the Marschallin in *Der Rosenkavalier*, although her wide repertory also embraced Verdi, Puccini and Viennese operetta. One of the greatest singers of the post-war era, she began as a COLORATURA, but soon moved to more lyrical roles. As well as possessing an exquisitely modulated voice, she was an artist of outstanding intelligence and musicianship, whose aristocracy of tone and style, combined with her personal beauty, made her one of the best-loved singers of her age. Also an exceptional lieder singer, the great refinement of her vocal technique occasionally lent a suggestion of artificiality and self-consciousness, but this seldom detracted from her great interpretative powers. She created Anne Truelove in *The Rake's Progress* and the Wife in Orff's *Trionfo d'Afrodite*. Her husband **Walter Legge** (1905–79) was artistic director of the Philharmonia Orchestra and a recording producer responsible for many famous operatic recordings for EMI. Schwarzkopf's memoirs of him, *On and Off the Record*, were published in 1982.

Schweigsame Frau, Die (*The Silent Woman*)
Comic opera in three acts by Strauss (Op 80). 1st perf Dresden, 24 June 1935; libr by Stefan Zweig, after Ben Jonson's *Epicoene*. Principal roles: Sir Morosus (bass), Aminta (sop), Henry (ten), Barber (bar), Housekeeper (mezzo). An extravagant and inventively written piece, whose plot is almost identical to that of *Don Pasquale*, it has for some reason never been particularly popular and is only infrequently performed.
Plot: London, *c* 1780. The bad-tempered former admiral Sir Morosus is unable to tolerate noise. His Barber suggests that he might achieve domestic harmony by marrying a silent woman, and undertakes to find him such a bride. Meanwhile, Morosus, furious to discover that his nephew Henry, who has joined a touring opera company, has married the singer Aminta, disinherits the young man. The Barber and Henry retaliate by duping Morosus into a supposed marriage with 'Timida', a silent woman, who is none other than Aminta in disguise. Immediately after the ceremony, 'Timida' becomes extremely noisy until Morosus will go to any lengths to get out of the marriage. The deception is revealed and Morosus, relieved to be rid of his 'wife', forgives all concerned. [R]

Schwertleite
Mezzo role in Wagner's *Die Walküre*. She is one of the Valkyries.

Scimone, Claudio (b 1934)
Italian conductor and musicologist, particularly associated with Rossini and with 18th-century Italian composers, especially Vivaldi. He has been responsible for notable performances and recordings in scholarly editions, many with the chamber orchestra I Solisti Veniti, which he founded in 1959.

Scintille diamant
Baritone aria (the Diamond Aria) for Dapertutto in the Giulietta Act of Offenbach's *Les Contes d'Hoffmann*, in which he addresses the diamond intended to enslave Giulietta. Offenbach incorporated it from his earlier *Le Voyage dans la Lune*.

Scipione
Opera in three acts by Händel. 1st perf London, 12 March 1726; libr by Paolo Antonio Rolli, after Antonio Salvi's *Publio Cornelio Scipione*. Principal roles: Scipione (c-ten), Berenice (sop), Lucejo (c-ten), Armira (mezzo), Lelio (ten), Ernando (bass). Dealing with an event in the life of the Roman Consul Publius Cornelius Scipio (237–183 BC), it is still performed from time to time.
Plot: Cartageña (Spain), 209 BC. Scipio arrives in triumph and falls in love with Berenice, daughter of Ernando, King of the Balaeric Islands, who has been rescued from the fighting by Scipio's general Lelio. Berenice, however, is betrothed to Lucejo. When Ernando arrives offering alliance with Rome, Scipio is unable to persuade him to give him Berenice's hand. Scipio eventually renounces his personal desires in the interests of peace and justice, and blesses Berenice's union with Lucejo. [R]

Sciutti, Graziella (b 1927)
Italian soprano, particularly associated with Mozart and with lighter 18th- and 19th-century Italian roles. One of the finest SOUBRETTES of the post-war era, her elegantly pointed singing, her fine diction and her charming and vivacious stage personality led to her being dubbed the 'Callas of the Piccola Scala'. She created the title-role in Sauget's *Les Caprices de Marianne* and Jenny Mere in Ghedini's *L'Ipocrita Felice*, and has also had considerable success as a producer.

Score
A term used to describe the written and ordered form of the various orchestral and vocal ingredients of a piece of music. Opera employs two types: **1** Vocal score: all the vocal parts (solo and chorus) with a piano reduction. **2** Full (or orchestral) score: all the vocal parts with the complete orchestral parts.

Scotland
see EDINBURGH FESTIVAL; SCOTTISH OPERA

Scott, Cyril (1879–1970)
British composer. Best known as an orchestral composer, he also wrote three operas, all to his own libretti. They are *The Alchemist* (Essen, 28 May 1925, composed 1917; libr after Ben Jonson), *The Saint of the Mountain* (1925) and *Maureen O'Mara* (1946). The last two have never been performed.

Scott, Sir Walter
see panel on page 505

Scotti, Antonio (1866–1936)
Italian baritone, particularly associated with the Italian repertory, especially Verdi roles and Scarpia. His voice, although not large, was used with outstanding artistry and he was one of the finest singing-actors of his day. He created Chim-Fen in Leoni's *L'Oracolo*. He formed the financially disastrous Scotti Grand Opera Company, which toured the USA and Canada between 1919 and 1922.

Scottish Opera
Founded by Sir Alexander Gibson in 1962, the company is based at the Theatre Royal, Glasgow (cap, 1,560) and tours throughout Scotland and northern and central England. The company soon established high artistic standards, and has been particularly noted for its Wagner and Britten productions. The annual season runs from September to June. Musical directors have been Gibson, John Mauceri and Richard Armstrong.

· Sir Walter Scott ·

The works of the Scottish poet and novelist Sir Walter Scott (1771–1832) have inspired some 60 operas, most of them written in the first half of the 19th century at the height of the romantic movement of which Scott was a leading exemplar. Below are listed, by work, those operas by composers with entries in this dictionary.

The Betrothed		
Pacini	*Il Contestabile di Chester*	1829
The Bride of Lammermoor		
Carafa	*Le Nozze di Lammermoor*	1829
Donizetti	*Lucia di Lammermoor*	1835
The Fair Maid of Perth		
Bizet	*La Jolie Fille de Perth*	1867
Guy Mannering		
Boïeldieu	*La Dame Blanche*	1825
The Heart of Midlothian		
Carafa	*La Prison d'Édimbourg*	1833
F. Ricci	*La Prigione d'Edimburgo*	1838
MacCunn	*Jeanie Deans*	1894
Ivanhoe		
Marschner	*Der Templer und die Jüdin*	1829
Pacini	*Ivanhoe*	1832
Nicolaï	*Il Templario*	1840
Sullivan	*Ivanhoe*	1891
Kenilworth		
Auber	*Leicester*	1823
Donizetti	*Il Castello di Kenilworth*	1829
Weyse	*The Feast at Kenilworth*	1836
Loewe	*Emmy*	1842
Lara	*Amy Robsart*	1893
The Lady of the Lake		
Rossini	*La Donna del Lago*	1819
Old Morality		
Bellini	*I Puritani*	1835
Rob Roy		
Flotow	*Rob Roy*	1836
The Talisman		
Riotte	*König Richard in Palästina*	1827
Pacini	*Il Talismano*	1829
Loewe	*Malekadhel*	1832
Costa	*Malekhadel*	1838
Adam	*Richard en Palestine*	1844
Balfe	*Il Talismano*	1874
Woodstock		
Flotow	*Alice*	1837
Pacini	*Allan Cameron*	1849

Scotto, Renata (b 1933)
Italian soprano, particularly associated with the Italian repertory. A singer of fine intelligence and artistry, she began in light lyric roles and was an especially successful Bellini interpreter. Later in her career, she turned to Puccini and still heavier roles such as Lady Macbeth in Verdi's *Macbeth*

and the title-role in Ponchielli's *La Gioconda*, which were exciting but which showed some signs of vocal strain. Her autobiography, *Scotto: More Than a Diva*, was published in 1984.

Scribe, Eugène (1791–1861)
French playwright and librettist. Author of over 300 plays and libretti (his collected works run to 76 volumes), he was the most prolific and successful librettist of the 19th century. The dominant writer at the Paris Opéra, his libretti epitomize the spectacular, theatrical, but often dramatically empty structure of French grand opera. His prodigous output, which led to snide references to the 'Scribe factory', included libretti for virtually every major composer of the period. He provided texts for Adam (seven, including *Giralda*), Auber (38, including *La Muette de Portici*, *Fra Diavolo*, *Le Cheval de Bronze*, *Le Domino Noir*, *Les Diamants de la Couronne* and *Manon Lescaut*), Audran, Balfe (*Le Puits d'Amour*), Boïeldieu (four, including *La Dame Blanche*), Carafa, Cherubini (*Ali Baba*), Donizetti (*Le Duc d'Albe*, *Dom Sébastien* and *Les Martyrs*), García, Gounod (*La Nonne Sanglante*), Halévy (six, including *La Juive* and *La Tempestà*), Hérold, Meyerbeer (*Robert le Diable*, *Les Huguenots*, *L'Étoile du Nord*, *Le Prophète* and *L'Africaine*), Monpou, Offenbach (*Barkouf*), Rossini (*Le Comte Ory*), Thomas and Verdi (*Les Vêpres Siciliennes*) amongst others. His works are also the source material for operas by Barbieri (*Los Diamantés de la Corona*), Bellini (*La Sonnambula*), Cilea (*Adriana Lecouvreur*), Donizetti (*L'Elisir d'Amore*), Gade (*Mariotta*), Gaztambide (*La Catalina*), MacFarren (*Jessy Lea*), Mendelssohn (*Die Beiden Pädagogen*), Mercadante (*Il Reggente*), Pavesi (*Fenella*), Ponchielli (*Il Figliuol Prodigo* and *I Mori di Valenza*), Rossini (*L'Occasione Fa il Ladro*), Suppé (*Fatinitza*), Verdi (*Un Ballo in Maschera*) and Zandonai (*La Via della Finestra*).

Scuoti o vento
Baritone aria for Rodolfo in Act IV of Leoncavallo's *La Bohème*, in which he says that the wind mirrors the poetry that he is writing.

Scylla et Glaucus
Opera in prologue and five acts by Leclair. 1st perf Paris, 4 Oct 1746; libr by d'Alberet, after Ovid's *Metamorphoses*. Principal roles: Scylla (sop), Glaucus (ten), Circé (sop), Témire (sop), Licas (bass), Vénus (sop). Leclair's only completed opera, it was unsuccessful at its appearance, despite its fine music, and it is only in the last 20 years that it has been at all performed.
Plot: Legendary Sicily. Rebuffed by Scylla, Glaucus seeks the aid of Circe, who falls in love with him. Glaucus escapes Circe's enchantments, and she vows revenge. Scylla's heart, meanwhile, has changed, and she and Glaucus are united. Circe summons Hecate, who gives her a vial of deadly poison. Circe puts it into the fountain by which Scylla and Glaucus first exchanged their vows. When Scylla looks into the fountain, she dies and is transformed into a rocky crag in the shape of a siren. Circe exults in her vengeance. [R]

Searle, Humphrey (1915–82)
British composer. He wrote three operas: *The Diary of a Madman* (Berlin, 3 Oct 1958; libr composer, after Nikolai Gogol), *The Photo of the Colonel* (BBC Radio, 8 Mar 1964; libr composer, after Eugène Ionesco's *The Killer*) and HAMLET.

Seattle Opera Association
Founded in 1965, the company gives an annual season from September to May at the Opera House (cap 3,017), which was built for the 1962 World Fair. Performances are given with international casts, and the repertory policy is adventurous. In addition, the company has since 1972 given two *Ring* cycles each summer, one in English and one in German.

Secco (Italian for 'dry')
A form of recitative, accompanied by the harpsichord, which is little more than pitched speech and which was used in 18th-century OPERA SERIA and in Italian OPERA BUFFA to carry forward the action between the formal musical numbers.

Secret, The (*Tajemství*)
Comic opera in three acts by Smetana. 1st perf Prague, 18 Aug 1878; libr by Eliška

Krásnohorská. Principal roles: Malina (sop), Róza (mezzo), Kalina (bar), Bonifác (bass), Blaženka (sop), Vít (ten), Skřivánek (ten). Notable for its fine ensemble writing and for its light and subtle characterization, it is still popular in the Czech lands but is rarely performed elsewhere.
Plot: Late-18th-century Bohemia. The rivalry between Kalina and Malina has prevented their children Vít and Blaženka from marrying, and has also stopped Malina's sister Róza from wedding the once-poor Kalina. The deceased friar Barnabáš had promised Kalina a secret which would enable him to marry Róza. This turns out to be the directions to a tunnel to her house, where both pairs of lovers are finally united. [R]

Secular oratorio
An 18th-century English theatrical form, which consisted of an oratorio on a non-religious subject. It was little different from opera, except that it employed a chorus. Much the best-known examples are by Händel, such as *Semele* and *Hercules*.

Seefried, Irmgard (1919–88)
German soprano, particularly associated with lighter Strauss and Mozart roles, especially Susanna in *Le Nozze di Figaro*. Largely based at the Vienna State Opera, she possessed a voice of great beauty, used with outstanding artistry, and was one of the finest Mozartians of the immediate post-war era. Her husband **Wolfgang Schneiderhahn** (*b* 1915) was a celebrated violinist who later in his career also conducted a number of operas.

Seelig, wie die Schöne
Soprano/mezzo/tenor/baritone/bass quintet for Eva, Magdalene, Walther von Stolzing, Hans Sachs and Veit Pogner in Act III of Wagner's *Die Meistersinger von Nürnberg*, in which they express their different feelings over the outcome of the forthcoming singing contest.

Segreto di Susanna, Il (*Susanna's Secret*)
Comic opera in one act by Wolf-Ferrari. 1st perf Munich, 4 Dec 1909; libr by Enrico Golisciani. Principal roles: Susanna (sop), Gil (bar), Sante (mute). Arguably Wolf-Ferrari's finest opera, it is based on the two-character 18th-century INTERMEZZI. An immediate success, it has remained popular ever since, especially its sparkling neo-classical overture.
Plot: Piedmont, 1840. Susanna's husband Count Gil, who strongly disapproves of smoking, returns home one day and smells tobacco. He works himself up into a fine rage, certain that the smoke indicates that his wife has been entertaining a lover. Susanna has to admit her guilty secret: she is herself a smoker. Gil confesses that actually he too enjoys it, and the couple enjoy a happy smoke-wreathed reconciliation. [R]

Segreto per esser felice, Il
Mezzo aria (the Brindisi) for Maffio Orsini in Act II of Donizetti's *Lucrezia Borgia*, sung to entertain his fellow dinner guests.

Seidl, Anton (1850–98)
Hungarian conductor, particularly associated with Wagner operas. One of the finest early Wagnerian interpreters, he was musical director of the Bremen Opera (1883–5) and from 1885 was based largely at the Metropolitan Opera, New York. His wife **Augusta Krauss** (1853–1939) was a successful soprano.

Sélika
Mezzo role in Meyerbeer's *L'Africaine*. She is an African slave loved by Nélusko.

Selim
Bass role in Rossini's *Il Turco in Italia*. He is the Turk of the opera's title.

Sellars, Peter (b 1957)
American producer. The *enfant terrible* of contemporary opera production, he shows great theatrical flair and perception, but his stagings often wilfully distort the plot in his attempts to make opera 'relevant' to modern audiences. His most controversial productions have included a drug-ridden *Don Giovanni* set in New York and his San Francisco flower-power *Die Zauberflöte* for Glyndebourne. He produced the first performances of Adams's *Nixon in China* and *The Death of Klinghoffer*.

Sellem
Tenor role in Stravinsky's *The Rake's Progress*. He is an auctioneer.

Sembrich, Marcella (b Praxsede Marcelline Kochańska) (1858–1935)
Polish soprano, particularly associated with Italian and French COLORATURA roles. Long based at the Metropolitan Opera, New York, she had a beautiful, brilliant and expressive voice with a range of c' to f''', which she used with an outstanding technique. She was also an accomplished violinist.

Semele
Secular oratorio in three acts by Händel. 1st perf London, 10 Feb 1744; libr by William Congreve, after Ovid's *Metamorphoses*. Principal roles: Semele (sop), Jupiter (ten), Juno (mezzo), Iris (sop), Somnus (bass), Athamus (c-ten), Ino (mezzo), Cadmus (bass), Apollo (ten). Although not strictly speaking an opera, it is the most popular and most frequently staged of all Händel's dramatic oratorios. Its glorious, sensuous music and its sharp sense of characterization make it one of the finest of all English musical stage works.
Plot: Legendary Thebes. Jupiter loves the beautiful but vain Semele, daughter of King Cadmus, much to the fury of his wife Juno. The disguised Juno persuades Semele to ask Jupiter to show himself to her in his full glory. This Jupiter does, burning Semele to a cinder in the process. [R]

Semeon Kotko
Opera in five acts by Prokofiev (Op 81). 1st perf Moscow, 23 June 1940; libr by the composer, after Valentin Katayev's *I, Son of the Working People*. Principal roles: Semeon (ten), Sofia (sop), Tkachenko (b-bar), Remenyek (bass), Klembovsky (ten). A nauseatingly patriotic work, with which Prokofiev temporarily found renewed favour with the Stalinist authorities, it is nowadays hardly ever performed.
Plot: Ukraine, 1918. Semeon returns home after fighting in the war. He wishes to marry Sofia, but her father, the wealthy landowner Tkachenko, refuses his consent. German soldiers destroy his home and Semeon escapes and forms a resistance movement. Subsequently returning home, he prevents Sofia's marriage to the rich Klembovsky by the expedient of blowing up the church. [R]

Semiramide
Opera in two acts by Rossini. 1st perf Venice, 3 Feb 1823; libr by Gaetano Rossi, after Voltaire's *Sémiramis*. Principal roles: Semiramide (sop), Arsace (mezzo), Assur (bass), Idreno (ten), Oroe (bass), Ghost of Nino (bass), Azema (sop). Rossini's last opera written for Italy, it contains some of his finest (and most demanding) music in serious vein. An immediate success, it is still regularly performed.
Plot: Babylon, 8th century BC. With the aid of her lover Assur, Queen Semiramide has murdered her husband Nino. Assur wishes to marry her, but she is attracted to the young soldier Arsace, ignorant of the fact that he is actually her son. Arsace, who loves the princess Azema, is informed of his relationship to Semiramide by the priest Oroe. Semiramide announces that she plans to marry Arsace, whereupon Nino's ghost appears and announces that Arsace will indeed be king, but only after crimes have been punished. Assur follows Arsace to Nino's tomb, intending to kill him, but Semiramide – now aware of Arsace's parentage – also goes, in order to protect him. Arsace kills Semiramide with a stroke intended for Assur. Nino's murder is thus expiated and Arsace ascends the throne and marries Azema. [R]

Sempre libera
Soprano cabaletta for Violetta Valéry in Act I of Verdi's *La Traviata*, in which she resolves always to live a life of pleasure.

Seneca
Bass role in Monteverdi's *L'Incoronazione di Poppea*. He is the historical stoic philosopher Lucius Annaeus Seneca (4 BC–AD 65).

Sénéchal, Michel (b 1927)
French tenor, particularly associated with French and Italian character roles. The leading French character singer of the post-war era, he had a fine voice of considerable range and an excellent stage presence. His large repertory ranged from baroque to contemporary, and he created Frère Élie in Messiaen's *Saint François d'Assise*, Fabien in Landowski's *Montségur* and Pope Leo X in Boehmer's *Docteur Faustus*. He enjoyed a remarkably long career, singing into his late 60s. Director of the Paris Opéra school (1980–).

Senesino (b Francesco Bernardi) (c 1680–c 1750)
Italian CASTRATO. Assumed by some to have been the greatest of all the castrati, his voice – of great beauty – was of contralto range, and was described by a contemporary as 'clear, penetrating and flexible, with faultless intonation and a perfect shake'. Notoriously temperamental, he enjoyed his greatest successes in London with Händel, with whom he worked from 1721 to 1728 and from 1730 to 1733, after which they quarrelled. He created Gualtiero in Bononcini's *Griselda* and, for Händel, roles in *Ottone, Flavio, Giulio Cesare, Tamerlano, Scipione, Rodelinda, Alessandro, Admeto, Riccardo Primo, Siroe, Tolomeo, Poro, Ezio, Sosarme* and *Orlando*. He should not be confused with the castrati **Giusto Fernandino Tenducci** (*c* 1736–90) and **Andrea Martini** (1761–1819), both of whom were also known as Senesino.

Senta
Soprano role in Wagner's *Der Fliegende Holländer*. She is Daland's daughter and the Dutchman's redemption.

Sento avvampar feroce
Tenor aria for Gabriele Adorno in Act II of Verdi's *Simon Boccanegra*, in which he expresses his jealousy of Boccanegra's closeness to Amelia.

Senza mamma
Soprano aria for Angelica in Puccini's *Suor Angelica*, in which she grieves over the death of her illegitimate child.

Septet
In opera, a musical number for seven solo singers, with or without chorus. There is a fine example in the prologue of Donizetti's *Lucrezia Borgia*.

Serafin, Tullio (1878–1968)
Italian conductor, particularly associated with the Italian repertory, especially Verdi. Largely based at La Scala, Milan, the Rome Opera, where he was artistic director (1934–43), and the Metropolitan Opera, New York, he was also an astute coach who encouraged young singers. He conducted the first performances of Gruenberg's *The Emperor Jones*, Alfano's *Risurrezione* and *Cyrano de Bergerac*, Taylor's *The King's Henchman* and *Peter Ibbetson*, Montemezzi's *L'Amore dei Tre Re* and *La Nave*, Pick-Mangiagalli's *Notturno Romantico* and Hanson's *Merry Mount*. His wife **Elena Rakowska** (1878–1964) was a successful Wagnerian soprano.

Seraglio, The
see ENTFÜHRUNG AUS DEM SERAIL, DIE

Serbia
see BELGRADE OPERA

Serbian opera composers
These include Isidor Bajič (1878–1915), Stanislav Binički (1872–1942), Petar Konjovič (1883–1970), Petar Krstić (1877–1957), Mihovil Logar (*b* 1902), Stanojlo Rajičić (*b* 1910) and Petar Stojanovič (1877–1957).

Serebrier, José (b 1938)
Uruguayan conductor and composer, particularly associated with the French repertory and with 20th-century works. Best known as an orchestral conductor, his operatic appearances have been intermittent. His wife **Carole Farley** (*b* 1946) is a soprano noted for her performances in 20th-century roles, notably the title-role in Berg's *Lulu*. She created the Bride in Chaynes's *Noces de Sange*.

Serena
Mezzo role in Gershwin's *Porgy and Bess*. She is Robbins's widow.

Serenade (from the Italian *serenata*, 'evening song')
A type of song – the opposite of an aubade which is a song for the morning – traditionally sung by a lover beneath his lady's window at night. The most famous operatic examples are Don Giovanni's 'Deh vieni' and Count Almaviva's 'Ecco ridente' in *Il Barbiere di Siviglia*.

Serenata (Italian for 'evening song')
The term has two meanings in opera: **1** A serenade (see above). **2** A term occasionally used in the 18th century to describe a short and often pastoral operatic work given to celebrate a royal or social event. Examples include Händel's *Acis and Galatea* and Gluck's *Le Cinesi*.

Sereni, Mario (b 1928)
Italian baritone, particularly associated with the Italian repertory. Resident at the Metropolitan Opera, New York, from 1957, he was a true Verdi baritone with a rich and beautiful voice, marred only by his frequent tendency to sing flat.

Sergei
Tenor role in Shostakovich's *Lady Macbeth of Mtsensk*. He is the labourer with whom Katerina falls in love.

Serial composition
see TWELVE-TONE OPERAS

Serov, Alexander (1820–71)
Russian composer and critic. Influenced by Verdi and the French school, and an opponent of the new Russian nationalist composers, his three operas met with great success in Russia, but are virtually unknown elsewhere. The fine JUDITH was followed by *Rogneda* (St Petersburg, 8 Nov 1865; libr composer and Dmitri Averkiyev, after Mikhail Zagoskin's *Ashkold's Tomb*) [R Exc] and the unfinished *The Power of Evil* (*Vrazhya Sila*, St Petersburg, 1 May 1871; libr composer, after Alexander Nikolayevich Ostrovsky), which was completed by Nikolai Solovyov. A difficult man, Serov was an acerbic but perceptive critic who supported the Liszt-Wagner school, although he himself was uninfluenced by Wagner. His wife **Valentina Bergmann** (1846–1924) was a pianist and composer, who wrote two operas: *Uriel Acosta* (Moscow, 15 Apr 1885; libr composer and P. Blaramberg, after C. von Grutschow) and *Ilya Mouromets* (Moscow, 22 Feb 1899; libr composer).

Serpina
Soprano role in Pergolesi's *La Serva Padrona*. She is the chambermaid who tricks her master into marrying her.

Serrano José (1873–1941)
Spanish composer. He wrote over 50 ZARZUELAS, of which the most successful include *La Reina Mora* (Madrid, 11 Dec 1903; libr Serafín and Joaquín Álvarez Quintero) [R], *La Canción del Olvido* (Valencia, 17 Nov 1916; libr Federico Romero and Carlos Fernández Shaw) [R], *Los de Aragon* (Madrid, 16 Apr 1927; libr Juan José Lorente) [R] and *La Dolorosa* (Madrid, 24 Oct 1930; libr Lorente) [R].

Serse (*Xerxes*)
Opera in prologue and three acts by Cavalli. 1st perf Venice, 12 Jan 1654; libr by Nicolò Minato. Principal roles: Serse (c-ten), Amastre (sop), Arsamene (c-ten), Romilda (sop), Adelanta (sop), Ariodate (ten), Eumene (ten). After nearly 300 years of complete neglect, it has received a few performances in the last decade. [R]

Serse (*Xerxes*)
Opera in three acts by Händel. 1st perf London, 15 April 1738; libr after Nicolò Minato's libretto for Cavalli. Principal roles: Serse (mezzo), Romilda (sop), Arsamene (c-ten), Amastre (mezzo), Atalanta (sop), Ariodate (bass), Elviro (bass). Always one of Händel's most popular operas, it is notable for its inclusion of some London street songs, and for containing in Elviro the only wholly comic character in a Händel opera.
Plot: Legendary Abydos. The Persian Emperor Xerxes is engaged to Amastris, but falls in love with his brother Arsamene's fiancée Romilda – daughter of Xerxes's general Ariodates – after hearing her sing. This generates much misunderstanding and jealousy, further complicated by the machinations of Romilda's sister Atalanta and by the incompetent behaviour of Arsamene's servant Elviro. Amastris views the proceedings in male disguise, finally revealing herself so as to bring Xerxes back to her. [R]

Serva Padrona, La (*The Maid-Mistress*)
INTERMEZZO in two parts by Pergolesi. 1st perf Naples, 28 Aug 1733; libr by Gennarantonio Federico, after Jacopo Angello Nelli's play. Principal roles: Serpina (sop), Uberto (bass), Vespone (mute). The most famous of all intermezzi and the work which precipitated the GUERRE DES BOUFFONS in Paris, it was originally given between the acts of the OPERA SERIA *Il Prigionier Superbo*.
Plot: Early-18th-century Italy. Serpina, employed as a maid by Uberto, tricks her master into marrying her by pretending to leave with a ferocious soldier – in fact the mute servant Vespone in disguise. [R]

Servilia
Soprano role in Mozart's *La Clemenza di Tito*. She is Sextus's sister.

Sessions, Roger (1896–1985)
American composer, whose style developed from neo-classicism through extended tonality to serialism. He wrote two operas: *The Trial of Lucullus* (Berkeley, 18 Apr 1947; libr after Bertolt Brecht) and the epic MONTEZUMA.

Seven Deadly Sins, The
see SIEBEN TODSÜNDEN, DIE

Se vuol ballare
Bass-baritone aria for Figaro in Act I of Mozart's *Le Nozze di Figaro*, in which he says that if the Count wishes to play games, he will remain in control.

Sextet
In opera, a musical number for six solo singers, with or without chorus. Much the most famous example is 'Chi mi frena' in Donizetti's *Lucia di Lammermoor*.

Sextus
Mezzo trouser role in: **1** Mozart's *La Clemenza di Tito*. He is Servilia's brother. **2** Händel's *Giulio Cesare*. He is Cornelia's son.

Seyfriend, Ignaz (1776–1841)
Austrian composer. He wrote many works in a variety of styles, including SINGSPIELS for Emanuel Schikaneder, parodies and biblical dramas, including *Saul* (Vienna, 7 Apr 1810) and *Die Makabäer* (Vienna, 21 Nov 1818). None of his works are nowadays remembered.

Shadow, Nick
Baritone role in Stravinsky's *The Rake's Progress*. He is the sinister figure who leads Tom to destruction.

Shadow Song
Soprano aria ('Ombre légère') for Dinorah in Act II of Meyerbeer's *Dinorah*, in which she expresses her love for the shadows cast by the moonlight.

Shakespearian operas
see panel on pages 512–4

Shamus O'Brien
Opera in two acts by Stanford (Op 61). 1st perf London, 2 March 1896; libr by George H. Jessop, after Sheridan le Fanu's poem. Principal roles: Shamus (bar), Kitty (sop), Murphy (ten), Capt Trevor (ten), Nora (mezzo), Fr O'Flynn (bass). Arguably Stanford's finest opera, it was successful at its appearance but is nowadays virtually forgotten.
Plot: Cork, 1798. Whilst Kitty O'Toole, the sister of the outlaw Shamus O'Brien's wife Nora, flirts with the Englishman Capt Trevor, Shamus himself eludes the British army. However, he is betrayed to the British by Mike Murphy, who loves Nora. With the aid of Father O'Flynn, Shamus escapes from the gallows and Murphy, pursuing him, is shot by the troops.

Shaporin, Yuri (1889–1966)
Russian composer. His one opera, the vast THE DECEMBRISTS, has proved to be arguably the finest stage work written in 'orthodox Soviet' style and has been widely performed.

Sharp
Written as the musical symbol ♯, sharp is the opposite of FLAT. It is a rising in pitch, either – intentionally – by a semitone, or – unintentionally – by an indeterminate amount, as when a singer accidentally sings above the written note.

Sharpless
Baritone role in Puccini's *Madama Butterfly*. He is the American Consul in Nagasaki.

Schedrin, Rodion (b 1932)
Russian composer. His three operas have met with some success. They are *Not Love Alone* (Moscow, 25 Dec 1961; libr V.A. Katanyan, after Sergei Antonov) [R], *Dead Souls* (Moscow, 7 June 1977; libr composer, after Nikolai Gogol) [R] and *Lolita* (Stockholm, 14 Dec 1994; libr composer, after Vladimir Nabokov).

Shebalin, Vissarion (1902–63)
Russian composer. He wrote two operas in 'orthodox Soviet' style which met with considerable success in Russia but which are unknown elsewhere. They are *The Taming of the Shrew* (*Ukroschcheniye Stroptivoy*, Moscow, 1 Oct 1955; libr

· Shakespearian Operas ·

The works of the English poet and playwright William Shakespeare (1564–1616) have inspired more musical works than those of any other writer; some 300 operas have been based wholly or in part on his plays. Shakespeare himself appears as a character in Thomas's *Le Songe d'une Nuit d'Été* (1850), Giuseppe Lillo's *La Gioventù di Shakespeare* (1851), Tomaso Benvenuti's *Guglielmo Shakespeare* (1861) and Serpette's *Shakespeare* (1899). Below are listed, by play, those operas based on his works by composers with entries in this dictionary. In addition, Berio's *Un Rè in Ascolto* and Tippett's *The Knot Garden* make extensive reference to *The Tempest.*

All's Well That Ends Well		
David	*Le Saphir*	1865
Audran	*Gillette de Narbonne*	1882
Castelnuovo-Tedesco	*Giglietta di Narbona*	1959
Antony and Cleopatra		
Malipiero	*Antonio e Cleopatra*	1938
Barber	*Antony and Cleopatra*	1966
Bondeville	*Antoine et Cléopâtre*	1974
As You Like It		
Veracini	*Rosalinda*	1744
The Comedy of Errors		
Storace	*Gli Equivoci*	1786
Krejčí	*The Tumult at Ephesus*	1946
Coriolanus		
Cikker	*Coriolanus*	1973
Cymbeline		
R. Kreutzer	*Imogène*	1796
Ostrčil	*Cymbelin*	1899 (U)
Hamlet		
Mercadante	*Amleto*	1822
Faccio	*Amleto*	1865
Thomas	*Hamlet*	1868
Zafred	*Amleto*	1961
Searle	*Hamlet*	1968
Szokolay	*Hamlet*	1969
Rihm	*Die Hamletmaschine*	1987
Slonimsky	*Gamlet*	1990
Julius Caesar		
J.C.F. Bach	*Brutus*	1774
Malipiero	*Giulio Cesare*	1936
Klebe	*Die Ermordrung Cäsars*	1959
King Henry IV		
Hérold	*La Gioventù di Enrico V*	1815
Pacini	*La Gioventù di Enrico V*	1820
Morlacchi	*La Gioventù di Enrico V*	1823
Mercadante	*La Gioventù di Enrico V*	1834
Holst	*At the Boar's Head*	1925
King Lear		
R. Kreutzer	*Cordelia*	1823

Gobatti	*Cordelia*	1881
Cagnoni	*Rè Lear*	1890
Litolff	*Le Roi Lear*	1890
Frazzi	*Rè Lear*	1939
Reimann	*Lear*	1978
Love's Labour's Lost		
Nabokov	*Love's Labour's Lost*	1973
Macbeth		
Verdi	*Macbeth*	1847/65
Rossi	*Biorn*	1877
Bloch	*Macbeth*	1910
Gatty	*Macbeth*	1920
Collingwood	*Macbeth*	1934
Measure for Measure		
Wagner	*Das Liebesverbot*	1836
The Merchant of Venice		
Foerster	*Jessika*	1905
Alpaerts	*Shylock*	1913
Hahn	*Le Marchand de Venise*	1935
Castelnuovo-Tedesco	*Il Mercante di Venezia*	1961
The Merry Wives of Windsor		
Philidor	*Herne le Chasseur*	1773
Dittersdorf	*Die Lustigen Weiber von Windsor*	1796
Salieri	*Falstaff*	1799
Balfe	*Falstaff*	1838
Nicolaï	*Die Lustigen Weiber von Windsor*	1849
Adam	*Falstaff*	1856
Verdi	*Falstaff*	1893
Vaughan Williams	*Sir John in Love*	1929
A Midsummer Night's Dream		
Purcell	*The Fairy Queen*	1692
Alyabyev	*The Enchanted Night*	1839
Mancinelli	*Un Sogno di una Notte d'Estato*	1917
Britten	*A Midsummer Night's Dream*	1960
Werle	*A Midsummer Night's Dream*	1985
Much Ado About Nothing		
Berlioz	*Béatrice et Bénédict*	1862
Stanford	*Much Ado About Nothing*	1901
Hahn	*Beaucoup de Bruit Pour Rien*	1936
Khrennikov	*Much Ado About Hearts*	1972
Othello		
Rossini	*Otello*	1816
Verdi	*Otello*	1887
Romeo and Juliet		
Benda	*Romeo und Julie*	1776
Dalayrac	*Tout Pour l'Amour*	1792
Zingarelli	*Giulietta e Romeo*	1796
Vaccai	*Giulietta e Romeo*	1825
Bellini	*I Capuleti e i Montecchi*	1830
Marchetti	*Romeo e Giulietta*	1865
Gounod	*Roméo et Juliette*	1867
Zandonai	*Giulietta e Romeo*	1922
Sutermeister	*Romeo und Julia*	1940

Blacher	*Romeo und Julia*	1950
Bernstein	*West Side Story*	1957
The Taming of the Shrew		
Götz	*Der Widerspänstigen Zähmung*	1874
Chapí	*Las Bravías*	1896
Wolf-Ferrari	*Sly* (Introduction only)	1927
Karel	*The Taming of the Shrew*	1939 (U)
Giannini	*The Taming of the Shrew*	1953
Shebalin	*The Taming of the Shrew*	1955
Argento	*Christopher Sly*	1963
The Tempest		
Locke	*The Tempest*	1674
Purcell	*The Tempest*	1695
Winter	*Der Sturm*	1798
Müller	*Der Sturm*	1798
Alyabyev	*The Tempest*	1835
Halévy	*La Tempestà*	1850
Fibich	*The Tempest*	1895
Gatty	*The Tempest*	1920
Lattuada	*La Tempestà*	1922
Sutermeister	*Die Zauberinsel*	1942
Atterberg	*Stormen*	1949
Martin	*Der Sturm*	1956
Eaton	*The Tempest*	1985
Timon of Athens		
Draghi	*Timone Misantropo*	1696
Oliver	*Timon of Athens*	1991
Twelfth Night		
Smetana	*Viola*	1883 (U)
Jírko	*Twelfth Night*	1964
A Winter's Tale		
Bruch	*Hermione*	1872
Goldmark	*Ein Wintermärchen*	1908

Abram Akimovich Gozenpud, after Shakespeare) [R] and *Sun Over the Steppe* (*Solntse ned Stepyu*, Moscow, 9 June 1958). He also produced an edition of Moussorgsky's unfinished *Sorochintsy Fair* in 1932.

Shepherds of the Delectable Mountains, The
see PILGRIM'S PROGRESS, THE

Shicoff, Neil (b 1949)
American tenor, particularly associated with Italian and French lyric roles. Possessing a clean and well-focused voice and a good stage presence, he is one of the most accomplished lyric tenors of the younger generation, although his performances are occasionally marred by a certain gracelessness and seeming off-handedness.

Shield, William (1748–1829)
British composer and violinist. He wrote over 50 light operas, including *The Flitch of Bacon* (London, 17 Aug 1778; libr Henry Bate), ROSINA, his only work still to be remembered, and *Robin Hood* (London, 17 Apr 1784; libr L. MacNally and E. Lysaght).

Shilling, Eric (b 1920)
British baritone, particularly associated with BUFFO roles, especially Sullivan and Offenbach and Col Frank in *Die Fledermaus*, which last was one of the classic buffo interpretations of modern times. Possessing good diction, great comic talent and a far better voice than most buffos, he enjoyed a remarkably long career, mainly with the English National Opera, singing into his mid-70s. He

created Three in Hopkins's *Three's Company*, the Bellboy in Bennett's *A Penny for a Song*, Hawthorne in Williamson's *Our Man in Havana*, Maj Braun in Crosse's *The Story of Vasco* and Screwtape in Holloway's *Clarissa*.

Shirley, George (b 1934)
American tenor, particularly associated with Mozart roles, especially the title-role in *Idomeneo, Rè di Creta*, and with Pelléas in Debussy's *Pelléas et Mélisander* and Loge in Wagner's *Das Rheingold*. He was the first male black singer to win a major international reputation in opera. His dark-toned but lyrical and flexible voice and his sense of classical phrasing, combined with his intelligence and keen dramatic sense, made him one of the most sensitive and compelling artists of the 1960s and 1970s.

Shirley-Quirk, John (b 1931)
British baritone, particularly associated with Mozart roles and with the English repertory, especially Britten. A firm-voiced singer of great intelligence and musicianship, his stage performances were notable for their intensity and dramatic commitment. He created Lev in *The Ice Break*, Coyle in *Owen Wingrave*, the Traveller in *Death in Venice*, Shadrach in *The Burning Fiery Furnace*, the Ferryman in *Curlew River* and the Father in *The Prodigal Son*.

Shostakovich, Dimitri (1906–75)
Russian composer. His first opera, the satirical THE NOSE, was written in the eccentric and experimental style common in Russia after the Revolution. His operatic reputation rests chiefly on THE LADY MACBETH OF THE MTSENSK DISTRICT. Perhaps the finest Russian opera of the 20th century, it provoked the Stalin-inspired attack on 'formalism' with the famous *Pravda* article of 28 Jan 1936 entitled 'Chaos Instead of Music'. The toned-down revised version of the opera, *Katerina Ismailova*, finally won acceptance in Russia, but the original version is much the greater opera. His other stage works are the unfinished THE GAMBLERS and the operetta *Moscow, Cheremushky* (Moscow, 24 Jan 1959; libr V. Mess and M. Chervinsky) [R], which is a satire on the housing question. He prepared new editions of *Boris Godunov* and *Khovanschina* in 1959 and 1960, and also completed his pupil Veniam Fleishman's unfinished *Rothschild's Violin* (Moscow, 20 June 1960, composed 1941; libr composer, after Anton Chekhov) [R]. His son **Maxim** (*b* 1938) is a successful conductor.

Shuard, Amy (1924–75)
British soprano. Beginning as a lyric soprano, she later undertook heavier roles, and developed into the finest British dramatic soprano of the 1960s. Her keen dramatic sense enabled her to excel in roles such as Lady Macbeth in Verdi's *Macbeth*, Kostelnička in Janáček's *Jenůfa* and, particularly, the title-role in *Turandot*.

Shuisky, Prince Vasili
Tenor role in Moussorgsky's *Boris Godunov* and baritone role in Dvořák's *Dimitrij*. A scheming boyar, he is a historical figure who subsequently had a brief reign as Tsar.

Shvanda the Bagpiper (*Švanda Dudák*)
Comic opera in two acts by Weinberger. 1st perf Prague, 27 April 1927; libr by Miloš Kareš and Max Brod, after J.K. Tyl's story. Principal roles: Shvanda (bar), Dorotka (sop), Queen Ice Heart (mezzo), Babinsky (ten), Devil (bass). Weinberger's first opera, and by far his most successful work, it is a folk opera of great charm which was widely performed in the inter-war period. Nowadays it is best remembered through concert hall performances of the famous polka and fugue.
Plot: Legendary Bohemia. The bagpiper Shvanda falls in with the robber Babinsky, under whose influence he has a series of not altogether pleasant adventures. He travels to the realm of Queen Ice Heart and then to Hell, from which Babinsky rescues him by winning a game of cards with the bored Devil. Eventually, Shvanda is reunited with his sweetheart Dorotka. [R]

Sibelius, Jean (1865–1957)
Finnish composer. Best known as one of the greatest of all symphonic composers, he also wrote one opera, the youthful THE MAIDEN IN THE TOWER. His brother-in-law was the conductor ARMAS JÄRNEFELT; his son-in-law **Jussi Jalas** (*b* 1908) was also a successful conductor.

Siberia
Opera in three acts by Giordano. 1st perf Milan, 19 Dec 1903; libr by Luigi Illica. Principal roles: Vassili (ten), Stefana (sop), Gleby (bar), Nikona (mezzo). A rough piece of VERISMO, it met with some initial success but is nowadays hardly ever performed.
Plot: Russia, 1850s. In a duel, Vassili injures Prince Alexis, whose mistress Stefana he loves. Exiled to Siberia, Vassili is joined by Stefana but, when they attempt to escape, she is fatally wounded by the guards. Before she dies, she succeeds in persuading the camp commander Gleby to release Vassili.

Sicilian Vespers, The
see VÊPRES SICILIENNES, LES

Sicily
see TEATRO MASSIMO, PALERMO; TEATRO MASSIMO BELLINI, CATANIA

Sid
Baritone role in Britten's *Albert Herring*. He is Nancy's boyfriend.

Siebel
Mezzo trouser role in Gounod's *Faust*. He is a youth in love with Marguerite.

Sieben Todsünden, Die (*The Seven Deadly Sins*)
Sung ballet in prologue, seven scenes and epilogue by Weill. 1st perf Paris, 7 June 1933; libr by Bertolt Brecht. Principal roles: Anna I (sop), Anna II (dancer), Father (ten), Mother (bass), Brothers (ten and bar). A bitingly satirical piece, with music modelled on popular song and dance idioms, it is not strictly speaking an opera, but several opera companies carry it in their repertories. [R]

Siège de Corinthe, Le
Opera in three acts by Rossini. 1st perf Paris, 9 Oct 1826; libr by Luigi Balocchi and Alexandre Soumet, after Voltaire's *Mahomet*. Principal roles: Pamira (sop), Néoclès (ten), Mahomet (bass), Cléomène (ten), Omar (bass). Rossini's first opera written for Paris, it is a revision of his earlier MAOMETTO SECONDO. Modern performances have tended to use a conflation of both versions. [R]

Siegfried
Opera in three acts by Wagner; part 3 of DER RING DES NIBELUNGEN. 1st perf Bayreuth, 16 Aug 1876 (composed 1869); libr by the composer, after the *Nibelungenlied*. Principal roles: Siegfried (ten), Wotan/Wanderer (bar), Brünnhilde (sop), Mime (ten), Erda (cont), Alberich (bar), Fafner (bass), Woodbird (sop). For plot see *Der Ring des Nibelungen*. [R]

Sieglinde
Soprano role in Wagner's *Die Walküre*. Married to Hunding, she is Siegmund's sister and eventual lover.

Siegmund
Tenor role in Wagner's *Die Walküre*. He is Sieglinde's brother and lover.

Siegrune
Mezzo role in Wagner's *Die Walküre*. She is one of the Valkyries.

Siepi, Cesare (b 1923)
Italian bass, particularly associated with Mozart roles and the Italian repertory, especially the title-roles in *Don Giovanni*, Boito's *Mefistofele*, and King Philip in Verdi's *Don Carlos*. Based mainly at La Scala, Milan, and, from 1950, at the Metropolitan Opera, New York, he was one of the finest basses of the post-war era. His rich and even-toned voice was of great beauty and was used with matchless style and musicianship and phenomenal breath control. His intelligence and his sharp dramatic sense made him an accomplished singing-actor. He created Nonno Innocenzo in Pizzetti's *L'Oro*.

Signor Bruschino, Il or **Il Figlio per Azzardo** (*The Son by Accident*)
Comic opera in one act by Rossini. 1st perf Venice, 27 Jan 1813; libr by Giuseppe Maria Foppa, after Alisan de Chazet and E.-T. Maurice Ourry's *Le Fils par Hazard ou Ruse et Folie*. Principal roles: Guadenzio (b-bar), Sofia (mezzo), Florville (ten), Bruschino (b-bar), Filiberto (bass). The last of Rossini's early little farces, it is still quite often performed and its overture is famous for Rossini's instruction to the violinists to strike their music stands with the wood of the bow.
Plot: 18th-century Italy. In order to marry

Sofia, Florville impersonates the son of Bruschino, the young man to whom she has been betrothed by her guardian Guadenzio, who has never seen him. When Bruschino arrives, he aids the lovers for his own reasons, and they manage to wed before the confusion is sorted out. [R]

Sigurd
Opera in five acts by Reyer. 1st perf Brussels, 7 Jan 1884; libr by Camille du Locle and Alfred Blau, after the Younger Edda. Principal roles: Sigurd (ten), Gunther (bar), Brunehild (sop), Hilda (sop), Hagen (bass), Uta (cont). Reyer's most successful opera, it is a lyrical treatment of the Siegfried episode in the Nibelung legend. It enjoyed great popularity in France at the height of the post-Wagnerian vogue for operas based on Nordic mythology, but it is nowadays only very rarely performed.
Plot: Legendary Rhineland. King Gunther's sister Hilda invokes the aid of the enchantress Uta to win the hero Sigurd. After drinking a drugged potion, Sigurd agrees to obtain Brunehild as Gunther's bride in exchange for the hand of Hilda. Disguised as Gunther, he seizes Brunehild, gives her to Gunther and marries Hilda. Brunehild, however, loves Sigurd, and when Hilda reveals the truth, he is released from the power of the potion and realizes that he returns Brunehild's affections. Sigurd is killed by Gunther's retainer Hagen, and Brunehild dies beside him. [R]

Si J'Étais Roi (*If I Were King*)
Opera in three acts by Adam. 1st perf Paris, 4 Sept 1852; libr by Adolphe Philippe d'Ennery and Jules Brésil. Principal roles: Nemea (sop), Zéphoris (ten), King (bar), Kadoor (bass), Zélida (sop). One of Adam's most successful works, nowadays only the delightful overture is at all remembered.
Plot: 16th-century Goa. The fisherman Zéphoris has rescued the princess Nemea from drowning and has fallen in love with her. Her father the King has Zéphoris brought to his castle to live in grand style, but has him thrown out when he becomes engaged to Nemea. The evil Prince Kadoor, who is plotting to kill the King and wed Nemea, challenges Zéphoris to a duel. The King appears, however, and banishes Kadoor and gives his consent to Zéphoris's marriage with Nemea. [R Exc]

Si la rigeur
Bass aria for Cardinal de Brogni in Act I of Halévy's *La Juive*, in which he decides that if harshness fails to convert unbelievers then mercy must be tried.

Silja, Anja (b 1940)
German soprano, particularly associated with Wagnerian roles and with 20th-century German operas, especially Berg. One of the finest operatic artists of the post-war era, she possesses a strong and firmly-placed voice and is a singing-actress of remarkable power and insight. Many of her finest early performances were given at Bayreuth in productions by WIELAND WAGNER, with whom she enjoyed a close artistic relationship. She created Luise in Einem's *Kabale und Liebe*. Married to the conductor CHRISTOPH VON DOHNÁNYI.

Silken Ladder, The
see SCALA DI SETA, LA

Silla
Opera in three acts by Händel. 1st perf London, 2 June 1713; libr by Giacomo Rossi, after Plutarch. Principal roles: Silla (c-ten), Metella (sop), Lepido (sop), Flavia (sop), Claudio (c-ten), Celia (sop). It tells of events in the life of the Roman Consul Lucius Cornelius Sulla (138–78 BC). One of Händel's earliest operas for London, much of the music was reused in *Amadigi di Gaula*. It is almost never performed.

Sills, Beverly (b Belle Silverman) (b 1929)
American soprano, particularly associated with Italian and French COLORATURA roles. Long resident at the New York City Opera, she had a small voice of exceptional agility, but her tone was often white and brittle and was aptly described by one critic as 'all icing sugar and no cake'. An outstanding singing-actress, she achieved greatest acclaim for her portrayal of Donizetti's three Tudor queens in *Anna Bolena*, *Maria Stuarda* and, particularly, *Roberto Devereux*. She created the Prima Donna in Weisgall's *Six Characters in*

Search of an Author. Possibly the most popular American singer since Grace Moore, she was director of the New York City Opera (1979–89). Her autobiography, *Beverly*, was published in 1987.

Silva, Don Ruy Gómez de
Bass role in Verdi's *Ernani*. He is a Spanish grandee in love with Elvira.

Silva, José da (1705–39)
Portuguese composer. He wrote five long-forgotten operas which were, in part, parodies of the Jesuit tragi-comedies so popular at that time. For his pains, he was burnt at the stake for heresy by order of the Inquisition.

Silveri, Paolo (b 1913)
Italian baritone, particularly associated with the Italian repertory, especially Verdi. Beginning as a bass, he enjoyed a short but brilliant career as one of the finest Verdi baritones of his time. In 1959, he made one excursion into the tenor repertory, singing the title-role in *Otello* in Dublin.

Silvio
Baritone role in Leoncavallo's *Pagliacci*. He is a farmer in love with Nedda.

Simionato, Giulietta (b 1910)
Italian mezzo, particularly associated with the Italian repertory. Perhaps the finest Italian mezzo of the post-war era, her rich and creamy voice was used with a technique and musicianship which enabled her to encompass both dramatic Verdi roles and COLORATURA Rossini roles. A fine singing-actress, she was ebullient in comedy and intense and commanding in tragedy. She created the Young Mother in Pizzetti's *Orsèolo*.

Simon Boccanegra
Opera in prologue and three acts by Verdi. 1st perf Venice, 12 March 1857; libr by Francesco Maria Piave, after Antonio García Gutiérrez's play. Revised version 1st perf Milan, 24 March 1881; libr revised by Arrigo Boito. Principal roles: Boccanegra (bar), Amelia (sop), Fiesco (bass), Gabriele (ten), Paolo (bar), Pietro (bass). Dealing with the historical Doge of Genoa (*c* 1301–69), it was musically and dramatically uneven in its original form, but Verdi revised it drastically at the height of his powers, expanding Paolo's role, adding the great Council Chamber Scene and building the Doge himself into one of the greatest musico-dramatic roles ever written for a baritone. Verdi's darkest and most sombre opera, for a century it was only very rarely performed, but in recent years its qualities have been appreciated and it is nowadays very popular.
Plot: Mid-14th-century Genoa. The corsair Boccanegra has had a daughter, whose whereabouts are now unknown, by the daughter of the patrician leader Jacopo Fiesco, who refuses to make peace with Boccanegra until the girl is found. The plebians under the leadership of the goldsmith Paolo Albiani engineer the election of Boccanegra as Doge, to the fury of Fiesco. Twenty years later, Boccanegra encounters the orphan Amelia, who has been brought up by Fiesco and who loves the patrician Gabriele Adorno. He discovers that she is in fact his long-lost daughter Maria. Paolo asks Boccanegra's permission to marry Amelia, but is rebuffed. Paolo has her abducted, but she escapes and Boccanegra, realizing Paolo's treachery, forces him to pronounce a curse upon himself in front of the Council. In retaliation, Paolo poisons Boccanegra's drink. Before he dies, Boccanegra is reconciled with Fiesco, blesses Amelia's union with Gabriele and names the latter as his successor. [R]

Simoneau, Léopold (b 1918)
Canadian tenor, particularly associated with Mozart roles and with the French repertory. A singer of outstanding style and refinement, he was arguably the finest interpreter of the French lyric repertory during the 1950s and early 1960s. He was artistic director of the Opéra de Québec for a brief period from 1971. His wife **Pierette Alarie** (*b* 1921) was a successful COLORATURA soprano.

Sinclair, Monica (b 1926)
British mezzo, particularly associated with Händel roles and with the British repertory. Possessing a rich and agile voice, she was also an accomplished singing-actress, being particularly successful in comedy. She created a

· *Singers in opera* ·

A number of opera singers have themselves subsequently appeared as operatic characters, including:

- Sophie Arnould in Pierné's *Sophie Arnould.*
- Faustina Bordoni in Louis Schubert's *Faustina Hasse.*
- Farinelli in Barnett's *Farinelli*, Auber's *La Part du Diable* and Bretón's *Farinelli.*
- Marie Favart in Offenbach's *Madame Favart.*
- Christine Nilsson in Björn Hallman's *Solitaire.*

Heavenly Being in Vaughan Williams's *The Pilgrim's Progress* and, for Walton, Evadne in *Troilus and Cressida* and Madame Popova in *The Bear.*

Sinding, Christian (1856–1941)
Norwegian composer. Although best known as a composer of piano music, he also wrote two operas: *Der Heilege Berg* (Dessau, 17 Apr 1914; libr Dora Duncker) [R] and the unperformed *Titandros* (libr Otto Sinding).

Sinfonia (Italian for 'symphony')
The term usually used by Italian composers to describe the overture to an opera.

Singher, Martial (1904–90)
French baritone, particularly associated with the French repertory. An elegantly-voiced singer, he was from 1943 largely resident at the Metropolitan Opera, New York. He created Bassanio in Hahn's *Le Marchand de Venise* and Bazaine in Milhaud's *Maximilien.* He was also a distinguished teacher, whose pupils included Jeannine Altmeyer, Judith Blegen, Donald Gramm, Thomas Hampson, James King, Louis Quilico, John Reardon, Thomas Moser and Benita Valente.

Singing-actor/actress
A term which has been much used in the post-war era to describe a singer whose operatic performances are as impressive for their dramatic interpretation as for their pure singing. Tito Gobbi and Maria Callas remain the most renowned examples.

Singspiel (German for 'song-play')
A form of opera which evolved in Germany and Austria in the second half of the 18th century in reaction against the rigid formality of OPERA SERIA and as an equivalent of French OPÉRA-COMIQUE. It consisted of self-contained musical numbers connected by spoken dialogue. Important early exponents of the genre were Hiller, Benda and Dittersdorf, and the form reached its apotheosis with Mozart's *Die Zauberflöte* and Beethoven's *Fidelio. See also* LIEDERSPIEL; SPIELOPER; ZAUBEROPER

Sinopoli, Giuseppe (b 1946)
Italian conductor and composer, particularly associated with the Italian repertory, especially Verdi and Puccini, and with Wagner. One of the most successful Italian conductors of the younger generation, his interpretations are always exciting, if occasionally hard-driven, but are sometimes of mind-bending idiosyncracy and are far from everybody's tastes, thereby causing much critical controversy. He was musical director of the Deutsche Oper, Berlin (1988–93). He has also composed one opera, *Lou Salomé* (Munich, 10 May 1981; libr Karl Dietrich Gräwe) [R Exc], which is written in post-expressionist style.

Sì pel ciel
Tenor/baritone duet (the Oath Duet) for Otello and Iago in Act II of Verdi's *Otello*, in which Iago vows to assist Otello in his vengeance.

Si può?
Baritone aria (the Prologue) for Tonio in Leoncavallo's *Pagliacci*, in which he

appears in front of the curtain and tells the audience that they are to witness a piece of real life.

Sir John in Love
Comic opera in four acts by Vaughan Williams. 1st perf London, 21 March 1929; libr by the composer, after William Shakespeare's *The Merry Wives of Windsor* and other sources. Principal roles: Falstaff (bar), Mistress Page (sop), Ann Page (sop), Page (bar), Mistress Ford (mezzo), Ford (bass), Fenton (ten), Mistress Quickly (mezzo), Pistol (bass), Slender (ten), Dr Caius (ten), Bardolph (ten). One of Vaughan Williams's finest works, unaccountably only very rarely performed, it combines folk-song idioms and some ardent love music in an opera of great charm and high spirits. [R]

Siroe, Rè di Persia (*Siroes, King of Persia*)
Opera in three acts by Händel. 1st perf London, 17 Feb 1729; libr by Nicola Francesco Haym, after Pietro Metastasio. Principal roles: Siroe (c-ten), Medarse (c-ten), Cosroe (bass), Emira (sop), Laodice (sop), Arasse (bass). Telling of events in the life of Chosroes II of Persia (reigned AD 591–628), it has never been one of Händel's more popular operas and is hardly ever performed.

Sitzprobe (German for 'sitting rehearsal')
The term used in Germany, Austria and Britain to describe the first complete rehearsal of an opera production in which the soloists and chorus join the orchestra. It is called *prova all'Italiana* in Italy.

Sì vendetta
Soprano/baritone duet for Gilda and Rigoletto in Act II of Verdi's *Rigoletto*, in which Rigoletto swears to have revenge on the Duke for dishonouring Gilda. One of opera's most powerful vengeance duets.

Six, Les
The name given to a group of young French composers, all of whom wrote operas, who came together in 1917 under the auspices of Satie and Jean Cocteau to promote the interests of their particular slick and witty style of modern music. The group comprised Auric, Louis Durey (1888–1979), Honegger, Milhaud, Poulenc and Germaine Tailleferre (1892–1983).

Škroup, František (1801–62)
Czech composer, conductor and singer. A crucial figure in the development of Czech opera (and the composer of the Czech national anthem), he was early drawn into the movement for Czech national music. His first opera *The Tinker* (*Drátenik*, Prague, 2 Feb 1826; libr Josef Chmelenský), in which he himself created the title-role, was the first opera written to a Czech libretto. His later works, all SINGSPIELS, were unsuccessful. They comprise seven works in German and a further two in Czech: *Oldřich and Božena* (Prague, 14 Dec 1828; libr Chmelenský) and *Libuše's Marriage* (*Libušin Sňatek*, Prague, 11 Apr 1835; libr Chmelenský). His brother **Jan Nepomuk** (1811–92) was also a composer, who wrote five operas.

Sleepwalking Scene
Soprano scene for: **1** Lady Macbeth ('Una maccia') in Act IV of Verdi's *Macbeth*. **2** Amina ('Ah! non credea mirarti') in Act II of Bellini's *La Sonnambula*.

Slezak, Leo (1873–1946)
Austrian tenor, particularly associated with heroic German and Italian roles, especially the title-role in Verdi's *Otello*. A singer of huge voice and physique, his vocal production was sometimes uneven, but this was more than compensated for by his magnificent phrasing, his excellent diction and his warm stage personality. After leaving the stage, he enjoyed a second career as a comedian in several Austrian films. His sense of humour was legendary: he once so dissolved the chorus at the Metropolitan Opera, New York, during a performance of *Aida* that they were all fined by the management – the fine was paid by Slezak. It was also Slezak who, accidentally failing to embark at the end of *Lohengrin*, enquired 'What time's the next swan?' His autobiography, *Song of Motley: Being the Reminiscences of a Hungry Tenor*, was published in 1938. His daughter **Margarete** (1901–53) was a successful soprano.

Slobodskaya, Oda (1888–1970)
Russian soprano, particularly associated

with the Russian repertory. From 1922, she was resident in Paris, where she created Parasha in Stravinsky's *Mavra*, and subsequently lived in London, where she also enjoyed great success as an operetta artist.

Slonimsky, Sergei (b 1932)
Russian composer. One of the earliest Russian composers to employ TWELVE-TONE techniques, he has written four operas. *Virineya* (Leningrad, 30 Sept 1967; libr Sergei Tsenin, after Lidyia Seyfullina; revised version Leningrad, Feb 1976) was followed by *The Master and Margarita* (Moscow, 20 May 1989, composed 1972; libr Yuri Dimitrin and V. Fialkovsky, after Mikhail Bulgakov), *Mariya Styuart* (Samara, 31 Jan 1981; libr Y.A. Gordin, after Stefan Zweig) and *Gamlet* (1990; libr Gordin, after Shakespeare's *Hamlet*).

Slovakia
see BRATISLAVA OPERA

Slovakian opera composers
see CIKKER; NEDBAL; SUCHOŇ
Other national opera composers include Jaraj Beneš (*b* 1940), Tibor Frešo (1918–67) and Ladislav Holoubek (*b* 1913).

Slovenian opera composers
These include Darjan Božič (*b* 1933), Davorin Jenko (1835–1914), Marij Kogoj (1895–1956), Marijan Kozina (1907–66), Gaspar Mašek (1794–1873), Jurij Mihevec (1805–82), Slavko Osterc (1895–1941), Franc Pollini (1762–1846), Risto Savin (*b* Friderik Širca) (1859–1948), Pavel Šivic (*b* 1908) and Jacob Zupan (1734–1810), whose *Belin* (*c* 1781) was the first opera written to a Slovenian text.

Sly
Opera in three acts by Wolf-Ferrari. 1st perf Milan, 29 Dec 1927; libr by Giovacchino Forzano, partly after William Shakespeare's *The Taming of the Shrew*. Principal roles: Sly (ten), Duke of Westmoreland (bar), Dolly (sop), John Plake (bar). Wolf-Ferrari's most ambitious opera, notable for its remarkable final scene, it deserves more than the very occasional performance which it currently receives.
Plot: London, 1603. At an inn, Sly antagonizes the Duke of Westmoreland. He is brought to the Duke's castle and is told that he is a nobleman recovering from an illness. The Duke's mistress Dolly is presented to him as his wife. When the two fall in love, the Duke has Sly thrown into a dungeon, where he expires. [R]

Smareglia, Antonio (1854–1929)
Italian composer. He wrote nine operas in a quasi-VERISMO style which was also influenced by Wagner. Several enjoyed great success in their time, especially in Germany, but they are nowadays – somewhat unjustly – largely forgotten. His first opera was the successful *Preziosa* (Milan, 20 Nov 1879; libr after Henry Longfellow's *The Spanish Student*). It was followed by *Bianca di Cervia* (Milan, 7 Feb 1882; libr F. Pozza), *Rè Nala* (Venice, 8 Feb 1887; libr V. Valle, after A. de Gubernatis's *Il Ritorno*), a failure which he later destroyed, *Il Vassallo di Szigeth* (Vienna, 18 June 1889; libr Pozza and Luigi Illica), *Cornil Schut* (Dresden, 6 June 1893; libr Illica), the successful *Nozze Istriane* (Trieste, 28 Mar 1895; libr Illica), *La Falena* (Venice, 6 Sept 1897; libr Silvio Benco), *Oceàna* (Milan, 20 Jan 1903; libr Benco), perhaps his finest opera, and *Abisso* (Milan, 10 Feb 1914; libr Benco). Totally blind by 1900, he was forced to dictate his last two operas.

Smetana, Bedřich (1824–84)
Czech composer. Regarded as the 'father of modern Czech music', his eight completed operas established a definitive groundwork of national music-dramas on which subsequent composers built, but which they seldom if ever surpassed. Notable for their prodigality of delightful melodies, for their remarkable ensembles, for their fine orchestration, for their choral writing and for their often deep psychological insight into character, his operas have (with one exception) been performed only infrequently outside the Czech lands, a neglect which is both unjust and inexplicable. The patriotic THE BRANDENBURGERS IN BOHEMIA was followed by his best-known opera, the ever-popular and ever-fresh THE BARTERED BRIDE. He next wrote the lofty and heroic DALIBOR, his masterpiece and arguably the greatest of all Czech operas. After the historical LIBUŠE (which is the Czech national opera

and which was written for the opening of the Prague National Theatre), he produced the light comedy THE TWO WIDOWS, THE KISS, THE SECRET and the richly-scored THE DEVIL'S WALL. The Shakespearian VIOLA was left unfinished.

Smeton
Mezzo trouser role in Donizetti's *Anna Bolena.* He is the historical Mark Smeaton (*d* 1536), a young musician in love with Anne.

Smyth, Dame Ethel (1858–1944)
British composer. The first woman composer of significance, she encountered a great deal of chauvanistic hostility, and played an important part in the campaign for women's suffrage. Her pure professionalism and her power-driver personality cut through all obstacles in her path, and she achieved the near-impossible feat of getting all of her operas performed in major houses during her own lifetime. She wrote six operas, whose style mixes late German romanticism with a breezy and irresistible Englishness. *Fantasio* (Weimar, 24 May 1898; libr composer and Harry Brewster, after Alfred de Musset) was followed by *The Forest* (Berlin, 9 Apr 1902; libr composer and Brewster), the highly successful THE WRECKERS, THE BOATSWAIN'S MATE, perhaps her finest opera, *Fête Galante* (Birmingham, 4 June 1923; libr Edward Shanks, after Maurice Baring) and *Entete Cordiale* (London, 22 July 1925; libr composer). After a period of complete neglect, there has recently been some revival of interest in her music. Her nine books include two volumes of autobiography, *Impressions That Remained* and *Streaks of Life*, which were published in 1919 and 1921.

Snow Maiden, The (*Snegourchka*)
Opera in prologue and four acts by Rimsky-Korsakov. 1st perf St Petersburg, 10 Feb 1882; libr by the composer, after Alexander Nikolayevich Ostrovsky's play. Principal roles: Snow Maiden (sop), Bobyl (ten), Lel (mezzo), Mizgir (bar), King Frost (bass), Spring (mezzo), Berendey (ten), Bobilyhka (mezzo), Kupava (sop). One of Rimsky's most successful fairy-tale operas, it combines the human and fantastic worlds in a charming manner, and boasts a score of delicacy and great orchestral brilliance. Still very popular in Russia, it is only infrequently performed elsewhere.
Plot: Legendary Russia. The Snow Maiden begs Spring to be allowed to remain, even though winter is ending. Mizgir falls in love with her, and his former love Kupava's complaints to Tsar Berendey achieve nothing, as the Tsar is captivated by the Snow Maiden's beauty. Terrified by Mizgir's passion, the Snow Maiden asks Spring to give her warmth of heart. This Spring agrees to, but warns her that she must keep it a secret from the sun. The sun finds out, however, and its rays melt the Snow Maiden. Mizgir drowns himself in despair. [R]

Sobinin
Tenor role in Glinka's *A Life for the Tsar.* Antonida's fiancé, he is Ivan's future son-in-law.

Sobinov, Leonid (1872–1934)
Russian tenor, particularly associated with lyrical Italian and Russian roles, especially Lensky. Regarded as the finest Russian tenor of the early 20th century, he was director of the Bolshoi Opera (1917–18 and 1921).

Söderblom, Ulf (b 1930)
Finnish conductor, particularly associated with the Finnish repertory. One of the leading figures in the remarkable contemporary operatic flowering in Finland, he was artistic director of the Finnish National Opera (1970–73) and conducted the first performances of Sallinen's *The Horseman* and *Kullervo*, Kokkonen's *The Last Temptations* and Heininen's *The Damask Drum* and *The Knife.*

Söderström, Elisabeth (b 1927)
Swedish soprano, particularly associated with Mozart, Strauss and Janáček roles. One of the most versatile operatic artists of the post-war era, she possessed a beautiful voice used with outstanding artistry and sensitivity, and was a singing-actress of uncommon insight and intensity, equally at home in serious or comic roles. Her remarkable versatility was amply demonstrated in 1959, when she sang the

Marschallin, Sophie and Octavian in *Der Rosenkavalier* within a year. She created Laura in Rosenberg's *The House With Two Entrances*, the title-role in Berwald's *The Queen of Golconda*, Juliana in Argento's *The Aspern Papers* and a role in Ligeti's *Le Grand Macabre*. Artistic director of the Drottningholm Castle Theatre (1990–). Her autobiography, *In My Own Key*, was published in 1979.

Sofia National Opera
Bulgaria's principal opera house (cap 1,200) replaced the previous theatre which had been destroyed in World War II. The annual season runs from September to June, and the repertory is strong in Russian and Italian works as well as native Bulgarian operas. Artistic directors have included the tenor Dimiter Uzunov and the bass Dimiter Petkov.

Sogno di Scipione, Il (*Scipio's Dream*)
Opera in one act by Mozart (K 126). 1st perf Salzburg, 29 April 1772; libr by Pietro Metastasio. Principal roles: Scipione (ten), Costanza (sop), Fortuna (sop), Publio (ten), Emilio (ten), Licenza (sop). It tells of the Roman Consul Publius Cornelius Scipio Africanus. One of Mozart's earliest stage works, described as a dramatic serenade, it is only very rarely performed.
Plot: North Africa, *c* 200 BC. The goddesses Fortune and Constancy appear to Scipio in a dream and demand that he chose between them. Fortune advocates the advantages of her changeability, whilst Constancy takes him to the Elysian Fields, where the spirits of his father Emilio and his grandfather Publius urge him to accept his earthly destiny and save Rome. Scipio choses Constancy. [R]

Sois immobile
Baritone aria for Tell in Act III of Rossini's *Guillaume Tell*, in which he urges Jemmy to remain still whilst he shoots the apple on his head.

Soldaten, Die (*The Soldiers*)
Opera in four acts by Zimmermann. 1st perf Cologne, 15 Feb 1965; libr by the composer, after Jakob Michael Lenz's play. Principal roles: Marie (sop), Stolzius (bar), Desportes (ten), Charlotte (mezzo), Countess de la Roche (mezzo), Wesener (bass). Zimmermann's only completed opera, it is written in serial style and employs jazz, film, dance, circus and electronic music, and several scenes take place simultaneously. One of the most controversial of all modern operas, it has been widely performed. The composer also arranged a vocal symphony from the music.
Plot: 18th-century Flanders. Marie is engaged to Stolzius, but allows herself to be seduced by Baron Desportes, a senior army officer. She subsequently takes a number of other lovers, and ends up as a soldier's prostitute. [R]

Soldiers' Chorus
1 'Gloire immortelle' in Act IV of Gounod's *Faust*. **2** 'Or co' dadi' in Act III of Verdi's *Il Trovatore*.

Solenne in quest' ora
Tenor/baritone duet for Don Alvaro and Don Carlo in Act III of Verdi's *La Forza del Destino*, in which they swear eternal friendship.

Solti, Sir Georg (b György) (b 1912)
Hungarian conductor and pianist, a British citizen since 1972. Particularly associated with Wagner, Strauss, Mozart and Verdi operas, he is one of the outstanding operatic conductors of the post-war era. His performances are notable for their precision, their great orchestral brilliance and their almost electric intensity and excitement. He was musical director of the Bavarian State Opera (1947–52), the Frankfurt Opera (1952–61), Covent Garden (1961–71) and the Salzburg Easter Festival (1992–3). Music director laureate of Covent Garden (1992–).

Sombre forêt
Soprano aria for Mathilde in Act II of Rossini's *Guillaume Tell*, in which she expresses her preference for the countryside over splendid palaces.

Song of the Flea
Bass-baritone aria ('Chanson de la Puce') for Méphistophélès in Part II of Berlioz's *La Damnation de Faust*, sung to entertain the students.

Song of the Viking Guest
Bass aria for the Viking Merchant in Scene IV of Rimsky-Korsakov's *Sadko*.

Son io dinanzi al Rè?
Bass/bass scene for King Philip and the Grand Inquisitor in Act IV of Verdi's *Don Carlos*, in which the Inquisitor accuses the King of permitting liberalism and demands of him the life of Posa. One of the most tremendous musico-dramatic scenes in all opera.

Son lo spirito che nega
Bass aria for Mefistofele in Act I of Boito's *Mefistofele*, in which he explains that he is the spirit of eternal negation.

Sonnambula, La (*The Sleepwalking Girl*)
Opera in two acts by Bellini. 1st perf Milan, 6 March 1831; libr by Felice Romani, after Eugène Scribe and J.-P. Aumer's ballet-pantomime *La Sonnambule ou L'Arrivé d'un Nouveau Seigneur*. Principal roles: Amina (sop), Elvino (ten), Rodolfo (bass), Lisa (sop), Teresa (mezzo). Bellini's most pastoral opera, it was an immediate success and is still regularly performed.
Plot: Early-19th-century Switzerland. Elvino is engaged to Amina, foster-daughter of Teresa. She is complimented by a stranger who is in fact the lord of the manor Count Rodolfo, returning after a long absence. The innkeeper Lisa, who also loves Elvino, visits the Count in his room, and when she hears a noise she runs away, dropping a handkerchief. Amina, sleepwalking, enters the Count's room. He tactfully leaves and she lies down to sleep. When she is found there the next day, Elvino refuses to believe the Count's explanation. He breaks off his engagement to Amina and decides to wed Lisa, but also breaks off that liaison when the handkerchief is found. Amina is later seen by everybody sleepwalking on the roof of the mill. When she has reached safety, Elvino wakes her and the two are reunited. [R]

Sophie
Soprano role in Strauss's *Der Rosenkavalier*. She is Faninal's daughter, betrothed to Baron Ochs.

Sophocles
see panel on page 525

Soprano
see panel on pages 526–7. See also COLORATURA SOPRANO; DUGAZON; FALCON; SOUBRETTE

Sorcerer, The
Operetta in two acts by Sullivan. 1st perf London, 17 Nov 1877; libr by W.S. Gilbert. Principal roles: J.W. Wells (bar), Aline (sop), Alexis (ten), Dr Daly (bar), Constance (sop), Lady Sangazure (mezzo), Sir Marmaduke (bass), Mrs Partlet (mezzo), Notary (bass). The first surviving full-length work of the Gilbert and Sullivan partnership, it is a satire on Victorian social conventions.
Plot: 19th-century England. Alexis is engaged to Aline, whilst their respective parents, Sir Marmaduke Pointdextre and Lady Sangazure, are also attracted to each other. Mrs Partlet's daughter Constance loves the curate Dr Daly, but dares not express her feelings. In futherance of his campaign to break down social barriers, Alexis hires the family sorcerer John Wellington Wells to distribute a love potion amongst the villagers which will cause the drinkers (if unmarried) to fall in love with the first person they see. The potion is duly administered, and everybody falls in love with the socially wrong people: Sir Marmaduke with Mrs Partlet, Aline with Dr Daly, Constance with the aged Notary and Lady Sangazure with Wells. Eventually, Wells offers himself up to the dark forces to break the spell, and everyone returns to their rightful partners. [R]

Sorceress, The
see ENCHANTRESS, THE

Sorochintsy Fair (*Sorochinskaya Yarmarka*)
Unfinished comic opera in three acts by Moussorgsky. 1st perf (in edition by Anatoly Liadov and Vyacheslav Karatygin) Moscow, 21 Oct 1913 (composed 1874); libr by the composer, after Nikolai Gogol's story. New realization by Cui 1st perf Petrograd, 26 Oct 1917; further version (that is now in usual usage) by Tcherepnin 1st perf Monte Carlo, 17 March 1923. Principal roles: Chervik (bass), Khivrya (mezzo), Parasya (sop), Gritzko (ten). A piece which makes

extensive use of Ukrainian folk melodies, Moussorgsky only completed about a third of the work before abandoning it. The opening of Act III is the famous NIGHT ON BARE MOUNTAIN.
Plot: 19th-century Ukraine. Parasya's disapproving stepmother Khivrya refuses permission for her to marry Gritzko. However, the discovery that Khivrya is having an adulterous affair with Chervik diminishes her authority, and the lovers are united. [R]

Sorozábal, Pablo (1897–1988)
Spanish composer and conductor. The last major composer of ZARZUELAS, his prolific output includes many works still popular in Spain. The most successful include *Katiuska* (Barcelona, 27 Jan 1931; libr Emilio González del Castillo and Manuel Martí Alonso) [R], *Adiós a la Bohemia* (Madrid, Dec 1933; libr Pío Baroja) [R], *La del Manojo de Rosas* (Madrid, 13 Nov 1934; libr Ramos de Castro) [R], *La Taberna del Puerto* (Barcelona, 1936; libr Carlos Fernández Shaw and Federico Romero) [R], *Don Manolito* (Madrid, 1943; libr Luis Fernández Sevilla and Anselmo C. Carreño) [R], *La Eterna Canción* (Barcelona, 27 Jan 1945; libr Fernández Sevilla) [R] and *Las de Caín* (Madrid, 1958; libr Serafín and Joaquín Álavarez Quintero) [R]. He also prepared a new edition of Albéniz's *Pepita Jiménez* in 1958. His autobiography, *Mi Vida y Mi Obra*, was published in 1986. His son **Pablo** is also a composer and conductor.

· Sophocles ·

The tragedies of the Greek dramatist Sophocles (495–406 BC) have inspired some 50 operas. Below are listed, by play, those operas by composers with entries in this dictionary.

Antigonae		
Traetta	*Antigonae*	1772
Zingarelli	*Antigone*	1790
Honegger	*Antigone*	1927
Krejčí	*Antigona*	1934
Orff	*Antigonae*	1949
Joubert	*Antigone*	1954
Elektra		
Haeffner	*Electra*	1787
Strauss	*Elektra*	1909
Ichneutae		
Roussel	*La Naissance de la Lyre*	1925
Oedipus the King		
Kovařovic	*Oedipus the King*	1894
Leoncavallo	*Edipo Rè*	1920
Stravinsky	*Oedipus Rex*	1927
Enescu	*Oedipe*	1936
Orff	*Oedipus der Tyrann*	1959
Oedipus at Colonus		
Sacchini	*Oedipe à Colone*	1786
Zingarelli	*Edipo a Colono*	1802
The Women of Thracis		
Händel	*Hercules*	1745
Saint-Saëns	*Déjanire*	1911
Eaton	*Heracles*	1964

· Soprano ·

Derived from the Italian *sopra* ('above'), soprano is the highest female vocal range. The term is also used to describe the highest artificial male voice (male soprano; *see* CASTRATO). Many different subdivisions of the soprano voice have evolved, particularly in Germany, France and Italy. They sometimes overlap and do not correspond precisely from one country to another. They are seldom used by composers, but are useful as an indication of the character of a role, if less so for its exact TESSITURA. The main French, German and Italian categories of soprano are as follows:

	Name	Range	Example
France	*soprano dramatique*	g to c'''	Valentine in *Les Huguenots*
	soprano lyrique	b♭ to c♯'''	Title-role in *Lakmé*
	Dugazon	a to c'''	Marguerite in *Richard Coeur de Lion*
	soubrette	b♭ to c'''	Zerlina in *Fra Diavolo*
	soprano demicaractère	a to c'''	Title-role in *Manon*
	Falcon	b to c♯'''	Alice in *Robert le Diable*
Germany	*dramatischer Sopran*	g to c'''	Brünnhilde in *Götterdämmerung*
	lyrische Sopran	b♭ to c'''	Title-role in *Arabella*
	hoher Sopran or *koloratur Sopran*	g to f'''	Zerbinetta in *Ariadne auf Naxos*
	soubrette	b♭ to c'''	Ännchen in *Der Freischütz*
Italy	*soprano drammatico*	g to c'''	Title-role in *Aida*
	soprano lirico	b♭ to c'''	Mimì in *La Bohème*
	soprano lirico spinto	a to c♯'''	Leonora in *Il Trovatore*
	soprano leggiero	g to f'''	Title-role in *Linda di Chamounix*

Below are listed the 242 sopranos with entries in this dictionary. Their nationalities are given in brackets afterwards.

Ackté, Aïno (Fin)
Albanese, Licia (It)
Albani, Dame Emma (Can)
Alda, Frances (NZ)
Amara, Lucine (US)
Ameling, Elly (Neth)
Anderson, June (US)
Angeles, Victoria de los (Sp)
Arnould, Sophie (Fr)
Arroyo, Martina (US)
Augér, Arleen (US)
Austral, Florence (Aust)
Baillie, Dame Isobel (Br)
Bampton, Rose (US)
Barstow, Josephine (Br)
Battle, Kathleen (US)
Begnis, Giuseppina Ronzi de (It)
Behrens, Hildegard (Ger)
Bellincioni, Gemma (It)
Beňačková, Gabriela (Slo)
Berger, Erna (Ger)
Bjoner, Ingrid (Nor)
Blegen, Judith (US)
Bordoni, Faustina (It)
Bori, Lucrezia (Sp)
Borkh, Inge (Swit)
Brouwenstijn, Gré (Neth)
Bumbry, Grace (US)
Burrowes, Norma (Br)
Caballé, Montserrat (Sp)
Callas, Maria (Gk)
Calvé, Emma (Fr)
Caniglia, Maria (It)
Carosio, Margherita (It)
Casa, Lisa della (Swit)
Cavalieri, Lina (It)
Cebotari, Maria (Russ)
Cerquetti, Anita (It)
Chiara, Maria (It)
Cigna, Gina (It)
Colbran, Isabella (Sp)
Collier, Marie (Aust)
Connell, Elizabeth (Ire)
Cotrubas, Ileana (Rom)
Crespin, Régine (Fr)
Cross, Joan (Br)
Cruz-Romo, Gilda (Mex)
Curtin, Phyllis (US)
Cuzzoni, Francesca (It)
Danco, Suzanne (Belg)
Darclée, Hariclea (Rom)
Dernesch, Helga (Aus)
Destinnová, Emmy (Cz)
Deutekom, Cristina (Neth)
Dimitrova, Ghena (Bulg)
Dobbs, Mattiwilda (US)
Donath, Helen (US)
Dugazon, Louise (Fr)
Duval, Denise (Fr)
Dvořková, Ludmila (Cz)
Eames, Emma (US)
Easton, Florence (Br)
Éda-Pierre, Christiane (Mart)
Evans, Anne (Br)
Falcon, Marie (Fr)
Farrar, Geraldine (US)
Farrell, Eileen (US)
Favero, Mafalda (It)
Figner, Medea (Russ)

Fisher, Sylvia (Aust)
Flagstad, Kerstin (Nor)
Fremstad, Olive (US)
Freni, Mirella (It)
Frezzolini, Erminia (It)
Galli-Curci, Amelita (It)
Garden, Mary (Br)
Gasdia, Cecilia (It)
Gayer, Catherine (US)
Gencer, Leyla (Turk)
Gluck, Alma (US)
Goltz, Christel (Ger)
Gomez, Jill (Br)
Gorchakova, Galina (Russ)
Grandi, Margherita (Aust)
Grisi, Giulia (It)
Grist, Reri (US)
Gruberová, Edita (Slo)
Grümmer, Elisabeth (Ger)
Gueden, Hilde (Aus)
Gustafson, Nancy (US)
Hammond, Dame Joan (NZ)
Harper, Heather (Br)
Harwood, Elizabeth (Br)
Hauk, Minnie (US)
Haymon, Cynthia (US)
Hempel, Frieda (Ger)
Hendricks, Barbara (US)
Hidalgo, Elvira de (Sp)
Hunter, Rita (Br)
Ivogün, Maria (Hung)
Janowitz, Gundula (Ger)
Jeritza, Maria (Cz)
Jones, Dame Gwyneth (Br)
Jurinac, Sena (Cro)
Kabaiwanska, Raina (Bulg)
Kanawa, Dame Kiri Te (NZ)
Kellogg, Clara Louise (US)
Kirsten, Dorothy (US)
Kniplová, Naděžda (Cz)
Konetzni, Hilde (Aus)
Köth, Erika (Ger)
Kubiak, Teresa (Pol)
Kupper, Annelies (Ger)
Kurz, Selma (Aus)
Kuznetsova, Maria (Russ)
László, Magda (Hung)
Lawrence, Marjorie (Aust)
Lear, Evelyn (US)
Lehmann, Lilli (Ger)
Lehmann, Lotte (Ger)
Leider, Frida (Ger)
Lemnitz, Tiana (Ger)
Lenya, Lotte (Aus)
Ligendza, Caterina (Swe)
Lind, Jenny (Swe)
Lindholm, Berit (Swe)
Litvinne, Félia (Fr)
Loose, Emmy (Aus)
Lorengar, Pilar (Sp)
Lott, Felicity (Br)
Malfitano, Catherine (US)
Martin, Janis (US)
Marton, Éva (Hung)
Masterson, Valerie (Br)
Mastilović, Daniča (Ser)
Mathis, Edith (Swit)
McNair, Sylvia (US)
McLaughlin, Marie (Br)
Melba, Dame Nellie (Aust)
Méric-Lalande, Henriette (Fr)
Mesplé, Mady (Fr)
Micheau, Janine (Fr)
Migenes, Julia (US)
Milanov, Zinka (Cro)
Mildmay, Audrey (Br)
Millo, Aprile (US)
Miolan-Carvalho, Marie (Fr)
Mitchell, Leona (US)
Miura, Tamaki (Jap)
Mödl, Martha (Ger)
Moffo, Anna (US)
Monte, Toti dal (It)
Moore, Grace (US)
Morison, Elsie (Aust)
Muzio, Claudia (It)
Neblett, Carol (US)
Németh, Mária (Hung)
Neway, Patricia (US)
Nilsson, Birgit (Swe)
Nilsson, Christine (Swe)
Noni, Alda (It)
Nordica, Lillian (US)
Norman, Jessye (US)
Novotná, Jarmila (Cz)
Olivero, Magda (It)
Pagliughi, Lina (It)
Pasta, Giuditta (It)
Patti, Adelina (It)
Pauly, Rosa (Hung)
Persiani, Fanny (It)
Peters, Roberta (US)
Petrella, Clara (It)
Pilarczyk, Helga (Ger)
Plowright, Rosalind (Br)
Pons, Lily (US)
Ponselle, Rosa (US)
Popp, Lucia (Slo)
Price, Leontyne (US)
Price, Dame Margaret (Br)
Raisa, Rosa (Pol)
Rethberg, Elisabeth (Ger)
Ricciarelli, Katia (It)
Rizza, Gilda dalla (It)
Robin, Mado (Fr)
Rothenberger, Anneliese (Ger)
Rysanek, Leonie (Aus)
Sanderson, Sybil (US)
Sass, Marie (Belg)
Sass, Sylvia (Hung)
Sayão, Bidú (Braz)
Schneider, Hortense (Fr)
Schröder-Devrient, Wilhelmine (Ger)
Schumann, Elisabeth (Ger)
Schwarzkopf, Elisabeth (Ger)
Sciutti, Graziella (It)
Scotto, Renata (It)
Seefried, Irmgard (Ger)
Sembrich, Marcella (Pol)
Shuard, Amy (Br)
Silja, Anja (Ger)
Sills, Beverly (US)
Slobodskaya, Oda (Russ)
Söderström, Elisabeth (Swe)
Souliotis, Elena (Gk)
Steber, Eleanor (US)
Stella, Antonietta (It)
Stich-Randall, Teresa (US)
Storace, Nancy (Br)
Storchio, Rosina (It)
Stratas, Teresa (Can)
Streich, Rita (Ger)
Strepponi, Giuseppina (It)
Studer, Cheryl (US)
Sutherland, Dame Joan (Aust)
Svobodová-Janků, Hana (Cz)
Tadolini, Eugenia (It)
Tebaldi, Renata (It)
Ternina, Milka (Cro)
Teschemacher, Marguerite (Ger)
Tetrazzini, Luisa (It)
Teyte, Dame Maggie (Br)
Tietjens, Teresa (Ger)
Tinsley, Pauline (Br)
Tomowa-Sintow, Anna (Bulg)
Traubel, Helen (US)
Turner, Dame Eva (Br)
Upshaw, Dawn (US)
Ursuleac, Viorica (Rom)
Vallin, Ninon (Fr)
Vaness, Carol (US)
Varady, Julia (Rom)
Varnay, Astrid (US)
Vaughan, Elizabeth (Br)
Vishnevskaya, Galina (Russ)
Vyvyan, Jennifer (Br)
Watson, Claire (US)
Watson, Lillian (Br)
Welitsch, Ljuba (Bulg)
Zampieri, Mara (It)
Zeani, Virginia (Rom)
Zylis-Gara, Teresa (Pol)

Sosarme, Rè di Media (*Sosarmes, King of Media*)
Opera in three acts by Händel. 1st perf London, 15 Feb 1732; libr after Antonio Salvi's *Dionisio Rè di Portogallo*, itself based on Matteo Noris's libretto for Antonio Pollarolo's *Alfonso Primo*. Principal roles: Sosarme (c-ten), Haliate (ten), Argone (bass), Altomaro (bass), Elmira (sop), Melo (mezzo), Erenice (mezzo).

Containing some of Händel finest operatic music, its highly muddled libretto has told against it and it is only infrequently performed.

Plot: Legendary Sardis (Lydia). Haliate and his son Argone are disputing the throne. The Median King Sosarmes, who is engaged to Argone's sister Elmira, unsuccessfully attempts to mediate in the dispute. The official Altomaro further exacerbates the situation by attempting to secure the throne for his grandson Melo, who is Haliate's illegitimate son. [R]

Sosostris
Contralto role in Tippett's *The Midsummer Marriage*. She is a seer.

Sotin, Hans (b 1939)
German bass, particularly associated with the German repertory, especially Wagner. One of the finest contemporary German basses, he has a rich and powerful voice, used with fine musicianship, and is an accomplished singing-actor, equally at home in serious or comic roles. He created Fr Rangier in Penderecki's *The Devils of Loudun*, Würfelspieler in Klebe's *Jakobowsky und der Oberst*, the Professor in Werle's *The Journey* and a role in Blacher's *Zwiehenfälle bei einer Nottlandung*.

Sotto voce (Italian for 'below the voice')
A direction to a singer to sing a phrase or passage quietly.

Soubrette (from the archaic French *soubret*, 'cunning')
Originally used to describe pert and scheming servant roles (such as Despina in *Cosi fan Tutte* and Serpina in *La Serva Padrona*), the term subsequently came to be used more generally to describe any light soprano comedy role. It is called *servetta* in Italy.

Souliotis, Elena (b 1943)
Greek soprano, particularly associated with dramatic Italian roles, especially Abigaille in Verdi's *Nabucco*. At her appearance she possessed one of the most abundant and exciting vocal and dramatic talents to have emerged for years, but within a very short time her recklessly undisciplined singing and her undertaking of heavy roles so young caused her voice to have deteriorated totally by the age of 30. Her powerful, dark, thrilling and resinous voice was strangely akin to that of Maria Callas, and she had a strong and committed stage presence. What might have been can be judged from her recording of Abigaille's cabaletta 'Salgo già il trono aurato' which, for all its technical faults, remains one of the most viscerally exciting pieces of dramatic singing ever committed to disc. She has recently re-emerged as a dramatic mezzo.

Sousa, John Philip (1854–1933)
American composer. Best known as a composer of military-style marches, he also wrote a number of operettas, of which the most successful was *El Capitán* (Boston, 13 Apr 1896; libr composer, C. Klein and T. Frost).

Soutullo, Reveriano (1884–1932)
Spanish composer. He wrote a number of ZARZUELAS, mostly in collaboration with Juan Vert Carbonell (1890–1931). The most successful were *La Leyenda del Beso* (Madrid, 18 Jan 1924; libr Enrique Reoyo, Antonio Paso and Silva Arambúru) [R] and *El Útimo Romántico* (Madrid, 9 Mar 1928; libr J. Tellaeche) [R].

Souzay, Gérard (b Tisserand) (b 1918)
French baritone, particularly associated with the French repertory and with baroque roles. One of the most stylish, intelligent and musicianly French singers of the post-war era, with superlative diction, he was best known as an outstanding lieder singer. His operatic appearances were sadly infrequent.

Sovrintendente (Italian for 'superintendent')
The title of the administrator of an Italian opera house.

Soyer, Roger (b 1939)
French bass, particularly associated with the French repertory and with Mozart roles, especially the title-role in *Don Giovanni*. His beautiful and smoothly produced voice, of considerable range, is used with great intelligence, and he has a strong stage presence. He created MacCreagh in Bécaud's *Opéra d'Aran*.

Spain
see TEATRO DE LA ZARZUELA, MADRID; TEATRO LICEO, BARCELONA

Spalanzani
Tenor role in Offenbach's *Les Contes d'Hoffmann*. An inventor, he is Olympia's 'father'.

Spanish opera composers
see ALBÉNIZ; ARRIAGA; ARRIETA; BARBIERI; BRETÓN; CABALLERO; CHAPÍ; CHUECA; FALLA; GAZTAMBIDE; GERHARD; GIMÉNEZ; GRANADOS; GUERRERO; GURIDI; LUNA; MARTÍN Y SOLER; PEDRELL; PENELLA; RODRÍGUEZ DE HITA; SERRANO; SOROZÁBAL; SOUTULLO; TORREJÓN; TORROBA; TURINA; USANDIZAGA; VALVERDE; VIVES

Sparafucile
Bass role in Verdi's *Rigoletto*. Maddalena's brother, he is a hired assassin.

Speziale, Lo (*The Apothecary*)
Comic opera in three acts by Haydn. 1st perf Esterháza, autumn 1768; libr by Carlo Goldoni. Principal roles: Sempronio (ten), Grilletta (sop), Mengone (ten), Volpino (sop). An entertaining little piece, it is still occasionally performed, although the music of Act III is lost.
Plot: 18th-century Italy. The newspaper-addicted old apothecary Sempronio wishes to marry his pretty young ward Grilletta. She is also courted by the serious-minded Mengone and by the light-hearted Volpino. After much intrigue, Mengone eventually wins her. [R]

Spieloper (German for 'opera-play')
A form of 19th-century German light opera, very similar to SINGSPIEL, which consisted of an opera on a comic subject and containing spoken dialogue. A number of Lortzing's works fall into this category.

Spinning Chorus
Women's chorus in Act II of Wagner's *Der Fliegende Holländer*.

Spinning Room, The (*Székely Fonó*)
Opera in one act by Kodály. 1st perf Budapest, 24 April 1932. Principal roles: Wife (mezzo), Lover (bar), Youth (ten), Neighbour (mezzo), Girl (sop). Described as 'lyric scenes with folk songs from Transylvania', it can barely be called an opera, the dramatic action being very tenuous. It is virtually unknown outside Hungary, but is notable for its fine choral writing. [R]

Spinto (Italian for 'pushed')
A description given to a voice or a role containing vigour and attack. Usually used only with reference to sopranos or tenors, it can be modified, as in soprano lirico spinto, which would describe Leonora in *Il Trovatore*.

Spirto gentil
see ANGE SI PURE

Spohr, Louis (1784–1859)
German composer, violinist and conductor. His music marks the link between the older classical composers and the new German romantic school, of which he is in effect the first exemplar. His first opera *Die Prüfung* (Gotha, 1806; libr E. Henke) made little impression. His first major success was his fourth opera FAUST, which was followed by ZEMIRE UND AZOR, JESSONDA, his finest opera, *Der Berggeist* (Kassel, 24 Mar 1823; libr Georg Döring), *Pietro von Abano* (Kassel, 13 Oct 1827; libr Karl Pfeiffer, after Ludwig Tieck), *Der Alchymist* (Kassel, 28 July 1830; libr Pfeiffer, after Washington Irving's *The Student of Salamanca*) and *Die Kreuzfahrer* (Kassel, 1 Jan 1845; libr composer and Marianne Spohr, after August von Kotzebue). He was musical director of the Kassel Staatstheater from 1847 and was perhaps the first modern-style conductor, introducing the use of the baton. He was also one of the earliest champions of Wagner. His autobiography was published in 1861.

Spoleto
see FESTIVAL OF TWO WORLDS, SPOLETO

Spoletta
Tenor COMPRIMARIO role in Puccini's *Tosca*. He is one of Scarpia's agents.

Spontini, Gasparo (1774–1851)
Italian composer, often referred to as 'the father of grand opera'. His first nine operas, beginning with *I Puntigli delle Donne* (Rome, 1796), are unremarkable essays in existing Italian styles. His success dated from his move to Paris in 1803, where he established his reputation with MILTON, his first major work, and *Julie* (Paris, 12 Mar 1805; libr A.G. Jars). Adopting, and intensifying, the classical features of Gluck, Méhul and Cherubini, he applied them to grandiose subjects with striking scenic effects, vast choruses and

much pageantry. The hugely successful LA VESTALE, his best-known opera, was followed by the equally successful FERNAND CORTEZ, OLYMPIE, *Nurmahal* (Berlin, 27 May 1822; libr Carl Alexander Herklotz, after Thomas Moore's *Lalla Rookh*), *Alcidor* (Berlin, 23 May 1825; libr G.M. Théaulon de Lambert, after Rochon de Chabannes) and AGNES VON HOHENSTAUFEN. His influence on the development of opera was enormous: Wagner regarded him highly, and he set the guidelines to which the whole subsequent French grand opera school of Meyerbeer and the rest conformed. A fine and currently underrated and neglected composer.

Sportin' Life
Tenor role in Gershwin's *Porgy and Bess*. He is Catfish Row's supplier of 'happy dust'.

Sposo Deluso, Lo (*The Deluded Husband*) or **La Rivalità di Tre Donne per un Solo Amante** (*The Rivalry of Three Women for a Single Lover*)
Unfinished comic opera in two acts by Mozart (K 430). Composed 1783; libr possibly by Lorenzo da Ponte. Principal roles: Bettina (sop), Pulchiero (ten), Bocconio (bass), Eugenia (sop), Asdrubale (ten). Only five numbers exist, three complete and the other two only sketched.
Plot: 18th-century Leghorn. The rich old bachelor Bocconio is awaiting his bride, the Roman noblewoman Eugenia. He is chided by his niece Bettina and her sweetheart Don Asdrubale, and his misogynist friend Pulchiero is scornful. Eugenia arrives but threatens to leave as she feels that she was not received with sufficient ceremony. She recognizes Asdrubale as her former lover and faints. While Bocconio goes for medicine, Asdrubale upbraids her for her infidelity. [R]

Sprechgesang (German for 'speech-song')
A type of vocal utterance originated by Schönberg, which is midway between singing and ordinary speech. The voice touches the note (which is usually marked in a special way in the score) but does not sustain it. It is employed in many TWELVE-TONE operas such as *Wozzeck*.

Sprechstimme (German for 'speaking voice')
A similar but earlier-derived form of vocal production to SPRECHGESANG, it was first used by Humperdinck in his original 1897 version of *Die Königskinder*, but was omitted in the revised 1910 version.

Squeak
Tenor role in Britten's *Billy Budd*. He is Claggart's below-decks informer.

Stabile, Mariano (1885–1968)
Italian baritone, particularly associated with the Italian repertory, especially Falstaff, which he sang over 1,000 times. His voice was good if never particularly beautiful, and it was used with style and intelligence. He had excellent diction and was an outstanding singing-actor, especially in comedy, and enjoyed a remarkably long career, singing into his early 70s. He created the title-role in Respighi's *Belfagor*.

Staccato (Italian for 'detatched')
A method of singing (an instruction for which is marked by a dot over the note in the score), whereby a note is shortened, and thus detatched from the following note, by being held for slightly less than its full value.

Stade, Frederica von (b 1945)
American mezzo, particularly associated with Mozart and Rossini roles and with the French repertory. One of the most accomplished contemporary lyric mezzos, she has a beautiful, agile and smoothly produced voice, used with intelligence and musicianship and a fine technique. She is a persuasive singing-actress, equally at home in serious or comic roles. She created Nina in Pasatieri's *The Seagull*, the title-role in Villa-Lobos's *Yerma*, Tina in Argento's *The Aspern Papers* and Merteuil in Conrad Susa's *Les Liaisons Dangereuses*.

Stagione (Italian for 'season')
The term has two meanings in opera:
1 The *stagione lirica* is the opera season in an Italian theatre. **2** The stagione system is the mounting of several performances of an opera production within a fairly short period and maintaining the same cast. Its opposite is the repertory system.

Stamitz, Karl (b Karel Stamic) (1745–1801)
Bohemian composer, son of the composer **Johann Stamitz**. Although best known as an orchestral composer, he also wrote two stage works: the SINGSPIEL *Der Verliebte Vormund* (*c* 1786) and the opera *Dardanens Sieg* (*c* 1800). The music for both works is lost.

Stanford, Sir Charles Villiers (1852–1924)
Irish composer. He wrote ten operas, several of which enjoyed considerable success in their time. He had a certain theatrical flair, and the almost total oblivion into which his stage works have fallen seems somewhat unjustified. His first opera *The Veiled Prophet of Khorassan* (Hanover, 6 Feb 1881; libr William Barclay Squire, after Thomas Moore's *Lalla Roukh*) was followed by *Savonarola* (Hamburg, 18 Apr 1884; libr Gilbert Arthur A'Beckett), THE CANTERBURY PILGRIMS, the unfinished *The Miner of Falun* (1888; libr Squire and H.F. Wilson, after E.T.A. Hoffmann's *Das Bergwerk zu Falun*), the unperformed *Lorenza* (1894; libr Antonio Ghislanzoni and Ferdinando Fontana), the once popular SHAMUS O'BRIEN, perhaps his finest opera, the unperformed *Christopher Patch* (1897; libr Benjamin Charles Stephenson and George H. Jessop), the Shakespearian MUCH ADO ABOUT NOTHING, the comedy THE CRITIC and the successful THE TRAVELLING COMPANION. He was also a noted teacher whose pupils included Benjamin, Bliss, Boughton, Bridge, Coleridge-Taylor, Holst, Howells, Ireland and Vaughan Williams.

Stanislavsky, Konstantin
see under NEMIROVICH-DANCHENKO, VLADIMIR

Stasov, Vladimir (1824–1906)
Russian critic. One of the most important critics in musical history, his friendship with and encouragement of the composers of the MIGHTY HANDFUL (a phrase which he coined) exerted an enormous influence on the development of the Russian nationalist school. He provided the scenario for *Prince Igor* and co-authored the libretto for *Khovanschina*, as well as writing important studies of Borodin, Cui, Glinka, Moussorgsky and Rimsky-Korsakov.

State Opera of South Australia
Based in Adelaide, the company was formed in 1974 and was originally called New Opera South Australia. It performs at either the Festival Theatre (cap 1,978), which opened in 1973, or at the Victorian Opera Theatre (cap 1,009), originally opened as the Tivoli Theatre in 1913. Musical directors have included Myer Fredman and Andrew Green.

Steber, Eleanor (1916–90)
American soprano, particularly associated with Verdi, Mozart and Puccini roles. Largely based at the Metropolitan Opera, New York, from 1940, she had a rich and firm voice of great beauty, which she used with fine musicianship. She created the title-role in Barber's *Vanessa*. Her autobiography was published in 1994.

Stefano, Giuseppe di (b 1921)
Italian tenor, particularly associated with the Italian repertory. Possessor of one of the smoothest, most beautiful and liquid tenor voices of the post-war era, he began by singing lighter lyric roles. He subsequently (and most unwisely) turned to heavier roles, which caused his voice to spread and coarsen. Despite the great natural beauty of his vocal instrument, he was an unsubtle and at times vulgar interpreter and had little dramatic ability. He created Giuliano in Pizzetti's *Il Calzare d'Argento*.

Steffani, Agostino (1654–1728)
Italian composer, cleric and diplomat. He wrote 16 operas, including *Niobe* (Munich, 1688; libr Luigi Orlandini), *Enrico Leone* (Hamburg, 30 Jan 1689; libr Ortensio Mauro) [R Exc] and *La Libertà Contenta* (Hanover, 3 Feb 1693; libr Mauro). He fulfilled a number of political duties at various German courts, including being Ambassador to Brussels in 1698.

Stein, Horst (b 1928)
German conductor, particularly associated with Wagner operas. A fine and sometimes underrated Wagnerian interpreter, he was musical director of the Mannhein Opera (1963–70) and the Hamburg Opera (1972–9). He conducted the first performance of Einem's *Der Besuch der Alten Dame*.

Stella, Antonietta (b 1929)
Italian soprano, particularly associated with the Italian repertory. One of the finest Italian sopranos of the 1950s, she had a voice of great beauty and considerable agility. Her fine technique allowed her to sing roles as diverse as the title-roles in Donizetti's *Linda di Chamounix* and Verdi's *Aida*. She created the title-role in de Bellis's *Maria Stuarda*.

Stenhammar, Wilhelm (1871–1927)
Swedish composer and conductor. Although best known as an orchestral composer, he also wrote two operas: *The Feast of Solhaug* (*Gildat på Solhaug*, Stuttgart, 12 Apr 1899, composed 1893; libr Borch, after Henrik Ibsen) and *Tirfing* (Stockholm, 9 Dec 1898; libr Anna Broberg).

Števa Buryja
Tenor role in Janáček's *Jenůfa*. He is Laca's drunken stepbrother.

Stevens, Risë (b Steenberg) (b 1913)
American mezzo, particularly associated with the French repertory, especially Carmen. Her warm and beautiful voice was allied to fine musicianship, outstanding dramatic talent and great personal beauty. She created Eriodade in Mortari's *La Figlia del Diavolo* and also appeared in a number of films, including *Going My Way* and *The Chocolate Soldier*. She was general manager of the Metropolitan National Touring Company (1965–7).

Stewart, Thomas (b 1928)
American baritone, particularly associated with Wagnerian roles, especially Wotan and the Dutchman (in *Der Fliegende Holländer*). Although not a true heroic baritone, his voice was well schooled and of considerable power and range, and he was a fine singing-actor. He created William in Blacher's *Rosamunde Floris* and Jupiter in Klebe's *Alkmene*. Married to the soprano EVELYN LEAR.

Stich-Randall, Teresa (b 1927)
American soprano, particularly associated with Mozart and lighter Verdi roles. She had an attractive, creamy voice and demonstrated great elegance of line and phrasing. The first American singer to be named an Austrian Kammersänger, she created Henrietta M. in Thomson's *The Mother of Us All*, the title-role in Luening's *Evangeline* and a role in Martin's *Le Mystère de la Nativité*.

Stiedry, Fritz (1883–1968)
Austrian conductor, particularly associated with Wagner and Verdi operas. He was musical director of the Vienna Volksoper (1924–8) and the Berlin State Opera (1929–33). After being forced to leave Germany by the Nazis, he became head of the German wing at the Metropolitan Opera, New York. He conducted the first performances of Weill's *Die Bürgschaft*, Schönberg's *Die Glückliche Hand* and Schmidt's *Fredegundis*.

Stiffelio
Opera in three acts by Verdi. 1st perf Trieste, 16 Nov 1850; libr by Francesco Maria Piave, after Émile Souvestre and Eugène Bourgeois's *Le Pasteur ou l'Évangile et le Foyer*. Principal roles: Stiffelio (ten), Lina (sop), Stankar (bar), Jorg (bass), Raffaele (ten). Revised version AROLDO, 1st perf Rimini, 16 Aug 1857. The last and one of the finest of Verdi's early period operas, it met with little success at its appearance, partly because Italian audiences found the idea of a priest's adulterous wife shocking – indeed, modern audiences still find the piece a little uncomfortable. Long believed lost, the orchestral score was rediscovered in 1968 and since then *Stiffelio* has usually been preferred to the revised *Aroldo*. A work of considerable dramatic power and insight, notable for its freedom of structure and for the declamatory intensity of Stiffelio's music, it is as yet only intermittently performed, but the revelatory Covent Garden production in 1993 is likely to change that.
Plot: Early-19th-century Austria. The evangelical Protestant minister Stiffelio returns home to discover that his wife Lina has been unfaithful. Her father Count Stankar tries to prevent him from learning the identity of the seducer, Raffaele, but provokes a duel with him. Stiffelio stops the fight, but learns the truth and offers Lina a divorce. Stankar kills Raffaele, and Stiffelio forgives Lina from the pulpit and takes her back. [R]

Stignani, Ebe (1903–74)
Italian mezzo, particularly associated with the Italian repertory. The leading mezzo of the inter-war period, she had a rich and powerful voice of remarkable range (f to c'''), which allowed her to sing some dramatic soprano roles. Her regal, opulent and committed singing distracted attention from the fact that her technique was not perfect and that her acting abilities were limited. She created the Voice in Respighi's *Lucrezia* and Cathos in Lattuada's *Le Preziose Ridicole*.

Stile rappresentativo (Italian for 'representational style')
The term used by the first opera composers of the FLORENTINE CAMERATA to describe the style of sung RECITATIVE which they introduced in 'representation' of speech.

Still, William Grant (1895–1978)
American composer, who employed Negro and American folk idioms in his music. The first black American composer to win serious recognition in opera, he wrote first in avant-garde style and later in a neo-romantic vein. His operas are the unperformed *Blue Steel* (1934; libr B. Forsythe, after C. Moss), *A Bayou Legend* (Jackson, 15 Nov 1974, composed 1941; libr V. Arvey), *Troubled Island* (New York, 31 Mar 1949, composed 1928; libr Arvey and Langston Hughes), his finest work, which is set in Haiti, *Costaso* (Pasadena, 23 May 1992, composed 1949; libr Arvey), the unperformed *Mota* (1951; libr Arvey) and *The Pillar* (1955; libr Arvey), *Minette Fontaine* (Baton Rouge, 24 Oct 1985, composed 1958; libr Arvey) and *Highway No 1 USA* (Miami, 11 May 1963; libr Arvey).

Stockhausen, Karlheinz (b 1928)
German composer. A leader of the extreme avant-garde, his one operatic work is the cycle LICHT, projected to comprise seven works, one for each day of the week. A vast undertaking of great technical difficulty and complexity, four operas have been performed to date.

Stockholm
see ROYAL OPERA, STOCKHOLM

Stokowski, Leopold (b Antoni Stanisław Bołesławowich) (1882–1977)
British-born American conductor. Best known as a symphonic conductor, his operatic appearances were extremely rare, but included the American premiere of *Wozzeck* and *Turandot* at the Metropolitan Opera, New York.

Stolz, Robert (1880–1975)
Austrian composer and conductor. He wrote some 65 operettas, of which the most successful include *Der Tanz ins Glück* (Vienna, 18 Nov 1921; libr Robert Bodanzky and B. Hardt-Warden), *Zwei Herzen in Drei-vierteltakt* (Zürich, 30 Sept 1933; libr Paul Knepler, Robert Gilbert and Ignaz Welleminsky), *Himmelblaue Träume* (Zürich, 30 Nov 1934; libr Gilbert and A.L. Robinson) [R Exc] and *Trauminsel* (Bregenz, 21 July 1962; libr Gilbert and Per Schwenzen) [R]. He conducted the first performance of O. Straus's *Der Tapfere Soldat*. His great-aunt **Teresa** (*b* Terezie Stolzová) (1834–1902) was a successful soprano, regarded by Verdi as one of the ideal interpreters of his later soprano roles, especially Aida.

Stolze, Gerhard (1926–79)
German tenor, particularly associated with German character roles, especially Mime and Herod, his psychopathic portrayal of the second being one of the most extraordinary operatic interpretations of modern times. One of the finest singing-actors of the post-war era (he had begun as a straight actor), his highly individual voice was far from beautiful but was used with musicianship and great intelligence, and its range was such that he was able to sing Oberon in *A Midsummer Night's Dream*. He created the title-role in Orff's *Oedipus der Tyrann*, the Colonel in Klebe's *Jakobowsky under der Oberst*, Forstmeister in Erbse's *Julietta*, Clestakov in Egk's *Der Revisor* and Satan in Martin's *Le Mystère de la Nativité*.

Stone Guest, The (*Kammeny Gost*)
Opera in three acts by Dargomijsky. 1st perf St Petersburg, 28 Feb 1872 (composed 1868); a setting of Alexander Pushkin's dramatic poem. Principal roles: Don Juan (ten), Leporello (bass), Donna Anna (sop), Laura (mezzo), Carlos (bar),

Monk (b-bar), Statue (bass). An historically important work, it employs dramatic RECITATIVE throughout and is the first opera of importance to set a literary work as it stands. It had a considerable influence on subsequent Russian composers, particularly Moussorgsky. Not quite finished at his death, it was completed by Cui and orchestrated by Rimsky-Korsakov. It is only rarely performed outside Russia.
Plot: 17th-century Spain. Don Juan, returned from exile with his servant Leporello, determines to seduce Donna Anna, widow of the Commander, who he has killed. Don Juan flippantly asks the Commander's statue to dine at Donna Anna's house. The statue accepts the invitation and drags Don Juan down to hell. [R]

Storace, Nancy (b Ann Selina) (1765–1817)
British soprano, sister of the composer STEPHEN STORACE and wife of the composer **John Abraham Fisher**. Perhaps the finest British singer of the late 18th century, she was an admired singing-actress, especially successful in comedy. She created Susanna in *Le Nozze di Figaro*, Lilla in Martín y Soler's *Una Cosa Rara*, the title-role in Cimarosa's *Artemisia* and, for Salieri, Eleonora in *Prima la Musica e Poi le Parole* and the Countess in *La Scuola dei Gelosi*.

Storace, Stephen (1762–96)
British composer, brother of the soprano NANCY STORACE. He wrote a number of stage works, several of which enjoyed great success in their time. They include *Gli Sposi Malcontenti* (Vienna, 1 June 1785; libr Gaetano Brunati), GLI EQUIVOCI, his only opera still to be remembered, *La Cameriera Astuta* (Vienna, 4 Mar 1788), *Dido* (London, 23 May 1792; libr Prince Hoare, after Pietro Metastasio) and *The Cherokee* (London, 20 Dec 1794; libr James Cobb).

Storchio, Rosina (1876–1945)
Italian soprano, particularly associated with lyrical Italian and French roles. She had a beautiful voice of considerable agility and a fragile and affecting stage presence. She created Cio-Cio-San in *Madama Butterfly*, the title-roles in Leoncavallo's *Zazà* and Mascagni's *Lodoletta*, Stefana in Giordano's *Siberia* and Musetta in Leoncavallo's *La Bohème*.

Story of a Real Man, The (*Povest o Nastoyashchem Cheloveke*)
Opera in three acts by Prokofiev (Op 117). 1st perf (privately) Leningrad, 3 Dec 1948; 1st public perf Moscow, 7 Oct 1960; libr by the composer and Mira Mendelson-Prokofieva, after Boris Polevoy's novella. Principal roles: Alexei (bar), Olga (sop), Andrei (bass), Commissar (bar). Prokofiev's last opera, it was the piece which he hoped (mistakenly) would bring him back to favour with the Stalinist authorities. It is only infrequently performed.
Plot: Russia, 1942. The aviator Alexei is shot down into deep forest, where he wanders for 18 days before being found. He is taken to hospital, where both his feet are amputated, and where he lies in delirium, horrified to think that he will never fly again. The Commissar tells him of an aviator who flew again after similar injuries, and Alexei resolves to do the same. After initially refusing, the medical team, impressed by his determination, allows him to fly again. Finally, he is reunited with his fiancée Olga. [R]

Stracciari, Riccardo (1875–1955)
Italian baritone, particularly associated with the Italian repertory, especially Rossini's Figaro, which he sang over 900 times. One of the finest baritones of the inter-war period, he possessed an imposing voice which he used with style and a fine technique. He was later a distinguished teacher, whose pupils included Paolo Silveri, Alexander Sved and Boris Christoff.

Stradella, Alessandro (1642–82)
Italian composer. He wrote a number of operas and INTERMEZZI which influenced the later Neapolitan school, but which are all now forgotten. They include *Il Trespolo Tutore* (Genoa, 30 Jan 1679; libr G. Villifranchi) and *Moro per Amore* (Genoa, 1681; libr Flavio Orsini). He led a colourful and adventurous life (he was murdered over an affair to which his mistress's brothers took exception), parts of which form the basis of Flotow's

ALESSANDRO STRADELLA and Louis Niedermeyer's *Stradella.*

Straniera, La (*The Foreign Woman*)
Opera in two acts by Bellini. 1st perf Milan, 14 Feb 1829; libr by Felice Romani, after Victor-Prévôt, Vicomte d'Arlincourt's *L'Étrangère*. Principal roles: Alaide (sop), Arturo (ten), Valdeburgo (bar), Isoletta (mezzo), Prior (bass). One of the least successful of Bellini's mature operas, it is only infrequently performed.
Plot: 14th-century Brittany. Arturo is engaged to Isoletta, but falls in love with the stranger Alaide, whom some believe to be a witch. Seeing her at a secret meeting with Valdeburgo (who is in fact her brother), Arturo challenges Valdeburgo to a duel during which the latter appears to slip and drown in a lake. Although Arturo attempts to take the blame, Alaide is accused of murder. However, Valdeburgo turns out to be alive and, at his insistence, Arturo agrees to go ahead with his marriage to Isoletta. However, when he finds out that Alaide is the unlawfully wedded wife of the French king, Arturo kills himself.

Strasbourg
see OPÉRA DU RHIN

Stratas, Teresa (b Anastasia Strataki) (b 1938)
Canadian soprano, with a wide-ranging repertory encompassing COLORATURA, lyrical and modern dramatic roles. Essentially a lyric soprano with a highly individual timbre, she sings with great intelligence and musicianship and is one of the finest contemporary singing-actresses. She played Violetta in Zeffirelli's film of *La Traviata* and created the title-role in the three-act version of *Lulu*, Queen Isabella in de Falla's *L'Atlántida*, the title-role in Glanville-Hicks's *Nausicaa* and Marie Antoinette in Corigliano's *The Ghosts of Versailles*.

Straus, Oscar (1870–1954)
Austrian composer. He wrote over 40 Viennese operettas, of which the most successful included EIN WALZERTRAUM, DER TAPFERE SOLDAT and *Drei Walzer* (Zürich, 5 Oct 1935; libr Paul Knepler and A. Robinson) [R]. His one serious opera, *Bozena* (Munich, 16 May 1952; libr Julius Brammer and Alfred Grünwald), was a failure.

Strauss, Johann (II) (1825–99)
Austrian composer and violinist, son of Johann Strauss I and brother of Josef and Eduard Strauss. Popularly known as the 'Waltz King', he wrote 16 operettas, establishing the classic form of the Viennese school of the genre. His first work *Indigo und die Vierzig Räuber* (Vienna, 10 Feb 1871; libr Maximilian Steiner) [R Exc] was reasonably successful, but its successor *Der Karneval in Rom* (Vienna, 1 Mar 1873; libr Josef Braun, after Victorien Sardou's *Piccolino*) [R Exc] was a failure. His third work was the immortal DIE FLEDERMAUS, the quintessential Viennese operetta and arguably the most enduringly popular of all light operas. His subsequent works include *Cagliostro in Wien* (Vienna, 27 Feb 1875; libr F. Zell and Richard Genée), *Prinz Methusalem* (Vienna, 3 Jan 1877; libr Carl Treumann, after Wilder and Delacour), *Blinde-Kuh* (Vienna, 18 Dec 1878; libr Rudolf Kneisel), *Das Spitzentuch der Königin* (Vienna, 1 Oct 1880; libr Genée and Heinrich Bohrmann-Riegen, after Miguel Cervantes), EINE NACHT IN VENEDIG, the highly successful DER ZIGEUNERBARON, the more serious *Ritter Pázmán* (Vienna, 1 Jan 1892; libr Lajos Dóczy, after J. Arany) and *Der Waldmeister* (Vienna, 4 Dec 1895; libr Gustav Davis). The successful WIENER BLUT is a pastiche arranged from his other works.

Strauss, Richard (1864–1949)
German composer and conductor. A disciple of Wagner, he was an infant prodigy, and his early orchestral tone poems established him as a leading modernist as regards harmonic audacity and orchestration, in which latter field he became one of the most brilliant exponents in musical history. His first two operas, GUNTRAM and FEUERSNOT, both heavily influenced by Wagner, met with little success, but the sensational SALOME established him at the forefront of contemporary opera composers. It was followed by the violent ELEKTRA, arguably his greatest opera, which marked the beginning of his partnership with HUGO

VON HOFMANNSTHAL. He then turned to a more lyrical and neo-classical style, inspired by his love of Mozart, with DER ROSENKAVALIER, his most popular opera. There followed ARIADNE AUF NAXOS, the vast DIE FRAU OHNE SCHATTEN, the autobiographical INTERMEZZO, DIE ÄGYPTISCHE HELENA, the successful ARABELLA, the comedy DIE SCHWEIGSAME FRAU, FRIEDENSTAG, the 'bucolic comedy' DAPHNE, DIE LIEBE DER DANAE and the brilliant conversation piece CAPRICCIO.

Strauss was also regarded as one of the finest opera conductors of his age, particularly in the German repertory. Working mainly in Munich, Weimar and at the Berlin State Opera (where he conducted nearly 1,200 performances), he conducted the first performances of *Hänsel und Gretel* and his own *Guntram*. His wife **Pauline de Ahna** (1863–1950) was a soprano, who created Freihild in *Guntram* and who is the inspiration of Christine in *Intermezzo*.

Stravinsky, Igor (1882–1971)
Russian composer, resident in Western Europe after the Russian Revolution. One of the greatest and most influential composers of the 20th century, his music (in a wide variety of styles) is notable for its rhythmic drive and variety and for its remarkable orchestral colours. His six operatic stage works are the beautiful fairy tale THE NIGHTINGALE, the burlesque RENARD, the conventional comedy MAVRA, the powerful opera-oratorio OEDIPUS REX, the neo-classical THE RAKE'S PROGRESS, one of the greatest of post-war operas, and the unsuccessful television opera *The Flood* (CBS, 14 June 1962), which is a setting in serial style of part of a York mystery play. His son **Soulima** (1910–94) was also a composer, and his father **Fyodor** (1843–1902) was a successful bass, who created Skula in *Prince Igor*, William the Conqueror in Nápravník's *Harold*, King Frost in *The Snow Maiden*, Golova in *May Night* and, for Tchaikovsky, Orlik in *Mazeppa*, the Royal Highness in *Vakula the Blacksmith*, Dunois in *The Maid of Orleans* and Mamirov in *The Enchantress*.

Street Scene
Opera in two acts by Weill. 1st perf Philadelphia, 16 Dec 1946; libr by Langston Hughes, after Elmer Rice's play. Principal roles: Anna, Frank and Rose Maurrant (sop, bass and sop), Sam Kaplan (ten), Olga Olsen (mezzo), Daniel Buchanan (ten), Lippo (ten), Greta (sop), Harry Easter (bass), Emma (mezzo). One of the most successful of Weill's later American works, it is written largely in Broadway musical idiom. It tells of everyday life in a New York tenement, culminating in murder and the heroine's decision to seek a new life elsewhere. [R]

Strehler, Giorgio (b 1921)
Italian producer. Beginning as an actor, he turned to opera production in 1947 and has been closely associated with La Scala, Milan, where his many notable productions have included *Simon Boccanegra* and *Don Giovanni*.

Streich, Rita (1920–87)
German soprano, particularly associated with Mozart and other German SOUBRETTE roles. One of the finest post-war lighter German lyric sopranos, her agile voice was used with musicianship and an assured technique, and she had a good stage presence, also being a successful exponent of Viennese operetta. She created the title-role in Erbse's *Julietta*.

Strepponi, Giuseppina (1815–97)
Italian soprano. She enjoyed a short but brilliant career in the 1830s and early 1840s as one of the leading lyrico-dramatic sopranos of her time. She created Abigaille in *Nabucco*, Federico in F. Ricci's *Luigi Rolla e Michelangelo* and the title-role in Donizetti's *Adelia*. She became Verdi's companion in 1847, and the two were married in 1859. Her father **Feliciano** (1797–1832) was a composer who wrote several operas.

Stretta (Italian for 'narrow')
A term used, especially in the 19th century, to describe the last, climactic section of an aria, duet or ensemble written in fast tempo so as to ensure a rousing finale.

Stride la vampa
Mezzo aria for Azucena in Act II of Verdi's *Il Trovatore*, in which she reflects on the terrible memories that come to her as she stares into the fire.

Strophic
A term which describes a song or aria in which the same music is repeated exactly (or nearly so) for each verse or stanza. It is the opposite of a song which is THROUGH-COMPOSED. Thus, to take two examples from Offenbach's *Les Contes d'Hoffmann*, the Doll's Song is strophic, whilst the Diamond Aria is through-composed.

Student Prince, The
Operetta in four acts by Romberg. 1st perf New York, 2 Dec 1924; libr by Dorothy Donnelly. Principal roles: Karl Franz (ten), Dr Engel (bar), Kathie (sop), Margaret (mezzo). Romberg's most successful work, given wide currency by the film starring Mario Lanza. [R]

Studer, Cheryl (b 1955)
American soprano, particularly associated with the Italian and German repertories. She possesses a warm and beautiful voice used with outstanding musicianship, and she has a good stage presence. An artist of remarkable versatility, her roles range from the title-roles in Donizetti's *Lucia di Lammermoor* to Strauss's *Salome*, by way of Mozart, Verdi and Wagner. One of the finest operatic artists to have come to the fore in recent years.

Sturm, Der (*The Tempest*)
Opera in three acts by Martin. 1st perf Vienna, 18 June 1956; a virtual word-for-word setting of August von Schlegel's translation of William Shakespeare's play. It is written in declamatory vocal style and incorporates jazz elements to portray the court society. It is hardly ever performed.

Stuttgart Opera
Opera in this German city in Baden-Württemberg is given at the Württembergisches Staatstheater (cap 1,400), which opened in 1912. The house has a strong Strauss and Wagner tradition, and the annual season runs from September to June. Musical directors have included Max von Schillings, Fritz Busch, Carl Leonhardt, Herbert Albert, Ferdinand Leitner, Václav Neumann, Silvio Varviso, Dennis Russell Davies, García Navarro and Gabriele Ferro.

Styx, John
Tenor role in Offenbach's *Orphée aux Enfers*. He is the slow-witted former King of Boetia.

Suchoň, Eugen (b 1908)
Slovakian composer. The first Slovak composer to win international recognition, he wrote two operas: the nationalist THE WHIRLPOOL and the TWELVE-TONE historical *Svätopluk* (Bratislava, 10 Mar 1960; libr composer, Ivan Stodola and Jela Krčméryová) [R].

Suder, Joseph (1892–1980)
German composer. He wrote one opera, *Kleider Machen Leute* (Coburg, 1964, composed 1934; libr composer, after Gottfried Keller) [R].

Suicidio!
Soprano aria for Gioconda in Act IV of Ponchielli's *La Gioconda*, in which she contemplates taking her life.

Suitner, Otmar (b 1922)
Austrian conductor, particularly associated with Mozart, Wagner and Strauss operas. A rock-solid, versatile and sometimes underrated conductor, he was musical director of the Kaiserslautern Opera (1957–60), the Dresden State Opera (1960–64) and the Berlin State Opera (1964–71 and 1975–90). He conducted the first performances of Dessau's *Puntila*, *Einstein* and *Leonce und Lena*.

Sullivan, Sir Arthur (1842–1900)
British composer. Despite his longing to be acknowledged as a composer of 'serious' music (which in operatic terms is exemplified by his one opera IVANHOE), he is principally famous as one of the greatest of all operetta composers, particularly through the 14 Savoy Operas written in collaboration with W.S. GILBERT. These works are noted for their sparkling melodies, for their subtle and often brilliant orchestration (especially for the woodwind), for their clever touches of musical satire and for their superb use of patter. His operettas are *The Sapphire Necklace* (London, 13 Apr 1867; libr Henry Fothergill Chorley), most of which is lost, the curtain-raiser COX AND BOX, *The Contrabandista* (London, 18 Dec 1867;

libr Francis Cowley Burnand; revised version *The Chieftain*, London, 12 Dec 1894), the largely lost THESPIS, his first collaboration with Gilbert, the brilliant TRIAL BY JURY, perhaps his masterpiece, THE ZOO, THE SORCERER, H.M.S. PINAFORE, THE PIRATES OF PENZANCE, PATIENCE, IOLANTHE, PRINCESS IDA, the immortal THE MIKADO, RUDDIGORE, the more serious THE YEOMEN OF THE GUARD, THE GONDOLIERS, HADDON HALL, UTOPIA LIMITED, THE GRAND DUKE, the more romantic *The Beauty Stone* (London, 28 May 1898; libr Joseph Comyns Carr and Arthur Wing Pinero), THE ROSE OF PERSIA and the unfinished THE EMERALD ISLE, which was completed by German.

Sulpice
Bass role in Donizetti's *La Fille du Régiment*. He is the regimental sergeant.

Summertime
Soprano aria for Clara in Act I of Gershwin's *Porgy and Bess*, sung as she rocks her baby.

Suoni la tromba
Baritone/bass duet for Riccardo and Giorgio in Act II of Bellini's *I Puritani*, in which they vow to fight for liberty.

Suor Angelica (*Sister Angelica*)
Opera in one act by Puccini. 1st perf New York, 14 Dec 1918; libr by Giovacchino Forzano. Principal roles: Angelica (sop), Princess (mezzo), Genevieve (sop). The central and least often performed panel of *Il Trittico*, it is notable for its all-female cast and for containing Puccini's only major mezzo role.
Plot: A convent near Siena, late 17th century. Angelica has taken the veil after bearing an illegitimate child. Her aunt, the Princess, visits her and asks her to renounce her share of the family estate. When Angelica asks about her child, the Princess brutally tells her that it is dead. Angelica takes poison and, as she dies, receives a vision of the Virgin bringing the child to her. [R]

Supernatural in opera
Apart from plots involving the supernatural which are drawn from classical or oriental mythology, few composers have tackled supernatural subjects. Those who did are largely from the German romantic school. Much the most important work is Weber's *Der Freischütz*; the Wolf's Glen Scene remains unsurpassed as a musical depiction of the macabre. Other works of this period include Marschner's *Der Vampyr* and Schubert's *Des Teufels Lustschloss*. Edgar Allan Poe has attracted many composers, but no major operas have been based on his horror stories; Debussy's unfinished *La Chûte de la Maison Usher* is the great might-have-been. More recently, Britten turned twice to Henry James ghost stories: to terrifying effect with *The Turn of the Screw* and rather less successfully with *Owen Wingrave*. The only important comic treatment of the supernatural is Sullivan's *Ruddigore*. Amongst the ghosts that appear in opera, the following spectral manifestations may be noted:

- The dead Louise in Charpentier's *Julien*.
- A dead wife in Korngold's *Die Tote Stadt*.
- Two former servants in Britten's *The Turn of the Screw*.
- A statue in Mozart's *Don Giovanni*, Dargomijsky's *The Stone Guest* and Hérold's *Zampa*.
- A dead opera singer in Offenbach's *Les Contes d'Hoffmann*.
- A jilted lover in Puccini's *Le Villi*.
- A murdered husband in Rossini's *Semiramide*.
- A murdered father-in-law in Shostakovich's *Lady Macbeth of Mtsensk*.
- The dead Oronte in Verdi's *I Lombardi*.
- Six dead poets in Thomson's *Lord Byron*.
- A soldier and a boy in Britten's *Owen Wingrave*.
- The dead Drago in Schumann's *Genoveva*.
- A friar in Smetana's *The Secret*.
- A bishop in Lalo's *Le Roi d'Ys*.
- A card-playing countess in Tchaikovsky's *The Queen of Spades*.
- An entire portrait gallery in Sullivan's *Ruddigore*.

Supervia, Conchita (b Concepción Supervía Pascual) (1895–1936)
Spanish mezzo, particularly associated with Rossini roles and with Carmen. The first modern-style COLORATURA mezzo, she had a warm and brilliant voice used with a fine

technique, which was marred only by her pronounced vibrato which at times approached a rattle. She had a delightful and mischievous stage personality.

Suppé, Franz von (b Francesco Ezechiele Ermenegildo Suppe Demelli) (1819–95)
Austrian composer. One of the earliest composers of Viennese operetta, his most successful works include *Das Mädchen von Lande* (Vienna, 7 Aug 1847; libr K. Elmar), DIE SCHÖNE GALATEA, *Die Leichte Kavallerie* (*Light Cavalry*, Vienna, 21 Mar 1866; libr C. Costa), with its famous overture, FATINITZA, the highly successful BOCCACCIO and DONNA JUANITA. Outside German-speaking countries, Suppé is nowadays remembered almost solely for his overtures, full of sparkling melodies but sometimes marred by his congenital inability to stop.

Surtitles
A projected translation in the language of the audience which appears on a screen at the top of the proscenium arch. Introduced in many houses in the late 1980s, they have been enormously helpful to audiences unfamiliar with the language of the opera, but have aroused controversy because they can be maddeningly distracting.

Susanna
Soprano role in: **1** Mozart's *Le Nozze di Figaro*. The Countess's maid, she is engaged to Figaro. **2** Wolf-Ferrari's *Il Segreto di Susanna*. She is Count Gil's wife. **3** Moussorgsky's *Khovanschina*. She is an Old Believer. **4** Hindemith's *Die Harmonie der Welt*. She is Kepler's second wife.

Susannah
Opera in two acts by Floyd. 1st perf Tallahassee (Florida), 24 Feb 1955; libr by the composer, after the Apocrypha. Principal roles: Susannah (sop), Blitch (bass), Sam (ten). Arguably Floyd's finest opera, it translates the biblical story to rural America and employs folk-like modality and simple vocal lines.
Plot: Tennessee, 1950s. The local elders consider Susannah Polk to be wanton for bathing in public. The itinerant evangelist Olin Blitch fails to convert her, but does succeed in falling in love with her. He confesses his love, and is killed by Susannah's brother Sam. She is left alone in bitterness. [R]

Susanna's Secret
see SEGRETO DI SUSANNA, IL

Süssmayr, Franz Xaver (b Francesco Saverio Dolcevillico) (1766–1803)
Austrian composer. Best known for his completion of his teacher Mozart's *Requiem*, he also wrote nearly 30 SINGSPIELS and OPERA BUFFAS, all of them now long forgotten. The most successful was *Der Spiegel von Arkadien* (Vienna, 14 Nov 1794; libr Emanuel Schikaneder).

Sutermeister, Heinrich (b 1910)
Swiss composer. He wrote 14 operas in a direct and readily accessible style, a number of which met with some success. They include ROMEO UND JULIA, *Die Zauberinsel* (Dresden, 30 Oct 1942; libr composer, after Shakespeare's *The Tempest*), the monodrama *Niobe* (Zürich, 22 June 1946; libr Peter Sutermeister), *Raskolnikoff* (Stockholm, 14 Oct 1948; libr Sutermeister, after Fyodor Dostoyevsky's *Crime and Punishment*), *Der Rote Stiefel* (Stockholm, 22 Nov 1951; libr composer, after W. Hauff), *Titus Feuerfuchs* (Basel, 14 Apr 1958; libr composer, after Johann Nestroy's *Der Talisman*), *Seraphine* (Swiss TV, 10 June 1959; libr composer, after François Rabelais), *Die Gespenst von Canterville* (Swiss TV, 6 Sept 1964; libr composer, after Oscar Wilde's *The Canterville Ghost*), *Madame Bovary* (Zürich, 26 May 1967; libr composer, after Gustave Flaubert) and *Le Roi Bérenger* (Munich, 22 July 1985; libr composer, after Eugène Ionesco).

Suthaus, Ludwig (1906–71)
German tenor, particularly associated with Wagnerian roles, especially Siegmund and Tristan. Possessing a strong voice of almost baritonal timbre, he was one of the leading HELDENTENORS of the immediate post-war era.

Sutherland, Dame Joan (b 1926)
Australian soprano, particularly associated with Händel and with French and Italian COLORATURA roles, especially the title-role in Donizetti's *Lucia di lammermoor*. One of

the greatest singers of the 20th century (dubbed 'La Stupenda' by the Italians), she possessed a voice of great beauty and far greater power than most coloraturas, combining extraordinary agility with flawless intonation and a phenomenal trill. Her total command of the Bellinian and Donizettian style was marred only by poor diction. On stage, she was a superb comedienne but sometimes rather less compelling an actress in serious roles. She created Jenifer in *The Midsummer Marriage*. Married to the conductor RICHARD BONYNGE.

Suzel
Soprano role in Mascagni's *L'Amico Fritz*. She is the daughter of one of Fritz's tenants.

Suzel, buon dì
Soprano/tenor duet (the Cherry Duet) for Suzel and Fritz in Act II of Mascagni's *L'Amico Fritz*, in which Suzel gives Fritz a gift of cherries which she has picked.

Suzuki
Mezzo role in Puccini's *Madama Butterfly*. She is Cio-Cio-San's maid.

Svanholm, Set (1904–64)
Swedish tenor, particularly associated with Wagnerian roles. Beginning as a baritone, he turned to tenor roles in 1936, and was one of the finest Wagnerian tenors of the immediate post-war period. His voice, if a little dry tonally, was used with great musicianship and intelligence, and he sang with much dramatic intensity. He created Erland in Frumerie's *Singoalla* and was artistic director of the Royal Opera, Stockholm (1956–63).

Svetlanov, Yevgeny (b 1928)
Russian conductor and composer, particularly associated with the Russian repertory, especially Tchaikovsky and Rimsky-Korsakov. Best known in the West as a symphonic conductor of great brilliance, excitement and showmanship, he has also conducted much opera in Russia, and was principal conductor of the Bolshoi Opera (1962–4). His wife **Larissa Avdeyeva** (*b* 1925) was a successful mezzo.

Svoboda, Josef (b 1920)
Czech designer. A qualified architect, he has been chief designer at the Prague National Theatre since 1948. His designs (often for productions by VÁCLAV KAŠLÍK) make extensive use of gauzes, staircases and large blocks which change smoothly into new shapes. He introduced into opera the 'Laterna Magica', which uses cinematographic projection on multiple screens. He has worked widely outside Prague, notably at Covent Garden (including a *Ring* cycle) and at the Metropolitan Opera, New York.

Svobodová-Janků, Hana (b 1940)
Czech soprano, particularly associated with heavier Italian and Czech roles. She possesses a rich and powerful lyrico-dramatic voice with a strong and vibrant lower register, and has a good stage presence.

· *Swedish royalty in opera* ·

The Swedish kings and queens who appear as operatic characters include:

- Gustavus I in Naumann's *Gustav Vasa*, Apolloni's *Gustavo Wasa*, Eyser's *The King of Hearts*, Marchetti's *Gustavo Wasa* and Berwald's unfinished *Gustav Vasa*.
- Erik XIV in Hallström's *Liten Karin*.
- Christina in Rossini's *Edoardo e Cristina* and Pavesi's *Odoardo e Cristina*.
- Charles XI in Pacius's *The Hunt of King Charles*.
- Gustavus III in Verdi's *Un Ballo in Maschera*, Auber's *Gustave III* and Werle's *Tintomara*.

Swallow
Bass role in Britten's *Peter Grimes*. He is a lawyer.

Sweden
see DROTTNINGHOLM CASTLE THEATRE; GÖTEBORG OPERA; ROYAL OPERA, STOCKHOLM

Swedish opera composers
see ATTERBERG; BERWALD; BLOMDAHL; FRUMERIE; HALLÉN; HALLSTRÖM; LIDHOLM; RANGSTRÖM; ROSENBERG; STENHAMMAR; WERLE

Other national opera composers include Sven-Erik Bäck (*b* 1919), Nathaniel Berg (1879–1957), Daniel Börtz (*b* 1943), Wilhelm Peterson-Berger (1867–1942), Andreas Randel (1806–64) and August Söderman (1832–76).

Swiss opera composers
see BLOCH; HONEGGER; LIEBERMANN; MARTIN; ROUSSEAU; SCHOECK; SUTERMEISTER

Other national opera composers include Volkmar Andreae (1879–1962), Willy Burkhard (1900–55), Hans Haug (1900–67), Rudolf Kelterborn (*b* 1931), Louis Niedermeyer (1802–61), Joachim Raff (1822–82), Meyer von Schauensee (1720–89) and Roger Vuataz (1898–1988).

Switzerland
see BASEL STADTTHEATER; BERNE STADTTHEATER; GRAND THÉÂTRE, GENEVA; LUZERN STADTTHEATER; ZÜRICH OPERNHAUS

Sydney Opera House
The home of the AUSTRALIAN OPERA, the theatre (cap 1,984) was designed by Jörn Utzon and opened on 20 Oct 1973. The long delays in its building and its vastly greater cost than originally thought, caused it to be regarded as something of a white elephant. Since its opening, however, its majestic if radical design and its breathtaking setting have led to its being viewed as one of the world's most beautiful modern buildings.

Széll, Georg (b György) (1897–1970)
Hungarian conductor, particularly associated with the German repertory. Noted for his painstaking preparation, for his sense of discipline and for his accuracy of orchestral detail, he was musical director of the Deutsches Theater, Prague (1929–37) and was resident in the United States from 1942. He conducted the first performances of Liebermann's *Penelope* and *The School for Wives*, Egk's *Irische Legende* and Krása's *Verlobung im Traum*.

Szokolay, Sándor (b 1931)
Hungarian composer. One of the most successful contemporary opera composers, with a strong theatrical sense, his five operas are the powerful BLOOD WEDDING, *Hamlet* (Budapest, 19 Oct 1968; libr composer and János Arany, after Shakespeare), *Sámson* (Budapest, 26 Oct 1973; libr composer, after László Németh) [R], *Ecce Homo* (Budapest, 25 Jan 1987; libr composer, after Nikos Kazantzakis's *Christ Recrucified*) and *Szávitri* (1988; libr composer, after E. Illés).

Szymanowski, Karol (1882–1937)
Polish composer. The most important 20th-century Polish composer, he wrote three stage works. The unperformed operetta *The Lottery for Men* (*Loteria na Mezów*, 1909; libr Juliusz Krzewiński-Haszyński) was followed by the locally successful *Hagith* (Warsaw, 13 May 1922, composed 1913; libr Stanisław Baracz, after Felix Dörmann) and his masterpiece, the magnificent KING ROGER.

T

Tabarro, Il (*The Cloak*)
Opera in one act by Puccini. 1st perf New York, 14 Dec 1918; libr by Giuseppe Adami, after Didier Gold's *La Houppelande*. Principal roles: Giorgetta (sop), Michele (bar), Luigi (ten), La Frugola (mezzo), Il Tinca (ten), Il Talpa (bass). The first panel of *Il Trittico*, it is the most truly VERISMO in style of Puccini's operas.
Plot: The Seine, 1910. The Parisian bargee Michele discovers that his wife Giorgetta is having an affair with the young stevedore Luigi. He kills Luigi as the latter is about to keep a rendezvous with Giorgetta, and presents her with the body wrapped in his cloak. [R]

Tacea la notte
Soprano aria for Leonora in Act I of Verdi's *Il Trovatore*, in which she tells Inez about the unknown troubador with whom she has fallen in love.

Taddei, Giuseppe (b 1916)
Italian baritone, particularly associated with Mozart, Donizetti and Verdi roles, especially the title-role in *Falstaff*. An outstanding singing-actor, equally at home in serious or comic roles, he had a fine voice of considerable power and range which he used with great intelligence. He continued singing into his late 70s.

Taddeo
Baritone role in Rossini's *L'Italiana in Algieri*. He is Isabella's ever-hopeful admirer.

Tadolini, Eugenia (b Savonari) (1809–c 70)
Italian soprano. One of the leading Italian lyric sopranos of the mid-19th century, she created Elvira in Mercadante's *Le Due Illustri Rivali* and the title-roles in *Linda di Chamounix*, *Maria di Rohan* and *Alzira*. Verdi rejected her as the first Lady Macbeth because he said that she sang too beautifully.

Tagliabue, Carlo (1898–1978)
Italian baritone, particularly associated with the Italian repertory, especially Verdi. One of the leading Italian baritones of the inter-war period, he had a warm and beautiful voice used with a fine technique, but his acting abilities were limited. He created Basilio in Respighi's *La Fiamma*.

Tagliavini, Ferruccio (1913–95)
Italian tenor, particularly associated with lighter Italian and French roles, especially Nemorino in Donizetti's *L'Elisir d'Amore*, the Duke of Mantua in Verdi's *Rigoletto* and the title-role in Massenet's *Werther*. He was the leading Italian TENORE DI GRAZIA of the immediate post-war period and was an accomplished comic actor. Married to the mezzo PIA TASSINARI.

Taille (French for 'edge' or 'cut')
A term used in late 17th- and early-18th-century French opera to describe the tenor voice. There were two types, *haute-taille* and *basse-taille*. The latter would nowadays be called a baritone.

Tajo, Italo (1915–93)
Italian bass, particularly associated with the Italian repertory. An outstanding singing-actor, particularly in comedy, he enjoyed a long career, singing into his mid-70s, latterly specializing in COMPRIMARIO roles. He created Il Torturato in Nono's *Intolleranza*, Agamennone in Malipiero's *Ecuba*, Schmuller in Tosatti's *Il Giudizio Universale*, Forlipopoli in Persico's *La Locandiera* and Mugnaio in Pizzetti's *L'Oro*. He also appeared in Broadway musicals and in three films.

Taktakishvili, Otar (1924–89)
Georgian composer and conductor. His operas, written in an eclectic and readily accessible style, are mainly on nationalist historical themes and sometimes employ traditional Georgian material. The most successful were *Mindiya* (Tbilsi, 21 June 1961; libr R. Tabukashvili) [R] and *Three*

Stories (*Sami Novela*, Tbilsi, 1967; libr composer, after M. Dzhavakhishvili and Galaktion Tabidze). He held a number of official positions, including Georgian Minister of Culture and membership of the praesidium of the UNESCO World Council. His father **Shalva** (1900–65) was also a composer, whose operas include *The Deputy* (Tbilsi, 5 May 1940; libr composer and A. Takayshvili).

Tal, Josef (b Grünthal) (b 1919)
Polish-born Israeli composer. Some of his operas have met with success not only in Israel, but also in Germany. They include *Saul at Endor* (Tel Aviv, 1957; libr composer), *Amnon and Tamar* (Jerusalem, 1961; libr R. Frier), *Ashmadei* (Hamburg, 9 Nov 1971; libr Israel Eliraz), *Masada 967* (Jerusalem, July 1973; libr Eliraz, after Josephus's *The Jewish War*), *Die Versuchung* (Munich, 26 July 1976; libr Eliraz), *Der Sturm* (Berlin, Sept 1987; libr Hans Keller), *Der Garten* (Hamburg, May 1988; libr Eliraz) and *Joseph* (Tel Aviv, 27 June 1995; libr Eliraz).

Talbot
1 Bass-baritone role in Donizetti's *Maria Stuarda*. Mary's jailer, he is the historical George Talbot, Earl of Shrewsbury. **2** Bass COMPRIMARIO role in Verdi's *Giovanna d'Arco*. He is the English commander.

Talbot, Howard (b Richard Lansdale Munkittrick) (1865–1928)
American-born British composer. He wrote, in whole or in part, a large number of operettas and musical comedies. Nowadays, he is largely remembered only for his collaboration with Monckton on THE ARCADIANS.

Tale of Tsar Saltan, The (*Skazka o Tsarie Saltanie*)
Opera in prologue and four acts by Rimsky-Korsakov. 1st perf Moscow, 3 Nov 1900; libr by Vladimir Ivanovich Belsky, after Alexander Pushkin's poem. Principal roles: Tsar Saltan (bass), Milistrisa (sop), Prince Gvidon (ten), Swan Princess (sop). Containing the famous 'Flight of the Bumblebee', it is one of Rimsky's most delightful and orchestrally brilliant fairy-tale operas. Still popular in Russia, it is only very rarely performed elsewhere.

Plot: Legendary Russia. As a result of the machinations of her jealous sisters, the Tsarina Milistrisa is set adrift in a cask with her son Gvidon. They are cast ashore on Buyan Island, where Gvidon rescues the Swan Princess. She turns him into a bee, and when Milistrisa's sisters try to stop Tsar Saltan visiting the island, he stings them. Gvidon turns the Swan back into a princess, and she returns Milistrisa to the Tsar. [R]

Tale of Two Cities, A
Opera in prologue and three acts by Benjamin. 1st perf BBC Radio, 1953; 1st stage perf London, 23 July 1957; libr by Cedric Cliffe, after Charles Dickens's novel. Principal roles: Charles Darnay (ten), Dr and Lucie Manette (ten and sop), Sydney Carton (bar), Madame Defarge (sop). Benjamin's finest opera (a joint winner of the Festival of British competition), it was successful at its appearance but is nowadays all but forgotten.

Tales of Hoffmann, The
see CONTES D'HOFFMANN, LES

Talich, Václav (1883–1961)
Czech conductor, particularly associated with the Czech repertory. The leading Czech conductor of his time, he was musical director of the Prague National Theatre (1935–47) and conducted the first performance of Martinů's *Julietta*. He was also a distinguished teacher, whose pupils included Jaroslav Krombholc and Sir Charles Mackerras.

Talvela, Martti (1935–89)
Finnish bass, particularly associated with Wagner, Mozart and Verdi roles and with the title-role in Moussorgsky's *Boris Godunov*. His enormous yet beautiful and refined voice, his intelligence and musicianship, his keen dramatic sense and his commanding stage presence – aided by his huge and powerful physique and his great height (6′ 8″) – all combined to make him one of the outstanding basses of the 20th century. A singing-actor of remarkable insight, he created Paavo Routsalainen in Kokkonen's *The Last Temptations*. He was artistic director of the Savonlinna Festival

(1972–9) and was named director of the Finnish National Opera shortly before his death.

Tamagno, Francesco (1850–1905)
Italian tenor with an extremely powerful, if not always particularly accurate or subtle voice, he is often regarded as the greatest TENORE DI FORZA of all time, thanks to his great dramatic intensity. In addition, his trumpet-like vocal quality was allied to an imposing stage presence. He created the title-role in *Otello*, Gabriele Adorno in the revised *Simon Boccanegra*, Fabiano in Gomes's *Maria Tudor*, a role in Leoncavallo's *I Medici*, Hélion in de Lara's *Messaline* and, for Ponchielli, Azael in *Il Figliuol Prodigo* and Didier in *Marion Delorme*.

Tamberlik, Enrico (1820–89)
Italian tenor, noted for his powerful declamation. Able to produce a high c♯ from the chest, he was the first singer to introduce the notorious high cs at the end of 'Di quella pira' in *Il Trovatore*. He created Don Alvaro in *La Forza del Destino* and the title role in Jullien's *Pietro il Grande*.

Tamburini, Antonio (1800–76)
Italian baritone. One of the finest baritones of the first half of the 19th century, he created, for Bellini, Ernesto in *Il Pirata*, Valdeburgo in *La Straniera* and Riccardo in *I Puritani*, Orosmene in Mercadante's *Zaira* and 11 roles for Donizetti, including Dr Malatesta in *Don Pasquale*, Constantine in *Fausta* and Israele in *Marino Faliero*.

Tamerlano (*Tamburlaine*)
Opera in three acts by Händel. 1st perf London, 31 Oct 1724; libr by Nicola Francesco Haym, after Agostino Piovene's libretto, itself based on Jacques Pradon's *Tamerlan ou la Mort de Bajazet* and Michel Ducas's *Historia Byzantina*. Principal roles: Tamerlano (c-ten), Bajazete (ten), Asteria (sop), Andronico (c-ten), Irene (mezzo), Leone (bass). Dealing with events in the life of the Tartar Emperor Tamburlaine (1358–1405), it is still performed from time to time.
Plot: Bithynia, 1402. Tamburlaine has defeated and captured the Turkish Emperor Bajazet. His Greek ally Andronicus loves Bajazet's daughter Asteria, whom Tamburlaine – although engaged to Irene – also loves. Asteria surprisingly accepts Tamburlaine, but when Bajazet threatens suicide, she throws a dagger at Tamburlaine's feet, saying that she had planned to kill him during their first embrace. Tamburlaine orders Bajazet and Asteria to be executed, but eventually relents because of the love between father and daughter. Finally, Tamburlaine kills himself. [R]

Taming of the Shrew, The
see GIANNINI; WIDERSPÄNSTIGEN ZÄHMUNG, DER

Tamino
Tenor role in Mozart's *Die Zauberflöte*. He is an oriental prince charged with rescuing Pamina.

Tancredi
Opera in two acts by Rossini. 1st perf Venice, 6 Feb 1813; libr by Gaetano Rossi, after Voltaire's *Tancrède* and Torquato Tasso's *Gerusalemme Liberata*. Principal roles: Tancredi (mezzo), Amenaida (sop), Argirio (ten), Orbazzano (bass), Isaura (mezzo). Telling of the Italian crusader Tancred (1077–1112), it is the opera which established Rossini's reputation. It is still quite often performed.
Plot: Syracuse, 1105. Tancredi returns home from exile and manages to prevent the marriage of his beloved Amenaida to his rival Orbazzano. Orbazzano intercepts a letter from Amenaida to Tancredi and presents it as addressed to the enemy Saracens. Amenaida is condemned to death for treason unless a champion will fight for her. Although he believes her to be guilty, Tancredi fights for her and wins and then goes on to defeat the Saracens. Orbazzano's perfidy is finally exposed and the lovers are reconciled. [R]

Taneyev, Sergei (1856–1915)
Russian composer. His only completed operatic work is the fine Aeschylean trilogy ORESTEIA. He toyed with several other operatic projects, but none of them came to more than sketches.

Tannhäuser Full title: **Tannhäuser und der Sangerkrieg auf der Wartburg** (*Tannhäuser and the Singing Contest at the Wartburg*)
Opera in three acts by Wagner. 1st perf Dresden, 19 Oct 1845; libr by the composer. Revised version 1st perf Paris, 13 March 1861. Principal roles: Tannhäuser (ten), Elisabeth (sop), Wolfram (bar), Venus (mezzo), Hermann (bass), Walther (ten), Reinmar (bass), Biterolf (bass), Heinrich (ten). Wagner's second 'canonical' opera, and the most old-fashioned of his mature works, both versions are still regularly performed.
Plot: Early-13th-century Eisenach. The minstrel-knight Tannhäuser has been seduced by the goddess Venus but, sated with physical pleasure, he calls upon the Virgin, who releases him from the Venusberg. He returns to his knightly comrades, led by his friend Wolfram von Eschenbach, and takes part with them in the minstrels' contest for the hand of Landgrave Hermann's daughter Elisabeth, who has long loved him. The words of his song in the contest betray his past carnal knowledge and he is ordered to undertake a pilgrimage to Rome to seek expiation from the Pope. He returns unshriven, but Elisabeth's self-sacrificing love finally redeems him, and he joins her in death on her funeral bier. [R both versions]

Tapfere Soldat, Der (*The Valiant Soldier*; usually given in English as *The Chocolate Soldier*)
Operetta in three acts by O. Straus. 1st perf Vienna, 14 Nov 1908; libr by Rudolf Bernauer and Leopold Jacobson, after George Bernard Shaw's *Arms and the Man*. Principal roles: Nadina (sop), Bumerli (ten), Mascha (sop), Alexius (bar). One of Straus's most successful works, set during the Serbo-Bulgarian War of 1885, it is still regularly performed. [R]

Tarantella
A fast Italian dance in 6/8 time with alternating major and minor sections. The name derives from the Italian town of Taranto, home of the tarantula: the dance was supposed to ward off the spider's poison. There are operatic examples in Sullivan's *Utopia Limited* and Donizetti's *Gianni di Parigi*.

Tarare
Opera in prologue and five acts by Salieri. 1st perf Paris, 8 June 1787; libr by Pierre Augustin Caron de Beaumarchais, after Hamilton's translation of a Persian story. Revised version *Axur, Rè d'Ormus*, 1st perf Vienna, 8 Jan 1788; libr revised by Lorenzo da Ponte. Principal roles (with *Tarare* first): Tarare/Axur (ten/bar), Astasie/Aspasia (sop), Atar (bass), Calpigi/Biscroma (ten). Often regarded as Salieri's masterpiece, it was sensationally successful at its appearance but is nowadays only rarely performed.
Plot: Ormus (Persia), 1680. King Atar is jealous of the popularity of his captain Tarare and unsuccessfully attempts to have him killed before carrying off Tarare's beloved Astasie. Tarare eventually rescues her with the aid of Calpigi. Following an insurrection in which Atar is killed, Tarare is proclaimed king.

Tarquinius
Baritone role in Britten's *The Rape of Lucretia* and Respighi's *Lucrezia*. He is the proud Prince of Rome.

Tartar opera composers
see ZHIGANOV
Other national opera composers include Sofia Gubaidulina (*b* 1931), Mansur Muzafarov (1902–66), Allagiar Valiullin (1924–72) and Mikhail Yudin (1893–1948).

Tassinari, Pia (1903–90)
Italian soprano and later mezzo, particularly associated with the Italian and French repertories. One of the leading Italian lyric sopranos of the 1930s, her voice later darkened and she became a successful mezzo. She created Lalla in Veretti's *Il Favorito del Rè*, Lucia in Zandonai's *La Farsa Amorosa* and Elisa in Pick-Mangiagalli's *Notturno Romantico*. Married to the tenor FERRUCCIO TAGLIAVINI.

Tate, Jeffrey (b 1943)
British conductor (and also a qualified doctor), particularly associated with the German repertory, especially Strauss and Mozart. One of the leading contemporary Mozartians, he overcame a severe spinal disability to become a conductor, and was

Covent Garden's first-ever principal conductor (1987–91). His performances are carefully prepared but can often seem sluggish. He conducted the first performance of Liebermann's *La Forêt*.

Tatyana
Soprano role in Tchaikovsky's *Eugene Onegin*. Madame Larina's daughter, she is Olga's sister.

Tauber, Richard (b Ernst Seiffert) (1891–1948)
Austrian tenor, particularly associated with Mozart and Lehár roles. One of the finest lyric tenors of the inter-war period, he sang with style, warmth and great elegance. He created several roles for Lehár, including Prince Sou-chong in *Das Land des Lächelns*, Goethe in *Friederike* and Octavio in *Giuditta*. He also conducted operetta, composed three operettas, including *Old Chelsea* (1942), and appeared in a number of films, including *Blossom Time* (1934). His first wife **Carlotta Vanconti** was a soprano; he later married the actress Diana Napier.

Tavener, John (b 1944)
British composer, whose more recent music has been strongly influenced by his Greek Orthodox faith. He has written three operas: *A Gentle Spirit* (Bath, 6 June 1977; libr Gerald McLarnon, after Fyodor Dostoyevsky), the unsuccessful *Thérèse* (London, 1 Oct 1979; libr McLarnnon) and *Mary of Egypt* (Aldeburgh, 19 June 1992; libr Mother Thekla) [R].

Taverner
Opera in two acts by Maxwell Davies. 1st perf London, 12 July 1972; libr by the composer. Principal roles: Taverner (ten), Jester (bar), White Abbot (b-bar), King (bass), Cardinal (ten), Rose Parrow (mezzo), Sir Richard Taverner (bass), Priest Confessor (c-ten). Maxwell Davies's first major operatic work, it deals with the English composer John Taverner (*c* 1495–1545) and his involvement in the political issues of his day.

Taylor, Deems (1885–1966)
American composer. He wrote in a readily accessible late-romantic style and many of his works met with considerable success in the United States in their time, but they are nowadays hardly ever performed. His first important opera THE KING'S HENCHMAN was followed by PETER IBBETSON, *Ramuntzko* (Philadelphia, 10 Feb 1942, composed 1937; libr composer, after Pierre Loti) and *The Dragon* (New York, 6 Feb 1958; libr composer, after A. Gregory), which was written for amateur performers.

Tbilsi Opera and Ballet Theatre
Georgia's principal opera house, in the city also known as Tiflis, the theatre (cap 1,061) was designed by V.A. Shretter and opened in 1896, replacing the previous theatre of 1851 which burnt down in 1874. The annual season runs from September to June, and the company has promoted the works of many Georgian composers.

Tchaikovsky, Modest (1850–1916)
Russian playwright and librettist, brother of the composer. As well as writing the libretti for his brother's *The Queen of Spades* and *Iolanta*, he also provided texts for Arensky (*Nal and Damayanti*), Nápravník (*Dubrovsky*) and Rachmaninov (*Francesca da Rimini*). He also wrote a three-volume biography of his brother.

Tchaikovsky, Pyotor Ilyich (1840–93)
Russian composer, who wrote 11 operas. Following some unfinished juvenilia, his first completed opera was THE VOYEVODA, which he subsequently abandoned, retaining the music for later incorporation into other works. His next opera, *Undine* (1869; libr Vladimir Sollogub, after Vasily Zhukovsky's translation of Friedrich Heinrich Carl de la Motte Fouqué's *Ondine*), he also abandoned after it was rejected for performance. His first opera to reach the stage was THE OPRICHNIK, in which his personal style can be discerned in embryo. His style becomes far more apparent in his next opera, the charming VAKULA THE BLACKSMITH. His lyrical love music, his orchestral mastery, his plangent and melancholic vocal lines and his exhilarating dance music all come together in EUGENE ONEGIN, which is usually regarded as his operatic masterpiece. Its successor, written in the hope of a Parisian success, was THE MAID OF ORLEANS, which

is cast in the form of French grand opera. For all but the last of his remaining operas, he returned to Russian subjects, sometimes evincing a more traditionally nationalist style than previously. This is especially the case with the powerful MAZEPPA, which was followed by *The Little Slippers* (a revision of *Vakula the Blacksmith*), the less successful THE ENCHANTRESS and the intense THE QUEEN OF SPADES. For his last opera, he returned to French sources with the medieval IOLANTA.

Standing somewhat outside the main stream of Russian nationalist musical development as exemplified by the MIGHTY HANDFUL, Tchaikovsky is perhaps the most international of 19th-century Russian composers. All of his mature operas are performed internationally, although only *Eugene Onegin* and *The Queen of Spades* have won a permanent place in Western repertories. His brother was the librettist MODEST TCHAIKOVSKY, and he is the subject of Peter Schat's *Symposion*.

Tcherepnin, Nikolai (1873–1945)
Russian composer and conductor. Best known as an orchestral composer, he also wrote two operas: *Poverty No Crime* (Paris, 1937, composed 1930; libr after Alexander Nikolayevich Ostrovsky) and *Vanka the Chancellor* (Belgrade, 1933; libr after Vladimir Sollogub). In addition, he produced in 1923 the completion now in general use of Moussorgsky's *Sorochintsy Fair*. His son **Alexander** (1899–1977) was also a composer, who wrote two operas: *01–01* (Weimar, 31 Jan 1928; libr after L. Andreiev) and *Die Hochzeit der Sobeide* (Vienna, 17 Mar 1933; libr after Hugo von Hofmannsthal).

Tear, Robert (b 1939)
British tenor, particularly associated with the British repertory and with German and Russian character roles, especially David in Wagner's *Die Meistersinger von Nürnberg*, Loge in *Das Rheingold* and Prince Shuisky in Moussorgsky's *Boris Godunov*. A versatile singing-actor of great intelligence and musicianship, he created Misael in *The Burning Fiery Furnace*, the title-role in *The Prodigal Son*, Dov in *The Knot Garden*, the Deserter in Henze's *We Come to the River*, the Painter in the three-act version of *Lulu*, Rimbaud in Tavener's *Thérèse* and the title-roles in Crosse's *The Grace of Todd* and Penderecki's *Ubu Rex*. He has recently also enjoyed some success as a conductor. His autobiography, *Tear Here*, was published in 1990.

Teatro alla Scala, Milan
Possibly the world's most famous opera house, it was designed by Giuseppe Piermarini and opened on 3 Aug 1778. After its partial destruction by bombs in Aug 1943, it was repaired and reopened (cap 3,600) in 1946. It is named after Regina della Scala, the wife of Bernabò Visconti, Duke of Milan. Musical directors have included Franco Faccio, Arturo Toscanini, Victor de Sabata, Franco Capuana, Claudio Abbado and Riccardo Muti. It has an associated chamber house, for 18th-century and contemporary works, LA PICCOLA SCALA.

Teatro Amazones, Manaus
Designed by Bernardo António Oliveira Braga, the theatre (cap 800) opened on 31 Dec 1896. Built at the height of the Brazilian rubber boom, no expense was spared to make it one of the world's most lavish opera houses. The vast fees offered lured many of the greatest singers of the time to undertake the 26-day trip up the Amazon to perform there. With the end of the rubber boom the house fell into disuse and decay, but it has recently been restored to its former glory.

Teatro Carlo Felice, Genoa
The opera house (cap 1,500) was designed by Carlo Barabino and opened on 7 April 1828. It was damaged by bombs in 1943, and reconstruction took many years; it finally reopened on 18 Oct 1991. The annual season runs from January to July. Musical directors have included Angelo Mariani and Fernando Previtali.

Teatro Colón, Buenos Aires
South America's most important opera house and one of the most lavish in the world, the present theatre (cap 2,478) opened on 25 May 1908. Its artistic standards have varied enormously, usually in direct relation to the degree of political

and economic stability in Argentina. At its best, it ranks as one of the world's greatest opera houses. The annual season runs from May to December. Musical directors have included Floro Ugarte and Juan Peter Franze.

Teatro Comunale, Bologna
The opera house (cap 1,500) was designed by Antonio Galli da Bibiena and opened in 1763. Since the mid-19th century, when it introduced Wagner to Italy, the theatre has pursued an adventurous repertory policy. Musical directors have included Angelo Mariani, Luigi Mancinelli, Franco Faccio and Riccardo Chailly.

Teatro Comunale, Florence
Originally called the Teatro Politeama Fiorentino Vittorio Emmanuele, the theatre opened in 1864. It acquired its present name in 1932 and reopened after modernization (cap 1,806) in 1961. As well as hosting performances by the MAGGIO MUSICALE FIORENTINO, it gives annual winter and summer seasons.

Teatro Comunale Giuseppe Verdi, Trieste
The present opera house, designed by Antonio Selva and Matteo Pertsch, opened on 21 April 1801 as the Teatro Nuovo, acquiring its present name in 1931. Under the artistic direction of Giuseppe Antonicelli (1936–45 and 1951–66) and Raffaelo de Banfield (1972–), it has become one of Italy's leading houses and is noted for its adventurous repertory policy.

Teatro de la Zarzuela, Madrid
Originally built to house ZARZUELAS, the theatre (cap 1,242) opened in 1856. It holds an international opera season from January to July. Musical directors have included Gerónimo Giménez and Antonio Ros-Marbá.

Teatro dell'Opera, Rome
The present opera house (cap 2,200), designed by Achille Sfondrini, opened on 27 Nov 1880 as the Teatro Costanzi. After extensive renovation and enlargement, it reopened as the Teatro Real dell'Opera on 28 Feb 1928; the 'Real' was dropped when Italy became a republic. Its greatest period was in the early 1940s, when it rivalled La Scala. Although it no longer enjoys such eminence, it still ranks as one of Italy's leading houses. Musical directors have included Gino Marinuzzi, Tullio Serafin, Gabriele Santini, Bruno Bartoletti, Gustav Kuhn and Daniel Oren.

Teatro Donizetti, Bergamo
The opera house in this city in Lombardy was first opened on 24 Aug 1791 as the Teatro Riccardi; it burnt down in 1797 but was rebuilt two years later. After extensive restructuring, it reopened (cap 2,000) in 1897 and was renamed after the city's most famous son. It is noted both for its performances of Donizetti and for its promotion of new operas. Its audience has a reputation of being extremely difficult to please.

Teatro la Fenice, Venice
Often regarded as the most beautiful opera house in the world, the theatre was designed by Antonio Selva and opened on 16 May 1792. Burnt down in Dec 1836, it was rebuilt from Selva's original ground plan and reopened on 26 Dec 1837. It reached its present form (cap 1,500) after alterations in 1938. It has recently been noted for important revivals of 19th-century Italian works. The annual season runs from December to May and there is also a summer festival devoted to 20th-century works. Musical directors have included John Fisher.

Teatro Liceo, Barcelona (*Gran Teatre del Liceu* in Catalan)
The first theatre of this name opened in 1847, but was destroyed by fire in 1861. The subsequent opera house (cap 3,000) was designed by José Oriol Mestres and opened on 20 April 1862. It burnt down on 31 Jan 1994. Spain's most important opera house, under normal circumstances it gives an annual season from November to June, and its charter requires it to give at least one Spanish opera each year. Musical directors have included Michelangelo Veltri.

Teatro Massimo, Palermo
Possessing the third-largest operatic stage in Europe, Sicily's principal opera house (cap 1,800) was designed by G.B.F. Basile

and opened in May 1897. It follows one of the most adventurous repertory policies of any Italian house.

Teatro Massimo Bellini, Catania
Named after the city's most famous son, this Sicilian opera house (cap 1,470) was designed by Carlo Sada and opened on 31 May 1890. It gives annual spring and summer seasons.

Teatro Municipal, Rio de Janeiro
The home of Brazil's national opera company, the theatre (cap 2,357) opened on 14 July 1909. The annual season runs from March to December.

Teatro Municipal, Santiago
Chile's principal opera house, the theatre (cap 1,420) opened in 1857. The annual season runs from March to December, and the repertory is predominantly French and Italian.

Teatro Municipale, Reggio Emilia
The opera house (cap 1,600) in this Italian town in Emilia-Romagna opened in 1857. Designed by Costa, it is widely regarded as one of the most beautiful theatres in Italy.

Teatro Petruzzelli, Bari
Named after the two brothers who planned it, the opera house (cap 2,000) in this Italian town in Puglia opened on 14 Feb 1903. It was largely destroyed by fire in Oct 1991.

Teatro Regio, Parma
The opera house (cap 1,200) in this Italian city in Emilia-Romagna was designed by Nicola Bettoli and opened on 16 May 1829. It has been closely associated with Verdi operas, and between 1843 and 1951 alone it gave 1,382 Verdi performances. Its audience has a reputation for being perhaps the most difficult in the world to please and for regarding itself as expert on all matters vocal. The annual season runs from January to April. Musical directors have included Peter Maag.

Teatro Regio, Turin
Designed by Benedetto Alfieri, the opera house in this Italian city in Piedmont opened on 26 Dec 1740. It was burnt down in Feb 1936 and did not reopen until 10 April 1973 after a rebuilding (cap 1,800) by Carlo Mollino and Marcello Zavalani Rossi. In the meantime, opera was given at Turin's second house, the Teatro Carignano (cap 1,000), also designed by Alfieri and which opened in 1753. Musical directors have included Arturo Toscanini, Fernando Previtali and Peter Maag.

Teatro San Carlo, Naples
One of the world's largest opera houses (cap 3,500), it was designed by Antonio Niccolini and opened in 1816, only six months after the previous theatre (dating from Nov 1737) had been destroyed by fire. Its greatest period was between 1809 and 1840 when DOMENICO BARBAIA was administrator and the theatre witnessed the premieres of many of the greatest operas of Rossini and Donizetti. Usually regarded as Italy's second most important house after La Scala, its recent fortunes have been variable, largely because of actute financial problems. Its audience has a not entirely undeserved reputation for conservatism, chauvinism and extremely vocal expression of its disapproval. Musical directors have included Salvatore Accardo. The theatre has an associated chamber house, the Teatro della Corte.

Teatro, São Carlos, Lisbon
Portugal's principal opera house (cap 1,148), it was designed by José da Costa in imitation of its namesake in Naples and opened on 17 June 1793. The annual season runs from September to July.

Tebaldi, Renata (b 1922)
Italian soprano, particularly associated with Verdi and Puccini roles and with the title-role in Cilea's *Adriana Lecouvreur*. The outstanding Italian lyric soprano of the post-war period, she possessed a voice of great beauty and considerable power, which she used with style, elegance and scrupulous good taste. Her radiant voice, her warm personality and her sympathetic stage presence combined to make her one of the best-loved singers of her time.

Tebaldo
1 Tenor role in Bellini's *I Capuleti e i Montecchi*. He is Giulietta's kinsman.

2 Mezzo trouser role in Verdi's *Don Carlos*. He is Elisabeth's page.

Te Deum
Scene for Baron Scarpia and the chorus which ends Act I of Puccini's *Tosca*.

Te Kanawa, Kiri
see KANAWA, DAME KIRI TE

Telemaco or **L'Isola di Circe** (*Circe's Island*)
Opera in two acts by Gluck. 1st perf Vienna, 30 Jan 1765; libr by Marco Coltellini, after Carlo Sigismondo Capece's libretto for A. Scarlatti, itself based on Homer's *The Odyssey*. Principal roles: Telemaco (mezzo), Ulisse (ten), Circe (sop), Asteria (sop), Merione (sop). After a long period of complete neglect, it has received a few performances in the last decade.
Plot: Legendary Greece. With the help of Asteria and Merione, Telemachus rescues his father Ulysses from the island of the sorceress Circe. In revenge, Circe sends Telemachus visions of his mother's death. However, all four succeed in escaping, and Circe turns the island into a desert.

Telemann, Georg Philipp (1681–1767)
German composer. Possibly the most prolific composer in the history of music, his output includes over 40 operas, including *Miriways* (Hamburg, 26 May 1728; libr J.S. Müller) and *Flavius Bertaridus* (Hamburg, 23 Nov 1729; libr C.G. Wendt, after S. Ghigi's *Flavio Pertarido*). Nowadays, his only two operas still to be remembered are the comedies DER GEDULDIGE SOCRATES and the intermezzo PIMPINONE.

Telephone, The or **L'Amour à Trois** (roughly *The Eternal Triangle*)
Comic opera in one act by Menotti. 1st perf New York, 18 Feb 1947; libr by the composer. Principal roles: Ben (bar), Lucy (sop). One of Menotti's most successful works, it is a descendant of the 18th-century Italian INTERMEZZI, with the telephone taking the place of the traditional mute player.
Plot: Mid-20th-century America. Lucy's addiction to talking on her new telephone sabotages Ben's intentions to propose marriage to her. Finally, unable to wait around for her calls to finish, he removes himself to a call box in order to propose by telephone. [R]

Television opera
The first televised opera transmission took place in 1936, when the BBC broadcast excerpts from Coates's *Pickwick*. The first broadcast in the United States was an abridged *Pagliacci* from Radio City in March 1941. In recent years, live broadcasts of opera from all over Europe have become frequent. In addition, there have also been many studio productions, of which the most successful has possibly been the BBC's *Der Fliegende Holländer*. Despite the obvious limitations of the small screen and of television's inferior sound quality, the medium has made opera available to millions who for financial or geographical reasons would otherwise be unable to see it, and it has done much to increase its popularity. The first opera specifically commissioned for television was Menotti's *Amahl and the Night Visitors* (NBC, 1951). Other television operas have included Foss's *Griffelkin*, Britten's *Owen Wingrave*, Fortner's *Der Wald*, Crosse's *Purgatory*, Křenek's *Der Zauberspiegel*, Bliss's *Tobias and the Angel* and Hoddinott's *Murder the Magician*.

Telramund, Friedrich von
Bass-baritone role in Wagner's *Lohengrin*. Ortrud's husband, he is the Count of Brabant.

Temirkanov, Yuri (b 1938)
Russian conductor and producer, particularly associated with the Russian repertory. Although best known in the West as a symphonic conductor, he was musical director of the Kirov Opera (1977–88), where he regularly acted as producer. He conducted the first performances of Shchedrin's *Dead Souls* and Petrov's *Peter I* and *Mayakovsky Comes Into Existence*.

Tempest, The or **The Enchanted Isle**
Opera in five acts by Purcell. 1st perf London, *c* 1695; libr by Thomas Shadwell and John Dryden, after William Shakespeare's play. It is really more incidental music or a quasi-MASQUE rather than a true opera. [R]

Tempest, The (*Bouře*)
Opera in three acts by Fibich (Op 40). 1st perf Prague, 1 March 1895; libr by Jaroslav Vrchlický, after William Shakespeare's play. Principal roles: Prospero (bass), Miranda (sop), Kaliban (bar), Fernando (ten), Ariel (mezzo). An imaginitive setting, it is still occasionally performed in the Czech lands but is virtually unknown elsewhere. [R Exc]

Templer und die Jüdin, Der (*The Templar and the Jewess*)
Opera in three acts by Marschner (Op 60). 1st perf Leipzig, 22 Dec 1829; libr by Wilhelm August Wohlbrück, after Sir Walter Scott's *Ivanhoe*. Principal roles: Ivanhoe (ten), Bois Guilbert (bar), Rowena (sop), Cedric (bass), Richard I (bar), Rebecca (sop), Friar Tuck (bass). One of Marschner's finest operas, it was very popular in the 19th century but nowadays it is unaccountably almost never performed. For plot see *Ivanhoe*.

Tender Land, The
Opera in three (originally two) acts by Copland. 1st perf New York, 1 April 1954; libr by Horace Everett, after James Agee's *Let Us Now Praise Famous Men*. Revised version 1st perf Berkshire, 2 Aug 1954. Principal roles: Laurie (sop), Martin (ten), Top (bar), Ma and Grandpa Moss (mezzo and bass). In this romantic pastoral opera, Copland evokes an unpretentious rustic atmosphere with the use of simple 'folksy' material. A beautiful work, it has been very successful in the United States but is only seldom performed elsewhere.
Plot: American mid-West, early 1930s. Carried away with the celebrations for her high school graduation, Laurie Moss falls in love with the drifting farm hand Martin and plans to run away with him. Martin has second thoughts about it and leaves without her, but Laurie nevertheless sets out on her own. [R]

Tennstedt, Klaus (b 1926)
German conductor, particularly associated with the German repertory, especially *Fidelio*. Best known as one of the outstanding contemporary symphonic conductors, he conducted much opera in the early part of his career (including a period as musical director of the Kiel Stadttheater), but recently his operatic appearances have been very rare. His career has been sadly interrupted in recent years by his long fight against throat cancer.

Tenor
see panel on pages 552–3. See also COUNTER-TENOR; HAUTE-CONTRE; HELDENTENOR; TAILLE; TENORE DI FORZA; TENORE DI GRAZIA; TENORINO; TRIAL

Tenor, The
Opera in one act by Weisgall. 1st perf Baltimore, 11 Feb 1952; libr by Karl Shapiro and Ernst Lert, after Frank Wedekind's *Der Kammersänger*. Principal roles: Gerardo (ten), Helen (sop), Maurice (bar), Young Girl (sop), Valet (bar), Bellboy (ten). Weisgall's most successful opera, it tells of a flamboyant dramatic tenor and his amorous entanglements and includes a number of quotations from *Tristan und Isolde*. [R]

Tenor all singers above, A
Tenor aria for Capt Fitzbattleaxe in Act II of Sullivan's *Utopia Limited*, in which he tells Zara that his love for her is adversely affecting his vocal prowess. The tenor has to crack deliberately on his high notes.

Tenore di forza (Italian for 'tenor of force')
Also known as *tenore robusto*, and roughly the Italian equivalent of the German HELDENTENOR, the term is used to describe a tenor with the sheer lung-power required to raise the roof in such heavy Italian roles as Manrico in Verdi's *Il Trovatore*, Calaf in Puccini's *Turandot* and, particularly, the title-role in Verdi's *Otello*. Epitomized by Francesco Tamagno, famous post-war tenore di forzas have included Franco Corelli, Mario del Monaco and Franco Bonisolli.

Tenore di grazia (Italian for 'tenor of grace')
A term which describes a tenor with the grace, agility and style required for the lighter Mozart, Rossini, Bellini and Donizetti roles. Recent leading tenore di grazias have included Ferruccio Tagliavini, Luigi Alva and Ugo Benelli.

· Tenor ·

The tenor is the highest natural male voice (both alto and counter-tenor being artificially produced). The word tenor is derived from the period at the end of the Middle Ages when polyphonic music emerged and when that voice's function was to 'hold' (Latin *tenere*) the tune whilst the other voices proceeded in counterpoint to it. The tenor's normal vocal range is roughly c to c'', although some Italian BEL CANTO roles go a little higher, and some exceptional Russian roles (such as the Astrologer in *The Golden Cockerel* and the Police Inspector in *The Nose*) require a range up to f''. Many different subdivisions of the tenor voice have evolved. They often overlap and do not correspond precisely from one country to another. They are seldom used by composers, but they are useful as an indication of the character of a role, if rather less so for its exact TESSITURA. The main French, German and Italian categories of tenor are as follows:

	Name	Range	Example
France	*haute-contre*	d to b''	Hippolytus in *Hippolyte et Aricie*
	Trial	c to b''	Franz in *Les Contes d'Hoffmann*
	ténor	c to c''	Title-role in *Faust*
	ténor-bouffe	c to c''	Paris in *La Belle Hélène*
Germany	*Spieltenor*	c to b♭''	Pedrillo in *Die Entführung aus dem Serail*
	Wagnerheldentenor	c to b''	Siegfried in *Götterdämmerung*
	hoher Tenor	c to c''	Brighella in *Ariadne auf Naxos*
	lyrischer Tenor	c to c''	Max in *Der Freischütz*
	Heldentenor	c to c''	Sir Huon in *Oberon*
Italy	*tenore-buffo*	c to b♭''	Bardolph in *Falstaff*
	tenore	c to c''	Gustavus in *Un Ballo in Maschera*
	tenore spinto	c to c''	Radamès in *Aida*
	tenore di forza	c to c''	Title-role in *Otello*
	tenore di grazia	c to d''	Elvino in *La Sonnambula*

Below are listed the 141 tenors with entries in this dictionary. Their nationalities are given in brackets afterwards.

Aler, John (US)
Alva, Luigi (Per)
Anders, Peter (Ger)
Aragall, Giacomo (Sp)
Araiza, Francisco (Mex)
Atlantov, Vladimir (Russ)
Benelli, Ugo (It)
Bergonzi, Carlo (It)
Björling, Jussi (Swe)
Blachut, Beno (Cz)
Bonci, Alessandro (It)
Bonisolli, Franco (It)
Borgatti, Giuseppe (It)
Borgioli, Dino (It)
Brilioth, Helge (Swe)
Burian, Karel (Cz)
Burrows, Stuart (Br)
Carreras, José (Sp)
Caruso, Enrico (It)
Cassilly, Richard (US)
Corelli, Franco (It)
Cossutta, Carlo (Arg)
Cox, Jean (US)
Craig, Charles (Br)
Crimi, Guilio (It)
Cuénod, Hugues (Swit)
Davide, Giovanni (It)
Davies, Ryland (Br)
Dermota, Anton (Slv)
Dickie, Murray (Br)
Dobson, John (Br)
Domingo, Plácido (Sp)
Donzelli, Domenico (It)
Duprez, Gilbert (Fr)
Dvorský, Peter (Slo)
Dyck, Ernest van (Belg)
Erb, Karl (Ger)
Ford, Bruce (US)
Fraschini, Gaetano (It)
García, Manuel I (Sp)
Gayarré, Julián (Sp)
Gedda, Nicolaï (Swe)
Giacomini, Giuseppe (It)
Gigli, Beniamino (It)
Hadley, Jerry (US)
Häfliger, Ernst (Swit)
Hislop, Joseph (Br)
Hofmann, Peter (Ger)

Holm, Richard (Ger)
Hopf, Hans (Ger)
Ilosfalvy, Róbert (Hung)
Jerusalem, Siegfried (Ger)
Jobin, Raoul (Can)
Johnson, Edward (Can)
Kelly, Michael (Ire)
King, James (US)
Kollo, René (Ger)
Kónya, Sándor (Hung)
Kozlovsky, Ivan (Ukr)
Kraus, Alfredo (Sp)
Langridge, Philip (Br)
Lauri-Volpi, Giacomo (It)
Lemeshev, Sergei (Russ)
Lewis, Richard (Br)
Lima, Luis (Arg)
Lorenz, Max (Ger)
Luchetti, Veriano (It)
Lucia, Fernando de (It)
McCormack, John (Ire)
McCracken, James (US)
Mario, Giovanni (It)
Martinelli, Giovanni (It)
Melchior, Lauritz (Den)
Merli, Francesco (It)
Merritt, Chris (US)
Mitchinson, John (Br)
Monaco, Mario del (It)
Mullings, Frank (Br)
Nash, Heddle (Br)
Nessi, Giuseppe (It)
Nourrit, Adolphe (Fr)
Oestvig, Karl (Nor)
Oncina, Juan (Sp)
O'Neill, Dennis (Br)
Palacios, Ernesto (Per)
Palma, Piero de (It)
Paolis, Alessio de (It)
Patzak, Julius (Aus)
Pavarotti, Luciano (It)
Pears, Sir Peter (Br)
Peerce, Jan (US)
Pertile, Aureliano (It)
Piccaver, Alfred (Br)
Picchi, Mirto (It)
Přibyl, Vilém (Cz)
Raimondi, Gianni (It)
Ralf, Torsten (Swe)
Randle, Thomas (US)
Reeves, Sims (Br)
Remedios, Alberto (Br)
Reszke, Jean de (Pol)
Riegel, Kenneth (US)
Rolfe-Johnson, Anthony (Br)
Roswaenge, Helge (Den)
Rubini, Giovanni Battista (It)
Schipa, Tito (It)
Schock, Rudolph (Ger)
Schreier, Peter (Ger)
Sénéchal, Michel (Fr)
Shicoff, Neil (US)
Shirley, George (US)
Simoneau, Léopold (Can)
Slezak, Leo (Aus)
Sobinov, Leonid (Russ)
Stefano, Giuseppe di (It)
Stolze, Gerhard (Ger)
Suthaus, Ludwig (Ger)
Svanholm, Set (Swe)
Tagliavini, Ferruccio (It)
Tamagno, Francesco (It)
Tamberlik, Enrico (It)
Tauber, Richard (Aus)
Tear, Robert (Br)
Thill, Georges (Fr)
Thomas, Jess (US)
Trial, Antoine (Fr)
Tucker, Richard (US)
Turp, André (Can)
Ulfung, Ragnar (Nor)
Unger, Gerhard (Ger)
Valletti, Cesare (It)
Vanzo, Alain (Fr)
Vickers, Jon (Can)
Vinay, Ramón (Chil)
Windgassen, Wolfgang (Ger)
Wunderlich, Fritz (Ger)
Young, Alexander (Br)
Zanelli, Renato (Chil)
Zednik, Heinz (Aus)
Zenatello, Giovanni (It)
Žídek, Ivo (Cz)

Tenorino (Italian for 'little tenor')
The term is sometimes used, usually rather disparagingly, to describe a tenor – generally a tenore di grazia – with a very small voice.

Tenuto (Italian for 'held')
An instruction to a singer in a vocal score telling him or her to hold a note for a fraction more than its full value. Most singers regard such an instruction as an open invitation to hold the note (especially if it is a high one) for as long as they wish, so as to make their effect.

Teresa
1 Soprano role in Berlioz's *Benvenuto Cellini*. Balducci's daughter, she is loved by Cellini and Fieramosca. **2** Mezzo role in Bellini's *La Sonnambula*. She is Amina's foster-mother.

Terfel, Bryn (b Terfel-Jones) (b 1965)
British baritone, particularly associated with Mozart and lighter Strauss roles. One of the finest singers to have emerged in recent years, he possesses a beautiful and perfectly placed voice of considerable range, used with musicianship, intelligence and a fine technique, and he has exemplary diction. A natural actor, he has a most engaging stage personality, especially in comedy. Perhaps the finest British singer to have appeared for 20 years.

Ternina, Milka (b Trnina) (1863–1941)
Croatian soprano, particularly associated with Wagnerian roles and with the title-role in *Tosca* and Leonore in *Fidelio*. One of the outstanding lyrico-dramatic sopranos of her time, she was also a fine singing-actress of great dramatic intensity. Henry James described her performance style as 'a devastating experience'. She was forced to retire in 1916 as a result of paralysis.

Terrasse, Claude (1867–1923)
French composer. He wrote several operettas, a number of which were successful in their time but which are nowadays seldom performed. They include *Les Travaux d'Hercule* (Paris, 7 Mar 1901;

libr Gaston de Caillavet and Roger de Flers), his most successful work, and *La Fiancée du Scaphandrier* (Paris, 8 Jan 1902; libr Franc-Noain).

Terzetto
A short trio, lacking the formal structure of a full-scale operatic trio.

Teschemacher, Marguerite (1903–59)
German soprano, particularly associated with the German repertory. Possessing a warm lyrico-dramatic voice and a good stage presence, she created the title-role in *Daphne* and Miranda in Sutermeister's *Die Zauberinsel*.

Teseo (*Theseus*)
Opera in five acts by Händel. 1st perf London, 10 Jan 1713; libr by Nicola Francesco Haym, after Philippe Quinault's libretto for Lully's *Thésée*. Principal roles: Teseo (c-ten), Medea (mezzo), Agilea (sop), Egeo (c-ten), Arcane (mezzo), Clizia (sop). Never one of Händel's more successful operas, it is only infrequently performed.
Plot: Legendary Athens. Theseus does not return the affections of the sorceress Medea. Her various plots to separate him from his beloved Agilea are frustrated, and Theseus is ultimately acknowledged as the long-lost son of King Aegeus. [R]

Tessitura (Italian for 'texture')
A term which describes the range or compass of a role or of a piece of music in relation to the vocal type for which it was written. Thus, for example, Verdi's baritone roles are said to have a particularly high tessitura.

Tetide in Sciro (*Thetis in Skyros*)
Opera in three acts by D. Scarlatti. 1st perf Rome, 10 Jan 1712; libr by Carlo Sigismondo Capece. Principal roles: Tetide (sop), Achille (ten), Deidamia (mezzo), Antiope (sop), Licomede (bass), Ulisse (bass). Perhaps Scarlatti's finest opera, it is an excellent example of early Italian OPERA SERIA.
Plot: Legendary Skyros. Much complication is caused by the relationship of two pairs of lovers: firstly, Achilles (disguised as a girl 'Arminda') and Deidamia, daughter of King Licomedes, and secondly, Antiope (disguised as Licomedes's page Filarte) and Licomedes himself, who falls for 'Arminda'. Antiope is torn between feelings of love, jealousy and revenge towards Licomedes, and becomes the object of Deidamia's affections. This arouses the fury of Licomedes, who orders Deidamia's execution. The situation is finally resolved by the intervention of Achilles's mother, the sea goddess Thetis. [R]

Tetrazzini, Luisa (1871–1940)
Italian soprano, particularly associated with Italian COLORATURA roles, especially Lucia and Violetta. Although her 'acting' was well-nigh non-existent, she was one of the highest paid singers in history, commanding $3,000 per performance in the early 1900s. Although reputed to have earned over $5 million in all, she died in poverty. Her autobiography, *My Life of Song*, was published in 1921. Her sister **Eva** (1872–1938) was also a successful soprano and was married to the conductor CLEOFONTE CAMPANINI.

Teufels Lustschloss, Des (*The Devil's Pleasuredrome*)
Opera in three acts by Schubert (D 84). 1st perf Vienna, 12 Dec 1879 (composed 1814); libr by August von Kotzebue. Principal roles: Oswald (ten), Luitgarde (sop). Schubert's first completed opera, written in SINGSPIEL form, it was composed at the age of 16. The music is charming, but the ludicrous farrago of a plot has ensured that it is virtually never performed.
Plot: Accompanied by his esquire, the brave knight Oswald goes to inspect a haunted castle. There, he is subjected to a number of ordeals in which he is joined by his faithful wife Luitgarde. Facing seemingly inevitable death, they are swept away to safety on a sudden flood.

Teyte, Dame Maggie (b Margaret Tate) (1888–1976)
British soprano, particularly associated with the Italian and French repertories, especially Mélisande in *Pelléas et Mélisande* and Cio-Cio-San in *Madama Butterfly*. A singer of outstanding artistry and vocal refinement, with an affecting stage presence, she created the Princess in Holst's *The Perfect Fool* and Glycère in

Hillemacher's *Circe*. Her autobiography, *A Star on the Door*, was published in 1958.

Thaïs
Opera in three acts by Massenet. 1st perf Paris, 16 March 1894; libr by Louis Gallet, after Anatole France's novel. Principal roles: Thaïs (sop), Athanaël (bar), Nicias (ten), Palémon (bass). One of Massenet's finest and most exotically scored operas, it is still quite often performed and is notable for the religio-erotic fervour of much of the music and for the famous *Méditation* with solo violin.
Plot: 4th-century Alexandria. The Coenobite monk Athanaël feels called upon to rescue the beautiful courtesan Thaïs from her life of physical pleasure. His friend Nicias, who has purchased Thaïs's love for a week, introduces him to her at a banquet. He attempts to convert her, and she agrees to enter a convent. However, Athanaël discovers to his horror that he has fallen in love with her. He goes to tell her of his love, only to find that she is dying. [R]

The
Titles beginning with the English definite article are listed under the letter of the first main word. For example, *The Mikado* is listed under M.

Thea
Mezzo role in Tippett's *The Knot Garden*. She is Faber's wife.

Theater an der Wien
Now the home of the annual Vienna Festival, the theatre (cap 1,232) was built by Emanuel Schikaneder and opened on 13 June 1801. Vienna's second most important opera house, and scene of the first performances of *Fidelio* and *Die Fledermaus*, it was totally renovated following its purchase by the city of Vienna on 30 May 1962.

Théâtre Bouffes-Parisiens
A theatre (cap 820) in the Champs-Élysées in Paris which was opened by Offenbach on May 1855. It still retains a strong operetta tradition.

Théâtre de l'Opéra, Nice
The present theatre (cap 1,230) in this city in Alpes-Maritimes (France) opened in Feb 1885. Musical directors have included Antonio de Almeida and Berislav Klobučar.

Théâtre des Arts, Rouen
The original opera house in this French city in Seine-et-Marne opened on 29 June 1776. It burnt down on 25 April 1876, reopening on 30 Sept 1882. Damaged by bombs in 1944, it was rebuilt (cap 1,460) and reopened on 11 Dec 1962.

Théâtre des Champs-Élysées, Paris
The theatre (cap 2,000) opened in 1913 and is the usual venue for performances by visiting companies.

Théâtre Municipal, Nancy
The present opera house (cap 1,310) in this city in Vosges (France) opened in 1919. Musical directors have included Jérôme Kaltenbach.

Théâtre Royal de la Monnaie, Brussels
Belgium's principal opera house, the present theatre (cap 1,140) was designed by Joseph Poelaert and opened in 1856, replacing the original theatre built in 1700. It takes its name from an *atelier monnetaire* which existed on the site in the 17th century. The annual season runs from September to July. Musical directors have included André Vandernoot, Sir John Pritchard, Sylvain Cambreling and Antonio Pappano.

Thebom, Blanche (b 1918)
American mezzo, particularly associated with Wagnerian roles. Based largely at the Metropolitan Opera, New York, from 1944, she was a rich-voiced singer with a good stage presence. In 1968, she became general manager of the short-lived Atlanta Opera Company.

Thérèse
Opera in two acts by Massenet. 1st perf Monte Carlo, 7 Feb 1907; libr by Jules Clarétie. Principal roles: Thérèse (mezzo), Armand (ten), André (bar). Never one of Massenet's more successful operas, it is only very rarely performed.
Plot: Versailles and Paris, 1792–3. The aristocratic soldier Armand de Clerval longs for his family home. This is owned

by André Thorel, son of the former concierge who bought it after Armand's father fled the Revolution. André hopes to return the château to Armand one day and is unaware that his wife Thérèse is Armand's former lover. She is shaken when Armand appears, but although she still loves him she decides to stay with André. Later, André and Thérèse hide Armand from the mob, and André gives him his own papers so that he may escape. Thérèse agrees to run away with Armand, but when she hears that André has been arrested and sees him in the tumbrill on his way to the guillotine, she realizes her duty and joins André on the way to execution. [R]

Theseus
The mythical Greek hero appears in many operas, including: **1** Bass-baritone role in Rameau's *Hippolyte et Aricie*. **2** Baritone role in Pizzetti's *Fedra*. **3** Counter-tenor role in Händel's *Teseo*. **4** Baritone role in Martinů's *Ariane*. **5** Baritone role in Enescu's *Oedipe*. **6** Counter-tenor role in Händel's *Arianna in Creta*. **7** Tenor role in Lully's *Thésée*. **8** Tenor role in Mayr's *Fedra*.

Thespis or **The Gods Grown Old**
Operetta in two acts by Sullivan. 1st perf London, 26 Dec 1871; libr by W.S. Gilbert. The first collaboration between Gilbert and Sullivan, all of the music is lost except for the tenor song 'Little maid of Arcady' and the chorus 'Climbing over rocky mountain', which Sullivan later reused in *The Pirates of Penzance*. Some attempts have been made to reconstruct the work, using other music by Sullivan. **Plot**: Mount Olympos. The ancient gods are old and decrepit and know that they are out of touch with the modern world. Thespis and his theatrical troupe arrive, and the gods accept his offer to take over the deities' duties whilst the gods visit the world incognito. Mercury is left to aid Thespis, but is never consulted. Thespis allows his actors to make any innovations they wish in the running of Olympos, with the result that chaos reigns in the world and Thespis is deluged with mortal complaints. The situation is only returned to normal when Jupiter returns and resumes his government.

Thieving Magpie, The
see GAZZA LADRA, LA

Thill, Georges (1897–1984)
French tenor, particularly associated with the French repertory, especially Julien in *Louise* (a part he also played in a film of the opera). One of the finest lyric tenors of the inter-war period, he combined an Italianate vocal style with an innate feel for the French musical idiom. He created the title-role in Canteloube's *Vercingétorix*.

Thomas, Ambroise (1811–96)
French composer. His 20 operas varied in style as he responded to the examples set by other more successful (and better) composers. His first opera *La Double Échelle* (Paris, 23 Aug 1837; libr François-Antoine-Eugène de Planard) was followed by 16 more or less successful OPÉRA-COMIQUES, written largely in imitation of Auber. They include *La Perroucquier de la Régence* (Paris, 30 Mar 1838; libr Planard and P. Dupont), *Angélique et Médor* (Paris, 10 May 1843; libr Thomas Sauvage, after Lodovico Ariosto's *Orlando Furioso*), *Le Caïd* (Paris, 3 Jan 1849; libr Sauvage), the Shakespearian *Le Songe d'une Nuit d'Été* (Paris, 20 Apr 1850; libr Adolphe de Leuven and Joseph Rosier), *Raymond* (Paris, 5 June 1851; libr de Leuven and Rosier, after Alexandre Dumas's *The Man in the Iron Mask*) and *Le Roman d'Elvire* (Paris, 4 Feb 1860; libr de Leuven and Dumas père). Turning to an imitation of Gounod's style, he produced his most successful works, MIGNON and HAMLET. His last opera *Françoise de Rimini* (Paris, 14 Apr 1882; libr Jules Barbier and Michel Carré, after Dante's *La Divina Commedia*) was a failure. Although he was a distinguished director of the Paris Conservatory from 1871, other composers had mixed feelings about him: Berlioz once remarked that there were three types of music – good music, bad music, and music by Ambroise Thomas!

Thomas, Arthur Goring (1850–92)
British composer, whose early insanity and death cut short a promising career. His five operas are the unfinished *Don Braggadocio* (libr C.I. Thomas), *The Light of the Harem* (London, 7 Nov 1879; libr C. Harrison, after Thomas Moore),

Esmeralda (London, 26 Mar 1883; libr T. Marzials and A. Randegger, after Victor Hugo's *Notre-Dame de Paris*), *Nadeshda* (London, 16 Oct 1885; libr Julian Russell Sturgis) and the unfinished comedy *The Golden Web* (Liverpool, 15 Feb 1893; libr F. Corder and Benjamin Charles Stephenson), which was completed by S.P. Waddington.

Thomas, Jess (1927–93)
American tenor, particularly associated with Wagnerian roles, especially Lohengrin. One of the leading Wagnerian tenors of the 1960s, if not a true HELDENTENOR, he was an artist of fine musicianship and intelligence. He created Octavius Caesar in Barber's *Antony and Cleopatra*.

Thomas and Sally or **The Sailor's Return**
Opera in three acts by Arne. 1st perf London, 28 Nov 1760; libr by Isaac Bickerstaffe. Principal roles: Sally (sop), Thomas (ten), Squire (ten), Dorcas (mezzo). One of Arne's most successful works, it is his only opera which is still occasionally performed.
Plot: 18th-century-England. Sally pines for her absent sailor husband Thomas. Dorcas tries unsuccessfully to persuade her to enjoy life and marry the Squire, but Sally rebuffs the Squire's advances, preferring virtue to his wealth. Thomas returns from his voyages just in time to send the Squire packing and praises the faithfulness of the 'British virgin'. [R]

Thomson, Virgil (1896–1989)
American composer and critic. His three operas are amongst the most important American operas and are written in a musical style which was heavily influenced by his friendships with the composer ÉRIK SATIE and the modernist writer Gertrude Stein. FOUR SAINTS IN THREE ACTS was followed by THE MOTHER OF US ALL and LORD BYRON. His 15 years with the *New York Herald Tribune* established him as one of the most perceptive and entertaining of American critics. His autobiography, *Virgil Thomson*, was published in 1966.

Three Church Parables
The collective title given by Britten to his three one-act operas, THE BURNING FIERY FURNACE, CURLEW RIVER and THE PRODIGAL SON, all of which are written for very small orchestral forces and which are intended for church performance.

Threepenny Opera, The
see DREIGROSCHENOPER, DIE

Through-composed
The term has three meanings in opera: **1** A song whose melody progresses continuously, as opposed to a STROPHIC song, in which the same music is repeated exactly (or almost so) for each verse or stanza. Thus, to take two examples from Sullivan's *Princess Ida*, 'O goddess wise' is through-composed and 'If you give me your attention' is strophic. **2** A musical stage work with no spoken dialogue in a genre (such as SINGSPIEL, operetta or ZARZUELA) which normally does contain spoken dialogue. An example is Sullivan's *Trial By Jury*. **3** A work in which each scene is a single, unbroken piece of music, as in Wagner's later operas. It is the opposite of NUMBER OPERA.

Tibbett, Lawrence (1896–1960)
American baritone, particularly associated with the Italian repertory, especially Verdi. Arguably the outstanding Verdi baritone of the inter-war period, he was a powerful singing-actor with a large, rich and truly magnificent voice. He created the title-roles in Gruenberg's *The Emperor Jones* and Goossens's *Don Juan de Mañara*, Wrestling Bradford in Hanson's *Merry Mount*, the Pasha in Seymour's *In the Pasha's Garden* and, for Taylor, Eadgar in *The King's Henchman* and Col Ibbetson in *Peter Ibbetson*. He also appeared in a number of films, including *The Rogue Song* and *The New Moon*. His autobiography, *The Glory Road*, was published in 1933.

Tichon
Tenor role in Janáček's *Káťa Kabanová*. Kabanicha's son, he is Káťa's husband.

Tiefland (*Lowland*)
Opera in prologue and three acts by d'Albert. 1st perf Prague, 15 Nov 1903; libr by Rudolph Lothar, after Angel Guimerá's *Terra Baixa*. Principal roles: Martha (sop), Pedro (ten), Sebastiano

(bar), Nuri (mezzo), Tommasso (bass). D'Albert's most successful and enduring opera, it is written in VERISMO style.
Plot: Late-19th-century Catalonia. The landowner Sebastiano, wishing to be rid of his unwilling mistress Martha, offers her as a bride to the shepherd Pedro. She distrusts Pedro, who turns on her at the instigation of the villagers, but eventually comes to realize that Pedro loves her. Pedro strangles Sebastiano and they return to the Pyrenees, whence Sebastiano had banished them to the lowlands. [R]

Tietjens, Therese (1831–77)
German soprano, particularly associated with the roles of Lucrezia Borgia, Donna Anna and Norma. Singing almost entirely in England, she was one of the finest sopranos of the mid-19th century, possessing a voice of great power and range which enabled her to encompass a wide variety of Italian and French roles. She created Louise in Lortzing's *Die Opernprobe*.

Tiflis
see TBILSI OPERA AND BALLET THEATRE

Tigranian, Armen (1879–1950)
Armenian composer. The most important Armenian opera composer, his operas do not employ specific examples of folk melody, but his extensive knowledge of traditional Armenian music and music-making is deeply embedded in the character of his stage works. His two most important operas are *Anush* (Alexandropol, 4 Aug 1912; libr composer, after Hovhannes Toumanian) [R] and *David-Beg* (Yerevan, 3 Dec 1950; libr composer) [R].

Timbre (French for 'chime-bell')
A French term, also used in Britain, for TONE-COLOUR.

Timur
Bass role in Puccini's *Turandot*. Calaf's father, he is the deposed King of Tartary.

Tinsley, Pauline (b 1928)
British soprano, particularly associated with dramatic Italian roles, especially Lady Macbeth, Abigaille and Turandot. A thrilling and often sadly underrated singer, she had a steely voice of great power and range and considerable agility which she used with fine musicianship and to exciting dramatic effect. She enjoyed a long career, singing into her mid-60s.

Tippett, Sir Michael (b 1905)
British composer. Widely regarded as one of the most important and original composers of the post-war era, his five operas are amongst the finest of the age. THE MIDSUMMER MARRIAGE, KING PRIAM, THE KNOT GARDEN, THE ICE BREAK and NEW YEAR exhibit great stylistic differences, but all share Tippett's strong humanism, his interest in contemporary social issues, and his almost mystical use of concepts and illusions. Less immediately theatrical and accessible than Britten's operas, Tippett's works have been slower to make their way internationally. His writings, particularly *Moving Into Aquarius* (1959), have exerted a considerable influence on contemporary developments in British music. His autobiography, *Those Twentieth-Century Blues*, was published in 1991.

Tiresias
The blind seer of Greek mythology appears in many operas, including: **1** Bass role in Stravinsky's *Oedipus Rex*. **2** Tenor role in Henze's *The Bassarids*. **3** Bass role in Honegger's *Antigone*. **4** Tenor role in Dallapiccola's *Ulisse*. **5** Tenor role in Orff's *Antigonae*. **6** Baritone role in Enescu's *Oedipe*. **7** Tenor role in Orff's *Oedipus der Tyrann*. **8** Bass role in Buller's *The Bacchae*. **9** Bass role in Leoncavallo's *Edipo Rè*.

Tirolese Landestheater, Innsbruck
The present opera house (cap 793) opened in Dec 1967, replacing the previous theatre originally built in 1653. Musical directors have included Siegfried Nessler and Kaspar de Roo.

Tisbe
Mezzo role in Rossini's *La Cenerentola*. She is one of the two ugly sisters.

Titurel
Bass role in Wagner's *Parsifal*. He is Amfortas's aged father.

Tobias Mill
Baritone role in Rossini's *La Cambiale di Matrimonio*. He is an English businessman.

· Tolstoy ·

The Russian novelist Count Lev Nikolayevich Tolstoy (1828–1910) strongly disliked all opera with the exception of *Don Giovanni* and *Der Freischütz*. He attempted to persuade Tchaikovsky to desist from operatic composition, and he mocked the form in *War and Peace*. Despite this, his works have often inspired composers. Some 20 operas have been based on his novels. Below are listed, by novel, those operas by composers with entries in this dictionary.

Anna Karenina		
Hamilton	*Anna Karenina*	1981
How Men Live		
Martinů	*What Men Live By*	1953
Resurrection		
Alfano	*Risurrezione*	1904
Cikker	*Resurrection*	1962
The Tale of Ivan the Jester		
Ostrčil	*Johnny's Kingdom*	1924
The Two Old Men		
Foerster	*Bloud*	1936
War and Peace		
Prokofiev	*War and Peace*	1946

Toczyska, Stefania (b 1943)
Polish mezzo, particularly associated with the Italian and Russian repertories. A dramatic mezzo in the grand tradition, she possesses a large and powerful voice with a strong lower register, and she has a good stage presence.

Todesverkündigung
Brünnhilde's announcement of Siegmund's death in Act II of Wagner's *Die Walküre*.

Tokyo Chamber Opera Group
Founded in 1969 by Ryosuke Hatanaka, it gives five productions a year. It has a wide-ranging repertory, and its artistic standards have been high.

Tolomeo, Rè di Egitto (*Ptolemy, King of Egypt*)
Opera in three acts by Händel. 1st perf London, 30 April 1728; libr by Nicola Francesco Haym, after Carlo Sigismondo Capece's libretto for D. Scarlatti's *Tolomeo e Alessandro*. Principal roles: Tolomeo (c-ten), Seleuce (sop), Elisa (sop), Alessandro (c-ten), Araspe (bass). Telling a fictitious story of Ptolemy VIII, it has never been one of Händel's more successful operas and is only very rarely performed.
Plot: Cyprus, 108 BC. The island is ruled by the tyrannical King Araspe, whose sister Elisa is in love with the exiled Ptolemy who, with his wife Seleuce, is living disguised as a shepherd. Arapse falls in love with Seleuce and attempts to win her. After much intrigue, Ptolemy is imprisoned, but is rescued by his brother Alexander, reunited with Seleuce and proclaimed King of Egypt.

Tolstoy
see panel above

Tom
Bass role in Verdi's *Un Ballo in Maschera*. Count Horn in the Swedish setting, he is one of the two conspirators.

Tomasi, Henri (1901–71)
French composer and conductor. His operas, little known outside France, include *Don Juan de Mañara* (Paris, 6 Nov 1952; libr composer, after Oscar Milosz), *L'Atlantide* (Mulhouse, 26 Feb 1954; libr

Francis Didelot, after Pierre Benoît), *Le Triomphe de Jeanne* (Rouen, 23 Mar 1956; libr composer), *Sampiero Corso* (Bordeaux, 6 May 1956; libr R. Cuttoli), *Princesse Pauline* (Paris, 11 Jan 1962; libr Didelot), *Le Silence de la Mer* (Strasbourg, 15 June 1963; libr composer, after Vercors) and *L'Élixir du Révérend Père Gaucher* (Toulouse, 3 Apr 1964; libr L. Bancal, after Alphonse Daudet). He was musical director of the Monte Carlo Opera (1946–50).

Tom Jones
Operetta in three acts by German. 1st perf Manchester, 3 April 1907; libr by Alexander M. Thompson, Robert Courtenidge and Charles H. Taylor, after Henry Fielding's novel. Principal roles: Tom Jones (bar), Sophia (sop), Honour (mezzo), Western (bar), Blifil (ten). Arguably German's finest stage work, it was enormously successful at its appearance but is nowadays only rarely performed.
Plot: 18th-century Somerset. Squire Western honours the foundling Tom Jones, adopted by Mr Allworthy, for saving the life of his only child Sophia. She and Tom fall in love, but Western wishes Sophia to marry Allworthy's nephew and heir Blifil, who Sophia loathes. Eventually, Western discovers that Tom is in fact Blifil's elder brother, and so has no objection to him as a son-in-law. [R Exc]

Tomlinson, John (b 1946)
British bass, particularly associated with Verdi, Mozart and Wagner roles, especially Wotan and Hagen (in *Götterdämmerung*). Possessing a large and rich voice of considerable power and range, he also has a strong stage presence. He created Villac Umu in Hamilton's *The Royal Hunt of the Sun* and the Green Knight in Birtwistle's *Gawain*.

Tomowa-Sintow, Anna (b 1941)
Bulgarian soprano, particularly associated with Mozart, Verdi and Strauss roles. Possessing a creamy lyrico-spinto voice, which she uses with style and great intelligence, she is an affecting singing-actress. She created a Sybil in Orff's *De Temporum Fine Comoedia*.

Tomsky, Count
Baritone role in Tchaikovsky's *The Queen of Spades*. He is a friend of Herman.

Tonadilla (Spanish for 'little tune')
A short comic opera in light style, similar to an Italian INTERMEZZO, given between the acts of an opera or play. It developed in Spain in the 18th century as a reaction against the increasing formality of ZARZUELA. Originally for two, three or four characters only and seldom exceeding 20 minutes' duration, the genre subsequently developed an independent life as *tonadillas generales*, employing up to ten characters. The leading tonadilla composers were Luis Misón (*d* 1766), Antonio Guerrero (1700–76), Pablo Esteve (*d* 1794), Ventura Galván (*fl* 1810), José Palomino (1755–1810) and Blas Laserna (1751–1816).

Tone-colour
The sound quality which distinguishes a note sung by one singer from the same note sung by a different one. It is also called timbre in France and Britain.

Tonie
Tenor role in Donizetti's *La Fille du Régiment*. He is a young Tyrolese in love with Marie.

Tonio
Baritone role in Leoncavallo's *Pagliacci*. He is the hunchbacked clown in Canio's troupe.

Tooley, Sir John (b 1924)
British administrator. He was general administrator of Covent Garden (1970–88), where he introduced the popular 'promenade' performances which are sometimes given at low prices to encourage young audiences.

Toreador's Song
Baritone aria ('Votre toast') for Escamillo in Act II of Bizet's *Carmen*.

Torna la pace
Tenor aria for Idomeneo in Act III of Mozart's *Idomeneo*, in which he welcomes the return of tranquility that will follow Idamante's assumption of the crown.

Tornami a dir
Soprano/tenor duet for Norina and Ernesto in Act III of Donizetti's *Don Pasquale*, in which they sing of their love.

Toronto
see CANADIAN OPERA COMPANY

Torquato Tasso
Opera in three acts by Donizetti. 1st perf Rome, 9 Sept 1833; libr by Jacopo Ferretti, after Giovanni Rosini's *Tasso*, Lord Byron's *The Lament of Tasso* and Johann von Goethe's *Tasso*. Principal roles: Tasso (bar), Eleonora (sop), Roberto (ten), Gherardo (bass), Scandiano (mezzo), Alfonso (bass). Dealing with events in the life of the Italian poet Torquato Tasso (1544–95), it is one of Donizetti's most adventurous operas. The chorus only comments on the action (as in a Greek drama), the villains are a tenor and a BASSO-BUFFO, and the enormously demanding title-role is for a baritone, prefiguring Verdi. Successful at its appearance, it is still performed from time to time.
Plot: Ferrara, 1579–86. The poet Tasso loves Eleonora, sister of Duke Alfonso d'Este. Don Gherardo believes that Tasso loves his own sweetheart Eleonora di Scandiano, and steals a poem of Tasso's in praise of Leonora. Gherardo's machinations lead to Tasso being declared insane and confined in an asylum for seven years. When he is released and told that his own Eleonora is dead, he really does go mad. However, he is persuaded to think only of his poetry and returns to his writing.

Torquemada
Tenor role in Ravel's *L'Heure Espagnole*. He is a clockmaker married to Concepción.

Torrejón y Velasco, Tomás de (1644–1728)
Spanish composer, resident in Peru from 1667. Most of his output was liturgical, but he also wrote one opera, *La Púrpura de la Rosa* (Lima, 19 Oct 1701; libr Pedro Calderón de la Barca), which was the first opera to be performed in South America.

Torroba, Federico Moreno (1891–1982)
Spanish composer and conductor. His stage works include LUISA FERNANDA, one of the most popular of all ZARZUELAS, the zarzuela *Maravilla* (Madrid, 12 Apr 1941; libr Antonio Quintero and Jesús María de Arozamena) [R Exc] and the unsuccessful opera *El Poeta* (Madrid, 19 June 1980; libr J.M. Herrera).

Torvaldo e Dorliska
Opera in two acts by Rossini. 1st perf Rome, 26 Dec 1815; libr by Cesare Sterbini, after Jean-Baptiste Louvet de Couvrai's *Les Amours du Chevalier de Faublas*. Principal roles: Dorliska (sop), Torvaldo (ten), Duke of Ordow (bass), Carlotta (mezzo), Giorgio (bar). Although it contains some fine music, it is only rarely performed, and only the overture is still remembered nowadays.
Plot: The tyrannical Duke of Ordow loves Torvaldo's wife Dorliska. He waylays them but fails to kill Torvaldo. Dorliska escapes and seeks shelter at a neighbouring castle. Unfortunately, it belongs to Ordow, who promptly makes her captive. Torvaldo gains entry to the castle in disguise, but is discovered and also made prisoner. With the aid of the Duke's servant Giorgio and his wife Carlotta, Torvaldo and Dorliska escape. Torvaldo takes the Duke captive to the acclaim of the oppressed populace.

Tosatti, Vieri (b 1920)
Italian composer. He has written seven operas, some of which have met with success in Italy but which are unknown elsewhere. They are the unperformed *Dionisio* (1946; libr composer), *Il Sistema della Dolcezza* (Bergamo, 25 Oct 1951; libr composer, after Edgar Allan Poe's *The System of Dr Tarr and Prof Fether*), the boxing opera *Partita a Pugni* (*Fist Fight*, Venice 1953), *Il Giudizio Universale* (Milan, 2 Apr 1955; libr Cesare Lodovici, after A. Bonacci), *L'Isola del Tesoro* (Bologna, 20 Nov 1958; libr composer, after Robert Louis Stevenson's *Treasure Island*), *La Fiora delle Meraviglie* (Rome, 30 Jan 1963; libr composer) and *Il Paradiso e il Poeta* (RAI, 3 Dec 1971; libr composer).

Tosca
Opera in three acts by Puccini. 1st perf Rome, 14 Jan 1900; libr by Giuseppe Giacosa and Luigi Illica, after Victorien Sardou's *La Tosca*. Principal roles: Tosca (sop), Scarpia (bar), Cavaradossi (ten), Angelotti (bass), Sacristan (b-bar). An instant success which has remained one of

the most enduringly popular of all operas, it gave to Maria Callas and Tito Gobbi their most thrilling roles, and their performances have become the yardstick by which all others are now measured.
Plot: Rome, June 1800. The artist and republican loyalist Mario Cavaradossi aids the escape of Cesare Angelotti, the former Consul of the Roman Republic. Baron Scarpia, the chief of police, lusts after Cavaradossi's lover, the singer Floria Tosca, and hopes to recapture Angelotti through her. He has Cavaradossi arrested and tortured until Tosca reveals Angelotti's hiding place. Scarpia agrees to release Cavaradossi and to provide him and Tosca with a safe-conduct after Cavaradossi has been through a mock execution. Scarpia's price is Tosca herself. She agrees, but stabs him with a knife from his own table when he begins to embrace her. Scarpia's 'mock' execution squad proves to have real bullets, and Cavaradossi is killed. By this time, Scarpia's murder has been discovered, and Tosca throws herself off the battlements. [R]

Tosca è un buon falco
Baritone aria for Baron Scarpia in Act II of Puccini's *Tosca*, in which he muses on his preference for violent sexual conquest.

Toscanini, Arturo (1867–1957)
Italian conductor, particularly associated with Verdi and Puccini operas. He began his career as a cellist (playing in the first performance of Verdi's *Otello*), making an unexpected conducting debut in Rio de Janeiro in 1886 when he replaced an unpopular colleague. Autocratic, even despotic, and given to severe outbursts of temper, he was nevertheless one of the greatest conductors of the early 20th century. His performances were noted for their scrupulous preparation, for their fiery excitement and for their sometimes idiosyncratic tempi, and he did more than any other single figure to raise the standards of operatic performance. He was musical director of the Teatro Regio, Turin (1895–98) and La Scala, Milan (1898–1903, 1906–8 and 1920–29). He conducted the first performances of *La Bohème*, *La Fanciulla del West*, *Turandot*, *Pagliacci*, *Zazà*, Pizzetti's *Dèbora e Jaéle* and *Fra Gherardo*, Zandonai's *I Cavalieri di Ekebù*, Mascagni's *Le Maschere*, Boito's *Nerone* (which he helped to complete), Giordano's *Madame Sans-Gêne*, Franchetti's *Germania*, Smareglia's *Oceàna* and Cilea's *Gloria*.

Toten Augen, Die (*The Blind Eyes*)
Opera in prologue and one act by d'Albert. 1st perf Dresden, 5 March 1916; libr by Hanns Heinz Ewers and Marc Henry, after the latter's *Les Yeux Morts*. Principal roles: Myrtocle (sop), Arcesius (bar), Galba (ten). One of d'Albert's best operas, notable for the sensuous power of its orchestration, it was successful at its appearance but is nowadays virtually forgotten.
Plot: Jerusalem, 1st century AD. The sight of Myrtocle, the blind wife of the Roman proconsul Arcesius, is miraculously restored. She discovers that Arcesius is hideously ugly, and believes the good-looking Capt Galba to be the man she had married. Galba is secretly in love with Myrtocle, but when she discovers the truth her love for Arcesius is renewed, and she prays to be blind once more. She looks full at the blazing sun and her prayer is answered.

Tote Stadt, Die (*The Dead City*)
Opera in three acts by Korngold (Op 12). 1st perf Hamburg and Cologne simultaneously, 4 Dec 1920; libr by the composer and his father Julius Korngold under the joint pen-name of Paul Schott, after Georges Rodenbach's *Bruges-la-Morte*. Principal roles: Paul (ten), Marietta (sop), Marie (sop), Frank (bar), Fritz (bar), Brigitta (mezzo). Korngold's most successful opera, still performed from time to time, it is written in a lush, late-romantic style. The two female roles are traditionally played by the same soprano.
Plot: Late-19th-century Bruges. Paul is in mourning for his late wife Marie. He meets the dancer Marietta, in whom he seems to see Marie. In a series of dream visions, he has various experiences with her, ending with her infidelity, which causes him to strangle her with her own hair. [R]

To this we've come
Soprano aria for Magda Sorel in Act II of Menotti's *The Consul*, in which she rails against the endless red tape of the consulate.

Tottola, Andrea Leone (d 1831)
Italian librettist. A typical example of the literary hacks who churned out vast numbers of libretti in early-19th-century Italy, he was based in Naples. He provided texts for Bellini (*Adelson e Salvini*), Carafa, Donizetti (*La Zingara*, *Alfredo il Grande*, *Il Fortunato Inganno*, *Il Castello di Kenilworth*, *Imelda de' Lambertazzi* and *Gabriella di Vergy*), Fioravanti, García, Generali, Guglielmi, Mayr (*Elena*), Mercadante, Pacini, Petrella, L. Ricci, Rossini (*La Donna del Lago*, *Mosè in Egitto*, *Zelmira*, *Ermione* and *Edoardo e Cristina*) and Vaccai amongst others.

Toulouse Capitole
The present opera house (cap 1,200) in this city in Haute-Garonne (France) opened in 1923, replacing the previous theatre of the same name which had dated from 1737. The name derives from the 12 consuls (*capitouls*) who ruled the city and who owned the original theatre. Particularly noted for its performances of the French repertory, the annual season runs from October to May. Since 1975, the company has shared productions with the Grand Théâtre, Bordeaux. Musical directors have included Louis Izar and Michel Plasson.

Tourangeau, Huguette (b 1938)
Canadian mezzo, particularly associated with Italian BEL CANTO roles and with the French repertory. She possesses a rich, agile and dark-toned voice, used with a good technique, and has an impressive (if much over-indulged) chest register.

Tourel, Jennie (b Davidovich) (1899–1973)
Canadian mezzo, particularly associated with the French repertory. Possessing a voice of remarkable range, which she used with an outstanding technique, she created Baba the Turk in *The Rake's Progress*. She was also a distinguished teacher, whose pupils included Maria Ewing and Barbara Hendricks.

Tous les trois réunis
Soprano/tenor/bass trio for Marie, Tonie and Sulpice in Act II of Donizetti's *La Fille du Régiment*, in which they express their joy at being together once again.

Tozzi, Giorgio (b George) (b 1923)
American bass, particularly associated with the Italian repertory. Starting as a baritone, he turned to bass roles in 1950, and from 1955 was largely resident at the Metropolitan Opera, New York. A rich-voiced and intelligent singer with an imposing stage presence, he created the Doctor in Barber's *Vanessa*.

Trabuco
Tenor role in Verdi's *La Forza del Destino*. He is a muleteer.

Tradito schernito
Tenor aria for Ferrando in Act II of Mozart's *Così fan Tutte*, in which he rages over Dorabella's betrayal of him. It is usually cut because of its formidable difficulty.

Traetta, Tommaso (1727–79)
Italian composer. His first opera *Il Farnace* (Naples, 4 Nov 1751; libr Antonio Maria Luchini, after Apostolo Zeno's *Mitridate*) was a success, and he soon became famous, writing operas for Italy, Austria, England and Russia. His most successful operas include *Ippolito ed Aricia* (Parma, 9 May 1759; libr C.I. Fruggoni, after Euripides's *Hippolytus*), *I Tintaridi* (Parma, Apr 1760; libr Fruggoni, after Pierre Joseph Bernard's *Castor et Pollux*), *Le Serve Rivali* (Venice, 1766; libr Pietro Chiari) and *Antigonae* (St Petersburg, 11 Nov 1772; libr Marco Coltellini, after Sophocles), usually regarded as his finest work. After a long period of complete neglect, there has recently been a minor revival of interest in his music.

Tragédie-lyrique (French for 'lyric tragedy')
The term used by Lully and Philippe Quinault to describe their stage works, in which epic or mythical subjects were intended to be treated with dramatic naturalness and to exhibit clarity of declamation. First used in 1673 to describe *Cadmus et Hermione*, the term later came into more general usage to describe the operas of Lully's successors, such as Rameau and Gluck.

Transcription
The arranging of a piece of music for an

instrument for which it was not originally written. In opera, the term is encountered only in reference to Liszt's many arrangements of operatic melodies for the piano.

Transposition
The performance of a piece of music in a key other than that in which it was originally written. Singers will sometimes transpose an aria (usually downwards), either to make specific high notes easier or because the general TESSITURA of the piece sits uncomfortably with their own vocal range.

Traubel, Helen (1899–1972)
American soprano, particularly associated with Wagnerian roles. Long resident at the Metropolitan Opera, New York, she left the house in 1953 after disagreements with Rudolf Bing over her nightclub appearances. Possessing a warm-toned voice of enormous proportions and superb projection, she created Mary in Damrosch's *The Man Without a Country*. She wrote a number of successful detective stories as well as her autobiography, *St Louis Woman*, which was published in 1959.

Traurigkeit
Soprano aria for Constanze in Act II of Mozart's *Die Entführung aus dem Serail*, in which she laments over her separation from Belmonte.

Traveller
Baritone role in: **1** Britten's *Death in Venice*. A multiple character who appears in seven different guises, he is the sinister figure who aids Aschenbach's destruction. **2** Holst's *The Perfect Fool*. **3** Britten's *Curlew River*.

Travelling Companion, The
Opera in four acts by Stanford (Op 146). 1st perf Bristol, 25 Oct 1926 (composed 1919); libr by Henry Newbolt, after Hans Christian Andersen's story. Principal roles: Companion (bar), Princess (sop), John (ten), King (b-bar), Wizard (bass). Stanford's last opera, produced posthumously, it was reasonably successful in its time but is nowadays virtually forgotten.

Travesti (from the Italian *travestire*, 'to disguise')
A term describing an operatic role which involves a singer portraying a character of the opposite sex. Although there are a few 'drag' roles for men (there is Mamm' Agata in Donizetti's *Le Convenienze ed Inconvenienze Teatrali*, and Wolf-Ferrari's *Il Campiello* contains a street fight for two old women played by tenors), most are for women playing male characters. Such characters are most often young men (such roles were called MUSICO in 19th-century Italy) or roles originally written for CASTRATI and now sung by mezzo-sopranos. Travesti parts are called *Hosenrolen* in Germany and trouser roles or breeches roles in Britain.

Traviata, La (roughly *The Fallen Woman*)
Opera in three acts by Verdi. 1st perf Venice, 6 March 1853; libr by Francesco Maria Piave, after Alexandre Dumas fils' *La Dame aux Camélias*. Principal roles: Violetta (sop), Alfredo and Giorgio Germont (ten and bar), Flora (mezzo). The most intimate of Verdi's operas, dealing with the historical demi-mondaine Marie Duplessis (1824–47), it was a failure at its premiere, but had established itself within a year and has remained ever since one of the best-loved and most frequently performed, recorded and filmed of all operas. Violetta remains one of the greatest musico-dramatic roles ever written for a lyric soprano, and the sometimes maligned role of Germont père is a fascinating study of a warm and kindly man, trapped by the social conventions of his class, attempting to come to terms with a situation outside his experience or comprehension.
Plot: Mid-19th-century Paris. The beautiful but consumptive demi-mondaine Violetta Valéry gives a lavish party at which Alfredo Germont, a young man of good family, is present. After the guests have departed, Alfredo – who has long loved Violetta from a distance – reveals his feelings and urges her to give up her brittle and shallow life and come to him. Realizing that this is her first and last chance of true love, Violetta brushes aside her misgivings and she and Alfredo go and live an idyllic life together in the country. Her happiness is shattered when,

during Alfredo's absence on an errand, his father Giorgio arrives to see her. He tells her that her liaison with his son is bringing dishonour to his family and is threatening his daughter's marriage prospects. He begs Violetta to give up Alfredo. Under the weight of his arguments, the distraught Violetta complies and leaves without explanation. In the company of her former protector Baron Douphol, to whom she has returned, Violetta attends a party given by her friend Flora Bervoix, where she encounters Alfredo. In his bitterness (and unaware of her sacrifice), he publicly insults her and she collapses. Violetta is now gravely ill and Germont, suffering remorse for the pain he has caused, tells Alfredo the truth about her departure and gives his blessing to their relationship. Alfredo rushes to Violetta but, after a joyous reunion, she dies in his arms. [R]

Treble
The unbroken voice of a child. It is most often used with reference to the male voice, and is sometimes called 'boy soprano'. Largely because a treble lacks the power and projection of a trained operatic voice, there are few major treble roles in opera; the most important are Miles in *The Turn of the Screw* and Amahl in *Amahl and the Night Visitors*.

Treemonisha
Opera in three acts by Joplin. 1st perf Atlanta, 28 Jan 1972 (composed 1911); libr by the composer. Principal roles: Treemonisha (mezzo), Monisha (sop), Remus (ten), Ned (bass), Zodzetrick (ten), Luddud (bar). Joplin's only surviving stage work, written in ragtime style, it is intended to be performed by an all-black cast. It has had a number of performances in recent years, in the arrangement by Gunther Schuller.
Plot: Arkansas, Sept 1884. Treemonisha upbraids the soothsayer Zodzetrick for spreading superstition amongst the plantation workers. In retaliation, Zodzetrick and his henchman Luddud abduct her. She is rescued by Remus, who frightens her abductors by disguising himself as the Devil. Returning to the village, Treemonisha agrees to become the community's leader. [R]

Treigle, Norman (1927–75)
American bass, particularly associated with the title-role in *Mefistofele*. Largely based at the New York City Opera, he was a magnificent singing-actor, both his stage personality and his powerful voice being highly individual. He created Granpa Moss in Copland's *The Tender Land*, John Hale in Ward's *The Crucible* and, for Floyd, Olin Blitch in *Susannah* and the title-roles in *The Passion of Jonathan Wade* and *Markheim*. He committed suicide.

Tremolo (Italian for 'shaking')
In singing, another term for VIBRATO.

Trial
A French term, named after the French tenor Antoine Trial (1736–95), which refers to a tenor more highly regarded for his dramatic abilities than for his singing.

Trial By Jury
Dramatic cantata in one act by Sullivan. 1st perf London, 25 March 1875; libr by W.S. Gilbert. Principal roles: Judge (bar), Defendant (ten), Plaintiff (sop), Counsel for Plaintiff (bar), Usher (bass). The first surviving work of the Gilbert and Sullivan partnership, it is really a comic opera rather than an operetta as it is entirely THROUGH-COMPOSED. A brilliant satire on the British legal system, it was an instant success which remains as fresh and delightful as ever, and it is sometimes regarded as Sullivan's masterpiece.
Plot: A 19th-century British law court. The Learned Judge hears a case for breach of promise of marriage brought by the Plaintiff Angelina against the Defendant Edwin. Judge, jury and everybody else in court make their partiality towards Angelina abundantly clear, and eventually the Judge decides to marry her himself. [R]

Trieste
see TEATRO COMUNALE GIUSEPPE VERDI, TRIESTE

Trill
A vocal ornament, also called a 'shake', which consists of the rapid alternation of the written note with its adjacent one

(usually the note above). Singers who have been especially renowned for their trill include Joan Sutherland and Selma Kurz.

Trillo
An obsolete vocal ornament, which consisted of a single note repeated with increasing rapidity.

Trimarchi, Domenico (b 1940)
Italian baritone, particularly associated with Italian BUFFO roles, especially Dr Bartolo in Rossini's *Il Barbiere di Siviglia*. One of the leading contemporary buffos, he has a good if not absolutely outstanding voice, abundant comic talent and superb diction.

Tringles des sistres tintaient, Les
Mezzo aria for Carmen in Act II of Bizet's *Carmen*. It is the gypsy song which she sings at Lilas Pastia's tavern.

Trinke, Liebchen
Tenor aria for Alfred in Act I of J. Strauss's *Die Fledermaus*, in which he invites Rosalinde to relax and drink with him.

Trio
In opera, a musical number for three solo singers, with or without chorus, in which the musical material is divided equally between the three soloists.

Trionfai
Soprano cabaletta for Lady Macbeth in Act II of the original 1847 version of Verdi's *Macbeth*, in which she exults over her triumph. It was cut in the revised version and replaced by 'La luce langue'.

Trionfi (*Triumphs*)
A theatrical triptych by Orff, comprising *Carmina Burana*, TRIONFO D'AFRODITE and *Catulli Carmina*. Only the second can be considered to be in any way operatic.

Trionfo d'Afrodite (*Triumph of Aphrodite*)
Scenic concerto in seven scenes by Orff. 1st perf Milan, 14 Feb 1953; libr by the composer, after Sappho, Euripides and Gaius Valerius Catullus. Principal roles: Bride (sop), Bridegroom (ten). The second panel of Orff's triptych *Trionfi*, it comprises various scenes in praise of love and marriage. [R]

Trionfo dell'Onore, Il (*The Triumph of Honour*) or **Il Dissoluto Pentito** (*The Repentant Rake*)
Comic opera in three acts by A. Scarlatti. 1st perf Naples, 26 Nov 1718; libr by Francesco Antonio Tullio. Principal roles: Riccardo (ten), Leonora (mezzo), Erminio (bass), Doralice (sop), Flaminio (ten), Cornelia (mezzo), Rosina (mezzo), Rodimarte (bar). Scarlatti's only wholly comic work, and the earliest surviving Neapolitan comic opera, it still receives a very occasional performance.
Plot: Early-18th-century Pisa. The dissolute Riccardo Alberoni has seduced and abandoned Leonora Dorini and is now pursuing Doralice Rossetti. With his friend Capt Rodimarte he comes to the house of his lecherous uncle Flaminio Castravacca, who is engaged to Doralice's aunt Cornelia Buffacci. Cornelia and her buxom maid Rosina Caruccia also arrive at the house, as do Leonora and her brother Erminio, Doralice's jilted lover. After much complicated amorous intrigue, Erminio challenges Riccardo to a duel. Riccardo is wounded and, perceiving the error of his ways, repents and asks Leonora to be his wife. Honour has triumphed. [R]

Triquet, Monsieur
Tenor role in Tchaikovsky's *Eugene Onegin*. He is Tatyana's French tutor.

Tristan und Isolde
Opera in three acts by Wagner. 1st perf Munich, 10 June 1865 (composed 1859); libr by the composer. Principal roles: Isolde (sop), Tristan (ten), Brangäne (mezzo), Kurwenal (bar), Marke (bass), Melot (bar). Wagner's most intense music-drama, in which he took chromatic harmony to new limits, it occupies a unique position in the repertory, both because of its overwhelming emotional impact and because of the enormous influence which it exerted on the subsequent development of music.
Plot: Legendary Cornwall and Brittany. Tristan, nephew of King Mark of Cornwall, has been despatched to fetch the Irish princess Isolde and bring her back as a wife for Mark. Tristan and Isolde had met previously, when he slew her intended husband, and she had tended his wounds. Each fell in love with the other, but each

kept silent, believing their feelings unrequited. Now, aboard the vessel from Ireland, they resolve to end their separate sufferings by taking poison. Knowing of this, Isolde's faithful companion Brangäne subsititutes a love potion, and the couple are overtaken by uncontrollable passion. Once in Cornwall, the lovers can only meet under cover of darkness. Betrayed by the knight Melot, they are discovered by Mark. Tristan is wounded by Melot and taken home to his own kingdom by his loyal esquire Kurwenal. Isolde follows him, arriving in time to join him in a mutual embrace of death. [R]

Tristram, Sir
Bass-baritone role in Flotow's *Martha*. He is Lady Harriet's ageing cousin and suitor.

Trittico, Il (*The Triptych*)
The title given by Puccini to his three contrasting one-act operas: IL TABARRO, SUOR ANGELICA and GIANNI SCHICCHI.

Triumph Scene
The title usually given to the great public scene (Act II Scene II) of Verdi's *Aida*.

Troilus and Cressida
Opera in three acts by Walton. 1st perf London, 3 Dec 1954; libr by Christopher Hassall, after Geoffrey Chaucer's *Troilus and Criseyde*. Revised version 1st perf London, 12 Nov 1976. Principal roles: Cressida (sop), Troilus (ten), Diomede (bar), Pandarus (ten), Calkas (bass), Evadne (mezzo), Antenor (bar), Horaste (bass). Written in Walton's most lyrical and romantic vein, it contains some of his finest music, but for some reason is only infrequently performed.
Plot: Legendary Troy. The high priest Calkas wishes his daughter Cressida to become a priestess. However, she responds to the love of Troilus, whose suit is pressed with the help of her uncle Pandarus. After the defection of Calkas to the Greeks, Cressida is exchanged for their prisoner Antenor, and agrees to marriage with Diomede. Troilus is stabbed in the back by Calkas whilst he is fighting Diomede. Cressida is ordered to remain with the Greeks as a prostitute, but she kills herself over Troilus's body. [R]

Trojans, The
see TROYENS, LES

Trompeter von Säckingen, Der (*The Trumpeter of Säckingen*)
Opera in four acts by Nessler. 1st perf Leipzig, 4 May 1884; libr by Rudolf Bunge, after Joseph von Scheffel's poem. Principal roles: Werner (ten), Maria (sop), Damian (bar), Schönau (bass). Nessler's finest opera, it was very successful in its time and is still occasionally performed in Germany.
Plot: Mid-17th-century Germany. Towards the end of the Thirty Years' War, the trumpeter Werner falls in love with the high-born Maria, whose father Baron von Schönau wishes her to marry the simpleton Damian. During an attack on the city, Damian proves himself to be a coward, whilst Werner behaves heroically. The discovery of a birthmark on his arm shows that he is of noble descent, and all objections to his marrying Maria are removed. [R Exc]

Troqueurs, Les (*The Barterers*)
Comic opera in one act by Dauvergne. 1st perf Foire St Laurent, 30 July 1753; libr by Jean-Joseph Vadé, after Jean de la Fontaine. Principal roles: Margot (sop), Fanchon (sop), Lubin (bar), Lucas (ten). A product of the GUERRE DES BOUFFONS, it is a historically important work in that it was the first French opera to be modelled on the Italian INTERMEZZO style, and may be said to be the first OPÉRA-COMIQUE.
Plot: 18th-century France. Lubin and Lucas are engaged to Margot and Fanchon, but are a little bored with their prospective mates and think that it would be a good idea to do a swap. The girls do not approve of this plan and decide to teach the boys a lesson. They pretend to agree, but then lead their new lovers such a dance that the two boys are only too happy to return to their original partners. [R]

Trouble in Tahiti
Comic opera in one act by Bernstein. 1st perf Waltham (Mass), 1 June 1952; libr by the composer. Principal roles: Dinah (mezzo), Sam (bar). A satirical domestic comedy about a bickering suburban couple, Bernstein later incorporated it into A QUIET PLACE. [R]

Trouser role
A term used to describe a soprano or mezzo singing a male role, usually a young man or boy. Famous trouser roles include Cherubino, Oscar, Octavian and Prince Orlofsky. They are called *Hosenrolen* in Germany, TRAVESTI in Italy, and the term breeches role is also sometimes used in Britain.

Trovatore, Il (*The Troubador*)
Opera in four acts by Verdi. 1st perf Rome, 19 Jan 1853; libr by Salvatore Cammarano (completed by Leone Emanuele Bardare), after Antonio García Gutiérrez's *El Trovador*. Principal roles: Manrico (ten), Leonora (sop), Conte di Luna (bar), Azucena (mezzo), Ferrando (bass). The apotheosis and epitome of Italian romantic and melodramatic opera, notable for its seemingly inexhaustible wealth of white-hot melody, it was an instant success and has remained ever since one of the most enduringly popular of all operas. The libretto is a byword for obscurity and confusion, but if the listener attends to Ferrando's narration in the first scene and bears in mind that the old gypsy Azucena is the central character, the action becomes rather more logical.
Plot: Vizcaya and Aragon, 1409. The troubador Manrico, leader of a rebel army, is believed to be the son of the gypsy Azucena. He loves Leonora, who is also loved by the Count of Luna, the leader of the royal army. Luna's men capture Azucena, and Luna's commander Ferrando recognizes her as the woman who caused the death of Luna's brother. Azucena is imprisoned and Manrico is captured during an attempt to rescue her. To secure Manrico's freedom, Leonora offers herself to Luna, taking a slow poison after he has agreed. Realizing that he has been tricked, Luna has Manrico executed. Azucena reveals that the child who died years ago was her own, and that Luna has just killed his own brother. [R]

Troyanos, Tatiana (1938–93)
American mezzo. An outstanding artist of great versatility, she possessed a rich, beautiful and flexible voice which she used with musicianship and great intelligence. She excelled in a wide range of music and styles, from Händel to Bernstein, by way of Bellini, Strauss and Britten. A powerful singing-actress, she created Jeanne des Anges in Penderecki's *The Devils of Loudun*, the title-role in Rachmaninov's *Monna Vanna* and Queen Isabella in Glass's *The Voyage*.

Troyens, Les (*The Trojans*)
Opera in two parts (five acts) by Berlioz. Part I *La Prise de Troie* (*The Capture of Troy*) 1st perf Karlsruhe, 6 Dec 1890 (composed 1862); Part II *Les Troyens à Carthage* (*The Trojans at Carthage*) 1st perf Paris, 4 Nov 1863; 1st complete uncut perf in French London, 17 Sept 1969; libr by the composer, after Virgil's *The Aeneid*. Principal roles: Énée (ten), Didon (mezzo), Cassandre (sop), Chorèbe (bar), Anna (mezzo), Narbal (bass), Iopas (ten), Panthée (bass), Ascagne (mezzo), Hylas (ten), Héctor (bass). Berlioz's masterpiece and one of the greatest of all French operas, it remained virtually unperformed for nearly a century, but has at last entered the repertory of most major opera houses. Once regarded (through ignorance) as a hopelessly-flawed white elephant, it is now appreciated to have a power, splendour and sense of vision unrivalled by almost any other opera. It is often split over two evenings (although its total length is less than Wagner's longest works), but Berlioz intended it to be performed on a single evening, and it is in that way that it makes its greatest effect.
Plot: Legendary Troy and Carthage. Despite the warnings of the prophetess Cassandra, the Trojans joyously escort the wooden horse into the city, allowing the Greeks to capture and sack Troy. After her betrothed Chorebus is killed, Cassandra leads the women in mass suicide, after foretelling that Aeneas will found a new Trojan city in Italy. Aeneas and his son Ascanius are thrown ashore with their ragged followers at Carthage, where they assist in repelling a Numidian attack. Aeneas falls in love with Queen Dido, to the distress of her sister Anna and her minister Narbal. Finally responding to the call of destiny, Aeneas abandons Dido and sets out for Italy. The grief-crazed Dido kills herself. [R]

Truelove
Roles in Stravinsky's *The Rake's Progress*:

Anne (sop), Tom's betrothed, and her father (bass).

Truffaldino
The Commedia dell'Arte character appears in a number of operas, including: **1** Bass role in Strauss's *Ariadne auf Naxos*. **2** Tenor role in Prokofiev's *The Love of Three Oranges*. **3** Tenor role in Busoni's *Turandot*.

Tsar Saltan
see TALE OF TSAR SALTAN, THE

Tsar's Bride, The (*Tsarskaya Nevesta*)
Opera in three acts by Rimsky-Korsakov. 1st perf Moscow, 3 Nov 1899; libr by the composer and Ilya Fyodorovich Tuymenev, after Lev Alexandrovich Mey's play. Principal roles: Marfa (sop), Grigori (bar), Lykov (ten), Lyubasha (mezzo), Sobakin (bass). Still popular in Russia, it is little known elsewhere, despite its colourful score.
Plot: Russia, 1572. Grigori Gryaznoy employs a love potion in his attempts to win the heart of Marfa, the fiancée of the boyar Ivan Lykov. The potion turns out to be a slow poison arranged by Grigori's former mistress Lyubasha. Ivan the Terrible choses Marfa as his wife, but she dies from the poison soon afterwards. Lyubasha confesses to the murder and is killed by Lykov. [R]

Tubin, Eduard (1905–82)
Estonian composer, resident in Sweden from 1944. He wrote four operas, the first two of which are unfinished. They are *Holy Lake* (*Pühajärv*, 1941), *Werewolf* (*Libahunt*, 1944), the successful *Barbara von Tisenhusen* (Tallinn, 4 Dec 1969; libr Jaan Kross, after Aïno Kallas) [R] and *The Priest of Reigi* (Tartu, 10 June 1979, composer 1971; libr Kross, after Kallas) [R].

Tu che la vanità
Soprano aria for Elisabetta in Act V of Verdi's *Don Carlos*, in which she bids farewell to her past hopes and pretensions.

Tucker, Richard (b Reuben Ticker) (1913–75)
American tenor, particularly associated with the Italian and French repertories. One of the finest of all American tenors, his full and strongly-projected voice was ideal for lyrico-dramatic roles, and was used with intelligence and unfailing musicianship. As the son of a Romanian Jew, his life's ambition was to sing Éléazar in *La Juive*, an ambition which he finally fulfilled in 1973. His brother-in-law was the tenor JAN PEERCE.

Tudor Ring
A collective title which has occasionally been given in recent years to Donizetti's three operas set in Tudor England: *Anna Bolena*, *Maria Stuarda* and *Roberto Devereux*. They are sometimes given as a cycle but are in no way interconnected.

Tu qui Santuzza?
Soprano/tenor duet for Santuzza and Turiddù in Mascagni's *Cavalleria Rusticana*, in which the jealous Santuzza accuses Turiddù of prefering Lola.

Turandot
Opera in two acts by Busoni. 1st perf Zürich, 11 May 1917; libr by the composer, after Carlo Gozzi's play. Principal roles: Turandot (sop), Kalaf (ten), Barak (bar), Adelma (mezzo), Truffaldino (ten), Pantalone (ten), Tartaglia (bass), Emperor Altoum (bass). A taut and economical setting, it has been much admired by musicians but is only very rarely performed. [R]

Turandot
Opera in three acts by Puccini. 1st perf Milan, 25 April 1926; libr by Renato Simone and Guiseppe Adami, after Carlo Gozzi's play. Principal roles: Turandot (sop), Calaf (ten), Liù (sop), Timur (bass), Ping (bar), Pang (ten), Pong (ten), Emperor Altoum (ten). Puccini's last opera and usually regarded as his masterpiece, it was left unfinished at his death and was completed by Alfano. It is notable for the exotic richness of its orchestration, for its unusually extensive choral writing and for providing one of the most severely demanding of all Italian dramatic soprano roles.
Plot: Legendary Peking. The icy Princess Turandot will wed the man who can answer her three riddles; anyone who fails must die. The unknown prince (Calaf), accompanied by his father Timur and the slave-girl Liù, arrives and accepts the

challenge. He solves the riddles correctly, and when Turandot is reluctant to wed him, gives her a day to discover his name; if she does, he will sacrifice his life. Turandot threatens to torture the name out of Liù, but she kills herself rather than betray Calaf. Finally, Calaf melts Turandot's resistance with a kiss and tells her his name. Accepting him, she announces that his name is 'love'. [R]

Turco in Italia, Il (*The Turk in Italy*)
Comic opera in two acts by Rossini. 1st perf Milan, 14 Aug 1814; libr by Felice Romani, after Caterino Mazzolà's libretto for Franz Seydelmann. Principal roles: Prosdocimo (bar), Fiorilla (sop), Selim (bass), Don Narciso (ten), Zaida (mezzo), Don Geronio (bass), Albazar (ten).
A quasi-Pirandellian story of a poet manipulating stock comic characters, it is a delightful work which has been regularly performed in recent years.
Plot: 18th-century Naples. The poet Prosdocimo is in search of a plot for an OPERA BUFFA. He comes up with a story of intrigues, disguises and misunderstandings involving Fiorilla, her admirer Don Narciso, her boring husband Geronio, Selim, a visiting Turk to whom Fiorilla is attracted, and Selim's old love Zaida. [R]

Turiddù
Tenor role in Mascagni's *Cavalleria Rusticana*. Mamma Lucia's son, he is a soldier loved by Santuzza.

Turin
see TEATRO REGIO, TURIN

Turina, Joaquín (1882–1949)
Spanish composer. He wrote four stage works: the ZARZUELAS *La Copla* (Seville, 24 Mar 1904; libr J. Labios and E. Lucuix) and *Fea y con Grazia* (Madrid, 3 May 1905; libr Serafín and Joaquín Álvarez Quintero) and the operas *Margot* (Madrid, 10 Oct 1914; libr Gregorio Martínez Sierra) and *Jardín de Oriente* (Madrid, 6 March 1923; libr Martínez Sierra).

Turkish opera composers
These include Kemal Resit Rey (1904–85), Muglis Sabahattin (1890–1947) and Ahmet Adnan Saygun (1907–91). *See also* ARMENIAN OPERA COMPOSERS

Turnage, Mark-Anthony (b 1960)
British composer. He has written one opera, the successful *Greek* (Munich, June 1988; libr composer and Jonathan Moore, after Steven Berkoff) [R], which is a reworking of the Oedipus myth set in the contemporary East End of London.

Turner, Dame Eva (1892–1990)
British soprano, particularly associated with Wagner and heavier Verdi roles and, especially, with the title-role in *Turandot.* Arguably the greatest dramatic soprano produced by Britain, she possessed a voice of great range and awesome power. Her somewhat cool and distant stage personality was ideally suited to Turandot. She was also a distinguished teacher, whose pupils included Amy Shuard, Dame Gwyneth Jones, Rita Hunter and Pauline Tinsley.

Turn of the Screw, The
Opera in prologue and two acts by Britten (Op 54). 1st perf Venice, 14 Sept 1954; libr by Myfanwy Piper, after Henry James's novella. Principal roles: Governess (sop), Peter Quint (ten), Miles (treble), Flora (sop), Mrs Grose (mezzo), Miss Jessel (sop), Prologue (ten). Britten's tautest opera, it is a work of great musical and structural complexity, achieved with the most economical of means and resources. One of the greatest operas of the post-war era, it is a deeply disturbing work (summed up by the interpolated Yeats line 'the ceremony of innocence is drowned'), which can have an overwhelming effect in the theatre.
Plot: Mid-19th-century England. The Governess arrives at the country house of Bly to take sole charge of the children Miles and Flora. She becomes convinced that the ghosts of two former servants, Peter Quint and her predecessor and Quint's mistress Miss Jessel, are attempting to corrupt the children. She determines to do battle with them and save the children's souls, and experiences a state of rising hysteria as the ghosts' power appears to wax. Eventually, Flora is sent away in the care of the housekeeper Mrs Grose, but Miles dies from the psychological strain imposed upon him by the conflicting demands of the Governess and Quint. [R]

Turp, André (1925–91)
Canadian tenor, particularly associated with the French and Italian repertories. He possessed a warm lyric tenor voice, used with considerable style, and had a good stage presence. An often underrated singer. His son **Richard** is also a tenor.

Tu sul labbro
Bass aria for Zaccaria in Act II of Verdi's *Nabucco*, in which he prays that Jehovah may triumph over the Assyrian gods.

Tutor
Bass role in Rossini's *Le Comte Ory*. He is Ory's long-suffering teacher.

Tutte le feste
Soprano/baritone duet for Gilda and Rigoletto in Act II of Verdi's *Rigoletto*, in which Gilda tells her father how she came to meet her seducer.

Tutto nel mondo è burla
The great comic fugue which ends Act III of Verdi's *Falstaff*, in which everyone agrees that all the world is a gigantic joke.

Twelve-tone operas
Twelve-tone (or dodecaphonic) describes a style of composition in which all 12 notes of the octave (on a piano the five black and seven white notes) are treated as equal, in other words they are subjected to an ordered relationship which establishes no 'heirarchy' of notes, unlike the traditional major/minor key system. Originally developed at the beginning of the 20th century by Schönberg as a standardization of atonal music, the style has since then also been employed alongside the traditional key system. The style is also known as 'serial composition', from the note-row or 'series' in which all 12 notes are placed in a particular predetermined order as the structural basis of the work. Many twelve-tone operas have been written, the first being Schönberg's *Von Heute auf Morgen*.

Twilight *(Daisi)*
Opera in three acts by Paliashvili. 1st perf Tbilsi, 19 Dec 1929; libr by V. Guniya. Principal roles: Maro (sop), Malkhaz (ten), Nano (mezzo), Kaizo (bar), Tsangala (bass). One of the earliest and finest operas by a Georgian composer, it is unknown outside the former Soviet Union.
Plot: Late-18th-century Georgia. Maro is engaged to the soldier Kaizo, but is in love with Malkhaz. When Malkhaz returns from abroad, Tsangala informs Kaizo of their relationship. Kaizo vows to be avenged, but is summoned to war to defend his country. He returns, however, and when Maro rejects him, he kills Malkhaz out of jealousy. [R]

Twilight of the Gods
see GÖTTERDÄMMERUNG

Two Widows, The *(Dvě Vodvy)*
Comic opera in two acts by Smetana. 1st perf Prague, 27 March 1874; libr by Emanuel Züngel, after Félicien Mallefille's *Les Deux Veuves*. Revised version 1st perf Prague, 15 March 1878. Principal roles: Karolina (sop), Anežka (mezzo), Ladislav (ten), Mumlal (bass), Toník (ten), Lidka (sop). Smetana's lightest opera, described as a conversation piece, it is still regularly performed in the Czech lands but is little known elsewhere.
Plot: 19th-century Bohemia. Ladislav Podhajský succeeds in meeting his old love Anežka, now a widow, by the expedient of having himself arrested by the gamekeeper Mumlal for poaching on the estate of Anežka's cousin, the widowed Karolina. Anežka initially rebuffs his advances, but urged on by Karolina the two are finally united. [R]

Tytania
Soprano role in Britten's *A Midsummer Night's Dream*. Oberon's wife, she is the queen of the fairies.

U

Uberto
Bass-baritone role in Pergolesi's *La Serva Padrona*. He is the master of the house who is tricked into marrying his servant.

Udite, udite o rustici
Bass aria for Dr Dulcamara in Act I of Donizetti's *L'Elisir d'Amore*, in which he reels off his miraculous nostrums.

Ugo Conte di Parigi (*Hugo Count of Paris*)
Opera in two acts by Donizetti. 1st perf Milan, 13 March 1832; libr by Felice Romani, after Hippolyte-Louis-Florent Bis's *Blanche d'Aquitaine*. Principal roles: Ugo (ten), Bianca (sop), Adelia (sop), Falco (bar), Emma (sop), Luigi (mezzo). Reasonably successful at its appearance, it is nowadays virtually never performed.
Plot: Late-10th-century Paris. Wishing the French crown to go to his own house of Anjou, Falco plans to provoke rivalry between the famous soldier Ugo and the newly-crowned Louis V, but Ugo remains loyal to Louis. Louis's betrothed Bianca hates her fiancé and secretly loves Ugo, as also does her sister Adelia. Ugo and Adelia become engaged, but the jealous Bianca declares her own love for Ugo. Louis, believing Ugo disloyal, has him arrested. Ugo resists Bianca's request for him to lead a revolt against Louis, but his troops start it without him. Ugo puts down the revolt and Louis is convinced of his loyalty. Ugo and Adelia are married, and the sound of the celebrations drives the outraged Bianca to take poison. [R]

Uhde, Hermann (1914–65)
German bass-baritone, particularly associated with Wagnerian roles, especially the Dutchman. A fine singing-actor with a powerful and incisive voice, he created Kreon in Orff's *Antigonae* and Elis in Wagner-Régeny's *Das Bergwerk zu Falun*. He died on stage in Copenhagen during a performance of Bentzon's *Faust III*.

Ukraine
see KIEV OPERA

Ukrainian opera composers
see BORTNYANSKY; DANKEVICH; LYSENKO
Other national opera composers include Nikolai Arkas (1853–1909), Semyon Gulak-Artemovsky (1813–73), Vitaly Kireyko (*b* 1926), Georgy Mayboroda (*b* 1913), Yuly Meytus (*b* 1903), Pyotr Sokalsky (1832–87) and Natal Vakhnyanin (1841–1908).

Ulfung, Ragnar (b 1927)
Norwegian tenor, particularly associated with German character roles, especially Mime and Herod. A versatile singing-actor with an incisive if not intrinsically beautiful voice, he had a wide-ranging repertory which included Gustavus III in Göran Gentele's controversial production of *Un Ballo in Maschera* and Monostatos in Ingmar Bergman's film of *Die Zauberflöte*. He created the Deaf Mute in Blomdahl's *Aniara*, the title-role in Maxwell Davies's *Taverner* and Christopher in Werle's *The Journey*. He has also produced a number of operas.

Ulisse (*Ulysses*)
Opera in prologue, two acts and epilogue by Dallapiccola. 1st perf Berlin, 29 Sept 1968; libr by the composer, after Homer's *The Odyssey*. Principal roles: Ulisse (bar), Nausicaa (sop), Circe/Melanto (mezzo), Telemaco (c-ten or mezzo), Demodoco/Tiresio (ten), Calypso/Penelope (sop), Eumete (ten). Dallapiccola's last and most ambitious opera, it deals with Ulysses's return to Ithaca after the Trojan War, with some of his adventures told in flashbacks. It is only very rarely performed.

Ullmann, Viktor (1898–1944)
Czech (Sudeten German) composer. A pupil of Schönberg, he is best known for his powerful DER KAISER VON ATLANTIS, written in a Nazi concentration camp. His other operas are the lost *Peer Gynt* (1928;

libr after Henrik Ibsen), *Der Sturtz des Antichrists* (Bielefeld, 7 Jan 1995, composed 1935; libr after Albert Steffen) and *Der Zerbrochene Krug* (1940; libr after Heinrich Wilhelm von Kleist). He was murdered by the Nazis in Auschwitz.

Ulm Stadttheater
The present opera house (cap 815) in this German town in Baden-Württemberg opened in Oct 1969, replacing the previous theatre built in 1781 but destroyed by bombs in 1944. Musical directors have included Robert Heger and Herbert von Karajan.

Ulrica
Contralto role in: **1** Verdi's *Un Ballo in Maschera*. Madame Arvidson in the Swedish setting, she is a fortune-teller. **2** Sullivan's *Ivanhoe*.

Ulster
see OPERA NORTHERN IRELAND

Ulysses
The mythical Homeric hero appears in many operas, including: **1** Tenor or baritone role in Monteverdi's *Il Ritorno d'Ulisse in Patria*. **2** Baritone role in Dallapiccola's *Ulisse*. **3** Baritone role in Liebermann's *Penelope*. **4** Tenor role in Egk's *Siebzehn Tage und Vier Minuten*. **5** Tenor role in Fauré's *Pénélope*. **6** Baritone role in Malipiero's *Ecuba*. **7** Bass role in D. Scarlatti's *Tetide in Sciro*. **8** Mezzo trouser role in Händel's *Deidamia*. **9** Tenor role in Gluck's *Telemaco*.

Un
Titles beginning with this form of the French, Italian and Spanish indefinite article are listed under the letter of the first main word. For example, *Un Ballo in Maschera* is listed under B.

Una
Titles beginning with the feminine form of the Italian and Spanish indefinite article are listed under the letter of the first main word. For example, *Una Cosa Rara* is listed under C.

Undine
Opera in three acts by E.T.A. Hoffmann. 1st perf Berlin, 3 Aug 1816; libr by the composer, after Friedrich Heinrich Carl de la Motte Fouqué's *Ondine*. Principal roles: Undine (sop), Huldbrand (bar), Berthalda (sop), Kühleborn (bass), Heilmann (bar). Hoffmann's most successful opera, nowadays only very rarely performed, it contains some striking prefigurements of the German romantic school. [R]

Undine
Opera in four acts by Lortzing. 1st perf Magdeburg, 21 April 1845; libr by the composer, after Friedrich Heinrich Carl de la Motte Fouqué's *Ondine*. Principal roles: Undine (sop), Hugo (ten), Kühleborn (bar), Veit (ten), Berthalda (sop), Tobias (bass). One of Lortzing's finest works, and his structurally most complex opera, it is still occasionally performed in Germany but is little known elsewhere.
Plot: Legendary Germany. Hugo falls in love with the nymph Undine, although his esquire Veit warns her father, the water-spirit Kühleborn, that Hugo may desert Undine for Berthalda, who is discovered to be the daughter of Undine's foster-father Tobias. Berthalda seduces Hugo, and Undine returns to her own land. Hugo is unable to forget Undine and when Veit opens a sealed well she emerges from it to take Hugo to her own kingdom as her husband. [R]

Une
Titles beginning with the feminine form of the French indefinite article are listed under the letter of the first main word. For example, *Une Éducation Manquée* is listed under E.

Unfinished operas
see panel on pages 574–6

Unger, Caroline (b Ungher) (1803–77)
Hungarian mezzo with a very wide range (a to d''') which also allowed her to sing soprano roles. She is famous in musical history for having turned round the deaf Beethoven at the end of the first performance of the Choral Symphony so that he could see the acclaim. One of the greatest singing-actresses of the 19th century, she created Bianca in Mercadante's *Le Due Illustri Rivali*, Isoletta in Bellini's *La Straniera* and, for Donizetti,

· *Unfinished Operas* ·

Many composers have left operas or operettas unfinished, either because of their death or simply because they lost interest in the work. The state of completion of such works varies enormously and often provides musicologists with severe problems. Some, such as Elgar's *The Spanish Lady*, amount to little more than sketches. Others, such as Weber's *Die Drei Pintos*, Debussy's *La Chûte de la Maison Usher* or Mozart's *Zaïde*, contain a considerable amount of finished work. Others again, such as Offenbach's *Les Contes d'Hoffmann* and Puccini's *Turandot*, are all but complete. Below are listed unfinished works by composers with entries in this dictionary; the completor or editor of the work is given where applicable.

Composer	**Work**	***Completor/Editor***
d'Albert	*Mister Wu*	Leo Blech
Alfano	*I Cavalieri e la Bella*	
Balfe	*Il Talismano*	MacFarren
Bellini	*Ernani*	
Benjamin	*Tartuffe*	Alan Boustead
Berg	*Lulu*	Cerha
Berkeley	*Faldon Park*	
Berlioz	*Les Francs Juges*	
Berwald	*Gustaf Vasa*	
Bizet	*La Coupe du Roi de Thulé*	
	Don Rodrigue	
Blitzstein	*Sacco and Vanzetti*	
Bloch	*Jézabel*	
Blodek	*Zítek*	F.X. Váňa
Blomdahl	*The Tale of the Big Computer*	
Boito	*Nerone*	Toscanini & Vincenzo Tommasini
Borodin	*Mlada*	
	Prince Igor	Glazunov & Rimsky-Korsakov
	The Tsar's Bride	
Busoni	*Doktor Faust*	Philipp Jarnach
Castro	*Cosecha Negra*	Eduardo Ogando
Cellier	*The Mountebanks*	Ivan Caryll
Chabrier	*Briséïs*	
	Fisch-Ton-Kan	
	Jean Hunyade	
	Vaucochard et Fils Premier	
Cherubini	*Marguerite d'Anjou*	
Cornelius	*Gunlöd*	Carl Hoffbauer
Dargomijsky	*The Stone Guest*	Cui & Rimsky-Korsakov
Debussy	*La Chûte de la Maison Usher*	Juan Allende-Blin
	Rodrigue et Chimène	Edison Denisov
Delibes	*Kassya*	Massenet
Dessau	*Giuditta*	
Donizetti	*L'Ange de Nisida*	
	Le Duc d'Albe	Matteo Salvi
	Ne M'Oubliez Pas	

Elgar	*The Spanish Lady*	Percy M. Young
de Falla	*L'Atlántida*	Ernesto Halffter
Fleishman	*Rothschild's Violin*	Shostakovich
Franck	*Ghisèle*	Chausson, d'Indy & 3 others
Ginastera	*Barrabas*	
Götz	*Francesca von Rimini*	Ernst Frank
Gounod	*Maître Pierre*	
Grieg	*Olav Trygvason*	
Guiraud	*Frédégonde*	Saint-Saëns & Dukas
Hadjibeyov	*Firuza*	
Halévy	*Noé*	Bizet
Hérold	*Ludovic*	Halévy
Hoffmann	*Julius Sabinus*	
Kálmán	*Arizona Lady*	Charles Kálmán
Karel	*The Taming of the Shrew*	
	Three Hairs of an Old Wise Man	Zbyněk Vostřák
Kovařovic	*Armida*	
	The Vow	
Lalo	*Le Jacquerie*	Arthur Coquard
Leoncavallo	*La Maschera Nuda*	Salvatore Allegra
Lully	*Achille et Polyxène*	Pascal Colasse
Martinů	*La Plainte Contre Inconnu*	
	Le Semaine de Bonté	
Méhul	*Valentine de Milan*	Louis Daussoigne-Méhul
Mendelssohn	*Loreley*	
Monpou	*Lambert Simnel*	Adam
Moussorgsky	*Khovanschina*	Rimsky-Korsakov
	The Marriage	Ippolitov-Ivanov
	Salammbô	Zoltán Peskó
	Sorochintsy Fair	Tcherepnin
Mozart	*L'Oca del Cairo*	Mortari
	Lo Sposo Deluso	
	Zaïde	Anton André
Offenbach	*Les Contes d'Hoffmann*	Guiraud
	Moucheron	Delibes
Ostrčil	*Cymbelin*	
	The Fishermen	
Pijper	*Merlijn*	
Pizzetti	*Gigliola*	
Planquette	*Le Paradis de Mahomet*	Ganné
Ponchielli	*I Mori di Venezia*	Arturo Cadore
Prokofiev	*Maddalena*	Edward Downes
Puccini	*Turandot*	Alfano
Rabaud	*Les Jeux de l'Amour et du Hasard*	Henri Busser & Max d'Ollone
Rachmaninov	*Monna Vanna*	Igor Bugetoff
Rameau	*Les Boréades*	John Eliot Gardiner
Rangström	*Gilgamesj*	John Fernström
Refice	*Il Mago*	
Respighi	*Lucrezia*	Elsa Respighi
Rousseau	*Daphnis et Chloé*	
Schönberg	*Moses und Aron*	
Schubert	*Die Bürgschaft*	
	Der Graf von Gleichen	
	Der Spiegelritter	

Schumann	*Der Korsar*	
Serov	*The Power of Evil*	Nikolai Solovyov
Shostakovich	*The Gamblers*	Krzysztof Meyer
Smetana	*Viola*	
Spontini	*Das Verlorence Paradies*	
Stanford	*The Miner of Falun*	
Storace	*Mahmoud*	Michael Kelly
Sullivan	*The Emerald Isle*	German
Suppé	*Das Modell*	Stern & Zamara
A.G. Thomas	*The Golden Web*	S.P. Waddington
Tubin	*Holy Lake*	
	Werewolf	
Usandizaga	*La Llama*	Ramón Usandizaga
Wallace	*Estrella*	
Weber	*Die Drei Pintos*	Mahler
	Rübezahl	
Wolf	*Manuel Venegas*	
Zandonai	*Il Bacio*	

Marietta in *Il Borgomastro di Saardam*, Antonina in *Belisario* and the title-roles in *Maria de Rudenz* and *Parisina d'Este*. Rossini described her as possessing 'a southern ardour, a northern energy, lungs of bronze, a voice of silver and a talent of gold'. Her most famous role was the title-role in Donizetti's *Lucrezia Borgia*, described by Chorley as being 'of serpentine and deep malevolence, subtly veiled at the moment when its most diabolical works were on foot'.

Unger, Gerhard (b 1916)
German tenor, particularly associated with German character roles, especially Pedrillo in Mozart's *Die Entführung aus dem Serail* and David in Wagner's *Die Meistersinger von Nürnberg*. A fine singing-actor, he had a far better voice than most German character tenors, which he used with musicianship and intelligence. He sang into his mid-60s.

United States of America
see AMERICAN OPERA SOCIETY; BALTIMORE CIVIC OPERA; CARAMOOR FESTIVAL; CHICAGO LYRIC OPERA; CINCINNATI OPERA ASSOCIATION; DALLAS CIVIC OPERA; HOUSTON GRAND OPERA ASSOCIATION; KANSAS CITY LYRIC THEATER; LINCOLN CENTER FOR THE PERFORMING ARTS; LOS ANGELES MUSIC CENTER OPERA; METROPOLITAN OPERA, NEW YORK; NEW ORLEANS OPERA HOUSE ASSOCIATION; NEW YORK CITY OPERA; OPERA COMPANY OF BOSTON; OPERA GUILD OF GREATER MIAMI; OPERA SOCIETY OF WASHINGTON; PHILADELPHIA OPERA COMPANY; SAN DIEGO OPERA GUILD; SAN FRANCISCO OPERA ASSOCIATION; SANTA FE OPERA; SEATTLE OPERA ASSOCIATION; VIRGINIA OPERA ASSOCIATION

Unterbrochene Opferfest, Das (*The Interrupted Sacrifice*)
Opera in two acts by Winter. 1st perf Vienna, 14 June 1796; libr by Franz Xaver Huber. Principal roles: Elvira (sop), Murney (ten), Villacuma (bass), Myrha (sop), Pedrillo (bass), Balisa (sop). Winter's most successful work, in German-speaking countries it was one of the most popular of all operas in the early 19th century. It is nowadays all but forgotten. **Plot**: Legendary Peru. An Inca sacrifice to the sun god is to be held. Elvira and Villacuma, wishing harm to Murney, imitate the god's voice at the preliminary ceremony and demand Murney as the human sacrifice. Murney, despite his longing to live with his beloved Myrha, resolves to accept his fate and to die bravely. However, the trick is discovered during the ceremony and Murney is saved.

Upfold, Mr
Tenor role in Britten's *Albert Herring*. He is the mayor of Loxford.

Uppman, Theodore (b 1920)
American baritone, particularly associated with the roles of Pelléas in *Pelléas et Mélisande* and Papageno in *Die Zauberflöte*. A warm-voiced singer and a fine singing-actor with a handsome stage presence, he created the title-role in *Billy Budd*, a role in Floyd's *The Passion of Jonathan Wade*, Víctor in Villa-Lobos's *Yerma*, Juan in Pasatieri's *Black Widow* and Bill in Bernstein's *A Quiet Place*.

Upshaw, Dawn (b 1960)
American soprano, particularly associated with Mozart and with lighter French and Italian roles. She possesses a warm and vibrant voice of individual timbre, used with great intelligence and musicianship, and she has a charming stage personality.

Urbain
Mezzo trouser role in Meyerbeer's *Les Huguenots*. He is Queen Marguerite's page.

Urna fatale
Baritone aria for Don Carlo in Act III of Verdi's *La Forza del Destino*, in which he agonizes over whether to open the casket entrusted to him by Don Alvaro.

Ursule
Mezzo role in Berlioz's *Béatrice et Bénédict*. She is Héro's companion.

Ursuleac, Viorica (1894–1985)
Romanian soprano, particularly associated with Strauss roles, for which Strauss himself considered her lyrico-dramatic voice ideal. She created Maria in *Friedenstag*, the title-role in *Arabella*, the Countess in *Capriccio* and roles in Křenek's *Der Diktator*, Sekles's *Die Zehn Küsse* and d'Albert's *Mister Wu*. Married to the conductor CLEMENS KRAUSS.

Uruguayan opera composers
These include Vicente Ascone (1897–1979), Alfonso Broqua (1867–1946), Eduardo Fabini (1883–1950), Carlos Pedrell (1878–1941), Juarés Lamarque Pons (*b* 1917) and Ramón Rodríguez Socas (1886–1957).

Usandizaga, José María (1887–1915)
Spanish composer. One of the leading Basque composers, his tragically early death cut short a highly promising career. He wrote three operas: *Mendi-Mendiyan* (*High in the Mountains*, Bilbao, 21 May 1910; libr José Power), *Las Golondrinas* (*The Swallows*, Madrid, 5 Feb 1914; libr Gregorio Martínez Sierra, after his *Teatro del Ensueño*) [R], his most successful work, and *La Llama* (*The Flame*, San Sebastián, 1918; libr Martínez Sierra), which was left unfinished at his death and which was completed by his brother Ramón.

Ustinov, Sir Peter (b 1921)
British actor, writer, producer and designer, great-nephew of the designer ALEXANDRE BENOIS. His main contribution to opera has been as a producer; he has directed operas at Covent Garden, the Hamburg State Opera, the Paris Opéra and the Edinburgh Festival. In addition, he is the narrator on the Decca recording of Kodály's *Háry János*.

Uthal
Opera in one act by Méhul. 1st perf Paris, 17 May 1806; libr by Jacques M.B. Bins de Saint-Victor, after James Macpherson's *Berrathan*. Principal roles: Uthal (ten), Malvina (sop), Larmor (bar). One of Méhul's finest operas, written 'in imitation of OSSIAN', it is notable for Méhul's extraordinary effect of totally omitting violins from the orchestra so as to produce a dark and 'Ossianic' colour. Successful at its appearance, it is nowadays unjustly neglected.
Plot: Legendary Scotland. King Larmor has been deposed by Uthal, the husband of his daughter Malvina. When troops loyal to Larmor defeat Uthal, Malvina is faced with a dilemma of divided loyalties. Despite her pleas, Uthal is sentenced to exile. Malvina's decision to accompany him so moves Uthal that he begs Larmor's forgiveness and the two men are reconciled.

Utopia Limited or **The Flowers of Progress**
Operetta in two acts by Sullivan. 1st perf London, 7 Oct 1893; libr by W.S. Gilbert. Principal roles: Paramount (bar), Zara (sop), Scaphio (bar), Phantis (b-bar), Fitzbattleaxe (ten), Lady Sophy (mezzo), Mr Goldbury (bar), Nekaya (sop), Kalyba (mezzo), Tarara (ten), Lord Drameleigh (bar), Capt Corcoran (bass), Sir Bailey

Barre (ten), Mr Blushington (bass). A satire on British capitalism and imperialism, the score is notable for the brilliant Christie Minstrels scene in which Sullivan succeeds in making the orchestral strings sound like banjos. Partly because of its large cast and lavish scenes, it is only intermittently performed.
Plot: The imaginary kingdom of Utopia (South Pacific), late 19th century. The Anglophile King Paramount is, in theory, an absolute despot, but in practice he is watched over by the wise men Scaphio and Phantis, who control his actions (even forcing him to write the scandal sheet 'The Palace Peeper'), and if he disobeys them will denounce him to the Public Exploder Tarara. His daughter Zara, who has been educated at Girton, returns with six Flowers of Progress, including Capt Fitzbattleaxe, with whom she is in love, and the company promoter Mr Goldbury. These representatives of British greatness proceed to remodel Utopia on English principles, but take these principles far further than in England itself. Paramount registers his crown and country under the Limited Liability Act. The King loves Lady Sophy, governess to his younger daughters Nekaya and Kalyba. She rebuffs him because of the scandalous allegations in the 'Peeper', but accepts him when he explains the way in which he is controlled by the wise men. The English reforms all prove far too successful and Utopia becomes 'swamped by dull prosperity' and rises in revolt at the instigation of Scaphio and Phantis. Zara remembers the one ingredient which she had omitted to introduce: a proper state of political chaos can only be achieved by having government by party. This is adopted, Scaphio and Phantis are foiled, and Utopia becomes a limited monarchy rather than a Monarchy Limited. [R]

Uttini, Francesco (1723–95)
Italian composer, largely resident in Sweden. He wrote 17 operas, mostly Metastasian OPERA SERIAS, beginning with *Alessandro nell'Indie* (Genoa, 1743). A number met with considerable success in their day but are all now largely forgotten. They include *L'Isola Disabitata* (Drottningholm, 1755; libr Pietro Metastasio), *Il Rè Pastore* (Drottningholm, 24 July 1755; libr Metastasio), *Psyché* (Drottningholm, 1766; libr Philippe Quinault, after Molière), *Thetis och Pelée* (Stockholm, 18 Jan 1773; libr Johan Wellander, after B.B. de Fontenelle) [R Exc], which was the first major opera written to a Swedish libretto, and *Alina, Queen of Golconda* (*Aline, Drottning uti Golconda*, Stockholm, 11 Jan 1776; libr C.B. Zibet, after Jean-Marie Sedaine). His wife **Sophia Liljegren** (1765–95) was a soprano.

Uzbek opera composers
These include Mukhtar Ashrafy (1912–75), Talib Sadykov (1907–57), Victor Uspensky (1879–1949), Sergey Vasilenko (1872–1956) and Suleiman Yudakov (*b* 1916).

V

Vaccai, Nicola (1790–1848)
Italian composer. He wrote 17 operas, largely in Rossinian style. Many of them met with considerable success in their day, but they are nowadays all largely forgotten. His operas include *Il Solitario di Scozia* (Naples, 18 Feb 1815; libr Andrea Leone Tottola, after Giovanni de Gamerra), *Il Lupo d'Ostenda* (Venice, 17 June 1818; libr Bartolomeo Merelli), GIULIETTA E ROMEO, his finest opera, *Bianca di Messina* (Turin, 20 Jan 1826; libr L. Piossasco), *Giovanna d'Arco* (Venice, 17 Feb 1827; libr Gaetano Rossi, after Friedrich von Schiller's *Die Jungfrau von Orleans*), *Giovanna Grey* (Milan, 23 Feb 1834; libr Carlo Pepoli), *Marco Visconti* (Turin, 27 Jan 1838; libr L. Toccagni) and *Virginia* (Rome, 14 Jan 1845; libr C. Giuliani).

Vada in fiamme
Baritone CABALETTA for Macbeth in Act III of the original 1847 version of Verdi's *Macbeth*, in which he vows to go to any lengths to secure the throne. Verdi's most powerful baritone cabaletta, it was cut in the revised version and replaced by the duet 'Ora di morte'.

V'adoro pupille
Soprano aria for Cleopatra in Act I of Händel's *Giulio Cesare*, in which she declares her love for Caesar.

Vainement ma bien-aimée
Tenor aria (the Aubade) for Mylio in Act III of Lalo's *Le Roi d'Ys*, in which he serenades Rozenn outside the door of her chamber.

Vakula the Blacksmith (*Vakula Kuznets*)
Opera in four acts by Tchaikovsky (Op 14). 1st perf St Petersburg, 6 Dec 1876; libr by Yakov Polonsky, after Nikolai Gogol's *Christmas Eve*. Revised version *The Little Slippers* (*Cherevichki*) 1st perf Moscow, 31 Jan 1887; libr revised by the composer. Principal roles: Vakula (ten), Oxana (sop), Solokha (mezzo), Devil (bar), Chub (bass), Panas (ten), Mayor (bass), Schoolteacher (ten). A delightful work, it is only very rarely performed outside Russia. For plot see *Christmas Eve*. [R]

Va! laisse les couleurs
Mezzo aria for Charlotte in Act III of Massenet's *Werther*, in which she says that she can no longer restrain her tears.

Valdegno, Giuseppe (b 1914)
Italian batitone, particularly associated with the Italian repertory, especially Verdi. Toscanini's favourite baritone in his later years, he was a rich-voiced and intelligent singing-actor. He created Alfieri in Rossellini's *Uno Sguardo dal Ponte* and played Antonio Scotti in the film *The Great Caruso*. His reminiscence of Toscanini, *Ho Cantato con Toscanini*, was published in 1962.

Valencienne
Soprano role in Lehár's *Die Lustige Witwe*. She is the 'highly respectable wife' of the Pontevedrian Ambassador. The role is occasionally sung by a mezzo.

Valentin
Baritone role in Gounod's *Faust*. He is Marguerite's soldier brother.

Valentine
Soprano role in Meyerbeer's *Les Huguenots*. She is Saint-Bris's daughter.

Valentini-Terrani, Lucia (b 1948)
Italian mezzo, particularly associated with the Italian repertory, especially Rossini. One of the leading COLORATURA mezzos of the 1980s, she had a rich, creamy and agile voice used with musicianship and a fine technique, and she had a good stage presence. Sadly, her voice declined early.

Valkyrie, The
see WALKÜRE, DIE

Valletti, Cesare (b 1922)
Italian tenor, particularly associated with Mozart, Donizetti and Rossini roles. A stylish and elegant singer of scrupulous good taste, he had a smallish but beautiful voice of considerable agility and he had a good stage presence.

Vallin, Ninon (b Eugénie) (1886–1961)
French soprano, particularly associated with the French repertory. The leading French soprano of the inter-war period, she was a sensitive and versatile singer with a warm voice of considerable power and range. She created roles in operas by Erlanger and Leroux.

Vallon sonore
Tenor aria for Hylas in Act V of Berlioz's *Les Troyens*, in which he expresses his homesickness.

Valverde Durán, Joaquín (1846–1910)
Spanish composer. He wrote over 30 ZARZUELAS, of which the most successful were *La Gran Vía* (Madrid, 2 July 1886; libr Felipe Pérez y González) [R] and *Agua* (Madrid, 1 Mar 1889; libr Ricardo de la Vega), which were written in collaboration with Chueca. His son **Joaquín Sanjuán** (1875–1918) was also a composer. Perhaps the most prolific of all zarzuela composers, he wrote his first work, *Con las de Caín* (1890), at the age of 15, and went on to write a further 250, often in collaboration with other composers. His most successful work was *La Marcha de Cádiz* (Madrid, 11 Oct 1896; libr C. Lucio and E. García Álvarez).

Valzacchi
Tenor role in Strauss's *Der Rosenkavalier*. Annina's accomplice, he is an Italian schemer.

Vampyr, Der (*The Vampire*)
Opera in two acts by Marschner (Op 42). 1st perf Leipzig, 29 March 1828; libr by Wilhelm August Wohlbrück, after John Polidori's *The Vampyre*. Principal roles: Sir Ruthven (bar), Aubry (ten), Janthe (sop), Emmy (sop), Malwina (sop), Sir Humphrey (bass). One of Marschner's finest works, even if heavily indebted to Weber, it was very popular throughout the 19th century and still receives an occassional performance, sometimes in the version prepared by Pfitzner in 1925.
Plot: 18th-century Scotland. The nobleman Sir Ruthven has become a vampire. The Devil will claim his soul unless he sacrifices three young maidens. His first victim is Janthe, but he himself is also killed. With the help of Edgar Aubry, to whom he reveals his secret, he is resuscitated in the moonlight. His second victim is the vampire-fascinated Emmy. Finally, he attempts to kill Aubry's fiancée Malwina, daughter of Sir Humphrey Davenaut, but is denounced by Aubry just as the clock strikes to mark the end of his period of respite. He descends back to hell. [R Exc]

Van
Names which contain this prefix are listed under the letter of the main surname. For example, Richard van Allan is listed under A.

Vancouver Opera Association
Founded in 1961, it gives an annual season from October to May at the Queen Elizabeth Theatre (cap 2,821). Artistic directors have included Irving Guttman, Anton Guadagno, Richard Bonynge and David Alger.

Vanda
Opera in five acts by Dvořák (Op 25). 1st perf Prague, 17 April 1876; libr by Václav Beneš–Šmavsky and František Zákrejs, after Julian Surzycki's story. Principal roles: Vanda (sop), Slavoj (ten), Roderich (bar), Božena (mezzo), Homena (mezzo), Lumír (bar), High Priest (bass). Dvořák's first mature opera, it is only very rarely performed, even in the Czech lands.
Plot: Legendary Poland. Queen Vanda, who loves the humbly-born warrior Slavoj, is courted by the German Prince Roderich, who is discovered to be in league with satanic forces. His troops invade Poland, and Vanda vows to offer up her life if her country is delivered. The Germans are defeated by the Polish army under Slavoj. In fulfilment of her vow, Vanda drowns herself in the River Vistula. [R]

Vaness, Carol (b 1952)
American soprano, particularly associated with Verdi and Mozart roles, especially

Vitellia. One of the finest American sopranos of the younger generation, she possesses a rich and beautiful voice used with fine musicianship, and she has a good stage presence.

Vanessa
Opera in four acts by Barber (Op 32). 1st perf New York, 15 Jan 1958; libr by Gian-Carlo Menotti. Principal roles: Vanessa (sop), Anatol (ten), Erika (mezzo), Old Countess (cont), Doctor (bass). Barber's finest opera, it is written in a lush and readily accessible late-romantic style.
Plot: Northern Europe, *c* 1905. Vanessa has waited for 20 years for her lover to return. His son Anatol arrives and informs her that her lover is dead. Anatol seduces Vanessa's niece Erika, but eventually marries Vanessa and goes to Paris to live with her. Erika realizes that she must now relive Vanessa's long vigil. [R]

Vanna Lupa (*The Vain She-Wolf*)
Opera in three acts by Pizzetti. 1st perf Florence, 4 May 1949; libr by the composer. Principal roles: Vanna Ricci (mezzo), Vieri (ten). Contrasting the political ambition and thirst for revenge of a woman (nicknamed Lupa) with her son's passion for freedom, it was reasonably successful at its appearance but is nowadays virtually forgotten.

Vanni-Marcoux
see MARCOUX, VANNI

Vanya
1 Mezzo trouser role in Glinka's *A Life for the Tsar*. He is Ivan's foster-son. **2** Tenor role in Janáček's *Káťa Kabanová*. He is a student in love with Varvara.

Vanzo, Alain (b 1928)
French tenor and composer, particularly associated with the French repertory. Virtually the only French tenor of international standing of the post-war era, he had a clean lyric voice, which was used with style, intelligence and musicianship. He has composed the operetta *Pêcheur d'Étoiles* (1972) and the opera *Les Chouans* (1982).

Va, pensiero
Chorus of Israelites in Act III of Verdi's *Nabucco*, in which they lament their Assyrian exile. Possibly the most famous of all operatic choruses.

Varady, Julia (b 1941)
Romanian soprano, particularly associated with Mozart, Verdi and Strauss roles. An accomplished and versatile singer with a strong stage presence, she possesses a rich, beautiful voice used with intelligence and outstanding musicianship. She created Cordelia in Reimann's *Lear*. Married to the baritone DIETRICH FISCHER–DIESKAU.

Varesi, Felice (1813–89)
Italian baritone. The leading Italian baritone of the mid-19th century and the first modern-style Verdian dramatic baritone, he created Antonio in *Linda di Chamounix*, the title-roles in *Macbeth* and *Rigoletto* and Giorgio Germont in *La Traviata*, which he foolishly considered unworthy of him. His daughter **Elena Boccabadati** (1844–1920) was a successful soprano.

Varlaam
Bass role in Moussorgsky's *Boris Godunov*. He is an itinerant monk.

Varnay, Astrid (b 1918)
Swedish-born American soprano and later mezzo, particularly associated with Wagner and Strauss roles, especially the title-role in *Elektra*. A powerful and intense singing-actress, who enjoyed a remarkably long career, she had a gleaming voice of great power and range, even if its production was occasionally a little uneven. She turned to mezzo roles in 1962 with equal success. She created Telea in Menotti's *The Island God*, the Grandmother in Banfield's *Lord Byron's Love-Letter* and Jocasta in Orff's *Oedipus der Tyrann*. Her husband **Hermann Weigert** (1890–1955) was a successful conductor.

Varney, Louis (1844–1908)
French composer. He wrote 37 operettas, of which the only two still to be remembered are LES MOUSQUETAIRES AU COUVENT, by far his most successful work, and *L'Amour Mouillé* (Paris, 25 Jan 1887; libr A. Liorat and Jules Prével).

Varvara
Mezzo role in Janáček's *Káťa Kabanová*. She is a foster-child in the Kabanov household.

Varviso, Silvio (b 1924)
Swiss conductor, particularly associated with the Italian and German repertories. A sometimes illuminating and sometimes curiously sluggish interpreter, he was musical director of the Basle Stadttheater (1958–62), the Royal Opera, Stockholm (1965–71), the Stuttgart Opera (1972–9) and the Paris Opéra (1980–81). He conducted the first performance of Sutermeister's *Titus Feuerfuchs*.

Vasco da Gama
Tenor role in Meyerbeer's *L'Africaine*. He is the historical Portuguese explorer (*c* 1469–1524).

Vašek
Tenor role in Smetana's *The Bartered Bride*. He is the shy son of Tobiaš Mícha who eventually joins the circus troupe.

Vaudeville (from the French *voix de ville*, 'town voices')
A French term which, in opera, refers to a style of finale in which each of the main characters sings a verse in turn, followed by a general refrain. The best known examples are the finales of *Die Entführung aus dem Serail* and *Il Barbiere di Siviglia*.

Vaughan, Elizabeth (b 1936)
British soprano, particularly associated with Verdi and Puccini roles, especially Cio-Cio-San in *Madama Butterfly*. One of the finest British *lirico spinto* sopranos (*see* SOPRANO) of the post-war era she had a fine and intelligently used voice and a strong stage presence. Later in her career she turned to mezzo roles.

Vaughan Williams, Ralph (1872–1958)
British composer. His six operas, although for some strange reason only infrequently performed nowadays, did much to assist the 20th-century revival of British opera. *The Shepherds of the Delectable Mountains* (London, 11 July 1922; libr composer, after John Bunyan's *The Pilgrim's Progress*) was followed by the ballad opera HUGH THE DROVER, the Shakespearian SIR JOHN IN LOVE and the powerful one-act RIDERS TO THE SEA, arguably his operatic masterpiece. The comedy THE POISONED KISS was less successful. Vaughan Williams set greatest store by the magnificent if somewhat unoperatic THE PILGRIM'S PROGRESS (into which he incorporated *The Shepherds of the Delectable Mountains*); its failure to win acceptance was his greatest artistic disappointment.

Va, vecchio John
Baritone arietta for Falstaff in Act II of Verdi's *Falstaff*, in which he pays a tender tribute to his old body.

Veasey, Josephine (b 1930)
British mezzo, particularly associated with Verdi, Wagner and Berlioz roles, especially Fricka in *Das Rheingold* and *Die Walküre* and Dido in Berlioz's *Les Troyens*. One of the finest British mezzos of the post-war period, with a strong stage presence, she created Helen in *King Priam* and the Emperor in Henze's *We Come to the River*.

Veau d'or, Le
Bass aria for Méphistophélès in Act II of Gounod's *Faust*, in which he mockingly tells the crowd of the Golden Calf.

Vecchi, Orazio (c 1550–1605)
Italian composer. His '*commedia harmonica*' L'AMFIPARNASO, which has occasionally been staged in recent years, is one of the most important 'proto-operas'.

Vecchia zimarra
Bass aria (the Coat Song) for Colline in Act IV of Puccini's *La Bohème*, in which he bids farewell to his old overcoat before selling it to help Mimì.

Vecchioto prender moglie, Il
Soprano aria for Berta in Act II of Rossini's *Il Barbiere di Siviglia*, in which she tells of the dangers of marrying in old age. The best-known example of an ARIA DEL SORBETTO.

Vedernikov, Alexander (b 1927)
Russian bass, particularly associated with the Russian repertory, especially Boris Godunov. A fine singing-actor, he had a dark and rich voice of considerable power and range which he used with unfailing musicianship.

Vedi le foschi
Chorus of gypsies (the Anvil Chorus) in Act II of Verdi's *Il Trovatore*, during which on-stage anvils are struck rhythmically.

Vedova Scaltra, La (*The Deceitful Widow*)
Comic opera in three acts by Wolf-Ferrari. 1st perf Rome, 5 March 1931; libr by Mario Ghisalberti, after Carlo Goldoni's play. Principal roles: Rosaura (sop), Runebif (bass), Marionette (sop), Arlecchino (bar), Bosco Nero (ten), Don Alvaro (bar), Le Bleau (ten). An elegant example of Wolf-Ferrari's neo-classical style, it was reasonably successful at its appearance but is nowadays only infrequently performed.
Plot: 18th-century Italy. The young and beautiful widow Rosaura has four suitors: the Italian Count Bosco Nero, the Frenchman Monsieur le Bleau, the Spaniard Don Alvaro and the Englishman Runebif. Each has one outstanding quality, but each also has one serious character flaw. To test their fidelity, Rosaura disguises herself and flirts with each of them. Only Bosco Nero rebuffs her advances because of his love for Rosaura. Rosaura has found the faithful husband she was seeking.

Vedrai carino
Soprano aria for Zerlina in Act II of Mozart's *Don Giovanni*, in which she comforts Masetto after his beating by Giovanni.

Vedrò mentr'io sospiro
Baritone aria for Count Almaviva in Act III of Mozart's *Le Nozze di Figaro*, in which he expresses his anger at the thought of being laughed at by his servant.

Veil Song
Mezzo aria ('Nel giardin del bello') for Eboli in Act II of Verdi's *Don Carlos*, in which she tells the story of a Saracen beauty.

Velluti, Giovanni Battista (1780–1861)
Italian CASTRATO. The last of the great castrati, he enjoyed great success initially, but later came to be regarded as a somewhat shocking oddity; Mendelssohn heard him and described the sound as 'distasteful'. He created Armando in Meyerbeer's *Il Crociato in Egitto*, the last major role written for the castrato voice, Arsace in Rossini's *Aureliano in Palmira* and, for Nicolini, Decebalo in *Trajano in Dacia* and the title-role in *Coriolano*.

Vendetta, La
Bass aria for Dr Bartolo in Act I of Mozart's *Le Nozze di Figaro*, in which he vows to have revenge on Figaro.

Venezuelan opera composers
see HAHN
Other national opera composers include José Angel Montero (1839–81), whose *Virginia* (Caracas, 26 Apr 1873) was the first Venezuelan opera.

Vengeance arias
A type of aria, especially popular in late-18th- and early-19th-century operas, in which a character determines to be avenged. The term refers only to the sentiment of the aria rather than to any formal structure. The most influential early example was 'Oui! Pour mon heureuse adresse' in Act III of Cherubini's *Lodoïska*. Although there are a few vengeance arias for women (of which the most famous is the Queen of the Night's 'Der Hölle Rache' in *Die Zauberflöte*), they are usually for men. A famous example is Don Pizarro's 'Ha! Welch' ein Augenblick' in *Fidelio*.

Vengeance duets
A popular device, especially favoured by 19th-century Italian composers, to end a scene in rousing style. Verdi wrote particularly fine examples in *Macbeth* ('Ora di morte'), *Rigoletto* ('Sì, vendetta') and *Otello* ('Sì, pel ciel').

Venice
see TEATRO LA FENICE, VENICE

Venite inginocchiatevi
Soprano aria for Susanna in Act II of Mozart's *Le Nozze di Figaro*, sung whilst she dresses up Cherubino.

Venti scudi
Tenor/baritone duet for Nemorino and Belcore in Act II of Donizetti's *L'Elisir d'Amore*, in which Nemorino enlists in the army to get money for the love potion.

Venus
The Graeco-Roman goddess of love appears in innumerable operas, including: **1** Mezzo role in Wagner's *Tannhäuser.* **2** Soprano role in Cavalli's *Ercole Amante.* **3** Soprano role in Blow's *Venus and Adonis.* **4** Soprano role in Rameau's *Dardanus.* **5** Soprano role in Offenbach's *Orphée aux Enfers.* **6** Soprano role in Mozart's *Ascanio in Alba.* **7** Mezzo role in Peri's *Euridice.* **8** Soprano role in Monteverdi's *L'Incoronazione di Poppea.* **9** Soprano role in Cherubini's *Anacréon.* **10** Soprano role in Leclair's *Scylla et Glaucus.* **11** Soprano role in Campra's *Idoménée.* **12** Mezzo role in Lully's *Thésée.* **13** Soprano role in Campra's *L'Europe Galante.*

Venus and Adonis
Opera in prologue and three acts by Blow. 1st perf London, 1684; librettist unknown. Principal roles: Venus (sop), Adonis (bar), Cupid (sop). Usually regarded as the earliest British opera, it is still performed from time to time.
Plot: Legendary Greece. Venus loves the huntsman Adonis and sends him off to demonstrate his skill in the chase. Cupid and the cherubs amuse themselves by tossing the alphabet around. Adonis is mortally wounded and Venus mourns over her dying beloved and all join in praise of his virtues. [R]

Vêpres Siciliennes, Les (*The Sicilian Vespers*)
Opera in five acts by Verdi. 1st perf Paris, 13 June 1855; libr by Eugène Scribe and Charles Duveyrier, after their libretto for Donizetti's *Le Duc d'Albe.* Principal roles: Hélène (sop), Henri (ten), Guy de Montfort (bar), Procida (bass). Verdi's first work written in French grand opera style, it is the least frequently performed of his mature works. Despite the rigid structure to which he was forced to conform, Verdi gave the work considerable dramatic interest and some splendid music, notably in the overture and in *Les Quatre Saisons*, arguably Verdi's finest ballet music. The story is based on an historical incident, when Sicilian patriots massacred the French on 30 March 1282.
Plot: Palermo, 1282. The revolutionary leader Giovanni da Procida, aided by the young Sicilian patriot Henri and by the Duchess Hélène, is planning an anti-French uprising with Spanish support. The tyrannical French governor Guy de Montfort discovers that Henri is his illegitimate son and tells him so. Although horrified at his parentage, Henri saves his father from an assassination attempt. The arrested conspirators repudiate Henri, but Hélène forgives him when he tells her of his dilemma. Henri persuades Montfort to pardon the conspirators and to agree to his marriage with Hélène. The implaccable Procida sees his chance: as the wedding bells sound, the Sicilians massacre the unarmed French. [R]

Veracini, Francesco Maria (1690–c 1770)
Italian composer and violinist, long resident in England. He wrote four operas, all of them now long forgotten. They are *Adriano in Siria* (London, 26 Nov 1735; libr M. Corri, after Pietro Metastasio), *La Clemenza di Tito* (London, 12 Apr 1737; libr Corri, after Metastasio), *Partenio* (London, 14 Mar 1738; libr Paolo Antonio Rolli) and *Rosalinda* (London, 31 Jan 1744; libr Rolli, after Shakespeare's *As You Like It*).

Vera Costanza, La (*True Constancy*)
Opera in three acts by Haydn. 1st perf Esterháza, 2 April 1779; libr by Francesco Puttini. Principal roles: Rosina (sop), Count Errico (ten), Villotto (bass), Lisetta (sop), Irene (sop), Masino (bar), Ernesto (ten). Although it contains some fine music it is only very rarely performed.
Plot: 18th-century Mediterranean. Irene, Ernesto, the fop Villotto and the maid Lisetta are shipwrecked on an island, where they encounter Rosina and her brother Masino. Irene recognizes Rosina as her nephew Errico's beloved and is unaware that the two are already married. Her attempts to marry off Rosina to Villotto lead to much confusion and amorous intrigue until she finally accepts Rosina as Errico's wife. [R]

Vera Storia, La (*The True Story*)
Opera in one act by Berio. 1st perf Milan, 9 March 1982; libr by Italo Calvino. Principal roles: Ada (mezzo), Leonora (sop), Luca (ten), Ivo (bar), Ugo (ten), Condemned Man (bass). A work of great musical complexity, it is a powerful

denunciation of political repression whose story-line partly follows that of Verdi's *Il Trovatore*.

Verbena de la Paloma, La (*The Feast of the Dove*)
ZARZUELA in three scenes by Bretón. 1st perf Madrid, 19 Feb 1894; libr by Ricardo de la Vega. Principal roles: Susana (sop), Don Hilarión (ten), Julián (bar). Written in GÉNERO CHICO style, it is one of the most enduringly popular of all zarzuelas. [R]

Verdi, Giuseppe (1813–1901)
Italian composer. Having been rejected by the Milan Conservatory as 'insufficiently talented', he studied privately, and composed his first opera *Rocester* (which is lost) in 1836. His first extant opera OBERTO, CONTE DI SAN BONIFACIO was a success, but its successor UN GIORNO DI REGNO, Verdi's only OPERA BUFFA, failed after a single performance. Coming at a time when he had lost both his wife and his baby daughter in quick succession, Verdi vowed to give up composition. Luckily, he was reluctantly persuaded to change his mind: the result was the triumphantly successful NABUCCO, which placed him at the forefront of Italian composers. I LOMBARDI confirmed his popularity, and the fine ERNANI established his European reputation. There followed, until 1850, what Verdi later referred to as his 'years in the galley', during which many operas of varying quality were written in rapid succession. These were the dark and sombre I DUE FOSCARI, GIOVANNA D'ARCO, ALZIRA, the energetic ATTILA, the powerful MACBETH, the finest of his early operas, I MASNADIERI, *Jérusalem* (a French revision of *I Lombardi*), IL CORSARO, the patriotic LA BATTAGLIA DI LEGNANO, the fine LUISA MILLER and the remarkably original STIFFELIO. In recent years, all of Verdi's early operas have received a number of performances, and *Nabucco*, *Ernani*, *Macbeth* and *Luisa Miller*, which stand head and shoulders above the others, have won a permanent place in the repertory.

Verdi's 'middle period' began in 1851 with RIGOLETTO, arguably the finest Italian music-drama since those of Monteverdi, and the work which prompted Rossini to observe (somewhat belatedly) 'at last I recognize Verdi's genius'. From this point onwards, each of Verdi's operas shows an increasing emphasis on the drama at the expense of musical structure or pure vocalism, each has its distinctive 'colour' and shows a growing mastery of orchestration, and each shows an increasing tendency to break up the formal components of Italian opera so as to achieve an uninterrupted dramatic flow. IL TROVATORE, with its white-hot melodic richness, marks the apotheosis of Italian romantic opera. Thereafter, Verdi forged his own musico-dramatic path: the intimate LA TRAVIATA was followed by the French grand opera LES VÊPRES SICILIENNES, AROLDO (a major revision of *Stiffelio*), SIMON BOCCANEGRA, his darkest opera, the finely balanced UN BALLO IN MASCHERA, the richly varied LA FORZA DEL DESTINO, a major revision of *Macbeth*, and his last and greatest middle-period operas: the vast political drama DON CARLOS and the ever-popular AIDA, which mark the transition to the full glories of his late works.

After the composition of his *Requiem Mass* in 1874, Verdi went into partial retirement, producing little new music. He enjoyed the life of a country gentleman at his farm at Sant'Agata with the soprano GIUSEPPINA STREPPONI, with whom he lived for many years before marrying her. The availability of ARRIGO BOITO as a librettist eventually persuaded Verdi to compose again. The results of their remarkable partnership were a major revision of *Simon Boccanegra* and Verdi's last two Shakespearian masterpieces, OTELLO and FALSTAFF, the two greatest Italian operas, in which Verdi – without any indebtedness to Wagner or his theories – at last achieved true music-drama. Verdi had a deep love for and understanding of Shakespeare and served him better than probably any other composer. However, a setting of *King Lear*, a project which obsessed Verdi for 50 years, unfortunately failed to materialize.

Particular Verdian features which may be found in many of his operas include patriotism, a burning anti-clericalism, a concern with the way in which personal interrelationships can affect the destinies of millions (especially notable in *Don Carlos*), the realization of the full musico-dramatic potential of the baritone voice, a dark and strikingly individual orchestral sound, and the relationship between father and daughter (a relationship which Verdi himself never experienced). An ardent Italian nationalist, Verdi lent his support to the Risorgimento, giving it its own opera in *La Battaglia di Legnano*. The popular slogan 'Viva Verdi' was universally known to stand for 'Viva Vittorio Emanuele Rè d'Italia'. Verdi was a deputy in the first parliament of united Italy in 1861, and was nominated a senator in 1874. In later life, Verdi engaged in much charitable work, including the endowment in 1899 of the still-functioning Casa di Riposo for retired musicians in Milan.

Verdi baritone
A term used to describe a baritone with the power and extension at the top of the voice necessary to sing Verdi's baritone roles. Most of these roles, especially Conte di Luna in *Il Trovatore*, have a cruelly high TESSITURA, often a minor third or more above other composers' baritone roles. True Verdi baritones (such as Leonard Warren, Robert Merrill, Peter Glossop or Leo Nucci), who have the upper notes whilst retaining a dark and rich baritone timbre, are extremely rare.

Verdi prati
Mezzo aria for Ruggiero in Act II of Händel's *Alcina*, in which he laments that the beautiful scene before him will soon revert to its previous horror.

Vere, Capt
Tenor role in Britten's *Billy Budd*. He is the commander of H.M.S. Indomitable.

Veretti, Antonio (1900–78)
Italian composer who wrote in many styles, including neo-classical, jazz and TWELVE-TONE. His operas include the unperformed *Il Medico Volante* (1923; libr Riccardo Bacchelli, after Molière's *L'Amour Volant*), *Il Favorito del Rè* (Milan, 17 Mar 1932; libr Arturo Rossato) and *Una Favola di Andersen* (Venice, Sept 1934; libr composer, after Hans Christian Andersen's *The Match Girl*).

Verismo (Italian for 'realism')
A term used to describe a style of Italian opera (largely pioneered by Mascagni), popular in the late 19th and early 20th centuries, which reproduced 'slices of life' rather than the idealized larger-than-life characters and subjects previously favoured. Sometimes regarded as the most coarse and vulgar genre of opera, its most important exponents were Alfano, Cilea, Franchetti, Giordano, Leoncavallo, Mascagni, Orefice, Puccini (only in part a verismo composer) and Zandonai. Some French and German composers imitated the style occasionally; examples include Massenet's *La Navarraise*, d'Albert's *Tiefland* and Schillings's *Mona Lisa*.

Verlobung in San Domingo, Die
(*The Betrothal in San Domingo*)
Opera in prologue and two acts by Egk. 1st perf Munich, 27 Nov 1963; libr by the composer, after Heinrich Wilhelm von Kleist's novella. Principal roles: Christoph (ten), Jeanne (sop), Hoango (bar), Babekan (mezzo). One of the most successful of Egk's later operas.
Plot: Hispaniola, 1803. During the slave revolt, Hoango and Babekan murder all white people coming to their house. When the French officer Christoph von Reid arrives, Babekan's daughter Jeanne falls in love with him and resolves to save him. Forced by Hoango to tie up Christoph, Jeanne later summons Christoph's followers, who release him. However, Jeanne is shot by Christoph who believes that she had deceived him. [R]

Verona Arena
A Roman amphitheatre (cap 16,663) in the Veneto in Italy, where open-air summer opera seasons have been given since 1913 (except during the two world wars). The repertory consists predominantly of 'spectacular' operas, such as *Aida*, *Turandot* and *Nabucco*. Top international casts are engaged, and the acoustics are superb.

Véronique
Operetta in three acts by Messager. 1st perf Paris, 10 Feb 1898; libr by Albert Vanloo and Georges Duval. Principal roles: Hélène (sop), Florestan (ten), Agathe (sop), Coquenard (bar), Ermerance (mezzo), Séraphin (bar). Usually regarded

as Messager's finest work, it is still regularly performed in France but unaccountably seldom elsewhere.
Plot: Early-19th-century Paris. Viscount Florestan de Valiancourt has so dissipated the family fortune that his options are either the debtors' prison or marriage to the unknown heiress Hélène de Solanges to whom he is engaged. He is attracted to a girl he has seen at a flower shop. The girl is Hélène herself, and she and her aunt Countess Ermerance decide to teach him a lesson. Disguising themselves as the flower girls Véronique and Estelle, they flirt with him until Florestan falls in love with 'Véronique'. After much intrigue, Florestan discovers that Véronique and Hélène are one and the same, and all ends happily. [R]

Verrett, Shirley (b 1931)
American mezzo, particularly associated with the Italian and French repertories, especially the title-role in *Carmen*. One of the finest mezzos of the 1970s, who also sang some soprano roles such as the title-role in *Tosca* and Lady Macbeth in Verdi's *Macbeth*, she had a rich and luscious voice of considerable power and range which she used with outstanding musicianship. She was an exciting stage performer, aided in roles such as Dalila in Saint-Saëns's *Samson et Dalila* by her great personal beauty. She created the title-role in Weisgall's *Athaliah* and in 1963 she became the first black singer ever to appear at the Bolshoi Opera.

Versailles
see SALLE DE L'OPÉRA, VERSAILLES

Verschworenen, Die (*The Conspirators*) or **Der Häusliche Krieg** (*Domestic War*)
Comic opera in one act by Schubert (D 787). 1st perf Frankfurt, 29 Aug 1861 (composed 1823); libr by Ignaz F. Castelli, after Aristophanes's *Lysistrata* and *Ecclesiazusae*. Principal roles: Heribert (bar), Ludmilla (sop), Udolin (ten), Helene (sop), Astolf (ten), Isella (mezzo). A delightful little SINGSPIEL, it is sadly only very rarely performed.
Plot: Medieval Vienna. Count Heribert and his nobles are away at the Crusades. His wife Ludmilla is angry that he should stay away so long and persuades the other wives to be cold and indifferent to their husbands when they return. Heribert's page Udolin hears of the plot through his sweetheart Isella and betrays it to his master. The nobles decide to use the women's own tactics against them. Both parties find the state of affairs intolerable until eventually the women all appear in full armour and the men declare themselves conquered. Domestic harmony is restored and Udolin and Isella are united. [R]

Verstovsky, Alexei (1799–1862)
Russian composer. His first two operas, the SINGSPIEL *Pan Tvardovski* (Moscow, 5 June 1828; libr Mikhail Nikolayevich Zagoskin) and *Vadim* (Moscow, 7 Dec 1832; libr S.P. Shevryov, after Vassily Zhukovsky), were unremarkable, but *Askold's Tomb* (Moscow, 28 Sept 1835; libr Zagoskin) [R Exc] was the most successful pre-Glinka Russian opera and had a considerable influence on the general development of Russian opera. His later operas, *Longing for the Homeland* (Moscow, 2 Sept 1839; libr Zagoskin), *Chur Valley* (Moscow, 28 Aug 1841; libr A.A. Shakhovsky) and *Gromoboy* (Moscow, 5 Feb 1858; libr D.T. Lensky, after Zhukovsky), were less successful.

Vert Carbonell, Juan
see under SOUTULLO, REVERIANO

Verurteilung or **Die Verhör des Lukullus**
(*The Sentencing*, or *Trial, of Lucullus*)
Opera in 12 scenes by Dessau. 1st perf Berlin, 17 March 1950; libr by Bertolt Brecht. Principal roles: Lukullus (ten), Tertullia (mezzo), King (bass), Fishwife (mezzo). Banned by the East German government after its premiere, it is an anti-war protest. It is Dessau's most successful opera, and has been widely performed.
Plot: The dead Lukullus arrives in the underworld and must stand trial before he is permitted to enter the Elysian Fields. He pleads worthiness to enter on the grounds of his great military victories. However, the jury rejects his arguments, and he is condemned because of the devastation caused by his military activities. [R]

Vespetta
Soprano role in Telemann's and mezzo

role in Albinoni's *Pimpinone*. She is a domineering housemaid.

Vespri Siciliani, I
see VÊPRES SICILIENNES, LES

Vestale, La (*The Vestal Virgin*)
Opera in three acts by Spontini. 1st perf Paris, 16 Dec 1807; libr by Victor Joseph Étienne de Jouy, partly after Johann Joachim Winckelmann's *Monumenti Antichi Inediti*. Principal roles: Julia (sop), Licinius (ten), High Priestess (mezzo), Cinna (bar), Pontifex Maximus (bass). Spontini's most successful and enduring opera, notable for its fine choruses, it is still quite often performed.
Plot: Legendary Rome. The vestal virgin Julia loves the general Licinius. He visits her during her vigil in the Temple of Vesta, and because of this distraction she allows the sacred flame to go out. She is about to be buried alive for her sacrilege when the flame is rekindled by divine intervention. She is released from her vows and united with Licinius. [R]

Vestale, La (*The Vestal Virgin*)
Opera in three acts by Mercadante. 1st perf Naples, 10 March 1840; libr by Salvatore Cammarano. Principal roles: Emilia (sop), Decio (ten), Publio (bar), Giunia (mezzo), Metello Pio (bass). One of Mercadante's finest operas, it was very successful in its time but is nowadays hardly ever performed.
Plot: Legendary Rome. Emilia, believing her beloved Decio killed in battle, has become a vestal virgin. However, Decio returns in triumph and Emilia has to crown him with the victor's laurels. To see Emilia, Decio enters the Temple of Vesta, where Emilia allows the sacred flame to go out. Decio is dragged away by his friend Publio, and despite an attempt by her friend Giunia to take the blame, Emilia is found guilty by the Senate. Decio's plea for clemency is ignored and he vows revenge. After the rejection of a further plea from Publio, Emilia bids farewell to Giunia and is locked into a tomb. Decio, arriving too late to save her, stabs himself.

Vesti la giubba
Tenor aria for Canio (often referred to in English as 'On with the motley') in Act I of Leoncavallo's *Pagliacci*, in which he says that he must go on for his performance whatever his private anguish.

V'ho ingannato
Soprano/baritone duet for Gilda and Rigoletto in Act III of Verdi's *Rigoletto*, in which the dying Gilda bids farewell to her father. The final scene of the opera.

Viaggio a Reims, Il (*The Journey to Rheims*) or **L'Albergo del Giglioli d'Oro** (*The Golden Lily Inn*)
Comic opera in one act by Rossini. 1st perf Paris, 19 June 1825; libr by Luigi Balocchi, partly after Anne-Louise de Staël's *Corinne ou l'Italie*. Principal roles: Corinna (sop), Madame Cortèse (sop), Melibea (mezzo), Countess Folleville (sop), Count Libenskof (ten), Don Profondo (bass), Lord Sydney (bass), Belfiore (ten), Baron Trombonok (bass), Don Alvaro (bar), Don Prudenzio (bass), Maddalena (mezzo). Possibly the most brilliant of all Rossini's comic scores, especially notable for its extraordinary 'Gran Pezzo Concertato a 14 Voci', it was written to celebrate the coronation of Charles X of France. Requiring ten front-rank singers, it remained totally unperformed for 150 years. Since the reconstruction of the score and its hugely successful revival at the 1985 Pesaro Festival, it has been widely performed. Rossini later incorporated much of the music into LE COMTE ORY.
Plot: Plombières, May 1825. An international group of travellers who are going to the coronation arrive at the inn run by Madame Cortèse to find both their journeys and their romantic intrigues interrupted by the lack of coach horses. They pass the time with songs and improvizations, and hold their own festival in honour of the coronation. [R]

Viardot-García, Pauline (1821–1910)
French mezzo and composer, daughter of MANUEL GARCÍA (I) and younger sister of MARÍA MALIBRAN and MANUEL GARCÍA (II) and also for many years the companion of the novelist Ivan Turgenev. One of the greatest singers of the 19th century, she created Fidès in *Le Prophète* and the title-role in Gounod's *Sapho*. She also composed a number of operettas,

including *Trop de Femmes* (1867; libr Turgenev), *Cendrillon* (1868), *Le Dernier Sorcier* (Weimar, 1869; libr Turgenev) and *L'Ogre* (1869; libr Turgenev).

Vibrato (Italian for 'vibrated')
A fluctuation in the pitch of the voice in a single note. Sometimes, as in a 'quick vibrato', it is correct and pleasing, but is more often unpleasant and is a serious vocal problem. In the latter case, it is also called tremolo, knock, beat or – more bluntly – wobble.

Vick, Graham (b 1953)
British producer. One of the most imaginative and thought-provoking of the younger generation of opera directors, his most notable productions have included *Un Rè in Ascolto* and *Mitridate Rè di Ponto* at Covent Garden. He was director of productions for Scottish Opera (1984–7) and the Glyndebourne Festival (1993–) and artistic director of the City of Birmingham Touring Opera (1987–).

Vickers, Jon (b Jonathan Stewart) (b 1926)
Canadian tenor, particularly associated with the roles of Florestan in *Fidelio*, Aeneas in Berlioz's *Les Troyens*, the title-role in Verdi's *Otello* (a part he also played in a film of the opera), Tristan in *Tristan und Isolde*, Radamès in *Aida* and the title-role in *Peter Grimes*. One of the greatest heroic tenors of the 20th century, with an incisive and powerful voice of highly individual timbre, he was also an intense and compelling singing-actor of remarkable commitment and dramatic insight.

Vida Breve, La (*Brief Life*)
Opera in two acts by de Falla. 1st perf Nice, 1 April 1913 (composed 1905); libr by Carlos Fernández Shaw. Principal roles: Salud (sop), Paco (ten), Carmela (mezzo), Uncle Salvador (bar), Grandmother (mezzo). De Falla's most successful stage work and the most important of all Spanish operas, it incorporates much traditional Andalusian music.
Plot: Granada, *c* 1900. The gypsy girl Salud loves Paco, who feigns to return her love, but who in reality is planning to marry Carmela. Salud discovers the truth, denounces Paco at the wedding ceremony and then, overcome by grief, falls dead at his feet. [R]

Video recordings
Since video cassettes became widely available in the early 1980s, many opera performances have been filmed, mostly on the VHS system. The majority have been live performances, including many from Covent Garden, the Verona Arena and the Glyndebourne Festival. There have, however, also been some studio recordings, such as the Brent Walker series of the Savoy Operas, and a few famous operatic films of the past (such as Tito Gobbi in *Rigoletto* and *Il Barbiere di Siviglia*) have also been made available.

Viene la sera
Soprano/tenor duet (the love duet) for Cio-Cio-San and Pinkerton in Act I of Puccini's *Madama Butterfly*.

Vieni, la mia vendetta
Bass aria for Alfonso d'Este in Act I of Donizetti's *Lucrezia Borgia*, in which he thinks of his planned vengeance on the man who his wife has been seeing.

Vieni, t'affretta
Soprano aria for Lady Macbeth in Act I of Verdi's *Macbeth*, in which she resolves to strengthen Macbeth's will and seize the throne.

Vienna
see THEATER AN DER WIEN, VIENNA; VIENNA CHAMBER OPERA; VIENNA STATE OPERA; VIENNA VOLKSOPER

Vienna Chamber Opera
The company was founded in 1953 by Prof Hans Gabor (1924–94) and has always maintained high artistic standards. The repertory consists largely of smaller-scale 18th- and 19th-century works, but also includes a number of contemporary operas.

Vienna State Opera
Called the Hofoper until 1918, the present theatre (cap 2,200) was designed by Eduard van der Nüll and August Siccard von Siccardsburg and opened on 25 May 1869. Destroyed by bombs in March

1945, it did not reopen until 5 Nov 1955; in the meantime, the company used the THEATER AN DER WIEN. One of the most prestigious and formal opera houses in the world, the annual season runs from September to June. Musical directors have included Mahler, Hans Richter, Felix Weingartner, Bruno Walter, Karl Böhm, Herbert von Karajan, Lorin Maazel and Claudio Abbado. The orchestra is the Vienna Philharmonic.

Vienna Volksoper
The theatre (cap 1,473) opened in Dec 1898 and began giving opera in 1904. The repertory is largely devoted to operetta and lighter operas, and the annual season runs from September to June. Musical directors have included Felix Weingartner, Fritz Stiedry and Leo Blech.

Vie Parisienne, La (*Parisian Life*)
Operetta in four acts by Offenbach. 1st perf Paris, 31 Oct 1868; libr by Henri Meilhac and Ludovic Halévy. Principal roles: Gabriele (sop), Brazilian (ten), Raoul (ten), Bobinet (bar), Métella (mezzo), Baron and Baroness Gondromark (bar and mezzo), Pauline (sop), Frick (bar), Alfred (bar). One of Offenbach's wittiest, most tuneful and most enduringly popular works, it is a satire on Second Empire morals (or lack of them).
Plot: Paris, 1867. The rakes Raoul de Gardefeu and Bobinet both love Métella but she rebuffs them. As they are both broke, they decide to try and make some money out of the visiting tourists, particularly the fast-living Brazilian millionaire and the Swedish Baron Gondromark, to whose wife Raoul takes a fancy. The Swedes are lodged at Raoul's house, which he tells them is a hotel, and the Baron is kept out of the way at a bibulous party given by Bobinet disguised as a Swiss admiral, with the chambermaid Pauline masquerading as his wife. Total confusion reigns at a masked ball given by the Brazilian, but eventually everything is sorted out, and the Brazilian decides to take the glovemaker Gabriele back home with him. [R]

Vierjährige Posten, Der (*The Four-Year Sentry Duty*)
Comic opera in one act by Schubert (D 190). 1st perf Dresden, 23 Sept 1896 (composed 1815); libr by Theodor Körner. Principal roles: Duval (ten), Käthchen (sop), Walther (bass), Captain (ten), Veit (ten). Like the rest of Schubert's early SINGSPIELS, it contains some delightful music, particularly the charming overture, but it is virtually never performed.
Plot: Franco-German border, early 19th century. The soldier Duval has deserted to wed his sweetheart, Walther's daughter Käthchen. He dons his uniform again when the army returns after four years, and escapes the death penalty for desertion by maintaining that he had remained on sentry duty for the entire time because nobody had relieved him. [R]

Vieuille, Félix (1872–1953)
French bass, particularly associated with the French repertory. Long resident at the Opéra-Comique, Paris, he had a rich and wide-ranging voice and was a fine singing-actor. He created Arkel in *Pelléas et Mélisande*, Eumée in Fauré's *Pénélope*, Bluebeard in Dukas's *Ariane et Barbe-Bleue*, the Father in Milhaud's *Le Pauvre Matelot*, the Sultan in Rabaud's *Mârouf* and Macduff in Bloch's *Macbeth*. His nephew **Jean** (1902–64) was a successful bass-baritone.

Vilja-Lied
Soprano aria for Hannah Glawari in Act II of Lehár's *Die Lustige Witwe*, in which she tells the story of a huntsman's unrequited love.

Village Romeo and Juliet, A
Opera in prologue and three acts by Delius. 1st perf Berlin, 21 Feb 1907; libr by the composer, after *Romeo und Julia auf dem Dorfe* in Gottfried Keller's *Die Leute von Seldwyla*. Principal roles: Sali (ten), Vrenchen (sop), Dark Fiddler (bar), Manz (bar), Marti (b-bar). Delius's most successful opera, notable for the instrumental 'Walk to the Paradise Garden', it is a lushly orchestrated work of great melodic beauty which for some reason is only infrequently performed.
Plot: Mid-19th-century Switzerland. The farmers Manz and Marti dispute a strip of land which rightfully belongs to the Dark Fiddler. Their children, Vrenchen and Sali, although forbidden by their fathers to meet because of the feud, fall in love. The feud exhausts both fathers' financial resources

and Sali attacks Vrenchen's father when the latter discovers the young couple together. The poverty-stricken lovers see no future and commit joint suicide by taking a barge out on to the river and sinking it. [R]

Villa-Lobos, Heitor (1887–1959)
Brazilian composer. He wrote nine operas, only three of which have ever been performed. They include *Izaht* (Rio de Janeiro, 6 Apr 1940, composed 1918; libr composer and Azevedo Júnior), an expansion of the earlier *Elisa* of 1910, *Malazarte* (1921; libr G. Aranha), the musical comedy *Magdalena* (Los Angeles, 26 July 1948) [R] and YERMA.

Villi, Le (*The Witches*)
Opera in two acts (originally one act) by Puccini. 1st perf Milan, 31 May 1884; libr by Ferdinando Fontana, after Alphonse Karr's *Les Willis*. Revised version 1st perf Turin, 26 Dec 1884. Principal roles: Anna (sop), Roberto (ten), Guglielmo (bar). Inspired by a folk legend and possibly also by Adam's ballet *Giselle* (to which the story bears more than a passing resemblance), it is Puccini's first opera. It still receives an occasional performance. **Plot**: Black Forest, Middle Ages. Anna is abandoned by her fiancé Roberto and dies of grief. Her spirit joins the Willis, the ghosts who haunt faithless lovers. Urged on by the prayers of her vengeful father Guglielmo Wulf, Anna's ghost appears before Roberto and draws him into a frenzied dance of death. [R]

Vinay, Ramón (b 1912)
Chilean tenor, particularly associated with the Italian repertory, especially the title-role in Verdi's *Otello*. Beginning as a baritone, he turned to tenor roles in 1943, becoming one of the finest HELDENTENORS of the immediate post-war period, enjoying equal success in Wagner and Verdi. He had a dark-toned voice of ringing power and was a singing-actor of great nobility and insight. He reverted to baritone roles in 1962 and also produced a number of operas.

Vincent
Tenor role in Gounod's *Mireille*. Ambroise's son, he loves Mireille.

Vinci, Leonardo (c 1690–1730)
Italian composer. He began by writing comic operas in Neapolitan dialect. His 12 works in this genre include *Lo Cecato Fauzo* (Naples, 19 Apr 1719; libr Aniello Piscopo) and *La Festa de Bacco* (Naples, 29 Aug 1722; libr Francesco Antonio Tullio). He later turned to OPERA SERIA, being one of the first to set Metastasian texts, and give the form greater flexibility by enriching the accompanied RECITATIVE and by loosening somewhat the strict Scarlattian aria structure. The most important of his 24 opera serias are *Didone Abbandonata* (Rome, 14 Jan 1726; libr Pietro Metastasio), *La Caduta de Decemviri* (Naples, 1 Oct 1727; libr Silvio Stampiglia), *Catone in Utica* (Rome, 19 Jan 1728; libr Metastasio), *Semiramide Riconosciuta* (Rome, 6 Feb 1729; libr Metastasio) and *Artaserse* (Rome, 4 Feb 1730; libr Metastasio), possibly his finest opera.

Vinco, Ivo (b 1928)
Italian bass, particularly associated with the Italian repertory, especially Verdi. He had a good, if not absolutely outstanding voice and had a fine stage presence. Married to the mezzo FIORENZA COSSOTTO.

Vin Herbé, Le (*The Drugged Wine*)
Dramatic oratorio in three parts by Martin. 1st perf Zürich, 26 March 1942; a virtual word-for-word setting of Joseph Bédier's *Tristan et Iseut*. Principal roles: Iseut (sop), Tristan (ten), Branhien (sop). One of Martin's finest stage works, written for 12 solo voices and seven string instruments, it is only very rarely performed. [R]

Viola
Unfinished opera in four scenes by Smetana. 1st perf Prague, 11 May 1924 (composed 1883); libr by Eliška Krásnohorská, after William Shakespeare's *Twelfth Night*. Principal roles: Viola (mezzo), Sebastian (mezzo), Antonio (bass), Marko (bass), Orsino (ten). Smetana only completed 365 bars of the music. [R]

Violanta
Opera in one act by Korngold (Op 8). 1st perf Munich, 28 March 1916; libr by Hans

Müller. Principal roles: Violanta (sop), Alfonso (ten), Trovai (bar), Bracca (ten), Barbara (mezzo). Korngold's first major success, it is nowadays only very rarely performed.
Plot: 15th-century Venice. Alfonso has seduced Violanta's sister. She entices him to her home so that her husband Simone Trovai can kill him. However, she falls in love with him and interposes herself between the two men. She is killed by her husband's dagger. [R]

Violetta
Soprano role in: **1** Verdi's *La Traviata*. Based on the historical Marie Duplessis (1824–47), with whom Alexandre Dumas fils had an affair, she is the consumptive demi-mondaine Violetta Valéry, the 'Lady of the Camellias'. **2** Mercadante's *Il Bravo*. She is Teodora's daughter.

Violins of St Jacques, The
Opera in three acts by Williamson. 1st perf London, 29 Nov 1966; libr by William Chappell, after Patrick Leigh Fermor's novel. Principal roles: Berthe (sop), Josephine (mezzo), Sosthène (ten), Marcel (bar), Countess Serindan (sop), Priestess (mezzo), Agenor (bass). Arguably Williamson's finest stage work, notable for its exotic orchestration, it is set on a Caribbean island shortly before a volcanic eruption.

Viozzi, Giulio (b 1912)
Italian composer. His operas, in late-romantic style and for all of which he wrote his own libretti, are the radio opera *Parete Bianca* (RAI, 1954), *Allamistakeo* (Bergamo, 26 Sept 1954; libr after Edgar Allan Poe's *Some Words With a Mummy*), *Un Intervento Notturno* (Trieste, 26 Jan 1957; libr after R.A. Bowen), *Il Sasso Pagano* (Trieste, 10 Mar 1962; libr after O. von Leitgeb), *La Giacca Dannata* (Trieste, 1967; libr after Dino Buzzati), *Elisabetta* (Trieste, 1971; libr after Guy de Maupassant) and the unperformed *L'Inverno* (libr after N. Spazzali).

Vi ravviso
Bass aria for Count Rodolfo in Act I of Bellini's *La Sonnambula*, in which he salutes the village on his return.

Virginia Opera Association
Based at the Norfolk Center Theater, this American company was founded in 1975 and has recently been closely associated with Musgrave's operas. The musical director is Peter Mark.

Visconti, Luchino (b Count Luchino Visconti di Modrone) (1906–76)
Italian producer, designer and film maker. One of the outstanding post-war opera directors, he was particularly associated with La Scala, Milan (where he directed *La Vestale*, *Anna Bolena*, *La Traviata*, *La Sonnambula* and *Iphigénie en Tauride*, all with Maria Callas) and with Covent Garden (where he directed *Don Carlos*, *La Traviata*, *Il Trovatore* and *Der Rosenkavalier*). His designs and stagings were notable for their strong sense of historical style – he occasionally went to the lengths of unearthing 19th-century scenery. He was also the co-author of the libretto of Franco Mannino's *Il Diavolo in Giardino*.

Vishnevskaya, Galina (b 1926)
Russian soprano, particularly associated with the Russian and Italian repertories, especially Tatyana in Tchaikovsky's *Eugene Onegin*, Katerina Ismailova in Skostakovich's *The Lady Macbeth of the Mtsensk District* and the title-roles in *Tosca* and *Aida*. A powerful dramatic performer (if sometimes in a style which Western audiences found rather old-fashioned), she had a rich voice of considerable power and range which she used with outstanding intelligence and musicianship. Married to the cellist and conductor MSTISLAV ROSTROPOVICH, she left the then USSR in 1974 and she and her husband were stripped of their Soviet citizenship for their befriending of the dissident novelist Alexander Solzhenitsyn. Her autobiography, *Galina: a Russian Story*, was published in 1984.

Vision fugitive
Baritone aria for Herod in Act II of Massenet's *Hérodiade*, in which he tells of the dreams of Salome's beauty which always haunt him.

Vissi d'arte
Soprano aria for Tosca in Act II of Puccini's *Tosca*, in which she says that she has lived only for love and for her art.

Vítek
Tenor role in: **1** Janáček's *The Macropolus Case*. Kristina's father, he is an old solicitor's clerk. **2** Smetana's *Dalibor*. He is in love with Jitka.

Vitellia
Soprano role in Mozart's *La Clemenza di Tito*. She loves the Emperor Titus.

Vittadini, Franco (1884–1948)
Italian composer. His six operas are the unperformed *Il Mare di Tiberiade* (1914; libr Luigi Illica), the highly successful ANIMA ALLEGRA, *Nazareth* (Pavia, 27 May 1925; libr Giuseppe Adami, after Selma Lagerlöf), *La Sagredo* (Milan, 29 Apr 1930; libr Adami), *Caracciolo* (Rome, 9 Feb 1938; libr Arturo Rossato) and *Fiametta e l'Avaro* (Brescia, Apr 1951; libr Adami and Giovacchino Forzano).

Vivaldi, Antonio (c 1678–1741)
Italian composer. He wrote 44 operas, many of them hastily put together from previous works. None of them has won a permanent place in the repertory. His more important operas include *L'Incoronazione di Dario* (Venice, 23 Jan 1717; libr Adriano Morselli) [R], *Tito Manlio* (Mantua, 1719; libr Matteo Noris) [R], *Giustino* (Rome, 1724; libr Nicolò Berengani), *Il Farnace* (Venice, 10 Feb 1727; libr Antonio Maria Lucchini), ORLANDO FURIOSO, perhaps his finest opera, *La Fida Ninfa* (Verona, 6 Jan 1732; libr Scipione Mattei) [R], L'OLIMPIADE, *La Griselda* (Venice, 18 May 1735; libr Apostolo Zeno) and *Catone in Utica* (Verona, May 1737; libr Pietro Metastasio) [R]. There has recently been some revival of interest in his stage works, and a few have been performed after nearly 250 years of neglect.

Viva il vino
Tenor aria (the Drinking Song) for Turiddù in Mascagni's *Cavalleria Rusticana*.

Vivat Bacchus
Tenor/bass duet for Pedrillo and Osmin in Act II of Mozart's *Die Entführung aus dem Serail*, in which they sing the praises of wine and women.

Vives, Amadeo (1871–1932)
Spanish composer. He began by writing operas, of which *Maruxa* (Madrid, 28 May 1914; libr Luis Pascual Frutos) [R] is still remembered in Spain. He subsequently turned to ZARZUELA, becoming one of the leading exponents of the genre, writing over 100 of them. The most successful include BOHEMIOS, *Los Viajes de Gulliver* (Madrid, 21 Feb 1911; libr Antonio Passo and Joaquín Abiati, after Jonathan Swift's *Gulliver's Travels*), which was written in collaboration with Giménez, *La Generala* (Madrid, 1912; libr Guillermo Perrin and Miguel de Palacios) [R], the popular DOÑA FRANCISQUITA and *La Villana* (Madrid, 1 Oct 1927; libr Federico Romero and Guillermo Fernández Shaw, after Félix Lope de Vega's *Peribañez*) [R].

Vivi, ingrato
Soprano aria for Elizabeth I in Act III of Donizetti's *Roberto Devereux*, in which she resolves to forgive Robert. Its cabaletta 'Quel sangue versato' is the final scene of the opera.

Vivi tu
Tenor aria for Riccardo Percy in Act II of Donizetti's *Anna Bolena*, in which he urges Rochfort to save his own life.

Vladimir
Tenor role in: **1** Borodin's *Prince Igor*. He is Igor's son. **2** Nápravník's *Dubrovsky*. He is in love with Masha.

Vocal competitions
Annual vocal competitions for young singers are held in a number of countries. Amongst the most prestigious are the Kathleen Ferrier Memorial Prize in Britain, the Voci Verdiani in Italy, the s'Hertogenbosch in the Netherlands, the Metropolitan Auditions of the Air in New York (now discontinued), the Cardiff Singer of the World in Wales (which is biannual) and those of Moscow, Toulouse and Barcelona.

Vocal ranges
see BARITONE; BASS; BASS-BARITONE; CASTRATO; CONTRALTO; COUNTER-TENOR; MEZZO-SOPRANO; SOPRANO; TENOR

Vocal score
The published music of an opera, showing all the vocal parts (solo and chorus) with a piano reduction for accompaniment.

Voce bianca (Italian for 'white voice')
A term used to describe singing in a vibratoless, 'straight' tone. It is usually employed to convey the impression of illness.

Voce di testa
The Italian term for HEAD VOICE.

Voce poco fa, Una
Mezzo aria for Rosina in Act I of Rossini's *Il Barbiere di Siviglia*, in which she says that she is obedient to her guardian only so long as she gets her own way.

Vogelfänger bin ich ja, Der
Baritone aria for Papageno in Act I of Mozart's *Die Zauberflöte*, in which he introduces himself to the audience.

Vogelgesang, Kunz
Tenor COMPRIMARIO role in Wagner's *Die Meistersinger von Nürnberg*. A furrier, he is one of the masters.

Vogelhändler, Der (*The Bird Seller*)
Operetta in three acts by Zeller. 1st perf Vienna, 10 Jan 1891; libr by Moritz Mitzelberger-West and Ludwig Held, after Varin and Biéville's *Ce Que Deviennent les Roses*. Principal roles: Adam (ten), Marie (sop), Stanislaus (ten), Christel (sop), Baron Weps (bar), Schneck (bar). By far Zeller's most successful and enduring work, it is still regularly performed in German-speaking countries.
Plot: Early-18th-century Rhineland Palatinate. The bird seller Adam is betrothed to the postmistress Christel, but they cannot afford to get married. The elector's wife Marie arrives in disguise and flirts with Adam. Count Stanislaus, nephew of the corrupt Master of the Hunt Baron Weps, disguises himself as the elector, and Christel obtains from him Adam's appointment as Menagerie Inspector. The various disguises cause much confusion and amorous misunderstanding, but all is eventually sorted out and Adam and Christel are able to marry. [R]

Voice of Ariadne, The
Opera in three acts by Musgrave. 1st perf Aldeburgh, 11 June 1974; libr by Amalia Elguera, after Henry James's *The Last of the Valerii*. Principal roles: Countess (sop), Valerio (bar), Bianca (sop), Mrs Tracy (mezzo), Baldovino (ten), Mr Lamb (bass). Musgrave's first major success, it is a chamber opera written for an orchestra of 13 players.
Plot: Rome, 1870s. Count Marco Valerio is fascinated by the legend of a statue buried in his garden. Excavation produces a pedestal inscribed 'Ariadne'. He imagines that he hears Ariadne's voice and becomes fixated on a vision of her, which estranges him from his wife. Finally, he recognizes the Countess as the embodiment of his vision and the source of all happiness, which he had been pursuing without realizing that he already possessed it.

Voices of the future
Large numbers of young singers.are always emerging with abundant vocal and dramatic talent. However, many fail to reach their full potential, often because they become 'sung out' through undertaking the wrong roles early in their careers. The blame for this can frequently be laid at the doors of agents, opera administrators and recording companies anxious to cash in on a new talent and giving little thought to nurturing it. In earlier days, young singers learnt their craft and tried out their roles in small houses out of the limelight and where they did not have to force their voices. Nowadays, with the major exception of Germany, this is seldom the case, and the lessons of the early decline of some exceptional voices – Elena Souliotis being the classic example – appear to have been ignored.

Voi che fausti
Tenor aria for Alessandro in Act II of Mozart's *Il Rè Pastore*, in which he begs the gods to smile on his plans.

Voi che sapete
Mezzo aria for Cherubino in Act II of Mozart's *Le Nozze di Figaro*, in which he sings a song of his own composition to the Countess.

Voilà donc la terrible cité
Baritone aria for Athanaël in Act II of Massenet's *Thaïs*, in which he condemns the moral corruption of Alexandria.

Voi lo sapete o mamma
Soprano aria for Santuzza in Mascagni's *Cavalleria Rusticana*, in which she tells Mamma Lucia of Turiddù's betrayal of her.

Voix Humaine, La (*The Human Voice*)
Opera in one act by Poulenc. 1st perf Paris, 6 Feb 1959; libr by Jean Cocteau. Principal role: Elle (sop). One of Poulenc's cleverest works, it is a 45-minute MONODRAMA for soprano, portraying a woman's conversation on the telephone with the lover who has jilted her. [R]

Volo di Notte (*Night Flight*)
Opera in one act by Dallapiccola. 1st perf Florence, 18 May 1940; libr by the composer, after Antoine de Saint-Exupéry's *Vol de Nuit*. Principal roles: Rivière (b-bar), Simona (sop), Radio Telephonist (ten), Laroux (bass). Dallapiccola's first opera, heavily influenced by Berg, it is only infrequently performed.
Plot: Buenos Aires, *c* 1930. In the control tower of the airport, the director Rivière plans dangerous night flights despite the loss of an aeroplane. The Radio Telephonist and Simona Fabien, whose pilot husband is expected on a night flight, gradually come to respect his attitude.

Voltaire
see panel on pages 596–7

Volta la terra
Soprano aria for Oscar in Act I of Verdi's *Un Ballo in Maschera*, in which he describes Ulrica's magic powers.

Vom Fischer un syner Fru (*Of the Fisherman and His Wife*)
Opera in one act by Schoeck (Op 43). 1st perf Dresden, 3 Oct 1930; libr (in Low German) by Philipp Otto Runge, after Jacob and Wilhelm Grimm's *Fairy Tales*. Principal roles: Wife (sop), Fisherman (ten), Turbot (bass). A tautly-written allegorical work, it is only very rarely performed.
Plot: The Fisherman catches a Turbot. He sets it free after the fish promises to grant his every wish. Urged on by his insatiably greedy wife, the Fisherman makes ever higher demands, until finally he wishes to be king, then emperor, then 'like the Lord'. At this last demand, chaos breaks loose and the Fisherman loses all that he had gained. [R]

Von
Names which contain this prefix are listed under the letter of the main surname. For example, Frederica von Stade is listed under S.

Von Heute auf Morgen (*From One Day Until Morning*)
Comic opera in one act by Schönberg (Op 32). 1st perf Frankfurt, 1 Feb 1930; libr by Schönberg's wife Gertrud Kolisch (under the pen-name of Max Blonda). Principal roles: Wife (sop), Husband (bar), Singer (ten), Friend (sop), Child (sop). The first TWELVE-TONE opera, it is supposedly based on an incident in the life of the composer Schreker.
Plot: The Wife and her Husband return from a party, where he was attracted to his Wife's Friend from her school days and his wife to the Singer. Stung that her Husband continually takes her for granted, the Wife changes into alluring night clothes and announces that she intends to lead a wild life, beginning with the Singer, who rings up to suggest continuing the party. Her attitude has the desired effect on her Husband, who confesses the error of his ways, and the two are reconciled. When the Singer and the Friend arrive, they mock the couple's old-fashioned attitude before leaving. Husband and Wife discuss the episode in new-found harmony over breakfast, and the Child asks, 'What's up-to-date people?'. [R]

Von Jugend auf in dem Kampfgefild'
Tenor aria (the Preghiera) for Sir Huon in Act I of Weber's *Oberon*, in which he says that love has replaced martial daring as his principal interest.

Vorspiel (German for 'fore-play')
The German term for an orchestral prelude.

Votre toast
Baritone aria (the Toreador's Song) for Escamillo in Act II of Bizet's *Carmen*.

Votto, Antonino (1896–1985)
Italian conductor, particularly associated with the Italian repertory. Long resident at La Scala, Milan, he was a rock-solid and often underrated Italian maestro of the old school. He conducted the first performance of Ghedini's *L'Ipocrata Felice*.

· Voltaire ·

The French philosopher, playwright and novelist Voltaire (*b* François Marie Arouet) (1694–1778) was himself keenly interested in opera. He wrote several opera libretti, including those for Rameau's *Samson, La Princesse de Navarre* and *Le Temple de la Gloire*. Voltaire appears as a character in Bernstein's *Candide* and in operas by two minor composers. Some 60 operas have been based on his writings. Below are listed, by work, those operas by composers with entries in this dictionary.

Adélaïde du Guesclin		
Mayr	*Adelaide di Guesclino*	1799
Alzire		
Zingarelli	*Alzira*	1794
Manfroce	*Alzira*	1810
Verdi	*Alzira*	1845
La Begueule		
Monsigny	*La Belle Arsène*	1773
Candide		
Bernstein	*Candide*	1958
Ce Qui plaît aux Dames		
Duni	*La Fée Urgèle*	1765
Gertrude		
Grétry	*Isabelle et Gertrude*	1766
L'Ingénu		
Grétry	*Le Huron*	1768
Leroux	*L'Ingénu*	1931
Mahomet		
Winter	*Maometto*	1817
Rossini	*Maometto Secondo/Le Siège de Corinthe*	1820/26
Mérope		
Graun	*Merope*	1756
Pacini	*Merope*	1847
Olympie		
Spontini	*Olympie*	1819
Mercadante	*Statira*	1853
L'Orphelin de la Chine		
Winter	*Tamerlan*	1802
Mayr	*Tamerlano*	1813
Samson		
Rameau	*Samson*	1732
Les Scythes		
Mayr	*Gli Sciti*	1800
Mercadante	*Gli Sciti*	1823
Sémiramis		
Portugal	*La Semiramide*	1806
Rossini	*Semiramide*	1823
Tancrède		
Rossini	*Tancredi*	1813

Zadig		
Vaccai	*Zadig ed Astartea*	1825
Zaïre		
Portugal	*Zaira*	1802
Winter	*Zaira*	1805
Bellini	*Zaira*	1829
Mercadante	*Zaira*	1831

Voyevoda, The
Opera in three acts by Tchaikovsky (Op 3). 1st perf Moscow, 11 Feb 1869; libr by the composer and Alexander Nikolayevich Ostrovsky, after the latter's *A Dream on the Volga*. Principal roles: Maria (sop), Bastryukov (ten), Dubrovin (bar), Shaligin (bass), Olyena (mezzo). Tchaikovsky's first opera, he discarded it and incorporated parts of it into later works.
Plot: 17th-century Russia. The voyevode (provincial governor) Shaligin is engaged to Praskovya, the elder daughter of the landowner Vlas Dyuzhoy, but falls in love with her sister Maria and abducts her. Maria's beloved Bastryukov meets Roman Dubrovin, earlier outlawed by Shaligin and whose wife Olyena the voyevode had abducted. They plan to rescue the two women. Their attempt is thwarted by Shaligin, who tries to stab Maria. However, at this very moment the Tsar's representative arrives and Shaligin is arrested. [R Exc]

Vrchlický, Jaroslav (b Emil Frída) (1853–1912)
Czech poet, playwright and librettist. He provided libretti for Chvála (*Záboj*), Dvořák (*Armida*), Fibich (*The Tempest* and the *Hippodamie* melodrama trilogy) and Foerster (*Jessika*). In addition, Novák's *A Night at Karlstein* and Fibich's *Šárka* are based on his plays.

Vyvyan, Jennifer (1925–74)
British soprano, particularly associated with Britten and Händel roles. A warm-voiced singer of fine musicianship, she had an affecting stage presence. She created, for Britten, Lady Penelope Rich in *Gloriana*, the Governess in *The Turn of the Screw*, Tytania in *A Midsummer Night's Dream* and Mrs Julian in *Owen Wingrave* and, for Williamson, Countess Serindan in *The Violins of St Jacques*, Agnes in *The Growing Castle* and several roles in *English Eccentrics*.

W

Wach' auf
Chorus in Act III Scene II of Wagner's *Die Meistersinger von Nürnberg*. Sung in honour of Hans Sachs, it is a modernization of the words with which the historical Sachs greeted Martin Luther and the Reformation.

Wächter, Eberhard (1929–92)
Austrian baritone, particularly associated with Wagner and Mozart roles, especially the title-role in *Don Giovanni*. An outstanding singing-actor with a fine and incisive voice used with style and great intelligence, he created Alfred in Einem's *Der Besuch der Alten Dame*. He was artistic director of the Vienna Volksoper (1986–92) and administrator of the Vienna State Opera (1991–2).

Waffenschmied, Der (*The Armourer*)
Opera in three acts by Lortzing. 1st perf Vienna, 31 May 1846; libr by the composer, after Friedrich Wilhelm von Ziegler's *Liebhaber und Nebenbuhler in einer Person*. Principal roles: Graf von Liebenau (bar), Marie (sop), Stadinger (bass), Georg (ten), Adelhof (bass), Irmentraut (mezzo). An engaging and tuneful work, it is still popular in Germany but is almost never performed elsewhere.
Plot: 16th-century Worms. Count von Liebenau loves Marie, daughter of the armourer Hans Stadinger. He woos her both as himself and in the guise of 'Conrad', a young apprentice. Marie falls in love with Conrad, but Stadinger wants her to wed the Count's manservant Georg. Georg declines her hand and Stadinger allows her to marry Conrad. The Count reveals that Conrad is actually himself and all ends happily. [R]

Wagner, Cosima (b Liszt) (1837–1930)
German administrator. Daughter of Liszt, she was married first to the conductor HANS VON BÜLOW, but left him for Wagner, whose second wife she became in 1870. She assisted Wagner in the establishment of the Bayreuth Festival, and was its artistic director (1883–1906), also acting as producer. Her diaries, first published in 1976, are a crucial if over-reverential source of information for Wagner's later years. Her son was the composer SIEGFRIED WAGNER and her grandson the producer WIELAND WAGNER.

Wagner, Richard (1813–83)
German composer, writer and theorist. The single most important and influential figure in the history of opera – indeed of all music – his theories (propounded in both his music-dramas and his writings) have had a profound influence on Western culture, affecting not only music, but also philosophy, literature, politics and drama. With the exceptions of Napoleon and Jesus of Nazareth, he is the most written-about individual in human history, and no artist has been more controversial or has produced such violent partisanship. The core of Wagner's musico-dramatic theories may be found in his concept of *Gesamtkunstwerk* ('unified work of art'), in which all aspects of the arts – music, poetry, drama and design – combine to form a single work of art: music-drama. On the purely musical level, this was achieved through a 'symphonic' conception of opera, produced by the development of LIETMOTIV. Wagner supervised every aspect of the production of his works and always wrote his own libretti.

His first stage work, *Die Hochzeit* (1832), is mainly lost. Neither of his first two extant operas are of great significance, nor do they give much indication of his future development; DIE FEEN remained unperformed until 1888 and the Shakespearian DAS LIEBESVERBOT met with little success. His first opera of importance, and his first definitive success, was the vast Meyerbeerian RIENZI. It was followed by DER FLIEGENDE HOLLÄNDER, nowadays regarded as his first 'canonical' work, TANNHÄUSER and LOHENGRIN, in which his theories first begin to find expression. Realizing that his ideas were best expressed through the medium of myth, Wagner turned to the *Nibelungenlied*. What began as a plan for a single opera, *Siegfrieds Tod*, developed into the tetralogy DER RING DES NIBELUNGEN, the longest and most complex work in the history of opera. After composing *Das Rheingold*, *Die Walküre* and the first two acts of *Siegfried*, Wagner laid the project aside for 12 years, turning to TRISTAN UND ISOLDE and the comedy DIE MEISTERSINGER VON NÜRNBERG, his only mature work to deal with historical figures. Returning to the tetralogy, he completed *Siegfried* and composed *Götterdämmerung*. The cycle received its first complete performance in 1876 at the opening of the Bayreuth Festpielhaus, designed by Wagner for the performance of his works. His last opera was the 'stage consecration festival play' PARSIFAL.

Wagner's voluminous (and usually turgid) writings include *Art and Revolution* (1849), *The Art-Work of the Future* (1849), the baleful *Jewry in Music* (1850), *Opera and Drama* (1851) and his somewhat tendentious autobiography *Mein Leben*.

Wagner's second wife was Liszt's daughter COSIMA. Their son was the composer SIEGFRIED WAGNER and their grandson the producer WIELAND WAGNER. Wagner's adopted niece **Johanna** (1826–94) was a successful soprano, who created Elisabeth in *Tannhäuser*. She lost her voice in 1861 and became a straight actress, but resumed singing (as a mezzo) in the 1870s and created the First Norn in *Götterdämmerung*.

Wagner, Siegfried (1869–1930)
German composer and conductor, son of RICHARD and COSIMA WAGNER. He wrote 15 operas in a conservative, late-romantic style, none of which achieved any lasting success. The most important are the once-popular *Der Bärenhäuter* (Munich, 22 Jan 1899; libr composer, after Grimms' *The Man in a Bear Skin*) [R], *Der Kobold* (Hamburg, 29 Jan 1904; libr composer), *Der Friedensengel* (Karlsruhe, 4 Mar 1914; libr composer) and *Der Schmied von Marienburg* (Rostock, 16 Dec 1923; libr composer). He was artistic director of the Bayreuth Festival (1906–30). His sons were the producers **Wolfgang** and WIELAND WAGNER.

Wagner, Wieland (1917–66)
German producer and designer, son of the composer SIEGFRIED WAGNER and grandson of RICHARD and COSIMA WAGNER. One of the most influential 20th-century German opera producers, his abstract and simplified Wagnerian productions, abandoning naturalism and pageantry, established a style of Wagnerian performance which lasted for 30 years. He described his aims as being to 'replace the production ideas of a century ago, now grown sterile, by a creative intellectual approach which goes back to the origins of the work itself. Every new production is a step on the way to an unknown goal'. He also made controversial productions of other composers' works, and frequently collaborated with the soprano ANJA SILJA, with whom he enjoyed a close artistic relationship. He was artistic director of the Bayreuth Festival (1951–66). His brother **Wolfgang** (*b* 1919) was co-director of the festival, becoming sole director on his brother's death. His autobiography, *Lebens-Akte*, was published in 1994.

Wagner-Régeny, Rudolf (1903–69)
Hungarian-born German composer. A number of his operas met with some success in Germany, but they are virtually unknown elsewhere. They include *Der Nackte König* (Gera, 1 Dec 1930; libr V. Braun, after Hans Christian Andersen's *The Emperor's New Clothes*), *Der Günstling* (Dresden, 20 Feb 1935; libr Caspar Neher, after Georg Büchner's version of Victor Hugo's *Marie* Tudor [R Exc], *Die Bürger von Calais* (Berlin, 28 Jan 1939; libr Neher, after Jean Froissart), *Johanna Balk* (Vienna, 4 Apr 1941; libr Neher), *Prometheus* (Kassel, 12 Sept 1959; libr composer, after Aeschylus) and *Das Bergwerk zu Falun* (Salzburg, 16 Apr 1961; libr composer, after Hugo von Hofmannsthal).

Wagner tuba
An instrument designed by Wagner for use in *Der Ring des Nibelungen*. More like a modified horn than the normal orchestral tuba, it is in two sizes, tenor and bass. It is mainly associated with Hunding in *Die Walküre*.

Wahn! Wahn!
Baritone monologue for Hans Sachs in Act III of Wagner's *Die Meistersinger von Nürnberg*, in which he broods over the idiocies of the world.

Waldner, Count
Bass role in Strauss's *Arabella*. Adelaide's husband, he is Arabella's and Zdenka's impoverished father.

Wales
see WELSH NATIONAL OPERA

Walker, Edyth (1867–1950)
American mezzo, particularly associated with Wagnerian roles. One of the first American singers to enjoy a major operatic career in Europe, she was later also a noted teacher, whose pupils included Irene Dalis and Blanche Thebom.

Walker, Sarah (b 1945)
British mezzo, particularly associated with Händel, Monteverdi and Berlioz roles and with 20th-century operas. One of the finest contemporary British operatic artists (and also a noted recitalist), her beautiful voice is used with great intelligence and musicianship and she is an outstanding singing-actress, equally at home in serious or comic roles. She created Suzanne in Blake's *Toussaint* and Agave in Buller's *The Bacchae*.

Walk to the Paradise Garden
Orchestral interlude in Scene V of Delius's *A Village Romeo and Juliet*, depicting the journey of Vrenchen and Sali to the garden.

Walküre, Die (*The Valkyrie*)
Opera in three acts by Wagner; Part 2 of DER RING DES NIBELUNGEN. 1st perf Munich, 26 June 1870 (composed 1856); libr by the composer, after the *Nibelungenlied*. Principal roles: Wotan (bar), Brünnhilde (sop), Sieglinde (sop), Siegmund (ten), Fricka (mezzo), Hunding (bass), Eight Valkyries (sop and mezzo). For plot see *Der Ring des Nibelungen*. [R]

Wallace, Ian (b 1919)
British bass, particularly associated with Rossini, Mozart and Sullivan roles. One of the finest and most popular post-war British BUFFOS, he had a good if not absolutely outstanding voice, allied to fine diction and an excellent stage presence. Later in his career, he also enjoyed success as a straight actor and as a broadcaster on musical programmes. His autobiography, *Promise Me You'll Sing Mud*, was published in 1975.

Wallace, Jake
Bass role in Puccini's *La Fanciulla del West*. He is an itinerant singer.

Wallace, Vincent (1812–65)
Irish composer. After an adventurous life in Australia, India, Chile and Mexico, he settled in London, where his six performed operas established him as one of the most successful 19th-century British composers. His operas, written on an ambitious scale in quasi-Meyerbeerian style, are MARITANA, by far his most successful work, *Matilda of Hungary* (London, 28 Feb 1847; libr Alfred Bunn), *Lurline* (London, 23 Feb 1860; libr Edward Fitzball, after *Loreley*), which was long popular, *The Amber Witch* (London, 28 Feb 1861; libr Henry Fothergill Chorley), *Love's Triumph* (London, 3 Nov 1862; libr James Robertson Planché) and *The Desert Flower* (London, 12 Oct 1864; libr Augustus Harris and T.J. Williams).

Wallberg, Heinz (b 1923)
German conductor, particularly associated with 19th-century German and Italian operas. A rock-solid German maestro of the old school, he was musical director of the Augsburg Stadttheater (1954), the Bremen Opera (1955–60), the Wiesbaden Opera (1960–75) and the Essen Opera (1975–85).

Wallmann, Margherita (1904–92)
Austrian producer. Originally a dancer and choreographer, she was especially associated with La Scala, Milan, where her productions included a number of world premieres, including Poulenc's *Dialogues des Carmélites* and Pizzetti's *L'Assassinio nella Cattedrale*. Her stagings, in traditional style, were notable for their superb handling of crowd scenes and for their fluidity of movement.

Wally, La
Opera in four acts by Catalani. 1st perf Milan, 20 Jan 1892; libr by Luigi Illica, after Wilhelmine von Hillern's *Die Geyer-Walley*. Principal roles: Wally (sop), Hagenbach (ten), Gellner (bar), Stromminger (bass), Afra (mezzo), Walther (sop). Catalani's last and finest opera, notable for its rich orchestration, it is still regularly performed in Italy but only infrequently elsewhere.
Plot: Swiss Tyrol, *c* 1800. Giuseppe Hagenbach does not return the love of the hoydenish girl Wally. He humiliates her and she plots to have him killed. Her suitor Vincenzo Gellner does this for her by pushing Hagenbach down a ravine. However, Wally is now repentant and rescues him. Hagenbach tells her that he does love her after all, but the two are killed in an avalanche. [R]

Walter, Bruno (b Schlesinger) (1876–1962)
German conductor, particularly associated with the German repertory. One of the finest operatic conductors of the 20th century, his lyrical and humane interpretations reflected his warm and sympathetic personality. He was musical director of the Munich Opera (1913–22) and the Vienna State Opera (1936–8). He conducted the first performances of Pfitzner's *Der Arme Heinrich* and *Palestrina*, Korngold's *Der Ring des Polykrates* and *Violanta* and Schreker's *Das Spielwerk*. His autobiography, *Theme and Variations*, was published in 1946.

Walther, Count
Bass role in Verdi's *Luisa Miller*. He is Rodolfo's father.

Walther von der Vogelweide
Tenor role in Wagner's *Tannhäuser*. He is the historical minstrel-knight (*c* 1170–*c* 1230).

Walther von Stolzing
Tenor role in Wagner's *Die Meistersinger von Nürnberg*. He is a Franconian knight in love with Eva.

Walton, Sir William (1902–83)
British composer. His two operas, neither of which is performed as often as their merits deserve, are the neo-classical TROILUS AND CRESSIDA and the witty one-act comedy THE BEAR.

Waltraute
Mezzo role in Wagner's *Die Walküre* and *Götterdämmerung*. She is one of the Valkyries.

Walzel, Camillo
see ZELL, F.

Walzertraum, Ein (*A Waltz Dream*)
Operetta in three acts by O. Straus. 1st perf Vienna, 2 March 1907; libr by Felix Dörmann and Leopold Jacobson, after Hans Müller's *Das Buch der Abenteuer*. Principal roles: Helene (sop), Niki (ten), Montschi (ten), Friederike (mezzo), Wendolin (bar), Franzi (sop). One of Straus's most successful works, it is still regularly performed in German-speaking countries.
Plot: The imaginary principality of Flausenthurn. Princess Helene, heiress to the throne, has secretly married the Viennese lieutenant Niki. A visit by his friend Montschi increases Niki's homesickness, and the two go to a park to hear a Viennese band. There, Niki meets and falls in love with the violinist Franzi. Helene realizes that only by becoming like the Viennese can she hope to regain Niki's love. She takes instruction from Franzi and is successful in winning Niki back. [R]

Wanda
Soprano role in Offenbach's *La Grande-Duchesse de Gérolstein*. She is Fritz's sweetheart.

Wanderer
Bass-baritone role in Wagner's *Siegfried*. He is Wotan in disguise.

Wandering Scholar, The
Opera in one act by Holst (Op 50). 1st perf Liverpool, 31 Jan 1934; libr by Clifford Bax, after Helen Waddell's *The Wandering Scholars*. Principal roles: Pierre (ten), Alison (sop), Fr Philippe (bass), Louis (bar). One of Holst's finest stage works, it is still occasionally performed, usually in the edition prepared in 1968 by Britten and Imogen Holst.
Plot: 13th-century France. Whilst her husband Louis is at the market, Alison receives the lecherous priest Philippe, but they are interrupted by the arrival of the scholar Pierre. They refuse him

refreshment and send him away. Pierre returns with Louis and relates a pointed story which leads to the discovery of Philippe under a pile of straw. [R]

War and Peace (*Voyna i Mir*)
Opera in two parts (five acts) by Prokofiev (Op 91). 1st perf Leningrad, 12 June 1946; libr by the composer and Mira Mendelson-Prokofieva, after Lev Tolstoy's novel. Revised version 1st perf Leningrad, 31 March 1955. Principal roles: Natasha (sop), Prince Andrei (bar), Marshal Kutuzov (b-bar), Pierre Bezukhov (ten), Prince Anatol (ten), Napoleon (bar), Dolokhov (bar), Sonya (mezzo), Count Rostov (bar), Akhrosimova (mezzo), Vaska Denisov (bar), Hélène Bezukhova (mezzo), Platon Karatayev (ten), Maria (mezzo). Arguably Prokofiev's finest opera, its carefully selected scenes from Tolstoy contrast public and private destinies against a backdrop of Russia under threat. The obvious analogy between 1812 and 1944 gave the work a particular relevance and impact at its appearance. Particularly notable for its superb choral writing and for its remarkable portrayal of Marshal Kutuzov, it requires vast forces and for that reason is not performed as often as it might be. [R]

Ward, David (1922–83)
British bass, particularly associated with Verdi and Wagner roles, especially Wotan. A singing-actor of great insight and humanity with a warm, rich and beautiful voice of considerable power and range, he created Capt Hardy in Berkeley's *Nelson*.

Ward, Robert (b 1917)
American composer. He has written six operas in a readily accessible style. They are *He Who Gets Slapped* (New York, 17 May 1956; libr Bernard Stambler, after Leonid Andreyev), the highly successful THE CRUCIBLE, *The Lady From Colorado* (Central City, 3 July 1964; libr Stambler, after Homer Croy; revised version *Lady Kate*, Ohio, 8 June 1994), *Claudia Legare* (Minneapolis, 14 Apr 1978; libr Stambler, after Henrik Ibsen's *Hedda Gabler*), *Abelard and Héloise* (Charlotte, 19 Feb 1982; libr Jan Hartman) and *Minutes Till Midnight* (Miami, 4 June 1982; libr Daniel Lang).

Warren, Leonard (b Warenoff) (1911–60)
American baritone, particularly associated with the Italian repertory, especially Verdi. One of the greatest of all Verdi baritones, his voice was large, rich, beautiful and powerful with a thrilling upper register. A forthright stage performer who also won great popularity as a radio and television singer, he created Ilo in Menotti's *The Island God*. He died on stage during a performance of *La Forza del Destino* at the Metropolitan Opera, New York.

Warsaw National Opera
Poland's principal opera company, it performs at the Teatr Wielki (Grand Theatre), which was designed by Antonio Corazzi and which is the world's largest theatre. Opened on 24 Sept 1833, it was largely destroyed by bombs in 1944; it reopened (cap 2,150) on 20 Nov 1965. Musical directors have included Karol Kurpiński, Tomasz Nidecki, Moniuszko, Cesare Tromboni, Emil Młynarski, Jerzy Semkow, Witold Rowicki, Jerzy Krenz, Robert Satanowski, Kazimierz Kord and Sł awomir Pietras. The theatre has an associated chamber opera company.

Washington
see OPERA SOCIETY OF WASHINGTON

Water Carrier, The
see DEUX JOURNÉES, LES

Watersprite
Bass role in Dvořák's *Rusalka*. He is Rusalka's father.

Watson, Claire (b McLamore) (1927–86)
American soprano, particularly associated with Mozart and Strauss roles. Her beautiful voice was allied to a fine technique, outstanding musicianship and a warm and charming stage personality.

Watson, Lillian (b 1947)
British soprano, particularly associated with Mozart and other SOUBRETTE roles. She possesses a bright voice of considerable agility which she uses intelligently and she has a captivating and delightful stage personality, especially in comedy.

Watts, Helen (b 1927)
British mezzo, particularly associated with Händel and Wagner roles. Possessor of a rich and beautiful voice used with outstanding musicianship and technique, she was best known as a concert artist. Her operatic appearances were sadly infrequent.

Wat Tyler
Opera in prologue and two acts by Bush. 1st perf Leipzig, 6 Sept 1953; libr by Nancy Bush. Principal roles: Wat Tyler (bar), Margaret (sop), John Ball (bass), Richard II (ten), Herdsman (bass), Bampton (bar), Minstrel (ten), Queen Mother (mezzo). Bush's finest opera, it tells (from a left-wing viewpoint) of events surrounding the Peasants' Revolt of 1381. It was a joint winner of the Arts Council's 1950 Festival of Britain competition.

Weber, Carl Maria von (1786–1826)
German composer. His first two operas were written in childhood: the first *Die Macht der Liebe und des Weins* (1798) was destroyed, and the second *Das Waldmädchen* (Freiburg, 24 Nov 1800; libr Carl von Steinsberg) was later reworked as *Silvana* (Frankfurt, 16 Sept 1810; libr Franz Carl Hiemer). Two further works, PETER SCHMOLL UND SEINE NACHBARN and the unfinished *Rübezahl* (1805; libr J.G. Rhode, after J.K.A. Musäus's *Volksmärchen der Deutschen*), followed before the SINGSPIEL ABU HASSAN, his first major success. In a review written in 1816, Weber referred to 'the kind of opera all Germans want – a self-contained work of art in which all elements, contributed by the arts in co-operation, disappear and re-emerge to create a new world'. His mature operas attempt to put this striking pre-vision of Wagner's theories into practice, and announce the birth of German romantic opera. The sensational success of DER FREISCHÜTZ marked a turning-point in German musical history. The THROUGH-COMPOSED EURYANTHE, although hampered by its dire libretto, represents a further advance, and OBERON, although written in a less complex style, contains some of his finest music. His other mature opera, the comedy DIE DREI PINTOS, was abandoned halfway through and was completed 60 years later by Mahler.

Weber's historical importance can hardly be overstated. His mature works laid the foundations of German national opera, influencing Marschner, Lortzing and, above all, Wagner, who developed Weber's techniques of LIETMOTIV, of dramatic recitative and of the symphonic use of the operatic orchestra. Weber was musical director at Dresden (1816–26), where he conducted the first performance of Spohr's *Faust*.

Weber, Ludwig (1899–1974)
Austrian bass, particularly associated with the German repertory, especially Wagner. Often regarded as the finest Wagnerian bass of the 20th century, he had a rich and warm voice of considerable power and had a sympathetic stage personality, especially as Gurnemanz and Rocco. He created Holsteiner in Strauss's *Friedenstag* and Saint Just in Einem's *Dantons Tod*.

Webster, Sir David (1903–71)
British administrator. A man of remarkable vision and judgement (with a shrewd nose for talent), he was general administrator of Covent Garden (1945–70). A tremendous showman, he nurtured and built up the infant company from nothing to a position in the late 1960s when many regarded it as the finest company in the world. He was also administrator of the London Opera Centre (1962–70).

We Come to the River
Opera in two acts by Henze. 1st perf London, 12 July 1976; libr by Edward Bond. Principal roles: General (bar), Governor (bar), Soldier 2 (ten), Old Woman (mezzo), Young Woman (sop), ADC (bass), Doctor (bass), Emperor (mezzo), Deserter (ten), Wife of Soldier 2 (sop), Rachel (sop). A vast (and, in the view of many, pretentious) work requiring over 50 soloists, it is an anti-war protest written from Henze's customary left-wing political viewpoint.

Weikl, Bernd (b 1942)
Austrian baritone, particularly associated with Mozart roles and with the German and Italian lyric repertories. He has a rich and warm voice used with fine musicianship and is an accomplished and

versatile singing-actor. He created Ferdinand in Einem's *Kabale und Liebe*.

Weill, Kurt (1900–50)
German composer. Writing in a light and satirical style, and often adopting popular musical forms and advocating left-wing political views, many of his stage works met with great success, particularly those written in collaboration with BERTOLT BRECHT. His first significant stage work DER PROTAGONIST was followed by *Royal Palace* (Berlin, 2 Mar 1927; libr Iwan Goll), DER ZAR LÄSST SICH PHOTOGRAPHIEREN, MAHAGONNY SONGSPIEL, DIE DREIGROSCHENOPER, AUFSTIEG UND FALL DER STADT MAHAGONNY, perhaps his most popular work, *Happy End* (Berlin, 2 Sept 1929; libr Brecht and Elisabeth Hauptmann) [R], DER JASAGER, *Die Bürgschaft* (Berlin, 10 Mar 1932; libr Caspar Neher, after J.G. Herder's *Der Afrikanische Rechtspruch*), *Der Silbersee* (Leipzig, Erfurt and Magdeburg, 18 Feb 1933; libr Georg Kaiser) [R] and the sung ballet DIE SIEBEN TODSÜNDEN, which is often staged as an opera.

Forced to leave Germany by the Nazis in 1935, Weill settled in the United States, where he wrote a number of further stage works, some of them in Broadway musical style. They include *Knickerbocker Holiday* (New York, 19 Oct 1938; libr Maxwell Anderson), STREET SCENE, DOWN IN THE VALLEY and *Lost in the Stars* (New York, 30 Oct 1949; libr Anderson, after Alan Paton's *Cry the Beloved Country*) [R]. Married to the singer LOTTE LENYA.

Weimar Opera
Opera in this German town in Thuringia is given at the Deutsches Nationaltheater (cap 857), which opened on 11 Jan 1908. Destroyed by bombs in 1945, it reopened on 28 Aug 1948. Musical directors have included Eduard Lassen.

Weinberger, Jaromír (1896–1967)
Czech composer. His first opera, written in Czech national style, was the highly successful SHVANDA THE BAGPIPER. None of his three other operas even began to approach this initial success. *Die Geliebte Stimme* (Munich, 28 Feb 1931; libr composer, after R. Michel), *The Outcasts of Poker Flat* (*Lidé z Pokerflatu*, Brno, 19 Nov 1932; libr Miloš Kareš, after Bret Harte) and the ambitious *Wallenstein* (*Valdštejn*, Vienna, 18 Nov 1937; libr Kareš, after Friedrich von Schiller) are all now forgotten. He committed suicide.

Weingartner, Felix von (1863–1942)
Austrian conductor and composer. One of the finest conductors of the early 20th century, particularly associated with the German repertory, he was musical director of the Mannheim Opera (1888–91), the Berlin State Opera (1891–8), the Vienna State Opera (1908–11 and 1935–6), the Hamburg Opera (1912–14), the Darmstadt Opera (1914–19) and the Vienna Volksoper (1919–24). He also composed 12 operas, including *Sakuntala* (Weimar, 23 Mar 1884; libr composer, after Kalidasa). Five times married, his autobiography, *Buffets and Rewards: a Musician's Reminiscences*, was published in 1937.

Weir, Judith (b 1954)
British composer. Her stage works, written in a eclectic and accessible style, include *A Night at the Chinese Opera* (Cheltenham, 8 July 1987; libr after C. Chun-Hsiang's *The Chao Family Orphan*), *The Vanishing Bridegroom* (Glasgow, 17 Oct 1990) and *Blond Eckbert* (London, 20 Apr 1994; libr composer, after Ludwig Tieck). [R]

Weisgall, Hugo (b 1912)
Czech-born American composer. His operas, written in both neo-classical and late expressionist style, are notable for their high literary quality. They are *The Night* (1932; libr after Sholem Asch), *Lillith* (1943; libr after Lois Elman), THE TENOR, arguably his finest opera, the MONODRAMA *The Stronger* (Westport, 9 Aug 1952; libr Richard Hart, after August Strindberg's *Den Starkare*; revised version New York, Jan 1955) [R], *Six Characters in Search of an Author* (New York, 26 Apr 1959; libr Denis Johnston, after Luigi Pirandello), *Purgatory* (Washington, 17 Feb 1961; libr after William Butler Yeats), *Athaliah* (New York, 17 Feb 1964; libr R.F. Goldman, after Jean Baptiste Racine's *Athalie*), *Nine Rivers From Jordan* (New York, 9 Oct 1968; libr Johnston), *Jennie, or the Hundred Nights* (New York, 22 Apr 1976; libr John Hollander, after Yukio Mishima), *Gardens of Adonis* (Omaha,

12 Sept 1992; libr John Olon-Scrymgeour, after André Obey) and *Esther* (New York, 8 Oct 1993; libr Kondek).

Weisse Rose, Die (*The White Rose*)
Opera in one act by U. Zimmermann. 1st perf Dresden, 17 June 1967; libr by Ingo Zimmermann. Revised version 1st perf Hamburg, 27 Feb 1986; libr revised by Wolfgang Willaschek. Principal roles: Sophie (sop), Hans (ten). It tells of Sophie and Hans Scholl, members of the Munich anti-Nazi resistance group, who were executed on 22 Feb 1943. Produced in over 30 cities within two years of its premiere, the revised version has proved to be one of the most successful chamber operas of recent years. [R]

Welche wonne, welche Lust
Soprano aria for Blönchen in Act II of Mozart's *Die Entführung aus dem Serail*, in which she expresses her delight on hearing of Belmonte's escape plan.

Welitsch, Ljuba (b Veličhkova) (b 1913)
Bulgarian soprano, particularly associated with dramatic Italian and German roles especially Salome. She had a silvery and sensuous voice with a soaring upper register, which was combined with a keen dramatic sense. Her prodigal use of her voice, combined with her fiery stage presence, made her one of the most thrilling operatic artists of the immediate post-war period. After 1959, she enjoyed a second career as an actress, appearing in a number of films.

Weller, Walter (b 1939)
Austrian conductor and violinist. Leader of the Vienna Philharmonic Orchestra from 1961, he turned to conducting in 1966. Since then, he has given notable performances of the German repertory, mainly at the Vienna State Opera. He was musical director of the Detmold Opera (1971–6) and the Basle Stadttheater (1994–). He conducted the first performance of Marcel Rubin's *Kleider Machen Leute*.

Wellesz, Egon (1885–1974)
Austrian composer and musicologist, resident in Britain after World War II. He wrote six operas, largely inspired by myth, in an eclectic style influenced both by Schönberg and by his researches into baroque opera. His most important operas are *Alkestis* (Mannheim, 20 Mar 1924; libr Hugo von Hofmannsthal, after Euripides) and the comedy *Incognita* (Oxford, 5 Dec 1951; libr E. Mackenzie, after William Congreve). His writings include *Essays on Opera* (1951).

Wellgunde
Mezzo role in Wagner's *Das Rheingold* and *Götterdämmerung*. She is one of the three Rhinemaidens.

Welser-Möst, Franz (b 1960)
Austrian conductor, particularly associated with 18th- and 19th-century German works, especially Mozart. Best known as an orchestral conductor, his operatic appearances have to date been sporadic and have sharply divided opinion. Musical director of the Zürich Opernhaus (1995–).

Welsh National Opera
Based at the New Theatre, Cardiff (cap 1,168) and touring throughout Wales and southern and central England, the company was formed in April 1946 by the baritone John Morgan, the conductor Idloes Owen and the businessman Dr Bill Smith. The company soon established a strong Verdi tradition, partly because of its superb chorus, which remained amateur until 1968. Recently, it has also been noted for its Janáček and Wagner performances and currently ranks as one of the most exciting and innovative European opera companies. Musical directors have been Idloes Owen, Leo Quayle, Frederick Berend, Vilém Tausky, Warwick Braithwaite, Sir Charles Groves, Bryan Balkwill, James Lockhart, Richard Armstrong, Sir Charles Mackerras and Carlo Rizzi.

Werle, Lars Johan (b 1926)
Swedish composer. He has written 12 operas in unconventional theatrical style, a number of which have met with considerable success in Sweden. They include the opera-in-the-round DREAMING ABOUT THÉRÈSE, *The Journey* (*Resan*, Hamburg, 2 Mar 1969; libr Lars Runsten, after P.C. Jersild's *Till Varmare Länder*), *Tintomara* (Stockholm, 18 Jan 1973; libr

Leif Söderström, after Carl Jonas Almqvist's *The Queen's Jewel*), *Medusa and the Devil* (*Medusan och Dvӓjulen*, Stockholm, 28 Nov 1973; libr composer, after E. Grave), *The Animals* (*Animalen*, Göteborg, 19 May 1975; libr Tage Danielsson), *Lionardo* (Stockholm, 31 Mar 1988; libr C. Fellborn), *The Ones Who Wait* (*Väntarna*, Stockholm, May 1990; libr I. Bergkwist, after Werner Aspenström) and *Hercules* (Stockholm, 24 Feb 1995).

Werther

Opera in four acts by Massenet. 1st perf Vienna, 16 Feb 1892; libr by Édouard Blau, Paul Milliet and Georges Hartmann, after Johann von Goethe's *Die Leiden des Jungen Werthers*. Principal roles: Werther (ten), Charlotte (mezzo), Sophie (sop), Albert (bar), Bailie (bass), Johann (bass), Schmidt (ten). Arguably Massenet's finest opera, its balance of dramatic urgency and irony with lyrical outpourings well catches the character of Goethe's hero.
Plot: Frankfurt, *c* 1780. The melancholy young poet Werther meets the Bailie's eldest daughter Charlotte and falls in love with her. He is distraught to learn that she is engaged to Albert. Obssessed with Charlotte, he decides to travel but keeps writing her impassioned letters while he is gone. Charlotte realizes that she feels something for Werther, and when he returns he extracts an admission of love from her before she orders him to leave. Albert suspects what has happened, and when a message arrives from Werther asking for the loan of his pistols, he agrees. Charlotte arrives to find that Werther has shot himself, and he dies in her arms. [R]

Werzlau, Joachim (b 1913)

German composer. His operas include *Regine* (Potsdam, 1964) and *Meister Röckle* (Berlin, 3 Oct 1976; libr Günther Deicke, after Ilse and Vilmós Korn's *Meister Röckle und Mister Flammfuss*) [R].

West Side Story

Musical in two acts by Bernstein. 1st perf Washington, 19 Aug 1957; libr by Arthur Laurents and Stephen Sondheim, after William Shakespeare's *Romeo and Juliet*. Principal roles: Maria (sop), Tony (ten), Anita (mezzo), Riff (bar). Bernstein's most successful stage work, it is written in Broadway musical idiom but is also regularly performed in the opera house.
Plot: New York, 1950s. The white Jets, led by Riff, and the Puerto Rican Sharks, led by Bernardo, are rival street gangs. Tony of the Jets meets Bernardo's sister Maria and the two fall in love. During an attempt to make peace between the two gangs, Tony accidentally kills Bernardo and is then himself killed by the Sharks. [R]

Wexford Festival

Founded by Dr T.J. Walsh (*d* 1988) in Oct 1951, this annual autumn opera festival in the Irish Republic is devoted to the performance of completely forgotten works. One of the most enterprising and popular European opera festivals, it has an enviable reputation for discovering major new vocal talent. The entire local community takes part in the mounting of the festival, which has a charming and welcoming atmosphere like no other. Three operas are given each year at the Theatre Royal (cap 555) and the orchestra is the Radio Telefis Eireann Symphony.

Weyse, Christoph (1774–1842)

German-born Danish composer. His tuneful operas, many in SINGSPIEL form, met with considerable success in their day but are now largely forgotten. They are *The Sleeping Draught* (*Sovedrikken*, Copenhagen, 21 Apr 1809; libr Adam Oehlenschläger, after Christoph Friedrich Bretzner), *Faruk* (Copenhagen, 30 Jan 1812; libr Oehlenschläger), *Ludlam's Cave* (Copenhagen, 30 Jan 1816; libr Oehlenschläger), *Floribella* (Copenhagen, 29 Jan 1825; libr C.J. Boye), the operetta *An Adventure in Rosenborg Garden* (*Et Eventyr i Rosenborg Have*, Copenhagen, 26 May 1827; libr J.L. Heiberg) and *The Feast at Kenilworth* (*Festen på Kenilworth*, Copenhagen, 6 Jan 1836; libr Hans Christian Andersen, after Sir Walter Scott's *Kenilworth*).

When I am laid in earth

Mezzo aria for Dido in Act III of Purcell's *Dido and Aeneas*, in which she takes leave of life.

Where e'er you walk

Tenor aria for Jupiter in Act II of Händel's *Semele*, in which he promises Semele that all nature will flourish wherever she goes.

Whirlpool, The (*Krútňava*)
Opera in six scenes by Suchoň. 1st perf Bratislava, 10 Dec 1949; libr by the composer and Štefan Hoza, after Milo Urban's *Over the Upper Mill*. Principal roles: Katrena (sop), Ondrej (ten), Štelina (bass), Zimoň (bass), Zimoňka (mezzo). The most successful of Suchoň's two operas, it is the only Slovak opera to have been performed internationally.
Plot: Early-20th-century Slovakia. Katrena's lover Jan has been murdered. She is reluctantly persuaded by her family to marry Ondrej, her previous admirer. In a drunken state, Ondrej admits to being Jan's murderer. He gives himself up and Jan's father Štelina agrees to care for Katrena and her child by Ondrej. [R]

White, Willard (b 1946)
Jamaican bass, particularly associated with Wagner and Mozart roles and with Golaud in *Pelléas et Mélisande* and Porgy in *Porgy and Bess*. He possesses a dark, rich and grainy voice of considerable power and range, used with fine musicianship and intelligence, and he has a commanding stage presence which is aided by his powerful physique. The first black singer to have developed a major career based in Britain, he is a singing-actor of outstanding ability and commitment. He created Boukman in Blake's *Toussaint* and has also played Othello for the Royal Shakespeare Company.

Widerspänstigen Zähmung, Der
(*The Wild Spinster Controlled*)
Comic opera in four acts by Götz. 1st perf Mannheim, 11 Oct 1874; libr by Joseph Victor Widmann, after William Shakespeare's *The Taming of the Shrew*. Principal roles: Katherina (sop), Lucentio (ten), Bianca (sop), Petruchio (bar), Baptista (bass). One of the most successful German comic operas of the second half of the 19th century, it is still quite often performed in German-speaking countries but is little known elsewhere.
Plot: 17th-century Padua. Lucentio loves Baptista's daughter Bianca, but Bianca's termagant elder sister Katherina is an obstacle to their marriage. To help the lovers, Petruchio agrees to marry Katharina. He woos her and eventually tames her. [R]

Widor, Charles Marie (1844–1937)
French composer and organist. Although best known as a composer of organ music, he also wrote four operas: *Maître Ambros* (Paris, 6 May 1886; libr A. Dorchain and François Coppée), *Le Capitaine Lys* (Lyon, 28 Mar 1900; libr E. Noel and L. d'Hève), *Les Pêcheurs de Saint-Jean* (Paris, 26 Dec 1905; libr Henri Cain) and *Nerto* (Paris, 27 Oct 1924; libr Maurice Léna, after Frédéric Mistral).

Wiener Blut (*Vienna Blood*)
Operetta in three acts by J. Strauss II. 1st perf Vienna, 25 Oct 1899; libr by Viktor Léon and Leo Stein. Principal roles: Gabriele (sop), Pepi (sop), Zedlau (ten), Franzi (sop), Josef (bar), Prime Minister (bar). A pastiche, it was arranged from other Strauss pieces by Adolf Müller Jr (1839–1901) and has always been one of the most popular Viennese operettas.
Plot: Vienna, 1815. During the Congress of Vienna, the ambassador Count Zedlau, although married to Gabriele, is having affairs with both the ballerina Franzi Cagliari and the model Pepi Pleininger, who is engaged to his valet Josef. His attempts to keep all these relationships going at once causes vast confusion, which is compounded by the intervention of the aged but amorous Prime Minister. After much intrigue, misunderstandings and false identities, Zedlau realizes that he still loves Gabriele and she forgives his peccadillos. [R]

Wiesbaden Opera
Opera in this German city in Hesse is given at the Grosses Haus (cap 1,041), which opened in Oct 1894. Always noted for its adventurous repertory policy, musical directors have included Otto Klemperer, Joseph Rosenstock, Karl Elmendorff, Wolfgang Sawallisch, Heinz Wallberg and Siegfried Köhler. The annual Wiesbaden May Festival dates originally from 1896; since 1950, it has been host to visiting companies from Eastern Europe.

Wilde, Oscar
see panel on page 608

Wildschütz, Der (*The Poacher*) or **Die Stimme der Natur** (*The Voice of Nature*)
Comic opera in three acts by Lortzing. 1st perf Leipzig, 31 Dec 1842; libr by the

· Oscar Wilde ·

The works of the Irish poet, playwright and novelist Oscar Fingal O'Flahertie Wilde (1856–1900) and the aesthetic movement of which he was the most famous exemplar form the subject of one of operetta's most devestating satires: Sullivan's *Patience.* Some 30 operas have been based on his writings. Below are listed, by work, those operas by composers with entries in this dictionary.

The Birthday of the Infanta		
Zemlinsky	*Der Geburstag der Infantin/Der Zwerg*	1922
The Canterville Ghost		
Křička	*The Gentleman in White*	1929
Sutermeister	*Das Gespenst von Canterville*	1964
Knaifel	*The Canterville Ghost*	1974
The Duchess of Padua		
Wagner-Régeny	*La Sainte Courtesane*	1930
A Florentine Tragedy		
Zemlinsky	*Eine Florentinische Tragödie*	1917
The Happy Prince		
Williamson	*The Happy Prince*	1965
The Importance of Being Ernest		
Castelnuovo-Tedesco	*L'Importanza di Esser Franco*	1962
Salomé		
Strauss	*Salome*	1905

composer, after August von Kotzebue's *Der Rehbock.* Principal roles: Baculus (bass), Gretchen (sop), Count Eberbach (bar), Baroness Freimann (sop), Nanette (sop), Baron Kronthal (ten), Countess (mezzo). Lortzing's most successful opera apart from *Zar und Zimmermann*, it remains very popular in Germany but is unaccountably almost never performed elsewhere.

Plot: Germany, 1803. The schoolteacher Baculus is caught accidentally poaching on Count Eberbach's estate. The Count's sister Baroness Freimann, disguised as a schoolboy, comes to his aid. She offers to disguise herself as Baculus's fiancée Gretchen and intercede with the Count on Baculus's behalf. After a great deal of intrigue and misunderstandings, Baculus is eventually forgiven. [R]

William Ratcliff

Opera in three acts by Cui. 1st perf St Petersburg, 26 Feb 1869; libr by the composer and Viktor Alexandrovich Krylov, after Alexei Nikolayevich Pleshcheyev's translation of Heinrich Heine's *Wilhelm Ratcliff.* Principal roles: Ratcliff (bar), Maria (sop), Douglas (ten), MacGregor (bass). Cui's most successful opera, it is nowadays all but forgotten, even in Russia. For plot see *Guglielmo Ratcliff.*

Williamson, Malcolm (b 1931)

Australian composer. His operas, written in a fluent and readily accessible style, have met with some success in Britain. They are OUR MAN IN HAVANA, *English Eccentrics* (Aldeburgh, 11 June 1964; libr Geoffrey Dunn, after Edith Sitwell), *The Happy Prince* (Farnham, 22 May 1965; libr composer, after Oscar Wilde) [R], the children's opera *Julius Caesar Jones* (London, 4 Jan 1966; libr Dunn) [R], THE VIOLINS OF ST JACQUES, perhaps his finest opera, *Dunstan and the Devil* (Cookham, 19 May 1967; libr Dunn), *The Growing Castle* (Dynevor, 13 Aug 1968; libr composer, after August Strindberg's *A Dream Play*), LUCKY PETER'S JOURNEY and *The Red Sea* (Dartington, 14 Apr 1972; libr composer).

William Tell
see GUILLAUME TELL

Willner, Alfred Maria (1859–1929)
Austrian librettist. He wrote, in whole or in part, many libretti, both operas and operettas. He provided texts for Fall (*Die Dollarprinzessin*), Goldmark (*Das Heimchen am Herd* and *Ein Wintermärchen*), Kálmán (*Die Faschingsfee*), Lehár (*Eva*, *Frasquita*, *Der Graf von Luxemburg*, *Wo die Lerche Singt* and *Zigeunerliebe*) and Nedbal (*Die Schöne Saskia*) amongst others. Puccini's *La Rondine* is based on one of his texts.

Willow Song ('Canzona del salice')
Soprano aria for Desdemona in: **1** Act III of Rossini's *Otello* ('Assisa al pie d'un salice'). **2** Act IV of Verdi's *Otello* ('Piangea cantando').

Wilson-Johnson, David (b 1950)
British baritone, particularly associated with 20th-century operas. He has a warm, beautiful and evenly produced voice which is used with great intelligence and musicianship. Best known as a concert artist, his operatic appearances have been intermittent but have included some notable performances in Russian opera and in modern works, notably as Messiaen's St Francis. He created Arthur in Maxwell Davies's *The Lighthouse*.

Windgassen, Wolfgang (1914–74)
German tenor, particularly associated with Wagnerian roles, especially Siegfried and Tristan. The leading HELDENTENOR of the post-war era, he was an artist of outstanding intelligence and musicianship, possessing a fine voice and an assured technique. He was director of the Stuttgart Opera (1972–4). His father **Fritz** (1883–1963) was also a tenor; his wife **Lore Wissmann** (*b* 1922) was a successful soprano.

Winter, Peter von (1754–1825)
German composer. He wrote 37 operas for Germany, Italy, Austria, London and Prague. Beginning by writing SINGSPIELS and ZAUBEROPERS, he later turned successfully to romantic opera. His most important works include DAS UNTERBROCHENE OPFERFEST, at one time one of the most popular of all German operas, *Das Labyrinth* (Vienna, 12 June 1798; libr Emanuel Schikaneder), which is a follow-up to *Die Zauberflöte*, *Zaira* (London, 29 Jan 1805; libr Filippo Pananti, after Voltaire's *Zaïre*), the Ossianic *Colmal* (Munich, 15 Sept 1809; libr M. von Collin) and *Maometto Secondo* (Milan, 28 Jan 1817; libr Felice Romani, after Voltaire's *Mahomet*).

Winterstürme
Tenor aria for Siegmund in Act I of Wagner's *Die Walküre*, in which he describes the succession of winter by spring.

Wishart, Peter (b 1921)
British composer. His five operas are *Two in the Bush* (Birmingham, 1959; libr Don Roberts), *The Captive* (Birmingham, 1960; libr Roberts), *The Clandestine Marriage* (Cambridge, 1 June 1971; libr Roberts, after David Garrick and George Coleman), *Clytemnestra* (London, 15 Feb 1974; libr Roberts) and *The Lady of the Inn* (Reading, 17 June 1983; libr Roberts, after Carlo Goldoni). His wife **Maureen Lehane** (*b* 1932) was a successful mezzo.

Witches' Sabbath
The title of Act II Scene II of Boito's *Mefistofele*.

Wixell, Ingvar (b 1931)
Swedish baritone, particularly associated with Mozart roles, the Italian repertory and with Mandryka in Strauss's *Arabella*. He possessed a bright and incisive voice of considerable power and had excellent diction and a good stage presence. Although he sang much Verdi, he was not a true Verdi baritone.

Woglinde
Soprano role in Wagner's *Das Rheingold* and *Götterdämmerung*. She is one of the three Rhinemaidens.

Wolf, Hugo (1860–1903)
Austrian composer. Although best known as a lieder composer (and also as a vitriolic critic), he also wrote two operas: the successful comedy DER CORREGIDOR and the unfinished *Manuel Venegas* (Mannheim, 1 Mar 1903, composed 1897; libr Moritz Hoernes, after Pedro de Alarcón's *El Niño de la Bola*).

Wolff, Albert (1884–1970)
French conductor and composer. One of the finest interpreters of the French repertory in the inter-war period, he was musical director of the Opéra-Comique, Paris (1921–4) and conducted the first performances of Poulenc's *Les Mamelles de Tirésias*, Milhaud's *La Brebis Égarée*, Bruneau's *Angélo Tyran de Padoue*, Ibert's *Angélique*, Charpentier's *Julien*, Laparra's *La Jota* and Bondeville's *Madame Bovary*. He also composed three operas: *Soeur Béatrice* (Nice, 1948, composed 1911; libr Maurice Maeterlinck), *Le Marchand des Masques* (Nice, 3 Apr 1914; libr L. Merlet and T. Salignac) and *L'Oiseau Bleu* (New York, 27 Dec 1919; libr Maeterlinck).

Wolf-Ferrari, Ermanno (1876–1948)
Italian composer. The principal figure of the early 20th-century Italian neo-classical school, his operas (nearly all drawn from Carlo Goldoni and other 18th-century comic writers) are notable for their grace, their rhythmic vitality, their charm and their sparkling orchestration. His first published opera *La Cenerentola* (Venice, 22 Feb 1901; libr M. Pezzè-Pascolato, after Charles Perrault's *Cendrillon*) was followed by LE DONNE CURIOSE, his first success, the popular I QUATRO RUSTEGHI, the one-act IL SEGRETO DI SUSANNA, perhaps his most enduring success, I GIOIELLI DELLA MADONNA, his one excursion into the VERISMO field, L'AMORE MEDICO, *Gli Amanti Sposi* (Venice, 19 Feb 1925; libr Giuseppe Pizzolato, Enrico Golisciani and Giovacchino Forzano, after Goldoni), *Das Himmelskleid* (Munich, 21 Apr 1927; libr composer, after Perrault), the remarkable SLY, his most ambitious opera, LA VEDOVA SCALTRA, the successful IL CAMPIELLO, LA DAMA BOBA and *Gli Dei a Tebe* (Hanover, 4 June 1943; libr L. Strecker and Mario Ghisalberti). His nephew **Manno** (1911–94) was a conductor.

Wolfram von Eschenbach
Baritone role in Wagner's *Tannhäuser*. Tannhäuser's friend, he is the historical minstrel-knight (*fl c* 1170–1220).

Wolf's Glen Scene
The title usually given to Act II Scene II of Weber's *Der Freischütz*, in which the free-shooting bullets are cast. It remains unsurpassed as a musical depiction of the macabre.

Wood, Sir Henry (1869–1944)
British conductor. He conducted a considerable amount of opera in the early part of his career, including the first performance of Standford's *Shamus O'Brien*, but later devoted himself entirely to the concert hall. The famous annual Promenade Concerts at London's Royal Albert Hall are his lasting memorial. His autobiography, *My Life of Music*, was published in 1938. His first wife **Olga Urussov** (*d* 1909) was a successful soprano.

Woodbird
Soprano role in Wagner's *Siegfried*.

Wordsworth, Miss
Soprano role in Britten's *Albert Herring*. She is the schoolmistress.

Workshop
A term which describes an organization devoted to teaching the techniques of operatic performance to students or amateurs by the preparation of operatic scenes. Opera workshops are most frequently found in the United States.

Wotan
Baritone role in Wagner's *Das Rheingold*, *Die Walküre* and *Siegfried* (in which last he is disguised as the Wanderer). Fricka's husband, he is the ruler of the gods.

Wotan's Farewell
The title usually given to Wotan's final monologue in Act III of Wagner's *Die Walküre*, in which he takes leave of Brünnhilde.

Wozzeck
Opera in three acts by Berg. 1st perf Berlin, 14 Dec 1925; libr by the composer, after Georg Büchner's *Woyzeck*. Principal roles: Wozzeck (bar), Marie (sop), Drum-Major (ten), Doctor (bass), Captain (ten), Margaret (mezzo), Andres (ten), Idiot (ten). Berg's first opera, sometimes regarded as the greatest of all 20th-century operas, it is an intense setting of Büchner's play, combining freely-conceived atonality

· *Writers as librettists* ·

Famous writers, poets and playwrights have turned their attention all too infrequently to the writing of operatic libretti. Those who have done so include:

- Hans Christian Andersen: Gläser's *The Watersprites* and *The Wedding on Lake Como*, Hartmann's *The Raven*, Weyse's *The Feast at Kenilworth* and Bredal's *The Bride of Lammermoor*.
- Gabriele d'Annunzio: Pizzetti's *Fedra* and Mascagni's *Parisina*.
- W.H. Auden: Britten's *Paul Bunyan*, Henze's *Elegie für Junge Liebende* and *The Bassarids*, Nabokov's *Love's Labour's Lost* and Stravinsky's *The Rake's Progress*.
- Pierre-Augustin Caron de Beaumarchais: Salieri's *Tarare*.
- Arnold Bennett: Goossens's *Judith* and *Don Juan de Mañara*.
- Bjørnstjerne Bjørnson: Grieg's *Olav Trygvason*.
- Pedro Calderón de la Barca: Hidalgo's *La Púrpura de la Rosa* and *Celos Aun del Aire Matan*.
- Italo Calvino: Berio's *La Vera Storia* and *Un Rè in Ascolto* and Liberovici's *La Panchina*.
- G.K. Chesterton: Holbrooke's *The Snob*.
- Paul Claudel: Milhaud's *Christophe Colomb* and *Les Choëphores* and Honegger's *Jeanne d'Arc au Bûcher*.
- Jean Cocteau: Honegger's *Antigone*, Stravinsky's *Oedipus Rex*, Poulenc's *Le Gendarme Incompris* and *La Voix Humaine* and Milhaud's *Le Pauvre Matelot*.
- Colette: Ravel's *L'Enfant et les Sortilèges*.
- Charles Dickens: Hullah's *The Village Coquettes*.
- John Dryden: Purcell's *The Indian Queen*, *King Arthur* and *The Tempest*.
- Alexandre Dumas père: Monpou's *Piquillo*.
- Umberto Eco: Berio's *Opera*.
- E.M. Forster: Britten's *Billy Budd*.
- Christopher Fry: Penderecki's *Paradise Lost*.
- John Gay: Händel's *Acis and Galatea* and Pepusch's *The Beggar's Opera* and *Polly*.
- Carlo Goldoni: Galuppi's *Il Filosofo di Campagna*, Piccinni's *La Buona Figliuola* and many others.
- A.P. Herbert: Holbrooke's *The Sailor's Arms* and Phyllis Tate's *The Policeman's Serenade*.
- Ted Hughes: Crosse's *The Story of Vasco*.
- Victor Hugo: Bertin's *Esmeralda*.
- Doris Lessing: Glass's *The Making of the Representative for Planet 8*.
- Maurice Maeterlinck: Dukas's *Ariane et Barbe-Bleue*.
- Iris Murdoch: William Mathias's *The Servants*.
- Dorothy Parker: Bernstein's *Candide*.
- J.B. Priestley: Bliss's *The Olympians*.
- Victorien Sardou: Offenbach's *Le Roi Carotte* and *Fantasio*, Saint-Saëns's *Les Barbares* and Bizet's unfinished *Grisélidis*.
- Gertrude Stein: Thomson's *Four Saints in Three Acts* and *The Mother of Us All*.
- Ivan Turgenev: Viardot-García's *Le Dernier Sorcier*, *L'Ogre* and *Trop de Femmes*.
- Paul Verlaine: Chabrier's *Vaucochard et Fils Premier* and *Fisch-Ton-Kan*.
- Voltaire: Rameau's *Samson*, *La Princesse de Navarre* and *Le Temple de la Gloire*.
- Tennessee Williams: Banfield's *Lord Byron's Love-Letter*.
- Émile Zola: Bruneau's *La Rêve*, *Lazare*, *Messidor*, *L'Ouragan*, *L'Enfant-Roi*, *Naïs Micoulin* and *Les Quatre Journées*.
- Stefan Zweig: Strauss's *Die Schweigsame Frau*.

see also BRECHT; GILBERT; GOETHE; HOFMANNSTHAL; MOLIÈRE; ROUSSEAU

with a highly complex formal structure. The title-role, described by Tito Gobbi as 'that tragic torn-off rag of humanity', is one of the most demanding musico-dramatic roles in the repertory.

Plot: Leipzig, 1821. To support the son whom he has had by his common-law wife Marie, the poor soldier Wozzeck shaves the Captain and submits to the Doctor's medical experiments. Wozzeck

· *Writers in opera* ·

A number of novelists, poets and playwrights appear as operatic characters, including:

- Anakreon in Cherubini's *Anacréon*, Grétry's *Anacréon chez Polycrate* and Rameau's *Anacréon*.
- Aristophanes in Telemann's *Der Geduldige Socrates*.
- Pierre-Augustin Caron de Beaumarchais in Corigliano's *The Ghosts of Versailles*.
- Giovanni Boccaccio in Suppé's *Boccaccio*.
- John Bunyan in Vaughan Williams's *The Pilgrim's Progress*.
- Lord Byron in Meale's *Mer de Glace* and Thomson's *Lord Byron*.
- Svatopluk Čech in Janáček's *The Excursions of Mr Brouček*.
- Miguel de Cervantes Saavedra in J. Strauss's *Das Spitzentuch der Königin*.
- Thomas Chatterton in Leoncavallo's *Chatterton*.
- André Chénier in Giordano's *Andrea Chénier*.
- George Crabbe in Britten's *Peter Grimes*.
- Dante Alighieri in Godard's *Dante et Béatrice* and Rachmaninov's *Francesca da Rimini*.
- Alexandre Dumas père in Giordano's *Andrea Chénier*.
- José Ignacio de Espronceda in Torroba's *El Poeta*.
- Jean Froissart in Sallinen's *The King Goes Forth to France*.
- Johann von Goethe in Lehár's *Friederike*.
- Ernest Hemingway in Yuri Ghazaryan's *Ernest Hemingway*.
- E.T.A. Hoffmann in Offenbach's *Les Contes d'Hoffmann*.
- Musa Jalil in Zhiganov's *Musa Jalil*.
- Jakob Michael Lenz in Lehár's *Friederike* and Rihm's *Jakob Lenz*.
- Lucan in Monteverdi's *L'Incoronazione di Poppea*.
- Martin Luther in Křenek's *Karl V*.
- John Milton in Spontini's *Milton*.
- Thomas Moore in Thomson's *Lord Byron*.
- Ovid in Gagliano's *La Dafne*.
- Petrarch in Granados's *Petrarca*.
- Edgar Allan Poe in Argento's *The Voyage of Edgar Allan Poe*.
- Marcel Proust in Schnittke's *Life With an Idiot*.
- Philippe Quinault in Isouard's *Lully et Quinault*.
- François Rabelais in Ganné's *Rabelais*.
- Arthur Rimbaud in Kevin Volans's *The Man Who Strides the Wind*.
- Jean-Jacques Rousseau in Dalayrac's *L'Enfance de Jean-Jacques Rousseau*.
- Sappho in Pacini's *Saffo* and Gounod's *Sapho*.
- William Shakespeare in Thomas's *Le Songe d'une Nuit d'Été*.
- Percy Bysshe Shelley in Meale's *Mer de Glace*.
- Torquato Tasso in Donizetti's *Torquato Tasso*, García's *La Mort de Tasse* and Pedrell's *Tasse à Ferrare*.
- Virgil in Rachmaninov's *Francesca da Rimini*.
- Voltaire in Bernstein's *Candide*.

discovers that the frustrated Marie has been having an affair with the Drum-Major, who taunts Wozzeck about it and beats him up. Wozzeck cuts Marie's throat in the woods and throws the dagger into a pond. Returning to the pond in search of the dagger, he wades in and drowns himself. Marie's body is discovered and the local children tell her uncomprehending child that his mother is dead. [R]

Wreckers, The
Opera in three acts by Smyth. 1st perf Leipzig, 1 Nov 1906; libr by Harry Brewster, after his own play. Principal roles: Thirza (mezzo), Mark (ten), Pascoe (bass), Avis (sop), Lawrence (bar). Often regarded as Smyth's finest opera, it was successful in its time but is nowadays virtually never performed.
Plot: Late-18th-century Cornwall. The local inhabitants pray for ships to be sent to the coast so that they can wreck and despoil them. Their savagery revolts Thirza, wife of the headman Pascoe. With her lover Mark (who has abandoned his former love Avis), she lights warning fires on the cliffs. They are discovered, however, and are locked in a cave where they will be drowned by the rising tide. [R]

Writers
see AESCHYLUS; ANDERSEN; ANNUNZIO; ARIOSTO; AUDEN; BEAUMARCHAIS; BRECHT; BYRON; CERVANTES; CHEKHOV; COCTEAU; CORNEILLE; DANTE; DICKENS; DOSTOYEVSKY; DUMAS; EURIPIDES; GILBERT; GOETHE; GOGOL; GOLDONI; GOZZI; HOFFMANN; HOFMANNSTHAL; HUGO; LORCA; LYTTON; MAETERLINCK; MÉRIMÉE; MOLIÈRE; OSTROVSKY; POE; PUSHKIN; RACINE; SARDOU; SCHILLER; SCOTT; SHAKESPEARE; SOPHOCLES; TOLSTOY; VOLTAIRE; WILDE; ZOLA

Wunderlich, Fritz (1930–66)
German tenor, particularly associated with Mozart and lyrical German roles and with Viennese operetta. The outstanding German lyric tenor of the post-war era, his career was cut short by his early death in an accident. He had a suave and beautiful voice used with outstanding musicianship, and he had a good stage presence. He created Tiresias in Orff's *Oedipus der Tyrann* and Christoph in Egk's *Die Verlobung in San Domingo*.

Wuppertal Opera
The opera house (cap 845) in this German town in North Rhine-Westphalia opened on 14 Oct 1956. The company is noted for its progressive repertory policy and for its encouragement of young talent. Musical directors have included Hans-Georg Ratjen, János Kulka and Peter Gülke.

Wurm
Bass role in Verdi's *Luisa Miller*. He is Count Walther's evil retainer.

Wuthering Heights
Opera in prologue and four acts by Herrmann. 1st perf Portland, 6 Nov 1982 (composed 1950); libr by Lucille Fletcher, after Emily Brontë's novel. Principal roles: Heathcliff (bar), Nelly (mezzo), Earnshaw (bar), Mr Lockwood (bass), Cathy (sop), Joseph (bass), Edgar and Isabella Linton (ten and mezzo). Herrmann's most ambitious composition, it is a straightforward setting of the novel. [R]

X

X: the Life and Times of Malcolm X
Opera in three acts by Davis. 1st perf New York, 28 Sept 1986; libr by Thulani Davis. Principal roles: Malcolm (bar), Elijah (ten), Ella (mezzo), Louise (sop), Reginald (b-bar). Davis's first opera, which incorporates jazz and rap idioms, it deals with the life of the radical black rights activist Malcolm X (1925–65). [R]

Xenakis, Iannis (b 1922)
Greek composer (and also an architect). An influential leader of the extreme avant-garde, his music is based on the mathematics of probability and chance, and employs computers. He has written a number of musical theatre pieces, mainly settings of Greek tragedies, of which the most nearly operatic is *The Bacchae* (London, 1 Sept 1993; a setting of C.K. Williams's translation of Euripides).

Xenia
The daughter of Tsar Boris, she appears as soprano role in: **1** Moussorgsky's *Boris Godunov*. **2** Dvořák's *Dimitrij*.

Xerxes
see SERSE

Ximena, Donna
Soprano role in Gazzaniga's *Don Giovanni*. She is a lady from Villena. She is the one character not used by Mozart and da Ponte in their version.

Xyndas, Spyridon (c 1812–96)
Greek composer. He wrote seven operas, of which the most important is the political satire *The Parliamentary Candidate* (*O Ypopifios Vouleftis*, Corfu, Oct 1867; libr I. Rinopoulos), which was the first opera written to a Greek libretto. Most of his music was destroyed in the bombing of Corfu during World War II.

Y

Yamadori, Prince
Baritone role in Puccini's *Madama Butterfly*. He is one of Cio-Cio-San's suitors.

Yan Tan Tethera
Opera in one act by Birtwistle. 1st perf London, 5 Aug 1986; libr by Tony Harrison. Principal roles: Alan (bar), Hannah (sop), Caleb (bar), Bad Un (ten), Ram (bass). Perhaps Birtwistle's most successful opera, it is a work of great orchestral complexity and of haunting, almost mesmeric beauty. Its title derives from an ancient counting mnemonic.
Plot: Legendary Wiltshire. The northern shepherd Alan has come south with his wife Hannah. The local shepherd Caleb Raven is jealous both of Alan's wife and of his growing flock, and seeks the aid of the Bad Un to drive Alan away. Alan is locked into a hill by the spell of the Bad Un's piping, and Hannah gives birth to twins which the Bad Un steals. For seven years, Hannah tends the flocks alone, rejecting Caleb's advances and offers of gold plundered from the hill graves. When Caleb uses one of Alan's spells to open the hill in which Alan is locked so as to steal the gold in it, Alan is released but Caleb is locked inside for ever. Alan and Hannah are reunited and their children are restored to them.

Yaroslavna
Soprano role in Borodin's *Prince Igor*. She is Igor's wife.

Yeletsky, Prince
Baritone role in Tchaikovsky's *The Queen of Spades*. He is Lisa's fiancé.

Yeomen of England, The
Baritone aria for the Earl of Essex in Act I of German's *Merrie England*, sung in praise of the sterling qualities of the yeoman class.

Yeomen of the Guard, The or **The Merryman and His Maid**
Operetta in two acts by Sullivan. 1st perf London, 30 Oct 1888; libr by W.S. Gilbert. Principal roles: Jack Point (bar), Elsie (sop), Fairfax (ten), Phoebe, Sgt and Leonard Meryll (mezzo, bass and ten), Shadbolt (b-bar), Dame Carruthers (mezzo), Sir Richard (b-bar), Kate (sop). One of the best-loved and much the most serious of the Savoy Operas, it was an instant success which enjoyed an initial run of over 450 performances. For it, Sullivan provided perhaps the finest operatic overture by any British composer.
Plot: Tower of London, 16th century. Col Fairfax is condemned to death. He tells the Lieutenant of the Tower, Sir Richard Cholmondeley, that he wishes to marry before his death in order to thwart the machinations of a relative. Sir Richard encounters the poor strolling players Jack Point and his sweetheart Elsie Maynard, and persuades Elsie to become a bride for one day. Meanwhile, Sgt Meryll is determined to engineer Fairfax's escape. His daughter Phoebe wheedles the key to Fairfax's cell from her admirer the jailer Wilfred Shadbolt, and Fairfax is disguised as Meryll's son Leonard, who has been appointed a yeoman but who is not known at the Tower. News arrives that Fairfax had been reprieved, but that the warrant had been deliberately held up by his relative. Fairfax reveals himself and claims Elsie as his wife. Having come to love him, Elsie readily accepts him. The heartbroken Point collapses at her feet. [R]

Yerma
Opera in three acts by Villa-Lobos. 1st perf Santa Fe, 12 Aug 1971 (composed 1956): a virtual word-for-word setting of Federico García Lorca's play. Principal roles: Yerma (sop), Juan (ten), Víctor (bar), María (mezzo), Dolores (mezzo). Arguably Villa-Lobos's finest opera, which incorporates folkloric elements and some exotic Brazilian instruments, it is only very rarely performed.
Plot: Early-20th-century Spain. Yerma assures her husband Juan of her love for

him, despite their lack of children. Her yearning for a child is heightened when her friend María joyously announces her pregnancy, and also when her childhood sweetheart Víctor appears. In desperation, she vainly seeks aid from the sorceress Dolores. Although her honour refuses to allow her to have a casual affair, Juan's inadequacy and indifference enrage her. In a fury, she strangles Juan, and then realizes that her chance of a child has been lost for ever.

Yniold
Soprano trouser role in Debussy's *Pelléas et Mélisande*. He is Golaud's young son. The role is occasionally sung by a treble.

Yodelling (from the German *jodel*)
A method of male vocal production which consists of frequent alterations between the natural voice and falsetto. Used for simple dance-like melodies, it is widely practised in the Austrian Tyrol. There are operatic examples of its use in Offenbach's *La Belle Hélène* and Rossini's *Il Viaggio a Reims*.

Yolanta
see IOLANTA

Young, Alexander (b 1920)
British tenor, particularly associated with Händel and Mozart roles and with Tom Rakewell. One of the most stylish and musicianly British tenors of the post-war era, he created Charles Darnay in Benjamin's *A Tale of Two Cities*, Philippe in Berkeley's *A Dinner Engagement*, Popristchin in Searle's *Diary of a Madman* and Cicero in Hamilton's *The Catiline Conspiracy*.

Ysaÿe, Eugène (1858–1931)
Belgian violinist, composer and conductor, brother of the pianist and composer Théophile Ysaÿe. Best known as a composer of violin music, he also wrote one opera (to his own libretto in Walloon), PETER THE MINER.

Yugoslavia
see BELGRADE OPERA

Yugoslavian opera composers
see CROATIAN OPERA COMPOSERS; SERBIAN OPERA COMPOSERS; SLOVENIAN OPERA COMPOSERS

Yuri
1 Baritone role in Tippett's *The Ice Break*. Lev and Nadia's son, he is Gayle's boyfriend. **2** Tenor role in Tchaikovsky's *The Enchantress*. He is Prince Nikita's son. **3** Bass role in Rimsky-Korsakov's *The Invisible City of Kitezh*. He is Prince Vsevelod's father. **4** Bass role in Rimsky-Korsakov's *The Maid of Pskov*. He is Olga's presumed father.

Yurisich, Gregory (b 1951)
Australian baritone, particularly associated with Mozart and Rossini roles, especially William Tell. He possesses a strong, gritty and incisive voice of considerable range which is used with intelligence and musicianship, and he has a good stage presence. He created Alcibiades in Oliver's *Timon of Athens* and Cadmus in Buller's *The Bacchae*.

Z

Zaccaria
Bass role in Verdi's *Nabucco*. The prophet of Israel, he is a conflation of the biblical Jeremiah and Ezekiel.

Zaccaria, Nicola (b Zachariou) (b 1923)
Greek bass, particularly associated with the Italian repertory. He possessed a rich and imposing voice of considerable power and had a good stage presence. He created the Third Tempter in Pizzetti's *L'Assassinio nella Cattedrale*. Married to the mezzo MARILYN HORNE.

Zafred, Mario (1922–87)
Italian composer and critic. His operas, similar in style to 'orthodox Soviet' music and reflecting his left-wing political views, include *Amleto* (Rome, 1961; libr composer and L. Zafred, after Shakespeare's *Hamlet*) and *Wallenstein* (Rome, 1965; libr composer and Zafred, after Friedrich von Schiller). He was artistic director of the Teatro Comunale Giuseppe Verdi, Trieste (1966) and the Rome Opera (1968–74) and was also music critic of the Rome *Unità* (1949–56).

Zagreb
see CROATIAN NATIONAL OPERA

Zagrosek, Lothar (b 1942)
German conductor, particularly associated with Mozart and with post-war operas, especially *Die Soldaten* by Zimmermann. One of the leading contemporary exponents of 20th century opera, he was musical director of the Krefeld Opera, the Paris Opéra (1986–8) and the Leipzig Opera (1990–). He conducted the first performances of Höller's *Der Meister und Margarita* and Jörg Herchet's *Nachtwache*.

Zaida
Mezzo role in Rossini's *Il Turco in Italia*. She is Selim's old love.

Zaïde
Unfinished opera in two acts by Mozart (K 344). 1st perf Frankfurt, 27 Jan 1866 (composed 1779); libr by Johann Andreas Schachtner, after Joseph von Friebert's libretto, itself based on Franz Josef Sebastiani's *Das Serail*. Principal roles: Zaïde (sop), Gometz (ten), Allazim (bass), Soliman (ten), Osmin (bar). The performing edition of this SINGSPIEL, elements of which hint at the later *Die Entführung aus dem Serail*, was prepared by Johann Anton André from the 15 musical numbers which survive.
Plot: 16th-century Turkey. Zaïde, the favourite of Sultan Soliman, takes pity on Gometz, the Sultan's European captive, and provides him with money for an escape. Gometz escapes with the aid of the Sultan's renegade servant Allazim, but is recaptured by the captain of the guard Osmin. [R]

Zaira
Opera in two acts by Bellini. 1st perf Parma, 16 May 1829; libr by Felice Romani, after Voltaire's *Zaïre*. Principal roles: Zaira (sop), Corasmino (ten), Orosmane (bass), Nerestano (mezzo), Lusignano (bass). The least successful of Bellini's mature operas and nowadays only very rarely performed, much of the music was incorporated into I CAPULETI E I MONTECCHI.
Plot: Jerusalem, Crusading times. The orphaned French slave Zaira is to wed the Sultan Orosmane. She is reunited with her father Lusignano and her brother Nerestano, who are horrified that her marriage involves the renunciation of her religion. Zaira promises the dying Lusignano that she will not abandon her faith. Orosmane thwarts her escape with Nerestano and – believing Nerestano to be Zaira's lover – he stabs them both. When the dying Zaira tells him the truth, Orosmane kills himself in remorse.

Zaïs
Opera-ballet in prologue and four acts by

Rameau. 1st perf Paris, 29 Feb 1748; libr by Louis de Cahusac. Principal roles: Zaïs (ten), Zélidie (sop), Oromasès (bass), Cindor (bass), Amour (mezzo). Described as a *ballet-héroïque*, it has recently received a few performances after over 200 years of complete neglect.
Plot: The genie of the air Zaïs loves the shepherdess Zélidie. Disguised as a shepherd, he finds his love returned, but feels that he must prove Zélidie's faithfulness. He transfers his powers to his confidant Cindor and orders him to seduce Zélidie. Despite the temptations offered by Cindor, she remains constant to Zaïs and the two are united. The pair experience destitution and suffering arising from Zaïs's loss of his powers. However, the king of the genies, Oromasès, restores Zaïs's powers and raises Zélidie to immortality. [R]

Zajc, Ivan (1832–1914)
Croatian composer. He was the leading figure behind the organization of the Zagreb Opera in 1870, and was one of the first composers to set Croatian libretti. His 21 operas include *Amelia* (Rijeka, 14 Apr 1860; libr after Friedrich von Schiller's *Die Räuber*), *Nikola Šubić Zrinjski* (Zagreb, 4 Nov 1876; libr Hugo Badalić, after Theodor Körner's *Zriny*) [R], his finest work, *Lizinka* (Zagreb, 12 Nov 1878; libr J.E. Tomić, after Alexander Pushkin's *Mistress Into Maid*) and *Our Father* (*Oče Naš*, Zagreb, 16 Dec 1911; libr J. Benešić, after François Coppée).

Zampa or **La Fiancée de Marbre** (*The Marble Fiancée*)
Opera in three acts by Hérold. 1st perf Paris, 3 May 1831; libr by Anne-Honoré Joseph de Mélesville. Principal roles: Zampa (bar), Camille (sop), Alphonse (ten), Rita (mezzo), Dandalo (bar), Daniel (bass). Hérold's most successful opera, it was enormously popular throughout the 19th century, but is nowadays only very rarely performed. The dashing overture is still popular in the concert hall.
Plot: 17th-century Sicily. The pirate chieftain Zampa attempts to abduct Camille, the fiancée of Alphonse de Monza – who is in fact Zampa's brother. He is foiled when a marble statue, inhabited by the spirit of his former wife Alice Manfredi, whose heart he broke, pulls him away and drowns him.

Zampieri, Mara (b 1941)
Italian soprano, particularly associated with Verdi and Puccini roles, especially the title-role in *Tosca* and Minnie in Puccini's *La Fanciulla del West*. One of the leading contemporary Italian sopranos, she possesses an exciting and intelligently-used *lirico spinto* voice and she has a fine stage presence.

Zancanaro, Giorgio (b 1939)
Italian baritone, particularly associated with the Italian repertory, especially Verdi. A true Verdi baritone, he possesses a dark, rich and velvety voice of considerable power and with an exciting upper register. He is a forthright if not especially subtle stage performer.

Zandonai, Riccardo (1883–1944)
Italian composer. One of the leading VERISMO composers, many of his 12 operas enjoyed considerable success in their day, and a few are still occasionally performed. His operas are the unperformed *La Coppa del Rè* (1906; libr G. Chiesa, after Friedrich von Schiller), *Il Grillo del Facolare* (Turin, 28 Nov 1908; libr Cesare Hanau, after Charles Dickens's *The Cricket on the Hearth*), *Conchita* (Milan, 14 Oct 1911; libr Maurice Vaucaire and Carlo Zangarini, after Pierre Louÿs's *La Femme et le Pantin*) [R Exc], which established his reputation, *Melenis* (Milan, 13 Nov 1912; libr Zangarini and M. Spiritini, after L. Bouillet), FRANCESCA DA RIMINI, his most successful and enduring opera, *La Via della Finestra* (Pesaro, 27 July 1919; libr Giuseppe Adami, after Eugène Scribe), the successful GIULIETTA E ROMEO, the once-popular I CAVALIERI DI EKEBÙ, *Giuliano* (Naples, 4 Feb 1928; libr Arturo Rossato, after J. da Varagine), *Una Partita* (Milan, 19 Jan 1933; libr Rossato, after Alexandre Dumas), *La Farsa Amorosa* (Rome, 22 Feb 1933; libr Rossato, after Pedro de Alarcón's *El Sombrero de Tres Picos*) and the unfinished *Il Bacio* (RAI, 10 Mar 1954, composed 1944; libr Rossato, after Gottfried Keller). His wife **Tarquinia Tarquini** (1883–1976) was a successful soprano, who created the title-role in *Conchita*.

Zanelli, Renato (b Morales) (1892–1935)
Chilean baritone and later tenor, particularly associated with dramatic German and Italian roles, especially the title-role in Verdi's *Otello*. Originally a successful baritone, he turned to tenor roles in 1924, and his early death from cancer cut short a brilliant career. He created the title-role in Pizzetti's *Lo Straniero*. His brother **Carlo Morelli** (1897–1970) was a successful baritone.

Zanetto
Opera in one act by Mascagni. 1st perf Pesaro, 2 March 1896; libr by Giovanni Targioni-Tozzetti and Guido Menasci, after François Coppée's *Le Passant*. Principal roles: Zanetto (mezzo), Silvia (sop). Moderately successful at its appearance, it is nowadays all but forgotten. It was originally written for performance by students at the Pesaro Conservatory.
Plot: 15th-century Italy. The noble Silvia meets and falls in love with the poor young wandering minstrel Zanetto. Despite the depth of their love, their social disparity is such that they realize that they must part for ever.

Zareska, Eugenia (1910–79)
Ukrainian mezzo, long resident at Covent Garden. Particularly associated with the French and Italian repertories, she had a good voice and was a fine singing-actress. She created a role in Martin's *Le Mystère de la Nativité*.

Zarewitsch, Der (*The Tsarevich*)
Operetta in three acts by Lehár. 1st perf Berlin, 21 Feb 1927; libr by Béla Jenbach and Heinrich Reichert, after Gabriele Zapolska-Scharlitt's play. Principal roles: Zarewitsch (ten), Sonja (sop), Mascha (sop), Iwan (ten). One of the most successful of Lehár's later works, it is still regularly performed in German-speaking countries.
Plot: Late-19th-century St Petersburg and Naples. Disguised as a Circassian soldier, the Russian ballerina Sonja overcomes both the anti-feminist and ascetic scruples of a young Russian prince. In Italy, the two fall in love. However, the prince is recalled to Russia to assume his public duties, and the lovers are parted for ever. [R]

Zar lässt sich Photographieren, Der
(*The Tsar Has His Photograph Taken*)
Opera in one act by Weill (Op 21). 1st perf Leipzig, 18 Feb 1928; libr by Georg Kaiser. Principal roles: Tsar (bar), Angèle (sop). A satire on anarchist conspiracy, it tells of the Tsar unwittingly foiling his would-be assassins during a visit to Paris. [R]

Zar und Zimmermann (*Tsar and Carpenter*) or **Die Zwei Peter** (*The Two Peters*)
Opera in three acts by Lortzing. 1st perf Leipzig, 22 Dec 1837; libr by the composer, after Georg Christian Römer's *Der Burgermeister von Saardam*, itself based on Anne-Honoré Joseph de Mélesville, Jean Toussaint Merle and Eugène Centiran de Boirie's *Le Bourgmestre de Sardam ou Les Deux Pierres*. Principal roles: Peter (bar), Peter Ivanov (ten), Marie (sop), van Bett (bass), Widow Browe (mezzo), Chateauneuf (ten). Lortzing's most successful and enduring opera, it is still regularly performed in German-speaking countries but for unaccountable reasons only seldom elsewhere.
Plot: Saardam (Holland), 1698. Peter the Great of Russia, disguised as Peter Michaelov, is working in the Dutch shipyards in order to learn nautical trades. He befriends the deserter Peter Ivanov, who is in love with Marie, daughter of the Bourgomaster van Bett. Asked whether Peter the Great is really in the shipyard, van Bett identifies the wrong Peter. The Russian and English Ambassadors are deceived, but the French Ambassador Marquis de Chateauneuf recognizes the real Tsar. Van Bett prepares to send Peter Ivanov home in state, whilst the real Tsar departs quietly for Russia. [R]

Zarzuela
see panel on page 620
see also SAINETE; TONADILLA

Zauberflöte, Die (*The Magic Flute*)
Opera in two acts by Mozart (K 620). 1st perf Vienna, 30 Sept 1791; libr by Emanuel Schikaneder, partly after Abbé Jean Terrasson's *Sethos*. Principal roles: Tamino (ten), Pamina (sop), Sarastro (bass), Papageno (bar), Queen of the Night (sop), Monostatos (ten), three

· *Zarzuela* ·

Similar to operetta, zarzuela is a Spanish musical stage work which often employs traditional Spanish material. It contains spoken dialogue and is usually of a comic nature. The term derives from the Spanish word *zarza* ('bramble'): its origins go back to the 17th century, when 'Fiestas de Zarzuela' were given at the Palacio la Zarzuela near Madrid; the palace took its name from the surrounding bramble bushes, and so the entertainments performed there were named after the palace. The earliest known zarzuela composer is Juan Hidalgo (*c* 1615–85), whose *Los Celos Hacen Estrellas* was first performed in *c* 1644. Librettists for early zarzuelas included both Pedro Calderón de la Barca and Félix Lope de Vega. During the 18th century, zarzuela became more formal (and much less popular), and the TONADILLA came into being as a reaction against this formality. In the mid-19th-century, zarzuela experienced a renaissance when Barbieri and other leading Spanish composers turned their attention to the genre, and its popularity became such that both the Teatro de la Zarzuela and the Teatro Apolo in Madrid were built to house it. There are a number of different varieties of zarzuela, of which the two most important are:

1 *Zarzuelita* or *género chico* (Spanish for 'little type'), which is in one act and is always on a comic subject.
2 *Zarzuela grande*, which is in three acts and often comes close to romantic opera in style and subject matter.

Still enormously popular in Spain, zarzuela has virtually never, however, been successfully exported. Perhaps the most successful of all zarzuelas are Barbieri's EL BARBERILLO DE LAVAPIÉS, Bretón's LA VERBENA DE LA PALOMA, Torroba's LUISA FERNANDA and Vives's BOHEMIOS and DOÑA FRANCISQUITA.

The following 22 zarzuela composers have entries in this dictionary:

Albéniz, Isaac
Arrieta y Corera, Emilio
Barbieri, Francisco
Bretón y Hernández, Tomás
Caballaro, Manuel Fernández
Chapí y Lorente, Ruperto
Chueca, Federico
Falla, Manuel de
Gatztambide, Joaquín
Giménez, Gerónimo
Granados, Enrique
Guerrero, Jacinto
Guridi, Jesús
Luna y Carné, Pablo
Panella, Manuel
Rodríguez de Hita, Antonio
Serrano, José
Sorozábal, Pablo
Soutullo, Reveriano
Torroba, Federico Moreno
Valverde Durán, Sanjuan
Vives, Amadeo

Ladies (sop, mezzo and mezzo), Speaker of the Temple (b-bar), Papagena (sop). Mozart's penultimate opera, it is a fairy-tale work overlaid with Masonic and humanist symbolism. The best-known example of ZAUBEROPER and the apotheosis of the SINGSPIEL form, it was an immediate success and has always remained one of the most popular of all operas.

Plot: Three Ladies save the prince Tamino from a monster and give him a portrait of Pamina, daughter of their mistress the Queen of the Night. He falls in love with Pamina's beauty, and the Queen charges him with rescuing her from the hands of the supposedly evil Sarastro, the priest of Isis. She gives him an enchanted flute to aid him through perils, and sends the bird-catcher Papageno with him as a guide. On arrival at the Temple of Isis, Tamino is told by the Speaker that only truth and wisdom reside within, and Sarastro bids him enter and learn. Pamina, lusted after by Sarastro's Moorish servant Monostatos, returns Tamino's love, and the two agree to undergo tests to prove their virtue and constancy. Papageno is also tested, and even though he makes a poor showing he is rewarded with Papagena. With the aid of the flute, Tamino and Pamina pass through the ordeals of fire and water. Sarastro gives Tamino the symbols of rule, and all celebrate the triumph of light over the powers of darkness represented by the defeated Queen of the Night. [R]

Zaubergeige, Die (*The Magic Fiddle*)
Opera in three acts by Egk. 1st perf Frankfurt, 22 May 1935; libr by the composer and Ludwig Andersen, after Count Franz Pocci's story. Revised version 1st perf Stuttgart, 2 May 1954. Principal roles: Kaspar (bar), Gretl (sop), Ninabella (sop), Amandus (ten), Guldensack (bass), Cuperus (bass). Egk's first opera, nowadays only rarely performed, it employs numbers based on popular melodies.
Plot: Legendary Germany. The serf Kaspar wishes to make his way in the world with his beloved Gretl, but lacks the money to buy his freedom. He encounters a beggar and is moved to give him the few coins that he has. The beggar turns out to be the earth spirit Cuperus, who gives Kaspar a magic fiddle whose power lasts so long as its owner renounces love. Kaspar becomes Spagatini, a rich and renowned virtuoso violinist. After a number of not always pleasant adventures, he returns the fiddle to Cuperus, prefering the faithful love of Gretl. [R Exc]

Zauberharfe, Die (*The Magic Harp*)
Melodrama in three acts by Schubert (D 644). 1st perf Vienna, 19 Aug 1820; libr by Georg von Hofmann. An ambitious MELODRAMA, and perhaps not strictly speaking an opera, it is nowadays all but forgotten, although the overture is well known as Schubert reused it for his incidental music to *Rosamunde*.

Zauberoper (German for 'magic opera')
A term used in Vienna in the late 18th and early 19th centuries to describe a type of SINGSPIEL which contained magic, sumptuous scenic effects, music by leading composers and ribald comedy. Fairy-tale themes, such as the Oberon story, were the most popular. Performances were given at the Theater auf der Weiden and later at Emanuel Schikaneder's Theater an der Wien. The best-known, and much the greatest example of the genre is Mozart's *Die Zauberflöte*.

Zazà
Opera in four acts by Leoncavallo. 1st perf Milan, 10 Nov 1900; libr by the composer, after Pierre Simon and Charles Berton's play. Principal roles: Zazà (sop), Milio (ten), Cascart (bar). Leoncavallo's most successful opera apart from *Pagliacci*, it is still performed from time to time.
Plot: St Étienne and Paris, 1890s. The music-hall singer Zazà falls in love with Milio Dufresne, having won his attentions on a bet. However, her partner Cascart, who is in love with her, leads her to the discovery that Milio is in fact already married and that he loves his wife. Realizing this, Zazà's affections turn to Cascart. [R]

Zazà, piccola zingara
Baritone aria for Cascart in Act IV of Leoncavallo's *Zazà*, in which he advises Zazà to return to her career.

Zdenka
Soprano trouser role in Strauss's *Arabella*. The Waldners' younger daughter, she has been brought up as a boy because her parents cannot afford to bring up two girls.

Zeani, Virginia (b Zehan) (b 1928)
Romanian soprano, particularly associated with the Italian repertory, especially Violetta in Verdi's *La Traviata*. A warm-voiced singer with an affecting stage presence, she won considerable success in BEL CANTO roles before turning to more dramatic roles. She created Blanche in Poulenc's *Dialogues des Carmélites* and the title-role in Banfield's *Alissa*. Married to the bass NICOLA ROSSI-LEMENI.

Zedda, Alberto (b 1928)
Italian conductor and musicologist, particularly associated with Rossini operas. He has produced outstanding critical editions, now in almost universal use, of a number of Rossini's major operas, notably *Il Barbiere di Siviglia*. He conducted the first performance of Viozzi's *La Giacca Dannata*. He was artistic director of La Scala, Milan (1992–93).

Zednik, Heinz (b 1940)
Austrian tenor, particularly associated with German character roles, especially Mime. Largely based at the Vienna State Opera from 1965, he is a fine singing-actor with a far better voice than most Germanic character tenors. He created the Regista in Berio's *Un Rè in Ascolto*, a role in Schnittke's *Gesualdo* and, for Einem, the Butler in *Der Besuch der Alten Dame* and Kalb in *Kabale und Liebe*.

Zeffirelli, Franco (b Gianfranco Corsi) (b 1923)
Italian producer, designer and film-maker. One of the leading post-war opera directors, he has been particularly associated with La Scala, Milan, and with Covent Garden, where he directed *Lucia di Lammermoor*, *Cavalleria Rusticana*, *Pagliacci*, *Alcina*, *Falstaff* and *Tosca*. He also directed the films of *La Traviata* (1983) and the controversial *Otello* (1986) and wrote the libretto for Barber's *Antony and Cleopatra*.

Zeffiretti lusinghieri
Soprano aria for Ilia in Act III of Mozart's *Idomeneo*, in which she begs the breezes go and tell Idamante of her love.

Zeit im Grunde, Die
Soprano monologue for the Marschallin in Act I of Strauss's *Der Rosenkavalier*, in which she muses on the effects of time.

Zeitoper (German for 'opera of the time')
A term used in Germany in the 1920s and 1930s to describe an opera which dealt – sometimes satirically – with contemporary themes and which often used or imitated current popular musical idioms. There are a number of examples by Weill, Hindemith and, particularly, Křenek.

Zeleński, Władysław (1837–1921)
Polish composer. The leading Polish opera composer after Moniuszko, his stage works, all of them unknown outside Poland, are nationalist in sentiment and make use of traditional Polish folk material. His four operas are *Konrad Wallenrod* (Lwów, 26 Feb 1885; libr Z. Sarnecki and W. Noskowski, after Adam Mickiewicz), *Goplana* (Cracow, 23 July 1896; libr L. German, after Julius Slowacki), *Janek* (Lwów, 4 Oct 1900; libr German) and *Old Fable* (*Stara Baśń*, Lwów, 14 Mar 1907; libr A. Bandrowski-Sas, after J.I. Kraszewski).

Zell, F. (b Camillo Walzel) (1829–95)
Austrian librettist. One of the most successful librettists of Viennese operetta, often writing in collaboration with RICHARD GENÉE, he provided texts for Genée (*Nanon* and *Der Seekadett*), Millöcker (*Der Bettelstudent*, *Gasparone* and *Gräfin Dubarry*), J. Strauss II (*Cagliostro in Wien*, *Die Lustige Krieg* and *Eine Nacht in Venedig*) and Suppé (*Boccaccio*, *Donna Juanita* and *Fatinitza*) amongst others.

Zeller, Carl (1842–98)
Austrian composer. He wrote one comic opera, but is best remembered for his six Viennese operettas, of which DER VOGELHÄNDLER remains widely popular. Of his other works, the most successful were *Der Vagabund* (Vienna, 30 Oct 1886; libr Moritz Mitzelberger-West and Ludwig Held) and *Der Obersteiger* (*The Master Miner*, Vienna, 5 Jan 1894; libr West and Held).

Zelmira
Opera in two acts by Rossini. 1st perf Naples, 16 Feb 1822; libr by Andrea Leone Tottola, after Dormont de Belloy's *Zelmire*. Principal roles: Zelmira (sop), Antenore (ten), Ilo (ten), Polidoro (bass), Emma (mezzo). Never one of Rossini's more successful operas, it is only very rarely performed.
Plot: Legendary Lesbos. Zelmira's father King Polidoro has been deposed. His usurper is killed and Antenore proclaims himself king and accuses Zelmira of having killed Polidoro – who is in fact hidden for safety in an underground vault. Zelmira's husband Ilo returns and is persuaded by lies to give credence to the charges against his wife. Ilo subsequently learns the truth and rescues Zelmira and Polidoro. Antenore is arrested and Polidoro is restored to his throne. [R]

Zémire et Azor
Opera in four acts by Grétry. 1st perf Fontainebleau, 9 Nov 1771; libr by Jean-Francois Marmontel, after Jeanne Marie le Prince de Beaumont's *La Belle et la Bête* and Pierre Claude Nivelle de la Chaussée's

Amour par Amour. Principal roles: Zémire (sop), Azor (ten), Sander (bar), Ali (ten), Fatme (mezzo), Lisbe (sop). Grétry's most successful opera, it is still occasionally performed.
Plot: Legendary Persia. Prince Azor has been given a beast's features by an evil fairy. The merchant Sander and his servant Ali are shipwrecked in a storm, losing all their goods. For cutting a rose at the harbour, Sander is arrested by Azor who demands the life of one of his three daughters, Zémire, Fatme and Lisbe. Zémire, the youngest of the three, resolves to give her own life, and goes to Azor's court. There, she learns that his normal appearance will only be restored when he can inspire love. Realizing his nobility, Zémire gradually comes to love him. The spell is broken and the two are united. [R]

Zemire und Azor
Opera in two acts by Spohr. 1st perf Frankfurt, 4 April 1819; libr by Johann Jakob Ihlée, after Jean-François Marmontel's libretto for Grétry. Principal roles: Zemire (sop), Azor (ten), Sander (bass), Ali (ten), Lisbe (sop), Fatme (sop). More serious than Grétry's version, it was successful in its time but nowadays – apart from the aria 'Rose softly blooming' – is all but forgotten. For plot see *Zémire et Azor*.

Zemlinsky, Alexander von (1871–1942)
Austrian composer and conductor. His eight operas, written in an orchestrally lush, late-romantic style, are *Sarema* (Munich, 10 Oct 1897; libr Adolf von Zemlinsky, after Rudolf von Gotschall's *Die Rose von Kaukasus*), *Es War Einmal* (*Once Upon a Time*, Vienna, 22 Jan 1900; libr Maximilian Singer, after Holger Drachmann's *Der var Engang*) [R], *Der Traumgörge* (Nürnberg, 11 Oct 1980, composed 1906; libr Leo Feld) [R], *Kleider Machen Leute* (Vienna, 2 Oct 1910; libr Ludwig Held, after Gottfried Keller) [R], EINE FLORENTINISCHE TRAGÖDIE, DER GEBURSTAG DER INFANTIN (or *Der Zwerg*), his finest opera, *Der Kreidekreis* (Zürich, 14 Oct 1933; libr composer, after Klabund) [R] and the unfinished *Der König Kandaules* (1935; libr Franz Blei, after André Gide's *Le Roi Candaule*). There has recently been a considerable revival of interest in his music, and performances are becoming more frequent. He was musical director of the Deutsches Theater, Prague (1911–27), where he conducted the first performance of *Erwartung*. He was also a distinguished teacher, whose pupils included Schönberg (later his brother-in-law) and Korngold.

Zenatello, Giovanni (1876–1949)
Italian tenor, particularly associated with heavier Italian roles, especially the title-role in Verdi's *Otello*. Beginning as a baritone, he turned to tenor roles within a year, and his powerful voice with its ringing high notes made him perhaps the finest Italian dramatic tenor of the early 20th century. He created Pinkerton in *Madama Butterfly*, Vassili in Giordano's *Siberia*, Lionetto de' Ricci in Cilea's *Gloria* and Aligi in Franchetti's *La Figlia di Iorio*. He instigitated the performance of opera at the Verona Arena, and in 1947 he was responsible for launching Maria Callas's international career. His wife **María Gay** (1879–1943) was a successful mezzo.

Zeno, Apostolo (1668–1750)
Italian poet and librettist, he was Pietro Metastasio's predecessor as court poet in Vienna. His many libretti, often on the theme of the conflict between passion and duty, and frequently written in collaboration with Pietro Pariati (1665–1733), were set by many composers. His texts were used by Albinoni, Bononcini, Bortnyansky, Caldara, Cherubini, Duni, Fux, Galuppi, Gasparini, Graun, Guglielmi, Händel, Hasse, Lotti, Mercadante Mysliveček, Paisiello, Pergolesi, Porpora, Sacchini, D. Scarlatti, Traetta, Vivaldi and Zingarelli amongst others.

Zerbinetta
Soprano role in Strauss's *Ariadne auf Naxos*. She is the star of the COMMEDIA DELL'ARTE troupe.

Zerlina
Soprano role in: **1** Mozart's *Don Giovanni*. She is a peasant girl engaged to Masetto. **2** Auber's *Fra Diavolo*. She is the daughter of the innkeeper Mathés.

Zhiganov, Nazib (b 1911)
Tartar composer. The leading Tartar composer, he was largely responsible for the establishment of a specifically Tartar

school of opera, employing indigenous folk styles and nationalist legendary or historical themes. His operas include *The Runaway* (*Kachkyn*, Kazan, 1939; libr Fayzy), *Freedom* (*Irek*, Kazan, 1940; libr Safin), *Tyulyak* (Kazan, 1945; libr Isanbet), *The Poet* (*Shagur*, Kazan, 1947; libr Fayzy) and *Musa Jalil* (Kazan, 1957; libr Fayzy), his finest opera which enjoyed considerable success in the former Soviet Union.

Ziani, Marc'Antonio (c 1653–1715)
Italian composer. He wrote over 40 operas, first for Venice and then for Vienna, all of which are nowadays forgotten. They include *La Pace Generosa* (Venice, 10 Feb 1700; libr Francesco Silvani, after Seneca's *Troades*) and *Caio Popilio* (Vienna, 9 June 1704; libr D. Cupeda). His uncle **Pietro Andrea** (1616–84) was also a composer who wrote 28 operas.

Žídek, Ivo (b 1926)
Czech tenor, particularly associated with the Czech repertory. One of the finest Czech tenors of the post-war period, he possessed a well-placed and firmly projected voice and had a good stage presence. He created Oleg Koševoj in Meytus's *The Young Guards* and the Inventor in Kašlík's *Krakatik*. He was administrator of the Prague National Theatre (1989–91).

Ziehrer, Carl Michael (1843–1922)
Austrian composer. Several of his many Viennese operettas were successful in their time but are nowadays only rarely performed. They include *Ein Deutschmeister* (Vienna, 30 Nov 1888; libr Richard Genée and B. Zappert), *Die Landstreicher* (*The Vagabonds*, Vienna, 26 July 1899; libr L. Krenn and C. Landau), his most successful work, *Der Fremdenführer* (*The Guide*, Vienna, 11 Oct 1902; libr Krenn and Landau) and *Der Schätzmeister* (*The Pawnbroker's Valuer*, Vienna, 10 Dec 1904; libr A. Engel and J. Horst).

Zigeunerbaron, Der (*The Gypsy Baron*)
Operetta in three acts by J. Strauss II. 1st perf Vienna, 24 Oct 1885; libr by Ignatz Schnitzler, after Maurus Jókai's *Saffi*. Principal roles: Barinkay (ten), Saffi (sop), Zsupán (bar), Arsena (sop), Czipra (mezzo), Ottokar (ten), Carnero (bar), Count Peter (bar), Mirabella (mezzo). An immediate success, it remains one of the most enduringly popular of all Viennese operettas.
Plot: Mid-18th-century Vienna and Banat (Hungary). Sándor Barinkay returns to claim his ancestral lands and finds that they have been occupied by gypsies. The irascible pig farmer Kálmán Zsupán hopes that Barinkay will marry his daughter Arsena, although she wishes to marry Mirabella's son Ottokar. However, Barinkay falls in love with the gypsy girl Saffi, foster-daughter of the fortune-teller Czipra. She turns out to be a princess and weds Barinkay, leaving Arsena free to marry Ottokar. [R]

Zigeunerliebe (*Gypsy Love*)
Operetta in three acts by Lehár. 1st perf Vienna, 8 Jan 1910; libr by Robert Bodanzky and Alfred Maria Willner. Principal roles: Jonel Bolescu (ten), Zorika (sop), Jozsi (ten), Ilona von Köröshaza (sop), Peter Dragotin (ten). Although never one of Lehár's most popular works, it is still occasionally performed in German-speaking countries. [R]

Zimmermann, Bernd-Alois (1918–70)
German composer, who wrote in atonal style. His only completed opera is the controversial and widely performed DIE SOLDATEN. A second opera, *Medea* (libr H.H. Jahnn), was left unfinished at the time of his suicide.

Zimmermann, Margarita (b 1942)
Argentinian mezzo, particularly associated with Mozart and Rossini roles and with the French repertory. She possesses a beautiful, rich and agile voice, used with a fine technique, and she has a good stage presence. She created the title-role in Piazzolla's *Maria di Buenos Aires*.

Zimmermann, Udo (b 1943)
German composer. His operas, written in serial style, have met with considerable success in Germany, particularly the chamber opera DIE WEISSE ROSE. His other stage works include *Levins Mühle* (Dresden, 27 Mar 1973; libr Ingo Zimmermann, after J. Brobowski), *Die Wundersame Schusterfrau* (Schwetzingen,

25 Apr 1982; libr composer and Eberhard Schmidt, after Federico García Lorca's *La Zapatiera Prodigosa*) and *Don Quichotte* (Berlin, 1992; libr after Miguel Cervantes). Administrator of the Leipzig Opera (1990–).

Zingara, La (*The Gypsy Girl*)
INTERMEZZO in two parts by Rinaldo da Capua. 1st perf Paris, 19 June 1753; librettist unknown. Principal roles: Nisa (sop), Tagliaborse (ten), Calcante (bass). Perhaps the finest 18th-century intermezzo apart from *La Serva Padrona*.
Plot: 18th-century Italy. The gypsy Nisa wishes to marry the rich old miser Calcante. She adopts several stratagems, including disguising her brother Tagliaborse as a bear, and is eventually successful. [R]

Zingarelli, Niccolò Antonio (1752–1837)
Italian composer. His first opera, the INTERMEZZO *I Quattro Pazzi* (Naples, 1768), was followed by 33 others, a number of which enjoyed great success in their day but which are all nowadays largely forgotten. His most important operas include *Montezuma* (Naples, 13 Aug 1781; libr Vittorio Amadeo Cigna-Santi), *Gli Orazi e i Curiazi* (Naples, 4 Nov 1795; libr C. Sernicola, after Pierre Corneille's *Horace*), *Giulietta e Romeo* (Milan, 30 Jan 1796; libr Giuseppe Maria Foppa, after Shakespeare's *Romeo and Juliet*), *Edipo a Colono* (Venice, 26 Dec 1802; libr Antonio Sografi, after Sophocles's *Oedipus at Colonus*), *Ines de Castro* (Milan, Sept 1803; libr Antonio Gasparini, after Antoine Houdart de la Motte) and *Berenice* (Rome, 12 Nov 1811; libr Jacopo Ferretti, after Apostolo Zeno's *Lucio Vero*), his finest opera. He was also a distinguished teacher, whose pupils included Bellini, Costa, Mercadante, Morlacchi, Petrella and F. Ricci.

Zinovy
Tenor role in Shostakovich's *Lady Macbeth of Mtsensk*. He is Katerina's ineffectual husband.

Zirkusprinzessin, Die (*The Circus Princess*)
Operetta in three acts by Kálmán. 1st perf Vienna, 26 March 1926; libr by Julius Brammer and Alfred Grünwald. Principal roles: Fedora (sop), Mr X (ten), Vladimir (bar), Toni (ten), Mabel Gibson (sop). Very successful at its appearance, it is still sometimes performed in German-speaking countries.
Plot: 19th-century St Petersburg. The mysterious Mr X's daredevil act is the sensation of the Stanislavsky Circus. Princess Fedora Palinska has rejected the advances of Prince Sergius Vladimir, who takes revenge by hiring Mr X to pose as an aristocrat and to woo and marry Fedora. X, however, is in reality Baron Korosov, disinherited after falling in love with his uncle's fiancée. That fiancée is Fedora herself, and the lovers are finally united. [R Exc]

Zítek, Vilém (1890–1956)
Czech bass, particularly associated with the Czech and German repertories. One of the finest basses of the inter-war period, he possessed a rich and dark voice and was an outstanding singing-actor, often considered to be in the same league as Fyodor Chaliapin. He created the title-role in Blodek's *Zítek*.

Zitti, zitti
1 Tenor/baritone duet for Don Ramiro and Dandini in Act II of Rossini's *La Cenerentola*, in which Dandini tells his master of the arrogance of the ugly sisters. **2** Mezzo/tenor/baritone trio for Rosina, Count Almaviva and Figaro in Act II of Rossini's *Il Barbiere di Siviglia*, in which they plan to escape via the ladder on the balcony. **3** Chorus of courtiers in Act I of Verdi's *Rigoletto*, in which they set about their abduction of Gilda.

Živný
Tenor role in Janáček's *Fate*. He is a composer married to Míla. The role contains autobiographical suggestions on Janáček's part.

Zola, Émile (1840–1902)
French novelist and librettist. A close friend of Bruneau, he wrote the libretti for his *La Rêve*, *Messidor*, *L'Ouragan*, *Lazare*, *L'Enfant-Roi*, *Naïs Micoulin* and *Les Quatre Journées*. Most of Bruneau's other operas, including *L'Attaque du Moulin*, are based on Zola's works, as is Werle's *Dreaming About Thérèse*.

Zoo, The
Operetta in one act by Sullivan. 1st perf London, 5 June 1875; libr by Benjamin Charles Stevenson. Principal roles: Thomas Brown (bar), Aesculapius (ten), Laetitia (sop), Eliza (sop), Mr Grinder (b-bar). Perhaps Sullivan's feeblest stage work, it is almost never performed.
Plot: Regent's Park Zoo, 19th century. Laetitia's father Mr Grinder has forbidden her to marry the apothecary Aesculapius Carboy, who therefore decides to hang himself near the zoo's refreshment stall. However, the stall-holder Eliza stops him. Eliza's admirer Thomas Brown is taken ill, and Aesculapius gives her a prescription. Mr Grinder seperates Laetitia from Aesculapius, who heads for the lions' den. However, it is revealed that Brown is in fact the Duke of Islington, and he persuades Mr Grinder to relent. [R]

Zorn, Balthazar
Tenor COMPRIMARIO role in Wagner's *Die Meistersinger von Nürnberg*. A pewter-worker, he is one of the masters.

Zoroastre
Opera in five acts by Rameau. 1st perf Paris, 5 Dec 1749; libr by Louis de Cahusac. Revised version 1st perf Paris, 19 Jan 1756. Principal roles: Zoroastre (ten), Amélite (sop), Erinice (mezzo), Oromasés (bass), Abramane (bass), Céphie (sop). Containing some of Rameau's finest music, much of it incorporated from his earlier *Samson*, it has received a number of performances in recent years. Set in legendary Bactria, it deals with the conflict between the magus Zoroaster (*c* 628–*c* 551 BC) and the evil priest Abramanes. [R]

Zsupán
1 Baritone role in J. Strauss's *Der Zigeunerbaron*. Arsena's father, he is a bad-tempered pig farmer. **2** Tenor role in Kálmán's *Gräfin Mariza*. He is a baron who becomes unexpectedly engaged to Mariza.

Zulma
Mezzo role in Rossini's *L'Italiana in Algieri*. She is Elvira's confidante.

Zuniga
Bass role in Bizet's *Carmen*. He is an army lieutenant.

Zurga
Baritone role in Bizet's *Les Pêcheurs de Perles*. He is the leader of the pearl fishers.

Zürich Opernhaus
The present theatre (cap 1,100) was designed by Fellner and Helmer and opened in 1891. One of Switzerland's two leading houses, it has recently been noted for its Mozart and Monteverdi performances. The annual season runs from September to June. Musical directors have included Robert Denzler, Otto Ackermann, Hans Rosbaud, Christian Vöchting, Ferdinand Leitner, Ralf Weikert and Franz Welser-Möst.

Zuzana Vojířovà
Opera in five scenes by Pauer. 1st perf Prague, 30 Dec 1958; libr by the composer, after Ján Bor's play. Principal roles: Zuzana (sop), Peter Vok (bar), Kateřina (mezzo), Ondrej Zachar (ten), Adam (bass). Pauer's most successful opera, it tells a partially fictitious story of events in the life of Peter Vok (1539–1611) the last of the Rožmberk rulers in southern Bohemia. It has been widely performed in the Czech lands, but is little known elsewhere. [R]

Zweihunderttausand Taler *(200,000 Thalers)*
Opera in three acts and epilogue by Blacher. 1st perf Berlin, 25 Sept 1969; libr after Sholom Aleichem's *The Two Hundred Thousand*. One of Blacher's most successful operas, it is an anti-capitalist comedy.

Zwerg, Der
see GEBURSTAG DER INFANTIN, DER

Zwillingsbrüder, Die (*The Twin Brothers*)
Comic opera in one act by Schubert (D 647). 1st perf Vienna, 14 June 1820; libr by Georg von Hofmann, after the anonymous French vaudeville *Les Deux Valentins*. Principal roles: Franz and Friedrich Spiess (bar and bar), Lieschen (sop), Anton (ten), Mayor (bass). A slight little SINGSPIEL, it is only very rarely performed. Traditionally, the two brothers are played by the same baritone.
Plot: 18th-century Germany. Lieschen is engaged to Anton, but had earlier been promised to Franz Spiess if he returned

from the Foreign Legion within a certain time. Franz returns at the last moment and claims Lieschen despite the entreaties of her father the Mayor. Franz goes to the magistrate to collect the dowry, and in the meantime his twin brother Friedrich (long believed dead) arrives and blesses Lieschen's marriage with Anton. Unaware of Friedrich's existence, everyone thinks that Franz is behaving oddly, and he is arrested for schizophrenia. However, Friedrich appears at the court and everything is sorted out. [R]

Zwischenspiel (German for 'twosome-play') The term used in Germany to describe an opera written in the style of an Italian INTERMEZZO, such as Telemann's *Pimpinone*.

Zylis-Gara, Teresa (b 1935) Polish soprano, particularly associated with Mozart and Verdi roles, especially Desdemona in Verdi's *Otello*. She possessed a beautiful lyric voice, used with intelligence and a fine technique, and she had an affecting stage presence.

· Appendix I ·

Opera on Record

This appendix provides a checklist, listed by composer, of the nearly 1,100 operas, operettas and zarzuelas which have been commercially recorded. It should be noted that some have never been released outside their country of origin, and that many others have been long unavailable. This listing does *not* include pirated recordings; although many are readily available; they are officially illegal.

ADAM	*Le Postillon de Longjumeau*
	Si J'Étais Roi (Exc)
ADAMS	*The Death of Klinghoffer*
	Nixon in China
ALBÉNIZ	*Pepita Jiménez*
ALBERT	*Die Abreise*
	Tiefland
ALBINONI	*Climene*
	Il Nascimento dell'Aurora
	Pimpinone
ALONSO	*La Parranda*
	La Picarona
ALWYN	*Miss Julie*
ARENSKY	*Raphael*
ARNE	*Comus*
	The Cooper
	Thomas and Sally
ARRIETA	*Marina*
AUBER	*Le Domino Noir*
	Fra Diavolo
	Manon Lescaut
	La Muette de Portici
AUDRAN	*La Mascotte*
J.C. BACH	*Amadis des Gaules*
BALASSA	*The Man Outside*
BALFE	*The Bohemian Girl*
BANFIELD	*Lord Byron's Love Letter*
BARBER	*Antony and Cleopatra*
	A Hand of Bridge
	Vanessa
BARBIERI	*El Barberillo de Lavapiés*
	Los Diamantés de la Corona
	Jugar con Fuego
BARTÓK	*Duke Bluebeard's Castle*
BARTON	*The Disappointment*
BATTIATO	*Gilgamesh*
BÉCAUD	*Opéra d'Aran*
BEESON	*Captain Jinks of the Horse Marines*
	Dr Heidegger's Fountain of Youth
	Hello Out There
	Lizzie Borden
	The Sweet Bye and Bye
BEETHOVEN	*Fidelio*
	Leonore
BELLINI	*Beatrice di Tenda*
	I Capuleti e i Montecchi
	Norma
	Il Pirata
	I Puritani
	La Sonnambula
BENATZKY	*Im Weissen Rössl*
BENDA	*Der Dorfjahrmarkt*
BENNETT	*All the King's Men*
BERG	*Lulu*
	Wozzeck
BERGMAN	*The Singing Tree*
BERKELEY	*Baa Baa Black Sheep*
BERLIOZ	*Béatrice et Bénédict*
	Benvenuto Cellini
	La Damnation de Faust
	Les Troyens
BERNSTEIN	*Candide*
	On the Town
	A Quiet Place
	Trouble in Tahiti
	West Side Story
BERWALD	*Estrella de Soria* (Exc)
BIBALO	*Ghosts*
BIRTWISTLE	*Punch and Judy*
BIZET	*Carmen*
	Djamileh
	Le Docteur Miracle
	Don Procopio
	Ivan IV (Exc)
	La Jolie Fille de Perth
	Les Pêcheurs de Perles
BLACHER	*Der Grossinquisitor*
BLACKFORD	*Sir Gawain and the Green Knight*
BLAVET	*Le Jaloux Corrigé*
BLITZSTEIN	*The Harpies*
	Regina
BLODEK	*In the Well*
	Zítek (Exc)

BLOMDAHL	*Aniara*
BLOW	*Venus and Adonis*
BOGUSŁAWSKI	*The Beelzebub Sonata*
BOÏELDIEU	*La Dame Blanche*
	Ma Tante Aurore
BOITO	*Mefistofele*
	Nerone
BONDEVILLE	*L'École des Maris* (Exc)
BONONCINI	*Griselda* (Exc)
BORODIN	*Prince Igor*
BORTNYANSKY	*The Falcon*
	The Rival Son
BÖRTZ	*The Bacchae*
BOUGHTON	*Bethlehem*
	The Immortal Hour
BOZAY	*Csongor and Tünde*
BRETÓN	*La Verbena de la Paloma*
BRIDGE	*The Christmas Rose*
BRITTEN	*Albert Herring*
	Billy Budd
	The Burning Fiery Furnace
	Curlew River
	Death in Venice
	Gloriana
	The Little Sweep
	A Midsummer Night's Dream
	Noye's Fludde
	Owen Wingrave
	Paul Bunyan
	Peter Grimes
	The Prodigal Son
	The Rape of Lucretia
	The Turn of the Screw
BUSONI	*Arlecchino*
	Doktor Faust
	Turandot
CABALLERO	*El Dúo de la Africana*
	Gigantes y Cabezudos
	Los Sobrinos del Capitán Grant
	La Viejecita
CAMPRA	*L'Europe Galante*
	Idoménée
	Tancrède
CASKEN	*Golem*
CATALANI	*La Wally*
CAVALIERI	*La Rappresentazione di Anima e Corpo*
CAVALLI	*La Calisto*
	L'Egisto
	Ercole Amante
	L'Erismena
	Giasone
	L'Ormindo
	Serse
CESTI	*Orontea*
CHABRIER	*Briséïs*
	Une Éducation Manquée
	L'Étoile
	Le Roi Malgré Lui
CHAPÍ	*El Barquillero*
	La Bruja
	El Punão de Rosas
	La Revoltosa
	El Rey que Rabió
	La Tempestad
CHARPENTIER	*Louise*
M. CHARPENTIER	*Actéon*
	David et Jonathas
	Le Malade Imaginaire
	Médée
CHAUSSON	*Le Roi Arthus*
CHAYNES	*Erzsebet*
CHERUBINI	*Lodoïska*
	Médée
CHRISTINÉ	*Phi-Phi*
CHUECA	*Agua*
	La Gran Vía
CIKKER	*Coriolanus*
	Resurrection
CILEA	*Adriana Lecouvreur*
	L'Arlesiana
CIMADORO	*Pimmalione*
CIMAROSA	*Il Maestro di Cappella*
	Il Matrimonio Segreto
	Il Pittor Parigino
COPLAND	*The Second Hurricane*
	The Tender Land
CORNELIUS	*Der Barbier von Bagdad*
CROSSE	*Purgatory*
DALLAPICCOLA	*Il Prigioniero*
DANKEVICH	*Bogdan Kmelnitsky*
DARGOMIJSKY	*Rusalka*
	The Stone Guest
DAUVERGNE	*La Coquette Trompée*
	Les Troqueurs
DAVIS	*X: the Life and Times of Malcolm X*
DEBUSSY	*La Chûte de la Maison Usher*
	Pelléas et Mélisande
	Rodrigue et Chimène
DELIBES	*Lakmé*
DELIUS	*Fennimore and Gerda*
	Irmelin
	Koanga
	The Magic Fountain
	Margot la Rouge
	A Village Romeo and Juliet
DESSAU	*Puntila*
	Die Verurteilung des Lukullus

DIBDIN	*The Ephesian Matron*
DONIZETTI	*L'Aio nell'Imbarazzo*
	Anna Bolena
	L'Assedio di Calais
	Betly
	Il Campanello di Notte
	Don Pasquale
	L'Elisir d'Amore
	Emilia di Liverpool
	La Favorite
	La Fille du Régiment
	Gabriella di Vergy
	Gemma di Vergy
	Linda di Chamounix
	Lucia di Lammermoor
	Lucrezia Borgia
	Maria de Rudenz
	Maria Padilla
	Maria Stuarda
	Ne M'Oubliez Pas
	Poliuto
	Rita
	Roberto Devereux
	Ugo Conte di Parigi
DOSTAL	*Die Ungarische Hochzeit* (Exc)
DUHAMEL	*Les Travaux d'Hercule*
DUKAS	*Ariane et Barbe-Bleue*
DUNAYEVSKY	*Free Wind*
	White Acacia
DVOŘÁK	*The Cunning Peasant*
	The Devil and Kate
	Dimitrij
	Jakobín
	Rusalka
	Vanda
EGK	*Peer Gynt*
	Die Verlobung in San Domingo
	Die Zaubergeige (Exc)
EINEM	*Der Besuch der Alten Dame*
	Dantons Tod
ELSNER	*The Echo in the Wood*
	King Loketiek
ENESCU	*Oedipe*
ERKEL	*Bánk Bán*
	László Hunyadi
EYSER	*The King of Hearts*
	The Last Voyage
FALL	*Die Dollarprinzessin* (Exc)
	Der Fidele Bauer (Exc)
	Die Rose von Stambul (Exc)
FALLA	*L'Atlántida*
	El Retablo de Maese Pedro
	La Vida Breve
FAURÉ	*Pénélope*
FÉNELON	*Le Chevalier Imaginaire*
FIBICH	*The Bride of Messina*
	Šárka
	The Tempest (Exc)
FIORAVANTI	*Le Cantatrici Villane* (Exc)
FLEISHMAN	*Rothschild's Violin*
FLIFLET–BRAIEN	*Anne Pedersdotter*
FLOTOW	*Martha*
FLOYD	*Susannah*
FOERSTER	*Eva*
FOMIN	*Les Cochers au Relais*
FRANÇAIX	*Le Diable Boîteux*
	Paris à Nous Deux
FRANCHETTI	*Cristoforo Colombo*
FRIED	*The Diary of Anne Frank*
FRUMERIE	*Singoalla*
GADE	*Fairy Spell*
GAGLIANO	*La Dafne*
GALUPPI	*Il Filosofo di Campagna*
GANNÉ	*Hans le Joueur de Flûte* (Exc)
	Les Saltimbanques
GAZZANIGA	*Don Giovanni*
GERHARD	*The Duenna*
GERMAN	*Merrie England*
	Tom Jones (Exc)
GERSHWIN	*Porgy and Bess*
GIANNINI	*The Taming of the Shrew*
GIMÉNEZ	*La Tempranica*
GINASTERA	*Bomarzo*
GIORDANO	*Andrea Chénier*
	Fedora
GLASS	*Akhnaten*
GLINKA	*A Life for the Tsar*
	Ruslan and Ludmila
GLUCK	*Alceste*
	Armide
	Le Cadi Dupé
	Le Cinesi
	La Corona
	La Danza
	Écho et Narcisse
	Iphigénie en Aulide
	Iphigénie en Tauride
	L'Ivrogne Corrigé
	Orfeo ed Euridice
	Paride ed Elena
	La Rencontre Imprévue
GOLDMARK	*Die Königin von Saba*
GOLDSCHMIDT	*Beatrice Cenci*
	Der Gewaltige Hahnrei
GOMES	*Il Guarany*
GOOSSENS	*Judith*

GOTOVAC	*Ero the Joker*
GÖTZ	*Der Widerspänstigen Zähmung*
GOUNOD	*Faust*
	Mireille
	Roméo et Juliette
	Sapho
GRANADOS	*Goyescas*
GRAUN	*Montezuma*
GRESNICK	*Le Baiser Donné et Rendu*
GRÉTRY	*L'Amant Jaloux*
	La Caravane du Caire
	Le Jugement de Midas (Exc)
	Lucile
	Richard Coeur de Lion
	Zémire et Azor
GRIEG	*Olav Trygvason*
GUERRERO	*La Alsaciana*
	Los Gavilanes
	El Huésped del Sevilliano
	La Montería
	La Rosa del Azafrán
GULAK–ARTEMOVSKY	*Cossack Beyond the Danube*
GURIDI	*El Caserío*
HÁBA	*The Mother*
HADJIBEYOV	*Kyor-Ogly*
HAEFFNER	*Electra*
HAHN	*Ciboulette*
HALÉVY	*La Juive*
HALLÉN	*Harald der Wiking* (Exc)
HÄNDEL	*Acis and Galatea*
	Admeto
	Agrippina
	Alcina
	Alessandro
	Amadigi di Gaula
	Ariodante
	Atalanta
	Athalia
	Belshazzar
	Flavio
	Floridante
	Giulio Cesare
	Giustino
	Hercules
	Jephtha
	Orlando
	Ottone
	Partenope
	Il Pastor Fido
	Poro
	Radamisto
	Rinaldo
	Rodelinda
	Samson
	Saul
	Scipione
	Semele
	Serse
	Sosarme
	Tamerlano
	Teseo
HARPER	*Fanny Robin*
HASSE	*Cleofide*
	Piramo e Tisbe
HAYDN	*Armida*
	La Fedeltà Premiata
	L'Incontro Improvviso
	L'Infedeltà Delusa
	L'Isola Disabitata
	Il Mondo della Luna
	Orfeo ed Euridice
	Orlando Paladino
	Philemon und Baucis
	Lo Speziale
	La Vera Costanza
HEININEN	*The Damask Drum*
HEISE	*King and Marshal*
HENZE	*The Bassarids*
	Elegie für Junge Liebende (Exc)
	The English Cat
	Der Junge Lord
	Rachel la Cubana
HÉROLD	*Le Pré aux Clercs* (Exc)
HERRMANN	*Wuthering Heights*
HERVÉ	*Mam'zelle Nitouche* (Exc)
HEUBERGER	*Der Opernball* (Exc)
HINDEMITH	*Cardillac*
	Hin und Zurück
	Mathis der Maler
	Mörder Hoffnung der Frauen
	Neues vom Tage
	Das Nusch-Nuschi
	Sancta Susanna
HOFFMANN	*Die Lustigen Musikanten* (Exc)
	Undine
HOLST	*At the Boar's Head*
	Sāvitri
	The Wandering Scholar
HONEGGER	*Les Aventures du Roi Pausole*
	Jeanne d'Arc au Bûcher
	Judith
	Nicolas de Flue
	Le Roi David
HOPKINS	*Three's Company*
HUMPERDINCK	*Hänsel und Gretel*

	Die Königskinder
JACOBI	*Sybill* (Exc)
JANÁČEK	*The Cunning Little Vixen*
	The Excursions of Mr Brouček
	Fate
	From the House of the Dead
	Jenůfa
	Káťa Kabanová
	The Macropolus Case
	Šárka
JESSEL	*Schwarzwaldmädel*
JOMMELLI	*Armida Abbandonata*
JOPLIN	*Treemonisha*
KABALEVSKY	*The Craftsman of Clamecy*
	The Family of Taras
KACSÓH	*János Vitéz*
KÁLMÁN	*Die Bajadere*
	Die Csárdásfürstin
	Gräfin Mariza
	Das Veilchen von Montmartre
	Die Zirkusprinzessin (Exc)
KALOMIRIS	*The Mother's Ring*
KARENTNIKOV	*Till Eulenspiegel*
KEISER	*Croesus* (Exc)
	Die Grossmüthige Tomyris
KETTING	*Ithaka*
KHRENNIKOV	*The Golden Calf*
	100 Devils and a Girl
	Into the Storm
	The Mother (Exc)
KIENZL	*Der Evangelimann*
KILLMAYER	*Yolimba*
KNAIFEL	*The Canterville Ghost*
KNUSSEN	*Where the Wild Things Are*
KODÁLY	*Háry János*
	The Spinning Room
KOKKONEN	*The Last Temptations*
KORNGOLD	*Die Tote Stadt*
	Violanta
	Das Wunder der Heliane
KORTEKANGAS	*Grand Hotel*
KOSMA	*Les Canuts*
KOVAŘOVIC	*The Dogheads* (Exc)
KRÁSA	*Brundibár*
KRAUS	*Proserpin*
	Soliman II
KŘENEK	*Jonny Spielt Auf*
KREUTZER	*Das Nachtlager von Granada*
KUHLAU	*The Elf's Hill*
	Lulu
KÜNNEKE	*Die Grosse Sünderin* (Exc)
	Traumland
	Der Vetter aus Dingsda
KURPIŃSKI	*The Charlatan* (Exc)
	Henry VI Hunting
KUSSER	*Erindo*
LALO	*Le Roi d'Ys*
LAMPE	*Pyramus and Thisbe*
LANDOWSKI	*Le Fou*
	Le Ventriloque
LECLAIR	*Scylla et Glaucus*
LECOCQ	*La Fille de Madame Angot*
	Le Petit Duc
LEHÁR	*Eva* (Exc)
	Frasquita (Exc)
	Friederike
	Giuditta
	Der Graf von Luxemburg
	Das Land des Lächelns
	Die Lustige Witwe
	Paganini
	Schön ist die Welt (Exc)
	Der Zarewitsch
	Zigeunerliebe
LEONCAVALLO	*La Bohème*
	Pagliacci
	Zazà
LEONI	*L'Oracolo*
LESUR	*Andrea del Sarto*
LIDHOLM	*A Dream Play*
LIEBERMANN	*Penelope*
LIGETI	*Le Grand Macabre*
LINCKE	*Frau Luna*
LISZT	*Don Sanche*
LLOYD	*Iernin*
	John Socman (Exc)
LOCKE	*Psyche*
	The Tempest
LORTZING	*Die Opernprobe*
	Undine
	Der Waffenschmied
	Der Wildschütz
	Zar und Zimmermann
LULLY	*Alceste*
	Armide et Renaud
	Atys
	Le Bourgeois Gentilhomme
	Isis (Exc)
	Phaëton
	Thésée (Exc)
LUNA	*El Asombro de Damasco*
	Los Cadetes de la Reina
	Los Molinos de Viento
	El Niño Judío
LYSENKO	*Natalka Poltavka*
	Taras Bulba
MADETOJA	*Juha*

	The Ostrobothnians
MAGNARD	*Guercoeur*
MARAIS	*Alcyone*
MARSCHNER	*Hans Heiling*
	Der Vampyr (Exc)
MARTIN	*Le Vin Herbé*
MARTINŮ	*Alexandre Bis*
	Ariane
	Comedy on the Bridge
	The Greek Passion
	Julietta
	The Miracle of Our Lady
MASSANA	*Canigó*
MASSÉ	*Les Noces de Jeanette*
MASSENET	*Cendrillon*
	Chérubin
	Le Cid
	Cléopâtre
	Don Quichotte
	Esclarmonde
	Grisélidis
	Hérodiade (Exc)
	Le Jongleur de Notre Dame
	Manon
	La Navarraise
	Le Roi de Lahore
	Sapho
	Thaïs
	Thérèse
	Werther
MATTHUS	*Judith*
MAXWELL DAVIES	*The Lighthouse*
	The Martyrdom of St Magnus
	Resurrection
MAYR	*Medea in Corinto*
MEALE	*Voss*
MENDELSSOHN	*Die Beiden Pädagogen*
	Die Heimkehr aus der Fremde
	Die Hochzeit des Camacho
MENOTTI	*Amahl and the Night Visitors*
	Amelia al Ballo
	The Boy Who Grew Too Fast
	The Consul
	Maria Golovin
	The Medium
	The Old Maid and the Thief
	The Saint of Bleecker Street
	The Telephone
	The Unicorn, the Gorgon and the Manticore
MERCADANTE	*Il Bravo*
	Orazi e Curiazi
MERIKANTO	*Juha*
MESSAGER	*La Basoche* (Exc)
	Fortunio
	Monsieur Beaucaire (Exc)
	Les P'tites Michu (Exc)
	Véronique
MESSIAEN	*Saint François d'Assise*
MEYERBEER	*L'Africaine* (Exc)
	Il Crociato in Egitto
	Dinorah
	Les Huguenots
	Le Prophète
MILHAUD	*Les Choëphores*
	Les Malheurs d'Orphée
	Opéras-minutes
	Le Pauvre Matelot
MILLÁN	*La Dogaresa*
MILLÖCKER	*Der Bettelstudent*
	Die Dubarry (Exc)
	Gasparone
MONIUSZKO	*The Countess* (Exc)
	Halka
	The Haunted Manor
	The Raftsman
	Verum Nobile
MONCKTON	*The Arcadians* (Exc)
MONDONVILLE	*Titon et l'Aurore*
MONTÉCLAIR	*Jephté*
MONTEMEZZI	*L'Amore dei Tre Re*
MONTEVERDI	*Il Ballo delle Ingrate*
	Il Combattimento di Tancredi e Clorinda
	La Favola d'Orfeo
	L'Incoronazione di Poppea
	Il Ritorno d'Ulisse in Patria
MOORE	*The Ballad of Baby Doe*
	Carry Nation
	The Devil and Daniel Webster
MOURET	*Les Amours de Ragonde*
MOUSSORGSKY	*Boris Godunov*
	Khovanschina
	The Marriage
	Salammbô
	Sorochintsy Fair
MOZART	*Apollo et Hyacinthus*
	Ascanio in Alba
	Bastien und Bastienne
	La Clemenza di Tito
	Così fan Tutte
	Don Giovanni
	Die Entführung aus dem Serail

La Finta Giardiniera
La Finta Semplice
Idomeneo
Lucio Silla
Mitridate Rè di Ponto
Le Nozze di Figaro
L'Oca del Cairo
Il Rè Pastore
Der Schauspieldirektor
Die Schuldigkeit des Ersten Gebotes
Il Sogno di Scipione
Lo Sposo Deluso
Zaïde
Die Zauberflöte

MUSGRAVE *A Christmas Carol*
Mary Queen of Scots

MYSLIVEČEK *Il Bellerofonte*

NÁPRAVNÍK *Dubrovsky*

NEDBAL *Polenblut* (Exc)

NESSLER *Der Trompeter von Säckingen* (Exc)

NICOLAÏ *Die Lustigen Weiber von Windsor*

NIELSEN *Maskarade*
Saul og David

NØRGÅRD *Gilgamesh*

NOVÁK *The Lantern*

NYMAN *The Man Who Mistook His Wife For a Hat*

OFFENBACH *Ba-Ta-Clan*
Les Bavards
La Belle Hélène
Les Brigands
Christopher Columbus
Les Contes d'Hoffmann
La Fille du Tambour-Major
La Grande-Duchesse de Gérolstein
Mesdames de la Halle
Monsieur Choufleuri Restera Chez-Lui
Orphée aux Enfers
La Périchole
Pomme d'Api
Robinson Crusoé
La Vie Parisienne

OHANA *Syllabaire Pour Phèdre*

ORFF *Antigonae*
Die Bernauerin
Die Kluge
Ludus de Nato Infante Mirificus
Der Mond
Oedipus der Tyrann
De Temporum Fine Comoedia
Trionfo d'Afrodite

PACIUS *The Hunt of King Charles*

PAER *Leonora*
Le Maître de Chapelle

PAISIELLO *Il Barbiere di Siviglia*
Il Duello
Nina
La Semiramide in Villa (Exc)

PALIASHVILI *Absalom and Etery*
Twilight

PARRY *Blodwen* (Exc)

PASHKEVICH *The Miser*

PAUER *The Hypochondriac* (Exc)
Zuzana Vojířová

PENDERECKI *The Devils of Loudun*

PENELLA *El Gato Montés*

PEPUSCH *The Beggar's Opera*

PERGOLESI *La Contadina Astuta*
Lo Frate 'Nnamorato
Il Geloso Schernito
Il Maestro di Musica
La Serva Padrona

PERI *Euridice*

PETERSON-BERGER *Arnljot*

PETROV *Mayakovsky Comes Into Existence*
Peter I

PETROVICS *C'Est la Guerre*
Crime and Punishment
Lysistrate

PFITZNER *Das Herz*
Palestrina

PIJPER *Halloween*

PLANQUETTE *Les Cloches de Corneville*
Rip (Exc)

PONCHIELLI *La Gioconda*

POULENC *Dialogues des Carmélites*
Les Mamelles de Tirésias
La Voix Humaine

PRODROMIDÈS *H.H. Ulysse*
Les Perses

PROKOFIEV *The Duenna*
The Fiery Angel
The Gambler
The Love of Three Oranges
Maddalena
Semeon Kotko
The Story of a Real Man
War and Peace

PUCCINI *La Bohème*
Edgar
La Fanciulla del West
Gianni Schicchi

	Madama Butterfly
	Manon Lescaut
	La Rondine
	Suor Angelica
	Il Tabarro
	Tosca
	Turandot
	Le Villi
PURCELL	*Dido and Aeneas*
	The Fairy Queen
	The Indian Queen
	King Arthur
	The Prophetess
	The Tempest
RABAUD	*Mârouf*
RACHMANINOV	*Aleko*
	The Covetous Knight
	Francesca da Rimini
	Monna Vanna (Exc)
RAMEAU	*Anacréon*
	Les Boréades
	Castor et Pollux
	Dardanus
	Les Fêtes d'Hébé (Exc)
	La Guirlande
	Hippolyte et Aricie
	Les Indes Galantes
	Naïs
	Nélée et Myrthis
	Les Paladins
	Platée
	La Princesse de Navarre (Exc)
	Pygmalion
	Le Temple de la Gloire
	Zaïs
	Zéphyre
	Zoroastre
RÁNKI	*The Tragedy of Man* (Exc)
RAUTAVAARA	*Thomas*
	Vincent
RAVEL	*L'Enfant et les Sortilèges*
	L'Heure Espagnole
REIMANN	*Lear*
	Troades
RESPIGHI	*Belfagor*
	La Fiamma
	Lucrezia
	Maria Egiziaca
	Semirâma
REYER	*Sigurd* (Exc)
RIHM	*Die Hamletmaschine*
	Jakob Lenz
RIMSKY-KORSAKOV	*Boyarina Vera Sheloga*
	Christmas Eve
	The Golden Cockerel
	The Invisible City of Kitezh
	Kashchey the Immortal
	The Maid of Pskov
	May Night
	Mlada
	Mozart and Salieri
	Pan Voyevoda
	Sadko
	The Snow Maiden
	The Tale of Tsar Saltan
	The Tsar's Bride
RINALDO	*La Zingara*
ROMBERG	*The Desert Song*
	The New Moon
	The Student Prince
ROSSI	*Orfeo*
ROSSINI	*Armida*
	Il Barbiere di Siviglia
	La Cambiale di Matrimonio
	La Cenerentola
	Le Comte Ory
	La Donna del Lago
	Elisabetta Regina d'Inghilterra
	Ermione
	La Gazza Ladra
	Guillaume Tell
	L'Inganno Felice
	L'Italiana in Algieri
	Maometto Secondo
	Mosè in Egitto
	L'Occasionne Fa il Ladro
	Otello
	La Pietra del Paragone
	La Scala di Seta
	Semiramide
	Le Siège de Corinthe
	Il Signor Bruschino
	Tancredi
	Il Turco in Italia
	Il Viaggio a Reims
	Zelmira
ROTA	*Il Cappello di Paglia di Firenze*
ROUSSEAU	*Le Devin du Village*
ROUSSEL	*Padmâvatî*
RUBINSTEIN	*The Demon*
RUDZIŃSKI	*The Dismissal of the Greek Envoys*
SAINT-SAËNS	*Samson et Dalila*
SALIERI	*Les Danaïdes*
	Falstaff
	Prima la Musica e Poi le Parole (Exc)

SALLINEN	*The Horseman*
	Kullervo
	The Red Line
SATIE	*Geneviève de Brabant*
	Le Piège de Méduse
	Socrate
SAUGET	*Tistou les Pouces Verts*
SAXTON	*Caritas*
A. SCARLATTI	*La Dama Spagnola e il Cavalier*
	Il Giardino di Amore
	Il Trionfo dell'Onore
D. SCARLATTI	*Tetide in Sciro*
SCHAT	*Houdini*
SCHMIDT	*Notre-Dame*
SCHNITTKE	*Life With an Idiot*
SHOECK	*Massimilla Doni*
	Penthesilea
	Venus
	Vom Fischer un syner Fru
SCHÖNBERG	*Erwartung*
	Die Glückliche Hand
	Moses und Aron
	Von Heute auf Morgen
SCHREKER	*Der Ferne Klang*
	Flammen
	Die Gezeichneten
	Der Schatzgräber
SCHUBERT	*Alfonso und Estrella*
	Fernando
	Fierrabras
	Die Freunde von Salamanka
	Der Spiegelritter
	Die Verschworenen
	Der Vierjährige Posten
	Die Zwillingsbrüder
SCHULTZE	*Schwarzer Peter*
SCHUMAN	*The Mighty Casey*
SCHUMAN	*Genoveva*
SEROV	*Judith*
	Rogneda (Exc)
SERRANO	*Alma de Dios*
	La Canción del Olvido
	Los Claveles
	La Dolorosa
	Los de Aragon
	La Reina Mora
SHAPORIN	*The Decembrists*
SHCHEDRIN	*Dead Souls*
	Not Love Alone
SHEBALIN	*The Taming of the Shrew*
SHIELD	*Rosina*
SHOSTAKOVICH	*The Gamblers*
	Lady Macbeth of Mtsensk
	Moscow Cherymouski
	The Nose
SIBELIUS	*The Maiden in the Tower*
SIKORA	*Ariadna*
SINDING	*Der Heilige Berg*
SINOPOLI	*Lou Salomé* (Exc)
ŠKROUP	*Columbus* (Exc)
SMETANA	*The Bartered Bride*
	The Brandenburgers in Bohemia
	Dalibor
	The Devil's Wall
	The Kiss
	Libuše
	The Secret
	The Two Widows
	Viola
SMYTH	*The Wreckers*
SOROZÁBAL	*Adiós a la Bohemia*
	Black
	Don Manolito
	La Eterna Canción
	Katiuska
	La del Manojo de Rosas
	Las de Caín
	La Taberna del Puerto
SOUTULLO	*La del Soto del Parral*
	La Leyenda del Beso
	El Último Romántico
SPOHR	*Faust*
	Jessonda
SPONTINI	*Olympie*
	La Vestale
STEFFANI	*Enrico Leone* (Exc)
STOCKHAUSEN	*Donnerstag aus Licht*
	Samstag aus Licht
STOLZ	*Fruhjährsparade* (Exc)
	Himmelblaue Träume (Exc)
	Die Rosen der Madonna
	Trauminsel
	Venus in Seide (Exc)
O. STRAUS	*Drei Walzer*
	Der Tapfere Soldat
	Ein Walzertraum
J. STRAUSS	*Die Fledermaus*
	Indigo und die Vierzig Räuber (Exc)
	Der Karneval in Rom (Exc)
	Die Lustige Krieg (Exc)
	Eine Nacht in Venedig
	Wiener Blut
	Der Zigeunerbaron
STRAUSS	*Die Ägyptische Helena*
	Arabella
	Ariadne auf Naxos

	Capriccio
	Daphne
	Elektra
	Feuersnot
	Die Frau ohne Schatten
	Friedenstag
	Guntram
	Intermezzo
	Die Liebe der Danae
	Der Rosenkavalier
	Salome
	Die Schweigsame Frau
STRAVINSKY	*Mavra*
	The Nightingale
	Oedipus Rex
	The Rake's Progress
	Renard
SUCHOŇ	*Svätopluk*
	The Whirlpool
SUDER	*Kleider Machen Leute*
SULLIVAN	*Cox and Box*
	The Gondoliers
	The Grand Duke
	H.M.S. Pinafore
	Iolanthe
	The Mikado
	Patience
	The Pirates of Penzance
	Princess Ida
	Ruddigore
	The Sorcerer
	Trial By Jury
	Utopia Limited
	The Yeomen of the Guard
	The Zoo
SUPPÉ	*Boccaccio*
	Die Schöne Galatea
SUTERMEISTER	*Romeo und Julia*
SZOKOLAY	*Blood Wedding*
	Sámson
SZYMANOWSKI	*King Roger*
TAKTAKISHVILI	*Mindiya*
TANEYEV	*Oresteia*
TAVENER	*Mary of Egypt*
TCHAIKOVSKY	*The Enchantress*
	Eugene Onegin
	Iolanta
	The Little Slippers
	The Maid of Orleans
	Mazeppa
	The Oprichnik
	The Queen of Spades
	The Voyevoda (Exc)
TELEMANN	*Der Geduldige Socrates*
	Pimpinone
TELLERÍA	*El Joven Piloto*
THOMAS	*Hamlet*
	Mignon
THOMSON	*Four Saints in Three Acts*
	Lord Byron
	The Mother of Us All
TIGRANIAN	*Anush*
	David-Beg
TIJARDOVIĆ	*Little Floramye*
TIPPETT	*The Ice Break*
	King Priam
	The Knot Garden
	The Midsummer Marriage
TORROBA	*Luisa Fernanda*
	Maravilla (Exc)
TUBIN	*Barbara von Tisenhusen*
	The Priest of Reigi
TURNAGE	*Greek*
ULLMANN	*Der Kaiser von Atlantis*
USANDIZAGA	*Las Golondrinas*
UTTINI	*Thetis and Peleus* (Exc)
VAJDA	*Mario and the Magician*
VALLS	*Cançó d'Amor i de Guerra*
VARNEY	*Les Mousquetaires au Couvent*
VAUGHAN WILLIAMS	*Hugh the Drover*
	The Pilgrim's Progress
	Riders to the Sea
	Sir John in Love
VECCHI	*L'Amfiparnaso*
VERDI	*Aida*
	Alzira
	Aroldo
	Attila
	Un Ballo in Maschera
	La Battaglia di Legnano
	Il Corsaro
	Don Carlos
	I Due Foscari
	Ernani
	Falstaff
	La Forza del Destino
	Un Giorno di Regno
	Giovanna d'Arco
	I Lombardi
	Luisa Miller
	Macbeth
	I Masnadieri
	Nabucco
	Oberto
	Otello
	Rigoletto
	Simon Boccanegra
	Stiffelio
	La Traviata
	Il Travatore
	Les Vêpres Siciliennes

VERSTOVSKY	*Askold's Tomb* (Exc)
VILLA-LOBOS	*Magdalena*
VIVALDI	*Catone in Utica*
	Dorilla in Tempe
	La Fida Ninfa
	L'Incoronazione di Dario
	Montezuma
	L'Olimpiade
	Orlando Furioso
	La Senna Festeggiante
	Tito Manlio
VIVES	*Bohemios*
	Doña Francisquita
	La Generala
	Maruxa
	La Villana
WAGNER	*Die Feen*
	Der Fliegende Holländer
	Götterdämmerung
	Lohengrin
	Die Meistersinger von Nürnberg
	Parsifal
	Das Rheingold
	Rienzi
	Siegfried
	Tannhäuser
	Tristan und Isolde
	Die Walküre
S. WAGNER	*Der Bärenhäuter*
WAGNER-RÉGENY	*Der Günstling* (Exc)
WALTON	*The Bear*
	Troilus and Cressida
WARD	*The Crucible*
WEBER	*Abu Hassan*
	Die Drei Pintos
	Euryanthe
	Der Freischütz
	Oberon
	Peter Schmoll
WEILL	*Aufstieg und Fall der Stadt Mahagonny*
	Down in the Valley
	Die Dreigroschenoper
	Happy End
	Der Jasager
	Johnny Johnson
	Der Kuhhandel (Exc)
	Lost in the Stars
	Mahagonny Songspiel
	Die Sieben Todsünden
	Der Silbersee
	Street Scene
	Der Zar lässt sich Photographieren
WEINBERGER	*Shvanda the Bagpiper*
WEIR	*Blond Eckbert*
WEISGALL	*The Stronger*
	The Tenor
WERLE	*Dreaming About Thérèse* (Exc)
WERZLAU	*Meister Röckle*
WILLIAMSON	*The Happy Prince*
	Julius Caesar Jones
WOLF	*Der Corregidor*
WOLF-FERRARI	*I Quatro Rusteghi*
	Il Segreto di Susanna
	Sly
WRIGHT	*Kismet*
	Song of Norway
ZAJC	*Nikola Šubić Zrinjski*
ZANDONAI	*Conchita* (Exc)
	Francesca da Rimini
	Giulietta e Romeo
ZELLER	*Der Vogelhändler*
ZEMLINSKY	*Es War Einmal*
	Eine Florentinische Trägodie
	Der Geburstag der Infantin
	Kleider Machen Leute
	Der Kreidekreis
	Der Traumgörge
ZIMMERMANN	*Die Soldaten*
U. ZIMMERMANN	*Die Weisse Rose*

· Appendix II ·

Operatic Chronology

1580s Florentine Camerata formed.
1597 Peri's *Dafne* – first opera.
1600 Peri's *Euridice* – earliest surviving opera.
1607 Monteverdi's *La Favola d'Orfeo*.
1608 Monteverdi's *Arianna* and *Il Ballo delle Ingrate*; Gagliano's *La Dafne*.
1624 Monteverdi's *Il Combattimento di Tancredi e Clorinda*.
1627 Schütz's *Dafne* – first German opera.
1633 Death of Peri.
1637 First public opera house opened in Venice.
1641 Monteverdi's *Il Ritorno d'Ulisse in Patria*.
1642 Monteverdi's *L'Incoronazione di Poppea*.
1643 Cavalli's *L'Egisto*. Deaths of Gagliano and Monteverdi.
1644 Cavalli's *L'Ormindo*; Hidalgo's *Los Celos Hacen Estrellas* – first zarzuela.
1649 Cavalli's *Giasone*.
1651 Cavalli's *La Calisto*.
1656 Cesti's *Orontea*.
1671 Cambert's *Pomone* – first French opera.
1672 Lully opens Académie Royale de Musique (Opéra) in Paris. Death of Schütz.
1674 Lully's *Alceste*.
1676 Death of Cavalli.
1679 Pistocchi's *Leandro* – first marionette opera.
1684 Blow's *Venus and Adonis* – first British opera; Lully's *Amadis*.
1687 Death of Lully.
1689 Purcell's *Dido and Aeneas*.
1692 Purcell's *The Fairy Queen*.
1695 Death of Purcell.
1704 Death of Charpentier.
1709 Händel's *Agrippina*.
1711 Händel's *Rinaldo*.
1712 Händel's *Il Pastor Fido*.
1713 Händel's *Teseo*.
1718 Händel's *Acis and Galatea*.
1720 Händel's *Radamisto*.
1723 Händel's *Ottone* and *Flavio*.
1724 Händel's *Giulio Cesare* and *Tamerlano*.
1725 Händel's *Rodelinda*; Telemann's *Pimpinone*. Death of A. Scarlatti.
1726 Händel's *Scipione* and *Alessandro*.
1728 Pepusch and Gay's *The Beggar's Opera*.
1730 Händel's *Partenope*.
1732 First theatre at Covent Garden opened. Händel's *Ezio* and *Sosarme*.
1733 Händel's *Orlando*; Pergolesi's *La Serva Padrona*; Rameau's *Hippolyte et Aricie*.
1735 Händel's *Ariodante* and *Alcina*; Rameau's *Les Indes Galantes*.
1736 Händel's *Atalanta*. Death of Pergolesi.
1737 First Teatro San Carlo opened in Naples. Händel's *Giustino* and *Berenice*; Rameau's *Castor et Pollux*.
1738 Händel's *Saul* and *Serse*.
1739 Rameau's *Dardanus*.
1741 Händel's *Deidamia*. Death of Vivaldi.
1743 Händel's *Samson*.
1744 Händel's *Semele*. Death of Campra.
1745 Händel's *Hercules* and *Belshazzar*; Rameau's *Platée*.
1746 Leclair's *Scylla et Glaucus*.
1747 Death of Bononcini.
1749 Rameau's *Zoroastre*.
1750 Death of Albinoni.
1752 Guerre des Bouffons starts in Paris. Rousseau's *Le Devin du Village*.
1757 Death of D. Scarlatti.
1759 Deaths of Graun and Händel.
1760 Piccinni's *La Buona Figliuola*.
1762 Gluck's *Orfeo ed Euridice*.
1763 Teatro Comunale opened in Bologna.
1764 Galuppi's *Il Filosofo di Campagna*. Death of Rameau.
1766 Present Drottningholm Castle Theatre opened.
1767 Gluck's *Alceste*; Mozart's *Apollo et Hyacinthus*. Death of Telemann.
1768 Mozart's *Bastien und Bastienne*.
1769 Mozart's *La Finta Semplice*.
1770 Salle de l'Opéra opened in

Versailles. Gluck's *Paride ed Elena*; Mozart's *Mitridate Rè di Ponto*.
1771 Grétry's *Zémire et Azor*.
1772 Mozart's *Lucio Silla*.
1773 Haydn's *L'Infedeltà Delusa*.
1774 Gluck's *Iphigénie en Aulide*. Death of Jommelli.
1775 Mozart's *La Finta Giardiniera* and *Il Rè Pastore*.
1777 Gluck's *Armide*; Haydn's *Il Mondo della Luna*.
1778 Teatro alla Scala opened in Milan. Death of Arne.
1779 Gluck's *Iphigénie en Tauride* and *Écho et Narcisse*; Mozart's *Zaïde*.
1781 Haydn's *La Fedeltà Premiata*; Mozart's *Idomeneo*.
1782 Haydn's *Orlando Paladino*; Mozart's *Die Entführung aus dem Serail*; Paisiello's *Il Barbiere di Siviglia*; Shield's *Rosina*. Deaths of J.C. Bach and Pietro Metastasio.
1783 Original Opéra-Comique opened in Paris. Death of Hasse.
1784 Grétry's *Richard Coeur de Lion*; Haydn's *Armida*; Salieri's *Les Danaïdes*.
1785 Death of Galuppi.
1786 Dittersdorf's *Doktor und Apotheker*; Martín y Soler's *Una Cosa Rara*; Mozart's *Der Schauspieldirektor* and *Le Nozze di Figaro*; Salieri's *Prima la Musica e Poi le Parole*. Death of Sacchini.
1787 Mozart's *Don Giovanni*; Salieri's *Tarare*. Death of Gluck.
1790 Mozart's *Così fan Tutte*.
1791 Mozart's *Die Zauberflöte* and *La Clemenza di Tito*; Cherubini's *Lodoïska*; Haydn's *Orfeo ed Euridice*. Death of Mozart.
1792 Teatro la Fenice opened in Venice. Cimarosa's *Il Matrimonio Segreto*.
1797 Cherubini's *Médée*.
1799 Fioravanti's *Le Cantatrici Villane*. Death of Dittersdorf.
1800 Boïeldieu's *Le Calife de Bagdad*; Cherubini's *Les Deux Journées*. Death of Piccinni.
1801 Theater an der Wien opened in Vienna. Death of Cimarosa.
1805 Beethoven's *Leonore*.
1807 Méhul's *Joseph*; Spontini's *La Vestale*.
1809 Spontini's *Fernand Cortez*. Death of Haydn.
1810 Rossini's *La Cambiale di Matrimonio*.
1811 Weber's *Abu Hassan*.
1812 Rossini's *La Scala di Seta* and *La Pietra del Paragone*.
1813 Mayr's *Medea in Corinto*; Rossini's *Il Signor Bruschino*, *Tancredi* and *L'Italiana in Algieri*. Death of Grétry.
1814 Beethoven's *Fidelio*; Rossini's *Il Turco in Italia*.
1815 Rossini's *Elisabetta Regina d'Inghilterra* and *Torvaldo e Dorliska*.
1816 Present Teatro San Carlo opened in Naples. Rossini's *Il Barbiere di Siviglia* and *Otello*; Spohr's *Faust*. Death of Paisiello.
1817 Rossini's *La Cenerentola*, *La Gazza Ladra* and *Armida*. Death of Méhul.
1818 Rossini's *Mosè in Egitto*.
1819 Rossini's *Ermione* and *La Donna del Lago*; Spontini's *Olympie*.
1820 Rossini's *Maometto Secondo*.
1821 Weber's *Der Freischütz* and *Die Drei Pintos*.
1822 Schubert's *Alfonso und Estrella*.
1823 Rossini's *Semiramide*; Schubert's *Fierrabras*; Spohr's *Jessonda*; Weber's *Euryanthe*.
1824 Boïeldieu's *La Dame Blanche*; Meyerbeer's *Il Crociato in Egitto*.
1825 Original Bolshoi Theatre opened in Moscow. Rossini's *Il Viaggio a Reims*. Death of Salieri.
1826 Weber's *Oberon*; Rossini's *Le Siège de Corinthe*. Death of Weber.
1827 Bellini's *Il Pirata*. Death of Beethoven.
1828 Auber's *La Muette de Portici*; Marschner's *Der Vampyr*; Rossini's *Le Comte Ory*. Death of Schubert.
1829 Rossini's *Guillaume Tell*; Spontini's *Agnes von Hohenstaufen*; Bellini's *Zaira* and *La Straniera*; Marschner's *Der Templer und die Jüdin*.
1830 Auber's *Fra Diavolo*; Bellini's *I Capuleti e i Montecchi*; Donizetti's *Anna Bolena*.
1831 Bellini's *La Sonnambula* and *Norma*; Hérold's *Zampa*; Meyerbeer's *Robert le Diable*.
1832 Donizetti's *L'Elisir d'Amore*; Hérold's *Le Pré aux Clercs*.
1833 Grand Theatre opened in Warsaw. Bellini's *Beatrice di Tenda*;

Donizetti's *Parisina d'Este*, *Torquato Tasso* and *Lucrezia Borgia*; Marschener's *Hans Heiling*. Death of Hérold.

1834 Donizetti's *Maria Stuarda* and *Gemma di Vergy*; Kreutzer's *Das Nachtlager von Granada*; Wagner's *Die Feen*. Death of Boïeldieu.

1835 Bellini's *I Puritani*; Auber's *Le Cheval de Bronze*; Donizetti's *Lucia di Lammermoor* and *Marino Faliero*; Halévy's *La Juive*. Death of Bellini.

1836 Adam's *Le Postillon de Longjumeau*; Donizetti's *Belisario*, *Betly* and *Il Campanello*; Glinka's *A Life for the Tsar*; Meyerbeer's *Les Huguenots*; Wagner's *Das Liebesverbot*.

1837 Auber's *Le Domino Noir*; Donizetti's *Roberto Devereux*; Lortzing's *Zar und Zimmermann*; Mercadante's *Il Giuramento*. Deaths of Fioravanti and Zingarelli.

1838 Berlioz's *Benvenuto Cellini*; Donizetti's *Poliuto*.

1839 Verdi's *Oberto*. Death of Paer.

1840 Donizetti's *La Fille du Régiment* and *La Favorite*; Verdi's *Un Giorno di Regno*.

1841 Auber's *Les Diamants de la Couronne*; Donizetti's *Rita*.

1842 Donizetti's *Linda di Chamounix*; Glinka's *Ruslan and Ludmila*; Lortzing's *Der Wildschütz*; Verdi's *Nabucco*; Wagner's *Rienzi*. Death of Cherubini.

1843 Balfe's *The Bohemian Girl*; Donizetti's *Don Pasquale*; Verdi's *I Lombardi*; Wagner's *Der Fliegende Holländer*.

1844 Erkel's *László Hunyadi*; Flotow's *Alessandro Stradella*; Verdi's *Ernani* and *I Due Foscari*.

1845 Lortzing's *Undine*; Verdi's *Giovanna d'Arco* and *Alzira*; Wallace's *Maritana*; Wagner's *Tannhäuser*. Death of Mayr.

1846 Berlioz's *La Damnation de Faust*; Lortzing's *Der Waffenschmied*; Verdi's *Attila*.

1847 Flotow's *Martha*; Verdi's *Macbeth* and *I Masnadieri*. Death of Mendelssohn.

1848 Moniuszko's *Halka*; Verdi's *Il Corsaro*. Death of Donizetti.

1849 Meyerbeer's *Le Prophète*; Nicolaï's *Die Lustigen Weiber von Windsor*; Verdi's *La Battaglia di Legnano* and *Luisa Miller*. Death of Nicolaï.

1850 Ricci's *Crispino e la Comare*; Schumann's *Genoveva*; Verdi's *Stiffelio*; Wagner's *Lohengrin*.

1851 Wagner publishes *Opera and Drama*. Verdi's *Rigoletto*; Gounod's *Sapho*. Deaths of Lortzing and Spontini.

1852 Adam's *Si J'Étais Roi*.

1853 Verdi's *Il Trovatore* and *La Traviata*.

1854 Wagner's *Das Rheingold*; Meyerbeer's *L'Étoile du Nord*.

1855 Verdi's *Les Vêpres Siciliennes*.

1856 Present Bolshoi Theatre opened in Moscow. Wagner's *Die Walküre*; Dargomijsky's *Rusalka*; Auber's *Manon Lescaut*. Deaths of Adam and Schumann.

1857 Verdi's *Aroldo* and *Simon Boccanegra*. Death of Glinka.

1858 Present theatre at Covent Garden opened. Cornelius's *Der Barbier von Bagdad*; Offenbach's *Orphée aux Enfers*; Gounod's *Le Médecin Malgré Lui*.

1859 Wagner's *Tristan und Isolde*; Verdi's *Un Ballo in Maschera*; Gounod's *Faust*; Bizet's *Don Procopio*; Meyerbeer's *Dinorah*. Death of Spohr.

1860 Maryinsky Theatre opened in St Petersburg. Gounod's *Philémon et Baucis*.

1861 Erkel's *Bánk Bán*. Death of Marschner.

1862 Teatro Liceo opened in Barcelona. Benedict's *The Lily of Killarney*; Berlioz's *Béatrice et Bénédict*; Bizet's *Ivan IV*; Gounod's *La Reine de Saba*. Death of Halévy.

1863 Berlioz's *Les Troyens*; Bizet's *Les Pêcheurs de Perles*; Serov's *Judith*.

1864 Teatro Comunale opened in Florence. Gounod's *Mireille*; Moussorgsky's *The Marriage*; Offenbach's *La Belle Hélène*. Death of Meyerbeer.

1865 Moniuszko's *The Haunted Manor*; Suppé's *Die Schöne Galatea*; Meyerbeer's *L'Africaine*.

1866 Offenbach's *Barbe-Bleue* and *La Vie Parisienne*; Smetana's *The Brandenburgers in Bohemia* and *The Bartered Bride*; Thomas's *Mignon*.

1867 Bizet's *La Jolie Fille de Perth*;

Gounod's *Roméo et Juliette*; Offenbach's *Robinson Crusoé* and *La Grande-Duchesse de Gérolstein*; Verdi's *Don Carlos*; Blodek's *In the Well*. Death of Pacini.

1868 Smetana's *Dalibor*; Wagner's *Die Meistersinger von Nürnberg*; Offenbach's *La Périchole*; Thomas's *Hamlet*. Deaths of Berwald and Rossini.

1869 Vienna State Opera opened. Borodin's *Prince Igor*; Verdi's *La Forza del Destino*; Moussorgsky's *Boris Godunov*; Wagner's *Siegfried*; Offenbach's *Les Brigands*. Deaths of Berlioz and Dargomijsky.

1870 Gomes's *Il Guarany*. Deaths of Balfe and Mercadante.

1871 Verdi's *Aida*. Death of Auber.

1872 Smetana's *Libuše*; Dargomijsky's *The Stone Guest*; Bizet's *Djamileh*.

1873 Moussorgsky's *Khovanschina*; Delibes's *Le Roi l'a Dit*; Rimsky-Korsakov's *The Maid of Pskov*.

1874 J. Strauss's *Die Fledermaus*; Wagner's *Götterdämmerung*; Smetana's *The Two Widows*; Tchaikovsky's *The Oprichnik*; Moussorgsky's *Sorochintsy Fair*.

1875 Paris Opéra (Salle Garnier) opened. Carl Rosa Opera Company founded. Bizet's *Carmen*; Boito's *Mefistofele*; Goldmark's *Die Königin von Saba*; Rubinstein's *The Demon*; Sullivan's *Trial By Jury*. Death of Bizet.

1876 D'Oyly Carte Opera Company formed. First complete performance of Wagner's *Der Ring des Nibelungen* at inaugural Bayreuth Festival. Ponchielli's *La Gioconda*; Smetana's *The Kiss*; Tchaikovsky's *Vakula the Blacksmith*. Death of Götz.

1877 Chabrier's *L'Étoile*; Massenet's *Le Roi de Lahore*; Planquette's *Les Cloches de Corneville*; Saint-Saëns's *Samson et Dalila*; Sullivan's *The Sorcerer*. Death of Borodin.

1878 Smetana's *The Secret*; Sullivan's *H.M.S. Pinafore*; Heise's *King and Marshal*.

1879 Monte Carlo Opera opened. Tchaikovsky's *Eugene Onegin*; Sullivan's *The Pirates of Penzance*; Suppé's *Boccaccio*.

1880 Teatro dell'Opera opened in Rome. Rimsky-Korsakov's *May Night*; Audran's *La Mascotte*. Death of Offenbach.

1881 Prague National Theatre opened. Massenet's *Hérodiade*; Offenbach's *Les Contes d'Hoffmann*; Sullivan's *Patience*; Tchaikovsky's *The Maid of Orleans*. Death of Moussorgsky.

1882 Wagner's *Parsifal*; Dvořák's *Dimitrij*; Millöcker's *Der Bettelstudent*; Rimsky-Korsakov's *The Snow Maiden*; Smetana's *The Devil's Wall*; Sullivan's *Iolanthe*.

1883 Original Metropolitan Opera House opened in New York. Delibes's *Lakmé*; J. Strauss's *Eine Nacht in Venedig*. Deaths of Wagner and Flotow.

1884 Massenet's *Manon*; Puccini's *Le Villi*; Reyer's *Sigurd*; Sullivan's *Princess Ida*; Tchaikovsky's *Mazeppa*. Death of Smetana.

1885 Sullivan's *The Mikado*; Massenet's *Le Cid*; J. Strauss's *Der Zigeunerbaron*.

1886 Chabrier's *Gwendoline*. Deaths of Liszt and Ponchielli.

1887 Verdi's *Otello*; Charbrier's *Le Roi Malgré Lui*; Sullivan's *Ruddigore*; Tchaikovsky's *The Enchantress*.

1888 Lalo's *Le Roi d'Ys*; Sullivan's *The Yeomen of the Guard*.

1889 Dvořák's *Jakobín*; Massenet's *Esclarmonde*; Puccini's *Edgar*; Sullivan's *The Gondoliers*.

1890 Mascagni's *Cavalleria Rusticana*; Tchaikovsky's *The Queen of Spades*; Catalani's *Loreley*. Death of Franck.

1891 Zürich Opernhaus opened. Mascagni's *L'Amico Fritz*; Sullivan's *Ivanhoe*; Zeller's *Der Vogelhändler*. Death of Delibes.

1892 Catalani's *La Wally*; Leoncavallo's *Pagliacci*; Massenet's *Werther*; Tchaikovsky's *Iolanta*. Death of Lalo.

1893 Royal Flemish Opera founded. Verdi's *Falstaff*; Humperdinck's *Hänsel und Gretel*; Puccini's *Manon Lescaut*; Rachmaninov's *Aleko*; Sullivan's *Utopia Limited*. Deaths of Catalani, Erkel, Gounod and Tchaikovsky.

1894 Massenet's *Thaïs* and *La Navarraise*; Rezniček's *Donna Diana*; Strauss's

Guntram. Deaths of Chabrier and Rubinstein.

1895 Chausson's *Le Roi Arthus*; Keinzl's *Der Evangelimann*; Rimsky-Korsakov's *Christmas Eve*; Taneyev's *Oresteia*. Death of Suppé.

1896 Puccini's *La Bohème*; Giordano's *Andrea Chénier*; Sibelius's *The Maiden in the Tower*; Wolf's *Der Corregidor*; Sullivan's *The Grand Duke*. Deaths of Gomes and Thomas.

1897 Fibich's *Šárka*; Leoncavallo's *La Bohème*; d'Indy's *Fervaal*; Massenet's *Sapho*.

1898 Present Royal Opera House opened in Stockholm; Vienna Volksoper opened. Mascagni's *Iris*; Giordano's *Fedora*; Messager's *Véronique*; Rimsky-Korsakov's *Sadko* and *Mozart and Salieri*.

1899 Dvořák's *The Devil and Kate*; Foerster's *Eva*; Massenet's *Cendrillon*; Rimsky-Korsakov's *The Tsar's Bride*; J. Strauss's *Wiener Blut*. Deaths of Chausson, Millöcker and J. Strauss.

1900 Charpentier's *Louise*; Leoncavallo's *Zazà*; Puccini's *Tosca*; Rimsky-Korsakov's *The Tale of Tsar Saltan*. Death of Sullivan.

1901 Dvořák's *Rusalka*; Strauss's *Feuersnot*; Massenet's *Grisélidis*. Death of Verdi.

1902 Debussy's *Pelléas et Mélisande*; Cilea's *Adriana Lecouvreur*; Nielsen's *Saul og David*; Massenet's *Le Jongleur de Notre Dame*; German's *Merrie England*; Rimsky-Korsakov's *Kashchey the Immortal*.

1903 First complete opera recording. Wolf-Ferrari's *Le Donne Curiose* and d'Albert's *Tiefland*. Deaths of Planquette and Wolf.

1904 Janáček's *Jenůfa* and *Fate*; Puccini's *Madama Butterfly*; Delius's *Koanga*. Death of Dvořák.

1905 Strauss's *Salome*; de Falla's *La Vida Breve*; Lehár's *Die Lustige Witwe*; Massenet's *Chérubin*.

1906 Rachmaninov's *The Covetous Knight* and *Francesca da Rimini*; Nielsen's *Maskarade*; Wolf-Ferrari's *I Quatro Rusteghi*; Smyth's *The Wreckers*.

1907 Delius's *A Village Romeo and Juliet*; Dukas's *Ariane et Barbe-Bleue*; Rimsky-Korsakov's *The Invisible City of Kitezh*; Ravel's *L'Heure Espagnole*; Messager's *Fortunio*.

1908 Present Teatro Colón opened in Buenos Aires. Death of Rimsky-Korsakov.

1909 Strauss's *Elektra*; Schönberg's *Erwartung*; Wolf-Ferrari's *Il Segreto di Susanna*; Rimsky-Korsakov's *The Golden Cockerel*; Lehár's *Der Graf von Luxemburg*.

1910 Humperdinck's *Die Königskinder*; Bloch's *Macbeth*; Delius's *Fennimore and Gerda*; Puccini's *La Fanciulla del West*; Massenet's *Don Quichotte*. Death of Fibich.

1911 Bartók's *Duke Bluebeard's Castle*; Strauss's *Der Rosenkavalier*; Wolf-Ferrari's *I Gioielli della Madonna*; Joplin's *Treemonisha*. Death of Mahler.

1912 Schreker's *Der Ferne Klang*. Death of Massenet.

1913 First opera performance at Verona Arena. Fauré's *Pénélope*; Montemezzi's *L'Amore dei Tre Re*.

1914 Finnish National Opera founded. Boughton's *The Immortal Hour*; Roussel's *Padmâvatî*; Schmidt's *Notre-Dame*; Stravinsky's *The Nightingale*; Vaughan Williams's *Hugh the Drover*; Zandonai's *Francesca da Rimini*.

1915 Kálmán's *Die Csárdásfürstin*. Death of Goldmark.

1916 Strauss's *Ariadne auf Naxos*; Granados's *Goyescas*; Holst's *Sāvitri*; Korngold's *Violanta*. Death of Granados.

1917 Busoni's *Arlecchino* and *Turandot*; Pfitzner's *Palestrina*; Puccini's *La Rondine*; Prokofiev's *The Gambler*; Schönberg's *Die Glückliche Hand*; Zemlinsky's *Eine Florentinische Tragödie*.

1918 Puccini's *Il Trittico*. Deaths of Boito, Cui, Debussy and Lecocq.

1919 Strauss's *Die Frau ohne Schatten*. Death of Leoncavallo.

1920 Janáček's *The Excursions of Mr Brouček*; Korngold's *Die Tote Stadt*. Death of Bruch.

1921 Salzburg Festival founded. Prokofiev's *The Love of Three Oranges*; Janáček's *Káťa Kabanová*; Honegger's *Le Roi David*. Deaths of

Humperdinck, Saint-Saëns and Enrico Caruso.

1922 Stravinsky's *Mavra* and *Renard*; Zemlinsky's *Der Geburstag der Infantin*.

1923 BBC gives first radio broadcast of an opera. San Francisco Opera Association founded. Hahn's *Ciboulette*; de Falla's *El Retablo de Maese Pedro*.

1924 Janáček's *The Cunning Little Vixen*; Boito's *Nerone*; Kálmán's *Gräfin Mariza*; Strauss's *Intermezzo*. Deaths of Busoni, Fauré, Puccini and Stanford.

1925 Berg's *Wozzeck*; Busoni's *Doktor Faust*; Ravel's *L'Enfant et les Sortilèges*; Holst's *At the Boar's Head*. Death of Satie.

1926 Puccini's *Turandot*; Hindemith's *Cardillac*; Janáček's *The Macropolus Case*; Kodály's *Háry János*; Milhaud's *Les Malheurs d'Orphée*; Szymanowski's *King Roger*.

1927 Prokofiev's *The Fiery Angel*; Křenek's *Jonny Spielt Auf*; Stravinsky's *Oedipus Rex*; Weinberger's *Shvanda the Bagpiper*; Wolf-Ferrari's *Sly*; Ibert's *Angélique*.

1928 First operatic sound film made. Strauss's *Die Ägyptische Helena*; Weill's *Die Dreigroschenoper*. Death of Janáček.

1929 Lehár's *Das Land des Lächelns*; Vaughan Williams's *Sir John in Love*. Death of Messager.

1930 Janáček's *From the House of the Dead*; Shostakovich's *The Nose*; Weill's *Aufstieg und Fall der Stadt Mahagonny*; Schönberg's *Von Heute auf Morgen*.

1931 Sadler's Wells Opera founded. Hába's *The Mother*. Deaths of d'Indy and Nielsen.

1932 Schönberg's *Moses und Aron*.

1933 Maggio Musicale Fiorentino founded. Strauss's *Arabella*; Thomson's *Four Saints in Three Acts*; Weill's *Die Seiben Todsünden*.

1934 Glyndebourne Festival founded. Hindemith's *Mathis der Maler*; Lehár's *Giuditta*; Holst's *The Wandering Scholar*; Shostakovich's *Lady Macbeth of Mtsensk*; Respighi's *La Fiamma*. Deaths of Bruneau, Delius and Holst.

1935 Strauss's *Die Schweigsame Frau*; Gershwin's *Porgy and Bess*. Deaths of Berg and Dukas.

1936 BBC gives first TV broadcast of an opera. Enescu's *Oedipe*; Wolf-Ferrari's *Il Campiello*. Deaths of German and Respighi.

1937 Berg's *Lulu*; Honegger and Ibert's *L'Aiglon*; Vaughan Williams's *Riders to the Sea*; Menotti's *Amelia al Ballo*. Deaths of Gershwin, Ravel, Roussel and Szymanowski.

1938 Strauss's *Friedenstag* and *Daphne*; Egk's *Peer Gynt*; Honegger's *Jeanne d'Arc au Bûcher*; Martinů's *Julietta*; Kabalevsky's *The Craftsman of Clamecy*.

1939 Orff's *Der Mond*.

1940 Prokofiev's *Semeon Kotko* and *The Duenna*; Dallapiccola's *Volo di Notte*; Strauss's *Die Liebe der Danae*.

1941 Britten's *Paul Bunyan*.

1942 Strauss's *Capriccio*. Deaths of Franchetti and Zemlinsky.

1943 Orff's *Die Kluge*. Death of Rachmaninov.

1944 New York City Opera founded. Ullmann's *Der Kaiser von Atlantis*. Death of Zandonai.

1945 Britten's *Peter Grimes* and *The Little Sweep*. Deaths of Bartók and Mascagni.

1946 Present Royal Opera company founded at Covent Garden; Netherlands Opera and English Opera Group founded. Prokofiev's *War and Peace*; Britten's *The Rape of Lucretia*; Menotti's *The Medium*; Weill's *Street Scene*. Death of de Falla.

1947 Komische Oper opened in East Berlin; Edinburgh Festival and Welsh National Opera founded. Britten's *Albert Herring*; Einem's *Dantons Tod*; Menotti's *The Telephone*; Poulenc's *Les Mamelles de Tirésias*; Thomson's *The Mother of Us All*.

1948 Aldeburgh and Aix-en-Provence Festivals founded. Prokofiev's *The Story of a Real Man*. Deaths of Giordano, Lehár and Wolf-Ferrari.

1949 Bliss's *The Olympians*; Dallapiccola's *Il Prigioniero*; Gerhard's *The Duenna*; Orff's

Antigonae; Suchoň's *The Whirlpool*. Deaths of Pfitzner and Strauss.
1950 Canadian Opera Company founded. Menotti's *The Consul*. Deaths of Cilea and Weill.
1951 Norwegian Opera and Wexford Festival founded. Stravinsky's *The Rake's Progress*; Britten's *Billy Budd*; Menotti's *Amahl and the Night Visitors*; Vaughan Williams's *The Pilgrim's Progress*. Deaths of Foerster and Schönberg.
1952 Henze's *Boulevard Solitude*; Bernstein's *Trouble in Tahiti*.
1953 Britten's *Gloriana*; Einem's *Der Prozess*; Shaporin's *The Decembrists*. Deaths of Kálmán and Prokofiev.
1954 Australian Opera and Chicago Lyric Opera founded. Britten's *The Turn of the Screw*; Copland's *The Tender Land*; Walton's *Troilus and Cressida*. Death of Alfano.
1955 La Piccola Scala opened in Milan. Tippett's *The Midsummer Marriage*; Rota's *Il Cappello di Paglia di Firenze*. Deaths of Enescu and Honegger.
1956 Bregenz Festival, Opera Society of Washington, Santa Fe Opera and Deutsche Oper am Rhein founded. Henze's *König Hirsch*; Bernstein's *Candide*; Moore's *The Ballad of Baby Doe*. Deaths of Charpentier and Glière.
1957 Dallas Civic Opera and Opera Company of Boston founded. Poulenc's *Dialogues des Carmélites*; Bernstein's *West Side Story*; Hindemith's *Die Harmonie der Welt*; Egk's *Der Revisor*. Deaths of Korngold, Sibelius and Toscanini.
1958 Barber's *Vanessa*; Pizzetti's *L'Assassinio nella Cattedrale*; Britten's *Noye's Fludde*; Menotti's *Maria Golovin*. Death of Vaughan Williams.
1959 Orff's *Oedipus der Tyrann*; Poulenc's *La Voix Humaine*. Deaths of Martinů and Villa-Lobos.
1960 Britten's *A Midsummer Night's Dream*; Henze's *Der Prinz von Homberg*. Death of Boughton.
1961 Henze's *Elegie für Junge Liebende*; Martinů's *The Greek Passion*; Nono's *Intolleranza*. Death of Sir Thomas Beecham.
1962 Scottish Opera founded. Tippett's *King Priam*; Ward's *The Crucible*. Death of Ibert.
1963 Deaths of Hindemith and Poulenc.
1964 Britten's *Curlew River*; Szokolay's *Blood Wedding*; Ginastera's *Don Rodrigo*.
1965 Henze's *Der Junge Lord*; Zimmermann's *Die Soldaten*.
1966 Present Metropolitan Opera in Lincoln Center opened in New York. Henze's *The Bassarids*; Britten's *The Burning Fiery Furnace*; Barber's *Antony and Cleopatra*.
1967 Salzburg Easter Festival founded. Ginastera's *Bomarzo*; Walton's *The Bear*; Goehr's *Arden Must Die*. Deaths of Kodály and Weinberger.
1968 Glyndebourne Touring Opera founded. Birtwistle's *Punch and Judy*; Britten's *The Prodigal Son*; Dallapiccola's *Ulisse*. Death of Pizzetti.
1969 Kent Opera founded. Penderecki's *The Devils of Loudun*; Tippett's *The Knot Garden*.
1971 Britten's *Owen Wingrave*; Einem's *Der Besuch der Alten Dame*; Ginastera's *Beatrix Cenci*. Death of Stravinsky.
1972 Opéra du Rhin and Moscow Chamber Opera founded. Maxwell Davies's *Taverner*.
1973 Sydney Opera House opened. Britten's *Death in Venice*. Death of Malipiero.
1974 Sadler's Wells Opera becomes English National Opera. Death of Milhaud.
1975 Sallinen's *The Horseman*; Kokkonen's *The Last Temptations*. Deaths of Bliss, Dallapiccola and Shostakovich.
1976 Henze's *We Come to the River*. Death of Britten.
1977 Tippett's *The Ice Break*; Musgrave's *Mary Queen of Scots*. Death of Maria Callas.
1978 Opera North founded. Ligeti's *Le Grand Macabre*; Reimann's *Lear*; Sallinen's *The Red Line*.
1979 Musgrave's *A Christmas Carol*.
1980 Maxwell Davies's *The Lighthouse*; Rihm's *Jakob Lenz*.
1981 Stockhausen's *Donnerstag aus Licht*. Death of Barber.
1982 Death of Orff.

1983 Messiaen's *Saint François d'Assise*; Bernstein's *A Quiet Place*; Henze's *The English Cat*. Deaths of Egk, Ginastera and Walton.

1984 Berio's *Un Rè in Ascolto*; Glass's *Akhnaten*; Sallinen's *The King Goes Forth to France*.

1986 Los Angeles Music Center Opera founded. Birtwistle's *Yan Tan Tethera*.

1987 Adams's *Nixon in China*. Deaths of Fortner and Kabalevsky.

1989 Opéra-Bastille opened in Paris. Tippett's *New Year*. Deaths of Thomson and Herbert von Karajan.

1990 Deaths of Bernstein, Copland and Nono.

1991 Birtwistle's *Gawain*. Death of Křenek.

1992 Sallinen's *Kullervo*. Death of Messiaen.

1994 Birtwistle's *The Second Mrs Kong*.

1995 Sallinen's *The Palace*.

· Bibliography ·

The following is only a selective bibliography. The literature on opera is vast, and this listing is intended to provide a representative selection of books in English, some of them designed for the general opera-goer and others intended for specialist musicians. In the sections for composers, conductors and singers, autobiographies are not listed as these are mentioned in the main text.

1 Opera – General

Adam, Nicky (ed) *Who's Who in British Opera* (Scolar Press, Aldershot, 1993)
Arblaster, Anthony *Viva la Libertà: Politics in Opera* (Verso, London, 1992)
Demuth, Norman *French Opera: its Development to the Revolution* (Artemis, Sussex, 1963)
Donnington, Robert *Opera and its Symbols: the Unity of Words, Music and Staging* (Yale University Press, New York, 1990)
— *The Rise of Opera* (Faber & Faber, London, 1981)
Eaton, Quaintance *Opera Production: a Handbook* (University of Minnesota Press, Minneapolis, 1974)
Fulcher, Jane *French Grand Opera as Politics and Politicised Art* (Cambridge University Press, 1987)
Grout, Donald Jay *A Short History of Opera* (3rd edition, Columbia University Press, New York, 1988)
Hamilton, David (ed) *The Metropolitan Opera Encyclopedia* (Thames & Hudson, London, 1987)
Harewood, Earl of (ed) *Kobbé's Complete Opera Book* (10th edition, Bodley Head, London, 1987)
Headington, Christopher *Opera: a History* (Bodley Head, London, 1987)
Heriot, Angus *The Castrati in Opera* (Secker & Warburg, London, 1956)
Hipsher, Edward Ellsworth *American Opera and its Composers* (Da Capo Press, New York, 1978)
Holden, Amanda (ed) *The Viking Opera Guide* (Viking, London, 1993)
Kerman, Joseph *Opera as Drama* (2nd edition, University of California Press, Los Angeles, 1988)
Kimbell, David *Italian Opera* (Cambridge University Press, 1991)
Larue, C. Steven (ed) *International Dictionary of Opera* (2 vols, St James Press, Detroit, 1993)
Loewenberg, Alfred *Annals of Opera 1597–1940* (3rd edition, John Calder, London, 1978)
Martin, George *The Companion to Twentieth Century Opera* (John Murray, London, 1989)
—*The Opera Companion* (Macmillan, London, 1962)
Mitchell, Jerome *The Walter Scott Operas* (University of Alabama Press, 1977)
Orrey, Leslie *The Encyclopedia of Opera* (Pitman, London, 1976)
Osborne, Charles *The Dictionary of Opera* (Macdonald, London, 1983)
Plant, Eric A. *Grand Opera: Mirror of the Western Mind* (Ivan R. Dee, Chicago, 1993)
Rosand, Ellen *Opera in Seventeenth Century Venice: the Creation of a Genre* (University of California Press, Los Angeles, 1991)
Rosselli, John *The Opera Industry in Italy from Cimarosa to Verdi: the Role of the Impresario* (Cambridge University Press, 1984)
Sadie, Stanley (ed) *History of Opera* (Macmillan, London, 1989)
— *The New Grove Dictionary of Opera* (4 vols, Macmillan, London, 1992)
Schmidgall, Gary *Literature as Opera* (Oxford University Press, New York, 1977)
— *Shakespeare and Opera* (Oxford University Press, New York, 1990)
Sternfeld, F.W. *The Birth of Opera* (Clarendon Press, Oxford, 1993)
Tyrrell, John *Czech Opera* (Cambridge University Press, 1988)

Warrack, John & West, Ewan *The Oxford Dictionary of Opera* (Oxford University Press, 1992)
Westerman, Gerhart von *Opera Guide* (Thames & Hudson, London, 1964)
White, Eric Walter *A History of English Opera* (Faber & Faber, London, 1983)

2 Operetta

Bordman, Gerald *American Operetta* (Oxford University Press, New York, 1981)
Harding, James *Folies de Paris: the Rise and Fall of French Operetta* (Chappell, London, 1979)
Hughes, Gervase *Composers of Operetta* (Macmillan, London, 1962)
Hyman, Alan *Sullivan and His Satellites: a Survey of English Operettas 1860–1914* (Chappell, London, 1978)
Lubbock, Mark *The Complete Book of Light Opera* (Putnam, London, 1962)
Traubner, Richard *Operetta: a Theatrical History* (Oxford University Press, 1983)

3 Opera Houses & Companies

Arruga, Lorenzo *La Scala* (Electa Editrice, Milan, 1975)
Arundell, Dennis *The Story of Sadler's Wells 1683–1977* (2nd edition, David & Charles, London, 1978)
Couch, John Philip *The Opera Lover's Guide to Europe* (Proscenium, New York, 1991)
Fawkes, Richard *Welsh National Opera* (Julia MacRae, London, 1986)
Gallup, Stephen *A History of the Salzburg Festival* (Weidenfeld & Nicolson, London, 1987)
Haltrecht, Montague *The Quiet Showman: Sir David Webster and the Royal Opera House* (Collins, London, 1975)
Hartford, Robert *Bayreuth: the Early Years* (Victor Gollancz, London, 1980)
Higgins, John (ed) *Glyndebourne: a Celebration* (Jonathan Cape, London, 1984)
Hughes, Spike *Glyndebourne* (2nd edition, David & Charles, London, 1981)
Rosenthal, Harold *Opera at Covent Garden: a Short History* (Victor Gollancz, London, 1967)
Sokol, Martin I. *The New York City Opera: an American Adventure* (Macmillan, New York, 1981)
Spotts, Frederic *Bayreuth: a History of the Wagner Festival* (Yale University Press, New York, 1994)
Turnbull, Robert *The Opera Gazatteer* (Trefoil, London, 1988)
Walsh, T.J. *Second Empire Opera: the Théâtre Lyrique Paris 1851–1870* (John Calder, London, 1981)

4 Librettists

FitzLyon, April *Lorenzo da Ponte* (John Calder, London, 1982)
Gilbert, W.S. *Complete Operas* (Random House, New York, 1932)
Hodges, Sheila *Lorenzo da Ponte: the Life and Times of Mozart's Librettist* (Granada, London, 1985)
Honolka, Kurt *Papageno: Emanuel Schikaneder: Man of the Theatre in Mozart's Time* (Amadeus Press, Portland, 1990)
Smith, Patrick J. *The Tenth Muse: a Historical Study of the Opera Libretto* (Victor Gollancz, London, 1971)

5 Producers

Fuchs, Peter Paul *The Music Theatre of Walter Felsenstein* (Quartet, London, 1991)
Hirst, David L. *Giorgio Strehler* (Cambridge University Press, 1993)
Romain, Michael *A Profile of Jonathan Miller* (Cambridge University Press, 1992)
Skelton, Geoffrey *Wieland Wagner: the Positive Sceptic* (Victor Gollancz, London, 1971)

6 Composers

Bellini
Orrey, Leslie *Bellini* (Master Musicians, J.M. Dent, London, 1969)
Osborne, Charles *The Bel Canto Operas of Rossini, Donizetti, Bellini* (Methuen, London, 1994)
Weinstock, Herbert *Vincenzo Bellini* (Methuen, London, 1971)
Berg
Perle, George *The Operas of Alban Berg* (2 vols, University of California Press, Los Angeles, 1980)
Schmalfeldt, Janet *Berg's Wozzeck: Harmonic Language and Dramatic Design* (Yale University Press, New Haven, 1983)
Berlioz
Cairns, David *Berlioz* (2 vols, André Deutsch, London, 1989)
Macdonald, Hugh *Berlioz* (Master Musicians, J.M. Dent, London, 1982)
Bizet
Dean, Winton *Georges Bizet: His Life and Work* (J.M. Dent, London, 1965)
Boughton
Hurd, Michael *Immortal Hour: the Life and Period of Rutland Boughton* (Routledge & Kegan Paul, London, 1962)
— *Rutland Boughton and the Glastonbury Festivals* (Clarendon Press, Oxford, 1993)
Britten
Banks, Paul (ed) *Britten's Gloriana* (Boydell Press, Woodbridge, 1993)
Herbert, David (ed) *The Operas of Benjamin Britten* (Hamish Hamilton, London, 1979)
Howard, Patricia *The Operas of Benjamin Britten* (Barrie & Rockliff, London, 1969)
Kennedy, Michael *Britten* (2nd edition, Master Musicians, J.M. Dent, London, 1993)
Cavalli
Glover, Jane *Cavalli* (Batsford, London, 1978)
Chabrier
Myers, Rollo *Emmanuel Chabrier and His Circle* (J.M. Dent, London, 1969)
Debussy
Orledge, Robert *Debussy and the Theatre* (Cambridge University Press, 1982)
Donizetti
Allitt, John Stewart *Donizetti* (Element, Rockport, 1991)
Ashbrook, William *Donizetti and His Operas* (Cambridge University Press, 1982)
Gossett, Philip *Anna Bolena and the Artistic Maturity of Gaetano Donizetti* (Clarendon Press, Oxford, 1985)
Osborne, Charles *The Bel Canto Operas of Rossini, Donizetti, Bellini* (Methuen, London, 1994)
Weinstock, Herbert *Donizetti* (Methuen, London, 1964)
Glinka
Brown, David *Mikhail Glinka* (Oxford University Press, 1974)
Gluck
Brown, Bruce Alan *Gluck and the French Theatre in Vienna* (Clarendon Press, Oxford, 1991)
Einstein, Alfred *Gluck* (Master Musicians, J.M. Dent, London, 1964)
Howard, Patricia *Gluck and the Birth of Modern Opera* (Barrie & Rockliff, London, 1963)
Newman, Ernest *Gluck and the Opera* (Victor Gollancz, London, 1964)
Gounod
Harding, James *Gounod* (Allen & Unwin, London, 1973)
Huebner, Steven *The Operas of Charles Gounod* (Clarendon Press, Oxford, 1990)
Grétry
Charlton, David *Grétry and the Growth of Opéra-Comique* (Cambridge University Press, 1986)
Halévy
Jordan, Ruth *Fromental Halévy: His Life and Music* (Kahn & Averill, London, 1994)
Händel
Dean, Winton *Handel and the Opera Seria* (University of California Press, Los Angeles, 1969)
— *Handel's Dramatic Oratorios and Masques* (Clarendon Press, Oxford, 1959)

Dean, Winton & Knapp, John Merrill *Handel's Operas 1704–26* (Clarendon Press, Oxford, 1987)
Harris, Ellen *Handel and the Pastoral Tradition* (Oxford University Press, London, 1980)
Hogwood, Christopher *Handel* (Thames & Hudson, London, 1984)
Keats, Jonathan *Handel: the Man and His Music* (Victor Gollancz, London, 1985)
Lang, Paul Henry *George Frideric Handel* (Faber & Faber, London, 1966)

Haydn

Robbins Landon, H.C. *Haydn: Chronicle and Works* (5 vols, Thames & Hudson, London, 1976–80)

Janáček

Chisholm, Erik *The Operas of Leoš Janáček* (Pergamon Press, Oxford, 1971)
Ewans, Michael *Janáček's Tragic Operas* (Faber & Faber, London, 1977)
Tyrrell, John *Janáček's Operas: a Documentary Account* (Faber & Faber, London, 1992)

Křenek

Cook, Susan S. *Opera for a New Republic: the Zeitopern of Krenek, Weill and Hindemith* (Ann Arbor, Michigan, 1988)
Stewart, John L. *Ernst Krenek: the Man and His Music* (University of California Press, Los Angeles, 1991)

Mascagni

Stivender, David *Mascagni* (Pro/Am Music Resources, New York, 1988)

Massenet

Harding, James *Massenet* (J.M. Dent, London, 1970)
Irvine, Demar *Massenet: a Chronicle of His Life and Times* (Amadeus Press, Portland, 1994)

Mayr

Allitt, John Stewart *J.S. Mayr: Father of 19th Century Italian Music* (Element, Shaftesbury, 1989)

Menotti

Gruen, John *Menotti: a Biography* (Macmillan, New York, 1978)

Meyerbeer

Becker, Heinz & Gudrum *Giacomo Meyerbeer: a Life in Letters* (Christopher Helm, London, 1989)

Moniuszko

Maciejewski, B.M. *Moniuszko: Father of Polish Opera* (Allegro, London, 1979)

Monteverdi

Arnold; Denis *Monteverdi* (3rd edition, Master Musicians, J.M. Dent, London, 1990)
Arnold, Denis & Fortune, Nigel (eds) *The New Monteverdi Companion* (Faber & Faber, London, 1985)

Moussorgsky

Calvocoressi, M.D. *Moussorgsky* (2nd edition, Master Musicians, J.M. Dent, London, 1974)
Leyda, Jay & Bertensson, Sergei (eds) *The Musorgsky Reader* (Da Capo, New York, 1970)

Mozart

Batley, E.M. *A Preface to the Magic Flute* (Dennis Dobson, London, 1969)
Brophy, Brigid *Mozart the Dramatist* (2nd edition, Libris, London, 1988)
Chailley, Jacques *The Magic Flute: Masonic Opera* (Victor Gollancz, London, 1972)
Dent, Edward J. *Mozart's Operas: a Critical Study* (2nd edition, Oxford University Press, 1947)
Ford, Charles *Così?: Sexual Politics in Mozart's Operas* (Manchester University Press, 1991)
Gianturco, Carolyn *Mozart's Early Operas* (Batsford, London, 1981)
Heartz, Daniel *Mozart's Operas* (University of California Press, Los Angeles, 1990)
Liebner, János *Mozart on the Stage* (Calder & Boyars, London, 1972)
Mann, William *The Operas of Mozart* (Cassell, London, 1977)
Osborne, Charles *The Complete Operas of Mozart: a Critical Guide* (Victor Gollancz, London, 1978)
Steptoe, Andrew *The Mozart-da Ponte Operas* (Clarendon, Oxford, 1988)
Till, Nicholas *Mozart and the Enlightenment: Truth, Virtue and Beauty in Mozart's Operas* (Faber & Faber, London, 1992)

Offenbach
Faris, Alexander *Jacques Offenbach* (Faber & Faber, London, 1980)
Gammond, Peter *Offenbach: His life and Times* (Midas Books, Tunbridge Wells, 1980)
Harding, James *Jacques Offenbach: a Biography* (John Calder, London, 1980)
Pfitzner
Williamson, John *The Music of Hans Pfitzner* (Clarendon Press, Oxford, 1992)
Prokofiev
Robinson, Harlow *Sergei Prokofiev* (Robert Hale, London, 1987)
Puccini
Ashbrook, William *The Operas of Puccini* (2nd edition, Oxford University Press, 1985)
Carner, Mosco *Puccini* (3rd edition, Duckworth, London, 1992)
Hughes, Spike *Famous Puccini Operas* (Robert Hale, London, 1959)
Jackson, Stanley *Monsieur Butterfly: the Story of Puccini* (W.H. Allen, London, 1974)
Macdonald, Ray S. *Puccini: King of Verismo* (Vantage Press, New York, 1973)
Osborne, Charles *The Complete Operas of Puccini* (Victor Gollancz, London, 1981)
Purcell
Harris, Ellen T. *Henry Purcell's Dido and Aeneas* (Clarendon Press, Oxford, 1987)
King, Robert *Henry Purcell* (Thames & Hudson, London, 1994)
Price, Curtis A. *Henry Purcell and the London Stage* (Cambridge University Press, 1984)
Rameau
Girdlestone, Cuthbert *Jean-Philippe Rameau: His Life and Work* (2nd edition, Dover, New York, 1969)
Rossini
Harding, James *Rossini* (Faber & Faber, London, 1971)
Kendall, Alan *Gioacchino Rossini: the Reluctant Hero* (Victor Gollancz, London, 1992)
Osborne, Charles *The Bel Canto Operas of Rossini, Donizetti, Bellini* (Methuen, London, 1994)
Osborne, Richard *Rossini* (Master Musicians, J.M. Dent, London, 1986)
Stendahl *Life of Rossini* (2nd edition, John Calder, London, 1956)
Till, Nicholas *Rossini: his Life and Times* (Midas Books, Tunbridge Wells, 1983)
Toye, Francis *Rossini: a Study in Tragi-Comedy*
Weinstock, Herbert *Rossini: a Biography* (Oxford University Press, London, 1968)
Salieri
Braunbehrens, Volkmar *Maligned Master: the Real Antonio Salieri* (Scolar Press, Aldershot, 1993)
Scarlatti
Grout, Donald Jay *Alessandro Scarlatti: an Introduction to His Operas* (University of California Press, Los Angeles, 1979)
Smetana
Large, Brian *Smetana* (Duckworth, London, 1970)
Nolan, Liam & Hutton, J. Bernard *The Pain and the Glory: the Life of Smetana* (Harrap, London, 1968)
Spohr
Brown, Clive *Louis Spohr: a Critical Biography* (Cambridge University Press, 1984)
Strauss
Gilliam, Bryan *Richard Strauss's Elektra* (Oxford University Press, New York, 1991)
Jeffersson, Alan *The Operas of Richard Strauss in Britain 1910–63* (Putnam, London, 1963)
Mar, Norman del *Richard Strauss* (3 vols, Barrie & Jenkins, London, 1962–72)
Osborne, Charles *The Complete Operas of Richard Strauss* (Michael O'Mara, London, 1988)
Sullivan
Ayre, Leslie *The Gilbert and Sullivan Companion* (W.H. Allen, London, 1972)
Baily, Leslie *The Gilbert and Sullivan Book* (2nd edition, Spring Books, London, 1966)
Eden, David *Gilbert and Sullivan: the Creative Conflict* (Fairleigh Dickinson University Press, New Jersey, 1986)
Ffinch, Michael *Gilbert and Sullivan* (Weidenfeld & Nicolson, London, 1993)
Hughes, Gervase *The Music of Arthur Sullivan* (Macmillan, London, 1960)
Jacobs, Arthur *Arthur Sullivan: a Victorian Musician* (2nd edition, Scolar Press, Aldershot, 1992)

Pearson, Hesketh *Gilbert and Sullivan* (Macdonald, London, 1975)
Smith, Geoffrey *The Savoy Operas: a New Guide to Gilbert and Sullivan* (Robert Hale, London, 1983)
Williamson, Audrey *Gilbert and Sullivan Opera: an Assessment* (Marion Boyars, London, 1982)
Young, Percy M. *Sir Arthur Sullivan* (J.M. Dent, London, 1971)

Tchaikovsky

Brown, David *Tchaikovsky: a Biographical and Critical Study* (4 vols, Victor Gollancz, London, 1981–91)
Garden, Edward *Tchaikovsky* (Master Musicians, J.M. Dent, London, 1973)

Tippett

White, Eric Walter *Tippett and His Operas* (Barrie & Jenkins, London, 1979)

Verdi

Budden, Julian *The Operas of Verdi* (3 vols, Cassell, London, 1973–81)
— *Verdi* (Master Musicians, J.M. Dent, London, 1985)
Busch, Hans (ed) *Verdi's Otello and Simon Boccanegra in Letters and Documents* (2 vols, Clarendon Press, Oxford, 1988)
Conati, Marcello & Medici, Mario (eds) *The Verdi-Boito Correspondence* (University of Chicago Press)
Godefroy, Vincent *The Dramatic Genius of Verdi: Studies of Selected Operas* (2 vols, Victor Gollancz, London, 1975–7)
Hughes, Spike *Famous Verdi Operas* (Robert Hale, London, 1968)
Kimbell, David R.B. *Verdi in the Age of Italian Romanticism* (Cambridge University Press, 1981)
Martin, George *Aspects of Verdi* (Robson Books, London, 1989)
Martin, George *Verdi: His Music, Life and Times* (Macmillan, London, 1965)
Osborne, Charles *The Complete Operas of Verdi: a Critical Guide* (Victor Gollancz, London, 1969)
— *Verdi: a Life in the Theatre* (Michael O'Mara, London, 1987)
Phillips-Matz, Mary Jane *Verdi: a Biography* (Oxford University Press, 1993)
Rosen, David & Porter, Andrew (eds) *Verdi's Macbeth: a Sourcebook* (Cambridge University Press, 1984)
Walker, Frank *The Man Verdi* (J.M. Dent, London, 1962)
Wechsberg, Joseph *Verdi* (Weidenfeld & Nicolson, London, 1974)

Vivaldi

Collins, Michael & Kirk, Elsie K. (eds) *Opera and Vivaldi* (University of Texas Press, Austin, 1994)

Wagner

Blyth, Alan *Wagner's Ring: an Introduction* (Hutchinson, London, 1980)
Chancellor, John *Wagner* (Weidenfeld & Nicolson, London, 1978)
Cooke, Deryck *I Saw the World End: a Study of Wagner's Ring* (Clarendon Press, Oxford, 1979)
Corse, Sandra *Wagner and the New Consciousness: Language and Love in the Ring* (Fairleigh Dickinson University Press, New Jersey, 1990)
Dahlhaus, Carl Richard *Wagner's Music Dramas* (Cambridge University Press, 1979)
Donnington, Robert *Wagner's Ring and its Symbols: the Myth and the Music* (Faber & Faber, London, 1963)
Ewans, Michael *Wagner and Aeschylus: the Ring and the Oresteia* (Faber & Faber, London, 1982)
Gutman, Robert W. *Richard Wagner: the Man, His Mind and His Music* (Secker & Warburg, London, 1968)
James, Burnett *Wagner and the Romantic Disaster* (Midas Books, New York, 1983)
Magee, Bryan *Aspects of Wagner* (Panther, London, 1972)
Mander, Raymond & Mitchenson, Joe *The Wagner Companion* (W.H. Allen, London, 1977)
Millington, Barry *Wagner* (Master Musicians, J.M. Dent, London, 1984)
Newman, Ernest *The Life of Richard Wagner* (3 vols, Cambridge University Press, 1937)

Osborne, Charles *The Complete Operas of Richard Wagner* (Michael O'Mara, London, 1990)
Skelton, Geoffrey *Richard and Cosima Wagner: Biography of a Marriage* (Victor Gollancz, London, 1982)
— *Wagner at Bayreuth* (Barrie & Rockliff, London, 1965)
Weber
Friese-Greene, Anthony *Weber* (Omnibus, London, 1991)
Tusa, Michael C. *Euryanthe and Carl Maria von Weber's Dramaturgy of German Opera* (Clarendon Press, Oxford, 1991)
Warrack, John *Carl Maria von Weber* (2nd edition, Cambridge University Press, 1976)

7 Singers

Adams, Brian *La Stupenda: a Biography of Joan Sutherland* (Hutchinson, Victoria, 1980)
Borovsky, Victor *Chaliapin: a Critical Biography* (Hamish Hamilton, London, 1988)
Bozhkoff, Atanas *Boris Christoff* (Robson, London, 1991)
Caruso, Enrico Jr & Farkas, Andrew *Enrico Caruso: My Father and My Family* (Amadeus, Portland, 1990)
Cone, John Frederick *Adelina Patti: Queen of Hearts* (Scolar Press, Aldershot, 1994)
Douglas, Nigel *Legendary Voices* (André Deutsch, London, 1992)
Emmons, Shirlee *Tristanissimo: the Authorised Biography of Heroic Tenor Lauritz Melchior* (Schirmer, New York, 1990)
Farkas, Andrew (ed) *Lawrence Tibbett: Singing Actor* (Amadeus Press, Portland, 1989)
FitzLyon, April *Maria Malibran: Diva of the Romantic Age* (Souvenir Press, London, 1987)
— *The Price of Genius: a Life of Pauline Viardot* (John Calder, London, 1964)
Forbes, Elizabeth *Mario and Grisi: a Biography* (Victor Gollancz, London, 1985)
Gobbi, Tito *World of Italian Opera* (Hamish Hamilton, London, 1984)
Fingleton, David *Kiri: a Biography of Kiri Te Kanawa* (Collins, London, 1982)
Headington, Christopher *Peter Pears: a Biography* (Faber & Faber, London, 1992)
Henstock, Michael *Fernando de Lucia* (Duckworth, London, 1990)
Hetherington, John *Melba: a Biography* (Faber & Faber, London, 1967)
Jefferson, Alan *Lotte Lehmann* (Julia MacRae, London, 1988)
Kesting, Jürgen *Maria Callas* (Quartet, London, 1992)
Leonard, Maurice *Slobodskaya* (Victor Gollancz, London, 1979)
MacDonald, Cheryl *Emma Albani: Victorian Diva* (Dundurn, Toronto, 1984)
Major, Norma *Joan Sutherland* (Macdonald, London, 1987)
O'Connor, Garry *The Pursuit of Perfection: a Life of Maggie Teyte* (Victor Gollancz, London, 1979)
Pullen, Robert & Taylor, Stephen *Montserrat Caballé: Casta Diva* (Victor Gollancz, London, 1994)
Puritz, Gerd *Elisabeth Schumann* (André Deutsch, London, 1993)
Rasponi, Lanfranco *The Last Prima Donnas* (Alfred A. Knopf, New York, 1982)
Roberts, Peter *Victoria de los Angeles* (Weidenfeld & Nicolson, London, 1982)
Rosselli, John *Singers of Italian Opera: the History of a Profession* (Cambridge University Press, 1992)
Scott, Michael *Maria Meneghini Callas* (Simon & Schuster, London, 1991)
Simpson, Harold *Singers to Remember* (Oakwood Press)
Stassinopoulos, Anna *Maria: Beyond the Callas Legend* (Weidenfeld & Nicolson, London, 1980)
Steane, J.B. *Voices: Singers and Critics* (Duckworth, London, 1982)
Turing, Penelope *Hans Hotter: Man and Artist* (John Calder, London, 1983)
Turnbull, Michael *Joseph Hislop* (Scolar Press, Aldershot, 1992)
Vogt, Howard *Flagstad* (Secker & Warburg, London, 1987)
Whitton, Kenneth S. *Dietrich Fischer-Dieskau: Mastersinger* (Oswald Wolff, London, 1981)

8 Conductors

Bookspan, Martin & Yockey, Ross *Zubin Mehta* (Robert Hale, London, 1978)

Burton, Humphrey *Leonard Bernstein* (Faber & Faber, London, 1994)

Conway, Helen *Sir John Pritchard: His Life in Music* (André Deutsch, London, 1994)

Fifield, Christopher *True Artist and True Friend: a Biography of Hans Richter* (Clarendon Press, Oxford, 1993)

Hart, Philip *Conductors: a New Generation* (Robson, London, 1980)

Horowitz, Joseph *Understanding Toscanini* (Faber & Faber, London, 1987)

Jefferson, Alan *Sir Thomas Beecham* (Macdonald, London, 1979)

Kennedy, Michael *Adrian Boult* (Hamish Hamilton, London, 1987)

Kenyon, Nicholas *Simon Rattle: the Making of a Conductor* (Faber & Faber, London, 1987)

Lucas, John *Reggie: The Life of Reginald Goodall* (Julia MacRae, London, 1993)

Mundy, Simon *Bernard Haitink: a Working Life* (Robson, London, 1987)

Phelan, Nancy *Charles Mackerras: a Musician's Musician* (Victor Gollancz, London, 1987)

Prieberg, Fred K. *Trial of Strength: Wilhelm Furtwängler and the Third Reich* (Quartet, London, 1991)

Reid, Charles *Malcolm Sargent: a Biography* (Hamish Hamilton, London, 1968)

Russell, John *Erich Kleiber: a Memoir* (André Deutsch, London, 1957)

Sachs, Harvey *Toscanini* (Weidenfeld & Nicolson, London, 1978)

Schönzeler, Hans-Hubert *Furtwängler* (Duckworth, London, 1990)

Secrest, Meryle *Leonard Bernstein* (Bloomsbury, London, 1995)

Shirakawa, Sam H. *The Devil's Music Master: the Controversial Life and Career of Wilhelm Furtwängler* (Oxford University Press, New York, 1992)

Vaughan, Roger *Herbert von Karajan: a Biographical Portrait* (Weidenfeld & Nicolson, London, 1982)

Wilson, Conrad *Alex: the Authorised Biography of Sir Alexander Gibson* (Mainstream, Edinburgh, 1993)